THE CANON AND MASORAH OF THE HEBREW BIBLE

An Introductory Reader

THE LIBRARY

OF

BIBLICAL STUDIES

Edited by

Harry M. Orlinsky

THE CANON AND MASORAH OF THE HEBREW BIBLE

An Introductory Reader

15758

Edited by Sid Z. Leiman

KTAV PUBLISHING HOUSE, INC.

NEW YORK

SBN 87068-164-8

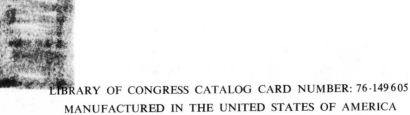

LIBRARY OF CONGRESS CATALOG CARD NUMBER: 76-149605
MANUFACTURED IN THE UNITED STATES OF AMERICA

CONTENTS

Preface

ix

CANON

MASORAH

PREFACE

This reader gathers together in one volume a select group of scholarly essays treating various aspects of Canon and Masorah. Its purpose is to contribute to the broadening of the scope of biblical studies by helping to bring about a better understanding of the problems of Canon and Masorah, wherever such studies—in however limited a fashion—are now pursued. It is also intended that the largely inaccessible secondary materials gathered here will serve students as guides to the primary sources, while forming a convenient point of departure for the serious study of Canon and Masorah in both the classroom and the study.

The need for an introductory reader which moves well beyond the standard biblical handbooks and introductions has long been felt in academic circles both here and abroad. Indeed, this volume grew out of a personal need felt by the writer when he offered a Canon and Masorah course in the Department of Religious Studies at Yale University. While no two editors will agree on what ought to be included in such a volume, I have chosen those studies which seem to:

    a. lead students to the primary sources.
    b. raise clearly specific issues, even when they are not resolved to my satisfaction.
    c. treat issues of sufficient broadness and depth so as to properly belong in an introductory reader.

Highly specialized and extraordinarily lengthy studies were excluded on those grounds alone; nor were selections from volumes readily available in most undergraduate libraries considered for inclusion.

Attempts to strike a balance between the Canon and Masorah sections of this volume were made in vain. The preponderance of studies in the latter section reflects the reality that more scholarly research has been expended on masoretic than on canonization studies. This is mostly due to the much longer time-span covered, and the larger number of issues explored, by masoretic studies. Also, the quantity and quality of tangible evidence available to masoretic scholars surpasses by far the sparse, and sometimes intractable evidence with which canonization scholars must struggle and speculate.

I wish to express my indebtedness and gratitude to the many authors, editors, and publishers whose collaboration made this volume possible. They did not merely lend their consent; they responded enthusiastically and with alacrity, making my task a pleasant one.

Sid Z. Leiman
Associate Professor of
    Religious Studies
Yale University

February, 1973

CANON

A. *Biblical Evidence.*

THE LAW AND THE PROPHETS

BY

DAVID NOEL FREEDMAN
Pittsburgh

The expression, "The Law and the Prophets", familiar to us from the New Testament [1]), refers to the first two major sections of the Hebrew Bible. Most Jews, including Pharisees and Essenes, and the followers of John and Jesus, accepted the authority of the Torah and the Nebi'im, and recognized their essential unity. These were the central core of Scripture, to which the Writings were subordinate, and upon which they were dependent. It will not be amiss in this assemblage, and especially at this time and place, to remind ourselves that Christianity and Judaism, in all their varied forms, are built upon the twin foundations of Law and Prophecy. Of their ultimate religious significance Jesus Christ is himself the chief witness: "Think not that I have come to abolish the law and the prophets; I have not come to abolish them, but to fulfil them. For truly I say to you, till heaven and earth pass away, not even the tittle on the *yod* will pass from the law until all is accomplished" (Mt. v 17-18).

In a similar fashion the story of the Transfiguration (Mk. ix 2-10 and parallels) emphasizes the close interrelationship between Law and Prophecy, symbolized by Moses and Elijah. These passages in turn may be connected with the closing verses of Malachi (H iii 22-23): "Remember the law of my servant Moses, the statutes and ordinances that I commanded him at Horeb for all Israel. Behold I will send you Elijah the prophet before the great and terrible day of the Lord comes [2])".

In this paper, our concern is with the literary history of the Law and the Prophets: the process of composition, compilation, edition, and publication. According to the common scholarly opinion, the literary process runs parallel to the cultural history of Israel. Thus a

---

[1]) Cf. Mt. v 17; vii 12; xi 13; xxii 40; Lk. xvi 16; Acts xiii 15; xxiv 14; xxviii 23; Rom. iii 21b.

[2]) Prof. David FLUSSER of Hebrew University has suggested that these verses constitute a poetic summation of the whole of the preceding portions of the Old Testament, the Law and the Prophets.

Reprinted from *Supplements to Vetus Testamentum* 9 (1962).

span of more than a thousand years is involved from the earliest oral sources until the final appearance of the Torah and Nebi'im as we have them. The long complicated story of the development and inter-relations of the sources, their adaptation, amalgamation, and editing into a single composition has been the subject of intensive study by scholars for more than 200 years, and it is not our intention to reca-pitulate their investigations at this point [1]). There is widespread agreement that the Pentateuch was formally published around 400 B.C., and that the Prophets received a similar imprimatur about 200 years later.

In our judgment, both dates are too low, whether they are taken to refer to the completion of the literary process of compilation and edition, or to the recognition of the authority of this literature in matters of faith and practice. The thesis which we advance here is that the literary process, strictly conceived, came to its conclusion at a much earlier date for both the Law and the Prophets, and that the question of authority is inseparable from that of formal publica-tion. We hold that the Law and the Former Prophets (which we desig-nate the Primary History, i.e., the books from Genesis through 2 Kings in the Hebrew Bible) comprise a literary unit which was compiled and published in its entirety by the middle of the 6th century B.C., [2]) and that the Latter Prophets (i.e., the books of Isaiah, Jeremiah, Ezekiel, and the twelve minor prophets) appeared in finished form toward the end of the 6th or in the early part of the 5th century B.C. We hold further that these were public documents, for which the highest religious authority was claimed, promulgated by an official ecclesiastical group in the Jewish community [3]). In

---

[1]) See the standard Introductions by EISSFELDT, WEISER, PFEIFFER and BENT-ZEN. For a survey of the literature and scholarly contributions toward a solution of Pentateuchal problems, see our article on the Pentateuch in *The Interpreter's Dictionary of the Bible*, New York 1962, Vol. III, pp. 711-27.

[2]) We wish to acknowledge the influence of Y. KAUFMANN's views and argu-ments in dating the Torah-literature, especially with respect to his case against a post-exilic date for the P source. At the same time we do not accept his reversal of the order of D and P, or his reconstruction of the pre-exilic history of the sources. Cf. his *Religion of Israel*, trans. by Moshe GREENBERG, Chicago, 1960, especially chap. v.

[3]) At the Congress, Prof. J. HEMPEL raised the question of the place of publi-cation of such a monumental work, and the nature of the group which could exercise the necessary authority to promulgate it. In our opinion the logical place to look for the publication of this work is Babylonia rather than Palestine. While the great concern for the holy land as the only suitable place to settle and worship in the one authorized temple might indicate a Palestinian location, even

short, these works constituted the authorized history of the people of God, along with relevant prophetic commentary, interpretation, and proclamation. The special status of the Torah was doubtless recognized from the beginning, but it was only later that the five books of Moses were set apart from the larger literary entity, resulting in the tripartite division we now have: Torah, Former and Latter Prophets.

In dealing with these portions of the Bible, we distinguish between their literary and textual history. The former is concerned primarily with the creative literary activity by which earlier oral traditions were shaped into a continuous record, the extensive editorial redaction of the different written sources, and the final compilation of available materials resulting in the appearance of the completed work. The latter is concerned with the transmission of the text and the process by which it was finally fixed. Together they constitute an account of the literature from its beginnings to its final form. With the formal promulgation of the work, in which contents, scope, and order of the parts are fixed, without further significant change, literary history comes to an end, and textual history, properly speaking, begins. The transmission of the text, with the development of recensional patterns, manuscript families, and the emergence of distinctive text-types, represents a phase in the history of biblical literature quite different from the preceding literary phase. Comparison of all existing manuscripts and versions of the books of both the Old and New Testaments reveals a relatively narrow range of variation, most of the alterations are of minor significance and belong to categories characteristic of scribal activity. Many of these are accidental, others are the result of grammatical, orthographic, or lexical revision. But creative literary work and extensive editorial revision belong to an earlier period before formal authoritative promulgation. We can trace the textual history of the Law and Prophets back to

---

greater emphasis is placed upon the twin themes of exile and return. It is repeatedly affirmed that the people will be taken from this holy land, and will be forced into captivity in foreign territories, where they must stay until God in his mercy restores them to their proper home. We would expect Palestinian Jews to emphasize rather the theme of continuous occupation of the land, even after the destruction of the temple. If a post-exilic date of publication were posited for the Primary History, then a Palestinian location would be perfectly in order. Such a line of reasoning would apply specifically to the Chronicler's History, which reflects the orientation of the Babylonian exiles, but was composed in Palestine (cf. our article, "The Chronicler's Purpose", *CBQ*, XXIII, 1961, pp. 436-42).

manuscripts of the 3rd century B.C., and we can make reasonable projections into the 4th and even the 5th century, to which we can assign the archetypal manuscripts which underlie all subsequent texts and versions [1]). It is also our opinion that the changes during the 6th-5th centuries were of the scribal-textual kind, rather than of the literary-editorial variety. But in order to determine the critical period when literary history ends and textual history begins, i.e., the point at which the literature becomes fixed in permanent and at least quasi-official form, it is necessary to examine the relevant criteria, as well as the principles and methods by which they are isolated and evaluated. It is to these matters that we now turn.

In attempting to determine the date of publication of a literary work, it is immediately clear that a terminus a quo is provided by the latest specific historical reference found in it. Under any circumstances, the work cannot be earlier than the date of such material. It is, of course, quite possible that such an historical note has been added to a previously completed entity, which except for the addendum should then be dated according to its other historical data. This appears to be the case with the last paragraph in 2 Kings (xxv 27-30), which stands apart from the narrative, and is to be dated at least 20 years later than any other historical reference in the Primary History. This possibility does not affect the principle involved, but points toward the determination of a terminus a quo for different parts of a composite work, using the same criterion.

In pursuing this line of inquiry it is important to distinguish between authentic predictive materials in the Old Testament, and the rare vaticinium ex eventu, which is to be classified with ordinary historical data. Specific information, giving names, dates, places, is to be treated historically. Thus the name "Josiah" in the well-known prophecy concerning the destruction of the temple at Bethel in 1 Kings xiii 2 must be a retrojection from the time of Josiah or later, though there may have been an authentic original prophecy couched in more general terms. In its present form, however, the terminus a quo for that passage is the last part of the 7th century B.C. General

---

[1]) See our article, "The Massoretic Text and the Qumran Scrolls: A Study in Orthography", *Textus* II 1962, pp. 87-102. Our conclusions agree substantially with those of Frank M. Cross, *The Ancient Library of Qumran and Modern Biblical Studies*, rev. ed., New York 1961, pp. 188-94. Cf. also, W. F. Albright, "New Light on Early Recensions of the Hebrew Bible", *BASOR* 140 (1955), pp. 27-33; and M. Greenberg, "The Stabilization of the Text of the Hebrew Bible ...", *JAOS*, LXXVI, 1956, pp. 157-67.

predictions of the collapse of the nation, the exile and return, do not necessarily presuppose these events, however. On the contrary, their vagueness, and notable divergence from the known course of history argue for their authenticity, and provide instead a terminus ante quem for the composition of this material [1]). The situation is well illustrated by the predictions in the books of Jeremiah and Ezekiel concerning the duration of the Exile [2]), and the manner of its termination. Far from reflecting the actual events, they can only be regarded as previsions of a course of history which followed the main outlines, but differed markedly in detail; and which were left undisturbed by subsequent editors and scribes.

In general, historical information helps to determine the terminus a quo for the completion of a literary work, but the terminus ante quem is fixed by other criteria. Thus the primary history could have been finished at any time after, say, 550 B.C.; the lower limit, strictly considered, would be fixed by the date of the oldest MS containing the completed work, or adequate evidence for the date of such a manuscript. No one would doubt now, on the basis of existing fragments from Qumran, and our knowledge of the Septuagint and its history, that the Primary History in substantially its present form, existed in the 3rd century, or even the 4th century B.C. But it is possible to make further use of the historical references in the work in narrowing the range between termini. It is universally recognized that historical works reflect not only the period of the subject matter, but also the time of composition. We all remember WELLHAUSEN'S dictum that the stories of Genesis tell us about the period of their authors rather than about the era of the patriarchs [3]). WELLHAUSEN

---

[1]) KAUFMANN, *op. cit.*, pp. 347-58, makes extensive and, in our judgment, generally effective use of this argument in connection with the prophetic writings.

[2]) Jeremiah's 70 years (xxv 11, 12) are to be dated from the 4th year of Jehoiakim, 605 B.C. The reference in xxix 10 (which may be dated about 10 years later) is to be interpreted in the light of the earlier passage. The starting point for the 40 years of Ezekiel (iv 6) is uncertain, but it must fall between the beginning of his ministry (593 B.C.) and the fall of Jerusalem (587 B.C.). The terminal dates for the fall of Babylon (Jeremiah) or the end of the exile (Ezekiel) differ somewhat, and neither coincides with the historical event (539 B.C.). It is to be noted that Ezekiel uses the same forty year pattern in predicting the downfall of Egypt (xxix 10-16), and its subsequent restoration. Here the results did not match expectations, and the chronology is left dangling. But all this is clear evidence that the prophecies antedated the events, and were not subsequently altered. Cf. G. A. Cooke, *The Book of Ezekiel* (*ICC*), New York 1937, II, pp. 328-29.

[3]) WELLHAUSEN'S language is characteristically strong: "Freilich über die Patriarchen ist hier kein historisches Wissen zu gewinnen, sondern nur über die

was perhaps too skeptical concerning the preservation of authentic traditions and reminiscences, and too ingenious in interpreting veiled allusions to contemporary situations. Nevertheless the principle is an important one. It is almost impossible for an author or editor to conceal entirely either his point of view or his historical position; clues to these will be found here and there throughout the work. Especially in the case of historical works, significant recent or contemporary events will inevitably find their way into the narrative. In the biblical histories there were compelling reasons for bringing the narrative up to date. For the biblical writer, Israel's history was its experience with God [1]). Events were the signs of his presence and embodied his activity. History was theologically conceived as a continuous chronological process, beginning with election (or creation), following the complex course of past events, leading to the present circumstances and experiences, and pointing to an as yet unfulfilled future. While chronicles and narratives can be of limited scope, sacred history can only have an eschatological terminus. The provisional stopping place in the sequence of historical events is fixed by the horizon of the author or compiler. We maintain therefore that if the last historical reference in such literary works as the Primary History is the terminus a quo, it also points to the date of composition within a few years of that event. The terminus ante quem is determined by the next significant historical event, known from other sources, which, so far as we can determine, would have figured in the historical account had the author or editor known of it. For the Primary History, these decisive events would be the fall of Babylon and the consequent return of the exiles. The fact that the Primary History comes to an end before these occurrences indicates that it was compiled and completed before that time.

More difficult to assess are obscure allusions and hidden references to current personalities and events. These abound in the late literature, especially of the Hellenistic era. The canonical book of Daniel and other apocalyptic books contain much material of this kind;

Zeit, in welcher die Erzählungen über sie im israelitischen Volke entstanden; diese spätere Zeit wird hier, nach ihren inneren und äusseren Grundzügen, absichtlos ins graue Altertum projicirt und spiegelt sich darin wie ein verklärtes Luftbild ab". *Prolegomena zur Geschichte Israels*, 4th ed., Berlin 1895, p. 322.

[1]) On the historical nature of biblical religion, see our article, "History and Eschatology", *Interpretation*, XIV, 1960, pp. 3-15; and G. E. WRIGHT, *God Who Acts*, London, 1952; and his "Faith of Israel", *The Interpreter's Bible*, New York 1952, I, 349-89.

the Qumran commentaries are especially rich in this respect. There is no doubt of the intent of the author to convey historical data, and it is only necessary to penetrate the disguise, which is frequently rendered more obscure by our lack of information about times, persons, and places. But there is little or none of this in the earlier biblical literature [1]).

Even more hazardous is the attempt to determine relative or absolute dating on the basis of a supposed evolution of ideas, institutions, or practices. Perhaps we do not sufficiently appreciate how much of Old Testament scholarship in the 19th and 20th centuries has been influenced by simple developmental formulas, or to what extent the modern reconstruction of Israelite literature, culture, and religion has been based upon such patterns. Thus the scholarly commonplace that the Priestly source of the Hexateuch (whatever ancient materials it may embody) deals with and reflects the post-exilic situation in Palestine, must be challenged on the grounds that verifying data have never been adduced [2]). While the theory has always been attractive, ingeniously argued, and embellished with numerous plausible connections between the P materials and post-exilic practice or purpose, it remains only an intriguing possibility. What is required is to demonstrate that post-exilic institutions and practices are antecedent to and reflected in P, and not influenced by or adapted from the material in P. It is not enough to show similarities, or even connections; it is necessary to demonstrate priority and the flow of influence; in short that P was produced by the post-exilic community.

---

[1]) It is only with the Babylonian exile that an underground literature begins to emerge, in which some measure of concealment, both of author and subject, was necessary. Note, e.g., the use of *athbash* for Babylon and the Chaldeans in the prophecies of Jeremiah li (vss. 1, 41); and the veiled references in Ezekiel xxxiv, xxxviii-xxxix, and Zechariah ix-xiv. Here our ignorance of the historical circumstances prevents us from making a reliable analysis of the material. We should be warned against the many ingenious connections suggested by scholars. At best they can only be possibilities, and what is required for the purpose of dating a composition is proof or high probability. In the nature of the case, allusive material can only offer tantalizing hints, and must be subject to the heavier weight of more objective and perspicuous data.

[2]) Cf. W. F. ALBRIGHT, *From the Stone Age to Christianity*, 2nd Anchor ed., New York, 1957, p. 345: "Since there is not a single passage in the whole Pentateuch which can be seriously considered as showing post-exilic influence either in form or in content, it is likely that the entire Pentateuch was compiled in substantially its present form before 522 B.C." See also E. A. SPEISER, "Leviticus and the Critics", *Yehezkel Kaufmann Jubilee Volume*, Jerusalem, 1960, pp. 29 45, esp. 41-45.

In applying these criteria to the question of the date of the Primary History, we note that the last dated reference is in the closing verses of 2 Kings. The date given is 561/60 B.C., but the statement also mentions the remaining years of Jehoiachin's life [1]). Since at that time, he was already 55 years old, an elderly man by ancient standards, we may assume that he did not long survive, but died within five or at most ten years. Since the event was of no great or lasting significance, it is likely that it was recorded within a short time. The next known events in the history of Israel, far more important than the pathetic notice of the king-in-exile, were the dramatic rise of Cyrus to world-suzerainty, his conquest of Babylon, and subsequent edict of release and return. It is difficult to imagine that the author or compiler would have closed his book so inconclusively and anticlimatically, had he known of the momentous events which took place in the succeeding decades, especially in view of the prophetic oracles about the end of the exile and return to the land. The argument would hold even more strongly if we suppose that the book originally ended with the report of the capture of Jerusalem and the exile to Babylon. If it is argued that the general predictions of exile and return which occur in Leviticus and Deuteronomy presuppose those events, then the omission of the historical fulfilment at the end of Kings is even more surprising [2]).

When we compare the Primary History with the Chronicler's History, we find in the latter precisely what we should expect in an historical account written after the return. There is explicit reference to Cyrus, the edict, and the return, as the fulfilment of prophetic expectation [3]). This is the way in which the narrative in Kings would have continued had it been written after those events. In fact, there is no allusion to any of them, explicit or veiled, in the entire corpus. We may go further and suggest that the reference to Jehoiachin in the last paragraph of 2 Kings is itself the postscript to an already

---

[1]) Cf. 2 Kgs. xxv 29, 30, where the expression "all the days of his life" occurs twice. Jer. lii 33, 34 retains the double reading, and adds in vs. 34, "until the day of his death". Apparently the notice was added after the death of Jehoiachin.

[2]) The compiler would hardly have missed the opportunity to stress the fulfilment of earlier predictions by adding the necessary historical information at the end of his account.

[3]) The Chronicler omits the episode concerning Awel-Marduk and Jehoiachin, presumably because of its unimportance, especially by contrast with the momentous events which followed. It is also possible that he used a text of Kings which did not include this addendum.

completed work. Thus the history proper concludes with the story
of the fall of Jerusalem, the exile, and aftermath ending with the
death of Gedaliah and flight to Egypt [1]). They may be dated approximately 587-582 B.C. and the whole of the Primary History, except
for the postscript, may be dated shortly thereafter, in the early stages
of the exile. The stereotyped references to the exile in the Primary
History do not reflect actual conditions and experiences, as do the
stories, for example, in the book of Ezekiel. We may conclude that
the compiler finished his work shortly after the events described,
and was not familiar with the subsequent experiences of the exiles.

The outlook and orientation of the compiler fit very well the
period immediately following the collapse of Judah. Throughout,
the work is in the form of a theodicy, a vindication of the creator
God who is at the same time the covenant deity of Israel. The catastrophe that has befallen his people is not due to his weakness, but
rather to his power: the inevitable consequence of covenant violation
and rebellion against his holy will. While most of the material belongs
to earlier sources, and traces the long course of salvation history,
the point of view of the editor has permeated the whole, which
serves as a paradigm for the current generation. His purpose is to
explain how it happened that the God who chose the people of Israel
in the Fathers, and saved them from bondage in Egypt through
Moses, who gave them the land through Joshua, and sovereignty
through Judges and Kings, could in these last days destroy their
nation, cast them from their land, and surrender them to the tyranny
of a new oppressor, the king of Babylon. The threat of doom, so
strongly articulated in the Deuteronomic sermons, is not lacking
elsewhere in the Primary History; prominent is the thread of tragedy,
foreseen but unavoidable [2]). Along with the mood of disaster is
confidence in the future: the certainty of a return and restoration,
which is rooted in the mystery of election. The God who has punished
the sinful nation in accordance with the conditions of the Sinai
covenant, is nevertheless committed irrevocably to his people, and
out of his inexhaustible grace will resettle the unworthy ones in the
promised land, even as they were torn from it for being unworthy.
It is clear, however, that the restoration has not yet taken place: there
is hope, even assurance, but not the exultation in the fact which we

---

[1]) The latter events are described in much greater detail in the book of Jeremiah, since the prophet played a central role in them.

[2]) Cf. e.g., Lev. xxvi, especially vss. 32 ff.

13

find in II Isaiah, or the explicit references to the event in Haggai, Zechariah, and the Chronicler's History. The prevailing mood is somber, as befits a community under judgment, enduring its days of punishment in exile.

The Latter Prophets present a more complex problem of dating, since we are dealing with a collection of works in which the process of organization and unification is incomplete. Nevertheless, there is a certain continuity of theme and treatment in the separate books; and it is of the collection as a whole that we wish to make the following observations: 1) That the Latter Prophets as a whole are to be dated toward the end of the 6th century, or roughly about 500 B.C.; and 2) that the bulk of the materials belong to an earlier collection which is to be dated to the middle of the 6th century, at about the same time as the final edition of the Primary History. 3) We hold further that the prophetic collection was organized as a supplement to the Primary History, and that the chronological and editorial links are deliberate. It has often been noted that the so-called literary prophets (i.e., those whose names are attached to books in the prophetic canon) have been largely ignored in the Primary History (only Isaiah and Jonah are mentioned), though there is great interest in prophecy in the Primary History, and much space is devoted to the earlier prophets like Samuel, Nathan, Elijah, Elisha, etc. We suggest that the existence of a prophetic corpus made unnecessary the kind of treatment accorded to the earlier prophets, for whom no extensive literary materials were available.

The bulk of the prophetic literature reflects the circumstances of the Babylonian exile, whatever may be the date of the original prophet and his oracles [1]). This is not only true of the 7th-6th century prophets like Jeremiah and Ezekiel, Habakkuk, and probably Obadiah, but also of the book, I Isaiah, which contains extensive materials from the Babylonian exile (e.g. chaps. xiii-xiv), and Micah, in which 8th century Assyrian oracles have been mingled with 6th century Babylonian material (chaps. iv-v). The same may be true of Amos and Hosea, though the evidence is less certain. If we add Nahum and Zephaniah, which are pre-exilic, we have a sizable collection of oracles, dating from the 8th to the 6th centuries, and bearing the marks of exilic editing. At the same time, there is nothing in the

---

[1]) In this collection we would include Isaiah i-xxxix (with the possible exception of xxxiv-xxxv), the whole of Jeremiah and Ezekiel, and the minor prophets Amos, Hosea, Micah, Nahum, Zephaniah, Habakkuk, and Obadiah.

literature mentioned which requires or implies a post-exilic date. Cyrus and the Persian Empire, the actual capture of Babylon and return of the exiles, are all beyond their horizon.

In the case of Ezekiel, we hold that the book is essentially a unity, that it derives in its entirety from the inspiration of the prophet, and is a product of the Babylonian exile [1]). In spite of numerous scholarly efforts to show that the book contains allusions to and reflections of the Persian and Greek periods, the evidence is at best ambiguous and the arguments unconvincing. Thus the passing references to Persian soldiers in association with those of Lud and Put (xxvii 10), or Cush and Put (xxxviii 5), are historically unexceptionable for that period, and far from reflecting the era of Persian supremacy, as TORREY among others supposed [2]), actually points to an earlier period [3]). Similarly the vision of the new Jerusalem in chaps. xl-xlviii, is an anticipation of the return and rebuilding of the temple, rather than a reflection of it.

The book of Jeremiah is likewise a product of the exilic period. Not everything in the book comes directly from the prophet or his biographer. There are substantial additions which are later than Jeremiah and the book has undergone extensive editorial revision. But there is nothing here or elsewhere in the book that presupposes or reflects the historical return from exile, or the events connected with it. In fact the prophecies concerning the impending destruction of Babylon (chaps. l-li) differ so markedly from the actual and comparatively peaceful capture of the city by Cyrus, that they must be assigned to the exilic period. A vaticinium ex eventu would have been more accurate in this respect. In I Isaiah the oracles on Babylon (e.g. chaps. xiii-xiv) must be assigned to the 6th century; but there is nothing of a later date in our opinion. The so-called apocalypse (xxiv-xxvii) is obscure, but that alone is no indication of date. Its affinities are chiefly with Ezekiel, and we believe that it belongs to the

---

[1]) There has been a significant reaction to the radical criticism of earlier decades, though the problem of the unity and date of the book of Ezekiel has not been entirely resolved. The differences in point of view are reflected in recent commentaries, e.g., by H. G. MAY in the *Interpreter's Bible*, and G. FOHRER and K. GALLING in the *Handbuch zum Alten Testament*.

[2]) Cf. C C. TORREY, *Pseudo-Ezekiel and the Original Prophecy*, New Haven 1930, p. 84.

[3]) Similarly the reference to the Chaldeans as desert marauders, in Job i 17, points to the period before the rise of the Neo-Babylonian empire in the last quarter of the 7th century B.C.

same general period [1]). The prevailing mood of the exilic collection
is the same as that of the Primary History: principal emphasis is upon
the threat and judgment of God, spelled out in terms of military
invasion, devastation of the land, and exile. It is this theme which
unites the prophets of the 8th and 7th-6th centuries; very little edito-
rializing was needed to make the 8th century speak to the 6th, or the
northern prophets to the south. But the prophets also spoke with
assurance of the ultimate future; hope and confidence in a return to
the land, and the restoration of the nation, are equally a part of
their message. Taken together, the collection reflects the situation
after the destruction of Jerusalem, but before the return.

In its present form, however, the collection has been supplemented
by a group of prophecies which belong to a later date, and which
refer directly to the return from exile and the rebuilding of the temple.
These are to be found in II Isaiah, Haggai, and Zechariah. Apart
from the authentic oracles of Haggai and Zechariah (i-viii), specific
attributions are impossible, and much of the material is shrouded in
historical obscurity (e.g., Zech. ix-xiv, Isa. lvi-lxvi). All the explicit
historical references in this material belong to the latter half of the
6th century; there is no compelling reason to assign any part of it to
a different period. If we could penetrate the obscurities of Zechariah
ix-xiv, we might be able to suggest a more definite date of composition, but perhaps the wisest procedure at present is to suspend
judgment [2]). With respect to Malachi, we agree with most scholars
in dating the book between the rebuilding of the temple and the
period of Ezra-Nehemiah. The marriage problems under discussion
in the different books are not precisely the same, though they may be
related [3]); otherwise the situation presupposed in Malachi more

---

[1]) Prof. G. W. ANDERSON read a paper at the Congress on Isa. xxiv-xxvii, and
made a convincing case for a 6th century date of composition, roughly in the
period of II Isaiah, Haggai, and Zechariah. While we lean toward a slightly
earlier date toward the end of the exile, it is to be recognized that the whole book
of Isaiah in its present form cannot be dated earlier than the last years of the 6th
century. Such passages as Isa. xxiv-xxvii and xxxiv-xxxv may have been composed
and inserted into the text in post-exilic times.

[2]) With regard to the date of Zech. ix-xiv, the reference to the Greeks in ix 13
does not reflect the period of Greek supremacy in the time of Alexander the Great
and his successors, any more than does the reference in Joel iv 6. What is described here is a conflict between the people of Zion and those of Yavan, treated
as approximately equal contestants. This would fit the 6th or early 5th centuries,
but hardly any later period; in the present state of our knowledge it is hazardous
to offer any date for this material.

[3]) Malachi is concerned primarily with the problem of divorce, though he

16

closely resembles that of Haggai and Zechariah. Joel may be dated with some confidence in the same general period, ca. 520 B.C. [1]). For Jonah the data are too limited to fix a date of composition. A reasonable estimate would place it also in the early post-exilic period, but more than this can hardly be claimed.

The last specific date we have in the Latter Prophets is the 4th year of Darius I, 518 B.C. [2]) A better knowledge of the period between the rebuilding of the temple and the age of Ezra-Nehemiah, along with a more accurate understanding of the obscure historical allusions in the post-exilic prophetic literature would permit a more precise dating of the corpus, which we set provisionally around 500 B.C. At the same time, the scope and orientation, the tone and outlook of this supplemental collection of prophecies fit very well with what we know of the early post-exilic community. The reason for the expanded collection is clear. In the sequence of events culminating in the return of the exiles, and the rebuilding of their community, former prophecies had been fulfilled; and new prophets had arisen to announce the purpose and promised actions of God to his people. Just as in the earlier period threat had been followed by judgment, so now promise was to be achieved in fulfilment. The principal theme of II Isaiah, Haggai, and Zechariah is the realization of prophecy and promise in the immediate historical situation. II Isaiah speaks of a recapitulation of salvation-history in terms of a second Exodus and permanent settlement in the holy land. Haggai and Zechariah concentrate attention on the second temple, and the revival of the house of David and the Zadokite priesthood, the traditional institutions of the divinely established community, and the marks of its legitimacy. There is an intimate association of monarchy and prophecy but especially of the house of David with the whole line of prophets from Samuel to Haggai/Zechariah. Regardless of their attitude toward particular kings, and this was often hostile, the prophets never abandoned confidence that the house of David would have its place of dignity and authority in the restored kingdom of God. But

---

makes passing reference to mixed marriages (cf. ii 10-16). Ezra and Nehemiah are concerned with the problem of mixed marriages in the Jewish community, and carry through a rigorous policy of excluding these foreign wives.

[1]) This is the conclusion of J. M. MYERS in a well-reasoned article, "Some Considerations Bearing on the Date of Joel", *ZAW* LXXIV 1962, pp. 177-95.

[2]) Zech. vii 1, the 4th day of the 9th month, apparently Dec. 8. Cf. R. A. PARKER and W. H. DUBBERSTEIN, *Babylonian Chronology 626 B.C.-A.D. 75*, Providence 1956, p. 30.

the prophetic-Davidic association continued only to the end of the 6th century B.C. [1]) in datable prophecies. Zerubbabel was the last of the line of David to figure significantly in the history of Judah; after his time we have only a list of his descendants. What happened to Zerubbabel and his successors of the line of David we do not know, but by the time of Ezra and Nehemiah, power and prestige had passed to other hands. There were prophets after Haggai, Zechariah, and Malachi; some of them are mentioned in Nehemiah, and others were doubtless active in that and even later periods. Since the house of David also survived, a connection between them may have persisted into late times. But of this there is no clear-cut evidence [2]). The sequence of prophetic oracles on the glorification of the Davidic dynasty reached a climax, and we believe a conclusion in the age of Zerubbabel, Haggai and Zechariah. Afterwards it was a matter of preserving the ancient traditions, and renewing hope of their fulfilment. But it was many centuries before Davidic messianism made an authentic historical appearance in Palestine.

It may be asked why, if the prophetic collection which first appeared in the course of the exile was brought up to date with the addition of the oracles of II Isaiah, Haggai, Zechariah, etc., no similar effort was made in connection with the Primary History. In its present form it ends rather inconsequentially; certainly the story of the return of the exiles and rebuilding of the temple would make a more fitting conclusion to the whole work. But this is precisely what has happened in the Chronicler's History, where the story of the return rounds out

---

[1]) The messianic or Davidic references in Zech. ix and xii-xiii cannot be dated with any assurance. We see no reason to date them later than the close of the 6th century.

[2]) The references in Nehemiah (vi 7 and 14) to various unnamed prophets and the prophetess Noadiah are of interest. In the first instance, Nehemiah denounces as false the rumor spread by Sanballat that Nehemiah had employed prophets to proclaim him king in Judah. We may infer that "king-making" was still considered a possible prerogative of the prophets, in the manner of ancient heroes like Samuel, Nathan, Elijah and Elisha. At the same time a true prophet presumably would restrict such activities to the house of David. In the second instance, Nehemiah complains about certain other prophets who along with the prophetess Noadiah tried to intimidate him. We may speculate that they objected to his exercise of temporal authority. Though legally authorized by the Persian king, Nehemiah may have been regarded as a usurper by the prophets, who would reserve such an office to the leader of the house of David. This would be in line with the tradition of Haggai and Zechariah in connection with Zerubbabel. In any case, Nehemiah dissociates himself entirely from the prophets, and their authority.

the narrative of the conquest of Judah and the captivity. At the same time, there was a drastic overhauling of the earlier history, especially in the account of David and Solomon. Whatever may have been the intention of the Chronicler with respect to the Primary History, his account did not displace the older compilation, nor were the two amalgamated into a single literary work [1]). It was ultimately accepted as a supplementary account, and preserved in the Writings. Most important is the fact that the Primary History escaped revision, even the slight addition which would have brought the story to a more satisfying conclusion. It would appear that the Primary History was no longer subject to this sort of literary modification because it was already the official record of Israel's experience.

We may summarize our proposed synthesis of the Law and the Prophets as follows:

I. In the course of the Babylonian Exile, roughly between 580 and 550 B.C., a great compilation of Israelite literature was made under appropriate authority and supervision. This collection included the whole of the Primary History as we know it (all the books from Genesis through 2 Kings in the Hebrew Bible), and a large selection of prophetic materials, including the bulk of I Isaiah, Jeremiah, Ezekiel, and the major portion of the minor prophets: Amos, Hosea, Micah, Nahum, Zephaniah, Habakkuk, and Obadiah.

II. After the Exile, and under the influence of new prophetic voices, who encouraged the return of the exiles and the rebuilding of the temple, a supplement to the prophetic collection was compiled, sometime between 518 and 450 B.C., perhaps around 500, including Isaiah xl-lxvi, Haggai, Zechariah i-viii, and Malachi; possibly also Joel, Zechariah ix-xiv, and Jonah, though these books are difficult to date and place, and we may wisely reserve judgment.

---

[1]) The Chronicler's History may have been intended as a supplement to the Primary History, rather than as a competing version of the same period of history (i.e., the monarchy). The extensive materials on David and Solomon are largely additions, while the stories in Samuel and Kings about these monarchs have been severely cut. Perhaps the objective was not so much to erase a previous picture of these kings, as to balance the existing picture with data not previously incorporated. Does the omission of almost the entire account of the northern kingdom imply that the Chronicler had no use for either the kingdom or its story, or simply that he had nothing to add or alter in the existing account? That the Chronicler meant for his work to be taken seriously, and to be regarded as official and authoritative is quite clear. But did he mean for it to replace the existing historical account (in Samuel and Kings), or to be regarded as a supplement of great if not equal value?

III. Thus we hold that the core of the Old Testament, the Law and the Prophets, emerged as a literary entity during a comparatively brief period in Israel's history, but a decisive one, during which the nation came to an end, and out of the trials of captivity a new community was born. The whole of the literature bears the stamp of this period, with its dramatic experience of death and resurrection.

20

B. *Extra-Talmudic Evidence.*

SOME LIGHT ON THE CANON OF THE QUMRAN SECT.

By Prof. Dr. I. H. Eybers, University of South Africa

Ever since the discovery of the manuscripts of the Qumran Sect (or "Dead Sea Scrolls"), interest centred upon the light which these documents could throw on the Bible. One point oi interest for Old Testament scholarship was possible information about the process of canonization[1] of the Scriptures of the Old Testament. In the very period of the sect's activity this process was drawing to a close, according to the opinion held by the majority of scholars.[2]. Since it is, however, fairly certain that the canonization of the *Tôrâ* and *N'bî'îm* had been completed by 200 B.C.,[3] we shall not discuss these books here, but in this study accept their canonicity without discussion.

For the purpose of this paper we also have to regard the texts discovered in the caves in the vicinity of Khirbet Quamran as documents which belonged to the sect which occupied the building between *c.* 130 B.C. and A.D. 70. We also have to accept the conclusion of a number of scholars that the Qumran sect separated from the rest of Judaism not later than *c.* 130 B.C. to form a distinct religious body, alienated from and opposed to the rest of the Jews.[4]

In an investigation of this kind, it should be clear that quotations from the Bible in the Qumran texts plays a very important rôle in determining the authority ascribed to a specific book, but that there is a limit to the value of the presence of texts and quotations. In the first place an argument, based on the absence of a specific text among the fragments and among the existing quotations, may prove to be invalid. Thus, for example, it would be wrong to deny the canonicity of the Biblical book of Haggai at Qumran simply because thus far no trace of this book has been found there: neither in the manuscripts nor in quotations or even in allusions.[5] It should be noted, too, that the quota-

---

1. The term "Canonization" is here used in the sense of recognition by the religious group (a sect or the synogogues) of certain writings as Divine revelation and therefore as normative in teaching and practice.
2. S. J. du Plessis (Jesus en die Kanon van die Ou Testament, p. 88), mentions e.g. R. H. Pfeiffer, F. Hölscher, F. Bleek, A. Dillmann, H. E. Ryle and probably also G. Ch. Aalders, H. L. Strack, cf. also S. Zeitlin, "An historical Study of the Canonization of the Hebrew Scripture," Proceedings of the American Academy for Jewish Research, 1932, p. 129, A. Weiser, Einleitung in das Alte Testament, (2nd Ed.) p. 252.
3. Cf. e.g. Weiser, op. cit. pp. 248-249, S. Zeitlin, op. cit. pp. 121-122 (where he speaks of pre-Maccabaean times), G. Ch. Aalders, Oud-Testamentische Kanoniek, pp. 35-39, A. H. Edelkoort, De Handschriften van de Doode Zee, (2nd Ed.) p. 65 and F. M. Cross, The Ancient Library of Qumrân and Modern Biblical Studies, pp. 120-121 (also quoted as Ancient Library). B. J. Roberts "The Dead Sea Scrolls and the Old Testament Scriptures," Bulletin of the John Rylands Library, XXXVI, p. 84 (henceforth quoted as BJRL states that the divine authority of the Law and Prophets at Qumran requires no demonstration. Cf. also W. F. Albright, Recent Discoveries in Bible Lands, p. 129, where he states "that most of the Old Testament canon was fixed in form by the end of the Persian period." cf. M. Burrows, More Light on the Dead Sea Scrolls, p. 159 (quoted here as More Light) where he refers to Albright's view that many of the Old Testament books were brought from Babylonia to Palestine in the 6th and 5th centuries B.C.
4. Our arguments in this connection may be traced in our Aspekte van die Organisasies en Rites van die Joodse Qoemraansekte, pp. 5-12, 37-38, 82-84, 97, 118-126, 137-148 (hereafter quot ed as AORQS). For the date cf. J. T. Milik, Ten Years of Discovery in the Wilderness of Judaea, pp. 4;-98 (especially pp. 80-87, also quoted as 10 Years), Cross, Ancient Library, pp. 80-119, cf. Burrows, More Light, pp. 191-249. We do not here enter into the discussion whether the sect is older by about another four decades, as proposed by H. H. Rowley (The Zadokite Fragments and the Dead Sea Scrolls, chapter III and Jewish Apocalyptic and the Dead Sea Scrolls, pp. 6 and 26), A. Michel, (Le Maître de Justice) and G. Vermès, Les Manuscrits du Désert de Juda, (2nd ed.) pp. 75 and 79. We find the above dates more acceptable than those of Dupont-Sommer, Brownlee, Elliger and F. F. Bruce (The Teacher of Righteousness in the Qumran Texts, pp. 21-25) who date the birth of the sect around 100 B.C. The theory of C. Roth c.s. who places the origin of the sect around the beginning of the first Christian century (c.f. his The Historical Background of the Dead Sea Scrolls, pp. 24-27, 70 etc.), we find entirely unacceptable.
5. It would have been strange indeed if this single book among the twelve "minor" prophets had been omitted at Qumran. The Twelve existed as a unity according to Ecclesiasticus 49:10(e.g. P. A. Verhoef, Ou Testamentiese Apokriewe, p. 163). cf. A. van Selms, De Rol der Lofprijzingen, p. 168, Albright, op. cit. p. 127 and Cross, Ancient Library, p. 34. It may be pointed out that cave 4Q produced no less than seven (or eight according to Cross, op. cit. p. 34) manuscripts of the minor prophets: Hosea being represented on manuscripts c, d and e, Joel and Amos on c, Jonah on f, Zachariah on e, and Malachi on c (cf. W.S. La Sor, Amazing Dead Sea Scrolls, p. 42). Therefore at least manuscripts c and e contained all twelve of the prophets. (Cf. regarding allusions C. F. Pfeiffer, The Dead Sea Scrolls, p. 101).

Reprinted from *Die Ou Testamentiese Werkgemeenskap in Suid-Afrika*, 1962.

tions depend upon the nature of the documents which contain them.[6] Thus practically all the quotations with an introductory formula occur in the Damascus-texts,[7] whereas such introductions never occur in the Hymn-scroll. Consequently a mere counting of the citations can easily produce a wrong impression.[8]

Now the question should also be considered whether the existence of a commentary on a book implies that it was regarded as canonical. *A priori* it seems quite probable, since only such books would be considered authoritative and sufficiently important to be commented on.[9] To this we may add that the commentaries which have come to light thus far,[10] and as a matter of fact also the paraphrases, have all been on parts of the *Tôrâ* or *Nᵉbî'îm* or the book of Psalms. Thus three or four commentaries on Psalms have been identified *viz.* on Ps. 37, 45, 57(?) and 68.[11] From this fact M. Burrows draws the conclusion that the whole of the present Psalter had "canonical status" at Qumran.[12]

Of the book of *Psalms* parts of eighteen manuscripts have been recovered.[13] This total means that this Biblical book, together with Deuteronomy, is the best represented among the identified fragmentary manuscripts of Qumran. However, it should be recalled that the book of Jeremiah and Psalms are the two largest books in the Bible, and therefore the probability of finding parts of these books among the fragments is statistically larger than in the case of a shorter book. In any case the finds have indicated that the compilation of the canonical Psalms

---

6. Cf. especially Van Selms, op. cit. pp. 168-169.
7. The "Damascus"-texts were mainly found in the Cairo Genizah and are indicated by the symbols CD. The main texts from Qumran are the Sèrèk or Manual of Discipline (1QS with additions 1QSa and 1QSb), the Milchamâ or Military Scrolls (1QM), the Hodayôt or Hymns (1QH), the pesharim or commentaries (e.g. 1QpHab on Habakkuk, and 4QpNah on Nahum) and an anthology, 4Q Florilegium. For the introductory fomulae cf. e.g. C. Rabin, Qumran Studies, pp. 96-97 (also quoted as QS).
8. If e.g. we compare the indices of Biblical quotations in 1QH, 1QS and 1QM as noted in the books in the series Studies on the Texts of the Desert of Judah (edited by J. van der Ploeg) we find that in all three manuscripts about second most of the texts come from the book of Isaiah, but the first and third positions are respectively taken by Psalms and Job in 1QH, by Psalms and Deutreonomy in 1QS and by Ezekiel and Deuteronomy in 1QM. According to Rabin's index (The Zadokite Documents, pp. 78-80 — also quoted as ZD) the three books occurring most in CD are Isaiah, Leviticus and Psalms. Moreover, in all four instances the books of Hosea and Daniel produce a very large number of similarities (to Qumran-texts) in relation to their actual size. This only indicates that the Biblical books mentioned in this note offered more comparative material than other books of the Bible (e.g. Job tor 1QH, Ezekiel for 1QM and Leviticus for CD).
9. F. F. Bruce (Biblical Exegesis in the Qumran Texts, p. 8 — hereafter quoted as Bruce, Exegesis) emphasizes the fact that in these circles a pèshèr is always an interpretation of a raz given by God (cf. op. cit. p. 17, La Sor, op. cit. p. 47, Pfeiffer, op. cit. p. 101 and Burrows, More Light, p. 171). Here the remark of B. J. Roberts (BJRL XXXVI, pp. 86-87) is relevant, where he declares: "What the Covenanters had as their source of inspiration was a traditionally treasured body of literature, which, possibly for centuries, had been regarded as the Word of God — divinely given oracles of salvation, and which were capable of application to times of woe" (our bold type). His remark (p. 77) that prophecy which has been authenticated (by fulfillment) was applied to a new situation, points in the same direction.
10. It is noteworthy that up to now only one copy of each commentary has appeared among the fragments, for in this matter, the book of Psalms need not be regarded as a unity. The conclusion that we therefore possess the autograph of the author (Milik, 10 Years, p. 41, and Cross according to Burrows, More L'ght, pp. 35-36 and 166) is rightly regarded as "rather precarious" by Burrows (loc. cit.). We note that the manuscripts of the commentaries are all relatively young (according to palaeographers, cf. Milik, op. cit. p. 41). However, this does not mean that the principle that the Biblical books are canonical and may therefore be interpreted, is not much older. In fact, various scholars regard this type of exegesis as originating from the Teacher of Righteousness (cf. 1Qp Hab vii 1-5) who is also regarded as the founder of the sect (cf. e.g. Bruce, Exegesis, p. 9 together with his The Teacher of Righteousness in the Qumran Texts, p. 7) contra H. J. Schonfield, Secrets of the Dead Sea Scrolls, p. 92.
11. The commentaries on Psalms 37 and 45 were found in cave 4Q, the one on Ps. 68 and the probable commentary on Ps. 57 in cave 1Q; cf. La Sor, op. cit. p. 47, Pfeiffer, op. cit. p. 101, Bruce, Exegesis, p. 7, M. Burrows, The Dead Sea Scrolls, p. 63 (also quoted as DSS) and his More Light, pp. 35 112, and 166. K. Scubert, Die Gemeinde vom Toten Meer, pp. 12 and 16, J. van der Plieg, Vondsten in de Woestijn van Juda, p. 149 and especially A. S. van der Woude, Bijbelcommentaren en Bijbelse Verhalen, pp. 61-64, and J. T. Milik, Qumran Cace I (Discoveries in the Judaean Desert — DJD — I) p. 81.
12. Cf. Burrows, More Light, p 171.
13. Milik, 10 Years, pp. 23 and 27, mentions "more than ten" and then "a dozen" of Psalm-mss. From 1Q we have three manuscripts (D. Barthelemy, Qumran Cave I, DJD, I pp. 69-72, Burrows, More Light, p. 141), from 2Q two mss, and form 3Q one ms., from 4Q ten mss. and from 5Q one (Burrows, loc. cit.) and from 11Q at least one (Milik, op. cit. pp. 27-28). Milik (loc. cit.) indicates that the sequence of the psalms in the 11Q and some 4Q mss. does not agree with the present arrangement, cf. also Burrows, op. cit. pp. 170-171 where examples of these differences are given, though he points out that the sequence nevertheless mostly agrees with the Massoretic one. In cave 4Q the number of Psalm-manuscripts is only exceeded by the Torah and Isaiah, cf. Albright, op. cit. p. 127, Cross op. cit. p. 34, Fritsch, op, cit. p. 45, Burrows DSS, p. 135.

had been completed in the Maccabaean period, making the presence of Maccabaean Psalms in our canon improbable.[14]

Hardly any definite quotations from the Psalms occur in the Qumran texts, although parts of Psalms 1 and 2 are quoted in 4Q Florilegium.[15] However, especially in the *Hôdāyôt*, numerous quotations and definite allusions to the Psalms occur, though they are not indicated as such.[16] Perhaps the most convincing example in this respect is the quotation of Ps. 31:19 in 1QH vii 11-12, but apart from this there are many more instances where texts from the Psalms are either verbally quoted, or directly determined or definitely influenced the choice of words in the Qumran documents. The following are some examples: Ps. 12:7 in 1QH v 16; Ps. 18:3 in 1QH ix 28-29; Ps. 22:14 possibly in 1QH xv 13; Ps. 41:10 practically verbally in 1QH v 24: Ps. 42:7 virtually quoted in 1QH ii 30; Ps. 33:15 in CD i 10; Ps. 37:23 in 1QH xv 13; Ps. 4:10 practically verbally in 1QH v 24: Ps. 42:7 and 43:5 in 1QH viii 32; Ps. 49:8 in 1QH xv 24; Ps. 51:7 in 1QH iv 29-30; influence of Ps. 57:5 in 1QH v 7 and 10; Ps. 59:4 in 1QH v 17; influence of Ps. 65:4 in 1QH iv 37; Ps. 69:22 in 1QH iv 11; Ps. 88:4-6 in 1QH viii 28-29; Ps. 89:29-30 in CD vii 6 = xix 1 as well as in CD xiv 2; Ps. 105:15 in CD ii 12 (as well as xii 23, xiv 19, xix 10, xx 1); Ps. 106:6 in CD xx 29; Ps. 106:25 in CD iii 7-8; Ps. 107:27 in 1QH iii 15; Ps. 107:29 in 1QH v 18 and a reference to the Septuagintal form of Ps. 145:7 in 1QS xi 14.

The indications thus seem to suffice for us to declare that the book of Psalms most probably had canonical authority at Qumran, especially in view of the surviving commentaries on some Psalms and the fact that the *Hôdāyôt* were demonstrably influenced by the Psalms, but were never intermingled with them.

As far as can be ascertained only one manuscript of the Biblical *Proverbs* has been recovered, namely among the fragments from 4Q. Nevertheless an important indication of the canonical authority of this book may be deduced from the fact that Prov. 15:8 is quoted in CD ix 20-21 (*cf.* 1QS ix 5), preceded by *kî kātûb*, which is virtually the same formula as that which introduces some *Torâ*-quotations.[17] Furthermore there are at least seven distinct references or definite allusions to Proverbs in the Qumran texts. We refer to Prov. 10:8, 10 in 1QH ii 18-19; Prov. 11:13 in 1QH v 25; Prov. 16:1 in 1QH ii 7; Prov. 17:15 in CD i 19; Prov. 18:20 in 1QH i 28; Prov. 25:3 in 1QH iii 20 and Prov. 27:12 in CD xiv 2.

Though we cannot be quite certain, it is highly probable that Proverbs also belonged to the sacred Scriptures of Qumran, especially in view of the introductry formula noted above.

The four manuscripts of *Job* which have been identified, are interesting because one was written in paleo-Hebrew

---

14. **Cf. e.g.** Cross, **op. cit.** p. 122 and Burrows, **More Light,** pp. 169-171.

15. **Cf.** Y. Yadin, "A Midrash on 2 Sam. vii and Ps. i-ii (4Q Florilegium)", **IEJ** IX, Burrows, **More Light,** p. 407 and Milik, **10 Years,** p. 41.

16. The absence of introductory formulae in 1QH is readily explained when we bear in mind that the Hymn-scroll contains poetical, and not legal material (as e.g. CD). **Cf.** also Burrows, **DSS,** p. 322.

17. **Cf.** the quotation of Lev. 23:38 in CD ix 18 and of Deut. 7:9 in CD xix 1-2 (where **kk** may represent k'shr ktwb or ky ktwb).

25

script, while another is virtually a Targum of Job.[18] Both the archaic script[19] and the use of Aramaic translations, are also known in manuscripts of the Pentateuch.[20] There are no quotations from Job, indicated as such, but Job 3:10 probably had direct influence upon 1QH xi 19 (and 1) and Job 31:22 upon 1QH viii 33. Especially in the Hymn-scroll there are many more possible allusions, but the nature of the book Job renders the possibility of numerous quotations slight. Nevertheless there are sufficient indications that the author of 1QH knew the book of Job very well, and also that this book possibly received special treatment at Qumran in matters of script and translation. Though we cannot prove the canonicity of Job at Qumran, it is quite possible that it was thus regarded.

The book *Ruth* is represented at Qumran by fragments of four manuscripts.[21] It is nowhere clearly cited in the Qumran literature, and the most probable cases of allusions are in CD i 7 (Ruth 1:6) and in 1QH ix 31 (Ruth 4:16). On this evidence we cannot be certain that the book of Ruth was regarded as Divine Word at Qumran, though there is no evidence at all to the contrary.

Of *Songs of Songs* remains of three manuscripts from Qumran have been identified.[22] Here too we have no definite quotations, but Song 4:15 possibly had some influence upon CD xix 34 (*cf.* iii 16 and vi 4). Concerning the canonicity of Canticles we therefore hold the same opinion as in the case of Ruth.

Fragments of two manuscripts of *Ecclesiastes* have been found at Qumran, one of which should be dated palaeographically around 150 B.C.[23] Proven quotations from Qohelet do not exist at Qumran, but M. Mansoor compares the expression "the way of Thy heart" in 1QH vi 7 with Eccl. 11:9 and then says: "This is a rare expression in the Bible but not in the *Hodayot*,"[24] justifying the opinion that we may have a derivation here. Eccl. 9:1 (and 2:19) probably had influence upon 1QS ix 22;[25] Eccl. 10:8 possibly upon 1QS iv 9 and Eccl. 11:9 and 12:14 perhaps upon 1QS xi 13-14.[26] Thus the position regarding the canonicity of Ecclesiastes is more or less the same as that of Canticles and Ruth.

The canonical status of *Lamentations* is only slightly more definite than the books just mentioned. Three fragmentary

18. Caves 2Q and 4Q each produced one ordinary manuscript of Job, and from 4Q a manuscript in "Phoenician" script was also recovered (La Sor, op. cit. p. 42, Burrows, More Light, p. 141, Milik, 10 Years, p. 27, cf. Cross, op. cit. p. 33). The Aramaic translation was found in cave 11Q (Burrows, More Light, p. 35 and Milik, 10 Years, pp. 27 and 31). Milik points out that scholars had previously been aware of the fact that the Targum of Job was very ancient. C. C. Torrey (The Apocryphal Literature, p. 142) had indicated that the pseudepigraphic "Testament of Job" which influenced the LXX of Job was "one of the most remarkable productions of the pre-Christian era." It would be interesting to compare this work with the Qumran-"pseudepigrapha," especially since Torrey regarded this Testament as originally written in Aramaic.

19 This was especially the case in some manuscripts of Leviticus and perhaps Numbers, cf. Barthélemey, op. cit .pp. 51-54 where (possibly two) manuscripts of Leviticus (and perhaps one of Numbers) in this script, from 1Q, are mentioned; cf. Burrows, More Light, pp. 136-137 and La Sor, op. cit. p. 41. One Leviticus manuscript in this script was also found in 6Q (La Sor and Burrows, loc. cit.).

20. Apart from Greek translations of some books (e.g. Exodus, Leviticus and Numbers) an Aramaic translation of Leviticus was identified among the fragments from 4Q. It contains a literal translation of Lev. 16:12-15, 18-21 (Milik, 10 Years, p. 31).

21. Two from 2Q and two from 4Q, cf. La Sor, op. cit. p. 43 and Y. Yadin, The Message of the Scrolls, p. 58.

22. Two come from 4Q (Burrows, More Light, p. 145 and La Sor, op. cit. p. 43) and one from 6Q (La Sor, loc. cit.).

23. Cf. La Sor, op. cit. p. 42, Burrows, More Light, pp. 35, 143 and 171, Albright, op. cit. p. 127, Cross, op. cit. p. 121 (dating it in 175-150 B.C.), Milik, 10 Years p. 123, Fritsch, op. cit. p. 45 and Van Selms, op. cit. p. 169.

2;. M. Mansoor, The Thanksgiving Hymns, p. 142. On the other hand Van Selms (op. cit. p. 169) states that Ecclesiastes is not quoted in 1QH.

25. P. Wernberg-Moller, The Manual of Discipline, p. 138 declares: "Some dependence . . . here is clear."

26. It is noteworthy that the word pèshèr which was used so often at Qumran, is a hapax legomenon in the Hebrew part of the Old Testament, appearing only in Ecclesiastes (8:1).

manuscripts containing the book have come to light.[27] Here too, there is no quotation indicated as such in the text, but there is a probable reference to Lam. 1:3 in 1QH v 29,[28] and possibly to Lam. 1:7 in 1QM i 6, to Lam 1:12 in 1QH viii 8, to Lam. 2:18 in 1QH ix 5, and perhaps to Lam. 2:19 in 1QS x 2. Among other texts which have been compared by scholars, the most important seem to be Lam. 2:3 and 17 with 1QM i 5. The information at our disposal does not warrant certainty that Lamentations was considered to be the Word of God at Qumran, but again there is complete silence to the contrary.

Of all the books of the Old Testament *Esther* alone has not been identified in a single fragment from Qumran.[29] Various explanations for this phenomenon have been offered, as e.g. that the book was only written after the founding of the Qumran sect,[30] or that it was rejected by the Qumran sect,[31] or that it was simply left out of their canon.[32] Other scholars regard the absence of Esther as mere chance.[33] At present, this last explanation seems safest and appeals most to us. If we recall that fragments of only three manuscripts of the large books of Kings and only one of the equally large work of Chronicles (and also of the somewhat shorter Proverbs) have been recovered at Qumran,[34] it seems almost self-evident that no recognizable fragment of the much shorter book of Esther has been preserved. Even if we add to this the fact that no clear quotation from, or reference to Esther has been found in the Qumran texts, it still does not prove that the book was not regarded as canonical,[35] since we would then have to remove the book of Haggai from the Qumran canon as well. Moreover, there are some possible references to Esther, of which we can mention 1QS ix 12-13, about which P. Wernberg-Moller states: "Our passage is dependent on Esther i 8, our author having taken $r\\d{s}wn$ absolutely as referring to God's will."[36] Among the other comparable texts it seems most probable that 1QH ii 5 and v 35 imply knowledge of Esther 9:22.

Yet it must be clear that, of all the books of the Hebrew Canon, Esther is the one which most probably was not considered as authoritative at Qumran, and if a strict criterion is applied,[37] then it must be stated that presently there are more indications

---

27. One each from 3Q, 4Q and 5Q, cf. Burrows, **More Light**, p. 154 and La Sor, **op. cit.** p. 43.
28. A. S. Van der Woude (**De Dankspalmen**, p. 91, cf. Mansoor, **op. cit.** p. 139) even speaks of "Quoted (aangehaald)" in this case.
29. Burrows, **More Light**, pp. 141 and 175, Cross, **op. cit.** pp. 31 and 121, Fritsch, **op. cit.** p. 45, Gaster, **op. cit.** p. 341 (where he adds that there is also no quotation from Esther in the Qumran literature), La Sor, **op. cit.** pp. 40 and 243, Milik, **op. cit.** p. 23, Pfeiffer, **op. cit.** pp. 15 and 101, Van der Ploeg, **op. cit.** p. 136 and Van Selms, **op. cit.** p. 169).
30. Thus probably P. Hyatt, "The Dear Sea Discoveries: Retrospect and Challenge," JBL, LXXVI, p. 4 and H. L. Ginsberg, "The Dead Sea Scrolls — Exciting for Jewish Scholarship," **The New Republic,** 9 April 1956, p. 25.
31. Cf. Roth, **op. cit.** p. 34, also mentioned by Burrows (**More Light**, pp. 175 and 271). Roth explains the absence of Esther as indication that the members of the sect were Zealots. The book was then rejected because it acknowledged foreign rule. A somewhat similar opinion was expressed by P. A. Verhoef when this paper was read, though he does not identify the sect with the Zealots. The sect was indeed extremely exclusive and according to the Military Scroll were to fight against all foreigners. Therefore it can be argued that Esther would have been unacceptable to them. (If it were true that the sect practised celibacy and shunned women — but cf. OARQS pp. 173-196 — they could have objected to Esther's attitude; but what then about Ruth?). Burrows (**loc. cit.**) also mentions Del Medico's explanation that Esther does not "soil the hands," and would therefore not be placed in a Geniza. This theory cannot be refuted here, but one of its most obvious weaknesses is the disregard of the pottery evidence which connects the scrolls with the building at Khirbet Qumran.
32. Van Selms, **op. cit.** p. 169, and with some doubt Cross, **op. cit.**, p. 121 and La Sor, **op. cit.** p. 243; also mentioned as a possibility by Hyatt (**loc. cit.**, cf. note 30).
33. This possibility is mentioned by Cross (**op. cit.** pp. 31 and 121), cf. P. Arbez ("The Dead Sea Scrolls — much is still obscure," **The New Republic**, 9 April 1956, p. 15) who also remarked that "the books of the Old Testament had been in their present form for quite a while."
34. Cf. Burrows, **More Light**, p. 141 and La Sor, **op. cit.** pp. 41-42.
35. Cf. Van Selms, **op. cit.**, p. 169.
36. Wernberg-Moller, **op. cit.** p. 136.
37. In the whole of this paper we try to apply the severest test of canonicity, before it is accepted. Therefore we generally do not reach definite conclusions, but have to be satisfied with various degrees of possibilities and probabilities.

that Esther was not regarded as canonical than indications of its canonicity. We should, however, bear in mind that, even if we deny canonical status to Esther, this view obviously does not imply that we decide against the *existence* of the book in this period. This question lies beyond the scope of our present study, but in this matter we can just note that a scholar like W. F. Albright declares that data from Qumran aids us in determining that only Ecclesiastes and Daniel of all the books of the Old Testament were written after about 330 B.C., and F.M. Cross states that probably no canonical book of the Old Testament was written after Maccabaean times.[38]

In the case of the book of *Daniel* the Qumran finds have rather surprised a number of scholars. No less than seven manuscripts of it have been identified among the fragments, one of which was written on papyrus.[39] This means that among the books of about the same size, it is the Old Testament book best represented among the Qumran fragments. On none of the fragments, however, have texts been found that correspond to the additions in the Septuagint of Daniel, thus rendering the possibility that they belonged to the book of Daniel in this period extremely slight.[40] Mention may here be made of the fact that one of these fragments is dated palaeographically before 100 B.C., therefore within about 50-60 years from the date mostly ascribed to the final form of this book.[41] Fragments also revealed the existence of the same changes in language in Dan. 2:7 and 8:1 as in the Massoretic text.

On the basis of the appearance of the Daniel fragments Barthélemy and others came to the conclusion that „certains indices permettraient de penser que Daniel n'etait peut-être pas considéré à Qumrâ comme un livres canonique;"[42] the reason being that the height of most of the manuscripts of canonical books was double the breadth of a column, whereas in the case of the Daniel-fragments the height and breadth were nearly equal. This criterion, however, is not decisive, for then *e.g.* 4Q Testimonia, 1QSa, 1QSb and 1QS i-iii would be canonical but 1QS iv-vi not at all. The script itself does not always give a good indication either, for in cave 4Q Biblical texts *in a cursive hand-writing* have been found.[13] Here it should be noted that Milik said: "At Qumran the Writings *(ktwbym)* are copied with more freedom than is found in other sections of the Bible."[11]

On the other hand there are definite indications that Daniel

---

38. Albright, **op. cit.** p. 129 and his "The Dead Sea Scrolls — Not likely to change beliefs" **The New Republic,** 9 April 1956, p. 12, and Cross, **op. cit.** p. 121, where he states that Esther is an exception **only in theory.** (Albright does not depend merely on data from Qumran, for if this were the case, it would be inconceivable to us that he reaches a date around 330 B.C., and why he excludes Ecclesiastes and Daniel).

39. Cave 1Q contained two manuscripts, 4Q four and 6Q one, cf. Burrows, **More Light,** p. 154, Milik, **10 Years,** p. 28 and La Sor, **op. cit.** p. 42 (who mentions three manuscripts from 4Q). The papyrus manuscript was found in cave 6Q, the same cave that produced the fragmentary papyrus-scroll of the book of Kings (La Sor, **loc. cit.**). The impression that a canonical book in Hebrew was not written on papyrus (D. Bathelemy, DJD, I, p. 150) therefore proved to be wrong, cf. F. M. Cross, "Qumran Cave I," JBL LXXV, p. 123 and Burrows, **More Light,** pp. 175-176.

40. Cf. Barthelemy, DJD, I, p. 151, Burrows, **More Light,** p. 176. Barthelemy points out that the "Song of the Three Men" should have been represented in the fragment from 1Q, if it had belonged to the text, since the point where it is included in the LXX is covered by the fragment.

;1. Cross, **Ancient Library,** p. 33, Burrows, **More Light,** p. 35, Milik, **10 Years,** p. 82 and G. E. Wright according to Fritsch, **op. cit.** p. 82 (cf. also Albright, **Recent Discoveries in Bible Lands,** p. 127).

42. D. Barthélemy, DJD, I. p. 150, cf. F. M. Cross, "Qumran Cave I," JBL, LXXV, p. 123, and for the reasons, cf. Barthélemy, **loc. cit.** and, in general terms, Cross, **Ancient Library,** p. 29, where he says: „Biblical fragments . . . usually . . . have a standard format."

43. Cross (**Ancient Library,** p. 29) says that "Scribal treatment of non-canonical works is rarely as careful or fine," but cf. the exceedingly elegant appearance of 1QM (plates by E. Sukenik, **The Dead Sea Scrolls of the Hebrew University)** and Cross's own remark that "the distinction in script does not always stand up" ("Qumran Cave I," JBL, LXXV, p. 123).

44. Milik, **10 Years,** p. 28.

was held in high esteem at Qumran. Witness to this fact comes not only from the relatively great number of manuscripts that have come to light, but also from the relatively many cases where influence from Daniel can be traced in the Qumran texts.[45] This is especially true of the Military Scroll, according to Van der Ploeg.[46] In addition there may be influence of Daniel on the Qumran Texts in the following cases: the use of the terms *rāz* and *pèšèr;*[47] the possible three times for daily prayer in 1QS x 1-3 may be compared with Dan. 6:11;[48] Dan. 4:9 (12 in translations) may have influenced 1QH viii 8, Dan. 6:23 1QH v 14, Dan. 9:7 1QH xvi 9, Dan. 10:16 1QH iii 7, Dan. 12:2 CD iii 20. The most important fact in this connection, however, is the fact that Daniel is quoted in 4Q Florilegium where, according to Milik, "texts are often quoted with the formula, 'As is written in the book of the prophet Isaiah, Daniel' etc."[49] Here the book of Daniel is practically placed on par with Isaiah; and this is even more significant if we accept the view of D. Flusser that 4QFlorilegium is probably "one of the early documents of the sect."[50]

Taking everything into consideration, and especially the quotation in the Florilegium text, it seems as if Daniel was regarded as an authoritative prophetic book at Qumran.[51]

The books *Ezra-Nehemiah* are represented by only one manuscript in the Qumran discoveries,[52] and are not quoted by name in any of the Qumran texts. There are however a number of fairly distinct references to these books in the Qumran literature of which we mention: reference to Ezra 2:63=Neh. 7:65 possibly in CD vi 10-11; to Ezra 9:14 in CD ii 6-7 and 1QS iv 14; to Ezra 10:2 in 1QH iii 20 and vi 6,[53] and to Neh 9:15 in CD iii 14. On these grounds we cannot be sure of the status of these books at Qumran, but the possibility that they were considered as Divinely inspired books, should not be overlooked, and becomes stronger if we couple these books with Chronicles.

Chronicles, in spite of its size, has been identified on only one fragmentary manuscript, though it is possible that the text called 1Q50 contains I Chron. 29:2.[54] Here, again, quotations indicated as such do not occur, and even allusions are relatively scarce or vague — the most probable reference seems to be to II Chron. 36:16 in CD vii 18. However, there is one decisive reference to Chronicles in the fact that the priestly *mišmārôt* of I Chron. 24:7-18 were mentioned and used in the *"mišmārôt"*-

45. Cf. at note 39 and note 8 above.
46. J. van der Ploeg, Le Rouleau de la Guerre, p. 20. Bruce (Biblical Exegesis, p. 63) refers especially to the influence of Dan. 11:40 ff. on 1QM.
47. Cf. Bruce, Biblical Exegesis, p. 59 (cf. p. 7). On p. 64 he says that Daniel also influenced the "Book of Mysteries" (1Q 27).
48. Cf. Gaster, op. cit., p. 203 (note 4). Van Selms (op. cit. pp. 110-111) sees reference to five set times for prayer in 1QH xii 4-7, but it may be argued that of these only three actually fall during the day, the other two during the night.
49. Milik, 10 Years, p. 41, cf. Burrows, More Light, p. 407.
50. D. Flusser, "Two Notes on the Midrash on 2 Sam, vii," IEJ, IX p. 109.
51. Van Selms (op. cit., p. 170) admits that this could be the case in the later period of Qumran, but then we should note his relatively early date for the beginning of the sect. (In this respect we might mention his references to Daniel in his commentary, pp. 33, 75 (N.B.), 93, 123, 127-128 (N.B.) and 162). Moreover, once the sect had broken with the rest of Judaism, acceptance by the sect of one of the non-sectarian books is hardly possible. When the paper was read, it was pointed out that the ideas of Daniel would have been approved by the Qumrun sect and would have led to its ready acceptance.
52. This is a part of Ezra from 4Q, cf. Burrows, More Light, p. 141 and La Sor, op. cit., p. 42.
53. Cf. Gaster, op. cit. p. 344. The word mqwh occurs with this meaning only twice in the Old Testament viz. in Ezra 10:2 (with ysh) and once in Nehemiah. Van Selms (op. cit. p. 186), however, says that Ezra-Nehemiah is not referred to in 1QH.
54. Cf. Burrows, More Light p. 141, La Sor, op cit., p. 42 and Milik, DJD, I, p. 145.

texts of which three have been discovered at Qumran.[55] This use of Chronicles is even more significant if we bear in mind that the division into twenty-four courses did not suit the solar calendar which was probably followed at Qumran.[56] Hence we may deduce that Chronicles had compelling authority, and must therefore probably be regarded as canonical.

On the whole it therefore appears that the sect of Qumran apparently knew all the writings of the Hebrew Canon, and probably accorded canonical authority to most of them, if not to all.[57] C. F. Pfeiffer indeed remarks that "the Old Testament as we have it, was regarded as sacred Scripture at Qumran."[58]

Whether the sect also accepted as Word of God other books, besides those in the Jewish Canon, depends partly upon the question whether all the manuscripts that were found in the caves associated with Qumran, must be regarded as acceptable to the sect? We consider that, in view of their aversion to everything that was foreign to the sect, this question should be answered in the affirmative;[59] *but,* in saying this, we emphasize that this does not imply that equal worth and sanctity were accorded to all these books, and almost certainly not all the books were regarded as canonical.[60] It therefore seems imperative to attempt to ascertain whether any books besides the present Jewish Holy Scriptures could have been authoritative to the sect.

As far as the *Apocrypha* or "deutero-canonical" books are concerned, it strikes the investigator that manuscripts of only Ecclesiasticus (Ben-Sira) and Tobia (Tobit) have been identified, namely two of the former and four of the latter — three in Aramaic and one in Hebrew.[61] Of the additions to Esther just as little has been found as of Esther itself; and the absence of the additions to Daniel in fragments where they should have appeared if they belonged to the text, has been noted.[62] The evidence in favour of a fragment of the Epistle of Jeremy in Greek from 7Q, is uncertain.[63]

There is no distinct quotation from any of the Apocrypha in

55. **Cf.** Milik, **10 Years,** p. 108 and E. Vogt, "Kalenderfragmente aus Qumran," Biblica, XXXIX, p. 76. These texts are important for the calendar of Qumran, **cf.** also J. van der Ploeg, **Vondsten in de Woestijn van Juda,** p. 160, Allegro, **op. cit.** p. 121, W. Baumgartner, "Neue Funde und Grabunge am Toten Meer," Archiv für Orientforschungen, XVII, p. 215. A. Jaubert, "Le calandrier de Jubilés et les jours liturgiques de la semaine," **VT,** VII, p. 61 and "Travail d'édition des fragments manuscrits de Qumrân," Revue Biblique, LXII, p. 61.

56. **Cf.** Jaubert, **op. cit.** p. 47, Yadin, **op. cit.** p. 140, Gaster, **op. cit.** p. 315, P. Winter, "Two non-allegorical expressions in the Dead Sea Scrolls," **PEQ,** XCI, pp. 43-44 and J. Obermann, "Calendaric Elements in the Dead Sea Scrolls," **JBL,** LXXV, p. 296.

57. Thus, with regard to 1QH, Van Selms (**op. cit.** p. 168) says that all three divisions of the Tenak are quoted and all three divisions were Sacred Scripture to the author, **cf.** Burrows, **DSS,** p. 246 where he adds that the sect "accepted all the books that were finally retained in the Jewish canon."

58. Pfeiffer, **op. cit.** p. 101, **cf.** R. H. Charles, **The Apocrypha and Pseudepigrapha of the Old Testament,** vol. II, p. 790 where he says that the owners of CD "acknowledged the canonicity of the Prophets and Hagiographa."

59. **Cf.** OARQS, p. 11 and Van der Ploeg, **op. cit.,** p. 134. Their books would reflect the opinions of the sect, but were probably not all produced at Qumran, **cf.** AORQS pp. 100 and 905-908, **cf.** Burrows, **DSS,** p. 63.

60. We may compare the relationship between the various confessional creeds and the Bible: all reflect the views of the specific church, but usually only the Bible is absolutely authoritative, **cf.** Pfeiffer, **op. cit.,** p. 100 (from whom we differ, however, as regards the **authority** of all the books represented) and Schubert, **op. cit.,** p. 19 (who also says the sect had no "profane" literature).

61. **Cf.** Burrows, **More Light,** pp. 35 and 177, Van der Ploeg, **op. cit.** p. 136 and Schubert, **op. cit.** p. 10. Milik (**10 Years,** pp. 31 and 139) points out that, of all the "Apocryphal" books a Hebrew (or Aramaic, in the case of Tobit) original is probable only in the cases of Tobit, Ecclesiasticus and I Maccabees. The fragments of Ecclesiasticus came from cave 2Q. **Cf.** AORQS, p. 933, Allegro, **op. cit.** p. 119, Milik, **10 Years,** p. 31, Schubert, **op. cit.,** p. 10, Van der Ploeg, **op. cit.,** p. 136 and Burrows, **More Light,** pp. 35 and 177 (who says these manuscripts are non-canonical in format and script.) In connection with Tobit **cf.** Milik, **10 Years,** p. 31 and AORQS, p. 933, Burrows, **More Light** pp. 35 and 177, (**cf.** his DSS, p. 63), La Sor, **op. cit.** p. 45, Schubert, **op. cit.,** p. 10 (the latter three mention one Aramaic text on papyrus) and Van der Ploeg, **op. cit.,** p. 136.

62. **Cf.** note 40 above. There is therefore no mere **argumentum e silentio** (**cf.** La Sor, **op. cit.,** p. 45).

63. **Cf.** Milik, **10 Years,** pp. 31-32, where he mentions small fragments which "seem" to be from this epistle.

the Qumran texts,[64] and though there may be references to Ecclesiasticus in the texts of Qumran, this is nowhere the case with Tobit. The only other book of the Apocrypha which, according to possible references, could have been used at Qumran, is the book "Wisdom of Solomon,"[65] but here, too, the points of comparison are not conclusive, and the Greek character of the book, renders it improbable that we must think of direct dependence (at least as far as Qumran is concerned) in these cases.

Of all the Apocrypha, as they appear in the Vulgate, it seems that only Ecclesiasticus could, with any degree of probability, have been considered as belonging to the canon at Qumran; and of the rest only Tobit seems to have been known.

If we turn to the large number of *Edifying Books* (among which we include the so-called "Pseudepigrapha"[66]) that have been found at Qumran, some new problems arise. Due to the fragmentary character of many of the manuscripts, the texts are often so broken that it is not quite clear whether we have quotations from or references to other works. In addition, the fragmentary state of the manuscripts, as well as other factors, make it exceedingly difficult to determine their date of composition, and, therefore, even if dependence of one text upon the other could be ascertained, it would often still be impossible to decide which is the original.[67] It may also happen that an idea or principle which was well-known in the circles in which the authors lived, occurs in different works, without indicating direct dependence.[68] It should also be borne in mind that some of these edifying books, as the Testaments of the Twelve Patriarchs and Enoch, as we know them, were probably re-written or re-cast by Christians,[69] so that we cannot always be sure what belonged to the original book.

There are a couple of hundreds of documents represented among the fragments from the Qumran caves; therefore it would be too tremendous a task to try to determine the "canonicity" of each fragment. In the light of what has just been said about the uncertainty of much of the information about these texts, such an attempt is in fact, impossible, even in theory. Therefore only a few of the best-known and larger works will be considered here.[70]

Of the book *Enoch* ("Ethiopic" or "I" Enoch) remains of

64. When B. J. Roberts (**BJRL**, XXXVI, pp. 84-86) frequently refers to "abundant quotations in the scrolls . . . from the present . . . Apocrypha" as distinct from the "Pseudepigrapha," and then decides that some of the books of the Apocrypha were probably included in "their Bible," one can only marvel at the fact that no attempt is made to prove the point, when the evidence is obviously vague or completely lacking.
65. Burrows (**More Light**, p. 35) and La Sor (**op. cit.**, p. 45) mention a Greek copy of this book discovered at Khirbet Mird, but this is entirely unrelated to Qumran. For the relation to Qumran cf. also **AORQS**, p. 194.
66. The term "Pseudepigrapha" is hardly appropriate for all these works — not even for those published by R. H. Charles (**op. cit.**, vol. II) under this name. cf. "Fragments of a Zadokite Work," Jubilees and perhaps the "Letter of Aristeas." These books can also not all be suitably classified as "apocalyptical" or "sectarian" works.
67. We may here refer to the well-known question about the authorship of Isaiah 2:2-4 and Micah 4:1-3.
68. This may be the case **e.g.** with many of the similarities between 1QS and CD. **e.g.** as listed by C. T. Fritsch, **The Qumran Community**, pp. 77-80, Burrows, **DSS**, pp. 188-190, cf. **AORQS** pp. 908-915.
69. Cf. Milik, **10 Years**, pp. 33-35, Cross, **op. cit.**, pp. 118 and 149, Burrows, **More Light**, p. 180, Schubert, **op. cit.**, p. 18 and **AORQS** pp. 100-101, 104-106 and 925-926. Especially in the case of the "Testaments" this opinion is fairly generally acepted, cf. the literature in the notes in **AORQS**, pp. 104-106.
70. Of the "Pseudepigrapha" published by R. H. Charles (**op. cit.**, vol II) fragments of only the Zadokite Work (CD), Enoch, Jubelees and sources of the Testaments of the Twelve Patriarchs have been identifide among the Qumran fragments, cf. Burrows, **More Light**, p. 36. For this reason books like the "Assumptio Mosis," "Psalms of Solomon," "Apocalypse of Abraham," "Apocalypse of Baruch," "Life of Adam and Eve," "Secrets of Enoch" and "Sibylline Oracles" are not discussed in this study on the canon of **Qumran**.

about ten manuscripts have been found at Qumran.[71] There are, also, a number of possible references or allusions to the contents of Enoch in the Qumran texts. Among these the most probable example is CD x 16, which could have been written under the influence of Enoch 72:3. We should also note that the calendar of Enoch is probably the one followed at Qumran[72] and that the book of Enoch — or large parts of it — was possibly written at Qumran.[73] However, it is nowhere indicated that Enoch had canonical authority at Qumran and we have no clear arguments in favour of such a view.

The book *Jubilees* is represented by some ten fragmentary manuscripts, one of which is a papyrus-manuscript.[74] The calendar of Jubilees was also most probably the one used at Qumran.[75] It also seems that Jub. 3:8-14 influenced a text in 4QD,[76] and Jub. 23:11 the text of CD x 8-10. There is a large number of less important references and allusions, but the decisive reference is found in CD xvi 2-4 where we read: "the exact interpretation of their periods — in view of the blindness of Israel at all these things — behold, it is determined in the Book of the Divisions of the Times according to their Jubilees and in their Weeks." This expression apparently refers to the book Jubilees;[77] and it is formulated in such a way that this book is indicated as authoritative.[78] It therefore seems that here we have a canonical or nearly canonical work of Qumran.

The *Testaments of the Twelve Patriarchs* has thus far appeared at Qumran only in the form of an Aramaic Testament of Levi and perhaps a Hebrew Testament of Naphtali.[79] Indications are therefore strong that it did not exist as a unity or even completely at Qumran. Numerous instances where comparison with the Qumran-texts are possible, must therefore be partly ascribed to common sources or a common background and partly to an author of the final "Testaments" who was saturated with Qumran ideas. It is therefore only the Testament of Levi which

---

71. Some ten manuscripts came from 4Q (cf. Millik, 10 Years, p. 33, Burrows, More Light, p. 180, Schubert, op. cit. p. 18), and in 1Q a text has been found which corresponds to Enoch 8:4-9:4 (cf. Milik, DJD, I, pp. 84 and 1952, cf. La Sor, op. cit. p. 46, who mentions eight manuscripts from 4Q). Burrows (More Light, pp. 36 and 407) mentions other sources of Enoch and similar works from 4Q and 6Q.

72. It is impossible to give a discussion of this problem here. We can only refer to J. Morgenstern, "The Calendar of the Book of Jubilees, its Origin and Character," VT, V. pp. 36-37, Jaubert, op. cit., p. 37, E. Vogt, "Antiquum Kalendarium sacerdotale," Biblica, XXXVI, p. 403, Dupont-Sommer, op. cit. p. 111, Fritsch, op. cit., p. 85, Pfeiffer, op. cit. p. 59 and M. Delcor, "Le Midrash d'Habacuc," RB LVIII, p. 537.

73. Of Chapters 37 to 71 (the second part of Enoch), however, no fragments have been identified at Qumran (cf. Millik, 10 Years, p. 33, Burrows, More Light, p. 180 and Schubert, op. cit. p. 18). For a further discussion cf. AORQS, pp. 99-101 and 923-926.

74. Cf. Burrows, More Light, pp. 178-179, Milik, 10 Years, p. 32; there were probably two from 1Q (La Sor, op. cit. p. 46, Milik, DJD, I, p. 83, cf. pp. 82-84 where parts of Jub. 27:19-21; 35:8-10 and 36:11? are mentioned), two from 2Q (La Sor, loc. cit., cf. Yadin, op. cit. p. 58) six from 4Q (Burrows, More Light, p. 408, one of these is on papyrus).

75. Cf. e.g. Jub. 6:22-38; 1QS x 3-8, i 11-15, 15-20, iii 9-11, ix 12-15; 1QH xii 3-11, iv 11-13; 1QpHab xi 2-8; CD vi 8, xvi 3-4; the so-called mishmarôt-texts from 4Q, and various studies, as e.g. those mentioned in note 72.

76. I.e. a "Damascus"-fragment from 4Q, cf. Milik, 10 Years p. 96.

77. Cf. R. H. Charles, op. cit., II, p. 833 (and p. 11 for the title of the book of Jubilees which differs from the reference, but contains similar elements, especially, "weeks (of years) and jubilees"), Burrows, DSS, p. 247, R. de Vaux, "A propos des manuscrits de la Mer Morte," RB, LVII, p. 246, Dupont-Sommer, op. cit., p. 108, Fritsch, op. cit., p. 85, Gaster, op. cit., p. 105, La Sor, op. cit., p. 92, Rabin, ZD, p. 75 (who says "there is no doubt that Jub. is meant") and his Qumran Studies, p. 78, Rowley, The Zadokite Fragments and the Dead Sea Scrolls, p. 28, S. Talmon, "Yom Hakkipurim in the Hab. Scroll," Bibl'ca, XXXII, p. 555, Vermès, op. cit., pp. 52 and 102, AORQS pp. 102-103 and 922-923. (In a note on CD xvi 1 Rabin writes, without any proof or apparent reason: "Quotation from a sectarian book, perhaps Jubilees" — ZD, p. 74).

78. G. Molin, Die Söhne des Lichtes, p. 162, AORQS pp. 945-946, Vogt, "Antiquum Kalendarium sacerdotale," Biblica, XXXVI, p. 404 and especially Schubert, op. cit., p. 20, where he says that Jubilees is perhaps indicated as canonical by this reference, since it also refers to Jub. 6:22-38 where it is stated that the calendar is written on heavenly tablets; cf. Talmon, op. cit., p. 555, where he says that Jubilees is thus equated to the Torah. Here we can leave in the midst the question whether Jubilees was actually written at Qumran, which seems quite possible to the present author, cf. Molin, loc. cit., and AORQS, pp. 919-923.

merits serious consideration as a possible canonical work at Qumran. Indeed, many scholars have found in CD iv 15 a definite allusion to this very Testament of Levi[80] where there is reference to "the three nets of Belial about which Levi, the son of Jacob, said that HE (the LORD) snatches Israel in them."[81] The theory that we have a reference to the Testament of Levi here, is, however, rendered highly improbable by the fact that no such reference to three nets (of Belial) is found in the extant Testament of Levi — the closest to it is the "net" of the "Spirit of Anger" in Testament of Dan 2:4.[82] We may have a reference to a text from another "Levi"-source, but then we are no longer discussing the Testaments of the Twelve Patriarchs, or a part thereof. In view of the uncertainty about the origin of the Testaments and about their existence at Qumran, it is doubtful whether this work was regarded as part of the canon at Qumran.

A book which was certainly highly esteemed at Qumran was the "Book of Meditation" (spr hhgy) which is mentioned in CD x 6, xiii 2 and probably in xiv 7-8, as well as in 1QS i 6, as a book which is important for the authorities of the sect.[83] However, it is completely uncertain whether this name indicates a book otherwise known to us or not. In replying to the question what book is meant, we almost find quot homines tot sententiae. It has been thought that the Torah is meant,[84] or the book of Haggai[85] or the Sèrèk Hayyahad (the "Manual of Discipline")[86] or the Hymns (1QH);[87] whereas others merely indicate the meaning of the name.[88] It does not seem, however, as if any of these suggestions to identify it with extant works are acceptable and agree with what is known about this book. On the other hand it is extremely strange that such an important book has not, as far as can be ascertained, been preserved among the fragments.[89] As a complete guess we may venture the suggestion that the book

---

79. Cf. Milik, 10 Years, p. 34, Schubert, op. cit., p. 18, AORQS, p. 104 and Burrows, More Light, pp. 36, 179-180, and 407-409, where he states that of T. Levi one copy was found in 1Q (cf. Milik, DJD, I pp. 87-91) and three copies in 4Q and that the probable copy of T. Naphtali comes fram 4Q.

80. Thus e.g. Molin, op. cit. p. 162, where he also considers this work as authoritative.

81. A reference to Ezek. 15:5 is clear, some scholars even regard the—text as a corrupt quotation (cf. L. Rost, Die Damaskusschrift, p. 12 and Rabin, ZD, p. 17). In Ezekiel the LORD is the subject, and this would be the most logical interpretation of hw' here (since yhwh was not written at Qumran except in Biblical manuscripts). Then the b in bysr'l may be the bêt of the direct object (cf. Ezek. 14:5) and the b in bhm may denote the instrument (and refer to "nets"), even though the gender differs.

82. Cf. Rabin, ZD, p. 16.

83. Rabin (ZD, pp. 76-77) thinks CD xvi 10 and ix 9 may be quotations from a book of short maxims. "The book of the Hagu (x.6) immediately comes to mind; but that seems to have been **a book for the learned only**" (our bold type), whereas the use of the expressions in CD implies that the expressions were generally known. (We think, however, that the quotation in CD xvi 10 is meant to be from Num. 30:9 in spite of differences).

84. Thus e.g. Yadin, op. cit., p. 125; but why would it be specifically stated that the authorities should be well-versed in this book — is the Torah not significant for everybody in the Sect?

85. R. H. Charles, op. cit., II, p. 825, but cf. the objections by H. N. Richardson, "Some Notes on 1QSa," JBL, LXXVI, p. 120, to which we may add: why would they single out this prophet who is never quoted or even referred to in the extant Qumran texts?

86. Cf. Dupon-Sommer, op. cit., p. 60, Fritsch, op. cit., p. 80, Pfeiffer, op. cit., p. 41, and mentioned by La Sor, op. cit., p. 82. It should be noted, however, that this name appears in 1QSa which formed an appendix to 1QS — therefore if this view is accepted, then the book is mentioned in its own appendix. Moreover, we have argued elsewhere that 1QSa is older than 1QS (cf. AORQS p. 22 etc.) and therefore the former cannot refer to the latter.

87. L. Rost, „Die anhänge der Ordensregel," TLZ, LXXXII, 699, also Bardtke, Molin and W. H. Brownlee, as quoted in AORQS, p. 22. The question is, however: what in the contents of 1QH would be so important to the sectarian authorities?

88. We prefer the suggestion that a book of "Meditation" is meant (cf. Richardson op. cit., p. 120 and Rost's reference to Ps. 9:4, Die Damaskusschrift, p. 19). Schonfield (op. cit., pp. 2-3) mentions the possibility that the title is the "Book of the holy one" (Greek: hagiou) referring to the Teachers of the sect; but Schonfield prefers to regard it as a case where the 'atbash-figure is used, and therefore he thinks it should be read as "Book of Testing" or Refining (srp). Rabin (ZD, p. 50) thinks it should be rendered "Book of Study" and that it contained halakâ.

89. Rowley (Jewish Apocalyptic and the Dead Sea Scrolls, p. 7) says the work has not been preserved, and this he explains by assuming that the book lost its importance. This explanation does not appeal to the present author. Could remains if not perhaps be among the fragmentary texts (cf. the next note, and the many unpublished texts).?

was an anthology of rules and passages from Scripture,[90] and if, indeed, it is not preserved among the fragments, it may be that the sectarians regarded this work as so important, and perhaps so secret, that they decided either to take all possible copies along when they fled,[91] or decided to destroy them to prevent any enemies from reading them. Otherwise we must decide that we face an unsolved puzzle.

Since we do not know the book, we cannot be sure it is quoted. Rabin points out that the phrase which occurs in both CD xii 20 and 1QS ix 12: "these are the ordinances for the teacher to walk in them . . . " is not a Biblical phrase, and therefore he thinks that it is possibly a quotation from the *spr hhgy;*[92] but we could also explain the similarity by regarding it as a coined phrase of the sect, or as a reference to 1QS in CD. At any rate, whichever book is indicated by this name, it certainly had considerable authority at Qumran,[93]

The book *Psalms of Joshua* is apparently quoted in 4Q Testimonia,[94] and a fragment of these psalms has also been identified among the Qumran finds.[95] This could be interpreted to mean that the *Psalms of Joshua* were as authoritative as the *Tôrâ* from which the other quotations in the Testimonia are derived, but it seems preferable to regard the quotation in 4Q Testimonia, introduced by the words "Joshua . . . said," as intending merely a quotation from Jos. 6:26, with the rest of the quotation incidentally added as a sort of *pèšèr*-explanation of the canonical text. This would then imply that Joshua is as important as the *Tôrâ*[96] but would not prove anything concerning the Psalms of Joshua.

It has been maintained that the *Sèrèk* (Manual of Discipline) and the Habakkuk Commentary was possibly used in the liturgy of the sect; but the arguments in favour of this view (*viz.* the marks in the margin of the manuscripts[97]) do not seem convincing at all. Use of the commentaries in the religious gatherings of the group, would not make them canonical, just as the Targumin were never regarded as the equal of the Scriptures they interpret. It should be noted that the *Hymns* (of 1QH etc.), too, could have played some part in the sect's liturgy.[98] If this was the case, then we would still prefer to compare it to a modern book of prayers or hymn-book, and therefore not regard it as necessarily canonical. The works just mentioned are not quoted elsewhere, as far as we know. Indeed, there are similarities and parallels, *e.g.* between 1QS x and 1QH (xii 3-7 etc.) or between 1QS and CD, but nowhere can quotation be proved; more probably we have the use of similar expressions among people closely associated. Moreover, we have indicated that before we can decide on quotation, we have to determine which work is the older one. We may therefore decide that some of the sect's

90. Perhaps it also contained eschatological passages, as the 4Q Florilegium and Testimonia texts. Cf. Vermès, **op. cit.**, p. 176.
91. Signs of a violent end to the sectarian settlement in the Qumran building have been found by the archaeologists, cf. R. de Vaux, "Fouille au Khirbet Qumran — rapport préliminaire sur la deuxième campagne," RB, LXI, pp. 213 and 234, and AORQS, p. 141.
92. Rabin, ZD, p. 63. This would be in agreement with the fact that this book was important to the leaders of the sect.
93. Cf. Burrows, DSS, p. 247 and AORQS, pp. 945-946.
94. Cf. J. M. Allegro, "Further Messianic References in Qumran Literature," JBL, LXXV, pp. 186-187 and Burrows, **More Light**, pp. 408-409. (Or have we here a quotation from the book of Hgy, cf. note 90?).
95. Cf. Milik, **10 Years**, pp. 36 and 125, Burrows, **More Light**, p. 408 and Bruce, **Biblical Exegesis**, p. 44.
96. This would certainly be a more reasonable view, and thus the existence of a "Commentary" on, or apocryphon to Joshua would also become obvious.
97. G. R. Driver, **The Hebrew Scrolls**, p. 13, A. P. Davies, **The Meaning of the Dead Sea Scrolls**, p. 19, cf. Burrows, DSS, p. 99. For objections cf. AORQS pp. 645-646.
98. Cf. AORQS, pp. 647-651, where it is, however, argued that possibly the Hymns were not sung. For the commentaries cf. AORQS pp. 646-647.

own books certainly had considerable influence on the group and its later writings, but the finds prove that these works were sometimes revised, and this renders their absolute authority, or canonity questionable.[99]

If we therefore regard any of the "Edifying Books" as canonical at Qumran, the book of Jubilees is clearly the most probable one, with the "Book HHGY", Enoch and the Testament of Levi as other possibilities.[100]

☆   ☆   ☆

There is one more important question which we have to attempt to answer, and that is whether the sect of Qumran had a well-defined canon at all.[101] It is not so much a question as to whether they had a term to denote their canonical scriptures — apparently no such term existed — for the Jews in the Mishna also do not speak in abstract terms, but only mention manuscripts that "soil the hands."[102] What is important, however, is whether we can determine what books the sectarians of Qumran regarded as authoritative Word of God. And, in the light of our preceding discussion, we can give no definite answer to this important question.

Still, our investigation was not in vain. We found valuable indications on the basis of which we may regard at least some books as canonical or probably canonical at Qumran. If we now proceed to compare these with the books included in the Jewish canon and with the Alexandrian "canon" as we find it in the Septuagint manuscripts and in the Vulgate, we can more or less determine the greatest common factor, which would then give us an indication of which books were considered normative (*i.e.* were included in the accepted "canon") at the time when the sect and the rest of the Jews parted company around 130 B.C., or earlier.[103]

To this common corpus undoubtedly belonged the *Tôrâ* and the *N^ebî'îm* of the Hebrew canon, as well as Psalms, Proverbs, Daniel and Chronicles, most probably also Job and Ezra-Nehemiah. Somewhat more uncertainty prevails about the five *m^egillôt*:

99. **Cf.** Burrows, **More Light,** p. 178 and Schubert, **op. cit.,** p. 19.
100. A number of scholars are of opinion that the Qumran sect acknowledged a more extensive canon than the rest of Judaism, e.g. Schubert, **op. cit.,** p. 19 La Sor, **op cit.** p. 92 (where he says that this would be the case if we use criteria: quotation and existence of a Hebrew text of the book) and p. 242 (where he expresses some doubt). M. Burrows (**DSS** pp. 246-247) feels uncertain about the matter, but says that the sect had a rather broad conception of Scripture (**DSS** p. 341). B. J. Roberts(**BJRL,** XXXVI pp. 85-86) is emphatic in stating that the Qumran sect recognized and used much of the "apocryphal" literature, the canonicity of which was never even discussed in Rabbinic circles. He even thinks it "possible that it was on this issue of accepting an apocalyptic interpretation to the scriptures, rather than a legalistic one, that tension between orthodox Judaism and Sectarians became acute; and the latter were expelled from the Synagogues" (p. 86). With the last part of this quotation, however, we do not agree, since we regard calendar disputes and the legitimacy of the priests as more direct causes of the origin of the sect (cf. **Studies on the Book of Ezekiel,** pp. 4-5 and 7-9).
101. **Cf.** K. Elliger, **Studien zum Habakuk-Kommentar vom Toten Meer,** p. 155 who thinks the Qumran Sect had a definite canon of Scripture, contra E. Osswald, „Zur Hermeneutik des Habakuk-Kommentars," **ZAW,** LXVIII p. 256 (but **cf.** note 59 and 60 above). La Sor (**op. cit.,** pp. 46-47) says we cannot be sure, but there are indications that the sect distinguished between "canonical" and "noncanonical." On the other hand R.B.Y. Scott maintains that "the limits of the 'canon' of authoritative scripture had not yet been settled" ("Christianity not born in a vacuum," **The New Republic,** 9 April 1956, p. 23. He is speaking of Judaism in general, but includes the Qumran sect. According to Pfeiffer (**op. cit.,** p. 100) and Schubert (**op. cit.** p. 19) no definite answer about the canon of Qumran is possible.
102. **Cf.** Burrows, **DSS,** pp. 247 and 341. B. J. Roberts (**BJRL,** XXXVI p. 86) thinks the Qumran sectarians did not even "spend their energies in arguments about whether or not that book 'defiled the hands' " and that they did not pay much attention to the question of canonicity. It may indeed be that they were not interested in a dogma about these matters, but the question had important practical imp'ications, e.g. as to which books should be commented upon, or should be used in different situations and disputes, or what procedure should be used in copying the texts (cf. Mishnah Yadaim 4:2-5 etc.). F. M. Cross (**op. cit.** p. 29) partly confirms this view by pointing out that scribal treatment of the manuscripts of the canonical books generally differs from others (cf. notes 42-44 above). Thus the extent of the canon indeed had practical implications to which the Qumran sectarians could not be indifferent.
103. **Contra** La Sor, **op. cit.,** p. 242. After the sect left Judaism they would not have accepted other literature, cf. note 4 above and G. Molin, **Die Söhne des Lichtes,** p. 162 where he emphasizes that the sect would not have accepted as authoritative a contemporary book from outside their group.

Ruth, Song of Songs, Ecclesiastes, Lamentations and Esther;[104] while Ecclesiasticus almost gains a place too. Apart from these there does not seem to be a book which is common to even *two of the three* "canons." And even if we were to add the New Testament, the picture hardly changes.[105]

Thus, on the basis of the information that is at our disposal, we may come to the conclusion[106] that, *not later than about 130* B.C. the "Law" and the "Prophets" (in the Hebrew sense of the word) and most of the "Writings" (Hagiographa) were accepted and *regarded as canonical* books, with *possibly* some doubt about Ecclesiastes, Canticles, Esther and Ecclesiasticus.

104. La Sor (**op. cit.**, p. 66) states that the Qumran sect was "devoted to the same Old Testament as we use today" and (on pp. 91-92) affirms that they "possessed" and "used" and "drew their theology" from what is the present Old Testament. If we were to apply the criteria he mentions on p. 242 to the book of Esther, however, we must decide that it was not canonical at Qumran.
105. If the quotations and possible references in the New Testament, as well as the transmission of manuscripts in the ancient Church were to be regarded as a fourth "canon," then we can compare the following four "canons": Jewish (i.e. **Tenak: Tôrâ, Nebi'im, Ketûbim),** Alexandrian (i.e. the present Roman Catholic canon), Qumran (as indicated in the above study) and the "enlarged canon" of the early Church, as just indicated. In this last mentioned group we leave out books like Ecclesiasticus and Tobit because they belonged to the LXX and were for that reason accepted by the early Church; moreover they are not quoted in the New Testament. The following could thus be regarded as common to the "enlarged canon" of the Church and the Qumran "canon": **Tenak** and the books Enoch, Jubilees and parts of the Testaments of the Twelve Patriarchs, although the latter two books are not quoted or referred to in the New Testament. Now it becomes apparent how vastly the body of literature **used** at Qumran differed from that used in the early Church. Apart from the Old Testament, **only three** of the hundreds of books that have appeared from the Qumran caves, were demonstrably known to the early Church, and of the whole New Testament **not a single fragment** has been found at Qumran, yea, not even a "source" or any part of the Gospels etc. This is remarkable if we bear in mind that not only the entire Pauline corpus, but some other N.T. books as well, not to mention the sources of the Gospels, obviously existed before the destruction of the Qumran settlement in about A.D. 70!
106. **If we use** the four "canons" mentioned in the previous note the position can be summarized thus:
    (i) **Books** common to all four "canons": probably **Tenak.**
    (ii) Book common to three of the "canons": **Tenak** (only).
    (iii) Books common to two of the "canons": **Tenak** plus probably Ecclesiasticus and Enoch, and possibly (though with much uncertainty) Tobit, Jubilees and a source of the Testaments of the Twelve Patriarchs.
From this summary the firm canonical position of the Old Testament, as accepted by Jews and Protestants, is clear.

Cave 11 Surprises

and

the Question of Canon *

J. A. SANDERS

I

THE last Qumran cave, the one designated Cave 11, has turned out to be a bonanza of surprises. Material from it first came into Jerusalem through the bedouin of the area in February of 1956. As the various pieces became identified and studied it became clear that new possibilities in Bible study, and in study of the Qumran sect, were opening up. For a variety of reasons, financial and otherwise, detailed scientific work did not begin on the Cave 11 materials until the fall of 1961. The preliminary reports published the following year, on the Psalms and on Job, provoked considerable interest and many questions.[1] Since 1962 a scroll of Ezekiel, three scroll texts of Psalms and a florilegium on the figure of Melchizedek have been published.[2] Only the Job and Ezekiel pieces have so far failed to generate some excitement: the Ezekiel because what little is legible from the ossified knot of leather on which it was written seems identical to the received text, and the targum of Job because it

---

*Abbreviations used in the notes include: *BA, The Biblical Archaeologist; BASOR, Bulletin of the American Schools of Oriental Research; CBQ, Catholic Biblical Quarterly; DJD, Discoveries in the Judaean Desert; HTR, Harvard Theological Review; JTS, Journal of Theological Studies, NTS, New Testament Studies; OS, Oudtestamentische Studiën; RB, Revue Biblique; RQ, Revue de Qumrân; VT, Vetus Testamentum.*

1. J. Van der Ploeg *Le Targum de Job de la grotte 11 de Qumrân* (1962); A. S. van der Woude, "Das Hiobtargum aus Qumran "Höhle XI," *VT* suppl ix (1963), pp. 322-32. J. A. Sanders, "The Scroll of Psalms (11QPss) from Cave 11: A Preliminary Report," *BASOR*, No. 165 (1962), pp. 11-15.
2. W. H. Brownlee, "The Scroll of Ezekiel from the Eleventh Qumran Cave," *RQ*, No. 13 (1963), pp. 11-28. J. A. Sanders, *The Psalms Scroll of Qumran Cave 11; DJD*, IV (1965); Sanders, *The Dead Sea Psalms Scroll* (1967). J. van der Ploeg, "Le Psaume XCI dans une recension de Qumrân," *RB*, lxxii (1965), pp. 219-17; van der Ploeg, "Fragments d'un manuscrit de psaumes de Qumrân (11QPs^b)," *RB*, lxxiv (1967), pp. 408-12. A. S. van der Woude, "Melchisedek als himmlische Erlösergestalt in den neugefundenen eschatologischen Midraschim aus Qumran Höhle XI," *OS*, xiv (1965), pp. 354-73.

Reprinted from *McCormick Quarterly* 21 (1968).

turns out to be a simple Aramaic translation rather than a full targum.[3]

The importance of the text dealing with Melchizedek, on the other hand, can hardly be exaggerated, for it reaches beyond the linguistics of New Testament study into its Christological thought forms. The preserved fragment is a midrash on a cluster of ten Old Testament passages centering in the jubilee-year text in Leviticus 25; but it also quotes, or alludes to, and interprets verses from Psalms 8 and 72 as well as Isaiah 52, 61 and Deuteronomy 15. It is a rich storehouse of material, along with similar texts from Cave 4, showing how some Palestinian Jews contemporized Old Testament texts. But its importance for Christianity, especially for understanding the Epistle to the Hebrews, is as yet beyond reckoning. Melchizedek is presented as a heavenly Redemption figure who will execute divine judgment and salvation in the drama to take place in the anticipated eschatological Jubilee year. He is presented as a member of the heavenly council of the holy ones of God and even exalted above them, fulfilling, in the judgment and salvation drama, the role later associated with the archangel Michael. In the same text the bearer of good tidings (Isaiah 52) appears to be identified with one anointed (a Messiah) by the Spirit (Isaiah 42 and 61). This same cluster of scriptural figures is, of course, related in the New Testament to Christ, but we have now in this very important Cave 11 fragment the evidence of their first being interwoven in this manner. The heavenly Son of God of Hebrews 7, who rules above all heavenly and earthly powers, and lives for ever to make intercession for those who put their trust in him, has his counterpart now in the heavenly Melchizedek at Qumran.[4]

There are still two manuscripts brought in from Cave 11 in 1956 which have not yet been worked on: a fragmentary copy of the Apocalypse of the New Jerusalem also known from Caves 1, 2, and 4; and fragments of the book of Leviticus written in the archaic Hebrew script. Professor David Noel Freedman, dean at the San

---

3. If the Job piece is the same as that interdicted by Rabban Gamaliel in the first century, as the Dutch scholars both think, it is something of a disappointment rather than an excitement. Its importance, however, along with the Genesis Apocryphon of Cave 1, as a primary source for study of the Palestinian Aramaic Jesus might have spoken, cannot be gainsaid; see now the excellent edition of the latter by J. A. Fitzmyer, *The Genesis Apocryphon of Qumran Cave 1* (1966), and especially pp. 17-25 and 171-206 on first-century Palestinian Aramaic.

4. M. de Jonge and A. S. van der Woude, "11Q Melchizedek and the New Testament," *NTS,* xii (1966), pp. 301-26, esp. pp. 322-23.

Francisco Theological Seminary, a Presbyterian scholar known to many readers of the *McCormick Quarterly,* is scheduled to begin work on the Leviticus materials as soon as the aftermath of the recent Six-Day War will permit.

But it was the war itself which brought further Cave 11 surprises. Professor Yigael Yadin, of the Hebrew University in Jerusalem, Israel, had somehow learned in the early nineteen-sixties about a cache of scrolls which were still in the hands of an antiquities dealer in Jordanian Palestine. While we are not absolutely certain, it is very highly probable that they were also part of the Cave 11 library. One of the scrolls turns out to be the largest yet found at Qumran, which Professor Yadin has entitled "The Temple Scroll." He reports that he acquired it in June "one day after the battle of Jerusalem was over." It contains some sixty-six columns covering four main subject matters: *halakot,* or religious rules of various types, especially ritual cleanliness; detailed listings of the proper sacrifices and offerings to have been made on the various festivals, following the Qumran-type calendar; detailed description of the temple which should have been in Jerusalem in place of the controversial Herod's Temple; and a final section on the mobilization plans to be followed "by the king" when the land of Israel was threatened. Apparently the scroll is quite different from the New Jerusalem texts and the Scroll of War between the Sons of Light and Sons of Darkness, of Caves 1 and 4, in that those are highly eschatological in tone whereas the Temple Scroll is written in this-worldly language. The excitement which Professor Yadin's acquisition has engendered about further scroll materials from Cave 11 coming to light, is already surpassed by the interest aroused by his preliminary report on the contents of the Temple Scroll.[5] Yadin promises a detailed preliminary publication on the scroll in the not too distant future. Whether that means a fuller preliminary report, a diplomatic edition of the text, or a full *editio princeps* is not clear. What is clear is the extent to which our appetites are whetted in anticipation.

II

But the greatest surprise provided by the amazing Cave 11 is in its Psalter materials. Three manuscripts of Cave 11 Psalms have been published to date, and they all three exhibit very interesting variations in the order and content of the psalms they include.[6] Two of the

5. Yigael Yadin, "The Temple Scroll," *BA,* xxx (1967), pp. 135-39. The announcement first appeared in the N. Y. *Times* 23 Oct. 67.
6. See above note 2 for bibliographic details: 11QPs^a (the large Psalms Scroll) Sanders; 11QPs^b (its identical mate but only parts of three columns preserved) J. van der Ploeg, in *RB* lxxiv; and 11QPsAp^a (or possibly 11QPs^e) J. van der Ploeg in *RB* lxxii.

manuscripts are copies of the same recension or edition of psalms; of the third so little has to date been published that it is difficult to judge whether it reflects the same edition, or collection, or not. The large Psalms Scroll from Cave 11 (11QPs^a) has been published in two editions, in 1965 and early in 1967; the other copy of the same recension (11QPs^b) has only just recently appeared in print. The fact that 11QPs^b where it is extant, duplicates 11QPs^a in both order and content of psalms is highly significant; it proves at the very least that the recension of psalms to which they witness was not a private or maverick collection. 11QPs^b includes psalms found in columns 16, 18, 19 and 23, of 11QPs^a. Column 23 of the larger scroll contains Pss 141, 133 and 144 in that order, and that is precisely the order of the same psalms on a single column in 11QPs^b. Just as interesting is the fact that in the very words of the psalms where 11QPs^a differs from the received Masoretic Text, 11QPs^b agrees with its Cave 11 companion. In fact, there is good reason to think that the 11Q texts were identical even where 11QPs^b has lacunae, except in the minor and obvious scribal errors.[7] Column 19 of the larger scroll contains a non-Masoretic and heretofore unknown psalm to which we have given the title, "Plea for Deliverance." 11QPs^b includes the same psalm in a more fragmentary form, except that it provides us now with a line at the top, which in the larger scroll was in the lost lower third of the previous column 18.[8] The two copies of the psalm are identical (even to the point of almost having the same line divisions on the leather) with the exception of two very minor and very similar orthographic variants.

Finally, column 16 of the larger scroll contains what is possibly a new non-Masoretic psalm composed of floating bits of liturgical material familiar from Psalms 118, 136 and elsewhere. In this regard it rather approximates the psalm in I Chronicles 16:8-36 which is itself a pastiche of Psalms 105:1-15; 96:1-13; 106:1 and 47-48. Its close relation in the scroll to Ps 136 reminds one of the very short Ps 117 which many scholars have suggested should be seen either as a coda to Ps 116 or an incipit to Ps 118; and it should be remembered that Ps 117 is itself reminiscent of Ps 67:4 and 103:11. Professor Peter

---

7. Careful measurements across fragments *d* and *e* of 11QPs^b (Plate XVIII) indicate, *pace* van der Ploeg, that *hayyim* was lacking in Ps 133:3b there as well as in 11QPs^a. (Note that it has long been questioned by scholarship because of scansion.) By contrast, 11QPs^b does not duplicate the obvious scribal goof of 11QPs^a in the following line (*ha-melammed* of 144:1). Finally, again *pace* van der Ploeg, I am not at all sure that MT *ledawyd* can be presumed in the immediately preceding lacuna where 11QPs^a lacks it.

8. *'ebyon/'any wedal 'anoky ky* . . . "Humble and poor am I, for . . ."

Ackroyd has made a very worthy translation of the little poem:

> Praise Yahweh for he is good,
>> his mercy is for ever.
>
> The sound of a shout of salvation
>> is in ˙the tents of the righteous.
>
> The right hand of Yahweh acts valiantly
>> the right hand of Yahweh is exalted
>>> the right hand of Yahweh acts in power.
>
> It is better to trust in Yahweh
>> than to trust in men.
>
> It is better to confide in Yahweh
>> than to trust in noble men.
>
> It is better to trust in Yahweh
>> than to trust in a whole army.
>
> Praise Yahweh for he is good,
>> his mercy is for ever.
>>> Hallelujah.[9]

This same new psalm also appears in 11QPs[b]. What is preserved of it in the smaller scroll is verbatim what appears in 11QPs[a] The sum of it is that our surprising Cave 11 contained two copies of the one really imposing witness to the Hebrew Psalter in pre-Masoretic times.[10]

The titular designation "Psalm of David" familiar from the 73 psalms where it appears in the Masoretic Psalter provides interesting

---

9. P. R. Ackroyd, "Notes and Studies," *JTS*, xvii (1966), pp. 396-99.
10. It should be very carefully noted, *pace* Yadin, *op. cit.*, p. 136, and S. Talmon, *Tarbiz*, xxxvii (1967), p. 100, that the tetragrammaton whether in archaic or block script is indeterminate for judging if a scroll was considered "canonical" at Qumran. Where 11QPs[a] always has it archaic, 11QPs[b] (identical otherwise) has it block (frag. *d*), 11QPsAp[a] (?11QPs[e]) apparently has it block, according to van der Ploeg, top p. 211; and 4QPs[f] has it block (columns vii 5, ix 5, ix 14, x 13) precisely in the non-Masoretic psalms. In point of fact, I am not actually disagreeing with Yadin's conclusion (see below n. 25); I would, however, disagree with Talmon's conclusion that the divine name in archaic script always indicated that the manuscript was considered somehow non-canonical at Qumran.

The simple fact of the matter is that we can no longer read our post-A.D. 70 concepts back into the earlier period at all points. *Contra* the conclusions of M. H. Goshen-Gottstein in *Textus*, v (1966), pp. 22-23, and S. Talmon in *Tarbiz*, xxxvii (1967), pp. 99-104, in this regard, see the more cautious remarks by P. R. Ackroyd, *op. cit.*, B. J. Roberts in *JTS*, xviii (1967), pp. 183-85, van der Ploeg in *RB*, lxxii (1965), pp. 216-17, and Sanders, *Dead Sea Psalms Scroll* (1967), pp. 156-58.

observations in the Qumran Psalter. It appears at the head of a non-Masoretic psalm in 11QPsAp[a], and a variant of it also appears in the first line of Psalm 151 in the large Psalms Scroll. Also in the larger scroll Psalms 104 and 123 begin "Psalm of David," whereas the Masoretic Psalter does not have the title for either. Conversely, the designation is lacking in the Psalms Scroll (11QPs[a]) for Ps 144; there is a lacuna at that point in 11QPs[b] and no secure way of knowing if it originally had the Davidic ascription, but the two scrolls are so identical in most other respects that it is best not to assume it simply because the received Masoretic Psalter has it. Similarly, the interjection, "Hallelujah," is omitted from the superscriptions in Pss 135, 148 and 150 where MT has it, but appears in Ps 93:1 where it does not. It appears, therefore, either that there was fluidity in the first century even in the Davidic ascriptions or that the Qumran Psalter represents, in complex ways, another text tradition or stage of Psalter canonization earlier than any we had heretofore. For, on the face of it, if there had already been a closed canon of Psalms since the fourth century, or since late Persian times, in which such matters were already invariable, even a "liturgical collection" of canonical and non-canonical psalms would surely reflect the accepted canon where it existed.[11] Composers of the pesharim and midrashim of the age did, apparently, "contemporize" biblical texts, and thus mold them to their convictions; but these Qumran Psalters are simply not sectarian in that sense, nor are they "sectarian" in any sense in which we have yet used that word in Qumran studies. To suggest that they are sectarian liturgical collections, forerunners of Jewish and Christian prayerbooks, far from being a simple, conservative, self-authenticating solution to the problem of Qumran psalmody, is a bold, venturous hypothesis fraught with as many difficulties as any other yet suggested.

The highly liturgical type materials in the Psalms Scroll which appear as addenda to known Masoretic psalms seem at first blush to lend themselves to the proto-prayerbook suggestion. The new psalm at the top of column 16, made up of many liturgical phrases from a number of sources, especially those familiar from Ps 118, has already been cited. Ps 135 has two apparent insertions, in verses 2 and 6, which commend themselves as cultic anacolutha. In italics

---

11. The suggestions that 11QPs[a] is to a "proper" Psalter what 1QapGen is to Genesis, and a pesher text to canonical texts, are comforting but misleading analogies. The matter is much more complex as we shall attempt to indicate. The suggestion that it is evidence of another "first," that is, a forerunner of later Jewish and Christian prayer books is so attractive in certain ways as to deserve careful criticism (Goshen-Gottstein, *op. cit.*).

in the following are the words peculiar to 11Q:

> What the Lord pleases he does in heaven,
>   and on earth *to do, he does;*
>   *there is none like the Lord,*
>   *there is none like the Lord,*
>   *and there is none who does as the King of gods,*
> in the seas and *in* all deeps (11Q Ps 135:6).

That is, of course, liturgical material very similar to what one finds in later Jewish prayers and songs. But it is also like what one finds in I Samuel 2:2, which is not better syntactically related to the rest of the Song of Hannah than the above italicized material to MT Ps 135:6.

> There is none holy like the Lord,
>   indeed there is none beside thee,
>   and there is no rock like our God (I Sam. 2:2).

There is a similar spate of material in 11Q Psalm 146 between verses 9 and 10 which is so poorly preserved that it is untranslatable but which reflects the same biblical-liturgical type literature. Other such bits and pieces should undoubtedly also be viewed in the same manner.[12]

The most interesting, perhaps, and the most obviously liturgical aspect of the scroll is in the refrain and the subscription to Ps 145. The subscription is very frustrating because in it we have, for the first time, a suggestion as to ancient categories of psalm types: in it Ps 145 is called a *zikkaron*, a "memorial psalm," but that is as far as the text goes at the bottom of the column of decomposed leather. We can imagine all sorts of possibilities, especially since the word *zikkaron* is so central to our current understanding of the theology of ancient Israel and her cultic life at all stages. But the refrain presents no difficulties in reading: after each verse of the psalm, as after each verse of Ps 145, a constant refrain recurs through all the verses, "Blessed be the Lord and blessed be his name for ever and ever." If one assumes an invariable canon of Psalms from the Persian period, then he is inclined to view this refrain as an addition to the Masoretic psalm, whereas the refrain to Ps 136 he is inclined to view as more ancient.[13] However, the problem is considerably more complicated, for verse 21 of the Masoretic recension of Ps 145 contains a clear historic memory of the refrain which the Qumran Psalter lacks precisely because it has the refrain. One wonders if the refrain now available for Ps 145 is not just as ancient as that all

---

12. Sanders, *Dead Sea Psalms Scroll*, pp. 15-21, 158-59.
13. J. van der Ploeg reports that 11QPsAp[a] has Ps 118 also with a constant refrain.

along available for Ps 136, relative only perhaps to the date of composition of the two psalms. Why, then, if the Masoretic Psalter has
a refrain to Ps 136, does it not have the refrain to Ps 145? At first
blush, one feels comforted to say that somebody at Qumran simply
added the Ps 145 refrain to an already set Psalter. And yet the
cautious student knows that he must leave wide open the possibility
that it was the Masoretic, or proto-Masoretic, tradition which omitted
the Ps 145 refrain because the refrain would have been retained in
liturgical memory and signaled otherwise in the psalm.[14] So far, only
Ps 136, of all Hebrew psalmody, has even the suggestion of a refrain
after each hemistich or colon rather than after a full bicolon. To
transmit Ps 136 without its refrain could have created a gross mis-
reading: the refrain in Ps 136 is integral to the scansion of the psalm
in a way not the case with Ps 145, or with any other psalm for which
we might posit an ancient refrain.

The greatest "addendum" of all in 11QPs[a] is in column 27, the
prose composition which says that David composed "through prophecy" 4,050 psalms and songs. The paragraph indicates the liturgical
usage of the songs (shir) which David composed, and follows the
calendar in use at Qumran and elsewhere in the late Second Temple
period. It might be comforting to suppose that all the non-Masoretic
materials in the Qumran Psalter could be relegated to the category
of "song" and thus dismiss the problem which it presents. No supposition could be more unscientific: there are songs so designated
in the Masoretic Psalter (cf. Pss 18, 92, 120-134, etc.). And 11QPs[a]
includes forty Masoretic psalms all from Books IV and V, or the last
third of Psalter.[15] To point out that later prayer books include forty

---

14. Precisely in the overloaded MT Ps 145:21. Note the presence of the enig-
matic Selah, after Ps 91:4 in 11QPsAp[a], lacking in MT 91:4.

15. As is carefully noted by Goshen-Gottstein, op. cit., p. 32, n. 42. A propos
Professor Goshen-Gottstein's further (less careful) remark on the same
page, n. 43, that the term Psalms Scroll itself uncritically influenced early
judgments, it should be noted that our first designation was "Scroll of
Psalms" and the first siglum assigned was 11QPss, as attested in BASOR,
No. 165 (1962), p. 11. Interesting in this regard is a conversation I had
in May 1963, with Professor Brownlee in Claremont. He asked, after a lecture
I gave on the non-Masoretic psalms, why I used the confusing siglum
11QPss, why not 11QPs[a]. I told him that the decision had since been made,
in conjunction with the Dutch, to use 11QPs[a]. I had decided that the
presence of 36 (now 40) Masoretic psalms in the scroll could not be
ignored, and that since the style of the non-Masoretic psalms was "biblical"
and not sectarian (cp. Hodayot), I had a complex problem on hand not
easily solved. The manuscript for DJD IV had already been mailed, and I
was content to have time to give the problem thought and to hear reactions.
My thinking at that time appeared later in tentative form in HTR, lix (1966),
pp. 83-94, after trying to collect the necessary data about all pre-Masoretic

psalms to be recited at a single service is less than illuminating, for no prayer book service would exclude all psalms from the first two-thirds of the Psalter. What is more than abundantly clear is that all Psalters are liturgical collections, Masoretic and non-Masoretic; that is not the point. The real question is whether the Qumran Psalter as we now have it is a variant form of that liturgical collection which came to be called Masoretic or is it an aberration from it, perhaps the earliest Jewish prayer book. Does it reflect on its past or anticipate its future?

III

The clue may lie just as much in how stable the first two-thirds of the Qumran Psalter appear to us, as in how unstable the last third (or slightly more) appears. The only really significant non-Masoretic features in the first half or so of the Qumran Psalter appear in two manuscripts from Cave 4, 4QPs[a] and Ps[q]. Both of them appear to omit Ps 32, and so far there is no explanation for the omissions. 4QPs[a] places Ps 71 after Ps 38, but this has been explained quite well by Monsignor Patrick W. Skehan as simply exhibiting the similarity which exists between Psalms 38 and 70; that particular scribe, on finishing copying Ps 38, would have erred in thinking he had just copied Ps 70 and thus went on to Ps 71, then later reverted to the received order. All the other variations in order of psalms at Qumran, even in Cave 11, appear in the last third of the Psalter, and all the non-Masoretic psalms in the Qumran Psalter show up in the same last third.

So far this observation is only a clue, but, as difficult as reviewing the "assured results" of scholarship may be, it of necessity requires that we think in ways we had not heretofore thought about the stages of stabilization of the Psalter.[16] The fluidity in the Qum-

---

psalms in *CBQ*, xxvii (1965), pp. 114-23 (now outdated). After all, the siglum includes always the preface 11Q; to have used 11QapPs, or some such designation would have prejudiced from the start the necessary discussions concerning canon. Even now, one must say, regret should be expressed rather against hastily conceived hypotheses than against patience. Concerning the column 27 prose section, see the tentative suggestions by W. H. Brownlee in *RQ*, No. 20 (1966), pp. 569-74.

16. Reviewing the various attempts to date the MT collection of 150 in Begrich, Schmidt, etc., one is struck by how uncertain the "assured results" are. The observation that I Maccabees 7:17 appears to quote a phrase from Ps 79:2-3 is simply no longer impressive in discussions of the date of the MT-150 collection, nor the mention in the prologue of Ben Sira of "the other books." B. J. Roberts has the right of it when he says. ". . . The departure from (MT) in the order of Pss., the presence of apocryphal Psalms and of pure Qumrân compositions in the same scroll needs to be explained, and the old question of canonicity to be reopened" (*op. cit.*, p. 185).

ran Psalter, aside from the two cases just noted, is in the last two Psalter books, IV and V, Pss 90 and following.[17] It has often been pointed out that it is this section of the MT Psalter which contains most of the highly liturgical psalms, whereas the early part of the Psalter contains mostly prayers for individuals. And this, too, may be a clue to the solutions we seek. We have for so long constructed theories about the canonization or stabilization of the Psalter on the idea of smaller collections being drawn together that we are reluctant to consider any of the smaller collections as fluid beyond a certain date. Books I to III contain three large collections, the 'psalms of David' (Pss 3-41), the 'Elohim' collection (42-83) and the so-called 'guilds' collection (84-89). But in the first group Pss 10 and 33 do not bear the name David; in the second the divine name Yahweh appears forty-three times; and even in the tiny 'guilds' grouping a "Psalm of David" appears (Ps 84). Over against a hypothetical Psalter of rigidly conceived groupings these Masoretic "aberrations" would have the same psychological effect on us that the Qumran Psalter has had.

We like to think that Books IV and V are composed of four smaller collections: "Pss 90-104, in which the individual psalms have no special features, but which is distinguished by the fact that the majority of the songs of 'Accession to the throne' are gathered together here. This collection is concluded with Pss 105-107." Pss 108-110, would appear to be "poems ascribed to David, concluding with Pss 111-118." Pss 120-134 include "the Songs of Ascents, concluded with Pss 135-136." And finally, Pss 138-145 would also appear to be "psalms ascribed to David, concluded with Pss 146-150." All of these observations are taken directly from Eissfeldt.[18] In the light now of the Qumran Psalter we simply must admit that the supposed "early collections" in the last third of the Psalter are more a product of the imagination of the rationalist mind than of realities in antiquity. Only the Songs of Ascents remains attractive as a grouping, but the decision as to whether songs of similar titles had always been grouped together must be made in the light of the fragile nature of all such groupings which have heretofore appealed to our modern minds. One might as easily suggest that such songs were pulled together artificially at a comparatively late date, as they were so neatly arranged early in the Second Temple period and then pulled apart for later, overriding liturgical reasons by the Qum-

---

17. See the full catalogue and index in Sanders, *Dead Sea Psalms Scroll*, pp. 143-49; the early effort in *CBQ*, xxvii (1965), pp. 114-23, is now outdated and misleading.
18. Eissfeldt, *Introduction* (1965), pp. 449-50.

ran sect (which reasons are not at all evident or even suggested in the supposed "rearrangement" of the Qumran Psalter).

Observations concerning such groupings, however, are somewhat more convincing for Books I to III than for Books IV and V—precisely the portion of the Psalter which at Qumran is most at variance with the Masoretic Psalter both in order and content. Where all such observations may lead is extremely difficult to say. Avi Hurvitz, of the Hebrew University in Jerusalem, will soon publish a treatise based on new methods of linguistic analysis of the Psalms in which he concludes that the ten Masoretic psalms whose language clearly reflects the post-exilic period are all in the last third of the Psalter.[19] It will be interesting to see if his results corroborate our observations about Books IV and V and the suggestion that "the last third of the Qumran Psalter indicates a still open-ended Psalter in the first century."[20] It is precisely to the first century (at least) that we must trace the various figures concerning how many psalms the Psalter contained, 150, 151, 155, 200, 3600 or 4,050![21] If the stabilization of Books I to III occurred earlier than the crystallization of Books IV and V, then the fluidity demanded by the desire to be faithful to the Davidic corpus or heritage had to be expressed in the later portions of the Psalter and threatened the earlier portions less and less as the desire and need for stabilization became greater. It must be remembered that the Psalter cannot be viewed in the same way other biblical books are viewed in the question of canonization. Each psalm is an independent entity and has its own existence in a way narratives, oracles, and even proverbs do not have within the books where they are located. The Psalter was more closely allied to the daily life of worship and piety of Israel and Judaism than any other biblical book. And a sect that owed its existence and identity to dissension from the establishment in Jerusalem would be more likely to maintain the fluidity than not.

Tentatively, one might suggest the hypothesis that the Qumran group arrested the process of stabilization as it was in the period before they left Jerusalem to seek their own identity, and in the then fluid third portion of the Psalter came to accept as "Davidic" what were actually Hasidic and proto-Essene (their own identity) poems, which were at least biblical in style (in contrast to the style of the Qumran sectarian hymns) and could on the face of it meet the basic

---

19. Hurvitz, *The Identification of Post-exilic Psalms by Means of Linguistic Criteria* to be published in Hebrew by the Magnes Press, Jerusalem. Herewith my gratitude to Dr. Hurvitz for this information in personal correspondence.
20. Sanders, *Dead Sea Psalms Scroll*, p. 158.
21. *Ibid.*, p. 157.

standards of canonical literature. The Jerusalem group, by contrast, would have tended to arrest the process of fluidity in the interests of stabilizing their own position and sponsoring the status quo. The more eschatological group would have had little interest whatever in encouraging stabilization. Those who look constantly to the heavens for the in-breaking drama of righteousness and vindication have little interest in five-year, or longer, programs and plans! The Psalter is also distinct, in this regard, because it bore the authority of the name David, comparable in the late Second Temple period to the authority of the name Moses. "The difference was perhaps somewhat the difference between the kinds of authority and loyalty which the names Moses and David elicited in the period in question: the one was the authority of Law, the other the authority of hope; the one represented God's theophany in the past, the other his theophany of the future, a future which in the Qumran period was believed imminent. David's name both stabilized Psalter collections and prohibited a universally invariable canon of Psalms. The tragedy of the destruction of the Second Temple in the failure of the First Jewish Revolt put an end to the fluidity of the Psalter, just as it eventually brought about a stabilization of the Hagiographa, the codification of Oral Law, the unification of Rabbinic Judaism, the writing of the Gospels, the eventual gathering and canonization of the New Testament, and the ultimate parting of the ways of Judaism and Christianity, the only two sects from Early Judaism to survive the tragedy."[22] For the Essenes, the open-ended Psalter was the more archaic Psalter, the preservation of an earlier stage of the stabilization process; just as their cultic calendar was for them the more archaic and authentic calendar.

Until the Temple Scroll is published and its relation to the Qumran Psalter is established, further discussion would be but premature. One may sincerely hope that the Temple Scroll, which Yadin[23] describes as believed at Qumran "to be a part of the Holy Scriptures *sensu stricto,*" will provide the conclusive clues to the canonical status at Qumran of the Qumran Psalter, and perhaps suggestive clues to the direction our thinking should now take on the general question of the Old Testament canon which is being reopened in our day in numerous ways.[24]

---

22. *Ibid.*, p. 158.
23. Yadin, *op. cit.*, p. 136.
24. Cf., e.g., W. H. Brownlee, *RB*, lxxiii (1966), pp. 178-85; B. J. Roberts, "The Old Testament Canon: a Suggestion," *Bulletin of John Rylands Library*, xlvi (1963-64), pp. 164-78; "A Symposium on the Canon of Scripture," *CBQ*, xxviii (1966), pp. 189-208.

IV

Besides the two major Psalter manuscripts from Cave 11 there are so far two others which also contain non-Masoretic psalms. The one is from Cave 11 as well and is designated at present by the siglum 11QPsAp[a], meaning "apocryphal psalms from Qumran Cave 11." Actually, all that is so far published of it is Psalm 91, but the editor reports that at least one of the non-Masoretic psalms in the scroll bears the "Psalm of David" title familiar to all Psalter traditions. He also reports that, like the non-Masoretic psalms in the other Cave 11 Psalters, the psalms in 11QPsAp[a] are "biblical" in style rather than of the hymnic style at Qumran familiar from the sectarian Thanksgiving Hymns. And he quite rightly suggests that the manuscript attests a more ancient stage of Psalter tradition than that of the Masoretic Psalter.[25] It is for this reason that I have proposed resignaling this particular manuscript 11QPs[e]. It is very difficult at this point to see why it must not be considered in the same light as the other Psalms texts from Cave 11.

There are a number of very interesting variants in the Cave 11 Psalm 91 which do not appear either in the received text of Psalms or in the Cave 4 text where Ps 91 also shows up in 4 QPs[b].[26] Since it has never to my knowledge been rendered into English, I shall append a translation here. Where it differs from the Masoretic psalm, I have indicated the variants in italics.

11Q Ps 91

He who dwells in the shelter of the Most High,
    who abides in the shadow of the Almighty
is he who says to the Lord, "My refuge and my fortress
        is my God,
    my confidence in whom I trust."
For he will deliver you from the snare of the fowler,
    from the deadly pestilence;
he will cover you with his pinions,
        and under his wings will you *dwell in his grace* . . . ,
        his truth your shield and buckler. *Selah.*
You need fear neither the fright of night
    nor arrows in flight by day,
neither scourge of destitution at noon,
    nor plague that stalks the gloom.

---

25. J. van der Ploeg, *RB*, lxxii (1965), pp. 210-17.
26. P. W. Skehan, *CBQ*, xxvi (1964), pp. 313-22.

Let a thousand fall at your side,
>   ten thousand on your right hand,
>   but you it cannot *touch*.
You will need but look with your own eyes
>   and see the *fate* of the wicked.
Because you have *invoked* the Lord *your* refuge,
>   and made the Most High your delight,
you will *behold* no evil,
>   no scourge *will touch* your tent.
But he will charge his angels for you
>   to guard you in all your ways.
They will carry you in their hands
>   lest your foot stub a stone.
On the adder and the asp shall you tread,
>   both young lion and serpent trample under foot.

The rest of the text, verses 14 to 16, is unfortunately mutilated, but we can be grateful that most of the psalm is fairly well preserved. While there is less of it preserved, the Cave 4 text of Ps 91 is identical with the Masoretic as over against our Cave 11 copy. What strikes one about the Cave 11 Ps 91 is that it relates to the Masoretic text of Ps 91 exactly as psalms in 11QPs[a] relate to their corresponding Masoretic psalms. That is, the variants exhibit no pattern or tendenz, and while a few appear to be errors, many of the variant readings commend themselves rather strongly. And if Professor van der Ploeg is right that this text attests a more ancient stage of Psalter transmission than the Masoretic text, *argumentum a fortiori* 11QPs[a].

The fourth Qumran Psalter manuscript which includes non-Masoretic psalms was found not in our Cave 11 of surprises, but in Cave 4. It was not until the Cave 11 Psalms Scroll was published that Father Jean Starcky identified the pertinent materials and took account of the fact that he was dealing also with a manuscript containing both Masoretic and non-Masoretic psalms. It is a text which apparently was continuous on one sheet of leather running from Ps 106 to 109, though only portions of Pss 107 and 109 are preserved in it. But beginning, apparently, on the same column where Ps 109 ends, and continuing through column 10, are three non-Masoretic psalms, the first of which is the "Apostrophe to Zion" of column 22 of 11QPs[a]. One must say "apparently" because unfortunately one cannot be absolutely certain, but Father Starcky seems confident that the fragment on which the "Apostrophe to Zion" begins is to be placed so as to form a lower part of the original full column 7. This re-identification was made in the summer of 1965, and it is not unreasonable to suppose that further such discoveries of non-Masoretic Psalter texts may be made when all the Cave 4 materials have been published (which are to fill some nine quarto-size volumes!).

An English translation of the "Apostrophe to Zion" has been published on the basis of the Cave 11 Psalms Scroll, and then a revision taking account of the variants between the Caves 4 and 11 copies.[27] There is, hence, no need to offer the "Apostrophe to Zion" here. But, to my knowledge, no translation has yet appeared in English of the two psalms which follow it in 4QPs^f. The second of the three may be titled Eschatological Hymn and the third Apostrophe to Judah.[28]

4Q Eschatological Hymn

. . .

Let the (congregation) praise the name of the Lord. . .
For he is coming to judge every deed,
    to destroy the wicked from the earth
    so that sons of iniquity will be no more.

The heavens (will bless with) their dew
    and no destruction will enter their borders.
The earth will yield its fruit in its season
    and its produce will never be wanting.
Fruit trees (will offer their figs)
    and springs will never fail.
Let the poor have their food
    and those who fear the Lord be satisfied. . .

4Q Apostrophe to Judah

. . .

Let then the heavens and the earth give praise together,
    let all the stars of evening sing praises!
Rejoice, O Judah, in your joy,
    rejoice your joy and exult your exultation!
Celebrate your festivals, fulfill your vows
    for no longer is Belial in your midst.
Lift up your hand, strengthen your right hand,
    behold your enemies go perishing
    and all workers of evil go scattering.
But thou, O Lord, thou art for ever,
    thy glory for e'er and aye.
    Hallelujah!

---

27. Sanders, *DJD* IV, pp. 85-89, and Sanders, *Dead Sea Psalms Scroll*, pp. 123-127.
28. Translated from the text of 4QPs^f in J. Starcky, *RB*, lxxiii (1966), pp. 356-57 (Plate XIII).

JEAN-PAUL AUDET

A HEBREW-ARAMAIC LIST OF BOOKS OF THE OLD TESTAMENT IN GREEK TRANSCRIPTION

THE list to which I invite attention was published by Bryennios more than sixty years ago, at the end of his introduction to the *editio princeps* of the Didache.[1] This list took up about twelve lines in the manuscript on fol. 76a, between the second Epistle of Clement and the Didache itself. From the outset Bryennios made every effort to produce an edition of the Didache worthy of the document which he was privileged to make known. He knew, or at least thought he knew, what he was dealing with.

Unfortunately, we cannot say the same of the list which is our concern here. Bryennios failed to grasp either its nature or its importance. He merely transcribed it—not too carefully—as if he were concerned solely with making known the content of his manuscript. Still, this transcription might of itself have been enough to provoke useful researches, were it not that Bryennios was led to present the list inaccurately. In the manuscript this list bears the following title: ὀνόματα τῶν βιβλίων παρ' ἑβραίοις. From παρ' ἑβραίοις, Bryennios straightway concluded that the list must be in Hebrew (transliterated into Greek). His interpretation of the title runs: τὰ ὀνόματα . . . τῶν τῆς παλαιᾶς Διαθήκης ἑβραιστὶ καὶ ἑλληνιστί (op. cit., προλεγ., p. ρμζ') a hasty deduction which could have been avoided by a small knowledge of Aramaic. Thus it came about that no one took notice of a list of Hebrew titles in a Greek manuscript of the eleventh century, for this was regarded as scarcely a matter of interest. We may add that the very considerable stir caused by the publication of the Didache was hardly likely to direct peoples' minds to what must have seemed a mere curio.

It is surprising, however, that Rendel Harris, who had delved much into manuscripts and old texts, should have failed to perceive the importance of the list.[2] But, at this time, he too had his attention drawn elsewhere. Lightfoot also failed in this. He gives the content of the manuscript, based on Bryennios' list, yet forgets to mention the list of Old Testament books;[3] and so the list came to be completely

[1] Ph. Bryennios, Διδαχὴ τῶν δώδεκα ἀποστόλων, Ἐν Κωνσταντινουπόλει, 1883, προλεγ., pp. ρμζ–ρμη'.
[2] J. Rendel Harris, *Three Pages of the Bryennios Manuscript*, Baltimore, 1885 (no pagination). Fol. 76a is one of the three pages reproduced.
[3] J. B. Lightfoot, *The Apostolic Fathers*, I, *St. Clement of Rome*, vol. i, p. 122.

[Journal of Theological Studies, N.S., Vol. I, Pt. 2, October 1950]

Reprinted from *Journal of Theological Studies* 1 (1950).

forgotten. In fact the same list, wholly recast, is in Epiphanius, but, as far as I know, no one except G. Card. Mercati has perceived the very special problems entailed.[1] He sought solutions, however, without attaining any positive results for the question as a whole. Because the list of the Jerusalem MS. was not at hand, the data were too slender for an explanation that would win conviction. But the list of the Jerusalem MS. completely alters the situation. Hence it is now opportune to discuss briefly some of the problems implied by its data.

For reasons which will appear later, pride of place must go to the text formerly published by Bryennios. It is in the manuscript now numbered 54 in the Greek Patriarchate Library in Jerusalem, fol. 76ʳᵒ. The manuscript is dated 6564 of the Greeks = A.D. 1056.[2] A transcription of the text as it stands, with numbers added to facilitate reference, will be given first.

·:· ὀνόματα τῶν βιβλίων παρ' ἑβραίοις :·

1. βρισίθ · γένεσις.   2. ἐλσιμόθ · ἔξοδος.   3. ὀδοικρά · λευϊτικόν.
4. διησοῦ · ἰησοῦ υἱοῦ ναυή.   5. ἐλεδεββαρί · δευτερονόμιον.   6. οὐιδαβίρ · ἀριθμοί.   7. δαρούθ · τῆς ῥούθ.   8. διώβ · τοῦ ἰώβ.   9. δάσοφτιμ̆ · τῶν κριτῶν.   10. σφερτελίμ · ψαλτήριον.   11. διεμμουήλ · βασιλειῶν α'.
12. διαδδουδεμουήλ · βασιλειῶν β'.   13. δαμαλαχήμ · βασιλειῶν γ'.
14. ἀμαλαχήμ · βασιλειῶν δ'.   15. δεβριαμίν · παραλειπομένων α'.
16. δεριαμίν · παραλειπομένων β'.   17. δαμαλεώθ · παροιμιῶν.   18. δακοέλεθ · ἐκκλησιαστής.   19. σιρὰ σιρίμ · ᾆσμα ᾀσμάτων.   20. διερέμ · ἱερεμίας.   21. δααθαρσιαρ̄ · δωδεκαπρόφητον.   22. δησαίου · ἠσαίου.
23. διεεζεκιήλ · ἰεζεκιήλ.   24. δαδανιήλ · δανιήλ.   25. δέσδρα · ἔσδρα α'.
26. δαδέσδρα · ἔσδρα β'.   27. δεσθής · ἐσθήρ.

My readings differ from those of Bryennios, here and there, on points of detail.

3. ὀδικρά (Br.) instead of ὀδοικρά, of this there can be no doubt; cf. Epiphanius, De mens. et pond., 23, οὐδωϊεκρά.   6. MS. οὐιδαβίρ instead of οὐϊδαβίρ (Br.).   9. MS. δάσοφτιμ̆. A letter is in fact written over the final *mu*; I read this letter as a *nu* (with Rendel Harris). Bryennios read it as an *eta*, and read δάσοφτιημ; but it is difficult to think that he is right. The shape of the letter rather suggests *nu*, though admittedly certitude on this point is impossible. I incline to think that the copyist queried the reading of his original, and accordingly wrote *nu* above *mu* as an

[1] G. Mercati, Note di letteratura biblica e cristiana antica (Studi e Testi, 5), Rome, 1901, pp. 17-27. Unfortunately, I came upon this essay too late to be able to use it.

[2] For the general description of the manuscript, see A. Papadopoulos-Kerameus, Ἱεροσολυμιτικὴ βιβλιοθήκη, Ἐν Πετρουπόλει, 1891, vol. i, pp. 134-7; for the list, p. 135. A very accessible phototype reproduction in Lightfoot, Apost. Fathers, I, St. Clement of Rome, vol. i, p. 474.

alternative. *Nu* fits in with the Aramaic form of the word (plural in *-in*). 23. διεεζεκιήλ instead of διεζεκιήλ (Br.). Bryennios may have wished to introduce a correction, but the manuscript reading is certain.

For the text of Epiphanius, I use Dindorf.[1] It is true that Paul de Lagarde produced a later edition of the *De mens*. But the only new elements for establishing the text consisted of two manuscripts (Brit. Mus., Or. add. 17148, seventh century, and Or. add. 14620, ninth century) of an old Syriac version of Epiphanius' *opusculum*.[2] Unfortunately, for the very special matter which concerns us, the Syriac version would serve only to mislead.

It is clear indeed that a Syriac translator (*a fortiori* a copyist after him, freed from all regard for the original Greek) would to some extent recognize the Aramaic forms of Epiphanius, and would be tempted to try to correct them where they seemed to him corrupt. Both translator and copyist did so. Two examples bring this out very clearly: thus δμεαλώθ, which is certainly a corruption, first of all slipped, unchanged, into the translation (ܠܡܐܬ). Then came a copyist who put in the margin *dm'th'lōth* (A, ܠܡܐܬܠ; B, ܠܡܐܬܠ). He realized that the word was short of the consonant T, since both Syriac and Aramaic derive a substantive from the same root MTL; and so, quite naturally, he supplied it in his own language. De Lagarde accepted the marginal reading as better in itself, and restored in the Greek δμεθαλώθ (Dean: *d^emethalōth*). So too with δαδουδεμουήλ. The translator simply transliterated as best as he could, ܠܐܡܘܪܘܠ. Such an unwonted form could hardly survive without the original text to vouch for it. A copyist (perhaps the same one) undertook a correction ܠܐܡܘܪܘܠ, and relegated to the margin the reading he had in his text, ܠܐܡܘܪܘܠ. But this marginal reading was once again corrupt, so that it is now in A, ܠܐܡܘܠܠ (notably, the third ܪ has been taken for ܪ *estrangelo*). De Lagarde kept the reading of the text, which seemed to him intrinsically better, and has restored in the Greek δαδουδεσαμουήλ (Dean: *dadūdh shamū'ēl*).

---

[1] *Epiphanii opera*, vol. iv, *De mens. et pond.*, 23; *P.G.* 43. 237 seq.

[2] P. de Lagarde, *Symmicta II*, Göttingen, 1880, pp. 150 seq. (Greek text with German translation); for the text of the Syriac version, see also P. de Lagarde, *Veteris Testamenti ab Origene recensiti fragmenta apud Syros servata quinque. Praemittitur Epiphanii de mensuris et ponderibus liber nunc primum integer et ipse syriacus*, Göttingen, 1880; or better, J. E. Dean, *Epiphanius' Treatise on Weights and Measures. The Syriac Version* (Stud. in Anc. Or. Civ., 11), Chicago, 1935. Dean adds to his English translation a phototype reproduction of MS. Or. add. 17148 (=A), with a collation of Or. add. 14620 (=B), and P. de Lagarde's previous edition. I am using Dean's edition here, as providing all the data required. In the manuscript reproduction, the list with which we are concerned is on fol. 60, cols. a–b; ed., p. 111; English translation and notes, p. 44.

It is, however, a mistake to correct the Greek by *a priori* methods from the Syriac, if we are seeking not the form which in itself is more correct, but the form which was in the version used by Epiphanius. There is no guarantee, indeed, that the corrections introduced by the version, and accepted by de Lagarde for the Greek text, are not related to corruptions which already existed in the text of the list incorporated by Epiphanius in his *opusculum*—supposing anyway that the list existed before him. Moreover, if it happens that a certain number of these corruptions appear to be common to both extant texts of the list, it is evident that such similarities can be important for establishing the literary relationship of one text to the other. It is therefore better in our particular question, to confine ourselves wholly to the Greek, in however corrupt a form the text has come to us.[1]

1. βρησὶθ, ἢ καλεῖται γένεσις κόσμου·
2. ἐλησιμὼθ, ἢ ἔξοδος τῶν υἱῶν ἰσραὴλ ἐξ αἰγύπτου·
3. οὐδωϊεκρὰ, ἢ ἑρμηνεύεται λευιτικόν·
4. ἰουδδαβὴρ, ἥ ἐστιν ἀριθμῶν·
5. ἐλλεδεβαρεὶμ, τὸ δευτερονόμιον·
6. διησοῦ, ἡ τοῦ ἰησοῦ τοῦ ναυῆ·
7. διὼβ, ἡ τοῦ ἰώβ·
8. διασωφτεὶμ, ἡ τῶν κριτῶν·
9. διαρούθ, ἡ τῆς ῥούθ·
10. σφερτελεὶμ, τὸ ψαλτήριον·
11. δεβριϊαμεὶμ, ἡ πρώτη τῶν παραλειπομένων·
12. δεβριϊαμεὶμ, παραλειπομένων δευτέρα·
13. δεμουὲλ, βασιλειῶν πρώτη·
14. δαδουδεμουὴλ, βασιλειῶν δευτέρα·
15. δμαλαχεὶ, βασιλειῶν τρίτη·
16. δμαλαχεὶ, βασιλειῶν τετάρτη·
17. δμεαλὼθ, ἡ παροιμιῶν·
18. δεκωέλεθ, ὁ ἐκκλησιαστής·
19. σιρασιρεὶμ, τὸ ᾆσμα τῶν ᾀσμάτων·
20. δαθαριασαρὰ, τὸ δωδεκαπρόφητον·
21. δησαΐου, τοῦ προφήτου ἠσαΐου·
22. διερεμίου, ἡ τοῦ ἱερεμίου·
23. διεζεκιὴλ, ἡ τοῦ ἰεζεκιήλ·
24. δδανιὴλ, ἡ τοῦ δανιήλ·
25. δδέσδρα, ἡ τοῦ ἔσδρα πρώτη·
26. δδέσδρα, ἡ τοῦ ἔσδρα δευτέρα·
27. δεσθὴρ, ἡ τῆς ἐσθήρ·

[1] On this last point, see K. Holl, 'Die handschriftliche Ueberlieferung des Epiphanius' (*T.U.* xxxvi. 2), Leipzig, 1920, pp. 87–95.

Before we embark on the literary question proper, a few preliminary remarks are necessary on the twofold text, that of the Jerusalem MS. and that of Epiphanius.

In both, transliterations have been much mangled by copyists, as has so often occurred in other cases. We may compare the apparatus of Schwartz in his critical edition of Eusebius' *Hist. eccl.*,[1] or that of the great Roman edition of the Vulgate,[2] and observe the fate of Origen's list, transliterated from Hebrew into Greek, or that of Jerome, transliterated from Hebrew into Latin.

But the essential elements remain and are perfectly recognizable. It is clear, first of all, that some of the titles maintain in transcription a purely Hebrew form, viz. the five books of the Pentateuch, Psalms, the Song of Songs, and the two books of Chronicles. In addition, both lists agree as regards the books transliterated from the Hebrew.

Hebrew	MS.	Epiphanius
בראשית	βρισίθ	βρησίθ
[ו]אלה שמות	ἐλσιμόθ	ἐλησιμώθ
ויקרא	ὀδοικρά	οὐδωϊεκρά
וידבר	οὐιδαβίρ	ἰουδδαβήρ
אלה הדברים	ἐλεδεββαρί	ἐλλεδεβαρείμ
[ספר] תהלים	σφερτελίμ	σφερτελείμ
שיר השירים	σιρὰ σιρίμ	σιρασιρείμ
דברי הימים	δεβριαμίν	δεβριαμείμ

No less clear than this first fact are the various Aramaic elements that come into the transliteration of all the other titles. Some must have disappeared in the course of transmission, or at least have been obscured, but enough is left to give us general certainty. Thus δάσοφτιν of the manuscript and διασωφτείμ of Epiphanius must both correspond to an Aramaic plural, *šāphʿṭīn*. So too δαμαλαχήμ of the manuscript, and δμαλαχεί of Epiphanius, because of the Aramaic genitive particle which is prefixed, must derive from *mᵉlākhīn* rather than *mᵉlakhīm*. Confusion of *mu* and *nu* was easy enough in such a case (cf. δάσοφτιν of the manuscript). 2 Sam. appears as: MS. διαδδουδεμουήλ; Epiphanius, δαδουδεμουήλ. The δου in both forms is none other than a Greek δύο, appearing in Aramaic in an apocopated form (*dū*) which is sometimes found in the language of the Targums.[3] δαμαλεώθ of the manuscript,

[1] 'Die Kirchengeschichte' (*G.C.S.* ix. 2), vi. 25, pp. 572 seq.

[2] *Biblia Sacra iuxta latinam Vulgatam versionem*, V, *Samuhel*, Rome, 1944, pp. 5–7; comp. G. Mercati, 'Il problema della colonna II dell' Esaplo', in *Biblica*, xxviii (1947), p. 10.

[3] See S. Krauss, *Griechische und lateinische Lehnwörter im Talmud, Midrasche und Targum*, I, *Grammatik*, §215, note 1; also §211; II, *Wörterbuch*, s.v.—Dean (op. cit., p. 44, note 269) has not succeeded in solving δαδουδεμουήλ, which he

and $\delta\mu\epsilon\alpha\lambda\dot\omega\theta$ of Epiphanius, suggest a feminine singular in $\bar{a}$', and so must be the Aramaic $math^ela$', which has been given a Hebraic plural in $\bar{o}th$. If we were concerned with a purely Hebraic form, the Greek should show at least something suggestive of $m^e\check{s}\bar{a}l\bar{\imath}m$. The form in our list is hybrid, half Aramaic half Hebrew, and indicates a mixed milieu wherein the languages play upon one another.

But the most obvious and significant element is of course the d prefixed to 18 out of 27 titles on the list. In four cases (Epiphanius, 15, 16, 17, 26), the d is followed by no vowel of its own. A few other instances are inconclusive, as the root word itself has an initial vowel. The remainder have as vowels a, e, i. There is thus considerable variation, but this is almost certainly partly due to transmission, as is clear if we compare the two extant texts. The original perhaps had simply $\delta\iota$, being the transliteration of the Aramaic genitive particle. It follows naturally that in every case a word is understood, such as 'the book of . . .', or, perhaps, 'the writings of . . .'. Side by side with this, it is noticeable that the Greek titles of the Jerusalem MS., though derived from the LXX, correspond in general to the form of Hebrew or Aramaic titles, the former being in the nominative, the latter in the genitive (where the latter occurs and where transmission has not disturbed the readings). As we shall see, Epiphanius' list has been recast as regards this point, although it maintains the general appearance of its original condition. This agreement of the Greek titles with Hebrew or Aramaic titles is an important element in the evaluation of all data. We have here a guarantee that the editor of the list was fully cognizant of the suitability of the various formulae which he used, and, beyond verbal forms, of the diversity of writings which they were meant to denote.

A genuinely Hebrew and Aramaic list of the books of the Old Testament is therefore what we have before us, preserved independ-

transcribes from the Syriac, *dadūdh shamū' ēl*. For *dadūdh* he proposes the Hebrew root עוּד, Syriac, ܥܽܘܕ. But עוֹד, in the meaning of 'still' here, hardly fits into any explanation; and the second d is not explained. The primitive Greek transcription appears to have been ΔΙΔΟΥΔΙϹΕΜΟΥΗΛ. There may be some doubt about the two I's; but it is clear enough that Ϲ has fallen out before the Ε, by haplographic assimilation, resulting finally in $\delta\alpha\delta\text{ου}\delta\epsilon\mu\text{ου}\acute\eta\lambda$. If we take דוּ ($=\delta\text{ου}$) as an ordinal, we get: [Book] of (דִי $=\delta\iota$) the second (דוּ $=\delta\text{ου}$) of (דִי $=\delta\iota$) Samuel (שְׁמוּאֵל $=\sigma\epsilon\mu\text{ου}\acute\eta\lambda$). An elliptic expression for: [Book] of the second [roll] of Samuel, or Book contained in the second scroll of Samuel. Those who hold that the division of certain books of the Old Testament is not an invention of the Alexandrine translators, might find here a point in their favour; cf. L. Blau, *Studien zum althebräischen Buchwesen und zur biblischen Literaturgeschichte*, Strasbourg, 1902, pp. 46 seq.; H. St. John Thackeray, *The Septuagint and the Jewish Worship* (Schweich Lectures 1920), App. IV: 'The Bisection of O.T. Books', pp. 131 seq.

ently in the Jerusalem MS., and embodied in the *De mens.* of Epiphanius. Any suspicion that it might be a late and artificial compilation is dispelled, first because the Greek titles are in general agreement with the Hebrew or Aramaic titles, and secondly because the assignment of Hebrew or Aramaic titles throughout the list (especially in the Jerusalem MS.) shows no trace of subsequent borrowing from different sources. The list we have in the Jerusalem MS., apart from minor corruptions in the course of transmission, is as it was drawn up; and for our part, we can but take it as it is, a document full of significant information about the state of affairs which gave it birth.

Only two texts, viz. that of the Jerusalem MS. and that of Epiphanius, are involved in the literary question. What is the literary relationship of these two texts, alike on some points, divergent on others? At the outset we can show that the former is not derived from the latter.

The two lists agree on the number (27) and the titles of the books listed, as well as on the proportion of Hebrew and Aramaic titles. But they differ in the order of listing. Taking as a basis Epiphanius' list, the Jerusalem MS. lists the items thus: 1, 2, 3, 6, 5, 4, 8, 9, 7, 10, 15, 16, 11, 12, 13, 14, 17, 18, 19, 21, 22, 20, 23, 24, 25, 26, 27. Only 13 books out of 27 are listed in the same numerical sequence in the two lists. The sequence in Epiphanius' list is manifestly better, both in itself and in relation to Church usage of the Old Testament. This being so, there is scarcely any possibility that a copyist borrowed Epiphanius' list from the *De mens.* and then jumbled the order at will. Such an action would be unparalleled. Canonical lists, at the end of the fourth century, have a *genre littéraire* admitting of very little liberty in the ordering of the sacred books.

The different formulations of the Greek titles in the two lists bring out the same conclusion. Epiphanius' titles are regularly more fullsome, affording a greater amount of detail, tending to smoothe out harsher phrases, and giving an appearance of more complex construction and more correct grammar. Had the Jerusalem MS. list been drawn from the *De mens.* of Epiphanius, there would have been no reason for not retaining precisely those elements which in fact made it more highly esteemed by everyone.

A number of forms in the Hebrew or Aramaic titles are pointers in the same direction. These forms are too divergent in details to allow us to suppose that all is due to accidents in transmission. In addition to two obvious mistakes of a copyist in the Jerusalem MS. ($\delta\iota\epsilon\epsilon\zeta\epsilon\kappa\iota\acute{\eta}\lambda$ for $\delta\iota\epsilon\zeta\epsilon\kappa\iota\acute{\eta}\lambda$, and $\delta\epsilon\sigma\theta\acute{\eta}s$ for $\delta\epsilon\sigma\theta\acute{\eta}\rho$, there are only 4 out of 27 titles which have exactly the same form in both lists, $\delta\iota\acute{\omega}\beta$, $\delta\eta\sigma\alpha\~{\iota}ov$, $\delta\iota\epsilon\zeta\epsilon\kappa\iota\acute{\eta}\lambda$, and δεσθήρ. It is also hard to imagine that a list like that of the Jerusalem MS. could have been in general circulation after the fourth century. The greater part of the divergences in form must date before that time. On the whole, therefore, it seems certain that the list of the Jerusalem MS. is not derived from the *De mens.* of Epiphanius.

On the other hand, if we suppose a remote common original source of both texts, then all is satisfactorily explained. There are positive hints of this. Thus several corruptions in the transliteration of Hebrew or Aramaic titles are identical in both texts, e.g. Epiphanius, οὐδωϊεκρά; MS. ὀδοικρά. The *delta* common to both forms corresponds to nothing in the Hebrew (*wayyiq'rā'*): it is a corruption. In the given circumstances it would be hard to assign it to chance. We must suppose a common source which was already corrupt at this place. Again, Epiphanius, δμεαλώθ; MS. δαμαλεώθ. The two extant forms suggest that a *thêta* in the original has fallen out, corresponding to the Aramaic *taw*, in a noun form derived from *m'thal*. Here again we can hardly argue that it is a chance corruption; there must be a common corrupt source. Thus it is likely that the nearest common ancestor of our texts was already corrupt in a number of places; and at the same time we can conclude that it must previously have had a relatively long history.

This being so, the list in the *De mens.*, in the order in which it exists, can only be derived from some recasting of the text preserved by the Jerusalem MS.

In general, in such a case as this, it is not the order that is intrinsically better which is necessarily older. Uniformity only came after a long process of revision which ancient lists underwent in the course of their long history. The *De mens.* list is simply an example of this, both in the order of the books and in the formulation of the Greek titles; it has been considerably altered and revised (cf., e.g., the order of the books of the Pentateuch in the two lists). Only the transliterations (by reason of their very nature) have escaped the reviser's zeal. Further, might the reviser have been Epiphanius himself? We cannot say: evidence is lacking. Could we do so, it would only help towards fixing a date in the history of the text; but we are already provided with a starting-point for our chronological inquiry.

The list is certainly very old. Epiphanius brings us to the fourth century. If there was, as we believe, a common ancestor older than the older of our two texts, we can work back from A.D. 392, but without knowing where to stop.

The list itself provides a number of chronological indications. First, the obvious fact that transliterations of the list in *De mens.*, as in the manuscript, are very corrupt, is evidence that there was a period of time and a milieu where the list was certainly known to a wide circle. On the other hand, the manuscript (as against the *De mens.*) is evidence that the list was current in an isolated form and owed its wide circulation to its own merits or usefulness, and not because it was associated with some great name. It is a mere accident in its history which led it to be incorporated in the *De mens.* of Epiphanius. Finally, it is immediately obvious that the order of titles as enumerated in the list, and as preserved in the Jerusalem MS., could not have of itself found favour in circles which gave birth to all the other lists of Old Testament books, from that of Melito of Sardis (*c.* A.D. 170) to the most recent.[1]

All these facts taken together would seem to argue that we should certainly go back at least as far as the second century for the origin of the list of the Jerusalem MS., and probably assign it to the first half of the century rather than to the second.

It is difficult to imagine how such a list could have been widely known at a later period. When it appears in the fourth century, it is already profoundly recast and is in line with accepted lists. And at that period, no doubt, the need for adaptation had long been felt. Moreover, before the second half of the third century another list of canonical books of the Old Testament, with Hebrew titles transliterated into Greek, was made familiar by Origen.[2] It is altogether more likely that the period when the list of the Jerusalem MS. was most widely known came before the establishment of Origen's influence in Palestine and in the Greek-speaking countries generally.

This general impression from a first survey of the facts is well confirmed by Melito of Sardis. Eusebius has preserved for us the letter by which the Bishop of Sardis presented to his 'brother' Onesimus the six books of *Extracts from the Law and the Prophets* which he had collected for him.[3] Who was this 'brother' Onesimus who so ardently desired a collection of *Testimonia* 'concerning our Saviour and the totality of our Faith'? We cannot be sure, but we gather naturally enough from the way in which Melito congratulates him on 'his zeal for the Faith and his love for the study of God's word' that Onesimus was also a bishop; a 'brother' therefore in the episcopate. However that may be, Onesimus earnestly requested that with the *Testimonia* asked for, he might be given a list of the 'ancient books', which would make certain of their number and precise order. If Onesimus thus

---

[1] Comparison easily made by referring to the tables in Swete, *Introd. to the O.T. in Greek*, pp. 198–214.

[2] In Ps. 1; *P.G.* 12. 1084; in Eusebius, *Hist. eccl.* vi. 25.

[3] *Hist. eccl.* iv. 26.

insists on the *order* as well as the exact number of books (ἔτι δὲ καὶ μαθεῖν τὴν τῶν παλαιῶν βιβλίων ἐβουλήθης ἀκρίβειαν, πόσα τὸν ἀριθμὸν καὶ ὁποῖα τὴν τάξιν εἶεν . . .), we gather at once that he is not satisfied with opinions prevalent in his own circles; and again, if Melito, leaving no stone unturned in this grave matter, purposely travels to Palestine to sound the best authorities (ἐσπούδασα τὸ τοιοῦτο πρᾶξαι . . . ἀνελθὼν οὖν . . .), we gather that he too is no more satisfied than Onesimus with the information which he has at hand. Does not all this suggest that at the time of Onesimus and Melito, in several churches of Asia Minor, lists were in circulation like that of our Jerusalem MS., equally 'unreliable' in the matter of the order of the books? Onesimus' request, Melito's inquiries, the order in the Jerusalem MS., are pointers that converge rather significantly, and show that it is at a period before the second half of the second century that we must look for the conditions required for the diffusion of a list such as ours.

Another line of argument leads to the same conclusion. As far as we can judge, the list is Greek and Christian as regards its range of diffusion. But what of its origin? We have before us a Greek transcription. In addition, the Greek titles are those of the Alexandrine translators. Thus, in its present state, and as a whole, the list purports to be useful to Greek readers, or hellenized readers, of the sacred books. But, basically, and forming a sort of norm for names, number, and order of the sacred books, we have a Hebrew-Aramaic list. Where can it come from?

We can only envisage a Jewish milieu, imbued with Judaism or Christianity. In either case, the title of the list (if original) makes reasonable sense: ὀνόματα τῶν βιβλίων παρ' ἑβραίοις. There is no other way of accounting for Aramaic titles among the Hebrew titles. Aramaic titles, as we shall see later, point to Aramaic Targums on the corresponding books of the Hebrew Old Testament. But these Targums could only be read by Jews or Jewish Christians. We must therefore ask ourselves at what period, either in Jewish or Christian circles, we can imagine the first dissemination of a list like that of the Jerusalem MS.

Unfortunately, we are very ill informed about the Christian communities of Palestine at the end of the first century or in the first half of the second century. Aramaic-speaking Christians—whom we need alone consider here—have left no direct evidence of their life and history. The slender information we have about them comes to us incidentally from Greek sources. Eusebius (*Hist. eccl.* iv. 5) notes *en passant*, that up to the time of Bar-Kochba (A.D. 132–5) 'the whole Church' ruled by the Jerusalem bishops was made up of 'Hebrews' (ἐξ ἑβραίων πιστῶν), a vague term, and, in the context, religious rather than linguistic. It is certain, however, that the fall of Jerusalem in A.D. 70 and the transference of the Christian community to Pella in Transjordan before the siege of the Holy City meant the complete cessation of all influence of Aramaic-speaking Christians on Gentile churches made up of hellenized Jews and converted pagans whose common idiom was Greek. Groups which survived the national disaster were reduced to living in narrow isolation, or unconsciously became contaminated by the Jewish sects all about them. Hegesippus (in Eus., *Hist. eccl.* iv. 22) and Justin (*Dial.* 47) could still, in the middle of the second century, have direct knowledge of them; but this marks the end of a period that was over. Such direct acquaintance with Aramaic Christians ceased. When, in the third quarter of the same century, Melito travelled to Palestine and made inquiries about the catalogue of the 'ancient books', it is more than likely that he was consulting Jews and not Christians. Origen, some fifty years later, did the same. There is no suggestion of any return, in this domain, to the traditions of Aramaic Christians of Palestine. This being so, if our list is from an Aramaic-speaking Christian milieu, then we must certainly put its origin very far back indeed—in all likelihood to the last part of the first century. The latest possible date still remains, however, the first half of the second century.

If we take the other supposition, viz. that the Hebrew-Aramaic substratum of the list is from a Jewish milieu properly speaking, then the still-discernible chronological hints point to the same period.

Note, first of all, that Daniel is placed among the Prophets. This was the old Jewish notion of the book, that which commonly obtained in Palestine in the time of Christ (Matt. 24[15]) or in the time of Josephus (*c.* A.D. 95; cf. *Contra Apionem*, 1, 8; *Antiquities*, x, 11, 17), and passed from Jewish to Christian tradition.[1] We know, however, that in Palestinian Judaism there was a change of opinion on this very point during the second century; and indeed the famous *Baraitha* attributed by the Talmud to R. Juda the Patriarch (*c.* end of second century), definitely places Daniel among the Hagiographa.[2] It is true that the utterances of R. Juda may at this point to some extent represent the special point of view of the prevalent Pharisee outlook, and that local variations may have remained for some time outside the orbit of a movement which tended to make Judaism as a whole more strictly unified. Allowing for

[1] Cf. R. D. Wilson, 'The Book of Daniel and the Canon', in the *Princeton Theological Review*, xiii (1915), pp. 352–408; especially pp. 402–6.
[2] Talm. bab., *Baba bathra* 14b–15a; on this text see G. Dalman's study, *Traditio rabbinorum veterrima de librorum V.T. ordine atque origine*, Leipzig, 1891, pp. 39 seq.

this, however, we still have some indication that our list, because it ranges Daniel among the Prophets, came before the end of the first century; it stands for the primitive point of view.

Besides, we might well be surprised by a composite list where original titles mingle with Targums, if we remember the very sensitive care which Judaism of the Mishnah and Talmud period gave to maintaining the unassailable dignity of an original text over and apart from all translations. The sacred character of God's Word extends to the language and the very signs themselves. For this reason, Targums must be preserved, not in the Synagogue chest, but in the Geniza (Talm. bab., *Shabb.* 115a; cf. Mishnah, *Yad.* 4, 5). Thus a complete list of Hebrew titles corresponding to the Targums would be intelligible enough. But a composite list as ours cannot be easily explained: it is only conceivable if we go back as far as the period before the definite establishment of the discipline already supposed by the Mishnah and more explicitly recorded in the Talmud, and the elimination of local variations. The indeterminate period lasting from the destruction of Jerusalem to the end of the first century furnishes the historical background which our list seems to require for its origin.

Finally, the very transliterations themselves provide a chronological hint which seems sufficiently clear to merit notice. The Massoretic ֻ appears to have been systematically transcribed by $\bar{a}$: thus, ὁδοικρά, ἐλεδεββάρι, δαδάνιήλ, δεσδρά. Two cases call for a special explanation. We have διερεμίου (Epiphanius) and δησαίου, and not ιερεμιά and ιεσσιά, as in Origen's transliteration. This last supposes יִרְמָיָה and יְשַׁעְיָא, respectively, which are simply the titles which are familiar to us (LXX, ἱερεμίας and ἠσαίας; Vulg., *Ieremias* and *Isaias*). But these titles are obviously later than the text of the books which they serve to denote. And in fact in the text we read the longer, older form, יִרְמְיָהוּ and יְשַׁעְיָהוּ. It is at once obvious that in this form the Massoretic vocalization gives an $\bar{a}$ which is not represented by the transcription of our list. διερεμιου and δησαιου presuppose the simplified pronunciation יִרְמִיהוּ and יְשַׁעְיָהוּ.

These facts are significant of their period. First, it is certain that of the two forms, יהו and יה, in proper names compounded of a verb, or a qualifying term, and the divine name, יהו is the older. It alone appears in the Lachish ostraka.[1] Old Hebrew inscriptions of Palestine (Samaria [יו], Ophel, jars, seals) almost without exception give the form יהו.[2]

[1] H. Torczyner, *Lachish I, The Lachish Letters*, London, 1938, p. 24; index, p. 198. I am using, in this paragraph, the editor's notes on the name *Gemaryahu* (i, 1), pp. 24-5.

[2] D. Diringer, *Le iscrizioni antico-ebraiche palestinesi*, Florence, 1934.

The popularity of the shortened form יה is post-exilic and must be due to Aramaic influence. The Aramaic papyri of Elephantine, with two exceptions, always give יה. The Bible makes use of both forms, shorter and longer, in about the same proportion, though there is a certain preponderance of יה over יהו in Chronicles, Ezra, and Nehemiah.

Transliterations developed along a parallel course. The longer form is represented in Assyrian transcriptions, sometimes by *i-a-a-u*, sometimes by *i-a-u*, and sometimes by *i-u*. This last transcription alone reappears in the LXX. Thus we have ηλιου (3 Kings 17¹, &c.), and οβδιου—αβδιου (3 Kings 18³, &c.). But these examples and a few others which might be adduced remain exceptions—at least in the present state of the text. The general tendency was towards an artificial transformation of the indeclinables in -ιου into genitives of a declinable form in -ιας, when once the translations had lost all contact with the original text. Thus ηλιου, which is indeclinable in the historic books (3 Kings 17¹, &c.) has become ηλιας in Mal. 4⁴ and in the New Testament (Matt. 11¹⁴, &c.). Of the two forms, indeclinable and declinable, there is no doubt that the former is older. And we might well wonder whether originally the transliteration of the form יהו, in the first Alexandrine translations, was not uniformly in -ιου, indeclinable. There is no obvious and direct passage from יהו to -ιας; but the indirect way seems likely: thus, a transcription in -ιου, first treated as indeclinable, and afterwards artificially looked upon as a genitive. Thus it was that Aquila, coming into contact with the original at a later period, put forward his own transcription: he wrote not -ιας nor -ιου but -ιαου.[1] The Greek transcription in -ιου, like the old Assyrian transcription in *i-u*, must therefore represent, beside -ιαου (for the Hebrew יהו), a real pronunciation יְהוּ, fairly widespread in the period of the first Greek translations of the Bible.

This being the general rule, the titles are but particular applications of it. The oldest lists and the oldest manuscripts explicitly read, or suppose, relatively late forms in יה = ιας (Origen, -ια). There is but one exception. According to all the great uncials (B א A), the title of the book of Obadiah is οβδ[ε]ιου (αβδ[ε]ιου), which corresponds to the older form עבדיהו, pronounced עָבְדִיהוּ, and not to עבדיה, our present Massoretic title: οβδιου can only be a survival of what must originally have been the general state of parallel forms.[2] If this title had been

[1] F. C. Burkitt, *Fragments of the Books of Kings according to the Translation of Aquila*, Cambridge, 1897, pp. 23-5.

[2] It is curious that this 'Greek' survival has an exact parallel in an 'Aramaic' survival in Egypt. The proper name *Abdyahu* is one of the two representatives of the ancient Hebrew form יהו, amongst all the names in יה in the Aramaic papyri found in Egypt (Cowley, *Aramaic Papyri*, no. 81, 22-3, dated by the editor, *c.* 300 B.C.).

influenced at a relatively late date by Aquila, we should read οβδιαου, and not οβδιου. Thus it is all the more striking that the two parallel forms in the list of the Jerusalem MS. are consonant with this old transcription in -ιου, and not with those of Aquila (-ιαου) or Origen (-ια). This is an excellent indication of antiquity. Of course, we must not confuse the relative age of certain transcriptions appearing in the list with the age of the list itself; at the same time, we cannot argue that they are completely unrelated. And indeed, as far as we can know, there are no other examples of the title of the books of Jeremiah and Isaiah in a form supposing ירמיהו and ישעיהו, rather than ירמיה and ישעיה (Talmud, Origen, Jerome, &c.). The document takes us back to a period previous to Aquila and probably a good deal previous to him.

Though, on the whole, this conclusion seems to have solid probability in its favour, yet the chronological question remains difficult. The oldest list which can be compared is that of Melito of Sardis. But if we are to go back very definitely farther, as we believe, then the list of the Jerusalem MS. becomes an isolated document. Points of reference enabling us to fix an upper limit for its origin become more vague. Where must we stop? If we must fix a period, we would choose the second half of the first century of our era.

Somewhat tentatively, I will attempt to assess the significance of the list in the Jerusalem MS. Its great antiquity isolates it in time; its nature also isolates it from all other canonical lists of the Old Testament. Yet certain facts are assured and can serve as a useful basis of discussion.

If we take the titles which are Aramaic in form in their most direct meaning, they point to Aramaic Targums just as the Hebrew titles can only refer to the originals in this tongue, and the Greek titles can only be related to the Greek translations of the corresponding books. If the list has historic significance, it lies here first. It must have historic significance, otherwise we cannot explain the wide diffusion which it certainly had originally. Only because the list had for a long time clear meaning and was commonly useful in a certain milieu, has it come down to us. The list has so little appearance of being interesting that no one has noticed it, though it was so long accessible to all.

That is the fundamental point. First of all, the list gives an impression of a mixed unstable milieu, rapidly evolving in respect of language for reading the sacred text. On the one hand, we have original titles mingled with Targum titles; on the other, Greek translations covering the whole collection. We could scarcely imagine a more interesting combination of evidence, pointing to the period suggested.

It will have been noticed that no book of the Pentateuch is presented in the Targum manner. We cannot conclude forthwith that no Targum on the Pentateuch existed at that time in any form at all. Rather, the list is in keeping with the conditions recently described by Professor Paul Kahle.[1] The Pentateuch must have had its written Targum, though in rather varying forms. But, on the other hand, the very special veneration which, in Jewish minds, should be given to the Law, tended to restrain or delay the official use of its Targum. The list seems to reflect this transition period.

It is noteworthy that the Psalms here are treated like the Pentateuch. This is intelligible if we bear in mind the place which this collection of traditional prayers occupied in the public and private devotions of the Jews. Repetition would have been enough to make them familiar in the original language for Jews whose daily idiom was Aramaic. It is interesting to note also that the Song of Songs is represented in Hebrew, just as the Psalms and the Pentateuch. The reasons for this are probably connected with the very special subject-matter of this little book. At the period which we believe to be that of the list, its literal interpretation was a difficult problem for Jewish exegesis. It is also not unnatural that Chronicles should appear in its original form; practically all its subject-matter (or equivalent material) was to be found in the other historical books, which already had Targums, viz. Samuel and Kings.

This dividing up between Targums and originals, fully in keeping with what we might expect on another score, very much strengthens our impression of the authenticity of the whole document. Its connexions with a determinate historic milieu are fairly clear.

It will be noted, in like manner, that the book of Job is represented by its Targum. We already know something of this Targum from various references in the Talmud.[2] A Tannaite tradition had it that the Targum on Job already existed in written form in the time of R. Gamaliel I (St. Paul's teacher), and that, after being withdrawn from circulation (relegated to Genizas), it reappeared in the time of his grandson Gamaliel II (*flor. c.* A.D. 90–130). It is also possible that the note appended to the book of Job in the LXX (according to all the great uncial manuscripts) refers in some way to the Aramaic Targum vouched for by the Jerusalem MS. list as by the Talmud. We read in effect, Job 42[17b] (text in Swete, *The O.T. in Greek*, ii, 602): 'This is translated from the Syriac book' (ἐκ τῆς συριακῆς βίβλου). This Syriac book can hardly be anything other than an Aramaic Targum.[3]

[1] *The Cairo Geniza* (Schweich Lectures 1941), pp. 117–32.

[2] Talm. bab., *Shabb.*, 115a; the other references in Kahle, *The Cairo Geniza*, p. 124, note 1.

[3] Thus Kahle, op. cit., p. 124; see also the notes of P. Dhorme, *Le livre de Job* (Études Bibliques), Paris, 1926, pp. xv–xvi.

The list comprises 27 books, but only by subdividing four of them and by separating Judges and Ruth. Basically, and in respect of content, it is really the Jewish canon of 22 books, as known to Josephus at the end of the first century of our era (*Contra Apionem*, 1, 8) and as still known to Epiphanius and Jerome at the end of the fourth century.[1] There is no point in discussing here the 22, or 24, or 27. More important and remarkable is the order in which the books are enumerated.

Even the Pentateuch is affected. We read: Gen.–Exod.–Lev. So far so good. But then, surprisingly, come Joshua, Deuteronomy, Numbers! Of all the lists known hitherto, only three offer a slight variation in the Pentateuch enumeration (inversion of Leviticus and Numbers): those given by Melito, Leontius of Byzantium, and Mommsen's Catalogue.[2] Moreover, it is very significant that the recasting of the Jerusalem MS. list which we find in Epiphanius (*De mens.* 23) has restored the usage of the Pentateuchal order and duly excluded Joshua. This 'restoration' occasions no surprise. Complete disorder follows: Ruth, Job, Judges, Psalms. All haphazard, as if intermediary books between Pentateuch and the series of Kings, from the point of view of historical sequence. But the historical books appear in good order, followed by Chronicles. So, too, Proverbs, Ecclesiastes, Canticles are in the same order as in the lists of Melito, Origen, &c. The prophets as a whole are grouped in a recognizable way. But note, in particular, that Jeremiah comes before Isaiah, and this order agrees with the Talmud, but would be without parallel in all the Christian lists.[3] But we have urged that our list is Jewish in origin. The Minor Prophets are strangely enough inserted between Jeremiah and Isaiah. Only Melito has a like grouping, viz.: Isaiah, Jeremiah, XII Minor Prophets, Daniel, Ezechiel. Epiphanius' version made away with this peculiarity. Daniel is in the usual place, according to the Christian lists. As for Esdras and Esther, the order is that of Melito (?), Epiphanius, &c.

What is to be made of this peculiar ordering? Let us first bear in mind that present-day order and permanence in the lists are a 'learned' product coming relatively late in the history of manuscript tradition as in the history of the canon of the Old Testament, later in the Prophets than in the Pentateuch, and later still in the Writings. The threefold division Law, Prophets, Writings, was known at Alexandria from the second century B.C. (Ecclus. Prol.). But Josephus, two centuries later, in Palestine, had an order of his own for the last two

[1] Epiphanius, *Panarion*, i. 1. 5; *De mens.* 4; Jerome, *Prologus galeatus.*

[2] Texts in Swete, *Introd. to the O.T. in Greek*, pp. 203, 207, 212.

[3] Talm. bab., *Baba bathra*, 15a; this order reappears in part of the manuscript tradition of our Massoretic text; cf. C. D. Ginsburg, *Introd. to the Massoretico-critical Edition of the Hebrew Bible*, p. 6.

groups (*Contra Apionem*, 1, 8). So we must beware of taking documents which merely present actual usage at various times, more or less common, advanced, or retrograde, as necessary rulings. Thus we can imagine a suitable place for a list such as ours. A tendency to group books as distinct unities made itself felt variously in the different milieux. Palestine was not bound to follow the example of Alexandria. Our list is, in its way, a more or less successful, and particular, example of early freedom.

Finally, the mention of two books of Esdras, both from the Aramaic and the Greek standpoint, might well be valuable evidence for the question of the origin and nature of 'Greek Esdras' (Esdras A of the LXX and III Esdras of the Vulgate). We cannot here discuss this at length; we would simply suggest a working hypothesis for further researches.

There is no satisfactory explanation of the origin of Greek Esdras— we hope we can say this without injustice to anyone. After fifty or sixty years of debate on this point, the work of Charles Torrey is particularly notable. We propose to summarize his conclusions before suggesting what we believe to be a better alternative.[1]

According to Torrey, there has never been a Hebrew-Aramaic fragment of the same dimensions as Esdras A (LXX). The latter is simply a fragment of some primitive Greek versions of the whole of the Chronicler's work (= Chronicles–Ezra–Nehemiah). Moreover, this version was a faithful representative of the Chronicler's work in the form in which it has been generally received right up to the beginning of our era; and there is no reason for supposing that any other existed at that time. But, on the other hand, the form of this section nowadays represented by Greek Esdras, was no longer in all particulars in conformity with the Chronicler's authentic narrative as it stood in the Hebrew-Aramaic original. For that narrative, before being translated into Greek, had undergone considerable literary transformations, especially as a result of the interpolation of an Aramaic tale of the Three Young Bodyguards at the court of Darius. It was a text recast in this way which is the immediate ancestor of our Greek fragment, Esdras A (LXX). The Chronicler's narrative, as interpolated, had little to

---

[1] Main references for Torrey's work are: *Ezra Studies*, Chicago, 1910, pp. 18–36; 'A Revised View of First Esdras', in *Louis Ginzberg Jubilee Volume*, New York, 1945, pp. 395–7. This latter article appreciably modifies Torrey's previous position, though the main elements relevant to our point remain unaltered. He writes: '. . . the true explanation of the First Esdras is that which is given in *Ezra Studies*, pp. 18 and 36' (op. cit., p. 395). Similarly, but with more restraint, the excellent introduction of S. A. Cook, in Charles, *The Apocrypha and Pseudepigrapha of the O.T.*, I, *Apocrypha*, pp. 1–20.

recommend it (Torrey: 'the impossible Hebrew text'), and was officially revised at the beginning of the second century of our era: this gave our Massoretic text of Ezra and Nehemiah (which is the basis of Esdras B of the LXX, and I and II Esdras of the Vulgate). The old Greek version of the Chronicler's work fell completely out of favour, and need began to be felt for a new translation in conformity with the revised Hebrew. Theodotion supplied this. But, subsequently, someone had the fortunate idea of salving from oblivion the ancient version. Two quires were extracted from a codex and preserved by a 'Jewish scholar', or possibly by a Christian. Anyway these quires came to the knowledge of and came to be owned by the Christians, who gave them pride of place in their LXX; hence Greek Esdras.

But at what date were the two quires extracted from the codex? Torrey does not say. But, following his own argument, we must conclude, not later than the end of the second century, that is, after Theodotion but a good number of years before Origen, who knew the two Esdrases of the LXX without appearing to have the least suspicion of the operation which put the first Esdras there. Thus, at the end of the second century A.D., it was hardly possible to obtain a codex of the ancient version. Unless perchance it had been the only codex to contain the work of the Chronicler, we must suppose that the other copies had perished through neglect and forgetfulness. And this is at the end of the second century! When then was the codex introduced in current usage for the transcription of the sacred books? The utmost goodwill on the part of palaeographers and papyrologists would hardly stretch as far back as Torrey's explanation demands.

But if this element in the argument be abandoned (it is important as showing the present dimensions of Greek Esdras), we get a succession of unlikely improbabilities as we go through the whole scheme of Torrey's explanation. Only some elements are valuable and must be retained.

The list which we have brought forward seems to furnish the element which explains all.

Corresponding to the Greek Esdrases of the LXX, we have not a *single* Hebrew Ezra—as Origen and Jerome's lists would suggest—but *two* Aramaic Targums. It follows (unless we suppose the impossible, viz. that Aramaic Targums conformed in their very origin to already existing Greek versions) that the first Greek Esdras must be descended directly from the Aramaic Targum. In the origin of the two Greek Esdrases, there is only one unknown quantity. As we know that Esdras B depends on the tradition of our Massoretic text, we can assume that the unknown quantity is precisely the Targum which the list relates to Esdras A.

All then is explained. There existed a Hebrew-Aramaic original, identical but for a few textual details with our Ezra–Nehemiah in the Massoretic text. Before the Chronicler's complete work was divided into its present-day parts, an Aramaic translator, only interested in one part of the story, handled the original narrative rather freely: he inserted a piece from his 'stock-in-trade' (the story of the Three Young Guardsmen, which Torrey recognizes as having been originally written in Aramaic), displaced other elements, recast the narrative. Towards the second century B.C., a Greek translation of the Aramaic Targum appeared probably in Palestine, which was thus an indirect and incomplete translation of the Chronicler's work. The version passed to Alexandria and entered the collection of translations already in use there. In addition, it was the Esdras used by Josephus in Palestine itself.

But such a translation, made from a Targum which openly differed from the Hebrew on a number of points, could not satisfy indefinitely. Thereupon a complete translation of the Chronicler's work based on the Hebrew was undertaken. In the interval, perhaps in Egypt, there may have arisen, in the transmission of the Hebrew text, a custom of writing the Chronicler's long story on three scrolls, instead of one only. That would mean that the text of the second scroll ended shortly after the point (2 Chron. 35[1]) where the Targumist had himself previously begun his own translation, thus unconsciously laying down for posterity the limits of the Greek version that would depend on him (Esdras A). The new translator, not necessarily Theodotion,[1] observed accepted

---

[1] We must not be misled by certain resemblances. Torrey's whole argument (*Ezra Studies*, pp. 66 seq.) amounts to assigning to Theodotion the transliterations which can be found in Chronicles–Ezra–Nehemiah. They would be sure evidence of his personal style as a translator. But we do not and cannot know how far the style is Theodotion's, if it is true that he merely revised, from the Hebrew, a collection of Greek versions that was already current in Asia Minor (see, on this, P. Kahle, *The Cairo Geniza*, pp. 168 seq., with T. W. Manson's comments in *Dominican Studies*, ii (1949), pp. 187 seq., reviewing Kahle's book). Of the 110 'Theodotion' transliterations counted by Field (*Origenis Hexapla*, i, pp. xl–xli), only six are from Daniel, whose whole text is extant, and is Theodotion's. We may explain this by saying that Daniel scarcely represents Theodotion's particular style; the translator was merely revising an old version. But the same argument would hold for other parts too, if not for all Theodotion's work. Were Torrey's argument valid, it would prove far too much. He puts before us a list of seventy transliterations from Chron.-Esdr.-Neh. Such a strong proportion causes him to think that it is an unmistakable work of Theodotion's style. But he fails to see that, just alongside, 3 and 4 Kings have much the same proportion of transliterations. C. F. Burney (*Note on the Hebrew Text of the Books of Kings*, Oxford, 1903, pp. xxviii seq.) gives a list of fifty transliterations for these two books alone (0·37 average per page of Swete's text, as against 0·39 for Chron.-Esdr.-Neh. of the same text). Nor has Torrey perceived that 4 Kings, taken alone, shows a proportion of transliterations nearly

usage in transmission as regards the respective lengths of the three sections of the book of the Chronicler. This gives us our Ezra–Nehemiah, which, in the Alexandrine collection, naturally took the name of Esdras B, coming after another Esdras whose complete elimination was not desired. The old Esdras maintained a priority because of its antiquity, and became Esdras A. Finally, the first part of the Chronicler's work, which had never as yet been translated (translation of the parallel historical books could at first suffice), took the distinctive name of παραλειπόμενα, i.e. 'that which is left aside' (in the present tense) *by the old translation.*[1] On the other hand, parallel to the new Greek translation of Ezra–Nehemiah, a new Aramaic Targum could well have appeared, characterized by a concern to be nearer to the Hebrew: it is the second Targum of Esdras in the list, corresponding to the Esdras B of the LXX.

But all this history may well have been forgotten by Christians long before Origen. Knowing only of one Hebrew Esdras for two Greek Esdras, they could not conceive where the first Esdras emanated from. Jerome called it apocryphal: his view obtained. But, in truth, it may well be the old Greek version of an Aramaic Targum which had itself long ago disappeared.[2]

This is but a working hypothesis, though so positively stated. Could it be more closely connected with known facts and be shown to harmonize with all their requirements, then the famous manuscript of the Didache, of Clement of Rome, of Ignatius of Antioch, will appear to have rendered us yet another great service, late in the day. The full historical significance of the list itself, as a whole, should also be put to its credit. *Pauca sed multum.*   JEAN-PAUL AUDET

double that of Chron.-Esdr.-Neh., viz. 0·63 as against 0·39. Must we then say that Kings are also Theodotion's? or where are we to stop? Torrey's hypothesis breaks down completely.

[1] The title 'Paralipomena' has no sure meaning when referred to the content of the work; but it is full of meaning when referred to the historical circumstances in which this part of the Chronicler's work appeared for the first time in Greek. Jerome substituted 'Chronicles' for 'Paralipomena': 'Verba dierum, quod significantius chronicon totius divinae historiae possumus appellare' (*Prol. galeat.*); but he was considering the *content* of the books (cf. Letter 53, *Ad Paulinum*, 7; *P.L.* 22. 548).

[2] For reasons why the old Palestinian Targums disappeared, see P. Kahle, *The Cairo Geniza*, p. 123. I must quote part of the text: 'Only when written in *Greek* were Jewish texts of this time preserved, and they were preserved not by Jews but by Christians who were interested in books like those of Philo and Josephus and similar texts. But Christians who might have been interested in texts written in *Aramaic* had lost their influence after the fall of Jerusalem in A.D. 70.' So with our case; fragments of the old Aramaic Targum of the Chronicler's work would never have come down to us, had they not been at an early period translated into Greek, and, in this tongue, in Christian keeping.

The Old Testament Canon in Palestine and Alexandria

by Peter Katz

(The Rev. Dr. W. Peter M. Walters: 59, Hinton Avenue, Cambridge, [England])

Georgio Cicestr: (1882 4/2 1957)

The textbooks on the Canon of the O. T. take it for granted that our Hebrew Bible preserves the original order of books which was subsequently changed to that of the "Alexandrian collection"[1]. While they are right in pointing out that evidence for the LXX is Christian and therefore comparatively late, they fail to point out that, apart from the mention of its three main groups, there is no pre-Christian evidence either for the "correct" Palestinian Bible and its revision in Alexandria. In fact the Hebrew selection of books is not attested earlier than the reconstitution of Judaism after the destruction of the Temple, and the attested order differs from that adopted in our printed Bibles. This is not surprising, for the canonization of the O. T.,

---

[1] O. Eissfeldt's *Einleitung in das Alte Testament*, Tübingen 1934, arranges the *Geschichte des Kanons* as follows: I. Der Palästinische Kanon §§ 67f. II. Sammlungen Heiliger Schriften des A. T.: § 69. Die Alexandrinische Sammlung. § 70. Andere Sammlungen. This arrangement was abandoned in the second edition (see note 19a below).

Reprinted from *Zeitschrift für die Neutestamentliche Wissenschaft* 47 (1956); 49 (1958).

together with the selection and arrangement of its books, is in itself
the most characteristic expression of this reconstitution.

There is no initial reason to expect much difference of attitude
toward the Bible between the Jewish homeland and its Dispersion
before the emergence of Christianity and the collapse of the Palestinian theocracy. Up to that time Jerusalem remained the centre of
production and assimilation from which Jewish influence radiated.
The Samaritans derived their Bible from Jerusalem and this was
identical in content with that of Jerusalem. Alexandria also received
from Jerusalem not only what are now regarded as the three classes of
canonical books, but also such apocrypha as were originally written
in Hebrew or Aramaic.

There is moreover nothing to prove that when taken over the
latter were passing from a lower canonical status to a higher one. At
that stage the question whether or to what extent they were "canonical" could not have arisen either in Jerusalem or abroad. Certainly
the "Law" was recognized, but not so much because it was laid down
in sacred writings as because of its content, the commandments and
injunctions to which the Jewish community as a whole felt themselves
pledged. The prestige of the "Law" was shared to a lesser degree by
two other groups of sacred writings, the "Prophets" and the "Writings". The authors of the former were considered the successors of
the Lawgiver and Prophet[2] whose books told the story both of mankind
and God's chosen people. The "former prophets," the historical books,
carried on the Pentateuchal narratives and it was perhaps not completely forgotten that these books had once formed a unity with
the Torah[3]. The "latter prophets," the Prophets proper, served as
God's mouthpiece, conveying his message, as Moses had done. The
"Writings", *viz* the Psalter and the sapiential books, were important
for public and private worship and for every day life, and they were
supported by the great names of David and Solomon. The "Prophets" and "Writings" were the halo around the centre, the cloud
of witnesses to the "Law". This much, and no more, can be safely
stated about the graduated esteem in which the three components
of the O. T. were held. The strict concept of canonicity, as we understand it, was still to emerge.

As to the difference of arrangement, there is nothing either to
prove that whatever order emerged from long vacillation was the

---

[2] The basic passage is Deut. xviii. 15 כָּמֹנִי ... וְבִיא, προφήτην ὡς ἐμέ. In
Sir. xlvi. 1 Joshua is מְשָׁרֵת מֹשֶׁה בִּנְבוּאָה, διάδοχος Μωυσῆ ἐν προφητείαις.

[3] In the LXX the Psalter and the other poetical books have their place between
the historical books and the Prophets. This may well be a primitive feature prior
to the formation of the group titles of the "former" and "latter" prophets and the
"Writings".

original which was deliberately altered in Alexandria. On the contrary, clear evidence points toward the reverse. Originally Chronicles and Ezra-Nehemiah, in this sequence, formed one work, compiled by the same author. Nothing could have been more artificial than its disruption in our Bible which has Ezra-Nehemiah first, and Chronicles following, as the last book of the Canon[4]. The theory behind this particular point of arrangement belongs essentially to the ideas guiding the synod of Jamnia about which less is known than is generally assumed. It can be understood only on the artificial premises on which it is based. To achieve this novel order a *terminus ad quem* had to be fixed and, to be workable, a number of dogmatic assumptions had to be introduced. These need no elaboration here but it is obvious that they were unreal and fictitious, designed to support a dubious construction. To exclude unsound apocalyptic speculations a *terminus a quo* had also to be established, as was seen by Hölscher. Since Moses was the first sacred author, there was no room for Enoch. Job and Daniel were a different matter. Where rigid rules clash with realities, a way can always be found.

The Hebrew arrangement is, as we have indicated, closely bound up with ideas and conditions peculiar to its late date of formation. It should not therefore be antedated by centuries. In fact these ideas were foreign even to the period immediately preceding, for the production of sacred writings had been going on steadily throughout the last centuries. It revealed Judaism as a continuous and aggressive missionary movement which looked toward the future, not merely to the past. There were degrees and nuances, as can be seen from Josephus. There was the Law, and the period of prophetic inspiration, the end of which was regretted. There was however no break in the production of poetic and sapiential literature. The place of prophecy was increasingly taken over by an apocalyptic literature.

Should we proceed to state that to collect and arrange this flowing production could be done appropriately in only one way, the "Alexandrian", as preserved in the LXX? There is much to favour this argument. This arrangement allowed each book the place within the whole for which it was intended, so much, indeed, that it is hard to imagine that it replaced an arrangement similar to our Hebrew. It bears the mark of life which knows of neither bias nor concern. The order of the LXX is natural and suitable and suggests a date even earlier than that of the translation of the LXX. And yet, to argue in this way would be rash. Surely, a demonstration that much in the arrangement of the Hebrew points to a late date, would not prove everything in the Greek original. Fortunately, however, we need not

---

[4] The transposition of Daniel is a further instance among many.

confine ourselves to inferences drawn from comparing the Hebrew and Greek Bibles in their present shape, for they are not the only ones about which we know. These early witnesses all have the Torah first, but show a wide variety as regards the remainder. The mere fact that they disagree as to the number and arrangement of the books and sets of books is apt to make us wary of rash assertions.

There is further evidence in the occasional references to the tripartite division of the Scriptures. These are (1) the threefold mention in the prologue of Ecclesiasticus (after 117 B. C.), (2) in Philo's *De vita contemplativa*[5] § 25 (ca 40 A. D.), with the same subdivision of the third group as in Josephus, (3) in the N. T., and (4) in Josephus' *Contra Apionem* I §§ 38ff., confirmed by shorter references elsewhere in his works. The N. T. frequently refers to the Law (or Moses) and the Prophets and Luke xxiv, 44 to the Law of Moses, the Prophets, and the Psalms[6]. *The Law, the Prophets, and the remainder* is a 'polar' expression for the Scriptures as a whole, in the typically Semitic way, just as *heaven and earth* for the universe and *the sun, the moon, and the stars* for heaven. The emphasis is on the whole and not on the parts. Similarly the Law can stand for the whole, a potiori. This 'whole', we should remember, was not a book, but a collection of many scrolls, and in practice the scroll was the thing that mattered. There is therefore nothing strange in what otherwise would be hard to understand, *viz* that vagueness obtained as regards the arrangement of the scrolls (except for the Law where, however, there also was some vacillation, cf. p. 206), while there was none about the tripartite division, in Egypt any more than in Palestine.

These early attestations of the three scriptural groups do not identify the components of the second and third groups and this reflects the fluid state still obtaining. Nevertheless, their emphasis is

---

[5] Its genuineness is no longer doubted.

[6] It has hitherto been usual to adduce Mt. xxiii. 35 = Luke xi. 50f. *from the blood of (righteous) Abel unto the blood of Zacharias (son of Barachias)* — the words in brackets are missing from Luke and the last are crucial. This saying may well survey the series of violent acts, mentioning the first and the last, but does not for that reason necessarily imply the masoretic book order. Its emphasis is on the events, not on their place in the Bible but rather in the history of the people. Jesus may very well have drawn on a Bible which had Chronicles immediately after Kings. Moreover, referring to W. Whiston's translation of Josephus, London, 1737, and to J. A. Osiander's Tübingen Thesis of 1744, Wellhausen has recalled Josephus' *Bellum* iv § 335 (*Ev. Mt.*, p. 120). If he was right, there would be neither a saying of our Lord nor any reference to Chronicles at all. The argument should not be stated without mentioning the difficulties with which it is beset. Neither the exact place of Zechariah's murder nor the name of his father, as found in Matthew, harmonize with II Chron. xxiv. 20f., but they do with the incident reported by Josephus from 67 or 68 A. D., before the siege of Jerusalem.

on the Law, and the practical use of Scripture in their quotations clearly indicates that a Canon was slowly evolving. Josephus takes us a step further. He states that the five books of Moses carried the legislation and history of creation as far as his death, covering a period of almost three thousand years, that the prophets after Moses continued this record in thirteen books down to Artaxerxes, son of Xerxes, and that four further books contain hymns and didactic writings (ὑποθήκας) as a guide for human conduct: in all, 22 books. His last group undoubtedly means the Psalter and the Solomonic books, his second includes some of our "Writings". The number of "reliable" books which allow for no alteration and are the code on which Jewish life is based, however, is final: *Prophetarum numerus clausus*, and a sharp line is drawn between them and the numerous records of the period after Artaxerxes which cannot be fully trusted owing to the extinction of the prophetic inspiration. This statement raises many questions. The number twenty-two doubtless implies that Ruth was appended to Judges, and Lamentations to Jeremiah, but does not necessarily imply that Josephus followed the LXX and that when he addressed the Western world he ignored a different order represented in the Hebrew text. Certainly his arrangement is not that of the LXX. The "memoirs of the Prophets after Moses" comprise the historical books: Job, Chronicles, Ezra, Esther, and the Prophets incl. Daniel, that is the "former" and "latter prophets", each group enlarged as in the LXX, and in addition Job which, like Daniel, was considered a history about, or an account written by, a prophet. Thus Josephus differs from the LXX in two points: by separating Job from his last group, as a "former prophet", and by having the Prophets proper immediately after the "former prophets", so that the hymnical and didactical books come after the prophetical as in our Hebrew Bible.

Since Josephus writes for a gentile public he does not give the titles of books[7], nor is it easy to tell to what extent his concept of official records written by those in a position of command is his own. It certainly had illustrious Roman parallels such as the *monumentum Ancyranum* of Augustus. There are, however, Jewish parallels, *e. g.* in the discussions preserved in Baba Bathra about the authorship of the several Biblical books. Therefore the point can be made that among many rival arrangements and traditions obtaining in Palestine he adopted one, possibly with modifications, which may be due to his task as a historian but can no longer be traced. We may speak with confidence about the number 22 of the books, about the seemingly

---

[7] In his exoteric treatises Philo's restraint goes still farther. In *De Abrahamo* the hero's name is mentioned as late as § 51 and Sarah's only in § 99 (*Philo's Bible*, pp. 156f.).

contradictory aspects of sharing the fuller groups of books with our Greek Bible and of placing the Prophets between the historical and poetical books like our Hebrew Bible. Not even the place assigned to Job need be peculiar to him.

A Jerusalemite by birth, and a priest and nobleman by tradition, he follows a pre-rabbinic order which combines characteristics of the final Greek and Hebrew arrangements and certainly is one of the various orders current in contemporary Palestine.

Much of it obviously survived Josephus by centuries as is clearly indicated by a review of subsequent witnesses[8]. Among them the place of honour belongs to the document discussed by Jean-Paul Audet[9], the early source both of fol. 76a of the Bryennios Manuscript of the *Didache* and of Epiphanius *De mens. et pond.* 23. In my opinion Audet convincingly dates this list, with its mixture of Hebrew and Aramaic titles, not later, and possibly earlier than the first half of the second century A. D. Behind its 27 titles there are the same 22 books as in Josephus, and the list is as obviously Jewish as that of Josephus[10].

The same must be said of those of Melito and Origen, who both went to Palestine with the set task of making sure about the number and arrangement of the books of the O. T.[11] According to Zahn "it is obvious that it was with his Greek Bible in hand that Melito gathered his information." In fact he drew up his list[12] so as to be understood by his Greek friend and brother (-bishop?) and therefore used the Greek titles and book divisions; for though he mentions no number his addressee who had expressly asked for the number could not but count 22. The expression τῶν δώδεκα ἐν μονοβίβλῳ indicates that Melito is satisfied to have given an unmistakable hint at the sum total. The number results by taking Samuel, Kings, and Chronicles as one each; Βασιλειῶν τέσσαρα, Παραλειπομένων δύο is merely a convenient reference to the Greek Bible intended to facilitate identification

---

[8] For the following I refer to the impressive chapter *Zählungen der biblischen Bücher* in Th. Zahn's *Geschichte des Nentestamentlichen Kanons* II 1, Erlangen und Leipzig, 1890, pp. 318ff.

[9] "A Hebrew-Aramaic List of Books of the Old Testament in Greek Transcription." *J. T. S.*, N. S. 1, 1950, pp. 135—54.

[10] There is a full discussion of Audet's essay in Excursus A.

[11] Th. Zahn never wrote his promised Beilage XV, 10 (p. 326) to prove that Melito consulted "*Jewish Christians* or Jews", but he is right in stating that Melito's list was not that "read in the services of the Christian congregations or the synagogues of Minor Asia but that of the O. T. books which the Jews *and Jewish Christians* (my italics) of the holy land recognized as such." Today we are less inclined to think of Jewish *Christians* in this connection.

[12] Eusebius, *H. E.* iv. 26, 13f.

without influencing the argument. Melito omits Esther which was slow to be accepted in some Palestinian circles but instead assigns a number of its own to Ruth (after Judges), probably following his authority who wished to retain the sum total of 22 books. Lamentations are not mentioned; they and perhaps also the other components of the *corpus Ieremianum* must be understood. He has Daniel before Ezekiel, an arrangement shared by others, though opposed to that of the LXX.

We would perhaps be less positive about Melito, had we not the distinct testimony of Origen[13]. What must be inferred in Melito is clear in Origen: he reflects traditions about which he had learned from Jewish scholars in Palestine; he even mentions a name and other particulars. Origen refers to the number 22 and equates it with the number of letters in the Hebrew alphabet. His list is studiously complete. Throughout he gives, first the Greek name of the book in question and then the Hebrew which he both transliterates and translates. He is at pains to note such peculiarities of the Hebrew arrangement and the content of its several scrolls as could not be inferred from the LXX. About Ruth he is clear: Κριταί, Ρουθ, παρ' αὐτοῖς ἐν ἑνί, Σωφτειμ. It is the same with Samuel: Βασιλειῶν α'β', παρ' αὐτοῖς ἐν, Kings: Βασιλειῶν γ'δ', ἐν ἑνί, Chronicles: Παραλειπομένων α'β', ἐν ἑνί, and with Ezra: Ἔζρας α'β' where I do not think it necessary to understand Ezra and Nehemiah. We have found so many peculiarities of the "Alexandrian" arrangement to be reflexions of the Hebrew, that it is quite possible that I Ezra, the Greek of which is undoubtedly an early translation from the Hebrew, was still current in Palestine, though perhaps not widely so. Furthermore he too has the order Daniel Ezekiel[13a]. The Minor Prophets dropped out in Eusebius at a very early date. Rufinus inserts them before Isaiah with a wording clearly secondary. In view of what is found in Melito, Leontius of Byzantium, and Canon Mommsen it is regrettable that we are unable to be definite about the place where Origen had them.

Three more among the early Fathers who were familiar with the Palestinian situation do not know about the number 24. Eusebius, Bishop of Caesarea, mentions Canticles as one of the 22 scriptures in which those ἐκ περιτομῆς believed as being inspired by God (*Eclog. proph.* ed. Gaisford, p. 106). Cyril, Bishop of Jerusalem, (*Catech.* 4 35) is very strict about the number 22 of the Hebrew Canon as normative for Christians. Epiphanius, though playing with the number 27,

---

[13] *Selecta in Psalmos*, II, 528 Delarue, condensed in Eusebius, *H. E.* vi. 25, 1f. The enumeration of the books is in Eusebius only.

[13a] Origen's order Dan. Ez. is reflected in the hexaplaric witnesses min. 88 (Chig. R. VII. 45) and the Syro-Hexaplaris, though as part of the peculiar sequence Jer. Dan. Ez. Is. (Rahlfs, *Verzeichnis*, p. 278; Ziegler, *Isaias*, p. 41).

and giving three different enumerations of the canonical books, throughout reckons with 22 books. Later lists that take this number from earlier authorities can safely be omitted here.

The assertion of H. L. Strack, and those following him, that wherever we find the number 22 it betrays Alexandrian influence, neglects several incontestable facts. (1) The sequence Daniel Ezekiel, as found in the two earliest witnesses, Melito and Origen, and later on in Hilary, the *Breviarium Hipponense* (419, reflecting definitions dating 393 and 397), Augustine, *doctr. Christ.* and elsewhere, and in Canon Mommsen, was met with independently in Palestine by Melito and Origen, and is otherwise attested by no Greek source. (2) The early place among the historical books as given to Job in the identical lists of the Bryennios MS and Epiphanius *mens.* 23, which reckon with 22 books, is equally Palestinian. Untouched by Greek influence, this tradition lived on in the African West. In the list of Innocent I (*Ep. ad Exsuperium*) we find, after a first section comprising the Hexateuch, Regnorum Ruth (with a position of Ruth after Regn. as repeatedly in Augustine who even commends it expressly, and in Canon Mommsen), and then, after the Prophets, five books of Solomon, and the Psalter, a second set of historical books, Job, Tobit, Esther, Judith, Maccabees, two books of Ezra, and Chronicles: Item Historiarum: Job ... Similarly in Canon. Mommsen (359 A. D., Zahn, p. 143), in the *Antiqua translatio* according to Cassiodorius, and in Augustine's earlier period previous to his *Speculum*, which stands for a later development under the influence of Jerome. Augustine discusses the point in *doctr. Christ.* 2 13. Here also a Palestinian tradition survived in Africa.

(3) More decisive than these stray observations is Jerome's canonical list. A. Kuenen is correct when he states that his witness cannot be discredited by assuming Alexandrian influence (*Onderzoek* I[1], 3, 1865, p. 450). He did not visit Palestine briefly for search, but lived there through many years and formed his opinions under the guidance of Jewish scholars. Jerome throughout numbers 22 books. His *prologus galeatus* mentions the habit of *nonnulli* to have "Ruth et Cinoth inter Hagiographa" and thus to count 24 books[14]; he even mentions that a connection was found with the 24 elders of the Apocalypse. His own count, however, is 22.

Jerome's *Epistle* 53 *to Paulinus* greatly differs in style and content from the former. It is rhetorical and less precise. In it he gives a list of the authors and their subjects, not primarily an enumeration of the scrolls. Thus each of the 12 Prophets has a paragraph to himself. If, however, we do the reckoning, as we have to do it in Melito and

---

[14] Others attain the number 24 by including Tobit and Judith.

elsewhere, we get 22. Job comes in immediately after the Pentateuch[15]. Ruth, after Judges, has its own paragraph and number. After Kings there follow the minor and major Prophets, Daniel as the last, and after the Psalter and the Solomonic writings Esther, Chronicles, and Ezra and Nehemiah. The sequence is peculiar, combining opposite tendencies, on the one hand some approximation to the final Hebrew arrangements, on the other peculiar aspects such as the place given to Job, a solution which requires to be seen in a wider context. There is nothing to mark Daniel as being of minor status. On the contrary: "Quartus vero, qui et extremus inter quatuor prophetas, temporum conscius, et totius mundi πολυΐστωρ, lapidem praecisum de monte sine manibus, et regna omnia subvertentem, claro sermone pronuntiat."

The *Prologus in Danielem* is also different. Jerome first mentions that the inadequate LXX translation was abandoned in favour of that of Theodotion. He professes not to know why this has been done, but expatiates upon the difficulties of the Aramaic and on rationalist strictures upon miraculous traits in the Prophets. "Deus scit." In this context he reminds the readers, leaving it all to them, "non haberi Danielem apud Hebraeos inter prophetas, sed inter eos qui hagiographa scripserunt." He continues: "In tres siquidem partes omnis ab eis Scriptura dividitur, in legem, in prophetas, et in hagiographa, id est in quinque, et octo, et in undecim libros; de quo non est huius temporis disserere. Quae autem ex hoc propheta, immo contra hunc librum, Porphyrius obiciat, testes sunt Methodius, Eusebius, et Apollinarius, qui multis versuum milibus eius vesaniae respondentes, nescio an curioso lectori satisfecerint." From this context it is obvious that Jerome, without in any way making the novel number and arrangement of the O. T. books his own, records it, because it might offer a solution to intellectual difficulties. Dubious apologetics, indeed! Jerome accepts the Jewish number of 22 books, but he knows another Jewish reckoning supported by a minority. At times it may have been useful to play with it, but it is not his and he is clearly averse to finding it in the Apocalypse though his aversion is expressed in non-committal language.

In conclusion Zahn, p. 336, rightly states that from 90 to 400 A. D. we have an almost unbroken chain of witnesses for the fact that the Palestinian Jews not only had a theory about the 22 books of the Canon, but also as a rule used a Bible consisting of 22 scrolls. As the only exception he notes that Melito follows Jewish contemporaries in excluding Esther and giving Ruth its own number to keep the number 22 unaltered, which confirms the part played by this number.

---

[15] For parallels to this arrangement see p. 208

We may add that Origen's giving Esther the last place in the list may indicate either slowness to acquiesce in it or its recovery.

Zahn is equally correct in making short shrift with the number 24. Its attestation is meagre, compared with 22. The first witness is IV Ezra xiv, contemporary with Josephus. IV Ezra is a fiction and the setting of the report about Ezra re-writing the Scriptures reflects the evaluation of Scripture in apocalyptic circles: the 24 books written first must be published and read by both worthy and unworthy; but the last 70 are to be guarded and transmitted only to the Initiated (Hölscher). For patristic references to this passage I again refer to Zahn, pp. 339f. He thinks it probable that Clement of Alexandria was among them and that he is the ultimate source of Victorinus of Pettau and other Occidentals. Further there is nothing in the Mishna proper, in earlier Midrashim (Mechilta, Sifra, Sifre), or in the Jerusalem Talmud; only Taanith fol. 8a (babyl. Talmud) and the report in Baba Bathra fol. 14b. 15a, a treatise of the Babylonian Talmud, which was not incorporated in the Mishna. It consists of a brief enumeration of the Prophets and Writings, each part followed by lengthy records of rabbinic discussions about particulars which, apart from characterizing its own period, are anything but material for writing history. To define its value it is sufficient to repeat from Marx's (Dalman's) authoritative commentary [16] that everything said is taken — or rather extracted — from the Scriptures as we have them. Moreover, the whole is not legislation but, at most, a programme. Apart from the number, nothing, not even the arrangement of the books, was settled. The next step toward this goal, the setting apart of the Megilloth, took place some centuries later. Only then the varying shapes of what we now call "our Hebrew Bible" could emerge [17].

---

[16] *Traditio Rabbinorum Veterrima de Librorum Veteris Testamenti Ordine atque Origine*, Lipsiae, 1884, p. 58.

[17] Although this latest stage is not within the scope of the present paper a few remarks which can easily be checked from Swete's convenient list (*Introduction*, p. 200) may be to the point. He puts side by side the Talmudic order, that of the Spanish, Franco-German, and of the masoretic MSS, and lastly that of the printed Bibles which, however, is no longer uniform since the Stuttgart *Biblia Hebraica*[3] has *Job* before the Proverbs, after its masoretic archetype, agreeing with the Talmud and the Spanish MSS, clearly an earlier order. Also, another difference in order is early. It is that of *Jeremiah* coming in as the first of the major Prophets, immediately after Kings with which it is more closely connected. In the Ketubim things become more difficult, as there is a bewildering variety of differences. It is sufficient to mention some instances. In the Talmudic order *Ruth* is the first of the Ketubim, not so much because earlier it had formed part of the former prophets, as an appendage to Judges (at times to Kings), as because it contains the genealogy of David with whose name the next book, the Psalter, is so closely connected. This was possible before the Megilloth were grouped together. It

To sum up, our decision about the number of books is easy. Once we dispense with the understandable propensity for considering our Hebrew Bible as reflecting the "original" at all points, we realize that neither its order nor its number of books can claim originality. The number 24 has scanty support. IV Ezra, which may be of Babylonian origin[18], is the first to suggest it, at the same time in which Josephus has the count 22, but probably later than Audet's Hebrew-Aramaic list. Some Occidental Christian authors before Jerome used the number 24, but as regards Palestine itself we have no witness except the Babylonian Baba Bathra which, to say the least, is not an encouraging document and, moreover, led to no practical measures. Life went on in neglect of it, as we see from Jerome. Neither Melito nor Origen nor the impressive ensemble of Bishops, stationed in Palestine or familiar with it, knew of it. Taanith also is Babylonian. 22 means Judges *plus* Ruth and Jeremiah *plus* Lamentations, each pair on a single scroll.

The number twenty-two is the sum total of the earliest arrangement of scrolls we are able to trace. It was not chosen to serve as an indication of anything else; it is not a symbol. As a matter of course, the identical number of letters of the Hebrew alphabet was snatched at in search for a deeper meaning. Who is likely to suppose that Homer aimed at writing as many books as represent the Greek alphabet? No more is the number twenty-four in any way symbolic. It was the mere result of transferring Ruth and Lamentations to the third group, within which they were later made to join the remaining three Megilloth to form a sub-group. Some Fathers attained the same object by adopting Tobit and Judith; they of course had Ruth and Lamentations in their original places.

---

may be worth recording that Ruth retained its leading position among the Megilloth in the Spanish and masoretic MSS and accordingly regained it in BH[3]. The same group of MSS, but in this instance without the following of BH[3], gives the first place to *Chronicles* which are thus found separated from Ezra-Nehemiah, the last in the list, by the whole of the remaining Ketubim. As to the motives responsible for this change from the Talmudic order our first impression is that this may go back to their original position among the historical books; but this can hardly be substantiated, since here, as in all other groups of MSS, the Prophets intervene. The place of *Daniel* after, instead of before, Esther (Talmud) is merely a consequence of the grouping of the Megilloth. The coincidence with the order of Chester Beatty 967, Ezekiel, Esther, Daniel, is incidental.

[18] "Attestation by the Babylonian Gemara and the late Midrashim which depend on it suggests an origin of this reckoning among the Jews of Mesopotamia. The fact that it occurs in IV. Ezra is not a counterargument, for we do not know the native country of its author. The choice of Ezra's rôle and the designation of his station Rome as Babel can reflect a piece of a life's story" (Zahn, p. 336).

There is no difficulty in tracing the twenty-two books in the LXX, as soon as it is remembered that the addition of books that were later precluded from the Canon points to an early period, to which the order of books could not imply a canonicity still non-existing. This formulation is meant to express the probability that the order of the LXX derived from Palestine and was one of the many orders obtaining there simultaneously. It may look rational, perhaps too much so, and even rationalistic, but our Excursus B indicates that much that we might call typically Alexandrian was quite as possible and real in Palestine. The division of Samuel, Kings, and Chronicles, on the other hand, appears to be late and Christian. We find it first in Melito and would connect it with the abandonment of scrolls for codices, one of the measures by which the early Church as the Israel in the Spirit marked her distance from the old Israel in the flesh[19]. Original components of a single scroll were separated only on theological grounds, as was done in Judaea. In contrast the division of the historical books was a matter of convenience.

Among the books with an uncertain position early witnesses assign Job to the former prophets and Daniel to the latter. Chronicles which headed the Ketubim in authoritative groups of Jewish MSS, among them the Masoretic, was firmly grounded among what was later called "former prophets" and at times moved forward to a place of honour. Very few of these features could rightly be styled Alexandrian or Greek, still less African or Western. Almost without exception it all derived from the Μήτηρ Σιων. It is owing to the LXX and the early Fathers that a prospect was kept open which the rabbis had done their utmost to obscure. In the decisive moment Jerusalem lost its grip of the Dispersion and when it was restored the Church kept aloof up to Origen. For this very reason many pre-rabbinic traditions outlived destruction, and their survival has kept alive a grand chapter of history which Palestinian Judaism in its hour of utter debacle and distress had to strike out for sheer survival. The rabbis must not be blamed for concentrating on what they considered the essentials. However, not even the most determined change of mind can ever undo realities.

What this paper urges is that much more attention should be given to the manifold pre-Talmudic aspects of the Canon in the making than has become usual; that the LXX and the early Fathers should be studied afresh with this end in view and, above all, that we should not read history backwards, taking our stand with a party which was proudly partisan and rightly so; for it had to turn its back to a past,

---

[19] Cf. my note "The early Christians' use of Codices instead of Rolls" in *J. T. S.* 46, 1945, pp. 63 ff.

its own past, in order to pave a way into a possible future. Once we own the bifurcation that has taken place in the shape of the Bible — and in the people of the Bible — we are in a position to evaluate the development of reconstituted Judaism on its own presuppositions and, equally, the development, which has its root in pre-rabbinic Judaism, but was by necessity eradicated in Palestine and Babylonia. To see in everything "Alexandrian" nothing but defection from Palestinian models and impulses is to antedate by centuries the situation of the first post-Christian centuries [19a].

The present paper has endeavoured to remain within the limits of the demonstrable or at least of the probable. Therefore points which could have been made with the same plausibility have been ignored. No survey of mistaken theories and presuppositions has been attempted. A book would have been required but, whether an essay or a book, there will always remain open questions, because at places the available evidence is too incomplete to afford valid answers [20].

[19a] I am happy to see that Dr. Eissfeldt now agrees to this statement. In a special contribution he explains how he came to accept the position set forth in the present paper, not without adding to its strength by his reference to the Qumrân scrolls: "The second edition (1956) of my *Einleitung in das Alte Testament* has abandoned the opinion that our Hebrew Bible preserved the original order of the books, and that the order in the »Alexandrian collection« was a transformation of this and merely secondary; and replaces it with the explanation that the extent of a collection of sacred writings as revealed in ⑤ is based on an older Jewish tradition which was later modified, particularly at the Council of Jamnia, by narrowing of the Canon. Apart from some critical scruples expressed by Johannes Goettsberger in his review of the first edition, my decision to abandon the position represented therein was due, firstly, to the relevant essays of P. Katz which the author rendered accessible to me, partly in manuscript, as well as manifold notes which he had gathered in the course of proof-correction of those parts of the new edition of the *Einleitung* which concern us here; and, secondly, to the textual discoveries made since 1947 in the Judaean desert, which clearly show that the indigenous Jewish community in and near the district of Khirbet Qumrân knew a collection of sacred writings similar in extent to the ⑤-Canon. In § 75, 4 ('Die von ⑤ und den Qumrân-Schriften repräsentierte Überlieferung') of the new edition, p. 706, it is said: 'However, the shape of the Canon depicted above, as fixed by the decree of Jamnia, is not the only one known to us. Far from it. In the tradition represented equally by ⑤ and by the Qumrân texts there has survived a type of Canon which, considered as the outcome of a stage of development antecedent to the verdict of Jamnia, is less rigid than the other and accordingly does not display one form, but several; in the way that the ⑤-MSS display manifold discrepancies both in the number of the O. T. books which they contain and in the arrangement of them, thereby undoubtedly continuing an older Jewish tradition.'" O. Eissfeldt.

[20] Two problems will continue exercising the minds of scholars. The first is the impossibility of circumscribing or eliminating Christian influence on the LXX in its pre-Christian form. The present paper, however, has indicated that, as in

Excursuses

A. On Audet's Hebrew-Aramaic list

The merit of Audet's essay is not confined to the attention which he has drawn to a neglected document, but extends to his treatment. Like a breath of fresh air it has changed a stale atmosphere. He points out that this ancient list is Jewish and has much in common with the Palestinian lists recorded by Melito and Origen. "Daniel is placed among the prophets. This was the old Jewish notion of the book, that which commonly obtained in Palestine in the time of Christ (Matt. 24 15) or in the time of Josephus (c. A. D. 95: cf. *Contra Apionem*, I 8; *Antiquities*, 10, II 17), and passed from Jewish to Christian tradition[21]." He mentions the primitive Jewish position of Jeremiah as the first of the prophets[22], and could have added that in the Bryennios list[23] which alone assigns this position to Jeremiah the latter does not follow Kings and Chronicles immediately, but is separated from them by Prov., Eccles., Cant. As he cannot agree with Torrey's theory about the two Ezra books, he offers a fresh solution.

Here and elsewhere, however, some points must be made by way of correction or supplement.

(1) There is nothing to justify Audet's assumption that the Aramaic book names point to books written in the Aramaic language and therefore to Targums. This assumption is at variance with all

Palestine, there was more than one grouping of the sacred scrolls in Alexandria. Our great uncials present no uniform order and many of their differences admit of explanation. Vat. B has the order of Athanasius' 39th Festal Letter. Sin. S, in spite of is textual affinity with B, has aberrations like assigning the last place to Job. There may have been more variety of order in the early Christian papyri than we can see today. Everything, including the early testimony of Melito and the others, points to a very wide diversity in all centres of Jewish learning and consequently among Christians. Perhaps our continued questions are less striking than the lack of answers and the explanation may be that the questions were gratuitous. The second problem may have been equally wrongly posed. How can we reconcile the two facts that there was a clear distinction between those books that came to be canonical and the others, and that they were mixed up in the order which now is that of the LXX? In other words: Is the order of the LXX due to Christian carelessness? The only satisfactory answer that can be given is that the order of books was not meant to indicate the esteem in which they were held, and that this attitude changed in Palestine too late to influence the Dispersion. This might well imply that much of what we are inclined to ascribe to Christian influence is in fact a survival from the pre-rabbinic period.

[21] p. 145, quoting R. D. Wilson's article in the *Princeton Theological Review* xiii, 1915, pp. 352—408, especially pp. 402—6.

[22] p. 150.

[23] Henceforth "Br." Epiphanius *De mens, et pond.* 23 is quoted as "Epiph." to indicate the list in common with Br.

that is known of the subject. What kind of a community would it suggest? If one remembers that there was strong prejudice against putting vernacular versions into writing so that the early existence of a written Targum of Job is expressly mentioned as an exception, there simply is no environment in which to locate such a Bible.

(2) The fact that the list is made up of Hebrew and Aramaic titles requires a more probable explanation. Why should not an Aramaic-speaking community use Aramaic names for their Hebrew books? Some exceptions are easily understood. The books of the Pentateuch were those regularly read in the services, the Psalter was the hymnal of the congregation designed for both public and private use. Their content was well known and their titles appropriate. The first explanation cannot be applied to δεβρι ιαμιμ and σιρ ασιριμ though Chronicles had a place of honour in the services of the Day of Atonement [23a]. As an alternative I would offer a grammatical explanation. Both are composite expressions in the construct state and it might have seemed awkward to prefix a genitive sign like שֶׁ or דִּ pointing to an understood סֵפֶר; no attempt therefore at translation was made. Perhaps also the titles were retained for their very expressiveness. Br. δααθαρσιαρ (δα[α]θαρισαρ = תְּרֵיסַר ?), Epiph. δαθαριασαρα do not constitute difficulties, because without a following נְבִיאִין they do not form a construct state. Moreover, with a following נְבִיאִין and a preceding סֵפֶר understood we should have a very complex construct state unlikely to be used, especially in post-Biblical Aramaic.

(3) In the remaining titles the Greek does not always express the Aramaic genitive. In this the two texts sometimes agree: δακοελεθ· (Epiph. ὁ) ἐκκλησιαστής; Br. διερεμ· Ιερεμίας, but Epiph. διερεμιου· ἡ τοῦ Ιερεμίου. Ezekiel, Daniel, I II Ezra, and Esther have the Greek name in its uninflected form as nominatives in Br., but all this is changed and detailed in Epiph. In δησαιου· Ησαιου Br. the Greek form need not be a genitive; analogy suggests that it is a transliteration. τοῦ προφήτου Ησαίου Epiph. is, of course, different. Audet prints ελησιμωθ, ἡ ἔξοδος τῶν υἱῶν Ισραηλ ἐξ Αἰγύπτου Epiph., but again analogy recommends ἡ, cf. τὸ ἆσμα τῶν ἀσμάτων. He pleads for the antiquity of the name forms in -ιου indecl. which he thinks were ousted from the LXX by those in -ίας. I feel on safer ground in noting that in an early text we should expect Ἐξαγωγή and not Ἔξοδος [24], but perhaps Ἔξοδος represents Palestinian usage.

(4) Audet's assumption [25] that I II Ezra are both translations of Aramaic Targums concedes too much to Torrey's solution which

---

[23a] A. Spiro, Samaritans, Tobiads, and Judahites in Pseudo-Philo, *Proceedings of the American Academy for Jewish Research* XX, 1951, n. 65 (pp. 303 ff.).

[24] Cf. *Philo's Bible*, p. 48; *Theol. Zeitschr.* 9, 1953, p. 231.

[25] p. 152.

Audet rightly rejects. He realizes that "Esdras A depends on the tradition of our Massoretic text", but this leaves no room for interposing a Targum. He further asserts that there is "only one unknown quantity in the origin of the two Greek Esdrases" and this he traces to "the Targum which the list relates to Esdras A". The list does nothing of the kind and the Achilles' heel in the whole argument is that it must date the apocryphal I Ezra later than the canonical II Ezra. In fact the loose and careless composition is bound to be the earlier. Moreover the Greek of I Ezra is early and certainly Alexandrian while II Ezra belongs to the translator of Chronicles, who is slavish and cannot therefore with certainty be localized. If it were Palestinian it would not stand alone among the later components of the LXX. Besides, would Audet seriously suggest that the twofold *corpus* as translated by the same author consisted of Chronicles in Hebrew and Ezra-Nehemiah all in Aramaic? Doubtless such an assumption would greatly add to the spice of the argument, as it would antedate by centuries[26] Audet's "Hebrew-Aramaic list". This, of course, is an aside, but it points to the risks of unguarded argument.

(6) More important is the question to what extent the order of books can be trusted. As a matter of course we must first correct distortions of the original order and this is made easy by the fact that they are confined to Br. Comparison with Epiph. reveals two corruptions in Nos 1—9 Br. Coming after 1. Genesis, 2. Exodus, 3. Leviticus, the three following entries, 4. Joshua, 5. Deuteronomy, 6. Numbers, are due to a mistaken βουστροφηδόν reading, 1→3, 4←6, a mishap that cannot be compared with the deliberate transposition: Numbers, Leviticus, Deuteronomy, in which Melito, Leontius of Byzantium, and the African Canon Mommsen of 359 A. D. agree. To correct a further mistake, 7. Ruth must be placed after the next two entries, 8. Job, 9. Judges, as in Epiph. The remaining divergences are due to intentional changes on the part of Epiphanius. After emendation there emerge several characteristic features.

(7) *Ruth* follows after Judges, and as soon we reduce, as we must, the pointless number of 27 books to 22 the two form part of a single scroll. The same can be safely assumed for Jeremiah and *Lamentations*; the latter are not even mentioned; considered to be Jeremiah's works they were assumed. Regrettably we cannot tell whether any more components of the little *corpus Ieremianum* lurk in this entry.

(8) The *Psalter* has its place immediately after Ruth as in Baba Bathra and for the same reason[27]. This remains true even though the

---

[26] I refer to the general argument sub (1). In addition we must keep in mind that use of the Greek Chronicles can be observed from about 150 B. C. onward (Schürer, *Geschichte des jüdischen Volkes im Zeitalter Jesu Christi*[4] III, Leipzig, 1909, p. 427).   [27] Cf. note 17 above.

connection of Ruth and the Psalter was no longer perceived; for the order of Baba Bathra was supposed to be the historical[28]. After Psalms follow Samuel, Kings, and Chronicles, and then Proverbs, Eccles, and the Song of Songs. Thus there is no solid block of either "Former Prophets" or "Writings"; as mentioned, Job comes in much earlier than even the Psalms, and the two Ezras and Esther occupy the last places. An unbiased critic might infer that the familiar division into three, though certainly known, did not influence the arrangement of the 22 scrolls in enumerating, grouping, or even committing them to writing in book form. We are not sufficiently informed of the rules prescribing a fixed order for depositing or locking up the scrolls: but the question became crucial when the early Christians abandoned scrolls for codices[29]. Since Christians spoke also of "The Law (Moses), the Prophets, and the other books", just as Ben Sira's grandson, but introduced or retained the traditional order in their Greek Bible, although this does not coincide with that division into three, the analogy of Audet's list serves as a useful parallel. We must never forget that the period which first understood the Bible as threefold did not employ the book form; what they express is a theory which could not be well applied to their 22 scrolls.

(9) Apart from the Pentateuch the only block observable is formed by the *Prophets* proper. In both lists *Daniel* follows Ezekiel. The fact that the next are the two Ezra books and Esther — the latter last as in Origen — does not affect the place of Daniel as the last among the prophets. Br. has *Jeremiah* first and the *Minor Prophets* next, Epiph. first the latter, then Isaiah. This early place of the Minor Prophets tallies with that in our LXX MSS. The leading position of Jeremiah, on the other hand, agrees with the Talmud and is found in the Spanish, Franco-German, and Masoretic MSS. Though early Palestinian and backed by argument (Baba Bathra), it is hardly more primitive than that of the LXX with Isaiah first after the Minor Prophets.

(10) In Epiph. *Chronicles* precede Samuel and Kings. This, however, is not a corruption, but one of Epiphanius' idiosyncrasies. He assigns the same positions in the list of *mens.* 4 with its artificial count of four "Pentateuchs", followed by the two remaining books[30], τοῦ Εσδρα δύο, μία λογιζομένη, and Esther. After the πέντε νομικαί = Torah there follow πέντε στιχήρεις, thirdly ἄλλη πεντάτευχος, τὰ καλούμενα Γραφεῖα, παρά τισι δὲ Ἁγιόγραφα λεγόμενα, and here

---

[28] "Samuel wrote his book and the book of Judges and Ruth. David wrote the book of Psalms ...".

[29] Cf. *J. T. S.* 46, 1945, pp. 63ff.

[30] John of Damascus has the same arrangement of four "Pentateuchs" plus two books, but eliminates Epiphanius' peculiarities.

Chronicles follow Joshua, Judges combined with Ruth and precede Samuel and Kings. His fourth "Pentateuch", ἡ προφητική π., has the grouping of *mens*. 23. In placing Chronicles at the head of the Ketubim (and earlier than Ezra-Nehemiah) the Spanish and Masoretic MSS present something comparable, different but as close an analogy as this late period could afford. The motive of Epiphanius' various attempts to assign an early place to Chronicles is not difficult to detect, in his observation that I Chronicles i—ix recapitulate the whole history down to David under the form of genealogical tables.

(11) Epiphanius' location of *Job* is still more vacillating. The artificial arrangement of *mens*. 4 enables him to assign to Job the earliest possible position, after Deuteronomy, as the first of the five στιχήρεις of the second "Pentateuch." Where he follows the emended Br., in *mens*. 23, he places Job after Joshua and in *haer*. I 15 he inserts Job, followed by the Psalter and the Solomonic writings, between Ruth and Samuel. These varying positions indicate that to Epiphanius Job was a "Former Prophet" contemporary with Moses (*mens*. 4) or his early successors, either Joshua (*mens*. 23 = Br.) or the Judges (*haer*. I 15). In this he does not stand alone. About no Biblical figure does Baba Bathra contain more conjectures than about Job. He never existed nor was ever created, he is a fable (משל). He was a Gentile — he was an Israelite. He entered Egypt with the Israelites and died when they left it. He was a contemporary of Isaac, Jacob, Moses, the Judges, David, the Kingdom of the Sabaeans, and of Ahasuerus. He accompanied those returning from the Exile and his academy was in Tiberias. He preached to the Gentiles. Moses wrote his book. This secured the place of the book of Job in the Canon. The other conjectures are all points of early discussion and based on adducing the most far-fetched Bible passages. Epiphanius relished improbabilities and was well at home in Palestine. Here was material on which to draw. Perhaps, however, his fertile mind was not in need of suggestions! There are many indications to show that Job conveyed an erratic impression among the Biblical books. In Sin. S it occupies the last place, after the two Wisdoms. The Synopsis published by Lagarde[31] places Job after Esther, Tobit, Judith. With some late Latin Fathers this seems to imply some devaluation. The last group of the list of Innocent I has them, together with I II Macc., I II Ezra, I II Chron., with the title *Historiarum*. Similarly Pseudo-Gelasius and Cassiodorius. In Isidore Job is missing, as in Pseudo-Chrysostom's *syn. script. sacr.* praef. (Swete, pp. 211f., 205). In Junilius and others it is the same, but here obviously under Syrian influence.

---

[31] *SeptuagintaStudien* II, Göttingen, 1892, pp. 60ff.

B. The "Alexandrian Doctrine of Inspiration"

One of the arguments for the inferiority of the tradition represented by the LXX is the assertion that there was an Alexandrian theory about inspiration which could not be reconciled with the Hebrew concept of prophecy as a divine gift bestowed only upon a classical period in the past. The proof for the existence of such a doctrine in Alexandria is found in Philo who is said to have claimed the gift of prophecy for himself[32]. The next step is to draw a parallel between Philo's claim and the fact that more books were considered prophetical in the LXX than in the Hebrew Bible. A looser kind of argument includes in this argument the *plus* of the LXX compared with the Hebrew even for non-prophetical texts. The Alexandrian doctrine of inspiration is made responsible for the larger collection of books in the LXX and the neglect of the borderline between the canonical and other books. All this, however, can be easily disproved.

(1) What is found in Philo has its exact parallels much earlier in Palestine. Rudolf Smend gives a picture of Ben Sira's argument which recalls Philo's[33]. In chs. xliv — xlix the Jewish belief in God is described in its cosmic aspect. In xlii. 15 — xliii. 33 the historical aspect is represented. "However, God's action in history essentially issues in the historical self-consciousness of the Jews[34]." "The glory of Israel is realized best in its Divine Services which are the best expression for the highest distinction of Israel, as the high-priestly garb is its highest title of glory. Therefore Moses is overshadowed by Aaron. David is primarily the sacred author of the Psalms and the originator of the music of the temple. And the eternal office of the High Priest of the house of Sadoc is more important than the Messiah from David's tribe. This glory will be completed only in the future. Therefore the summit is the apostrophe to Elijah who waits in the heavenly chamber to bring about the last days. Therefore apocalyptic interest and eschatological speculation make themselves sometimes felt. The truth is guaranteed to Israel by the prophetic succession, but above all in its holy scriptures. However, even present teachers proclaim the truth by divine inspiration, but essentially Revelation lies behind[35]". All this sounds like Philo *minus* Plato, but transposed. Behind the unmistakable enthusiasm for God's own history of salvation as manifested in the people of Israel there is a centring on inspiration which, while doubtless verging on secularizing the ancient concept of prophecy, never loses contact with its theological source[36]. Ben Sira

---

[32] The passage most frequently quoted is *cherub.* § 27.

[33] *Die Weisheit des Jesus Sirach erklärt*, Berlin, 1906.

[34] p. 412.   [35] pp. 413f.

[36] Recognition of the prophetic succession was one thing, applying the title "prophet" to great men outside this succession another. For this there is Biblical.

wrote in Palestine more than two hundred years before Philo who knew his book [37].

There are striking similarities between Philo and Ben Sira. The latter's description [38] of how the waters of inspiration, first modestly termed an irrigation ditch and "a conduit into a garden" (A. V.), became an inundating stream, nay, a sea is in the Philonic vein [39] and, at the same time, is Palestinian literature of the early second century B. C. There are close parallels even in the particular way of arguing by giving special prominence to what in the context of a Bible quotation is but an accessory. Philo is a past master in the art of basing amazingly far-reaching statements upon some incidental words taken from a context which does not bear out his inferences. Similarly Ben Sira puts side by side two heroes of the past on whom God had conferred unique distinctions [40]: Enoch was translated to heaven, but Joseph's bones were "visited". Here the Greek spoils the meaning of the Hebrew: *Few* were created like Enoch, *none* like Joseph. This is a climax; to be taken to heaven seems a small thing in comparison with God's care for Joseph's very bones in arranging for their burial in Canaan. "Ben Sira is here no longer far from Alexandrian exegesis [41]." We might well reverse this statement to: We thus learn where the so-called Alexandrian exegesis originated. It was in Palestine that the sacred history and text first became flexible tools in the hands of ingenious interpreters (cf. *Philo's Bible* p. 120). Our last point is slightly different, as it concerns a resemblance between Philo and the Greek Sira which here corrects the Hebrew characteristically. To Philo Enoch stands for repentance. For this there are parallels in Jewish sources and a reflection in the Epistle of Jude

precedent. In Ps. cv. 16 Abraham is called a prophet after Gen. xx. 7. To Ben Sira, as later on to Josephus, Job is a prophet and the book of Job a prophetic book. In xilx 9 he places him between Ezekiel (8) and the Twelve (10). To this exception was taken, as can be seen from the Hebrew MS and the translations. In the Cambridge MS which alone has preserved this passage נביא was corrected to נשיא. The Syriac makes Ezekiel to mention Job and omits the word נָבִיא. The Greek changed, or found changed, אִיּוֹב to אוֹיֵב and, in addition, derived נָבִיא from נבע, as in l. 27 and elsewhere (Smend). At first sight no one would identify ἐμνήσθη τῶν ἐχθρῶν ἐν ὄμβρῳ with *I mention Job as a prophet* (אוכיר את איוב נ[ב]יא)!

[37] The Palestinian Josephus describes Hyrcanus as a prophet.

[38] xxiv. 30f.

[39] Though the imagery differs it calls to mind Philo's renowned passage about his unfailing remedy for barrenness: as soon as he turns to renewed study of the Scriptures, release is at hand and, with it, a streaming wealth of inspiration. The last couplet of Ben Sira's stanza is to the point: *I will yet pour out doctrine as prophecy, and leave it to all ages for ever.*

[40] xlix. 14f.

[41] Smend, p. 476.

14f. = Enoch i. 9. This is explained by a corruption of Gen. v 22 in the Hebrew. The whole set-up of this genealogical chapter would lead us to expect "Enoch *lived* after he had begat Methuselah," but the text has "Enoch *walked with God,*" an obvious anticipation of verse 24. From the text as it stands, however, it was inferred that Enoch "became pleasing to God" (according to the Greek) not before becoming a father and that at this date a change of ways by way of repentance is bound to have taken place [42]. This explains the translation of Sir. xliv. 16. While the Hebrew reads, "Enoch walked with the Lord, the marvel of learning (אוֹת דַּעַת) for all generations", the Greek has ὑπόδειγμα μετανοίας. The Jewish parallels indicate that this agreement of Ecclesiasticus and Philo represents Palestinian teaching, and not Alexandrian. In so far it supports our argument.

(2) The "Alexandrian doctrine of inspiration" is a dubious bequest from Hegelian writers of more than a hundred years ago [43]. Dähne goes a long way in using Philo as a clue to the LXX and explains variants from the Hebrew as mere consequences of Philonic "philosophy". This has been largely forgotten but never properly refuted, and therefore exercises its subterranean influence. I adduce one instance which at first sight might appear to be valid, because it seems to be confirmed by a further difference from the Hebrew. In Gen. ii. 5 the LXX translates טֶרֶם *there was not* by its connotation *not yet* with the nonsensical result that (God created) "every plant of the field *before* it was in the earth, and every herb in the field *before* it grew", to quote from the A. V. which followed Jerome in this mistranslation. Philo seized this translation with enthusiasm, for it brought the Bible into agreement with his beloved Plato's doctrine that previous to creation there existed the idea of the thing to be created. Gfrörer and Dähne proceed to teach the existence of an Alexandrian philosophy centuries before Philo, assuming that this philosophy was at the basis of this translation and similar instances which they unearth. As corroborative evidence Dähne adduces verse 9 where the LXX has an unanimous ἐξανέτειλεν ὁ θεὸς ἔτι ἐκ τῆς γῆς πᾶν ξύλον and and interprets ἔτι = in addition to the creation of its idea. This ἔτι presents a real difficulty. There are, however, two ways of resolving it. It could be an early dittograph [ετι] εκ. Or it could be due to an early interpolator who, perhaps without any knowledge of "Alexan-

---

[42] I refer to my comment on Philo's *Quaestiones in Genesin* I 82—5 in a review of R. Marcus' translation of the Armenian *Quaestiones et solutiones* (*Gnomon* 26, 1954, p. 226).

[43] August Gfrörer, *Philo und die alexandrinische Theosophie*, 2 vols, Stuttgart, 1831, and August Ferdinand Dähne, *Geschichtliche Darstellung der jüdisch-alexandrinischen Religions-Philosophie*, 2 vols, Halle, 1834.

drian Philosophy" or Philo, supplied it in accordance with the mistranslation of verse 5.

(3) Neither the misinterpretation of septuagintal blunders nor reference to (Pseudo-)Aristobulus justifies the assumption of a succession of Jewish philosophical schools and teachers in Alexandria, of whom Philo is the summit. Nor does even Bousset's idea [44] of a wealth of Philonic references to generations of predecessors any longer find support. The fact is that the translators were blunderers and that Philo's work does not rest upon a long succession of "philosophers".

The upshot of the whole is that there is no "Alexandrian doctrine of inspiration" from which to explain what is different in the arrangement of the LXX. If there are no better arguments, the idea of the LXX as an offshoot from "philosophy" should be abandoned.

C. About the History of the Problem

In conclusion, a word about the history of our problem may not be out of place. None of our current Introductions or books on the O. T. Canon deal with it. From them we get the impression that their complete unanimity prevailed in the past. This paper was drafted without reference to modern authors. Zahn's *Geschichte des neutestamentlichen* Kanons vol. II,1, 1890, however, contains a very full treatment of the sources of the history of the Canon. It does not include the O. T. in its title and has been completely neglected by students of the O. T., though they could have learned much from it. Most of my points have been anticipated by Zahn, and I therefore decided to consult the earlier literature. This proved unexpectedly rewarding. Far from being confined to a particular school of thought, my view proved to have been shared by strict Lutherans, such as Chr. Fr. Schmid [45] and G. Chr. Storr [46], the Roman F. K. Movers [47], and the Dutch Liberal A. Kuenen [48]. Its radical reversal was due to H. L. Strack in his article *Kanon des Alten Testamentes*, first [49] in *RE²*

[44] W. Bousset, *Jüdisch-Christlicher Schulbetrieb in Alexandria und Rom*, Göttingen, 1915.

[45] Christiani Friderici Schmidii *Historia Antiqua et Vindicatio Canonis Sacri Veteris Novique Testamenti*, 736 pp., Lipsiae, MDCCLXXV.

[46] Gottlob Christian Storr, Über die älteste Einteilung der Bücher des Alten Bundes, in Paulus' *Neues Repertorium*, 2. Teil, Jena, 1790, pp. 225—47.

[47] Franciscus Carolus Movers, *Loci quidam Historiae Canonis Veteris Testamenti Illustrati*, Vratislaviae (1842).

[48] Abraham Kuenen, *Historisch-Kritisch Onderzoek naar het Ontstaan en de Verzameling van de Boeken des Ouden Verbonds*, Derde Deel, Leiden, 1865. Tweede Deel, pp. 394—450.

[49] An article by Strack in *Zeitschrift für Lutherische Theologie*, 1875, is quoted by Wellhausen in Friedrich Bleek's *Einleitung in das Alte Testament⁴*, 1878, p. 547.

VII, 1880, pp. 412—51[50]. In its re-edition in *RE*³ IX, 1901, pp.741—68 his decisive points are made still more rigidly in an attempt to refute the earlier consensus and Zahn who, oddly enough, is the author of the next article in this encyclopedia, *viz* on *Kanon des Neuen Testamentes*. Strack whose extensive knowledge of his special subject by far exceeded his power of judgment was too deeply immersed in his Jewish sources to be unbiased. He therefore was unable to reach an impartial decision whenever it was a question of the contradicting claims of rabbinic and non-rabbinic authorities. Although his article on the Talmud[51] dates and characterizes correctly its earlier and later parts, scholarly caution is thrown to the winds in his article òn the Canon. "The history of the origin of the Canon", he asserts[52], "gives rise to number 24 canonical books". His first piece of evidence is Baba Bathra, and he goes on to state "This number is maintained by the entire Jewish tradition, so far as it is not influenced by the Alexandrians". To the usual numbering of 22 books he objects that, however great the number of witnesses to it, "they must not be counted, but above all weighed. Those numbering 22 follow the LXX. However, as regards the Canon the Alexandrians cannot be accepted as authoritative; for they delt with the LXX in a cavalier manner both by changing the order and arrangement of the Biblical books, and by appending completely new books to the collection translated from the Hebrew Canon"[53]. In this way he too readily disposes of Josephus, Melito, Origen, and the rest. He then passes on to IV Ezra xiv which is followed by numerous quotations from the post-Biblical Jewish literature, but fails to distinguish between Palestinian and Babylonian, early and late. More than half his texts are taken from Exod. and Num. Rabba, the late date of which is admitted in his own article on the Talmud where much of this literature is characterized as homiletic. Strack's proof texts consist mainly in comparisons of anything mentioned in the Bible confirming the number 24 with the number of canonical books. Once this number was generally accepted, however, i. e. after the Tannaitic period, its edifying application ceases to be probative for the earlier centuries. Most of it therefore was not taken over by other authors on the Canon.

The same sort of argument is well known from H. E. Ryle's often reprinted monograph[54]. Its preface refers to S. R. Driver. It can,

---

[50] J. J. Herzog, *Realencyklopädie für die protestantische Theologie und Kirche* 2. A.; 3. A. by A. Hauck.

[51] *RE*³, XIX, pp. 31—4.

[52] p. 756.   [53] p. 757.

[54] Herbert Edward Ryle, *The Canon of the Old Testament*. An Essay on the Gradual Growth and Formation of the Hebrew Canon of Scripture, 2ⁿᵈ edition London, 1904 (first in 1892).

however, hardly be doubted that Driver would have written a very different book, had he ever considered this problem. Ryle too proclaims that the number 22 is Alexandrian. No one is likely to consider his 316 pages too few but they contain no full quotation of Origen's statement, recorded in Euseb. *H. E.* vi. 25. Every word in Origen's description of the Jewish Canon in comparison with the Greek Bible counts, but Ryle is satisfied to quote "ἡ παρ' ἡμῖν Γένεσις κ. τ. λ. ... 'Εσθήρ"! Earlier in the book[55] he paraphrases Melito's and Origen's lists; he records that Origen gives the Hebrew names of the books as well as the Greek and that his object is to give the names and the number of the Hebrew books; "and he enumerates them, following the Alexandrine order". This and the remark that the Greek titles are an indication of Greek influence is mere bias, however subconscious. Hence the reader can nowhere get a true impression of Origen's record quoted by Eusebius which is first-hand evidence.

Strack and Ryle both set the tune to which we have been dancing for seventy-five years. The only book that breaks the spell is G. Hölscher's early work *Kanonisch und Apokryph*, Naumburg a. S., 1905. In it he makes the excellent point that the grouping of Hebrew literature into three classes and even the recognition of their content as authoritative should not be confused with canonization. The latter implies the actual exclusion of other books. Hölscher is even in a position to determine the tendencies pro and con which sharpened the final conflict of opinions. The tendency against which canonization was used effectively was apocalypticism. The goal was to put an end to the placing of fictitious pre-Mosaic authors above Moses and his succession. The struggle against Gnosticism as the final impulse in circumscribing the N. T. Canon forms a true parallel.

We may now turn to those early authors who were eclipsed by Strack, confining ourselves to Schmid, Movers and Kuenen. Schmid presents a curious mixture of naïve presuppositions and true insight. He endorses the Judaistic turn towards the Hebrew Bible as a model which begins with Origen and Jerome. Accordingly some problems are solved in a trice: the earliest form of the Alexandrian Bible contained only the books of the Hebrew canon. The Jews had some more books for reading purposes but did not consider them divine or prophetic. The Church adopted them and called them apocrypha, thus giving the word a new meaning. Clement of Alexandria used a more complete codex which his pupil Origen abandoned, knowing more about Judaica. Origen's defence of Susanna as inspired derives from early impressions acquired in Clement's school. Schmid emphasizes the long succession of witnesses to 22 books in the Palestinian Bible

---

[55] pp. 225 f.

as the only legitimate one; he comments on the absence of Esther in Melito and others and the inclusion of the Epistle of Jeremiah and Baruch *de more seculi quod a Ieremia propheta scripta crederentur*. He is unambiguous about the original position of Ruth, Lamentations, and Daniel among the prophets. Taken all in all, this early contribution commands respect.

Movers' inaugural essay as Professor, consisting of thirty-two pages in Latin, is packed with evidence and argument. It is a fine example of the liberal Roman Catholic scholarship of the time. Movers freely quotes Eichhorn and de Wette, and combats mistaken assumptions from which we are now free. He cannot understand how an antagonism between Jewry in the Dispersion[56] and in Jerusalem can be assumed. In all matters there was the closest connection between the two centres. When doubts arose, the priests in Jerusalem were consulted[57]. They gladly looked to Jerusalem for their sacred scriptures[58], including translations[59]. As they included books which were later excluded from the Canon, it is certain that these were not distinguished from the canonical books, and that at this period the Canon was not completely closed even in Palestine. On the contrary, the Canon was not yet fixed in the first century A. D., either among Christians or Jews. Both whole books and additions were taken over with a good conscience. It was only in the third century that the Christian Church, unduly influenced by the novel Jewish theories, began to follow their stricter view concerning canonicity. Recognition of these facts, Movers goes on to say, has been unfortunately prevented by the theory about Ezra as the originator of the Canon. When it comes to identifying the thirteen prophets of Josephus *Ap.* I 40, Movers is misled by the fact that his text read ἀπὸ δὲ Μωυσέως τελευτῆς μέχρι τῆς Ἀρταξέρξου τοῦ μετὰ Ξέρξην Περσῶν βασιλέως ἀρχῆς. He takes ἀρχῆς as *beginning*, using τελευτῆς as a pointer, and must therefore exclude Esther which, as he points out, was barred by some Jews and many Christians from inclusion in the Canon. He fills its place by assigning a number each to Ezra and to Nehemiah[60]. Did Josephus make use of the apocrypha? Against Eichhorn he argues that Josephus quotes I Ezra whereas certain proof for his use of II Ezra cannot be found. Baruch and the Epistle of Jeremiah must be understood to be included as part of "Jeremiah". The Christian

---

[56] He mentions Egypt and Babylon.

[57] Josephus, *Contra Apionem* I, 30—6, about priestly genealogies.

[58] Movers adduces II Maccabees ii. 14 f.

[59] For the latter he quotes the last verse of the Greek Esther.

[60] A. Kuenen, p. 412, translates ἀρχή by *reign*. We know from Niese's edition that ἀρχῆς was interpolated by the editor of the *editio princeps* against the unanimous evidence.

Church in Palestine retained them in accordance with the practice of contemporary Judaism, as is proved for the Jews by Origen in Eusebius. In the third century they were still canonical and used as lessons[61]. Some Oriental Churches went too far in yielding to Jewish pressure. This able essay has been forgotten, unfortunately, like many other occasional papers.

The same cannot be said about A. Kuenen's monumental work which reached a second edition and was translated into more than one language[62]. His presentation and discussion of the evidence is fuller than is possible in modern handbooks and his decisions are models of circumspection. Strictly speaking, he says, Josephus is the only one to make a more extended use of the Apocrypha[63]; but his Canon was ours, consisting of 22 books[64]. The Egyptian Jews never stated expressly that they acknowledged other than the 22 books as canonical. However, in limitation of O. Fritzsche's categorical assertion[65] that "only the 22 books of the O. T. constituted the Canon proper and not even the Alexandrians judged otherwise", as could be seen in Philo and Josephus, Kuenen retorts, "for this proposition there is not a single proof; Philo is silent, and Josephus was born and formed in Palestine. The addition of apocryphal books may be rightly ascribed to arbitrariness on the part of the translators of the O. T. or of the owners of this translation, but does not this very arbitrariness indicate that by then the Canon was not yet strictly circumscribed? It must not be forgotten that (1) post-Christian witnesses are not evidence for an earlier period; too much had changed in the meantime, especially after the destruction of Jerusalem, and (2) that the Christians were not the first to put the Alexandrian additions on the same footing as the books acknowledged as canonical in Palestine[66]. Josephus had already done so by using the additions to Esther[67]." "Our Canon cannot be as early as some believe; for not before the fourth and fifth centuries were Ruth and Lamentations placed among the Writings, a fact which should not be explained by subtle or over-refined distinctions, but by pointing out the facts of history. Neither the LXX nor Josephus separated the historical works which at a later date were placed either among the Prophets or the Writings; still less did they assign a special place to Daniel. Our inference is not that the distribution known to us did not yet exist, but that the

---

[61] The reliability of Const. Apostol. v. 20 is now doubted.

[62] The second edition is inaccessible to me.

[63] p. 406.

[64] p. 447.

[65] *RE¹, art.* Canon des Alten Testamentes, p. 230.

[66] p. 437.

[67] Kuenen refers to his p. 410.

Hellenists stressed it weakly or not at all[68]." "Neither the Talmudic nor the Masoretic arrangement is primary, as is seen from the Fathers; to them Ruth and Lamentations belong to the second group of the O. T.[69]." "Even if all the others were influenced by Egypt, Jerome certainly was not. By his time the old order still existed and the new was emerging only slowly[70]."

Zahn's treatment is still valid and the present paper derives much from him, as will others when Strack and Ryle have been outdated. In conclusion, I would again emphasize the great value of Hölscher's book, an inaugural dissertation as Lecturer whose wealth of fruitful suggestions is out of proportion to its seventy-seven pages.

(Completed Dec. 1955)

Retractatio

On p. 206 (top), ZNW 47, 1956, an error in quoting J.-P. Audet's p. 152 (below) necessitates rewriting most of the paragraph:

He realizes that "Esdras B depends on the tradition of our Massoretic text." He further asserts that there is "only one unknown quantity in the origin of the two Greek Esdrases" and this he traces to "the Targum which the list relates to Esdras A." In fact, in the late II Ezra the Greek follows the Hebrew so meticulously that it is as meaningless to interpose a Targum as it would be in Chronicles which are the work of the same, perhaps Palestinian, translator. In contrast, the Greek of the much earlier I Ezra is unfettered, idiomatic, and certainly Alexandrian. Neither can be traced to on Aramaic Targum. The obvious fact that the two books are opposites in every respect makes it impossible to place them under this common denominator. Therefore the inference that the book titles must point to Aramaic Targums, because they are given in Aramaic, proves unjustified — and Audet offers no other proof. Besides, would Audet seriously suggest . . .

Cambridge (England) *P. Katz*

98

THE "OLD TESTAMENT": A CHRISTIAN CANON*

If my hearer has read what has been printed of my views on the Old Testament canon in the church, he could reply to what I am about to say that it is the same game of chess. And from the start I openly confess that I have recruited no new pawns; the pieces are the same and the game is the same—certainly the middle game. There is only a slight variation in the opening and in the end game. I have previously applied the recent re-examination of the history of the OT canon in the early church to the question of the OT canon in Protestantism.[1] The results are, perhaps, better known among Roman Catholics than are the reasons. And the results are surprisingly conciliatory to Roman Catholics and their definition of the OT canon. Therefore, I hope it will not appear unfriendly or tendentious if, on this occasion, I attempt to relate that same history of the OT canon to Roman Catholic teaching on the subject.

Actually, Roman Catholic teaching and the Protestant view on the OT canon are surprisingly similar. Both have held that the Jewish canon was in fact already formed before the days of Jesus and the rise of Christianity.[1a] Both have held that the early church adopted an Alexandrian or Septuagint canon from diaspora Judaism which, in addition to the books of the Hebrew or Palestinian canon, included the literature known as deuterocanonical among Roman Catholics. Both make a distinction between the status of the books of the Hebrew canon and the additional books and

---

* A lecture delivered at l'École Biblique, Jerusalem, Jordan, May 25, 1967, with some revisions for publication.

[1] "A Symposium on the Canon of Scripture: 2 The Protestant Old Testament Canon: Should it Be Re-examined?" *CBQ* 28 (1966) 194-203.

[1a] This, of course, is not to say that every Protestant or every Roman Catholic has held this or the following positions. This, however, has been the predominant position in both groups. On the Protestant side see Sundberg, *op. cit.*, 194-199. On the Roman Catholic side see L. F. Hartman, *Encyclopedic Dictionary of the Bible* (A Translation and Adaption of A. van den Born's Bijbels Woordenboek, second rev. ed., 1954-1957; New York, 1963), p. 310; A. Robert and A. Tricot, *Guide to the Bible* (second ed.; Paris, 1960), I, 72f., 81ff.; A. Suelzer, "Old Testament Literature," *NCE* (New York, 1966), X, 676f.; J. C. Turro, "Bible III. 2. History of the Old Testament Canon," *ibid.*, II, 387-391; A. Wikenhauser, *New Testament Introduction*, trans. J. Cunningham (Freiburg, 1958), p. 21. The positions expressed in these works I take to be substantially parallel to the *de facto* pre-Jamnia Palestinian canon held by R. H. Pfeiffer, *Introduction to the Old Testament* (New York, 1941), pp. 50-70. J. L. McKenzie, *Dictionary of the Bible* (Milwaukee, 1965), pp. 118ff. and A. Robert and A. Feuillet, *Introduction à la Bible* (Tournai, 1959), pp. 35-38, reflect a more open situation with respect to the Writings-collection in Palestine prior to Jamnia.

Reprinted from *Catholic Biblical Quarterly* 30 (1968).

writings; and, as we shall see, the differences between Roman Catholics and Protestants on this point have been greatly exaggerated. Both have defined canonicity in relation to inspiration. Thus, for me to discuss these matters, even within the context of Roman Catholic teaching, is not to give voice again to carping sectarianism. Rather, my studies on *The Old Testament of the Early Church*,[2] while not undertaken for this purpose, may provide a basis for greater understanding and unanimity among Christians on the canon of the OT.

The first two items mentioned above are relatively recent innovations in Catholic teaching on the OT. In the early polemic, it was the Protestants, having received the Talmudic tradition through Elias Levita that the canon had been closed by Ezra and the men of the Great Synagogue, who argued that the canon of Jesus and the apostles was the canon of the church.[3] And after two centuries, when tensions had eased sufficiently, so that some could admit that the NT contained quotations and allusions to scripture beyond the Jewish canon, it was this position that forced the Protestants to look elsewhere for an explanation for this wider usage. John Salomo Semler, a professor of theology at Halle, in 1771 turned to the Letter of Aristeas and found there the authority for a wider canon.[4] He extended the activity of the seventy in translation to the Prophets and the Writings, as well as the Law. And, noting that the seventy were inspired men, gave their authority of inspiration to the wider canon in Greek. Thus was born the Alexandrian or Septuagint canon hypotheses that came to be accepted, almost universally, among Protestant scholars by the last quarter of the nineteenth century. But tensions had eased on both sides of the old barrier. When Protestants admitted that a wider OT canon had been received by the early church, Roman Catholics reciprocated by accepting the Protestant theory of an inspired Jewish Septuagint canon.

The difficulty with this reciprocity, however, is that the Protestant theory of a Septuagint canon has proved wrong. The bases upon which the Septuagint canon hypothesis was built have each been shown to be fallacious.[5] But, since the history of the hypothesis had been forgotten, no one

---

[2] Harvard Theological Studies XX (Cambridge, 1964).

[3] Cf. for example, J. Cosin, *A Scholastical History of the Canon of Holy Scripture* (London, 1657).

[4] *Abhandlung von freier Untersuchung des Canon* I (Halle, 1771). Semler was preceded by J. E. Grabe (W. R. Churton, *The Uncanonical and Apocryphal Scriptures* [London, 1884] p. 12) and T. Lewis (J. E. Grabe, *The History of the Seventy-two Interpreters*, trans. T. Lewis [London, 1715] preface) in postulating an Alexandrian canon. However, these played no role in the acceptance of this hypothesis by modern Biblical scholarship.

[5] Sundberg, *OT Canon*, pp. 51-79.

knew that the theory had been destroyed. As late as 1884 W. R. Churton still held, as had Semler, that the deuterocanonical books had been composed in Greek;[6] whereas it is now recognized that only Wisdom, 2 Maccabees, and additions to Esther (13,1-7; 16,1-24) were originally written in Greek. And the notion of Greek: diaspora/Hebrew: Palestine in matters of canon has been controverted by clear evidence of the circulation of the Septuagint in Palestine, and even a Palestinian revision of the Septuagint now seems probable. The statements in the prologue of Sirach indicate both that the Law and the Prophets were recognized collections among Alexandrian Jews (supported by 2 Mc 15,9) and that the collection of the Writings was not yet defined (supported by Philo, *De Vita Contemplativa* III 25; 2 Mc 15,9). Moreover, the demise of the Great Synagogue at the hands of A. Kuenen in 1876[7] made possible the full acceptance of the fact that the Jewish canon did not receive its final definition until about the end of the first century A.D. And, since there is no evidence of any interest to define the third collection in the Jewish canon until after A.D. 70,[8] it has become impossible to maintain even a *de facto* canon for Palestine in the days of Jesus and the primitive church.

The Septuagint canon hypothesis was a rationalization that was intended to explain the use of a wider literature in the NT than that contained in the Jewish canon. But from its inception it should have been clear that the blanket did not cover the bed. Not only are there allusions to the deuterocanonical literature in the NT. There are direct quotations and numerous allusions to the apocryphal writings as well and it is impossible to arrive at a plausible explanation of the history of the OT canon in the church without attention to this fact. Yet one can read on OT canon in standard Roman Catholic works and find no mention of the relation of apocrypha to canon.[9] But this fact must be faced squarely before any

---

[6] *Op. cit.*, p. 12.

[7] "Over de mannen des Groote Synagoge," *Verslagen en Mededeeligen der Koninklijke Akademie van Wetenschappen* (Amsterdam, 1876), pp. 207-248. German trans., "Über die Männer der grossen Synagoge," trans. K. Budde, *Gesammelte Abhandlungen zur biblischen Wissenschaft von Dr. Abraham Kuenen* (Freiburg i. B., 1894), pp. 125-160.

[8] Sundberg, *OT Canon*, pp. 113-128. Cf. J. P. Lewis, "What do We Mean by Jabneh?" *JBR* XXXII (1964), 125-132.

[9] Hartman, *op. cit.*, pp. 311f.; McKenzie, *op. cit.*, pp. 118f.; Robert and Feuillet, *op. cit.*, pp. 37-39; Robert and Tricot, *op. cit.*, pp. 79-84; Suelzer, *op. cit.*, pp. 676f.; J. E. Steinmueller, *A Companion to Scripture Studies* (rev. ed.; New York, 1962), I, 86f.; Turro, *op. cit.*, p. 387. The reason for this oversight is due to the widely held theory that the early Christian church adopted an Alexandrian or Septuagint canon that included the deuterocanonical books. But cf., Sundberg, *OT Canon*, pp. 51-79.

101

progress can be made. It is not possible to differentiate in the NT usage
between the deuterocanonical and the apocryphal literature; both are used
and only prejudice would deny that their usage implies a sense of religious
authority.[9a] Here, where Protestants have gone wrong with respect to the
whole deuterocanonical/apocryphal literature, Roman Catholics have ignored the implications of the use of the apocryphal books for the history
of the canon. Now, with the publication of the Qumrân texts, it has become
possible to gain an understanding of this unwanted and embarrassing
phenomenon.

At Qumrân it has become clear that the gamut of deuterocanonical/
apocryphal literature was collected and used. And, as is observed in the
usage of the NT, it is not possible to distinguish in the usage of the sectarian writings from Qumrân between the books included in the Jewish
canon and the deuterocanonical/apocryphal writings.[10] That is to say the
terms "deuterocanonical" and "apocryphal" have no meaning with respect
to the usage either of the NT writers or the sectarian Jews at Qumrân. It
is also to note that while the books later distinguished as "Writings,"
"deuterocanonical," and "apocryphal" were used by the NT writers and
by the Qumrân sectarians, there is no distinction that can be observed
among these two groups of writers between these groups of books. Thus,
in a Jewish sectarian group that came to an end in Palestine about A.D.
68 and in primitive Christianity that arose within Judaism in Palestine
subsequent to A.D. 30 we find a similar treatment of Jewish religious
literature. Collections of Law and Prophets were recognized. And a large,
undifferentiated group of non-sectarian religious writings that included
the books later called "Writings," "deuterocanonical," and "apocrypha"
was also used as in some sense authoritative, the Qumrân sectarians using
this literature almost exclusively in Hebrew and Aramaic and the Christians from very early in their history using it almost exclusively in Greek.
When we compare this parallel usage and its relation to the closing of the
Jewish canon about A.D. 90, its importance to the question of canon becomes evident. It does not seem likely that the Christians received their
usage of this literature by direct transference from the Qumrân sectarians.
So, for example, the Christians used the books of Maccabees, which appear
to have been eschewed at Qumrân. And the Enoch literature and the Testament of the Twelve Patriarchs seem to have been used by Christians in a

---

[9a] *Ibid.*, pp. 52f.

[10] B. J. Roberts, "The Dead Sea Scrolls and the Old Testament Scriptures," *BJRL*
XXXVI (1953/54), 84; J. Carmignac, "Les citations de l'Ancien Testament dans 'la
Guerre des Fils de Lumière contre les Fils de Ténèbres,'" *RB* LXIII (1956), 234-260,
375-390.

different form than that used at Qumrân. Hence, we have here "in the mouth of two witnesses" evidence of the use of a larger literature than that ultimately gathered into the collection of the "Writings" of the Jewish canon. And since this usage in both instances finds its locale in Palestine, it is possible to posit that this wider literature was used throughout Judaism before the movement toward the closing of the Jewish canon set in following A.D. 70. This is confirmed by the translation of this larger literature into Greek for circulation among Greek speaking Jews in Palestine as well as in the diaspora. And since there was no restriction against the usage of this larger literature in Judaism before A.D. 70, Jewish religious writings composed in Greek came to be used without any stigma of unacceptability by Jews who read Greek. These were the circumstances that obtained in Judaism at the time when Christianity arose until it became almost entirely separated from Judaism by Jewish exclusion and persecution. And these were the circumstances that passed into Christianity and that eventuated in the church's finding it necessary to define the canon of the OT for herself.[10a]

Here it is necessary to pause for a moment for a clarification of terms. In the past the terms "scripture" and "canon" have been used synonymously. By "scripture" we have also meant religious writings that are in some sense authoritative. And in the past authoritative religious writing has meant canon. This has been the result of inaccurate analysis. We need now to differentiate between the terms "scripture" and "canon," understanding by "scripture" religious writing that is in some sense authoritative, and by "canon" a closed collection of scripture. That this is necessary is clear from our previous discussion. It is clear that more writings than the Law and the Prophets were used in Judaism in the first century A.D. and used in an authoritative way. And it is also clear that no collection of Writings had yet been formed and no closed canon had been defined. In Judaism canonization did not occur until the end of the first century A.D. And, yet, the church did receive the "scriptures" from Judaism. Thus, when we read about the "scriptures" in the NT, it is inaccurate to understand thereby "canon."[11] The Jewish "canon" had not yet been defined. And when Judaism did define its canon about A.D. 90, the church had already been separated from Judaism by exclusion and persecution. Thus, the Jewish canon cannot be said to have any authority for the church. The authority that has been previously attributed to it by Christians, whether church fathers or Protestants or Roman Catholics, has been based

---

[10a] For a full statement of this case see Sundberg, *OT Canon*, pp. 81-103.

[11] E.g., Lk 24,27; Acts 17,11; 18,24.28; Gal 3,8; 2 Tm 3,16.

on the erroneous assumption that the Jewish canon was closed in the days of Jesus and the apostles. When the theory of canonization by Ezra and the Great Synagogue proved wrong, rather than carefully re-examining the matter, scholars assumed a *de facto* canon. But that has proved wrong as well. And we need to adjust our thinking about "scripture" and "canon" accordingly.

So then, the church received the scriptures from Palestinian Judaism: a closed collection of Law, a closed collection of Prophets, and an undefined body of literature that included the "Writings" (defined as a collection at Jamnia), the "deuterocanonical" and the "apocryphal" books. The usage of the Apostolic Fathers and of the early fathers of the church, both East and West, confirms this, except that the Jewish divisions were soon lost in the church; everything became "prophets." And the books now called "deuterocanonical" and "apocryphal" were used in ways indistinguishable from the usage of the books included in the Jewish canon.[11a] In our extant Christian literature there is no cognizance of the closing of the Jewish canon until some eight decades after the event, when Melito, after repeated questioning by his brother, Onesimus, went to the East to "the place where these things were preached and done" and brought back what appears to have been intended as a twenty-two-book list,[12] a clear evidence of the influence of the Jewish canon. Origen forthrightly acknowledges Jewish influence. Introducing his OT list, he says, "But it should be known that there are twenty-two canonical books, as the Hebrews have handed them down; the same as the number of the letters of their alphabet . . . . These are the twenty-two books according to the Hebrews . . ." (Euseb., H. E. VI.xxv), and he goes on to list the books. In the past it has been held that all the books listed by Origen were actually contained in a Jewish canon. But this is certainly not the case. The canon Origen received from the Jews is found in the twenty-one Hebrew names. His intention is expressly a twenty-two book list and he has inadvertently overlooked naming the Book of the Twelve. But Origen drew a distinction between "their scriptures" (i.e., of the Jews) and "our scriptures" (i.e., of the church) both with respect to the reading of the text (for him, "our scriptures" were the Greek translation; as to passages missing in the Hebrew text, he wrote, ". . . I think no other supposition is possible than that they who had the reputation of wisdom and the rulers and elders took

---

11a Steinmueller, *op. cit.*, pp. 88f., for the deuterocanonical books in early Christian authors. See the introductions to each of the books in R. H. Charles, *Apocrypha and Pseudepigrapha of the Old Testament* II (Oxford, 1913) for Christian use of the apocryphal literature.

12 Eusebius, H. E. IV.xxvi.13.

away from the people every passage which might bring discredit among the people" [*Ad Africanum* ix]) and with respect to books, noting that the Jews did not use, for example, Judith and Tobit but the church did. Thus, we are able to understand that, while the Hebrew names given in Origen's OT list are the Jewish canon, the Greek names represent the Greek Septuagint recension in Christian use and include those books that tradition attributed to authors of the Jewish list.[13]

The Jewish list, with its *a priori* claim to correctness, exerted an increasing pressure on the church in the East. Thus, when Jerome, who had apparently concurred with Western usage until that time, moved east, he soon was championing the Jewish canon as the definition of the OT for the church.[14] Conversely, Rufinus, dominated by the Jewish canon while living in the East, moved west and soon was writing with biting sarcasm of Jerome, having him say, "And though he, a Jew hired from the synagogue of Satan, sell his remarks for a price, nevertheless he is my master and should be preferred above all others, for among them alone is the truth of the scriptures perdurable" (*Apology* 11:30). But, despite Origen's publication of the Hexapala that confronted Christian usage with the Hebrew text, the Jewish canon made its impact upon the church as a list of books, not as a canonical text. And, confronted with the Jewish list (the church fathers show no knowledge that the Jewish canonical list was not defined until about the end of the first century A.D.), the resultant in the East shows that the fathers as much as possible preserved what had been Christian usage within the strictures of that list, as observed in Origen. Thus Athanasius (A.D. 295-373), who first urged the Jewish canon on the church, listed four books of Kings after the Christian Septuagint usage, and included Ezra-Nehemiah and IV Esdras under one title, and Jeremiah included Baruch, Lamentations and the Epistle of Jeremy.[15] A similar circumstance prevailed in the East until the Council of Laodicea (between A.D. 343 and 381) which named an OT following the Jewish list but according to the Christian Septuagint recension. Epiphanius (d. A.D. 403) shows the extent of the effort to preserve Christian usage against the impact of the Jewish canon when, acknowledging the exclusion of Sirach and Wisdom of Solomon from the Old, he included them in the New Testament.[16]

The impact of the Jewish canon was felt not only in the East but in the West as well. Proximity, however, played an important role with

---

[13] Sundberg, *OT Canon*, pp. 134-138.
[14] *Ibid.*, pp. 148-153.
[15] *Ep. Fest.* xxxix.
[16] *Heresies* lxxvi.

respect to both the time and the stringency of that impact. Farther removed from the concentration of Jewish population in Palestine, the earliest reflection of the impact of the Jewish canon in the West is in Hilary of Poitiers (d. A.D. 368). H. H. Howorth has shown that, while Hilary probably was following Origen's list of the Jewish canon when enumerating the books of the OT, elsewhere in his writings he made use of Judith, Tobit, Wisdom, Baruch, and Susanna in a way corresponding to his use of the Jewish canonical scriptures.[17] Thus his list probably reflects a transition he himself has made under the influence of Origen's list and the claims of the Jewish canon wherein his earlier use of a wider OT was exchanged for a more limited list, as is observed in the Eastern fathers from Athanasius.[18] Jerome became the champion of the Jewish canon in the West though, as remarked above, only after his removal to Bethlehem. He collected the citations of the OT in the Gospels and Epistles that depended on the Hebrew text and argued therefrom that Jesus and the apostles had sanctioned the Jewish canon.[19] Conversely, Rufinus, on moving West and adopting the Western point of view, collected the OT passages in Gospels and Epistles that depended on the Greek text and argued therefrom the apostolic authority of the Septuagint, including the deuterocanonical books.[20] Certainly it was not the superiority of Rufinus' argumentation or prestige that won the day for his position; Jerome made a far greater and enduring impression on the church. But Rufinus' position coincided with the position in the West whence he learned it. Augustine (A.D. 354-430) added the weight of his tremendous influence to the Western usage and gave it a rationale. While it played no part in the formulation and acceptance of the modern theory, Augustine actually propounded the first Alexandrian Septuagint canon hypothesis. Finding it impossible to escape the claim to authenticity of the Jewish canon and unwilling to deny authenticity to the tradition of the church, he proposed:

If anything is in the Hebrew copies and not in the version of the Septuagint, the Spirit of God did not choose to say it through them, but only through the prophets. But whatever is in the Septuagint and not in the Hebrew copies, the same Spirit chose rather to say through the latter, thus showing that both were prophets. (*City of God* xviii. 42-43)

Thus Augustine postulated an equal and identical divine inspiration for both the Jewish canon and the Christian OT. He did not view them as

[17] "The Influence of St. Jerome on the Canon of the Western Church, II," *JTS* XI (1909/10), 323ff.
[18] Sundberg, *OT Canon*, pp. 140-148.
[19] *Ibid.*, pp. 148-153.
[20] *Ibid.*, pp. 153-155.

competitive but supplementary in authority: the Hebrew was appropriate for its time; the Septuagint was appropriate for the church. In this theory of inspiration, Augustine recognized the difference between the Jewish and the Christian canons. Thus, in postulating that the material contained in the Septuagint and not in the Hebrew was composed by the Seventy under the same authoritative inspiration that had inspired the writers of the Hebrew canon, more than a millennium before Semler we have in Augustine an Alexandrian Septuagint canon hypothesis.[21]

Church councils toward the end of the fourth and early in the fifth centuries confirmed the practice of the church in the West as witnessed by Augustine. Three councils in North Africa (at Hippo in 393,[22] and two at Carthage in A.D. 397[23] and 419[24]) included in their definitions of the OT both the protocanonical and the deuterocanonical books, making no distinction between them. It is to be observed that in the West, as in the East, it was the new knowledge of a closed Jewish canon that differed markedly from Christian usage of OT literature that raised the question of OT canon among the fathers and that led to conciliar decisions on the matter. Likewise, as the resulting OT canon in the East was an accommodation of Christian usage to the Jewish list, similarly the Western OT canon appears to have been an accommodation within the broadest scope of Jewish practice. Of course, it was the Christian recension of the Septuagint that was employed in the West. Thus 1 Esdras was included under Ezra, and the Epistle of Jeremy and Baruch were included with Lamentations under Jeremiah. And Esther and Daniel continued to be used in the longer Greek forms. Augustine suggested that Wisdom and Sirach were similarly agglomerated under Solomonic writings.[25] However, the case for them is not so strong since they were not so agglomerated in the East. How then did the church differentiate between Sirach, Wisdom, the Maccabees, Tobit, and Judith and the apocryphal books? There is one factor that is common to each of these remaining deuterocanonical books that does not obtain for the apocryphal books. There is evidence that each of these continued to circulate in Judaism even after the closing of the Jewish canon. Sirach is twice quoted in the Talmud by name, and a third

---

[21] *Ibid.*, pp. 175f.

[22] G. D. Mansi, *Sacrorum conciliorum nova et amplissima collectio* (Florentiae, 1759-1792) III, 850.

[23] *Ibid.*, IV, 430; C. J. Hefele, *A History of the Councils of the Church* II, trans. H. H. Oxenham (Edinburgh, 1876) 407f.

[24] Mansi, op. cit., IV, 430; C. J. Costello, *St. Augustine's Doctrine of the Inspiration and Canonicity of Scripture* (Washington, D.C., 1930) p. 68.

[25] *On Christian Doctrine* II.13.

time a passage from Sirach is cited as from the Writings.[26] That Origen knew a Hebrew name for the books of Maccabees is evidence that a Hebrew original of 1 Maccabees existed in the third century A.D.[27] There is little doubt but that such a manuscript was in Jewish hands. Jerome was able to obtain the books of Tobit and Judith in Aramaic, from which he hurriedly translated them into Latin.[28] Again, these Aramaic copies were obtained from the Jews. There is no early evidence of the circulation of Wisdom after Jamnia. However, Moses ben Nahman (Nachmanides, c. 1194-1270) knew and used an Aramaic text of Wisdom.[29] I know of no similar mitigating factor for a single book of the Apocrypha. These circumstances suggest that the impact of the *a priori* claims of the Jewish canon were softened with respect to these books, since they continued to circulate in Judaism after Jamnia. Whatever arguments Christians were able to derive from them probably met little resistance from Jews on the grounds that they were depending upon noncanonical writings.

The apocryphal literature enjoyed a high esteem in the church, similar to the other Jewish religious literature, until about the third century A.D. Thereafter these writings were subjected to attack and eventual withdrawal from the scriptures of the church. It appears that the principal reason for the loss of authority suffered by them was that when the Jewish canon became known in the church it was assumed, *a priori*, that the Jewish canon was determinative for the OT of the church. The period of attack upon these books among Christian writers coincides with the tendency in the church toward conformity to the Jewish canon. So then, the forming of the Christian OT canon from the larger literature received from Judaism appears to have been the result of the impact of the closed Jewish canon of Jamnia upon the more inclusive practice of the church. But it is also clear that the church did not inherit a canon of scriptures from Judaism. The church was forced to determine her OT for herself. The OT, thus, is seen to be a Christian canon.[29a]

---

[26] Hagigah 13a; Yebamoth 63b; Baba Kamma 92b.

[27] Eusebius, H. E. VI.xxv.2; J. E. L. Oulton, *Eusebius' Ecclesiastical History with an English Translation* (Loeb Classical Library, Cambridge, Massachusetts, 1953), II, 74f., n.1.

[28] Preface to Tobit.

[29] A. Marx, "An Aramaic Fragment of the Wisdom of Solomon," *JBL* XL (1921), 57-69.

[29a] J. C. Turro, in his otherwise excellent article, "Bible III (Canon), 2. History of the Old Testament Canon," *NCE* II, 387-391, having agreed that diaspora Judaism never took an independent stand on canon but "turned to Jerusalem for their Scriptures," still clings to the idea that the Septuagint included both the proto- and the deuterocanonical books and represented a (Jewish) tradition that is older than the

We are now prepared to discuss the division in the Christian OT between the proto- and the deuterocanonical books in the light of the history of the OT canon in the early church. Martin Luther had denied the canonical status of the deuterocanonical books in his debates with Johann Maier of Eck in 1519.[30] While Luther appears to have been pressed into his initial statement by the exigencies of the debate, his statement became Protestant doctrine. It is interesting to note that most of the participants in the Council of Trent were initially prepared to support an undivided OT.[31] The Council was keenly aware that defense against the Protestant position was at stake. And this pressed some of the members of the Council who were well aware of the difficulties raised by Jerome to prefer to pass over them. Thus Bishop Marco Vigerio of Senigillia explained his vote, saying,

Although there is a certain distinction between the Sacred Books, yet for good reasons "placet" that this be not expressed, and that all be "absolutely" accepted as authored by the Holy Ghost, and as books in which there is no falsity or suspicion, without distinction.[32]

Cardinal Pacheco feared that "our adversaries would be able to boast that their arguments had made us doubt our truths and the traditions of our fathers."[33] And it was sentiments such as these that carried the day and eventuated in the promulgation of an undivided OT canon. Still it is informative to note how closely some of the discussion in the Council came to the language employed by the Protestants. Cardinal Madruzzo had argued "that a distinction be made between the books, by which those that are truly sacred and upon which our dogmas are founded, be separated from those that are made to instruct youth and for the sake of history, according to the view of Jerome and Augustine."[34] And the Cardinal Legates' report of Feb. 12 had called some books canonical and others

---

Jewish canon. Whereas, the only evidence we have on the contents of the Septuagint is from Christian sources. In previous discussions Alexandrian and Septuagint canon have been synonymous terms so that to question the Alexandrian canon, on the one hand, and to maintain that the Septuagint formed a recognized collection antedating Jamnia, on the other, is a contradiction in terms. No Septuagint or Alexandrian canon or collection (including the proto- and deuterocanonical books) ever existed in Jewish hands prior to Jamnia.

[30] J. K. F. Knaake, et al., D. Martin Luthers Werke (Weimar, 1883-1939), II, 275-279.

[31] P. G. Duncker has collected the principal evidence from the primary sources in his article "The Canon of the Old Testament at the Council of Trent," CBQ 15 (1953) 277-299. I quote his translations.

[32] Societas Goerresiana, Concilium Tridentinum (Friburgi Brisgoviae, Torn. I, 1901), V, 55 No. 13; Duncker, op. cit., p. 297.

[33] CT, I, 31-33; Duncker, op. cit., p. 288.

[34] CT, I, 38; Duncker, op. cit., p. 297.

only "agiographi."[35] Now, Andreas Bodenstein of Karlstadt in his *De Canonicis Scripturis Libellus,* published in 1520 apparently to clarify Luther's precarious position on OT canon, had called Wisdom, Sirach, Judith, Tobit, and two books of Maccabees "apocryphi, that is, outside the Hebrew canon, but they are, nevertheless, agiographi,"[36] the same word used by the Cardinal Legates. And in Luther's German Bible of 1534 the deuterocanonical books were retained; they were called "Apocrypha. Das sind Bücher, so der H. Schrifft nich gleich gehalte u doch nützlich und gut zu lesen."[37]

Now that the heat has gone from the arguments and positions of those days, it is possible to see how near the discussions at Trent were to the position held by the Protestants. Both were troubled by the Jewish canonical list and especially Jerome's support of it. Both had been affected by the new humanism and its concern for original texts. And it is interesting to note that, despite the blanket pronouncement of Trent, the OT continues to be divided in Roman Catholic discussion into proto- and deuterocanonical books. While this distinction is primarily historical, denoting the books about which there was no question in the church concerning canonical status, on the one hand, and the books whose canonical status was at one time questioned, on the other,[38] apparently for some this division still carries doubts engendered by Jerome because of the impact of the Jewish canon. At least that appears to be the point of P. G. Duncker's attack in his article "The Canon of the Old Testament at the Council of Trent"; his conclusions are clearly an apology for the inspiration and canonicity of the deuterocanonical books and asserting their dogmatic usability on a par with the protocanonical.[39] That is, despite the pronouncement of Trent, Duncker apparently finds it necessary to counter a Jerome remainder.

Now the history of the OT in the early church enables us to make one further statement. Jerome's premise was wrong.[40] The Jewish canon was not the canon of Jesus and the apostles; in the days of Jesus and the apostles no closed canon of Jewish scriptures had yet been formulated, whether Palestinian or Alexandrian, whether Hebrew or Septuagint. The church received from Judaism closed collections of Law and Prophets

[35] Letter No. 298, *CT,* X, 397, 1-4; Duncker, *op. cit.,* p. 286.

[36] Reprinted in K. A. Credner, *Zur Geschichte des Kanons* (Halle, 1847), pp. 316-412, cf. p. 389.

[37] *Biblia, das ist: die ganze heilige Schrift altes und neues Testaments, ubersetzung d. M. Luthers* (Germantown, 1763).

[38] Robert and Tricot, *op. cit.,* p. 70; Steinmueller, *op. cit.,* pp. 61f., etc.

[39] *Op. cit.,* pp. 297-299.

[40] Sundberg, Protestant OT, pp. 199-202.

and an undefined group of religious writings that included books later defined in Judaism as Writings and in the Western church as deutero-canonical and apocryphal. And it was from this total legacy from its Jewish origins that the church came to define her OT for herself. I have previously urged Protestants that, in view of that fact, they ought either to accept the OT canon of the Western church or they must develop a new apologetic for continued support of the Jewish canon.[41] It is now clear that the OT of the early church was distinctly a Christian canon. And there remains no longer any reason to differentiate among the books of that canon because of Jerome's doubts. The deuterocanonical books are the books that were not received in the Jewish canon but were fully accepted in the OT of the early church. And it is now possible for Roman Catholics and Protestants to accept that fact in a mutual, undivided OT Christian canon.

Albert C. Sundberg, Jr.
American School of Oriental Research
Jerusalem, Jordan

[41] *Ibid.*, p. 203.

C. *Talmudic and Midrashic Evidence.*

THE DEFINITION OF THE JEWISH CANON AND THE REPUDIATION OF CHRISTIAN SCRIPTURES

By George F. Moore

At the beginning of the Christian era, lessons from the Pentateuch were read in the synagogue on the Sabbath, the book being for this purpose divided in such a way that it was read through in course in three years. This first lesson was followed by a second, selected from the Prophets, under which name the books of Joshua, Judges, Samuel, and Kings are included. These scriptures were given by God; their authors were divinely inspired, and divine authority resided in their every word.

Besides the Law and the Prophets there were several books to which the same character was ascribed: the Psalms—whose author, David, was, indeed, a prophet—Job, the Proverbs of Solomon, Ecclesiastes, the Song of Songs, Esther, Daniel, and others. These books, for which no specific name existed, were not read in the synagogue; it was not necessary, therefore, that the synagogue should possess a complete collection of them, and perhaps few private scholars had copies of them all. What books belonged to the Law and the Prophets every one knew; that was determined by the prescription of immemorial liturgical use and by long-standing methods of study in the schools. What books were comprised in the third class, "the scriptures," was not so determined. In regard to most of them there was, indeed, unanimous agreement; but others were not universally accepted: Ecclesiastes, the Song of Songs, and Esther, in particular were antilegomena; and on the other hand some reckoned Sirach among the inspired books. The question had, however, no great practical importance, and it does not appear that any attempt was made to settle it by drawing up a list of the 'scriptures.'

Reprinted from *C. A. Briggs Testimonial* (*Essays in Modern Theology*), New York, 1911.

In the Christian church it was not the differences about anti-legomena, such as the smaller Catholic Epistles and the Apocalypse, that compelled a definition of the canon of the New Testament, but the rise of heresies, particularly gnostic, whose writings, pretending to the authority of scripture, disseminated doctrines at war with catholic tradition and in the eyes of the catholic leaders subversive of the foundations of religion—writings doubly seductive because they professed to present the perfection of Christianity.   The orthodox bishops were constrained, therefore, not only to unmask these insidious errors, but to publish for the guidance of the faithful lists of the books which the Church received as its inspired Scriptures, and to denounce as spurious the writings of the heretics.*

The so-called Muratorian canon is peculiarly instructive here, not only because it is the oldest list of this kind which has come down to us,† but because the specification of rejected writings shews clearly what were the heresies which gave its author the greatest concern.   Thus, at the end of the enumeration of the Pauline Epistles we read: ‡ Fertur etiam ad Laudecenses alia ad Alexandrinos Pauli nomine finctae ad heresim Marcionis, et alia plura, quae in catholicam ecclesiam recipi non potest; fel enim cum melle misceri non congruit.   Epistola sane Iudae et superscriptio Iohannis duas in catholica habentur, et Sapientia ab amicis Salomonis in honorem ipsius scripta.   Apocalypses etiam Iohannis et Petri tantum recipimus, quam quidam ex nostris legi in ecclesia nolunt.   Pastorem vero nuperrime temporibus nostris in urbe Roma Herma conscripsit, sedente cathedra urbis Romae ecclesiae Pio episcopo fratre eius, et ideo legi eum quidem oportet, se publicare vero in ecclesia populo neque inter prophetas completum numero neque inter apostolos in finem temporum potest.   Arsinoi autem seu Valentini, vel Mitiadis [?] nihil in totum recipimus.   Qui etiam novum Psalmorum librum Marcioni conscripserunt una cum Basilide, Assianum cataphrygum constitutorem. . . ..

The text is in more than one point obscure, but the names of

---

* This motive is set forth at some length by Athanasius at the beginning of the 39th Festal Epistle (A.D. 367).

† Drawn up probably in Rome near the close of the second century.

‡ The text is based on Preuschen, Analecta (1893), p. 129 ff., with correction of manifest orthographical errors and the introduction of the punctuation.

Marcion, of Valentinus and Basilides, and of the founder of the cataphrygian heresy, suffice to render the situation clear.

Similarly in the Jewish church: it was not the diversity of opinion in the schools about Ecclesiastes and the Song of Songs that first made deliverances about the 'scriptures' necessary, but the rise of the Christian heresy and the circulation of Christian writings. Older than any catalogue of the canonical books which has been preserved * are specific decisions that certain books are not inspired scripture, and among these repudiated books the Gospels stand in the front rank.

The earliest deliverance of this kind is in the Tosephta,† Jadaim, 2¹³:

הגליונים וספרי המינין אינן מטמאין ‡ את הידים . ספרי בן סירא
וכל ספרים שנכתבו מכאן ואילך אינן מטמאין את הידים:

"The Gospels § and the books of the heretics are not holy scripture; ‖ the books of the son of Sirach and all books that have been written since his time are not holy scripture."

To the same effect is the decision in Tos. Sabbath, 13 (14)⁵. The question here under consideration is: What things may be rescued from a burning building on the Sabbath? ¶ The general principle is that holy scriptures (expressly including the hagiographa) should be saved;** but "the Gospels and the books of the heretics may not be saved"—they are not holy scriptures. The passage is so important that it must be quoted entire.

הגליונים וספרי מינין אין מצילין אותן אלא נשרפין †† במקומן הן
ואזכרותיהם . רבי יוסי הגלילי אומר בחול קורע ‡‡ את האזכרות וגונז
ושורף את השאר . אמר רבי טרפון אקפח את בניי שאם יבואו לידי

* The oldest (before 200 A.D.) is a Baraitha in Baba Bathra, 14ᵇ, on the proper order of the Prophets and the Hagiographa.
† Ed. Zuckermandel, Pasewalk, 1881.
‡ Ed. מטמאות.
§ That *gilion* here and in the following quotations is εὐαγγέλιον will be proved below.
‖ Literally, "do not make the hands unclean"; the principle being, "All holy scriptures make the hands unclean." See below, p. 119.
¶ It being under ordinary circumstances a breach of the Sabbath to carry anything out of a building on that day; Tos. Sabbath, 1, Mishna Sabbath, 1.
** M. Sabbath 16¹.
†† + הן Ed.
‡‡ So Jer. Sabb. 16¹ (ed. Venet. f. 13ᶜ). Zuckermandel, with cod. Erfurt., קורא: other MSS. and edd. of the Tosephta, Bab. Sabb. 116ᵃ, Sifrè, Num. § 16 (on 5²³) קויר; Tanchuma, Buber, Korah, App. 1, קורט.

שאני שורפן הן ואזכרותיהן שאלו הרודף רודף אחריי נכנסתי לבית עבודה
זרה ואיני נכנס לבתיהן שעובדי עבודה זרה אין מכירין אותו וכופרין
בו והללו מכירין אותו וכופרין בו ועליהם הכתוב אומר ואחר הדלת
והמזוזה שמת זכרונך. אמר רבי ישמאל ומה אם לעשות שלום בין
איש לאשתו אמר המקום שמי שנכתב בקדושה ימחה על המים ספרי
מינין שמטילין איבה וקנאה ותחרות בין ישראל לאביהם שבשמים על
אחת כמה וכמה שיפרקו הן ואזכרותיהם ואליהם הכתוב אומר הלוא
משנאיך יי אשנא ובתקוממיך אתקוטט תכלית שנאה שנאתים לאויבים
היו לי. וכשם שאין מצילין אותן מפני הדליקה כך אין מצילין אותן
מפני המפלות ולא מפני המים ולא מכל דבר המאבדון:

"The Gospels and the books of heretics are not to be rescued,
but allowed to burn where they are, names of God and all.*
Rabbi Jose the Galilean says:† On a week day one should tear
out the names of God and put them away in safe keeping, and
burn the rest. Rabbi Tarphon said: May I lose my children,‡
but if these books came into my hands, I would burn them, names
of God and all! If a pursuer were after me, I would take refuge
in a heathen temple and not in their conventicles; for the heathen
deny God without knowing him, but these know him and yet
deny him. Of them the scripture says: "Behind the door and
the door post thou hast set up thy memorial."§ Rabbi Ishmael
said: ‖ If, to make peace between a man and his wife, God commanded, 'Let my name, which is written in holiness, be wiped
off into the water,' how much more should the books of the
heretics, who bring enmity and jealousy and strife between Israel
and their father in heaven, be put out of the way, names of God
and all. Of them the scripture says: "Do not I hate them, O
Lord, that hate thee? Do not I loathe them that oppose thee?
I hate them with perfect hatred; I count them my enemies." ¶
And as they are not to be saved from a fire, so they are not to be

---

* A pious man might scruple to allow the divine names to be destroyed,
even in a context that richly merited destruction.—The same rule applies to
written prayers and to amulets: "though they may contain the letters of the
divine name and many sentences of the law," they are to be left to burn.
Tos. Sabb. 13⁴; Jer. Sabb. 16¹; Sabb. 61ᵇ, 115ᵇ.

† In Sifrè, Num. § 16, the view here attributed to Jose is maintained by
Ishmael; Akiba says, One should burn the whole of it, because it was not
written in holiness.

‡ A favorite oath of Tarphon; see e. g., Tos. Hagiga 3³ᵃ.

§ Isa. 57⁸.

‖ See also Sifrè, Num. § 16.   ¶ Ps. 139²¹ ᶠ.

saved from the fall of a building, or from flood, or from any other destroying agency."

The whole passage is repeated—with minor variations which do not affect the sense—in Jer. Sabbath 16[1] * and in the Babylonian Talmud, Sabbath 116[a].† In the latter the question is thereupon raised whether the books of "Be Abidan" fall in the category of heretical writings which may not be saved; and further (a propos of Tarphon's violent words about the conventicles of heretics), whether it is proper to visit the "Be Abidan" and the "Be Nizrephi."‡ Rabbi Abbahu, to whom the inquiry was addressed, was not certain; precedents are quoted on both sides.

After this digression the Babylonian Talmud resumes the subject of the Gospels. In the current editions, since that of Basel (1578–1581), the text has been so mutilated by the censors that neither the connection nor the significance of the passage is recognizable. The subjoined text is that of the first complete edition of the Talmud, published at Venice by Bomberg in 1520.§ The most important variations of the Munich manuscript (M) and of an Oxford manuscript (O) are noted after Rabbinowicz, *Dikduke Sopherim.*

רבי מאיר קרי ליה און גיליון ' יוחנן קרי ליה עון גליון . אימא
שלום דביתהו דרבי אליעזר אחתיה דרבן ' גמליאל הואי הוה ' ההוא
פילוספא דשיבבותיה דהוה שקיל שמא דלא מקבל שוחדא בעו לאחוכי
ביה אעיילה ליה שרנא דדהבא ואזול ' לקמיה אמרה ליה ' בעינא דניפלגי
לי בנכסי דבי נשי ' אמר להו פלוגו אמר ליה כתיב לן ' דבמקום ברא
ברתא לא תירות אמר להו מן יומא דגליתון מארעכון איתנטלית אורייתא
דמשה ויאתיהיבת עון גיליון ' וכתיב ביה ברא וברתא כחדא ירתון
למחר הדר עייל ליה איהו חמרא לובא אמר להו שפילית לסיפיה דעון
גיליון וכתיב ביה אנא עון גיליון לא למיפחת מן אורייתא דמשה אתיתי
אלא ' לאוספי על אורייתא דמשה ' אתיתי וכתיב ביה במקום ברא

---

* In his edition of the Midrash Tanchuma, Buber inserts the passage—which is not found in the common recension—at the end of the Parasha Korah, from a Roman codex, in which, as Buber shows, it is derived from the lost Midrash Jelamedenu.

† Quoted in full from the Babylonian Talmud in Jalkut, II, § 488, on Isa. 57.

‡ What these assemblies were is a question that need not detain us here.

§ From a copy in the library of Union Theological Seminary, New York. The text of this edition is reprinted by L. Goldschmidt, Der Babylonische Talmud, 1897 sqq., with *variae lectiones* and translation.

בְרָתָא לֹא תִירוּת אָמְרָה לֵיהּ נְהוֹר נְהוֹרֵיךְ כְּשַׁרְנָא אָמַר לֵיהּ רַבָּן גַמְלִיאֵל
אָתָא חֲמָרָא וּבְטַשׁ לְשַׁרְנָא:

O וְהָיָה לֵהּ־דִּינָא בַּהֲדֵי דְּרַ״ג וְאָתָא קְמֵיהּ דַּחֲוָיָא +³   M שִׁמְעוֹן בֶּן +²   M   רַבִּי +¹
O נְשִׂיא ⁶   M   M >⁵   וְאָזְלָה ⁴
אִיתַנְטְלִית אוֹרַיְיתָא דְּמֹשֶׁה Modern edd.—O reads: אוֹרַיְיתָא אַחֲרִיתִי ⁸   M   בְּאוֹרַיְיתָא ⁷
מִינְּכוֹן וְאִיתְיְהִיבַת לְכוֹן אוֹרַיְיתָא דְּעוֹן גִּלְיוֹן.
וְלֹא ⁹ Modern edd.
¹⁰ The three preceding words > M and earliest edd.

' "Rabbi Meir called it 'awen gilion, Rabbi Johanan called it
'awon gilion.*

Imma Shalom, the wife of Rabbi Eliezer and sister of Rabban
Gamaliel, had in her neighborhood a certain philosopher † who
had the reputation there of not taking bribes. They wished to
bring him into ridicule, so she brought him a gold lamp, appeared
before him and said: I want to have a share in the division of
the patriarch's estate.‡ He said to them, Divide it, then!
Rabban Gamaliel replied, It is written for us that where there
is a son, a daughter does not inherit.§ The judge answered,
From the time when you lost your independence the law of
Moses was done away, and the gospel ($\epsilon\dot{v}a\gamma\gamma\epsilon\lambda\iota o\nu$) was given;
and therein it is written, 'Son and daughter shall inherit alike.'
On the following day, Rabban Gamaliel brought him a Libyan
ass. The judge said to them, I have looked further down to
the end of the Gospel, and there it is written, 'I, Gospel, did not
come to take away from the law of Moses, but to add to the law
of Moses I came'; ‖ and it is written in it, 'Where there is a
son, a daughter does not inherit.' Imma Shalom said to him,

---

* אָוֶן and עָוֹן are both words of evil association in the Old Testament,
especially connected with religious defection; בֵּית אָוֶן is Hosea's opprobrious
name for Bethel (4¹⁵, 5⁸, 10⁵); for עָוֹן cf. Hos. 5⁴, 14², etc.

† I. e., heretic. Jebamoth 102ᵇ, "A heretic (מִינָא) asked R. Gamaliel,"
etc.; in Midr. Tehillim on Ps. 10 near the end, the questioner is a 'philosopher.'

‡ The estate of their father.—Cf. the request addressed to Jesus, Bid my
brother divide the inheritance with me, Luke 12¹³.

§ See Num. 27⁸.—The Sadducees (Tosephta, "Boethusians") held that a
daughter could inherit from her father, inasmuch as a granddaughter whose
father was dead inherited from her grandfather. Tos. Jadaim 2²⁰, Baba
Bathra 115ᵇ.

‖ Cf. Matt. 5²¹ ᶠ. The reading אֶלָּא is original; it was changed to וְלֹא by
editors, who made the superficial observation that the following quotation
from the Gospel is identical with Gamaliel's from that law.

May thy light shine like the lamp! Rabban Gamaliel rejoined, The ass came and kicked over the lamp!" *

The story of Imma Shalom has no pertinence to the subject of Sabbath 16; it is brought in here because the judge in his decisions cites the *'awon gilion*. That this name is a perversion of εὐαγγέλιον † is put beyond question by the quotation of an utterance of Jesus which we read in the Gospel of Matthew, 5¹⁷.‡

The rabbinical puns attach themselves to the word *gilion* in the preceding passage—"R. Meir called it *'awen gilion*," etc. *Gilion* itself,§ as a name for the gospel, is another example of the same kind of wit; the word properly signifies a *blank*, writing material not written on, as the margins of a manuscript or blank spaces in one; ‖ the εὐαγγέλιον is nothing but a *gilion*, a blank.

Constantly coupled with the gospel in the passages we have before us are the ספרי המינין. *Minim* is the common name in the Talmuds and Midrashim for heretics; that is, Jews who maintained opinions or practised rites and customs at variance

---

* Substantially the same story, without any names, is told in Pesikta, Echa (ed. Buber, p. 122ᵇ,) and from the Pesikta in Jalkut on Isa. 1 (§ 391), as an illustration of the venality denounced in Isa. 1²³. The bribes are respectively a *silver* lamp and a little *golden* ass (asses colt); the last words are כפה סיח את המנורה. This apparently proverbial expression occurs in another story of the venality of the priests of the second temple in Jer. Joma 1¹, Sifrè, Num. § 131 (on 25¹²), Pesikta, Aḥarè (ed. Buber, f. 177ᵃ, Wayikra Rabba 21ˣ, Jalkut, Aḥarè, near the beginning.

† Cf. Rashi on Sabb. 116 (in uncastrated editions) ר׳ מאיר קרי ליה לספרי המינין און גליון לפי שהן קורין אותו אונגילא (*Evangile*).

‡ Imma Shalom's words: "May thy light shine like the lamp," not improbably contain an allusion to Matt. 5¹⁶, "Let your light so shine before men," etc. Güdemann (Religionsgeschichtliche Studien, 1876, pp. 79 ff.), comparing the groups of stories about bribery cited in note* above, conjectures that in the original version Gamaliel's present was not an ass (חמור) but a measure (חֹמר) of gold—an allusion to the lamp under the bushel, Matt. 5¹⁵.

§ Cod. M consistently גליון (sing.); Tos., and edd. in Sabb. *l. c.* have the plural.

‖ *E. g.* M. Jadaim 3⁴.—It is evident that the Babylonian Amoraim who discuss the Baraitha in Sabb. 116ᵇ were ignorant of the origin of the name; they know only the ordinary meaning of the word, 'blank, margin.' But the contradictions which this involves bring them very close to the true explanation: The sense must be, the books of the heretics are like blank pages. The mutilation or perversion of names as a testimony of pious abhorrence is common in the Old Testament, and is explicitly enjoined, *e. g.* in Tos. Aboda Zara, 6⁴.

with the standards of the community at large and the teaching of its recognized authorities.* The term conveyed the same reprobation as its Christian equivalent, and was as freely applied. The vexatious questioners who bring up the difficulties of scripture are called *minim*, even when their questions betray no tendency more dangerous than a disposition to pester the rabbis.† It may be suspected that they are sometimes fictitious interlocutors, put on the stage only to give the doctors an opportunity to show how easily such captious questions can be disposed of; the audience of pupils not infrequently intimate their dissatisfaction with the evasive answer, and ask for themselves a serious solution.

The heretics with whom the rabbis of the first centuries of the Christian era had to do were not a single school or sect, much less were they exponents of a coherent and consequent system of thought; they represent all the varying tendencies which in that age led individuals or groups to diverge more or less widely from the high road of sound doctrine and correct usage.‡ There are heretics who deny the resurrection of the dead, or at least that the belief has any foundation in scripture; and to the same class belong those who affirm that there is only one world.§ Some deny that there is any divine retribution; others, at the opposite extreme, deny that God receives the penitent.

There are heretics who deny revelation—"the law is not from heaven." In the damnation of these infidels the rabbis include those who impugn a single word in the written law or the most subtle point in the deductions of the learned.‖ Those who ignore "the seasons and equinoxes"—that is, the rabbinical determination of the calendar, are also heretics; singularities in the form of the phylacteries or the manner of wearing them are "heretical ways"; turning the face to the East in prayer is a heretical custom. In particular, certain peculiarities in the

* Cf. Rashi on Gittin 45[b]: מין. יהודי שאינו מאמין לדברי רז"ל.

† Sadducees, Samaritans, Romans—especially emperors—philosophers and unbelievers, miscellaneously play the same rôle and propound the same questions.

‡ See Jer. Sanhedrin 10[5] (Johanan): "Israel was not exiled until there were formed twenty-four sects of heretics."

§ M. Berakoth 9[5].

‖ Sanhedrin 99[a], cf. Tanchuma, Ki Tissa 17.

slaughtering of animals are condemned as the practise of the heretics.

A heresy of a different type was the recognition of "two authorities," or powers (שני רשויות), or, as it is sometimes expressed, of more than one divinity (אלהות), especially in the creation of the world. According to Tosephta Sanhedrin 8⁷, Adam was created at the end, "in order that the heretics might not say that God had a helper in his work." * These allusions do not disclose the meaning or motive of the heretical contention. It is only enveloping obscurity in confusion to label their error with names so charged with foreign connotation as dualism or gnosticism.† That they were influenced by conceptions of a godhead too exalted to do things himself—conceptions which were then everywhere in the air, and, as we see in Philo, found acceptance among Hellenistic Jews—may reasonably be surmised, but cannot be proved. No less uncertain is the common assumption that the heretics to whom the Tosephta and Mishna refer in the places quoted were Christians. Nothing that we know about the Jewish Christianity of the second century would lead us to think that the part of Christ in creation was a salient feature of their apologetic, nor is there anything distinctively Christian in the belief that God had a helper in creation.

From a much later time—the second half of the third and the first quarter of the fourth century ‡—are the discussions in which the *minim* bring a long array of biblical texts to prove a plurality

---

* Adam was not created an ordinary man, but a being of superhuman dimensions and intelligence. Cf. M. Sanhedrin 4⁵; Adam was created single (*i. e.,* only one man was created), "in order that the heretics might not say that there is more than one power in heaven" (הרבה רשויות בשמים). Bereshith Rabba 1³: all agree that the angels were not created on the first day, that it might not be said that Michael and Gabriel assisted in stretching out the heavens. Therefore angels are not to be adored.

† Elisha ben Abuya (Aḥer) is said to have been led to believe in "two authorities" by seeing, in one of his raptures, the "Metatron".; but we are none the wiser for this information (Ḥagiga 15ª). The restrictions put on the study of the first chapters of Genesis and Ezekiel (M. Ḥagiga 2¹) imply that secret cosmological and theosophic speculations, perilous for common minds, were rife.

‡ The rabbis who take part in these controversies are Johanan (d. ca. 279), Simlai, and Abbahu (d. ca. 320). See Sanhedrin 38ᵇ; Jer. Berakoth 9¹, and parallels; and for Abbahu, the passages collected by Bacher, Agada der Palästinischen Amoräer, II, 115 ff.

in the godhead, such as the plural אלהים in Gen. 1; "let us make man in our image" (Gen. 1²⁶); "let us go down and confound their speech" (Gen. 11⁷); the plurals in Gen. 35⁷, כי שם נגלו אליו האלהים; "thrones were set" (Dan. 7⁹), and similar expressions. That the disputants who cite these passages are Christians is altogether probable. Johanan, the respondent in the earliest of these controversies, had studied in Caesarea under Hoshaia, who may very well have been acquainted with Origen during his residence in that city.* Abbahu, the most distinguished pupil of Johanan, taught in Caesarea, where he was for a time contemporary with Eusebius; his familiarity with Greek is repeatedly attested. Simlai's school was in Lydda, which was a Christian bishopric certainly in 325 and probably earlier. We seem to hear a distinctively Christian note when the *minim* ask R. Simlai the significance of the *three* divine names אל אלהים יהוה in Jos. 22²² and Ps. 50¹.† The Christians in these controversies are, however, not representatives of Jewish, but of Catholic, Christianity.‡ The discussions are, in any case, much too late to throw any light on the beliefs of the heretics whose books are condemned in the Tosephta.

That among the heretics of the second century Jewish Christians had the place of eminence is proved by many stories of the relations of distinguished rabbis to them. Rabbi Eliezer (ben Hyrcanus),§ the brother-in-law of Rabban Gamaliel II, was once arrested on the ground of heresy (that is, as the sequel shows, on the charge of being a Christian), and brought before a Roman magistrate, who said to him, An old man like

---

* Origen was in Caesarea for two or three years from 215, and from 231 on it was his home. He frequently consulted Jewish teachers about points of exegesis. It has been surmised that the "Patriarchus Huillus" whom he quotes as authority for certain interpretations was Hillel II.

† Unmistakable is also the point of Abbahu's polemic (against unnamed opponents) in Shemoth Rabba 29⁴: An earthly king has a father or a son or a brother; but God is not so (Isa. 44⁶): "I am the first"—I have no father—and "I am the last"—I have no son—"and beside me there is no god"—I have no brother.

‡ As in the second century Jewish Christianity was *the* heresy, the name *min*, 'heretic,' was ordinarily equivalent to Christian, and later was applied to Gentile Christians as well. Occasionally Christians of the uncircumcision are distinguished, as in Aboda Zara 65ᵃ: a proselyte who lets twelve months pass without being circumcised is כסין שכאומות; cf. Ḥullin 13ᵇ.

§ Tos. Ḥullin 2²⁴.

you occupying yourself with these things! Eliezer replied,
One whom I can trust is my judge! The magistrate applied
these words to himself (whereas Eliezer meant his father in
heaven), and said, Since you show confidence in me, very well.
I thought perhaps these errorists had seduced * you in these
matters. You are acquitted. When he was dismissed from
court he was much distressed because he had been arrested for
heresy. His disciples came to console him, but he refused to be
comforted. Then Rabbi Akiba came and said, Rabbi, may I
speak without offence? He replied, Say on! Akiba said, Is it
possible that one of the heretics repeated to you some heretical
utterance and you were pleased with it? Eliezer responded,
Heaven! you remind me. Once I was walking in the main street
of Sepphoris, and met [one of the disciples of Jesus the Nazarene]†
Jacob of Kefar Siknin, who repeated to me a heretical saying in
the name of Jesus ben Pantera which pleased me well.‡ I have
been arrested for heresy, because I transgressed the injunction
of scripture, "Remove thy way far from her, and come not near
the door of her abode; for she has laid low many slain" (Prov.
5⁸ + 7²⁶).§

In the corresponding passage, Aboda Zara 16ᵇ–17ᵃ, the conversation between Jacob and Eliezer is reported by the latter,
as follows: [Jacob asked] It is written in your law, "Thou
shalt not bring the hire of a harlot into the house of thy God"
(Deut. 23¹⁹). Is it permissible to use it to build a privy for the
high priest? I had no answer for him.‖ He continued: Thus
did Jesus the Nazarene¶ teach me, "From the hire of a harlot
she gathered it; to the hire of a harlot they shall return" (Mic. 1⁷).
From a filthy place they came, to a filthy place they shall go.

---

* Reading by conjecture, הסיתו; the text has הסיבו. Cf. Sanhedrin 43ᵃ, 107ᵇ
(of Jesus) הסית ימסית.

† These words are found in the parallel text, Aboda Zara 17ᵃ.

‡ The curious halaka quoted below was perhaps not the only saying of
Jesus that pleased Eliezer well. His words in Sotah 48ᵇ, "A man who has
a piece of bread in his basket and says, What shall I eat tomorrow? is one
of them of little faith," sound like an echo of Matt. 6³¹.—My attention was
called to this saying some years ago by Professor G. Deutsch.

§ The warning of the proverb against harlotry applied to heresy. Similarly Eccles. 7²⁶ is interpreted in Koheleth Rabba.

‖ In Koheleth Rabba (on 1⁸) Eliezer gives the opinion that it is prohibited.

¶ In Koheleth Rabba "So and So," as frequently to avoid the name Jesus.

Rabbi Eleazer ben Dama,* a nephew of Rabbi Ishmael, was bitten by a serpent, and Jacob of Kefar Sekania† came to cure him in the name of Jesus ben Pantera, but Rabbi Ishmael would not permit him, saying, You have no right to do it, Ben Dama.‡ The latter replied, I can bring you a verse to prove that he may heal me; but he died before he had time to adduce his proof-text. Ishmael exclaimed, Blessed art thou, Beñ Dama, that thou didst depart in peace, and didst not break through the ordinance of .the sages, etc.

The heresy that could bring so eminently conservative a teacher as Rabbi Eliezer into trouble had plainly a perilous fascination.§ Beside Ishmael's nephew, Eleazer ben Dama, several other rabbis are named who had singed their wings in fluttering around it.‖ To guard against its seductive attractions, it was forbidden to enter into discussion with the heretics or have any intercourse with them.¶ The ordinance is introduced in the Tosephta in connection with the prohibition of a certain mode of slaughtering animals (bleeding them over a hole in the ground), which is said to be in accordance with the ritual rules of the heretics. The edict then proceeds:**

"It is permitted to derive profit from flesh which is in the possession of a gentile (גוי), but forbidden in the case of a heretic (מין); flesh from an heathen temple is the flesh of sacrifices to the dead. For the authorities say: The slaughtering of a heretic is heathen (עבודה זרה), their food is Samaritan food, their wine is libation wine,†† their fruits are treated as untithed, their books are books of magic (ספרי קוסמין), and their children are bastards (ממזרין). It is forbidden to sell to them or to buy

* Tosephta Ḥullin 2²²ᶠ·, immediately preceding the story of Eliezer ben Hyrcanus; Jer. Aboda Zara 2², Jer. Sabbath 14, end; Aboda Zara 27ᵇ.

† So in Aboda Zara 27ᵃ. The Palestinian tradition, כפר סמא, "Poison Town."

‡ It is forbidden to employ heretics as healers either for man or beast (Tos. Ḥullin 2²¹). The Mishna allows them veterinary practice.

§ So it is expressly said in Aboda Zara 17ᵃ.

‖ See Koheleth Rabba on 1⁸; Weiss, Dor wa-Dor, I⁴, p. 222; Bacher, Agada der Palästinischen Amoräer, III, 711.

¶ Tos. Ḥullin 2²⁰; cf. Sanhedrin 38ᵇ. The rabbinical prohibition of discussion with Christians is cited by Trypho in Justin's Dialogue, c. 38.

** Tos. Ḥullin 2²⁰ᶠ·; cf. Ḥullin 13ᵃ·ᵇ.

†† Wine of *idolatrous* libations.

from them, to enter into argument with them, to teach their children a trade, to allow them to heal man or beast."

The stringency of this interdict and the violence of the language in which it is couched show how critical the situation was felt to be. To emphasize the danger of having anything to do with the heretics, the Tosephta proceeds to narrate the stories of Eleazer ben Dama and Eliezer ben Hyrcanus which I have translated above; and these examples show plainly that the heresy which gave the authorities the greatest cause for apprehension was Christianity.

The heretics are excluded from the society of the good not only in this world but in the other. Their torment in hell is eternal: * "The wicked of Israel in their bodies and the wicked of the gentiles in their bodies go down to hell and are punished there for twelve months. At the end of twelve months their souls cease to be; their bodies are consumed, and hell spews them out and they turn to ashes which the wind scatters and strews beneath the feet of the righteous (Mal. 3²¹). But the heretics and the apostates and the informers and the Epicureans,† and those who deny the scriptures, those who separate themselves from the customs of the community, and those who deny the resurrection of the dead, and every one who sins and makes others sin, like Jeroboam and Ahab, and those who create a reign of terror in the land of the living, and those who lay hands on the temple—hell will be locked on them, and they will be punished in it for all generations (Isa. 66²⁴)." ‡

Beside the interdict on all intercourse with the heretics, another measure adopted to check the spread of heresy was the insertion in the Eighteen Benedictions of a prayer for the perdition of the heretics. The Palestinian recension of this petition, in the oldest form in which it is preserved, runs as follows: §
"For the apostates let there be no hope, and may the proud

---

* Tos. Sanhedrin 13⁴⁻⁵; see also Rosh ha-Shana 17ª.

† There is reason to suspect that this catalogue of candidates for hell has been amplified in the course of time; but the beginning is indubitably authentic, and that the heretics take precedence even of apostates to heathenism is significant.

‡ Rosh ha-Shana adds: "Hell shall come to an end, but not they!"

§ Schechter, Jewish Quarterly Review, X (1898), pp. 654–659; from manuscripts found in a *geniza* in Cairo.

kingdom be speedily uprooted in our days. And may the Nazarenes and the heretics perish in a moment." In the Babylonian tradition:* "For the apostates let there be no hope; and may all the heretics and the informers perish in a moment; † and may the proud kingdom be uprooted and demolished speedily, in our days."

To the use of this prayer Jerome in all probability refers in a letter to Augustine (Ep. 112 § 13): Usque hodie per totas Orientis synagogas inter Judaeos haeresis est, qui dicitur Minaeorum, et a Pharisaeis nunc usque damnatur: quos vulgo Nazaraeos nuncupant, etc.

The introduction of this petition is ascribed to the Patriarch Gamaliel II and his college at Jamnia; the formulation, to Samuel ha-Katon.‡ The motive was perhaps not so much to relieve the pious feeling which the orthodox of all creeds and times have cherished toward misbelievers as to serve as a touchstone for heretics; § for we learn in the sequel of the passage just cited from Berakoth,‖ that if the leader in public prayer made a mistake in reciting any of the other petitions, he was allowed to proceed, but if he stumbled in the petition against heretics, he was called down, because it was to be suspected that he was himself a heretic.

The "books of the heretics" which, according to Tosephta Jadaim 2¹³, are not holy scripture, and, according to Tosephta Sabbath 13⁵, so far from being rescued from fire on the Sabbath, are rather to be burned on a week day, may therefore be—or at least include—Christian scriptures ¶; and the standing association with the gospel suggests that Christian scriptures were primarily aimed at in these deliverances.** The violent antipa-

---

* See Dalman, Worte Jesu, 1898, pp. 301 f.

† Compare the constellation of heretics, apostates, and informers in Aboda Zara 26ᵇ.

‡ Berakoth 28ᵇ–29ᵃ; cf. Megilla 17ᵇ.

§ Like the recitation of a creed in the liturgy.

‖ The authority is Rab, quoted by Rab Judah.

¶ The Christians were, of course, not the only sect that had books.

** Taken by themselves, the words ספרי המינים might mean manuscripts of biblical books copied by the heretics, as ספרי כותים in Sanhedrin 90ᵇ (Sota 33ᵇ; Sifrè, § 112, on Num. 15³¹; cf., however, Jer. Sota 7ᵃ, סופרי כותים, and see Levy, NHWb. I, 530) are Samaritan copies of the Pentateuch, which the Samaritans are accused of falsifying. According to Gittin 45ᵇ a Pentateuch

thy which Tarphon and Ishmael manifest toward these writings and their possessors reminds us of the hostility toward the Christians and their books which breathes in every line of the interdict in Tosephta Hullin 2[20-22], and makes it reasonable to infer that this intensity of feeling was aroused by the same danger.

In Mishna Sanhedrin 10[1] the classes of Israelites are enumerated who have no lot in the world to come—the man who denies that the resurrection of the dead can be proved from the law; * he who denies that the law is from heaven; and the 'Epicurean.' † "Rabbi Akiba says, Also he who reads in the outside books (ספרים החיצונים); and he who murmurs as an incantation over an ailment the words of Exodus 15[26b]."

On the words ספרים החיצונים the Babylonian Talmud comments: תנא בספרי מינים. רב יוסת אמר בספר בן סירא נמי אסור למקרי. "Tradition ‡ says, the books of the heretics. Rab Joseph § said, It is also forbidden to read in the book of Sirach." In the corresponding passage in the Palestinian Talmud we read: "'Also he who reads in the outside books,' such as the books of Sirach and the books of Ben Laana." ‖ Koheleth Rabba, on Eccles. 12[12], declares that he who brings into his house more than the twenty-four canonical books brings in confusion, "for example, the book of Sirach and the book of Ben Tigla." ¶

copied by a heretic is to be burned; one that had been in the possession of a heretic is to be carefully preserved (גנז), but not used. The greater severity of these regulations as compared with those concerning a copy made by a gentile (Tos. Aboda Zara 3[7]; Jer. Aboda Zara 2[2], end; see also Menaḥoth 42[b], top) are probably attributable to the suspicion that the heretic might falsify the text in the interest of his errors, while the gentile, who made copies only to sell to Jews, presumably had no such motive.

Rashi (on Sabbath 116[a]) understands ספרי המינים in this sense—copies of Old Testament books made by heretics. So also L. Löw, Graphische Requisiten, II, 19, and many others, among whom Bacher is to be especially mentioned. But for the reasons indicated above this interpretation is improbable.

* The oldest statement probably was: "he who denies the resurrection of the dead."

† The Epicurean in this context is perhaps a man who denies providence and retribution; cf. Josephus, Antt. X, 11, 7.

‡ That is, authoritative Palestinian tradition earlier than 220 A.D.

§ Rab Joseph bar Hiyya, Babylonian Amora; died ca. 330.

‖ On the whole passage, see below, pp. 116 f., where it will be shown that the inclusion of Sirach in this condemnation is the result of a scribal error.

¶ The first vowel is uncertain. See further below, p. 117*.

In the light of these passages the words of Akiba have commonly been taken to mean, "books outside the Jewish canon,"
more particularly, as the mention of Sirach suggests, books of
the class which we call apocrypha. In support of this explanation is cited the analogous phrase משנה החיצונה (Bamidbar
Rabba 18¹⁷) the Hebrew equivalent of the common *Baraitha*
(ברייתא), a Mishnic tradition outside the Mishna of the Patriarch Judah.

This interpretation is, however, beset by grave difficulties.
Why should the reading of a book like Sirach be condemned in
this fashion? The question was discussed in the Babylonian
schools; * Abbaye quotes some sayings in the book to which
objection might be raised, but has no difficulty in discovering
good biblical or rabbinical parallels to them. The one indefen-
sible utterance he singles out ("The thin-bearded man is crafty;
the thick-bearded man is stupid; he who blows the foam from
his cup is not thirsty; from him who says, What shall I eat for
a relish with my bread? his bread shall be taken away; the
whole world is no match for the man with a forked beard")
shows how hard he was put to it to explain why Sirach should be
on the Index Librorum Prohibitorum. In fact, the objections
made to Sirach on internal grounds are far from being as serious
as those which are brought up against the Proverbs of Solomon,†
not to speak of Ecclesiastes.

Rab Joseph, who attests the fact that Sirach was on the Index,
himself says in the course of the discussion, "We make homiletical use of the excellent sayings that are found in this book,"
and adduces many such. Authorities of unimpeachable correctness in all periods—including Akiba himself—quote Sirach without suspicion that it is an interdicted book. Mediaeval quotations, and the recovery in recent years of a considerable part of
the Hebrew text from fragments of several manuscripts, prove
that the popularity of Sirach continued unabated.

To remove this evident contradiction it has been suggested
that what was condemned was not private reading, but the public
reading of passages from Sirach and other Apocrypha in the
synagogue, whereby the distinction between inspired and uninspired writings was obscured. The principle seems, however,

* Sanhedrin 100ᵇ.   † Sabbath 30ᵇ.

to have been early established that even the acknowledged hagiographa should not be read in the synagogue; * and if the public
reading of uncanonical books had become in the second century
an evil that needed to be checked, we should expect to find somewhere an express prohibition of the practice.

It is to be noted, further, that Akiba couples with the reading
of the "outside" books the use of Exod. 15²⁶ as a charm. He
excludes from the world to come "the man who murmurs (לֹחֵשׁ)
over an ailment the words, 'None of the diseases which I inflicted
on the Egyptians will I inflict on thee: I am the Lord, thy
healer.' " † The use of verses of the Bible in connection with
medication or with what we should call magical healing was
common and pious practice; the most orthodox rabbis had no
scruples about it. Akiba does not condemn biblical incantations
in general, but a specific formula, and one which in itself appears
to be wholly unobjectionable. Why should the use of this particular verse deserve eternal perdition?

The hypothesis which seems best to account for Akiba's abhorrence is that this formula was employed by a class of healers
whom he deemed especially pernicious. We know that in his
time the Christian healers gave the authorities much trouble.‡
The employment of these heretics to practice on man or beast
was prohibited; yet only Ishmael's prompt and positive inter-
vention kept his nephew Eleazer ben Dama from letting a Christian cure him of a snake bite in the name of Jesus; and he
might, in spite of his uncle's protests, have broken through the
ordinance of the sages with a proof-text in his mouth, if timely
death had not saved him from mortal sin. In the same context
in the Palestinian Talmud in which Ben Dama's case is reported,
another instance is cited, from a time a century later, in which
a Christian healer was called in to the family of one of the most

---

* Tos. Sabbath 13¹; cf. M. Sabbath 16¹. The different reasons for the
rule in the two codes warrant the inference that the rule itself was not a new
one.

† Tos. Sanhedrin 12¹⁰ adds the words, "and spits" (a magical averruncation). R. Johanan (Sanhedrin 101ᵃ) sees in the spitting a profanation of
the divine name; in the recitation of the verse itself he finds no sin. See
Blau, Altjüdisches Zauberwesen, 68 f.

‡ Precisely as the healers of certain modern sects give concern to the conservators of ecclesiastical order.

famous teachers of his generation.* "A grandson of Rabbi
Joshua ben Levi got something stuck in his throat. A man
came and murmured a charm (לחש) to him in the name of Jesus
Pandera, and he recovered. When the healer came out, he was
asked, What did you murmur to him? He replied, A word of
So and So (Jesus). Joshua exclaimed, It would have been
better for him to die than to have such a thing happen to him!"
It is not a remote surmise that certain of these Christians may
have made use in their incantations of Exod. 15²⁶, combining it
in some way with the name of Jesus—perhaps even inserting his
name in the efficacious part of the formula, so that it sounded,
I am the Lord *Jesus*, thy healer.

This is, of course, pure guessing; but independent of all
guesses remains the strong probability that Akiba's twofold
anathema was launched against heretical books and heretical
practices, rather than against liturgical irregularities or abuse of
scripture in orthodox circles. This conclusion, so far as the
books are concerned, is in conformity with the old Palestinian
tradition as recorded in the Babylonian Talmud, according to
which the "outside" books are the "books of the heretics."

The impossibility of identifying the "outside books" with
apocryphal books such as Sirach appears conclusively when the
context in Jer. Sanhedrin is considered. The whole passage
is as follows:

רבי עקיבא אומר אף הקורא בספרים החיצונים כגון ספרי בן סירא
וספרי בן לענה אבל ספרי המירם וכל ספרים שנכתבו מיכן והילך
הקורא בהן כקורא באיגרת: †

"Rabbi Akiba says: 'Also he who reads in the outside books.'—
Such as the books of Sirach and the books of Ben Laana; but
the books of המירם, and all books that have been written since
then, he who reads in them is as one who reads in a letter.—
What does this mean? 'And as to what is beyond these, my

---

* Jer. Sabbath 14⁴; cf. Jer. Aboda Zara 2ª; Koheleth Rabba 10⁷. The text
of the current editions is castrated out of respect for the censorship; see
Aruch s. v. בלע.—In Koheleth Rabba the sufferer is a *son* of R. Joshua b.
Levi; the rabbi himself fetches the healer—"one of those of Bar Pandera."
In answer to Joshua's question what charm he used, he replies: "A verse of
So and So after So and So " (Jesus).

† For a reconstruction of the text, see below, p. 121.

son, be warned' (Eccles. 12¹²); they were given for reading merely, not [like the scriptures] for laborious study." *

If any demonstration were needed that the text is in disorder the labors of the interpreters would furnish it. With Tosephta Jadaim 2¹³ before us, it is manifest that בן סירא and המירם have exchanged places; the last clause should read: "But the book[s] of Sirach and all books that have been written since— he who reads in them is as one who reads in a letter"; † that is, they are purely secular writings (cf. Tosephta, "they are not holy scripture"), which may be read as such, but are not a proper object of that reverent and laborious study—a religious observ- ance and a meritorious work—which is the prerogative of the scriptures.

The dislocation of בן סירא and המירם, which must have occurred very early, ‡ is the root of all the difficulties in which Babylonian Amoraim and modern scholars have found themselves to explain why Sirach should be so signally damned. § With the restoration of the true order the only colorable ground for inter- preting חיצונים, 'books outside the canon, apocrypha,' vanishes.

In Mishna Megilla 4⁸ the word החיצונים is used of persons, and stands in close connection with מינות, 'heresy.' If a man wears his phylacteries on his forehead or on the palm of his hand, this is the way of heresy (הרי זה דרך המינות); if he covers his phylacteries with gold and puts them on his sleeve, הרי זה דרך

---

* In Kohéleth Rabba the midrash plays on מֵהֵמָּה־מַהֵמָּה: Every one who brings into his house more than the twenty-four canonical books brings in confusion, for instance, the book of Sirach and the book of Ben Tigla.— From the following words, ולהג הרבה יגיעת בשר (E. V. "much study is a weariness of the flesh ") the midrash extracts: להגות ניתנו ליגיעת בשר לא ניתנו, "they were given merely to read; for a weariness of the flesh (i. e. for severe study) they were not given."—Cf. Berakoth 28ᵇ, among Eliezer's counsels to his disciples: "Restrain your sons from mere reading" (of the scriptures). In Midrash Tehillim on Ps. 1⁸ (ed. Buber, f. 5ᵃ), Ps. 19¹⁶ is explained: David prays that his words may endure to remote generations, and that men may not read them as they read בספרי מריס, that is, as secular books, but may study them as scripture. The dependence on Jer. Sanhedrin 10¹ is evident.

† Joel, Blicke in die Religionsgeschichte, I, 72 ff., brought Sirach over into the right company; but left "המירס" ("Tagebücher" = ἡμέρας, after Grätz) unmolested.

‡ It is presupposed in Koh. Rabba on 12¹². The transposition is probably a transcriptional error of a common kind, due to the frequent occurrence of ספרי.

§ See Dei Rossi, Meor 'Enayim, Wilna, 1866, p. 83 ff.

החיצונים.* The term is here in effect synonymous with מינים, but evidently carries a stronger reprobation. The *Minim* took Deut. 6⁸ literally, disregarding the prescriptions of scribes (Menaḥoth 37ᵇ); † whereas the חיצונים had no authority for their practise either in the written or the oral law ‡—it was, as the Munich manuscript has it, מינות והונה חיצונה, 'heresy and extraneous speculation.' So also the Talmud (Megilla 24ᵇ): "What is the meaning [of דרך החיצונים]? We suspect that he is inoculated with heresy (מינות)." The *Ḥiṣonim* are, therefore, persons wholly 'outside' the fences of orthodoxy, heretics of the most radical type. In the same sense the word is used by Akiba in Mishna Sanhedrin 10¹: ספרים החיצונים is a more emphatic expression for heretical books—they are books outside the pale, not of the canon, but of Judaism.

As types of these books, the reading of which shuts a Jew out of his birthright in the world to come, Jer. Sanhedrin 10¹ § names ספרי בן לענה וספרי המירם.‖ On these enigmatical names there is a literature more voluminous than illuminating. Limits of space precludes a discussion of the many fanciful identifications that have been put forward. It must suffice here to pursue our investigation of the sources.

For ספרי המירם the Aruch cites, besides Mishna Jadaim 4ˢ and Jer. Sanhedrin 10¹, Hullin 60ᵇ, which is quoted as follows: "Rabbi Simeon ben Lakish said, There are many verses in the Pentateuch which seem fit to be burned *like the books of* מירון, ¶

---

* The reading דרך החיצון, attested in the Aruch, is also found in a manuscript of the Talmud.

† See Sanhedrin 88ᵇ, where the principle that the regulations of the scribes have stronger sanctions than the words of the written law is exemplified by the case of the phylacteries.

‡ So Maimonides in his commentary on the Mishna; Rashi on Megilla 24ᵇ.

§ As emended above, p. 117; cf. p. 121.

‖ The best attested spelling is המירם; there are many variations in manuscripts, editions, commentators, and lexicographers, chiefly affecting the vowels. Hai Gaon (on M. Jadaim 4ᵉ) reads המרום, and takes this for *Homeros;* his explanation is cited, with others, by Nathan ben Jeḥiel in the Aruch, and was adopted by Mussafia in his supplements to the Aruch. It has been repeated by many since. The reading מירם is found also in Midrash Tehillim on Ps. 1ˢ (see below); but the forms ending in ם apparently have no support in known manuscripts or in editions of the Talmud.

¶ So Kohut, on manuscript authority; the first printed edition has מרון. Other manuscripts have המירום, etc.

and yet they are essential parts of the law." The italicised words are lacking in the current editions of the Talmud, doubtless because the censors smelt a reference to Christianity. The first edition, however (Venice, 1520), and the Munich codex have ספרי המינים, and the unmistakable allusion to deliverances about burning the books of heretics such as are reported in Sabbath 116 * makes it certain that this is the original reading, for which, at a comparatively late time, מירון or something of the kind was substituted.

In Mishna Jadaim 4⁶ the Sadducees are represented as deriding certain Pharisaic decrees: We object to you Pharisees because you say, 'The holy scriptures make the hands unclean; the books of המירם do not make the hands unclean.' Rabbi Johanan ben Zakkai replied, Is this the only thing we have against the Pharisees? They also say that the bones of an ass are clean, but the bones of Johanan the high priest are unclean.† The Sadducees answered, Their uncleanness is in proportion to the affection in which they are held. . . . He replied, Just so with the holy scriptures, their uncleanness is in proportion to the affection in which they are held.‡ The ספרי המירם, for which we have no love, do not make the hands unclean.§

The general rule which the Sadducees quote, 'Holy scriptures make the hands unclean,' is stated in Mishna Jadaim 3⁵ (cf. Mishna Kelim 15⁶), and is assumed throughout in Tosephta Jadaim 2¹⁰ ff., cf. 2¹⁹; to show the absurdity of the rule they adduce a Pharisaic decision which corresponds word for word to Tosephta Jadaim 2¹³,‖ ספרי המינין אינן מטמאין את הידים, 'the books of the heretics do not make the hands unclean,' except that for המינים the Mishna has המירם. The commentators on the Mishna Jadaim 4⁶ interpret ספרי המירם as writings of Jewish heretics; those who attempt an explanation of the word regard it as a disparaging term, which they etymologize as if it were coined *ad hoc*.¶ However unconvincing we may

---

* See above, pp. 101 ff.   † Cf. Nidda 55ᵃ.

‡ Cf. Tos. Jadaim 2¹⁹. For כתבי הקודש the Vienna manuscript of the Tosephta has ספרי המורים ! (Zuckermandel, in loc.)

§ Johanan's answer is an argumentum ad hominem.   ‖ Above, p. 101.

¶ R. Simson of Sens (12th century) says: "These are the books of the Sadducees [substitution of צדוקים for מינים, as often], of which it is said in Sabbath 116 that they ought to be burned." Maimonides: "Books which con-

find these etymologies, we must give its due to the exegetical
insight which recognized that the context in the Mishna demands "the heretics," the *minim*; and since, in the deliverance
which the Sadducees quote, the Tosephta actually has המינים,
the inference can hardly be avoided that המירם in the Mishna
is either a corruption or, more probably, a sophistication of
המינים,* as it demonstrably is in Ḥullin 60ᵇ.

There remains Jer. Sanhedrin 10¹, where "the books of Ben
Laana and the books of המירם" are cited as examples of the
writings which are the object of Akiba's commination.—We
have seen that Akiba's contemporaries manifest a peculiarly
violent animosity toward "the gospels and the books of the heretics," and there is a strong presumption that the ultra-heretical
writings against which Akiba fulminates are the same that aroused
the ire of his colleagues. This presumption is strengthened by
a confrontation of Jer. Sanhedrin 10¹ with Tosephta Jadaim
2¹³: in the former, "The books of Ben Laana and the books of
המירם . . . Sirach and all the books that have been written
since," etc.; in the latter, "The gospels and the books of the
heretics . . . Sirach and all the books that have been written
since," etc. The correspondence of the formulation suggests
that the same books are meant in both cases.†

In the other places where המירם occurs it has been shown
that המינים is demanded either by manuscript evidence or by
the context and parallels, and the same is true here. "The
books of Ben Laana" we shall then take to be, not obscure
apocrypha of which nothing is elsewhere heard, but the gospels.
Ben Laana (Son of Wormwood‡) has not the look of a real

---

travene our law and set forth dissident views about it. They are called ספרי
מירם, as if to say, May God thrust them away and banish them from existence !
meaning, destroy them, as the house in which they assemble for such purposes
is called Beth Abidan, meaning a house which may God cut off."—Bertinoro's
comment is: "The books of the heretics (ספרי המינים); they are called ספרי
המירם because they have exchanged (המירו) the true law for falsehoods."

* Compare *gilion, 'awen gilion, 'awon gilion* for εὐαγγέλιον, above, p. 105.

† It is the correspondence of the formulation that is significant; that in
the Tosephta Sirach is put with the gospels in the category of uninspired
scriptures, while in Jer. Sanhedrin, Sirach as a secular book is contrasted with
the heretical books is here irrelevant.

‡ Heb. לענה is a bitter and poisonous herb; the conventional rendering
'wormwood' is not meant to imply identification with *Artemisia absinthium*,
L. The same reservation must be made about the translation ' hemlock ' below.

name or a parody on a name, but rather of an opprobrious nickname, conveying an allusion to something in the character or
history of the person decorated with it. The point of the allusion lies, if I mistake not, in the association of לענה in the Old
Testament with apostasy and the fate of apostates. In Deut.
29¹⁷, for example, the Israelite who turns away from the Lord
to follow the gods of the idolatrous peoples becomes "a root
bearing hemlock and wormwood" (ראש ולענה);* Jer. 9¹²⁻¹⁴ "Because they have forsaken my law. . . . I will make this people
eat wormwood and drink hemlock." Most pertinent of all
these passages is Jer. 23¹⁵:† "Therefore thus saith the Lord of
Hosts concerning the prophets; I will make them eat wormwood
and drink hemlock, for from the prophets of Jerusalem defection (חנופה, religious defection) is gone abroad into all the
land." The application of such utterances to Christianity and
its founder lay near at hand. Rabbi Jonathan teaches that wherever the Bible speaks of defection (חנופה, often with the connotation of hypocrisy) it means heresy (מינות). Jesus was in
the eyes of the orthodox a seducer of the people,‡ a false prophet;
he appears in the Talmud as Balaam, the type of the false prophets.§ From this point of view Ben Laana, "Wormwood Man,"
is a cognomen as apt as it is pointed.‖ The "books of Ben
Laana" would then be the gospels; compare Mark 1¹, The
beginning of the Gospel of Jesus Christ.¶

The text of the much vexed passage, Jer. Sanhedrin 10¹, is
accordingly to be restored as follows:

הקורא בספרים החיצונים . כגון ספרי בן לענה וספרי המינים
אבל ספרי בן סירא וכל ספרים שנכתבו מיכן והילך הקורא בהן
כקורא באגרת:

---

* Note the use of this verse in Heb. 12¹⁵; cf. Acts 8²³.

† See the whole of this drastic oracle against the false prophets, Jer. 23⁹⁻⁴⁰.

‡ Sanhedrin 43ᵃ, 107ᵇ; cf. Deut. 13.

§ E. g. Sanhedrin 106ᵇ.

‖ If Ben Laana is meant for Jesus, the probability is strong that Ben
Tigla in Koheleth Rabba is another nickname.

¶ Another possible association of the name may perhaps be suggested.
The story of Imma Shalom gives evidence that the Jews were acquainted
with a Hebrew gospel related in some degree to our Matthew. In the account
of the crucifixion in Matt. 27³⁴ we read that they offered Jesus οἶνον μετὰ χολῆς,
μεμιγμένον. By χολή some bitter drug is doubtless intended. In the Greek
Bible χολή sometimes translates לענה (Prov. 5⁴, Lam. 3¹⁵; it more frequently

"'He who reads in the arch-heretical books.'—Such as the books of Ben Laana [Gospels] and the books of the heretics [Christians]. But as for the books of Ben Sira and all books that have been written since his time, he who reads in them is as one who reads in a letter."

It is evident from the texts that have been discussed that there was a time when Christianity had for many Jews a dangerous attraction, and when the circulation among Jews of the gospels and other Christian books gave the teachers of the synagogue serious apprehension. The earliest mention of the ordinance against "the books of the heretics" is in Mishna Jadaim 4⁶, in a tilt between the Sadducees and Johanan ben Zakkai, which may have occurred before the war of 66–70, and cannot be more than a decade or two later. Johanan's successor at the head of the college and council at Jámnia, Rabban Gamaliel II, caused the petition for the downfall of the heretics to be inserted in the prescribed form of prayer; he and his sister Imma Shalom, the wife of Eliezer ben Hyrcanus, figure in the story of the Christian judge who quotes the gospel; in the same time falls the intercourse of Eliezer ben Hyrcanus with Jacob of Kefar Sekania, "a disciple of Jesus the Nazarene." In the second and third decades of the second century the situation becomes more strained; all the great leaders of Judaism—Ishmael,* Akiba, Tarphon, Jose the Galilean—inveigh against the heretics and their scriptures with a violence which shows how serious the evil was.† Tarphon would flee to a heathen temple sooner than to a meeting house of those worse-than-heathen whose denial of God is without the excuse of ignorance; the usually mild-mannered Ishmael finds pious utterance for his antipathy, like many another godly man, in an imprecatory Psalm: "Do not I hate them, O Lord, that hate thee? . . . I hate them with perfect hatred." Akiba, who was never a man of measured words,

stands for ראש). It is conceivable, therefore, that in the passage corresponding to Matt. 27³⁴ the Hebrew gospel read: יין מזוג בלענה. If so, the Jewish reader might well be pardoned for seeing in the narrative a signal fulfilment of prophecy. No such fulfilment would be necessary, however, to bring to mind the words of Jeremiah.

* See also Ishmael's interpretation of the dreams of a heretic, Berakoth 56ᵇ.

† Just as in the Church Fathers, the increasing vehemence of their objurgations of heresy corresponds to the alarming progress gnosticism was making.

consigns to eternal perdition the Jew who reads their books. The rigorous interdict on all association with the Christians * breathes the same truculent spirit; it bears every mark of having been framed in the same age and by the same hands, as does also the anathema which condemns the heretics, before all the rest, to eternal torment in hell.†

In the second half of the century the polemic against Christianity abruptly ceases. From Akiba's most distinguished pupil and spiritual heir, Rabbi Meir, nothing more serious is reported than his witticism on the name of the gospel — εὐαγγέλιον ʿawon gilion; from Nehemiah, only that among the signs of the coming of the Messiah he included the conversion of the whole empire to Christianity.‡ Of the other great teachers of the generation no antichristian utterances are preserved. What is much more significant, at the close of the century the Mishna of the Patriarch Judah embodies none of the defensive ordinances against heresy which we find in the Tosephta and the Talmudic Baraithas.§ The decision that the Gospels and the books of the heretics are not holy scripture is not repeated in the Mishna; it deals only with the Jewish antilegomena, Ecclesiastes and the Song of Songs, the long-standing differences about which were passed on by a council about the beginning of the second century—a decision which did not, however, prevent the differences from lasting through the century.‖ The only mention of heretical writings is preserved as a mere matter of history in the account of the Johanan ben Zakkai's defense of the Pharisaic ordinances against the criticisms of the Sadducees.

We shall hardly err if we see in all this an indication that the danger had passed which in the early decades of the century was so acute. The expansion of Christianity had not been checked, nor was the attitude of the Jewish authorities to it more favorable than before; but with the definitive separation of the Jewish Christians from the synagogue they ceased to be a spreading leaven of heresy in the midst of the orthodox community, and

---

* Tos. Hullin 2²⁰ ᵃ·; above, pp. 110 f.   † Above, p. 111.
‡ Sanhedrin 97ᵃ, and parallels.
§ If M. Hullin 2⁹ be regarded as an exception, it is an exception that proves the rule; cf. Tosephta Hullin 2¹⁹⁻²⁰.
‖ M. Jadaim 3⁵.

became a distinct religious sect outside the pale of Judaism. The complete and final separation was brought about by the rebellion of the Jews in the reign of Hadrian. This rebellion was not merely a national uprising, but a messianic movement. Its leader was hailed as the "star out of Jacob" predicted by Balaam (Num. 24[17]),* and Bar Coziba became Bar Cocheba. In such a movement the Christians could not join without denying their own Messiah, Jesus, the signs of whose imminent return they doubtless discerned in the commotions of the time. They stood aloof from the life-and-death struggle of their people, and incurred the double resentment of their countrymen as not only heretics but traitors.† Before this storm they retreated to regions beyond the Jordan, where their neighborhood was heathen. In the eyes of the government, however, they were Jews; and the edicts excluding all Jews from residence in the new city, Aelia Capitolina, ended the succession of Jewish bishops of Jerusalem; henceforth the church was a church of gentile Christians, with Greek bishops. From that time Jewish Christianity, deprived of the prestige which the see of the mother church gave it, left behind with its primitive ideas by the development of Catholic doctrine—trying to be both Jew and Christian, and succeeding in being neither, as Jerome puts it—stigmatized as heresy by both camps, languished and dwindled in the corners in which it had taken refuge.

The Catholic Christianity which succeeded it in the centres of Palestine was essentially a foreign religion, and had little attraction for Jews. By its side Judaism could live, as it did by the side of a dozen other foreign religions, not without controversy,‡ but without fear that it would spread like a pestilence in the orthodox community. The Patriarch had no need, therefore, to repeat in his Mishna the deliverances against heresy which had been so necessary seventy-five or a hundred years earlier. But the memory of the crisis and the stringent measures it demanded were perpetuated in codifications of the oral law

---

* This application of the prophecy is attributed to Akiba.

† There is no reason whatever to question the assertion of Justin Martyr, a contemporary, that efforts were made to force them into line.

‡ On the controversies of the end of the third and beginning of the fourth century, see above, pp. 107 f.

and traditions less exclusively dominated than his by a practical end.*

Not the least interesting result of an examination of these sources is the fact that the attempt authoritatively to define the Jewish canon of the Hagiographa begins with the exclusion by name of Christian scriptures.

CAMBRIDGE, MASS.,
September, 1910.

* It is perhaps not without a bearing on this point, that a prominent part in the redaction of the Tosephta is attributed to Hoshaia, who, at Caesarea, was in close contact with a vigorous and aggressive Christianity.

SOME OBSERVATIONS ON THE ATTITUDE OF THE SYNAGOGUE TOWARDS THE APOCALYPTIC-ESCHATOLOGICAL WRITINGS

LOUIS GINZBERG

JEWISH THEOLOGICAL SEMINARY OF AMERICA

THE attractiveness of the novel is responsible not only for the lively interest in the Apocalyptic-eschatological literature noticeable among all students of the origins of Christianity, but also for the exaggerated claims advanced by some scholars for these literary productions of a handful of Jewish visionaries. Many an apocalypse has been discovered or made accessible only in recent times and scholars are human enough to be dazzled by sudden light. A picture drawn by artificial light will never be true to nature, great as the skill of the artist may be, and hence the failure of some really great scholars to give us a true picture of the religious life of Israel at the time of the rise of Christianity. A history of Judaism based on the Pseudepigrapha and particularly the visions of the apocalypses could but be a visionary pseudo-history. It would, however, be impossible within the compass of anything less than a substantial volume to present an adequate criticism of the view which sees in the so-called popular literature of the Jews the true mirror of the religion of the Jewish people. In the following few remarks I intend to give some facts about the attitude of the Synagogue towards the apocalyptic writings which I hope may throw some light on the very intricate problems connected with the eschatological doctrines and beliefs of the Jews at the time of the Apostles and Apostolic Fathers.

Reprinted from *Journal of Biblical Literature* 41 (1922).   8*

It is a well-known fact that none of the apocalyptic books with the exception of Daniel was received by the Synagogue.[1] The preservation of this literature is exclusively due to the efforts of the early Church. With equal certainty one may state that there is not one quotation from the now extant apocalyptic writings in the vast Rabbinic literature extending over the first six centuries of the common era. One might cite numerous parallels to the statements, legends or phrases of the apocalyptic authors from the Rabbinic writings, but these parallels are never of a nature that would indicate a literary dependence of the one kind of literature upon the other. This is best proved by the fact that the Rabbis never mention by name any apocalyptic writing. It is true Dr. Kohler (J. Q. R. V., pp. 400—401) finds in an ancient Tannaitic tradition a direct reference to the Testaments of the Twelve Patriarchs. Not having however the vision of an apocalyptic writer I fail to detect in the passages indicated by Dr. Kohler the slightest reference to the Testaments. The assertion of Dr. Kohler is based on an arbitrarily construed text and on the impossible translation thereof. He quotes from the Talmud the text dealing with the nature of the admonition addressed by the court to the woman suspected of adultery; the text as given by Dr. Kohler reads:

דברי הגדה מעשים שאירעו בכתובים הראשונים

כגון מעשה ראובן בבלהה ומעשה יהודה בתמר אשר חכמים יגידו

אלו ראובן ויהודה

The translation of this text by Dr. Kohler is: Words of the Haggadah, historical facts which occur in the early writings as the story of Reuben regarding Bilhah and of Judah regarding Tamar, as it says in Job XV. 18 "The wise ones confess and conceal it not; these are Reuben and Judah." The early writings, according to Dr. Kohler, are the Testaments where the confessions of Reuben and Judah are found. We thus learn from this tradition of the Tannaim the very interesting fact that one of the apocalypses at least, for some time, enjoyed almost canonical dignity among the Rabbis. Before giving the true text

[1] The apocalyptic literature of the Gaonic period is neither in form nor in matter a direct development of the pre-Talmudic Apocalypse.

as found in the Rabbinic sources I want to call attention to the
very strange translation[2] by Dr. Kohler of the imaginary one.
Misled by the English expression "occur in a book" he renders
שאירעו בכתובים by "which occur in the writings". But אירע ב'
has never any other meaning than "it happened to"—generally
something evil or unpleasant[3]—and accordingly our text would
speak of something that happened to the ancient writings!

Dr. Kohler, though giving three sources for the text quoted
did not state that in none of them "his" text is found.[4] Sifre,
Numbers 12 has not the sentence from מעשה to בתמר; after
כגון follows the quotation from Job;[5] in Babli, Sotah 7b where
this sentence is found it follows after the quotation from Job,
while in Yerushalmi, Sotah I, 16b the text begins with כגון as
a comment upon the words of the Mishna I, 4 and hence may
entirely be ignored in the discussion of the meaning of כתובים
הראש' found in the two other sources. The text as given in
Sifre and Babli admits two explanations. דברי הגדה ומעשים
may be taken as ἐν διὰ δυοῖν, the Haggadah concerning the events
that happened and כתובים הראשונים stands for Job which, according to the Rabbis, is the third[6] in the order of the eleven
Hagiographa. The passage is consequently to be rendered: "The

---

[2] Dr. Charles, who, in the introduction to his translations of the
Testaments, quotes Dr. Kohler's view with approval very likely did not
take the trouble to look up the passages quoted by him.

[3] The "happenings" consequently refer to the sins and not the confessions; why then quote the Testaments and not Genesis?

[4] The text given by Dr. Kohler is that emended by Guedemann,
Zunz — Jubelschrift, 116, in accordance with his view that Haggadah
means "story". Bacher, *Tannaiten*, II. 451, has disposed of the "story"
and also of the emendation.

[5] In Sifre מעשם without ו, which is probably due to some "learned"
copyist who omitted this letter on account of his inability to explain the
construction of the sentence. The reading with ו as given in the editions
of Babli is found also in Rashi, *ad loc.*, Yalkut, I, 707, on Num. 5 15
(in the first edition: בכתובות comp. note 10), Ibn Masnut in his commentary
on Job 15 18 and in the Munich Ms. of the Talmud.

[6] According to the Massorah the three first Hagiographa are "Psalms,
Proverbs and Job", while the Tannaitic tradition in Baba Batra, 14b, gives
the order as, "Ruth, Psalms and Job". Comp. also Berakot, 57b, beginning,
"The three big Hagiographa—Psalms, Proverbs and Job".

Haggadah found in the first Hagiographa concerning the events that happened, for example: which wise men have told etc." The verse of Job is quite correctly described as a Haggadah on the narratives of Genesis about the sins of Reuben and Judah. The other explanation presupposes that the text of the Talmud though fuller than that of the Sifre is not quite complete, the words ומעשה דוד בבת שבע being omitted out of respect for the pious king. If this assumption be correct כתובים הראשו' stand for the Pentateuch,[7] where the sins of Reuben and Judah are told and the Book of Samuel, where the story of David's sin is given. The woman is thus admonished to confession by the court who put before her in an elaborate way, or, as the Rabbis say, in Haggadic style, the events narrated in the earlier parts of Scripture, i. e. Genesis and Samuel.[8] The second explanation has much in its favour, especially as it does away with a very great difficulty. The incident of David with Bath-Sheba and the confession of his sin by the pious king is certainly the most natural thing that we would expect the court to dwell upon in addressing the woman suspected of adultery. The omission of the reference to David in our texts can easily be explained, as according to the regulations laid down in Mishnah, Megillah, end, the "story of David" is not to be read in the Synagogue and still less to be translated by the Meturgeman, while the "story of Reuben" may be read, though not translated, the "story of Judah" only is permitted to be read and translated.[9]

Attention should also be called to the fact that the text of Yerushalmi as given in Midrash Haggadol, Num. 5, 19 (in

[7] Rashi, *ad loc.*, understands בכתובים הר' to refer to the Pentateuch which however is very unlikely, as we certainly would expect בתורה, the usual term for this part of the Bible. Of course Rashi does not commit the error of making בכתובים dependent on שארעו but takes it to stand for שבכתובים which is quite possible.

[8] The order of the Prophets is, "Joshua, Judges, Samuel" (Baba Batra 14b) and it is quite natural to describe the first and fourth books of the Bible as the first writings.

[9] This is in accordance with the readings of the editions. See, however, *Variae Lectiones*, Megillah, 25 a, note 60. It is very likely that, according to the Mishnah, the paraphrase by the Meturgeman only was prohibited, while later this prohibition was extended to the reading too.

manuscript) has ומעשה אמנון באחותו after יהודה בתמר. This
reading[10] can hardly be justified, as Amnon does not belong
to the repentant sinners and it can be explained only by the
assumption that the original reading was: מעשה ראובן ... בתמר
ומעשה דוד בבת שבע as in Mishnah Megillah, end. When the
reference to David was omitted the one concerning Amnon was
substituted to make our Baraita agree as far as possible with
the phraseology of the Mishnah. It may be mentioned in passing
that the confessions of Reuben and Judah are a very favorite
subject with the Tannaim and Amoraim, comp. e. g. Pesikta
Buber XXV, 159 a—159 b, Sifre Deut. 348, Midrash Tannaim 214.

On כתובים as name for Pentateuch and Prophets comp. Blau,
Zur Einleitung, p. 28 sq. His explanation of the later use of the
term כתובים = Hagiographa as an abbreviation of שאר כתובים is
supported by the very same development of the use of ספרי "Sifre"
from שאר ספרי דבי רב; comp. RSBM on Baba Batra 124 b.[11]

The only quotation from an apocalypse in the Talmud[12] is
found Sanhedrin 97 b and reads: "Four thousand two hundred
and ninety years after "creation" the world will become or-
phaned;[13] the wars of the dragons (תנינים, a mythological-
eschatological word!) will then take place as well as the wars of
Gog and Magog and after these events the days of the Messiah,
but the renewal[14] of the world by God will take place after

---

[10] Comp. Schechter in the introduction to his *Sectaries*, I, 27, note 65.
The emendation לאבות הראשונים suggested by him is not acceptable. It is
true אבות is sometimes applied to prominent men of biblical times (comp.
Ginzberg, "*Eine Unbekannte Jüdische Sekte*", 295, note 2), but Amnon is
certainly more of an infamous person than a famous one. In Yalkut ed.
princeps בכתובות (comp. note 5) is a corruption of בכתובים, not of לאבות.

[11] The objections raised by Hoffmann, *Zur Einleitung*, 40, note 1,
against this explanation of R. S. B. M. are not very strong, but it would
lead me too far to discuss them here.

[12] Prof. Israel Levi, R. E. J. I, 108 seq. has collected a number of
apocalyptic passages—but not all of them—found in the Talmud. His
view, however, that they prove the composition of apocalyptic writings
by the Amoraim is far from convincing.

[13] I. e. there will be no pious and good men left; comp. Mekilta,
Bo 16, 18 b, and parallel passages given by Friedmann.

[14] חדש admits two meanings, "to renew" and "to create anew", comp.
Ps. 51 12 where חדש is = ברא.

146

seven thousand years". This passage is quoted in the Talmud
from a Scroll "written in Assyrian script (= square) and in
Hebrew language" which a Jewish soldier is said to have found
about 300 c. e. in the archives of Rome.

The description of this apocalyptic Scroll as having been
"written in Assyrian script and in Hebrew language" is very
interesting. What is meant by this characterization of the
apocalyptic writing is that it had the make-up of a Biblical
book. Scripture defiles the hands only when written in Hebrew
language and in Assyrian script (Yadaim IV, 5), and similarly
the scroll of Esther used for public reading on the feast of
Purim had to be written in the same way, comp. Megillah I, 8;
II, 1. The claim made accordingly for the apocalyptic scroll
was that it was, if not of a canonical, at least of semi-canonical
character, written for the purpose of public reading and study.
The question whether this claim was justified does not need to
detain us since we know nothing about its merits. It is, however,
very significant that as late as the fourth century such a claim
could be raised for a non-canonical book.

This leads us to the very crucial question: did the Synagogue
at some time or another, at the joint conference of the schools
of Shammai and Hillel about 66 c. e., or later in Jabne about
120,[15] take steps to prohibit the reading of the Pseudepigrapha
and particularly the Apocalypses. This is not the place to discuss
the difficult problems connected with the history of the Canon,
but it is evident that we shall never understand the attitude of
the Synagogue towards these "outside writings" as long as we
do not know what the Tannaim have to say on this subject. The
very learned and stimulating essay by Professor George F. Moore
"The Definition of the Jewish Canon and the Repudiation of
Christian Scriptures"[16] represents the last word of Biblical
scholarship on the final delineation of the Canon. I regret however that I cannot accept the conclusion which this distinguished
scholar has reached.

The result of the thorough examination by Prof. Moore of

[15] Comp. Graetz, Kohelet 166 seq.
[16] Published in "Essays in Modern Theology and Related Subjects",
N. Y., 1911.

the Tannaitic sources bearing upon this question may be briefly
summed up as follows: The ספרים החיצונים the reading of which
is strongly condemned [17] by Rabbi Akiba, Sanhedrin X, 1 refer
to the heretical, in particular to the early Christian writings.
The ספרי המירם spoken of by Rabban Johanan ben Zakkai,
Yaddaim IV, 6 in connection with the defilement of the hands
and the reading of which books is permitted in Yerushalmi,
Sanhedrin X, 28a owe their existence to a scribal error; המירם
is nothing but a corruption of המינים. Consequently the text of
Yerushalmi is to be emended to read as follows: הקורא בספרים
החיצונים כגון ספרי בן לענה וספרי המינים אבל ספר(י) בן סירא וגו'".
The translation of this passage as given by Prof. Moore reads:
"He who reads in the arch-heretical books, such as the books of
Ben-Laana (Gospels) [18] and the books of the heretics (Christians).

---

[17] The words of R. Akiba are "Also he who reads in the outside
books has no share in the world to come". It may not be out of place to
remark that the rabbis were often in the habit of using emphatic language.
That the losing of the share in the world to come is not always to be taken
literally can easily be seen from the remark, Abot R. Nathan, XXXVI,
108, about the seven professions—very honorable ones—whose members
are declared to forfeit their share in the world to come; comp. also,
ibid. XXVII.

[18] The reading Laana is very doubtful. The only MS. of this part of
the Yerushalmi has לענא (comp. Ginzberg, *Yerushalmi Fragments*, 262)
and this is very likely the correct reading, as Kohelet R. XII, 12, in a
passage undoubtedly dependent on Yerushalmi has תנלא and this is much
nearer to לענא than to לענה of the editions. The identification of Laana
with Jesus by Prof. Moore is neither better nor worse than the half
dozen other identifications of this name recorded by me in *Jewish Encyclopedia*, s. v. Ben Laana. When, however, Prof. Moore, in support of
his identification, points to another nickname for Jesus found in the
Mishnah I must say with the Rabbis of old: "An error once entered
remains." A Babylonian Amora in the second half of the third century,
who very likely never in his life saw a Christian nor knew anything about
Christianity had the ingenuity to find in בן סטרא—a sorcerer mentioned
in the Tannaitic source, Tosefta Shabbat, XI, 15—a nickname for Jesus.
The identification is not only without any sound basis, but hardly possible,
as has been conclusively shown by Derenbourg, *Essai*, 460 seq. and
especially Chajes in the Hebrew periodical, Ha—Goren, IV, 33—37. The
hunt for nicknames, however, continues merrily and soberminded scholars
speak seriously of Balaam, Doeg, Ahitophel, and Gehazi as being the
nicknames which the Mishnah Sanhedrin, X, 1, uses for Jesus and three

But as for the books of Ben-Sira and all books that have been written since his time, he who reads in them is as one who reads in a letter". The inference which Prof. Moore draws from these premises is that the attempt authoritatively to define the Canon of the Hagiographa was dictated by the danger that threatened the Synagogue from the circulation among Jews of the Gospels and other Christian books.

Personally I am firmly convinced that there never was a time when the Synagogue had to carry on a fight against the canonicity of the Gospels,[19] but, as this is rather a matter which

---

of his disciples. If these scholars were consistent they ought to try to identify the three kings—Jeroboam, Ahab, and Manasseh—with three Christian emperors, since the four "private persons" mentioned and the "three kings" are said in the Mishnah to form one class of grave sinners. What a pity that there were no Christian emperors at the time of the Mishnah! Numerous legends concerning these seven sinners are given in both Talmuds in connection with the statement of the Mishnah concerning them, and these legends can by no stretch of imagination be made to apply to other persons than to those who bear these names in the Bible. They show not only how the Amoraim understood this statement of the Mishnah, but also how much the lives of these Biblical persons occupied the fancy of the Jewish people. One may therefore state with absolute certainty that the entire Talmudic-Midrashic literature does not know of any nicknames for Jesus or his disciples. I may add that גליונים = εὐαγγέλιον must not be taken as a mutilation or perversion, but is a very common form of apheresis, comp. the remark on page 128 about מירום = Homer. By the way, if Ben Laana is a nickname for Jesus why not take it as an equivalent for בן מרים, the son of Miriam? According to the Rabbis, the name Miriam denotes "bitterness" (Seder Olam R., III, and the parallel passages given by Ratner), and לענה "wormwood" is used in Hebrew to describe something very bitter. Of course I do not consider this etymology seriously. Jesus is never named in old sources otherwise than יהושע, ישו, ישוע or Jesus the son of Pantera. Origen. C. Cels. I, 70, shows that Pantera (= פנתירא i. e. πάνθηρ) is a real name and not a nickname.

[19] The passage Tosefta Yadaim, III, 4, "The Gospels and the other heretical books do not defile the hands" has been frequently misunderstood. The defiling of the hands by a book being equal to our way of saying that such a book is canonical, this statement of the Tosefta was taken to mean that it needed a special ruling to declare these books as non-canonical. The truth of the matter, however, is, that the Halakah had to consider the possibility of the defilement by these books not on

can neither be proved nor disproved, I shall limit myself to an examination of the premises which led Prof. Moore to his conclusions. I fully agree with the view which finds in the Mishna Sanhedrin a statement by R. Akiba directed against Christians. The severe condemnation by Rabbi Akiba of the use of Exodus 15 26 in connection with medication is certainly directed against certain Christian healers,[20] as has been felt by many scholars, though they were unable to explain why just this Biblical verse was so opprobrious to the Rabbis. The answer to this question is very simple. The last three words of this verse רפאך יהוה אני have the same numerical value (three hundred eighty eight plus three for the three words = three hundred ninety one) as the name of Jesus (יהושע = three hundred ninety one). It is not unlikely that some crypto-Christians who were afraid to openly perform

account of their own merits but because of the numerous quotations from Scriptures they contain. This paragraph of the Tosefta is, as one easily sees, not a comment upon Mishnah Yad. IV, 6, where the defilement by Scripture is discussed between Rabban Johanan ben Zakkai and the Sadducees, but on Yad. III, 5, where the law is laid down that even a very small fragment of a canonical book defiles the hands. In view of this ruling the question had to be discussed what to do with those heretical writings containing copious quotations from Scriptures. The final decision was that even the most extensive quotations from Scripture lose their holy quality if embedded in an heretical writing or in a prayer book; prayers should not be written down, but recited by heart. The far fetched interpretation of גליונים in Tosefta as "margins" given in Shabbat 116a shows rather the acquaintance of the Babylonian Amoraim with the Gospels than their ignorance of the true meaning of גליונים = εὐαγγέλιον. They knew that there is no continuous quotation containing 85 letters from the Hebrew Bible in the Gospels, which number is the minimum of a fragment that might defile the hands. Accordingly the Amoraim found the statement concerning the Gospels, גליונים, given in Tosefta entirely superfluous, and solved the difficulty by explaining גליונים as margins. The Tosefta however either mentioned גליונים on account of the other heretical books with which the Gospels are ordinarily coupled together (and there very likely were heretical books that contained quotations from the Bible of more than 85 letters), or the Tosefta dates from a time when the minimum was less than 85 letters.

[20] The magical averruncation mentioned in Tosefta Sanhedrin, XII, 10, and Abot R. Nathan, XXVI in connection with this mode of healing is said in Mark 7 33, 8 23, John 9 6, to have been employed by Jesus.

cures "in the name of Jesus" would use this verse in which they found his name indicated. Professor Moore, however, does in-justice to the Rabbis when he maintains that they had no scruples about using verses of the Bible in connection with medication. The prohibition against "healing by the words of the Torah" is given in the Babylonian as well as in the Palestinian Talmud (comp. Shebuot 15 b, Yerushalmi Shabbat VI, 8 b), and the numerous magical formulas in the Talmudim, with one ex-ception (Shabbat 67 a, top), contain no Biblical verses. The very strong condemnation of the use of Exodus 15 26 cannot, however, be explained otherwise than on account of the favour this verse enjoyed among the Christian healers. But the coupling by R. Akiba of the prohibition against the outside books with that against the use of Exodus 15 26 as a charm does not indicate that both prohibitions are directed against Christians. Tosefta Sanhedrin XII, 10 and Aboth R. Nathan XXXVI, end, add another statement concerning the Canon by R. Akiba which by no stretch of imagination can be made to refer to some Christian heresy or practice. In these sources the man who sings the Song of Songs at festival gatherings— i. e. who treats this Biblical book as if it were of a secular character—is classed among those who have no share in the world to come. We know from many other places that Rabbi Akiba was the valiant champion of the canonicity of this Biblical book, but the opposition he had to combat he met among his own colleagues and friends.[21]

The meaning of חיצונים in the statement of Rabbi Akiba is the crucial point in the entire discussion. I shall therefore try to establish its true meaning. The word occurs nowhere else; Mishna Megillah IV, 8 דרך החיצון is in the correct reading[22] while החיצונים of the editions is undoubtedly due to החיצונים in R. Akiba's famous statement. The meaning of דרך החיצון is

---

[21] Comp. Yadaim, III, 5.

[22] This is the reading of Ms. Munich, Aruk s. v. אונקלי, Meïri, and R. Nissim Gerondi (*Jerusalem*, 1884) ad loc. Aruk s. v. חצון, agree with the editions, but this is certainly a copyist's error, since the explanation of the phrase given in this passage does not admit any other reading than that given in the first passage.

easily established if one considers it in connection with the expressions כשורה and לפנים משורת הדין. A correct action is כשורה, literally "according to the line"—of the law, לפנים משורת הדין "within the line" describes a pious action which the strict law does not directly command and accordingly דרך החיצון is "outside the line"—the exact regulation of the law.[23] To say with Prof. Moore that the term חיצונים is synonymous with מינים, but evidently carries a stronger reprobation, would be far from the mark, even if the reading החיצונים were the correct one. The covering of the phylacteries with gold[24] or putting them on the sleeve instead of on the bare arm is characterized as דרך החיצונים. Now, while these practices are not quite correct they are not at all a serious break of the Law, as pointed out by R. Nissim Gerondi in his commentary on *Al-Fasi* ad loc. and consequently, though censured as incorrect, are never said to be heretical. On the other hand, the putting of the phylacteries not on the part of the body prescribed for this practice is declared to be an outright heresy. If therefore the reading החיצונים in Megillah were correct it would furnish the strongest proof against taking החיצונים in Sanhedrin in the sense of heretics. Prof. Moore quotes Talmud Megillah 24b to the effect that the persons described as החיצונים in the Mishna are such as are suspected to be inoculated with heresy. The Talmud, however, offers no comment whatever on this part of the Mishnah. The words quoted from the Talmud by Prof. Moore refer to something entirely different. The Mishna *ibid.* reads: "He who says 'I refuse to step before the Tebah (perform the public service in the Synagogue) in coloured garments' is not permitted to do it in white gowns". The comment of the Talmud on this Mishnah is: Because we suspect that he is inoculated with heresy. Clemens Alexandrinus, *Instructor* II, 11, 12, as well as III, 11 likewise mentions the custom of the early Christians to dress in white, and consequently the heresy spoken of by the Talmud in

---

[23] Comp. Aruk, s. v. חצון whose words are: לא עבד כדין וכשורה.

[24] This custom reminds one of the use of chrysography for the divine names in the Holy Scrolls by the Alexandrian Jews, which was likewise censured by the Rabbis. Comp. Shabbat, 103 b, Masseket Soferim, I, 10.

this connection refers to Christianity.[25] Professor Moore quotes
further the reading מינות הוגה חיצונה from the Munich manuscript
which he renders by "heresy and extraneous speculation". No
such reading is found there, nor does הוגה "speculation" occur anywhere else in the Rabbinic literature. The copyist of the MS.
made a mistake and wrote מינות which word he had before him
in the first clause of the Mishnah, but noticing his error he corrected it to חיצונה. Rabbinovicz, the author of *Variae Lectiones*,
thus remarks: written מינות but "corrected" הוגה to חיצונה.
The photograph of this manuscript is before me and I find that
this statement of Rabbinovicz is correct.

We may then state with certainty that there is no such
word as חיצונים "heretics" in the entire Talmudic-Midrashic
literature, and that judging by the use of the singular חיצון the
plural חיצונים could not have been used in the sense supposed
by Prof. Moore. But even granted the equation מינים=חיצונים, the
expression ספרים החיצונים "heretical books" is hardly possible
in Talmudic Hebrew. We have ספרי מינים "heretical books",
ספרי קוסמים "magical books",[26] and consequently we would
expect ספרי חיצונים the "books of the heretics" and not ספרים
החיצונים as we have it in R. Akiba's Mishnah. It is true, the
Babylonian Talmud, Sanhedrin 100b explains ספרים החיצונים
by ספרי מינים "heretical books", but the Palestinian Talmud,
Sanhedrin X, 28a, which is by far a safer guide in historical or
linguistic matters than the Babli, quite explicitly states that
Ben Sira is included among the ספרים החיצונים and thus clearly
takes ס' החיצונים to mean books "outside of the Canon", though
not of a heretical character. The attempt made by many scholars
to reconstruct the text of Yerushalmi so as to agree with Babli
is decidedly a vain effort. Before entering, however, upon the
discussion of this point it is necessary to know what ס' המירם
stand for in this passage of the Yerushalmi, as a good deal
depends upon the correct understanding of this term.

Professor Moore gets rid of this inconvenient term by emending it to ס' מינים, but while there may be some doubt as to the

[25] Comp. also Goldfahn, Monatsschrift 1870, 174.
[26] Yerushalmi Maaserot, I, 51a.

exact meaning of this obscure word,[27] no doubt is possible as
to its genuineness. Midrash Tehillim, I, 9 in commenting upon
Ps. 19 15 remarks: David prayed to God that men may not
read his words as they read the books of מירום, but that they
may read them and meditate [28] over them so that they receive
reward for doing it as if they would study the most difficult
parts of the Tora ואל יהו קורין בהם כקורין בספרי מירוס אלא יהו
קורין בהם והוגין בהם ונוטלין עליהן שכר כנגעים ואהלות [29] וגו'.
It is evident that מירום is the same as המירום in Yaddaim IV, 6
and in our passage of the Yerushalmi and that by it the Midrash
understands books of a secular nature which one may read
without doing damage to one's salvation though the reading is
without spiritual benefit; one "reads them, but does not meditate
or ponder over them". To make David pray that the Psalms
may not be read by men "like heretical books" would be the
height of absurdity. A careful reading of the Mishna Yaddaim
leads to the same conclusion as to the meaning of המירם ס'.
The books which according to Rabban Johanan ben Zakkai do
not defile the hands "because they are not precious" can only
be secular books but not heretical ones. The description of
heretical books by the leader of the Pharisees as "not precious"
would be as inept as such a characterization of the Thesis of
Luther by the head of the *Index Expurgatorius*.

The earliest commentary on the Mishnah composed in the
ninth or tenth century by one of the Babylonian Gaonim—
perhaps Saadia[30]—takes המירם to be "Homer" and this is very
likely the correct interpretation of this word. Of course, we

---

[27] There are numerous etymologies of this word; comp. Graetz, Monatsschrift, 1870, 139 seq., Perles R. E. J. III, 114, Weil, *ibid.* 278, Kohut,
J. Q. R. III, 546, Kohler, *ibid.* V, 415, Jastrow, *Dictionary*, 355 b. Not
one of these etymologies deserves serious consideration; on the traditional
explanation of המירס == Homer see text.

[28] This passage shows conclusively that הגה is not "read" but "study"
or "meditate", comp. note 40.

[29] These laws form a very difficult section of the Mishnah and hence
are often used to describe the most important parts of the Halakah;
comp. for instance Hagīgāh, 14 a.

[30] Comp. Ginzberg, *Geonica*, 172 seq. and Epstein, *Der Gaonäische
Kommentar*, 29 seq.

must not think of a translation of Homer into Hebrew—the discussion about the "defiling of the hands" could only refer to Hebrew books—but the books of Homer[31] stand for "light literature", books one may read but which are "not precious". The apheresis of Greek loan words is quite common in Jewish writings and the forms מירוס and מירון (accusative!) offer no difficulty.[32] That some of the copyists who undoubtedly never had heard of Homer wrote המירם is not in the least surprising, if one considers that ληστής "thief" is regularly mispelled as ליסטים, though its meaning must have been known as it occurs hundreds of times in the Talmudic-Midrashic literature.

We shall now proceed to examine the text of the Yerushalmi. We have seen that המירם must not be amended and that by it secular literature is meant, the reading of which is permitted in contrast to that of the Book of Ben Sira which is said to belong to the prohibited books. The question is of course very puzzling how to harmonize this interdict by Rabbi Akiba[33] with the fact that, of all the Apocrypha, Ben Sira is the only one quoted by the rabbis. A great Talmudist at the end of the sixteenth century[34] suggested the following emendation of the Yerushalmi: (.r :ספר) כגון ספרי המירם וספרי בן לענה אבל ספרי בן סירא וכל ספרים שנכתבו מיכן והילך הקורא בהן כקורא באיגרת. Among modern scholars it was Graetz (*Kohelet* 166) who

---

[31] In the Ms. of the Yerushalmi reproduced by me in *Yerushalmi Fragments*, 36 b, this word is vocalized as הומירם Homeras, comp. note 27.

[32] In Hullin, 60 b, two manuscripts have מירום, Aruk מרון, מירון, המירום and R. Samson of Sens, in his commentary on Yadaim, III, 5, מידם which is very likely a corruption of מירום. The reading of the Editions ספרי מינים is quite impossible as no one would ever have dared to say that there are verses in Scripture which seem fit to be burned like heretical books. The names and histories of certain nations who lived in pre-Mosaic times mentioned in Genesis—these are the verses spoken of as the Talmud explicitly states—might be said to be superfluous, but certainly not heretical and deserving to be burned. The original reading was ס' [ה]מירום "like story books" and as מירום was later understood by many to mean heretical, a pious copyist added the words ראוין לישרף, and still later מינים was substituted for מירום. Comp., however, Baba Batra 91 a.

[33] R. Akiba himself shows acquaintance with this book; comp. Graetz, *Gnosticismus*, 119, and Bacher, *Tannaiten*[2] I, 269, note 2.

[34] R. Issachar Baer Eulenburg in his *Novellae on Sanhedrin*, 100 b.

independently proposed the same emendation which was later accepted by Perles (R. E. J. III, 116), Joel (*Blicke* I, 75) and Professor Moore. I do not think however that this emendation is acceptable. The statement of R. Joseph, Sanhedrin 100b, that one is prohibited to read the book of Ben Sira is certainly based upon a Tannaitic tradition which counted Ben Sira among the prohibited books. In other words this Babylonian Amora, celebrated for his great knowledge of Tannaitic traditions (comp. Berakot 64a, Horayyot, end) agrees with the view given in our text of the Yerushalmi and it would therefore be against all canons of criticism to emend it against such high authority for its genuineness. It is true the discussion between R. Joseph and his pupil Abbay shows that even the master was unable to explain the reason of the interdict against the reading of Ben Sira and driven into a lurch he had to admit: Were it not for the prohibition against Ben Sira by the Rabbis we would lecture on the book.[35] This, however, corroborates our view that Rabbi Joseph was acquainted with the Tannaitic tradition that counted Ben Sira among the ס' החיצונים and *nolens volens* he had to submit to the authority of the Tannaim. He could not, of course, explain this Palestinian view which is based upon a different interpretation of ס' חיצונים from that prevailing in the Babylonian academies. The Babylonians identified ס' חיצונים with ס' מינים "heretical books" and Ben Sira could not well be described as heretical, while the Palestinian authorities correctly explain the term used by Rabbi Akiba as referring to "outside books" i. e. Apocrypha, especially those among them which were very popular, like Ben Sira.

The above quoted remark of Rabbi Joseph with regard to the use of Ben Sira in public lectures shows at the same time what is meant by the reading of the "outside books". Not the reading of the Apocrypha was prohibited by Rabbi Akiba, but their use in the Synagogues and houses of study for public service or instruction. More than twenty years ago I wrote: "Akiba protested strongly against the canonicity of certain of the Apocrypha, Ecclesiasticus for instance (Sanhedrin X, 1,

---

[35] The corruption of the text in the Editions is obvious. Read with R. Meir Abulafia, *ad loc.*: אי לאו דנגנוזה רבנן להאי סיפרא הוה דרש' וגו'.

9

Babli *ibid.* 100b, Yerushalmi *ibid.* X, 28a) in which passages קורא is to be explained according to Kiddushin 49a and חיצונים according to its Aramaic equivalent[36] ברייתא so that Akiba's utterance reads: "He who reads aloud in the Synagogue from books not belonging to the Canon as if they were canonical" etc. I have little to add to it, except that by reading aloud in the Synagogue I meant public study too and not liturgical recitation only. The objection raised by Prof. Moore against this interpretation of R. Akiba's statement can be easily refuted; he writes: "The principle, however, seems to have been early established that even the acknowledged Hagiographa should not be read in the Synagogue". But the very sources[37] quoted by him (Mishna, Shabbat XVI, 1 and Tosefta XIII, 1) show clearly that it needed a special ruling of the Rabbis to prohibit the public reading of the Hagiographa on Sabbath afternoon.[38] Accordingly these sources assume that but for this ordinance the reading of the Hagiographa—i. e. public study—would have been quite the thing to be expected. The interpretation of the statement of R. Akiba as given in Yerushalmi is therefore not only from the philological point of view, but also from the historical one by far preferable to that of Babli. The identification of חיצונים with מינים is, as we have seen, hardly possible and an interdict against the private reading of heretical books by R. Akiba is not very likely. Of his colleague Elisha ben Abbuyah[39] it is told that he was a passionate reader of heretical books. Later when he became an apostate his unwholesome reading was made responsible for his apostasy, but there is not the slightest indication that he was censured for his reading. The Palestinian Midrashim, even those of comparatively late

---

[36] On ברייתא see my article in the Jewish Encyclopedia, *s. v.* where the origin of this term is explained differently from the traditional one. The Hebrew משנה חיצונה occurs only in late writings.

[37] Comp. also the passage quoted above, page 118, from Mishnah Megillah, end; the reading of the story of Amnon undoubtedly refers not to liturgical use of this section of the Bible but to its public study.

[38] Comp. Shabbat, 116b, where the view of Rab is given that the Mishnah refers exclusively to public reading.

[39] Hagigah; Elisha ben Abbuyah was a younger contemporary of R. Akibah.

origin, like the Tanhumas have still the old Palestinian tradition that the interdict against the הסיצונים 'ס is directed against the Apocrypha and not against "heretical books", comp. Tanhuma Buber IV,59, Tanhuma Behaaloteka 15, Bamidbar R. XIV,4 and Kohelet[40] R. XII, 12. The last Midrash influenced by Babli warns against taking into the house any other book than the Bible. Pesikta Rabba III, 9a is likewise partly dependent upon the Babli and hence distinguishes between the non-canonical and the ספרים החיצונים. One of the outstanding features of the later Midrashim is the harmonizing of the Palestinian with the Babylonian traditions.

By an *argumentum ex silentio* one might prove too much. We have seen that in the entire Rabbinic literature of the first six centuries of the Common Era there is not one quotation from the now extant apocalyptic literature, and an easy explanation is at hand. The Jewish schools at Jabneh and Tiberias whose literary activities resulted in the production of Talmud and Midrash deliberately ignored the writings of their opponents, the so-called apocalyptic Pharisees. But how about the many other apocryphal writings, not of an apocalyptic nature of which not the slightest trace is to be found in the Rabbinical literature? Did the Rabbis at Jabneh detect the hidden Sadduceeism of the First Book of the Maccabees and withdraw it from circulation? They were certainly not Sadducees who, two centuries later,

---

[40] The present text of the Midrash is corrupt as it contains a self contradictory statement. If the "taking into the house" of any other book than the Bible "brings confusion", it is absurd to say that non-Biblical books were given for "reading and not for serious study"; books that one is not to take into the house were certainly not given for reading. In Yerushalmi Sanhedrin, the source of Kohelet Rabba, the translation of להגיון by "for reading" would give a satisfactory sense, as nothing is said there about not taking into the house any non-canonical books. I have elsewhere conclusively shown (comp. *Eine unbekannte Jüdische Sekte*, 70, 71; see also above note 28) that הגה is always "intensive study" or "meditation". The manuscript of the Yerushalmi in my "Yerushalmi Fragments", 262, has the correct reading להגיון נתנו ליגיעת וגו'. The Haggadic interpretation of Eccles. 12 12 takes this verse to refer to Scripture which alone is said to have been given for meditation and serious study—with the exclusion of all other writings which are not a subject for study. Targum paraphrases this verse in a very similar manner—on להג comp. Erubin, 21 b.

9*

showed the Hebrew text of this apocryphal book to Origen and
Jerome. It may be profitable to remember that in the entire
Tannaitic literature only two non-Biblical books are mentioned
by name: Megillat Taanit (Mishna Taanit II, 8) and Megillat
Hassidim or Harissim (Sifre, Deut. 48 and Midrash Tannaim 42);
the former thanks to its Halakhic contents is still extant, and the
latter no longer so. The disappearance of the apocalyptic literature from among the Jews shows as little opposition on the
part of the Rabbis to it as the disappearance of the Book of
Judith shows any opposition of the Rabbis against this genuinely
Pharisaic writing. The Synagogue at the time of the Tannaim
did not use any book younger than Daniel and there is not one
apocalyptic writing that antedates this Biblical book. One might
add that, disregarding Ben Sira, which really enjoyed, at least
for a time a semi-canonical character, it would be as difficult
to prove the existence of a pre-Maccabean Apocryphon as that
of a post-Maccabean Biblical book. There is therefore very
little probability in the assumption that the Jewish schools that
survived the destruction of Jerusalem rejected writings "which
played an important part in the older religious life of Jerusalem
and the dominions of Herod Antipas in the days when the Temple
was yet standing and the Jewish state was still a reality".[41] The
Rabbis of Jabneh would never have hit upon the time of the
Maccabean revolution as the end of the period of inspiration.
This distinction must have been conferred upon the time of the
Maccabees at a very early date. It is perhaps not superfluous
to call attention to the fact that the discussion at the school
of Jabneh concerning the Canon points in the direction of a
rather liberal attitude towards it, by far more so, than that
taken by the schools of Shammai and Hillel at the time of the
Jewish state. Ecclesiastes, Esther and Song of Songs were denied
admission into the Canon by these schools, while the scholars at
Jabneh declared them canonical. But there is no book mentioned
that was excluded at Jabneh from the Canon and there is not
the least likelihood that there ever existed such a one.[42]

[41] Prof. Burkitt, "*Jewish and Christian Apocalypses*", 10.

[42] That Ben Sira was a very popular book, no one would deny, but
where are the proofs that it was considered canonical by Palestinian Jewry?

Professor Burkitt in his highly instructive lectures on *"Jewish and Christian Apocalypses"* quotes a saying by Rabban Johanan ben Zakkai which, he believes, really implies the renunciation of the apocalyptic idea, the notion that the Kingdom of God was an external state of things, which was just upon the point of being manifested and (as a corollary) that the person of insight could know something about it beforehand. This saying of Rabban Johanan reads: God revealed to Abram this world, but the world to come he did not reveal to him. In a note Professor Burkitt remarks that according to Rabbi Akiba, on the contrary, God revealed to Abram both this world and that which is to come. But, adds Professor Burkitt, Akiba unlike Johanan ben Zakkai believed that the Kingdom of God was at hand.[43]

If this however be so, one might as well quote R. Akiba's view to prove the predilection of the Rabbis for the apocalyptic idea as that of Rabbi Johanan in proof of their opposition to it. We know for certain that at the final delineation of the Canon Rabban Johanan was no longer living, while Rabbi Akiba took a very important part in the deliberations leading to it. Accordingly we certainly would expect a much more favorable attitude towards the apocalyptic writings from the school of Jabneh than from the schools of Shammai and Hillel in the year 66. That Rabbi Akiba did not stand isolated in his expectation of the imminent manifestation of the Kingdom of God is clearly shown by the "small apocalypse" found in the Mishna Sota, end, the only one of its kind in the entire Tannaitic literature. The author or transmitter of this apocalypse was no other than "Rabbi

---

[43] Genesis R. XLIV, 22, states only that R. Johanan and R. Akiba differ as to the nature of the revelation, at the "covenant between the pieces", but there is no way of telling who holds the one view and who the other, and one may doubt whether the saying attributed to R. Johanan by Prof. Burkitt does not really belong to R. Akiba. By the way, the difference of opinion between these Tannaim is of a purely exegetical nature, based upon the different interpretation of the כ in Genesis 15 18. II Baruch 4 4, and IV Ezra 3 13, 14 agree with the view that the time to come was shown to Abram, while among the Amoraim both views are represented; comp. Genesis R. l. c.

Eleazar the Great",[44] the favorite disciple of Rabban Johanan ben Zakkai. But even the master himself counted upon the speedy appearance of the Messiah with such certainty that one of his ordinances regulating a certain religious ceremony had its reason in this expectation.[45]

It would therefore not be true to the ascertainable facts to maintain that for the leading Rabbis in the first and the second generations after the destruction of the Temple the Messianic hopes were not as actual and real as they were for the generation living at the time of the great catastrophe or shortly before it.

A saying by Rabban Johanan ben Zakkai truly characteristic of the attitude of the Rabbis towards the apocalyptic idea is the following one; he said: "If thou hast a sapling in thy hands and thou art told: Behold, the Messiah has come, plant thy sapling and then go to meet him".[46] The Apocalyptics cut loose from life, the Rabbis were the guardians and leaders of a nation and they did not fail to see in the wild and vague visions of those dreamers a true menace to the physical and spiritual welfare of Israel.[47] Ethics is, if not entirely, at all events preeminently social ethics and the apocalyptic movement that flung itself with unrestrained imagination upon the future caring nothing for the present concerns and perils of the individual and the community was not only anti-social but also anti-ethical. If the Prophets had any successors they were not the Apocalyptics who forgot this world and with it men, but the Rabbis for whom the center of gravity of religion was not in a world beyond—important as that thought was—but in the actual life of man on earth. It is true, the ethical element was not ignored by the apocalyptic writers; with some of them it even played an important part.

[44] The reading: R. Joshua ben Hananaiah—another favored pupil of R. Johanan—is not based on good authority.

[45] Comp. Rosh Hashanah, 30 a, "speedily the temple will be erected". By "speedily" is meant there, as the content shows, the very next year. Comp. also Taanit 17 a: אסור.

[46] II Abot. R. Nathan, XXX, 67. Read מֶלֶךְ instead of לְךָ.

[47] It would be very difficult to prove the contention that the attitude of the apocalyptic authors toward the Torah was different from that taken by the Rabbis.

This, however, must not deceive us, any more than it did the great Rabbis, who clearly perceived that the apocalyptic view, which lacked touch with the vital problems of man, really endangered the moral element in the Jewish religion.

The "end" is the outstanding feature of the apocalyptic writings and one is apt to forget of what great importance the "beginning" was to these authors. Yet very likely the vagaries and fantasmagoria of the apocalypses about creation or, to use the term of the Rabbis, "the works at the beginning", were primarily responsible for the disappearance of this kind of literature from among the Jews. As early as the time of Rabban Johanan ben Zakkai we meet with the prohibition against discussing the "beginning" with more than one person and this prohibition was the death knell for a goodly number of the apocalypses. A matter not to be discussed becomes quickly a matter not to be read.[48]

The demonology and angelology of the apocalypses not rarely discussed by them in connection with the story of creation were again of a nature that could not but repulse those who were not blind to the danger lurking in the attempt to turn popular fancy into a system of theology. The Rabbis and, of course, still more so the people undoubtedly believed in the existence of angels and demons. But like many other popular beliefs, they meant very little in the religious life of the people and still less in that of the Rabbis. The apocalyptic writings began to make wide use of these popular beliefs, first for purely literary reasons. In describing, for instance, an ascension to Heaven one could not well dispose of the angels or the description would have fallen flat; when God commands man can only obey, with an angel one can argue and dispute. Nor are the demons to be neglected, if one strives to achieve dramatic effects, as, for instance, the author of the book of Enoch in describing the depravity of mankind at the time of the deluge. What at the beginning was merely literary form gradually became theology, angels and demons began to be considered from a speculative point of view.

[48] Comp. Mishnah Hagigah II, 1, and Tosefta, II, 1. It is worth while noticing that Daniel is one of the very few apocalypses that does not contain cosmological speculations, and this apocalypse is the only one admitted into the canon.

The true leaders of Judaism saw the danger and therefore avoided as far as possible in their sayings and writings even the mentioning of angels and demons. It is certainly not an accident that the Mishna never speaks of angels or demons and that in the other Tannaitic sources they are very rarely referred to.

Of course, it would be an error to infer from it any disregard for angels and demons on the part of the Rabbis. But it is a far more grievous error to see in the widely developed demonology and angelology of the apocalypses the religious conceptions and sentiments of the people (Volksfrömmigkeit), in opposition to the teachings of the scribes (Schriftgelehrtentum) as found in the Tannaitic literature. Whatever the Rabbis might have been, we must not think of them as a class by themselves separated from the people; they were neither monks nor professors. They were of the people, lived with the people and worked for the people. Accordingly the most pronounced feature of the Haggadah of the Tannaim is its popular character, a great part thereof being the spoken word addressed by the Rabbis to the people. The apocalyptic writings by their fixed literary forms and their obscurities were not meant for the people, but for the initiated ones. The true mirror of the religious life of the Jews we find therefore in the homely and simple sayings and the teachings of the Rabbis and not in the literary productions of the Apocalyptic writers who wrote primarily for a "class" of men like themselves and not for the people.

163

AN HISTORICAL STUDY
OF THE CANONIZATION OF THE HEBREW SCRIPTURES

By Solomon Zeitlin

I

The Canonization of the Prophetic Books

Though the word "canon" or a word similar to it, is never used in rabbinic literature with reference to the Bible, the principle of canonization, however, is quite applicable. The term "canon" is used mainly with reference to books which are considered divine, therefore authoritative; whereas the books which are not canonized are not only of no authority and hence not binding, but are not allowed to be read.

The Hebrew Bible is divided into three sections: תורה Laws, נביאים Prophets, כתובים Hagiographa,—Scriptures. The first section, the Pentateuch, according to the opinion of most scholars, was already canonized at the time of Ezra.[1] The second section, the Prophets, likewise, was canonized in the early Hellenistic period. Ben Sira, in enumerating the number of the Prophets, mentions the twelve minor prophets as contained in one book.[2] The author of the second book of Maccabees also tells us that Nehemiah "collected the books about the Kings, the prophets, and the books of David . . . so did Judas collect all the writings."[3] That the second section of the Bible, namely the Prophets, was canonized in the pre-Maccabean period, can be shown from a

---

[1] See H. E. Ryle, *The Canon of the Old Testament*, London, 1892; Buhl, *Kanon u. Text des Alten Testamentes*, Leipzig, 1891; Comp. also Wood's article on the Old Testament in Hasting's Dictionary of the Bible. Also J. Fürst, Der Canon des Alten Testament, Leipzig, 1868; G. Wildeboer, The Origin of the Canon of the Old Testament, London, 1895.

[2] Ben Sira XLIX, 10. Comp. Ryle, *Ibid.*

[3] II Maccabees 1, 13, 15.

Reprinted from *Proceedings of the American Academy for Jewish Research* 3 (1931-1932).

passage in the early Tannaitic Literature, where it is stated that
Shammai (Shemaiah) in his endeavor to introduce a new law,
cited for his support a verse from the book of Samuel.[4] This means
of deriving a new law could not have been followed unless the
book of Samuel had already been canonized, for those books
which were not canonized were not authoritative, and no new
laws could have their validity based on such non-authoritative
works.

Some scholars are of the opinion that the Prophets might have
been canonized much before the destruction of the Temple.
Nevertheless, there was not an unanimous agreement on some of
the Prophetic books. The Book of Ezekiel was in danger of being
removed from the Canon.[5] These scholars base their assumption
on the Talmudic passage: had it not been for Hananiah ben
Hezekiah, the book of Ezekiel would have been withdrawn, נגנז,
because its words conflicted with the words of the Torah.[6] From
the Sifre we learn some of the points of disagreement between
the Prophet and the Pentateuch. The Prophet Ezekiel states,
"That the meal offering shall be an ephah, for a bullock, and a
ephah for a ram, and for a lamb."[7] According to the Pentateuch,
however, the meal offering for a bullock was to be three tenth
deals; for a ram, two tenths deals, and one tenth deal for a lamb.[8]
Hananiah ben Hezekiah succeeded in reconciling this seeming
contradiction by stating that Ezekiel wished to teach that any
measure, whether large or small is called ephah.[9] Another discrepancy between Ezekiel and the Pentateuch is given in the
Tractate *Menaḥot*. Ezekiel states "in the first day of the first

---

[4] Kid. שמאי [שמעיה] אומר משום חני הנביא שולחיו חייב שנאמר אותו הרנת בחרב בני עמון
43a, See S. Zeitlin, The Semikah Controversy between the Zugoth, *J.Q.R.N.S. VII.*

[5] Bertholet, *Das Buch Hesekiel*; Ryle, Ibid.; Graetz, *Geschichte*, III; Dẹrenbourg,
Essai p. 296.

[6] ברם זכור אותו האיש לטוב [אלעזר בן] וחנינה בן חזקיה שמו שאלמלא הוא נגנז ספר יחזקאל
שהיו דבריו סותרין דברי תורה Shab. 13b.

[7] Ezek. XLVI, 11.

[8] Num. XXVIII.

[9] רבי אלעזר בן חנינה בן חזקיה אומר איפה לפר ואיפה לאיל ואיפה לכבש וכי מידת אילים
Comp. Men. 45a. וכבשים אחת היא אלא מלמד שאיפה גדולה ואיפה קטנה קרויה איפה
איפה לפר . . . אמר ר' שמעון וכי מידת פרים ואלים אחת היא אלא שאם היו להם פרים
מרובין ולא היו נסכים יבאו פר אחד ונסכיו . . .

165

month thou shalt take a young bullock, without blemish, and cleanse therewith the sanctuary."[10] From the Pentateuch, however, we learn, that on the new moon a bullock was to be offered as a burnt offering,[11] which is obviously in contradiction with Ezekiel's passage where the bullock was not a burnt offering but a sin offering. Rabbi Judah being perplexed with these conflicting passages said that only Elijah would be able to interpret this passage of Ezekiel. Rabbi Jose's opinion was that there is no discrepancy between the Torah and Ezekiel, and the passage in Ezekiel has no bearing upon the new month sacrifice. He refers to the sin offering of the dedication of the second Temple, which was celebrated on the new moon of the first month (Nisan).[12]

The prevailing opinion among the modern scholars is that the early teachers of the Talmud were not only opposed to the last chapters of Ezekiel because of the evident halakic conflict with the Torah, but also for his theosophical speculations related in the first chapter, namely his description of the Chariot (Markaba).[13] Here again Hananiah ben Hezekiah was the man who was responsible for having Ezekiel retained in the canonical books. It once happened, we are told in the Talmud, that a lad was reading in his teacher's house (school) in the Book of Ezekiel, and so absorbed himself in the *Hasmal*, that a fire came out from the *Hasmal* and consumed him. Therefore, the Rabbis sought to withdraw, לגנו, the book of Ezekiel. But Hananiah ben Hezekiah said to them, "If he (the lad) was wise, are then all wise?"[14] Consequently, through the efforts of Hananiah ben Hezekiah the book was not excluded from the canon. Professor Torrey goes a little farther and maintains that the objection of the Jewish Teachers to the book of Ezekiel was not because of its conflict with the

---

[10] Ezek. XLV, 18. בראשון באחד תיקח פר בן בקר וחטאת את המקדש.

[11] Num. XXVIII, 11.

[12] ר' יהודה אומר פרשה זו אליהו עתיד לדורשה אמר לו ר' יוסי מילואים הקריבו בימי עזרא כדרך שהקריבו בימי משה, וכל נבלה וטרפה מן העוף . . . . . לא יאכלו הכהנים כהנים הוא . . . Men. 45a הא ישראל אכלי . . . אליהו עתיד לדורשה

[13] Ryle, The Canon, p. 193.

[14] ת"ר מעשה בתינוק אחד שהיה קורא בבית רבו בספר יחזקאל והיה מבין בחשמל ויצאה אש מחשמל ושרפתו ובקשו לגנוז ספר יחזקאל אמר להם חנינה בן חזקיה אם זה חכם הכל חכמים Hag. 13a.

words of the Torah. "The real cause of the controversy" according
to Torrey, "was hidden and that out of necessity under a mere
pretext." The entire story as given in Shabbat is "good humor
camouflaged, nothing else." He is of the opinion that the real
cause for the objection to the Book of Ezekiel lies in the fact
that the book is not the product of the prophet Ezekiel, but was
compiled much later. The entire book is pseudo-Ezekiel.[15]

The theory that the book of Ezekiel was in danger of being
excluded from the canonical books, is based entirely on the talmudic
passage where it is stated בקשו לגנו. The word גנז has different
meanings. It may mean "to store away" some very precious
thing,[16] or it may mean "to store away from the possibility of
destruction." This latter definition of the word גנז is frequently
found in the Talmud.[17]

Many scholars have rendered the Hebrew word גנז wrongly by
interpreting it as "hidden": בקשו לגנוז ספר יחזקאל they wanted to
remove the Book of Ezekiel from the Canon, that is, to declare it
an Apocryphal book. The word גנז never occurs in the Talmudic
literature in that sense. It occurs only in the sense of storing
something away because of its great value; or it refers to a book
which is not fit for public reading any more, and which should
not, however, willfully be destroyed. This is indicated by a
story related in the tractate *Shabbat*. Once R. Gamaliel was
standing on the hill of the Temple, and a translation of the Book
of Job was brought before him. He said to one of the masons:
"store it away under the rubble," (so acc. to Tal. Jer. ibid.).
R. Jose, the son of Juda, says that a trough of mud was
put upon the book. But Rabbi did not accept this testimony
of R. Jose, giving two objections for not accepting the validity

---

[15] C. Torrey, *Pseudo-Ezekiel and the Original Prophecy*; Comp. also Budde,
Zum Eingang des Buches Ezechiel, *Journal of Biblical Literature*; 1931, 20ff.,
S. Spiegel, Ezekiel or Pseudo-Ezekiel, *The Harvard Theological Review*, Oct. 1931.
[16] Pes. 119a; גנוזה לצדיקים לעתיד לבא B. B. 11a; אבוחי גנוז למטה ואני גנוחי למעלה
Yom. 52b. Comp. II Maccabees, II, "Jeremiah found טשננו הארון גנוז עמו צנצנת המן
a cavernous chamber, in which he placed the tabernacle, and the ark, and the altar
of incense; and he made fast the door." ובאוצרות בית המלך Pes. 56a. גנז ספר רפואת
II Kings, XVIII, 15, the Targum has ובנזי בית מלכא; see ibid., XX, 17.
[17] חשמישי קדושה גנזין Meg. 26b and passim.

of the story.   First, there was no mud on the Temple Mount;
secondly, the book could not be destroyed willfully.[18]   From
here we can see that the word נגנ must be interpreted in the
sense of preserving as opposed to destruction.   Again, in the
Talmud it is stated that the Holy Scriptures, when translated into
one of the foreign languages, although they were not supposed
to be read on the Sabbath; nevertheless, in case of a fire, such books
were to be saved, regardless of the Sabbath.[19]   Books in such a
class were to be stored away from destruction.   On the other hand,
the heretical books, which had the name of the Deity written
in them did not have to be saved, and were to be burned immediately even though the divine name was in them.   But Rabbi
Jose of Galilee says "on week days, one may examine the portion
where the name of the Deity appears, and this part is to be stored
away from destruction, while the rest should be burned."[20]   Here
again, we see the word נגנ is in opposition to שרף used to denote
destruction by burning.   The same thought is expressed frequently
in the Talmud.   A Scroll which is in a state of decay נונגין should
be buried by the side of a scholar.[21]   Another Rabbi said that
the wrappings of the scrolls which were in a state of decay should
be used as shrouds.[22]   Here again we see the word נגנ is applied
to those sacred books which could not be used any more for
public reading because they were in a state of decay.   Such books
had to be buried, but not destroyed.   Similarly a scroll in which
the name of the Deity was written in gold must be stored away.[23]
Such a scroll may not be used in the synagogue, as the law states

[18] מעשה באבא חלפתא שהלך אצל רבן גמליאל ברבי לטבריא ומצאו שהיה יושב על שלחנו
של (יוחנן הנזוף) ובידו ספר איוב תרגום וקרא בו אמר לו זכור אני ברבן גמליאל אבי אביך
שהיה עומד ע"נ מעלה בהר הבית והביאו לפניו ספר איוב תרגום ואמר לבנאי]וגנזו תחת
הנדבך[ר' יוסי בר' יהודה אומר,ערובה,של טיט כפו עליו אמר ר' שתי תשובות יש בדבר ...
וכי מותר לאבדן ביד Shab. 115a.
[19] Ibid. היו כתובים תרגום וכל לשון מצילין אותן מפני הדליקה... אין מצילין ואפילו הכי.
מצילין אותן וגונזן אותן Comp. Tosefta, Ibid. XIII. נגיזה בעו.
[20] Tosefta, Ibid. ספרי מינין אין מצילין אותן אלא נשרפין הן במקומן הן ואזכרותיהם
ר' יוסי הגלילי אומ' בחול קורא את האזכרות וגונז ושורף את השאר.
[21] Meg. 26b. ספר תורה שבלה גונגין אותו אצל תלמיד חכם.
[22] Ibid. מטפחות ספרים שבלו עושין אותן תכריכין למת מצוה וזו היא גניזתן.
[23] Trac. Sef. I, 9. מעשה בתורתו של אלכסנדרים שהיו כל אזכרותיה כתובות בזהב ובא
מעשה לפני חכמים וגנזו.

that letters of the Deity must not be written in gold.[24] Since the name of God, however, is found in the scroll, it should not be destroyed, and must be stored away.

The word גנז is found in tannaitic literature in reference to sacred objects which for one reason or another became unfit for use. Such objects had to be stored away in a particular place and could not be destroyed. A Mishna tells us that the stones of the altar which were defiled, were stored away in the Temple area by the Hasmoneans.[25] According to the first book of the Maccabees, the stones were stored away in the Mountain of the House until a prophet should come to decide concerning them.[26] The altar which was profaned by the Syrians could not be used further. On the other hand, the stones could not be destroyed. Similarly the knives which were used in the Temple, when they became unfit for further use, were not thrown away, but were stored away in a particular place in the Temple.[27] In the same manner, if a book of the Bible which was found by the rabbis not fit to be used in the synagogue for some reason or other, because it contradicted other canonical books of the Bible,[28] or if it contradicted itself[29], or if there were found in it some heretical ideas,[30] such a book had to be stored away and could not be used further in the synagogue, but that did not mean that the book was excluded from the canon. If we should say that the word גנז is to be interpreted as meaning exclusion of the book from the canon and to make it as ספרים חצונים, that would be the same as saying that they are profane and should be destroyed, as ספרים חצונים were not allowed to be used even privately[31] and had to be destroyed.

The very passage from which the scholars want to deduce that the Book of Ezekiel was to be classified among the apocryphal

---

[24] Ibid.

[25] Mid. I, 6. ‏בה גנזו בני חשמונאי את אבני המזבח ששקצום מלכי יון‎.

[26] I Mac. IV, 46.

[27] Mid. IV, 7. Zeb. 88. ‏ששם גונזים את הסכינים, סכין מטרפת . . . ונגנזה‎.

[28] Shab. 13b. ‏גנגז ספר יחזקאל שדבריו סותרין דברי תורה‎.

[29] Shab. 30b. ‏בקשו חכמים לגנוז ספר קהלת מפני שדברין סותרין זה את זה‎.

[30] Mid. R. Q. I ‏בקשו חכמים לגנוז ספר קהלת מפני שמצאו בו דברים מטין לצד מינות‎;

[31] San. X, 1.

books, is based entirely on a faulty reading. The story relates that a youth who was reading in his teacher's house (school) in the book of Ezekiel, and absorbed in the Hasmal, when a fire came out from Hasmal, and consumed him. Therefore they sought to withdraw the book of Ezekiel. Hananiah ben Hezekiah said to them, "If he (the lad) was wise, are then all wise?"[32] In En Jacob the reading is יהושע בן גמליאל instead of חנינה בן חזקיה. Rabinowitz in his Variae Lectiones, דקדוקי ספרים, substitutes שמעון בן גמליאל Simon ben Gamaliel, for he says that there is no rabbi by the name of Joshua ben Gamaliel.

I believe, however, that the original reading was יהושע בן גמלא Joshua ben Gamala. We recall, that this man, according to the Talmud, was responsible for instituting the public schools in Palestine and in some way made the study of Hebrew letters compulsory.[33] When the Rabbis sought to remove the book of Ezekiel from being studied in the schools, Joshua ben Gamala opposed them, and argued that the study of the book of Ezekiel in the public schools is not dangerous. "If he (the lad) was wise, are then all wise?"

Since the name of Joshua ben Gamala rarely occurs in the Talmud, and was quite unknown to the scribes of the Talmud, some scribe changed the name to Joshua ben Gamaliel. While other scribes, being unfamiliar with the name of Joshua ben Gamala, and knowing that the book of Ezekiel was quite frequently connected in the Talmud with the name of Hananiah ben Hezekiah, consequently changed the name in this passage from Joshua ben Gamala to Hananiah ben Hezekiah. Undoubtedly the original text had Joshua ben Gamala, and not Hananiah ben Hezekiah, for if the text had Hananiah ben Hezekiah, no scribe would have amended it to read יהושע בן גמליאל Joshua ben Gamaliel (or יהושע בן גמלא Joshua ben Gamala), as Joshua ben Gamala was hardly known to the scribes of the Talmud and there was no man by the name of יהושע בן גמליאל.

The word גנז in relation to Ezekiel should be interpreted as stored away from public reading; that is, it should not be studied

---

[32] Hag. 13a.

[33] B. B. 21a. יהושע בן גמלא שמו שאלמלא הוא נשתכחה תורה מישראל .... תיקן שהיו מושיבין מלמדי תינוקות.

and interpreted in the academies of learning. The story which is recorded in Talmud Chagiga illustrates this idea quite clearly. When the lad tried to interpret the matter of the Hasmal the rabbis decided to store away this book from further study in the schools. In the tractate Shabbat we are told that the rabbis were of the opinion that the Book of Ezekiel should not be studied in the academies, "for its words conflict with the words of the Pentateuch."

The entire tannaitic literature gives us no inkling whatsoever that the Book of Ezekiel was threatened with being withdrawn from the canon and declared an apocryphal book, in which case it would be forbidden to be read. Of all the portions of the Bible, which, according to the Mishna and *Tosefta* of *Megillah*, were not allowed to be read,[34] the book of Ezekiel is not even mentioned. From this we may conclude that the rabbis did not oppose the reading of Ezekiel. We do find, however, a statement that the first chapter of Ezekiel, the *Markaba*, was read publicly,[35] which shows clearly that the rabbis had no objection at all to the first chapter of Ezekiel. What they maintained was that this chapter should be interpreted and discussed only by men who were both mature and scholarly.[36] Some rabbis were of the opinion that the first chapter of Ezekiel should not be read as *Haftarah*. Rabbi Judah, however, maintained that the first chapter can be used even as an *Haftarah*.[37] It is out of the question to assume that the rabbis at this late date dared to declare the Book of Ezekiel apocryphal, for the Prophets were already canonized, and the rabbis did not possess the authority of withdrawing any book from the Canon. Ben Sira had Ezekiel already in his list of the Prophets, and the order of the Prophets as given by Ben Sira is almost identical with the record in the Talmud.[38]

---

[34] See Mishna, Meg. IV, 10; Tosefta, Ibid. IV.

[35] Tosefta, Ibid. והמרכבה קורין אותה לרבים.

[36] Hag. II, 1, אין דורשין .... במרכבה ביחיד.

[37] M. Meg. IV, 10. אין מפטירין במרכבה ור' יהודה מתיר.

[38] Ben Sira, XLVIII–XLIX; Isaiah, Jeremiah, Ezekiel and the Twelve Prophets. According to the Talmud the order was Jeremiah, Ezekiel, Isaiah and the Twelve Prophets. However, in our Masoretic Bibles is in the same order as that which Ben Sira gives.

II

THE CANONIZATION OF THE SCRIPTURES

The third part of the Bible is the Scriptures—Hagiographa. This section of the Bible is likewise authoritative. The *Tannaim* in expounding the Law many a time quote the *Ketubim* in support, which meant that the words of the Scriptures were authoritative, and upon their passages, new laws were based. The question now arises, was this group, called the *Ketubim*, canonized at the same time with the group called Prophets, or was this group canonized at a later period, and if so, when?

Ben Sira in giving the list of the Prophets does not mention by name any of the books of the Scriptures.[39] We may assume from this that although the books of the Scriptures may already have been written, they were not yet canonized. Josephus in his book "Against Apion" stated that the Jews had twenty-two books. Of these, five are the books of Moses, thirteen are the prophetic ones, and the remaining four books contained the Hymns to God and the precepts.[40] So in the time of Josephus the Bible was already canonized and contained twenty-two books, divided into three parts, the Pentateuch, the Prophets, and a third part comprising four books of Hymns and precepts. A *Baraita* in the Talmud, however, gives the canon as consisting of twenty-four books, the prophetic books being eight in number, and the Scriptures consisting of eleven.[41]

The question is, which of the books that the Talmud had in the third group, the Hagiographa, did Josephus place in the second group, the Prophets. This cannot be ascertained, and many speculations have been offered by students of the Bible. Many scholars are of the opinion that Josephus probably had in his Canon, among the Prophets, the Books of Daniel, Ezra, Nehemiah, Chronicles, and Job, while in the third group, the Hagiographa, he had the remaining four books: Song of Songs, Psalms, Ecclesiastes,

[39] Although Ben Sira may have quoted some phrases or passages from the books which are known to us as Kethubim, he does not refer to them by name. Comp. S. Schechter, The Wisdom of Ben Sira, Cambridge, 1899.

[40] *Against Apion*, I, 8.

[41] B. B. 14b.

and the Proverbs. The Book of Ruth was added to Judges and
Lamentations to Jeremiah.[42]

The fact remains that Josephus had in his Canon, twenty-two
books, instead of twenty-four. Did he append two books of the
Scriptures to the Prophets, namely, Ruth to Judges, and Lamentations to Jeremiah, as many scholars maintain? On the other hand,
should we assume that the Hebrew Canon at the time of Josephus
consisted of only twenty-two books, while two more books were
added at a later period, which made the Hebrew Canon consist
of twenty-four books, and this final canonization of the Bible
is recorded in the Baraita? The latter hypothesis is, I believe,
the correct one, namely that the Jewish Bible at the time of the
destruction of the Temple consisted of twenty-two books and
the Books of Ecclesiastes and Esther were added later.[43]

From tannaitic literature we learn that there were varying
opinions in reference to the Book of Ecclesiastes in relation to
the defilement of the hands. Rabbi Judah said that "the Book
of *Kohelet* defiles not the hands, and with respect to Song of Songs,
there was a difference of opinion." Rabbi Jose said "Song of Songs
defiles the hands, and with respect to Kohelet there is a dispute."[44]
From all the passages we learn that the rabbis differed as to the
Book of Ecclesiastes. According to everyone, the Song of Songs
defiles the hands. From this we may safely conclude that the

---

[42] Comp. Ryle, *The Canon*, p. 165; W. Robertson Smith, *The Old Testament*,
London, 1892, p. 164. Comp., also, Thackeray, Josephus, The Man and the
Historian, 1929, p. 79.

[43] Josephus had in his Canon the Five Books of Moses, Thirteen Prophets,
1. Joshua, 2. Judges, 3. Samuel, 4. Kings, 5. Isaiah, 6. Jeremiah, 7. Ezekiel,
8. The Twelve Minor Prophets, 9. Ezra and Nehemiah, 10. Job, 11. Daniel,
12. Chronicles, 13. Psalms. In the third group, the Scriptures, he placed: 1. Proverbs,
2. Song of Songs, 3. Ruth, 4. Lamentations. αἱ δὲ λοιπαὶ τέσσαρες ὕμνους εἰς
τὸν θεὸν καὶ τοῖς ἀνθρώποις ὑποθήκας τοῦ βίου περιέχουσιν. With ὕμνους
εἰς τὸν θεὸν he refered to the Song of Songs, and with ὑποθήκας he refers to
Proverbs, in which advice is given for the conduct of human life.

[44] M. Yad. III, 5. ר׳ יהודה (מאיר) אומר שיר השירים מטמא את הידים וקהלת מחלוקת
ר׳ יוסי אומר קהלת אינו מטמא את הידים ושיר השירים מחלוקת אמר ר׳ עקיבא חס ושלום לא
נחלק אדם מישראל על שיר השירים שלא תטמא את הידים שאין כל העולם כדאי כיום שניתן
בו שיר השירים לישראל שכל הכתובים קדש ושיר השירים קדש קדשים ואם נחלקו לא נחלקו
אלא על קהלת אמר ר׳ יוחנן בן יהושע בן חמיו של ר׳ עקיבא כדברי בן עזאי כך נחלקו וכך
נמרו. Comp. reading in Meg. 7a; see additional note.

Song of Songs was canonized before the time of Akiba. The only difference of opinion among the early Tannaim was concentrated on the Book of Ecclesiastes. Some were of the opinion that the Book of Ecclesiastes does not defile the hands, therefore was not included in the Canon, while others maintain that there was a dispute among the early rabbis in reference to this Book, but there is no positive statement found to the effect that the Book of Ecclesiastes defiles the hands. In other words, there is no statement found in the controversy between the Tannaim that the Book of Ecclesiastes defiles the hands, which means that *Kohelet* was not included in the Canon at the time of the destruction of the Temple.

The difference of opinion between Rabbi Judah and Rabbi Jose can be summarized as follows: Rabbi Jose states that the Book of 'Song of Songs' was unanimously accepted in the Canon and hence defiled the hands, while the Book of Ecclesiastes was rejected, but after a dispute between the Schools of Shammai and Hillel, the Shammaites being against and the Hillelites for. The Shammaites won because they had a majority in the Assembly when the eighteen measures were adopted. Rabbi Judah, on the other hand, was of the opinion that 'Ecclesiastes' was unanimously rejected, while 'Song of Songs' was accepted only after a discussion.

In the famous gathering of the Shammaites and Hillelites which took place in the house of Hananiah ben Hezekiah, a few years before the destruction of the Temple, the question arose as to which of the books of the Scriptures should be canonized and should defile the hands and which should not; the status of the Book of *Kohelet* was discussed, the Hillelites maintaining that Ecclesiastes should be included in the Canon and hence defile the hands, while the Shammaites were against the defilement of the hands. At this gathering the Shammaites were victorious and all the amendmends of the Hillelites were rejected and therefore Koheleth was not included in the Canon. Thus Rabbi Simon says that the Book of Kohelet is ר' שמעון אומר קהלת] מקולי בית שמאי ומחומרי בית הלל[i.e. [45] Kohelet, according to the Shammaites, does not defile the hands, as this Book is not sacred. From this we may further infer that

[45] Ibid.

174

the canonization of the third group, Hagiographa, did not take place before the year sixty-five, and only in that gathering Kethubim was added to the Bible.

The Book of Esther was likewise added to the Canon much later. According to the Talmud the Book of Esther also does not defile the hands,[46] which means that the Book was not canonized. That the Book of Esther was not included among the Scriptures which were canonized in the year sixty-five can be proved from the fact that in Megillat Taanit, where all the semi-holidays are recorded, the Festival of Purim is among them.[47] Had the Book of Esther been canonized, the holiday of Purim would not have been placed in the Megillat Taanit. The author of this chronicle in giving the list of the semi-holidays, states that fasting is prohibited on the holidays and on the days before them. If the Book of Esther was already canonized in the year sixty-five, it would have been unnecessary for the author of the Megillat Taanit to state that on the day of Purim fasting is prohibited. He does not mention the day of the New Moon when fasting is likewise prohibited, because the feast of the New Moon is mentioned in the Bible. Furthermore, when the Tannaim wanted to prove that the day of Purim is a day of rejoicing and that no Jew is allowed to fast on that day, they inferred this from the Megillat Taanit.[48] It would not have become necessary for the Tannaim to infer this law from the Megillat Taanit if they had had the Book of Esther in the Bible. The rabbis of the later period, however, when they wanted to prove that the day of Purim is a festival and that no Jew is allowed to work on this day, they inferred this law from the Book of Esther itself,[49] which goes to show that at the time of the early Tannaim, although the day of Purim was observed, the Book of Esther was not yet canonized. The Book of Esther was canonized at a much later period, some time after the Hadrianic period. Public opinion was primarily responsible for the canonization of

[46] Meg. 7a. ‎.אסתר אינה מטמא את הידים

[47] ‎באים פוריא עשר ובחמשה עשר ביה יומי ארבעת‎. Comp. S. Zeitlin Meg. Taanit, pp. 65–68.

[48] Yer. Meg. 70–71. Comp., also, B. T. 18b. Meg. 5b.

[49] Meg. 5b.

this Book.   The rabbis were never anxious to have this book
among the Hebrew Scriptures, but the Festival of Purim was
celebrated for many centuries before the destruction of the Temple;
already at the time of the Maccabees Purim was a holiday.   The
author of the second book of the Maccabees called it the Festival
of Mordecai.[50]   The Book of Esther was recited annually on Purim,
but nevertheless it was not considered "inspired" and so was
not included in the Scriptures.[51]   The rabbis, however, after the
Hadrianic period could not keep this Book out of the Canon any
longer, due to the importance which was laid on the reading of
the Megillah on the Festival of Purim, and thus they were compelled to include it in the Bible.   The canonicity of Esther was
due, therefore, to pressure of public opinion, and did not originate
at the academies.   This idea is borne out in the Talmud, where it
is related that Esther sent to the scholars and said: "Inscribe
my Book for posterity".[52]   The scholars were at first reluctant to
accept it, but finally yielded, and we may say that the canonicity
of the Book of Esther was forced on the rabbis.   Therefore as
late as the third century, it was recorded in the name of Samuel
that Esther does not defile the hands—that is, Esther does not
belong to the Canon.   "The Book of Esther was inspired that it

[50] II Maccabees, XV, 36. The author of I Maccabees in recording that Nicanor
was slain on the 13th of Adar, does not mention that it was a day before Purim.
From this many scholars deduce that the Festival of Purim was not observed in
Palestine during the Second Commonwealth and was brought over from the
Diaspora at a much later period. This theory is erroneous. Elsewhere I have
shown that the year 152 A.S., 161 B.C.E. was a leap year, that is, the Jews had
two months of Adar. Nicanor was killed on the 13th of Adar and therefore the
author of I Maccabees who wrote this book shortly after the Hasmonean victory,
knew quite well that Nicanor was killed on the first Adar, which was not a day
before Purim. On the other hand, the author of II Maccabees, who drew his
material from the books of Jason of Cyrene and compiled his work in the Diaspora
at a much later period, not knowing that the year when Nicanor was killed had two
Adars and having before him only the material of Jason, where it was recorded
that Nicanor was beheaded on the 13th of Adar though that it was an ordinary
year and added the words "the day before Mordecai," and that is the reason why
we have the day of Mordecai mentioned in the second book, while it is entirely
passed over in the first book. Comp. S. Zeitlin, Meg. Tannit, P. 118.

[51] Meg. 7a. אסתר ברוח הקודש ... נאמרה לקרות ולא נאמרה לכתוב.

[52] Ibid. שלחה להם אסתר לחכמים קבעוני לדורות.

should be read on Purim, but it was not inspired to be written down." According to Eusebius, Melito, Bishop of Sardis, in the third quarter of the Second Century journeyed to Palestine to learn the exact number of the books of the Hebrew Canon. In his list Lamentations and Esther were not yet included, as Lamentations was probably added to Jeremiah, while Esther was probably not yet included in the Canon.[53]

The Hebrew Canon consisted of three parts, Torah, תורה Prophets, נביאים, and Hagiography, כתובים. Each of these had not only different degrees of sanctity,[54] but they were also canonized at different periods, the Torah at the time of Ezra, the Prophets some time in the Hellenistic period before the Maccabeans; they consisted of eight books, Joshua, Judges, Samuel, Kings, Isaiah, Jeremiah, Ezekiel, and the twelve Minor Prophets, and the Hagiographa were canonized in the year sixty-five, five years before the Temple was destroyed, and comprised the following nine books: Psalms, Proverbs, Job, Daniel, Ezra-Nehemiah, Chronicles, Ruth, Lamentations and the Song of Songs. The book of *Kohelet* was added some time in the beginning of the Second Century in the Academy of Jabneh.[55] Esther was added later in the Academy of Oushah. Although the Kethubim were compiled before the Roman period, and were known to the people, and the Psalms were chanted by the Levites in the Temple, and some of them may even have been translated into Greek nevertheless, the canonization of Kethubim came at a much later period, namely, in the year Sixty-five. The author of the Prologue to Ecclesiasticus refers to the books of the third group as other books—thus he says: "My grandfather, Jesus,

[53] Eus., *The Church History*, IV, 26; Ibid. VI, 25. The Church Fathers had different books and in different order in the Hebrew Canon. Their testimony must, however, be taken with a grain of salt, as they were outsiders' and most likely they followed the order of the Septuagint. For more about the Hebrew canon, according to the Church Fathers, comp. Ryle, *The Canon*. (According to IV Ezra, 14, there were twenty-four books in the Bible, while another reading has ninety-four.)

[54] Tos. Meg. IV, 20.

[55] Yad. III, 5. אר׳ש ב׳ע מקובל אני מפי ע׳ב זקנים ביום שהושיבו את ראב׳ע בישיבה. מורה נבוכי הזמן שער י׳א, Comp. also, Krochmal. ששיר השירים וקהלת מטמאים את הידים. Graetz, Kohelet, 1871.

seeing he had much given himself to the reading of the Law and
to the Prophets and the other books of the Fathers."[56] In the
year 132 B.C.E. when the grandson of Joshua ben Sirach wrote
his Prologue to "The Wisdom of Sirach," the Hebrew Canon
was not yet tripartite, as Kethubim was not yet canonized.

III

"THE HOLY SCRIPTURES DEFILES THE HANDS"

In the preceding pages we pointed out that books which were
canonized defiled the hands. The question now arises why a book
of the Scriptures defiled the hands. What is the underlying
reason for such laws? The whole subject of the "Defilement of
the Hands" presents many difficulties. The Sadducees indeed
questioned the law, as to the reason why the Holy Scriptures
should defile the hands.[57] The answer which was given by Jochanan
ben Zakai to the Sadducees[58] does not throw much light on the
origin of this Halakah. There is another problem which has to
be solved. Why should the hands be defiled, and not the whole
body? From what we know about the Laws of defilement in the
Pentateuch, we learn that if any part of the body—a hand or leg
touched any unclean thing, the person is considered defiled, and
must go through all the laws of Purification.

The laws of Levitical cleanliness are the most complicated in
the Talmud. Therefore, to understand the expression that the
Holy Scriptures defile the hands, we believe it would not be out
of place to give a short survey of the Laws of Impurity, and their
development. According to the Biblical Laws, if a person touched
a dead body, he is unclean for seven days, and for that period of
time he must leave the camp. At the end of the seven days, he

---

[56] ὁ πάππος μου Ἰησοῦς ἐπί πλεῖον ἑαυτὸν δοὺς εἴς τε τὴν τοῦ νόμου καὶ
τῶν προφητῶν καὶ τῶν ἄλλων πατρίων βιβλίων ἀνάγνωσιν. In the same
Prologue the author refers again to the third group as 'others,' "The Prophets
and the others who followed after them." "The Prophecies and the rest of the
books."

[57] Yad. IV, 6. אומרים צדוקים קובלין אנו עליכם פרושים שאתם אומרים כתבי הקודש
מטמאים את הידים.

[58] Ibid. לפי חבתן היא מטמאתן.

must bring a sacrifice.[59] Any person who comes in contact with this man must leave the camp for one day, and he can only return to the camp after sunset, and after he has taken the prescribed bath. Likewise, the man who experienced pollution had to undergo the same grades of purification.[60] They are all called in the tannaitic literature ראשון לטומאה, which is the first degree of uncleanliness. A ראשון לטומאה can transmit its impurity, and any object which comes in contact with this "first degree" becomes a "second," but the "second" can not transmit any further. However, if the "second" comes in contact with Terumah, the Terumah becomes a "third" and it is unfit to eat, and must be burned.[61] Terumah which is unclean in the "third degree" can not transmit its impurity to others. If it comes, however, in contact with an object which is "sacred" the latter is defiled.[62]

The Tannaim who strove to bring religion into agreement with life, amended to the Laws of "impurity." They interpreted the word מחנה to mean Camp of God, or Camp of the Levites.[63] By this amendment the laws of temporary banishment for the "first degree" could only apply to the Sanctuary proper, and to the "Azarah" (the camp of the Levites) but the unclean person is not banished from the City.

The person who was unclean in the "first degree" had still to wait until the evening, and mere bathing of the body in water would not be sufficient to render the person pure. This was a great hardship for the Jews during the Second Commonwealth, as it hampered them in their daily life. So the Tannaim further amended the Laws of Impurity. They explained that the biblical law, which says that a man who is unclean must wait until sunset, refers only to the priests in the case of eating Terumah.[64] Otherwise mere washing of the body suffices to make a person pure, and it was not necessary for him to wait until sunset.

---

[59] Num. XIX, 11.
[60] Ibid. XIX, Deut. XXIII.
[61] M. P., XI, 4. Hag. 24.
[62] Ibid., Pes. 18b.
[63] Ibid., 68a. See S. Zeitlin, Les Dix-huit Mesures. R.E.J., Vol. 68.
[64] Sifra Shemine. יטמא עד הערב ... טהור לחולין מבעוד יום ולתרומה משתחשך. See Idem, Takkanot Ezra, J. Q. R., N. S. VIII.

Even the prerequisite of washing the body to render the person clean, the early Tannaim considered a hardship, and they modified the law by instituting the *washing of the hands* as a sufficient substitute to render the person pure. This Takkana the Talmud ascribed to Solomon, who instituted "washing the hands."[65] On the other hand, according to the Talmud, Shammai and Hillel decreed the "defilement of the hands." The Talmudist[66] as well as the modern scholar[67] interchanged the Takkana of Solomon of washing the hands with G'zerah of Shammai and Hillel, "The defilement of the hands," and so complicated the entire subject of "washing the hands" and "The defilement of the hands."

I have shown elsewhere that the washing of the hands, and the defilement of the hands had nothing to do with each other. The former is a Takkana, an amendment of the early law, while the latter is a decree.[68]

The G'zerah of the defilement of the hands, according to the Talmud, was decreed by Shammai and Hillel. This decree was aimed particularly against the Priests. A Mishna in Hagigah tells us that after every holiday, all the vessels of the Azarah were dipped in water. The Priests said to the worshippers "Be careful

---

[65] Shab. 14b. Idem. The Halaka in the Gospels and its Relation to the Jewish Law in the Time of Jesus, H. U. C. A. Vol. 1. בשעה שתיקן שלמה עירובין ונטילת ידים.

[66] Shab. 14b. ואכתי שלמה גזר .... בשעה שתיקן שלמה.

[67] Comp. הגרון איש שלום in II–V.

[68] According to Shab. 14b. Solomon instituted the Takkanah of washing the hands בשעה שתיקן שלמה עירובין ונטילת ידים while Shammai and Hillel decreed defilement of the hands שמאי והלל גזרו טומאה על הידים. Dr. Klausner in the second edition of his book מפני הדברים הברורים ש.שמאי והלל גזרו' על נטילת ידים says on p. 492 ישו הנוצרי (שבת י"ד ע"ב) .... בטלה דעתו של ש' ציטלין שנטילת ידים היא מי"ח דבר שנתקנו רק ביםי החורבן. If Dr. Klausner would be careful in the subject matter which he treats, he would find out that there is no mention made anywhere in the Talmud that שמאי והלל גזרו על נטילת ידים Shammai and Hillel decreed washing of the hands. What they really decreed was defilement of the hands שמאי—שמאי והלל גזרו טומאה על הידים Yer. Sh. 3d, והלל גזרו על טהרת ידים. Any student of the Talmud is aware of the difference between נטילת ידים and גזרו טומאה על הידים. Furthermore, error follows error. He wrongly ascribes to me that I said that washing of the hands is one of the eighteen measures which were adopted shortly before the destruction. What I really said was the defilement of the hands is one of the eighteen measures which were adopted before the destruction.

not to touch the vessels that can not be readily dipped, such as golden altar, or the candelabra."[69] The reason for dipping all the vessels in water after every holiday was due to the fear that the Israelites who came for the holidays to worship, might have handled the vessels in the Azarah. Therefore the priests insisted that the vessels should be purified. However, such vessels which were handled only by the Priests did not need purification. The Pharisees who strongly opposed any distinction between Priests and Israelites, insisted that even vessels touched by the Priests required purification. This is undoubtedly the decree of defilement of the hands which the Talmud ascribed to Shammai and Hillel; namely vessels touched by Priests in the Temple are defiled, just as when they were touched by the Israelites.[70]

Some Tannaim objected to the decree that any vessel of the Temple touched by the hands requires purification. This disapproval is well borne out by Rabbi Akiba's statement in which he declares: "We can prove our point that there is no defilement of the hands in the sanctuary,"[71] as Rabbi Akiba was likewise opposed to the decree that the hands defile the vessels in the Temple.

In the previous pages we believe we have shown the underlying reasons of the Takkana of washing the hands, as well as the decree of the defilement of the hands. We shall now endeavor to show the meaning of the statement that the Holy Scriptures defiled the hands. The decree of the defilement of the hands was aimed chiefly against the priests, just as were most of the other eighteen decrees which the schools of Shammai and Hillel adopted in the year sixty-five.[72] The purpose of these decrees was to make it impossible for the priests to eat the Terumah. One of these measures was Sefer,[73] The Book, i. e., that if Sefer "The Book" came in contact with Terumah, the Terumah became defiled and could not be eaten by the priests, but had to be burned. This decree was directed against the Priests and the Sadducees. The

[69] Hag. III, 7-8. ‎[ובמנורה] ‎ואומרין להם הזהרו שלא תגעו בשלחן.
[70] S. Zeitlin, The Halakah in the Gospels, H. U. C. A., Vol. 1.
[71] Pes. 19a. ‎אמר ר' עקיבא זכינו טומאת ידים שאין במקדש.
[72] S. Zeitlin, Les Dix huit Mesures, R. E. J., 68.
[73] ‎הספר ... אלו פוסלין את התרומה ..... שמונה עשר דבר גזרו.

Sadducees accepted only the laws of the Pentateuch and rejected the Oral Law. The Pharisees who stressed the Oral Law very much and were anxious that the Oral Law should be studied in the Academies in preference to the Written Law,[74] declared that "The Book," the Pentateuch, or any other Books which are canonized, i. e. Holy Scriptures, if they touch Terumah, the latter is rendered unfit for use. With this decree they made it impossible for the Priests to read the Pentateuch, and to eat Terumah, as the latter would be unfit for use. According to the Talmud "The Book" does not defile but only renders the Terumah unfit.[75] Thus the Book was put in the "second degree" of defilement which only makes Terumah unfit, and not ordinary food. With the decree that "The Book" makes Terumah unfit, the Pharisees did not gain their entire end, as the Priests could avoid contact of the "Sefer" with Terumah. So they decreed that "The Book" which is only of the "second degree" of defilement, makes the hands which touch the book not impure in the "third degree" but in the "second degree."[76] Therefore the hands which touch "The Book", as well as the "Sefer" itself make the Terumah unfit for eating. With this they accomplished their end, i. e., that the Priests could not read "The Book" and if they read it, the hands that touched it were declared in the "second degree," and hence they could not touch Terumah until evening, as washing the body was not sufficient to render them pure in connection with Terumah.[77]

So the book which is considered sacred in order that it should not be used was declared by the early Tannaim as defiling the hands. In consequence of this decree any sacred thing which cannot be used defiles the hands. For example, any part of the pascal lamb which was left over until after midnight defiled the hands, and so נותר portions of sacrifices left over beyond the

[74] Yer. Shab. 15c. שהמשנה קודמת למקרא ... העוסק במקרא מידה שאינה מידה.
[75] Shab. 13b. פוסלין את התרומה.
[76] Yad. III, 2. כל הפוסל את התרומה מטמא את הידים להיות שניות .... כתבי הקדש שניים מטמאים את הידים.
[77] Comp. also B. K. 114b. תרומה משתחשך. מעשה באדם אחד שהיה מסיח לפי תומו שאמר זכורני כשאני תינוק ומורכבני על כתיפו של אבא והוציאני מבית הספר והפשיטני את כתנתי והטבילוני לאכל בתרומה לערב.

182

legal time, defiled the hands, פסח אחר חצות and נותר are holy, but cannot be used by anyone and therefore defile the hands.[77a]

Only the "Book," the Torah, which was in the Azarah[78] (otherwise called ספר עזרא[79]) did not defile the hands, the reason most likely for this being that it should not defile the High Priest when he read the Torah on the Day of Atonement.[80] However, if this "Torah" was taken out from the Azarah, then it did defile the hands just as all the "Books" did. On the other hand, if somebody brought into the Azarah any of the Prophetic books, or any part of the Pentateuch or other books, they did defile the hands,[81] as only the Sefer of the Azarah was excluded from the decree of defilement of the hands.

When the "Scriptures" were canonized, they were considered holy and were placed with the first two sections, namely, the Pentateuch and the Prophets. As "The Book," i. e., The Pentateuch and the Prophets, which according to the decree of the "eighteen measures," defiles the hands, so the "Holy Scriptures" also, as a part of the Hebrew Canon, defile the hands. Scriptures which were written before the Maccabean period and were popular among the Jews much before the destruction of the Temple, like

---

[77a] M. Pes. X, 9. הפסח אחר חצות מטמא הידים הפגול והנותר מטמא את הידים.

[78] Kelim 15, 6. כל הספרים מטמאין את הידים חוץ מספר העזרה.

[79] Tos. Ibid. B. M., V. 8. The Pentateuch which was kept in the Azarah was sometimes called the book of Ezra, as the belief apparently was that Ezra, who was a scribe, עזרא הסופר not only canonized the Five Books of Moses, but wrote the copy of the Pentateuch which was in the Azarah. Comp. also M. K., 111, 4, Jer. Tan. 68a.

[80] Yom. VII, 1. חזן הכנסת נוטל ספר תורה . . . . וכהן הגדול עומד ומקבל וקורא. Anything which was in use in the Temple did not defile other objects. Ordinary liquids are susceptible to Levitical uncleanliness, but wine and oil which are used in connection with the sacrifices are not susceptible to Levitical uncleanliness. M. Kelim, 15, 6. ונבלי בני לוי טהורין, כל המשקין טמאין ומשקה בית מטבחייא טהורין.

[81] Tosefta, Kelim, B. M. 15, 8; ספר עזרא שיצא לחוץ מטמא את הידים ולא ספר עזרא בלבד. וספר אחר. The expression אלא אפילו נביאים וחומשים וספר אחר שנכנס לשם מטמא את הידים. used in this Tos. refers most probably to the Kethubim. It is interesting to note that the translator of Ben Sira used the identical expression ἄλλων πατρίων βιβλίων in connection with the Kethubim. This particular Tosefta was compiled apparently before the Kethubim were canonized and therefore he used the expression ספר אחר in referring to the books which later became known as Kethubim. Comp. Jer. Meg. 70d בספר אילו הכתובים.

Ben Sira, etc. do not defile the hands, since they were not included in the Canon.[82] Hence any book that defiles the hands is canonized. The book which does not defile the hands is not sacred, and is not included in the Canon. The Tannaim opposed the reading of the Kethubim on Saturday, and they declared that the "Holy Scriptures" should not be read on Saturday before Minhah.[83] This law, that the "Scriptures" should not be read on Saturday, was followed even in the later periods. A story is told that once when Purim fell on Saturday, the Megillah was read after Minhah.[84] From another story we learn, when the eve of the fast of the Ninth of Ab fell on Saturday, the Book of Lamentations was likewise read after Minhah,[85] as neither the Book of Esther which the Jews read annually on the Feast of Purim, nor the Book of Lamentations, which was read annually on the fast day of Ab, could be read at the proper time, when these days fell on Saturday.

IV

The Reason for the Exclusion of Jubilees, Ben Sira, etc. from the Hebrew Canon

In the previous pages we tried to show that the "Scriptures" were added to the Hebrew Canon in as late a period as the year sixty-five. We are now confronted with the following problem: Why were books like the Jubilees, Ben Sira, Tobit, Susanna, Judith, written in the Pharisaic spirit before the Maccabean period, not included in the Canon? In order to understand why these books were not included in the Canon, we shall take each book up separately and show the reasons why the Tannaim declared these as extra canonical.

[82] Tos. Yad. II, 13. ספרי בן סירא וכל ספרים שנכתבו מכאן ואילך אינן מטמאין את הידים.

[83] Tos. Shab. XIII, 1; Yer. Ibid. 15c.

[84] Yer. Meg. 74b.

[85] Yer. Shab. 15c. דלמא רבי ור' חיא רבא . . . . פושטין במגילת קינות ערב תשעה באב שחל להיות בשבת מן המנחה ולמעלה . . . למדנו שלשה דברים . . . אין קורין בכתבי הקודש אלא מן המנחה ולמעלה.

Jubilees.[86] The Book of Jubilees, or the Little Genesis, as it is sometimes called, contains the history from the Creation to the Exodus, dividing it into Jubilee periods of forty-nine years each. This Book was written, according to some scholars, between the year 135 and 105 B.C.E., that is before the rupture between John Hyrcanus and the Pharisees. This date of the compilation of the Book of Jubilees is not supported by the contents of the Book. From internal evidence we will be able to show that this Book was written at a much earlier period. First, the Laws of Sabbath are very strict and primitive and not at all according to the Pharisees of the period of John Hyrcanus. Again, the Book is divided into cycles of forty-nine years, called Jubilees. We are at a loss to understand why an author should write a book, call the book Jubilees and stress so much the observance of the Jubilees, when for many centuries Jubilees were no longer in existence among the Jews. Furthermore, the author complains against the leaders of the Jews for changing the calendar from a solar to a lunar-solar one, and thus disturbing the seasons, and making the year ten days shorter. The author bitterly complains that with this change the Jubilee years will be destroyed and profane days will become holidays. This, we believe, is sufficient evidence that the Book of Jubilees was written at a very early period when the Jews changed the solar calendar to a lunar-solar one, and many of the Jews opposed this innovation. The author expresses his opposition in the book: "And command thou the children of Israel that they observe the years according to this reckoning—three hundred and sixty-four days, and (these) will constitute a complete year, and they will not disturb its time from its days and from its feasts; for everything will fall out in them according to their testimony, and they will not leave out any day nor disturb any feasts . . . And all the children of Israel will forget, and will not find the path of the years, and will forget the new moons, and seasons, and sabbaths, and they will go wrong as to all the order of the years. For I know and from henceforth will I declare it unto thee, and it is not of my own

[86] On the literature, and text, editions, of the Book of Jubilees, consult Schürer, Gesch. Vol. III; Charles, *The Apocrypha and Pseudepigrapha of the Old Testament*, Vol. II, p. 1–10.

devising; for the book (lies) written before me, and on the heavenly tablets the division of days is ordained, lest they forget the feasts of the covenant and walk according to the feasts of the Gentiles after their error and after their ignorance. For there will be those who will assuredly make observations of the new moon—how (it) disturbs the seasons and comes in from year to year ten days too soon. For this reason the years will come upon them when they will disturb (the order), and make an abominable (day) the day of testimony, and an unclean day a feast day, and they will confound all the days, the holy with the unclean, and the unclean day with the holy; for they will go wrong as to the months and sabbaths and feasts and jubilees. For this reason I command and testify to thee that thou mayst testify to them; for after thy death thy children will disturb (them), so that they will not make the year three hundred and sixty-four days only, and for this reason they will go wrong as to the new moons and seasons and sabbaths and festivals, and they will eat all kinds of blood with all kinds of flesh."[87]

The above quotation shows quite clearly that the Book of Jubilees was written when the question of the change in the calendar was still an issue among the Jewish people.[88] Otherwise, we couldn't account for the author arguing so forcibly against the change in the calendar, if this question had already been settled centuries before. To say that the Book of Jubilees was written in the second century before the Common Era is as utterly out of the question as to presume that anyone should

[87] Jubilees, VI, 32–38.
[88] See S. Zeitlin, *Some Stages of the Jewish Calendar*, 1929; Idem. Notes relatives au calendrier juif, *R. E. J.*, Vol. 89, 1930. In these essays I have shown that the Jubilee Year consisted of forty-nine days, which were added after seven cycles of seven years. These days were called the Jubilee Year. They began with the Sunday after the Day of Atonement up to the day before the Festival of Succoth. As to the question whether the Jews observed the Jubilee Year or whether it was economically possible for the Jews to keep the laws connected with the Jubilee Year, that is another matter; but one thing, I believe, is sure and that is, that the Jews had the Jubilee Year, as well as the Sabbatical Years at one time before the change of the calendar from the solar system to solar-lunar system occurred. It is most likely that the Jews did not observe the laws of the Jubilee Year, as they did not observe at the time of the first Temple many laws which we have in the Pentateuch.

write a book now in refutation of Sabbatai Zevi as the true Messiah. The issue of Sabbatai Zevi is dead for centuries and no man would raise this question again.

How can it be possible for an author so forcibly to argue against a calendar which for many centuries had already been discarded? The Book of Jubilees, in my opinion, is one of the earliest books /of Jewish literature. The idea of the author was to give the history of the Creation and the laws in a Midrashic form, and it was written at a time when the change in the Jewish calendar occurred. The author being a very conservative Jew, opposed this change very bitterly, since with this change the Jubilee year disappeared from the Jewish calendar. We may classify this book as apocryphal to the Pentateuch. When the Pentateuch was canonized this book (and many like it) was excluded. And hence there could be no question about the canonization of this book in the year sixty-five, when the "Scriptures" were canonized.

There is no inkling found in the entire tannaitic literature to the effect that there was a controversy between the Pharisees and Sadducees on the question of the calendar. The controversy between the Pharisees and the Sadducees in relation to the Festival of Pentecost has no bearing whatsoever on the calendar. The Sadducees maintained that the Festival of Pentecost should be on a Sunday, since the Bible has ממחרת השבת, the morrow after the Saturday, regardless of the day of the month, while the Pharisees, on the other hand, maintained that the Pentecost should always fall on the fiftieth day after the first day of Passover, regardless of what day of the week it was. The phrase ממחרת השבת was interpreted as referring to the morrow of the first day of Passover.[89] The notion of the scholars that the Pharisees were against having Pentecost on Sunday is untenable, as this view is not borne out by the sources. The Pharisees maintained that the day of the Omer should always be on the sixteenth of Nisan, regardless of the day of the week and so Pentecost should always be on the fiftieth day after the Omer was sacrificed, i. e. the sixteenth of Nisan, again regardless of the day of the week.[90]

[89] Men. 65a.

[90] The reader will find a more detailed discussion of the controversy between the Pharisees and Sadducees on the question of Pentacost in an article by the

Ben Sira.[91] The reason why the rabbis did not include Ben Sira among the Scriptures is given in *Tosefta Yadayim*, where it is stated ספרי בן סירא וכל ספרים שנכתבו מכאן ואילך אינן מטמאין את הידים Ben Sira and all the books which were written from that time on do not defile the hands. The reason why the books which were written מכאן ואילך do not defile the hands is due to the fact that the rabbis were of the opinion that prophecy ceased from Israel after Daniel in the Persian period.[92] Therefore all the books written after that time cannot be considered a part of the Holy Scriptures. The Book of Ben Sira was written in the Hellenistic period and that was the reason for its exclusion from the cannon.

Ben Sira gives a description of a high priest Simon. With whom is this Simon to be identified? Some scholars are of the opinion that the high priest mentioned in the book refers to the Simon who flourished from 300 to 270 B.C.E.,[93] while others are of the opinion that it refers to Simon who was high priest of the Jews in 219–179.[94] The translator of the Book of Ben Sira, in his Prologue, calls the author of the original version his ὁ πάππος. If we should take the term ὁ πάππος in its usual sense of grandfather, then we would say that the Simon who is mentioned in Ben Sira refers to Simon II, and the original version of Ben Sira was written between 185–75 B.C.E. On the other hand, if we should assume that the word ὁ πάππος means ancestor, then Ben Sira could have lived many generations before the translator, and the Simon mentioned in the book may refer to Simon I, and the composition of the original book of Ben Sira may therefore be assigned to the first half of the third century B.C.E. Elsewhere we have pointed out that the Simon referred to by Ben Sira is the second one.[95] We may further substantiate this theory by a

---

writer, entitled, "The Date of the Crucifixion According to the Fourth Gospel" in the *Journal of Biblical Literature* 1932, pp. 266–77.

[91] On the text, editions, and Bibliography, consult Charles, *Apocrypha*, Vol. I, pp. 268–315.

[92] Seder Olam Rabba, XXX.

[93] Graetz, Gesch. III.

[94] Derenbourg, Essai; III, Krochmal תורה נבוכי הזמן שערי'.

[95] נר מערבי 1924.

passage from Ben Sira. In chapter 50:24 we read as follows: "May His mercy be established with Simeon,

And may He raise up for him the covenant of Phinehas; May one never be cut off from him;

And as to his seed, (may it be) as the days of heaven." This can be applied only to the time from 180–175 B.C.E., when the sons of Joseph (who was a grandson of Simon I and a priest also), Simon and Menelaus, tried to usurp the office of high priest from Onias the son of Simon II.[96] Ben Sira, as a pious Jew and much devoted to Simon II, prays to God that the priesthood should not cease from Simon's lineage and that the covenant of Phinehas should never be broken with Simon's children.

Tobit.[97] The story of this Book is as follows: Tobit, a pious Jew, of the tribe of Naphtali, with his wife Anna and his son Tobias, was taken into captivity by the Assyrians to Nineveh. Even in captivity Tobit was very scrupulous with regard to the Jewish laws and customs. He took particular pains in burying the bodies of his countrymen who had been put to death by the Assyrians and were not allowed by the Government to be buried. Once on the Feast of Pentecost Tobit sent out his son to bring some poor Jew to partake of the holiday meal with him. Tobias returned saying that there was a Jew lying in the street strangled. Tobit rose at once from his table without finishing his meal, hid the man, and at night buried him, for which the king ordered that he be put to death. Instead of being rewarded for his praiseworthy. deeds, he was visited with a great] affliction, and upon returning from burying the dead, he lay down to sleep in his courtyard. Then a sparrow's dung fell upon his eyes, and in consequence he became blind. Helpless and reduced to poverty, his wife, Anna, reproached him for the misery which they had to endure. One day under such provocation Tobit prayed to God that he should die. At the same time there lived in Ecbatana in Media, a pious

---

[96] That Simon, Menelaus and Lysimachus were priests and that they were the sons of Joseph of Tobias, the writer will endeavor to show in a separate essay.

[97] On the texts, editions, and literature see Schürer, *Gesch.* III; Charles, *Apocrypha*, Vol. I, pp. 174–201. See also the article by Marshall in Hasting's Dictionary of the Bible.

Jewess, called Sarah, the daughter of Raguel, who had been married seven times, and all her husbands had died on the bridal night by the evil spirit Asmodeus. Sarah was reproached by her maid for having slain them. She likewise prayed for death. The prayers of both were heard and the angel Raphael was sent to deliver both from their affliction. The aged Tobit recalled in the midst of his distress that he had once left ten talents of silver with Gabael of Rages in Media, and he sent his son, Tobias, for the money. When Tobias sought a guide, the angel Raphael offered his services, pretending to be a man by the name of Azarias, and these two set out on their journey to Media with a favorite dog. On the way, while Tobias was bathing in the River Tigris, a great fish leaped up out of the water and he caught it. Upon the advise of Raphael, he cut out its heart, liver and gall, to be used as a medicament later on. Passing through Ecbatana they stopped at Raguel's house, and Tobias asked for Sarah in marriage. Raguel consented, and he wrote an instrument of cohabitation, even that he gave her to him to wife according to the decree of the Law of Moses. In the evening, as the newly married couple entered the bridal chamber, Tobit acting under the instructions of Raphael, burned the heart and the liver of the fish and this odor caused Asmodeus to disappear. The wedding was celebrated for fourteen days. Thus, during the fourteen days, Raphael took the opportunity to go to Rages to take the money from Gabael. After the marriage festivities were over, Tobit returned to Nineveh to his parents, accompanied by Raphael, and took half of his father-in-law's wealth with him. Tobias, upon meeting his father, applied the gall of the fish to his father's eyes, and his sight was instantly restored. Tobit wished to reward the faithful Azarias, whereupon the latter disclosed his identity, and returned to heaven. Full of gratitude to God, Tobit chanted a song of thanksgiving to God. He continued to live in health and prosperity for many more years.

From the contents of the Book we can safely say that the Book was written by a very pious Jew, who stressed the observance of the Jewish Law and particularly those relating to burying the dead. He also wants to show that God may test a man, as he tested Abraham and Job. He may even give power to Asmodeus

190

to test the man, as he tested Job, but in the end He will reward the righteous man.

As to the time of the composition of this Book, various dates have been advanced by scholars. Schürer is of the opinion that the Book was written in the course of the last two centuries before Christ. Ewald fixes it around 350 B.C.E.[98] On the other hand, Graetz[99] ascribes it to the period of Bar Kokba, and Kohut goes a little further and believes that the Book was written some time in the year 226 of the Common Era.[100] The chief reason for which Graetz places the composition of this Book at such a late date is that the principal object of the Book is to stress the duty for every pious Jew to bury the dead, even at the risk of his own life, as God would in the end reward him for it, and such a time in Jewish history, according to Graetz, was in the period of Hadrian, when those of the slain in Bettar were not allowed to be buried. We believe, however, that Graetz's theory is quite untenable, as his chief argument for giving such a late period of the Book of Tobit, is that Hadrian did not allow those Jews slain in battle to be buried. This custom of not allowing enemies to be buried prevailed among all the nations. Josephus tells us that during the civil war in Jerusalem, when the Zealots slew their enemies, they left them without burial, and any relative who buried his kin was punishable by death.[101] And so the Psalmist complains that "the bodies of thy servants have they given to be meat unto the fowls of the heaven, the flesh of thy saints unto the beasts of the earth. Their blood have they shed like water round about Jerusalem; and there was none to bury them."[102]

We believe that Schürer is quite right in saying that the Book was written in the course of the two centuries before C. E. To be more exact, we would say that the Book was written during

[98] *History of Israel*, Vol. V, 209.

[99] *Monatschrift f. Gud. Jud.*, 1879.

[100] Geiger's, Z. vol. X. 49.

[101] B. J. IV, 6, 3; "They left the dead putrefying in the sun. For burying a relative, as for desertion, the penalty was death."

[102] Psalms LXXIX, 2–3. נתנו את נבלת עבדיך מאכל לעוף השמים בשר חסידך לחיתו ארץ שפכו דמם כמים סביבות ירושלים ואין קובר.

the revolt against the Syrians when many pious Jews were slain and their bodies were left unburied.

Furthermore from internal evidence, namely the Halakah recorded in this Book, we may conclude that it was written in an early period. The author relates that when Raguel gave his daughter in marriage to Tobias, he wrote an instrument of cohabitation,[103] which means he wrote a document (shtar) in giving away his daughter. This is the old Halakah, which says that a` woman may be acquired as a wife by "shtar."[104] This law, however, was later amended. Instead of the "shtar" which had to be written by the father of the bride, a Ketubah was introduced, which was to be written by the groom. The Talmud ascribes this amendment to Simon ben Shetach.[105] In the Book of Tobit, we are told, however, that Raguel, the father, wrote the "shtar," and not Tobias, the husband. This indicates clearly that the Book was written before the time of Simon. It must, therefore, have been written either before the Maccabean period, or at the very latest in the early Maccabean period.

Now, if we are correct in assuming that the book was written in such an early period, why was it not included among the Kethubim when the latter were canonized in the year sixty-five? This difficulty is easily removed if we recall that "Tobit" still had the old Halakah which was already modified at the time of the canonization of the Kethubim. If there was a disagreement between a Prophetic book and the Pentateuch, the rabbis tried to reconcile it, but they would never canonize a book which was in direct contradiction with their Halakah. That is sufficient reason for not including the Book of Tobit among the Kethubim.

Susanna.[106] The contents of the book of Susanna is as follows: In the early period of the captivity in Babylon, there lived a woman named Susanna, beautiful, virtuous, and pious, a daughter

---

[103] VII, 11–13.

[104] Kid. I, 1. ‏האשה נקנית בשלשה דרכים בכסף בשטר ובביאה.‏

[105] Shab. 14b. ‏שמעון בן שטח תיקן כתובה לאשה.‏ Comp. Yer. Ket. 32c; Tos. Ibid. XII, 1. A more detailed discussion of the origin of the Ketubah, will be found in an article by the writer, entitled, "The Origin of the Ketubah," which will appear shortly in the *J.Q.R.*

[106] On the texts, editions, and literature, comp. Charles, Vol. I, pp. 638–646.

of a priest. She was married to a man by the name of Joakim, who was rich and very much respected in the community. There were two elders in Babylon who were also judges. One evening they saw Susanna walking in her husband's garden, and their passion for her was aroused, and they tried to coerce her to lie with them, saying to her, "if you will not consent to our lust, we shall say that we saw you sin with a young man." But Susanna repulsed them with scorn and said that she would rather die than sin against God. The two judges to protect themselves accused Susanna, and summoned her to appear before the assembly. The two elders appeared as witnesses, telling the people that they saw Susanna lying in the park with a young man, who managed to escape before he could be arrested. Susanna protested her innocence, but the people of the assembly had to take the evidence of the two witnesses and condemned Susanna to death. As they were leaving the assembly house to lead her to be executed, a young man, by the name of Daniel, reproached the community, by saying that, without any examination or knowledge of the truth, they had condemned a daughter of Israel, and he undertook to prove the innocence of Susanna. He cross-examined the two elders separately, and put the same question to each, and asked them under what kind of tree did the adultery occur. Each gave the name of a different tree. The people being convinced of the innocence of Susanna and the malevolence of the two judges, put the two elders to death.

The author may not have had any motive in writing this story, but he certainly reflects his theological point of view; a man should rather prefer death to sinning against God, and he who trusts in the Lord, will be rewarded by him in the end. On the other hand, hypocrisy, as practiced by the judges, will meet with a just penalty.

As to the date of the composition of Susanna, we shall endeavor to establish this from the contents. The author of this book, in giving the story of Susanna, would certainly present the institutions and laws as they existed in his time. We are told in the book that Susanna was summoned before the assembly of the people. Apparently the institution of the Sanhedrin was not yet in existence at that time, otherwise the author would certainly have mentioned the fact that Susanna was summoned to appear before the Sanhedrin. This proves that the story was written before the existence of the Sanhedrin, which means that it was written before the time of Simon II. Furthermore, Daniel in cross-examining the witnesses, asked the name of the tree under which the act of adultery was committed. In giving different trees, (which according to the Tannaim was called הכחשה) Susanna was not only acquitted, but the witnesses were put to death. This is the biblical law: "Then shall ye do unto him, as he had thought to have done unto his brother."[107]

The early Tannaim maintained that false witnesses can be put to death only in the case of an alibi, that is, if other witnesses come to testify that the said witnesses were together with them in a different place at the time that the supposed crime took place. If, however, their testimony does not agree, as in the case of the trial of Susanna, the defendent cannot be convicted, and the witnesses are free from punishment.[108] This law was already in existence at the time of Simon ben Shetach.[109] The author of the book tells us that when Daniel found that the two witnesses were not in agreement about the tree, they were put to death. This clearly shows that the book was written before the time of Simon ben Shetach.

The reason why the book "Susanna" was not included among the Scriptures can be readily understood, for the Halakah recorded in "Susanna" is early Halakah and did not agree with the Halakah which existed in the year sixty-five. This was sufficient reason for excluding this book from the Scriptures, just as the book of Tobit was excluded.

Judith.[110] The following is a brief account of the Book of Judith: Nebuchadnezzar, after conquering Media, sent a large force, under the leadership of his general Holofernes to take vengeance on Judea because the Jews had not come to his aid. Holofernes laid waste the various countries, demolished their temples, and their

[107] Deut. XIX, 19.
[108] M. Mak. I; Comp. M. San. V, 11.
[109] Comp. Mak. 5b; Tos. San. VI, 6.
[110] On the texts, editions, and literature see Charles, pp. 242–247; Schürer, *Gesch*. III.

gods, and demanded that Nebudhadnezzar alone should be worshipped as God. The Jews who had but lately returned from the Exile, resolved to resist Nebuchadnezzar with all their might and to defend their country and their religion. Joakim, the high priest in Jerusalem, sent instructions to Bethulia to stop the passes leading to the Capital. Holofernes called a council of officers to decide how to proceed with the campaign against the Jews. One officer, called Achior, an Ammonite, warned Holofernes that God in Heaven protects the Jews and no one can do them any harm unless they sin. This speech displeased Holofernes, and Achior was delivered to the enemy in Bethulia. Holofernes then laid siege to Bethulia. After this had lasted for forty-seven days, the water supply of the city gave out, and the inhabitants of the city suffering very severely, demanded that their leaders surrender the city to the enemy. When the distress in the city had reached a climax, a wealthy, beautiful and very pious widow, by the name of Judith, resolved to save her people by a great act of daring. Prepared by praying and strict observance of the Jewish law, she made her way to the camp of the enemy, taking a single maid servant with her and a bag of "pure" food. Holofernes was captivated by her beauty, and he invited her to his camp. On the evening of the fourth day, Judith was invited to participate at a banquet, which was given in her honor. After the guests had departed, she was left alone with Holofernes. When the general was lying intoxicated upon his bed, Judith decided that this was the most opportune moment for carrying out her design. She took his sword and cut off his head. Then she and her maid servant managed to leave the camp without being observed and made their way to Bethulia, taking the head of Holofernes with them. When the enemy discovered that their general had been betrayed by the Jewess, they fled in all directions, hotly pursued by the Jews, who killed a great number of them. Achior, seeing the wonders of God, had himself circumcized and became converted to Judaism. The Jews celebrated this great victory with sacrifices to God and with great rejoicing.

The author believed that Israel's troubles were due to their sins, and if the Jews would follow God's commandments and observe the laws, he would deliver them from all their enemies

195

who threatened their religion and their country. Judith, because she was devoted to God, and because she strictly observed the dietary laws, was able with God's help, to conquer Holofernes.

The original language of this book is commonly accepted to have been Hebrew. Schürer rightly points out that Judith was written in the Hellenistic period when the Jewish religion, as well as their country, were threatened by the Syrians.[111]

Graetz's opinion that the book of Judith was written at the time of Trajan,[112] is not even to be considered, as Clement of Rome, who died before Trajan, already in his Epistle to the Corinthians, gives an account of the Book of Judith. He says: "The blessed Judith, when her city was besieged, asked the elders to suffer her to go out into the camp of the strangers. So she gave herself up to danger, and went forth for love of her country and her people in their siege, and the Lord delivered over Holofernes by the hand of a woman. Not less did Esther also, who was perfect in faith, deliver herself to danger, that she might rescue the nation of Israel from the destruction that awaited it; for with fasting and humiliation she besought the all-seeing Master of the Ages."[113] Furthermore, the author of the Book of Judith relates that when Achior was converted to Judaism, he was circumcised. If the book had been written after the destruction of the Temple, as Graetz assumes, then why does the author fail to mention that Achior was baptized, for baptism was already a necessary requirement for proselytes.[114] We must, therefore, assume that the book

---

[111] Schürer, Ibid.

[112] *Gesch*. III.

[113] LV.

[114] The institution of baptism for proselytes came into existence in the year sixty-five, when the Gentiles were declared in a state of בו. Büchler, in an article in the *J.Q.R.*, 1926, entitled, "*The Levitical Impurity of the Gentile in Palestine before the Year Seventy*," does not accept the date of the year sixty-five as a terminus *a quo* for this institution. He claims that in the year 17–18 the Gentiles were already considered unclean. His argument is based on a statement found in the Talmud: Yom. 47a אמרו עליו על ר' ישמעאל בן קמחית פעם אחת סיפר דברים עם ערבי שיצא Tos. Yom. IV, 20 אחד בשוק וניתזה צינורא מפיו על בגדיו ונכנס ישבב אחיו ושמש תחתיו צינורא וניחזה ערבי המלך עם לדבר. According to Büchler the high priest concerned here was Simon (Ishmael), the son of Kamethis, who was appointed by Gratus in the year 17–18, and so at that time the Gentiles were already considered in a state

was written before the destruction of the Temple, when baptism was not yet a requisite for conversion to Judaism.

In order to understand why Judith was not included in the Scriptures it is only necessary to recall that the Book of Esther which is quite similar to it, was not included in the Canon until a very late period, for the rabbis had been opposed to the inclusion of the Book of Esther in the Canon. Only through pressure of public opinion was this book finally included, as the Book of Esther had been read for centuries on the festival of Purim. It may be true that the Book of Judith was connected with the festival of Hannukah[115] and may have been read during the days of Hannukah, but the festival of Hannukah itself was not very popular among the Jews during the Second Commonwealth, when the Hasmonean dynasty was overthrown by Herod. Moreover a statement is found in tannaitic literature that a fast was declared on Hannukah.[116] The festival of Purim, however, was always very popular with the Jews. The Book of Jubilees, Ben Sira, Tobit, Susanna, Judith, and other similar books, such as, First Maccabees, the Wisdom of Solomon, or books of an Apoca-

---

of Levitical impurity. However, after critical examination of all the passages in the tannaitic literature, relating to this episode, we believe that Dr. Büchler's theory is not acceptable. The story recorded in the Palestinian Talmud reads as follows: שיצא לדבר עם המלך ערב יום הכפורים וניתזה צינורא של ריק ספיו על בנדיו וטימאחו וגכנס יהודה אחיו ושיטש תחתיו. This version is found several times in the Palestinian Talmud, and it is undoubtedly the correct one. It is hardly conceivable that the high priest would go out from the Temple on the Day of Atonement to take a promenade with an Arab—or to talk over matters with him. The text in the Babylonian Talmud is corrupt. In place of ערב it has ערבי. Dr. Büchler furthermore quotes the following passage from the Talmud to prove his point: כי אתא רב דימי Ab. Zarah, 36b אמר בית דין של חשמונאי נזרו ישראל הבא על הנכריה חייב משום נש'נא. But Rav Dima was an Amora who lived in the fourth century and hence his statement cannot overthrow my thesis, as we have shown from many passages of tannaitic literature that Gentiles were not subject to Levitical impurity and do not transmit it. הבהמה והגוים אין Tos. Oh. I, 4, הגוי והבהמה הנוגעים במת כלים הנוגעים בהן טהורין. מקבלים טומאה Tos Neg. VII, 10, הגוים והגר התושב אינן מטמאין בזיבה Tos. Zab. II, 1. There is no reference found anywhere in the Tannaitic literature or in the Hellenistic literature before the destruction of the Temple that baptism was a requisite for conversion to Judaism. See also Craetz, III, n. 19.

[115] See Zunz, *Gottesdienstliche Vortrage*, p. 131.

[116] Yer. Tan. 70d. מעשה שנזרו תענית בחנוכה בלוד.

lyptic nature, which were written in the Hebrew language, or in the Greek language, were considered ספרים חצונים and these books were prohibited from being read, and anyone who read these, according to the rabbis, would not share a portion in the world to come, while such books which have no connection whatsoever with Judaism,[117] as the books of Hamerum (Homer), were not prohibited from being read.

The early Jewish literature may be divided into two sections כתבי הקודש the Holy Scriptures, and the Extra-Canonical Books ספרים חצונים. The term ספרים גנוזים which occurs in modern Hebrew literature, and is used quite frequently by modern scholars, is an erroneous one, as no such term is found in the Talmud, and there were no books of that name.[118]

The Jewish tradition connects the canonization of the Hebrew Scriptures with the Great Synagogue. This Essay, I believe, supports this tradition. Many scholars have denied the existence of the Great Synagogue. They considered it a rabbinical fiction.[119] I believe, that of the scholars who dealt with the historical question of the Great Synagogue, some did not penetrate into the history of that period, while others did not fully comprehend the sources in the original language. Had they made a thorough investigation of the tannaitic literature, they would not have come to such a hasty conclusion. The institution of the Great Synagogue was not a myth and the rabbis did not invent it. It was a reality and it had great influence in helping to shape the history of the Jews during the Second Commonwealth.

---

[117] M. San. X, 1. ואלו שאין להם חלק לעולם הבא . . . ר' עקיבא אומר אף הקורא בספרים כגון סיפרי בן סירא וספרי בן לענה, אבל ספרי המירם . . . הקורא .Yer. ibid. 28a ;החיצונים בהן כקורא באיגרת.

[118] Comp. Charles, *Apocrypha* V. I, p. VII,

[119] Kuenen, Over de mannen der groote Synagogue 1876; Robertson Smith, The Old Testament, p. 169; "It has been proved in the clearest manner that the origin of the legend of the Great Synagogue lies in the account given in Neh. viii.–x . . . and everything that is told about it, except what we read in Nehemiah, is pure fable of the later Jews." Compare also H. E. Ryle: The Canon of the Old Testament, Excursus A. Kohler, H. U. C. A., Vol. I, p. 388, "Without going into detail, it can be positively asserted that the organization is a fictitious product of the Rabbinical schools."

The Great Synagogue was not a permanent institution which existed at the time of Ezra only and lasted up to the time of Simon the Just but it was something like a constitutional assembly which gathered from time to time when the need for such assemblies arose. `One such assembly met at the time of Ezra upon the return from the Exile. Another one met at the time of Simon the Priest II (The Just); while another such assembly met in the year 141 B. C. E. when the High Priesthood was given to the family of the Hasmonaim.[120] Still another Great Synagogue assembled in the year 65 C. E., after the great victory which the Jews had over the Roman general Cestius, when a new government was established and a constitution was drafted, and in that period the Hebrew Scriptures, that is, the last part, the Kethubim, were canonized.[121]

[120] See S. Zeitlin, The Origin of the Synagogue, Proceedings of the American Academy for Jewish Research, 1930–31. Comp. George F. Moore, Judaism, III, p. 10.

[121] Idem. Megillah Taanit, p. 108.

ADDITIONAL NOTE

כל כתבי הקדש מטמאין את הידים שיר השירים וקהלת מטמאין את הידים ר' יהודה (מאיר)
אומר קהלת אינו מטמא את הידים ומחלוקת בשיר השירים ר' יוסי אומר שיר השירים מטמא את
הידים ומחלוקת בקהלת ר' שמעון אומר קהלת מקולי בית שמאי ומחומרי בית הלל (so according
to Meg. 7a) אמר ר' שמעון בן עזאי מקובל אני מפי ע'ב זקן ביום שהושיבו את ר'אב'ע בישיבה
ששיר השירים וקהלת מטמאים את הידים אר'ע חס ושלום לא נחלק אדם מישראל על שיר השירים
שלא תטמא את הידים שאין כל העולם כלו כדאי כיום שניתן בו שיר השירים לישראל שכל הכתובים
קדש ושיר השירים קדש קדשים ואם נחלקו לא נחלקו אלא על קהלת א'ר יוחנן בן יהושע בן חתיו
של ר'ע כדברי בן עזאי כן נחלקו וכך נמרו. M. Yad. III, 5.

"All Holy Scriptures defile the hands. The 'Song of Songs' and 'Ecclesiastes'
defile the hands. Rabbi Judah said,—'Ecclesiastes' does not defile the hands
but as to the 'Song of Songs,' there was a difference of opinion. Rabbi Jose said
'Song of Songs' defiles the hands but in the matter of Ecclesiastes there was a
controversy." (So according to the reading in Meg. 7a which undoubtedly is the
correct one). Rabbi Simon, (a Hillelite) said "Kohelet is מקולי בית שמאי and ומחומרי
בית הלל." (According to the school of Shammai, Kohelet does not defile the hands.
This corresponds to the statement of Rabbi Jose, a Hillelite, that 'Kohelet' was
rejected, but only after a dispute between the schools of Shammai and Hillel).

Rabbi Simon ben Azzai said, "I have a tradition received from the 72 elders that
on the day when R. Eleazar ben Azariah was made president, it was determined
that the 'Song of Songs' and 'Kohelet' defile the hands." Rabbi Akiba denied
that there had ever been a controversy with respect to the book of Song of Songs.
If ever there had been a controversy, he said, it was only in the matter of the book
of 'Ecclesiastes.' From this statement of Rabbi Akiba we may deduce that the Song
of Songs was accepted into the Canon before the destruction of the Temple. This
agrees with the opinion of Rabbi Jose that שיר השירים מטמא את הידים. Rabbi Johanan
the son of Joshua, the son of Rabbi Akiba's father-in-law concurs in Ben Azzai's
statement that the Court of Jabneh decreed that 'Kohelet' as well as 'Song of
Songs' defile the hands. This means that the Book of Kohelet was added to the
Hebrew Scriptures then.

It has been shown in Chap. III that anything which is sacred but cannot be used
is מטמא את הידים defiles the hands. With this view in mind, we can understand the
underlying reason for the decree that בשר תאוה מטמא את הידים. The Tosefta of Ma'aser
Sheni 1, 8 read as follows: משנורו (אבל לא לובחי שלמים) לוקחין חיה ועוף לבשר תאוה
שיהא בשר תאוה מטמא את הידים אמרו אין לוקחין חיה לבשר תאוה אבל לוקחין העוף לבשר
תאוה. One may buy with the money which was redeemed *Ma'aser Sheni* any
בשר תאוה i. e. flesh of חיה ועוף לבשר תאוה. Since the decree that בשר תאוה מטמא את הידים
the animal which was bought with the money with which the *Ma'aser Sheni* was
redeemed, defiles the hands, one may not purchase any beast. The reason for
this is quite clear since בשר תאוה is still sacred but yet cannot be used for secular
purposes, one may not purchase with this money any beast which is not fit for
the altar הלוקח בהמה לבשר תאוה. (Comp. M. Ma'aser Sheni 1, 3 אין לוקחין חיה לבשר תאוה.
שלמים או חיה לבשר תאוה יצא העור לחולין. This Mishna most likely dates back to

the period before the decree בשר תאוה defiles the hands.)   One may however buy a
fowl for בשר תאוה since a fowl is permitted as a sacrifice אבל לוקחין העוף לבשר תאוה.
Comp. Jer. ibid. Chap. 1, 52ⅆ, particularly the statement בראשונה היו אומרין לוקחין
בהמה לבשר תאוה והיו מבריחין אותו מעל גבי המזבח חזרו לומר לא יקחו אפילו חיה אפילו
עופות.   Comp. also ibid. 1, 15, הלוקח בהמה לובחי שלמים בשוגג יחזרו דמיה למקומה
במזיד תעלה ותאכל במקום, בזמן הזה תמות.   אסר ר' יהודה במה דברים אמורים בזמן שמתכוין
ולקחה בתחילה לשום שלמים אבל בסתכוין להוציא מעות של מעשר לחולין בין בשוגג בין במזיד
יחזרו דמים למקומן.   More on the question of redemption of Ma'aser Sheni or בשר תאוה
will be discussed at length in my forthcoming book on the development of the
Halakah.

201

"OUTSIDE BOOKS"

By Joshua Bloch

Very little is known of the procedures followed in fixing the collection of Hebrew Scriptures. Such early rabbinic passages as bear on the subject are too few in number and too vague in content. The information they yield is scanty and the knowledge they convey on the canon is virtually nil. Such references as they contain on the inclusion or exclusion of certain books have nothing to do with the establishment of a canon of Hebrew Scriptures. They merely refer to the use of the books in question for liturgical or instructional purposes. It is, indeed, very doubtful whether there ever was a formal canonization by any competent authority in Judaism of the books comprising the Hebrew Bible. Gradually and through usage only the collection of Hebrew Scriptures acquired a recognized authoritative position. The biblical books that were studied in the schools and read in the synagogues on Sabbath, festive and fast days as well as on other appropriate occasions were regarded as God-given: their authors were divinely inspired and divine authority resided in their every word. Not so with other books containing Jewish religious teachings. The rabbis were not concerned so much with fixing the number of books comprising the collection of Scripture as with formulating regulations designed to preserve the integrity of its text and teachings. The Hebrew Bible acquired its "sanctity" because it presents the basis for authoritative religious instruction and belief. Indeed, "all the books of the canon of Jewish Scriptures were considered of equal importance as the source and expression of divine Law. As to prophetic teachings — ethical, messianic and theological — it has rightly been maintained that they became part and parcel of the rabbinic doctrine."[1]

All discussions dealing with problems connected with what is called canonicity of the Hebrew Scriptures must of necessity take cognizance of a number of pertinent passages in early rabbinic texts.

---

[1] N. N. Glatzer, "Talmudic Interpretation of Prophecy," in *Review of Religion*, New York, January, 1946, v. 10, p. 118. Cf. Louis Ginzberg, *Eine unbekannte juedische Sekte*, New York, 1922, pp. 265 and 275; מקומה של ההלכה, Jerusalem, 1931, p. 11 and Ch. Tchernowitz, תולדות ההלכה, New York, 1934, v. 1, p. 306.

Reprinted from *Mordecai M. Kaplan Jubilee Volume*, English Section, New York, 1953.

Among such passages there are several which record well-established and other traditions in which mere opinions are attributed to eminent rabbis. Some of those rabbis played a notable.role in the formation of teachings which have become basic in the development of Judaism as a religious system. Not the least of such rabbis is the eminent and eloquent Rabbi Akiba ben Joseph, who, perhaps more than any other of the early rabbis, contributed to the formation, maintenance and perpetuation of Judaism as a religion which draws upon Scripture for authoritative support of its teachings and practices. Mindful of the admonition of the Men of the Great Synagogue[2] to "make a fence around the Torah"[3] he and his circle became very much concerned with the protection of the integrity of the text of the Hebrew Scriptures; they feared the misuse and misinterpretation of Scripture, especially when applied to teachings regarded as questionable, inimical or foreign to the spirit of Judaism.

Often spoken of as the father of rabbinical Judaism,[4] Rabbi Akiba formulated rules and regulations governing the study and interpretation of the text of Hebrew Scripture. According to some recorded tradition Rabbi Akiba inspired Aquila[5] and Onkelos[6] to undertake the preparation of new Greek and Aramaic versions of the Hebrew Scriptures in conformity with the rabbinic traditions which he represented. These were to replace existing versions in those languages, which were evidently being used with advantage to their cause by men who were then occupied with gaining converts to the messianic and other beliefs of the early Jewish Christians (i. e. the Nazarenes). Such texts of the Bible as were then current and served the theological needs of the Nazarenes were not free of errors and inaccuracies which often distorted the actual meaning of Scripture. Moreover they were frequently employed in "arguments against the Jews by Christians."[7] The Nazarenes "numbered, from the first, a very considerable body of those who were fully persuaded that Jesus was the predicted

---

[2] On the role of the Men of the Great Synagogue in fixing the collection of Hebrew Scripture, see L. Finkelstein, הפרושים ואנשי כנסת הגדולה, New York, 1950, pp. 74 ff.

[3] M. Ab. 1.1.

[4] Yer. Sheḳ. 3.47b; R. H. 1.56d. Cf. L. Ginzberg, in *Jewish Encyclopedia*, New York, 1901, v. 1, p. 304.

[5] See Jerome on Isa. 8:14, Yer. Ḳid. 1.59a.

[6] F. Rosenthal (in בית תלמוד, Wien, 1882, v. 2, p. 280) has shown that the basic layer of Targum Onkelos in all matters of Halakah reflects the opinions of Rabbi Akiba.

[7] Louis Ginzberg, in *Jewish Encyclopedia*, v. 1, p. 306a.

Messiah."[8] In other ways too Rabbi Akiba resisted the impact of Christian ideas upon Jews. His persistent opposition to Christian doctrines is evident in some of his teachings. His opposition to the Christian notions of the sinfulness and depravity of man was vigorous; he derided those who offered as reason for man's sins the supposed innate depravity.[9]

Scholars are generally agreed that the tripartite division of the Hebrew Bible was attained in stages and that in its present form it was already completed at the time when Christianity began to make its inroads into the religious life of the Jews.[10] The admission then of any new book to the collection of Hebrew Scripture would have met

[8] C. C. Torrey, *Our Translated Gospels*, New York, 1936, p. XXXVII.

[9] Ḳid. 81a; cf. F. Rosenthal, *Vier Apokryphische Bücher*, etc., Leipzig, 1885, pp. 95–103, 124–131.

[10] See Robert Pfeiffer, *Introduction to the Old Testament*, New York, 1941, pp. 74 ff., and M. L. Margolis, *The Hebrew Scriptures in the Making*, Philadelphia, 1922. Franz Buhl, *Canon and Text of the Old Testament*, Edinburgh, 1892, p. 25 ff., has shown that the collection of books comprising the Hebrew Bible in its present form was already in existence prior to the destruction of the Temple and that before the first century even that group of books known as the Hagiographa was already in a finally fixed state. The collection of Hebrew Scriptures was already then virtually the same as the one extant now. It was believed to be divinely inspired, and follows the familiar division into the Torah, Prophets and Writings. "The Bible of the Jews in our Lord's time," says Professor George Adam Smith (see his *Modern Criticism and the Preaching of the Old Testament*, New York, 1901, p. 11), "was practically our Old Testament." There is a passage in Josephus (*Against Apion*, H. St. J. Thackeray's translation, 1, 8) which gives early and eloquent testimony to this fact. It reads: "we do not possess myriads of inconsistent books, conflicting with each other. Our books, those which are justly accredited, are but two and twenty, and contain the record of all time. Of these, five are the books of Moses, comprising the laws and the traditional history from the birth of man down to the death of the lawgiver. This period falls only a little short of three thousand years. From the death of Moses until Artaxerxes, who succeeded Xerxes as king of Persia, the prophets subsequent to Moses wrote the history of the events of their own times in thirteen books. The remaining four books contain hymns to God and precepts for the conduct of human life. From Artaxerxes to our own time the complete history has been written, but has not been deemed worthy of equal credit with the earlier records, because of the failure of the exact succession of the prophets." The division of Hebrew Scripture into twenty-two books (with slight variation of enumeration) was followed by several Church Fathers such as Origen and Melito of Sardis (who received it from Jews) and by Jerome, who, however, knew of and mentions the Rabbinical division into twenty-four books. Ben Sira, too, testifies to a threefold division of Hebrew Scripture giving the impression that already in his day the collection of Torah, prophets and other sacred writings was already old, a fact borne out by the Septuagint. The fact that the "canonicity" of Esther and Kohelet was a subject of rabbinic discussion is no argument against the view that the collection

with formidable obstacles.[11] It was then that leading rabbis felt the need of establishing a fixed text of Hebrew Scripture. "At that time two factors contributed to focus attention on the dangers lurking in the variety of textual recensions: the controversy with the Christians and primarily the recognition that the whole system of Jewish faith and practice rested on the authority of the Scriptures — on the very letter of the sacred texts."[12]

Fear that the Gospels, the teachings of which they did not regard as of the authentic Jewish grain, may in the course of time assume a position equal with that held by the Hebrew Bible prompted the early rabbis to discourage their reading and ultimately to deny them a place in the national literature of the Jews by banning them from the body of Jewish literature. Already in the year 90 C. E. leading rabbis meeting at Jamnia declared that "the Gospels and the books of the Minim are not sacred Scripture."[13] They thus denied them a position in Jewish literature equal with that occupied by the books comprising the Hebrew Bible. Evidently they regarded those books

of Hebrew Scripture in its present form was already fixed in the second century when the "outside books" were outlawed.

[11] It is true that the Greek Bible in existence at the time of the rise of Christianity included not only the books extant in the Hebrew Bible, but also some, at least, of those which are now familiar as apocryphal. There is no evidence in rabbinical literature that those books were ever recognized as Scriptural. Some of the Church Fathers, too, refused to treat them as such. In fact those books never came within the purview of Jewish religious authorities in their discussions about books which do or do not "defile the hands."

[12] R. Pfeiffer, *op. cit.*, p. 75.

[13] הגליונים וספרי המינים אינן מטמאות את הידים ספרי בן סירא וכל ספרים שנכתבו מכאן ואילך אינן מטמאין את הידים. Tos. Yad. 2.13. Cf. Tos. Shab. 13 (14) 5 and see G. F. Moore, *Judaism*, Cambridge, 1927, v. 1, p. 243. The process of growth and the formation of a fixed collection of sacred literature was a slow one. The crystallization of Hebrew Scriptures into the now familiar tripartite collection was imperceptibly going on during a period extending over several pre-Christian centuries, with the final results appearing after the test of long usage. In all decisions or discussions of the rabbis declaring "admissibility" into the collection of Hebrew Scripture of one book or the rejection of another the well-known phrase מטמאין את הידים "defiling of the hands" merely expressed conformity to existing custom in the matter. Indeed, the rabbinic discussions as to which books "defile the hands" because of their sacredness are the early references to the acceptance of the books in question as part of the fixed collection of Hebrew Scripture. The discussions were informal ones and tended to strengthen the traditional Jewish attitude to certain biblical books. All references in rabbinical literature to Ezekiel (B. Shab. 13b), Kohelet and Shir ha-Shirim (M. Yad. 3.5) are found not in connection with discussions as to whether or not they should have been given a place in Scripture but rather as to whether they ought to have been included at the time when they were.

as pernicious, certainly erroneous, writings. In spite of this declaration against their authoritative writings the Nazarenes continued to worship with their fellow Jews in the synagogues and to preach messianic doctrines, finding support for them in passages drawn from the Hebrew Bible. In fact they shared a common faith in the messianic teachings of the Hebrew prophets. In this faith there was no line that could be drawn. The major argument of the Nazarenes was always concerning the person of the messiah and never concerning the role he is destined to play. Their claims for the messiahship of Jesus rested upon their own interpretation of scriptural passages. Moreover they insisted upon regarding the destruction of Jerusalem in the year 70 C. E. as divine punishment for the Jewish rejection of their messianic beliefs.

To avoid misuse and misinterpretation of the text of Hebrew Scripture the rabbis formulated rules of interpreting it. Hillel is credited with seven such rules and in the early days of the second century Rabbi Ishmael expanded them into thirteen. By applying the method of interpreting Scripture employed by his teacher Nahum of Gimzo, Rabbi Akiba with great ingenuity detected hidden meanings even in obviously insignificant particles,[14] and declared that "Masorah (i. e. the transmission of the correct Scriptural text) is a fence for the Torah".[15] His rules and regulations for the study and elucidation of the Scriptures contributed in a very large measure to the fixation of the definitive text of the Hebrew Bible.

While accepting the denial to some books of a position in Jewish literature alongside with those occupied by them in the Hebrew Bible, Rabbi Akiba defended Kohelet and Shir ha-Shirim against questions raised as to the validity of their place in Scripture.[16] But to those books which he denied a place in Jewish literature he objected most vigorously and, no doubt, justifiably. They were neither the apocryphal nor the pseudepigraphic books, many of which, while current in his day, were, for one reason or another, not regarded as Scriptural. Rabbi Akiba certainly had no objection to the private reading of apocryphal books as is evident from the fact that he himself made frequent use of Ben Sira,[17] an apocryphal book, rich in ethical teach-

---

[14] See I. H. Weiss, דור דור ודורשיו, Berlin, 1924, v. 2, pp. 101–118; G. F. Moore, *Judaism*, Cambridge, 1930, v. 3, p. 76; L. Ginzberg, *Legends of the Jews*, Philadelphia, 1910–11, v. 2, p. 325 f., v. 3, p. 115. Cf. R. Pfeiffer, *op. cit.*, p. 76.

[15] מסורת סיג לתורה, Ab. 3.18.

[16] M. Yad. 3:5. Cf. Tos. Yad. 2.14.

[17] See W. Bacher, *Agada der Tannaiten*, Strassburg, 1903, v. 1, p. 218 f.; H. Grätz, *Gnosticismus und Judenthum*, Krotoschin, 1846, p. 120.

ings and wisdom, which had been given a place in the early lectionary of the Synagogue. Ben Sira and similar writings were regarded as secular books which might be read with impunity. Ben Sira certainly enjoyed considerable popularity in rabbinic circles. Among leading Amoraim there were men who made advantageous use of its teachings. Thus, for instance, when (Rab) Abba Arika, the founder of the Academy at Sura (d. 247) warned his disciple Hamnunah against unjustifiable asceticism he quoted advice contained in Ben Sira: that, considering the transitoriness of human life,[18] one should not despise the good things of this world. Another eminent Babylonian Amora, Abaye, had occasion to defend Ben Sira by quoting from it several edifying passages and thus arguing that it did not belong to the kind of books which are forbidden, and even persuaded his teacher Rabbi Joseph bar Hama, head of the Academy at Pumbedita, to admit that quotations from it might be used advantageously for homiletical purposes.[19] This and the other familiar apocryphal works could not have been among the "outside books" to which Rabbi Akiba's interdict applies.

When Rabbi Akiba declared that among those who have no part in the World to Come is "he who reads in the outside books,"[20] he merely gave expression to his antagonism not only to books decidedly Christian in character but also to the Nazarenes who cherished such books, and who claimed for them Scriptural standing and authority. Originally written in Aramaic, those books have come down among the

---

[18] 'Er. 54a.

[19] Sanh. 100b.

[20] הקורא בספרים החיצונים . . . אין לו חלק לעולם הבא, Sanh. 10.1, Y. Sanh. 10.1, 28a; B. Sanh. 100b identifies "outside books" as "books of the Minim," see *Encyclopaedia Judaica*, Berlin, 1931, v. 7, col. 85. "It is true, the Babylonian Talmud, (Sanh. 100b) explains ספרים החיצונים by ספרי מינים 'heretical books,' but the Palestinian Talmud, Sanh. X, 28a, which is by far a safer guide in historical or linguistic matters than the Babli, quite explicitly states that Ben Sira is included among the ספרים החיצונים and thus clearly takes ס' החיצונים to mean books 'outside of the Canon', [i. e. national Jewish literature] though not of a heretical character" (Louis Ginzberg, in *Journal of Biblical Literature*, 1922, v. 41, p. 126). Rabbi Akiba's damnatory sentence is probably aimed at reading from such books in the Synagogue, הקורא בהם בצבור. See Nachman Krochmal, מורה נבוכי הזמן, in כתבי נחמן קרוכמאל, ed. S. Rawidowicz, Berlin, 1924, p. 119 f. Professor Solomon Zeitlin has convincingly shown (in *Proceedings of the American Academy for Jewish Research*, New York, 1933, v. 3, p. 124 ff.) that בקשו לגנוז often taken as a technical term "sought to declare uncanonical" should be rendered "sought to store away from public reading, so as not to be studied and interpreted in the academies." Cf. my *On the Apocalyptic in Judaism*, Philadelphia, 1952, p. 85.

essential portions of the Gospels.[21] They were the "outside books" upon which the Nazarenes depended for the dissemination of their teachings. In his attitude to the Nazarenes and to such of their books for which they claimed Scriptural standing Rabbi Akiba was not alone; his attitude was shared by many of the early rabbis. A Palestinian sage of a later day gave expression to it by declaring that "whoever brings together in his house more than twenty-four (Scriptural) books introduces confusion."[22] They regarded the teachings contained in the books of the Nazarenes as injurious to the spirit and basic doctrines of Judaism.

No doubt there were extraordinary circumstances and very potent reasons, political and religious, for the stand which Rabbi Akiba had taken against the "outside books." Rabbi Akiba himself, as is well-known, "took a leading part in the war of Bar Kokba, which was entirely a messianic effort inspired by apocalyptic ideas of which Akiba himself was the most distinguished preacher."[23] He could not possibly have objected to books containing such ideas. Indeed, it is hardly conceivable that any of the Tannaim could have taken such violent exception to the teachings of the Jewish apocalyptic books current in their day. Such works as the Apocalypse of Baruch and the Apocalypse of Ezra are rich in ethical and religious teachings;[24] they are certainly free of what could be regarded as heretical. One is therefore entirely at a loss to understand the reasons that prompted so competent and brilliant a scholar as Professor Charles C. Torrey to advance the opinion,[25] without the slightest proof to justify it, that in the days of Akiba all of "the extra-canonical [i. e. the apocryphal and pseudepigraphic] writings in Hebrew or Aramaic, disappeared absolutely and finally," and "that all the extra-canonical Scriptures existing in either Aramaic or Hebrew were systematically destroyed by official Jewish order near the end of the first century C. E." No record of such an order is extant.

The Nazarenes and their teachings presented a stumbling block, if

---

[21] A very stimulating discussion of the "Aramaic Gospels in the Synagogue" is offered by Professor C. C. Torrey in his *Documents of the Primitive Church*, New York, 1941, pp. 90–111.

[22] Koh. Rab. 116a: ‏כל המכניס בתוך ביתו יותר מכ'ד ספרים מהומה הוא מכניס בביתו.

[23] T. R. Herford, *The Pharisees*, New York, 1924, p. 179.

[24] See Joseph Klausner, *Jesus of Nazareth*, New York, 1925, p. 72. Cf. his article on the apocryphal and pseudepigraphic books in ‏אוצר היהדות, חוברת לדוגמא, Warsaw, 1906, pp. 95–96.

[25] See his "The Hebrew of the Geniza Sirach," in *Alexander Marx Jubilee Volume*, New York, 1950, English Section, p. 598.

not an affront, even a challenge to the advancement of the political and religious aspirations of the Jews in Palestine living under Roman oppression. The Jews were then a vassal people; they had been subjected successively to the Achaemenides (with a Persian governor in Palestine), the Seleucids and the Romans. Under the definite promise of God through his prophets, they were accustomed to look eagerly for the day when they should proclaim a king of their own, rise in successful rebellion and drive the foreign oppressors out of the holy city. Much of their spiritual life revolved around this hope. Now under the rule of Hadrian the persecution of the Jews was aimed at the utter destruction of their spiritual life.[26] Jewish religious practices were forbidden under severe penalties and the direst punishment awaited those who occupied themselves with the study of Torah.[27] Rabbi Akiba was also jealous for the preservation of the purity of the idea of the oneness of God;[28] to keep the Jewish conception of God free from the taint of Christian ideas. The Nazarenes accepting Jesus of Nazareth as the long-awaited messiah had claimed divine inspiration for their Gospels (Mark, Matthew and John) then current in Aramaic.[29] When fear arose that these books were aspiring to a place equal with the writings of the Hebrew prophets and especially with the books of Ezekiel and Daniel, so rich in apocalyptic ideas,[30] Rabbi Akiba and his circle became apprehensive. Seeing that the teachings contained in them were rapidly gaining followers and that the ranks of the Nazarenes were being swelled by the influx of many of the common people, Rabbi Akiba denounced those who indulged in the reading and study of "outside books." Rabbi Yohanan

[26] The late Prof. Max Radin's (*The Jews Among the Greeks and Romans*, Philadelphia, 1915, p. 343) effort to absolve Hadrian of the guilt of having attempted "to root out Judaism as Antiochus had done," found no acceptance in the circles of the learned.

[27] For a description of the extent to which Jewish observances were prohibited by Hadrian see H. Grätz, *Geschichte der Juden*, v. 4, Leipzig, 1908, 4th ed., ed. by S. Horovitz, pp. 135–167.

[28] On the resistance to Dualism in Judaism see G. F. Moore, *op. cit.*, v. 1, p. 364 f., and v. 3, p. 115, note 110.

[29] See G. F. Moore, *op. cit.*, v. 1, pp. 184 f., 189 and 244. The vernacular of Palestine was then Aramaic. Not only the Gospels but also the classical apocalyptic works of that day were written in that language. Incidentally, the book of Job, too, was already then available in Aramaic. See Tosefta, Shab., c. 14. Cf. F. Rosenthal, *op. cit.*, p. 11 and in בית תלמוד, Wien, 1882, v. 2, p. 268 ff., and A. Berliner, *Targum Onkeles*, Berlin, 1882, v. 2, p. 91.

[30] Certainly the Revelation of John lays claim to "prophecy," both at the beginning (1.3) and at the end (22.7 ff.). See Charles C. Torrey, *Documents*, etc., pp. 165–173 and 225–244.

ben Zakkai had performed a similar act in an earlier day when he declared that "the Gospels and the books of the Minim[31] do not defile the hands" i. e., they are not spritural in character.[32] The Nazarenes and their books became objectionable not so much because of their belief about the role of Jesus but because of their persistent attempt to exalt him to a position almost equal with that of God.[33] While in the days of Rabbi Yohanan ben Zakkai the early teachings of the Nazarenes were apparently harmless they evidently became quite dangerous in the days of Rabbi Akiba. In all likelihood Rabbi Akiba and his circle regarded the teachings of the Christian books current in their day about the 'divinity' of Jesus of Nazareth, as a serious infringement of the belief in the Divine Unity, the idea of the One Sole God, Supreme and Undivided, to which Jews have always clung most tenaciously.

The close of the first century found the Jews and the Nazarenes going further and further apart. The 'anathema' on the Nazarenes pronounced about the year 80 by Rabban Gamaliel applies also to any one who ventures to indulge in the reading or studying of their books.[34] It at once created a strained relationship between the Jews and the Nazarenes. The fall of Jerusalem had given a new impetus to the apocalyptic writings in Judaism. Stirring men's imagination and whipping them up to action, their teachings assumed significance; they lent new messianic inspiration to various ventures, even to so daring an uprising as that of Simon Bar Kokba and they touched the life of the Jews in other ways as well. The Jews had been goaded by Hadrianic edicts of violence and oppression into open revolt. With a desperate but ill-fated heroism Bar Kokba launched a struggle for the

---

[31] Whenever Minim is mentioned in early rabbinical texts, it usually refers to the early Jewish Christians, the Nazarenes. Among the Church Fathers Epiphanius (4th cent.), bishop of the Oriental Church who was a native of Palestine, employed Nazarenes as the designation of the Jewish-Christians whom the Palestinian rabbis called Minim and Jerome likens the Nazarenes to the Minim, both the former and the latter being Jewish-Christians. T. R. Herford discusses the term Minim in his *Christianity in Talmud and Midrash*, London, 1903, pp. 97-341 and 361-397, in which he disposes of Moritz Friedländer's theory that Minim refers to the Gnostics. Cf. W. Bacher's review of the book in *Jewish Quarterly Review*, London, 1904-1905, v. 17, pp. 171-183 and G. F. Moore, *op. cit.*, v. 3, p. 68 f. "On the meaning of Minim" is the title of another study by T. R. Herford, in *Jewish Studies* in memory of George Alexander Kohut, New York, 1935, pp. 359-369, in which he points out the few exceptional instances in which Minim does not refer to Jewish-Christians.

[32] See above note 5.

[33] T. R. Herford, in *Jewish Studies*, p. 368.

[34] See below note 45.

attainment of political independence and for religious freedom similar
to the Maccabean revolt in earlier days. He led his people to war on
the all-conquering power of the Roman empire. It was a very determined effort on the part of the Jews to regain their freedom. The
occasion for the uprising is variously given but, in the eyes of those
that fought in it, the struggle was vastly more than an attempt to
shake off a foreign yoke. This is shown by the messiahship to which
Bar Kokba openly laid claim and for which he had the support of the
passionate Rabbi Akiba.[35] Bar Kokba was a revolutionary influenced
by apocalyptic ideas and hopes; he was also a soldier and strategist
whose early victories aroused wild enthusiasm among the people.
Rabbi Akiba had enormous faith in him; he saw in him not only a
second Maccabee but the promised Messiah[36] as well. Inspired by
apocalyptic hopes and convinced that the advent of the Messiah was
at hand, Rabbi Akiba could not resist the contagious influence of
Messianism. When he saw the Roman legions yield to Bar Kokba's
forces, much hope blossomed in his heart. "Yet once, it is a little
while," he quoted an apocalyptic passage from the prophet Haggai
(2.6), "and I will shake the heavens and the earth, and the sea, and
the dry land."[37]

The uprising of Bar Kokba in the days of Hadrian gained the
support not only of Rabbi Akiba, who saw in him the deliverer, but
of many other leaders in Jewry including Elazar of Modi'im. Inspired
by apocalyptic teachings, they were all carried away by national
passion and aspirations. From every corner of Palestine and from
other countries too Jews flocked to Bar Kokba's standard. Even
Samaritans made common cause with them: only the Nazarenes held
aloof; they were not willing to join the forces which Bar Kokba led
against the Roman legions. The Jews fought their enemy by themselves. The Nazarenes were thus disloyal to the Jewish national cause.
Regarding them as blasphemous and as spies and therefore guilty of
treason, Bar Kokba made them pay dearly. Because they refused
to take part in the national war — they were only idle onlookers at
the fearful spectacle — he displayed considerable hostility against

---

[35] Y. Ta'an. 4.7; Ekah Rab. 2.1. The messianic claims of Bar Kokba were
resented by the rabbis. For his pretentious claim to messiahship he was executed.
When "he said to the rabbis 'I am Messiah,' they answered him, 'It is written of
Messiah that he discerns and judges; let us see if he can do so.' When they found
this beyond his power they put him to death." Sanh. 93b; see S. Yeivin's admirable
study מלחמת בר-כוכבא, Jerusalem, 1946.

[36] Y. Ta'an. 4.68d.

[37] Sanh. 97b. Cf. Louis Finkelstein, *Akiba*, New York, 1936, p. 269.

them. Gradually his hatred for them increased and many of them
were put to death. Those who survived were, for one reason or another,
forced to withdraw gradually from the Jewish community.

It is not unlikely that the Nazarenes were guided by a strong
religious or ethical reason for their determination not to share in the
Bar Kokba uprising against the Romans. Because of the emphasis
their teachings gave to the idea of resisting evil the Nazarenes did not
believe that fighting for freedom and independence of the nation
against the religious, political and economic oppression of Rome was
a worthy cause.[38] It was in desperate revolt against such oppression
that the Bar Kokba uprising was launched. The Nazarenes, guided
by the Gospel teaching: "give unto Caesar that which is Caesar's,
and unto God that which is God's," refused to lend a helping hand in
the venture. Such teachings as "resist no evil" and when one is
struck on the left cheek — to retaliate by offering the right cheek
also (Matthew 5:39–48) are, to say the least, impractical, certainly
unworkable. Moreover, they are out of harmony with the principle
of absolute justice stressed so strongly in the teachings of Judaism.
Such teachings helped to justify the aloofness of the Nazarenes from
the cause championed by Bar Kokba. In these and in some other
teachings of the Gospels Rabbi Akiba and his colleagues saw grave
danger lurking for Judaism, certainly for the Jewish people; they saw
in them the negation of Jewish national life and the ultimate destruction of the Jewish state. Such teachings were not only inconsistent
with sound Jewish ethical and legal doctrine but, inasmuch as they
opposed the struggle against evil, they were also incompatible with the
best interests of the Jewish people. Writings containing such teachings[39] are altogether out of place in a body of literature which presents
the authentic doctrine and the record of the historical experience of
the nation. No wonder Rabbi Akiba declared them to be "outside
books," that is books not legitimately belonging within but standing
outside of the body of Jewish literature. Moreover those who adhered
to the teachings they contain were to be regarded as standing outside
of the pale of Judaism. In the circumstances it is not at all surprising
to find that just as the Nazarenes were ultimately completely removed
from the body of Israel so were their books entirely eliminated from

[38] See Kirsopp Lake and F. J. Foakes Jackson, *Beginnings of Christianity*,
London, 1920, v. 1, pp. 318–320.

[39] On points of opposition between Judaism and the teachings of Jesus as reported
in the Gospels see Joseph Klausner, *Jesus*, pp. 369–376 and especially Gerald Fried-
laender, *Jewish Sources of the Sermon on the Mount*, London, 1911.

the body of the national Jewish literature. Any Jew who read them *aloud*[40] is assured of no share in the World to Come. Rabbi Akiba saw in them the negation of every thing that tended to vitalize Jewish life. As Dr. Joseph Klausner has so well put it:[41] "The Judaism of that time, however, had no other aim than to save the tiny nation, the guardian of great ideals, from sinking into the broad sea of heathen culture and enable it, slowly and gradually, to realize the moral teaching of the Prophets in *civil life* and in the *present world* of the Jewish state and nation." Any group within Jewry that then advocated teachings and ideas which tended to counteract the efforts of patriotic Jews to attain the desired end was a cancer on the body of Israel.

Before the Bar Kokba uprising the Nazarenes were regarded as good and loyal Jews; their faith was that of contemporary Judaism, except in the matter of belief as to the advent of the messiah. The Gospel in their hands constituted an instrument designed to bring about the acceptance by the Jews of the belief that Jesus of Nazareth was the promised messiah. It is quite understandable, indeed, that they could not accept the messianic claims made for Bar Kokba, who, according to Rabbi Akiba was the "star out of Jacob" of Balaam's prophecy (Num. 24:17), a militant messiah who should triumph over Edom.[42] The war lasted three years and a half and ended in bloody failure in 134/135 with the fall of Bether, a few miles from Jerusalem. The disillusion was stunning. The Nazarenes regarded the disastrous end of the Bar Kokba uprising as a judgment on the Jews for their rejection of the messianic claims made for Jesus. There were Jews to whom this view was not altogether without merit but Rabbi Akiba and his colleagues sensed danger in it. Regarding it as a serious threat to the destiny of the Jews and of Judaism, they resented it. The tide of indignation was now rising high against the Nazarenes. Their role in the Jewish community was now looked upon with definite disapproval and with increasing apprehension. Rabbi Akiba and his followers sought appropriate means to diminish whatever influence the Nazarenes[43] and their teachings still wielded, thus demonstrating

---

[40] Sanh. 10.1; B. Sanh. 100b; Y. Sanh. 10.28a in which passage קורא is to be explained according to Ḳid. 49a: "He who reads *aloud* in the Synagogue from 'outside books'," etc. See Louis Ginzberg, *Journal of Biblical Literature*, 1922, v. 41, p. 126 and Solomon Zeitlin, in *Jewish Quarterly Review*, 1947, v. 37, pp. 219 ff.

[41] *Op. cit.*, p. 376.

[42] Num. 24:17–19. The point lies in verse 18, Edom (Rome) shall be conquered, etc.

[43] See G. F. Moore, *op. cit.*, v. 1, p. 243 f., cf. p. 90 f.

that it was hardly possible for them to maintain that as Jews they can also be Christians at the same time. The breach became conspicuous. Rabbi Akiba endeavored to bring about a severance in whatever connection there still existed between the Jews and the Nazarenes. He banned them from the Jewish community and accompanied that act with the rejection of their books as well; their books were now "outside books."

There is no doubt that in the days of Rabbi Akiba the circulation of Christian writings in Hebrew or Aramaic became an increasing menace to the religious teachings of Judaism. An attitude of toleration maintained heretofore toward the Nazarenes and their teachings was now abandoned. Not alone were they ousted from the Jewish community but their books and the teachings they contained were likewise repudiated. In maintaining that those who indulge in the reading of "outside books" have no portion in the World to Come Rabbi Akiba made a significant contribution to the various measures then taken by authoritative Jewish leaders to bring about "the final separation of the Nazarenes from the rest of the Jews. Hitherto these 'disciples of Jesus the Nazarene' had been a conventicle within the synagogue, rather than a sect."[44] Bar Kokba and Rabbi Akiba, each one in his own way, effected the complete break of the Nazarenes from Judaism. No alternative was now open to them but to merge themselves into the Christian body and thus seal their complete severance from the Jews and from Judaism.

Indeed, long before this had occurred Jewish leaders were very apprehensive of the position the Nazarenes occupied in the community of Israel. There was a growing feeling against them even prior to the Bar Kokba uprising. So strong was that feeling that it became necessary to warn the people against the role the Nazarenes and their teachings played. Rabbi Samuel the younger, at the request of Rabbi Gamaliel II, had composed a prayer against the Sadducees, but before long it was employed against the Nazarenes and was given a place in the Prayer Book.[45] Directed primarily against the

---

[44] *Ibid.*, p. 90.

[45] ת"ר . . . אמר להם רבן גמליאל, כלום יש אדם שיודע לתקן ברכת הצדוקים. עמד שמואל הקטן ותקנה. Ber. 28b; Meg. 17b; Y. Ber. 4.3. It refers to the Birkat ha-Minim, the twelfth of the Eighteen Benedictions, to the use of which Epiphanius (Haer. 29.9) and Jerome (on Isa. 5:18 f.; 49:7; 52:4 f.) refer; in both the Nazarenes are specifically named. The text from the Genizah which Schechter published (*Jewish Quarterly Review*, London, 1898, v. 10, pp. 654–659) is directed against "the Notzerim and the Minim," which Marcel Simon (*Verus Israel*, Paris, 1948, p. 236) translated by "the Nazarenes and the other Minim." In the wording of the prayer as it is now familiar

Minim[46] within the Synagogue, the insertion of that prayer in the Jewish liturgy was one of the means designed to effect the complete severance of the Nazarenes from Judaism.[47] The rabbis sought protection against heterodox manifestations in the Synagogue. The prayer "was aimed at the Judeo-Christians who during the first half of the Second Century C. E. stood up against the Synagogue."[48] .

It served as an effective measure in counteracting the influence of the teachings and practices of the "new and even more dangerous enemies of official Judaism [who] engaged in the polemical — and liturgical — preoccupations. At the same time it was necessary to remove from the Synagogue the Judeo-Christians who may have slipped in among the faithful and whose propaganda may have been feared."[49] It was evidently intended to exclude the Nazarenes from playing any role in the Synagogue. No longer was one of their ranks able to lead Jews in congregational worship for he could not very well recite a prayer containing an imprecatory phrase aimed at him and his fellow Nazarenes while the worshippers approvingly answer Amen. Thus the Nazarenes and their books were henceforth excluded from the Congregation of Israel. Their primary books were their "Gospels," for which they had claimed a position of recognition similar to that given to the books of the Hebrew Bible.[50] Heretofore they, like any

ולמלשינים is substituted for מינים. The text of the prayer in current prayer books has the appearance of having been modified more than once in the course of centuries and adapted to new conditions and surroundings (see S. Baer, *Abodat Yisrael*, p. 93 f.; Singer, *Authorized Daily Prayer Book*, p. 48 with I. Abrahams' note, p. LXIV f. Cf. G. F. Moore, *op. cit.*, v. 1, p. 292 and v. 3, p. 97, note 68 and S. Krauss, "Imprecations against the *Minim* in the Synagogue," in *Jewish Quarterly Review*, April, 1897, v. 9, pp. 515–518.

[46] The assertion, made first by Justin Martyr, that it represents an imprecation against Christians in general is without foundation in fact. See M. Joel, *Blicke in die Religionsgeschichte*, Breslau, 1880, v. 1, pp. 26, 29; H. Grätz, *Geschichte*, v. 4, note 11.

[47] See I. Elbogen, *Der Juedische Gottesdienst*, etc., Leipzig, 1913, p. 36 ff.

[48] M. Liber, *Jewish Quarterly Review*, April, 1950, v. 40, p. 349.

[49] *Ibid.*, p. 349.

[50] In rabbinical literature the Gospels are usually spoken of as הגליונים with the definite article, the name by which they were known to such rabbis as Tarfon, Ishmael and Jose the Galilean, who flourished in the period between the destruction of the Temple and the Hadrianic war; they were called *evangelion* and by this name or punning distortions of it (עון גליון, און גליון, גליון, Shab. 116a). See H. Grätz, *Geschichte der Juden*, 5ed. ed. by M. Brann, Leipzig, 1906, v. 3², p. 759. For other explanations of the term see G. F. Moore, *Judaism*, v. 3, p. 67. Cf. S. Krauss, *Griechische und Lateinische Lehnwörter im Talmud*, Berlin, 1898–99, v. 2, p. 21. For parallels see H. L. Strack and Paul Billerbeck, *Kommentar zum Neuen Testament aus Talmud und Midrasch*, München, 1926, v. 3, p. 11. Strack does not accept the suggestion

other Jews, were permitted to share in all religious and communal functions in the Jewish community. It was, however, in the days of Akiba after the Bar Kokba uprising and the war under Hadrian that the separation of the Nazarenes from the Jewish community and the exclusion of their books from Jewish literature was completely effected. But the struggle against those books and the teachings they contained was a long one. It began in an earlier day; perhaps even earlier than the war under Titus, not possibly more than a decade or two later.[51] When Rabbi Yohanan ben Zakkai declared that "the gilyonim and the writings of Minim[52] do not defile the hands"[53] he denied their claim to Scriptural status as he did when he declared: "the writings of Ben Sira and whatever books have been written since his time, do not defile the hands."[54]

Circumstances were such as to have prompted Rabbi Yohanan ben Zakkai to issue his mild yet decisive declaration against the literature of the Nazarenes. Like Rabbi Akiba, in a later day, he too was concerned with the preservation of the religion of Israel in its purity and with maintaining its authority as derived from Hebrew Scripture. The encroachment of other writings upon its sphere of influence constituted a threat to the future of Judaism. His declaration was aimed at diverting it and every effort was exerted to prevent the books of the Nazarenes from acquiring Scriptural status. Any attempt to gain for them such recognition was vigorously resisted. "It was a literary age in Palestine and a wide-awake literary people, but this was not all. The Israelites were 'a people of the Book' (to use Mohammed's term); meaning, that their faith was based on a

that גליונים in Y. Shab. 15.5 refers to Evangelion (W. Bacher, *Agada der Tannaiten*, Strassburg, 1890, v. 2, p. 258). He takes the Talmudic formula הגליונים וספרי המינים אינן מטמאות את הידיים (Shab. 116a) to mean that the books of the *Minim* are to be treated like the *gilyonim*, to which also applies the injunction that they be burned etc., etc. Cf. J. Jocz, *The Jewish People and Jesus Christ*, London, 1949, pp. 332, 374 and 376. Cf. above Note 13.

[51] C. C. Torrey, *Our Translated Gospels*, etc., p. XL.

[52] When the phrase ספרי המינים is associated with הגליונים it designates or embraces all Christian writings which were known and acknowledged to be authoritative works of the Nazarenes. (See G. F. Moore in *Essays in Modern Theology and related subjects* etc., New York, 1911, p. 112 f.) "The Gilyonim and the books of the Minim were a well-known group: Aramaic writings which had been put forth with the claim to prophetic inspiration, Messianic scriptures designed to show a new era of divine revelation and to supplement the older sacred books of Israel." (C. C. Torrey, *Documents of the Primitive Church*, New York, 1941, p. 111).

[53] "Do not defile the hands" is a technical phrase the usage of which is equivalent to "are not holy scripture." See above note 13.

[54] Tosefta, Yad. 2.13, ed. Zuckermandl-Lieberman, p. 683.

divine revelation which was written down."[55] The Nazarenes wanted
to enlarge upon this record of revelation by adding to it "their 'Gospel'
for which they evidently claimed the character of sacred Scripture."[56]
This claim they pressed with vigor. Never wavering in their endeavors
to resist the efforts of infusing Judaism with the teachings of the
Nazarenes, the rabbis took appropriate measures to outlaw them and
their books. To counteract the strong impression which the Nazarene
Gospels were making and to discourage frequent use of their teachings,
Rabbi Akiba declared them to be "outside books" (ספרים חיצונים) that
is, the kind of books which were not indigenous to the spirit of the
national literature of the Jews; they were therefore not to be given
a place of recognition either in the Synagogue for public reading or
in the school for study. His declaration served a warning that any
one reading them will thereby be deprived of a portion in the World
to Come. Not the Jewish apocalyptic books but the Gospels of the
Nazarenes and other early Christian writings fell under his ban. It
seems that in spite of Rabbi Yohanan ben Zakkai's declaration against
them and Rabbi Gamaliel's prayer, which held no hopes for the
Minim, the Nazarene writings continued to be read by Jews until
the time when, under the authoritative leadership of Rabbi Akiba,
the Nazarenes were definitely thrust out of the Jewish community
and their literature "by which many a teacher was fascinated condemned exactly as were their cures in the name of the Nazarene."[57]
If, as it is assumed, the elimination of "outside books" from the body
of Jewish literature was prompted by the desire to remove every
vestige of early Christian influence upon Jews it certainly did not
concern itself with the apocalyptic books, for they were not used by
Christians in the advancement of their cause. The Hebrew Bible and
the Gospels served their need adequately. In fact there is no record
of early Christians in the Jewish community ever having drawn upon
the apocryphal, especially the apocalyptic, books for "proof" in
support of their teachings. The "outside books" to which Rabbi Akiba
and other rabbis took such vigorous exception were no other than the
Gospels. Whatever else was included in the "outside books" the
apocalyptic writings certainly formed no part of it.

The assumption that the term "outside books" was applied by
Rabbi Akiba to the Jewish apocalyptic books current in his day is
not well founded. It can not gain for itself unqualified acceptance.

[55] C. C. Torrey, *ibid.*, p. 95 f.

[56] G. F. Moore, *Judaism*, v. 1, p. 244.

[57] M. L. Margolis, *The Hebrew Scriptures in the Making*; cf. G. F. Moore, *Judaism*, v. 2, p. 388, and v. 3, p. 71.

It has been used as an argument to support the contention that the
teachings contained in the Jewish apocalyptic writings have exerted
no influence upon Judaism.[58] Whatever merit this argument has,
it tends, in a measure, to strengthen the widespread assumption that
the early rabbinical writings reveal best the essential teachings and
spirit of Judaism in the days of the Second Commonwealth. The
assumption that Rabbi Akiba, the most eminent of the Tannaim,
speaks of them as "outside books" is not tenable. No convincing
proof in support of it has thus far been adduced from early rabbinic
texts or from any other trustworthy source. The fact that none of
the known early Jewish apocalyptic works is mentioned in early
rabbinic literature has no bearing whatsoever on the meaning of the
term "outside books" as employed by Rabbi Akiba.[59]

Strong as the feeling of the Jewish sages was against the Nazarenes
it was twice as strong against their books. This is apparent from a
rabbinic discussion as to books which may be rescued from fire on the
Sabbath; the Gospels are excluded though they contain the name of
God. As to what things may be rescued from burning on Sabbath,
the general rule is, that it is not lawful to carry out anything from a
building on that day. The Sacred Scriptures which contain the names
of God and other references to the deity, form an exception: they may
be rescued. In this connection the Christian books come up for
consideration, since they too contain the Holy Names. The decision
is: "The Gospels and the books of the Minim[60] are not to be saved;
they are to be allowed to burn where they are, names of God and
all."[61] This decision represents the opinion of Rabbi Tarfon. Though
he often engaged in halakic controversies with Rabbi Akiba he

[58] See, for instance, Solomon Schechter, *Some Aspects of Rabbinic Theology*,
New York, 1909, Preface, p. IX f.

[59] The arguments of H. Grätz (*Monatsschrift für Geschichte und Wissenschaft
des Judenthums*, 1886, v. 35, p. 285 ff.) against the reading of the passage M. Sanh.
10.1; Sanh. 100b and Y. Sanh. 28a are quite cogent. By combining it with Tos.
Yad. 2.13, ed. Zuckermandl, p. 683, 10 he constructs it to read: "Rabbi Akiba said:
Whoever reads in the outside (חיצונים) i. e., Nazarene writings (cf. Rabbinovicz,
דקדוקי סופרים) has no share in the World to Come. On the other hand, books, like
Ben Sira, Ben Laanah and other such which were written after the age of the prophets
has been concluded (מכאן ואילך) may be read just like one reads a letter" etc. But
see M. Joel, *Blicke in die Religionsgeschichte*, 1880, v. 1, p. 73 ff., who incidentally
identifies בן סטרא with Christian writings.

[60] הגליונים וספרי מינין אין מצילין אותן מפני הדליקה בשבת, Tos. Shab. 13 (14).5 and
parallels.

[61] Tos. Yad. 2.13 ed. Zuckermandl-Lieberman, p. 683, reports that Rabbi Jose
the Galilean (ca. 110) held that if the burning of the Gilyonim takes place on a
week day the names (האזכרות) of God may be cut out and stored away (וגונז).

evidently shared his attitude to the Nazarenes and to their books. So intense was Rabbi Tarfon's feeling about their books that he had no scruples against their destruction even though the name of God frequently occurs in them.[62] Rabbi Ishmael, too, suggested that the Gospels and the books of the Nazarenes be not saved from burning because they cast enmity, hatred and strife between Israel and their heavenly father.

It is not likely that Rabbi Akiba's interdict against "outside books" was aimed at the apocryphal books, especially at those of an apocalyptic character, because not only was Rabbi Akiba himself familiar with the nature of the apocalyptic, he was often under its spell. His famous visit to Paradise,[63] whatever it was, had been inspired by apocalyptic teachings. The role he played in the uprising of Bar Kokba was a significant one; in its messianic character it was likewise inspired by apocalyptic teachings. The examples cited in connection with the "outside books" in the passage attributed to Rabbi Akiba are certainly not taken from the now extant Jewish apocalyptic writings which were current in his day. Such titles as Ben-Laanah and Homerus are clearly those of works which are not familiar in Jewish literature. Moses Maimonides[64] seems to imply that Rabbi Akiba used the term "outside books" as applicable to idolatrous, "non-Jewish" writings. He regarded the Gospels as such. It certainly does not apply to any of those works now considered as early Jewish apocalyptic writings. Many a scholar has endeavored to identify Rabbi Akiba's "outside books" with apocryphal writings not in the collection of Hebrew Scriptures, especially such as were popular, like the Wisdom of Ben Sira.[65] Professor Louis Ginzberg is among the more recent ones to do so. From the words of Rabbi Joseph bar Hiyya,[66] a learned Babylonian Amora of the early fourth century, and in the light of other considerations Professor Ginzberg concluded that "not the reading of the Apocrypha was prohibited by Rabbi Akiba, but their use in the Synagogue and houses of study for public service or instruction."[67] In this view Professor Ginzberg was already

[62] Shab. 116a.
[63] Ḥag. 14b.
[64] Yad. הלכות עבודה זרה, 2.2.
[65] L. Ginzberg, in *Journal of Biblical Literature*, 1922, v. 41, p. 129.
[66] Sanh. 100b. It seems that according to Rabbi Joseph bar Ḥiyya, the prohibition against the reading of "outside books" was still effective in his day and that it had been instituted by Rabbi Akiba and his associates. See Louis Ginzberg, *ibid.*, and C. C. Torrey, *Documents*, etc., p. 109, and in *Alexander Marx Jubilee Volume*, English Section, p. 597 ff.
[67] *Op. cit.*, p. 129.

anticipated by Nachman Krochmal.[68] They were not to be read in public and verses from them were not to be expounded publicly by preachers. Moreover they were not to be drawn upon for authoritative support of religious opinions, beliefs and practices as is often done with Scriptural passages. This makes sense and certainly holds true of books not in the recognized collection of Hebrew Scriptures for which Scriptural standing was claimed. There is no evidence to show that such claim was ever made in Jewry for either the books of the Apocrypha or for the early Jewish apocalyptic writings. At any rate rabbinical literature fails to reveal such evidence. On the other hand the Minim (Nazarenes) did treat their scriptures (gospels) as if they were equal with any or all that comprise the Hebrew Bible and did draw upon them for authoritative support of their beliefs in certain messianic ideas which did not conform to those then held by the rank and file of Jewry. Politically and religiously the "outside books" and their sponsors constituted a veritable threat to the integrity of Judaism and to the welfare of Jewry. Incompatible with the theological doctrines of Judaism, their teachings were subversive of the national and religious aspirations of the Jewish people. They, therefore, had to be removed from the body of Israel's literature; they are "outside books" and do not form an integral part of the national literature of the Jews. This separation was accomplished by Rabbi Akiba's denial of a portion in the World to Come to those in the Jewish Community who indulge in the reading and study of the Gospels.

Some years ago Professor George F. Moore advanced the notion that the interdict of Rabbi Akiba against those who read "outside books" was aimed at the elimination of the reading *in private* of heretical books and especially of Christian authoritative writings current in his day. In a remarkable essay,[69] he endeavored to prove that Rabbi Akiba used the term "outside books" as a designation for heretical, in particular, the early Christian writings. While in a general way he was right in identifying the type of literature Rabbi Akiba had in mind, Professor Moore was wrong in the assumption that the intention of the interdict was to discourage their reading *in private*. As already indicated above, this was not the case, Rabbi Akiba's objective was a double one: prevent the Christian writings from gaining a place of recognition in the national literature of the Jews

---

[68] הקורא בספרים החיצונים, Sanh. 11.1 is explained by him in the light of קורין in Shab. 16.1: הק״ד כמו מכחוב' ראיה מהם כמו כמו מביא ומביא פסוקיהם ודורש בצבור בהם הקורא. See N. Krochmal, *op. cit.*, p. 119 f.

[69] In *Essays in Modern Theology and Related Subjects* gathered . . . as a testimonial to Charles Augustus Briggs, New York, 1911, pp. 99–125.

and to deny the teachings they contain such Scriptural authority as their followers claimed for them. This was accomplished not only by discouraging their reading in private but also by prohibiting their use in the Synagogue and in the Jewish religious schools.

The conclusion attained by Professor Moore was based on a Talmudic passage in which, as Professor Ginzberg has well pointed out, he ventured to introduce rather unnecessarily a slight emendation and thus was able to translate it: "He who reads in the arch-heretical books such as the books of Ben-Laanah[70] (Gospels) and the books of the heretics[71] (Christians). But as for the books of Ben-Sira and all books that have been written since his time, he who reads in them is as one who reads in a letter." The weakness inherent in Professor Moore's handling of this text has been shown in Professor Ginzberg's analysis of it. In questioning the validity of Moore's inference from the Tannaitic pronouncement against the Gospels and Ben Sira, Professor Ginzberg offered conjectures of his own and corrected some details in Moore's interpretation of several phrases in the Talmudic passage.[72] Moreover, he also demonstrated that "an interdict against the private reading of heretical books by Rabbi Akiba is not very likely," and that the phrase ספרים חיצונים in the sense of "heretical books" is hardly possible in Talmudic Hebrew.[73] The Gospels were not heretical books; they were declared to be "outside books," i. e. foreign to the character and content of the Jewish Scriptures. They are books outside the pale not merely of Scripture but of Judaism as well.

An entirely new, but not quite convincing explanation of the circumstances which led to Rabbi Akiba's interdict is offered by A. Marmorstein who suggested that, in all likelihood, it was directed against dualists who believed in two gods, for instance Heaven and Earth.[74] This explanation implies that Rabbi Akiba was very much

---

[70] In Koh. Rab. on Eccl. 12:12, in place of Ben Laanah the name is given as Ben Tagla. Neither of these names is mentioned elsewhere in rabbinical literature.

[71] Assuming that המירם is a scribal error for המינים = Christians.

[72] In *Journal of Biblical Literature*, 1922, v. 41, p. 120 ff.

[73] *Ibid.*, p. 130. C. C. Torrey has pointed out (in his *Documents*, etc., p. 94) that while in general terms Professor Moore (*Judaism*, v. 3, pp. 34 f., and 67–69) accepted Professor Ginzberg's corrections he seems to have been inclined not to abandon his main contention.

[74] See the discussion of Rabbi Ishmael and Rabbi Akiba on the phrase את השמים (Gen. 1:1) as reported in Gen. Rab. 1.19: ר' ישמעאל שאל את ר' עקיבא א'ל ... א'ל. ואת הארץ הדין את דכתוב הכא מה הוא? א'ל אילו נאמר בראשית ברא אלהים שמים וארץ היינו אומרים השמים והארץ אלוהות הן. Cf. Tanhuma, ed. Buber, 1, 5 f., and Midrash Abkir, ed. Marmorstein, in דביר, Berlin, 1923, v. 1, p. 126 f. For a discussion of this and other like

concerned with the impact upon Jewish thinking of Greek ideas of the deity. He evidently regarded some of the theories of the pre-socratic and Aristotelian schools as dangerous to the teachings of Judaism, especially those which considered heaven and earth as deities who created the universe. In combatting such theories Rabbi Akiba also endeavored to counteract the view of the sun-worshippers by implying that they were also created. A created thing, however, can not be a creator; it can not be a god.[75] In so far as such teachings are similar to some which are utterly incompatible with the Jewish conception of the oneness of God, Rabbi Akiba was naturally opposed to them. Books containing such or like teachings were abhorrent to him. But such books, as far as it is known today, were not among the Jewish apocalyptic writings.

Whatever merit is attached to Dr. Marmorstein's theory, it rests upon late Midrashic[76] texts and lacks additional support, literary or historical, to sustain it. At any rate it hardly tends to strengthen the view that when Rabbi Akiba denied a portion in the World to Come to one who reads "outside books" he aimed at the outlawing of the Jewish apocalyptic writings current in his day. Certainly those books now regarded as belonging to that class contain no reference to either sun worship or to heaven and earth as deities who created the universe. In so far as it tends to reject the notion of plurality of deities it certainly supports the assumption that the "outside books" which Rabbi Akiba outlawed are the Gospels, in which the idea of the trinity plays its familiar Christian role. The circumstances which led to Rabbi Akiba's action are known and understandable. They are quite well-established in history. Concerned solely with the elimination of the Nazarenes and their influence from Jewish national life, he declared their books to be "outside books" the reading of which deprives one of a portion in the World to Come.

Efforts to consider the bearing of Rabbi Akiba's interdict upon the so-called canonization of the Hebrew Scriptures are futile, for in his day the Hebrew Bible had already been fixed and existed virtually in the same form in which it is known today. Such discussions by the rabbis as to how or why a given biblical text had found its way into the fixed collection of Hebrew Scriptures were never intended to bring

passages see A. Marmorstein, *Studies in Jewish Theology*, ed. by J. Rabbinowitz and M. S. Lew, Oxford, 1950, pp. 6 f., and 88 ff.

[75] See A. Marmorstein, *ibid.*, p. 89. V. Aptowitzer, *Monatsschrift für Geschichte und Wissenschaft des Judenthums*, Breslau, 1929, v. 73, p. 14, sees in this discussion an allusion to the Christian doctrine of the Trinity.

[76] Gen. Rab. 1.13 and Esth. Rab. 3.

about its inclusion in or elimination from the collection; they are merely
expressive of an effort to confirm the position the books in question
have already gained for themselves in the existing collection of Hebrew
Scriptures. The significance of Rabbi Akiba's interdict lies elsewhere:
in the direction of strengthening the position of Judaism and the purity
and nobility of its teachings. And when Rabbi Akiba coined the term
"outside books" and applied it to the books of the Nazarenes he did
it in order to stigmatize as un-Jewish certain writings for which
Scriptural authority was claimed by those who accepted their teachings. To discourage the use of those writings in and their influence
upon Jewry he declared that any one reading in them is thereby
deprived of a portion in the World to Come. In so doing Rabbi Akiba
made a significant contribution to the development of Judaism the
effect of which has not yet been fully appraised.

SUMMARIES

PROBLEMS OF THE CANONIZATION OF SCRIPTURE

by MENAHEM HARAN *(pp. 245—271)*

This is the first part of a series on problems of the canonization of the Bible, and includes three sections:

I. The place of B e n S i r a *in the History of the Canonization of the Bible.*

The contradictory opinions about *Ben Sira* as set forth in the Talmudic sources are dealt with here. On the one hand, the Rabbis expound the book's sayings, and indicate their reliance upon its authenticity with such introductory formulas as "as it is said" or "as it is written", as though it were canonized. On the other hand, however, Talmudic law prescribes that *Ben Sira* is to be classified with the books which do not "defile the hands" (cf. *Tosephta Yadayim* 11:13), and, further, includes it among those volumes the reading of which is prohibited (*Sanhedrin* 100b; *Jer. Sanhedrin* X:1).

In order to explain this contradiction, the writer first elucidates the meaning of the concept *Qeri'ah* — usually translated as "reading" or "recitation" — as used in the Talmudic sources, and comes to the conclusion that it was not understood as consisting of silent reading or of simple oral recitation, as common in Western countries, but rather was always accompanied by a *chant or melody*. as is also common in the East today. Scholars in ancient times could not even imagine any other kind of "reading". The ban on reading *Ben Sira* was not directed, therefore, against utilizing its sayings, but against that particular kind of loud reading which was accompanied by a chant (using cantillation notes!). This is not to say, however, that the reading of *Ben Sira* *without* cantillation was permitted, for as it was not customary during the Talmudic period to use books in this way, the matter was not taken into account. Thus, such a prohibition was bound to result in the removal of *Ben Sira* from the jurisdiction of the *baale miqrah* (i. e., the masters of the art of Scripture-reading) and in its being placed outside of the area of utilization.

Why was the reading of *Ben Sira* prohibited? It would seem that the reading of a canonical book implied an attitude of holiness toward it, and that such a ceremony had as its purpose the imparting of a spirit of solemnity and even a liturgical tendency. But it is evident from the Talmudic law that the Rabbis were opposed to such an estimate of *Ben Sira*. and therefore ruled against its being read.

This conception of *Ben Sira*. which made it out to be a canonical book, did indeed enter in occasionally into the Talmudic jurisprudence. In the opinion of the writer, however, this idea had its source not in the society of scholars but rather in the people themselves. From a careful study of all the passages in the Talmudic literature which quote from *Ben Sira*. it becomes evident that only in Amoraic sources — and then not in all of them — can there be discerned an attitude of canonical holiness toward that book. In general, *Ben Sira* was considered by the *tannaim* and many of the *amoraim* to be simply a book of ethical maxims, or else was thought of as a kind of "midrash" on the Bible — to be sure, of very early vintage, pre-dating the Talmudic literature, but a midrash nevertheless, whose purpose, as

224

it were, was to offer novel interpretations for Biblical passages, but which could not make the claim to stand on the same level with them.

The following is then the picture we have of *Ben Sira* as derived from the Talmudic sources: 1) A certain degree of holiness is at times ascribed to this book even in the Talmudic sources, but it is a kind of intermediate holiness, which is present to some extent but is not in the same class with the canonized Biblical literature. Its place is in the gradual transition from the holy to the profane. From this point of view, its importance rests in the fact that it is the one specimen we have, of intermediate books of this kind which comes from the ranks of the popular-Pharisaic Judaism of Palestine and Babylonia. The other intermediate books of this type, which in part made their way into the Christian canonical literature, were preserved and hallowed only in the sectarian Judaism of Palestine or in the Hellenistic Judaism. 2) It is no mere accident, furthermore, that there are no signs in the pre-Amoraic sources of an attitude of holiness toward this book; for such an attitude toward a literary work — especially one akin to the books included in the Hagiographa — can come to the fore only after a considerable period of time has elapsed. 3) These two considerations lead to a further one, namely, that the canonization of the Hagiographa was not accomplished through a series of decisions at a particular time and place, that is to say, for example, at the Synod of Jabneh or any previous one. The esteem for books was not forced upon the people from above, but grew up from below. With regard to most of the books included in the Hagiographa, there was undoubtedly a *process* of sanctification and canonization, whose standard-bearers were the great masses of the people and whose main instrument was time. (This is not true, however, of the pentateuchal and prophetic literatures, whose sanctification followed immediately upon their being produced).

II. The Scriptures as "Defiling the Hands".

As is well known, Talmudic sources consider the books of the Bible as capable of "defiling the hands". This is a very strange phenomenon, for it cannot be compared to the transmissible holiness which P and Ezek. XL—XLVIII attribute to the Temple and its various parts, nor to the transmissible impurity known throughout the ancient world. For with respect to the Biblical books the assumption in the Talmud is not that they transmit holiness by being touched, but rather that they render one impure. The explanations offered for this phenomenon by R. Mesharshya (*Shabbath* 14a) and by R. Yohanan b. Zakkai (*Yadayim* IV:1, *Tosephta ibid.* II:19) appear to be a later rationalization — and they can serve to demonstrate that the true causes were no longer known in the Talmudic period.

Modern research tends to consider this matter as a Rabbinical ordinance. It seems likelier, however, that this was not an ordinance but an old custom which the Rabbis accepted ready-made. All of the Talmudic sources accept it as if it were something self-understood, and when they differ at all it is only as to whether certain books defile or not. It therefore seems reasonable to assume that this is a vestige of folk-ritual from the pre-Talmudic period.

It should further be emphasized that defilement of the hands served principally as a sign of recognition of the holiness of the parchment on which the composition was written, and not of the holiness of the composition itself. Indeed, the fact that certain books were considered as not defiling the hands did not necessarily mean that any aura of holiness surrounding them had to be abolished. For that reason, this idea probably belongs to the realm of folk-ritual, which has its foundation in certain non-rational habits and conventions, and is therefore rather irrelevant to the problem of the canonization of the Bible.

III. *The Holiness of Books and Their Consignment to Storage in* G e n i z o t h

Here again a gradual transition from the more weighty to the less weighty degrees of book-holiness is indicated; but unlike the case mentioned above in Section I, we are dealing here only with an external and formalistic aspect of the problem. In this sense, the various degrees are: books written in "Assyrian" (i. e., in the original language of the Bible and in Aramaic square characters); translations into Greek; translations into other languages. In this case, however, even in the latter category, while there is only a minimum of holiness, there is still no complete annulment of it, since these too are Biblical books; if they are no longer in use, a *genizah* must be set aside for them.

The second part of the discussion deals with problems connected with the *genizah* and with the relation of the latter to the idea of holiness. From the evidence at hand it may be concluded that a *genizah* could not include profane objects, but only sacred ones. It is set aside if the conclusion is reached that it is no longer possible to use those sacred objects for any of several reasons. It was for this reason that the Talmudic sages sought to consign Ezekiel, Ecclesiastes, and Proverbs to the *genizah*. The reason was not that they had doubts about the holiness of these writings, but just the opposite: their sacredness was a matter that was self-understood and on which all were in complete agreement, but it was difficult to use these books because of the many baffling passages in them which either contradicted one another or the express words of the Pentateuch, or else contained "hidden secrets of the Torah" (*sithre torah*) or other such passages. The holiness of a particular thing, in the last analysis, was the very reason for its being stored away — if indeed it was judged to be in need of being stored.

It may also be shown that the prohibition against "reading" can in itself not be identified with the idea of storing holy writ in a *genizah*. In reality, these are two entirely different things; of course, writings which are stored cannot be read — but at the same time various books the reading of which was prohibited were not consigned to a *genizah* at all. *Ben Sira* was never thus consigned. On the contrary, it was in use (in partial use, to be sure) for hundreds of years until the end of the Geonic period; and it was not stored precisely because it was not sufficiently holy. Therefore the prohibition against reading *Ben Sira* — a prohibition which indicates the *opposition* to its being esteemed as a holy book — is in this particular case consonant with the fact that the Rabbis *did not* deem it correct to consign it to a *genizah*.

מבעיות הקנוניזציה של המקרא

מאת מנחם הרן

א. מקומו של ס׳ בן סירא בתולדות הקנוניזציה של המקרא

1. ס׳ בן סירא (להלן: ב״ס) זוכה במקורות התלמודיים לשתי הערכות סותרות. מצד אחד דורשים את פסוקיו ומסתמכים עליו במלות־ההצעה שנאמר, דכתיב, כאילו הוא אחד מספרי המקרא; במאמרו של האמורא הבבלי רבה בר מרי אף נחשב ספר זה במפורש כאחד מספרי הכתובים (ראה להלן). אבל מצד שני מוציאה אותו ההלכה מגדר הספרים שנכתבו ברוח־הקדש. שלא כמו ביחס לרוב ספרי המקרא, נקבע והוסכם כי "ספרי בן סירא וכל הספרים שנכתבו מכאן ואילך אינן מטמאין את הידים" (תוספתא ידים ב׳ יג)[1]. ולא עוד אלא שההלכה כוללת את ס׳ ב״ס במפורש בין הספרים האסורים בקריאה. על דבריו של רבי עקיבא במשנת סנהדרין "אף הקורא בספרים החיצונים [אין לו חלק לעולם הבא]" — מוסיף הירושלמי: "כגון ספרי בן סירא וספרי בן לענה, אבל ספרי המירם [צ״ל המירס] וכל ספרים שנכתבו מיכן והילך[2] הקורא בהן כקורא באיגרת" (ירו׳ סנהדרין י׳ ה״א). משמע שאפילו דין ספרי הומירוס הוקל מבחינה זו מדינו של ב״ס — הללו שהם ספרי אלילות גמורות, הקריאה בהם לא נאסרה והקורא בהם נתפס כקורא סתם בעלמא, כקורא באיגרת, ואילו הקורא בב״ס גדון כאן כמי שכופר בתורה מן השמים. אף בבבלי מסמיך רב יוסף הלכה זו לדבריו של רבי עקיבא, "בספר בן סירא נמי אסור למיקרי". אך רב יוסף זה עצמו הוא גם שקובע שם בהמשך הסוגיא כי "מילי מעלייתא דאית ביה דרשינן להו" (סנהדרין ק׳ ע״ב). זאת אומרת, ש"מילי מעלייתא" הנמצאים בס׳ ב״ס נחשבים אף לרב יוסף כ"כתוב" מן המקרא שאפשר לדרוש בו[3] — ואילו הקריאה בספר בכללו, כפי שמוסכם גם אצלו, אסורה. אין לך דוגמא מובהקת יותר להערכות הסותרות שס׳ ב״ס זכה להן מאשר היחס הכפול שבא לידי ביטוי בדבריו של אמורא אחד זה. שהרי האיסור לקרוא, איסור המלווה באיום כה חמור כאיבוד עולם הבא, מתכוון ללא ספק להיות מוחלט. איסור זה צריך הלא להקיף גם "מילי מעלייתא" שלכאורה

<hr>

1. על מהותו של טימוי ידים והקשר שלו לקדושת הספרים, ראה להלן במאמר ב.
2. על משמעו של הביטוי "מיכן והילך" (ובבבלי: "מכאן ואילך"), שהוא מציין את הסתלקות רוח הקדש מישראל בזמן הופעת אלכסנדר — עי׳ Graetz, Der Abschluss des Kanons des AT, MGWJ 35 (1886), S. 284—285; וכן מ. צ. סגל, מבוא המקרא, ספר ד׳ (ירושלים תש״י: להלן: מבוא), עמ׳ 816, 819, 822. הש׳ גם ש. ליברמן, תוספת ראשונים, ד׳, עמ׳ 157; א. א. אורבך, מתי פסקה הנבואה?, "תרביץ" י״ז (תש״ז), עמ׳ 3־2, 6—7.
3. וזהו פשט משמעם של דברי רב יוסף, "דרשינן להו". ולא כמו שפירש רש״י, "אמרינן להו בפרקא ומשמעינן להו לכולי עלמא". וכך קיבל פרופ׳ סגל, ספר בן סירא השלם (ירושלים תשי״ג; להלן: בן סירא), עמ׳ 41 והע׳ 12. אבל פירוש זה כבר מתכוון ליישב את הסתירה שבדברי רב יוסף מתוך מגמה הרמוניסטית.

Reprinted from *Tarbiz* (1956).

נמצאו בו בס׳ ב״ס. אך אם יש בספר דברים הראויים להידרש כמקראות, ואם מסוגל היה אחד האמוראים לחשבו לספר בין ספרי הכתובים — קשה להעלות על הדעת שהוא יורד למטה מדרגת ספרי הומירוס, עד כדי כך שאפילו הקריאה בו תיאסר.

בקושי זה כבר נגע אחד מן הראשונים ותירץ ששני ספרים הם, האחד נקרא ״משלי בן סירא״ ובו מותר לקרוא והשני ״ספר בן סירא״ והוא שהעיד עליו רב יוסף שאסור לקרוא בו[4]. אין צריך לומר שתירוץ זה הוא דחוק ביותר, חוץ ממה שמתעלם הוא מן העובדה, שסוף סוף במקומות רבים בתלמוד הספר נדרש ונקרא ״ספר בן סירא״ דוקא. רמז לקושי זה גם מן האחרונים[5]. ופרופ׳ סגל השתדל לתפוס את האיסור של רב יוסף כעין תקנה של שעה, כלומר, לא שראו בו פגם כלשהו בס׳ ב״ס כשלעצמו, אלא ״שהנוסחה של הספר שהיתה אז בבבל הכילה את דברי הבאי״. בכלל מניח פרופ׳ סגל שבידי רב יוסף ואביי (הנושא־ונותן עמו באותה הסוגיא) היתה מהדורה מיוחדת של ס׳ ב״ס, מהדורה המונית ומרובת גיבובים[6]. ברם, כשרב יוסף אוסר את הקריאה בספר בן סירא הלא אין הוא משמיע סברה מדעתו. אין ספק שזוהי הלכה שכבר נקבעה לפניו והיא רק הגיעה אליו במסורת בית המדרש. אף אביי אינו חולק עליו בדבר זה, אלא לפי דרכם הם רק מחפשים נימוק להלכה שכבר מקובלת בידם. ואכן, כהלכה זו ממש נמסרה גם בירושלמי: ״אף הקורא בספרים החיצונים, כגון ספרי בן סירא וספרי בן לענה. אבל ספרי המירס וכו׳״ והיא שם אולי ברייתא ולא סתם־גמרא. אין לנו טעם להניח שגם לפני זמנם של רב יוסף ואביי היתה הנוסחה של ס׳ ב״ס קלוקלת, וודאי שקשה לומר כי עובדה זו היא שגרמה לאיסור הקריאה בספר בדורות שקדמו לשני אמוראים אלה. ובאמת בירושלמי הרי לא מצינו שהאיסור לקרוא בס׳ ב״ס יהיה מנומק על־ידי מהדורה המונית מיוחדת שהכילה דברי הבאי[7]. חוץ מזה מניח הפרופ׳ סגל, שהאיסור לקרוא בס׳ ב״ס

4. S. Schechter, A Further Fragment of Ben Sira, JQR 12(1900), p. 461; מובא גם אצל מ. צ. סגל, שם, עמ׳ 12.

5. עי׳ למשל בסלפולא חריפתא ליו״ט ליסמאן הלר על הרא״ש, סדר נזיקין, לסנהדרין ק׳ ע״ב : ״לפי שיש בהן דברים של הבל — לכאורה משמע דמש״ה (דמשום הכי) אפי׳ בדברים טובים שבהם נמי אסור לקרות, ותמיה לי דבהדיא אי׳ בגמרא דרב יוסף עצמו אמר דמילי מעליותא דאית ביה דרשינן״. וראה גם הע׳ 21 להלן.

6. מ. צ. סגל, בן סירא, עמ׳ 46, הש׳ עמ׳ 40—41!.

7. על דברי הירושלמי ״כגון ספרי בן סירא וכו׳״ אומר הפרופ׳ סגל כי ״פירוש זה [של הירושלמי] הוא קשה מאד״, ״דעה זו אי אפשר להתאים לשימוש הרב בס׳ ב״ס שהשתמשו בו חכמי ישראל (וביניהם גם רבי עקיבא עצמו) במשך דורות רבים״ (שם, עמ׳ 46). אך הוא הדבר, שברור כי פירוש זה של הירושלמי קדום הוא למדי ואינו תלוי בדברי רב יוסף שבבבלי ועל־כן הוא גם מחזק אותם. להלן נאמר שם בירושלמי : ״מאי טעמא ? ויותר מהנה בני היזהר וגו׳, להגיון ניתנו ליגיעה לא ניתנו״. בעל פני משה על הירושלמי מפרש שהדברים אלה מוסבים על ספרי הומירוס ; וכך מקבל פרופ׳ סגל וכמוהו שהוא נוטה לבטל את דברי הירושלמי מכל וכל לטובת הגירסה של מדרש זה שבקהלת רבה. ״ובאמת בקהלת רבה (י״ב יב) פירשו את הכתוב ״ויותר מהמה בני הזהר״, לא על ספרי הומירס.

היה מכוון לטובת ההמון. חוששים היו שהעם לא יידע להבחין בין דברי ההבאי לבין
הדברים של ממש באותה מהדורה קלוקלת שהיתה בידו[8]. אך מסתבר יותר שאיסור זה
הוא עצמי וסיבתו איננה "תועלתנית". הוא לא נקבע לתקנת ההמון, אלא גם, כביכול,
לתקנת היחיד. שהרי ההלכה אינה מבחינה כאן בין תלמידי־חכמים היודעים להבדיל מהו
תפל ועיקר לבין ההמון שאינו יודע להבדיל. גם ת"ח שקורא בספר זה לעצמו, מבלי
שישמיע אותו באזני אחרים — אין ספק כי לפי ההלכה "אין לו חלק לעולם הבא"[9].
ועוד, הרי בירושלמי הנימוק של דברי הבאי אינו קיים כלל, ואף־על־פי־כן האיסור לקרוא
בס' ב"ס מצוי אף שם, וטעמו — משום שבן סירא איננו בכלל כ"ד ספרים.

‫2.‬ סבורני שכדי להבין איסור זה של ההלכה לקרוא בס' ב"ס, חובה עלינו לדייק,
קודם כל, במשמעות המושג "קריאה". "קריאה" בספר לפי מושגי חז"ל אינה מתכוונת
לעיון רגיל באותו ספר, כדרך שאנו נוהגים לקרוא ספרים ומשתמשים בפועל קרא. עיון
בעלמא בס' ב"ס לא נאסר, לכאורה, כלל — נאסרה הקריאה בו. והקריאה, לפי מושגי
חז"ל, נעשית על־פי כללים קבועים ומתבצעת בצורה מסויימת, כך שיכולים לשוות
למעשה זה ערך ידוע של קדושה מצד עצמו. קריאה — הרי זה לא רק מעשה חגיגי,
אלא גם מעשה שיכולה להיות בו משמעות ליטורגית[10]. כך, למשל, יכולים אנו
לראות מדברי שמואל על אסתר, שהיא "נאמרה [ברוח הקדש] לקרות ולא נאמרה ליכתוב"
(מגילה ז' ע"א). פירוש הדבר: קדושתה מצומצמת רק בקריאה שלה, ומשום כך יש כאן,
במקרה זה, מעשה בעל ערך ליטורגי — אבל במגילת העור עצמה, שבה כתוב החיבור,

אלא על ס' ב"ס: '(מהמה) מהומה בתוך ביתו יותר מכ"ד ספרים מהומה הוא מכניס
בביתו, כגון ספור בן סירא וספר בן תגלא. והגות הרבה יגיעת בשר — להגות ניתנו ולא ליגיעת בשר
ניתנו'" (שם, שם). אבל לאמיתו של דבר, גם הדברים שבירושלמי מוסבים על ספרי בן סירא. "מאי
טעמא" שם משמעו: על שום מה הקורא בספרי בן סירא אין לו חלק לעולם הבא — ולא: על שום
מה הקורא בספרי הומירס ובספרים שנכתבו מכאן ואילך כקורא באיגרת. ברור שהדברים בירושלמי
אינם אלא מעין נוסח מקוצר לאותו מדרש ממש המובא גם בקהל"ר. ודברי הירושלמי, האוסרים את
הקריאה בספרי בן סירא, עדיין צריכים הסבר. אף אין שום אפשרות לקבל, למשל, את תיקונו של
גרץ (במאמרו הנזכר, עמ' 285—289) לנוסח הירושלמי כאן: "הקורא בספרים החיצונים כגון ספרי
המינים, אבל ספרי בן סירא וכפרי בן לענה וכל ספרים שנכתבו מכאן ואילך מותר לקרות
בו" (!). פתרון כזה נראה לנו קל מכדי שיוכל להיות נכון. לניתוח פיסקה זו בירושלמי והסברתה
עי' עוד S. Lieberman, Hellenism in Jewish Palestine (N. Y. 1950), pp. 108—109

‫8.‬ בן סירא, עמ' 41: "...שאיסור לעם [דגישה שלי, מ. ה.] לקרוא בס' ב"ס". ושם, עמ' 46.
‫9.‬ והשווה רש"י בסנהדרין ק' ע"ב, על דברי רב יוסף: "ובא עליהם [על דברי ההבאי שיש בספר]
לידי ביטול תורה". היינו, אף כשהוא קורא לעצמו.
‫10.‬ בדיעבד עיינתי בערך Apokryphen של J[echezkel] K[aufmann], בתוך Encyclopaedia
Judaica כרך ב'. שם, עמ' 1166 למטה, צויינו במשפט אחד דברים הקרובים למדי אל רעיון זה.
ושמחתי שבפרט הנזכר כיוונתי קרוב למחשבתו. והש' (כמסומן שם) גם בדברי הרנ"ק, מונה"ז, שער
י"א סימן ה' (= מהדורת ראבידוביץ, עמ' קיט—קכ).

אין לנהוג קדושה לפי שיטת שמואל. ואמנם הוא טוען שאין היא מטמאה את הידים (שם
שם). אבל היתה גם השקפה אחרת, שאסתר "ניתנה לכתוב" (יומא כ"ט ע"א).

כיצד היתה הקריאה נעשית? השמעת הטכסט לא היתה נעשית כדיקלום גרידא, אלא
לעולם היא היתה מלווה בניגון. דבר זה אנו למדים מן המונחים טעמים, פיסוק טעמים,
סימני טעמים, שנזכרו הרבה בספרות התלמודית (ירו' מגילה ד' ה"א והמקבילות, עירובין
כ"א ע"ב ועוד) ואף המונח נעימה הנרדף לטעמים (מגילה ל"ב ע"א ועוד) [11]. המלמדים
מקרא לתינוקות היו נוהגים לקבל "שכר פיסוק טעמים" (נדרים ל"ז ע"א). בשעת הקריאה
היו נוהגים להראות את הטעמים על־ידי תנועת יד ימין (ברכות ס"ב ע"א) וזוהי כנראה
המשמעות של "סימני טעמים", שהרי בתקופת התלמוד לא היו הטעמים מסומנים
בגוף הטכסט. טעמים וﬞﬨ נעימה וסימנים היו צמודים לא רק לקריאה של פרקי תורה
ונביאים, אלא לכל פרק ופסוק בכתבי־הקדש, כולל כל ספרי הכתובים. דבר זה יכולים
אנו ללמוד, למשל, מדברי הברייתא: "ה ק ו ר א פסוק של שיר השירים ועושה אותו כמין
זמר והקורא פסוק בבית משתאות בלא זמנו, מביא רעה לעולם" (סנהדרין ק"א ע"א).
פירוש הדבר: הוא קורא אמנם אותו פסוק של שיר־השירים בטעמיו ובנעימתו, אלא שהוא
מתייחס אליו כאל זמר של חולין [12]. אך עם זאת מיוסדים דברים אלה של הברייתא על
ההנחה, ש"הקורא פסוק" מבצע זאת ממילא ובהכרח בלוויית נעימה ולַחַן, שהרי אם לא
כן לא היתה יכולה להֵינתן לו לאותו פסוק צורה של "זמר". זה הכלל: "קריאה" של ספר
בלשון חז"ל אינה רק השמעת הדברים בקול, אלא גם בניגון ובנעימה מגובשת. "קריאה"
באופן אחר מתוך כתבים אף לא תיארו הקדמונים לעצמם. קריאה דוממת "בעיניים",
כדרך שנהוג בעולם המערבי, וכן גם אמנות של דיקלום מילולי בלי ניגון — שתי אלו
לא היו מוכרות להם כלל. וכך אתה מוצא שגם במזרח של היום, ואף במסורת הקריאה
של תלמודי־התורה והישיבות היהודיות (אפילו בטכסטים תלמודיים) — אין קריאה אלא
זו שנעשית בניגון קולני.

צורת הקריאה בכתבי־הקדש, בטעמים ובנעימה, שבתקופת התלמוד היתה מסורת
הנשמרת בעל־פה בחוגים של סופרים ובעלי־מקרא, היא שהועברה בהמשכיות רצופה
לתקופת הגאונים ורק אז נקבעו לה שיטות שונות של סימנים ד י א ק ר י ט י י ם מוסכמים
בגוף הטכסט. משום כך, אגב, צריכים אנו לומר (שלא כפי שמניחים חוקרים אחדים), כי
הסימנים הדיאקריטיים של הטעמים באו לעולם כרוכים יחד עם סימני הניקוד. המצאה של
דור אחד הם, אותם המניעים יצרו את שניהם, ואין הצדקה להניח כי אלה הומצאו לאחר
אלה. כי באותה שעה שנקבעו סימנים דיאקריטיים לווֹקאליזציה השלמה של הטכסט, צריך

11. למשמעות המונח נעימה הנרדף לטעם, עי' סגל, מבוא, ספר ד', עמ' 888, הערה 30. ולאמור
להלן בפנים על "סימני טעמים", הש' עוד שם, עמ' 876.

12. אין שום צורך לפרש "שקורא" בנעימה אחרת שאינו נקוד בה" (רש"י, שם). דבר זה לא נרמז
במלות הברייתא. נאמר "הקורא פסוק" בסתם, משמע — כדרכו.

היה לקבוע גם את סימני ניגונו, שהרי לא יכול היה לעלות על דעתם שיהגו את מלות
המקרא ללא הנעימה הקבועה המצורפת להן. ואכן, סימני הטעמים, ממש כסימני הניקוד,
מכסים את כל ספרי המקרא, מ״בראשית ברא״ עד ״ויעל״; הדבר מאשר, שוב, כי הם לא
דימו כלל, שאפשר לקרוא קריאה לגיטימית אפילו קטע אחד מכתבי-הקדש ללא נעימה
קולנית. — ויתכן שאף ספרי הומירוס, כלומר, טכסטים פיוטיים ונערצים מחוג התרבות
ההלניסטית, היו נקראים אצל הקדמונים בניגון חגיגי. אלא שבתלמוד לא יכלו, כמובן, לייחס
להם שום ערך של קדושה ומשום כך אמרו שהקורא בהם כקורא באיגרת.

פרשיות התורה ופרקי נביאים, יודעים אנו באלו מסיבות ליטורגיות היו נקראים (וכך
עד היום) — בתפילות שחרית של שני וחמישי ושבת, ובמנחה של שבת. קטע נבחר מן
התורה, הוא קריאת שמע, נהגו להשמיע אף פעמים בכל יום. אך גם קריאה מיוחדת זו של
שמע מלכתחילה היתה נעשית, כנראה, בצורה דומה מאד לקריאת התורה, עם ניגונה
וטעמיה. כמה מאמרים בהלכות קריאת שמע (כגון: ״הקורא [את ק״ש] מכאן ואילך [היינו,
לאחר גמר זמנה] לא הפסיד, כאדם הקורא בתורה״, מ׳ ברכות פ״א ב; ועוד) נותנים מקום
להניח, שבתקופות קדומות היתה קריאה זו נעשית בדרך כלל כקריאת התורה, באותה
הנעימה ובקול רם, וכלפי חוץ כמעט שלא היה הבדל ביניהן. אמנם בקריאה זו דעת הסתם-
משנה היא, ש״הקורא את שמע ולא השמיע לאזנו, יצא״ (שם פ״ב ג); אבל אפילו פירוט
מיוחד זה באמת יש בו כדי לאשר כי דרך העולם היתה שהקורא בעלמא היה ״משמיע
לאזנו״ דוקא, ואילו הקריאה שאינה קולנית היא שהיתה יוצאת-דופן12א. קטעים מספרי
כתובים נהגו בכמה מקומות לקרוא בשבת מן המנחה ולמעלה (שבת קט״ז ע״א13, והש׳
ירו׳ שבת ט״ז ה״א ומס׳ סופרים פט״ו ג) והקורא בכתובים היה מברך ברכה מיוחדת (שם
פי״ד ד). וגם פרקי ההלל שהיו נאמרים בימים מסויימים בשנה היו נקראים בנעימה (שם
פכ״ב ט), כלומר, באותה קריאה מוטעמת של ספרי הכתובים. אלא שמסתבר כי טעמי הקריאה
של התורה, והנביאים, וספרי אמ״ת, ושאר ספרי הכתובים, היו מיוחדים ושונים זה מזה

12א. כיוצא בזה, המאמר של ר׳ שפטיה משם ר׳ יוחנן, ״כל הקורא בלא נעימה ושונה בלא זמרה
עליו הכתוב אומר ׳וגם אני נתתי להם חוקים לא טובים׳ וגו׳ [יחז׳ כ׳ כה]״ (מגילה ל״ב ע״א) —
באמת יש בו כדי לאשר שצורת הקריאה בלא נעימה היא שהיתה נדירה, באופן יחסי, ויוצאת-דופן,
שלא כדרך העולם. וראה להלן בפנים.

13. ״בנהרדעא פסקי סידרא בכתובים במנחתא דשבתא״. ואין זה כהפטרה לקריאת התורה דוקא,
כמו שייעבו התוספות במגילה כ״א ע״ה ואין מפטירין בנביא, ובשבת כ״ד ע״א ד״ה שאלמלא.
באמת נהגו בכמה מקומות להפטיר בנביא אף במנחה בשבת. השווה דברי רש״י, שבת כ״ד ע״א ד״ה
המפטיר בנביא: ״מצאתי בתשובת הגאונים שהיו רגילים לקרות בנביא בשבתות במנחה עשרה
פסוקים ובימי פרס״ים [הכוונה לפרסים הסאסאנידים, כששלטו בבבל] גזרו גזרה שלא לעשות וכיון
שנסתלקו נסתלקו״. דברים אלה של רש״י מתאשרים ע״י המובא באוצר הגאונים למס׳ שבת, עמ׳ 26,
102 (הנני מודה לד״ר א. א. אורבך שהעירני על מקום זה, כשם שהעיר כמה הערות חשובות נוספות
אגב עיון במאמרי).

כבר בתקופת התלמוד, כפי שהם נשתמרו בייחודם בתקופות שלאחרי כן. אבל ערך ליטורגי
ידוע היה לכל קריאה מתוך כתבי-הקדש באלו מסיבות שהן, ואפילו כשאדם קורא לעצמו
ואפילו תינוק הקורא בבית רבו (הש' הברייתא בחגיגה י״ג ע״א: "מעשה בתינוק אחד
שהיה קורא בבית רבו בספר יחזקאל" וכו').

האיסור לקרוא בס' ב״ש אינו מתכוון, אם כן, לעיון בעלמא ול"שימוש" בספר זה, אלא
ל ק ר י א ה בו. וסתם קריאה לפי מושגי חז״ל היא זו שנעשית בקול רם ובחגיגיות, בניגון
ובטעמים. שקריאה כזאת בס' ב״ש, בטעמים, אמנם אפשרית היתה, אנו למדים מן העדות
המעניינת של רב סעדיה גאון, שמעיד על ספר זה כי הוא "דומה לספר משלי בפרשיותיו
ופסוקיו ועשאו [המחבר] מס'מן ומוטעם" ("וגעלה מסמנג מטעמא") [14]. זאת אומרת,
שלעיני רס״ג עדיין מצוי היה טופס של ס' ב״ש שכולו היה מחולק לפרשיות וכל פסוקיו
היו מוטעמים. ולא עוד אלא שרס״ג מעיד כי בצורה הזאת, עם חלוקה לפרשיות ולפסוקים
ועם סימני נקודות ו ט ע מ י ם, היו כתובים ספרים נוספים שמחוץ לכתה״ק, והם: ספר חכמה
שחיבר אלעזר בן עיראי "הדומה לספר קהלת"; מה "שכתבו בני חשמנאי יהודה ושמעון
ויוחנן ויונתן ואלעזר בני מתיה ספר במה שעבר עליהם, הדומה לספר דניאל בלשון
הכשדים". ואפילו ספרים נמלצים שנתחברו ב ת ק ו פ ת ו ש ל ר ס ״ ג היו נכתבים לפעמים
כדרך ספרי המקרא, עם פיסוק לפסוקים ועם סימני טעמים. כאלה נ ז כ ר י ם אצל הרס״ג
ארבעה: ספר נמל״ץ בעברית שחיברו אנשי קירואן "ממה שנמצא אצלם מן שעדי הנוצרי";
ושלושה ספרים שחיבר הוא עצמו בעברית — "ספר המועדים"; "ספר במה שראיתי מן
האנשים שתחסרנה להם הבחינה וההשתדלות"; וכן גם המהדורה הראשונה של ספר הגלוי,
שהיתה כתובה בעברית נמלצת [15]. לגבי ספר אחד מספרי רס״ג אין אנו צריכים לעדות, כי
הוא גופו נתגלה בצורה זו: ההקדמה העברית לספר האגרון, הכתובה בסגנון פיוטי,
מועתקת לא רק עם נקודות אלא גם עם טעמים, בדיוק כמו פסוקי המקרא המשובצים

14. עי' הרכבי, זכרון לראשונים, מחברת חמישית: זכרון הגאון רב סעדיה אלפיומי וספריו
(פטרבורג תרנ״ב), עמ' קנ—קנא.

15. עי' הרכבי, שם, עמ' קמב, קנ—קנג, קס—קסא. להלן מביא הגאון כמה ציטאטות מן הספרים
שהוא מזכיר. לבעית זהותו של אלעזר בן עיראי עי' מ. צ. סגל, קובץ רס״ג בעריכת י״ל הכהן פישמן
(ירושלים תש״ג), עמ' קה—קז; הנ״ל, קרית ספר" כ' (תש״ג-תש״ד), עמ' 247—248. ב"ספר בני
חשמנאי" אפשר שכוונת הגאון לנוסח ארמי של ס' החשמונאים א', שהיה לנגד עיניו. ביחס ל"ספר
הבחינה וההשתדלות" שיער הרכבי (עמ' קנב, הערה ב) שכוונתו לס' האגרון. אבל הגאון פורט שם
(עמ' קנב—קנד) את תוכן עשרת שערי הספר, ומהם מסתבר שעיקרו רצוף דברי מוסר והטפה. רק
תכנם של שלושת השערים האחרונים ("השערים הכלליים", כנגד שבעת "השערים הפרטיים"
הראשונים) חופף לתכנו לס' האגרון, כפי שהוא אומר שם: "כאשר ביארתי ש ל ו ש ת ה ע נ י נ י ם
ה א ל ה בספר השיר העברי" (עמ' קנד, שו' 8—9), שהוא ס' האגרון. חוץ מזה, על ס' הבחינה
וההשתדלות אומר הגאון שכולו היה כתוב עברית וכולו מפוסק ומוטעם — ולא הקדמתו בלבד, כפי
שהיה בס' האגרון. משום כך אין לזהות את שני אלה.

בהקדמה הערבית [16]. ואילו עדותו של רס״ג לגבי ס׳ ב״ס עשויה גם היא להתאשר עכשיו באופן מוחשי: אף כתבי־היד העבריים של ס׳ ב״ס שהגיעו לידינו עדיין מכילים כמה פסוקים שאינם מנוקדים בלבד, אלא גם מוטעמים [17]. סימני טעמים מצויים, כידוע, אף בכמה כתבי־יד ודפוסים ראשונים של משנה ומדרשים. ושוב, טעם הדבר מסתבר על נקלה: כיון שגם הטכסטים הללו (לאחר שכבר התירו לכתבם בספרים) היו נקראים ב נ י ג ו ן, אם כי בניגון שהיה שונה שונה מניגוני הקריאה של התנ״ך על חלקיו השונים. והראיה, שבתלמוד (מגילה ל״ב ע״א) אמרו על ״ ה ק ו ר א ״ — בלא נעימה ״, אבל על ״השונה — בלא זמרה ״. משמע שהם עצמם הבחינו בין ניגונו של הקורא לזה של השונה. וגם בתחום הלשון הסורית באים הטעמים לפעמים לידי שימוש, כידוע, מחוץ לספרי המקרא והברית החדשה.

אבל עם זאת עלינו להדגיש, שאם מוצאים אנו כי אסרו את הקריאה בס׳ ב״ס, אין זאת אומרת ש״התירו״ לעיין בו, כלומר, להשתמש בו ב ל א קריאה מוטעמת. כי למעשה, כאמור, עיון־סתם בעצם לא הובא כאן בחשבון כלל; שימוש כזה, שאינו מלווה בקריאה ממש, לא היה מדרכם של בעלי־הספרים בתקופת התלמוד. לא היתה כאן ברירה בין קריאה לעיון, אלא בין קריאה לאי־שימוש גמור. איסור הקריאה צריך היה להשמיט ספר זה ממילא מתחת ידם של ״בעלי מקרא״ ולהוציאו מחוץ לגדר השימוש.

3. למה נאסרה הקריאה בס׳ ב״ס? אין ספק שהטעם המובא בירושלמי, שאין להכניס יותר מכ״ד ספרים, צופן בתוכו את הסיבה הממשית לכך. קריאה של ספר — אם אחד מכתבי־הקודש הוא — מבליעה בתוכה יחס של קדושה כלפי אותו ספר ויש בה, כאמור, יסוד ליטורגי. אבל בעלי ההלכה התנגדו להערכה זו של ס׳ ב״ס ומשום כך גם גזרו שלא לקרות בו. עובדה זו מתבררת, למשל, מתוך השוואת ס׳ ב״ס לכתבי־הקדש האמיתיים, שדינם מזכיר לכאורה במשהו את דינו, כמו ששנו בברייתא, שבת קט״ז ע״ב: ״אע״פ שאמרו כתבי הקדש אין קורין בהן [18], אבל שונין בהן ודורשים בהן, נצרך לפסוק מביא ורואה בו״. משמע שבשניהם, גם בס׳ ב״ס וגם בכתה״ק, מותר לשנות ולדרוש ויחד עם זאת בשניהם ״אין קורין״. אלא שיש כאן הבדל גדול במעלה. בכתה״ק אין זו אלא תקנה, או לכל היותר סייג — מפני ביטול בית המדרש (כמו שאמרו במ׳ שבת פט״ז א), או מחשש שמא יבואו לקרוא בשבת בשטרי הדיוטות (כמו שאומר ר׳ נחמיה באותה הברייתא). אין

16. עי׳ הרכבי, שם, עמ׳ לט, נב —נז. בדפוס השאיר הרכבי רק סימני אס״ף, וכן את המקף.

17. עי׳ תיאור חמשת כתבי־היד אצל מ. צ. סגל, בן סירא, עמ׳ 49—53. כ״י א מכיל לפחות שבעה פסוקים בניקוד ובטעמים (ט׳ ג—ה, י׳ ג, י״א ז—ט) וכ״י ד פסוק אחד (ל״ז ג). רישומים של שיטת טעמים שלמה יש בכ״י ה. בכלל יש בכתבי־יד אלה פה ושם סממנים הטופים של כתבי־יד מקראיים: פרשיות פתוחות או סתומות, כתיב וקרי, שיטין מסורגלות, כתיבה בשורות רצופות — אך גם במסורגות (אריח על גבי אריח ולבנה על גבי לבנה). כמו ספרי שירה של נביאים וכתובים וכתובים בהרבה כתבי־יד מימי הביניים.

18. היינו אלא מן המנחה ולמעלה, הש׳ ירו׳ שבת ט״ז ה״א, מגילה ג׳ ה״ה ומס׳ סופרים פט״ו ג.

כאן שום פגם בגוף הכתבים, שקדושתם אינה עומדת כלל בויכוח. ואילו הקריאה בס׳ ב״ס
היא איסור חמור שהעובר עליו, בין ב ש ב ת בין ב ח ו ל, "אין לו חלק לעולם הבא".
ערכם המקודש של כתה״ק הוא בבחינת מובן־מאליו ואילו האפשרות של הערכה דומה לס׳
ב״ס מעוררת מצד ההלכה הרשמית ה ת נ ג ד ו ת נמרצת. ועלינו לזכור כי העובדה שס׳ ב״ס
אינו נחשב כמטמא את הידים, כשלעצמה, אינה יכולה לבטל את ערך קדושתו לחלוטין.
מבחינה זו תופס ס׳ ב״ס דרגת ביניים בין אסתר (בהתאם להשקפת שמואל) מזה, לבין
הספרים "שנכתבו מכאן ואילך" מזה. שלושת סוגי הספרים האלה — אסתר, ב״ס והספרים
שנכתבו מכאן ואילך — כולם כאחד אינם מטמאים את הידים[19]. אבל אסתר[20] "נאמרה
לקרות", כלומר, בקריאתה יש קדושה ליטורגית של ממש, ומשום כך היא כלולה בכל זאת
בכ״ד ספרים. הספרים שנכתבו מכאן ואילך לא נתקדשו ביהדות הארצישראלית מכל וכל,
ומשום כך הקורא בהם נחשב כ"קורא באיגרת" וקריאתם לא נאסרה כלל. מעיקרם הם
נשארו — לפחות בארץ־ישראל — בגדר חולין ולא היה בה כל מקום לחשוש מפני יחס ליטורגי
כלפיהם. ואילו ס׳ ב״ס לא היה חול גמור, אך עדיין גם לא הגיע לכלל כ״ד ספרים. בחוגים
רחבים בעם הוא נחשב בחזקת כתבי־קדש ואת ההערכה ה ז א ת כלפיו שאפה ההלכה
הרשמית לדחות ולבטל. כל קריאה שלו לא יכלה להתפרש כקריאת דברים בעלמא, אלא
בהכרח עישויים היו להתבטא בה יחס ליטורגי והערכה של קדושה כלשהי. משום כך לא
יכלו בעלי ההלכה להישאר אדישים לקריאה בו ואסרו אותה[21].

שאמנם הערכה כזאת של ס׳ ב״ס, שתפסה אותו ככתב־קדש, מצויה היתה בעם — דבר זה
אנו רואים מן העובדה המופלאה, שהיא חדרה אפילו לתוך התלמוד עצמו! אלא שכאן עלינו

---

19. שהספרים שנכתבו מכאן ואילך, יחד עם ב״ס, אינם מטמאים את הידים — ר׳ המובאה לעיל
בפנים, עמ׳ 245, מתוספתא ידים ב׳ יג. גם הגליונים וספרי המינים (שם, שם) וספרי הומירוס (מ׳ ידים
פ״ד ו) אינם מטמאים את הידים.

20. וכמוהו ודאי גם ספרים אחרים מכתבי־הקדש, במידה שסבירים היו כי הם אינם מטמאים
את הידים.

21. גורל זה של ס׳ ב״ס יכול להעלות על הדעת, שנהגו בו דין ש ל ג נ י ז ה. אך באמת אין זו
גניזה, כי גניזה נאמרה רק בספרים שקדושתם ודאית. לעניין זה ראה לדי״ן במאמר ג. ומעניין שאחרי
המלים "אמר רב יוסף" בסנהדרין ק׳ ע״ב, נוספו בכ״י מינכן בשולי הגליון (בכתב יותר מאוחר) מלים
אלו : "אי לאו דגנזוה רבנן להאי סיפרא כי הני [מילי מעלייתא דאית ביה דרשינן להו]". וביד
רמה על מס׳ סנהדרין לר׳ מאיר הלוי אבולעפיא הוא כותב למקום זה : "אמר רב יוסף אי לא
דגנזוה רבנן להאי סיפרא הוה דרשי׳ להו להני מילי מעלייתא דאית ביה, כלומר הוה מפרשינן להו
לפום דרשייהו, ואיכא דאמרי דהוה דרשי׳ להו בפירקא ומשמע׳ להו לכ״ע (לכולי עלמא), ומאי נינהו
אשה טובה וכו׳". כוונת הרמ״ה ב"איכא דאמרי" היא, כמובן, לפירוש רש״י כאן (הש׳ הערה 3 לעיל),
אך מן החלק הראשון של דבריו מתברר שהיו עיניו לנגד כדברי התוספת של כ״י מינכן.
והשווה דק״ס למקום זה (עמ׳ 304) וכמסומן אצל S. Schechter, JQR 3 (1891), p. 700 n. 30.
אף־על־פי־כן ברור שאין מלים אלו יכולות להיות עיקר וכל כוונתן ליישב את הסתירה שבדברי
רב יוסף. והראיה, שס׳ ב״ס נדרש בתלמוד לא על־ידי רב יוסף בלבד ובאמת הוא ל א נגנז.

לדייק, שוב, מהו הקפה של התפיסה הזאת לס׳ ב״ס במקורות התלמודיים ובאיזה דור היא מתחילה.

4. בירושלמי ובמדרשים מובאת אגדה אחת בגירסאות שונות, על שלוש מאות נזירים שעלו לירושלים בימי שמעון בן שטח להקריב את קרבנם, ומסופר שם כיצד שמעון בן שטח בדבריו אל ינאי המלך, מסתמך על פסוקים שונים מכתבי־הקדש ובין השאר הוא מביא אף פסוק מס׳ ב״ס בלשון כתיב (ירו׳ ברכות ז׳ ה״ב, נזיר ה׳ ה״ה, בר׳ רבה פצ״א, קהל״ר פ״ז כד). ה״פסוק״ המיוחס שם לב״ס הוא ״סלסליה ותרוממך ובין נגידים תושיביך״, והוא אינו אלא צירוף של משלי ד׳ ח עם ב״ס י״א א [22]. אבל מכאן אין ללמוד, כמובן, שאמנם שמעון בן שטח דיבר דברים אלה אל המלך ושעל פסוקים אלה ממש הוא הסתמך לפניו. המאמר כולו מלא נופך דמיוני ומה שאפשר לכל היותר ללמוד ממנו מבחינה זו, הריהי העובדה, שבימי ב ע ל י האגדה הזאת — והם ראשוני האמוראים — כבר נהגו להסתמך על ס׳ ב״ס כאחד מספרי הקדש. ובאמת אין לחשוב כלל שאחד מן הזוגות מסוגל היה להתייחס בצורה כזאת אל ס׳ ב״ס. הראשון בספרות התלמודית שמביא פסוק מפסוקי ס׳ ב״ס הוא רבי לויטס איש יבנה, כנראה בן דורו של ר׳ עקיבא (אבות פ״ד ד). אך הוא א י נ ו דורש אותו ואינו מזכיר אותו כלקוח מכתבי־הקדש, אלא רק מצטט את המלים, והן ב״ס ז׳ יז, כאילו מורגלות בפיו. שימוש זה בס׳ ב״ס אינו מוכרח להוציא אותו מגדר ספר־מוסר או ספר־משלים רגיל, בלא כל תוקף של קדושה. ואמנם לפי אבות דר״נ פכ״ד ד משתמש אלישע בן אבויה, גם הוא בן דורו של ר׳ עקיבא, בפסוק מב״ס, כ״ב ב, ובפירושו הוא מציע אותו במלים וכן מתלא אומר. במלים של הצעה כאלה משתמשים אף מקורות אמוראים לגבי שני פסוקים אחרים מס׳ ב״ס [23]. שלושה פסוקים אחרים מס׳ ב״ס מובאים בברייתות הפתוחות ״תנו רבנן״ או ״תניא״, ושוב, בלא שום מלים של הצעה, כאילו הם סתם דברים של חכמים ואף אינם ציטאטים מספר אחר. אלה הם: פסים קי״ג ע״ב (ב״ס כ״ה ג—ד) [24],

---

22. במקבילה בבבלי, ברכות מ״ה ע״א, מובא בדפוסים הפסוק ממשלי בלבד. אך אין ספק שזהו שיבוש ע״פ דברי רש״י, ואילו הגירסה המקורית היתה אף כאן ״ובין נגידים (או: נדיבים) תושיביך״. עי׳ בחידושי אגדות למהרש״א וכמסומן בהגהות הש״ס כאן.

23. שמ׳ רבה פכ״א ז: ״המשל אומר כבד את רופאך״ וכו׳. תנחומא חקת א: ״מתלא אמר בן סירא״ וכו׳. במקבילות למדרש הראשון (מסומנות אצל מ. צ. סגל, בן סירא׳, עמ׳ 38, רמה) מוצע הפסוק, והוא ל״ח א, על־ידי המלים ״כתוב בספר בן סירא״, או שהוא מובא בשם רבי לעזר ובארמית. במקבילות למדרש השני (מסומנות שם, עמ׳ 40, הע׳ 10) מוצע הפסוק על־ידי המלים אינון אמרין, מתלא אמרי, הדא דבריתא אמרין. ור׳ גם המובאה שם, עמ׳ 41, הע׳ 14: ״ועוד בחכמת חכמים״. (מראי המקומות מס׳ ב״ס עשויים בכל המאמר הזה לפי הסימון של סגל).

24. ת״ר ארבעה אין בדעת סובלתן, אלו הן דל גאה ועשיר מכחש״ וכו׳. ״פסוק״ זה מובא בתוך סידרה של ברייתות שכולן מכילות משלים מספריים: שלושה שונאין זה את זה, שלושה אוהבין זה את זה, חמישה דברים ציוה כנען את בניו, ששה דברים נאמרים בסוס, וכיוצא באלה. וברור שאותו

ביצה ל"ב ע"ב (הש' ב"ס מ' לד) [25], ב"מ קי"ב ע"א (הש' ב"ס ל"ד כג, והקשר רופף למדי) [26].

נוסף על כך קיימת אפילו במקורות א מ ו ר א י י ם התופעה, שמביאים אמנם דברים מס' ב"ס ובשמו, אך דברי ב"ס עצמם אינם נתפסים כ"כתוב" אלא רק כ"מדרש" על כתוב אחר מן המקרא המובא לפניהם או לאחריהם. במקרים כאלה נסמכים דברי ב"ס תמיד לפסוק אמיתי מכתבי־הקדש והם משמשים לו רק הסבר והארה. סגנון ההבאות הוא מעין זה: בפסוק פלוני מן המקרא כתוב כך וכך – "בן סירא אומר" כך וכך. לדוגמא: "כל ימי עני ורעים' [משלי ט"ו טו], בן סירא אומר אף לילות, בשפל גגים גגו ובמרום הרים כרמו וכו'" (כתובות ק"י ע"ב והמקבילות). כיוצא בזה, "'וירא יעקב את פני לבן' [בראש' ל"א ב], בר סירא אמר לב אדם ישנה פניו בין לטוב בין לרע וכו'" (בר' רבה פע"ג). או, שוב לדוגמא: "אמר בן סירא בטרם תדור הכן נדריך בל תהיה כמתעה, 'אל תתן את פיך לחטיא את בשרך' [קהלת ה' ה]" (תנחומא וישלח, בסוף) [27]. וכיוצא בזה אף הבאה מעין זו: "כדכתיב בספר בן סירא הכל שקלתי בכף מאזנים ולא מצאתי קל מסובין, וכל מסובין חתן הדר בבית חמיו, וכל מחתן אורח מכניס אורח, וכל מאורח משיב דבר בטרם ישמע, ש נ א מ ר 'משיב דבר בטרם ישמע אולת היא לו וכלמה' [משלי י"ח יג]" (ב"ב צ"ח ע"ב). שימוש כזה בפסוקי ס' ב"ס, בין בפסוקים ממשיים מתוכו ובין בפסוקים פיקטיביים, מרובה בספרות התלמודית [28]. ובכל ההבאות האלה נחשבים דבריו של ב"ס לא בחזקת "מקרא

משל אשר יש לי מקבילה בס' ב"ס אינו לקוח -- היינו, לפי תודעת בעלי הברייתות -- מעם דוקא. היא אינו נחשב כאן בגדר "כתוב", אלא משל בין משלים אחרים של ר ב נ ן.

25. "ת"ר שלשה חייהן אינם חיים, ואלו הן המצפה לשלחן חבירו" וכו'. אף ברייתא זו שייכת מעיקרה לסידרה הקדומה של משלים מספריים. ובאבות דר"נ פכ"ה ה מובא משל זה בשמו של בן עזאי. גם הוא בן דורו של ר' עקיבא.

26. באמת יש כאן מדרש על דכתיב בתורה: "לכדתניא... 'ואליו הוא נושא את נפשו' [דבר' כ"ד טו], כל הכובש שכר שכיר כאילו נוטל נפשו ממנו". וראה הנאמר להלן בפנים.

27. זהו הנוסח השלם של המאמר ואין לקטעו. לפני הפסוק מקהלת מתבקשת כלת הצעה מעין "שנאמר", "דכתיב" וכדומה.

28. עי' מראי־המקומות אצל מ. צ. סגל, בן סירא, עמ' 28—39 (וכן שם, עמ' 68, סעיף 91) ובפירושים לפסוקים המתאימים. מסתבר שההקף של תופעה זו הוא הרבה יותר ניכר מכפי שהפרופ' סגל מציין. על ב"ס כ"ה יג כפי שמובא בבויק"ר פל"ג, הוא אמנם אומר כי צורתו מדרש למשלי י"ח כא: וכן על שתי מובאות אחרות מב"ס בדברי רז"ל. אך גם ב"ס ל"א א, למשל, המצוטט ע"י רבי לעזר בארמית או ר' אלעזר בן פדת בעברית, משמש להם מדרש על הכתוב על בצר וכל מאמצי כח" (איוב ל"ו יט); עי' מתנות כהונה בשם' רבה פכ"א ז, והש' סנהדרין מ"ד ע"ב. "בר סירא אמר אלה העלה סמים מן הארץ" וכו' (ב"ס ל"ה ד) מובא בבר' רבה פ"י ו כמדרש על הכתוב "וכל צבאם" (בראש' ב' א); עי' בחידושי הרד"ל שם (דפוס ווילנא תרע"א, דף כ"ו ע"א). "בן סירא אומר... הדר בני אדם כסותן" נתפס כמדרש עה"כ "קח את הבגדים" (ויק' ח' ב); עי' בית המדרש לאהרן ילינק, ו' (ירושלים תרצ"ח), עמ' 85. ובשבלי הלקט מהדורת בובר (ווילנא תרמ"ז),

כתוב״ אלא בחזקת מ ד ר ש — אמנם מדרש עתיק ביותר, מלפני היות היצירה התלמודית,
ובכל זאת הוא מדרש שבא, כביכול, רק לגלות פנים חדשות בפסוקי המקרא ואינו מתיימר
כלל לעמוד על מישור אחד אתם.

כמו כן צריך לציין כי מצינו שגם אמוראים משתמשים לפעמים בדברי ב״ס כאילו הם
סתם דברים של חכמה המורגלים בפיהם ואינם דוקא ציטאטים מתוך כתבי־הקדש. בדרך זו
מובאים, למשל, פסוקים של ב״ס משמו של רב, בשני מקומות (עירובין נ״ד ע״א — ב״ס
י״ד יב, כ—כא; שבת י״א ע״א — ב״ס כ״ה טז). והאמורא הארציישראלי רבי אלעזר מביא
דברים ״בשם בר סירה״ (ירו׳ חגיגה ב׳ ה״א, בר׳ רבה פ״ח). לא מצינו שבצורה זו, ״בשם
וכו׳״, יובאו דברים מתוך כתבי־הקדש.

אבל מצויים כמה מקומות בתלמוד שבהם נתפסים דברי ב״ס כפסוקים מן המקרא ממש.
הם מובאים שם בצורות האפייניות: כתיב, דכתיב, שנאמר, ואין מסמיכים אותם לפסוק אחר
מן המקרא, אלא הם עצמם נחשבים בחזקת כתבי־קדש. תופעה כזאת קיימת רק במקורות
אמוראיים — במקורות שמלפני כן אין לה זכר. כך עושים בשמו של רב (עירובין ס״ה ע״א[^])
ומעין זה עושה רבי חנינא (שם שם) וגם רב אחא בר יעקב, בן הדור הרביעי לאמוראי
ארץ־ישראל (חגיגה י״ג ע״א). רבה בר מרי, בן הדור הרביעי לאמוראי בבל, משמיע את
המאמר המופלא: ״...דבר זה כתוב בתורה, שנוי בנביאים ומשולש בכתובים״ — וכ״כתובים״
משמש לו פסוק מס׳ ב״ס (ב״ב צ״ב ע״ב). דברי ב״ס מובאים גם על־ידי סתמא דגמרא
בלשון כתיב (יבמות ס״ג ע״ב[^30], ועי׳ מס׳ כלה רבתי פ״ג). אף על פי כן, לכשתבחן תמצא

דף כ״ג ע״א. המובאה מס׳ ב״ס ״שלשה שנאתי וארבעה לא אהבתי, שר הנרגל בבית המשתאות״ וכו׳
משמשת לרבי יוחנן (נדה ט״ז ע״ב) מצע למדרש עה״כ ״בוזה דרכיו ימות״ (משלי י״ט טז). וראה
מ. היגר, מסכתות זעירות, עמ׳ 10—11 (המובאה מכ״י אדלר 1446). וראה גם בהערה הבאה. על
דוגמאות אלו אפשר להוסיף עוד, חוץ מאותן שכבר סומנו בפנים. שימוש זה של בעלי התלמוד בס׳
ב״ס יוכל אולי להסביר לנו את הופעת קטעי הפסוקים המקראיים, המשובצים במובאות המרובות מס׳
ב״ס שבסנהדרין ק׳ ע״ב: הם משמשים ״נקודות אחיזה״ לדברי ב״ס שנתפסו כמדרש על כתובים.
בדוק ותראה שכל פסוק שם מאוחה עם דברים משל ב״ס הדנים ב א ו ת ו ע נ י ן. ״כי בתואר אשה
יפה רבים הושחתו, ׳ועצומים כל הרוגיה׳ [משלי ז׳ כו]״. ״המרגילים לדבר ערוה כניצוץ מבעיר
גחלת, ׳כלוב מלא עוף כן בתיהם מלאים מרמה׳ [ירמ׳ ה׳ כז]״; כך צריך לפסְ־ ובתיהם שבפסוק
חוזר אל המרגילים. ״רבים יהיו דורשי שלומך גלה סוד לאחד מאלף, ׳משוכבת חיקך שמור פתחי
פיך׳ [מיכה ז׳ ה]״. בכל מקום כזה מתבקשת לפני הבאת הפסוק מלת הצעה מעין ״שנאמר״, ״דכתיב״
וכדומה. אמנם הפסוק מירמ׳ ה׳ כז מעולב גם בנוסח הספר שלפנינו, ב״ס י״א לז.

29. הפסוק המובא כאן, בלשון שנאמר, הוא ״בצר אל יורה״. וראה רש״י. וכבר ציין צונץ כי יש
להשוותו לב״ס ז׳ י (יא); עי׳ הדרשות בישראל וכו׳, מהדורת אלבעק, עמ׳ 282. אבל בירו׳ ברכות
ה׳ ז״א (בראש) מובאים דברים מעין אלה כמדרש עה״כ ״לכן שמעי נא זאת עניה, ושכורת ולא
מיין״ (ישע׳ נ״א כא). ועי׳ בתוספות כאן, עירובין ס״ה ע״א, ד״ה בצר. (והש׳ עכשיו גם א. א.
אורבך, בעלי התוספות, עמ׳ 539, הע׳ 28).

30. הדברים המסומנים על־ידי רב יוסף בסנהדרין ק׳ ע״ב כמילי מעליתא הראויים להידרש,

שבכל המקומות האלה מובאים דברי ב״ס בכל זאת לשם עניינים שמבחינת ההלכה אין להם
חשיבות יתרה. הדברים נתפסים אמנם כמקראות, ובכל זאת רחוקים הם מלשמש בסיס
לעניינים בעלי אופי לגליסטי ממש, אלא הם באים רק לאשש מימרות מקובלות, פתגמי
חכמים ופתגמים עממיים, עצות מן הסוג השגור כיצד להתנהג וכל כיוצא בזה. מאמרו של
רבה בר מרי מתכוון להביא דברי ראיה ל״מילתא דאמרי אינשי, מטייל ואזיל ואזיל דיקלא בישא גבי
קינא דשרכי״, כשם שכל הסוגיא שם אינה אלא מחרוזת של דברי משל מחודדים כאלה,
שהאמורא מבקש להם ראיה במקראות. ולא עוד אלא שעל פתגם עממי זה הוא מכריז כי
יש לו סמך לא מן התורה, הנביאים והכתובים בלבד, אלא גם — ״ותנן במתניתין ותניתא
בברייתא״; והוא ממשיך שם ומביא ראיות גם מהן. טבעי הדבר, שבמקום כזה הוא לא
יקפיד על הקפם המדוייק של הכתובים ומבחינה זו יספיקו לו כראיה אף דברים מתוך ס׳
ב״ס. כיוצא בזה, בשביל רב משמש הפסוק מב״ס ראיה למנהג ש״כל שאין דעתו מיושבת
עליו אל יתפלל״. וכך היה מתנהג גם רבי חנינא — ״ביומא דרתח לא מצלי״.

5. כללו של דבר, לס׳ ב״ס מיוחסת לפעמים מידה מסויימת של קדושה ״קנונית״ אפילו
בספרות התלמודית, אך זוהי מעין קדושה של ביניים, קדושה שאינה מתעלה לדרגה
מקראית־קנונית אמיתית וגם אינה נעדרת לחלוטין, כבספרים שנכתבו מכאן ואילך. ס׳ ב״ס
שייך לפֶּרִיפֶריה של המקרא — אך שייכותו למקום זה נקבעת רק מבחינת המעלה
היחסית של קדושתו. מבחינת צורתו הספרותית, סגנון כתיבתו ומושגיו הכלליים, אולי לא
היתה צריכה להימצא שום מניעה מלשייך אותו לגדר הספרות המקראית ממש[31]. חסרון
מסויים היה רק בערך הקדושה שייחסו לו. במובן זה המעבר בין קדש לחול לא היה נמרץ
וחד־משמעי, אלא רצוף ומודרג. היו גם ספרים שמקומם באמצע, שלא היו קדש גמור וגם
לא חול גמור, אלא שתי ההערכות מתרוצצות יחד והאחת אינה דוחה את השניה לחלוטין.
חשיבותו של ב״ס בכך, שהוא בעצם הדוגמא ה י ח י ד ה שיש לנו מטיפוס זה של ספרי־
ביניים — הדוגמא היחידה מחוג היהדות הפרושית־העממית של ארץ־ישראל ובכל בתקופת
התלמוד. ספרי בן לענה (בקטעי הגניזה: בן לעגא) ובן תגלא, שנזכרו יחד אתו, אין אנו
יודעים מה הם, ולאלה גם לא נמצאה לנו שום ראיה שהסתמכו עליהם כעל כתבי־קדש.
כמה וכמה יצירות אמנם הגיעו לידינו מטיפוס זה של ספרי־ביניים, אבל הללו נקלטו
ונתקדשו בחוג היהדות ה ס ק ט נ ט י ת של ארץ־ישראל (כגון ספרי חנוך, היובלים, צוואת
השבטים ודומיהם, ואף טוביה ויהודית), או בחוג היהדות ההלניסטית של מצרים, צפון־
אפריקה ואסיה הקטנה, יהדות ששפת דיבורה היתה יוונית (כגון איגרת אריסטיאס, ספרי
חשמונאים ב׳—ד׳, חזיונות הסבילות ודומיהם). משם עברו ספרים אלה אל הקנונים של

מובאים כאן בלשון כתיב. ועם זאת ראוי לציין, שאף דברי ההבאי אשר אביי מצטט בסנהדרין שם,
מוצעים על־ידי המלה דכתיב! וכן גם בכמה מאותם המקומות שדברי ב״ס נחשבים בהם כמדרש.

31. למרות זאת לא נרמזה שייכותו של ס׳ ב״ס למקרא בשום מקום ב ת ו כ ו. ולא כפי שמבקשים
הפרשנים למצוא. לענין זה ראה להלן בנספח.

הנצרות. בחוג היהדות הפרושית־העממית של ארץ־ישראל נחשבו הללו, כנראה, כ"חיצונים"
ודחויים. סוג אחר של ספרים, אותם "שנכתבו מכאן ואילך", נשארו בחוג היהדות הפרושית־
העממית של ארץ־ישראל חולין מעיקרם, כאמור. ס' ב"ס לבדו ידוע לנו מבין אלה שזכו
לעלות ביהדות זו על דרך ההתקדשות, ולא זו בלבד אלא שהוא היחיד אשר זכה כי הערכה
של קדושה או קדושה־למחצה תינתן לו פה ושם אפילו בספרות התלמודית.

מקומו של ס' ב"ס כיצירת־ביניים בין כתבי־הקדש האמיתיים לבין ספרים של חולין,
יוכל להסביר לנו את השינויים הטכסטואליים הניכרים שחלו בו ואת הגירסאות שבהן הוא
נמסר בספרות התלמודית. המקורות העבריים שהיו לעיני המתרגם היוני הראשון, לעיני
בעל נוסח התרגום היוני של כ״י 248, לעיני המתרגם הסורי, הנוסחים העבריים כפי שהגיעו
אלינו מכתבי־היד של הגניזה — כל אלה מסמנים שלבים של הידרדרות טכסטואלית
שהמרחק ביניהם גדול למדי [32]. אך יותר מכל אלה מפתיעות הגירסאות המובאות בספרות
התלמודית. הללו בעצם אינן ציטאטות מס' ב"ס, אלא פאראפראזות כמעט חפשיות. את
הסגנון המקראי המובהק, הנמלץ והפיוטי, הבנוי אברים אברים לפי עקרונות התקבולת,
מתירים חז"ל לעצמם לפעמים אפילו לרדד לצורה של לשון חכמים, לפי מיטב המתכונת
של העברית המשנאית. דבר כזה לא היה נעשה בשום אופן אילו הגיע ס' ב"ס למעלת
כתבי־הקדש האמיתיים. ודאי שיש הבדלים דקים גם בין הנוסח של כ״ד ספרים לפי
המסורה לבין הגירסאות המובאות מהם בתלמוד — אך הבדלים אלה אינם יכולים להשתוות
כלל אל ההבדל ה מ כ ר י ע שיש מבחינה זו לגבי ס' ב"ס. נראה שספר זה, אף־על־פי שהיה
נקרא (במידה שנקרא) בנעימה ובטעמים, כדרך ספרים מקראיים, לא זכה שתיעשה לו
מסורה מדוקדקת של פסוקים ותיבות ואותיות — שוב, מפני שמקומו נשאר בין התחומים.
מצד שני ראוי לציין כי פסוקים שונים ממנו מובאים בספרות התלמודית בתרגום ארמי.
רשות ניתנה להניח, שאנו עדים כאן לעצם התהוותו של תרגום ארמי לס' ב"ס, כדרך שלכל
ספרי המקרא נעשו תרגומים ארמיים, ובספרי הכתובים במיוחד הם קיבלו לפעמים צורה
חפשית ביותר עם נופך מדרשי [33].

העובדה שערך של קדושה "קנונית", ולו גם באופן חלקי, ניתן במקורות לס' ב"ס לא
לפני תקופת האמוראים, ודאי אינה מקרה. יחס של קדושה כלפי ספר עשוי להתגבר
ולהתעצם רק תוך מרחק של זמנים ; וביחוד אמור דבר זה ביחס לספרים שמן הרגע הראשון
של יצירתם אינם נתפסים כמחוברים דוקא ברוח־הקדש (מה שאין כן ספרות התורה
והנבואה, שקדושתן באה להן עם בריאתן). בסוג זה של ספרים, שאליו שייכים, כנראה,

32. בעיות אלו נבחנו ונתבררו בפרוטרוט על־ידי מ. צ. סגל, בן סירא, עמ' 53—69.

33. על אפשרות מעין זו כבר רמז צונץ בשעתו. עי' צונץ, הדרשות בישראל וכו', מהדורת
אלבעק, עמ' 50. אבל המחקרים של קאהלה על דרך התהוות התרגומים למקרא (Kahle, The
Cairo Geniza, London 1947, Third Lecture) מקרבים אפשרות זו באופן שונה מכפי שעלתה
במחשבתו של צונץ.

רובם של ספרי הכתובים, רק הדרת־העתיקות שבאה עם חלוף התקופות יכולה לשוות להם
ארשת של קדושה ולבסוף גם לכללם במסגרת הקנונית[34]. בתקופת התנאים עדיין לא
נעשה ס' ב"ס ראוי לעלות על דרך זו. בתקופת האמוראים הוא רק ה ח ל להתקדש —
וביתר דיוק: בתקופה זו רק החלה הכרת קדושתו לחדור לחוגי החכמים בעלי־ההלכה ולקבל
כאילו את הסכמתם למעשה.

עוד ענין אחד יכול להתאשר לנו, על כן, מס' ב"ס, מעצם היותו ספר־ביניים ומן העובדה
שיחס כל־שהו של קדושה החל להתבטא כלפיו רק בימי האמוראים: שמקור ההערכה
של קדושה למקרא ומקור הקנוניזציה של ספריו היה לא בחוגי החכמים בעלי־ההלכה, אלא
ב ע.מ. הקנוניזציה של הכתובים אפילו לא נתאשרה ולא נקבעה סופית ב"סינוד" של יבנה —
כפי שהניחו החוקרים במאה שעברה וכפי שעדיין מקובל אצל רבים[35] — ולא בשום "סינוד"
שמלפניו כן. חוץ ממה שאין לנו במקורות שום עדות ממשית לכך, הרי גם טבען של החלטות
סינודיות כזה, שצריכה להיות בהן הכרעה ברורה לצד אחד —קדש או חול; אבל
עצם מציאותם של ספרי־ביניים המהווים מעבר מודרג מן הקדש אל החול, ומה גם דורות
רבים א ח ר י יבנה, סותר את ההנחה על קנוניזציה בעזרת "החלטות". ובכלל הלא כבר
כמעט שהוסכם, כי שום החלטה חד־פעמית בכנסיה של חכמים לא יכלה לטבוע גושפנקה
של קדושה בספר מן הספרים, אלא אם כן קדמה לה ההערכה בנטיתו הכללית של
העם. לגבי רוב ספרי הכתובים היה זה ללא ספק ת ה ל י ך של התקדשות וקנוניזציה,
שנושאיו העיקריים היו בדרך כלל השכבות הרחבות של העם והמעמיד העיקרי שלו היה
הזמן. ההערכה לספרים לא נכפתה מלמעלה, אלא צמחה מלמטה. באמת בדרך זו נוטים
עכשיו החוקרים לתאר אף את תהליך ההתקדשות והקנוניזציה של כ"ז ספרי הברית
החדשה[36]. ההלכה הרשמית יכולה היתה להתנגד להערכה המקובלת ביחס לספרים
מסויימים, או שיכלה לעודד אותה ולהסתמך עליה——מבחינה זו יכולה היתה ההלכה

34. התקדשות של יצירה ספרותית וקנוניזציה שלה אינן היינו הך. דברי התורה והנביאים נחשבו
ללא ספק לקדושים מרגע יצירתם, אבל רק בתקופות מאוחרות יותר הפכה ספרות קדושה זו — או
חלק ממנה — לאותו דבר שנקרא אצל אבות הכנסיה "קנון". ביחס לרובם של ספרי הכתובים היה
ענין זה שונה במקצת. הללו לא יכלו לדתקדש אלא במרוצת הזמן, אך הקנוניזציה שלהם נעשתה,
כנראה, תקופה קצרה לאחר התקדשותם הגמורה. דברים נכונים על ההבדל שבין התקדשות לקנוניזציה,
הן ביחס למקרא והן ביחס לברית־החדש, מצויים. למשל, אצל
F. F. Bruce, The Books and the
Parchments (London 1950), pp. 94—95.

35. דעה זו עדיין תמצא באפנים שונים. למשל, במבואות של בֶּנטצֶן (I, 1948), עמ' 28—29:
אייספלדט (1934), עמ' 624 ; פפייפֶר (1948), עמ' 64, אם כי גם הללו מודים באופי הסטיכי של
הקנוניזציה ; ואף ביסוד מאמרו של ציטלין, המסומן להלן בהע' 37.

36. ראה, למשל, את הסיכום בספרו הנזכר של F. F. Bruce, עמ' 111, והציטאטה מדברי
Foackes—Jackson המובאת שם: "הכנסיה בודאי לא יצרה את הברית החדשה ; השתים צמחו
יחד".

הרשמית להאיץ את התהליך, או לעכב אותו — אך אין זה משנה מן העובדה שההתהליך עצמו לא נבע ממנה. בס׳ ב״ס אנו רואים בעליל כיצד נוטה ההלכה הרשמית לעצור ולבטל את יחס הקדושה שהחל להסתמן כלפיו. ויחד עם זאת אנו רואים כיצד בשלבים מאוחרים יותר היא נגררת פה ושם אחרי היחס הזה עצמו. אבל ההתנגדות בסופו של דבר עשתה את שלה: אחרי תקופת התלמוד פסקה הערכת הקדושה לס׳ ב״ס כאילו לפתע, בתקופת הגאונים הוא לא יצא מגדר ספר־מוסר רגיל ובסופה של תקופה זו הוא אבד לחלוטין.[36א]

ב. כתבי־הקדש כמטמאי ידים

טימוי ידים שימש, כידוע, אחד מסימני־ההכר לקדושתם של ספרים. ביתר דיוק: לדעתנו הוא שימש גילוי מובהק ביותר לקדושתן של מגילות־הספרים, שבהן נכתב החיבור (וכיוצא בזה לקדושת התיקים שבהם הספרים מונחים ולקדושת המטפחות שבהן הם עטופים)[37].

תופעה זו, שכתבי־הקדש היו [א] פוסלים במגעם את התרומה ו[ב] מטמאים את הידים, היא מופלאה ותמוהה ביותר. ודאי שאין לדמות אותה — כשם שעשו בטעות כמה חוקרים מודרניים — לקדושה המדבקת, המיוחסת בס״כ (P = המקור) ובס׳ יחז׳ מ׳—מ״ח למקדש ולאביזריו; ולא לטומאה המדבקת הרווחת במקרא ומוכרת בכל העולם העתיק. כי אובייקט־טים קדושים מעבירים קדושה על־ידי מגע, וכן אבות־טומאה מעבירים טומאה — אבל כאן מניחים שאובייקט קדוש מ ט מ א על־ידי מגע. תופעה זו היא מיוחדת במינה וכבר לראשוני

36א. בערך הנזכר של פרופ׳ קויפמן, Encyclopaedia Judaica, כרך ב׳, עמ׳ 1168, מפורשת סיבה נוספת, אחרונה, לאבדנו של ס׳ ב״ס (יחד עם כל הספרים החיצוניים): הללו לא יכלו להיקלט במסגרת התורה שבע״פ, מחמת צורתם הפורמאלית שהיתה שונה מצורתה של זו. שכן, גם התורה שבע״פ נחשבה אצל היהדות כקדושה, לא פחות מן התורה שבכתב, אם כי באופן שונה ממנה. וכיון שס׳ ב״ס גם לא הפך לאחת מיצירותיה של התורה שבע״פ, לכן נעשה חולין. במאמר זה לא טיפלנו בגורלו הכללי של ס׳ ב״ס, אלא רק בבעית הקנוניזציה שלו, כלומר, ביחסו אל התורה ש ב כ ת ב דוקא. העובדה, שהוא לא הצליח להיכלל במסגרת הקנונית — והיא שעניינה אותנו כאן — שימשה, גם היא סיבה ראשונה לאבדנו. אך מעניין הדבר שהמקורות התלמודיים מייחסים לס׳ ב״ס גם משהו מן הערך של ״מדרש״, כפי שקבענו למעלה (עמ׳ 254—255). משמע שגם לגבי התורה שבע״פ תפס ספר זה מעין עמדה של בינים: הוא החל כביכול להשתלב בה, אך לא נשתלב ממש.

37. ענין טימוי הידים נדון הרבה בספרים המיוחדים לבעית הקנון, בעיקר מן המאה שעברה (של Buhl, Ryle, Wildeboer, Budde ואחרים). אצל אלה ניטשטש לעתים ההבדל שבין ענין טימוי הידים לענין הגניזה. יעויין כמו כן ביחוד אצל G. F. Moore, Judaism in the First Centuries of the Christian Era, vol. I pp. 242 ff., vol. III pp. 65—69; במאמר של ר׳ מאיר איש שלום, הנזכר להלן; מ. צ. סגל, מבוא, ספר ד׳, עמ׳ 819—832; S. Zeitlin, An Historical Study of the Canonization of the Hebrew Scriptures, Proceedings of the American Academy for Jewish Research 3(1931-2), pp. 130—134, 138—141; וכן גם במבואות הישנים והחדשים למקרא, בפרק על הקנון. כל אלה כבר נהגו לציין את המקורות העיקריים.

התנאים לא היתה מובנת, כי ההסברים הניתנים לה בספרות התלמודית אינם אלא טעם
"מושכל" בדיעבד, ולא סיבתו הראשונה והממשית של המנהג. העובדה שהספר פוסל את
התרומה במגע מוסברת בבבלי על-ידי רב משרשיא בעזרת התירוץ, שבתחילה היו מצניעים
תרומה אצל ס"ת והספרים היו מתקלקלים (היינו, מחמת מציאות עכברים, כרש"י) ומשום כך
גזרו רבנן, כביכול, טומאה בספרים — כדי שלא יבואו להצניע בהם דברי אוכל (שבת י"ד
ע"א). ואילו העובדה שכתבי-הקדש מטמאין את הידים מוסברת על-ידי ר' יוחנן בן זכאי
משום ש"לפי חבתן היא טומאתן" (מ' ידים פ"ד ו), "שלא יעשה אותן שטיחים לבהמה"
(תוספתא ידים ב' יט). ואין שום הכרח לומר כי אלה הם דברי אירוניה וליצנות כלפי
הצדוקים, כמו שהניח הרמב"ם בפירושו למשנת ידים ופרשנים אחרים בעקבותיו. והשווה
בפירושי הרא"ש ור"ש משאנ"ץ שם.

תירוצו של רב משרשיא, אף-על-פי שמלאכותי הוא ובשום אופן אינו יכול לחשוף את
השורש האמיתי של תופעה זו, לא היתה בו מניעה שיתקבל על דעתם של פרשני המשנה
הישנים[38]. ור' מאיר איש שלום[39] הודה כי "אין לתלות הדבר בעכברים" והדגיש, שהטעמים
שהמציאו האמוראים לגזירות הקדמוניות אינם "מסורת וקבלה, אלא השערות וסברות הן
לשכך את הלב". אך לפי דרכו שיער גם הוא את טעם הדברים והסביר אותם כגזירה קדומה
להגדיל את כבודו של ספר העזרה, גזירה שנתרחבה אחרי-כן על כל ספרי התורה והנביאים
כדי לעשות סייג כנגד הצדוקים, מתוך "שרצו למנוע את הבנים מלקרות התורה שבכתב
מעצמם, שלא יהא לבם נוטה אחר פשוטן של המקראות"[40]. עד שלבסוף נתרחבה הגזירה
גם על ספרי הכתובים. גזירה זו הוא תופס כעין צורה מתונה של גניזת ספרים.

בעינינו נראה שאין כאן שום "גזירה" במובן של תקנת חכמים, לא כסייג כלפי הצדוקים
ולא כסייג נגד הפסד ספרים. מסתבר שאין זה אלא גילוי מיוחד-במינו של מנהג מיושן,
שמטעו הן אמונות-עם וספירתו הן מוסכמות והרגלים, שלעתים קרובות יכולים להיות אי-
רציונאליים. דבריהם של ריב"ז ורב משרשיא כאחד אינם אלא רציונאליזציה מאוחרת והם
עצמם מוכיחים שהמניעים האמיתיים של מושג זה כבר היו רחוקים מהם. אמנם על הספר
שהוא פוסל את התרומה נאמר, שהוא מי"ח דברים שנאמרו בעלית חנניה בן חזקיה בן גרון
(שבת י"ג ע"ב, פסחים י"ט ע"ט ע"ב והמקבילות). אבל על כתבי-הקדש שהם מטמאים את הידים
לא נרמז כלל שהם מי"ח דברים שנאמרו בו ביום[41]. לאמיתו של דבר, כל המקורות שבמשנה

38. וכך אף אצל מ. צ. סגל, מבוא, ספר ד', עמ' 821.

39. במאמרו "גלגול טומאת ידים בכלל וע"י מגע בכתבי-הקדש בפרט", "הגרן" ג', עמ' 30—39.

40. שם, עמ' 32.

41. בעלית חנניה בן חזקיה גזרו שנוסף על הספר, גם הידים (רש"י: "סתמן קודם נטילתן") פוסלות
את התרומה, כאחד מי"ח הדברים (שבת י"ג ע"ב). עובדה זו עומדת בקו אחד עם אותה מסורת
שקובעת כי "שמאי והלל גזרו טומאה על הידים" (שם י"ד ע"ב). אך בגמרא (שם שם ע"א) הוסיפו
לזה "אף ידים הבאות מחמת ספר פוסלות את התרומה" (ואגב כך הביאו נימוק נוסף לטימוי ידים

מקבלים את התופעה הזאת, שבכתבי־הקדש יש "טומאה" מסויימת, לתומם, כאילו היא מובנת מאליה. בית־שמאי ובית־הלל כאחד מסכימים, שכתבי־הקדש בדרך כלל צריכים לטמא את הידים, ואם נחלקו לא נחלקו אלא על ספרים מ ס ו י י מ י ם אם מטמאים הם או לא. יתר על כן: אף י"ח הדברים שנאמרו בו ביום היו מכוונים סוף סוף כלפי ה ת ר ו מ ה. לא ש"גזרו" טומאה בספר, אלא הכריזו כי הספר — בין שאר דברים — יש בו כדי לפסול את התרומה. האמונה המוסכמת שבספר יש משהו מן ה"טומאה" קדמה כאן להכרזת הפיסול של התרומה. נראה שאמונה תמוהה וישנה זו נתגלגלה למנהיגיהם של הפרושים ונשתלבה בהם, אך הצדוקים לא קיבלוה. מוצאה לפחות מימי הזוגות, ואולי אף מן התקופה הטרום־ הלניסטית, תקופה אפלה בתולדות הבית השני, שאין אנו יודעים עליה כמעט ולא כלום.

כן יש להטעים, שטימוי ידים שימש סימן הכר בעיקר לקדושתה של מגילת־העור, שבה נכתבו הדברים, ולא לקדושתו של החיבור עצמו. אף ספרים שהוחלט עליהם כי אינם מטמאים את הידים, עדיין לא היתה קדושתם מוכרחת לפקוע לחלוטין. המחלוקת ביחס לטימוי ידים נסבה רק על חיבורים מבין ח מ ש ה מ ג י ל ו ת: שיה"ש, קהלת ואסתר. יתכן שהיתה מחלוקת אף על מגילת רות. כך לפחות משתמע מנוסח הברייתא, מגילה ז' ע"א: "ר' שמעון אומר... אבל ר ו ת ושיר השירים ואסתר מטמאין את הידים". עובדה זו, שהמחלוקת הצטמצמה רק על חיבורים מבין חמש המגילות, ודאי איננה מקרה. מן הסתם יש לה אחיזה בצורות הכתיבה וההחזקה של החיבורים באותו הזמן. אך אפילו החליטו שחיבור מסויים מבין אלה אינו מטמא את הידים — אין זאת אומרת, שהדבר יכול היה לעשותו חול גמור. דבר זה יכול היה בעיקר להורות, שאין לנהוג קדושה בגוף הספר שבו כתוב החיבור, בגוויליו, אבל לא שדברי החיבור עצמם הם נטולי קדושה. מובן שחיבור אשר החליטו עליו כי לא נאמר ברוח הקדש, ממילא לא יוכל לטמא את הידים — אבל חיבור שאינו מטמא את הידים עדיין א י נ ו מ ו כ ר ח להיות אמור שלא ברוח־הקדש. ביחס למגילת אסתר קובע שמואל במפורש, שאף־על־פי שאינה מטמאה את הידים, בכל זאת היא נאמרה ברוח־הקדש — "לקרות" בלבד (מגילה ז' ע"א).[42] סיוע כלשהו להבחנתנו אפשר למצוא גם בעובדה, שעל הדעה כי קהלת אינה מטמאה את הידים אמרו שהיא "מ ק ו ל י

על־ידי ספר: משׁום דר' פרנך, שחובה לאחוז ס"ת במטפחת ולא בידים). אלא שגם ההלכה הזאת, ש"ידים הבאות מ ח מ ת ס פ ר פוסלות את התרומה", ש ה ג מ ר א משחילה שם, לא נאמרה כלל בעלית חנניה בן חזקיה. וע'י בתוספות שם, ד"ה אף הידים. ואפילו נניח שההלכה הנוספת הזאת נאמרה בעלית חנניה בן חזקיה הרי גם אז טומאת הספר עצמו באמת ק ד מ ה ל"גזירה" זו והיתה לגביה כמובנת מאליה. משנת ידים פ"ג ב ("כל הפוסל את התרומה מטמא את הידים להיות עניות"), ולהלן המחלוקת בין ר' יהושע וחכמים) אף היא אינה קשורה בעלית חנניה בן חזקיה. כל שנלמד ממנה מבחינה זו לגבי טימוי ידים ע"י ספר הריהו רק ספר העובדה, שהענין הוא מדברי סופרים ולא מדברי תורה.

42. ונוסח דבריו של ר' שמעון בן מנסיא בתוספתא ידים ב' יד (הש' מגילה ז' ע"א) אינו מספיק כדי לבטל את ההנחה הזאת.

בית שמאי" ועל הדעה ההפוכה אמרו שהיא "מ ח ו מ ר י בית הלל" (מ' עדיות פ"ה ג,
ידים פ"ג ה, מגילה ז' ע"א). אילו הדעה שקהלת אינה מטמאה את הידים היתה מתכוונת
לכפור בקדושת החיבור מכל וכל, הרי לשון זה של "קולא" לא היה מתאים לכאן. אבל לשון
זה הולם יפה את הענין אם נניח, שדעת בית שמאי אמנם אינה מתכוונת לבטל לחלוטין
את קדושת ס' קהלת, אלא רק ל ה ק ל בקדושתי, באשר הם סבורים כי אין צורך לנהוג
קדושה י ת ר ה בגוויליו. ואילו בית הלל מחמירים במקרה זה, באשר הם טוענים כי קדושה
מן הסוג החמור ביותר, קדושה כמעט "חמרית", צריך לייחס אפילו לגוויליו, כמו בכל שאר
כ"ד הספרים.

רק מתוך הבחנה זו בין ערכו הסקרלי הכללי של החיבור (שלא עמד בוויכוח) לבין
הקדושה שצריך לנהוג בגוויליו, נוכל להבין כיצד נחלקו תנאים ואמוראים אם ספר פלוני
מטמא את הידים — בשעה שמחלוקת זו ממש כבר הוכרעה לכאורה דורות רבים לפניהם.
להבחנה זו רמזתי בכמה מקומות במאמר א, וראה גם במאמר הבא.

ג. קדושת ספרים וגניזת ספרים

1. כמה דרגות קיימות לפי המקורות התלמודיים בקדושת הספרים. אלא שדרגות אלו
מסתבכות ומסתעפות עוד יותר בגלל הערכות סותרות ודברי מחלוקת הנכרכים לעתים
סביב אותו הספר שנכתב באותו האופן.

הצורה החמורה ביותר בקדושת ספר, אם לא להביא בחשבון את ספר העזרה שדינו יוצא
מן הכלל (כלים פט"ו ו), הרי זה כשיש בו באותו ספר כדי לטמא את הידים. צורה זו
קיימת בכל כתבי-הקדש, אבל רק כשהם כתובים בלשונם המקורית—היינו עברית, וכל אותם
קטעים בעזרא ובדניאל (עם הפסוק הבודד ירמ' י' יא) שלשונם ארמית במקורה —
וכשהכתב הוא אשורי ועשוי על העור ובדיו (מ' ידים פ"ד ה, מגילה ח' ע"ב והמקבילות).
ולא עוד אלא שגם רצועות התפילין, וגם "גליון שבבספר שמלמעלן ושמלמטן", שלא נכתב
עליו כלום, וגם "ספר שנמחק ונשתייר בו שמונים וחמש אותיות" — כל אלה מטמאים את
הידים (מ' ידים פ"ג ג—ה). וכיוצא בזה אף כל אביזריהם של הספרים, התיק והמטיבה
והמטפחות, מטמאים את הידים (תוספתא ידים ב' יב). סוג לעצמם יוצרים כאן אותם
החיבורים מבין חמש המגילות, שמבחינה זו היו שנויים במחלוקת: שיר-השירים, קהלת,
אסתר וכנראה גם רות. אך אין ספק שגם אותם חכמים שנחלקו על קדושת הגוויליים במקרה
זה, לא כפרו בקדושת החיבורים כשלעצמם, כאמור במאמר הקודם, וודאי שאיש מהם לא
נתכוון לומר, שהחיבורים האלה (אף שגוויליהם אינם מטמאים את הידים) לא ניתנו לקרות
בהם. מיד נראה שהיתה דעה כי אפילו ספרים שנכתבו בכל לשון — שעליהם איש לא
נחלק כי אינם מטמאים את הידים — בכל זאת גם הם ניתנו לקרות וקדושה מסויימת
היתה בהם.

הספרים שנכתבו בכל לשון חוץ מן העברית-האשורית (עם הקטעים הארמיים המקוריים),

מהווים דרגה אחרת של קדושה, למטה מן הקודמת. מה היה דינם של אלה? היתה השקפה
אחת, "שהספרים נכתבין בכל לשון" (מ' מגילה פ"א ח, שבת קט"ו ע"ב), זאת אומרת,
שניתנו לקרות בהן. אף היה מעשה ברבן גמליאל השני, בטבריה, שנמצא יושב עם ספר
איוב תרגום בידו והוא קורא בו (שבת קט"ו ע"א). אם כי ברור שאיש מן החכמים לא
העלה על דעתו שהללו יטמאו את הידים. והיתה השקפה אחרת, זו שנתבטאה על-ידי רבן
שמעון בן גמליאל, שבספרים התירו שיכתבו, בצד העברית-האשורית, יונית בלבד (מ'
מגילה פ"א ח). בגמרא פסקו שההלכה כרשב"ג. הטעם להעדפה מיוחדת זו של היונית נעוץ,
כמובן, במציאות החברתית-התרבותית של אותה תקופה, שהיונית היתה רווחת ומכובדת
הרבה ואפילו בבית רבי היו כרוכים אחריה. ברייתא אחת מצמצמת את ההתר האכסקלוסיבי
הזה לגבי היונית על התורה בלבד: "אף כשהתירו רבותינו יונית לא התירו אלא בספר
תורה, ומשום מעשה דתלמי המלך". ואגב כך מציינים המקורות עשרה או שלושה-עשר
דברים שאותם ע"ב זקנים שינו בתורה (מגילה ט' ע"א ובירו' א' הי"א, מס' סופרים פ"א ח,
והש' תנחומא שמות כב [43] ועוד). ומעין זה התירו לפי דעה אחת, שקריאת המגילה תיעשה
בלעז, אבל רק ללועזות (מ' מגילה פ"ב א), והלעז במשנה זו משמעו, כנראה, באמת יונית
דוקא, כמו שפירשו רב ושמואל בגמרא שם [44]. אך היתה עוד השקפה שלישית קיצונית,
שאין לכתוב ספרים אלא עברית ובכתב אשורי בלבד. "היו כותבין גיפטית [= קופטית],
מדית, עיברית [= בכתב עברי עתיק], עילמית, יוונית... לא ניתנו לקרות בהן" (שבת קט"ו
ע"א, הש' מס' סופרים פ"א ו) [45]. מעין ההשקפה הקיצונית הזאת אמרו סוף סוף גם במשנת
מגילה פ"ב ב: "קראה תרגום [= ארמית], בכל לשון, לא יצא". ועל כתיבת התורה ביונית
מספר מקור אחד, כידוע, כי "היה היום קשה לישראל כיום שנעשה העגל" (שם שם ז). —
למחלוקת זו ביחס לקריאה הנכונה של ספרים, אפשר להקביל אף את המחלוקת בנוגע
לקריאת שמע, אם זו יכולה להיעשות בכל לשון או ככתבה בלבד (ברכות י"ג ע"א ועוד).

כלום נחשבו כל הספרים האלה, שנכתבו בכל לשון, כנטולי קדושה לחלוטין? שום
נקודת-מוצא אינה מניחה לענות על השאלה הזאת בחיוב. אלא שכאן, שוב, האפשרויות
מסתעפות ומסתבכות קמעה, בהתאם להשקפות השונות.

---

43. יש גורסים בכמה מקומות שמונה עשר במקום עשרה, מתוך ההנחה שהמלה שמונה נשמטה.
עי' במה שמביא בעל פי' עץ יוסף למקום זה בתנחומא, בשם בעל יפה תואר. אבל נראה יותר
שהעיקר שלשה עשר והמלה שלשה היא שנשמטה, או שנסתרסה בכמה מקומות לשמונה.

44. ושם בגמרא, י"ח ע"א, הגיעו לבסוף לומר שאליבא דרב ושמואל "לעז יווני לכל כשר"
ושדינו הושווה למעשה אל האשורית. וכך פירש הרמב"ם את משנתנו בפירושו.

45. לברייתא זו יש להקיש את הברייתא המובאת במגילה י"ח ע"א: "קראה גיפטית, עברית,
עילמית, מדית, יוונית, לא יצא". פשט משמעה של זו הוא, שקריאת המגילה צריכה להיעשות
מתוך אשורית דוקא, ואם היתה כתובה בכל לשון ובכל כתבים לא יוכל לצאת ידי חובת קריאה. ולא
כפי שהסבירוה בגמרא שם, "גיפטית לגיפטים, עברית לעברים, עילמית לעילמים וכו' יצא" — מתוך
הרמוניזציה עם ההתר המיוחד שנאמר במשנת מגילה פ"ב א: "אבל קורין אותה ללועזות בלעז".

אותם שסבורים היו כי הספרים ניתנו לקרות בהן כשהם כתובים בכל לשון, לא פיקפקו,
כמובן, שיש בהם קדושה של ממש ושמשום כך יש גם להציל אותם בשבת מפני הדליקה
(עי' בגמרא שבת קט"ו ע"א ; וזוהי דעת הת"ק בברייתא המובאת שם : "היו כתובין תרגום
ובכל לשון, מצילין אותן מפני הדליקה"). אך גם אותם חכמים שסבורים היו כי הללו לא
ניתנו לקרות בהן — גם הם לא תיארו כלל, שקדושת הספרים האלה בטלה מכל וכל. גם
בין אלה היתה, בכל זאת, דעה (והיא דעת "תנא דגיפטית" בברייתא המובאת שם, ודעת
רב חסדא, ולפי הפשט אף דעת תנא דמתניתין שם), שצריך להציל את הספרים הללו
בשבת מפני הדליקה. ואפילו לפי ההשקפה הקיצונית-שבקיצונית, היא ההשקפה הגורסת
כי ספרים שנכתבו בכל לשון לא ניתנו לקרות בהן וכי אין מצילין אותם בשבת מפני
הדליקה (לדעת ר' יוסי בברייתא המובאת שם, וכדעת רב הונא) — הרי גם לפי ההשקפה
הזאת עדיין הכל מסכימים, שלפחות צריך לגנוז את הספרים [46]. גניזת הספרים אינה
יכולה להיעשות אלא מתוך ההנחה שיש בהם קדושה.

לפנינו, אם כן, שוב מעין סולם יורד, או מעבר מודרג מן הצורות החמורות אל הצורות
הקלות של קדושת ספרים — בדומה למעבר המודרג והרצוף שהזכרנו במאמר א, מכ"ד
הספרים שקדושתם ודאית (ואף בתוכם מצוי דירוג במעלות הקדושה: תורה, נביאים,
כתובים) אל הספרים שנכתבו מכאן ואילך, שנחשבו חולין גמורים. אבל יש להיזהר מפני
השוואה נחפזת. הסולם האחד (הוא שנדון במאמר זה עד כאן) מיוסד על בחינה צורנית
גרידא, השני (הוא שטיפלנו בו במאמר א) — על בחינה תכנית-מהותית. במקרה האחד
אנו דנים בכ"ד הספרים בלבד, שקדושת-יצירתם כשלעצמה אינה מפוקפקת, אלא שחומרתם
מתמעטת ככל שהם כתובים ב צ ו ר ה אחרת: אשורית על העור ובדיו, יונית, בכל לשון, על
דפתרא ועל גבי נייר, בסם ובסיקרא, בסם ודומיהם. במקרה השני מוריד אותנו הסולם אל הספרים
ש מ ח ו ץ לגדר כתבי-הקדש האמיתיים, שעצם הקדושה של יצירתם נעשית מסופקת,
ואפילו הם כתובים בצורה הלגיטימית ביותר — אשורית על העור ובדיו. לפיכך אתה מוצא
שבמקרה האחד לעולם אין הקדושה של הספרים מתבטלת לחלוטין: כ"ד הספרים, גם
כשלא ניתנו לקרות בהם ואין להצילם בשבת מפני הדליקה, לעולם נשארת בהם קדושה
ובמצב "הגרוע ביותר" צריך לגנזם. ואילו במקרה השני מוריד אותנו הסולם אל הביטול
הגמור, אל היצירות שמעיקרן הן חילוניות. ולא עוד אלא שברגע שאנו חורגים שם מכלל

---

46. עי' בסיפור המובא על-ידי ר' יוסי בברייתא שם, בשם חלפתא אביו, ושכבר צויין בפנים. סופו
של המעשה היה, לדברי ר' יוסי, ש"אף הוא [רבן גמליאל השני, בטבריה] צוה עליו [על ס' איוב
תרגום] וגנזו". וראה דברי רב הונא באותה הסוגיא: "ואפילו הכי [שאין מצילין אותן] גניזה בעו".
לפי הפשט, תנא דמתניתין מניה כי ספרים שנכתבו בכל לשון אמנם אין קורין בהן — אבל מ צ י ל י ן
אותן מפני הדליקה. ואף הוא מסכים כי הללו "טעונים גניזה", כפי שאמנם אומר שם. לשיטתו צריך
לגנזם בדרך מכובדת ולא להפקירם לאש.

כ״ד הספרים, שוב אין מקום לדבר על גניזת ספרים, כי קדושתם של אלה כבר היתה רופפת ומפוקפקת מכדי שאפשר יהיה לנהוג בהם ג נ י ז ה.

2. בעית הגניזה כבר נדונה אצל חוקרים הרבה, ישנים וחדשים, אם כי אף המובהקים שבהם לא נצרכו למצות את העדויות על מנת להבהיר מהותו של מושג זה [47]. לעניננו כאן חשוב להטעים בעיקר את זיקתה הפנימית של הגניזה ל ק ד ו ש ת הספרים.

הבחינה יכולה להוכיח שהמקורות התלמודיים מזכירים גניזה, לפי הפשט, רק בקשר עם אובייקטים של קדושה שלא ניתנו לשימוש: אין גניזה נעשית אלא באובייקטים כאלה. והמניעה מלהשתמש בהם יכולה להיות אובייקטיבית (למשל, במידה שהם נפסדים ומתקלקלים) וגם ״סובייקטיבית״, היינו, באשר יש איסור מדאורייתא או מדרבנן. חזקיהו ואנשיו גנזו את כלי השרת שהוזנחו על-ידי אחז (ע״ז נ״ב ע״ב). בית חשמונאי גנזו את אבני המזבח ששקצום מלכי יון (מדות פ״א ו). אנטונינוס ששאל לרבי מהו לבנות מזבח, נענה: ״בניהו וגנוז אבניו״ (ירו' מגילה א' הי״ג). חכמים אמנם ״ביקשו לגנוז כל כסף וזהב שבעולם״ — אבל היה זה ״מפני כספה וזהבה של ירושלים״, שהוא של הקדש (בכורות נ' ע״א, ועי' רש״י). על עצי ירושלים אמרו שהן ״של קינמון היו, ובשעה שהיו מסיקין מהן ריחן נודף בכל ארץ ישראל, ומשחרבה ירושלים נגנזו״ (שבת ס״ג ע״א; הכוונה ודאי לעצים שהיו מסיקין מהן במקדש ושל הקדש היו. האפר של תרומת הדשן טעון גניזה, ואליבא דרבנן גם בגדי לבן של כהן גדול (כריתות ו' ע״א, פסחים כ״ו ע״א והמקבילות; לדעת רבי דוסא הם כשרים לכהן הדיוט). התלמוד מניח שלאחר שלאחר שנבנה בית ראשון ״נגנז אהל מועד, קרשיו, קרסיו, בריחיו, ועמודיו, ואדניו״ (סוטה ט' ע״א). ביחס לגורלו הסופי של הארון יש דעה כי הוא לא גלה לבבל, אלא ״במקומו נגנז״ (יומא נ״ג ע״ב, נ״ד ע״א, הש' מ' שקלים פ״ו א—ב, תוספתא סוטה י״ג א). לדברי אבא שאול גנזו כהנים סכין מטרפת שהיתה במקדש (זבחים פ״ח ע״א). תרומה שהופרשה על-ידי עכו״ם שלא בדעת ישראל טעונה גניזה, ועכו״ם שהתנדב קורה לבנין בית-הכנסת קורתו טעונה גניזה, כיון שבכל אלו חוששים ״שמא בלבו לשמים״ והתכוון לעשותן הקדש (ערכין ו' ע״א, הש' תוספתא מגילה ג' ה). מעשר שני וכתבי-הקדש של עיר הנידחת טעונים גניזה (מ' סנהדרין פ״י ו). כיוצא בזה נאמרה גניזה לגבי ס״ת שבלה ואינו ראוי לשימוש, מטפחות ספרים שבלו (מגילה כ״ו ע״ב), ס״ת שיש בו שלוש או ארבע טעויות בכל דף

47. השווה כמסומן בהערה 37. בספרו של מור, Judaism, כרך ג', ביחוד עמ' 70—72; במאמרו של ר' מאיר איש שלום, ״גלגול טומאת ידים וכו'״ — בחלק השלישי: ״הגרן״ ד', עמ' 5—12; אצל מ. צ. סגל, מבוא, ספר ד', עמ' 823—826. הש' גם Max L. Margolis, The Hebrew Scrip- tures in the Making (Philadelphia 1943), pp. 85—90; והערך של W. Bacher בתוך Hastings' Encyclopaedia of Religion and Ethics, VI, pp. 187—189 ובמיוחד בערך של J. K[aufmann], Encyclopaedia Judaica, II, S. 1164—1165; ובמאמר הנזכר של צייטלין, עמ' 124—128, 155 (אף הוא נזדמן לידי בדיעבד).

ודף (מנחות כ"ט ע"ב), מקק ספרים ומקק מטפחותיהם (שבת צ' ע"א[48]). הדין הוא
ש"תשמישי מצוה נזרקין, תשמישי קדושה נגנזין"; באחרונים הכוונה לתפילין, מזוזות,
דלוסקמי ספרים, תיק של ס"ת וכדומה (מגילה כ"ו ע"ב). ולא עוד אלא שגונזים ספרים
שלא ניתנו לקרות בהם, אם מפני שנכתבו בכל לשון (לעיל והערה 46), אם מפני שנכתבו
שלא כהלכה — למשל, כשהאזכרות נכתבו בהם בזהב (מס' סופרים פ"א ט, הש' שבת
ק"ג ע"ב) — ואם מפני שהספר נכתב על-ידי עכו"ם, או שנמצא ביד מין (עי' גיטין
מ"ה ע"ב). אמרה הסוטה "איני שותה" עד שלא נמחקה המגילה, מגילתה נגנזת (מ' סוטה
פ"ג ג)[49]. יש דעה שאפילו צריך לקדור את האזכרות מתוך ספרי מינים ולגנזן (שבת
קט"ז ע"א), כמו שגורדים גם את השם שהיה כתוב על ידות הכלים, על קרן הפרה ועל
כרעי המיטה, לשם קמיע, וגונזים אותו, ואם היה כתוב על האבן, שומטה וגונזה (שם
ס"א ע"ב, הש' מס' סופרים פ"ה יג). ועל דוגמאות אלו ודאי שאפשר להוסיף עוד כהנה.

בכל הגניזות האלה הכוונה היא בדרך כלל להטמנה של אותו אובייקט מקודש במקום
סגור ונסתר, על מנת שיהיה נפסד שם מאליו בדרך מכובדת ויישאר מחוץ לאפשרות
ההשגה על-ידי הציבור. בית חשמונאי גנזו את אבני המזבח באחת הלשכות שבבית
המוקד. רבן גמליאל הראשון גנז ספר איוב תרגום על-ידי שביקש את אחד הבנאים
ושיקעו תחת הנדבך בהר הבית (ירו' שבת ט"ז ה"א, הש' ב' קט"ו ע"א). הסכינים (מסתבר:
לכשיצאו מכלל שימוש) היו נגנזות בבית החליפות שמשני צדי האולם (מדות פ"ד ז).
מטפחות ספרים נגנזות על-ידי שעושים אותן תכריכין למת מצוה, ס"ת שבלה גונזים
אותו בקבר של תלמיד חכם (מגילה כ"ו ע"ב) ומגילת הסוטה נגנזת תחת צירו של היכל
(תוספתא סוטה ב' ב—ג)[50].

48. (המשנה). וראה רש"י שם: "שכל דבר קדש טעון גניזה", היינו, לכשיצא מכלל שימוש. והש'
סוטה מ"ט ע"ב: "משמת רבי אליעזר נגנז ס"ת" — מכל שורת המאמרים הסטיריאוטיפיים המובאים
שם נאמר לשון גניזה רק לגבי ס"ת.

49. וראה רש"י בפירושו בגמרא (סוטה כ' ע"א): "דכל כתבי הקדש שאינן ראויין לקרות בהן
נגנזין, שלא יתבזו".

50. באגדות ובמדרשים אנו מוצאים לעתים קרובות שימוש מושאל למושג ה"גניזה". כך אמרו
על התורה שהיא "חמודה גנוזה", שהיתה גנוזה תשע מאות ושבעים וארבעה דורות קודם שנברא
העולם והקב"ה היד משתעשע בה בכל יום, עד שבא משה וקיבלה (שבת פ"ח ע"ב, פ"ט ע"א). על
השבת מודיע הקב"ה, "מתנה טובה יש לי בבית גנזי ושבת שמה ואני מבקש ליתנה לישראל וכו'"
(ביצה ט"ז ע"א). במדרש מסוגלים אפילו לדבר על "גניזה" של אליהו (תוספתא סוטה י"ב ה,
הש' סדר עולם רבה פי"ז). וכך אמרו גם על נשמותיהם של צדיקים שהן „גנוזות תחת כסא הכבוד"
(שבת קנ"ב ע"ב). אור שברא הקב"ה ביום ראשון "עמד וגנזו... לצדיקים לעתיד לבא" (חגיגה י"ב
ע"א). ובמקרים רבים מדובר על "גניזה" של ענינים שהם מופשטים כמעט לחלוטין וגם קדושה
שלישית אין בהם, אלא שיש בהם זיקה קרובה לקדושה ומשום כך הם בבחינת סינונימים שלה: כגון
צדקה, טהרה, יראת שמים וכדומה. כך יכולים לדבר על גניזה של אוצרות צדקה על-ידי מונבז המלך
(ב"ב י"א ע"א, תוספתא פאה ד' יח), על גנזי חיים וגנזי שלום וגנזי ברכה השמורים עם הקב"ה (חגיגה

וכך אנו רואים שלפעמים ניסו לגנוז גם חיבורים מסוימים מתוך כתבי־הקדש.
הנימוקים לכך יכלו להיות: (1) שדבריו של אותו חיבור מכילים סתרי תורה, (2) או שהם
סותרים דברי תורה, (3) או שהם סותרים זה את זה, (4) או שהם מטים לצד מינות. מן
הטעמים האלה ניסו, כידוע, לגנוז את ספרי יחזקאל (שבת י״ג ע״ב והמקבילות, חגיגה
י״ג ע״א: מעשה בתינוק אחד וכו׳), קהלת ומשלי (שבת ל׳ ע״ב, קהל״ר פ״א ד) 51.
גניזה זו של חיבורים אין לנו להבין כ״עירעור״ על קדושתם, כשם שנטו חוקרים רבים
להניח. אדרבא, קדושת החיבורים האלה היתה מובנת מאליה ואיש לא פיקפק בה אפילו
במשהו, אלא שהם נראו בלתי־ניתנים לשימוש מחמת דבריהם הקשים. וגניזת חיבורים
מסוימים מתוך כתבי־הקדש, כמו גם גניזת אובייקטים מוחשיים, יכלה להתבטא ללא
ספק רק על־ידי העלמתם המוחלטת־למעשה והוצאתם מחוץ לאפשרות השימוש על־ידי
הציבור. רחוקה היא הדעה המניחה, למשל, כי ״גניזת ספר הוא שלא יהא מסור בידי העם
כי אם ליחידים הראויים לכך״, או המגדירה את הנסיון לגנוז את ספר יחזקאל ככוונה
״שלא יהא בכלל ספרי הנביאים כי אם בכלל הכתובים, כספר דניאל״ 52. אילו כזה היה
המעשה לגבי החיבורים, לא יכול היה להיטיב בו אותו המונח שנטבע לגבי האובייקטים
המוחשיים — גניזה. ברור שבשני המקרים האלה כוונת הגניזה ביסודה צריכה להיות
אחת, והיא להרחיק אותו דבר — בין שהוא אובייקט מוחשי ובין שהוא חיבור מקודש —
מיכולת ההשגה של הציבור, היחידים והקהל כאחד. ולדברי אבא שאול רצו לגנוז את
משלי, שיר־השירים וקהלת גם בתקופה קדומה ביותר: לא בסוף ימי הבית השני, כפי
שמציינים המאמרים הקודמים המדברים בגניזת חיבורים (הנסיון לגנוז את ספר יחזקאל
נתארע בימי חנניה בן חזקיה בן גרון), אלא עוד בימי הבית הראשון, וחזקיהו המלך וסיעתו

<hr>

י״ב ע״ב), על אוצר של יראת שמים שיש לו להקב״ה בבית גנזיו (ברכות ל״ג ע״ב), וכן ״כל
המוריד דמעות על אדם כשר הקב״ה סופרן ומניחן בבית גנזיו״ (שבת ק״ה ע״א). למעשה כל דבר
השמור לצדיקים לעתיד לבוא יכול שייאמר עליו בדרך האסימילאציה הלשונית, שהוא ״גנוז״:
״שלש מטמוניות הטמין יוסף במצרים, אחת נתגלה לקרח, ואחת נתגלה לאנטונינוס בן אסוירוס, ואחת
גנוזה לצדיקים לעתיד לבא״ (פסחים קי״ט ע״א). בקשר עם הענינים האלה נזכר תכופות ״בית
גנזים״, או ״בית גניזה״, והוא כנראה מונח מוגדר מצד עצמו עם אחיזה במציאות הריאלית. ״לא
יאצר״ [ישע׳ כ״ג יח] זה בית אוצר, ׳ולא יחסן׳ זה בית גניזה״ (שם קי״ח ע״ב). השימושים המוש־
אלים למושגנו רווחים הרבה בספרות המדרשית. יעוינו גם במובאות שבמלונים התלמודיים. אבל כדי
לעמוד על המשמעות הראשונית של המושג אי אפשר, כמובן, לצאת מתוך השימושים האלה. לשם
כך חובה עלינו לצאת מתוך השימושים הלגליסטיים, שהם הצופנים בקרבם ללא ספק את המשמעות
הראשונית והקונקריטית למושג ה״גניזה״.

51. לנסיון הגניזה של ס׳ קהלת יש זכר גם בדברי הירונימוס, ששמע ענין זה מפי רבותיו היהודיים.
ראה הציטאטה המובאת אצל מור, Judaism, כרך ג׳, עמ׳ 66—67 (הערה 10).
52. ר׳ מאיר איש שלום, במאמרו הנזכר, עמ׳ 11, 16.

הם שהצילו את הספרים האלה מן הגניזה על־ידי ש״פירשו״ אותם (אבות דר״נ פ״א ד) [53].

אפשר לראות, איפוא, שגניזה נעשית רק באובייקטים ובחיבורים שיש בהם קדושה. קדושתם של הללו צריכה להיות ברורה ובלתי־מפוקפקת, ולא זו בלבד אלא שקדושתם ממשמשת סוף סוף סיבה אחרונה לגניזתם. אובייקטים של חולין או של טומאה אינם יכוליכ להיגנז מפני שמלכתחילה אין הם תואמים את המושג הזה: אפשר לאסור את השימוש בהם, אך לעולם אי אפשר לנהוג בהם דין של גניזה. אמנם מצויים במקורות התלמודיים שני עניינים שלכאורה יש בהם כדי להפריך את הנחתנו, שגניזה יכולה להיעשות רק בדברי קדש. אבל היא הנותנת, שהקשר בין הגניזה לבין הקדושה הוא שצריך לשמש לנו נקודת מוצא כדי להסביר את המוקשה גם בעניינים האלה.

53. גירסת המאמר קשה ומבולבלת. בדפוסים (= נוסחה א במהדורת שכטר) גורסים כך : ״...שכל הממתינין בדין מיושב בדין, שנאמר 'גם אלה משלי שלמה אשר העתיקו אנשי חזקיה מלך יהודה׳ [משלי כ״ה א] ולא שדעתיקו אלא שהמתינו. אבא שאול אומר לא שהמתינו אלא שפירשו : בראשונה היו אומרים משלי ושיר השירים וקהלת גנוזים היו שהם היו אומרים משלות ואינן מן הכתובים ועמדו וגנזו אותם. עד שבאו אנשי כנסת הגדולה ופירשו אותם, שנאמר 'וארא בפתאים אבינה בבנים נער חסר לב׳' וכו' (משלי ז' ז, מצוטט למקוטעין עד פס' כ). נוסחה ב שונה כאן בהרבה; עי' בהוצאת ש. שכטר, וינא תרמ״ז. לגופי הדברים השווה גם המובא בילקוט שמעוני למשלי כ״ה, ברמז תתקס״א. להלן עוד מצטט שם אבא שאול את שיה״ש ז' יב—יג, קהלת י״א ט, שיה״ש ז' יא (לפי נוסחת הגר״א יש למחוק פסוק אחרון זה). מדוגמאות אלו מסתבר שכוונתו לומר כי יש בהן משום הטיה לצד מינות, באשר הדברים נראים כדברי קלות ראש ופיתוי — אלא ש״אנשי כנסת הגדולה״ ״פירשו״ אותם. היינו, שגילו בהם משמעות של צניעות ודבקות בקב״ה, מעין המדרש שרבא דורש לשיה״ש ז' יב—יג בעירובין כ״א ע״ב. קהלת י״א ט משמש ראיה לביישוב הספר גם במאמרו של ר' שמואל בר יצחק, בקהל״ר פ״א ד : ״...כיון שאמר 'ודע כי על כל אלה יביאך האלהים במשפט' אמרו יפה אמר שלמה״. בין כך ובין כך ברור שקדושתם של הספרים לא היתה מעוררת אפילו במשהו, אלא שכדי להציל מן הגניזה הם נצרכו ל״פירוש״. המלים אנשי כנסת הגדולה הנזכרות בנוסחה זו אינם יכולות להיות עיקר, שהרי מדובר כאן בחזקיהו וסיעתו ולא בהם. וכך הרגישו נכון רוב פרשני המסכת, עי' למשל בדברי בעל כסא רחמים ואצל פרשנים אחרים (בנוסחה ב אנשי כנסת הגדולה לא נזכרו כלל). במקום המלים גנוזים היו שבראשית דברי אבא שאול צ״ל לפי נוסחת הגר״א : ״יגנזו, שהם היו אומרים״ וכו'. היתה, אם כן, רק כוונה לגנוז את הספרים ולא שהספיקו לגנזם ממש. ולבי אומר כי אף המלים ועמדו וגנזו אותם אינן יכולות להיות עיקר, ומכל מקום קשה להלמן. כי בשום מקום לא מצינו שאובייקט כלשהו אשר כבר נגנז יוכל להיות מוחזר לשימוש הציבור וגניזתו תבוטל. גם על נסיונות הגניזה של ספרי יחזקאל, קהלת ומשלי בסוף ימי הבית השני נאמר שחכמים רק ״ביקשו לגנוז״ ולא שגנזו ממש. הדעת נותנת שאילו ביצעו את הגניזה, שוב לא היו יכולים לחזור בהם ו״להחיות״ את הספרים מתוך הטמיון. דבר כזה נוגד כל הגיון וכל נוהג של חיי דת. (ומה שנעשה בספר התורה במקדש ירושלים, שנתגלה בימי יאשיהו, כמסופר במל״ב כ״ב, לא היה, כמובן, ״גניזה״, במובנה של היהדות המאוחרת. מושג הגניזה, המודע והמכוונת, לאובייקטים מקודשים, נוצר על רקע ההוויה הדתית שלאחר המקרא, כמו גם שיטת הקנוניזציה של כתבי־הקדש, שיטת הגיור הדתי ועוד).

הענין האחד הוא המסופר על חזקיהו המלך, ש"גנז ספר רפואות" (ברכות י' ע"ב והמקבילות, ובמ' פסחים פ"ד ט). אין בידינו לדעת מהו ספר רפואות זה. בירושלמי מדובר לא על ספר אלא על "טבלה של רפואות" (ירו' נדרים ו' הי"ג, פסחים ט' ה"א). אך תהא זו טבלה או ספר, אין ספק שהוא נחשב לקדוש בעיני העם וגם בעיני החכמים בעלי־ההלכה, וקדושתו לא הועמדה כלל בויכוח. ויתכן שכבר בתקופת התלמוד לא ידעו את מהותו בדיוק, אלא רק זכר מטושטש נשאר לו במדרש או במסורת. יש לשים לב שהמדובר הוא לא בגניזה מאוחרת, אלא, שוב, בגניזה שזמנה חל כבר בימי הבית הראשון. משמע שהם לפחות הניחו כי יצירתו של הספר קדמה אף לימי חזקיהו המלך. הרמב"ם בפירושו למשנת פסחים פ"ד מוסר שמועה ששמע, שספר רפואות חובר על־ידי שלמה.[54] בכל אופן ברור שהכוונה כאן ליצירה שנחשבה לעתיקה ביותר, לא כספרים שנכתבו "מכאן ואילך" ואפילו לא כספרים שנכתבו על־ידי אנשי כנסת הגדולה, אלא מימי הנביאים הראשונים, כשרוח־הקדש עדיין היתה שורה בכל תקפה.

הענין האחר הם שני המאמרים המ־פלאים והמוקשים בבבלי, הקובעים כי "עכו"ם של ישראל טעונה גניזה" (ע"ז נ"ב ע"א). רבי יצחק לומד ענין זה מתוך מדרש הכתוב "ושם בסתר" (דבר' כ"ז טו); רב חסדא משמיה של רב לומדו מן הכתוב "לא תטע לך אשרה כל עץ אצל מזבח" (שם ט"ז כא), "מה מזבח טעון גניזה אף אשרה טעונה גניזה". דברים אלה הם כולם תמיהה. בדרך כלל מוסכם בתלמוד שעבי־ם של ישראל אין לה ביטול לעולם, אבל כיצד זה הגיעו אל הסברה שהיא טעונה גניזה? שהרי הדעת נותנת כי היא צריכה ביעור גמור ומוחלט, כמו שעשה משה לעגל, ששרף אותו וטחן וזרה על־פני המים — או שצריך "להוליכה לים המלח", כמו שאמרו על המוצא כלים של עבודה זרה (מ' ע"ז פ"ג ג). ואמנם בירושלמי מ־דגש שעכו"ם של ישראל אין לה ביטול, אבל שם לא אמרו בשום מקום כי היא טעונה גניזה. רש"י פירש כי "כשהיא שלמה גונזה בקרקע" (ע"ז נ"ב ע"א, ד"ה שטעונה, והש' הגהות הב"ח), אך פירוש זה אינו מסיר את הקושי, כי השאלה היא על שום מה הוא צריך להשאיר א־תה במצב של שלמות דוקא ובכלל מה ענין גניזה לכאן. התוספות הניחו ש"גניזה" במקום זה משמעו "ביעור בלא הנאה, כמו עגל ששחקוהו וזרוהו" (שם, ד"ה מה מזבח). אך גם תירוץ זה דחוק הוא, כי אין שום אפשרות לפרש מעשה כזה כ"גניזה". הרמב"ם, בהלכות עכו"ם פ"ח ה"ט, חזר על דברי התלמוד הבבלי, ש"עבודת כוכבים של ישראל... טעונה גניזה". ובעל כסף משנה הרגיש שם בתמיהה שבצירוף דברים

54. לשמועה זו יש להשוות מה שמספר אצל יוספוס על שלמה, שידע לרפא בני אדם על־ידי גירוש שדים והשאיר אחריו נוסחאות מיוחדות לכך (קדמוניות ח', ב, 5). בספר היובלים י' יג נאמר על נח שכתב ספר רפואות. וע' במובא אצל Ginzberg, The Legends of the Jews, VI, p. 369 n. 40 מתוך פירושו של חיד"א לאבות דר"נ. חיד"א מצטט שם מתוך כ"י של ר' אלעזר מוורמס, שה"ספר" שחזקיהו גנז היה רשימה מפורטת של מעינות־רפואה, ורשימה זו היתה נמסרת מדור לדור החל מימיו של נח.

משוּנה זה, שעכו"ם נידונה לא לאיבוד אלא לגניזה, ופטר את הענין בצריך עיון. נראה שאין לנו דרך אלא לקבוע, שהמאמרים בתלמוד הבבלי נגררו כאן אחרי שגרת־הלכות שאיננה במקומה, או אולי שאלו מושג קרוב והשתמשו בו אף־על־פי שאינו חופף את כוונתם בדיוק. מסתבר שבעלי המאמרים הניחו כי אי אפשר לשחוק־ולזרות את העכו"ם של ישראל משום החשש ש"אף היא נעשית זבל", ואילו למעשה מעין ה"הולכה לים המלח" הם קראו "גניזה" (עי' מ' ע"ז פ"ג ג). אך מקרה בודד זה, שכולו פרובלמאטי ויוצא־דופן, אינו יכול, לדעתנו, לשמש נקודת־מוצא להסברת מהותה של הגניזה, כמו שהוא שימש לר' מאיר איש שלום. ועל כל פנים, אין מקרה זה מספיק כדי לדחות את הקשר המהותי שבין הקדושה לבין הגניזה, ואין הוא יכול לבטל את העדויות שהגניזה נעשית רק בדברים מקודשים.

על ס' ב"ס לא נאמר בשום מקום שהוא נדון לגניזה או שביקשו לגנזו. נאמר שאסור לקרות בו, אבל איסור־הקריאה, כשלעצמו, אינו יכול להזדהות עם גניזה. באמת גם כאן קיימות כמה אפשרויות בהתאם לאבחנת איכותם של הספרים. חיבורים קדושים ממש, שהם כ"ד ספרים, נקראים, או שהם יכולים מטעמים שונים להיגנז, ואז אי אפשר יהיה לקרות בהם. אם הללו כתובים בצורה שאינה לגיטימית, יש דעה שאסור לקרות בהם, וגוייליהם טעונים גניזה. ספרים חיצוניים וס' ב"ס נאסרו לקרות בהם, אבל איש לא טען שראוי לגנזם. הספרים שנכתבו מכאן ואילך, כמו גם ספרי הומירוס, איש לא אסר לקרות בהם, כי העושה זאת נחשב כקורא באיגרת, ואיש לא העלה על דעתו שיש צורך לגנזם, מאחר שהיו חולין גמורים. ספרי מינים נאסרו לקרות בהם, אבל חובה היתה לא לגנזם אלא לשרפם ולאבדם (שבת קט"ז ע"א, ובירו' ט"ז ה"א). זאת אומרת, איסור הקריאה אינו מוכרח להיות קשור בגניזה והוא גופו איננו גניזה.

שס' ב"ס לא נגנז כלל — דבר זה אנו רואים מן העובדה החותכת, שבמשך מאות שנים הוא נמצא בשימוש, עד סוף תקופת הגאונים. ואין ספק שהוא לא נגנז מפני שלא היה קדוש כל צרכו. כמו הקריאה הליטורגית בספר כך גם גניזה של ספר צריכה להיות מיוסדת על ההנחה, שבאותו ספר יש קדושה של ממש. אבל ס' ב"ס הגיע למעלת כתבי־קדש אמיתיים, לא יכול להיות נגנז. עצם האיסור לקרות בו, אפילו כשאינו מתורגם ואינו כתוב בכתב אחר מאשר אשורית, וכשצורתו הולמת לכל התביעות החוקיות — עצם האיסור הזה מביע בתוכו התנגדות להערכתו כחיבור קדוש. מכאן שהאיסור לקרות בו, בסופו של דבר, מתאים במקרה זה יפה לעובדה, שבספר זה מעולם לא נעשה דין של גניזה.

נספח למאמר א: ב"ס כ"ד לד—לה, ל"ג יט—כ

אף־על־פי שמבחינת צורתו וטבעו הספרותי אפשר לשייך את ב"ס לספרי המקרא, לא נרמזה השתייכות זו בשום מקום בגופי דבריו. שני מקומות מצויים בס' ב"ס, שהחוקרים נוהגים לפרשם כך

כאילו הכריז בהם ב״ס שיצירתו היא המשך רצוף לספרות המקראית[55]. אבל חוץ ממה שאפשרות זו, כשלעצמה, נראית דחוקה למדי — מעולם לא מצינו שסופר יבוא ויעיד על כתביו כי הם חלק מן המקרא — הרי גם עיון באותם הפסוקים יעלה לנו מיד שמשמעם איננו כזה. ואלה הם שני המקומות.

ב״ס כ״ד לד—לה :   עֹוד מוּסָר כַּבֹּקֶר אָאִיר   וְאַזְרִיחֶנּוּ עַד לְמֵרָחֹוק

          עֹוד לֶקַח כִּנְבוּאָה אֶשְׁפֹּךְ   וְאַשְׁאִירֶנּוּ לְדֹורֹות עֹולָם

אבל דברים אלה אינם של המשורר כלל, אלא הם מן הסיום של נאום ה ח כ מ ה. כל פרק כ״ד שם הוא, כידוע, נאום, נאום ודברי השתבחות של החכמה. אלא שנאום החכמה מתמשך גם מעבר לפס׳ כה, במקום שהיא עוברת לדבר בשבח ה ת ו ר ה (הַמְּלֵאָה כְּפִישֹׁון חָכְמָה / וּכְחִדֶּקֶל בִּימֵי אָבִיב וכו׳). אחרי כן היא מכריזה שלתורה אין שיעור וחקר (כט : לֹא כִלָּה הָרִאשֹׁון לְדַעְתָּהּ / וְגַם הָאַחֲרֹון לֹא יַחְקְרֶנָּה). ולהלל היא מעידה על עצמה, שהיא, החכמה, נובעת גם־כן מן התורה ״כנחל מנהר״, אם כי היא גדלה והתעצמה עד כדי כך שהיה ״הנחל לנהר״ והנהר לים (לא—לג). אך ההתעצמות הזאת לא באה לריק ; תכליתה לזכות את הרבים. וכאן באים דברי ההתפארות וההבטחה המתגדלת : ״עֹוד מוסר כבקר אאיר״ וכו׳. דברים כאלה לא יתכן שיהיו מושמים בפיו של הממשל הצנוע, אבל הם משתלבים כאן יפה בדברי החכמה והולמים את תכונתה, שכבר העידה על עצמה כי יצאה מפי עליון ושכנה תחת כסא כבודה. כן לא יתכן שהממשל הצנוע ידמה את לקחו לנבואה (אפילו לא נגרוס כמו בסורי בנבואה, אלא לפי היוני : כנבואה). אבל דימוי כזה יתכן בפי החכמה, יחד עם ההזהרה שהלקח שלה ישאר ״לדורות עולם״. הפסוק האחרון בפרק זה חותם את נאום החכמה : רְאו כִּי לֹא לְבַדִּי עָמָלְתִּי / כִּי לְכָל מְבַקְשֶׁיהָ. לֹא לבדי — משמע, לא למען עצמי, שהחכמה כשלעצמה ארטילאית היא ; לכל מבקשיה — משמעו לכל מבקשי ה ת ו ר ה, כל גדולתה של החכמה לא באה אלא לשם גדלות התורה. (פסוק אחרון זה עוד משולב בהמשך אחר, ל״ג כא, אבל שם הוא מנאום המשורר ; ופסוק זה יכול להשתלב גם בנאום המשורר, שהרי תכנו דברים של ענוה וצניעות).

ב״ס ל״ג יט—כ :   גַּם אֲנִי אַחֲרֹון שָׁקַדְתִּי   וּכְמֹו עֹולֵל אַחֲרֵי בֹוצְרִים

          בְּנִרְכַב אֶל גַּם אֲנִי קִדַּמְתִּי   וּכְבוֹצֵר מִלֵּאתִי יָקֶב

בדברים אלה מתבטאת הרגשתא הרגשת האפיגון, המסתפק בעוללות, לעומת הראשונים, שהיו בוצרים ממש. אבל כנגד משמעו של הניב אחרון אין לנו להעמיד את יוצרי הספרות המקראית. ב״ס הוא ״אחרון״ ל ח כ מ י ם. פסוקים אלה משמשים חתימה מיוחדת לפרשה מיוחדת שבעיקרה דנה בחכם, ובהיפוכו חֵלֶךְ (ל״ב יט — ל״ג כב). לפי הלך המחשבה האפייני מזדהה כאן חכם גם עם דורש התורה, ירא ה׳, שומר מצוה והאיש הטוב. במובן זה מציג זה מציג ב״ס עצמו את עצמו כאחרון למבקשי חכמה, שבברכת האל הצליח בכל זאת למלא את יקבו. ״אחרון״ זה יש להשוות אל ״הראשון״ ו״האחרון״ שנזכרו בנאום החכמה לעיל, כ״ד כט, והוצגו כמבקשים לדעת ולחקור את התורה. בין ה״ראשונים״ כלולים ודאי, לפי תפיסת ב״ס, גם בעלי החכמה המקראית — אך אין הם יוצרי הספרות המקראית בכללה. על כן נראה לנו, שאף מפסוקים אלה אי אפשר סוף סוף להוכיח כי ב״ס ה כ ר י ז על עצמו שהוא ממשיך ישיר של הספרות המקראית, גם אם היה כזה למעשה.

55. ובאופן זה גם אצל מ. צ. סגל, בן סירא, עמ׳ 15, 36, קנא ; ובמבוא, ספר ד׳, עמ׳ 826.

What Do We Mean By Jabneh?[1]

JACK P. LEWIS

PRIOR to the period of critical scholarship, the formation of the canon was attributed to Ezra,[2] Nehemiah,[3] or the men of the Great Assembly.[4] Many scholars have repudiated these traditions and have affirmed that a meeting held in Jabneh, often dated simply "ca. A.D. 90," closed the canon.[5]

Older handbooks like those of Ryle[6] and Buhl[7] reflect varying degrees of uncertainty in treating the character and significance of the Jabneh meeting. With the passing of years, however, assertions concerning its activities have grown increasingly more positive. We are told that the rabbis "fixed for all time the canon of scriptures."[8] We are further informed that the apocrypha were definitely excluded at this meeting.[9] On the other hand, other scholars question whether we should speak of such a council at all.[10] In the midst

JACK P. LEWIS is Professor of Bible at Harding College Graduate School of Bible and Religion, Memphis, Tennessee. He holds Ph.D. degrees from both Harvard and Hebrew Union College. His article is a paper read before the Annual Meeting of the Society of Biblical Literature at Union Theological Seminary, New York, December 28, 1962.

[1] In Christian writings this town is usually called Jamnia.

[2] IV Ezra 14:38 ff.; *Baba Bathra* 14b; Patristic echoes of this legend are given by H. E. Ryle, *The Canon of the Old Testament*, London: Macmillan and Company, 1904, pp. 253–61.

[3] II Macc. 2:13.

[4] *ARN.* 1; *Baba Bathra* 14b. The work of this body does not extend in *Baba Bathra* 14 beyond Ezra's time and is limited to four books: Ezekiel, the Twelve Prophets, Daniel, and Esther; but the statement was enlarged in the seventeenth and eighteenth centuries upon the basis of a case made by Elias Levita to include the whole canon of Scripture. The history of this theory is summarized by H. E. Ryle, *op. cit.*, pp. 261 ff. and G. F. Moore, *Judaism*, Cambridge, Mass.: Harvard University Press, 1930, III, 7–11. Since the time of Kuenen the idea has been rejected, but S. Zeitlin, "An Historical Study of the Canonization of the Hebrew Scriptures," *Proceedings of the American Academy for Jewish Research*, 1931–1932, Philadelphia: American Academy for Jewish Research, 1933, p. 35, has argued that scholars have been too hasty in dismissing the Great Synagogue.

[5] This case seems to have been first presented by H. Graetz, *Kohélet oder der Solomonische Prediger*, Anhang I, "Der alttestamentliche Kanon und sein Abschluss," Leipzig: C. F. Winter, 1871, pp. 147–73; among others cf. also R. Gordis, *Koheleth, The Man and His World*, New York: Jewish Theological Seminary of America, 1951, p. 41; R. H. Pfeiffer, *Introduction to the Old Testament*, New York: Harper and Brothers, 1941, p. 75.

[6] H. E. Ryle, *op. cit.*, pp. 182–83.

[7] F. Buhl, *Canon and Text of the Old Testament*, translated by J. MacPherson, Edinburgh: T. and T. Clark, 1892, pp. 24–25.

[8] R. H. Pfeiffer, *op. cit.*, p. 64; cf. also W. O. E. Oesterley, *An Introduction to the Books of the Apocrypha*, London: Society for Promoting Christian Knowledge, 1953, p. 4, who suggests that the canon was formed "in one act" at Jamnia; and B. W. Anderson, *Understanding the Old Testament*, Englewood Cliffs, N. J.: Prentice-Hall, 1957, pp. 535–36.

[9] See C. T. Fritsch, "Apocrypha," *The Interpreter's Dictionary of the Bible*, Nashville: Abingdon Press, 1962, I, 163; cf. also B. Metzger, *An Introduction to the Apocrypha*, New York: Oxford University Press, 1957, p. 8.

[10] H. H. Rowley, *The Growth of the Old Testament*, London: Hutchinson University Library, 1950, reprinted 1960, p. 170: "It is, indeed, doubtful how far it is correct to speak of the Council of Jamnia. We know of discussions that took place there amongst the Rabbis, but we know of no formal or binding decisions that were made, and it is probable that the discussions were informal, though none the less helping to

Reprinted from *Journal of Bible and Religion* 32 (1964).

of this variety of opinion the careful student who strives to gain a clear view of this council experiences frustration. Definite texts describing it prove to be few and elusive. The present lack of consensus regarding Jabneh compels us to investigate the problem again and to try to assemble the available materials in a clear form.

I. The Establishment of the Center in Jabneh

When R. Johanan b. Zakkai escaped from the siege of Jerusalem, he is said to have asked permission of the Roman general to reestablish his school at Jabneh.[11] This college, without assuming the name of Sanhedrin,[12] began to exercise legal functions, replacing the great law court in Jerusalem. It was ordained that certain privileges which previously had been peculiar to Jerusalem should be transferred to Jabneh.[13]

Johanan probably lived a decade after the destruction of the temple. The sources record a debate between him and certain Sadducees over whether the Scriptures "defile the hands,"[14] and it is likely that the first occurrence of this phrase is from his mouth.[15] It has been hinted by Burkitt that Johanan's contention that God revealed to Abram this world, but that he did not reveal to him the world to come, reflects an opposition to apocalyptic that might have contributed to the rejection of this literature by the rabbis.[16] The sources, however, do not preserve a record of any official canonical debate at Jabneh during Johanan's leadership.

The date when Gamaliel II succeeded Johanan as leader of the group at Jabneh and assumed the title of "Nasi"[17] is not certain, but during the period ca. A.D. 80–117, Gamaliel was the recognized leader.[18] The earliest known use of the term Kethubim for the third section of scripture occurs in his answer to the Sadducees about where scripture taught the resurrection of the dead. He replied: "in the law, prophets, and writings."[19] Motivated by a desire to eliminate factions in Israel, Gamaliel strengthened his own authority and that of the assembly. His leadership was recognized by the Romans.[20] He forced Joshua b. Hananiah to accept his calendar for the day of Atonement.[21] The ban was used to enforce decisions against Eliezer b. Hyrcanus.[22] Long standing issues between Beth Hillel and Beth Shammai were resolved by the bath kol which declared that though both schools taught the

---

crystallize and to fix more firmly the Jewish tradition." Cf. also R. Abba, *The Nature and Authority of the Bible*, Philadelphia: Muhlenberg Press, 1958, p. 33 n.; G. W. Anderson, *A Critical Introduction to the Old Testament*, London: Gerald Duckworth and Company, 1959, pp. 12–13.

[11] Gittin 56a–b: חן לי יבנה וחכמיה, cf. *Lam. R.* 1:5; *ARN.* 4.

[12] G. F. Moore, *op. cit.*, I, 85; S. B. Hoenig, *The Great Sanhedrin*, Philadelphia: Dropsie College, 1953, pp. 10, 146.

[13] M. *Rosh Ha-Shanah* 4:1, 3.

[14] M. *Yad.* 4:6.

[15] T. *Yad.* 2:19 f. (Zuckermandel, Vol. II, p. 684), cited in G. Hölscher, *Kanonisch und Apokryph*, Leipzig: A. Deichert'sche Verlagsbuchhandlung, 1905, p. 6.

[16] F. C. Burkitt, *Jewish and Christian Apocalypses*, London: H. Milford, 1914, p. 12, commenting on *B.R.* 44 on Gen. 15:18. But for the converse, see L. Ginzberg, "Some Observations on the Attitude of the Synagogue towards the Apocalyptic-Eschatological Writings," *Journal of Biblical Literature*, XLI (1922), 133.

[17] But see S. B. Hoenig, *op. cit.*, pp. 64, 253, n. 15a.

[18] The dates are cited from Graetz as given in H. Mantel, *Studies in the History of the Sanhedrin*, Cambridge, Mass., Harvard University Press, 1961, p. 2, n. 4.

[19] *Sanh.* 90b.

[20] S. B. Hoenig, *op. cit.*, p. 64; M. *Eduyoth* 7:7.

[21] M. *Rosh Ha-Shanah* 2:9; *Rosh Ha-Shanah* 25a, b.

[22] *Baba Metzia* 59b.

voice of the Living God, the *halakhah* was to be according to the practices of Beth Hillel.[23] It would take us too far afield to attempt to survey all the *halakhoth* set forth at this period.

There were seventy-two judges in the assembly,[24] which was frequently referred to as "the vineyard at Jabneh."[25] The Gemara interprets the phrase to refer to the seating of the disciples in rows, but it may mean that the meetings were actually held in a vineyard.[26] The experts who attended the meetings are called *ḥakhamim*[27] and *zeḳenim*.[28]

A further attack on Joshua b. Hananiah by Gamaliel aroused the anger of the sages so that Gamaliel was relieved of his leadership of the *yeshiva* and Eleazar b. Azariah was appointed to this position.[29] It is to the day of this action that the tradition traces the decision of the group on certain biblical books as well as upon many other items.[30] We shall return to this matter shortly.

With the accession of Eleazar, the portals of the academy were thrown open to all who sought admission.[31] The deposition of Gamaliel was temporary, and later Eleazar shared the leadership of the academy and lectured every fourth sabbath,[32] while Gamaliel lectured three sabbaths as *Nasi*.[33] Younger members of the gatherings in Jabneh were R. Akiba, R. Jose the Galilean, Simeon ben 'Azzai, and R. Ishmael.[34] Many other learned men of the day attended sessions there during the period that it served as the center of Judaism. The tradition speaks of an alternation of the court from Jabneh to Usha, and back to Jabneh, before the end of the Jabneh period which came with the war under Hadrian. After the war, the academy was reestablished at Usha.[35]

II. TERMINOLOGY

The first problem with the gathering at Jabneh is one of terminology. In the sources the terms *beth din*,[36] *methivta*,[37] *yeshiva*,[38] and *beth ha-midrash*[39] are used to designate the meetings in addition to the phrase already noticed, "in the vineyards of Jabneh."[40] In dis-

---

[23] G. F. Moore, *op. cit.*, I, 85, citing Yer. *Ber.* 7:1, 3b end; *Erub.* 13b.

[24] S. B. Hoenig, *op. cit.*, pp. 62, 65; see H. Mantel, *op. cit.*, p. 209 for other numbers given in other sources.

[25] M. *Eduyoth* 2:4; M. *Ketub.* 4:6.

[26] I. Abrahams, *Studies in Pharisaism and the Gospels*, Cambridge: The University Press, 1924, Vol. II, p. 211, citing Yer. *Ber.* 4:1, 7d end; cf. S. B. Hoenig, *op. cit.*, p. 56.

[27] M. *Bekhoroth* 6:8; M. *Eduyoth* 2:4.

[28] M. *Yad.* 3:5.

[29] W. Bacher, "Gamaliel II," *Jewish Encyclopaedia*, Vol. V, p. 560.

[30] The Mishna phrase to designate these decisions is: בו ביום, M. *Yad.* 4:1, 2, 3; M. *Zeb.* 1:3; cf. *Ber.* 28a: תנא עדיות בו ביום נשנית וכל היכא דאמרינן בו ביום ההוא יומא הוה ולא היתה הלכה שהיתה תלויה בבית המדרש שלא פירשוה.

[31] *Ber.* 28a.   [32] S. B. Hoenig, *op. cit.*, pp. 65, 68.

[33] *Ber.* 28a; see S. B. Hoenig, *op. cit.*, p. 194.

[34] See B. W. Helfgott, *The Doctrine of Election in Tannaitic Literature*, New York: King's Crown Press, 1954, pp. 51–75.

[35] *Rosh Ha-Shanah* 31a–b; *Cant. R.* II:5, 3. Despite the testimony of the text, H. Mantel, *op. cit.*, pp. xiii, 140 ff., questions the alternation.

[36] T. *Ber.* ii:6; M. *Rosh Ha-Shanah* 4:1–2; M. *Sanh.* 11:4: בית דין.

[37] *Ber.* 27b: מתיבתא; see S. B. Hoenig, *op. cit.*, p. 292, n. 4.

[38] M. *Zeb.* 1:3; Yer. *Ber.* 4:1, 7b: ישיבה; S. B. Hoenig, *op. cit.*, p. 292, n. 5.

[39] *Ber.* 28a. בית המדרש is of course to be distinguished from בית דין.
   M. *Eduyoth* 2:4; M. *Ketub.* 4:6.

cussions of the Jabneh gatherings where the canon is not concerned, these terms are commonly translated "academy," "court," or "school." When, however, canon is under consideration, the group suddenly becomes a "council" or "synod." Though these are legitimate renderings of these terms, sixteen hundred years of ecclesiastical usage and twenty-one ecumenical councils have given these latter words certain ecclesiastical connotations of officially assembled authoritative bodies of delegates which rule and settle questions. These titles are not appropriate for Judaism. One's mind immediately thinks of gatherings such as Nicea, Hippo, or Trent. It is a fallacy to superimpose such Christian concepts upon Judaism. It is proposed that the terms "court," "school," or "assembly" would more nearly convey the true nature of the body at Jabneh than would terms like "council" or "synod."

III. The Decision at Jabneh

The second problem is to attempt to evaluate the decision of the group in Jabneh. In doing this, there are eight items to consider:

1. Jabneh did not initiate a new division of the canon, for a canon of *Kethubim* existed prior to the time of Jabneh. No list of books from this period survives. One cannot be dogmatic about the extent of the canon, but there are witnesses to the threefold division of scripture: The prologue to Ecclesiasticus, Luke 24:44, and Josephus, *Apion* I:8. There are manuscripts of books from the Dead Sea Caves and quotations in Philo, the New Testament,[41] and Josephus, showing that most books had beyond doubt attained canonical standing prior to A.D. 90.[42] Any activity at Jabneh could only be the affirmation of established usage.[43]

2. The fact that the number of biblical books is described by Josephus as twenty-two[44] and given as twenty-four by IV Ezra would imply a fairly well defined canon.[45] Josephus claims to be a Pharisee, representing a Pharisaic viewpoint. There is not, however, any definite reason for supposing that either Josephus or IV Ezra is an echo of a binding decision made in Jabneh in A.D. 90.[46] Rather, the passage from Josephus, dating from the latter part of the first century A.D., implies that the canon was already of long standing.[47] The Baraita preserved in Baba Bathra 14b also reflects a tendency to date the close of the canon back to remote times and contains no direct allusion to a decision in Jabneh.

3. Jewish sources contain echoes of debate over biblical books in which canonicity was not the issue, debate which is not to be connected with Jabneh.

First, there are texts that speak of some scholars "seeking to store up" (*ganaz*)[48]

---

[41] Matt. 23:35 has been thought to indicate a canon of extent from Gen. to II Chron., see A. Bentzen, *Introduction to the Old Testament*, Copenhagen: G. E. C. Gads Forlag, 1948, I, 28.

[42] Only Koheleth, Song of Songs, and Esther are still under dispute in some circles, while other circles had considered each of these canonical. See *infra*, sections 4 and 5.

[43] Cf. A. Bentzen, *op. cit.*, I, 31: "The synod at Jamnia did not define the Canon, but undertook a revision. The Canon in reality was finished before the time of the synod, but perhaps more in the character of a collection grown out of practical use. The synod of rabbis tries to account for the right of the books to be parts of the Book."

[44] Josephus, *Apion* I.8, has five books of law, thirteen books of prophets, and four books containing hymns to God and precepts for the conduct of human life.

[45] K. Budde, "Canon," *Encyclopaedia Biblica*, I, 672; H. E. Ryle, *op. cit.*, pp. 174, 177.

[46] F. Buhl, *op. cit.*, p. 25.

[47] H. St. John Thackeray, *Josephus, The Man and the Historian*, New York: Jewish Institute of Religion Press, 1929, p. 79.

[48] בקשו לגנות.

certain books, among them Ezekiel. The debate over Ezekiel is reported in the Talmud but not preserved in Tannaitic sources, and no scholars urging its withdrawal are named. One objection centered around contradictions between the prophet and the Law. Hananiah ben Hezekiah expended three hundred jars of oil harmonizing the book with the Pentateuch.[49] Another objection was based on the fear that the chariot material would stimulate speculation, a fear increased by the unfortunate episode of the lad who understood the *hashmal*. This problem is also said to have been settled by the same authority.[50] Hananiah was of the school of Shammai in the generation before the fall of Jerusalem. Certain people would have "stored up" Proverbs,[51] but in post-Talmudic times it was said that the men of the Great Synagogue justified it; thus the controversy is in the tradition transferred to remote antiquity.[52] Ecclesiastes[53] and the Song of Songs[54] are also included in passages using *ganaz*.

Second, there is controversy echoed where *ganaz* is not used. The affirmation of the canonicity of Ruth by R. Simeon (ca. 150) implies that some challenged it.[55] One passage speaks of "eleven minor prophets, excluding Jonah which is a book by itself."[56] A late midrash speaks of scholars who say in the name of Rab (ca. A.D. 250) that Chronicles "was not given except as a Midrash."[57] In the matter of these disputes, other than in the cases of Hananiah ben Hezekiah and Rab, the authorities cited are anonymous *hakhamim* with no specific indication of date or place. There is no valid reason for connecting them with Jabneh.

Furthermore, Moore[58] and Zeitlin[59] have shown that *ganaz* is not the opposite of "defile the hands."[60] *Ganaz* is not applied in rabbinic literature to any of the apocrypha known to

---

[49] *Shab.* 13b; *Hag.* 13a; *Men.* 45a; see G. F. Moore, *op. cit.*, I, 247, n. 1.

[50] Jerome, *Ep.* 53.8 (*NPNF.*[2] VI. 101), reports problems continuing into his own time: "The beginning and end of Ezekiel . . . are involved in so great obscurity, that like the commencement of Genesis they are not studied by the Hebrews until they are thirty years old."

[51] *Shab.* 30b: Rab Judah, son of R. Samuel b. Shilath in Rab's (ca. 247) name said: "The Book of Proverbs too they desired to hide because its statements are self contradictory. Yet why did they not hide it? They said, Did we not examine the Book of Ecclesiastes and find a reconciliation? So here let us make a search. And how are its statements self-contradictory? It is written, Answer not a fool according to his folly; yet it is also written, answer a fool according to his folly. There is no difficulty: the one refers to matters of learning; the other to general matters." (English translations are from the Soncino edition).

[52] *ARN.* 1 (Goldin translation): "Originally it is said, Proverbs, Song of Songs, and Koheleth were suppressed: for since they were held to be mere parables and not part of the Holy Writings (the religious authorities) arose and suppressed them; (and so they remained) until the men of Hezekiah [the Great Assembly] came and interpreted them."

[53] *Shab.* 30b; "Rab Judah, son of R. Samuel b. Shilath (ca. 300) said in Rab's name (ca. 247): The sages wished to hide the Book of Ecclesiastes, because its words are self contradictory; yet why did they not hide it? Because its beginning is religious teaching and its end is religious teaching. Its beginning is religious teaching, as it is written, 'What profit hath man of all his labour wherein he laboureth under the sun?'" See also *ARN.* 1; and *Mid. R. Qoh.* I.3.1.

[54] *ARN.* 1.

[55] *Meg.* 7a.

[56] *Num. Rabbah* 18:21: ‏י"א מן תרי עשר חוץ מן יונה שהיא בפני עצמו‎.

[57] *Midrash Vayyik.* 3, cited by W. M. Christie, "The Jamnia Period in Jewish History," *Journal of Theological Studies*, XXVI (July, 1925), 355.

[58] G. F. Moore, *op. cit.*, I, 247; III, 70–72; cf. also R. H. Charles, *Apocrypha and Pseudepigrapha of the Old Testament*, Oxford: Clarendon Press, 1913, I, vii.

[59] S. Zeitlin, *op. cit.*, pp. 3–7.

[60] Nevertheless, Strack-Billerbeck, *Kommentar zum Neuen Testament*, München: C. H. Beck'sche Verlagsbuchhandlung, 1928, Vol. IV, 1, pp. 425, 426, renders the phrase: "für apokryph erklärt."

us. Canonicity is not the issue in these discussions; rather the issue is that the books should not be studied in the academies. No text uses *ganaz* in connection with decisions made at Jabneh; hence these texts about books the wise sought to "store up" or "reserve" are not relevant to our study and should not be cited as evidence for activities of that gathering.[61]

4. There is no evidence to support the assumption sometimes made that Esther came to the attention of the Jabneh gathering.[62] Evidence that Esther circulated before the Jabneh period is to be seen in the phrase "Day before Mordecai's Day" of II Macc. 15:36; in the fact that the Greek subscript to the book of Esther attributes the translation to a man from Jerusalem, Lysimachus, son of Ptolemy, whom some have estimated to have lived 114–113 B.C.;[63] and in the fact that the book was known to Josephus. Despite this earlier usage of the book and despite the fact that an entire tractate of the Mishna is devoted to Esther (M. *Megilla*), dispute over the book arose in the second century after the Jabneh period.[64] R. Simeon (ca. 150) asserts that Esther defiles the hands.[65] R. Eleazer, R. Akiba, R. Meir, and R. Jose b. Durmaskith all assert that the book was composed under the Holy Spirit and give proof texts.[66] No opposition is cited to these matters.

In the third century Rab Judah in the name of R. Samuel (ca. 254) argues that the book is not canonical, but in apology for his attitude others explained that he meant that the material was intended to be recited by heart and not to be written.[67] On the other hand, Simeon b. Laḳish, in the same third century, exalted Esther by arguing that even in the days of the Messiah the scroll of Esther would not pass away.[68] In the light of these facts, it is not needful to discuss Esther further in evaluating Jabneh. No text specifically affirms that Esther was debated there.

5. A specific canonical discussion at Jabneh is attested only for Koheleth and the Song of Songs. Both of these books had circulated earlier than the Jabneh period. The evidence for Koheleth includes the Koheleth scroll from Cave IV at Qumran[69] and definite citations as scripture in the Gemara attributed to Simeon b. Sheṭaḥ (ca. 104–79 B.C.),[70] Baba Ben Buta of the time of Herod,[71] and a disciple of Gamaliel I (ca. A.D. 44).[72] Evidence for the Song of Songs is the citation by Johanan b. Zakkai.[73] There had been, nevertheless, vigorous debate between Beth Shammai and Beth Hillel over both Koheleth and the Song of Songs. The latter group affirmed that both books "defile the hands."[74]

---

[61] A. Bentzen, *op. cit.*, p. 29, assumes in error that Jamnia dealt with Ezekiel, Proverbs, Song of Songs, and Esther.

[62] L. H. Brockington, *A Critical Introduction to the Apocrypha*, London: Gerald Duckworth and Company, 1961, p. 135, asserts that Esther was considered at Jabneh; S. Zeitlin, "Jewish Apocryphal Literature," *Jewish Quarterly Review*, XL (Jan., 1950), 229, on the other hand, without giving proof, asserts that it was the academy at Usha that canonized Esther.

[63] L. B. Paton, *The Book of Esther* (International Critical Commentary), Edinburgh: T. and T. Clark, 1908, p. 30.

[64] *Sanh.* 100a.

[65] *Meg.* 7a.   [66] *Meg.* 7a.

[67] *Meg.* 7a.

[68] Yer. *Meg.* 1:1; 70d, cited in G. F. Moore, *op. cit.*, Vol. I, p. 245.

[69] J. Muilenburg, "A Qoheleth Scroll from Qumran," *Bulletin of the American Schools of Oriental Research*, 135 (Oct., 1954), 20–28.

[70] Yer. *Ber.* 7:2, 11b.

[71] *Baba Bathra* 4a.

[72] *Shab.* 30b.

[73] *Mek. Ex.* 19:1, II, 193 ff.

[74] "R. Simeon (ca. 150) [variant text: Ishmael] reports three opinions in which the School of Shammai

The one text that clearly speaks of official action at Jabneh, after a blanket statement that "all Holy Scripture defiles the hands," adds debate over these two books, and then continues: "R. Simeon b. 'Azzai said: I have heard a tradition from the seventy-two elders on the day when they made R. Eleazar b. Azariah head of the college, that the Song of Songs and Koheleth both render the hands unclean" (M. *Yadayim* 3:5). The passage continues with Akiba denying that the controversy included the Song of Songs, but with R. Johanan b. Joshua insisting that the controversy existed and that the decision was made.[75]

All indications would be that the decision settled nothing, for immediately one is confronted with additional debate about these same two books. R. Meir (ca. 150);[76] R. Jose (ca. 150);[77] and R. Simeon b. Menasya (ca. 180)[78] declare that Koheleth is not canonical, while R. Judah (ca. 150)[79] admits that there is debate over it. No individual authority is cited as saying, in these disputes, that it does not defile the hands. Echoes of debate are found as late as the time of Jerome.[80] No specific opponents are given for the Song of Songs, but R. Judah (ca. 150),[81] R. Akiba (ca. 135),[82] R. Simeon (ca. 150),[83] and R. Simeon b. Menasya (ca. 180)[84] affirm its canonicity. R. Jose (ca. 150)[85] admits that there has been debate, as does R. Meir.[86] The force of this added debate is usually dealt with by those exalting Jabneh by saying that it was merely academic in nature.[87]

6. Of the apocryphal books, only Ben Sira is mentioned by name in rabbinic sources. This would be true of both pre- and post-Jabneh sources. Ben Sira continued to be circulated, quoted,[88] and copied, for we have a Hebrew text of this work later than Jabneh. Though it is often assumed that apocrypha were excluded at that time,[89] no text specifically attributes a discussion of the apocryphal books to Jabneh. That the apocrypha were discussed by the gathering is a conjecture incapable of proof. For that matter, no book is mentioned in the sources as being excluded from the canon at Jabneh.[90]

---

follows the more lenient and the School of Hillel the more stringent ruling. According to the School of Shammai the book of Ecclesiastes does not render the hands unclean. And the School of Hillel says: It renders the hands unclean." M. *Eduyoth* 5:3: רבי [שמעון] ישמעאל אמר שלשה דברים מקולי ב'ש ומחומרי ב'ה קהלת אינו. מטמא את הידים כדברי ב'ש וב'ה אומרים מטמא את ידים. Parallel to M. *Yad.* 3:5; T. *Eduyoth* 2:7 (458), *Meg.* 7a.

[75] M. *Yad.* 3:5: כל כתבי הקדש מטמאין את הידים. שיר השירים וקהלת מטמאים את הידים....אר'ש ב'ע מקובל....אני מפי ע'ב זקן ביום שהושיבו את ראב'ע בישיבה ששיר השירים וקהלת מטמאים את הידים....א'ר יוחנן בן יהושע בן חמיו של ר'ע כדברי בן עזאי כך נחלק וכן נמרו.

[76] *Meg.* 7a.

[77] M. *Yad.* 3:5.

[78] T. *Yad.* 2:14; *Meg.* 7a.

[79] M. *Yad.* 3:5.

[80] *Comm. in Eccl.* 12:13 f., cited in G. F. Moore, *op. cit.*, Vol. I, p. 243.

[81] M. *Yad.* 3:5.

[82] M. *Yad.* 3:5.

[83] *Meg.* 7a.

[84] T. *Yad.* 2:14.

[85] M. *Yad.* 3:5; but in *Meg.* 7a he affirms its canonicity.

[86] *Meg.* 7a.

[87] B. M. Metzger, *op. cit.*, p. 8.

[88] *Baba Qamma* 92b; *BR.* 91:3; also the article "Sirach" in *Jewish Encyclopaedia*, XI, 390.

[89] S. Zeitlin, "Jewish Apocryphal Literature," *Jewish Quarterly Review* XL (Jan., 1950), 23, asserts: "There must have been opposition to other books of which we have no historical records. On the other hand there must have been many in favor of the inclusion of a number of the books in the canon which are now commonly called apocrypha, particularly those books which bore such titles as Enoch, Ezra, Wisdom of Solomon, Baruch, etc."

[90] L. Ginzberg, *op. cit.*, p. 132; S. Zeitlin, *op. cit.*, p. 230.

The text usually invoked to establish that a decision was made is T. *Yadayim* 2:13: "The Gilyonim and the books of the Minim do not defile the hands. The books of Ben Sira and all the books which are written since that time do not defile the hands."[91] The text does not give a date or occasion for this decision. The effort to equate *Gilyonim* with apocrypha has failed.[92]

7. The sources quote individual opinions on certain biblical books by authorities of the Jabneh period, both pro and con. Rabbi Akiba, who argues that the earlier debate did not include the Song of Songs,[93] vigorously opposed the reading of "outside books," threatening exclusion from the world to come.[94] The statement is further commented on in the Gemara. The Babylonian academies identified these books with heretical books, while the Palestinian academies identified them with outside books like Ben Sira.[95] Both Moore[96] and Ginzberg[97] see in Akiba's statement a polemic against Christian writings rather than against apocrypha as such. The statement is not presented in the sources as an official decision of the Jabneh group and need not be so considered.

8. Near the end of the second century the authorities became explicit in giving the number of biblical books as twenty-two or as twenty-four. This evidence begins with the list of books of Melito,[98] but is also continued in Church Fathers like Origen[99] and Jerome[100] who were directly influenced by Palestinian sources. The Baraita, Baba Bathra 14–15, and a host of Midrashic texts also speak of twenty-four books.[101] These would prohibit our thinking of an open canon as late as the latest Talmudic discussions.

From these phenomena, it would appear that the frequently made assertion that a binding decision was made at Jabneh covering all scripture is conjectural at best. The current certainty on the matter appears to be one of those things that has come to be true due to frequent repetition of the assertion rather than to its being actually supported by the evidence. In the absence of evidence, it would be sounder scholarship to admit ignorance and to allow the question to remain as vague as the sources are. We can say that certain books came before the gathering at Jabneh; that debate continued after that time; and that opinion about the extent of the canon crystallized in the Tannaitic period. Beyond this, we cannot be certain.

---

[91] ‏הגיליונים וספרי המינים אינן מטמאות את הידים ספר בן סירא וכל ספרים שנכתבו מכאן ואילך אינן מטמאין את הידים.‏ Parallel texts are: Yer. *Sanh.* 10:1, 28a.

[92] For an equation of *Gilyonim* with "Gospels," see G. F. Moore, *Judaism*, I, 244; III, 67; L. Ginzberg, *op. cit.*, p. 123. For a bibliography on the word see B. W. Helfgott, *op. cit.*, p. 168, n. 87.

[93] M. *Yad.* 3:5.

[94] M. *Sanh.* 10:1: ‏ואלו שאין להם חלק לעוה"ב .... ר' עקיבא אומר אף הקורא בספרים החצונים.‏ cf. *Sanh.* 90a; 100b.

[95] L. Ginzberg, *op. cit.*, pp. 126, 129.

[96] G. F. Moore, "The Definition of the Jewish Canon and the Repudiation of Christian Scriptures," in *Essays in Modern Theology and Related Subjects: A Testimonial to C. A. Briggs*, New York: Charles Scribner's Sons, 1911, p. 114.

[97] L. Ginzberg, *op. cit.*, p. 126.

[98] Euseb., *H. E.*, iv. 26, 14.

[99] Euseb., *H. E.*, vi. 25, 1–2.

[100] *Praefat. in libr. Samuel et Malachim.*

[101] The sources are given in Strack-Billerbeck, *op. cit.*, Vol. IV.1, p. 419.

THE SONG OF SONGS AND THE
JEWISH RELIGIOUS MENTALITY

Gerson D. Cohen

I

Sometime around the year 100, the supreme council of
rabbis in Jamnia took up the question of the canonicity of
certain books of the Bible. Among the legacies of earlier generations was the sanctity of such books as the Song of Songs
and Ecclesiastes. According to the reports of one of the earliest
of the Tannaim: "Originally, Proverbs, Song of Songs, and
Ecclesiastes were suppressed; since they were held to be mere
parables and not part of the Holy Writings, [the religious au-
thorities] arose and suppressed them; [and so they remained]
until the men of Hezekiah came and interpreted them."[1]

Indeed, some of these verses must have required a good deal
of interpretation, for their plain sense did not exactly commend
them as Holy Writ. How could the same category of sanctity be
applied to the Psalms, Job, Lamentations, and Chronicles —
let alone the Pentateuch and the Prophets — as to verses such
as these:

> Come, my beloved, let us go forth into the field
> Let us sit among the henna flowers
> Let us get up early to the vineyards
> Let us see whether the vine hath budded
> Whether the vine blossom be opened
> And the pomegranates be in flower;
> There will I give thee my love [Song of Songs 7:2-13].

Reprinted from *The Samuel Friedland Lectures*, New York, 1962.

Need we wonder that despite the belief that these verses were the products of Solomon's pen, some were skeptical of their sanctity? This uneasiness about the book must have continued down to the end of the first century, for even as late as the convocation at Jamnia some still expressed doubts on the true nature of the book. Against these doubts, Rabbi Akiba protested vehemently and cried: "Heaven forbid! No Jew ever questioned the sanctity of the Song of Songs; for all of creation does not compare in worth to the day on which the Song of Songs was given to Israel. Indeed, all Scripture is holy, but the Song of Songs is the holiest of the holy."[2]

Ironically, modern students of Scripture have vindicated the misgivings of Rabbi Akiba's opponents, for they have unanimously dismissed the theory that the Song of Songs was originally a religious work. However, even this "modern" view had adherents in the days of Rabbi Akiba. Indeed, he himself pronounced an anathema against those who crooned the verses of the Song of Songs as erotic jingles.[3] To be sure, modern critics are well aware of the position of Rabbi Akiba, which was accepted by all subsequent schools of traditional Judaism. Modern exegetes, accordingly, respectfully indicate that the Song was included in the canon only because it was believed to be an allegory of the dialogue of love between God and Israel and then turn around and interpret the text quite literally.

Let us, therefore, ask the historical question that needs to be asked. The rabbis of the first and second century, like the intelligent ancients generally, were as sensitive to words and the meaning of poetry as we are. How, then, could they have been duped — or better yet, have deluded themselves and others — into regarding a piece of erotica as genuine religious literature, as the holy of holies! Should not the requirements of elementary common sense give us reason for pause and doubt? Perhaps, after all, the poem was known to them as a religious work; or — granted that modern literary criticism is correct in its appraisal — perhaps, many of its earliest readers felt that the Song, with all its direct and uninhibited expressions of sensual love, best expressed their highest and most profound religious sentiments. Perhaps they seized upon it — regardless of the intentions of its author(s) — as a work of authentic religious expression. If so, why? Why should ancient Jews, who after all were quite modest and socially correct, expose themselves and their most precious book to the kind of 'misuse' and misunderstanding that ancients and moderns alike have manifested?

To answer glibly that the work was accepted as an allegory merely evades the basic issue. The problem is, really, why anyone should have thought of treating the work as an allegory in the first place. There must have been works aplenty that were excluded from the canon and that were not reinterpreted. One must, therefore, ask why the scales were tipped in favor of this particular poem that was *a priori* so religiously questionable.

The problem is all the more serious when the Jewish reverence for the Song of Songs is studied against the background of the ancient world. The ancient Israelites and Jews were, of course, sufficiently familiar with idolatrous rites and, above all, with the significant role fertility cults and sacred prostitution played in neighboring cultures. Their religious authorities were horrified by them. This is manifested by the Pentateuchal prohibition not only of sacred prostitution itself, but even of the contribution of a whore's price to the Temple of the Lord; by the repeated prophetic denunciations of anything that remotely smacked of such rites and by the total elimination of the fairer sex from any official role in the Temple; indeed by the prohibition against women even entering the inner courtyard of the Temple. The institution of "sacred marriage" would have been unthinkable to the Hebrew king or priest. Why, then, did a theme such as that of the Song of Songs come to represent a conversation of love between Israel and its God? Note that the very same circles that were insistent on the most scrupulous observance of the prohibition against representing God by any image or likeness not only admitted, but *advocated* the canonization of a work whose idiom makes anthropomorphism a triviality by comparison!

The conclusion is inescapable that the work filled a gap, a void no other work in the Bible could fill. Its very daring vocabulary best expressed, and was, perhaps, the only way of expressing what the Jew felt to be the holiest and loftiest dimension of religion — the bond of love between God and His people. In the final analysis, it is not the canonization of the Song of Songs that needs to be explained but the Jewish conception of the bond of love between God and Israel that made the canonization possible.

II

The explanation, paradoxically enough, is to be sought in the type of religious expression current in the ancient Near Eastern milieu out of which Israelite religion sprang. In the ancient Near East, men spoke of, and to, their gods in terms that were projections of relationships that obtained between humans on earth, most often in terms that reflected — and extended — their relationships with their own rulers. Like the Israelite, the Sumerian, Egyptian, Hittite, Babylonian, and Canaanite of ancient times often addressed his god(s) "by lik'ning spiritual to corporal forms" (Milton), as creator, master, king, source of life, revealer of law, healer of the sick, guardian of the orphan and widow, protector of the righteous, and so on and on. The attributes of the ancient gods expressed the functions their worshippers hoped these kings and deities would fulfill.[4]

Indeed, there are even expressions of intense affection on the part of the worshipper toward his god. However, one metaphor that cannot be found in the literature of any ancient religion outside of Israel is the description of the god as lover or husband of his *people*.[5] This seems odd, for an examination of the myth and rituals of these other religions will reveal a profound paradox about the pagan renunciation and the Israelite adoption of such a metaphor. The ancient peoples had many graphic myths about the lives, struggles, and loves of their gods — myths which ancient teachers like Plato found most objectionable on moral grounds. What is more, the ancient peoples of the Mediterranean world, Semitic as well as Hellenic, regularly celebrated rites of fertility in which carnal union with the gods was enacted in the temple or sacred grove. On the other hand, the religion of Israel alone had no myth, no account of the struggle of God against the forces of chaos, and no sexual ritual. The Lord was master of fertility as he was master of the universe and the fullness thereof. However, the Hebrew God was inscrutable and could not be worshipped by rites that were magical and coercive. Whenever some Israelites did attempt from time to time to introduce rites that smacked of fertility cults, they immediately evoked the wrath and excoriation of those jealous guardians of Israelite faith — the prophets. And yet, after all this, the Hebrew God alone was spoken of as the lover and husband of his people, and only the house of Israel spoke of itself as the bride of the Almighty.

It goes without saying that the source of the metaphor of God as husband of Israel cannot be located in the Canaanite Baalistic rituals in which some, or even many, Israelites may have participated. In the first place, as we have indicated, pagan rituals expressed no such relationship. But even if they had, we would still have to explain how fanatical monotheists, who would have no truck with such rituals or with terms associated with them, could have made peace with such a figure of speech and then proceed to make it central in their thought.

The solution must be sought within Israelite religion itself. A reconsideration of the terms and metaphors employed in this connection suggests that they derive from the very heart of the Jewish religion itself and are actually a midrashic development from the very first prohibition of the Decalogue, "You shall have no other gods beside Me." Absolute fidelity on the part of Israel to one God, come what may, is the sum and substance of the message of the Bible. Now in the life of the ancient Israelite there was only one situation reflecting that kind of absolute relationship, and that was the vow of fidelity of a woman to her husband. Infidelity is a euphemism for adultery, promiscuity, looseness, and prostitution, and it is precisely in these terms that the prophets, from Amos to Ezekiel, represent the hankering after, or the adoption of, the ways of the pagans. The sixteenth chapter of Ezekiel is a religious indictment of the people in terms that even by the canons of ancient tastes must have sounded as quite prurient. And yet its imagery does not seem to have shocked the faithful Jew of Babylon, or of later generations, for it was but a forthright and graphic expression of the theological relationship as the Jew understood it. The promiscuity portrayed by Ezekiel was principally religious infidelity and a violation of the vows of a "religious marriage." The jealousy of God, which the prophet assumes, is properly characteristic of a husband. The very same commandment that forbids the worship of other gods or the making of graven images concludes with a thundering warning: "For I the Lord your God am an impassioned God." The identical root *qana*, impassioned or jealous, is used elsewhere in the Pentateuch, Numbers 15:14, in the technical sense of a husband who is jealous of his wife. In other words, the earliest documents of Israelite religion had already expressed the requirement of religious fidelity in the terms employed for the demands of marital fidelity.

No other ancient people entertained such notions or metaphors of its gods, for no ancient people conceived of itself as having the same intense, personal, and exclusive relationship with its god that Israel did. The God of Israel was not merely the God of earth, of the Land of Promise, and the Lord of the Heavens. He was specifically the God of Israel, the Lord and Master of a particular group, who, in turn, owed Him special

267

marks of duty, the duty of the most intense loyalty, that of a wife to her husband. Ergo, the God of Israel, who would brook no fealty or service to other gods, became the husband of Israel, and the people became His bride.[6]

There can be no more doubt about the antiquity of this conception than there can be of its general acceptance in all circles of ancient Israelite religious leadership. The Bible is replete with more than mere hints of this conception of the relationship between God and Israel. For instance,

> You must not worship any other god, because the Lord, whose name is Impassioned [*qana* = 'jealous'], is an impassioned [*qana*] God. You must not make a covenant with the inhabitants of the land, for they will lust [*we-zanu* = 'whore'] after their gods and sacrifice to their gods. . . . And when you take wives from among their daughters for your sons, their daughters will lust [*we-zanu*] after their gods and will cause your sons to lust [*we-hiznu* = 'seduce'] after their gods [Exodus 34:14-15].

Or, to quote from a historical work: "And they hearkened not unto their judges, for they went astray [*zanu* = 'whored'] after other gods, and worshipped [Judges 2:17]." The instances we have cited could be multiplied many times, and if we cite one more it is only because of the familiarity it ultimately gained as part of the liturgy of the *Shema'*. In the final section of this recitation from Scripture, the fringes were ordered to be worn on the corners of garments, "so that you do not follow your heart and eyes in your *lustful urge* [Numbers 15:39]." That the lust here is not merely sexual is clear from the following verse: "Thus shall you be reminded *to observe all My commandments* and to be holy to your God."

As there is a positive aspect to the relationship between husband and wife, so, too, there was in the Israelite conception of the relationship between God and His people. It is, therefore, most significant to establish that this positive aspect, namely the

loyalty of Israel to its God, was expressed in terms that implied
fidelity and love in the very same ancient strata of the Bible that
proclaim the negative formulative of jealousy we have been em-
phasizing. To return again to the Decalogue: "For I the Lord
your God am an impassioned God, visiting the guilt of the
fathers upon the children, upon the third and fourth generation
of those who reject me, but showing kindness to the thousandth
generation of those who *love* Me and keep My commandments." Note that already the Decalogue couples, and in a sense
thus defines, loyalty to God with love of God and with the faithful observance of His commandments. If one, therefore,
wonders what is meant by the moving verses of Deuteronomy,
"You must love the Lord your God with all your heart and with
all your soul, and with all your might [Deuteronomy 6:5]," one
need only look elsewhere in the same book to find the content
of this ostensibly platitudinous phrase clearly spelled out: "And
now, O Israel, what is it that the Lord your God demands of
you? It is to revere the Lord your God, to walk *only* in *His*
paths, to love Him, and to serve the Lord your God with all your
heart and soul [Deuteronomy 10:12]." And shortly after that:
"Love, therefore, the Lord your God and always keep His
charge, His laws, His norms, and His commandments [Deu-
teronomy 11:1]." Clearly, if disloyalty was whoring, obedience
and observance of the commandments were the concrete expressions of fidelity; in the language of the metaphorical relationship, of love.

Thus far we have made almost exclusive reference to documents stemming from the legal and priestly circles of ancient
Israel. We have done so deliberately, to emphasize that neither
the conception of the relationship between God and Israel nor
the key terms in which it was later expressed were the exclusive
contribution of the prophets. The latter, to be sure, spelled it
out, amplified it and gave it a new intensity. However, they had
inherited it from more ancient circles of popular and priestly
monotheism.

269

III

No student of the Bible can fail to be shaken by the pathos and rage of the prophecies of Hosea, who drew much of his imagery and religious insights from his picture of a tragic experience of marital love.[7]

In Hosea's chastisement, the totality of Israel — what the rabbis call *knesset* Israel — is represented by the mother-wife figure, while the individuals of Israel are designated as the children. The mother has been seeking false and foreign lovers, but in the end she will say: "I will go and return to my first husband; for then it was better with me than now [Hosea 2:9]." Here, God is openly and forthrightly — unabashedly anthropomorphically — represented as Israel's husband.

Even if we should grant that Hosea's prophecies were based on his own experience, we must still wonder whether Hosea presumed to construct a religious allegory merely out of his personal frustrations. Is all that we have in the message of Hosea the transference of his own experience to a theological plane? Would it not be more correct to say that Hosea saw a religious message in his own experience, or as is more likely, deliberately enacted a religious allegory, *because* his Israelite mind had been taught from childhood to think of the relationship between God and Israel in terms of marital fidelity, in terms of love! That is indeed the case, and it is significant that Hosea's imagery added nothing to what is already *implied* in the Decalogue. Harlotry meant to him principally religious infidelity, idolatry, worship of strange gods. The greatness of his message thus lies not in the originality of its concepts, but in their direct and poetic formulation. Hosea's poetic power lay not only in his raging passion against the infidelity of Israel, but in his promise of restitution in the same figure of speech:

> And I will *betroth* thee unto Me forever, yea, I will *betroth* thee unto Me in righteousness and in justice, in loyal-

270

ty and in *love*. And I will *betroth* thee unto Me in faithful-
ness; and thou shalt know the Lord [Hosea 2:21-22].

This is a promise not of a new relationship, but of a restitution,
of repair and restoration to an *original* form.

Nevertheless, in the final analysis, Hosea did contribute
something new to the literature and vocabulary of Israel. Hosea
made explicit, put into bold relief, a motif that had hitherto
been but one among several expressing the relationship between
God and Israel. Hosea was the first and for that matter the only
one to prophesy daringly: "And it shall come to pass on that
day, saith the Lord, that you shall call me 'My husband', and
you shall not call me any longer 'My Baal' [Hosea 2:18]" — a
word having the *double-entendre* of mastery and idolatry. No
less daring was the *double-entendre* of his vision of the time
when Israel would "know the Lord" alone, for in the context
of the promise of betrothal the phrase, which to Hosea meant
obedience,[8] had distinct overtones of marital union. What had
been merely implicit in the speech of the past, Hosea brought
out to the full light of day.

Henceforth, this motif was to appear again and again in the
speech of the prophets. Jeremiah, the prophet of doom and consolation, took up both aspects of the imagery and gave them
renewed poignancy. As modern critics have often noted,
Jeremiah was a careful student of the prophecies of Hosea and
had been deeply influenced by them. "Thus saith the Lord," he
proclaims, "I recall the devotion of your youth, your bridal love,
how you followed me through the wilderness, in a land that was
not sown [Jeremiah 2:2]." To Jeremiah the idyllic beginnings
of Israel's history were the days of the espousals of Israel to its
God in a troth of law and love. Accordingly, Israel's turning its
back on the covenant is portrayed in similar terms: "Can a maid
forget her ornaments, or a bride her attire? Yet My people
have forgotten Me days without number [*Ibid.* 2:32]." There is
no need to refer to the many further instances of the usage in

Jeremiah and especially in the prophecies of his disciple, Ezekiel. They are legion and familiar. What it has been our purpose to stress is the direct and continuing chain of the imagery of Israel the wife and God the husband, and in Jeremiah's turn of phrase, of Israel the bride and God the lover. Each of the prophets contributed his own poetic variation on this motif, but the theme itself was a classical one even in ancient times, integral to the Hebrew concept of religion.

The identical theme was taken up by the anonymous prophet of the exilic period commonly referred to as the Second Isaiah. However, in the work of this prophet of hope and consolation, it is the vision of the restitution of the ancient relationship that is graphically portrayed. To the Second Isaiah, Jerusalem is a widow, a picture he may well have appropriated from the author of Lamentations: "How doth the city sit solitary that was full of people! How she is become as a widow [Lamentations 1:1]." In the context of Lamentations, of course, the widowhood of Jerusalem represents despoliation, depopulation, and desolation. But "Isaiah" quickly turned a figure of speech into a symbol: "Fear not," he cries to Zion the desolate,

> for thou shalt not be ashamed. Neither be thou confounded, for thou shalt not be put to shame; for thou shalt forget the shame of thy youth, and the reproach of thy *widowhood* shalt thou remember no more. For thy Maker is thy husband, the Lord of hosts is His name; and the Holy One of Israel is thy redeemer, the God of the whole earth shall He be called. For the Lord hath called thee as a wife forsaken and grieved in spirit; and a wife of youth, can she be rejected? saith thy God. For a small moment have I forsaken thee. But with great compassion will I bring thee back to Me [Isaiah 54:4-7].

This is a very delicate transition from the popular metaphor of a land widowed of her inhabitants to a land whose reunion will be with her Maker as husband. Isaiah carefully refrains from ever stating the metaphor too positively. In this, as in a subsequent passage, he cautiously shifts from one meaning to another:

> Thou shalt no more be termed Forsaken. [We would say 'divorced;' and once again I must stress that the addressee of his speech is the Land rather than the people]. Neither shall thy land any more be termed desolate; but thou shalt be called, My delight is in her [a term for marital love][9] and My land, Espoused; for the Lord delighteth in thee, and thy land shall be espoused. For as a young man espouseth a virgin, so shall thy sons espouse thee; and as the bridegroom rejoiceth over the bride, so shall thy God rejoice over thee [Isaiah 62:4-5].

Since in the prophecy of Second Isaiah, this is a return, a restoration, we need hardly wonder that later rabbinic exegetes, who fondly searched every word of the Bible for new and undiscovered meaning, would seek to locate in Scripture the exact time of the consecration of this marriage between the bride of Israel and its God. What better occasion could be, and indeed was, selected for this than the theophany at Sinai, when the daughter of Jacob, the house of Israel, was given the Torah as its marriage-ring?[10] What was specifically rabbinic in this interpretation of the narrative in Exodus was the play on words and consequent reading of a metaphor into verses where it was conspicuously absent. But once again, the rabbis were merely amplifying what they had already found in Scripture. To the rabbinic Jew, the Bible was a unit. What was stated in one book could be and should be found elsewhere, even where it is not explicit in the plain sense of the text. Since the theme of an inseparable marital bond between Israel and its God appeared implicitly in the Pentateuch and explicitly in the prophets, the historical beginning for the relationship had to be located.

IV

It is against this background that we are able to understand the pattern of mind that could see in the Song of Songs the very type of expression that would convey positively and fully what was implicitly or but briefly stated in the works of the prophets. Or, to put the matter differently, from the point of view of the Jews of early rabbinic times, without such a work as the Song of Songs the Bible was not quite complete. The prophetic metaphor had been employed either as an admonition against idolatry or as an eschatological vision of the restoration of Israel to its proper relátoinship with God and to its reunion with its bereaved country. But what of the believing and faithfully observant Jew of rabbinic times? How was he to articulate in the here and now his affirmation of, and his delight in, God's love, his satisfaction in the unique relationship between God and Israel expressed through the Torah and its commandments?

A glance at the book of Psalms is most instructive in this connection, not for what it has but for what it lacks. On the one hand, no other book of the Bible is so continual a paean of love to the Almighty as the book of Psalms. And yet, despite all of its affirmations of submission and devotion, the book of Psalms lacks one quality that the Song of Songs does possess, and that to the rabbinic Jew was all-important: the assurance of the inseverable *marital union* between God and Israel.

The Psalmists speak to and of God as Lord, King, Master, Creator, Father, and so on; they address Him directly and familiarly, but they do not turn to Him as a lover, as the bridegroom of Israel. This omission is probably no accident and has left its mark on subsequent Jewish liturgy. Whatever the reason for this, what is important to stress at this point is that the most challenging figure of speech employed by the prophets was conspicuously missing in the Psalms. Was it indeed impossible to assert somehow what the Jew had come to feel, his yearning and love for his lover, for the One who had designated His name over His people? The Song of Songs filled this gap, and in a way that satisfied religious needs.

Here I will let the ancient students of Scripture speak for themselves: "Why is the work called the Song of Songs? To indicate," the rabbis say, "that the Song is really a collection of songs responding to each other."

> In all other hymns [in the Bible] either the Almighty sings the praises of Israel, or Israel sing the praises of the Almighty. . . . However, only here in the Song of Songs their hymn to God is answered by a hymn to them. Thus, God praises Israel, saying [Song 1:15]: "Behold, thou art fair, my love; behold thou art fair;" and Israel responds with a paean to Him [with the words of the very next verse]: "Behold, Thou art fair, my Beloved, yea, pleasant."[11]

In other words, whereas the other books of the Bible do indeed proclaim the bond of love between Israel and the Lord, only the Song of Songs is a *dialogue* of love, a conversation between man and God that gives religious faith a kind of intensity no other form of expression can.

These then were some of the needs that the Song of Songs filled. As the work of Solomon it was prophetic revelation. As revelation it was the truth. But it was truth in a special sense. It was the most intimate of truths, the type that was vouchsafed only to the true believer. As the ultimate form of theological expression, it was comparable to the one moment in the year when the high-priest entered the royal chamber, as it were, the Holy of Holies, and confronted his God privately on behalf of the house of Israel. It was this moment of supreme religious experience to which Rabbi Akiba compared the effulgence of emotion evoked by the Song of Songs when he said that all the Scriptures are holy, but the Song of Songs — the Holy of Holies.

For an appreciation of the role the Song of Songs played in the canon, it matters not at all who really composed the Song and when. What counted for the Jews who sanctified it was that

275

they believed it to be of Solomon's pen. And this they could readily believe, for the Song was in keeping with a metaphorical usage found and even spelled out, as we have seen, in the Torah and the prophets.

V

It is significant that of all the rabbis who should so vigorously express the importance and unique sanctity of the Song, it should be Rabbi Akiba. It was he, who is represented in rabbinic literature as being one of the four types of ancient Jews who indulged in mystical speculation. It is further reported that of the four only Rabbi Akiba emerged as sound in his faith as he had been when he entered.[12] What this report emphasizes is the precipitous height of such an ascent to God — its glories and its dangers. Intense religious passion is risky, for its symbolism can easily be cheapened to the *risqué*. Long after it had been accepted into the canon, the Song of Songs, or at least its interpretation, was accordingly reserved for the elite, for the select few, who had proven their trustworthiness through maturity and their way of life.[13] And even when it was taught publicly, the allegorical interpretation was carefully sifted to avoid open discussion of the mystical states and doctrines the knowledgeable considered to be embedded in it. It was an *allegory* of love, and it was enough for the average man to know that only in the most general terms. To the extent that the Song was interpreted publicly, its verses were represented as being allegories of Jewish history, of the publicly documented contacts between the collectivity of Israel and the divine command. The profoundest secrets of the Song, of its innermost allegory, were restricted to the few, to select individuals, who entered the chambers of mystical knowledge in solitude.[14]

VI

In the final analysis, all that we have really explained up to this point is why the Song of Songs *could* have been admitted

276

into religious Jewish literature. What remains to be explained is why the work was published and allegorized at the time in history that it was.

Scholars are for the most part in accord that while the Song of Songs may contain very ancient strata, the work as we have it now cannot have been completed before the Macedonian conquest of the Near East and the rise of Hellenistic culture. In other words, both the work itself and the rabbinic allegory must be considered as aspects of the Jewish culture that emerged as a consequence of the impact, and under the influence, of Hellenism.[15]

In all likelihood, the allegorizing activity took place not long after the Song itself was compiled and both the book (understood quite sensually) as well as the religious interpretation of it reflect two sides of the identical cultural temper. The motif underlying both of these is Love. To the literalist, it is love in a sensual sense, while to the religious exegete it is love in a spiritual, *meta*-physical sense. Now Love-fulfilled, as an *abstraction*, as the highest and therefore the most desirable human experience, was a subject placed in the forefront of the intellectual agenda by the Platonic dialogues. It is from these dialogues, the textbook of the ancient intelligentsia, that the meaning of true love came to be discussed throughout the Hellenistic world. Wherever Greek literature and philosophy went, the problems of Beauty and Love went with them. Literature and artifacts of the early Hellenistic period reflect a considerable increase in the uninhibited concentration on erotic subjects, this interest being expressed in the religious sphere by a growing emphasis on the person of Aphrodite. In the latter half of the fourth century B.C.E., the Greek temple in Knidos displayed for the first time in history a nude Aphrodite, attracting world-wide attention for the daring innovation in the representation of the goddess no less than for the artistic masterpiece of its sculptor, Praxiteles.[16] Hellenistic civilization, it will be recalled, was the soil out of which arose many schools of ethics and thought, each purporting to teach the true, the pure, the noble, the beautiful. For virtually all of these schools Plato's *Phaedrus* and *Symposium* had provided an ultimate goal, an expression of the highest human emotion and state.[17] Indeed, the fixation on, and the definition of, the proper human motives and emotions, are two of the characteristic contributions of Hellenistic thought. Inevitably, Jewish teachers and thinkers, who claimed that their own tradition possessed the sum and substance of all truth, beauty and goodness, would have to show how their way of life met the needs and demands of the religious spirit. Hence, it is no accident that in this very period many circles in Judaism first reflected deep concern with the intentions of the heart, with purity of thought, with chastity of motives, with love.

Love was thus in the air of Hellenistic civilization, and so were the many programs for the attainment of love. Some of them were quite carnal, the objects of contempt of the philosopher no less than of the rabbi. But other forms were quite the vogue in certain religious-philosophical circles, and to the rabbi these forms were frequently no less repugnant, indeed religiously even more dangerous than the vulgar, carnal type. No rabbi could tolerate the type of "enthusiasm," the spiritual ascent to and the union with the deity, that these forms bespoke. However, if love could not be ignored, it could be channeled, reformulated and controlled, and this is precisely what the rabbinic allegory of the Song of Songs attempted to achieve.[18]

In the Song itself, the love between male and female is never consummated,[19] and throughout the rabbinic interpretations of the Song, one is aware of a marital relationship between two individual entities that are never united as one flesh. Israel and God are always distinct beings, and never can the twain unite. What binds them in their relationship is the *contract*, but Israel never becomes the mystical body of its deity. The Jewish mystic of ancient times may rise to Heaven and *behold* the glory of the throne, but he will never cease to be an onlooker from the outside, a human whose being and essence can never be altered.

The very rapture of the Song became a prophylaxis against the pantheistic enthusiasm and knowledge (*gnosis*) that the Jew must have known from the world about him.[20]

Ultimately then, the Song of Songs bespeaks the great paradox of the biblical metaphor of God as the bridegroom or husband of Israel. On the one hand, the tabu against representation of the deity precluded the attribution to him of any sexuality; and this was buttressed by the prohibition of any cultic sexual rites. On the other hand, the Bible unquestionably affirmed the masculinity of God and spoke of Him graphically as the husband. Both sides of the paradox were fruitful in producing the unique totality that is rabbinic religion. By denying the sexuality of God, Judaism affirmed His utter transcendence, His absolute freedom from the drives and passions that beset the gods of mythical religions and that made of them but *super*-men. By proclaiming His masculinity, on the other hand, Judaism affirmed His reality and, equally important, His potency. It thus avoided the pitfall of the impersonal deity of the Greek philosophical monotheists, on the one hand, and the mythically anthropomorphic deity of paganism on the other. To go one step further, by denying his sexuality, it eliminated the possibility of a magical and coercive (homeopathic) ritual. By conversely acknowledging His masculinity, it contended that God was a person to whom one could turn with a *supplicatory* ritual. To such a person one could proclaim fealty, submission, and love. However, let it not be forgotten, this love could reach the pitch of ecstasy, but never the stage of mystical *union*. The latter form, the neo-Platonic-Plotinian ecstasy, was but the other (and philosophical) side of the pagan coin of a mythical man-like god. The Hebrew husband-wife metaphor insisted to the last on reaffirming the God of Moses, Hosea, Jeremiah and the Second Isaiah, who could only be heard or seen, and even then only by the elect.

279

NOTES

1. *The Fathers According to Rabbi Nathan,* Ch. 1 (Translated by J. Goldin. New Haven, 1955), p. 5.

2. *M.* Yadayyim 3:5, and see S. Lieberman, "Mishnat Shir ha-Shririm" in G. Scholem, *Jewish Gnosticism, Markabah Mysticism and Talmudic Tradition* (New York, 1960), pp. 118 f.

3. *Tosef.* Sanhedrin 12:10 (ed. Zuckermandel), p. 433.

4. See M. Smith, "The Common Theology of the Ancient Near East," *JBL,* LXXI (1952), 135 f. and especially 141 f. I owe the quotation from Milton, *Paradise Lost,* V, 573 to E. Bevan, *Symbolism and Belief.* (Boston, 1938), p. 15; cf. also Bevan's own formulation on p. 30.

5. Smith, *loc. cit.* See also T. Ohm, *Die Liebe zu Gott in den nichtchristlichen Religionen* (Krailling vor Munich, 1950); J. Moffatt, *Love in the New Testament* (London, 1930), pp. 9 f.

6. For similar, but by no means identical explanations of the origins of the marriage motif and its relationship to the allegory on the Song of Songs, cf. D. Buzy, "L'Allégorie Matrimoniale de Jahve et d'Israel et la Cantique des Cantiques," *Vivre et Penser.* III (1945), 79 f.; U. Cassuto, *A Commentary on The Book of Exodus* (in Hebrew) (Jerusalem, 1959), p. 163 (brought to my attention by Prof. J. Goldin); C. Spicq, *Agapé* (Leiden, 1955—*Studia Hellenistica,* No. 10), p. 113 nn. 3-4; E. A. Synan, "The Covenant of Husband and Wife," *The Bridge,* IV (1962), 150. The crucial distinction between "marriage" of the god to the land and a marital relationship between God and the people of Israel is made by A. Roifer in *Tarbiz,* XXXI (1960-61), 140 n. 80.

7. On Hosea's marriage imagery, see H. L. Ginsberg, "Studies in Hosea 1-3," *Yehezkel Kaufman Jubilee Volume* (Jerusalem, 1960), pp. 50 f.

8. Cf. Y. Kaufmann, *The Religion of Israel* (Trans. by M. Greenberg. Chicago, 1960), pp. 372 f.; *idem, Toledot ha-Emunah ha-Yisraelit,* VI, 113.

9. Cf. Genesis 34:19; Deuteronomy 21:14 etc.

10. See L. Ginzberg, *Legends of the Jews,* VI, 36 n. 200. Cf. also I. Heinemann, *Altjuedische Allegoristik* (Baselau, 1936), p. 31, par. b. For customs in early modern times based on this concept, cf. A. Ben-Ezra in *Hadoar,* 4 Sivan 5721 (1961), p. 473.

11. Midrash Shir ha-Shirim 1:11 to Song of Songs 1:1.

12. *Tosef.* Ḥagiga 2:3-4 (ed. Lieberman), p. 381.

13. Scholem, *op. cit.,* pp. 14 f., 36 f.

14. Lieberman, *ibid.,* p. 125.

15. See M. Rozelaar, "Shir ha-Shirim 'al Reqa' ha-Shirah ha Erotit ha-Yevanit ha-Hellenistit," *Eshkolot* (Scholia), I (1954), 33 f. That allegorical interpretation is one of the hallmarks of Hellenistic literary exegesis is too well known to need belaboring. Whatever distinctions are pertinent between Greek and Jewish allegorization with respect to other Biblical books, in the case of the Song of Songs the Hellenistic features are quite apparent; for in this instance, the allegorical interpretation was doubtless regarded as the true meaning by those persons or circles who read it as Scripture. Cf. Heninermann, *op. cit.,* p. 64 f. This does not mean to say that many persons did not read the book in its literal sense, or even that strictly religiously oriented groups regarded the literal meaning as false. To them the plain sense of the verses was specious, but could be cited as evidence for "archeological" data. Thus, Heinemann's contention in *The Methods of the Aggadah* (in Hebrew) (Jerusalem, 1949), p. 156, that Eupolemos cited Song 4:4 in its literal meaning is misleading, for Eupolemos did not cite the verse so much as glean historical information from it; cf. J. Freudenthal, *Hellenistische Studien,* II (Breslau, 1875), pp. 114 (bot.), 229 lines 21-24. More recently, Professor E. E. Urbach has argued that the allegorical interpretation of the Song cannot be traced to much before the destruction of the Second Temple, and that the mystical interpretation was probably the contribution of R. Akiba. He further points to *M.* Ta anit 4:8 as clear evidence for an earlier sensual understanding of the Song, presumably even in orthodox circles. Cf. E. E. Urbach, "Rabbinic Exegesis and Origenes' Commentaries on the Song of Songs and Jewish-Christian Polemics" (in Hebrew), *Tarbiz,* XXX (1960-61), 148 f. However, neither the citation in the Mishna nor the lateness of the dateable statements of allegorical interpretations are really any proof that the work had not been studied esoterically much earlier. The mere fact that the work was housed in the library of the Dead Sea Sect is sufficient evidence to warrant the conclusion that the work was not regarded as an erotic one long before the destruction of the Temple. Moreover, the exact point of the citation in M. Ta'an. 4:8 is obscure. In all likelihood it is a later gloss that was appended because of the *religious-allegorical* significance associated with the verses; cf. C. Albeck's note in his commentary to *Mishna Seder Moed,* p. 498. However, even if the verse was indeed part of the cele-

bration described in the Mishna—as contended by J. N. Epstein, *Mavo le-Nusaḥ ha-Mishna*, II, 686 f. — it may have been taken out of an "original" religious context for this dance. In conclusion, it must be emphasized that no one—not even R. Akiba—ever claimed that many ancient readers did not understand and recite the book in its sensual sense. But that is not really the issue. The question is whether those circles who were responsible for its preservation as a record of revelation did so. We think the logic of the evidence points to a negative answer.

16. For these observations I am indebted to Professor Elias Bickerman, who also referred me to M.H. Chehab, "Les Terres Cuites de Kharayeb," *Bulletin du Musée de Beyrouth*, X (1951-52), XI (1953-54); cf. especially X, 79 f., where the frequency of Hellenistic erotic figurines illustrates the new trend in popular religion. Cf. also G.M.A. Richter, *The Sculpture and Sculptors of the Greeks* (Revised ed. New Haven, 1950). pp. 54, 58 f., 100 f., 260 f.; K. Clark, *The Nude* (New York, 1959), pp. 109 f.

17. Cf. A. E. Taylor, *Plato, the Man and His Work* (New York, 1956), p. 226; *idem, Platonism and Its Influence* (Boston, 1924), p. 9. On Eros as the object of man's yearning for the good and the beautiful as well as for immortality, cf. W. Jaeger, *Paideia*, II, 189 f.; F. M. Cornford, *From Religion to Philosophy* (New York, 1957), pp. 230 f; A.J. Festugière, *Epicurus and His Gods* (Oxford, 1955), pp. 17, 62. On Love as an epithet for the divine (Isis), see S. Lieberman, *Greek in Jewish Palestine* (New York, 1942), p. 140. On the permeation of the "symposial" genre into Jewish literature, cf. M. Stein, *Dat va-Da' at* (Cracow, 1937-8), p. 61; on the influence of Greek doctrines of love on Jewish thought, *ibid,* pp 142 f.

18. Taylor, *Plato*, p. 209, notes the affinity between the *amor mysticus* of Eros to the allegorical interpretation of the Song of Songs.

19. M. H. Segal, "The Song of Songs," *Vetus Testamentum*, XII (1962), 475 takes Song 4:16 and 5:1 to signify consummation. Whether or not that is the meaning of these verses, the ancient allegorists certainly did not understand them that way. Indeed, the phraseology is sufficiently metaphorical to enable avoidance of any real sexual interpretation.

20. See S. Lieberman, "How Much Greek in Jewish Palestine?" *Biblical and Other Studies* (Edited by A. Altmann. Cambridge, Mass., 1963). pp. 135 f.

MASORAH

A. *Pre-Tannaitic Evidence:*
The Emergence of the Textus Receptus.

THE PROMULGATION OF THE AUTHORITATIVE
TEXT OF THE HEBREW BIBLE

M. H. SEGAL

HEBREW UNIVERSITY, JERUSALEM

I

THE Dead Sea Scrolls have revealed to us two texts of the Book of Isaiah. One, written in an archaic square script, deviates considerably from our MT in spelling, in grammar and in contents;[1] the other, written in a later square script, is practically identical with MT, to judge from the scanty specimens so far published.[2] The deviations of this younger text from MT are such as often occur in two copies of the same MS, and as are found also in medieval copies of MT. Evidently this later text of DSIb is much younger than the earlier text of DSIa (to give them the designations proposed by the editor of the older text).[3] It may be surmised that the sect of Hayyaḥad prepared the later text to replace the older text, either because the older text had become worn out by much use,[4] or because the older text was no longer considered satisfactory. We may plausibly conjecture that in the interval of time between the writing of DSIa and DSIb an authoritative text of the Scriptures had been promulgated and generally accepted in the learned circles of Judea, and that even the dissenting sect of Hayyaḥad had felt constrained to recognize its superior authority, and therefore it prepared a new text of Isaiah in conformity with this new authoritative text.

Our conjecture is confirmed by the evidence of some of the additions and corrections by a later hand which are found in DSIa. Thus, Isa 38 21-22 was absent from the original copy of DSIa (Pl. xxxii), and rightly so, for the verses are a late and clumsy interpolation in Isaiah from II Kings 20 7-8, which was misplaced by the interpolator at the end of the chapter instead of before v. 7.[5] But the spelling of the interpolation agrees with the spelling of MT, and not with the spelling of DSIa. Thus, in v. 21: ישעיהו instead of ישעיה, as everywhere else in DSIa, and in v. 22: ויאמר, instead of ויואמר, or ויאומר; חזקיה, instead of the usual

---

[1] Millar Burrows, *The Dead Sea Scrolls of St. Mark's Monastery*, New Haven, 1950.

[2] אלעזר ליפא סוקניק, מגילות גנוזות, סקירה שנייה, ירושלים, Plates xvii–xviii.

[3] Burrows, *loc. cit.*, p. xi.

[4] Cf. Burrows, *ibid.*, p. xv.

[5] Cf. A. Dillmann, *Jesaia*, 1890, p. 312; K. Marti, *Jesaia*, 1900, p. 265. LXX sought to overcome the difficulty by rendering מה: τοῦτο.

Reprinted from *Journal of Biblical Literature* 72 (1953).

יחיזקיה (but also חזקיה); כי, instead of כיא.[6] So also in the addition in DSIa 34 17 (Pl. xxviii): ישכנו, instead of ישכונו, as in v. 11; 35 1: פרח, instead of פרוח; אלהינו, instead of אלוהינו; 66 20 (Pl. liv): מכל, instead of מכול. This spelling proves that the later scribe copied his additions out of a text which was similar to our MT and to DSIb. In other words, this scribe had already before him the authoritative text which became the common ancestor of DSIb and of MT, and he respected its authority to correct by it the older and no doubt venerated text of DSIa. Moreover, it may be shown that the author of the Habakkuk "Commentary" also possessed a copy of this new text, and that he too recognized its authority, though he still transcribed his citations of Habakkuk from the older divergent text. Only thus can we explain his citing in Hab 1 11 the older and undoubtedly more original reading וישם, but basing his comment בית אשמה on the corrupt MT reading ואשם. Again in Hab 2 16, he cites the older and original reading והרעל, but comments on the later and inferior reading of MT: עורלת לבו: והערל.[7] Evidently he regarded both variants as authoritative, just as the ancient rabbis regarded the Kethîb-Qerê variants as equally authoritative, using now the one, now the other for their midrashic expositions.

Assuming our conjecture to be well-founded, we may next inquire: what was the date of the promulgation of this new authoritative text? If we could fix the date of the respective writing of the two Isaiah scrolls, we might be able to answer this question with some approximate definiteness. The present writer has endeavoured elsewhere to connect the activity of the Hayyaḥad sect with the anti-Hasmonean movement in the reigns of John Hyrcanus and his son Jannaeus (*JBL*, LXX, pp. 131–147). This theory would enable us to identify the age and the generation, if not the exact date, of the various literary products in the possession of the sect. But the whole problem of the Hayyaḥad sect is still a subject of keen controversy among scholars. It may therefore be desirable to approach from a different angle, and independent of the scrolls, the question of the date of the authoritative text of the Hebrew bible, the promulgation of which, according to our conjecture, intervened between the writing of the two Isaiah scrolls. A satisfactory answer to this question may also prove helpful to the solution of the problem of the scrolls and their owners.

II

Writers on the history of the Hebrew text have observed that the later Greek versions of the second century *post*, those of Aquila and Theodotion and Symmachus, all reflect a Hebrew original similar to

---

[6] Burrows *ibid.* Plate xxxii. The transliteration כיא עלה is a misprint for כי אעלה.

[7] Burrows, *ibid.* Plate lvi, col. iv; lx, col. xi. Cf. W. H. Brownlee, *BASOR*, 112, p. 17, 18, notes 31, 70.

MT, if not identical with it in all details. From this observation the conclusion has been drawn that early in that second century a standard Hebrew text was formed and fixed by the learned rabbis which ultimately developed into our MT. The fixation of this standard text has been connected with the Synod of Jabneh (c. 100 *post*), where it is alleged the Hebrew canon was finally fixed and closed, and again with the exegesis of R. Akiba which utilized particles and even single letters of the Hebrew for deducing therefrom *Halachoth* and moral lessons.[8] But these connections rest upon a misunderstanding of the rabbinic sources. The synod of Jabneh did not deal with the question of the canon as such. It only touched incidentally on the sanctity of two late books of the Hagiography, Koheleth and Canticles, in connection with the discussion of the application of the so-called decree of the uncleanness of the hands (טומאת ידים), viz. that the touch of a scroll of scripture by the hands required the hands to be washed before they could handle produce of the priestly heave-offering (תרומה). A controversy on the subject in reference to Koheleth arose already between Beth Shammai and Beth Hillel before 70 *post*, and as soon as the decree was enacted.[9] The controversy regarding Koheleth was continued at Jabneh in the following generation and extended also to Canticles, but it was not finally settled at Jabneh. It was resumed by rabbis of the following generations, and later extended also to the Book of Esther.[10] So there can be no talk of the fixation of a standard text at Jabneh as a result of a fixing and a closing of the canon. As for the minute exegesis of R. Akiba which is said to have necessitated the fixing by him or by his contemporaries of a standard text, that exegesis was not the invention of R. Akiba or of his generation. He learnt it from his master Nahum of Gimzo, of whom it is related that he subjected every particle את to a special exposition.[11] Likewise an older contemporary of this Nahum, Zachariah ben Haqqaẓẓab who ministered as a priest in the second Temple, deduced *halachoth* from the conjunction *waw*.[12] And their great contemporary Rabban Joḥanan ben Zakkai is said to have been an adept in this method of exegesis.[13] Thus this method had a somewhat long history before R. Akiba, and it could not therefore have been responsible for the fixation of the text in the generation of R. Akiba. It is certainly true that this method required for its development a fixed and generally accepted standard text, but since the method was already practised by the rabbis of the middle of the first century *post*,

---

[8] Cf., among others, W. Robertson Smith, *The OT in the Jewish Church*, 1892, p. 63 ff.; F. Buhl, *Kanon und Text*, 1891, p. 258; C. H. Cornill, *Einleitung*, 1913, p. 292; C. Steuernagel, *Einleitung*, 1912, p. 20; R. H. Pfeiffer, *Introduction to the OT*, p. 76 ff.

[9] Mishnah 'Eduyyoth 5, 3. Cf. on the whole subject my סבוא המקרא, iv, p. 819 ff.

[10] Mishnah Yadaim 3, 5; Tosephta Yadaim 2, 14; Bab. Megillah 7a.

[11] Bab. Ḥagigah 12a and parallels.

[12] Mishnah Sotah 5, 1; cf. Mishnah Ketuboth 2, 9.

[13] דקדוקי תורה, Bab. Sukkah 28a and Rashi *ad loc.*

it follows that the fixation of the text must have taken place some considerable time before the age of those rabbis, and long before the age of Jabneh and R. Akiba.

That in the generation of the destruction of the second Temple the Hebrew text was already fixed and sacrosanct is also attested by Josephus. Speaking of the reliability of the biblical books as compared with the untrustworthiness of Greek books, Josephus says:

> "For during so many ages as have already passed, no one has been so bold as either to add anything to them, to take anything from them, or to make any change in them."[14]

Obviously these words refer to the Hebrew text of the biblical books, and they prove beyond a doubt that in the days of Josephus the Hebrew text had been consecrated by the veneration of generations, and was regarded as fixed unalterably. This testimony of Josephus is supported by rabbinic statements. Thus we learn from a tradition reported by rabbis of the third century *post* that during the existence of the second Temple there was in Jerusalem a group of official correctors of biblical MSS:

> "Rabba bar bar Ḥanah reported in the name of R. Joḥanan that the correctors of biblical books in Jerusalem received their wages out of the apportionment from the fund of the shekel-chamber in the Temple."[15]

What the character of the work of these official correctors or revisers was we can only guess at. Most probably they confined their work to biblical MSS used in the public worship of the synagogues and in the teaching of the schools. But at any rate their work presupposes the existence of a recognized and authoritative standard text with which all copies had to conform.

Another very ancient rabbinic tradition says:

> "For this reason were the ancients (הראשונים) called sopherim, because they used to number[16] all the letters of the Torah. For they used to say the *waw*[17] of נחון (Lev 11 42) marks the end of half the letters of the Book of the Torah; דרש דרש (Lev 10 16) marks the end of half the words of the Torah; והתגלח[17] (Lev 13 33) marks the end of half the verses of the Torah; the *'ayin*[18] in יער (Psa 80 14) marks the end of half of the Psalms in respect of the letters; והוא רחום (Psa 78 38) marks its half in verses."[19]

---

[14] *Con. Ap.* I, § 42: τοσούτε γὰρ αἰῶνος ἤδη παρῳχηκότος οὔτε προσθεῖναι τις οὐδὲν οὔτε ἀφελεῖν αὐτοῖς οὔτε μεταθεῖναι τετόλμηκεν.

[15] Bab. Ketuboth 106a: אמר רבה בר בר חנה אמר רבי יוחנן מגיהי ספרים שבירושלים היו נוטלין שכרן מתרומת הלשכה.

[16] Deriving the noun סופרים from the verb סָפַר, and not from the noun סָפָר.

[17] Marked in the Masorah by a big letter.

[18] Marked in the Masorah by a suspended letter.

[19] Bab. Qiddushin 30a: לפיכך נקראו ראשונים סופרים שהיו סופרים כל אותיות שבתורה, שהיו אומרים ואו דנחון חציין של אותיות של ספר תורה, דרש דרש חציין של תיבות, והתגלח חציין של פסוקים, יכרסמנה חזיר מיער עין דיער חציין של תהלים, והוא רחום יכפר עון חציין דפסוקים.

This statement speaks only of the most important books of the Hebrew scriptures, but it is no doubt an abbreviation of a longer statement embracing all the books of the Hebrew bible. We learn from it that already in the age of the sopherim, the predecessors of the first Tannaitic rabbis, there existed a fixed authoritative text, the letters and words and verses of which were numbered in the same way as the medieval masoretes numbered them in their notes at the end of each biblical book.

III

The inference, however, that the sopherim possessed a fixed and authoritative text cannot be true of all the sopherim throughout the four centuries of their activity from the generation following Ezra down to the age of the Tannaim at the beginning of the Christian era. We have conclusive evidence, both internal and external, that for a long time in the age of the sopherim the text was in a fluid condition, and that scribes were not tied to a standard model text. There is much indisputable evidence in the text of editorial activity by the scribes, such as additions and interpolations and omissions, and various other editorial changes, such as the substitution of *Elohim* for *JHWH* in the second and third books of the Psalms, of *bosheth* for *ba'al* and similar other changes. There is also the persistent rabbinic tradition that the scribes introduced changes in the text in a number of passages in various books of the bible, including the Torah. These are the so-called *tiḳḳune sopherim*, the number of which fluctuates between 11 and 18 in the lists recorded in various rabbinic sources,[20] and the lists are certainly not exhaustive. Then there are the textual divergencies exhibited by duplicate passages like II Sam 22 and Psa 18, Psa 14 and 53, the duplicates in Jeremiah, and others of a like nature. Finally we have the external evidence of the textual differences between MT and LXX and the Samaritan Pentateuch, to which must now be added the differences between MT and DSIa and the citations in the Habakkuk "Commentary," all of which prove conclusively that during a very considerable portion of the sopheric period different recensions of biblical books were in circulation, and each of them enjoyed equal authority in their particular localities or circles. It is clear therefore that at some point of time in the long sopheric period a stop was put to the laxity and arbitrariness of the scribes, and a text was issued with the sanction of some authority which gained general acceptance as a standard text, resulting in the rejection and eventual suppression of the older recensions. When did this memorable event take place? What was the occasion which brought it about? What were

---

[20] Cf. A. Geiger, *Urschrift*, 1928, p. 309 f.; C. D. Ginsburg, *Introduction*, p. 347 ff.; Segal, סבוא המקרא, iv, p. 859 ff.

the motives which moved the learned scribes in Jerusalem to undertake the heavy task of formulating an official text and circulating it in the Jewish communities?

I submit that the answer to these questions is to be found in the circumstances described in the First Book of the Maccabees. We read there:

> "And they rent in pieces the books of the law which they found, and set them on fire. And wheresoever was found with any a book of the covenant, and if any consented to the law, the king's sentence delivered him to death. Thus did they in their might unto Israel, to those that were found month by month in the cities" (I Macc 1 56–58).

The passage speaks of a monthly inquisition and burning of the book of the law, the book of the covenant, but no doubt other biblical books shared the same fate as the holy Torah. Compare also I Macc 3 48, from where it appears that the heathen defiled the holy scrolls by depicting upon them the likenesses of their idols.[21] The destruction and defilement of the holy scrolls must have resulted in a great scarcity of the books of scripture in Judea. It stands to reason that after the Maccabean victory, when divine service was restored at the Temple and at the synagogues, and when the schools and the colleges were reopened for an intensified study of the scriptures, a great need arose for new copies of biblical books, and that the scribes must have set about to satisfy that need. It may be presumed that the scribes worked with the authority of Judas Maccabaeus himself, who seems to have been a devout student of the scriptures, as appears from the references to biblical history attributed to him in the first and second books of the Maccabees;[22] and that at his orders a stock of new copies of biblical books was accumulated for distribution among the Jewish communities. This seems to be implied in the following statement in the second epistle from Jerusalem to Alexandria which prefaces the second book of the Maccabees:

> "And in like manner Judas also gathered together for us all those writings that had been scattered by reason of the war that befell and they are with us. If therefore ye have need thereof, send some to fetch them unto you" (II Macc 2 14–15).

The statement that Judas collected the books which had been scattered during the war does not quite tally with the undoubtedly historical report in I Maccabees that the books of the Law were destroyed or defiled by the servants of Antiochus, but nevertheless both statements may be correct. Some copies were no doubt concealed by their owners and thus escaped destruction and defilement. Some copies may have been saved by the Assideans who fled from Jerusalem and took refuge

---

[21] Following the reading of cod. 55 and other cursives: τὰ ἔθνη] τοῦ ἐπιγράφειν ἐπ' αὐτῶν κτλ.

[22] Cf. I Macc 4 30; 7 41; II Macc 8 19, 23; 15 22.

in the caves of the desert (I Macc 2 29 ff.). One of the scrolls thus rescued
may have been the scroll of DSIa (Cf. *JBL*, LXX, p. 140). A few other
copies may have been hidden in the Temple precincts.

It may be assumed that the official body of scribes engaged in the
task of supplying new copies of the scriptures for the use of Temple and
synagogues and schools did not work with the carelessness and arbitrariness which characterized the individual and unofficial scribes working
each for himself in previous generations. The scribes of the Maccabees
must have consulted the few codices that had escaped destruction by
the pagan persecutors, and finding that in certain passages the codices
presented variant readings the scribes had to decide which reading to
adopt. A reminiscence of this procedure has been preserved in the well-
known rabbinic tradition concerning three codices that had been discovered in the Temple court:

> "Three books they found in the Temple court, the book מעוני,[23] and the book
> זעטוטי, and the book היא. In the one they found written מעון and in the two they
> found written מעונה (Deut 33 27), and they upheld the two and set aside the one.
> In the one they found written זעטוטי and in the two they found written נערי (Exod
> 24 5), and they upheld the two and set aside the one. In the one they found written
> nine times היא, and in the two they found written eleven times היא, and they upheld
> the two and set aside the one."[24]

The first variants מעון, מעונה, are to be explained by the application
of both these forms to God in Ps 71 3; 90 1 and 76 3. The reading
זעטוטי (or זאטוטי) is a Mishnaic or Aramaic form derived from the Aramaic
זוטא, small, young (or according to others from the Greek ζητητής),
a strange neologism which another rabbinic tradition ascribes to the
Hebrew original of LXX in Exod 24 11 for אצילי.[25] The last variant deals
with the number of times the regular form for the third person feminine
singular היא occurs in the Pentateuch, instead of the usually anomalous
form הוא. The contents of the passage make it clear that the discovery
of the codices was not accidental, but the result of a search for old MSS
which had been made for the purpose of establishing a new and correct
text, and we are justified in ascribing this search to the official scribes
after the Maccabean victory. The rule followed by the scribes in this
story of adopting the majority reading is in accord with the established

---

[23] Better: מעון.

[24] Siphre Deut 33 27; Yer. Taanith 4, 2, and parallels: ''שלשה ספרים מצאו בעזרה
ספר מעוני וספר זעטוטי וספר היא, באחד מצאו כתוב מעון אלהי קדם ובשנים כתוב מעונה אלהי קדם
וקיימו שנים וביטלו אחד, באחד מצאו כתוב וישלח את זעטוטי בני ישראל ובשנים כתוב וישלח את נערי בני
ישראל וקיימו שנים וביטלו אחד, באחד מצאו כתוב תשע היא ובשנים כתיב אחת עשרה היא וקיימו שנים
וביטלו אחד.'' Cf. Geiger, *ibid.*, p. 232 ff.; M. Friedmann, *Onkelos und Akylas*, p. 23;
Segal, *ibid.*, p. 867.

[25] Cf. Bab. Megillah 9a; Sopherim 1, 9; Z. Frankel, *Vorstudien z. d. LXX*, p. 25 ff.;
Segal, *ibid.*, p. 929.

rabbinic rule of adopting the opinion of the majority in case of a disputed *halacha*.[26]

But whatever the numbers and character of the MSS consulted by these scribes, they seem to have chosen to follow some old authentic MS which was distinguished by its usually defective spelling and its primitive arrangement of the text. These characteristics have been preserved to this day in the hand-written parchment scrolls which alone are permitted to be used in the public worship of the synagogue. Where however the defective spelling may involve a possible misunderstanding of the correct meaning of the word, the scribes handed down orally the correct pronunciation.[27] And so they handed down orally the division of the paragraph into verses. But they did not permit themselves to introduce changes into the text, as their predecessors had done. They did however mark some readings which they considered doubtful by dots above and below the letters. To this practice refers the rabbinic tradition anent these dots which have been preserved also in the synagogue scrolls:

> "Wherefore are the dots? Nay, thus said Ezra: If Elijah will come and say, why didst thou write them?, I shall say unto him: I have already put dots over them. And if he will say, thou hast written well, I shall remove the dots from over them."[28]

Ezra was the ideal scribe to whom tradition attributed the text and its peculiarities, while the prophet Elijah was traditionally destined to reappear and announce the advent of the Messiah and to solve all outstanding doubts and problems (Cf. Mal 3 23, and Mishnah 'Eduyyoth 8, 7).

The work of compiling the authoritative text must have begun immediately after the restoration of the Temple service in 164 *ante*. The first part of the text issued was undoubtedly the Torah, and in fact the story of the three codices found in the Temple court speaks only of codices of the Torah. Then followed other books as demanded by the religious needs of the people. One of the first after the Torah must have been the Psalter, which was needed for use in the service of the Temple and the synagogue. Then came the books of the prophets, and finally such of the Hagiography as had already acquired in the synagogue and in the schools the character of inspired scripture. I conjecture that the authoritative text of the Torah issued by these official scribes was laid down in the codex known in early rabbinic literature as "The Book of the

---

[26] Bab. Berachoth 9a: "יחיד ורבים הלכה כרבים."

[27] This oral tradition was known as מקרא סופרים, Bab. Nedarim 37b. It was a comprehensive term embracing the oral pronunciation of all peculiar forms, including also the ordinary Kethîb-Qerê.

[28] Numbers Rabbah § 3 (towards the end); Aboth d'R. Nathan 34: "?למה נקוד אלא כך אמר עזרא, אם יבוא אליהו ויאמר למה כתבת אותן? אומר לו כבר נקדתי עליהם, ואם יאמר לי יפה כתבת, כבר אמחוק נקודותיהן מעליהן." A similar use of dots is found in DSIa; Burrows, p. xv.

Temple Court" (ספר העזרה),[29] and which contained only the Pentateuch. This celebrated MS was preserved in the Temple court as a model codex for the revision of new copies. Thus we are told that the Torah which the king of Israel had to write for himself, in accordance with the command in Deut 17 18, was revised in conformity with the book of the Temple court under the authority of the court of seventy-one, i. e. of the Great Sanhedrin.[30] Historically the king spoken of in this passage refers to the kings of the Hasmonean and Herodian dynasties, though the later rabbis understood it to refer also to the kings of the biblical monarchy. At any rate the passage proves that this codex was in existence in pre-Christian times. Rashi reports,[31] no doubt on the authority of a credible tradition which he derived from a written source, that this Temple codex was used in the ceremony of the reading of the Law by the king in the Temple on the feast of Tabernacles following the Sabbatical year, as enjoined in Deut 31 12 and as described in Mishnah Sotah 7, 8; and further that it was used in the reading of the Law in the Temple by the high priest on the Day of Atonement, as described *ibid.* 7, 7, and in Mishnah Yoma 7, 1. The high veneration in which this codex was held is further attested by the *halacha* that unlike other books of scripture, the touch of the book of the Temple court does not render the hands unclean for handling produce of the priestly heave-offering.[32] For the decree was originally enacted in order to put a stop to the popular custom of placing the holy produce of the heave-offering by the side of the holy books because of their common sanctity, and thus attracting rats which gnawed the holy books together with the produce.[33] But there was no fear of such produce being put near the venerated book of the Temple court. Further proof of the special sanctity of this book is afforded by the *halacha* which lays down that "on the intermediate days of the festival (of Tabernacles and Passover) one may not correct (or perhaps: re-ink) a single letter, not even in the book of the Temple court."[34]

The promulgation of the official text gradually superseded the few older pre-Maccabean texts, but did not for a long time completely suppress them, especially in the communities of the great Jewish diaspora.

[29] This is the correct spelling, and not ספר עזרא, Ezra's book, as in some editions.
[30] Yer. Sanhedrin 2, 6: "ומגיהין אותו מספר העזרה על פי בית דין של שבעים ואחד".
[31] Bab. Baba Bathra 14b, s. v. ספר עזרה   This statement is repeated by other commentators. Cf. also Rashi, Bab. Mo'ed Qatan 18b, s. v. אפילו.
[32] Mishnah Kelim 15, 6: כל הספרים מטמאין את הידים חוץ מספר העזרה"; cf. Maimonides *ad loc.*
[33] Cf. Bab. Sabbath 14a. This is the true reason for the seemingly strange but really wise hygienic enactment. The reasons given by Rabban Johanan ben Zakkai in Mishnah Yadaim 4, 6; Tos. Yadaim 2, 19, were not meant to be taken seriously; cf. Maimonides, *ad loc.*
[34] Mishnah Mo'ed Qatan 3, 4. The hiph'il הגיה may mean here and elsewhere "to make bright," or legible, by re-inking.

Some of the variant and more original readings of the Hebrew text preserved in the post-Christian versions may ultimately have been derived from such older pre-Maccabean texts. We have now a striking example of the preservation of an older text beside the new official text in the two Dead Sea scrolls of the book of Isaiah. No doubt only the new text was permitted to be used in public worship and in the teaching of the schools. In this way the new text acquired its authority and secured the veneration of the people, as reported by Josephus in the passage cited above from *Against Apion* (p. 38). It may be that the authorities in Jerusalem sought to induce the Jewish communities in the diaspora to discard their old texts in favour of the new text. Such an attempt seems to be implied in the above-mentioned second epistle from Jerusalem to Alexandria, II Macc 2 15, cited above (p. 40): "If therefore ye have need thereof (of the writings gathered by Judas), send some to fetch them unto you." This may be interpreted as a polite invitation to the Alexandrian community to adopt the new text of the scriptures sponsored by Judas in the place of the older but, in the opinion of Jerusalem, incorrect Hebrew text underlying the Alexandrian Greek version of the Septuagint. For there can be no doubt that the Jews in Alexandria, like their brethren in Babylon and elsewhere in the diaspora, continued for a very long time to read in their public worship the Hebrew text of the Torah alongside of the Septuagint, which merely served as a Targum in the Greek vernacular. This is proved by the Nash Papyrus which contains the Decalogue and the Shema' in Hebrew, and which was undoubtedly written for liturgical use in Egypt when the Decalogue was still recited daily before the Shema' (Cf. Mishnah Tamid 5, 1). In a study of the text of the papyrus in comparison with LXX and MT,[35] I have shown that the papyrus agrees in every detail with LXX against MT, from which may be inferred that the papyrus contains an excerpt from the Hebrew Pentateuch current in Alexandria which served as the original for the authors of the LXX version of the Pentateuch. The papyrus is certainly pre-Maccabean, as rightly held formerly by Albright on palaeographical grounds.[36]

The authenticity of the epistle in II Maccabees cited above, and its connection with the main body of the book, are a subject of dispute among scholars. There is however a general agreement that II Macc 1 10b — 2 18 was originally composed in Hebrew (or Aramaic) and by a Pharisee, but the date of this Pharisee composition which glorifies Judas Maccabaeus cannot be later than the rupture between the Pharisees and

---

[35] לשוננו, vol. xv (Jerusalem, 1947), pp. 27–36.

[36] *JBL*, LVI, pp. 145–170. Dr. S. A. Birnbaum (in a private communication to the writer) assigns the writing of the Nash Papyrus to the first quarter of the second century *ante*.

John Hyrcanus. After the rupture no Pharisee would have thus exalted a Maccabee, placing him in the same rank of national heroes as Moses and Solomon and Nehemiah. Nor would an author living long after Judas have described him simply as Judas without the epithet "the Maccabee" (Cf. *ibid*. 2 19; 5 27; 8 1). Perhaps after all the date in *ibid*. 2 10a of 188 of the Seleucid era, corresponding to 125/4 *ante*, really belongs to this second epistle, and thus the second epistle was written when the Pharisees were still loyal to the Hasmoneans. By that time the new authoritative text of the whole Bible had long been completed and promulgated, and accepted by all sections of the Jewish public in Judea, including also the dissident sect of Ḥayyaḥad, as attested by DSIb, and then was the invitation extended to the Alexandrian community that they too should accept the holy books of the collection made under the authority of the great Judas.

IV

In conclusion, reference may be made here to a tradition of the existence of another codex of the Torah anterior to the destruction of the Temple in 70 *post*, which differed both in spelling and in reading from the official text. This is the codex which is said to have been preserved at the Severus Synagogue in Rome, apparently so named after Alexander Severus (222–235), one of the few Roman emperors who were friendly to the Jews. Rabbinic literature records a number of variant readings in the MS of R. Me'îr, the celebrated disciple of R. Ishmael and R. Akiba in the second century *post*, who was also famous as a professional scribe of biblical books. For טוב מאד (Gen 1 31) R. Me'ir's MS had טוב מות מות (=מָוֶת=). For כתנות עור (Gen 3 21) R. Me'ir's MS had כתנות אור. For משא דומה (Isa 21 11) it had משא רומי (=רומא=רומה, 'Ρώμη; or in accordance with the equation of אדום=דומה, derived from the following משעיר, found in LXX and in Jewish tradition, cf. Rashi ad loc.). These readings may have been merely marginal notes of a homiletical character. A real variant in R. Me'ir's MS was ובן דן, for ובני דן (Gen 46 23).[37] Finally another reading of R. Me'ir's MS is recorded in a medieval midrashic compilation by the name of *Bereshith Rabbathi*,[38] viz. Gen 45 8: וישני לאב, for וישמני לאב=וישימני לאב. This is explained there (apparently not by R. Me'ir himself) as related to אשר ישה ברעהו (Deut 15 2), i. e. as derived from the root נשה=נשא, and meaning: And he lent me as a father. The

---

[37] This reading is preserved in the Masora as סבירין.
[38] בראשית רבתי, (to be distinguished from the ancient בראשית רבה), edited by Ch. Albek, Jerusalem, 1940.

midrash then continues in Aramaic, evidently citing an old Masoretic source:

> "This is one of the words which were written in the Torah which came out of Jerusalem in captivity, and went up to Rome and was stored in the synagogue of Severus."[39]

If we are to credit this statement, then the codex was part of the loot from Jerusalem brought by Titus to Rome. Josephus relates that in the triumphal pageants in honour of Vespasian and Titus, the conquerors of Jerusalem, the last of the spoils carried in procession was the Law of the Jews, and that after the celebrations of the triumph the Law and the veils were laid up in the palace of Vespasian as the property of the emperor (*Wars*, VII, §§ 150, 162). Perhaps it was this very codex of our midrash which was carried in procession, and subsequently came into the possession of the later emperor Severus, who presented it to the synagogue which bore his name as its patron.

The Aramaic introductory sentence in our midrash is then followed by a list of 32 variant readings from the codex Severus. The text of the list is badly corrupt, but it can be corrected by the two MSS mentioned in the note above, though the text of those MSS is also badly preserved. The 32 variants may be classified under three heads.

1. *Scribal errors*:

Gen 25 33, (מכרתו) מכירתו, for בכרתו. The change of מ — ב is common, especially between MT and LXX.[40]

Gen 45 8, וישני, for וישימני, וישמני, cited above from R. Me'ir's MS. The change is due to the accidental omission of מ.

Exod 12 37, מרמסס for מרעמסס, omission of the guttural ע, which probably was not pronounced by the scribe.

Num 31 2, אשר, for אחר, change of ח — ש.

Deut 29 22, שרפת, for שרפה, change of ה — ת.

Deut 22 6, האבנים, for הבנים, addition of א.

Exod 19 3, לבית ישראל, for לבני ישראל, caused by the preceding לבית.

Exod 26 27, omission of second בריחים.

Lev 14 10, בת שנתה תמימים, for תמימה, caused by the preceding תמימם.

Lev 15 8, במים חיים, an addition derived from v. 13.

---

39 דין הוא מן מליא דכתיבן באוריתא דנפקת מן ירושלם בשביתא וסלקת לרומי והות גניזא בכנישתא
דאסוירוש, p. 209; cf. Albek's notes and the literature cited there. Two other medieval MSS give the passage in a less original form: "These are the verses which were written in the Book of the Torah, and it is stored and closed at the synagogue of Severus with a change of letters and words."

40 Cf. S. R. Driver, *Notes on . . . . the Books of Samuel*, 1913, p. lxiv.

Num 36 1, בן יוסף, caused by preceding בן (or perhaps defective spelling,
בני = בנ = בן).

Deut 29 22, כמהפכת א ל ה י ם, an addition derived from Isa 13 19;
Jer 50 40; Amos 4 11.

2. *Variant spelling*:

מ for final ם, Gen 27 2, מותי יום; 48 7, שם; Lev 4 34, מדם; Deut 1 26, אביתם;
3 20, הם. Similarly, Gen 36 10, בנעדה = בן עדה (Cf. מנ, Job 38 1; 40 6
in the Kethîb).

Gen 36 5, 14, יעיש, like Kethîb for Qerê יעוש.

Deut 32 26, אף איהם, for אפאיהם.[41]

Gen 27 27, סדה, for שדה, an Aramaic spelling.

Num 15 21, (לְדָרִיכם) לדריכם, for לדרתיכם, an Aramaized form.

Deut 1 27, האמר, for האמרי, a defective spelling.

3. *Textual variants*:

Gen 1 31, טוב מות, for טוב מאד; 3 21, כתנות אור, for כתנות עור, as in R. Me'ir's
MS.[42]

Gen 18 21, הכצעקתם, for הכצעקתה. So also LXX, Aquila and the Aramaic
Targums.

Gen 24 7, לקחני מבית אבי ומארץ מולדתי, for לקחני מביתי ומארצי, a deliberate
change because Harran was not Abraham's paternal home and the
land of his birth.[43]

Gen 43 15, מצרימה, for מצרים. And conversely, Gen 46 8, מצרים, for מצרימה.

Num 4 3, כל הבא לצבא, for כל בא לצבא, as in vv. 23, 30. So also the
Samaritan.

Num 13 26, ואל עדת, for ואל כל עדת, as in Num 31 12.

The list concludes with these words in Aramaic: "Thus were they
written in the Torah which came out of Jerusalem."[44]

We may suppose that this list, like similar other lists in rabbinic
literature, is not exhaustive, and if it be true that the codex was plundered
from the Temple, it may have been written before the promulgation of
the authoritative text under Judas Maccabaeus. Perhaps it was one
of the MSS which the official scribes consulted in the preparation of their
new text.

[41] Cf. Siphrê *ad loc.*: אמרתי באפי איה הם. Similarly some ancient versions. See S. R.
Driver, *Deuteronomy*, 1902, p. 369.

[42] These changes may have been caused by faulty hearing. But cf. A. Sperber,
HUCA, XII–XIII, p. 146.

[43] Cf. Rashi and Nachmanides *ad loc.*

[44] P. 212: כן הוו כתיבין באוריתא דנפקת מירושלם. Cf. now also A. M. Habermann, *Sinai*,
XXXII (Jerusalem, 1953), pp. 161–167.

THE STABILIZATION OF THE TEXT OF THE HEBREW BIBLE, REVIEWED IN THE LIGHT OF THE BIBLICAL MATERIALS FROM THE JUDEAN DESERT *

MOSHE GREENBERG

UNIVERSITY OF PENNSYLVANIA

THE REMARKABLE CACHES of ancient documents discovered in the Wilderness of Judah enable us for the first time to see what the text of the Hebrew Bible looked like at about the turn of the Era. What was formerly a matter largely of inference from early translations and the testimony of Rabbinic literature can now be controlled by manuscript evidence. The material is extensive, and will take years to publish; yet a sufficient amount has already been made available to make some tentative judgments possible, and, indeed, necessary. The following is an attempt to sketch the effect of the new material on our understanding of the old, and to outline some major stages in the formation of the received Hebrew text from the early Hellenistic period onward.

Reprinted from *Journal of the American Oriental Society* 76 (1956).

The text of the Hebrew Bible is made up of three historically distinct elements: in order of antiquity and stability they are the consonants, the vowel letters, and the system of diacritical marks for vowels and cantillation. The present system of diacritical marks was developed by the Massoretes —the preservers of the text tradition—of the Palestinian school at Tiberias in the 9th century. It is the product of two centuries of intensive text-critical work in the schools of Palestine and Babylonia, whose object was the establishment of the correct pronunciation and text.[1] The Massoretic ideal remained, however, unachieved. For in the consonantal text—let alone the diacritical marks— thousands of minute differences touching the vowel letters, particles, the copula, singular and plural, and the like, remained. Massoretic manuals listed many of these differences but did not resolve them. The text of our Western Bibles is substantially that of Jacob ben Ḥayyim, the editor of the second Rabbinic Bible published by Daniel Bomberg at Venice in 1524/5. His harmonizing efforts were supplemented by others; later editions, for example, have incorporated the text-critical commentary of Jedidiah Solomon Norzi (*Minḥat Shay*, 1626). The difficulties these men faced can be gathered from their prefatory remarks; Jacob ben Ḥayyim writes:

[Bomberg] bent every effort, sending throughout all these countries to search out what could be found of Massoretic manuals . . . After I saw these manuals and examined them I discovered that they were extremely confused and corrupt . . . In places where there was an omission . . . I searched the manuals and corrected

accordingly; where I found them mutually contradictory
I have recorded the conflicting statements . . . Where
one book was self-contradictory, or in error, I investigated until I found what appeared to me to be the
truth; at times, however, I left the matter unsettled . . .
God knows how I labored on this.[2]

Jedidiah Solomon recounts the types of dissensions
the books of his time contained:

Conflicts are legion; the Torah has become, not two
Torot, but numberless Torot owing to the great number
of variations found in our local books—old and new
alike—throughout the entire Bible. There is not a passage which is clear of confusion and errors in the vowel
letters, in accents and vowel signs, in the qrē and kṯīb,
in dāḡēš and rāfe . . . Nor have the Massoretic manuals
escaped the same fate in several places . . . so that if a
man undertake to write a Torah scroll according to law,
he must necessarily err in respect of the vowel letters,
and be like a blind man groping in pitch darkness.[3]

It is owing to the energy of Paul Kahle in publishing great quantities of early manuscripts, primarily from the Cairo Genizah, that we have today
a clearer picture of the work of the Palestinian
and Babylonian Massoretes of the 7th-9th centuries. We now see that the bewildering variety of
Massoretic notes confronting the later editors had
its roots in the differences among and within these
schools.[4] Thanks to Kahle a manuscript dated to
1008/9 copied from a codex made by Aaron ben
Moses ben Asher—the last of the Tiberian Massoretes—was published as the text of the third and
subsequent editions of Kittel's *Biblia Hebraica*.
Thus for the first time a genuine Massoretic text—
not *the* Massoretic text, which is now recognized as
a will-o'-the-wisp, but the text of one famous Massorete—was made available. If Kahle is right

300

against Cassuto, this is a copy of the very ben-Asher text utilized and recommended by Maimonides.[5]

The Genizah manuscripts, like those confronting the later editors, show many small disagreements in vowel letters, diacritical marks, particles, and the like. After discounting copyists' errors and unwitting alterations, the real variants are negligible. To regard the Massoretes as having created a new recension is true only insofar as their fixing of certain orthographic and diacritical details.[6] It is perfectly plain that all the Genizah manuscripts belong to the same consonantal recension, and that this was made long before the Massoretes. For the history of that recension we must look to our early sources and the newly discovered manuscripts.

II

Jewish tradition attributes several types of textual activity to the *sōfrīm*—the 'bookmen' of the Persian and Hellenistic period—and especially to the archetypal *sōfēr* Ezra. The change from paleo-Hebrew to the so-called square script in writing the Torah is dated to the time of Ezra.[7] Text-critical activity of a sort is also ascribed to him:

There are ten dotted places in the Torah . . . For Ezra thought, 'If Elijah should come and ask, "Why did you write these?" I can answer, "I have already marked them with dots"; and if he should say, "You did well in so writing" I shall remove the dots.'[8]

This is a picturesque way of saying that the text in ten places was suspect, and, following a practice which was common to the Alexandrian Greek grammarians, these doubtful passages were marked with dots. It was doubtless on the evidence of

301

other manuscripts that they were so marked; in four cases out of the ten the dotted matter is lacking in the Septuagint or the Samaritan Pentateuch.[9]

Another parallel to Greek text-critical marks are the *sīmāniyyōṯ* 'marks' (Hebraized from Greek *sēmeia*) placed before and after Numbers 10: 35-6.[10] From the recorded forms of these signs Lieberman has argued to identify them with the Alexandrian *antisigma*; like the latter the *sīmāniyyōṯ* were understood to mark a transposition of verses.[11] Tradition ascribes the introduction of the *sīmāniyyōṯ* into the text to God himself; at any rate it is clear that they must have been found in Torah scrolls at a very early date.

Two other types of text-critical activity by the *sōfrīm* are specified: they are termed *tiqqūn sōfrīm* 'emendation of the bookmen' and *'iṭṭūr sōfrīm* 'deletion of the bookmen.' Some Rabbinic sources list eleven, others eighteen, cases of 'emendation' in the Bible.[12] In all but one case the alteration of a single letter is involved—the one exception involves a change in the word order—in passages which unemended would have been theologically offensive. Lieberman has suggested that the principle behind this procedure lurks in an expression now found only as a figure of speech in Rabbinic texts: 'Better that one letter be removed from the Torah than that the Divine Name be publicly profaned.'[13]

Five examples of 'deletion' are given, drawn from the Torah and Psalms; in each case the copula *waw* is deleted, thus creating an asyndeton.[14] An 11th century Talmudic thesaurus gives this interesting explanation of the deletions:

It would appear that anciently the village people were not careful in their Bibles, and read [the copula in each of these cases] . . . They fell into error at these places in that time, thinking that they were right because it made good sense . . . And when the bookmen saw this they removed these *waws*, and called these instances 'deletions of the bookmen' . . . And until quite recently people were similarly erring and reading (in Ex. 23: 13) '*and* it shall not be heard in thy mouth' . . .[15]

That is to say, the readings with the copula were popular smoothing of the text; such vulgar readings were recognized by the bookmen as they were by the 11th century lexicographer, and, accordingly, expunged from authoritative manuscripts.

Rabbinic literature reserves the name *sōfrīm* for scholars of the period between Ezra and Simon the Just, i.e. from about the middle of the 5th to the beginning of the 2nd century B. C. At what time the editorial activity ascribed to them took place we cannot say. But it is implied that by Maccabean times the text had been largely stabilized—at least that of the Torah, Prophets, and Psalms. To be sure, since Lagarde the fixing of the text has been placed in the first part of the 2nd century A. D., as if it was inspired by Rabbi Aqiba's minute exegesis which involve every jot and tittle of the text.[16] But it has been pointed out several times—most recently by Segal [17]—that Aqiba was not the innovator of this method. He learned it from his teacher, Nahum of Gimzo, and as early as the time of Herod Hillel the Elder was already utilizing hermeneutical methods which presuppose a text verbally stable.[18] Moreover Josephus, writing toward the end of the 1st century A. D. writes of the Scriptures that

during so many ages as have already passed, no one has been so bold as either to add anything to them, to take anything from them, or to make any change in them.[19]

Literary sources, then, suggest a date well before the end of the first Christian century for the stabilization of the Bible text. Now this was the period of the Hasmonean dynasty, whose rise gave birth to a cultural as well as a political renascence among the Jews. The literature and architecture of the period testify to the flourishing of Hebraic arts, and there is good reason to look for the origins of Mishnic Hebrew in the legal and chancery style of the Hasmonean palace.[20] Hasmonean interest in reestablishing the Temple archives, which had been destroyed during the Syrian persecution (cf. I Macc. 1:56), is reflected in an incidental notice in the 'Hanukka letter' sent by the Jerusalem community to the Jews of Alexandria in 143 B.C.:

Even so did Judah the Maccabee collect for us all the writings which had been scattered owing to the outbreak of war, and they are with us still.[21]

For Pseudo-Aristeas, writing perhaps a decade later,[22] the authority of the Septuagint rests, in the first place, on its having been translated from a copy of the Torah sent from Jerusalem by the High Priest himself;[23] and Josephus likewise appeals to 'books deposited in the Temple' for confirmation of his Biblical history.[24] The existence of a temple library in which official copies of sacred documents were preserved is a commonplace in the ancient Near East; indeed; it would have been odd had the Jews not had such an archive at Jerusalem. Several scholars have plausibly suggested that the stabilizing of the biblical text is to be associated with this renovation of the Temple library made after the success of Maccabean arms.[25] As we shall see, there may be other signs which point the same way.

304

Rabbinic sources also make mention of the 'book of the Temple Court,' apparently a standard scroll used for public reading on holydays. Books of the Prophets—possibly including some of the Hagiographa as well—are likewise mentioned as belonging to the Temple Court.[26] We are warned, however, against considering the text even of the Temple books as finally fixed in every detail by two circumstances: There were 'correctors of the book of the Temple Court' maintained out of the public treasury.[27] These were not merely correctors of exemplars made from the Temple book, for one passage explicitly speaks of correcting the Temple scroll itself.[28] What such correction might have entailed is related elsewhere thus:

Three scrolls were found in the Temple Court: the scroll *m'ōn*, the scroll *za'ṭūṭē* and the scroll *hī'*. In one scroll they found written *m'ōn* (in Deut. 33:27), in the other two *m'ōnā*; the sages discarded the reading of the one and adopted the reading of the two. In one they found written *za'ṭūṭē*, in the other two *na'rē* (in Ex. 24:5) . . . In one they found nine occurrences of *hī'* (spelled *hy'*), in the other two eleven; they discarded the reading of the one and adopted the reading of the two.[29]

There thus appear to have been several authoritative Torah scrolls in the archive, and the editorial activity on them was a continuing process. The Bibles of the people and even of the local synagogues could hardly have kept pace with the continuing refinement of the standard scrolls,[30] and it should occasion no surprise that evidence is at hand to show that deviations in detail were current even in synagogue manuscripts at the turn of the Era. An interesting case in point is the so-called Codex Severus referred to in an 11th century midrash as 'having been captured in Jerusalem and brought to Rome, and there stored away in the

Synagogue of Severus.' The midrash lists 29 variant readings contained in this scroll, presumably taken as part of Titus' plunder in 70 A. D. These variants consist of scribal errors, orthographic peculiarities reflecting earlier practice, Aramaized spellings, and a few altered readings—smoothings or expansions on the basis of parallel passages.[31] The midrash states that this scroll was 'stored away' (*gnūzā ūsṯūmā*), meaning that it was later withdrawn from public use because of its deviations. This withdrawal reflects the increased weight of Rabbinic authority among Jews after the fall of Jerusalem, when the economy of crisis forced Judaism into a more rigid mold in which there was no room for deviations. Thus Aquiba exhorts his disciple from prison, 'When you teach your son, teach only from a corrected text,'[32] and a later authority applies Job 11:13 'Let not evil dwell in thy tents' to the retention beyond thirty days of uncorrected books in one's home.[33] But the presence of vulgata containing small deviations is demonstrable from citations throughout Rabbinic literature; it has even been suggested that these deviant citations point to the use of the vulgata by the Rabbis in their preaching, in spite of their differing from the standard text.[34]

The final stage in the fixing of the Bible text seems thus to have been arrived at gradually by the successive refinement of a selected recension during the last pre-Christian centuries. The impetus to this may well have been the reorganization of the Temple library following the Maccabean victory. The editorial work of the bookmen did not immediately affect the Bibles in the hands of the people. Only after the consolidation of Rabbinic Judaism between the two revolts (70-

132) did a more thorough supervision of the text on the basis of the standard became possible. But while the standard was made to prevail at this time, vulgar readings cropping up throughout Rabbinic literature testify to the tenacity of the hold the popular texts had.

III

The received text is the end result of work on one recension. Two other recensions of the Torah attest to the type of text which was set aside by that of the bookmen: the Samaritan Pentateuch and the Hebrew *Vorlage* of the Septuagint.

The Samaritan Pentateuch has been made available in an eclectic edition by von Gall.[35] Although von Gall failed to utilize the earliest manuscripts, and conformed his text to the Jewish Torah in some ways,[36] we can still utilize his work to get a reasonably good conception of the distinctive features of this recension. The Samaritan Pentateuch is less asyndetic than the Jewish. Those passages of the Torah which the Talmud enumerates as bearing 'deletions of the bookmen' show up here with the copula. Unusual expressions are replaced by more common ones. Archaic grammatical forms found in the Jewish text are replaced with later forms. Words and phrases are added, drawn as a rule from similar or parallel passages. The effect is to make the text smoother and more repetitive without altering the meaning. A good instance is the account of the theophany at Sinai in Ex. 20. Deut. 5 contains a different version of the event; in the Samaritan, however, the accounts of Exodus and Deuteronomy are neatly combined, giving a fully harmonized story. Here and there an explanatory remark is found;

e. g. following the prohibition of cooking a kid in its mother's milk in Ex. 23 : 19 we read, ' Whoever does this is like one who sacrifices a *škḥ* (?) ; it is sin to the God of Jacob.'

These features of typical of later Jewish popular translations of the Bible, such as the Aramaic Targums or Saadya's Arabic Bible. The antiquity of the Samaritan text has, accordingly, been questioned. The Samaritans broke away from the Jews during the 5th-4th centuries B. C., before the change from paleo-Hebrew to the square character was made; accordingly their Torah is still written in a form of paleo-Hebrew, and separates words by dots—the custom of very early times. The oldest manuscript is in Nablus and has been seen by few scholars. Moses Gaster, who was an enthusiastic advocate of Samaritan tradition, saw it and dated it no later than the first Christian century; [37] his date has not been generally accepted though few, indeed, are qualified to speak on the matter. Support for the Samaritan, however, is forthcoming from a source of undisputed antiquity, the Septuagint. Cases of agreement between the Septuagint and the Samaritan against the received Hebrew in their additions and divergent readings are so numerous as to require the assumption of some relationship. In earlier days this agreement served the ends of theological polemic: the Catholic Church sought to discredit the received Hebrew on the basis of the Septuagint and Samaritan; the Protestants defended the Hebrew denigrating the value of the other two. Bizarre theories have been spun to explain this agreement: One held that the Samaritan and the Septuagint were translations of an Aramaic version of the original Hebrew. Another was that the Samaritan was a Hebrew rendering of the Septuagint. The first sober verdict was given by Gesenius in 1815 who maintained that the two must have originated in a Hebrew text earlier than the fixing of our Massoretic text.[38]

The matter is more complicated, however. For in spite of their many agreements the Septuagint is not nearly as full as the Samaritan. None of the large scale harmonizing and transposing of verses of the Samaritan appears in the Greek. Does this mean that, as suspected, the Samaritan is a later conflation?

We are indebted to Kahle for pointing to the indications that the Septuagint as we have it may not have been the first Greek translation of the Torah, but a revision of earlier translations. Pseudo-Aristeas explicitly refers to earlier translations of the Law, made before the Seventy.[39] Inquiring after possible remains and reflexes of these superseded translations Kahle noted that some Torah citations in the New Testament which conflict with our Septuagint agree with the readings of the Samaritan Pentateuch. Moreover he noted that readings of certain Septuagintal manuscripts agreed with the Samaritan not only in their similar readings, but even in their having that fuller text to characteristically Samaritan and unlike our Septuagint.[40]

We are thus led to think that—allowing for certain obvious dogmatic changes—the Samaritan represents an early Hebrew text type. Its fulness, its harmonizations and levellings will be part of its popular character, as a text in circulation from times before the text-criticism of the bookmen provoked the search for better, less expanded (and therefore less popular) recensions.[41] There seems to be no reason to exclude the origin of this text type from as early as the 4th century B. C. Remains of early Greek translations preserved in out of the way places appear to reflect a Samaritan-like Hebrew *Vorlage*. At some time toward the middle of the 2nd century B. C., before Pseudo-Aristeas, a new Greek translation of the Torah was produced. It is reasonable to suppose that one of the purposes of this undertaking was to adapt the Greek version in accordance with the best Hebrew text of the time; hence Pseudo-Aristeas' stress on the fact that the scroll from which the translation was made came from Jerusalem's High Priest. Interestingly enough the early Hasmonean Hebrew text reflected in the Septuagint *Vorlage* shows, in relation to the Samaritan, a considerable amount of pruning and editing. This accords with the view set forth above that the final phase of the fixing of the text had begun by early Hasmonean times. Thus the Septuagint *Vorlage* will represent an intermediate stage between the full Samaritan and the pruned received Hebrew. In the Septuagint *Vorlage* we are probably to see an early product of the text-critical endeavors of the *sōfrīm* to establish an authentic Torah on the basis of older, less edited manuscripts than those in circulation among the people.

IV

The materials from the Wilderness of Judah now enable us to see at first hand some of the types of biblical texts which were current in Palestine in the centuries just before and after the turn of the Era.

The settlement at Khirbet Qumran belonged to a community which had broken with the authorities in Jerusalem. It was a religious order organized along communistic lines, with a rigidly graded structure: priests, Levites, and lay members with various further subdivisions involving seniority. It saw itself as Israel in miniature, as true Israel, and looked for the day when God would lead its army in successful battle against the heathens and apostate Jews.[42] The abandonment of the settlement has been dated to the period of the First Revolt (66-70) on the basis of dated coins, pottery, and the type of manuscript remains found: the latter consist of biblical, apocryphal-eschatological, and liturgical works written on skins; some papyrus fragments were found too, but no paper and no codices. Ten caves have thus far been found to contain manuscript fragments; those of Cave I have recently been published, while specimens of the far richer store of Cave IV had been published previously.[43]

The biblical fragments in square script have been examined by F. M. Cross with a view to their paleography. His conclusions are that the vast majority fall in the Hasmonean period, especially the latter half, and the Herodian period, again especially the latter part; a few are dated to the end of the 3rd century B. C.[44] Fragments in paleo-Hebrew were also found, including an Exodus manuscript, largely intact. These have been variously dated from the 5th to the 1st centuries B. C.[45] It is best, therefore, to await further publication of this material and refrain at present from drawing the far-reaching conclusions that an early date would permit.

There is a great variety in the orthography of the fragments. Some are written with a profusion of vowel letters—although it must be stressed that this fulness is essentially different from that of medieval Jewish manuscripts.[46] Manuscript fragments of this type of orthography may be considered as vulgata. In the case of Isaiah a [47] we are dealing with a careless copyist (or copyists) ; the scroll abounds in errors, smoothings, paraphrases, and conjectural filling-in.[48] Orlinsky, who has published the only detailed studies of individual variants in the scroll, characterizes its text as ' an oral variation on the theme of the text tradition which came to be known . . . as Masoretic.' ' Its text is worthless to the student who wishes to get behind the Masoretic text or to recover the Hebrew *Vorlage* of the ancient primary versions; it is a vulgar text, largely, if not wholly, orally contrived.' [49] This severe judgment is stated in perhaps overly drastic terms; it is justifiable as a much needed corrective to the text-critical conclusions which have been drawn from hasty and unmethodical work.[50] But that even vulgar texts may on occasion preserve more original readings is a possibility which must be allowed.[51]

To this category belongs also Deuteronomy *a*, a fragment containing some inferior variants and a misspelling due to the current pronunciation of Hebrew in which laryngals appear to have lost their distinctive pronunciation. It is of interest to note that the practice of crossing out errors rather than erasing them—a practice not permitted in the writing of authorized texts—has been found so far only in this type of text.[52]

The orthographic and grammatical peculiarities of the vulgata reflect a type of Hebrew strongly influenced by Aramaic and similar in several respects to the Hebrew known from Samaritan sources. This is significant support for the authenticity of the Samaritan tradition: it now appears to have retained features of early popular Hebrew which were modified in later development.[53]

Another series of fragments have an orthography generally similar to, occasionally slightly fuller than, that of late Biblical books. These have readings now like the Septuagint, now like the Samaritan (in the Pentateuch), now like the Massoretic text against them both, and sometimes a reading otherwise unattested. Of particular interest is an Exodus manuscript having throughout additional verses and expansions often identical with those of the Samaritan Pentateuch.[54] Fragments of Samuel and Deuteronomy from the same cave (IV) show variations and additions with Septuagintal affinities.[55]

Finally there are some manuscripts with the standard biblical orthography. The Isaiah scroll *b* is such a text,[56] as are the fragments of Psalter *a*. To be sure, there are many slight deviations from the Massoretic text, but these are almost always of the type which keep occurring throughout the history of biblical manuscripts.

Thus the Qumran material witnesses to a variety of text types all current contemporaneously. This is an important point. It is not possible to set up a line of development of text forms from this material, so that the form closest to our Hebrew be the latest. Three Psalter fragments which do not appear to have been written at any considerable interval run the orthographic gamut from exceptional fulness to Massoretic leanness. Of the two Deuteronomy fragments the one whose orthography is closest to Massoretic shows two variants with Septuagint parallels.

It would thus appear that the forerunner of our received text was extant and current during the last pre-Christian centuries. The Isaiah *b* scroll and Psalter *a* testify to that. But in the Qumran community other texts were also current: the Samaritan type of Torah, and manuscripts with Septuagint-like readings in the Torah and Prophets. There is no standard text at Qumran. While this at first may seem strange it is not really so. Piety is not always accompanied by a critical sense. To the devout reader a text giving the substance of the sacred message is not invalidated by slight verbal divergences from other texts. It must be also kept in mind that no binding laws were derived at Qumran from the letters of Scripture. Examples are ready at hand of pious indifference to textual considerations among Jews of later ages. The position of the "received" Talmud text studied in the *yeshiva* has not been affected to any large degree by the great corpus of variant readings collected by Rabbinovicz over seventy years ago. Nor has the impetus to publish critical texts of Rabbinic writings always come from circles marked by piety. Kahle's resuscitation of a genuine ben Asher manuscript of the Bible has not been met by acclamation outside of academic circles, despite the endorsement given it by Maimonides (if Kahle's identification be correct). Just so the verbal and orthographic divergences which rarely affected the meaning, the additional phrases and verses which were based on parallels or traditional interpretations—these need not have troubled the Qumran pietists any more than they do those of a later day.

What is exceedingly valuable in these manuscripts and fragments is their evidence for the an-

314

tiquity and reality of variants whose existence, attested to heretofore only by the versions, had been questionable. The Greek Samuel, so different at times from our Hebrew, seems now to have a relative in the Samuel manuscript of Cave IV. The antiquity of the Samaritan Pentateuch, whose extraordinary conflateness had been taken as a sign of lateness, is now supported by a Qumran Exodus manuscript. At the same time the received Hebrew is shown to have had early representatives, although at Qumran, at least it had not gained dominance.

But the peculiar nature of the Qumran community prohibits us from drawing conclusions confidently as to the state of affairs in Jerusalem. What the official priesthood and bookmen had achieved in stabilizing the text need not have been reflected in this community which had cut itself off from the rest of Judea, and was irreconcilably hostile to Jerusalem and its authority. Hence we must consider the possibility that just as the Samaritan tradition froze the Torah in a relatively unedited and uncritical form, and did not share in the successive refinement that resulted in the received text, so too the Qumran manuscripts may show an uncritical acceptance of all types of texts. But their attitude need not have reflected the state of affairs in official Jewish circles.

The state of the text in the first and second Christian centuries can be seen from the finds in Wadi Murabba'āt, some twenty kilometers south of Qumran. Here several dated documents show the main post-Exilic settlement to have been that of a Jewish military post in the mid-second century, followed by some decades of Roman occupation. The Jews appear to have been an outpost of

Bar-Kochba's rebel army. Now, since the spiritual leaders of this Second Revolt against Rome (132-5) were some of the most eminent Rabbis, there is no question as to the orthodoxy of this group. Accordingly we do not find any heterodox literature at Murabba'āt as was found at Qumran. Moreover the biblical fragments—remnants of the Torah and Isaiah—agree in every detail with our text.[57] Equally interesting is what Barthelemy regards as a Jewish Greek prototype of Aquila, Symmachus, and Theodotian dating from the first century—i. e. from approximately the same time as the latest Qumran materials. In six out of eight cases where comparison with Qumran texts is possible the Murabba'āt Greek agrees with the Massoretic text where the Qumran text agrees with the Septuagint.[58] This is, to be sure, not much to go by, but it may be a hint that the Qumran community showed a lag in its textual level as compared with the Jewish orthodoxy.

To sum up then: It would appear that at the beginning of the Hellenistic period biblical texts were extant in two main types, a fuller and a shorter text. The longer texts were the popular ones; in the Torah they are represented by the Samaritan tradition which broke away from the line of further evolution at this time. During the Ptolemaic period the text-critical work of the *sōfrīm* began, accelerated, probably, under the Hasmonean renascence. Their effort was directed toward selecting the manuscripts reflecting the oldest tradition, and to make them standard. In the case of the Torah it was the shorter text, with its earlier orthography and older linguistic forms which was made the norm.[59] The editing was a continuing process which reached its end by the first Christian century, well before the First Revolt. The standard became all prevalent, however, only after the fall of Jerusalem, when Rabbinic Judaism came into exclusive hegemony. Previously the various stages of the text work coexisted in the Bibles of the people. While types modelled after the evolving standard trickled down from Jerusalem, they had to compete with older, less edited texts, and with such as were written in a fuller, vulgar orthography. The prevalence of the standard, not its creation, came after 70 A. D., and is the necessary precondition of the highly literal exegesis which flourished in the Tannaitic academies. Such an exegesis, undertaken in all seriousness by earnest men is inconceivable had the text not been hallowed in its letter well beforehand.

V

It is instructive to compare the evolution of the Biblical text with that of the Greek classics, as we can now see it thanks to the discovery of the papyri.

With the aid of the papyri it is possible to get behind the text of the 10th-15th century vellums to as early as the 3rd century B. C. It can be seen that by the 1st century A. D. the texts of the chief prose authors, without being altogether uniform, were, by and large, in the form they appear in the medieval manuscripts. But the Homer and Plato fragments of the early Ptolemaic period reveal a text in a decidedly unsettled condition. The Homeric fragments contain a striking amount of additional matter, consisting chiefly of tags from parallel passages. Kenyon observed that 'with hardly an exception they add nothing substantial to the poem, but are just such additions as a rhap-

317

sodist might make who was anxious to extend the bulk of his recitation.' (One might say, a ' Samaritan recension ' of Homer.) It was during the 2nd century B. C. that the shorter, esthetically superior text came to prevail; the outcome, it would appear, of the text-critical work of the Alexandrians. During this time many transition forms are found side by side (much as our Qumran material reflects the contemporaneous currency of various text types during this very period in Judea).[60]

The concurrence of Jewish textual activity with the work of the Alexandrian grammarians is suggestive. That the *sōfrīm* utilized critical marks strikingly similar to those of the Greeks lends plausibility to the assumption of a connection between the two. To be sure, the methods of the Greeks and their attitude toward their classics differed fundamentally from the methods and attitudes of the Jews.[61] Nonetheless it would appear likely that some of the techniques of criticism, if not the very stimulus to undertake it, came to Judea from abroad. The editing and standardization of the biblical text thus has a claim to be regarded among the several phenomena which, while thoroughly Judaized, had their roots at least in part in the Hellenistic world.[62]

* A paper presented to the Oriental Club of Philadelphia. In the course of revision I had the benefit of discussing the major points with Professor Harry M. Orlinsky. Professor Orlinsky also made available to me his as yet unpublished contribution to the Irwin *Festschrift*. I wish to acknowledge here his courtesy and valuable criticism.

[1] A concise survey of the work of the Massoretes is B. J. Roberts, " The Emergence of the Tiberian Massoretic Text," *Journal of Theological Studies*, XLIX (1948), 8 ff.

[2] C. D. Ginsburg, *Jacob ben Chajim ben Adonijah's Introduction . . .*[2] London, 1867, 77 f. On ben Ḥayyim's eclectic method see also Sperber, " Problems of the Masora," *HUCA*, XVII (1943), 370 ff. It is important to note that ben Ḥayyim's editorial activity does not go beyond selecting one of the given variants. He does not invent readings; in this he may well serve as a representative of Massoretic conservatism.

[3] Introduction to *Minḥat Shay*, reprinted in Shulsinger's *Pentateuch* (Hebrew), VI 8 f.

[4] Kahle has summarized this aspect of his life work in his *The Cairo Genizah* (hereafter cited as *CG*) (London, 1947), 36 ff.

[5] Maimonides *Code, Sefer Torah* 8, 4; cf. Kahle, " The Hebrew ben Asher Bible Manuscripts," *Vetus Testamentum*, 1 (1951), 161 ff.

[6] See Orlinsky's remarks in *JAOS* LXI (1941), 84 ff., and compare the more detailed treatment of Roberts in *Journal of Jewish Studies*, I (1949), 147 ff., where, on p. 152, the same conclusion is reached regarding the single consonantal recension.

[7] *Tosefta Sanhedrin* 4, 7; *Bab. Sanhedrin* 22a.

319

⁸ *Aboth de Rabbi Nathan* I 34, II 37 (translated by J. Goldin, *The Fathers According to Rabbi Nathan, Yale Judaica Series X*, 138 f.). On these and other critical marks discussed below see the fundamental study by S. Lieberman, *Hellenism in Jewish Palestine* (New York, 1950), 38 ff.

⁹ The second *y* of *wbynyk* (Gen. 16: 5) lacking in Sam.; *wyšqhw* (Gen. 33: 4) lacking in Sept.; *w'hrn* (Nu. 3: 39) lacking in Sam.; *r* of *'sr* (Nu. 21: 30) lacking in both Sam. and Sept.

¹⁰ *Sifre* I 84; *Aboth de R. Nathan* I 34 (tr. Goldin 137).

¹¹ See Lieberman's discussion, *op. cit.* 39 ff.

¹² *Ibid.* 28 ff.

¹³ *Ibid.* 35 f.

¹⁴ *Bab. Nedarim* 37b.

¹⁵ Nathan ben Yeḥiel, *Sefer he'ārūḵ*, s. v. *'āṭar*; cited by Jacob ben Ḥayyim in *Introduction*, ed. Ginsburg 66 f.

¹⁶ Cf. e. g. Pfeiffer, *Introduction to the Old Testament*, (New York, 1948), 76 f.

¹⁷ M. H. Segal, "The Promulgation of the Authoritative Text of the Hebrew Bible," *JBL*, LXXII (1953), 36 f.

¹⁸ See, e. g. the two Talmuds to *Pesaḥim* 6, 1 where Hillel argues from a *gzērā šāwā* (verbal analogy, on which cf. Lieberman, *op. cit.* 58 ff.), a hermeneutic which could not have developed before the fixing of the text.

¹⁹ *Against Apion* I 42.

²⁰ J. Klausner, *The Second Temple at its Height* (Hebrew), Tel-Aviv, 1930, 148 ff. M. H. Segal (*Grammar of Mishnic Hebrew* (Hebrew), Tel-Aviv, 1936, 13) argues for an earlier origin but agrees that the Hasmonean period saw the 'expansion and enrichment' of Mishnic.

²¹ *II Maccabees* 2: 14; on this letter cf. Bickermann, *Zeitschrift f. d. neutest. Wissenschaft*, XXXII (1933), 254.

²² For the most recent discussion of the date of Ps.-Aristeas see M. Hadas, *Aristeas to Philocrates*, New York, 1951. On p. 54 he decides for the approximate date 130 B. C. For an earlier date (before 170 B. C.) cf. Orlinsky, *Crozer Quarterly*, XXIX (1952), 202 ff.

²³ *Ps.-Aristeas* 176, on which see Bickerman, *JBL*, LXIII (1944), 343.

²⁴ *Antiquities* V 1, 17; III 1, 7; see also *War* VII 5, 5.

25 M. Gaster, *The Samaritans* (London, 1925), 132; Segal, *JBL*, LXXII (1953), 40.

26 References to the books of the Temple Court are collected and fully discussed in L. Blau, *Studien zum althebräischen Buchwesen* (Budapest, 1902), 107 ff. That Hagiographia may be included under the rubric Prophets in Jewish sources is shown *ibid.* 63.

27 *Pal. Sheqalim* 48a; Blau, *op. cit.* 107.

28 *Mishna Mo'ed Qaṭan* 3, 4. The verb *higgīᵃh*, which elsewhere means 'correct (a manuscript),' proof-read,' is sometimes taken to mean 're-ink' in this one passage (Jastrow, *Dictionary* 872; Segal, *ibid.* 43). But 're-ink' is expressed otherwise (*heʿeḇīr qulmus 'al, ḥiddēš*; cf. Rashi, *Bab. Shabbat* 104b, s. v. *kāṯaḇ al gaḇ hakkṯāḇ*); as for instances of correcting the Temple scroll, see ahead in the text.

29 *Sifre* II 356, *Aboth de R. Nathan* II 46, *Soferim* 4, 4; see Lieberman, *op. cit.* 21 f. and references there.

30 Note the allegation by Ps.-Aristeas (30) that the Hebrew copies of the Torah current in Alexandria were corrupt; for this meaning cf. Bickerman, *JBL*, LXIII (1944), 343 n. 24.

31 Published and discussed by A. Epstein in *Chwolson Festschrift* 49 f.; Sperber gives the variants, *op. cit.* 333 f., as does Segal, *op. cit.* 46 f. See also Lieberman, *op. cit.* 23 f.

32 *Bab. Pesaḥim* 112a.

33 *Bab. Kethubboth* 19b.

34 Lieberman, *op. cit.* 26. The most thorough collection of Biblical variants found in Rabbinic literature is by V. Aptowitzer, *Das Schriftwort in der Rabbinischen Literatur* (Vienna, 1906-15). His material covers only Joshua, Judges, and Samuel. Despite Aptowitzer's care much of it can not be said to reflect real text variants, but is rather to be explained by the Rabbinic practice of citing memoriter or in paraphrase. Aptowitzer has set forth the Rabbinic methods of citation in excellent summary in Pt. I of his work, 21 ff.

35 August Freiherr von Gall, *Der Hebräische Pentateuch der Samaritaner* (Giessen, 1914-18).

36 On manuscripts see *CG* 50 n. 1; on von Gall's editorial method, see his *Vorwort* lxviii.

37 *The Samaritans* 108.

38 A survey of the shifting opinions concerning the

value of the Samaritan Torah is found in Geiger, *Urschrift und Übersetzungen der Bibel* (Breslau, 1857), 14 ff.; Montgomery, *The Samaritans* (Philadelphia, 1907), 286 ff.

[39] The clear statement of Ps.-Aristeas 314, where the writer tells us that Theopompus (early 4th century B. C.) 'had been driven out of his mind for more than thirty days because he intended to insert in his history some of the incidents from the earlier and somewhat unreliable translations of the law' (so rendered by Andrews in Charles, *Apocrypha* II 121). It is true that that *episphalesteron* may be taken rather with *prosistorein* (see Andrews' note), and the passage rendered '. . . when he was too rashly intending to introduce into his history some of the incidents of the law which had been previously translated' (Thackery *apud* Andrews, similarly Hadas). But even so the fact of previous translation still stands, although the need to *revise* 'somewhat unreliable translations' is more obvious. Yet even following Trackery and Hadas the necessity for making a new translation is best explained as due to the desire to revise previously existing efforts. Thus even if Kahle's argument from par. 30 is rejected—and it would appear from Orlinsky, *Crozer Quarterly*, XXIX (1952), 205 that it must be—the evidence of par. 314 is clearly in favor of a pre-Septuagint Greek translation.

[40] *CG* 132 ff., and especially 144 ff.

[41] *Ibid.* 147 f., but so already Gaster, *The Samaritans* 123 ff. On the popular character of the Samaritan see further S. Talmon, *Journal of Jewish Studies* II (1951), 144 ff.

[42] The ideology of the community is set forth well in their various writings, for a provisional translation of which see the selection in Burrows, *The Dead Sea Scrolls* (New York, 1955).

[43] The materials of Cave I have been published by D. Barthelemy and J. T. Milik, with contributions by R. de Vaux *et al.* in *Discoveries in the Judaean Desert I. Qumran Cave* I (Oxford, 1955). References to Qumran material are to this publication unless otherwise noted.

The following have been published from Cave IV

a. F. M. Cross, Jr., "A New Qumran Biblical Fragment Related to the Original Hebrew Underlying the Septuagint," *BASOR*, CXXXII (1953), 15 ff.

b. J. Muilenberg, "A Qoheleth Scroll from Qumran," *BASOR*, CXXXV (1954), 20 ff.

c. *Idem*, "Fragments of Another Qumran Isaiah Scroll," *ibid*. 28 ff.

d. P. W. Skehan, "A Fragment of the 'Song of Moses' . . . ," *BASOR* (1954), 12 ff.

e. F. M. Cross, Jr., "The Oldest Manuscripts from Qumran," *JBL*, LXXIV (1955), 165 ff.

f. P. W. Skehan, "Exodus in the Samaritan Recension from Qumran," *ibid*. 182 ff.

The latest comprehensive report of the work being done on the Qumran finds at the Palestine Archaeological Museum is in *RB*, LXIII (1956), 49 ff.; a brief survey is given by Cross in *BASOR*, CXLI (1956), 9 ff.

[44] See e in the preceding note.

[45] The Leviticus fragments of Cave I have been dated to the second half of the 5th c. (Birnbaum, *BASOR*, CXVIII [1950], 27); late 4th-early 3rd c. (Diringer, *BA*, XIII [1950], 93 ff.); 4th c. (de Vaux, *RB*, LVI [1949], 600 ff.); 2nd-1st cc. (Yeivin, *BASOR*, CXVIII [1950], 28 ff., Cross, *JBL*, LXXIV [1955], 147 n. 1 ['archaizing,' so too Albright, *BASOR*, CXL [1955], 33 n. 29]). The Samaritan-type Exodus manuscript, and with it all other paleo-Hebrew fragments, are dated to 'the normal period of Qumran cursive documents' by Skehan, *RB*, LXIII (1956), 58; cf. *JBL*, LXXIV 182 f.

[46] As shown by H. Yalon in *Kirjath Sepher*, XXVII (1951), 164 f., from which I quote the following 'This fulness involves only *he* and *waw* . . . *yod* is treated as it is in Massoretic orthography, never occurring before strong-*dāḡēš* or before quiescent *šwā* [in contrast to medieval orthography where it frequently does occur in these positions] . . . In the Isaiah *a* scroll there is not a single instance of a double consonantal *waw*, which is the normal way of indicating consonantal *waw* in medieval writing.' Cf. also *Kirjath Sepher*, XXVIII (1952), 65.

[47] Published in *The Dead Sea Scrolls of St. Mark's Monastery*, Vol. I, ed. M. Burrows (New Haven, 1950).

[48] Listed by Burrows in *BASOR*, CXI (1948), 16 ff.; CXIII (1949), 24 ff.

[49] These judgments will be found respectively in his Studies in the St. Mark's Isaiah Scroll, *JBL*, LXIX (1950), 157, *JQR*, XLIII (1952-3), 338. Further installments of Orlinsky's studies are in *Journal of Jewish*

Studies, II (1951), 151 ff., *JNES*, XI (1952), 153 ff., *IEJ*, IV (1954), 5 ff., *Tarbiz*, XXIV (1954), 4 ff. (see the full English summary pp. i-ii), *HUCA*, XXV (1954), 85 ff.

[50] See Orlinsky's strong critique, Notes on the Present State of the Textual Criticism of the Judean Biblical Cave Scrolls, to appear in the forthcoming *Irwin Festschrift*. The especial merit of his studies lies in the painstaking care and rigorous method with which they are pursued, and of which they are indeed models.

[51] That Orlinsky may have overstated the case against the textual value of the Isaiah *a* scroll appears to be indicated by the occasional, rare reading which is original and seems superior both to the received Hebrew and the Greek. One such is *ymrw* (*yimrū*) 'they shall feed' for received *wmry'* (*ūmrī*) 'and a fatling' at 11: 6; the Greek here is conflate and in disorder (cf. Gray, *Isaiah* in *ICC ad loc.*). Another case occurs at 37: 27b-28a, where the scroll's *hnšdf lfny qdym*; *qwmkh* (*hannišdāf lifnē qādīm; qūmkā*) 'which is parched by the east-wind; thy rising etc.' makes original good sense out of unintelligible Hebrew; the Greek had the same Hebrew before it. On this passage cf. Burrows, *BASOR*, CXI (1948), 23 and CXIII (1949), 28 (toward the bottom). As to the scroll's reflecting the Greek's Hebrew *Vorlage*, two instances may be cited: 51: 23a where the scroll's plus *wm'ynk*, and 53: 11a where its plus *'wr* are both represented in the Greek (the latter plus is found even in Isaiah *b*, which hews so closely to our received text).

[52] In Isaiah *a* (see list on p. xv, bottom), and the Qoheleth fragment (note 37 *b*, above) at 6: 4.

[53] Yalon, *Kirjath Sepher*, XXVII (1951), 170 f. Gaster's feeling that the language of the 'Zadokite Documents' —seven manuscripts of which have now been found at Qumran (see Milik's report in *RB* LXIII [1956], 61)— had its closest affinities with Samaritan Hebrew (*Samaritans* 100) is thus strikingly borne out.

[54] See note 37 f.

[55] See note 37 d e.

[56] The bulk of Isaiah *b* was published in *ōṣar hammgillōt haggnūzōt* (*Treasury of Cached Scrolls*), ed. Sukenik (Jerusalem, 1954). Some additional bits are published in Barthelemy-Milik, *Discoveries*.

[57] See the preliminary report of de Vaux, *RB* LX (1953), 245 ff.

[58] D. Barthélemy, "Redécouverte d'un chainon manquant de l'histoire de la Septante," *ibid.* 18 ff.

[59] In other cases, however, it was not the shorter text that was finally adopted. The Greek Job, for example, seems to reflect a *Vorlage* shorter by at least one-sixth than the received Hebrew (see Gray in the *ICC* on Job, lxxiv n. 1). But the nature of the Greek's omissions supports the overall priority of the Hebrew; e. g. in many cases the omission destroys the poetic parallelism (*ibid.*). The Greek Jeremiah is one-eighth shorter than the Hebrew, and has, in addition, some considerable transpositions. 'The variations of the LXX are in part " recensional," *i. e.* they are due to the fact that the Hebrew text used by the translators deviated in some particulars from that which we at present possess; but in part, also, they are due to the faulty manner in which the translators executed their work . . . *on the whole* the Massoretic text deserves the preference; but it is impossible to uphold the unconditional superiority of either' (Driver, *Introduction to the Literature of the OT*[9] 270).

In those frequent cases in which the translators appear merely to have condensed the Hebrew, there is the likelihood that they were adjusting the text to Greek taste. Similarly, the contemporary Alexandrian grammarians appear to have eliminated a considerable amount of the repetitions found in early Ptolemaic texts of Homer; see the next note.

[60] The value of the papyri for the text-criticism of Greek literature presents several relevant considerations to the student of the Judean Desert material. See the following surveys: F. G. Kenyon, *Proceedings of the British Academy* 1903-4, 141 ff.; B. P. Grenfell, *Journal of Hellenic Studies*, XXXIX (1919), 16 ff.; W. Schubart, *Einführung in die Papyruskunde* (Berlin, 1918), ch. V.

Whether the received, shorter Homer text is older and closer to the original than the longer, early Ptolemaic text is discussed by Grenfell, who tended to doubt it. If the Alexandrians had a hand in creating the received text we have here an example of the differing approaches of Greek and Jewish criticism: The Greeks worked on their text creatively, making it meet criteria of reason and taste (see the next note); the Jews refined their text on the basis of what they judged to be the best available manuscripts and the best attested readings. Aside from the recognized 'emendations of the bookmen' there is no objective evidence of deliberate text alteration by the *sōfrīm*. That this has not stood in the way of scholarly conjecture can be seen from, e. g. Pfeiffer, *Introduction to the OT* 86 ff. Ancient cacophemisms (the substitution of *bōšet* for *baʿal* in proper names, already attested to in the Greek), ancient euphemisms (substituting 'less' for 'curse God,' already in the Greek), and changes to be made in recitation—not in the body of the text—are here combined and ascribed to the history of the text during the period 135-500 A. D.

[61] See Lieberman, *op. cit.* 27, especially n. 34.

[62] On the Hellenistic infiltration of Judaism during the Hasmonean period see the suggestive remarks of Bickerman in *The Maccabees* (New York, 1947), 83 ff., 113 ff., and *The Jews*, ed. L. Finkelstein, 109 f.

NEW LIGHT ON EARLY RECENSIONS OF THE HEBREW BIBLE

W. F. ALBRIGHT

The publication of the Dead Sea Scrolls, though still in an early stage, has now reached a point where we can begin to discuss recensional problems in the early Hebrew text of many books of the Bible. In this brief article I wish to point out certain directions along which future research will have to move; it is thus programmatic and lays no claim to being anything but a pioneer attempt. Now that the chronology of the principal types of script used in the Qumran scrolls and fragments is pretty well established, thanks especially to the recent work of Frank M. Cross,

Reprinted from *Bulletin of the American Schools of Oriental Research* 140 (1955).

Jr.,[1] refining and extending the results of John C. Trever,[2] the writer,[3] and especially of S. A. Birnbaum,[4] we can attack the recensional problems with more confidence.

Recognition of the existence of early Hebrew recensions is not new. Though there has never hitherto been any clear evidence for different recensions in the extant Hebrew and Samaritan manuscripts, the text of some of the Greek books differs so widely from the Massoretic Hebrew tradition that divergent Hebrew recensions must be assumed.[5] Thus H. M. Orlinsky wrote in his analysis of the present state of Septuagintal studies, published nearly fifteen years ago: " Of course there was at one time more than one text-tradition of the Hebrew Bible. The Hebrew manuscripts used by the several Septuagint translators of the various books in the Old Testament differ at times not in minor details alone, but, as is the case in such books as Jeremiah, Job, Esther, *recensionally* from the masoretic text-tradition. But these text-traditions have long perished . . ."[6]

The greatest textual surprise of the Qumran finds has probably been the fact that most of the scrolls and fragments present a consonantal text which is virtually indistinguishable from the text of corresponding passages in our Massoretic Bible. The new material carries Hebrew examples of the proto-Massoretic text back into the second century B. C., and there are many Qumran manuscripts, long and short, of this type from the last century and a half of the Second Temple, as well as Murabba'ât texts of Massoretic type from the late first and early second centuries A. D.[7] The complete Isaiah Scroll (1QIs^a), now in Israel, is written in a text which belongs to the proto-Massoretic type, though

---

[1] See especially his splendid paper in *Jour. Bib. Lit.*, LXXIV (1955), pp. 147-165; I have no suggestions for revision of his chronology.

[2] See BULLETIN, No. 113 (1949), pp. 6-23, and for his important subsequent studies and photographic experiments see *Proc. Amer. Philos. Soc.*, 97 (1953), pp. 184-193, and the revised reprint of the latter in *The Smithsonian Report*, 1953, pp. 425-435.

[3] See most recently BULLETIN, No. 115 (1949), pp. 10-19, in which I referred to most of the material I had been gathering since 1937 for a new study of the palaeography of the Nash Papyrus. It is interesting to note that my original preference for the first half of the period to which I had assigned this papyrus (placed in 1937 somewhere between cir. 150 and 50 B. C., but in no case later than the accession of Herod the Great in 37 B. C.) is now shown by Cross to be better than my 1949 date in the second half of this period.

[4] See especially his monograph, *The Qumran (Dead Sea) Scrolls and Palaeography* (BULLETIN, *Supplementary Studies*, Nos. 13-14, 1952), and his great work, *The Hebrew Scripts* (London, 1955—), now in its second fascicle (for a notice of the first see BULLETIN, No. 139, p. 24).

[5] A beginning along this line was made by the late A. T. Olmstead in his papers in *Am. Jour. Sem. Lang.*, XXX (1913), pp. 1-35, and XXXI (1915), pp. 169-214, with considerable acumen but with very questionable method; against his views see J. A. Montgomery's commentary on *Kings* (ICC, 1951), pp. 251 f., and my comments in *Jour. Bib. Lit.*, LXXI (1952), p. 250. The trouble with Olmstead's treatment is that he assumed a series of late revisions of the *Hebrew*, as well as of the Greek text even *after* the original LXX translation. The Jeroboam story of LXX he considered to go back to a Hebrew original antedating our MT.

[6] *Jour. Amer. Orient. Soc.*, LXI (1941), p. 85b.

[7] This point has been emphasized by the scholars working on the Scrolls; cf. n. 15 below.

it has a much fuller vocalization with the aid of *waw* and *yodh* [8] and does have a few very useful variants, as well as a great many careless readings.[9]

Only a little less surprising than the new evidence for the great age of the consonantal tradition on which the Massoretic text depends, is the discovery of portions of Exodus, Deuteronomy, and especially of Samuel in recensions which are much closer to the LXX than they are to MT, though they usually differ from both and sometimes exhibit a text which is obviously older than either.[10] The earliest so far found fragments of this type seem to go back into the late third century B. C. and are in any case pre-Maccabaean.[11] The new texts of Samuel, especially 4QSam[a] which represents portions of the text of at least two-thirds of the chapters in I and II Samuel, show that Wellhausen and Driver were entirely wrong in considering the LXX translation as so free as often to be a paraphrase of its Hebrew prototype; actually its fidelity to the Hebrew prototype is much greater than has often been assumed. We now know that in the fragments so far described from the Pentateuch and the Former Prophets (Joshua-Judges-Samuel-Kings) the Greek translators were almost slavish in their literalism (though they seldom pushed it to the point of absurdity, as later done by Aquila). When we find sections preserved in the LXX (i. e., in the Egyptian recension of Codex B and its congeners) that are missing in MT, as well as completely different forms of names, we may thus be reasonably certain that they are not inner Greek additions or corruptions, but go back to an older Hebrew recension which differed from MT.

Returning to our proto-Massoretic texts from Qumran, we can now revert to the position shared by tradition and by scholars of the Wellhausen and related schools of criticism, that many of the older books of our Hebrew Bible were edited in approximately their present form in Babylonia and were then brought back to Palestine by the returning exiles during the late sixth and the fifth centuries B. C. This point of view, once taken for granted by most conservatives and liberals alike, has been rejected by many recent students, but is strongly supported by archaeological evidence.[12] We now have most striking confirmatory evidence from the first Qumran Isaiah Scroll, referred to above. In this text we have a number of correct vocalizations of Assyro-Babylonian words and names: *Šar'uṣur* (*ŠR'WṢR*) for MT *Šar'éṣer* and LXX

[8] See Dewey M. Beegle, BULLETIN, No. 123 (1951), pp. 26-30; Millar Burrows, BULLETIN, No. 124, pp. 18-20.

[9] See Burrows, *The Dead Sea Scrolls* (New York, 1955), pp. 303-314. However, Burrows's extremely judicious selection by no means exhausts the list of important variants in this scroll, which I have studied repeatedly with my students.

[10] See especially Cross, BULLETIN, No. 132 (1953), pp. 15-26, and *Jour. Bib. Lit.*, LXXIV, pp. 165-172 (cf. *Christian Century*, Aug. 10, 1955, p. 921); Patrick W. Skehan, BULLETIN, No. 136 (1954), pp. 12-15 (cf. n. 27).

[11] See Cross, *Jour. Bib. Lit.*, LXXIV, p. 164.

[12] For the evidence supporting the completeness of the devastation of Judah in the early sixth century and the historicity of the Exile and Restoration see most recently the references in Albright, *The Bible after Twenty Years of Archaeology* (1932-1952), reprinted by the Biblical Colloquium (Pittsburgh, 1955), *Notes*, p. 3.

Sarasar; turtân (*TWRTN*) for MT *tartān* and LXX *Tanathan*, etc.; *'Urarat* (*'WRRT*) for MT *'Arārāt* and Greek *Ararath*. There are many similar correct occurrences of the vowel-letter *W* for *u, o* in 1QIs[a], including a considerable number which are not in Beegle's excellent paper,[13] but these correct vocalizations of Assyro-Babylonian words are particularly striking. In a text handed down in Babylonia such precise tradition is not at all surprising, since we know from the work of O. Neugebauer and A. J. Sachs that cuneiform scribes were still active in the latter part of the first century A. D. In the West it would be very unlikely *a priori*, and the LXX transcriptions from the second (or even late third) century B. C. prove that there was no such fixed tradition.

I have maintained for several years that the prototype of the first Isaiah Scroll came from Babylonia, probably in the second half of the second century B. C. There is supporting evidence, into which we have no room to go here.[14] 1QIs[a] is thus an offshoot of the proto-Massoretic text-tradition in Babylonia, where it may have developed further for several centuries after the ancestral Hebrew text was taken by the returning exiles to Palestine; this would help to explain some divergences from MT, as well as the generally inferior character of the text when compared with the proto-Massoretic of the second Isaiah Scroll (1QIs[b]), etc., which is virtually identical with MT.[15]

Returning now to the Egyptian recension of the LXX, we note that there is much evidence of pre-Septuagintal Egyptian influence on the text of several books. I formerly thought that this evidence of Egyptian influence on the LXX pointed to the translators themselves, in the third century B. C.[16] However, in a period of such strong Greek influence on the Egyptian Jews, many of whom had been brought to Egypt by the Lagides as captives or had recently come as traders, it is scarcely likely that the Jews would have treated the Hebrew consonantal text with such freedom merely to exhibit their knowledge of native Egyptian. Moreover, we are in a position to demonstrate from the Qumran fragments so far published that the translators were extremely careful not to depart from the Hebrew text that lay before them. We are, therefore, compelled

---

[13] BULLETIN, No. 123 (1951), pp. 26-30.

[14] Suffice it to say here that this evidence is partly derived from Essene beliefs and practices, such as the strong Mazdayasnian and specifically Zervanite dualism (to which attention has been drawn particularly by K. G. Kuhn, A. Dupont-Sommer, and Henri Michaud), and the emphasis placed on lustration by water (as still in Mandaeanism) as well as upon quasi-science (according to Josephus). There are also historical arguments pointing to a movement from Babylonia in the second century B. C. (cf. the Damascus Document, i).

[15] On the other Isaiah scroll and fragments so far published see most recently Burrows, *The Dead Sea Scrolls*, pp. 314 f.; F. M. Cross in the *Christian Century*, August 10, 1955, pp. 920. The original publications by the Hebrew University on behalf of the late E. L. Sukenik, *Ôṣār ham-megillôt hag-genûzôt* (Jerusalem, 1954), by James Muilenburg, BULLETIN, No. 135, pp. 28-32, and by P. W. Skehan, *Cath. Bib. Quar.*, XVII (1955), pp. 158-163, provide all the supporting evidence necessary. There is already a respectable literature on the second Isaiah scroll alone.

[16] Cf. my *Archaeology of Palestine and the Bible* (1932), p. 143, and my observations in *The Biblical Period* (in Louis Finkelstein, *The Jews*, 1949), p. 6.

to reckon with the probability that the translators dealt piously with a text which had been handed down for generations in Egypt itself. We can probably fix the time at which the Egyptian recensions of the Pentateuch and Samuel-Kings were edited about the fifth century B. C. (presumably not before the sixth century or after the fourth in any book).

I shall limit myself to a few examples. The Egyptian name of Joseph appears as *ṢPNTP'NḤ* which, as long ago pointed out by Spiegelberg, stands for an Egyptian *Ḍd-p₃-nṭr-iw.f-'nḫ*, pronounced in the early first millennium approximately *Čepnū-tef'anḫ*.[17] This name belongs to a type which was in common use about the tenth century B. C. However, the Greek equivalent in Gen. 41:45 is *Psonthomphanech* for a Late Egyptian **Psontenpa'anḫ*, "The Creator (or Sustainer) of Life,"[18] obviously substituted for a somewhat different consonantal form which had become unintelligible by the Achaemenian period (even assuming that MT had been transmitted correctly to Egypt). The new form of the word made such excellent sense as an appellation of Joseph that we can be quite certain that the editor of the Egyptian recension or a precursor knew Egyptian very well and considered it important to show that he did. There is even more striking evidence in Genesis. We may expect the correct equivalents Heliopolis and Heroönpolis for On and Pithom,[19] respectively, but it is much more remarkable to find Heb. *Gōšen*, "Goshen," replaced by "Arabian Gesem" in two passages (Gen. 45:10 and 46:34). A year ago Dr. Isaac Rabinowitz pointed out to the Society of Biblical Literature that the peculiar Greek form *Gesem* for *Gōšen* evidently goes back to the famous Arabian king Geshem, Nehemiah's foe, mentioned on silver bowls found at or near Tell el-Maskhûṭah, ancient Pithom-Heroönpolis.[20] Since Geshem's rule extended from the eastern Delta of Egypt to the frontier of Judaea on the northeast and at least as far as Dedan (el-'Ulā) in the south,[21] he was a very important chieftain who must have made a name for himself in the half-century immediately preceding the restoration of Egyptian independence under Amyrtaeus (cir. 400 B. C.). Rabinowitz is undoubtedly right in explaining *Gesem Arabías* for Heb. *Gōšen* as a reminiscence of the Arabian prince Geshem. This makes it difficult to date the editing of the Egyptian recension of Genesis before about 400 (Geshem presumably reigned between 450 and 420 B. C.) or after the beginning of the Greek period (330 B. C.). A very interesting example of the difference between the Egyptian and Babylonian recensions of Genesis is the fact that the former substitutes "land of the Chaldaeans" for "Ur of the Chaldaeans" in the story of Abram. As suggested by the Book of Jubilees (probably from the first quarter of the second century B. C.) the original Hebrew text included the words rendered "Ur in the land of the Chaldaeans" (*'R B-'RṢ H-KŚDYM*), which the Babylonian Jewish scribes (who knew Ur very well) corrupted by haplography to *'R H-KŚDYM*, "Ur of the Chaldaeans," while the Egyptian Jews (who knew nothing of Ur) corrupted the original text, by the alter-

---

[17] This explanation we owe to Spiegelberg, *Zeits. f. ägypt. Spr.*, XXVII, pp. 41 f.; XXX, pp. 50 ff.; for names of the same formation see the long list in H. Ranke, *Die ägyptischen Personennamen*, pp. 409-412, who attributes them to the outgoing New Kingdom (specifically to the XXth Dynasty), and especially to the XXIst Dynasty and the following period.

[18] For this explanation see *Jour. Bib. Lit.*, XXXVII (1918), p. 132, where I was wrong in regarding the LXX form as original.

[19] In Gen. 46:28 f., we have a very remarkable substitution in the Egyptian recension of LXX (fortunately B is extant here). Where MT twice offers *Gōšenāh*, "to Goshen," the LXX has "by way of Heroönpolis," which the derived Coptic correctly rendered by "Pithom"; where MT has *'arṣāh Gōšen*, the LXX substitutes "to the land of Ramesses" (just as both versions offer in Gen. 47:11). The mention of Pithom and Rameses evidently goes back to the Hebrew prototype of LXX.

[20] Cf. provisionally F. M. Cross, *Biblical Archaeologist*, XVIII (1955), pp. 46 f., and my remarks on the chronology in BULLETIN, No. 139, p. 19.

[21] For our previous knowledge of Geshem and the extent of his power see especially my discussion in the Alt *Festschrift* (*Geschichte und Altes Testament*, 1953), pp. 4 ff.

native haplography, to *'RṢ H-KŚDYM*, "land of the Chaldaeans." One might adduce other illustrations, but we have no space.

In Kings we have two very interesting forms of an Egyptian personal name which reflect quite different Egyptian originals. I Kings 11: 19 f. mentions the name of an Egyptian queen of the late XXIst Dynasty, about the second quarter of the tenth century B. C., as *Taḥpenēs* (*TḤPNYS*); this the Greek reproduces as *Thekemina*, which obviously reflects an entirely different Egyptian name, since there is no indication of inner Greek corruption. While the MT form of the name does look suspiciously like *TḤPNḤS*, Greek Daphne in the northeastern Delta,[22] there is no reason to doubt that the name has been correctly transmitted. If so, it may stand for an Egyptian **T₃-ḥn.t-p₃* (or *pr*)-*nsw*, "She Whom the King (or Palace) Protects,"[23] to be pronounced something like **Taḥnepinse*, or **Taḥepinse* with dissimilation of the first *n*. However, the name may be corrupt, and there are many long names from the XXlst and XXIInd Dynasties which begin and end with the same consonants.[24] *Thekemina*, on the other hand, seems rather transparent; I should identify it provisionally with an Egyptian **T₃-k₃i-(n.t)-mn*, "The Female Attendant (or the like) of Min," which would be pronounced something like **Tekemin*. In Late Egyptian we have a name with the same meaning and form in *T₃-ḥnr.t-(n.t)-mn*, "The Concubine of Min."[25] Min, the god of Koptos, was renowned for his role as an ithyphallic producer of life. The pejorative sense which could be attributed to *k₃i* (translated by German scholars as "Dirne")[26] can scarcely have been overlooked by the editors of the Hebrew prototype of the Greek Kings.

It must be emphasized strongly that the Egyptian editions of different biblical books may have quite different recensional backgrounds, and that we know far too little to be dogmatic. I should be inclined to consider the Egyptian Pentateuch as essentially of Babylonian origin, i. e., it generally reflects the text which had probably been established in Babylonia during the sixth century B. C. This text was brought back to Judah and may have become canonical under Ezra's influence in the late fifth century. There are, of course, other possibilities. Some of the sharp deviations which we find, for instance, in Deut. 32, especially in verse 43 where the Greek has eight cola as against four in MT and six in the Qumran fragment recently published by Mgr. Skehan,[27] warn us

[22] On this see my observations in the Bertholet *Festschrift* (1950), pp. 13 f., with references to the literature.

[23] For names of this formation see H. Ranke, *op. cit.*, p. 365: 24 f., both from the XXIst Dynasty, and for the substitution of a word for "the king" or "house of the king (*pr-nsw*)" see *ibid.*, p. 355: 23, again from the XXIst Dynasty.

[24] The original Egyptian name may have begun with the feminine article, *t₃*, and have ended with (*n.t*)-*ist*, "of Isis," like various names from the same general period cited by Ranke, but this explanation seems less likely.

[25] Ranke, *op. cit.*, p. 367: 2.

[26] There are quite a number of names formed with the word *k₃r.t*, *k₃i*, *kry*, which is treated by Erman-Grapow, *Wörterbuch der ägyptischen Sprache*, V, p. 101; it may go back to the classical Egyptian word *k₃.t*, "vulva" (cf. Heb. *raḥam*) and it is always feminine in personal names, whether it has the feminine ending or not. From the XIXth and XXth Dynasty come names like *T₃-k₃r.t*, etc. (Ranke, *loc. cit.*, p. 370: 21, 371: 5-6, 8, 11, 14-15) and much later names like *T₃-kr-hb* or *T₃-kr-Dḥw.ty* (*ibid.*, p. 371: 12 f.), "The Concubine of Thoth." Note that the vocalization of the word for "Dirne" seems to have been originally *ku'e*, *kuya* and would have become approximately *ke* in later times. Observe further that the attribution of a name with such definitely pejorative connotation (for the Jews) to the sister-in-law of the Edomite rebel would be on a par with the statement in the Egyptian recension of Kings that Jeroboam's mother was a harlot.

[27] I should propose the following tentative original Hebrew form of the Egyptian

not to underestimate the possibility that the Egyptian Hebrew prototype had been influenced by Palestinian MS readings handed down independently of the Babylonian text-tradition. The complex situation in the earliest fragments of Samuel from Qumran, with which Frank M. Cross is dealing, suggests a basic form of text antedating sixth-century Babylonian copies. Such MSS as 4QSam[a] and 4QSam[b] reflect a text which antedates both the Hebrew prototype of the LXX and the proto-Massoretic text,[28] and may thus preserve textual elements going directly back to the original Deuteronomic Samuel, compiled toward the end of the seventh century B. C. We must patiently await the results of Cross's work before jumping at conclusions.

Other biblical books must eventually be restudied in the light of this program; we may mention particularly the Egyptian Isaiah, which perhaps separated recensionally from the proto-Massoretic text as late as the third century B. C., and Jeremiah, which presumably circulated in Egypt as early as the sixth century—thus perhaps accounting for the drastic divergences in content and order between LXX and MT. All such suggestions must await detailed study of the thousands of unpublished fragments from Qumran IV.[29]

---

recension, on the basis of MT and the new fragment (a word which departs from the Greek translation is marked by an asterisk) :

Harnînû šāmáyim 'immô	*we-hištaḥawû lô benê 'Elôhîm*
Harnînû gôyîm *'et le'ummô*	*we-hitḥazzeqû lô ( ) maḻ'akê 'El*
kî dam **'abādāw yiqqôm*	we-nāqām yāšîb le-ṣārāw
u-le-meśanne'âw yešallēm	we-kipper ( ) 'admat 'ammô

The words which are preserved in MT are not italicized but left in Roman type. The new fragment has the first, third, and fourth bicolon substantially as given above, though with two verbal and one morphemic difference. The parallelism in the Egyptian recension is much better than in MT, so there can be little doubt that this text is very ancient. In such cases, where we may have to do with orally transmitted texts, it is dangerous to speak of relative originality of recensions. However, my own impression is that the Egyptian recension, after a few minor corrections on the basis of the other two recensions, presents a satisfactory archaic text.

[28] See above, note 10.

[29] We have not discussed the extremely interesting publication by Mgr. Skehan of a recension of Exodus which conforms closely to the Samaritan text and is actually written in proto-Samaritan script (resembling the latest preëxilic cursive, but not directly derived from it). My long-standing opinion that both the Samaritan and proto-Samaritan scripts are archaizing rather than archaic is shared by S. Yeivin and now by Cross: cf. my remarks in *From the Stone Age to Christianity* (1940), pp. 266, 336, and BULLETIN, No. 115, p. 14; Yeivin, BULLETIN, No. 118, pp. 28-30; Cross, *Jour. Bib. Lit.*, LXXIV, p. 147, n. 1. I doubt whether any of the fragments in proto-Samaritan script antedate the last century B. C. The recension differs only slightly from MT, and it obviously springs from the proto-Massoretic of Qumran.

The Contribution of
the Qumrân Discoveries to the Study of
the Biblical Text*

F. M. CROSS, Jr.

Harvard University

I.

THE most striking feature of the biblical manuscripts found in the vicinity of Qumrân is the diversity of their textual traditions. We refer, not to the multiplicity of individual variant readings within manuscripts nor to the variety of orthographic traditions in which copies of biblical works are inscribed, but to the plurality of distinct text types preserved.[1]

This plurality of textual families was not immediately manifest owing to the happenstance of discovery which directed attention first to the text of Isaiah at Qumrân. The two great scrolls from Cave I, together with the dozen or so fragmentary scrolls of Isaiah from Cave IV, proved on careful analysis to belong precisely to the Proto-Massoretic tradition, that is to the textual family from

---

* Address delivered on the occasion of the dedication of The Shrine of the Book, April 21, 1965.
[1] See most recently, F. M. Cross: The History of the Biblical Text in the Light of the Discoveries in the Judean Desert, *Harvard Theological Review* 57 (1964), pp. 281-299; S. Talmon: Aspects of the Textual Transmission of the Bible in the Light of the Qumrân Manuscripts, *Textus* 4 (1964), pp. 95-132; P. Wernberg-Moller: The Contribution of the *Hodayot* to Biblical Textual Criticism, *Textus* 4 (1964), pp. 133-175; P. W. Skehan: The Biblical Scrolls from Qumrân and the Text of the Old Testament, *BA* 28 (1965), pp. 87-100.

Reprinted from *Israel Exploration Journal* 16 (1966).

which our received text derived.[2] The text of Isaiah at Qumrân gave an important and unambiguous witness to the antiquity of the Proto-Massoretic tradition, and the several manuscripts illustrated vividly the range of variation and development within a textual family at home in Palestine in the last two centuries of the Second Commonwealth.[3]

Non-traditional text types were first recognized when study was directed to the biblical manuscripts of Cave IV. An excellent example is the text of Jeremiah. A Hasmonaean manuscript, 4QJer[b], contains the so-called short recension of Jeremiah,[4] a text type identical with that which underlies the Old Greek (Septuagint) translation. The latter is about one-eighth shorter than the received text. The Proto-Massoretic family is also represented at Qumrân, especially well in 4QJer[a], a manuscript from ca. 200 B. C.[5] Study of the two textual traditions in the light of the new data makes clear that the Proto-Massoretic text was expansionist, and settles an old controversy. Those who have defended the originality of the traditional text by arguing that the Greek translator abbreviated the Hebrew text before him are proved wrong. The Septuagint faithfully reflects a conservative Hebrew textual family. On the contrary, the Proto-Massoretic and Massoretic family is marked by editorial reworking and conflation, the secondary filling out of names and epithets, expansion from parallel passages, and even glosses from biblical passages outside Jeremiah.[6]

---

[2] The literature on the Isaiah scrolls is immense and growing; for recent discussions and bibliography, one may note the following: P. W. Skehan: The Qumrân Scrolls and Textual Criticism, *VT* Supplement IV (1957), pp. 148-160; H. M. Orlinsky: The Textual Criticism of the Old Testament, *The Bible and the Ancient Near East*, New York, 1961, pp. 113-132; F. M. Cross: *The Ancient Library of Qumrân*, New York, 2nd ed., 1961, pp. 177 ff. (hereafter *ALQ²*); J. Ziegler: Die Vorlage der Isaias—Septuaginta (LXX) und die erste Isaias-Rolle von Qumrân (IQIs[a]); *JBL* 78 (1959), pp. 34-59; S. Talmon: DSIs[a] as a Witness to Ancient Exegesis of the Book of Isaiah, *Annual of the Swedish Theological Institute* 1 (1962), pp. 62-72; E. Y. Kutscher: *The Language and Linguistic Background of the Isaiah Scroll* (Hebrew), Jerusalem, 1959; M. H. Goshen-Gottstein: Theory and Practice of Textual Criticism, *Textus* 3 (1963), pp. 130-158; and *The Book of Isaiah: Sample Edition with Introduction*, Jerusalem, 1965.

[3] On the Palestinian origin of the Proto-Massoretic text of Isaiah, Jeremiah, and certain other books, see below.

[4] A fragment of the poorly preserved manuscript is cited in Cross: *ALQ²*, p. 187, n. 38.

[5] On the script and date of this manuscript, see Cross: The Development of the Jewish Scripts, *The Bible and the Ancient Near East*, Fig. 1, line 5, and pp. 136-160. On the orthography of this manuscript, see D. N. Freedman: The Massoretic Text and the Qumrân Scrolls, A Study in Orthography, *Textus* 2 (1962), pp. 87-102.

[6] For detailed documentation, see the forthcoming Harvard dissertation on the two recensions of Jeremiah by Mr. J. G. Janzen. As instances of glosses from outside Jeremiah, he cites Jer. 28:16, 29: 32, and 48:45-6 (all omitted in the Old Greek). In analyzing several categories of conflation in the

The text of Samuel found in three manuscripts from Cave IV is non-Massoretic. 4QSamᵃ, an extensively-preserved manuscript of ca. 50-25 B.C.,[7] contains a text-type closely related to the *Vorlage* of the Septuagint.[8] Its precise textual relationships can be defined even more narrowly. It is allied with the text of Samuel used by the Chronicler about 400 B. C. It is even more closely allied to the Greek text of Samuel used by Josephus, and surviving in a substratum of the Lucianic recension of the Septuagint. In short, its textual family is Palestinian, and corresponds to the Greek recension usually called Proto-Lucianic.[9] 4QSamᶜ, written by the same scribe who copied the *Sérek Hay-yáḥad* (1QS), preserves the same Palestinian text-type. The archaic manuscript of Samuel from Cave IV (4QSamᵇ), dating from the third century B. C.,[10] belongs to an early stage of this Palestinian tradition.

Divergent textual families are represented also in the Pentateuch. A palaeo-Hebrew manuscript of Exodus (4QpalaeoExᵐ),[11] and a Herodian scroll of Numbers (4QNumᵇ)[12] present a textual tradition closely allied to the Samaritan, a Palestinian text-form characterized by wide-spread glosses, expansions from parallel passages, and like editorial activity.[13] We note that these textual traits of the Proto-Samaritan family are remarkably similar to those of the Proto-Massoretic (and Massoretic) text of such books as Jeremiah described above, and Isaiah, to be discussed below. In contrast to these expansionistic texts, however, the Massoretic text of the Pentateuch was remarkably short and conservative. One other manuscript may be cited to illustrate these deviant textual families found at Qumrân: 4QExᵃ.[14] This Herodian exemplar stands

---

Massoretic tradition, Janzen concludes that 'in the number of expansions from parallel passages [in Jeremiah], M[assoretic] exceeds G[reek] by a ratio of 6:1'.

[7] On the dating, see Cross: The Development of the Jewish Scripts, Fig. 2, line 3, and pp. 166-181.

[8] See provisionally, F. M. Cross: A New Qumrân Biblical Fragment Related to the Original Hebrew Underlying the Septuagint, *BASOR*, 132 (1953), pp. 15-26; and the corrections in *JBL* 74 (1955), p. 165, n. 40.

[9] On the 'Proto-Lucianic' and Palestinian character of the text of Samuel at Qumrân, see the writer's detailed discussion: *Harvard Theological Review*, 57 (1964), pp. 292-299 (hereafter *HTR*).

[10] Cf. Cross: The Oldest Manuscript from Qumrân, *JBL* 74 (1955), pp. 147-172; and The Development of the Jewish Scripts, pp. 145-158, and Fig. 1, line 4.

[11] Parts of this manuscript, formerly labeled 4QExα, were published by P. W. Skehan: Exodus in the Samaritan Recension from Qumran, *JBL* 74 (1955), pp. 182-187.

[12] See provisionally, Cross: *HTR* 57 (1964), p. 287 and n. 27. [13] Cf. the older studies of P. Kahle: Untersuchungen zur Geschichte des Pentateuchtextes, *Opera Minora* (1956), pp. 5-26; S. Talmon: The Samaritan Pentateuch, *Journal of Jewish Studies* 2 (1951), pp. 144-150; and the forthcoming Harvard dissertation by Bruce Waltke on the textual character of the Samaritan Pentateuch. [14] See provisionally the fragment published in *ALQ*², Pl. opposite p. 141, and p. 184, n. 31.

very close to the Hebrew text used in Egypt by the Greek translator of the Septuagint.[15]

II.

The plurality of textual types from the Judean Desert fall into distinct families limited in number. Their diversity is not fluid or chaotic but conforms to a clear and simple pattern.[16] In the Pentateuch and Former Prophets, all textual traditions known from Qumrân and from the southern Judean Desert belong to three families. In the Latter Prophets only two families are extant. Moreover, none of these text-types is unknown. They have left their witnesses in textual traditions available before the discovery of the caves of Qumrân, in the received text, in the Septuagint and its recensions, in apocryphal Jewish works, in the New Testament, in the Samaritan Pentateuch, and in Josephus.

The Hebrew textual families have left clearest traces in the Greek Bible. We are able to trace a series of as many as three stages in the recensional history of the Septuagint before the emergence of the Massoretic text. The Old Greek preserves a non-traditional text-type which is represented at Qumrân, for example, by 4QExᵃ and especially 4QJerᵇ. In the second or first century B. C., the Septuagint was revised in Palestine to conform to a Hebrew text then current, represented at Qumrân by the manuscripts of Samuel from Cave IV; this is the Proto-Lucianic recension of the Greek Bible best known, perhaps, from Josephus, and the special readings of a small group of Greek witnesses.[17] No

---

15 4QExᵃ also exhibits readings which are clearly 'Palestinian,' however, and we may observe that the Old Palestinian text of Exodus (i.e., the text of the fourth-third centuries B. C.) stood far closer to the *Vorlage* of the Septuagint than to the Samaritan text (*sensu stricto*). This is to be expected, however, if we are correct in describing the Egyptian text as a branch of the Old Palestinian, and if the recent analysis of Waltke is sound, showing that the Samaritan recension was influenced secondarily by the developed Massoretic tradition.

16 Within a textual family, there is, if course, a considerable range of minor variation, especially in texts of an expansionist character. An example of 'minor variations' are those found in certain Palestinian texts owing to the introduction of new, so-called *plene* orthographic style in the Maccabaean and Hasmonaean periods, an innovation that affected only a part of the texts in this tradition (see below).

17 The clearest witness to the Proto-Lucianic text actually is to be found in the sixth column of the Hexapla to 2 Sam.11:2-1; Kgs.2:11 (normally Theodothionic elsewhere). It is found as the substratum of the Lucianic Recension (hence 'Proto-Lucian') of Samuel-Kings, in the cursives boc₂e₂, in Joshua-Judges in the groups K gn dpt, and more faintly in the Pentateuch in the families gn dpt and (in Deuteronomy) θ. In the Former Prophets, especially, the Old Latin also is often a witness to the Proto-Lucianic recension. See the discussion with references to the literature in the writer's paper in *HTR* 57 (1964), pp. 292-297.

later than the beginning of the first century A. D., portions of the Greek Bible were revised a second time, this time to the Proto-Massoretic text. This Greek recension, called Proto-Theodotian or καίγε, is extensively preserved in a manuscript of the Minor Prophets from the Naḥal Ḥever.[18] In Jeremiah its text-type is preserved in Hebrew in 4QJer^a, in Greek in the supplementary additions to the Old Greek. In Samuel-Kings it has replaced the Old Greek in most witnesses in the section II Samuel 11:2-I Kings 2:11 and in II Kings.[19] These three stages in the history of the Greek Bible, the Old Greek, the Proto-Lucianic recension, and the καίγε recension reflect in turn the three families of the Hebrew text isolated in the finds at Qumrân.[20] If one distinguished the fully developed Massoretic text from the Proto-Massoretic, a fourth stage may be discerned, represented by the Hebrew text-type found, for example, at Murabba'ât and Maṣada, reflected in Greek in the revision of the καίγε recension prepared by Aquila in ca. 130 A. D.

III.

Any reconstruction of the history of the biblical text before the establishment of the traditional text in the first century A. D., must comprehend this evidence: the plurality of text-types, the limited number of distinct textual families, and the homogeneity of each of these textual families over several centuries of time. We are required by these data, it seems to me, to recognize the existence of local texts which developed in the main centers of Jewish life in the Persian and Hellenistic age.[21]

---

[18] This manuscript has now been published by D. Barthélemy: *Les devanciers d'Aquila,* Leiden, 1963.

[19] Cf. Barthélemy, *op. cit.* (above, n. 18); Cross: *HTR* 57 (1964), pp. 281-299; and S. Jellicoe: *JAOS* 84 (1964), pp. 178-182.

[20] It need scarcely be said that these stages are not found for every book in the Hebrew Bible, either in Hebrew or Greek, and in the case of many books, especially those which became canonical late, never existed.

[21] A theory of local texts was adumbrated by W. F. Albright in his study, New Light on Early Recensions of the Hebrew Bible, *BASOR* 140 (1955), pp. 27-33. Against Albright, we should argue, however, that the local textual families in questions are not properly called 'recensions'. They are the product of natural growth or development in the process of scribal transmission, not of conscious or controlled textual recension. The steady accumulation of evidence from the Desert of Judah has enabled us to elaborate a 'general theory' and to document it in considerable detail. See the chapter on The Old Testament at Qumrân in *ALQ*², and The History of the Biblical Text in *HTR* 57 (1964), pp. 281-299. A similar approach is presented in the forthcoming article of P.W. Skehan on Bible. Texts and Versions in the *New Catholic Encyclopedia,* and in the Harvard dissertation of J. D. Shenkel: *Chronology and Recensional Development in the Greek Text of Kings,* 1964.

We may sketch the history of the local texts as follows. Three textual families appear to have developed slowly between the fifth and first centuries B. C., in Palestine, in Egypt, and in a third locality, presumably Babylon. The Palestinian family is characterized by conflation, glosses, synoptic additions and other evidences of intense scribal activity, and can be defined as 'expansionistic'. The Egyptian text-type is often but not always a full text. In the Pentateuch, for example, it has not suffered the extensive synoptic additions which mark the late Palestinian text, but is not so short or pristine as the third or Babylonian family. The Egyptian and Palestinian families are closely related. Early exemplars of the Palestinian text in the Former Prophets, and Pentateuchal texts which reflect an early stage of the Palestinian tradition, so nearly merge with the Egyptian, that we are warranted in describing the Egyptian text-type as a branch of the Old Palestinian family. The Babylonian text-type when extant is a short text. Thus far it is known only in the Pentateuch and Former Prophets. In the Pentateuch it is a conservative, often pristine text, which shows relatively little expansion, and a few traces of revision and modernizing. In the books of Samuel, on the contrary, it is a poor text, marked by extensive haplography and corruption. While it is not expansionistic, it is normally inferior to the Old Palestinian tradition preserved in 4QSam[b], and often to the Egyptian despite the more conflate traits of the latter.[22] It is not without significance that the oldest manuscripts from Qumrân are uniformly of the Palestinian family, or rarely, of Egyptian provenience. The first appearance of what we term the Babylonian text-type appears in the Former Prophets in the Proto-Theodotionic (καίγε) recension of the Greek Bible, and at Qumrân not at all. The evidence is more complex in the Pentateuch, but I am now inclined to believe that genuine exemplars of the Babylonian text-form at Qumrân are exceedingly rare, and late in date.

The grounds for the localization of these textual families are both theoretical and specific. In the textual criticism of ancient works, it is an axiom that texts which develop over a long span of time in geographical isolation tend to

---

22 Cf. the conclusions reached by the writer in his paper. The Oldest Manuscripts from Qumrân, pp. 165-172. A study of an additional column of this text will be published shortly.

23 Several old manuscripts of Pentateuchal books have escaped the severe reworking that produced the late Palestinian or Proto-Samaritan text, e. g., the early Hasmonaean text of Genesis-Exodus (4Q Gen[a] = 4Q Ex[b]). However, in key readings these manuscripts sometimes display Palestinian or Egyptian readings. Perhaps their assigment to a textual family should be left *sub judice*. Earlier the writer had assigned them to the Proto-Massortic tradition.

develop special characteristics, corrupt or secondary readings, haplographies and expansions, recalculated numbers and chronologies, etc., as well as preserving a pattern of primitive readings. These traits and peculiarities are transmitted producing series of filiated readings which distinguish the family. In turn, when textual families are detected, each with a particular series of special readings or traits, it must be postulated that such textual families arose in separate localities, or in any case, in complete isolation. Distinct textual families take centuries to develop but are fragile creations. When manuscripts stemming from different textual traditions come into contact, the result is their dissolution into a mixed text, or the precipitation of textual crisis which results in recensional activity, and often in the fixing of a uniform or standard text.

Our new evidence for Hebrew textual families yields, on examination, specific grounds for assigning each tradition to a certain locality, to Egypt, to Palestine, and to Babylon. The Hebrew text-type which was used by the Alexandrian translators of the Septuagint may be attributed to Egypt. Supporting such an attribution is not merely the provenience of the Old Greek text. W. F. Albright has collected evidence of pre-Septuagintal Egyptian influence on the text of the Pentateuch and Former Prophets.[24] We have noted above that frequently the Egyptian text-type is closely allied with the Palestinian family, precisely the relationship which might have been posited of an Egyptian local text on *a priori* grounds. It should be said, however, that the range of agreement between the Egyptian and Palestinian text fluctuates rather widely in different biblical books. In the Pentateuch it is only in the earlier stages of the Palestinian text that there is a real convergence of the two traditions, suggesting that the Egyptian text separated relatively early, no later than the fourth century B. C., from the main Palestinian stream. In Samuel, the two families are much more closely related, suggesting that the archetype of the Egyptian text split off no earlier than the fourth century. In Jeremiah, on the other hand, the Egyptian text is to the farthest degree unrelated, requiring a special explanation, namely that the text of Jeremiah at home in Egypt derived from a time near or before the beginning of the special development of the Palestinian family, thus in the fifth or even the sixth century B. C. In Isaiah, or in certain of the later books, where the Egyptian tradition is virtually identical with the Palestinian, we are led to conclude that the Hebrew text underlying the Old

---

[24] See his discussion in *BASOR* 140 (1955), pp. 30-33.

Greek separated from the Palestinian quite late, or indeed that a Palestinian Hebrew manuscript was used for the Greek translation.

By far the majority of the Hebrew witnesses from Qumrân belong to the Palestinian family. The evidence for the identification of the Palestinian family is most easily delineated in Samuel. The three manuscripts of Samuel from Cave IV, while not directly filiated, contain a single textual tradition, known at Qumrân as early as the third century (4QSam^b), the early first century B.C., (4QSam^c), and in the late first century B. C., (4QSam^a). The earliest distinctive witness to a text of the type of these manuscripts is found in the Chronicler. As has been shown elsewhere, the Chronicler, shortly after 400 B. C., cited a text of Samuel which stands in close agreement with the manuscripts of Qumrân, but, as is well known, sharply diverges from the received text.[25] In the second or early first century B. C., the same Palestinian text-form was used to revise the Septuagint: the Proto-Lucianic recension. Finally Josephus at the end of the first century A. D., made use of this Palestinian Greek recension in writing his *Antiquities*. The Proto-Massoretic tradition appears in no witness to the text of Samuel before the early first century A. D., and then in the second Palestinian recension of the Septuagint, 'Proto-Theodotion.' In the Pentateuch, the evidence is closely parallel. It has been observed that in the Chronicler's citations from the Pentateuch, his text stands closer to the Samaritan recension than to the Massoretic.[26] There can be little doubt, I believe, that he utilized the prevailing Palestinian text. At Qumrân two stages of the Palestinian text are represented, an early form and the Proto-Samaritan form, the former standing closer to the *Vorlage* of the Septuagint, the latter more expansive including long synoptic interpolations found also in the Samaritan Pentateuch. The Samaritan Pentateuch, as we have shown elsewhere, derives from the Palestinian family, separating from the common Palestinian not earlier than the Hasmonaean era.[27] Other witnesses to this non-traditional, Palestinian textual family are scattered through Jewish apocryphal works and the New Testament. An especially useful example is the book of Jubilees. In its scriptural cita-

---

[25] See Cross: *ALQ²*, pp. 188 f. and n. 40a; *HTR* 57 (1964), pp. 292-297; and the forthcoming paper of Werner Lemke: The Synoptic Problem in the Chronicler's History, *HTR* 58 (1965), pp. 349-363.

[26] Cf. G. Gerleman: *Synoptic Studies in the Old Testament*, Lund, 1948, pp. 9-12, and especially S. Talmon: *op. cit.* (above, n. 13), pp. 146-150.

[27] See Cross: The Development of the Jewish Scripts, p. 189, n. 4; and the Harvard dissertation of J. D. Purvis: *The Samaritan Pentateuch and the Origin of the Samaritan Sect*, 1964, shortly to be published in monograph form; and Cross: *HTR* 59 (1966), pp. 201-211.

tions,[28] it regularly sides with the Septuagint and the Samaritan (most often with the former), and in its readings in common with the Massoretic text, it is regularly joined by the Samaritan. This is, of course, precisely the pattern of the earlier forms of the Palestinian text. Charles in his analysis of the biblical text used by the author of Jubilees notes also its frequent alignment with the Syriac Bible.[29] This datum is also significant since in the Former Prophets and in the Pentateuch, the Syriac is often a witness to Palestinian readings.

A word may be said about the orthography and script used in manuscripts of the Palestinian textual family.

Hasmonaean and Herodian exemplars of the Palestinian family often exhibit a *plene* style of orthography, far fuller than that we are accustomed to in the Massoretic text. The introduction of this new style[30] began sporadically in the third century, but was developed systematically in the Maccabaean era, and reached its most extreme form in the Hasmonaean age. The extreme, or baroque phase of the style is often associated with archaizing or, most often, pseudo-archaic grammatical forms. The best known text in this style is, of course, the great Isaiah scroll (1QIsᵃ). The extreme form of the style is, however, relatively rare. In its milder, dominant form, it appears regularly in texts inscribed in the Palaeo-Hebrew script, and in modified form is the style surviving in the Samaritan Pentateuch. The emergence of the style is most likely to be attributed to the literary activity which attended the nationalistic revival of the Maccabaean Age.

All manuscripts, so far as I am aware, inscribed in the new Palestinian orthography contain a text-type which on other grounds must be called Palestinian.[31] The same is true of manuscripts written in the Palaeo-Hebrew character. Script and orthography thus may be useful clues in assigning texts to the Palestinian family. Of course, the great majority of our witnesses to the Palestinian text-form are not written in Palaeo-Hebrew script, and many in every period are inscribed, not in the new, or Maccabaean style but, in a more archaic, or archaizing orthography. We may cite again the Palestinian texts of the three

---

[28] See provisionally, R. H. Charles: *The Book of Jubilees,* Oxford, 1902, pp. xxxiii-xxxix, for analysis of the textual affinities of Ethiopic Jubilees. [29] *Ibid.*
[30] Its primary trait is the use of *waw* to mark ō derived from etymological ā. Earlier orthographies restricted the use of *waw* to signify ū, and later ō derived from the diphthong -aw. See Cross and Freedman: *Early Hebrew Orthography,* New Haven, 1952, pp. 69 f.; and D. N. Freedman: *Textus* 2 (1962), pp. 87-102. [31] We cannot agree with the view of W. F. Albright: *BASOR* 140 (1955), pp. 29 f., that the text of 1QIsᵃ is Babylonian.

Samuel manuscripts from Cave IV. 4QSam^b, the archaic Samuel, is written in
an orthography which is not only defective, but which has no parallel after
the fourth century B. C. Long-*ō* is marked by *waw* only when it derives ethmo-
logically from the diphthong -*aw*.[32] Massoretic orthography is typologically
much more developed and hence later. 4QSam^c is inscribed in the baroque new
style, replete with such forms as *hw'h* and *mw'dh*. 4QSam^a, from the early
Herodian period is written in the standard form of the new orthography.

The third or Babylonian textual family cannot be localized on the basis of
direct evidence. We have described its traits which are very different from those
of the Palestinian and Egyptian textual families, and have noted that it has
appeared so far only in the Pentateuch and in the Former Prophets, and then
only in relatively late witnesses. Texts of this family are never found inscribed
either in Palaeo-Hebrew script or in the new orthography developed in Palestine in the Maccabaean Era. Its orthographic tradition is not especially early,
however, deriving in the main from orthographic usage which was first established in the third century B. C., and which continued to be widely used until
the end of the Second Commonwealth.

The assignment of the family to Babylon rests on several lines of argument.
It is a distinctive text-type, distant from both the Egyptian and Palestinian
families. It must have arisen in isolation. On the one hand it cannot have arisen
in a late eclectic recension to judge from the pattern of its superior readings
(especially in the Pentateuch). This would be too much to ask of the text-
critical skills of the Rabbis. On the other hand, it is not a text drawn from a
single or several old manuscripts, so archaic as to escape or predate the development of the Palestinian and Egyptian families. It is a text-type with a long
independent history to judge from its special set of secondary readings (especially in Samuel-Kings).[33] Since we know well the textual families of Palestine and
Egypt, we must look elsewhere for its locale, most naturally to Babylon. Further, examination of the Palestinian witnesses to the text at Qumrân and in
citations in Palestinian Jewish literature in no way prepares us for the sudden

---

[32] Occasionally very archaic orthographic practices appear in 4QSam^b. An example is the 'pre-Exilic'
use of *he* for the 3.m.s. suffix -*ô* (<-uh <uhu), found in the following reading in 1 Sam. 20:38:
ᶜlmh, LXX τοῦ παιδαρίου αὐτοῦ, revised in MT to *hnᶜr*.

[33] James D. Shenkel has shown (see above, n. 21) that in one section of the chronology of the
Kingdom, the Egyptian and Palestinian tradition is based on one set of calculations, the Massoretic
and Proto-Massoretic on another, the latter demonstrably secondary. The secondary system first appears in Kings in the καίγε recension, in our extant witnesses.

emergence of this text-type as a signifiant, much less dominant or standard text. Its choice in the time of Hillel as the textual base of a new revision of the Septuagint is the first hint of its coming importance. By the end of the first century A. D., it has become dominant, or in any case standard, to judge from its exclusive use in the texts from Maṣada, Murabbaᶜât, and the Naḥal Ḥever. The simplest explanation of these data, it seems to me, is found in placing the development of this text-type in Babylon during the interval between the fifth century and the second century B. C., and to fix the time of its reintroduction into Palestine no earlier than the Maccabaean period, no later than the era of Hillel.

IV.

Before sketching the history of the biblical text from the time of its separation into textual families until the establishment of the Massoretic recension, it will be useful to analyze briefly an alternate theory of the development of the biblical text. This is the view which attempts to explain the complex data we have presented in terms of a distinction between a standard text and vulgar texts. In application, the Massoretic text is deemed 'standard', all non-traditional text-types 'vulgar'.

I have often argued that the terms *standard* and *vulgar* are anachronistic. Both imply that a standard exists, either that authorities have designated one text-type as standard, or to say the same thing, that an official recension has been promulgated. But this is precisely not the case in the period under discussion. There is no tendency toward the stabilization of the text at Qumrân, no drift toward the traditional text. Indeed neither in the Palestinian Greek witnesses nor in the citations of Jewish works composed in this era is there any evidence earlier than the time of Hillel that the recensional activities had begun which would ultimately establish an authoritative text.

Let us suppose, however, that our analysis is wrong, and that a standard text did exist in Palestine alongside vulgar text types over these early centuries. What kind of picture emerges? As for the Pentateuch and the Former Prophets, we must say that no one used the standard text. The Chronicler used a vulgar text in the composition of his history. The author of Jubilees ignored the standard text. Palestinian revisers of the Greek translation chose, not the standard Hebrew text but the vulgar for their important labours. The Zadokite priests[34]

---

[34] Cf. Cross: *BA* 26 (1963), p. 121.

of Samaria chose the vulgar text for their official recension... *mirabile dictu*. From a text-critical point of view, it is even more extraordinary that the standard text exercised no influence on the vulgar text. That there was no mixing, no contact, could be explained only, I believe, if the 'standard' text were the property of a tiny cabal, secretly preserved, copied, and nourished. Moreover, even if all this were true, we should have to ask, why do the vulgar texts fall into two distinct, homogeneous families?—that is, if one wishes to dispose entirely of resort to an explanation in terms of local texts. Such a picture of the textual situation can only be described as bizarre, and we are left wondering why the little circle who hid the standard text away for these centuries suddenly decided to publish it.

Perhaps there are other grounds upon which we may legitimately label Massoretic or Proto-Massoretic texts 'standard', non-traditional text-forms 'vulgar'. Our criterion might be one particular characteristic of the text itself. Since the Pentateuch and Former Prophets in the received text are clearly short texts, perhaps we may discover here a valid criterion to distinguish the standard from the vulgar text-forms. As is well-known, the Alexandrian grammarians based their recension of Homer on the principle of the superiority of the short reading. While haplography also produces short readings, and the text of Samuel is demonstrably defective by reason of extensive haplography, there can be no denying that the received text of the Pentateuch is a marvelously compact and well-preserved text, from the point of view of the modern textual critic. The difficulty arises when we look at the received text outside the Pentateuch and the Former Prophets. The traditional texts of Isaiah, Jeremiah and Ezekiel, for example, are notoriously expansionistic, marked by conflations, readings added from parallel passages, and harmonizing. The Egyptian text of Jeremiah and 4QJer[b] contains a text tradition which is drastically shorter as well as far superior to the Massoretic text. Indeed the texts of these books possess all the expansionistic traits charateristic of the 'vulgar' (Palestinian) textual family. This is true of the Proto-Massoretic texts of Isaiah, Jeremiah, and Ezekiel at Qumrân; it is also true of the developed Massoretic texts of these books.[35] In short, the criterion cannot be sustained.

---

[35] It may be observed that the Proto-Massoretic text of 1QIs[a], and the Egyptian Hebrew text underlying the Septuagint, often go beyond the other Proto-Massoretic texts of Qumrân, as well as the Massoretic text in the extent of their expansionistic character (cf. P. W. Skehan: *VT* Supplement IV [1957], p. 152). However, the expansions, happily, are not always the same as those in MT, and we are given some control of the additions, double readings, etc., in the Massoretic text.

The criteria of orthographic or linguistic development have occasionally been used to ferret out 'vulgar' text forms. It is true that the Rabbis chose an orthographic and linguistic tradition which by-passed the innovations of Maccabaean orthography, and the archaizing and modernizing features preserved in this orthography. But as we have seen, Proto-Massoretic manuscripts may appear in late orthography, non-traditional manuscripts in the most archaic. The same must be said for late or early, archaic or modernizing grammatical forms. It was probably the choice of the Pentateuch text which established orthographic principles for the remainder of the Bible, not the selection of an orthographic tradition which determined the choice of text.

These criteria will not justify the use of the distinction *standard/vulgar* in describing the text-forms later to be selected and established as the Massoretic recension. This is because no one textual family was selected by the Rabbis or scribes when the era of textual crisis and recension arrived. In the Pentateuch, a Babylonian, or in any case, non-Palestinian textual tradition was chosen, in the Latter Prophets a Palestinian.

v.

If we put together all the evidence now at hand, woven together, to be sure, with occasional skeins of speculation, I believe that the history of the biblical text can be outlined as follows. Sometime in the Persian period, probably in the fifth century B. C., local texts began to diverge and develop in Palestine and Babylon. Certainly the Priestly edition of the Tetrateuch and the Deuteronomic edition of the Former Prophets cannot antedate the late sixth century B. C. Presumably the local texts stem from copies of the Law and Former Prophets whose literary complexes had come into final form in Babylon in the sixth century, and which were then brought back to Palestine. The traditions concerning the text of Ezra may reflect these circumstances.[36] In any case we must project the 'archetype' of all surviving local texts of these books roughly to the time of the Restoration.

In the early fourth century, the Chronicler used an early form of the developing Palestinian text, and sometime about this time the Egyptian text of the

---

[36] See D. N. Freedman: The Law and Prophets, *VT* Supplement IX (1962), pp. 250-265. With possible exception of the short text of Jeremiah, we know no evidence of the survival of Exilic editions of a biblical work surviving independently in Palestine.

Pentateuch broke off from the Old Palestinian text, to begin its independent development. The separation of an Egyptian text of Jeremiah was probably earlier, that of the text of the Former Prophets rather later. Meanwhile in Babylon the third of the incipient textual families was developing, continuing in isolation until its reintroduction into Palestine, perhaps in the Maccabaean era when longings for Zion and Parthian expulsions coincided to bring large numbers of the Jews to Palestine, or perhaps later in the second or first century B. C. At all events, the Babylonian textual family was not selected for the early (Proto-Lucianic) revision made in the second or early first century B. C. It was taken up in the Proto-Theodotionic reworking of the Old Greek translation prepared in Palestine at the beginning of the first century A. D.

Probably the Proto-Theodotionic recension of the Old Greek coincided with earliest recensional endeavours on the Hebrew text of the Pentateuch and Prophets. In any case between the era of Hillel and the first Jewish Revolt the Massoretic text came into being. The principles which guided the scholars who prepared the recension were unusual. The recension was not characterized by wholesale revision and emendation, nor by eclectic or conflating procedures. Nor was a single, local textual family chosen. In the Pentateuch the current Palestinian text-type was rejected, and along with it the Palaeo-Hebrew script and orthographic innovations that marked certain of its exemplars. Rather the conservative, superb text of Babylonian origin, recently introduced into Palestine, was selected for the standard text. In the Former Prophets, the same pattern was followed, a Babylonian text was chosen, despite the existence of the superior Old Palestinian textual family. Presumably the pattern was set by the selection of the Pentateuch. In the Latter Prophets, the scholars shifted textual families. In these books a Palestinian text was chosen, perhaps because Babylonian texts were not available. However that may be, the orthographic type chosen was not the new *plene* style common in many Palestinian manuscripts beginning in Maccabaean times.

The process of recension was basically one of selecting traditions deriving from two old textual families available in Palestine in the first century A. D.

There was some leveling through, not always successful, of the conservative orthographic style chosen, and some revision, within narrow limits, was undertaken.[37] The process was not evolutionary or adventitious, but one of careful

---

[37] Cf. *ALQ*², p. 191 and n. 45.

selection between sharply differing traditions. It was in short a systematic if not radical process of recension.

The promulgation of the new, standard recension evidently took place sometime near the mid-first century A. D. The text used to prepare the καίγε recension at the beginning of the century is Proto-Massoretic, not Massoretic. Readings which differ both from the older Greek, and from the developed Massoretic text are not few or insignificant, especially in Samuel and Kings. While the Proto-Massoretic text is well-known in many books at Qumrân, there is no exemplar of the Massoretic text, and no evidence of its influence. On the other hand, the Rabbinic recension appears to have been the accepted text in other circles by 70 A. D., and in the interval between the Jewish Revolts against Rome, became the reigning text in all surviving Jewish communities. Its victory was complete and rival textual traditions shortly died out, except as they were preserved frozen in ancient translations or survived in the text of an isolated sect such as the Samaritans.

B. *Talmudic and Midrashic Evidence:*
The Stabilization of the Textus Receptus.

ספר תורה שהיה גנוז בבית כנסת סוירוס ברומא

—יחסו אל מגילות ישעיהו ממדבר יהודה ואל "תורתו של רבי מאיר"—

מאת

ד . ש . לוינגר

מוקדש לכבוד מר זלמן שזר, נשיא
מדינת ישראל, למלאות שמונים שנה לחייו
המבורכים

א. מבוא

גדולי חוקרי נוסח המקרא והבלשנות העברית בתקופתנו עסקו ברשימת השינויים
שהורכבה על יסוד ספר תורה זה. השתדלו לקבוע חשיבותם של שינויים אלה ומקומם
בתולדות הנוסח העברי של התנ"ך, אולם לא השיגו מטרתם מסבות שונות:

1. לא הגיעו אליהם המקורות המוסמכים המכילים רשימת השינויים.
2. גם אחרי הופעת המקורות האמתיים לא פנו אליהם והמשיכו משום־מה להשתמש
   במקורות המשובשים.
3. לא הבדילו בין המקורות לפי ערכם הממשי.

לכן הכרחי הוא היום להציג לפני הקוראים את כל המקורות בשלמותם ובצורתם
העיקרית, בליווי פקסימילים המאפשרים קביעת המצב האמיתי.

סקירת־ביקורת על הפירסומים, שהוקדשו במלואם או באופן חלקי לבעיה זאת,
תלמד אותנו: איך משפיעה לרעה אפילו על מחקריהם של אנשי מדע מוכרים בצדק
במקצוע זה, ההסתמכות־יתר על השערות וקביעות בלתי מבוססות של קודמיהם.
במיוחד יש להצביע על ליקויים אלה, אם מדובר על בירור בעיות הקשורות במגי־
לות מדבר יהודה שפתחו לנו בעשרים השנים שעברו חלונות אטומים בחקר
המקרא.

במשך הסקירה נעמוד בעיקר על הדוגמה השנייה שברשימתנו, כי קביעת נוסחתה
האמיתית מכרעת היא גם בפתרון בעיה אחרת, שגם היא העסיקה במידה מרובה את
החוקרים בזמננו, והיא שאלת השינויים המובאים בספרותנו בשם רבי מאיר.

1. א. עפשטיין היה הראשון שפירסם [1] את כל הרשימה הזאת על יסוד
העתק, של "בראשית רבתי", כתב־יד פראג שבספריית "תלמוד תורה" [2] שם. אמנם
היתה זאת רשימה מקוטעת מאד, כי הושמטו ממנה כל המקומות מדובר בהם על

Ein von Titus nach Rom gebrachter Pentateuch-Codex und seine Varianten 1
(MGWJ, XXXIV, 1885, pp. 332—351). בעתיד נביא את המאמר הזה כעפשטיין א, ואת
מאמרו המסכם הנזכר בהערה 9 כעפשטיין ב.

H. Brody Die Handschriften der Prager jüd. Gemeinde, Prag 1913, pp. 11-12 2

Reprinted from *Beth Mikra* 42 (1970).

שנויי אורתוגרפיה בקשר לתיפעות שלא היו ידועות בתקופה זאת. צורתן של שה
הדוגמאות הראשונות היתה בה:
וירא אלהים את כל אשר עשה והנה טוב מאד (ברא' א', לא)
לאדם ולאשתו כתנות עור (שם ג' כא).

כן מכל הפסוקים שבהם יש רק שינוי אורתוגרפי בלבד מביא "בראשית רבתי"
את נוסח המסורה, אבל עפשטיין ניסה לנחש מה הם השינויים שהושמטו ?

מאחר שהיה מדובר בהתחלת הרשימה על פסוקים שבקשר אתם היו ידועים
מבראשית רבה גרסאות שהובאו בשם ר' מאיר, אין פלא שניסה לחפש קרבה בין
השינויים הידועים בשם ר' מאיר לבין השינויים שהיו צריכים להיות בנוסח המקורי של
רשימה זאת. בנוגע לדוגמה 1 אמנם חשב על "מאוד" במקום "מאד", למרות שהוא
ידע על פירוש בראשית של רד"ק[3] המביא את פתיחתה של רשימה זאת, יחד עב
השינוי "מות" ומתייחס כבר אל הגרסה הדומה של ר' מאיר, אבל בקשר עם הדוגמה
2 הוא נוטה לתקן מן "עור" שברשימה ל־"אור" ואז תהיה פה הקבלה לגרסת רבי
מאיר.

כמו שהשערה זאת לא התאמתה, כך לא אושרו הנחותיו בקשר עם שאר המקומות
בהם הובא ב"בראשית רבתי" נוסח המסורה בלבד[4].

2. כ. ד. גינצבורג[5] כבר באותה שנה כלל באוספו גם רשימה זאת, אמנם
בסימן שאלה הוא מביא חלק מהשערותיו של עפשטיין בתוך הטכסט והקורא אינו
יכול לדעת על מה היה מדובר בנוסח הרשימה עצמה. על כל פנים להדפסת טכסט
המשבש את המקוטע אין ערך מדעי.

3. א. נויבואר[6] הצליח לגלות את הרשימה הזאת בצורתה העיקרית בסיף
כתב־היד של המקרא בפריס (הספריה הלאומית, מס' 31 משנת 1404). במקור זה
מופיעים כל השינויים במלואם : ברובריקה הראשונה נוסח המסורה ואחריו כל פעם
השינוי בלי להתחשב בזה, אם מדובר על שינויי אורתוגרפיה או גרסה ממשית, אולם
גם הוא לא הבין את תוכנה של דוגמה 2 ובהערותיו — בהשפעת עפשטיין — הוא
מעלה את הרעיון שיש פה קלקול בטכסט ואולי מסתתרת פה קריאה המזדהית עם
גרסתו של רבי מאיר *[6]. בכל זאת הוא מדפיס את הנוסח כמו שמופיע במקור, רק
במקומות אחדים בקשר עם תיפעות אורתוגרפיות בלתי שכיחות משתמש הוא בסימן־
שאלה.

4. א. א. הרכבי בעת ביקורו בדמשק מצא כתב־יד מקראי יותר קדום
שהועתק בשנת 1382 ועל יסודו פירסם[7] שוב פעם את כל הרשימה, וכנראה, בהשפעת

3 נדפס בפרסבורג, תר"ב: הפירוש האליגורי להתחלת בראשית פורסם ע"י א"א פינקלשטיין
The Commentary of David Kimhi on Isaiah, (New York, 1926) Appendix I,
Kimhi's Allegorical Commentary on Genesis.
4 לפי השערתו היתה בדוגמה 7 במקום "שדה" "שדה מלא", כמו בשומרוני או בתרגום השב־
עים: בדוגמה 27 היה "המה" במקים "הם", ועוד.
5 The Massorah, Vol. III, p. 19.
6 Der Pentateuch der sogenanten Severus-Synagoge (MGWJ, XXXVI, 1877,
pp. 508-509).
6* איר Wahrscheinlich zu lesen.
7 הפסגה, קיבץ ראשין, תרנ"ה, עמ' 58—59 = הדשים גם ישנים, בס' 6, עמ' 4—5.

קדמיו, הוא מיטעה ומטעה גם אחרים באשר מביא את הדוגמה 2 בצירה כזאת שהיי
קורא מקבל את הרושם: אמנם נמצאת דוגמה זאת במקור עתיק זה. מכיון שהספק
נעשה פה לודאי, מתחזקת בין החוקרים הבאים אחריו ההנחה שקריאה "כתנוד"
בכ"י פריס 31 היא המשובשת ויש לגרוס: "כתנור".

5. נוסח כ"י פריס 31 ג"כ מצא מקום במבואו של כ. ד. גינצבורג[3]. בדרך
כלל העתק זה נאמן לנוסח, אולם בדוגמה 31 המציא קריאה חדשה "כמפכת" במקום
"כמהפת" שבנוסח כ"י זה, ומייצר על ידי כך "מקור" חדש לשגיאה: לדאבוננו
הגרסה שהומצאה על ידו נהפכת למקורית ותופסת את מקומה של העיקרית בדיונים
בלשנים רציניים. בהערותיו גם הוא מבטל את הגרסה "כתנוד" ורואה בה שגיאת
מעתיק גרידה.

6. א. עפשטיין — , על יסוד פרסומיהם של נויבואר והרכבי הוא משתדל
לתקן את שגיאותיו הקודמות במאמר מסכם[9]. כמובן, הוא כבר מנסה לשחזר את
הדוגמה 2 בהתאם להעתקתו של הרכבי וזה נוסחתו: "כתנות איר (עור l.) כתנור
(כתנות אור l.) כתיב".

7. מפירסום הקטלוג של ד. ש. ששון[10] היו יכולים לקבל הדרכה מתאי־
מה החוקרים שעסקי ברשימה זאת: ממנו אפשר היה ללמוד שכ"י דמשק — שהיה
לפני הרכבי בשעתו — עבר לידי משפחת ששון (בליתשוורת) ובו נמצאת רשימה זאת
פעמים בשלמותה[11] וכדאי היה לשאוב מהמקור עצמו ולא מהעתקתו של הרכבי,
שנחשב בדרך כלל אמנם לדייקן בעניינים אלה, רק במקרה זה, כנראה, מחמת הזמן
הקצר שעמד לרשותו בדמשק לא דייק ואף נעלם ממנו הדף השני[12] בו ג"כ מופיעה
רשימה זאת. אם היו רואים חוקרי רשימה זאת שבשתי הוריאציאות אלה הנוסח של
דוגמה 2 הוא "כתנוד", כמו בכ"י פריס 31 ושאר הקריאות בקשר עם דוגמה זאת הן
רק הנחות בלבד, בודאי לא היו בונים עליהן.

8. חנוך אלבעק כשפרסם את המדרש "בראשית רבתי"[13] שהעתק ממנו
עמד פעם לרשותו של עפשטיין, היה בודאי מפיק תועלת רבה משימושו במקור של
כ"י דמשק ובלא ספק היה מוותר על חלק ניכר מהערותיו שאינן הולמות את
המציאות. למשל, מה שנאמר אצלו בפירושו[14] על דוגמה 2: "1. כתנות עיר. צ"ל
כתנות אור, ובכי"פ וכי"ד: כתנור כתיב (היה כתוב)". כמובן, אין צורך "לתקן"
טכסט כזה ולא להביא נוסח ע"פ כי"י שאינו מופיע באף אחד משלוש הוריאציאות
שנשמרו ממנו במקורות אלה.

8 Introduction to the Massoretico-critical Edition of the Hebrew Bible, London
1897, p. 411.

9 Biblische Textkritik bei den Rabbinen (Recueil des travaux rédigés en
mémorie du Jubilé Scientifique de M. Daniel Chwolson), Berlin, 1899, pp. 42-56.
= לחם חמדות לדניאל איש חמדות.

10 Descriptiv catalogue of the Hebrew and Samaritan manuscripts in אהל דוד
the Sassoon library, London, 5692—1932, N. 368, pp. 6-14.

11 בפעם ראשונה בדף 146.

12 בדף 403.

13 ירושלים, ת"ש (הוצ' מקיצי נרדמים בסיוע מוסד הרב קוק).

14 עמ' 210, הערה לשורה 1.

9. א. שפרבר במחקרו על בעיות המסורה[15] מקדיש לנושא זה פרק קצר ומתייחס
לאותן דוגמאות שבקשר אתן הוא יכול להצביע על מחקריו בשטחים אלה[16]. יש
להצטער שהוא ניתן בהקדמה סיכום המקורות עם שיבושים כבדים: אין לכתוב
שעפשטיין במחקרו הנ"ל (תחת מס' 6) הפנה את תשומת לב החוקרים לרשימה
זאת ולא לספר שרשימה זאת מופיעה בכמה בכמה כתבי יד של "בראשית רבה". גם אין
להשוות תופעה ושאינה במקורות רק בהערות או בהשערות, אל אלה שבהם מדובר
באמת על ענין זה (עור—אור).

10. ש. ליברמן בספרו "יוונית ויוונות בארץ־ישראל"[17] דן ג"כ בכמה
דוגמאות ברשימתנו וביניהן גם בדוגמה 2. התעניינותו מופנית בעיקר אל בעיית
גרסאותיו של רבי מאיר ואנו בטוחים שלאור המקורות הניתנים פה ישנה במהדורה
חדשה של חיבורו אחדות מקביעותיו.

11. מ. צ. סגל במבואו למקרא[18] מנתח את רשימתנו, אולם גם הוא חושב
שדוגמה 2 מקשרת רשימה זאת עם סדרת השינויים מתורתו של רבי מאיר ובכלל
אינו מתייחס אל הקריאה "כתנוד" שבמקורות המוסמכים.

12. נ. ה. טור־סיני בחיבורו "הלשון והספר"[19] כשעוסק בבעית ש־
האותיות מנצפ"ך דן גם על דוגמאות אחדות ברשימתנו. השערותיו בשטח זה אינן
מתאימות ע"י המגילות הגנוזות ואף ההבאה מירושלמי[20] שמדובר עליו גם בספרי
הנ"ל של ליברמן[21], טעונות תיקון.

13. א. מ. הברמן ניגש לבירור בעיות רשימה זאת על יסוד פרסום כל
הטכסטים הידועים לו[22], יחד עם פירוש. לדאבוננו לפעמים גם הוא מביא אותם
הנוסחים שהיו כבר בצורה נכונה או קרובה אל המציאות לפני חוקרים אחרים
בצורה משובשת מצד אחד ונותן פירושים המשמשים מקור־טעויות להולכים
בעקבותיו. דוקא בדוגמאות שיש להן קשרים עם המגילות הגנוזות נפלו אצלו
שגיאות שאפשר היה להימנע מהן. דוגמה 2 אצלו לפי כתב־יד פריס: "כתנות אור
וילבשם, כתנוד היה כתיב". אם הוא מדפיס "אור" במקום "עור" שבכ"י זה[23], יכל
להיחשב אולי כשגיאת דפוס, אולם מה שנמצא בהערותיו הם דברים שאינם מתקבלים

15 Problems of the Masora (HUCA, XVII, 1943, pp. 293--394) = A Historical
Grammar of Biblical Hebrew (Leiden, 1966, pp. 493-562).

16 Hebrew based upon Greek and Latin Transliterations (HUCA, XII-XIII,
1937-38 = TRL); Hebrew based on upon Biblical Passages in Paralell Transmissions (HUCA, XIV, 1939 = HPT).

17 מחקרים באורחות־חיים בארץ־ישראל בתקופת המשנה והתלמוד. ירושלים, תשכ"ב (הוצאת מוס־
ביאליק) וזה תרגום של שני ספריו -Greek in Jewish Palestine, New York, 1942. Helle
nism in Jewish Palestine, New York, 1950.

18 ירושלים, תשכ"ה (מהדורה ראשונה בשנת תש"ו—תש"י), עמ' 88—883.

19 בעיות יסוד במדע הלשון ובמקורותיה בספרות: כרך הלשין, ירושלים תשי"ד (היצא־
ראשונה בשנת תש"ח).

20 מגילה א, ט.

21 עמ' 166.

22 סיני, לב, תשי"ג, עמ' קכא—קכז: "ספר אירייתא דאשתכח ברומא", נספח למאמרו "עיונים
במגילות מדבר יהודה".

23 שם עמ' קסג.

על הדעת: "אבל נראה לי כי עיקר השינוי בנוסח הוא כאן כתנור (ולֹא כתנוד)...
ומסתבר כי מן הנוסח 'כתנור' נתפתח גם הנוסח 'אור' מ'עור'". הקושי העיקרי פה
שבשום מקור לא נמצא לא הגרסה "אור" ולא "כתנור". שגיאה דומה נעשתה על ידו
בנוגע לדוגמה 31: במקום לעיין היטב בפרסום נויבואר שהודפס בירחון האשכנזי
הוא מסתמך על נוסחא המשוחזב של כ. ד. גינצבורג ומדפיס כקריאת כ"י פריס 31
"כמפכת" במקום "כמהפת" לפי כ"י פריס ופרסומו של נויבאר הנ"ל. בפירושו[24]
הוא גם מברר את העניין: "ועי' גם בנוסח כ"י פאריז. 'כמפכת' בחסרון הה"א אחרי
המי"ם מצווי, עי' מגילת ישעיה א, ז (כמפכת ואל"ף תלויה), ו—י"ג, יט (כמ־
אפכ]ת) ... נויבאואר: כמהפת". מאיזו מקור שאב שיש הבדל בין גרסת נויבאואר
לבין כתב-היד עצמו? מן הפקסימיל אפשר בקלות להיווכח שאין להבחנה זאת
יסוד.

14. י. קוטשר בספרו "הלשון והרקע הלשוני של מגילת ישעיהו השלמה
ממגילת ים המלח"[25] בונה, לא בצדק, על נוסחיו ופירושיו של הברמן. למשל
בפירושו על דוגמה 2: "כתנות אור" בהערה 39: "כ"י אחד גורס "כתנור' (הברמן
עמ' קס"ג, הערה 2). פירוש הדבר לדעתי, כי הוא גרס 'כתן' (='כתנת' בארמית)
+ 'עור' בהבלעת הע' (='כתנור', כמו המג' לעתים, ראה לעיל עמ' 42)". "ושוב
אין זה מקרה מן הסתם, כי לפי גרסה אחת נמצאת צורת 'מפכת' בספר אסוירוס",
הערה 70. "הברמן, אסוירוס, עמ' קסז"[26].

על כל פנים אין להשוות תופעות שהן תוצאתו של שגיאות מעתיקים מהמאה
הי"ט אל נוסחאות של המגילות הגנוזות.

15. ש. טלמון במאמרו "שלשה ספרים מצאו בעזרה"[27] מביא מבחר דוגמ־
אות מרשימתנו בצורה בלתי נכונה: יש להיזהר מלהביא כנוסח מסורה
טכסטים שלא בצורה זאת ידועים לנו וגם לא למרכיב הרשימה: (בר' מג, טו)
בנוסח הרשימה לפי כ"י פריס 31[28] ; "ויקמו וירדו מצרימה. מצרים היה כתוב",
כלומר, הצורה המקוצרת היא של נוסח סוירוס. כן הוא בשלושת המקורות גם
יחד[29] ; על כ"י פראג אין להסתמך בלי הסתייגות, כי זה פשוט מביא פה את
נוסח המסורה שלפניו; בוי' ד', לד נוסח המסורה: "ולקח הכהן מדם" ולא "ויקח הכהן
מדמה", בבראשית רבתי באמת מובא הנוסח של פסוק ל' מאותו פרק: "ולקח
הכהן מדמה"[30]: כמו כן יש להבחין בין נוסח הרשימה ופירושים מודרניים
לרשימה: חבל שהשתרבב מפירוש אלבעק משפט שלם לתוך הרשימה בלי להצביע
על זאת: יוממיתי כתיב... והיינו שהמ"ם אינה סתימה וכתובות בתיבה אחת.

24 שם הערה 28.

25 ירושלים, תשי"ט (הוצאת ספרים ע"ש י"ל מאגנס, האוניברסיטה העברית), עמ' 64—65.

26 עמ' 190.

27 ספר סגל מוגש לכבוד פרופ' משה צבי סגל. ירושלים, תשכ"ה (הוצאת החברה לחקר
המקרא בישראל) עמ' 252—265. = The Three Scrolls of the Law that were Found in
the Temple Court (Textus, II, 1964, pp. 14—28)

28 עמ' 259.

29 כי"פ+כיש"ד.

30 גם בקשר ההבאה מן דב' ג', ח היה צריך להעיר לעיר שבכ"י פראג הגירסה הנכונה; בכי"פ
יכשי"ד בטעות "ויעשו" במקום "וירשו".

(=אצל אלבעק: "והיינו שהמ"ם אינה סתומה (סופית), וכתובות בתיבה אחד".

16. במחקרי, המופיע השנה באנגלית כפרוליגומנון להוצאת צילום של יצירת א. אפטוביצר על שינויי נוסח המקרא בספרות הרבנית[31], דן אני בבעיית שינויי נוסח התנכי"ים בתלמוד, במדרש ובספרות המסורה, ומקדיש פרק גם לרשימתני אולם שם בגלל המקום המצומצם שעמד לרשותי לא יכולתי לתת רק תוכן רשימ" סוירוס, יחד עם בירור בעיות מסוימות הקשורות אתה, פה אני מדפיס את כל המקורות בהם מופיעה רשימה זאת בשלמותם, עם הסברים וליבון בעיותיהם.

כנוסח א אדפיס את שלושת המקורות ה ס פ ר ד י י ם שהם קרובים זה לזה. כפנים אתן את נוסח כ"י פריס 31 (=כי"פ) ובאפראט את השינויים הנובעים משתי הואריאציאות בכ"י ששון (=כיש"ד). מן האפראט אפשר גם להיווכח שלמעשה שתי הרשימות הכלולים בכיש"ד מיוסדות על אותו מקור: אין ביניהן הבדלים יסודיים. האופי המשותף בהם הוא שהן מקצרות את הפסוקים בהשוואה אל כי"פ ודוגמה אחת בשתיהן חסרות (19). בנוגע לדוגמה 31 סוטות הן מכי"פ. על כ" פנים על יסודן אפשר גם לתקן שגיאות־העתקה אחדות בכי"פ (דוגמה 3 ו־11: הכצעקתם; בן עדה). כדי להקל על הקורא תקנתי שגיאות אלה כבר בנוסח הפנים אולם העירותי על זאת באפראט.

כנוסח ב אני מדפיס את רשימות "בראשית רבתי", כי זאת היא מהדורה מיוחדת שהיתה נפוצה ב פ ר ו ב א נ ס (נרבונה). ההבדל העיקרי הוא בין נוסח זה לבין הנוסח הקודם שפה לפנינו רשימה מקוטעת ומסורסת מצד אחד ומצד שני מופיעים ברשימה זאת שינויים לגמרי חדשים שהוכנסו בה מן הגליון, וכנראה, אין להם שייכות לרשימת סוירוס. חלק מהדוגמאות החדשות הן "אורחות" שדחפו את רגלי השינויים העיקריים.

בכל אופן על ידי הפרדה בין שני מקורות אלה אפשר יהיה לקבל תמונה יותר בהירה על החומר כולו.

אין שום ספק שנוסח ב מ ש נ י הוא ומותר לנו להתייחס בחשד אל כל שינוי המופיע ר ק בנוסח זה: קרוב לודאי שכל ההבדלים אלה נבעו ממקורות אחרים.

עלינו להביא בחשבון שנוסח ב הוא תוצאה של עריכה חדשה. קשה לקבוע אם עורכו של "בראשית רבתי" שינה את צורתה העיקרית או שהיתה כבר לפני" רשימה מוזרה כזאת. מתקבלת יותר על הדעת ההשערה שלפניו מונחת כבר רשימה מקוטעת, עם הוספות מסוימות. כי אם לא: קשה לתאר לעצמנו למה לא הצביע כבר בדוגמה 1 על הקשר בין תוכן רשימתנו לבין השינוי המובא בשם רבי מאיר. כמו שעושה זאת הרד"ק המדגיש את ההקבלה הזאת באופן טבעי בקשר עם דוגמה זאת, ומחכה עד בר' מח, ח (וישימני—וישני) ?

כנראה, בפרובאנס היו חוגים שלא הכירו בקיומם של שינויי אירתוגרפיה ומביניהם קם "עורך" אשר השמיט את אלה וכתחליף להם רשם "שינויים" ממשיים נוספים הקשורים באותם פסוקים בהם ישנם שינויים בקודכס סוירוס (דוגמה

Das Schriftwort in der rabbinischen Literatur, Wien 1905—1906, I—V. 31
The Library of Biblical Studies. Edited by H. M. Orlinsky, "Ktav Publishing House Inc.", New York 1970)

4, 15, 18, 25, 28 (28) ובמקרה אחד גם שינוי הקשור עם פסוק שאינו בין אלה המנויים ברשימתנו : דוגמה a10.

בכל אופן אחר החלטתו הברורה לא להזכיר שינויי אורתוגרפיה, היה רצוי לא להזכיר בכלל פסוקים אלה, כי על ידי כך שבמקרים אלה הוא מצטט את חלקי פסוקים כמו שהם מופיעים בנוסח המסורה, הוא מכניס בלבול. הקוראים בימי הביניים לא ידעו מה לעשות עם פסוקים אלה ואף החוקרים המודרניים לא הבינו מה מסתתרת מאחורי ההבאות הללו, עד שהופיעו המקורות השלמים.

בהדפסת נוסח ב אנו אמנם הולכים בעקבות מהדורת "בראשית רבתי" של אלבעק, אולם מרשים לעצמנו לסטות משיטתו בשתי נקודות :

1. אנו שמים קו־קיצור בין אותן מלים שיש להניח : זאת היתה כוונת עורך הרשימה.

2. מציינים בנקודות אותם המקומות בהם הושמטו מלים או מלה מתוך ההבאות. על ידי כך אנו ממעיטים את השגיאות בטכסט זה ואין צורך אחר כך להעיר באפרט מה צ"ל לפי נוסח המסורה. לעומת מקומות אלה, בהסברים, הצבענו על הקריאות ברשימה זאת אשר בלי ספק שגיאות העתקה הן, כמו בדוגמה 8 (ואהליבה) ; 9 (בן ענה) ; 21 (בקרות).

לנוסח ב לא צרפנו אפראט, כי יחיד הוא ואין אל מה להשוותו : הסתפקנו בזה שאחרי מספרים סידורים ברשימה זאת ציינו את המספר הסידורי של נוסח א ובנוסח זה הוספנו את המספר המקביל בנוסח ב. בהסברים השייכים לשני הנוסחים עמדנו על ההבדלים ביניהם במדה שהיה צורך בכך.

לפני הדפסת הנוסח עלי להודות מקרב לב להרב ס. ד. ש ש ו ן, בעל כיש"ד, שנתן לי באדיבותו רשות לפרסם את שתי היאריאציאות של כ"י זה, יחד עם הפקסימילים, כמו כן להביע תודתי לידידי הפרופ' י. א. ו ו א י ד ה מפריס שהעמיד לרשותי את צילום הרשימה מן כי"פ.

ב הנוסחים

נוסח א

(כי"פ + כיש"ד)

אלין פסוקיא דהוו כתיבין בספר אוריתא דאישתכח ברומי והיא גנוזה וסתימא בכנסתא דסירוס בשנוי אותיות ותיבות

(1=)1   בר' א, לא
וירא אלהים את כל אשר עשה והנה טוב מאד — מ ו ת היה כתוב
(2=)2   שם ג, כא
כתנות עור וילבשם — כ ת נ ו ד היה כתוב
(3=)3   שם יח, כא
הכצעקתה הבאה אלי עשו כלה — ה כ צ ע ק ת ם היה כתוב
(4=)4   שם כד, ז
ואמר י"י אלהי אדני אברהם — ו מ א ר ע היה כתוב

357

5 (5=)   שם כה, לג
וימכר את בכורתו ליעקב — מ כ ר ת ו היה כתו'

6 (6=)   שם כז, ב
הנה נא זקנתי — י ו מ מ ת י היה כתוב

7 (7=)   שם שם כז
ראה ריח בני כריח שדה — ס ד ה היה כתוב

8 (8=)   שם לו, ה
יעוש דואהליבמה ילדה — י ע י ש היה כתוב

9 (10=)   שם שם יד
וכן דואלה היו בני יעוש [—י ע י ש] היה כתוב

10 (10=)   שם מג, טו
ויקמו וירדו מצרימה — מ צ ר י ם היה כתוב

11 (9=)   שם לו, י
אליפז בן עדה — ב נ ע ד ה היה כתוב

12 (13=)   שם מה, ח
וישימני לאב לפרעה — פ ר ע ה היה כתוב

13 (12=)   שם מח, ז
ואקברה שם — ש מ היה כתוב

14 (14=)   שמ' א, א (=בר' מו, ח)
ואלה שמות בני ישראל הבאים מצרימה — מ צ ר י ם היה כתוב

15 (16=)   שם יב, ל'
ויסעו בני ישראל מרעמסס — מ ר ע מ ס היה כתוב

16 (15=)   שם יט, ג
כה תאמר לבית יעקב ותגיד לבני ישראל — ל ב י ת היה כתו' תרויהֻ

17 (17=)   שם כו, כז
וחמשה בריחים לקרשי — לא היה כתוב ב ר י ח י ם

18 (18=)   וי' ד, לד
ולקח הכהן מדם — מ ד מ היה כתוב

19 (19=)   שם טו, ח
וכי ירק הזב — במים ח י י ם היה כתוב

20 (20=)   שם יד, י
וכבשה אחת בת שנתה תמימה — ת מ י מ י ם היה כתוב

21 (21=)   במ' ד, ג
כל בא לצבא דקהת — ה ב א היה כתוב

22 (22=)   שם טו, כא
מראשית עריסותיכם לדרתיכם — ל ד ר י כ ם היה כתוב

23 (23=)   שם לא, ב
נקם נקמת בני ישראל מאת המדינים אחר תאסף — א ש ר היה כהֵיב

24 (24=)   שם לא, יב
ויבאו אל משה... ואל כ ל עדת — לא היה כתו' בו כל

25 (25 =)   שם לו, א

ויקרבו ראשי ... בני יוסף — ב ן יוסף היה כתוב

26 (26 =)   דב' א, כו

ולא אביתם לעלות — א ב י ת ם היה כתוב

27 (27 =)   שם ג, כ

ויעשו גם הם — ה ם היה כתוב

28 (28 =)   שם א, כז

לתת אותנו ביד האמרי — ה א מ ו ר היה כתוב

29 (29 =)   שם כב, ו

לא תקח האם על הבנים — ה א ב נ י ם היה כתוב

30 (30 =)   שם כט, כב

גפרית ומלח שרפה — ש ר פ ת היה כתוב

31 (31 =)   שם שם שם

כמהפכת אלהים את סדום — כ מ ה פ ת היה כתו'

32 (32 =)   שם לב, כו

אמרתי אפיהם — א ף א י ה ם היה כתוב

ויבא מורה צדק במהרה בימינו ויאמר לנו

א פ ר א ט

דברי פתיחה:

אלין / אין ב־כיש״ד 2. כתיבין / כיש״ד 2: כתבין. דאישתכח / כיש״ד 1: דאשתכח; כיש״ד 2: ראשכח. ברומי / כיש״ד: ברומא. והיא / כיש״ד 1: והי. וסתומא / כיש״ד: וסתימא. בכנשתא / כיש״ד 2: בכנישתא. דסירוס / כיש״ד: דסוירוס.

2   וילבשם / אין ב־כיש״ד. היה כתוב / ב־כיש״ד: כתי' (וכן גם בדוגמאות הבאות).

3   הבאה ... כלה / אין ב־כיש״ד. הכצעקתם / בכי״פ: הכצעקתס (תקננו על יסוד כיש״ד 1); כיש״ד 2: הקצעקתם (!).

4   י״י / כיש״ד 2: יה.   5   וימכר / אין ב־כיש״ד. בכורתו / כיש״ד 1: בכרתי.

6   יוממתי / כיש״ד 2: יוממת.   7   ראה / אין ב־כיש״ד.

8   ילדה / אין ב־כיש״ד.   9   [—יעיש] / אין בכי״פ (והשלמנו על יסוד כיש״ד).

10   ויקמו / כיש״ד: ויקומו.   11   בן עדה / כי״פ: בן ערה; תקנו על יסוד כיש״ד: בן עדה.

12   וישימיני / אין ב־כיש״ד.   13   שם / כיש״ד 2: שמ. שמ / כיש״ד 1: שם.

15   ויסעו ... ישראל / אין ב־כיש״ד.

16   כה תאמר / אין ב־כיש״ד. ותגיד / כיש״ד 1: ודגיד(!); כיש״ד 2: ותגד.

17   היה כתוב / כיש״ד 1: היו כתי'; כיש״ד 2: היה כתו' בי.

18   מדם / כיש״ד 1: מ(פ)ר.   19   דוגמה זאת הסרה ב־כיש״ד.

20   תמימה / כיש״ד 1: תמימת.

22   מראשית / אין ב־כיש״ד. לדרתיכם / כיש״ד: לדרותיכם.

23   נקם ... ישראל / אין ב־כיש״ד.

24   ויבאו / כיש״ד 2: ויביאו. כתו' / אין ב־כיש״ד.   26   לעלות / אין ב־כיש״ד.

28   לתת / אין ב־כיש״ד. האמור / כיש״ד: האמר.   30   גפרית / אין ב־כיש״ד.

31   אהים את / אין ב־כיש״ד. סדום / כיש״ד 1: סדב. כמהפת / כיש״ד: כמהפכת אלהים.

32   אי הם / כיש״ד: איהם.

הסיום: ויבא / כיש״ד: יבא. במהרה ... לנו / כיש״ד 1: ויאמר אלינו בימינ[ו]; כיש״ד 2: במהרה בימינו אמן.

נוסח ב

(בראשית רבתי)

וישימני לאב לפרעה. שאני כנושה עליו כד״א לא תשימון עליו נשך (שמ׳ כב
כד), מה דרכו של נושה, עבד לוה לאיש מלוה (מש׳ כב׳ ז). בספרו של ר׳ מאי״ר
כתוב וישני לאב [48], שנאמר אשר ישה ברעהו (דב׳ טו, ב). דין הוא מן מלי׳א
דכתיבן באורייתא דנפקת מן ירושלם בשביתא וסלקת לרומי [50] והות גניזא בכנישת׳א
דאסוירוס.

1(1=)	וירא אליהם את כל אשר עשה והנה טוב מאד
2(2=)	לאדם ולאשתו כתנות עור
3(3=)	ארדה נא ואראה ה כ צ ע ק ת ם
4(4=)	ה׳ אשר לקחני מ ב י ת י ו מ א ר צ י
5(5=)	וימכור את מ כ י ר ת ו
6(6=)	הנה נא זקנתי לא ידעתי יום מותי
7(7=)	כריח שדה אשר ברכו ה׳
8(8=)	ו א ה ל י ב ה ילדה את יעוש
9(11=)	אליפז בן ע נ ה
10(9=)	ואלה היו בני אהליבמה יעוש
11(10=)	ויקומו וירדו מצרימה
12(13=)	ואקברה שם בדרך
13(12=)	ו י ש נ י לאב לפרעה
14(14=)	ואלה שמות... הבאים מצרימה
15(16=)	כה תאמר ל ב נ י יעקב ותגד לבני ישראל
16(15=)	ויסעו בני ישראל מרעמסס
16א(=)	כי אות ה י א ביני (שמ׳ לא, יג)
17(17=)	חמש׳ לקרש׳ צלע, תנינא לית בה ב ר ח י ם
18(18=)	ולקח הכהן מ ד מ ה , דאם כבש
19(19=)	וכי יטהר הזב... במים חיים (וי׳ טו, יג)
20(20=)	וכבשה אחת בת... ת מ י מ י ם
21(21=)	וכל ה ב א לצבא, בקרות בה
22(22=)	מראשית עריס׳ תתנו... ל ד ר י כ ם
23(23=)	נקום נקמת... א ש ר
24(24=)	ויבאו אל משה... ואל ע ד ת בני ישראל
25(25=)	ויקרבו ראש׳...ממשפחת ב י ת יוסף
26(26=)	ולא אבית׳ לעלות
27(27=)	וירשו גם הם את הארץ
28(28=)	לתת אותנו ביד ה א מ ו ר י ם
29(29=)	ולא תקח האם ע ל ה א ב נ י ם
30(30=)	גפרית ומלח ש ר פ ת

31(= 31) **כמהפכת סדום ועמורה**

32(= 32) **אמרתי אף איהם**

כן הוו כתיבין באורייתא דנפקת מירושלם

נוסח ג

פירוש רד"ק לבראשית (כ"י פריס 193)

...ולזה פרש ר' מאיר והנה טוב מאד והנה טוב מות וכן מצאנו בבראשית רבה
בתורתו של רבי מאיר מצאו כתוב והנה טוב מות ואני מצאתי כתוב דהוה
כת' באורייתא דאישתביאת לרומי והיא פי' גניזא וסתימא בכנישתא דסויירוס והנה
טוב מית.

ג. הסברים

נוסח א

1. זאת היא הדוגמה ה י ח י ד ה המזדהית במלואה עם הגרסה המובאת בשם
ר' מאיר, בה מדובר על שתי תופעות: החלפת ד' בת' ושימוש בו' במקום א'.
על יסוד הקבלה זאת בודאי אין לחשוב על קשר ממשי בין שתי הרשימות אלה,
כי זאת היא תופעה שכיחה בהרבה מקורות. שד"ל קבע כבר ש"לצית" בתרגומים
התפתחה מן "לציד" [1]. שפרבר [2] מצא את התופעה הזאת בתעתיקי המקרא: זבוד =
ζαβουδ; כבוד = χαβωδ; עובד = obeth; היגיד = αιεγγιδ; פחד = faath.
קוטשר הקדיש לזאת בספרו את הסעיף 12 בחלק ו': "דל"ת בסוף תיבה ביצ'עה:
תי'ו"[3]. הוא מביא השלמות השובות לחומר שהיה ידוע לו, בעיקר על יסוד מגילת
ישעיה א: מס' תחד = תחת (יד, כ); לעד = לעת (סד, ח).

גם לתופעה שנייה ישנן הקבלות במקורות אהרים. שפרבר [4] מצביע על הרוברריקה
השנייה של הששיה לאוריגנס: מאד (תה' מו, ב) = δωθ; מות (שם מט' טו) =
θωμ. קוטשר בספרו [5] מוסיף בקשר עם תופעה זאת חומר מעניין מתוך מגילת
ישעיה א: כעת נוכל להצביע על מקור חדש במגילות: אזכירך לברכה בכל מודי
(= מאדי)[6].

2. בדוגמה זאת לפנינו תופעה הפוכה. מעתיק ספר תורה של סויירוס גורס פה
ד' במקום ת'. הבל, שלפני קוטשר לא היה הנוסח הנכון של דוגמה זאת, כי
במקרה זה היה יכול למצוא הקבלה מצוינת למגילת ישעיהו א הגורס במקום
"גת" (שבמס' סג, ב) "גד". הדוגמה "כתנוד" במקום "כתנות", בידאי מחזק
את קביעתו "כיון שדדל"ת ותי"ו בסוף התיבה הומיפוגיניות היו, הרי מופיעה 'גד'
במקום 'גת'"[7].

1 אוהב גר, עמ' 199: ע"ע לוי, מלון לתרגומים, ערך "צית".

2 TRL, עמ' 128.

3 עמ' 408.

4 TRL עמ' 146—147; ראה הערה 16 רבבוא.

5 עמ' 408—409.

6 J. A. Sanders, The Psalms Scroll of Qumran Cave 11, p. 86, Oxford 1965

7 עמ' 409.

על כל פנים יש לבטל אצלו ואצל כל המחברים את הפירושים המבוססים על
הקריאה "אור" במקום "עור" שבנוסחה המסורה, השייכת לגרסאות "תורתו של
ר' מאיר": לפסוק זה היו שייכים שני שינויי נוסח שונים, בלי קשר ביניהם.

3. גם לפני התרגומים היוונים וארמיים היתה גרסה כזאת. לא מן הנמנע
שהמעתיק הושפע ע"י הפסוק הקודם (וחטאתם—הכצעקתם) כמו שעפשטיין[8] מעיר
על זאת, אולם אפשר גם להביא בחשבון שבאמת יש להוסיף את הדוגמה הזאת
לאלה המנויות ע"י שפרבר[9]; הברמן[10] מצביע על בראשית רבה פמ"ט: "הכצעקתם
אינו אומר [הכתוב] אלא הכצעקתה", שלנערה.

4. כמובן, אין צורך ב"תיקון"[11] דוגמה זאת על יסוד בראשית רבתי. אפשר לחשוב
על ארמיזם (הברמן[12]—קוטשר[13]), אולם לפי השערתי מתקבלת יותר על הדעת
ההנחה שלפני מרכיב הרשימה הזאת היה "ומארץ", כלומר צ' אמצעית במקום צ'
סופית. תופעה זאת שכיחה במגילת ישעיהו א, ומצורה זאת התפתחה: ומארא:
אני רואים במגילת ישעיהו א שכמעט בלתי אפשרי במקרים מסוימים להבחין בין
צ' וע', למשל, מגיעי־מציגי (ה, ח).

5. כמו שאין פתרון בדוגמה הקודמת בתיקון הטקסט, כן אין לחפש פה את
משמעות השינוי[14]. גם בעניינהם של אלבק[15] והברמן[16] אינה נראית השערתו של
עפשטיין המשתדל לפרש דוגמה זאת: מכרתו=חרבו. מתקבל על הדעת הנחתו של
הברמן "שיש כאן החלפת בי"ת במי"ם. ראה גם החומר המובא ע"י שפרבר[17]
ורשימת אכלה ואכלה מס' 154—155[18].

6. הבעיה העיקרית היא פה צירוף שתי מלים ביחד, כמו בדוגמה 11. בכל אופן
אין להביא את השינוי בצורה שאינה מופיעה במקורות (יום מותי, בן עדה) כמו
שעושה שפרבר[19] ובודאי אין צורך בפירושים שניתנו למספר זה ע"י הרכבי[20]
(יוממתי כתיב / מן בא בימים/) ואף אין הצדקה בדרישתו של הברמן[21]: "שיש
להכניס את הפעל 'יוממתי' למלון העברי". לעומתם צודקים גינצבורג[22] ואלבק[23]
שחושבים פה על תופעה אורתוגרפית בלבד. על בעיית המנהג בחוגים מסוימים
להשתמש במ"ם אמצעית במקום מ"ם סופית נעמוד בדיוננו על מס' 13, 18, 26,
27). פה נביא הקבלות ממגילות ישעיהו א וב לצירוף שתי מלים ביחד.

8   א, עמ' 344, מס' 3.
9   HPT, § 6, 32; ראה הערה 16 למבוא.
10   עמ' קסג, הערה 3.
11   עפשטיין ב, עמ' 52, מס' 4.
11•   עפשטיין ב, עמ' 52, מס' 4.
12   עמ' קסג־ד, הערה 4.   13   עמ' 65.
14   עפשטיין ב, עמ' 52, מס' 5.   15   עמ' 210, הערה לשורה 2.
16   עמ' קסד, הערה 5.
17   HPT, § 70a, 12; ראה הערה 16 למבוא.
18   ע"צ סגל, עמ' 882, הערה 10.
19   Problems, עמ' 333.
20   חדשים גם ישנים, חוב' 6, עמ' 5.
21   עמ' קסד, הערה 6.
22   Introduction, עמ' 413.
23   עמ' 210, הערה לשורה 3.

גם מעתיק מגילת ישעיהו ב, השומר בדרך כלל על חוקי האורתוגרפיה המקובלים
אצלנו בנוגע למנצפ״ך סוטה מהנהוג באשר מצרף לפעמים שתי מלים [24] :

מג, ב : במואש=במו־אש

מו, יג : לאתאחר=לא תאחר

נא, ו : כמוכן=כמו־כן

נג, ח : ואתדורו=ואת־דורו

נה, יב : כיבשמחה=כי־בשמחה

סו, ח : מיראה=מי ראה

רובן של מלים אלה קשורות בנוסח המסורה במקף, וכנראה, צירוף המלים הוא
למעשה תחליף לסימון זה.

גם במגילת ישעיהו א אנו נפגשים בתופעה זאת ; שם ג״כ כתובות הרבה
פעמים ביחד שתי מלים לא לבד בסוף השורה, אלא אף באמצעה, אולם יש במגילה
זאת גם גורם נוסף : השימוש במ״ם אמצעית בסוף המלה, מעתיקה מתעלם בכלל
מהחוק המקובל בחוגים מסורתיים ואינו מבחין בין הצורה הסופית לבין האמצעית.
נביא כמה דוגמאות :

ח, יט : עמאל=עם אל

מ, כו : בשמיקרא=בשם יקרא

נא, ז : עמתורתי=עם תורתי

נה, יא : אמעשה=אם־עשה

נו, ו : שמיהוה=שם יהוה

נח, יג : אמתשיב=אם־תשיב

אמנם מעניין שדווקא בקשר עם השם ״יום״ אינו עקיב מעתיק זה, למשל : כיא יים
ליהוה (ב, יב) ; ביום אחד (ט, יג) ; כי קרוב יום יהוה ; הנה יום יהוה (יג, ו. ט ; בשני
מקרים אלה השם ״יום״ בסוף השורה) ; כי יום מהומה (כב, ה) ; כיא יום נקם ליהוה
(לד, ח) ; יום צרה ותוכחה (לז, ג) ; ולפני יום לוא שמעתים (מח, ז) ; היום ומחר
(נו, יב) ; אותי יום ויום ידרושו ; צום אבחרהו יום ענות אדם (נח, ב. ה) ; כיא
יום נקם בלבי (סג, ד).

[ו]

במיוחד ראויה לתשומת לב יש׳ ט, ו : למ רבה המשרה=לםרבה המשרה ;
כמו כן יש להסתכל בשני פסוקים באיוב : מן הסערה (לח, א) ; מן סערה (מ, ו) ;
אין כל ספק שנוסח המסורה המקורי היה ״מנהסערה״ או ״מנסערה״ שתוקן
בשלב ראשון ל־מן הסערה או ל־מן סערה ורק בשלב שני התפתח הקרי ל־מן הסערה
או מן סערה.

7. סדה=שדה. זאת היא תופעה שכיחה ועמדו על כך ; ראה דברי קוטשר
בעיקר בקשר עם מגילת ישעיהו א׳, עמ׳ 139, שם הוא מצביע גם על רשימת
סוירוס ; כמובן, מיותרת הערת עפשטיין [25] שחיפש פה הקבלה מתרגום השבעים.

8. בהילוף של י׳ ו׳ אין חידוש, אילם עלינו לקבוע פה שלפני מרכיב רשימת
שינויים אלה היה נוסח מסורה שאינו מזדהה עם המקובל. בנוסח המסורה
מופיעה יעיש שתיקנה אחר כך ל־יעוש.

24 ראה מאמרי The Variants of DSI II (Vetus Testamentum, IV, 1954) עמ׳ 156.

25 א, עמ׳ 345, מס׳ 7.

9.   פה אנו נתקלים באותה תופעה, המסבירה לנו את הקלקול של כי״פ שתקני
על יסוד שתי הואריאציאות בכיש״ד.

10.   גם בדוגמה זאת היה לפני מרכיב הרשימה נוסח אחר ממה שמצוי אצלנו
לכן הוא מכניסה ברשימת השינויים: לוא נמצא לפניו הנוסח שלנו היה מוותר על
דוגמה זאת.

11.   בקשר עם דוגמה זאת ראה את הסברנו למס׳ 6.

12.   עפשטיין [26] כבר מצביע על כך שבכ״י קניקוט 155 מופיע ג״כ שינוי זה.

13.   זאת היא הדוגמה הראשונה בסדרה בה מופיעה מ״ם אמצעית במקום
מי״ם סופית ואינה מצורפת למלה שלאחריה, לכן כדאי לעמוד עליה במיוחד.
במגילת ישעיהו א עשר פעמים משתמש המעתיק בקשר עם מלה זאת במ״ם
אמצעית בסוף המלה (שם) ז, כג; כ, ו; כג, יב; כח, י (פעמיים); כח, יג; לג; כא;
לז, לג; נז, ז; כז, י; אולם בפסוק זה הוא מחליף את השיטה ומשתמש גם במ״ם
סופית, כמו בפרק יג, כא (שם); במספר מקומות יש בהעתק זה צורה מאורכת (שמה=
משמה) במקום ״שם״ או ״משם״ שלנו: יג, כ; לד, יב. יד. טו; לה, ח. ט; מח, טז;
נב, ד; סה, כ (משמה=משם) ובמקום אחד (נב, יא) משמה—משם.

כנראה שלא היו ביד המעתיקים גם בקרב אנשי הכת חוקים קבועים בענין זה,
כמו שהיו כאלה ביד הסופרים השייכים לחוג המסורתי. על כל פנים לאור הממצאים
אלה עלינו לעיין שוב בהבאה מן התלמוד הירושלמי שדנו עליה גם טור־סיני [28]
וליברמן [29]. שניהם מקבלים כנכון את פירושו של בעל ״קרבן העדה״ לעומת
פירוש ״פני משה״.

״ר׳ סימון ור׳ שמואל בר נחמן תריהון אמרין אנשי ירושלים היו כותבין ירושלים
ירושלימה ולא היו מקפידין ודכותה צפון צפונה תימן תימנה״ [29a].

פני משה: ״ירושלים. אף במקום שנכתב ירושלים היו כותבין ירושלימה וכן
להפך ולא היו מקפידים על כך ודכוותה וכו׳״.

קרבן העדה: ירושלימה. כיון דמשמעות הענין אינו משתנה לא היו מקפידין
א״נ ה״ג ירושלים צפון תימן וה״פ באותיות כפופי׳ בסוף וכ״נ עיקר דירושלימה הרי
הענין משתנה דהוי כמו לירושלים שכל תיבה שצריכה למ״ד בתחלתה הטל לה
ה״א בסופה״.

לי נראה [30] יותר הפירוש הקודם מטעמים הבאים:

א. אין לתאר שדווקא אנשי ירושלים לא יקפידו על חוקים אורתוגרפיים כאלה,
כמו השימוש בצורות הסופיות בקשר עם מנצפ״ך, הלוא אלו יוחסו כבר לנביאים [31].

ב. לא היה השש שהענין משתנה בגלל הוספת או הסרת ההה״א, כי מתוך ההקשר
כבר הבינו, אם מדובר על כיוון או לא, כמו שראינו במס׳ 10 ויקמו וירדו מצרים

26   ב, עמ׳ 53, מס׳ 13.   27   עמ׳ 13, הערה 2.

28   עמ׳ 166: ״אנשי ירושלים היו כותבים [בספרי התורה שלהם] ירושלים ירושלמה [ירושלמ(ה)]
ולא היו מקפידין, כלומר לא היו מבחינים ביןם ל־מ וזהו והיו משתמשין בהן לסירוגין״.

29   ירוש׳ מגילה א, ט.

30   ראה מאמרי ״שרידי הניב המאורך במגילת ישעיהו הראשונה ובנוסח המסורה״ (מחקרים
במגילות גנוזות — ספר זכרון לא. ל. סוקניק ז״ל), ירושלים תשכ״א, עמ׳ 151.

31   ראה טור־סיני, הלשון והספר, עמ׳ 4 והלאה: א. מנצפ״ך צופים אמרום.

(בר' מג, טו) ולא היה צורך להשתמש בצורה הארוכה, כדי שידעו למה מתכוון הפסוק.
אף היו שתי צורות של נוסח המסורה עצמו מופצות "מצרימה—מצרים" במס' 14 :
להבאים מצרימה=מצרים.

ג. גם אם מצאו בטכסט ה"א בסוף המלה לא חשבו תמיד על כיוון. דוגמה טובה
לזאת מעון—מעונה (דב' לג, כז).

ד. בנוגע לצפונה—צפונה מספיק להצביע על כמה מקרים במקרא בהם משתמשים
בצורה "צפונה" או "צפון" בלי להתכוון לסמן את הכיוון, למשל, "לפאת צפון" (שמ' כו,
כ. לו, כה; שמ' כז, יא. לח, יא, ועוד) מול "לפאת צפונה" (יהו' טו, ה. יח, יב;
הבדלים מבחינה זאת קיימים בין נוסח המסורה לבין השומרוני המשתמש בצורה
ארוכה "צפונה" במקום "צפון" (שמ' כו, כ. לה; כז, יא; לו, כה; לח, יא). במיוחד
כדאי להסתכל ביחזקאל מ—מח (ראה דוגמאות שהובאו במאמרי הנזכר בהערה 30,
עמ' 147—149 בקשר עם השמות "חצר", "שער") בהם אנו נתקלים בתוך
נוסח המסורה בתנודות גם בנוגע לצפון: כי' מימי הבינים מנסים בכמה מקרים
להתגבר על קשיים מסוג זה ע"י כך שמתקנים את תופעתו המוזרות בעיניהם: מ, מ
"ואל הכתף מחוצה (כ"י קנ' 154, 89; מחוץ) לפתח השער הצפונה (קנ' 154 : הצפון)
שנים שלחנות האחרת" (קנ' 28 : האחת); מו, ט: "דרך שער צפון", "דרך שער
צפונה" (באותו פסוק); מז, טו: "לפאת צפונה" (קנ' 4 : צפון); במיוחד ראוי
לתשומת לב הפסוק יז בפרק זה בו, כנראה, נכנס התיקון "וצפון" מן הגליון ונוצרה:
"גבול דמשק וצפן וצפונה". תנודות דומות שכיחות גם ביר' א, טו : "משפחות
ממלכת צפונה"; כג, ח : "מארץ צפונה", ועוד.

ה. בקשר עם הצורה תימן־תימנה אין לפנינו הוכחות ברורות, אבל במסירת
בת־זוגה "נגב־נגבה" ישנם הבדלים הן בנוסח המסורה עצמה (למשל, "לפאת נגבה
תימנה", שמ' כו, יח; מול "לפאת נגב־תימנה" (שם כז, ט), הן בנוסח השומרוני
הגורס לפעמים "נגבה" במקום "נגב" שלנו. וכי' עבריים מימי הביניים שג"כ
"מתקנים" במקומות אחדים את הצורה "נגב" ל"נגבה" (שמ' כז, ט. קנ' 95; שם
לו, כג, קנ' 253).

על כל פנים נראית קרובה יותר אל האמת ההשערה שבעל המאמר בירושלמי
הג"ל על תנודות מסוגם של אלו התכוון, מאשר על השימוש בנו"ן או מ"ם אמצעית
בסופי המלים [32].

14. ראה הפירוש למס' הקודם.

15. מתקבלת השערתו של פולוצקי (מובא אצל הברמן [33]) שאמנם "נודע שם
פרטי רע'מס במצרית", אולם לזה אין קשר עם הקריאה שלנו. גם הברמן מסתייג מקשר
זה ומצביע על עפשטיין [34] המזכיר שבתרגום השבעים מצויה צורה דומה. גינצ־
בורג [35] מוכיח בצדק שזאת היא תופעה שכיחה גם בכי' מקראים שמקצרים את

---

32 אין להניח שאנשי ירושלים מתעלמים, או שלא היו מקפידים די הצורך על דברים שקבעו
חכמינו בעניני מנצפ"ך "כל האותות הכפולים באל"ף בי"ת כותב הראשונים בתחילת התיבה
:ובאמצע התיבה ואת האחרונים בסופה ואם שינה פסול" (ירו' מגילה א, ט).

33 עמ' קסה, הערה 14; אצל סגל, עמ' 882, יש לתקן את ההבאה מן "מרמסס" ל"מרעבמס".

34 ב, ע"ב 53, מס' 16.   35 Introduction עמ' 416.

המלים בצורות משונות: קניקוטו, שאינו יודע על רשימתנו עדיין, מתאר כ"י
מקראי המקצר בין השאר גם מלה זאת: מרעמס[36].

16.   האפשרות לטעות פה קרובה מאד; ראה גם בנוסח ב: שם יש במקום "לבית"
"לבני".

17.   פה נוסח ב ברור יותר באשר מוסיף: "תנינא לית בה ברחים".

18.   ראויה לתשומת לב מיוחדת שבמגילת ישעיהו א רק פעמים מופיעה בסוף
המלה מ"ם אמצעית בקשר עם השם "דם": ודם (א, יא); דמחוזיר (סו, ג), אולם
בזאת האחרונה יש גם צירוף של שתי מלים; שאר המקומות (טו, ט; לד, ו. נט, ז:
(דם); נט, ג (בדם); לד, ז (מדם) הם לפי המקובל.

19.   עצם העובדה שזאת היא הדוגמה היחידה שאינה מופיעה בשתי הואריאצי'
אות של כיש"ד ובנוסח ב יש פסוק אחר מאותו פרק, אומר דרשני: אין מן הנמנע'
שמדובר פה על הוספה שנכנסה לרשימת כי"פ מן הגליון. אין שום מקור שידבר ע'
מים חיים[37], לכן קל יותר לתאר שהיתה גרסה "במים חיים" במקום "במים"
בלבד בנוסח המקובל.

20.   אולי לא היתה המלה "תמימים" בכ"י סוירוס אחרי "כבשים", כמו בק:
200, רק אחרי "שנתה" במקום "תמימה": יקח שני כבשים וכבשה אחת בת שנתה
תמימים.

21.   "הבא" היא גרסה המצויה בנוסח השומרוני וגם בכי"י עבריים כקרי וכסבי'
רין; ע"ע בפסוקים כג. ל. לה. לט. מג. מז בפרק זה.

22.   המעתיק השמיט אולי בטעות את התי"ו, וישנם שחושבים על ארמיז
(הברמן[38]).

23.   תרגומים וכי"י עבריים אחדים גורסים פה "ואחר" במקום "אחר". אפשר
גם להניח שיש פה טעות גראפית גרידה: המעתיק קרא בטעות "אשר", שאין ל'
משמעות, במקום "אחר".

24.   גם בנוסח המסורה המקובלת אצלנו הגרסה כמו בכ"י סוירוס (ואל עדת
אולם לפני מרכיב רשימה זאת היה נוסח מסורתי אחר, הנמצא בהרבה כי"י עברייב
וגם בתרגומים.

25.   ראה גם התרגום הסורי וכי"י עבריים: מנשה בן[39] יוסף: תרגום יונתן
בר יוסף.

26.   כדאי להעיר שבמגילת ישעיהו א מופיעה מלה זאת דוקא במ"ם סופית
אביתם (ל, טו); אמנם מעתיק מגילה זאת משתמש לפעמים, כמובן, גם בקשר עם מל'ב
מסוג זה במ"ם אמצעית בסופי המלים.

27.   בנוסח ב גרסה נכונה "וירשו" במקום "ויעשו"; הצורות הם—והם במגיל'ת
ישעיהו א תמיד מאורכות הם (=הם, המה) לעומת שם—דם שחלק מהם גורסיב
בסוף המלה מ"ם אמצעית או צורות מאורכות (שמה במקום שם), אולם אין בז'
חיקיות, כי באותם פסוקים או בסביבתם משתמש מעתיק זה במ"ם אמצעית בסופ'
המלים, למשל נז, ו (גמ); ל, ו (עמ); שם ט (עמ), שם יב (מאסכם).

36   מס' 155 (קרלסרוה), אולם באפאראט השינויים איגו מזכיר קריאה זאת.
37   אלבעק, עמ' 211, הערה לשורה 2.   38   עמ' קסי, הערה 21; ראה עיד סגל, עמ' 883
39   אצל סגל, עמ' 883 יש לגרוס במקום "בן-בני" "בן-בני".

28. גם פה מדובר על קיצור בלי שום משמעות מיוחדת, כמו שאנו רואים
בכתבי יד מקראיים מימי הביניים שמטעמים שונים ובמיוחד בסוף השורות גומרים
אותה במלים קטועות ואת ההשלמה כותבים על הגליון קצת רחוק מן המלה בצורה
כזאת שהמעתיק השני אינו מבין את התופעה המוזרה הזאת ואת ההוספה אינו מכניס
בטכסט: גינצבורג במבואו [40] מצביע על כתבי־יד מקראיים שנקטו בשיטה זאת,
כגון כ"י וינא 15 שבין השאר את השם הזה מביא בצורה כזאת: האמ רי (בר' י, טז)
או מאותה ספריה כ"י מס' 5 (יהו' ו, יב: הכהני ם); אין כל ספק שלפני מעתיק קודקס
סוירוס היה כ"י מקראי שהשתמש בשיטה זאת שהוליכתהו שולל ולכן גרס האמור
במקום האמורי. אין מתקבלת על הדעת השערת הברמן [41] לפיה: "האמר" כאן הוא
כמו "אמר" ביחז' כה, ח [42].

29. אין מן הנמנע שהמעתיק חשב על הקבלה בשמ' א, טז. הברמן [43] מצביע
על צורות מקביליות במגילת ישעיה א: יאתום (א, יז. כג) תתיאמרו (סא, י)
קוטשר [44] מוצא הקבלה עוד יותר מתאימה "האזורה" במקום "הזורה" שבנוסח
המסורה (נט' ה).

30. הגרסה הזאת בודאי תוצאה של החלפת ה' בת' בטעות.

31. ראה בקשר עם דוגמה זאת מה שאמרנו על נקודה זאת בסקירת הספרות
כשהבאנו פירושיו של הברמן [45]; יש להבליט שבנוגע למהות שינוי זה יש
הבדל בין כי"פ ושתי הואריאציאות בכי"ד: לפי הראשון ההבדל הוא "כמהפכת =
כמהפת" ובשני ההבדל הוא במלים: במקום "כמהפכת סדום" גרס כ"י סוירוס:
כמהפכת אלהים / את סדום /; לפי כי"פ היה לפני מרכיב רשימת סוירוס נוסח מסורה
השונה מהמקובל: כמהפכת אלהים את סדום.

32. גם בנוגע לדוגמה זאת יש הבדל בין נוסח א לבין נוסח ב כמו כן בין כי"פ
לבין כיש"ד ונוסח ב: שלושת המקורות אלו קבלו רשימה בה יש פה שתי מלים
שצריך לגרוס אותם במקום נוסח המסורה (אפיהם=אף איהם) ולא שלושה כמו
שמופיעה בכי"פ (אף אי הם). כבר בנוסח השומרוני (אפי הם) גם בתרגומים משתקפות
חילוקי דעות בנוגע למלה זאת [46] ואף המפרשים היהודיים מימי הביניים מביאים דעות,
לפיהם אפשר לחלק להלק מלה זאת: "ואונקלוס תרגם [47] — אחר לשון הברייתא השנויה
בספרי [48] — החולקת תיבה זאת לג' תיבות אמרתי אף אי הם אמרתי באפי אתנם כאילי
אינם" (רש"י): "יש אומרים שהם שלוש מלות והנכון שאין לו ריע וטעמו כמו
אשחיתם" (ראב"ע). הרשימה נגמרת בדוגמה שבה נוסח המסורה מצרף שתי אי
שלוש מלים, כמו שראינו במס' 6: (יוממתי [49] או 11 (בנעדה) בהם מעתיק קודקס

40   עמ' 166—167.

41   עמ' קסו, הערה 25.

42   גם השערתו של גרינץ בנוגע לתרגום השבעים ליש' יז, ט (והאמיר = האמורי, המובאה אצל
הברמן בתחתית עמ' קסז כהוספה להערה 25 (קסו), אינה מתקבלת על הדעת.

43   עמ' קסז, הערה 26.

44   עמ' 64.   45   עמ' קסז, הערה 28.

46   ראה קיטל-קאהלה לפסוק זה.

47   איחול רוגזי עליהון; ת"י: למיכלי מנהון רוח קדשי.

48   ראה מהדורת פינקלשטיין לפסוק זה. ברלין, ת"ש, עמ' 370, פיסקא שבב.

49   ראה ההסברים למס' זה.

סיירוס מצרף מלים שהן בנוסח המסורה נפרדות וראויה לתשומת לב שבכל מקרים אלה יש השלכה על אופן השימוש של מנצפ״ך, כלומר אם מצרפים את המלים, נהפכות האיתיות הסופיות לאמצעיות, או להפך.

נוסח ב

1. את ההוספה "מות היה כתוב" משמיט מעתיק זה כי מדובר פה על שינוי אורתוגרפי שאינו מעניין אותו או שלא הבינו; אמנם לפני הרד״ק , היתה גם הרוב־ ריקה השניה עם הקריאה "מות". לכן הוא מזכיר את קשר רשימה זאת עם השינוי המובא בבראשית רבה בשם רבי מאיר בניגוד לבראשית רבתי שאינו מזכיר — כאמור — את הקרבה בין שתי רשימות אלה רק כשהגיע אל בר׳ מ״ה, ח (וישימני—וישני).

2. לפני עורך בראשית רבתי היה, כנראה, הנוסח המקוטע שאינו מדבר על שינויי אורתוגרפיה. אולם מעצם העובדה שאינו מזכיר בכלל שינוי בקשר עם פסוק זה, אפשר ללמוד שלא היה לפניו שינוי כמו עור—אור, כי במקרה כזה היה מביאו, מאחר שהוא אינו רואה פסול בהבאת שינויים בהחלפת אותיות במדה שיש בהם משמעות כלשהי, כגון הכצעקתה—הכצעקתם. הוכחה אחרת שברשימה העיקרית שהיתה ידועה בנרבונה הופיעה "כתנוד" על בראשית מוזכר השינוי עור—אור היא שבפירוש השני של הרד״ק ולא שינוי אחר הקשור עם רבי מאיר בשם רבי מאיר, אולם אינו מזכיר את רשימת סוירוס[51], כלומר לפניו השינוי "כתנוד" שאינו מזדהה עם השינוי של רבי מאיר ומאחר שהוא אינו עוסק בשינויים אורתוגר־ פיים כאלה אך ורק כשיש להם משמעות מיוחדת וקשורה בהקבלה ידועה.

3. ראה ההסבר לנוסח א.

4. אין מן הנמנע שהיה נפוץ גם שינוי כזה והיה על הגליון של רשימת סוירוס (ומארץ או ומארע) וזה דחק רגלו של המקורי שלא הבינו את תוכנו; יש להביא בחשבון גם את הקשים שכבר נזכרו ע״י עפשטיין[52] בנוסח המסורה, שם כתוב מבית אבי וארץ מולדתי.

5. מכירתו=מכורתו, כמו בנוסח א, וכן צריך להיות.

7—6. השינויים הושמטו מאחר שהם אורתיגרפיים.

8. ואהליבה=ואהליבמה; יעוש: בנוסח המסורת של מעתיק זה היה "יעוש" או שמביא את הקרי.

9. ענה=עדה[53].

10. ראה ההערה למס׳ 8.

11. אפשר שגם לפניו נוסח מסורה: מצרימה ולא מצרים.

12. שינוי כזה אינו ראוי שייזכר לפי השקפת המקצר.

13. גם במקרה זה השינוי שהוכנס מן הגליון דוחק רגלו של המקורי (לפרעה— פרעה), מאחר שזה היה ביחד עם "פירוש" במדרש "שנאמר אשר ישה ברעהו": קרוב לודאי שלפני עורך מדרש "בראשית רבתי" היתה כבר רשימה שלא הופיע בה רק גרסה זאת.

59 ראה העיר 3 לעיכא.   51 ראה הוצאת פינקלשטיין הנזכרת בהערה הנ״ל.
52 א, עמ׳ 344, מס׳ 3.   53 בעניין שגם בכ״פ נפלה פה טעות וגורם "ערה" במקום "עדה".

14. פה גם נוסח המסורה הוא "מצרימה" ולכן מעדיף — כמובן — להזכיר רק את זאת.

15. כנראה, על הגליון של רשימת סוירוס היה שינוי אחר, לפיו בשני המקומות יש לגרוס "לבני" ולא "לבית" וזה היה המנצח[54].

16. גרסת סוירוס גם פה הושמטה, כי אין לה משמעות.

16א. בנוסח המסורה "הוא", אמנם מנוקד הוא: אפשר שאחד המעתיקים רשם בהקשר זה על הגליון כקרי במקום הכתיב "הוא" שהוכנס אחר כך בתוך הרשימה[55].

17. כמו שאמרנו בהסבר נוסח א, יש פה ניסוח ברור יותר, מאחר שקובע איזו מן שתי האפשרויות באה בחשבון.

18. בדוגמה זאת ג"כ גרסת נוסח זה ברורה יותר מצד אהד, כי נוסף "דאם כבש", אולם מצד שני הוא מביא את הפסוק שלפניו "ולקח הכהן מדמה" (ל)[56]. אבל ניסה א נראה מקורי יותר, מכיון שזה נותן את תוכן השינוי "מדמ" במקום "מדם" באותוגרפיה המקובלת.

יש להניח שמעתיק נוסח ב מאחר שכוונתו לא להביא שינויי אורתוגרפיה, לוקה פסוק שלפניו: אפשרות אחרת היא שהיה לפניו כ"י מקרא בו הגרסה גם בפסוק לד "ולקח הכהן מדמה" במקום "ולקח הכהן מדם חטאת"; בפסוק ל גורס "ולקח הכהן מדם חטאת" במקום "ולקח הכהן מדמה" שבנוסח המקובל.

19. פה פותר המעתיק את הקושי של השינוי בצורה אחרת באשר הוא מביא נוסח שבו מופיע כבר הנוסח של קודקס סוירוס בתוך הרשימה ולא את הפסוק ח בו נוסף המסורה "במים", בלי התוספת "חיים"; בכל זאת ראויה לתשומת לב הנחתו של אלבעק שמדובר פה על שינוי אורתוגרפי "במים חיים"[57], לפי זה יהיה זה בפסוק אחד שתי מלים הכתובות לפי האורתוגרפיה המשונה. על כל פנים קשה להסביר מפני מה אינם יודעים על זאת שלושת המקורות (כי"פ+כיש"ד) של נוסח א.

24—20. הם שינויים המקובלים על דעת מעתיק מקור זה ומביאם כמו שאר המקורות[58].

25. בניגוד לנוסח א נרשמה פה גרסה "בית יוסף"; ראה למעלה מס' 15 ובו "לבני" בנוסח ב פעמים במקום "לבית" שבנוסח א.

26. פה מצא מעתיק נוסח זה שיטה חדשה להעלים את התופעה האורתוגרפית זרה בעניניו: "אבית" במקום "אביתם" או "אביתם"[59].

27. פה הבאת הפסוק עצמו יותר מדויק מאשר בנוסח א, כי המלים "גם הם"

---

54 אין מן הנמנע שלפני בעל רשימה זאת היתה גרסה ...את בנוסח המסורה שלפני: כדאי להזכיר שכ"י קניקוט 109 (=בריטיש מוזיאום, מס' 170) גורס "לבית לבני", אולם שב בודאי נכנס מן הגליון שהכיל את המלה "לבית" הלקוחה מתרגום יונתן המשתמש בה במקום "לבני", כלומר קריאה זהה עם קודקס סוירוס.

55 אלבעק, עמ' 210, הערה לשורה 8.

56 יש להביא בחשבון גם את האפשרות שאחד ...יקי נוסח ב של רשימתנו "תיקן" את "מדמ" ל"מדמה", בלי להתחשב אם מדובר על הפסקה "דאם כבש", או לא.

57 עמ' 211, הערה לשורה 2; ראה עוד מה שאמרנו בהסבר נוסח א בקשר עם דוגמה זאת.

58 "בקרות בה" בדוגמה 21 היא קלקול מן "דקהת—הבא".

59 כדאי להזכיר השערת עפשטיין א (עמ' 349, מס' 27) שחשב בתחילה שפה מדובר על שינוי במלא וחסר: לעלת = לעלות.

מופיעות יחד עם "ויירשו" ולא עם "ויעשו"; אולם את התופעה "הם" אינו מזכיר
מעתיק זה, כמנהגו.

28. צורה כזאת אינה מופיעה במקרא וגם שאר המקורות של רשימתנו אינב
יודעים עליה; אפשר להניח שיש פה טעות המעתיק בלבד.

29—30. בשתי דוגמאות אלה מביא מעתיק זה את השינויים כמו בנוסח א.

31. פה הוא כנהוג אצלו, מביא את נוסח המסורה.

32. פה מזדהית קריאתו עם כיש"ד ולא עם כי"פ.

ד. יחס רשימתנו אל מגילות ישעיהו

ממדבר יהודה

מן ההסברים לנוסח א ומן ההקבלות שהובאו שם התברר שם שלספר התורה על
יסודו הורכבה רשימה זאת שייך לסוג של המגילות ואף אין מן הנמנע שהיה פעם
בידי אנשי כת יהודית הקרובה לאלה שברשותן היו המגילות הגנוזות ממדבר יהודה.
הנימוקים:

א. מעתיקו אינו שומר על האורתוגרפיה המקובלת בחוגים המסורתיים ומשתמש
לפעמים באותיות אמצעיות בסופי המלים: שם (13); מדם (18); אביתם (26):
הם (27).

ב. לפעמים הוא מצרף שתי מלים שבנוסח המסורה מופיעות בנפרד: יוממתי (6):
בנעדה (11), או מחלק מלה אחת, שהיא בנוסח המסורה מופיעה כיחידה אחת.
לשתים או לשלוש: אף איהם, אף אי הם (32).

ג. הוא משתמש בא' כאם קריאה אחרי ה' הידיעה: האבנים (29).

ד. מחליף בסופי המלים ד' בת' (1) או להפך ת' בד' (2).

ה. הוא משתמש אולי גם בארמיזמים: ומארע (4); לדריכם (22).

ו. מחליף אותיות, משמיט או מוסיף: הכצעקתם (3); מכרתו (5); סדה (7);
יעיש (8—9); מצרים (14. 10); מרעמס (15); תמימים (20); הבא (21); אשר
(23); בן (25): האמור (28); שרפת (30); כמהפת (31).

ז. גורס מלה אחרת במקום המקובלת: לבית (16).

ח. מחסיר (בריחים, 17, כל, 24) או מוסיף מלה (חיים, 19).

אמת, התופעות המנויות במס' ו—ח, אינן נדירות גם בכי"י שבדרך כלל
שומרים על המנהגים המקובלים, בכל זאת משלימות הן את התמונה שאנו מקבלים
על האכסמפלר המשונה הזה.

עלינו עוד להדגיש שמספר שינויים אלה קטן הוא מדי ביחס הרשימה העשירה
של אלה מה שאפשר להרכיב כתוצאה של השוואת שתי המגילות של ישעיהו ממדבר
יהודה אל נוסח המסורה, אולם בכל זאת גם ספר תורה זה היה נדון לגניזה בחוגים
מסורתיים בגלל השנויים המצויים בו.

לבסוף עלינו לברר את בעיית ירושלמיותו של קודכס סוירוס. כבר עפשטיין
במאמרו הראשון [1] מעלה את האפשרות שיש לכ"י זה קשר עם האכסמפלר שהובא

ע"י טיטוס מירושלים לרומא, אמנם אין בידו הוכחות ממשיות. הוא בונה על
הביטוי הנמצא בבראשית רבתי המסבר בתוך דברי הפתיחה לרשימתנו: "דנפקת
מן ירושלם בשביתא וסלקת לרומי" (= שיצא מירושלים בשבי ועלה לרומא),
אבל שאר המקורות, לרבות נוסח הרד"ק בפירושו לבראשית, אינם מדברים על
זאת: דאישתכח [דאשתכח—דאשכח] ברומי" (כי"פ+כי"ד); "דאישתביאת לרומי"
(רד"ק). אפשר להניח שההתיחסות אל ירושלים במקור זה היא רק תוספת
מאוחרת, כמו שאר ההוספות שהוכנסה, לפי הנראה, מן הגליון בתוך הרשימה
ואינן מקוריות. גם העובדה שבמדרש זה נמצאת בסוף הרשימה ההוספה: "כך הוו
כתיבין באורייתא דנפקת מירושלם", אינה מוכיחה את מקוריותה[3].

הסיום של שאר מקורות, שאמנם ג"כ לא הגיע לידינו בצורה מליאה, נראה
יותר אבטנטי: אולי גם הזכרת "מורה צדק" בהערה זאת רומזת על מוצאו הכתתי,
מאחר שביטוי זה שכיח בספרי הכת של מדבר יהודה.

בנוגע להבאה מהירושלמי עליה דנו בהסברנו לנוסח א[1], באנו לידי מסקנה ששם
לא מדובר על מעתיקים שלא נזהרו בשימושם באותיות הסופיות אלא שלא הקפידו על
השימוש בה' הכיוון[5]. לאור שימוש ספר סוירוס בשני מקרים (14. 10 : מצרים)
דוקא בצורה המקיצרת אפשר יותר לערער על ירושלמיותו של ספר תורה
של סוירוס.

כמובן למרות שישתי כדוגמאות אלה אינן מחזקות את ההשערה שמוצאו מירושלים
אין מן הנמנע שהוא מאותה הסביבה כמו מגילת ישעיהו א, בקשר עמה קובע קוטשר
"לפיכך לא מן הנמנע הוא — אף שאין ראויות בטוחות לכך — כי לפנינו ניב
עברי-ארמי משלהי הבית השני, שהיה אחד הניבים העממים של בירת הארץ —
ירושלים"[6]. אבל אין לאפשרות זאת ערך מכריע במכלול הבעיות הקשור ברשימתנו.

ה. "תורתו של רבי מאיר"

מספר השינויים המובאים מספרי ר' מאיר (תורה, ישעיהו, תהלים) קטן מאד,
באופן יחסי אל רשימת סוירוס. אין כל ספק שעל יסודם קשה לעמוד על אפיו של
האכסמפלר ממנו לקוחים שינויים אלה. נעשו נסיונות רבים לפתור את הבעיה
הזאת וכדי להגיע למסקנה המתקבלת על הדעת השתמשו הרבה גם ברשימת סוירוס
משתי סבות:

2 ראה נוסח ג'.

3 הוספה זאת חזרה על מה שאמור בדברי הפתיחה ונוספה על ידי עורך בראשית רבתי.

4 בקשר עם דוגמה 13.

5 בודאי אין להביא בחשבון שמדובר פה על "ספרי התורה שלהם" (ליברמן, עמ' 166), הלוא
השם ירושלים בכלל אינו מוזכר בתורה לעומת תימן וצפון שכ׳ נזכרים. אמנם אין לשכוח שגם
אם אנו מקבלים את דעת "פני משה" שאין הכונה לשימוש במ"ם אמצעית במקום המ"ם סופית, אלא
על ה"א הכיוון, אין להאמין שריקא "אנשי ירושלים" לא הקפידו בענינים אלה, הלוא בקשר מעון—
מעונה קבעו כבר איזו מהן תהיה הגרסה הנכונה, כלומר שגם בענינים אלה היתה החלטה; יש
להזכיר שבניסוח האנגלי של ליברמן כתוב "scrolls" שיכול להיות "מגילות", נניח נביאים, ולא
דוקא "ספר-תורה".

6 עמ' 70.

1. מבין 32 הדוגמאות המופיעות בנוסח א של רשימתנו היו שתים הראשונות
מזדהות עם אותם השינויים הנזכרים בשם רבי מאיר.

2. על שתים אלה נוספה שלישית: האמינו שהדוגמה המובאה מרשימת סיירוס
בבראשית רבתי (וישני, בר׳ מה, ח) ג״כ מקורית היא, כלומר מחצית הדוגמאות
המובאות בשם ר׳ מאיר היו זהית בשתי הרשימות.

אמנם אחרי קביעת הנוסח האמתי של רשימת סיירוס לפי המקורות המוסמכים
יצא שהדוגמה השנייה היא בדויה ע״י החוקרים ואין לה שום קשר עם השינוי
המובא ייחוותו של רבי מאיר ומהערכת המקורות מבחינת נאמנותם התברר, שיכול
להיות ואולי קרוב לודאי שהדוגמה השלישית לקוחה אמנם מספרו של רבי מאיר.
אולם לרשימתנו הוכנסה בטעות מעל הגליון.

נשארה רק דוגמה אחת בלבד שהיא משותפת בשתי הסדרות, אולם גם זאת
תופעה אורתוגרפית כללית היא שבמקרה מופיעה בשתיהן גם יחד [1].

בכל זאת שתי רשימות אלה משתלבות כל אחת לחוד בתולדות נוסח המקרא
וכדאי לברר עניני שינויי רבי מאיר כשלעצמם בלי להביא בחשבון יחסם האמיתי
אל הרשימה של ספר התורה שהיה גנוז בבית כנסת סיירוס ברומא:

אלו הן ההבאות מתורתו או מספרי רבי מאיר:

1. בתורתו של רבי מאיר מצאו כתוב והנה טוב מאד, והנה טוב מות
(בראשית רבה לבר׳ א, לא) [2].

2. בתורתו של רבי מאיר מצאו כתוב כתנות אור (שם לבר׳ ג, כא).

3. בתורתו של רבי מאיר מצאו כתוב ובן דן חשים (שם לבר׳ מו, כג).

4. בספרו [3] של רבי מאיר כתוב וישני לאב (בראשית רבתי לבר׳ מה, ח).

5. בספרו של רבי מאיר מצאו כתוב משא דומה, משא רומי (ירוש׳ תענית א, א,
ליש׳ כא, יא).

6. וירדו ראמים עמם, אמר רבי מאיר וירדו רומים עמם (פסיקתא דרב כהנא,
פסקא ז, ויהי בחצי הלילה, מהדורת ד. מנדלבוים, נויארק, תשכ״ב (עמ׳ 134).

7. אם יתן לי אדם ספר תילים של רבי מאיר מוחק אני את כל הללויה שבו
שלא נתכוון לקדשן [4] (ירוש׳ סוכה ג, יב).

זה המקום האחרון למעשה אינו שינוי מסוג ששת הקודמים, כי מדובר בה
על תיפעה של צירוף מלים שגם בחוגים מסורתיים לא היתה דעה אחידה בענין זה.
ביטוי זה מופיע 24 פעמים בתהלים ואפילו בכתבי יד עתיקים ומדויקים ישנם
הבדלים מבחינת כתיבתו ביחד או בנפרד [5], כמו כן יש אם לקשר שתי מלים אלה

---

1 כדאי לקרוא דברי הרמב״ן המובאים בעפשטיין ב (עמ׳ 49, הערה 1): "ואמרו בתורתו של
ר׳ מאיר מצאו כתוב והנה טוב מאד והנה טוב מות, כי ר׳ מאיר היה לבלר ובשכתבו ס״ת אחד היה
מחשב בלבו כי הנה טוב מאד ירמוז אפילו למות ולאפיסת כוחם והלך ידי אחר לבו וטעה וכתב
בספר התורה והנה טוב מאד והנה טוב מות כמו שהיה מחשב בלבו" (הודפס מדרשת הרמב״ן
ע״י ברלינר מכ״י מינכן 327 בהלבנון, ה, עמ׳ 469).

2 ראה הערות במהדורת טעאדור—אלבעק גם למקומות הבאים מבראשית רבה.

3 ראוי לתשומת לב מיוחדת שבעל המדרש הזה אינו משתמש במלת "בתורתו".

4 או "לקדשו" (ירוש׳ מגילה א, ט); ע״ע בבלי פסחים קיז, ב.

5 ע״ע י. ייבין, כתר ארם-צובה, ירושלים תשכ״ט, עמ׳ 80—81.

במקף או לא׳ כלומר ויכוח עתיק שלא הוכרע גם בימי הנקדנים המפורסמים בטבריה.

מהות שינויים אלה:

1. החלפת אותיות (ת׳ במקום ד׳, דוגמה 1 ; א׳ במקום ע׳, דוגמה 2 ; ר׳ במקום ד׳, דוגמה 5 ; ו׳ במקום א׳, דוגמה 1+6).

2. הסרת אות (בני—בן, דוגמה 3 ; וישמני—וישני, דוגמה 4).

תופעות דומות שכיחות גם ברשימת סוירוס ואף במגילות מדבר יהודה.

אמנם יש הבדל מהותי ביניהן: בו בזמן שהדוגמאות 1—2 ; 4—6 מתנגדות לקריאות המסורתיות ולכן לא זכו אפילו להזכרה באפּרַאט המסורה המקובלת ורק אחת מהן (מס׳ 3) נזכרת בגליוני כתבי יד מאוחרים כסבירין, מאחר שיש בקריאה המסורתית קושי פרשני [6].

על כל פנים בתקופתו של ר׳ מאיר היו כבר הטכסטים המקראיים, בעיקר נוסח ספר התורה, קבועים ולא היתה אפשרות של הסתננות חומר העומד מחוץ למסגרת לתוך הטכסט. לכן אם אנו מקבלים את השערתו של ליברמן שהיו עדיין בתקופות מאוחרות נפוצים בקרב הקהל טכסטים השייכים לסוג של הוולגטה, עלינו להסתייג מכמה הנחותיו הקשורות עם בעיית ספריו של ר׳ מאיר, במיוחד לאור המגילות הגנוזות שלא היו עוד ידועות בעת כתיבת כרכיו על ״יוונית ויוונות בארץ ישראל״, שפתחתו תקופה חדשה בחקר בעיות אלה וערכם לא יופחת על ידי תיקונים המחייבים המקורות החדשים שנתגלו בעשרים שנה שעברו [7].

איננו יכולים להצטרף אל קביעתו: ״הביטוי ׳ספרו של ר׳ מאיר׳ הובן כרגיל בהוראת ספר שהיה קנינו הפרטי של ר׳ מאיר. דבר זה נכון הוא בלי ספק, הואיל וכמה שינויי־גירסאות נראה שהיו הערות שהוסיף ר׳ מאיר בשולי הגליונות, אך מלבדם היו גם בגוף הספר הזה גירסאות שונות מאלו המצויות בטפסים המקובלים בידנו, כפי שמוכיחות המובאות מספר־התורה של בית הכנסת של אסוירוס״ [8] אמנם ברור, האקסמפלר שעל גליונו הופיעו הגרסאות הסוטות מהמקובל היו ״קנינו הפרטי״, כלומר לא היה מכוון להפצה ברבים, אולם אין להעלות על הדעת שהכניס אפילו א ח ת מגרסאות אלה לתוך הטכסט עצמו, הלוא על ידי כך היה מטעה אחרים שבאו אחריו ולא היו תופסים מהות השינוי.

כמו כן טעון תיקון מה שאמור אצלו בהמשך דבריו: ״במשמעות זו יש לפרש את הציון ׳ספרו של ר׳ מאיר׳. ר׳ מאיר היה סופר לפי מקצועו: ׳כתבן טב מובחר׳, והרשות לנו להניח שהספרים שהעתיק נקראו על שמו ... ר׳ מאיר לבלר היה (librarius) ועל מלאכתו זו פרנסתו ; הוא העתיק ספרים לתינוקות של בית רבן ולצורך יחידים. לפיכך העתיק את ה־vulgata, את הנוסח שהציבור רגיל בו ... ספרי ירושלים, שרבות מגירסותיהם זהות עם אלה שבספרי ר׳ מאיר, היו מן הסתם סוג מסוים של נוסח עממי״ [9].

אף אינה מתקבלת על הדעת סברתו: ״כנגד זה המגילות שכתב ר׳ מאיר היו

<hr/>

6 ע״ע פירוש הראב״ע והסבריו של נורצי במנחת שי לפסוק זה.
7 ספריו באנגלית על נושא זה הופיעו בשנת 1942, 1950, ויש להצטער שבתרגים העברי לא התחשבו במסקנות הנובעות מהמגילות הגנוזות.
8 עמ׳ 167.   9 עמ׳ 168.

העתקים מדוייקים של טופסי ה־vulgata,   השגורים בסוג הירושלמי, לנוסח
מסוג זה התייחסו בודאי כאל נוסח שראוי לסמוך עליו, ועל כל פנים, לצרכי
דרוש״ [10].

מה שנוסף על קביעת ליברמן בידי חוקרים דגולים אחרים שרצו לחזק
השערותיו, ג״כ אינו מ־שכנע, למשל, דברי גורדיס: ״הכנת כתב־יד מוגה ומדויק
לכל פרטיו היתה מפעל קשה ומסובך וכרוך בהוצאות מרובות. לכן אין לתמוה
שגם החכמים היו מסתפקים בכתבי־יד ״עממיים״ בלתי־מוגהים לשם קריאה פרטית.
בכך מתבארים חילופי הגירסה הנמצאים בספרים ידועים, כגון ״ספר תורה של ר׳
מאיר״ והמובאות הרבות בספרות התלמודית שאינן מסכימות עם הטכסט המקובל״ [11].

גם אינם מתקבלות על הדעת דבריו של קוטשר בנושא זה: ״מתורתו של רבי
מאיר מצטטים המקורות כמה פסוקים המעידים, כי תורה זו שונה בנוסחתה
כין הנוסחה המסורתית. רבי מאיר, בן המאה השנייה לסה״נ, סופר היה, והיו כנראה
בידו ספרים, שהושפעו מספרים בעלי הכתיב העממי״ [12] ובהערותיו הוא מוסיף:
״כנראה קיים בידו ספר זה (או ספרים אלה) לשם דרש״ [13].

כדי שנקבל תמונה בהירה על המצב של הטכסטים המקובלים בתקופה זאת מספיק
להשוות את ההבדלים של נוסח התפילין שנשמרו בקומראן [14] אל אלה שמוצאן
בוואדי מרבעת [15]. אלו הראשונים באמת נותנות לנו טכסטים של פרשיות התפילין
הסוטים מכל הבחינות מהמקובל [16], לעומתם אם אנו מסתכלים בנוסח הפרשיות של
אלה האחרונות, נוכל להוכח שבחוגים מסורתיים בתקופתם של רבי עקיבא ורבי
ישמעאל, רבותיו של ר׳ מאיר, היו מגובשים וקבועים הנוסחים אפילו בנוגע למלאים
וחסרים [17], כמו שמוכרים לנו מתקופתם של נקדני טבריה [18].

את התמונה הזאת משלימים המאמרים המצוטטים בנושא זה בשם מוריו המובה־

10   עמ׳ 169.

11   ״קדמותה של המסורה לאור ספרות חז״ל ומגילות ים המלח״ (תרביץ כז, תשי״ח, עמ׳ 458).

12   עמ׳ 63.

13   שם, הערה 34.

14   ראה: י. ידין, תפילין של ראש מקומראן (תדפיס מן ״ארץ ישראל״ כרך ט, ״ספר אולברייט״)
בהוצאת החברה לחקירת ארץ ישראל ועתיקותיה והיכל הספר, ירושלים תשכ״ט, שם הובאה כל
הספרות הקשורה בנושא זה.

15   ראה מסוג זה את הטכסט המודפס ע״י י. ט. מליק: Les Grottes de Murabba'at
(Discoveries in the Judean Desert. II. Oxford 1961).

16   הן מבחינה טכסטואלית הן מבחינת השמירה על חקי ומנהגי האורתוגרפיה המקובלת בחוגים
מסורתיים.

17   אם אנו משום למשל את הטכסטים המובאים ע״י מיליק אל הפרשה המתאימה במשנה תורה,
אהבה, הלכות תפילין, מזוזה וספר תורה (פרק ב, ד—ז), רואים אנו שבמאה השנייה היו הטכסטים
האלה כבר מגובשים מכל הבחינות.

18   בכתר ארם־צובה לא נשמרו פרשיות אלה (החלק של התורה הנמצא בארץ ישראל, ושמור
במכון בן־צבי, מתחיל בדב׳ כח, סו), אולם הרמב״ם הכין את רשימתו על יסוד כ״י של ר׳ אהרן
בן־אשר, כמו שהוא מעיד על זאת במשנה תורה (אהבה, הלכות תפילין וכו׳ פרק ז, ד: ״וספר
שסמכנו עליו בדברים אלו הוא הספר הידוע ... שהגיהו בן־אשר״): ראה על בעיות אלו: מחקרים
בכתר ארם־צובה מאת י. בן־צבי, מ. גושן־גוטשטיין, ד. ש. לוינגר (כתבי מפעל המקרא של האוני־
ברסיטה העברית) ירושלים תש״ך, ובאחרונה: ד. ש. לוינגר וא. קופפר ״תיקון ספר תורה של ר׳
יום ט״ב ליפמן מילהויזן״ (סיני, ס, תשכ״ז), במבוא, עמ׳ רלח—רמס.

קים של ר' מאיר: "כשאתה מלמד את בנך למדהו בספר מוגה" [19] (הזהרתו של רבי
עקיבא אל תלמידו ר' יוחנן): "הוי זהיר במלאכתך שמלאכתך מלאכת שמים היא
שמא אתה מחסר או מייתר אות אחת נמצאת מחריב את כל העולם כולו" [20]. (דברי
רבי ישמעאל אל רבי מאיר כשנודע לו שהוא מתפרנס מהעתקת ספרי קודש
לבלר).

איך אפשר להניח שרבי מאיר יעתיק לצרכי תינוקות של בית־רבן או לצרכי הקהל
טכסטים העשויים להטעותם וליצר ניגודים המכניסים מבוכה בלבם: הלוא אגדות
יהלכות היו בנויות גב על עניני מלא וחסר. אין ספק שייסדו גם על הקרי והכתיב
הלכות ואגדות [1ג]. אולם במקרים אלה הם מדגישים את העובדות אלה וידעו היטיב
להבחין בין שני הסוגים.

נימוקו של גורדיס [22] בקשר עם הקשיים הקשורים עם הכנת טכסט מוגה ומדויק
ג"כ אינם עומדים לפני הבקורת: הלוא לא יותר קשה הוא להעתיק טכסט פחות
מדויק מאשר טכסט מושלם; במשך הדורות עד ימינו אנו סופרי סת"ם יודעים
להעתיק במדויק ספרי תורה לצרכי שימוש בבית הכנסת; אף אם לפעמים נופלים
שגיאות בהעתקם, למרות כוונתם הטובה, מתקנים את אלה בלי קשיים.

אף אין לקבל לקבל השערתו של קוטשר [23] שבידי רבי מאיר הועתקו ספרי תורה
שהושפעו על ידי אכסמפלרים "מספרים בעלי הכתיב העממי או שהעתיק
אכסמפלרים לשם דרש".

לפי עניות דעתנו אנו מגיעים לפתרון מתאים יותר אם אנו מפרידים בין פעולתו
של רבי מאיר כסופר וכחכם: "איסי בן יהודה היה מונה שבחן של חכמים: רבי מאיר
חכם וסופר" [24].

כסופר היה בוודאי רבי מאיר זהיר ככל בעל מקצוע בדורו ואולי עוד
יותר להעתיק ספרי תורה מדוייקים בהחלטיות גמורה ובודאי לא סטה מן המקובל.
אכסמפלרים אלה לא היו מסומנים בשמו. אפשר בכל זאת שבגלל דייקנותם המיוחדת
יפעמים היו מדברים עליהם וכמובן, בלי להזכיר דוגמאות מהם, אולם התפרסם
האכסמפלר שלו שעל ג ל י ו נ ו הוא אסף גרסאות מיוחדות שמצא בהן ענין מאיזו
סיבה שהיא.

אפשר להניח שבתקופתו פנו אליו בשאלות מסוג זה, מאחר שהאכסספלרים שהיו
שמורים בבית המקדש כשהיה קיים נעלמו והיו מקרים שרצו לקבל חוות דעת
ממומחה מקצועי; אליו פנו בקשר עם קריאות פרובלימטיות. אולי גם לא מקרה
הוא שבטבריה נוסד מרכז רוחני שהחזיק מעמד במשך הדורות עד תום פעולתם
של אנשי משפחת בן־אשר וגם אחריהם [25]. מקומו של "העזרה" נתפס אולי ע"י בית
מדרש בטבריה שהיה מוקדש לבעיה זאת.

19 פסחים קיב, א; כתובות יט, ב.   20 עירובין יג, א; סוטה כ, א.
21 ראה ליברמן, עמ' 169, הערה 49.   22 ראה הערה 11.   23 ראה הערה 12.
24 גיטין סז, ב; ע"ע א. א. אורבך "הדרשה כיסוד ההלכה ובעית הסופרים" (תרביץ, כז, תשי"ח,
עמ' 166־182).
25 גם בית מדרש סורא שנוסד ע"י רב בהתחלת המאה השלישית החזיק מעמד עד
המאה הי"א (1037); אין ספק שהוקדשה בטבריה תשומת לב מיוחדת לבעיות נוסח המקרא
ומסורתו כבר בתקופת ר' מאיר ולא פסקה ההתעניינות בהן עד חורבנה ע"י הצלבנים.

עלינו עוד להביא בחשבון שבתקופה זאת — חוץ מהנוצרית־יהודית — כתות
שונות אחרות, השומרונים, ועוד, התחזקו בארץ ישראל והיו בעיות עם ספריהם
וגרסותיהם המיוחדות גם בקשר עם הפולמוס עמהן. הכרחי היה למצוא איש מקצוע
שיכול היה להכריע בבעיות המסובכות אלה.

כמו בתקופות הקודמת היתה לחקר הבלשני היוני השפעה מכריעה על הטיפול
בטכסטים המקראיים, שהוכחו בעליל במחקריו של ליברמן הנ״ל, כך יש לתאר
שהשפעה זאת התגברה דוקא בתקופתו של רבי מאיר.

לא לבד בקרב היהודים השפיעו שיטות מדעיות אלה על הטיפול בחקר נוסח
המקרא, אלא גם בקרב חוגים נוצריים. תקופת עבודתו ומקום פעילותו של אריגנס [?]
בעל ״הששיה״ קרובים הם מבחינות הזמן והמקום אל מקום ומועד פעילותו של
רבי מאיר.

בקשר עם שיטת סידורו של חומר ההלכה נסינו להוכיח שהשפעתו של אלישע בן
אבויה גדולה היתה על רבי מאיר [?]. אם בשטח ההלכה לא היסס ללמוד מרבו
״השלישי״ הזה את שיטת הסידור היונית, כך אפשר להניח שלמד אצלו גם השיטה
הבלשנית איך לטפל בטכסטים מקראיים בהתאם לדרישות המיוחדות בזמנו.

אמנם בשטח המקרא היו הנושאים רגישים יותר מאשר בקשר עם סידור חומר ההלכה.
ראשית כל מאחר שמבחינה ההלכה לא היו דפוסים מגובשים כל כך [?]. כמובן, עצם
התקשרותו של ר׳ מאיר עם אלישע בן אבויה עוררה חשד בחוגים רחבים ואינם
נלאים אנשי שני התלמודים והמדרשים למצוא הצדקה לקשר זה, ואין ספק שהיו
מסתייגים ממנו החוגים השמרנים בארץ ישראל, ולא לדבר על בבל, אם היה
מדובר בבעיות הקשורות בנוסח המקרא. על כן מובן, שכל העניינים הקשורים
בגרסאות שונות של התירה או בישעיהו לא מצאו הדים במקורות בבליים [?]. אולם
גם במדרשי אגדה של ארץ ישראל לא נכנסו רק אותם ״שינויי גרסה״ שהיה להן
איזו קשר עם יחסם אל הרומאים [?]. אפשר גם לתאר שבקרב הקהל הארציישראלי
היו נפוצים במיוחד שינויי גרסאות מסוג מדיני כאוסף מיוחד והדיהם של אלה
נשמרו בספרות המקובלת בארץ ישראל.

גם בימי הבינים הפיצו כיחידה נפרדת קטעים הקשורים עם בעיית תקופתם,
בלי שום קשר עם הנושא של תוכן כתב־היד העתיקו טכסטים כאלו בראשי או בסופי

---

26 פעל בקיסריה כמה עשרות שנים אחרי תקופת ר׳ מאיר.

27 Entwicklung unsere Traditionsliteratur mit Beruecksichtigung der juedischen
und der griechischen Kultur. Stellung M. Guttmanns in der juedischen Geistes-
geschichte (Jewish Studies in Memory of M. Gutmann, pp. XIII—XXXII),
Budapest 1946.

28 אופן סידור חומר ההלכה לא גובש עדיין במאות אלה ויש להניח שגם בתקופות הקודמות
היו נסיונות שג״כ הושפעו במקצת ע״י השיטה המדעית היוונית.

29 אין מן הנמנע שבכוונה התעלמו עורכי המקורות שמוצאם בבבל מחומר שלא היתה בהתאמה
לגישתם לבעיות נוסח המקרא; לפי הנחתנו גם סידור המשנה לפי שיטה חדשה לא היה לפי רוחם.
אולם מזה לא יכלו להתעלם בגלל תוכן הדברים והאישים הבולטים בשמם היה קשור אוסף זה.

30 גם במקומות שלא נזכרו במפורש הרומאים, כמו אלה הקשורים בתורה ואינם מזכירים שם
שאפשר היה לשנותו כדי שיצא ממנו רומא או רומי, מצאו קשר אחר שהיה מובן להם, למשל, אם
מדברים על פרעה (בר׳ מה, ח) או אם ראו את הגזמה בביטוי ״טוב מאד״ בקשר עם בריאת האדם
בראותם את אכזריותם ורשעתם של הרומאים בתקופתם.

האוספים. דוגמה טובה היא ההבאה הקטנה הקשורה באיכה ד, כא—כב: "שישי
ושמחי בת אדום... פקד עונך בת אדם: ק ו ש ט נ ט י נ א קרתא דאדום רשיעא
דמתבניאה בארץ א ר מ י נ י א ה בסגיאין אוכלסין דמן עמא דאדום... רומי
רשעא דמתבניאה ב א י ט ל י א ה ומליאה אוכלוסין מבני אדום..."[31] קטע זה
הופצה גם בשם "נבואה"[32].

אין פלא שכל רמז שהיה, יכולים ללמוד ממנו על מפלת אויבי נפשם בעתיד
משכה את לב הקוראים הן בארץ ישראל בימי שלטון הרומאים — בתקופת ר' מאיר
ואחריה — הן בגלות אדום בימי הבינים[33].

אולם אין כל ספק שחוץ משימנים אלה הקשורים עם הבעיות היומיומיות, היי
בספרו של רבי מאיר רשומים על הגליון גם גרסאות שלא היה להן קשר עם
שום בעיה מדינית: הוא אספם מאחר שמצא בהן ענין: אולי רק העדיף לרשום
בעיקר כאלה שהיו קשורים בעניני מדיניות או פולמוס עם כתות שונות?

ו. סיכום

ריבוי החומר, שמקורו אינו בקרב החוגים המסורתיים, מרשה לנו היום יותר
מאשר בעבר לגשת אל פתרון הבעיות מנקודות־ראות חדשה. כמו כן השגת מקורות
"פנימים", כמו רשימת שינויי ספר־התורה של בית כנסת סוירוס ברומא, שנשמרה
לפחות בסופי העתקי מקרא מקובלים, מאפשרת לנו הפרדת המקורות ולתפוס עמדה
חדשה לבעיותיהם.

אין כל ספק שגם בעיית בירור שינויי נוסח המובאים בשם רבי מאיר יקבל:
אור חדש על ידי מקורות "חיצוניים", כמו המגילות הגנוזות, אבל גם בספרות
התלמוד והמדרש ימצאו עוד החוקרים חומר חדש שיאפשר לנו לסקור את ההתפתחות
בתקופת תנאי ואמוראי ארץ ישראל. תחת השלטון הרומאי היתה בודאי גם ההשפעה
התרבותית היונית מכרעת שלא נחקרה עדיין די הצורך: על כל פנים מבחינה זאת
יש הבדלים יסודיים בין ארץ ישראל ובבל.

במיוחד יהיה מעניין אם יעלו רעיונות שישפכו אור על התפתחות חקר נוסח
המקרא בארץ ישראל בפרט ובכלל בטבריה, עיר שנעשתה בתקופת הנקדנים
כל כך בולטת מבחינת מסורת המקרא.

31 בדפוסים הנפוצים לא נשמר הטכסט הזה במהרתו, לכן הדפסנוהו פה על יסוד כ"י אורבינטי
מס' 1 שבואטיקן.

32 בהתחלת כ"י הספריה הלאומית בפריס, מס' 1178 משנת 1455, המכיל חיבור רפואי: הנה
אליו תשומת־לבי חברי, מר ב. ריצלר.

33 בסוף ס' תהלים, כ"י מס' 480 בפרמא שהועתק בשנת 1321.

378

ANCIENT CORRECTIONS IN THE TEXT OF THE OLD TESTAMENT (*Tikkun Sopherim*).

THE student of the Old Testament is so much accustomed to the story of the scrupulous care with which the Scribes guarded the Sacred Text, counting even its letters, that it comes as a shock to him to be told that, according to Jewish tradition, he has before him in eighteen places of his Hebrew Bible not the original text, but a text altered by the Scribes! In these eighteen passages, if we may believe a statement which has been frequently made, and perhaps never fully disproved, the original reading was altogether displaced from the MSS, as being unbecoming (or, indeed, in some cases, almost blasphemous), and a Scribes' emendation took its place, the memory of the original reading being preserved in tradition only.

The fullest account of the matter in English is to be found in Dr. Ginsburg's *Introduction to the Hebrew Bible*[1]; and Mr. T. H. Weir devotes some pages to it in his *Short History of the Hebrew Text of the Old Testament*. Dr. Buhl (*Kanon und Text des A. T.*, 1891) deals with the subject (pp. 103–105), and to some extent[2] accepts the theory (pp. 251 ff.). The 'Scribes' corrections,' in short, still attract considerable attention, and some of them are accepted by serious scholars.

Yet the evidence alleged for the theory is very thin. The early evidence is ambiguous, while what is unambiguous is too late to be of any real value. A Midrashic fancy; an ambiguous phrase; a misinterpretation; such seems to be the history of the growth of the doctrine of Scribes' emendation.

In the present paper I propose to examine the evidence with

---

[1] In which the theory of emendation is fully accepted.

[2] As far as regards the following passages:—Num. xi 15; 1 Sam. iii 13 (in part); Ezek. viii 17; Hab. i 12; Zech. ii 8 [12]; Job vii 20; Lam. iii 20.

Reprinted from *Journal of Theological Studies* 1 (1900).

regard to the eighteen passages, in order to discover whether it is sufficient to prove that our present text is indeed an altered text, and that the original readings are really preserved in our 'traditional' sources.

The evidence which is to be the subject of this inquiry is derived from authorities which may be divided into three classes, viz. the Midrashic, the Masoretic, and the Exegetical (commentators).

(A.) MIDRASHIM. (These may be roughly described as homiletic commentaries on books of the Old Testament. They are broadly distinguished from later exegetical works, such as those of Rashi, Aben Ezra, and Ḳimḥi, by their lack of literal and grammatical exegesis and of purely critical matter.) Those useful for the present inquiry are:—

(i) *Siphrē* (ed. Friedmann, Vienna, 1864, p. 22 b), a very early work, revised in the second century of the Christian era, and again in the third [1].

(ii) *Mechilta* (ed. Friedmann, Vienna, 1870, p. 39 a), composed in the second century, and revised perhaps towards the close of the same century [1].

(iii) Midrash *Tanḥuma* (Mantua, anno 323 = 1563 A.D., p. 32 b, col. 2), a late work in which *Mechilta* and an earlier Midrash *Tanḥuma* were used. The earlier *Tanḥuma* [2] (ed. S. Buber, Wilna, 1885) belongs to the fifth or sixth century.

To these some writers would add:—

(iv) *Yalkut Shimeoni* (ed. B. Lorje, Zolkiew, 1859), a compilation by R. Simon of Frankfort (1200–1250 A.D.) from the Midrashim. [Its evidence has not been cited in the important Table VI (below) owing to its secondary character.]

(B.) MASORETIC WORKS. (These deal with the text of the Old Testament, but rather as a fixed thing to be guarded in its integrity, than as subject to correction and improvement.) The chief of these are:—

(i) The printed Masorah found in Rabbinic Bibles (Bomberg's and Buxtorf's). (See the passage at the head of the book of Numbers, repeated in the margin of Ps. cvi 20.) Cited below as '*Masorah* (printed).'

[1] According to Schiller-Szinessy (*Encl. Brit.* MISHNAH) neither *Siphrī* nor *Mechilta* was written down before the sixth century A.D.

[2] According to Eppstein Buber's is the later recension. It does *not* contain the list of *tiḳḳun* passages.

(ii) The *Ochlah w'ochlah* (ed. Frensdorff, Hannover, 1864). There are two MSS of this work, one at Paris, from which Frensdorff printed his edition, containing four hundred articles, and one at Halle[1], containing over a thousand. This second MS, however, does not contain the list of *tikkun sopherim* passages, so that there is grave doubt whether the list belongs to the original form of the book *Ochlah*. The book in one form or another is older than Ḳimḥi (1155–1235 A.D.) who quotes it by name.

(iii) The Masorah found in Yemen MSS (B. M. Orient. 1379 of the fifteenth or sixteenth century, and 2349 of the year 1469 A.D., in the margin of Num. xii 12 (cf. Ginsburg, *Introduction to the Hebrew Bible*, p. 350).

(iv) The Masorah given at the foot of the page containing Zech. ii 12 [8] in the Codex *Petropolitanus Babylonicus* of the year 916 A.D., reproduced in facsimile by Herm. Strack, 1876.

(v) The list published from the Baer MS by S. Baer and H. Strack as an Appendix ('Anhang') to their edition of Ben Asher's Masoretic work *Dikdukē ha-teamim*. The editors seem to think (p. 44, note) that the list may be the work of Ben Asher himself, who flourished in the first half of the tenth century. It is cited in this paper as Ben Asher.

To the Masoretic lists may be added the isolated marginal notes attached to particular passages in Biblical MSS, asserting in each case that the particular passage is '*tikkun sopherim*,' or 'one of the eighteen *tikkun sopherim*.' From the mass of MSS I have singled out a few. Each contains Masorah, and is representative of an important or seemingly important class of MSS.

(*a*) Camb. Univ. Add. 465. Sephardic of the twelfth or thirteenth century. Contains the whole Bible. Valuable for its Masorah; cf. Schiller-Szinessy, *Catalogue of Hebrew MSS in Camb. Univ. Library*, pp. 18, 19.

(*b*) Brit. Mus. Orient. 2349. Yemenite of A.D. 1469. Contains the Pentateuch. Sometimes supposed to be valuable on account of its South Arabian origin.

(*c*) Brit. Mus. Orient. 1379 of the fifteenth or sixteenth century. Contains the Pentateuch. Probably also Yemenite.

(*d*) Codex *Babylonicus Petropolitanus* (quoted from Strack's facsimile edition of 1876). Finished in the year 916 A.D. Contains the 'Later Prophets' (i.e. Isaiah to Malachi). Valuable as being pointed[2] on the

---

[1] Described by H. Hupfeld in *ZDMG* xxi 201–220.
[2] Three or four columns are left unpointed; see Zech. xiv 5; Mal. i 5.

supralinear system and therefore as being probably different in *provenance* from the bulk of Biblical MSS. (The supposition, however, implied in the title 'Babylonicus' that it has any connexion with Babylon, or with some other place situated equally far towards the East, lacks sufficient support to be probable.)

(*e*) Camb. Univ. Taylor-Schechter Collection, Job ᵃ. A quarto fragment (centim. 37·5 × 38) of six leaves containing the beginning of Job. North African; 'very old' (Dr. Schechter). From the Genizah at Cairo.

(*f*) Camb. Univ. Taylor-Schechter Collection, Job ᵇ. A quarto (or folio) fragment consisting of the lower part of two leaves (centim. ? × 31). Contains some later verses of Job. Also from the Cairo Genizah [1].

(C.) COMMENTATORS.

(i) Rashi (obiit 1105 A.D.) of Troyes. I have compared the printed text of the Pentateuch as given in the Vienna Pentateuch (5 vols. 4to, 1859) with Camb. Univ. Add. 626, an important MS (fourteenth century) not used by Berliner for his edition (Berlin, 1866); see Schiller-Szinessy, *Catalogue*, p. 50. For the Prophets (Earlier and Later) I have compared the text printed in Bomberg's Bible (Venice, ed. 2) with Brit. Mus. Harley 150 of A.D. 1257, a MS which contains some important variations from the common text.

(ii) Aben Ezra (1090–1168 A.D.) of Toledo. I have compared the printed text in Job and Psalms with Brit. Mus. Add. 24896 (fifteenth century), and in Genesis and Numbers with Brit. Mus. Add. 26880 (A. D. 1401).

(iii) R. David Ḳimḥi (1155–1235 A. D.) of Narbonne.

Before tabulating and summarizing the evidence of the authorities specified above, I give two of the passages (one Midrashic from *Mechilta*, and one Masoretic from Cod. *Babyl. Petropol.*) in full, in order to illustrate the nature of this evidence.

(*a*) *Mechilta* (ed. Friedmann, 1870, p. 39 a) :—

'*And in the greatness of thine excellency thou overthrowest them that rise up against thee* [Ex. xv 7] that is "thou hast greatly magnified thyself against him who rose up against thee." And who are they who rose up against thee? They who rose up against thy sons. "Thou overthrowest them that rise up against *us*" is not written here, but "Thou overthrowest them that rise up against *thee*." It sheweth that every one

---

[1] Dr. Schechter most kindly called my attention to (*e*), and I am indebted to him and to the Master of St. John's College for permission to examine (*f*).

who riseth up against Israel is as if he rose up against the Holy One (Blessed be He!) . . . And similarly it saith (וכה"א), *And he that toucheth them* (בהם) *is as he that toucheth the apple of his eye* [Zech. ii 8, not M.T.]. Rabbi Jehudah[1] saith, "The apple of an eye" it saith not, but "The apple of his eye" is written; it concerns (if such a thing may be said) the Exalted One, but the Scripture has employed euphemism (אלא שכינה הכתוב). Of the same class (כיוצא בו) is [the passage], *Ye say also, Behold what a weariness is it! and ye have snuffed at it* [Mal. i 13], but the Scripture has employed euphemism. Of the same class is, *For the iniquity which he knew, because his sons did bring a curse upon themselves*[2], &c. [1 Sam. iii 13], but the Scripture has employed euphemism. Of the same class is, *Why hast thou set me as a mark for thee, so that I am a burden to myself* [Job vii 20]: the Scripture has employed euphemism. Of the same class is, *Art not thou my king from everlasting, O Lord God, that we die not*[3] (ולא נמות) [Hab. i 12, not M.T.]: the Scripture has employed euphemism. Of the same class is, *Hath a nation changed their gods which yet are no gods? but my people have changed their glory* [Jer. ii 11]: the Scripture has employed euphemism. Of the same class is, *Thus they changed their glory for the likeness of an ox* [Ps. cvi 20]: the Scripture has employed euphemism. [4]*And let me not see my wretchedness* [Num. xi 15]: the Scripture has employed euphemism. Of the same class is, *We have no portion in David . . . every man to his tents, O Israel* [2 Sam. xx 1]: the Scripture has employed euphemism. *And, lo, they put the branch to their nose* [Ezek. viii 17]: the Scripture has employed euphemism. *When he cometh out of his mother's womb* [Num. xii 12]: (*from our mother's womb* one should have said:) the Scripture has employed euphemism. Also here thou sayest, *He that toucheth him* (בו) *is as he that toucheth the apple of his eye*. The Scripture speaketh (if such a thing may be said) concerning the Exalted One, but the Scripture has employed euphemism.'

(The passage from *Siphrē* reckoned above among the authorities for this paper is closely parallel, but offers a shorter text.)

It may be remarked on the passage from *Mechilta*:

(1) that the *Ṭikkun* list seems to be ascribed to R. Jehudah

---

[1] R. Jehudah ben Ilai (first half of second century A. D.).

[2] Quoted from the R.V., which is used as far as possible for the quotations given in this paper.

[3] *Siphrē* (in the parallel place) reads, *that I die not* (ולא אמות), though otherwise it agrees with M.T.

[4] The usual formula seems to have fallen out.

ben Ilai, the pupil of R. Akiva and of R. Tarphon. (Notice the return to Zech. ii. 8 [12] at the close.)

(2) that the isolated emendation given, viz. that on Num. xii 12 is not free from suspicion of interpolation. It is indeed found in *Siphrē*; but here it reads like an addition to the original text. The text of most Midrashim seems to have been in a 'fluid' state during the early centuries.

(*b*) Cod. *Babylonicus Petropolitanus* (in a footnote referring to Zech. ii 8 [12]):—

'Eighteen words are *tikkun sopherim*: *But Abraham* [Gen. xviii 22]: *My wretchedness* [Num. xi 15]: *Out of his mother's womb* [Num. xii 12]: *Did bring a curse* [1 Sam. iii 13]: *The branch* [Ezek. viii 17]: *We shall not die* [Hab. i 12]: *Have changed their glory* [Jer. ii 11]: *Each man*[1] *to your tents, O Israel* [1 Kings xii 16], twice in the verse; and the parallel passage of Chronicles, twice in the verse: *And yet had condemned* [Job xxxii 3]: *So that I am* [Job vii 20]: *Profane*[2] [Mal. i 12]: *And ye have snuffed* [Mal. i 13]: *Thus they changed* [Ps. cvi 20]: *Rob* [Mal. iii 8, 9]: *The apple of his eye* [Zech. ii 8].

This is the oldest Masoretic reference which we can date to *tikkun sopherim*. It may be remarked:—

(1) No kind of hint is given as to the nature of the process called *tikkun sopherim*.

(2) The list of passages differs from other lists of eighteen.

(3) No alternative reading is given in any passage.

Thus it can be seen that the ancient evidence of *Mechilta* and the Codex *Babylonicus* goes very little way indeed towards supporting the common theory of Scribes' emendation. We have two lists of Biblical passages, one of eleven, which speaks of the employment of euphemism in Scripture, the other of sixteen, which speaks of *tikkun sopherim* without giving any explanation of the phrase. The two lists between them suggest *at the most* one possible various reading. Not a promising beginning for those who wish to establish the common theory!

Most of the evidence which remains exists in a form similar to one or other of the two forms already given. For presenting this remainder tabular statements are most convenient, and

---

[1] The word ‏אִישׁ‎, 'each man,' belongs rightly to 2 Sam. xx 1.

[2] A verb.

accordingly six tables are given here, viz. (I) a table of the number of passages affected by *tikkun sopherim*, according to different authorities; (II) the identification of the passages according to Midrashic sources; (III) the same according to Masoretic sources; (IV) the same according to marginal notes in Biblical MSS; (V) the same according to the commentators Rashi and Aben Ezra; (VI) a table of the passages, their supposed 'original readings,' and the authorities for and against.

TABLE I.

The number of tikkun sopherim *according to different authorities.*

Siphrē	7[1]
[Yalkut]	10[2]
[Midrash Haggadol]	10[3]
Mechilta	11
Rashi	11[4]
Masorah (printed)	[16[5]]
Tanhuma (later form)[6]	18[7]
Masorah of Codex *Petropolitanus*	18[8]
Ochlah (Paris MS)[9]	18
Kimhi	18[10]
Masorah of Yemenite MSS	18[11]
Ben Asher	18

[1] *Seven* instances (*eight* reckoning two in Num. xii 12) are given in Friedmann's edition, and Rashi (according to Brit. Mus. Harley 150, though not according to printed editions) says on Hab. i 12 that *seven* instances of *tikkun* are found in *Siphrē*.

[2] Job vii 20 is omitted, perhaps through homoeoteleuton; otherwise the list is the same as in *Mechilta*.

[3] Num. xi 15 is omitted.

[4] On Mal. i 13 (printed text = B. M. Harley 150).

[5] Seventeen, if two instances are to be counted in Num. xii 12; eighteen according to the heading of the list.

[6] The passage giving a list of *tikkun sopherim* is absent from the (probably) earlier recension of *Tanhuma* published by S. Buber.

[7] Counting two instances in Num. xii 12.

[8] Counting two *tikkun* in Malachi not given in other sources, except that one appears in Ben Asher.

[9] The list of *tikkun sopherim* is absent from the Halle MS of *Ochlah*.

[10] On Ezek. viii 17.

[11] The list is the same in contents, but not in arrangement, with that in *Ochlah* (Paris MS).

TABLE II.

Midrashic Lists.

Second or third century. *Siphrē.*	Second century. *Mechilta*[1] (= *Yalkut*).	Century ? *Tanḥuma* (common recension).
Zech. ii 12 [8]	Zech. ii 12 [8]	Zech. ii 12 [8][2]
Job vii 20	Mal. i 13	Mal. i 13[2]
Ezek. viii 17	1 Sam. iii 13	1 Sam. iii 13
Hab. i 12	[Job vii 20][3]	Job vii 20[2]
Ps. cvi 20	Hab. i 12	Hab. i 12[4]
Num. xi 15	Jer. ii 11	Jer. ii 11[2]
Num. xii 12	Ps. cvi 20	Ps. cvi 20[2]
	Num. xi 15	Hos. iv 7[2]
	2 Sam. xx 1	Job xxxii 3
	Ezek. viii 17[5]	Gen. xviii 22
	Num. xii 12[5]	Num. xi 15
		Num. xii 12[2]
		1 Kings xii 16
Sixth century. *Breshith Rabba.*		2 Chron. x 16
Gen. xviii 22		Lam. iii 20
		2 Sam. xvi 12[2]
		Ezek. viii 17[2]

[1] Rashi (on Mal. i 13) speaks of *eleven* words of 'ס 'ת, but he includes (elsewhere) Gen. xviii 22 and Job xxxii 3, which do not appear among the eleven instances of *Mechilta*. For *Mid. Gad.* see Note II at the end of this article.

[2] Quoted according to the supposed original reading.

[3] Omitted (perhaps through homoeoteleuton) in *Yalkut*.

[4] Quoted with the reading ימות.

[5] Transposed in *Yalkut*.

TABLE III. *Masoretic Lists.*

Sixteenth century. *Masorah interior.* Printed in the Bibles of Bomberg and Buxtorf.	Fifteenth century. *Yemen Masorah.* (B.M. Orient. 1379 and 2349.)	916 A.D. *Masorah.* (Cod. *Petropolitanus Babylonicus.*)	Twelfth century? *Ochlah w'ochlah.* (Paris MS¹.)	[Tenth?] Century? Ben Asher (Baer MS²).
Gen. xviii 22	Gen. xviii 22	Gen. xviii 22	Gen. xviii 22	Gen. xviii 22
Num. xi 15	Num. xi 15	Num. xi 15	Num. xi 15	Num. xi 15
Num. xii 12 (*semel*, בבא אשר)	Num. xii 12 (*bis*)	Num. xii 12 (*semel*, מברכ אשר)	Num. xii 12 (*bis*)	Num. xii 12 (*bis*)
1 Sam. iii 13	1 Sam. iii 13	1 Sam. iii 13	1 Sam. iii 13	1 Sam. iii 13
2 Sam. xvi 12	2 Sam. xvi 12	Ezek. viii 17	2 Sam. xvi 12	2 Sam. xvi 12
2 Sam. xx 1	1 Kings xii 16 (*bis*)	Hab. i 12	1 Kings xii 16 (*semel*)	1 Kings xii 16 (*semel* vid.)
Ezek. viii 17	2 Chron. x 16 (*bis*)	Jer. ii 11	2 Chron. x 16 (*semel*)	2 Chron. x 16 (*semel* vid.)
Hab. i 12	Ezek. viii 17	1 Kings xii 16 (*bis*)	Jer. ii 11	Hab. i 12
Mal. i 13	Mal. i 13	2 Chron. x 16 (*bis*)	Ezek. viii 17	Mal. i 12
Zech. ii 12 [8]	Zech. ii 12 [8]	Job xxxii 3	Hos. iv 7	Mal. i 13
Jer. ii 11	Jer. ii 11	Job vii 20	Hab. i 12	Zech. ii 12 [8]
Job vii 20	Hos. iv 7	Mal. i 12	Zech. ii 12 [8]	Jer. ii 11
Hos. iv 7	Hab. i 12	Mal. i 13	Mal. i 13	Ps. cvi 20
Job xxxii 3	Job vii 20	Ps. cvi 20	Ps. cvi 20	Job vii 20
Lam. iii 20	Job xxxii 3	Mal. iii 8, 9	Job vii 20	Job xxxii 3
Ps. cvi 20	Lam. iii 20	Zech. ii 12 [8]	Job xxxii 3	Lam. iii 20
	Ps. cvi 20		Lam. iii 20	Hos. iv 7

¹ This list is wanting in the Halle MS.
² This list is published as an appendix to Baer and Strack's edition (1879) of Ben Asher's *Diḳduḳē ha-ṭ'amim* (tenth century).

TABLE IV.

Passages to which the note 'ס 'ח, or the like, is added in specified Biblical MSS.

Num. xi 15 (*a*) (*b*) (*c*)	Mal. i 12 (*d*)
Num. xii 12 (*b*) (*c*)	Mal. i 13 (*d*)
Ezek. viii 17 (*d*)	Job vii 20 (*e*)
Zech. ii 12 [8] (*d*)	Job xxxii 3 (*a*) (*f*)

(*a*) Camb. Univ. Add. 465 (whole Bible). (*b*) Brit. Mus. Orient. 2349 (Pentateuch). (*c*) Brit. Mus. Orient. 1379 (Pentateuch). (*d*) *Babylonicus Petropolitanus* (Later Prophets). (*e*) Camb. Univ. Taylor-Schechter Collection, Job ᵃ. (*f*) Camb. Univ. T.-S. Collection, Job ᵇ.

*** This Table is intended to illustrate the unsystematic way in which the note 'ס 'ח is added in the margin in MSS well furnished with Masorah. The results for (*d*) and still more for (*a*) are striking.

TABLE V.

Passages mentioned by Rashi and Aben Ezra [1] *in reference to* tiḳḳun ṣopherim.

Rashi (asserts *tiḳḳun*).	Aben Ezra [2] (repudiates *tiḳḳun*).
Gen. xviii 22	Gen. xviii 22
Num. xi 15	Num. xi 15
Num. xii 12 [3]	Num. xii 12
[1 Sam. iii 13] [4]	[Ps. cvi 20 [5]]
Hab. i 12	Job vii 20
Mal. i 13	Job xxxii 3
Ps. cvi 20 [6]	Hab. i 12 [7]
Job xxxii 3 [8]	

[1] I have not examined fully the evidence of Ḳimḥi, whose later date makes him of less importance as a witness, but according to the printed text he does not notice *tiḳḳun* in connexion with Jer. ii 11 ; Hos. iv 7 ; Zech. ii 12 (*in locis*).

[2] Aben Ezra rejects the ordinary theory of *tiḳḳun ṣopherim* in the *Sepher Çahoth* ; and in his Commentaries he nowhere (so far as I can discover) accepts the *tiḳḳun* tradition as yielding trustworthy textual evidence.

[3] Two instances according to the printed text, one only (אמנו for אמו) in C. U. Add. 626.

[4] In the printed text, but omitted in B. M. Harley 150.

[5] Aben Ezra deals with this passage as an instance of כינוי , comparing 2 Sam. xii 14, but he does not use the term 'ס 'ח in connexion with it.

[6] Not mentioned *in loco*, but cited on Job xxxii 3, according to the common texts, but not according to the Mendelssohnian Bible (Fürth, anno 565 [1805]).

[7] In the *Sepher Çahoth* p. 74 b.

[8] I have not been able to consult any MS with which to check the printed text, though the passage is an important one.

TABLE VI. *The tikkun passages and their emendations.*

Passage according to M. T.	Alternative 'reading' supposed to be original.	Authorities giving the alternative reading.	Authorities giving no alternative reading, but applying the terms 'ח"ס or 'ח"ל to the passage.	Authorities silent altogether as to the existence of an alternative.
(1) Gen. xviii 22, 'But Abraham stood yet before the Lord.'	'But the Lord stood yet before Abraham.'	Rashi. Ben Asher. *Ochlah.* Yemen Masorah.	*Tanḥuma; Bresh. R. Masorah*(of Cod. Bab. Pet. and printed). [Aben Ezra, 'No need for 'ת 'ס.']	*Siphrē; Mechilta. Mid. Gad.*
(2) Num. xi 15, 'And let me not look upon my wretchedness' ('evil,' בְּרָעָתִי).	'And let me not look upon thy evil' (בְּרָעָתֶךָ).	Rashi (on Job xxxii 3). Ben Asher. *Ochlah.* Yemen Masorah.	*Siphrē; Mechilta. Tanḥuma. Masorah* (printed). [Aben Ezra, 'No need for 'ת 'ה.']	(For *Mid. Gad.* see Note II at the end of this article.)
	'And let me not look upon their evil' (בְּרָעָתָם).	Rashi, *in loco.*		
(3) Num. xii 12, 'Let her not be as one born dead, whose flesh is half consumed when he cometh forth from his mother's womb.'	'Let her not be as one born dead when he cometh out of our mother's womb, so that half of our flesh should be consumed.'	[*Mechilta*[1]]; *Tan-ḥuma*[2]; *Mid. Gad.*[1] Rashi[2]. Ben Asher.[2] *Ochlah*[2]. Yemen Masorah[2]. [2] Double tikkun.	*Siphrē*[2]. *Masorah*(of Cod. Bab. Pet. and printed[3]). [Aben Ezra, 'No need for 'ת 'ה.']	[3] Single tikkun ('Our flesh').

[1] Single tikkun ('Our mother').

[2] Double tikkun.

TABLE VI (continued).

Passage according to M.T.	Alternative 'reading' supposed to be original.	Authorities giving the alternative reading.	Authorities giving no alternative reading, but applying the terms ק'ח or ה דל' to the passage.	Authorities silent altogether as to the existence of an alternative.
(4) 1 Sam. iii 13, 'For the iniquity which he knoweth, because his sons were cursing themselves' (מקללים להם).	'For the iniquity which he knoweth, because his sons were cursing me' (מק' לי).	[Rashi(in loco ק'ל'ה).] Ochlah. Mid. Gad.	Mechilta. Tanḥuma. Masorah(of Cod. Bab. Pet. and printed).	Siphrē.
	'... were cursing him.'	Ben Asher (vid.). Yemen Masorah.		
(5) 2 Sam. xvi 12, 'It may be that the Lord will look upon my eye' (בעיני).[1]	'...will look with his eyes' (בעינו).	Tanḥuma, Stettin edition, anno 624 [1864].	Masorah (printed).	Rashi, in loco. Siphrē. Mechilta. Cod. Bab. Pet.
	'...will look upon my trouble' (בעניי).	Masorah (printed). B. M. Orient. 1379.		
	'...will look with his eye' (בעינו).	Tanḥuma, Mantua edition, anno 323 [1563]. Ben Asher; Ochlah.		
(6) 2 Sam. xx 1, 'Every man to his tents (לאהליו), O Israel.'	[vide infra.]		Mechilta. Masorah (printed).	All other authorities.

¹ So Kri; 'on the wrong done unto me' R.V. following the C'thib, בעיני.

TABLE VI (*continued*).

1 Kings xii 16, 'So Israel departed unto his tents' (לאהליו).	['So Israel departed unto his gods' (לאלהיו)¹.]	Ben Asher, *Ochlah*, *Yemen Masorah*, *Tanḥuma*²(all supplying same *tikkun* in Chron.).	*Cod. Bab. Pet.*	*Siphrē*. *Mechilta*. Rashi, *in loco*.
(7) Ezek. viii 17, 'And, lo, they put the branch to their nose' (אפם אל).	'And, lo, they put the branch to my nose' (אפי אל). '... his nose' (אל אפו).	*Tanḥuma*; *Mid. Gad.* *Yemen Masorah*. R. D. Ķimḥi. *Ochlah*.	*Siphrē*; *Mechilta*. *Masorah*(of *Cod. Bab. Pet.* and printed).	Rashi, *in loco*. Ben Asher.
(8) Hab. i 12, 'Art not thou from everlasting, O Lord, my God, my Holy One? we shall not die' (נמות אל).	'... my Holy One, [who] diest not' (תמות). '... my Holy One, he who dieth not' (ימות).	Rashi, *in loco*. Ben Asher. *Ochlah*. *Yemen Masorah*. *Mid. Gad.* *Tanḥuma*.	*Siphrē*; *Mechilta*. *Masorah*(of *Cod. Bab. Pet.* and printed).	
(9) Mal. i 13, 'And ye have snuffed at it' (אותו).	'And ye have snuffed at me' (אתי).	Rashi, *in loco*. *Tanḥuma*; *Mid. Gad.* Ben Asher. *Ochlah* and *Yemen Masorah*.	*Mechilta*. *Masorah*(of *Cod. Bab. Pet.* and printed).	*Siphrē*.

¹ The *Masorah* (of *Yemen* and of *Cod. Bab. Pet.*) has, it appears, a double *tikkun*, 'To thy gods' only, and has no mention of Chron.
² Bible text influenced by 2 Sam. xx 1. 'To thy gods . . . unto his gods.' *Mid. Gad.* has 'To 2 Sam. xx 1.

TABLE VI (continued).

Passage according to M.T.	Alternative 'reading' supposed to be original.	Authorities giving the alternative reading.	Authorities giving no alternative reading, but applying the terms 'כנה or 'ת to the passage.	Authorities silent altogether as to the existence of an alternative.
(10) Zech. ii 12 [8], 'Thus saith the Lord of hosts, ... He that toucheth you toucheth the apple of his eye' (עינו).	'... He that toucheth you toucheth the apple of my eye' (עיני).	*Tanḥuma; Mid. Gad.* Ben Asher. Ochlah. *Yemen Masorah?* Shemoth R. (§ 13).	*Siphrē.* [*Mechilta* [1]] *Masorah*(of Cod.*Bab. Pet.* and printed).	Rashi, *in loco.* R. D. Kimḥi, *in loco.*
(11) Jer. ii 11, 'But my people have changed their glory (כבודו) for that which doth not profit.'	'... my glory (כבודי) ...'	*Tanḥuma; Mid. Gad.* Ben Asher. Ochlah. *Yemen Masorah.*	*Mechilta.* *Masorah*(of Cod.*Bab. Pet.* and printed).	Rashi. R. D. Kimḥi. *Siphrē.*
(12) Job vii 20, 'Why hast thou set me as a mark for thee, so that I am a burden to myself?' (עלי).	'...So that I am a burden to thee' (עליך).	*Tanḥuma; Mid. Gad.* Ben Asher. Ochlah. *Yemen Masorah.*	[Aben Ezra [3].] *Siphrē; Mechilta.* *Masorah*(of Cod.*Bab. Pet.* and printed).	Rashi, *in loco.*
(13) Hos. iv 7, 'I will change their glory (כבודם) into shame.'	'... my glory (כבודי) ...'	*Tanḥuma.* Ben Asher. Ochlah. *Yemen Masorah.*	*Masorah* (printed).	Rashi; R. D. Kimḥi. *Siphrē; Mechilta. Cod. Bab. Pet.*
(14) Job xxxii 3, 'And yet they had condemned God' (or 'the Lord'	'... condemned God' (or 'the Lord'	[Rashi, *in loco* [4].]	*Masorah* (printed). *Tanḥuma.*	*Siphrē; Mechilta. Cod. Bab. Pet.*

[1] See above, p. 391.   [3] See below, p. 412.

[2] B. M. Orient. 1379 is defective here.   [4] See below, p. 412.

TABLE VI (continued).

Job' (יראו את אלהים).	or — euphemistically —'the Judgement').	Ben Asher. [Yemen Masorah and Ochlah,'condemned the Judgement,' an euphemism.]		[Aben Ezra, i. l.]
(15) Lam. iii 20, 'And my soul sinketh down upon thee' (עלי).	'And my soul (נפשי) is bowed down within me' (עלי). 'And thy soul(נפשך) will mourn over me' (עלי)[1].	Ben Asher. Ochlah. Yemen Masorah.	Masorah (printed). Tanḥuma.	Siphrē; Mechilta. Rashi; Aben Ezra. Cod. Bab. Pet.
(16) Ps. cvi 20, 'Thus they changed their glory (כבודם) for the likeness of an ox.'	'. . . my glory (כבודי) . . .'	Ben Asher. Ochlah. Yemen Masorah. Tanḥuma; Mid. Gad.	Siphrē; Mechilta. Masorah(of Cod. Bab. Pet. and printed).	[Rashi[2].] Aben Ezra[3].
(17) Mal. i 12, 'But ye profane it' (אותו).	'But ye profane me' (אותי).	Ben Asher.	Masorah(of Cod. Bab. Pet.).	Rashi. Siphrē; Mechilta. Tanḥuma. Ochlah. Masorah (Yemen, and printed).
(18) Mal. iii 8, 9, 'Ye rob me' (bis).	[Not known.]	[No authorities.]	Masorah(of Cod. Bab. Pet.).	All other authorities.

[1] So Dr. Ginsburg, Introduction to the Hebrew Bible, p. 361; Dr. Buhl, Kanon des A. T., p. 105.
[2] See below, p. 411.
[3] See below, p. 411.

VOL. I.

D d

393

From a study of the contents of the foregoing tables we may draw several deductions :—

(1) The *tiḳḳun* tradition lacks definiteness as to (i) the number of passages affected, (ii) the identity of the passages, (iii) the nature of the change made or supposed to be made in the text.

(2) The tradition (in one form or another) is a favourite element in the Midrashim, including the earliest known.

(3) The tradition has not an undisputed position in the *Masorah*, as the following facts show :—

   (a) It is doubtful if it had a place in Ben Asher's *Diḳduḳē*.

   (b) It is not found in the Halle MS of *Ochlah*.

   (c) It is only casually noted in Biblical MSS which are provided with *Masorah*.

   (d) The authority of the printed *Masorah* (in which the *tiḳḳun* list is found) is doubtful, for it is not known whether it rests on direct authority of MSS or not.

(4) The two earliest commentators of greatest name either fail to support the tradition in its fullness (Rashi), or treat it as a thing which may be set aside (Aben Ezra).

From the first three of these deductions we may, I think, tentatively draw a fresh conclusion, viz. *The tiḳḳun tradition belongs rather to Midrash than to Masorah*, i.e. its true bearing is on exegesis, not on textual criticism ; the *tiḳḳunē ṣopherim* are interpretations not readings. This conclusion can, I believe, be verified (i) by an examination of the terms used in the oldest authorities in rendering the tradition, (ii) by a detailed examination of the evidence alleged for each case of *tiḳḳun*.

(i) The terms used in our authorities with regard to these passages are many ; *tiḳḳun ṣopherim* is only one form out of a dozen. Yet a careful scrutiny leaves us with two formulas only which are ancient, from which all the rest appear to be derived ; these two formulas are כינה הכתוב ('the Scripture has employed euphemism ')[1] and תיקון סופרים ('scribes' correction')[2]. Now the first thing to be noted is that the latter formula is ambiguous, while the former bears an unmistakable meaning.

[1] *Siphrī*; *Mechiltā*; *Ochlah*; Ben Asher; [*Yemen Masorah*; *Tanḥuma*].
[2] *Breshith Rabba*; *Masorah* of Cod. *Bab. Pet.* [and of Yemen]; printed *Masorah*; [*Tanḥuma*].

The phrase 'the Scripture[1] has employed euphemism' is irreconcilable with the theory that the text of Scripture has been
altered by transcribers. It means not that a euphemism has
been introduced into Scripture, but that it was already found
there and noted. The second phrase 'ס 'ת 'scribes' correction'
stands on different ground. It is ambiguous, and *two* views of its
meaning seem to have been taken by the Jews themselves.

According to one view *tikkun sopherim* was a *viva voce*
correction (or modification) of Scriptural language authorized
for homiletic purposes by the Scribes. This seems to be the
meaning of the phrase adopted in the printed Masorah and
in Ben Asher. The printed Masorah heads its list with the
title י"ח מלין בקריאה תקון סופרים, 'the eighteen expressions [which]
in reading [are] *tikkun sopherim*.' Similarly Ben Asher introduces his list with the remark that *They are not written
according to their tikkun, but the wise men of Israel read them
with tikkun sopherim* (קורין אותם בת' ס'[2]). The scribes interpret
a supposed euphemism, and their interpretation is called *tikkun
sopherim*.

The other sense given to the phrase *tikkun sopherim* seems
to be that of a 'change' (mental, not written) made by the
original writers or redactors of Scripture. 'Our Rabboth' writes
Rashi[3] 'turned back in writing thus' (on Gen. xviii 22), i.e. they
recoiled from putting into writing a thought which some of their
readers might expect them to express. A number of phrases in
which the *tikkun* is connected with Ezra and the Great Synagogue
arise, it seems, from this view.

Such phrases are :—

(1) '*Tikkun* of Ezra' (margin of Yemenite Masorah).
(2) '*Tikkun* of Ezra and the scribes' (Cod. Taylor-Schechter, Job [b]).
(3) '*Tikkun* of Ezra and Nehemiah and Zechariah and Haggai and
Baruch' (Cod. Taylor-Schechter, Job [a]).
(4) '*Tikkun* of the scribes, even of the men of the Great Synagogue'
(*Tanhuma*).
(5) '*Tikkun* of the scribes, or as some say *Tikkun* of Ezra' (*Yemen
Masorah*).

---

[1] The Heb. הכתוב corresponds with the Greek τὸ γεγραμμένον or τὸ γραφέν.
[2] Surely not ' call them *tikkun sopherim*.'
[3] Or the editor of Rashi's Commentary, see below, p. 405.

To these may be added :—

(6) 'Ezra made a *tikkun*' (תקן עזרא; *Ochlah* in its heading to the passages).

(7) 'The scribes made a *tikkun*' (Rashi on Job xxxii 3)[1].

Probably the *tikkun* tradition is connected with the tradition which ascribes the redaction of several books of Scripture to the Great Synagogue. According to 4 Esdras xiv 19 ff., Ezra, with five companions, re-wrote under inspiration the Law (the whole Old Testament apparently ; *omne quod factum est in saeculo ab initio, quae erant in lege tua inscripta*) which had been burnt, presumably by the Chaldeans. This tradition was a favourite one with the Fathers, from Irenaeus downwards (Bensly-James, *Fourth Book of Ezra, Texts and Studies*, vol. iii, no. 2, p. xxxvii), but in origin it is almost certainly Jewish. Certainly those scholars who disbelieve in the existence of the Great Synagogue ought to feel their belief in the ordinary doctrine of *tikkun sopherim* shaken.

(ii) It now remains to examine each instance of *tikkun sopherim* by itself, in order to decide by a consideration of external evidence, and of internal probability, whether it is likely that our present text is an altered form, and that the original form is preserved in the *tikkun* tradition.

The first passage to be examined is Gen. xviii 22. It is not marked as *tikkun* in the earliest Midrashim, *Siphrē* and *Mechilta*, but the *Breshith Rabba* (sixth century) xlix 7, has the remark, 'R. Simon said, This is *tikkun sopherim*, for the Shechinah was tarrying for Abraham.' The fuller form of the same comment is preserved in the *Midrash Shemoth* (not earlier than the tenth century ?) xli 4, 'R. Simon said, Come and see what is written, *And the men rose up from thence and looked toward Sodom* (Gen. xviii 16), &c. It was due [for the Scripture] to say (לא היה צריך לומר אלא), *And the Lord stood yet before Abraham*, but it is *tikkun sopherim*.' The tradition quoted in the name

---

[1] The terms in which *tikkun* (or *kinnui*, as the writer prefers to call it) is described in Ben Asher are at first sight mutually contradictory. The list itself begins thus :—'*And Abraham stood yet.* "And the Lord stood yet" it was, but the Scripture has employed euphemism.' The phrase ' it was ' (היה) is, however, probably an abbreviation of the phrase used in *Ochlah*, 'One should have said' (הצ"ל). [Cf. the היה לו ומר of *Mechilta* (on Num. xii 12).] The preface to the list denies that the *sopherim* ' blotted out and wrote afresh.'

of R. Simon is to the effect that the author of the text quoted wrote one thing, when it was to be expected that he would have written quite another. He employed euphemism. There is nothing here of a transcriber emending the text which lay before him. The comment of Rashi on this place is based upon R. Simon's tradition, but it is somewhat fuller in wording. Its conclusion runs thus, 'This is *tiḳḳun ṣopherim* : [for our Rabboth made a change ("turned back") in writing thus (שהפכו רבות לכתוב כן[1])].' The bracketed words (the genuineness of which is doubtful), though at first sight they seem to favour the common theory of *tiḳḳun ṣopherim*, will nevertheless bear an explanation which yields no support to the theory. 'Our Rabboth' may be identified with the *ṣopherim* just mentioned, and by the *ṣopherim* we may understand, as has been said above, the original writers or redactors of books of Scripture. The statement that these writers or redactors 'made a change' or 'turned back' in writing ver. 22 b is easy of explanation. After writing that '*the* [*three*] *men' went towards Sodom*, the natural continuation was to write, *But the Lord stood yet by* (על[2]) *Abraham*. But something checked the pen before it could write the bold words ; there was a *change*, and the Scripture ran, *But Abraham stood yet before the Lord*. Thus since the meaning of the clause is ambiguous and its genuineness doubtful, this comment does not justify us in counting Rashi as a witness for the common theory of *tiḳḳun ṣopherim*. It may be added that the versions (Targum, Peshitta, LXX [3], Vulgate) give no hint of the supposed 'original reading.' A' Σ' Θ' in Field's *Hexapla* are silent. Kautzsch and Socin in their German edition of Genesis (1888), in which the 'Quellenschriften' are distinguished typographically, take the 'original reading' into the text. Delitzsch, however, who had more Rabbinical learning than Kautzsch and Socin, rejects it.

The next instance is Num. xi 15. Here *Siphrē* (ed. Friedmann, p. 25 a) gives the paraphrase, 'Let me not look upon the retribution which is to come *upon them.*' Rashi accordingly writes *in loco*, ' *Their wretchedness* (or "*their evil*" ברעתם) one should have written, but the Scripture has employed

---

[1] Quoted from C. U. Add. 626 ; the clause is omitted in some MSS, cf. Berliner, *in loco*.

[2] So Rashi (according to C. U. Add. 626).   [3] Cod. A ; Lucian ; *hiat* B.

euphemism; and this is one of the *tikkunē sopherim*[1] for the euphemizing and correction (תקון) of the language.' The same writer, however (on Job xxxii 3), has a different remark on the text of Num. xi 15. He writes: '*Thy wretchedness* (or "*Thy evil*" ברעתך) one should have written, but the Scripture has employed euphemism.' Thus we have two 'original readings' offered us by one authority in the place of the present Masoretic reading, *My wretchedness*. The inference can hardly be avoided that *Siphrē* and Rashi are not stating facts, but offering suggestions; they are as it were playing with the text in order to point out that Moses' evil was the people's evil, and that a people's evil was their God's evil. This is plainly the view of Aben Ezra (*in loco*) who points out that the reading *My wretchedness* gives good sense, and then adds 'and there is no need for *tikkun sopherim*.' This is not the way in which one would speak of a real variant. Again the versions (Targum, Peshitta[2], Vulgate[3]) give no support to the 'original reading.' LXX B has τὴν κάκωσιν *sine add.*, a reading which may be significant, but cod. A and Lucian have μου, and the Lyons Pentateuch (O. L.) *meam*, in agreement with the M.T. A' Σ' Θ' in Field are silent. The common interpretation of the *tikkun* tradition breaks down hopelessly in this instance. The evidence for classing Num. xi 15 among the *tikkun* (or *kinnui*) passages is very early (*Siphrē* and *Mechilta*), but early evidence fails to prove that a genuine various reading of this verse has been preserved by tradition.

Num. xii 12. On this passage *Siphrē* (ed. Friedmann, p. 28 a) comments as follows : —

'*From the womb of his mother.* [It should be,] "From the womb of *our* mother," but the Scripture has employed euphemism in respect to this phrase. *And half of his flesh is consumed.* "Half of *our* flesh" ought to have been said (היה צריך לומר) in the sense in which that expression is used in the passage, *For he is our brother, our flesh.*'

Rashi (*in loco*) has a similar comment, based no doubt on *Siphrē*. But it is important to note that there is no assertion either in Rashi or in the *Siphrē* of an alteration of the text by early transcribers. The *Siphrē* simply points out that a certain

---

[1] I omit the word בתורה, 'in the Law,' with C. U. Add. 626.
[2] Verified. *Lee* = B. M. Add. 14425 (A. D. 464); Cod. Ambrosianus; edition of Urmi.
[3] *Ne tantis afficiar malis.*

passage would yield good sense, if read differently from the traditional reading. Such remarks on the text are not uncommon in Midrashim and in the Talmud[1]. That the *tiḳḳun* tradition has here preserved a true various reading is a statement wholly devoid of support. No version preserves the supposed 'original reading.' The *wĕlā nehwē*, with which the Peshitta[2] renders אל תהי, comes probably from the μὴ γένηται of the LXX (which often influences the present text of the Peshitta), and should not be rendered (as in Walton's Polyglot) by *et non simus*. The ἐκ μήτρας μητρός *sine add.* and the σαρκῶν αὐτῆς of the LXX and the paraphrase of the Targum ('Pray now for the dead flesh which is in her') in no way suggest the בשרנו of the *tiḳḳun*, though they show that the אמו and בשרו of the M.T. gave trouble to translators.

I Sam. iii 13. Here neither the *Mechilta* nor Rashi asserts that the scribes made an alteration in the text. The latter writes, *in loco* :—

'*Because his sons were cursing them* (להם). *Cursing me* (לי) one ought to have said (היה לו לומר), but the Scripture has employed an euphemism.' [The comment is absent from B. M. Harley 150.]

In this instance the versions offer readings which need some consideration. The Peshitta[3], either paraphrasing להם or reading לעם, gives *were reviling the people*. The Greek (Codd. AB and Lucian), however, is more suggestive ; it reads κακολογοῦντες θεὸν [οἱ] υἱοὶ αὐτοῦ. Similarly Lucifer of Cagliari (a valuable authority for the Old Latin), as cited by Sabatier, gives *Quoniam contemnentes Dominum mala locuti sunt filii eius.* Thus we have Rashi, the LXX, and Lucifer agreeing that the object of the verb *were reviling* is not להם. On the other hand the difference between Rashi and the LXX, and again between the LXX and Lucifer, as to the actual word to be supplied, shows us

---

[1] 'PLAYING' WITH THE TEXT.—Bab. Talm. *Ḥăgigah* (fol. 13 a) on Prov. xxvii 26 (*The lambs are for thy clothing*) :—' Do not read it *lambs* (כבשים), but *hidden things* (כבושים).'

Bab. Talm. *Shabbath* (fol. 55 a) on Ezek. ix 6 (*and begin at my sanctuary*) :—' Do not read it *at my sanctuary* (ממקדשי) but *at my sanctified ones* (ממקודשי).'

In neither case is the ' emendation' put forward as an existing variant, but simply as an occasion for a particular lesson to be enforced.

[2] Verified. *Lee* = B. M. Add. 14425 ; Cod. Ambrosianus ; edition of Urmi.

[3] *Lee* = Cod. Ambrosianus ; C. U. Add. 1964 ; edition of Urmi.

that their agreement is on a matter of interpretation, not of reading. We can read neither לי with Rashi, nor θεόν with the LXX ; evidence such as this does not carry us behind the reading מקללים להם.

2 Sam. xvi 12. Rashi's comment on this passage is simply, ' *The Lord will look upon my eye*, i. e. upon the tears of my eye' (so Targum). Clearly the commentator did not include this passage in his list of *tikkun sopherim*. Neither do the versions testify to the supposed original reading of the passage. LXX (codd. A B [Lucian]) gives ἐν τῇ ταπεινώσει μου (i. e. בעניי [1] for בעיני). Field gives no variants from LXX. The Masorah itself, as represented by the Kri and C'thib, reads for the former *upon my eye*, and for the latter *upon my iniquity* (or *upon my punishment*), and altogether ignores such a reading as *with his eye*. Peshitta [2] and Vulgate agree with LXX.

On 2 Sam. xx 1 Rashi has no note at all. The Peshitta [3], Targum, LXX, and Vulgate, agree with the M.T. No variation from the ordinary text is cited in Field. In 1 Kings xii 16, and in the passage parallel with it, 2 Chron. x 16, the Peshitta [3], Targum, LXX, and Vulgate, give no hint of any reading 'gods' for 'tents.' Field cites no variant from the later Greek versions. Rashi is silent on 1 Kings xii 16 ; on 2 Chron. x. 16 he has a note, but no mention of *tikkun sopherim*.

On Jer. ii 11 neither Rashi nor Ḳimḥi [4] has any note. The LXX, Peshitta [5], Vulgate, and Aquila *apud* Field, agree with the M.T. Theodotion and Symmachus are not cited. The rendering of the Targum seems to represent the כבודו of the M.T., ' They have forsaken my service for the sake of which I bring upon them glory.'

Ezek. viii 17. Rashi has a long note on this passage, but makes no mention of *tikkun*. Ḳimḥi, however, remarks ' *Their nose*: it means (רוצה לומר) *my nose*, but the Scripture has employed

---

[1] So the printed *Masorah* in quoting this passage among the eighteen, though it does not profess to give the 'original reading' of any passage affected by *tikkun sopherim*. B. M. Orient. 1379 also has בעניי.

[2] *Lee* = Cod. Ambrosianus ; C. U. Add. 1964 ; edition of Urmi.

[3] *Lee* (1 Kings xii 16) = Cod. Ambrosianus ; C. U. Add. 1964 ; edition of Urmi.

[4] Aben Ezra seems not to have commented on Jeremiah.

[5] The reading of *Lee* (here and in the instances in Ezek., Hos., Hab., Zech., and Mal.) has been verified by comparison with Cod. Ambrosianus; C. U. ' Ll. 2. 4 ' (Edessa, 1173 A. D.) ; and C. U. Add. 1965 (Nestorian, fifteenth century).

euphemism, and it is one of the eighteen words which are *tikkun
ṣopherim*.' The versions give no support to a reading אפי. The
LXX (ὡς μυκτηρίζοντες) is perhaps too free a rendering for
absolute certainty, but the three later Greek versions *apud*
Field, and the Peshitta[1], Targum, and Vulgate support אפם
without doubt.

Hos. iv 7. Neither Rashi nor Ḳimḥi makes any mention
of a variation here. The LXX and Vulg. agree with the M.T.
No variation from the M.T. is recorded in Field from Aquila,
Symmachus, and Theodotion. On the other hand the Targum
(with which the Peshitta[2] agrees almost *ad literam*) has what is
almost a *tikkun* of its own, יקרהון בקלנא חליפו ' they changed their
glory for shame.'

Hab. i 12. Rashi writes :—

'The prophet says, And thou, wherefore dost thou keep silence at all
this? *Art not thou from everlasting, my God, my Holy One, who diest
not* (אשר לא תמות). And this which is written *We shall not die* (לא נמות)
is one of the *tikkunē ṣopherim* which are in Scripture, for the Scripture
has employed euphemism ; cp. (וכן), *And ye have snuffed at it* [Mal. i 13],
and there are seven[3] similar instances which are set forth in *Siphrē*. And
according to the *tikkun ṣopherim* the interpretation is this, *Art thou not
my God from everlasting? My Holy One, give me not for death into
his hand.*'

Again LXX and Vulg. agree with M.T., except that with
Siphrē and *Mechilta* they read ולא for לא. Field gives no Greek
variant, but Symmachus, quoted by Jerome, gives ' ut non
moreremur' an idiomatic rendering of the Masoretic text.
The Targum, however, reads מימרך קיים לעלמין, which is a paraphrase of לא תמות. [The Peshitta[4], דלא נמוס ('without law !'), is
probably a corruption of דלא נמות, which should be taken in
agreement with the M.T. as a first person plural.] Lastly, it
must be noted that *Siphrē* quotes the passage with ולא אמות
for לא נמות. If the text were otherwise settled, we might
pass over this fresh reading as due simply to inaccurate
quotation, but under the circumstances we are bound to take
note of it. We are left, then, with three possible readings

---

[1] Verified ; *cf.* note [5], p. 408.   [2] Verified.
[3] B. M. Harley 150 reads המה ו וכן for the הורבה וכן of the printed text.
[4] Verified.

(1) נמות M.T., LXX, Vulg. [Pesh. ?] ; (2) תמות Targum ; (3) אמות
Siphrē. To these must perhaps be added (4) ימות Tanḥuma[1].
It must be confessed that the weight of the evidence thus
displayed is decidedly in favour of the נמות of the M.T., and
the tiḳḳun tradition does not turn the scale in favour of תמות·
The Targum contains a Midrashic element, and its reading here
is not improbably a Midrashic play on the original reading, viz.
that of the Masoretic Text. It should be mentioned here that
the tendency to avoid anthropomorphism is far from universal
in Talmudic and Rabbinic literature. Sometimes an exactly
opposite tendency makes itself strongly felt. Thus in Siphrē
(ed. Friedmann, 22 b) it is said that when Israel went into exile
to 'Edom,' the Shechinah was with them, and when they
return *the Shechinah will return* with them.

Zech. ii 12 [8]. Neither Rashi nor Ḳimḥi mentions *tiḳḳun*
in connexion with this passage. LXX and Peshitta read
עינו 'his eye,' Targum עיניו 'his eyes.' The Vulgate, however (as
printed in Stier and Theile), has 'tangit pupillam oculi mei' (i. e.
עיני the alleged 'original reading'), but some MSS (affected,
perhaps, by the LXX through the Old Latin) read *eius* or *sui*
for *mei*. Field cites nothing here from the later Greek versions.
It is not uninteresting that *Siphrē, Mechilta, Shemoth R.* (§ 13),
and the printed *Masorah*, together with five [seven] MSS cited
by Kennicott, give כנונע for נוגע, and that LXX has ὡς ἁπτόμενος,
and the Targum כדמושיט ידיה למיקרב. One spirit of glossing inspired
them all.

Mal. i 12. This instance is without visible means of support
from versions and commentators. As an interpretation it is
correct : *Ye profane it* means *Ye profane my name, Ye profane me.*

Mal. i 13. Rashi[2] writes (*in loco*) :—

'*Ye say also, Behold a weariness,* i. e. a lean beast and one driven
away (ונהלאה), for we were poor and there was no power in our hands to
vow choice offerings ; and in this sense Jonathan has interpreted, *Behold
we brought our fulness* ("the best that we had"). *And ye have snuffed
at it* (והפחתם אותו). This is one of the eleven words of *tiḳḳun*. *At
me* they pointed [the word] (נקרו[2]), but the Scripture has employed

---

[1] In *Tanḥuma* most of the passages are quoted in their 'original' form, so that
ימה is strictly speaking a variant of תמות.

[2] Emended from B. M. Harley 150, which varies considerably from Bomberg's
text (2nd edit.).

euphemism, and *at it* is written (וכחו׳ אותו). *And ye have snuffed* [*at it*], i.e. "and ye have made [it] waste away"; [הפחתם] is in the sense of blowing away with the breath. [*Ye have snuffed*] *at me* and at my table.'

This passage suggests no alteration of the consonantal text at all. It tells us that *punctators* (all or some only?) added a point to suggest the reading of י for ו. The written text, however, is clearly stated to be אותו (*at it*); the אותי (*at me*) is simply an unveiling of a supposed euphemism of Scripture. The versions here give an uncertain sound. The Targum, the Vulgate, and Cod. א and Cod. 311 (according to H. P.) of the LXX as well as the Complutensian edition support the Masoretic Text. On the other hand the Peshitta has *w'nephḥēth b'hōn* (Cod. Ambros.), 'And I rejected them' (the sacrificers), or (C. U. 'Ll. 2. 4'; C. U. Add. 1965) *b'hēn* 'them' (the sacrifices). Similarly LXX (ABQΓ) has ἐξεφύσησα αὐτά.

Mal. iii 8, 9. Here the expression אתם קבעים 'ye rob' (R.V.) is supposed to be substituted for the original reading, and it has been supposed that the πτερνίζετε (=אתם עקבים) 'ye attack in the rear' or 'ye trip up' of the LXX represents this original reading. But the supposition lacks support; one only of our authorities mentions Mal. iii 8, 9, as a *tiḳḳun* passage at all, and even that one does not give us the alleged displaced reading. It seems, in fact, that the LXX guessed, as do the rest of the versions, at the meaning of a rare and obscure word. A΄Σ΄Θ΄ give ἀποστερεῖτε; Vulgate *configitis*; Peshitta *ṭāl'min* 'ye injure'; Targum מרגזין קדמי 'ye provoke me.' From a passage so obscure it is well to keep out the obscure subject of *tiḳḳun*, since there is so little authority for introducing it.

Ps. cvi 20. Here Rashi (*in loco*) gives no hint of any variation [1], but Aben Ezra writes:—

'*Thus they changed their glory.* An euphemism for *the glory of the Name* [2]; cp. [2 Sam. xii 14] *Because thou hast verily despised* [*the enemies of the Lord*]. And there the euphemistic expression is in reference to David the king by way of reproof; and he said not to him, *Because thou hast verily despised the Name.*'

With this note of Aben Ezra agrees the Targum ופרגנו ית איקר ריבוניהון, 'and they changed the glory of their Lord,' but the

[1] But see his comment (quoted below) on Job xxxii 3.
[2] i.e. 'the glory of Jehovah.'

agreement need not necessarily be more than an agreement in interpretation. Aben Ezra does not say anything about a change of *reading*. LXX B, Peshitta, and Vulgate support the M.T. The LXX variant τὴν δόξαν αὐτοῦ (א ᶜˑᵃ ART) is probably a corruption introduced from the parallel place (Jer. ii 11). Field is silent.

Job vii 20. On this passage Rashi mentions no variant, but Aben Ezra writes :—

'*So that I am a burden to myself* (עלי). A *tikkun sopherim* although the interpretation is certain (נכון) without a *tikkun*.'

The LXX here stands alone among the versions in supporting the alleged original reading ; it reads εἰμὶ δὲ ἐπὶ σοὶ (=עליך) φορτίον. (This σοὶ may, however, be derived from the σοῦ of the previous clause.) Peshitta, Targum, and Vulgate agree with the M.T. Field is silent.

Job xxxii 3. Here Rashi writes :—

'*And yet they had condemned Job*. This is one of the verses in which the scribes have corrected (תקנו סופרים) the language of Scripture ; *and they passed by their silence a condemnatory judgement in reference to the Omnipresent* (וירשיעו כלפי המקום) one ought to have written, but the Scripture has employed euphemism (כינה הכתוב). Compare [Ps. cvi 20], *Thus they changed their glory for the likeness of an ox ; my glory* one ought to have written, but the Scripture has employed euphemism[1]. Compare also [Num. xi 15], *And let me not look upon my wretchedness* ("my evil") ; *on thy evil* one ought to have written, but the Scripture has employed euphemism. Compare also many places [cited] in *Siphrē* and in the Masorah *magna*.'

Aben Ezra on the other hand (*in loco*) writes :—

'And it is written (וכתוב) that it is an instance of *tikkun sopherim*, but they who say so, know that which has been hidden from me.'

Three of the versions (Peshitta, Targum, and Vulgate) reproduce the M.T., while the LXX gives no support to the supposed original reading, for it has καὶ ἔθεντο αὐτὸν εἶναι ἀσεβῆ, with the variant εὐσεβῆ, which is plainly a secondary reading. A'Σ'Θ' *apud* Field are silent.

Lam. iii 20. Neither Rashi nor Aben Ezra (whose commentary on Lamentations, however, is rather slight) mentions

---

[1] This whole sentence is omitted in the *Fürth* Bible (anno 565 = 1805 A. D.).

a variant. The versions, Peshitta, Targum, LXX, and Vulgate, support the M.T. There is nothing in Field to support the *tikkun*.

CONCLUSION.

I have already drawn tentatively (p. 402) the conclusion that the *tikkun* tradition is not Masoretic (i. e. textual), but Midrashic (i. e. exegetical or, more accurately, homiletic). This conclusion was based on the nature of the documents in which the *data* of the subject are contained ; it is supported further by the consideration of each passage in detail. There is no confirmatory evidence in favour of the 'original reading' of Gen. xviii 22. Of Num. xi 15 the utmost which can be said is that the reading of LXX B throws a slight doubt on the M. T. In Num. xii 12 the two 'original readings' are impossible as readings, possible only as flights of homiletic fancy. In 1 Sam. iii 13 the M. T. is probably corrupt, and the tradition of the *sopherim* may be said to be no worse than the emendations of the Peshitta and the A. V. The reading restored in 2 Sam. xvi 12 is simply a homiletic fancy. The 'original reading' alleged in the group of passages consisting of 2 Sam. xx 1 ; 1 Kings xii 16 ; 2 Chron. x 16 is merely a theological reflexion. A similar remark may be made regarding the group, Jer. ii 11 ; Hos. iv 7 ; Ps. cvi 20. In Ezek. viii 17 the obscurity of the heathen rite alluded to has opened the door to the play of fancy. In Hab. i 12 we get a very early and very daring homiletic flight ; that is all. In Zech. ii 12 [8] the meaning of the M. T. and of the 'original reading' is the same in substance, only if we read עיני we introduce a change of speaker between שלחני and the end of the verse ; no 'reverence' is saved by the עינו of the M. T. As regards Mal. i 12 and 13 and Job xxxii. 3 the *tikkun* tradition is simply theological comment. Mal. iii 8, 9 is an instance too obscure to be discussed further. Job vii 20 is a difficult passage which the 'original reading' makes more difficult still. Lam. iii 20, according to the M.T., yields satisfactory sense, no other reading has any support from the versions.

The whole evidence leads us back to the play of homiletic fancy on Zech. ii 12 [8] (*Siphrē, Mechilta, Tanhuma*, Cod.*Bab. Pet.*) and to a parallel play of the same fancy on Num. xi 15 ; xii 12 (printed and Yemen *Masorah*). The homiletic commentators found parallels for these first three passages, and passage was linked with passage until the chain was long. Next the purpose of the list was misunderstood in some quarters and the list was introduced (but by no means invariably [1]) into Masoretic works, at first as an appendix [2]. Scholars like Aben Ezra, Ben Asher, and Ben Addereth protested against popular notions regarding *tikkun sopherim*, but the list when once placed among the traditions of *Masorah* continued to be misunderstood and the effects of the mistake are with us to-day.

W. EMERY BARNES.

---

[1] *Not* in the Halle MS. of *Ochlah*. [2] Ben Asher.

NOTE I. Dr. Schechter has pointed out to me that the number 'eighteen' appears in *Shemoth Rabba* v 5 as the number of the places which the LXX translators 'changed for Ptolemy the king.' Elsewhere these alterations are reckoned at 'thirteen' or 'fifteen,' and not more than *fifteen* instances are ever specified. From this and many other like facts 'eighteen' would seem to be a merely symbolic number.

NOTE II. Dr. Schechter kindly allows me to make use of a MS in his own possession (*Bamidbar*, paper, 23 lines to a page, $10\frac{1}{2}$ in. × $7\frac{5}{8}$in., foll. 242) of the *Midrash Haggadol*, of which he is preparing an edition ('*M. H.* edited from Yemen MSS by S. S., Camb. University Press'). It is cited in Table VI as *Mid. Gad.* It agrees in the list (foll. 70 b, 71 a) of *tikkun* passages in contents (but not in order) with *Mechilta*, except that it has 1 Kings xii 16 instead of 2 Sam. xx 1, and that it omits Num. xi 15. This last passage should perhaps be added to the text of *Mid. Gad.* to make up the number *eleven*, for the Midrash *in loco* (fol. 62 a, line 7) seems to base its comment on the reading ברעתם. Unlike *Mechilta* the *Midrash Haggadol* adds in its list the 'original reading' of each passage. Like *Yalkut* it cites with the formula, 'Similarly thou sayest' (כיוצא בו אתה אומ).

THE ORIGIN OF THE KETHIB-QERE SYSTEM:
A NEW APPROACH

BY

HARRY M. ORLINSKY

New York

The present paper began as a study of the masoretic text of the Hebrew Bible, to determine whether there was such a thing as *the* masoretic text, or, if not, whether such a text could be achieved; in other words, whether *the* (as against *a*) masoretic text was really but a scholarly fiction. However, this paper soon became involved, as inevitably it should have, in the matter of the Kethib-Qere variants, to the point where this special problem consumed the entire half-hour at my disposal for the problem as a whole. Accordingly, the present paper will deal with the Kethib-Qere phenomenon, and propose a new theory concerning its origin and character. The larger problem ("The Masoretic Text—A Scholarly Fiction?" [1]), meanwhile, having waited almost a millennium and a half for analysis, will patiently wait a few years longer.

There are between some 1,000 and 1,500 instances of Kethib-Qere in the Bible, [2] where in such standard editions as those of BAER, GINSBURG, LETTERIS, KITTEL (either the second or the third editions of *Biblia Hebraica*), or in the Rabbinic Bibles published in Vilna and Warsaw, the consonants of one word are written

---

[1] The title of the paper originally scheduled to be read at the Oxford Congress.

[2] Different manuscripts and masoretic lists are responsible for this difference in totals. It is no longer possible, short of discovering the manuscripts used by the Masoretes who introduced vocalization, to determine the earliest total. Many of the Kethib-Qere are patently of later origin; cf. ORLINSKY, "The Import of the Kethib-Kere and the Masoretic Note on *Lᵉḳâḥ*, Judges 19.13, "*J.Q.R.*, XXXI, 1940-41, pp. 59ff.; "The Biblical Prepositions תַּחַת, בֵּין, בַּעַד, and Pronouns אָנוּ (or אָֽנוּ), זאתָה, "*H.U.C.A.*, XXVII, 1942-43, pp. 267-292 (cf., e.g., p. 277, ". . . as to when such forms like תֶּחְתּוֹ, עָלוֹ, אֵלִי, אַחֲרוֹ, and the other 150 cases of K-Q of the same kind, first came into existence, even if incorrectly and without proper authority, it would appear that they originated after the time of David Qimhi, who died in 1235 . . ."). Cf. the statement in C. D. GINSBURG, *Introduction to the Massoretico-Critical Edition of the Hebrew Bible* (London-Vienna, 1897), pp. 185 f.

Reprinted from *Supplements to Vetus Testamentum* 7 (1959).

(*Kethib*) in the text proper, but together with the vowels of another word or of another form of the same root, with the consonants of the other word, or form, written in the margin, the vowels in the text and the consonants in the margin being read together, to form the *Qere*. It is true that other means, variations on this theme, used to be employed in recording the Kethib and Qere; but the principle was essentially the same as the one incorporated in today's widespread procedure. [1]

It has long been the general concensus of scholarly opinion that the Qere readings frequently represent corrections of the Kethib; that is to say, that the Jewish scholars responsible for the Kethib-Qere system— (or, הַמַּסֹרֶת) בַּעֲלֵי הַמָּסֹרֶת, "Masoretes," they came to be called [2])—finding in their text readings that were, in their judgment, erroneous, corrected them, the corrected forms constituting the Qere. Thus S. R. DRIVER, in the valuable "Introduction" of his excellent *Notes on the Hebrew Text and the Topography of the Books of Samuel* (2nd ed., 1913, pp. lxii-lxiii; and cf., e.g., the reference on p. xxviii to § *c* on p. xxix), asserts that "The omission was in some cases made good by the Massorites in the Qrê, but not always," and "The correction is made in the Qrê."

Yet there have never been lacking some scholars who have held that the Qere readings were not corrections—i.e., emendations, inventions—on the part of the Masoretes, but rather actual textual variant readings, which the Masoretes incorporated into the text. Neither of these two theories, in the manner presented by their proponents and adherants, has been without serious defect, or has lacked cogent objection. [3]

Those scholars who have dealt directly with the Kethib-Qere recognize the significant fact that apart from those very many instances where the Kethib-Qere readings are equally acceptable to the textual critic, the Kethib reading is acceptable where the Qere is not, almost as often as the Qere is acceptable where its Kethib

---

[1] Cf. GINSBURG, *op. cit.*, pp. 183 f.

[2] On such forms as מָסֹרָה, מַסֹרָה, מָסֹרֶת, and מַסֹרֶת, deriving from the root אסר or מסר, cf. conveniently B. J. ROBERTS, *The Old Testament Text and Versions* (Cardiff, 1951), pp. 40-42.

[3] A reliable analytical survey of these and other views of the origin of the Kethib-Qere system is still a desideratum; cf. ORLINSKY, "Problems of the Kethib-Qere", *J.A.O.S.*, LX, 1940, p. 44, § 7; see for the present, R. GORDIS, *The Biblical Text in the Making: A Study of the Kethib-Qere* (Philadelphia, 1937), pp. 7 ff.

correspondent is not. In other words, if the Masoretes responsible for the Kethib-Qere system were correctors, and corrected unacceptable Kethibs into acceptable Qeres, why then is the Qere reading so frequently not acceptable where the Kethib is?

On the other hand, if the Masoretes were not correctors at all, but selectors, selecting as the better reading what they designated as the Qere, why did they so frequently select as the Kethib—or what came to be designated as the Kethib—the reading which was obviously the superior? Clearly the Masoretes were neither correctors nor selectors; i.e., they did not deal with the Hebrew text of the Bible subjectively, *ad hoc*, deciding each reading within its context. That is why the very first Kethib-Qere in the Bible, in Gen. viii 17, exhibits the anomalous, quite incorrect form הַיְצֵא, the alleged hiph'il imperative of the root יצא, as the Qere, and the patently correct and expected form, הוֹצֵא, as the Kethib. The verse reads: "God spoke to Noah, saying, 'Come out of the ark . . . and bring out (Qere הַיְצֵא, Kethib הוצא) with you every living thing . . .' "

A new approach to the circumstances under which the Kethib-Qere system came into being would appear to offer a clear and consistent explanation where the other hypotheses do not. It is well known that two significant developments in the *Überlieferungsgeschichte* of the Hebrew text of the Bible took place early in the second half of the first millennium A.D. I refer to the development of symbols for the Hebrew vowels, and to the system known as Kethib-Qere. The chronology is certain enough: neither the Babylonian nor the Palestinian Talmud makes any mention at all of either of these two phenomena or contains any reference to their technical terminology [1]); and St. Jerome, who evinced an especial interest in the Hebrew text and commented on its peculiarities freely, knows nothing about vowel symbols or the Kethib-Qere system.

---

[1]) The fact that the Talmud will make mention of such terms as כתיב . . . קרינן (cf. e.g., H. L. STRACK, *Prolegomena Critica in Vetus Testamentum Hebraicum*, etc. [Lipsiae, 1873] § II, pp. 80 ff.) does not mean at all—as some have gratuitously assumed (e.g., S. BAMBERGER, "Die Bedeutung der Qeri Kethib, ein Beitrag zur Geschichte der Exegese," in *Jahrbuch der Jüdisch-Literarischen Gesellschaft*, XV, 1923, pp. 217-265; § II. "Q. und K. im Talmud," pp. 232-243)— that a Kethib-Qere system was in vogue already before about 600 A.D. By the same token, the fact that the Septuagint, or Aquila, etc., had before them a reading that many centuries later became a member of the Kethib-Qere system, does not imply that these early translators recognized a Kethib-Qere system. Cf. "Problems of Kethib-Qere," § 8, pp. 44 f.; and the references in n. 2 above, p. 185.

When Jewish scholars after about 600 A.D. decided to introduce vowel symbols into the hitherto unvocalized consonantal text of the Hebrew Bible, they had, first of all, to select some manuscripts to vocalize. Then, when the manuscripts differed among each other, they had to select the variant reading which they proceeded to vocalize. [1]) What procedure did the Masoretes follow in making the selection and achieving the Kethib-Qere system?

It is our hypothesis that the Masoretes first selected the three best manuscripts of the Hebrew Bible available to them. Where the three manuscripts had no variant readings, no difficulty was experienced in vocalizing the text. But where the manuscripts differed, the Masoretes accepted the reading of the majority and vocalized it; that reading became the Qere. The reading of the minority was left unvocalized, and became the Kethib. On this view, the Masoretes did not select or correct any reading; rather, automatically and objectively, regardless of personal opinion or predilection, the three selected manuscripts themselves, by a vote of two to one, determined the Kethib-Qere system. That is why in many scores of instances, far more than one would expect and many more than is generally realized, the reading of the Kethib is clearly superior to that of the Qere, and yet it was the latter that became the accepted reading. No Masorete would have picked הַיְצֵא in preference to הוֹצֵא, or fail to correct the former into the latter, if he were at liberty to practice selection or emendation. On our view, the Masoretes had no choice; they had to accept the reading of the majority, and vocalize it.

Again, this hypothesis accounts readily, and naturally, for the interesting fact that not a single instance of Kethib-Qere involves the *scriptio plena* and *defectiva*. There can be little doubt that in this respect the manuscripts must have differed not infrequently. But since this orthographic phenomenon presented no problem in vocalization, no Kethib-Qere category arose for them. Thus, whether the form *yōsheḇîm* ('dwelling; sitting") was written entirely *plene* (יושבים), or entirely *defective* (ישבם), or partially *defective* (ישבים; יושבם), no problem

---

[1]) J. WELLHAUSEN made specifically chronological connection between the beginnings of the Kethib-Qere system and the introduction of vocalization, but he did not pursue the matter; cf. F. BLEEK-J. WELLHAUSEN, *Einleitung in das Alte Testament*, 6th ed. (Berlin, 1893), § 264, pp. 572 f., ". . . Keri und Ketib . . . reichen in die Anfänge der synagogalen Vorlesung herauf, sind aber natürlich . . . erst nach der Enstehung der Punktation schriftlich angemerkt worden und zwar in immer wachsendem Umfange, von den elementaren Hauptsachen an bis ins kleinste Detail."

was involved in vocalizing with the symbols for the *ḥolɛm* and the *ḥirɛq*. [1])

Furthermore, it is reasonable to assume that the three carefully selected manuscripts differed among themselves only relatively infrequently, and then usually in the manner that a scribe can accidentally be responsible for; virtually all Kethib-Qere readings fall into this category. They are textual variants of the kind that scribes bring into being unintentionally.

Our theory, moreover, accounts perfectly for the significant fact that time and again there is a Kethib-Qere for a word in one passage and not in another. Thus in Judg. ix 8, 12 there are the Qere readings מָלְכָה and מָלְכִי, respectively the masculine and feminine forms of the 2nd person singular Qal imperative of the root מלך, "rule," for which the unvocalized Kethibs read מלוכה and מלוכי, usually vocalized מְלוֹכָה and מְלוֹכִי. Yet exactly between these two verses, in v. 10, in precisely the same context, occurs the form מָלְכִי, with no Kethib-Qere reading involved. (The context involves Jotham's famous parable in which the trees went about seeking a king to rule over them.) As in scores of other instances, the two most popular theories concerning the origin of the Kethib-Qere system, according to which the Masoretes selected or corrected readings that they designated as the Qere, this too would be an example of masoretic carelessness or inconsistency in having failed to do with מָלְכִי in v. 10 what they did with מָלְכָה and מָלְכִי in vv. 8 and 12. On our hypothesis, however, the Masoretes did not select or invent any variants, and were not guilty of such extraordinary carelessness or inconsistency: in the three manuscripts they were working on, they found variant readings in vv. 8 and 12 and vocalized the reading of the majority as the Qere; in v. 10, however, they found no variant reading, and so no Kethib-Qere resulted.

There is, further, the significant fact that not only the ordinary but even the extraordinary cases of *scriptio plena* and *defectiva* are notable

---

[1]) It may be noted that there are numerous instances of Kethib-Qere involving the letters *waw* and *yodh*, but only when they are consonants, or when the *yodh* is the orthographic residue of its originally consonantal use, and indicates the *qāmeṣ* vowel in the 3rd person singular masc. pronominal suffix, e.g., יָדָיו "his hands," בָּנָיו "his sons"; never, however, when they are *matres lectionis* indicating the *ḥolem* and *ḥireq* pronunciation. Cf. further, "The Biblical Prepositions," etc. *passim*.

for their absence from the Kethib-Qere system. Thus, e.g., in Deut. iii 21 and Judg. ii 7, the unusual *plena* form of Joshua's Hebrew name, יְהוֹשׁוּעַ, is found, with a masoretic note on the *plena*; but since the absence or presence of the two *waws* did not interfere with the vocalization of the word, no Kethih-Qere reading arose from the unusual orthography. The same is true of the spelling וּבֹרֹת, "and cisterns," in Deut. vi 11, where the Masoretes noted the unusual *defective* form, but where, again, no Kethib-Qere reading arose. There are dozens of such extraordinary spellings noted in the masoretic lists, none with Kethib-Qere association.

Related to this category are the scores of instances of unusual spelling, e.g., מָצָתִי, "I have found," in Num. xi 11, with the masoretic *caveat*: א חסר "it is written (anomalously) without the א"; or the masoretic note on the word וּשְׂמֹאול in Num. xx 17, viz., יתיר ו, "the *waw* is superfluous." In all these cases, the Masoretes did not correct these peculiar forms, or substitute a correct variant for them; they permitted them to stand as they were. And neither did these forms become members of the Kethib-Qere system, for the Masoretes found no difficulty in vocalizing these forms, whether they read מצתי or מצאתי, ושמאל or ושמאול. They contented themselves with what might be described as the scholarly use of Latin *"sic!"* within brackets. Theirs was not to reason why, to select or to correct, but faithfully to receive, and record, and transmit.

Our proposition gains considerable prestige from an important independent source. In the Palestinian Talmud, Ta'anit iv 2, with parallel passages in the extra-canonical talmudic tractates, *Masechet Soferim*[1]) (Chap. VI, Halakah 4) and *Abot de-Rabbi Nathan* (ed. Schechter, Version 2, Chap. IV end), we read that Rabbi Simon ben Laqish, a third century Palestinian Amora, said, "Three scrolls (ספרים) were on file (lit., were found, מָצְאוּ/נִמְצְאוּ) in the Temple Court (בָּעֲזָרָה): the scroll called מָעוֹן, the scroll called זַעֲטוּטֵי, and the scroll called הִיא." The statement continues:

באחד מצאו כתוב "מעון" ובשנים כתוב "מעונה" אלהי קדם: וקייׂמו שנים
ובטלו אחד. באחד מצאו כתוב "וישלח את-זעטוטי בני-ישראל" ובשנים
מצאו כתוב "וישלח את-נערי בני-ישראל"; וקיימו שנים ובטלו אחד. באחד
מצאו כתוב אחד-עשר "הוא" ובשנים מצאו כתוב אחד-עשר "היא"; וקיימו
שנים ובטלו אחד.

---

[1]) Ed. J. Müller (Leipzig, 1878), p. XII, with the editor's commentary on pp. 90 ff.

'In one scroll (at Deut. xxxiii 27) they found written מָעוֹן אֱלֹהֵי קֶדֶם (traditionally rendered: The eternal [or, ancient] God is a dwelling place) and in two scrolls was written מְעוֹנָה; they confirmed (the reading of) the two (מעונה) and rejected (the reading of) the one (מען). In one (at Ex. xxiv 5) they found written, "And he (viz., Moses) sent the זְעַטוּטֵי (Aramaic for "young men") of the Israelites," and in two they found written, "And he sent the נַעֲרֵי (Hebrew for "young men") of the Israelites"; they confirmed (the reading of) the two (נערי) and rejected (the reading of) the one (זעטוטי). [1] In one they found written 11 times the spelling הוּא, [2] and in two they found written 11 times הִיא; they confirmed (the reading of) the two (היא) and rejected (the reading of) the one (הוא).'

Whether there really were three scrolls of the Torah in the Temple and with such readings, especially with Aramaic זעטוטי for Hebrew נערי, can hardly be determined. But whether this was so or not, is fortunately no immediate problem for our own purpose. For us it is sufficient to recognize the important fact that already in the third century it was believed that three scrolls, the minimum that would permit a majority decision, were on file in the Temple, and that whenever they differed in a reading, the majority prevailed automatically, 2 : 1. The Temple authorities did not wight the relative merits of מָעוֹן as against מְעוֹנָה, or of זְעַטוּטֵי as against נַעֲרֵי, or of הוא as against היא, and make selection on that basis; neither are they said to have emended הוא into היא, or substituted נערי for זעטוטי.

In other words, the Temple authorities neither selected nor corrected. They simply let the three manuscripts themselves determine the correct reading. This is precisely what our own hypothesis has assumed, and what the masoretic data, the non-Kethib-Qere as well as the Kethib-Qere, independently and inductively have led to. That the reading of the majority in the three Temple scrolls pushed out the minority reading altogether—unless these scrolls with the minority reading had never really existed—is evident from the fact that neither מען nor זעטוטי has been preserved in the Hebrew tradition; and even the 4 occurrences of הוּא (with the *waw*, as witness the masoretic

---

[1]) There is also the spelling זאטוטי (apart from conflated זעאטוטי); see *Masechet Soferim*, ed. MÜLLER, p. 92, note 17.

[2]) Whether pronounced הוא or היא is not indicated, though the latter is probable.

note at Gen. xxiii 15 [1]) may well have nothing to do with the 11 that our rabbinic source mentions. [2])

Yet the Masoretes of the sixth-seventh centuries could not follow completely the procedure of their predecessors in the Temple over half-a-millennium earlier. They could hardly assume responsibility for the obliteration of an existing reading. So that while they adopted for vocalization, as the Qere, the reading of the majority, they preserved the reading of the minority, as the Kethib, without vocalizing it at all. That is why every attempt at vocalizing the consonants of the Kethib is purely subjective, and without authority, be it in such editions as GINSBURG's and KITTEL's, or in the grammars of Biblical Hebrew. Such attempts in the past have resulted in "Jehovah" for Qere אֲדֹנָי and Kethib (unvocalized) יהוה; and, more recently, in vocalizing the root שׁגל as qal or niph'al by quite gratuitously combining the vowels of Qere שׁכב with the consonants of Kethib שׁגל. [3])

In retrospect, the number "3" becomes even clearer and more logical for the number of manuscripts selected by the Masoretes for vocalization purpose: 3 is the minimum number for a majority; neither 1 nor 2 satisfies this desideratum, in manuscripts of the Bible any more than in judges of the court. The even number 4 could not always produce a majority; and 5 manuscripts, or more, not only lacked precedent but would too often produce more than 2 variant readings and no clear-cut majority. On all counts, it is only the number 3 that is satisfactory *per se* and has excellent precedent in the statement in the talmudic statement of Rabbi Simon ben Laqish.

A question that may fairly be asked is: What did the Masoretes do when their 3 selected manuscripts came up with 3 variants? Clearly, there could hardly be many instances where the 3 manuscripts presented 3 different readings of such nature that no single vocalization

---

[1]) Incidentally, there is much unclarity about this (cf., e.g., MÜLLER, n. 18, pp. 92 f.), even after S. FRENSDORFF, in his useful work on *The Massora Magna* (Hannover und Leipzig, 1876), p. 233, s. הוא, has clarified some of the problems.

[2]) It may be noted that neither מעון nor זעטוטי ever became Kethib-Qere; in all probability, they had vanished from the textual scene by the time the Kethib-Qere system came into being.

[3]) Cf. C. D. GINSBURG, *Introduction*, etc., p. 184, "I know that some critics may in sundry cases differ from me as to the proper pointing of the *Kethiv*, but in the absence of all MS. authority I could do it only according to the best of my judgment." On the vocalization לְךָ (rather than the generally accepted לָךְ of GINS-

BURG KAHLE, and others) for Kethib לך in Judg. xix 13 (where the Qere is לְכָה), see ORLINSKY, "The Import of the Kethib-Kere," etc., pp. 63-66.

could be applied to at least 2 of them so that they constituted a majority, But if, and when, such an instance did occur, what did the Masoretes do? No specific answer can be given to this question. Yet a plausible answer may readily be induced from the statement by Simon ben Laqish. What did the Temple authorities do when, and if, they were confronted by such a circumstance? Simon's statement does not mention such an occasion. We should have to assume that if such an occasion actually did arise, that the Temple authorities—and the Masoretes after them—simply, and justifiably, ignored the least likely reading among the 3 variant readings.

THE THREE BOOKS FOUND IN THE TEMPLE AT JERUSALEM

By Jacob Z. Lauterbach, Hebrew Union College.

An ancient tradition, preserved in the talmudic literature, speaks of three certain books which were found in
the Temple at Jerusalem. Each one of these three books
is mentioned under a special name, by which it was called,
and which, no doubt, was meant to designate its peculiar
character. The report of this tradition is very brief, and
reads as follows: שלשה ספרים מצאו בעזרה ספר מעוני ספר זעטוטי
וספר היא (p. Taanit 68 a, 47 ff.). In Sifre Deut. § 356 (ed.
Friedmann, p. 148 b) the wording of this report is slightly
different. There it reads thus: שלשה ספרים נמצאו בעזרה,
אחד של מעונים ואחד של היא היא ואחד שנקרא ספר זעטוטים [1].

There is no reason whatever to question the historic
character of this report or doubt the correctness of its
statements. Its brief form and concise language mark it

---

[1] It should be stated at the outset that these ten words in the Pal.
Talmud, or the fifteen words in the Sifre, constitute the complete text of the
report. What follows these first ten, resp. fifteen words in the Pal. Talmud
and in the Sifre, beginning with באחד מצאו, is no more part of the report
itself, but later additions which seek to explain the meaning of the old
report.

This report is also found in Abot d. R. Nathan, version B, ch. 46, ed.
Schechter, p. 65 a, and in tractate Sopherim, VI, 4, where it is quoted by
R. Simon b. Lakish (or R. Judah b. Lakish (?), see below, note 4). The text
of the report, as given in these two last works, shows but a few slight
variants, as מעונה instead of מעוני or מעונים, and זעטוטה (in tractate
Soferim זאטוטי) instead of זעטוטי or זעטוטים.

Reprinted from *Jewish Quarterly Review* 8 (1917-18).

as a historic document, and not as a mere legendary report.

The date of this report is very old. This is evident from the very language it employs. The terms used in it seem to be archaic; at least, we do not find them used elsewhere in the talmudic literature. The manner and form in which the report is expressed also point to a very early date. The author of this report seems to speak of a contemporaneous fact, or at least of something well known to the people of his time. He seems to take it for granted that the main character and the contents of these books are known to all, and that therefore he need only state their number and mention the specific names which designate the special distinction or peculiar feature of each one of them. For he did not deem it necessary, except by merely giving their names, to describe these books in detail, or to say something more about their contents.

That this report represents an ancient tradition and is of a very early date is further evidenced by the fact that its real contents and their correct meaning were no longer known to the later talmudic teachers, the younger Amoraim. For, as will be shown in the course of this essay, the later talmudic teachers, especially the redactors of the Abot d. R. Nathan and of the Palestinian Talmud, who preserved this report to us with additions and comments of their own, have altogether misconstrued the purport of this report and misunderstood the meaning of its statements. It is hardly possible to assume that these teachers could have made such blunders if they had been discussing and interpreting statements of a contemporary author or even of one near to their own time. Such mistakes in the interpretation of an historical report on the part of the later teachers

417

can be explained only on the supposition that a long period of time separated the author of the report from the teachers who tried to interpret it. In the course of such a long time, which also brought about radical changes in the conditions of life, it could well have happened that the actual facts to which the report referred, and the conditions which it presupposed, should have become entirely forgotten, so that the correct meaning of the report was no longer known. The later teachers, who found the brief statements of this old report without any comment to it, could only guess at its meaning. They may have considered it from a wrong point of view, in that they looked at it in the light of the conditions of their own time, and thus could easily misunderstand and misinterpret it.

It may, accordingly, be assumed with reasonable certainty that our report originated at a very early date, possibly during the time when the Temple was still in existence; at least, not long after its destruction. At that time the conditions which prevailed in the Temple and the nature of the books which were kept there were still well known to the people. The author of our report, therefore, could well content himself with merely stating the number of these books and designating each by its characteristically significant name.

Now, what are the contents and the real purport of this report? What was the character common to all these three books, found in the Temple? What was the special feature of each one of them, and how is this special feature of each indicated in the distinct name given to it in our report?

In all the four works (Sifre, Abot d. R. Nathan,

D d 2

Palestinian Talmud, and the tractate Soferim) containing our report, there are also found accompanying it a few additions by later teachers, consisting of explanatory remarks which constitute a sort of a commentary to the original report.[2] From these additions it is evident that

---

[2] These explanatory remarks are different in the different works and partly contradict one another. In order to be able to show the origin of this Talmudic commentary on our report and trace its changes and gradual developments into its present various forms, which will be attempted at the end of this essay, I will quote here this talmudic commentary as found in the different works. In the Pal. Talmud, *loc. cit.*, the explanatory remarks to our report read as follows : באחד מצאו כתוב מעון אלהי קדם ובשנים כתוב מעונה אלהי קדם וקיימו שנים וביטלו אחד באחד מצאו כתוב וישלח את. זעטוטי בני ישראל ובשנים כתוב וישלח את נערי בני ישראל וקיימו שנים וביטלו אחד באחד מצאו כתוב תשע היא ובשנים כתוב אחת עשרה היא וקיימו שנים וביטלו אחד.

It should be noticed that, according to this explanation, the name of the first book ought to have been called, after its peculiar variant, ספר מעון and not אחד של מעונים or ספר מעוני, since neither one of these last two forms was, according to the commentary, found in the text of this book.

In Abot d. R. Nathan, *loc. cit.*, the additions to our report read as follows : ספר מעונה [באחד היה כתוב מעון אלהי קדם ובאחד היה מעונה בטלו האחד וקיימו השנים, אמר רבי יוסי זה הוא ספר שנמצא בבית מעון ספר זעטוטי] באחד היה כתוב זעטוטי בני ישראל ובשנים כתוב וישלה את נערי בני ישראל בטלו את האחד וקיימו את השנים ספר היא בכל מקום שהיה כתוב היא היו קורין (אותו) הוא, ויש אומרים אחד עשר יודידיות היא שבתורה בטלו את האחד וקיימו את השנים.

Here we are not told in what form the word מעון or מעונה was found in the third book. On the other hand, there are two different explanations offered for the meaning of the name of the third book היא. Neither one of these two explanations, however, is sufficiently clear ; see Schechter's remark, note 11.

In tractate Soferim the explanatory remarks to our report read as follows : באחד מצאו כתוב מעון אלהי קדם ובשנים כתוב מעונה אלהי קדם וקיימו שנים ובטלו אחד, באחד מצאו כתוב וישלח את זעאטוטי בני ישראל ובשנים מצאו כתוב וישלח את נערי בני ישראל וקיימו שנים ובטלו אחד, באחד כתוב אחד עשר הוא ובשנים מצאו כתוב אחד עשר היא וקיימו שנים ובטלו אחד.

the authors of these explanatory notes, or, at any rate, the respective redactors of these four talmudic works, who added these notes to our report, understood the latter to have reference to the Books of the Law or Torah scrolls. According to this commentary of the later talmudic teachers, our report tells us about three model Torah scrolls or standard copies of the Pentateuch which were kept in the Temple, and from which a correct text for all other copies of the Torah was established. Each one of these standard copies is said to have been marked by just one special peculiarity in the writing of a certain word. From this characteristic peculiarity, which distinguished it from the two others, each one of these three copies is supposed to have derived its distinct name.

The one copy is described as having contained a peculiar variant of the word מעונה, occurring in Deut. 33. 27, and hence it was called ספר מעוני. The other copy is said to have contained the foreign word זעטוטי instead of the Hebrew word נערי in Exod. 24. 5. For this reason it was called ספר זעטוטי. The third copy again was distinguished from the others by the peculiarity which it showed in the spelling of the personal pronoun third person feminine. In all the passages where this word occurs—or, according to the other

The Sifre contains but one short comment, explaining the meaning of the name of but one book. It reads as follows: באחד כתוב מעון קדם ובשניה כתיב מעונה אלהי קדם ובטלו חכמים את האחד וקיימו השנים (instead of ובשניה should perhaps be read ובשנים). No explanation is given of the meaning of the other two books.

It should further be noticed that the commentary in its various forms, the short comment of the Sifre included, is based upon the version of our report as given in the Pal. Talmud and not upon the version of the Sifre. ספר מעוני and ספר זעטוטי can be interpreted to mean, the book containing the variant מעוני or זעטוטי. But the version אחד של מעונים וכו׳ does not permit the possibility of such an interpretation.

version of the commentary, only in eleven (nine) passages—
this copy had the correct form היא instead of the form הוא
which the other two copies had. Because of this peculiarity
this third copy was called ספר היא.

Although the three different versions of the commentary
on the report differ from one another very much in details
and partly conflict with one another, yet in the main question as to the contents of our report they all agree in their
interpretation that the books described in it were Torah
scrolls. This interpretation of the meaning of our report
has also been accepted by all modern scholars. To my
knowledge, at least, no one has questioned the correctness
of the assumption that our report speaks about Torah
scrolls.

This supposition, however, is full of difficulties and
obviously untenable. The objections to the report, as
understood by the talmudic commentary, are so many
and the arguments against its correctness are so strong
that one is constrained either to reject the whole report as
unreliable and legendary, or to ignore the talmudic glosses
altogether, and seek to understand this report and interpret
it independently of the commentary given to it by later
talmudic teachers.

Professor L. Blau [3] pointed out the many difficulties

[3] *Studien zum althebräischen Buchwesen* (Budapest, 1902), pp. 102 ff.
To the difficulties involved in the talmudic conception of our report, mentioned by Blau, there is to be added the following main difficulty, namely,
that the explanations offered by this talmudic commentary on our report
do not explain the report and are altogether out of accord with the statement they are to explain. Thus, according to this commentary, the one
book is said to have contained the variant מעון instead of מעונה, which the
other two books had. We would accordingly expect, if the book was
called after the peculiarity found in its text, that this book should be called
ספר מעון, but this is not the case. No version of the report has this form

421

inherent in this report, as understood by the talmudic
commentary, and he also mentions the strong objections
which must be raised against the supposition that our
report refers to three Books of the Law or Torah scrolls,
found in the Temple at Jerusalem, which differed from one
another only in the writing or peculiar spelling of just these
three words but otherwise were perfectly alike and had no
other peculiarities to distinguish them from one another.
On the ground of all these difficulties found in the talmudic
conception of our report, Blau has rightly rejected the com-

of the name. The Pal. Talmud has מעוני and the Sifre has מעונים, while
the Abot d. R. Nathan and tractate Soferim have the name of this book as
ספר מעונה, according to the form of this word which was correctly written
in the two other copies. It is true, the Yalkut to Deuteronomy, § 964,
quotes the text of our report as stating that the book was called ספר מעון,
but this is merely a correction in the text of our report made by the Yalkut
to harmonize it with the talmudic explanation of the meaning of ספר מעוני.
The same is also to be said about the Midrash Tannaim (ed. Hoffmann,
p. 222), where alongside of the form ספר מעונו is also found the corrected
reading ספור מען.

In the interpretation of the name of the book היא the different versions
of the commentary conflict with one another and none of them explains the
name sufficiently. According to the Pal. Talmud, the book so designated
contained only nine times the word היא spelled with Yod, while the other
two books contained this word in the form spelled with Yod eleven times.
The difference between the books, then, was merely in the number of times
this peculiarity was found in them. And it is rather strange that a book
should be designated after the peculiarity in the spelling of a certain word
when it shows this peculiarity in less instances than the other books.
Again, according to tractate Soferim the peculiarity of this book was that
in eleven instances it contained the word הוא in the form spelled with Waw
instead of with Yod, while the other books had the word in the same eleven
instances in the form היא spelled with Yod. Then we would expect this
book to be designated ספר הוא after its peculiarity in the spelling of this
word. Of the two explanations offered in the Abot d. R. Nathan, the one
is apparently identical with the explanation given in tractate Soferim and
presents the same difficulty, while the other does not at all state clearly
wherein the peculiarity of the ספר היא consisted. See above, note 2.

mentary, given to our report in the talmudic glosses, as incorrect. He substitutes a theory of his own whereby to explain the contents and the meaning of this ancient report. But the theory which he advances and the explanations which he offers for the names of the three books and their origin are, to say the least, not better than the theory and the interpretations contained in the talmudic glosses.

According to Blau, this report is not a very ancient report. It does not represent a record of the time of the existence of the Temple or of the period immediately following it. Perhaps it is not even a Baraita. It did not originate in the tannaitic period. Its date is a late one. It comes originally from the third century (p. 106) and speaks of three Torah scrolls of the third century which it compares with one another and the peculiarities of which it records. These three Torah scrolls were merely believed to have originally come from the Temple in Jerusalem. They may have been found somewhere (where?) by Jews or bought by them from the Roman spoilers who had carried them away from Jerusalem (p. 104).

The designation of these three names are, according to Blau, very aptly chosen. In one case, the designation is after the place where the book was found; in the other it gives the name of the owner of the very valuable copy; and finally, in the third case, it gives a characteristic description of the form and size of the book. Thus, (1) The ספר מעוני was a Torah scroll which was found and kept in the place Beth Maon, briefly called Maon, which is in the neighbourhood of Tiberias. This Torah copy was perhaps saved from the Temple by exiles from Jerusalem who brought it with them to this place Maon (p. 105). It was accordingly designated after the place in which it had been preserved, ' The Book

of Maon' or ' Maoni-Codex '. (2) The ספר היא or ספר היא היא
was a Torah copy which was in the possession of a gentle-
man by the name of He or He-he. It was therefore called
after its owner, ' The Book of He' or ' The He-Codex '.
(3) The ספר זעטוטי, finally, was so designated because of
its very small size. In the tractate Soferim this name
Zatuti is found in the form זאטוטי instead of זעטוטי. A comparison of this form זאטוטי with the word זוטא, which means
'small', suggests to Blau that the former is a Katlul-form
of the latter and means accordingly ' very small '. The
book thus designated was, accordingly, very small in size,
or its writing was in very small characters (pp. 105–6).

This theory of Blau, however, is merely an unfounded
conjecture. In the first place, it is altogether against the
plain meaning of the words of our report. For the report
distinctly speaks of books which were found in the Temple,
and which, already at the time when they were found in the
Temple, had been designated by the names מעוני זעטוטי and
היא respectively. It can therefore not be interpreted to
have reference to books which merely were believed to
have come from the Temple and which were subsequently
designated by these names. Besides, this theory represents
many difficulties and inconsistencies, and is even contradictory in itself. I shall point out only some of the
incredibilities and contradictions contained in this theory
of Blau.

On p. 103, Blau correctly distinguishes between the
original text of our report and the later additions made
to it. He rightly states that the older text of the original
report consisted only of the first ten words, closing with
the word היא, as given in the version of the Pal. Talmud
Taanit. All the rest which follows this, beginning with

the word באחד, is later addition and forms a commentary to the older original report. But at the same time he also assumes that these later additions, or the commentary which gives the explanations to these three names, originated with the Palestinian Amora Simon b. Lakish or with one of his teachers. If, however, the original report originated in the third century, as Blau assumes on p. 106, and the author of the commentary was the Amora Simon b. Lakish, who lived in the first half of the third century, or one of his teachers who must have lived at a still earlier time, then we are confronted with the preposterous conclusion that the original text of the older report, dealing, as Blau assumes, with Torah copies of the third century, must have been younger than the commentary given to it. At any rate it could not have been older, so that one cannot speak, as Blau himself does, of an earlier report and a later commentary on it.

Furthermore, if the report merely compares three Torah copies of the third century, of which the one existed in Maon near Tiberias, and the other was in the possession of a person named He, and the third was of very small size, how could Simon b. Lakish, who lived in Tiberias, have made such an egregious blunder in the interpretation of this report as to reduce the well-known neighbouring town Maon and the owner of the second copy by the name of He, who must have been not less well known, to mere variants in the spelling of certain words? While we grant that it could have happened, and in fact did happen, that the later Amoraim sometimes misunderstood an older Mishnah or misinterpreted an old traditional report when after the lapse of a long period of time the correct meaning was lost to them, it is almost inconceivable that a prominent

425

teacher, such as Simon b. Lakish was, should have so utterly misunderstood a contemporary report, describing a well-known copy of the Pentateuch extant in his own time and in a town so very near his own place of residence. This is all the more strange, if we should assume with Blau that another teacher R. Jose (Abot d. R. Nathan, *loc. cit.*), whom Blau takes to have been an Amora younger than Simon b. Lakish (p. 105, note 3), has known that Sefer Maoni really meant a Torah copy preserved in the town of Beth Maon. How then could this supposedly well-known fact, mentioned by the younger R. Jose, have escaped the notice of the older teacher Simon b. Lakish ?

Blau must have realized this difficulty, and it seems that he hesitated somewhat to ascribe to Simon b. Lakish such a blunder in the interpretation of well-known names of persons and places. To account for the possibility of such a mistake on the part of Simon b. Lakish, Blau offers the following explanation according to which Simon b. Lakish's supposed interpretation of our report was after all not entirely wrong, and his alleged mistake perhaps no mistake at all.

In the case of the copy of the man He, Blau suggests that it might have actually had a peculiar way of spelling the word היא, the very word which sounds like the name of the owner. Of course, it may also have had other characteristics and different peculiarities in the spelling of other words, but these were not noticed or at least not commented upon. Blau does not find it strange on the part of ancient writers to thus have ignored all other characteristic peculiarities and to have reported only this one variant. He explains it as follows : ' Since this copy was called by the name of ספר הי and the ancient teachers did not consider

names as merely accidental but rather had a special fondness
for interpreting them, it can well be understood why they
just set out to search after the variants in the writing of
the word היא and why they reported only these variants'
(p. 105)

In the case of the copy supposed to have been found in
the town of Beth Maon, Blau seems likewise to assume that
by a strange coincidence it also contained the variant מעון
instead of the form מעונה in the passage of Deut. 33. 27.
For he remarks on p. 105, 'Whether in this copy the ה of
the word מעינה had been originally missing or merely faded
away, is not of any importance'.

One might as well add a third miracle by assuming
that in the third copy, the one which was of very small
size, by a strange coincidence actually had instead of the
word נערי in the passage of Exod. 24. 5 the foreign word
זאטוטי, which sounds so much like זוטא 'small', a description
which just fits the peculiar characteristic of this copy.   In
this manner both theories, the one advanced by Blau himself, and the one ascribed by him to the Amora Simon
b. Lakish, could well be harmonized.

However, even if one could bring himself to believe
in all these miraculous coincidences and accept the far-
fetched and forced explanations of the difficulties inherent
in both these theories, one would still be compelled, by
reasons about to be stated, to reject their commentary on
our report.   For this commentary is based on an altogether
unwarranted supposition which entirely misunderstood the
nature of our report and mistook its purport.

To save the reputation of Simon b. Lakish, I wish to
state first that he is not guilty of any of the grievous
mistakes pointed out above, as he is not responsible for the

427

theory ascribed to him by Blau. He is neither the author of our report nor did the commentary on this report, as given in the talmudic glosses, originate with him or his teacher, as Blau erroneously assumes. If the name of Simon b. Lakish [4] is mentioned in the tractate Soferim in connexion with our report, it is not to be interpreted, as Blau does, that Simon b. Lakish was the author of our report, as well as of the explanatory remarks and additions which follow it in the text of the tractate Soferim. Simon b. Lakish is mentioned there merely as one who cited or transmitted the old report. To this old report, cited by Simon b. Lakish, the redactor of the tractate Soferim added the explanatory remarks which he found in the Palestinian Talmud or possibly gathered from other sources.

These explanatory remarks and additions, however, were the work of later teachers who tried to explain the meaning of the old report. We have seen that their interpretations are not satisfactory. It is evident that they merely guessed at its meaning and guessed wrongly. To understand correctly this ancient report we must try to find its real meaning independently of these explanatory remarks of the later teachers. We must even be careful not to allow ourselves to be biased by their guesses in favour of their supposition. The proper way to proceed, then, would be to ignore their commentary altogether and consider only the text of the report itself.

Now, if we consider the text of the report itself we have no reason whatever to assume that it refers to Books of the

---

[4] The suggestion of V. Aptowitzer (*Hakedem*, 1908, p. 103) that in the passage of the tractate Soferim the name of the Tanna R. Judah b. Lakish, a pupil of R. Akiba, should be substituted for the name of the Amora Simon b. Lakish, seems to me to be very plausible.

Law, or Torah scrolls at all. This idea about our report
viz. that it speaks of copies of the Torah, was given to us
only by the commentary of the later teachers, which commentary we have found to be unsatisfactory. Having
rejected their commentary as unsatisfactory, there is no
reason why we should still retain the supposition upon
which their whole theory was based, as such a supposition
is altogether unwarranted by the words of the text of the
report. Nay, even more, such a supposition is disproved
by the terminology used in the text.

As we have seen above, the text of the report consists
of only ten words, and reads as follows: ג' ספרים מצאו בעזרה
ספר מעוני ספר זעטוטי וספר היא. Now, if we consider this
report without any preconceptions as to its contents and
do not read into it what it does not expressly say, then this
report tells us merely about books found in the Temple,
but not about sacred books, and certainly not about books
of the Pentateuch or Torah scrolls. For to the latter the
designation ספרים could hardly have been applied by the
author of this report. During the Temple times, when our
report most probably originated, and even later on throughout the period of the Mishnah, the name used as a designation for the Pentateuch was תורה [5] and not ספר or ספרים. In
contradistinction with the Pentateuch, the other books of
holy Scriptures are designated ספרים (M. Megillah III, 1).
Whether this designation ספרים was applied only to prophetical books or was also used to designate the Hagiographa
as well, does not concern us here. This much, however, is
certain, that the designation ספרים could have been applied

[5] It is also found in the plural to designate Torah scrolls, as in the
passage of the Pesikta d. R. K. 32 (Buber, p. 197 a) has שלש עשרה תורות
כתב משה, where it means copies of the whole Pentateuch.

429

only to biblical books outside the Pentateuch—prophetical
or both prophetical and hagiographical—but not to the
Pentateuch which had its special name : Torah. Consequently, the author of our report, who certainly was not
later than the Mishnah period, in speaking about books,
found in the Temple, and using the term *sefarim*, could
not have meant copies of the Pentateuch to which this term
was not applied in his time.

It is likewise evident that the author of our report did
not mean any of the other sacred books of the Bible outside
the Pentateuch. For even though the sacred books of
Scripture outside of the Pentateuch were designated by
the term ספרים, this latter term had not lost its original
simple meaning, denoting books in general. The term
ספרים was used both in a broader (general) and in a narrower
(technical) sense. When used as a technical term to denote
the books of holy Scripture, the books *par excellence*, no
additional phrase or comment was necessary to characterize
the books or to describe their contents. When, however,
the term was used in its simple meaning and in the broader
sense to denote books in general, there was usually added
another term, or a phrase to characterize and describe more
accurately the nature of the books referred to, what kind of
books they were and what they contained. Thus, e.g. when
it is said in the Talmud (R. H. 17 b) that on New Year's
Day there are three books opened שלשה ספרים נפתחין בראש
השנה, there is immediately added a description of these
books, to tell us what kind they were and what they contained, namely, אחד של רשעים גמורים ואחד של צדיקים גמורים ואחד
של בינונים. This is also the case with the statement made
in our report. The author of our report does not speak of
sacred books. He uses the term ספרים in its broader sense

to denote books in general. After stating that there were
three books found in the Temple, he felt the necessity of
characterizing and describing these books. He therefore
goes on immediately to tell us what kind of books they
were and what they contained. The words in our report
ספר מעוני וגו', or, as the more correct version in Sifre reads,
אחד של מעונים וגו', must therefore not be understood as
merely describing certain peculiarities of each book, like
the peculiar spelling of a certain word, or the extremely
small size of the characters in which it was written, or the
name of the owner, or the place where it was kept. For then
the most essential thing in the description of these books,
namely, what they really were, would be missing. Like the
words אחד של רשעים גמורים וגו' in the statement about the
books that are opened on New Year's Day, the words אחד של
מעונים וגו' in our report tell us the main thing about these
three books found or kept in the Temple, namely, what
kind of books they were and of what their contents consisted. By ascertaining the correct meaning of these words
of description in our report and interpreting them without
any preconceived notions, we shall be able to find out what
books our report has reference to. The first part of this
report tells us that these three books were found in the
Temple of Jerusalem. This does not mean that these books
were accidentally found in the Temple, but it means rather
that these books were found in the Temple, because the
Temple (i. e. its archives) was the place where these books
were always kept and preserved. This gives us a clue to
the meaning of these descriptions of the three books. We
have only to find out what kind of books were especially
preserved and kept in the Temple archives.

Whether there were kept in the Temple such standard

431

Torah scrolls which served as model copies from which the text of all other Torah copies was corrected, is, to say the least, historically not quite certain. For our purpose a discussion of this question is irrelevant. For, even if we should grant that there were such model copies of the Pentateuch preserved in the Temple, it would not alter the fact that our report does not refer to them. For our report speaks of books ספרים, and not of Books of the Law ספרי תורה, or Torah scrolls תורות.

The books which our report has reference to were books of a character altogether different from books of the sacred Scriptures. They were books about which we know with all certainty from other historical sources that they were kept and preserved in the Temple at Jerusalem. These books kept in the Temple and referred to in our report were ספרי יוחסין, Books of Genealogies, containing the genealogical lists of various classes of the people, or family records.

In order to be able to prove my thesis that our report speaks about these genealogical books, and to show how these genealogical books are unmistakably mentioned and aptly described in our report, I must first state briefly the character of these family records and what we know about them from other historic sources.

Josephus (*Contra Apionem*, I, 7) reports the fact that in the archives of the Temple at Jerusalem exact and careful records of the genealogies of the priestly families were kept. When giving his own aristocratic family tree, he emphatically states that he had set down the record of the genealogy of his own family as he had found it described in the public records (*Vita*, I). These records, of course, contained not only the lists of the families of the

VOL. VIII.   E e

priests but also those of the Levites, the minor priests. This fact is also confirmed by reports found in rabbinic literature. In Mishnah Middot, V, 4, we are told that in the Lishkat ha-gazit (one of the halls in the Temple at Jerusalem) a tribunal of the great Sanhedrin would hold their sessions for the purpose of judging and deciding about the family purity of the priesthood and of the Levites. See Tosafot Yom Tob *ad loc*. Cp. also Tosefta Hagigah, II, 9 and Tosefta Sanhedrin, VII, 1.

This statement is repeated in the Talmud (b. Ḳiddushin 76 b), and the members of the tribunal who attended to this work are designated as מיחסי כהונה ומיחסי לויה, the examiners of the Genealogies of the Priests and Levites. These judges about the purity of descent of the Priests and Levites must have had before them records in which they could trace the pedigree of each Priest or Levite. This presupposes not only the existence of such records from which proofs for the pure descent of the Priests and Levites could be obtained, but also that such records were kept in the Temple, where this tribunal held its sessions, and where they were at hand for the consultation by the members of this tribunal, holding their session in the Temple.

Besides these records which contained the lists of the families of Priests and Levites, there was also a special register of all the non-priestly Israelitish families of purely Jewish descent, such as could intermarry with the priestly families, the משפחות המשיאות לכהונה. This record was likewise kept in the Temple and had frequently to be consulted by the Judges who decided upon the purity of the priests, as, for instance, in the cases of priests whose mothers were Israelitish women, not of priestly family. It was from this record that they could prove that there was no stain in their family.

Josephus presupposes such records for Israelitish families when he says (*Contra Apionem, loc. cit.*) that the priest before marrying must examine the character of his wife's family and take her genealogy from the archives, thus to make sure that she is, if not of priestly, at least of pure Jewish descent. Such records are also presupposed by the Mishnah (Ḳiddushin, IV, 4), where it is prescribed that one need not search [in the genealogies] farther than the altar (in the case of priests) or the Dukan (in the case of Levites), or than membership in the Sanhedrin (in the case of Israelites).[6] These genealogies were supposed to have their origin in the book of genealogies ספר היחש, which contained the lists of the families of the returned exiles (Ezra 8. 1–15; Neh. 7. 5 ff.). The ספרי יוחסין, or Books of Genealogies kept in the Temple, which contained the families of Priests, Levites, and Israelites, were probably believed to have been the continuation of the book or register first begun by Ezra. Beside these registers,

---

[6] אין בודקין לא מן המזבח ולמעלה ולא מן הדוכן ולמעלה ולא מן סנהדרין ולמעלה. The meaning of this regulation is that in searching the genealogical records to examine the purity of descent of a certain person, we need only establish the fact that one of the progenitors of the person in question held one of these three offices unchallenged. For then we are assured of the purity of descent of that progenitor, for, before admitting him to the office, the authorities of that time must have convinced themselves of his being of legitimate birth and of pure descent. If, therefore, nothing derogatory is found in the record of the genealogies between that ancestor and the person now on trial, the purity of descent of the latter is established. The altar is the test for the priests, the Dukan for the Levites, and membership in the Sanhedrin is the test of the aristocratic Israelites of purely Jewish descent, for only Israelites of blameless families and purely Jewish descent were eligible to an office in the Sanhedrin (see Mishnah Sanhedrin IV, 2, Horayot I, 4, and Talmud Sanhedrin 36 b).

E e 2

containing all the classes of the Jewish nation, it became necessary, already at a very early time in the history of the restored community, to have another register containing the Proselytes that joined the community and the families which descended from them.

The prohibition against intermarriage, even in its most rigorous interpretation as given by Ezra, could not be so applied as to exclude marriages with proselytes altogether. It certainly did not prevent marriages with sincere proselytes from such nations whose admission into the community of God is expressly permitted in the Law, as e. g. the Egyptians and Edomites of the third generation (Deut. 23. 8). Such marriages no doubt were contracted, more or less frequently, soon after the time of Ezra. Whether this was due to a reaction against Ezra's rigid reforms, or was not considered to be incompatible even with Ezra's conception of the Law, is for our purpose irrelevant. Suffice it to say that the fact of such marriages having taken place soon after the time of Ezra cannot be denied. This, of course, made it necessary to keep special records of such proselyte families from which each proselyte could obtain proof as to his or her status and furnish such information as was necessary in order to decide whether or not he or she might be permitted to marry into the Jewish community, as for instance from what nation he was descendant, and in what generation he was. Such information was necessary both for priests, who were not permitted to marry any proselyte of the first generation, as well as for Israelites, who were prohibited from marrying proselytes from certain nations.

Indeed, we have evidence that in the later times of the second Temple such records of proselyte families were kept

435

and preserved in the Temple at Jerusalem. Eusebius (*Church History*, I, ch. vii. 3) reports from an old tradition that up to the time of Herod there were kept in the archives of the Temple at Jerusalem genealogical books in which the families of the Israelites as well as of the proselytes were recorded, and those descended from proselytes.[7]   From the Zadokite fragment published by Schechter, which, even if it be not a document originating in Temple times, at least records conditions of Temple times, we likewise learn that the custom prevailed to record the people according to four distinct groups, Priests, Levites, Israelites, and Proselytes, and that the persons or families belonging to each of these four classes were recorded by name in their special register.[8]   From many passages and discussions in the Talmud it is likewise evident that there existed such lists or registers for proselyte families from which each proselyte could prove his origin, descent, and status in regard to his admission into the community.

An indication of the existence of such a special register for the families of the proselytes kept in the Temple is, in my opinion, found already in the book of Malachi.

---

[7] According to the tradition reported by Eusebius, Herod is said to have destroyed these registers for the purpose of hiding his own non-Jewish origin. With no record to prove his descent from Proselytes, he could claim to come from Jewish ancestors. This tradition has some connexion with the report in the Talmud (Pesaḥim 62) about the suffering of the teachers in connexion with the hiding away of the ספר יוחסין. I expect to treat all the talmudic reports about family records ספר יוחסין and מגלת יוחסין in a special essay.

[8] *Documents of Jewish Sectaries* (Cambridge, 1910), vol. I, p. 14. The passage reads as follows: וסרך מושב כל המחנות יפקדו כלם בשמותיהם הכהנים לראשונה והלוים שנים ובני ישראל שלשתם והגר רביע ויכתבו בשמותיהם איש אחר אחיהו הכהנים לראשונה והלוים שנים ובני ישראל שלישתם והגר רביע.

The rigour with which Ezra and Nehemiah proceeded against intermarriage preventing the neighbouring nations from joining the Jewish community, had frightened away many sincerely pious and God-fearing proselytes. These pious proselytes, even though remaining true to the religion which they had sincerely adopted, were, nevertheless, very much disheartened and discouraged by the treatment accorded them by the Jewish rigorists. They complained very bitterly about the injustice done them by expelling them from the community which they earnestly wished to join and excluding them from the people of God with whom they anxiously sought to be identified. The justice of their complaint was recognized by the more liberal elements in the Jewish community who did not approve of the rigid policy of exclusion. These liberal advocates of universalistic tendencies among the Jews encouraged the proselytes to remain true to their adopted faith, for the God of Israel whom they serve accepts them fully as His own people. We hear the anonymous prophet offering such a comforting message to the despairing proselytes. ' Neither let the son of the stranger that hath joined himself to the Lord speak, saying, the Lord hath utterly separated me from His people. . . . For thus saith the Lord . . . Also the sons of the stranger, that join themselves to the Lord, to serve Him and to love the name of the Lord, to be His servants. . . . Even then will I bring to my holy mountain and make them joyful in my house of prayer . . . for mine house shall be called an house of prayer for all people. The Lord God which gathereth the outcasts of Israel saith, Yet will I gather others to him besides those that are gathered unto him' (Isa. 56. 3, 6-8). A reaction soon set in against the rigid policy of indiscriminately excluding the stranger from the community.

The prophet Malachi (3. 13–15) rebukes those people
who, if not in actual words, yet by their conduct and
attitude towards the proselytes declare that it is in vain
for the stranger to serve God, and that it would not profit
them to keep His ordinances, since in spite of their piety
they will not be accepted into the community but will be
refused the privilege of being registered and have a זכרון
mention of their names in the lists of the members of the
community, while on the other hand wicked and proud
people—if they be of Jewish descent—are made happy and
set up as acceptable among the members of the community.
The prophet recognizes the justice of the complaint of the
proselytes who would speak among themselves of this unjust
attitude towards the stranger on the part of the Jews. The
prophet goes on to say: 'When they [the proselytes] that
feared the Lord spoke often one to another [complaining
about their being thus unjustly discriminated against] then
God hearkened to them and listened and there was written
before Him a book of remembrances for them that
feared the Lord and that thought upon His name. And
they [these strangers] shall be mine saith the Lord of
hosts. . . . Then shall ye return and discern [that distinction should be made only] between the righteous and
the wicked, between him that serveth God and him that
serveth Him not [but not between the born Jew and the
proselyte]' (ibid., vers. 16–18). The passage ויכתב ספר זכרון
לפניו ליראי אדני is to be taken in a very plain sense to mean,
simply, that a book mentioning the names of the יראי אדני,
the proselytes who fear God, was written and kept before
God, not in heaven, but in His sanctuary.[9]

---

[9] There is no reason for assuming that in this passage of the book of
Malachi reference is made to a mystic book in heaven. The term לפני ד'

We have in this passage a statement of the fact that
the reaction against the rigid policy of excluding the
stranger resulted in the recognition on the part of the
official leaders of the community of, at least, the sincerely
pious and God-fearing among the proselytes. We are
accordingly justified in assuming that already at a very
early time in the history of the restored community
the re-admission of the truly pious proselytes into the community took place. A special book was then opened for
them and kept in the sanctuary, before God, i. e. in the
archives of the Temple. In this book all the names of
proselytes and their families descended from them were
recorded and found mention. By this official recognition
the proselytes became an integral part of the community,
which now consisted of *four* distinct groups or classes, viz.
Priests, Levites, Israelites, and Proselytes. The latter were
called by the name of יראי אדני ' Those who fear the Lord '.
Such a division of the community into four distinct classes,
of which the proselytes were one, is already found in the
Psalms. Here the proselytes, under the name of יראי אדני
' Those who fear the Lord ', are mentioned together with
the Priests בית אהרן, the Levites בית הלוי, and the Israelites
בית ישראל (Ps. 135. 12–13).

This division of the community into special classes was
also maintained in the books of the genealogical records.
Each one of these four classes had a special register of its
own. The proselytes had their separate register called

' Before the Lord' means in the Sanctuary, where His presence is especially
manifested. Thus, a jar containing an omerful of manna was laid up before
the Lord, i. e. in His sanctuary (Exod. 16. 33); Moses laid up the rods
before the Lord in the tent of the testimony (Num. 17. 22), and Samuel
wrote down the manner of the kingdom in a book and laid it up before
the Lord, i. e. in the sanctuary (1 Sam. 10. 25).

ספר זכרון ליראי אדני 'The Book of Remembrance for those who fear the Lord', or shortened ספר יראי אדני 'The Book of those who fear the Lord'. The Israelitish families of pure Jewish descent, i.e. the genuine Israel, had their own register, originally called כתב בית ישראל 'The record of the House of Israel'. The lists of this record were traced back to the lists of the families kept already in exilic times, and referred to in Ezek. 13. 9, hence it was called by the name given to this record in Ezekiel. The Priests and Levites, finally, also had their special registers, which, as we have seen, were frequently consulted by the members of the Tribunal sitting in the Lishkat ha-gazit and examining the purity of the descent of the Priests and Levites.

There seems, however, to have been a tendency already in early times to consider these two classes, Priests and Levites, as one. Thus in Psalms 115. 12–13 and 118. 2–4, only three classes of the community are mentioned, viz.: Proselytes, or those who fear the Lord, Israelites, and the House of Aaron, בית אהרן. Here evidently the Levites together with the Priests are included in the House of Aaron. Ezekiel also classes Priests and Levites together (45. 15), as is also done in Deut. 18. 1, and the Talmud speaks of twenty-four passages in the Bible where the Priests are called Levites (Yebamot 86 b). We cannot here enter into a discussion of the relative position of the Priests and Levites, whether they were at one time equals and then distinguished from one another, and then again made equals. But without discussing these mooted questions it may be safely stated that the majority of the Rabbis considered Priests and Levites as in a certain sense one class. It may be reasonably assumed that the registers for Priests

and Levites, even if they were kept separately, were regarded
by the Rabbis as one.   It is, however, more likely that in
later times, when the Levites obtained more recognition of
their equality to the Priests, there was actually kept only
one register for both Priests and Levites.

After this digression, describing the genealogical records
kept in the Temple, we shall now proceed to interpret our
report about the three books and we shall have no difficulty
at all.

As already stated, the report, in my opinion, speaks
about these very genealogical records.   I may further add
that our report, emanating from a rabbinical source, represents the opinion of the majority of the Rabbis who regard
the two priestly classes, Priests and Levites, as one, or
considers the two distinct records, if they were kept distinct,
as one.

The report tells us first that three such books were found
in the Temple שלשה ספרים נמצאו בעזרה.   Then it proceeds to
give us the character and contents of each one of them.
אחד של מעונים, one book, was the Book of the 'Templars', i.e.
of those belonging to the Temple or connected with its service.
The Temple was called מעון, and those connected with it
are called Meonim, or in the shorter form Meone.   This
ספר מעוני, then, is the book in which the genealogical records
of the Priests and Levites were kept.

The second book was the record of the noble families
of pure Jewish descent.   This was called ספר זעטוטים.   In
Talmud b. Megillah 9 a, we are told that the elders who
translated the Torah for King Ptolemy used the word זעטוטי
for the word אצילי in Exod. 24. 2.   From this we learn that
the word זעטוטי, like אצילי, was understood to mean 'the
nobles', 'the distinguished ones'.   For this reason these

translators are also said to have used the same word זעטוטי
for the word נערי in Exod. 24. 5, to indicate that those who
were sent to sacrifice and officiate were not mere youths
נערי, but the nobles, men of high rank.

As has already been said above, this record of the
Israelites was originally called by the name כתב בית ישראל.
However, since this record furnished the proofs for the pure
descent and the nobility of the families recorded in it, it
was subsequently called ספר זעטוטים 'The Book of the
Nobles or Aristocrats'. This is indicated especially in the
version of our report as found in Sifre. There the statement
reads ואחד שנקרא ספר זעטוטים 'And one that was called the
Book of Zaatutim'. The phrase 'that was called' implies
that this was not its original name. It may be that this
name was used by the people ironically to indicate by it
that the book is of interest and benefit only to the aristocratic families. This also explains the use of the foreign
word, Zaatutim, because it was the name given to this
book by the people who could well use such a foreign
word.[10]

The third book was the record of the families of the

---

[10] Whatever this foreign word may have meant, it described the character
of the book adequately. If we accept the explanation of Perles (*Beiträge
zur Rabb. Sprach- und Sagenkunde*, p. 5) that it comes from the word *zata*
in the Zend language, which means 'born', then Zatutim would simply mean,
those born, that is, born of Jewish parents. זעטוטי בני ישראל would be
like תולדות בני ישראל, and would designate those born of purely Jewish
families. The book may have received this name already in the Persian
period instead of the name כתב בית ישראל, with which these genealogical
lists were designated in the exile. And if we assume that the word
זעטוטי is the Greek ζητητής, which means, the wise men, or, the searchers,
the name ספר זעטוטי would also adequately describe the character of this
book, in which were recorded those people from which alone the wise
judges and members of the Sanhedrin could be chosen; see above, note 6.

God-fearing proselytes who, as we have seen, were designated by the name ירְאֵי אדני ' Those who fear the Lord '. This record of the proselytes was originally called by the name suggested by the passage in Malachi ספר זכרון ליראי אדני. In a shorter form it was called ספר יראי אדני. As יראי אדני is a compound word, used as a designation for a special class of people, it could well receive the article ה.[11]

The record of the proselytes was therefore called ספר הַיִּרְאֵי אדני.. Some people may have called it more explicitly ספר הגרים יראי אדני ' The record of the truly God-fearing proselytes'. Abbreviated, this title was written הי"ר,[12] which stands for הַיִּרְאֵי אדני or יראי אדני הגרים. The abbreviation marks, if ever such were used in ancient times, were by mistake dropped or ignored. And the abbreviation הַיִּרְאֵי אדני became merely the word היא, which caused

---

[11] The use of the article ה before such compound words is not infrequently found, as e. g. Ezek. 45. 16 הָעָם הָאָרֶץ, and Judges 16. 14 הַיָתֵד הָאָרֶג. It is of interest in this connexion to notice that the teacher בר הי הי mentioned in the Talmud (Ḥagigah 9 b) was, according to tradition, the son of a proselyte; the name, accordingly, also contains the abbreviated form הי for יי הירא and not as Tossafot, ad loc., explains the same. See Bacher, *Agada der Tannaiten*, I, p. 11.

[12] Such abbreviations are not infrequently found in the Talmud, as e. g. מנ"ח in Megillah 21 b, נש"גן in Sanhedrin 82 a, and גב"ם חנ"בי אב"יי אב"יי in Yoma 18 a. In the latter passage it is evident that the abbreviations were used in the Baraita already, for the Gemara there explains what each abbreviation means. How such abbreviations could sometimes be misunderstood is best shown in the case of Mishnah Abot IV, 19. Here the phrase שמואל הקטן אומר is, as Bacher (*Agada der Tannaiten*, I, p. 370) has shown, the result of an erroneous dissolution of the abbreviation שה"א which stood for the phrase שהרי הכתוב אומר, introducing the Scriptural proof (Prov. 24. 17) for the saying of R. Simon b. Eleazar in the preceding paragraph.

a great deal of misunderstanding in the interpretation of our report.

According to this interpretation, our report presents no difficulties at all. It is clear in its statements and plain in its meaning. All the difficulties in our report, caused merely by the false interpretation given to it in the talmudic glosses, disappear in the light of my theory. This in itself is a strong recommendation, and speaks for the correctness of this theory.

The following observation about the position of our report in the context of the Pal. Talmud will further confirm our theory that the report deals with genealogical records and not with Torah scrolls. As already stated, the text of the original report, as given in the Pal. Talmud, consists of the first ten words, beginning with the words שלשה ספרים on line 47, and closing with the word היא on l. 48. All that follows, beginning with the word באחד on l. 48 and ending with the word אחד on l. 53, is, as we have seen, a later addition and forms a commentary on the original report. Close upon this commentary, right after its last word אחד, there follows in the text of the Pal. Talmud a statement by R. Levi about the מגלת יוחסין, or a scroll containing genealogical lists, which was found in Jerusalem. Now, if we eliminate the commentary on our report which extends from l. 48 to l. 53, as a later addition, or an interpolation, then we have in that passage two statements about the family registers which were kept in the Temple at Jerusalem, the one giving the general information that the three classes or groups were recorded in three separate books, and the other quoting a fragment of such a record which was found in Jerusalem and which probably came from the Temple archives. Although we cannot apply the method

444

of סמוכים to the interpretation of the Talmud, yet the close contact of these two statements in the context of the passage strongly suggests also a close relationship between their contents. And we may consider this as a סמך, an additional support for our theory.

In this connexion I would further state that, as it seems to me, these two sayings belonging to one another and furnishing information about the genealogical records, are both placed in the wrong section of the Pal. Gemara, as we have it now. Such a misplacement of sayings is not infrequently found in the Pal. Talmud (see Frankel, *Mebo Hayerushalmi*, pp. 39–40). These two intimately connected sayings properly belong to the section of the Gemara, commenting upon paragraph six of the fourth chapter of the Mishnah Taanit, in which there is mentioned a list of many old families who in the respective dates assigned to them brought the wood-offerings. In a collection of Amoraic sayings and explanations to the Mishnah, or, as I would call it, in an early Gemara, which was subsequently made use of by the redactor of our Yerushalmi, the comment to paragraph six of the Mishnah contained these two sayings. In connexion with the names of the families enumerated in the Mishnah reference was given to the sources whence such lists of ancient families could be obtained, or where these families were recorded. So, there was first stated that three books containing such lists of families were found in the Temple at Jerusalem. And then a fragment of such a list was cited in which some of the families referred to in the Mishnah are actually recorded (compare the names of the families בן יהודה and יונדב בן רכב mentioned in the Mishnah and also given in the fragment of the מגלת יוחסין cited by Levi). This was the point of contact between the

445

Mishnah and the comment of the Gemara, stating where these families were actually recorded, and incidentally giving us also general information about the three records. At the redaction of the Pal. Talmud, the comment containing these two sayings, viz. the ancient report about the three books and the saying of Levi about the fragment of such records, was erroneously transferred from the Gemara discussion of paragraph six to the one pertaining to paragraph two in the Mishnah. The mention made in the latter paragraph of the Mishnah of the priestly divisions and their corresponding Israelitish divisions כ״ד משמרות ומעמדות, suggested to the redactor the idea of connecting with it the comment of the Gemara containing the statement about the three books, in one of which, the Sefer Meoni, the priestly divisions were recorded. This was but a slight mistake of arrangement made by the redactor and is rather pardonable. Of course, he could have placed the report about the three books in the section discussing paragraph two and the saying of Levi in the section discussing paragraph six of the Mishnah. He would have thus maintained in each case the point of contact and the connexion between the Mishnah and the Gemara comment on it. But, as already stated, the two sayings have both been taken over from one source, an earlier Gemara, and were inseparably connected with one another, so that with the transfer of one the other was also transferred.

In this manner the saying of Levi with the quotation from the מגלת יוחסין came into the wrong section of the Gemara, simply because it was so closely connected with the report about the three books. Later on, in the course of time, after the true meaning of this report had been forgotten and its statements misinterpreted, a later inter-

polater inserted the false commentary on the report right
next to its text, thus separating the words of the report
from the saying of Levi with which it had before been so
closely connected. The origin of this later interpolation
I shall now discuss briefly.

We have found that the commentary contained in the
talmudic glosses on our report altogether misunderstood
the purport of the report and gave it a false interpretation.
Now, it is true that the later Amoraim sometimes misunderstood old tannaitic statements, especially such as deal
with ancient problems, long forgotten, or refer to conditions
of earlier times which were no more known to the younger
Amoraim. For this reason, we find not infrequently that
some of the interpretations given by the later Amoraim to
older Mishnahs are not correct. Accordingly, there would
be nothing unusual in the supposition that the false interpretations given to our report in the talmudic glosses
originated with some of the younger Amoraim. However,
I am inclined to think that the false commentary to our
report as found in the Pal. Talmud, is not an interpretation
of the Amoraim but rather a later interpolation, as we find
many such interpolations in the text of the Pal. Talmud
(see Frankel, *op. cit.*, p. 38). Furthermore, it may be
reasonably assumed as plausible that the false conception
of our report as given in this commentary did not originate
wholly in one teacher's mind. It is not one mistake made
by one individual teacher. It is rather the result of a few
minor mistakes and slight misunderstandings made by many
different persons. Each one of these minor mistakes is in
itself pardonable and can be easily explained. But the
repetition and cumulation of these slight misunderstandings
gradually led to graver mistakes, and finally resulted in

that altogether false commentary given in these talmudic glosses.

The very fact that there are different, and partly contradictory, versions of this commentary supports such a supposition. For the existence of these conflicting versions of the commentary can be explained only by the supposition that they are modifications and enlargements of an earlier commentary. If we could distinguish in each one of the versions the additional elements to the earlier commentary, and if we could also recognize the slight changes and modifications which each version made in the original commentary, then we might be able, by a process of elimination, to restore the original commentary or earlier interpretation of the report. We could then decide whether the report has been misunderstood by its very first commentator, or its misinterpretation be due to a series of mistakes made by those responsible for the different versions which changed the original commentary beyond recognition.

I believe the latter to be the case, and in the following I shall attempt to trace the various misunderstandings through the whole process which resulted in the different and conflicting versions of the commentary.

I offer the following theory merely as a hypothesis. The original commentary to the report read as follows: באחד כתוב מעונים ובאחד כתוב זעטוטי בני ישראל ובאחד כתוב הגרים יראי אדני. Using the abbreviation י"א for יראי אדני, the last sentence read ובאחד כתוב י"א or ובאחד כתוב הי"א. The term כתוב was used here in the sense of ' was inscribed ' or ' was recorded '. This furnished a correct explanation of the meaning of the report, telling us that in each book was registered or recorded a special group or class of families

which constituted the Jewish community. This commentary
probably originated with R. Jose b. Ḥalafta, the reputed
author of the Seder Olam, who as an historian correctly
understood this ancient report.

This explanation of R. Jose, like so many other teachings and Halakot, was written down by students in their
private scrolls or note-books. These private scrolls were
not intended for publication, but merely to assist the memory
of the student. The students would therefore not always
record the sayings or teachings, which they embodied in
their note-books, in the exact wording in which they
heard them from their teachers. They would very often
record the gist of the saying or express it in their own
words and add a brief remark of their own. We need
therefore not be surprised if some of the students in recording this commentary of R. Jose in their note-books made
some slight changes in it or added a short explanation to
it, so as to make its idea clearer to themselves. One of the
students, in copying the brief explanation to the third
book, wrote down in his note-book instead of באחד כתוב הי"א
the words באחד כתוב טה"יא, which is the abbreviation of
טהרת הגרים י"א or טהרת הי"א, thus indicating to what purpose
these lists of families were recorded, namely, to prove them
pure without any stain and consequently eligible to be permitted into the community.[13]   This is a slight change in
the wording of the original commentary, but can certainly
be excused as it gives a fuller explanation. Another student
in copying the commentary into his note-book wrote about
the first book ספר של מי שנמצא במעון, the book of those who

---

[13] The use of the term טהר in the sense of purity of descent is frequently used in the Talmud, as e. g. Ķiddushin 72 b ממזרי ונתיני עתידין
למהר, and M. Eduyot, V, 7 אין אליהו בא לטמא ולטהר.

are found in or belong to the Temple, thus explaining the term מעונים to mean Priests and Levites who are connected with the Temple service.

The collections of such sayings contained in the note-books of students were copied and used by later students, and subsequently used by the later compilers or redactors of the talmudic works. In the process of copying these notes many mistakes naturally occurred. It is out of such errors and mistakes, made by later copyists, that the various versions of our commentary gradually grew. A copyist who found in one collection the comment באחד כתוב טהי"א, with an indication that the letters טהיא are an abbreviation, misunderstood the significance of the abbreviation. He erroneously took it to stand for ט' היא, i. e. nine times the word היא. To avoid any possible mistakes he wished to make the meaning of the expression clear. He therefore wrote down in his own collection, instead of the abbreviated form טהיא, the full words באחד כתוב תשע היא. Another copyist made a similar mistake with the simple statement found in the other collections reading באחד כתוב יא, where the abbreviation יא stood, as we have seen, for יראי אדני. The copyist erroneously took the two letters here to stand for their numerical value. Taking י"א to mean eleven, he accordingly understood the comment to say that in this one book were written *eleven*. Having in mind the Massoretic notice that there are eleven passages in the Torah in which the word היא is written in this form, he associated this comment with the remark about the י"א יודות שבתורה and explained it to say that this one book was a Torah scroll or Pentateuch copy, which contained this peculiarity eleven times as distinguished from the other copies which had it only nine times, ט' היא. Thus developed

F f 2

450

the false interpretations of this part of the report as referring
to Pentateuch copies. Still another later copyist tried to
indicate this false interpretation into the very text of the
ancient report itself. After the book mentioned in the
report had been understood to be the Pentateuch copy
with the peculiarity of the היא, and finding in an older text
of our report the words ספר הי״א with some indication that
the letters היא are an abbreviation, he took it to mean the
book of the eleven and believed that the word היא ought to
be added to the letters היא, standing for eleven, to indicate
what is meant, namely, the eleven times of the word היא
written in this form. In this manner originated the slight
change in the text of our report as found in Sifre ספר היא היא,
the abbreviation marks over the first הי״א, if such were used,
having been dropped.

The same misunderstanding probably took place in
regard to the comment about the second book; at least,
we can see how easily it could have been made. The
phrase זעטוטי בני ישראל was familiar to the copyist. He
remembered the talmudic report that this phrase was used
by those who translated the Torah for Ptolemy, as a substitute for נערי בני ישראל in Exod. 24. 5. When reading
this comment that in one of the books were written the
זעטוטי בני ישראל, he could easily make the mistake to believe
that this had reference to a Pentateuch copy in which this
phrase, supposed to have been used in the translation
prepared for Ptolemy, actually occurred in the text itself
instead of the word נערי as written in the others. To the
original comment, reading באחד כתוב זעטוטי בני ישראל, he
therefore added the explanatory words ובשנים כתוב וישלח את
נערי בני ישראל to indicate plainly in what this copy was
distinguished from the other two.

451

Thus far the mistakes could easily be made. All that was necessary was to start wrongly and give to the word כתוב the meaning of 'In the text was written' instead of 'In it was inscribed or recorded'.

In the case of the first book, it is true, the mistake cannot so easily be explained. However, once the mistake was made to interpret the phrase כתוב to mean 'in the text of one was written' instead of 'in one was recorded' they necessarily had to interpret the phrase in the same sense also in regard to this case, and take the word Meonim or the shorter form Meoni as a word which was found written in the text of this book, instead of some other word. Having taken the other two books for Torah copies, the first was likewise taken for a Torah copy and the word Meoni as a variant to the passage in Deut. 33. 27, where a similarly sounding word Meonah occurs, which in the mistaken opinion of this compiler could have been the one in regard to which the copies differed, although the supposed reading in the text מעון אלהי קדם does not quite satisfactorily explain the name Meoni.[14]

[14] It is probably due to such a misunderstanding on the part of a later interpolator that our report was inserted into the Sifre to the very passage, of which one of the three books was supposed to have contained a different reading.

It is, however, more plausible to assume that the text of our report was originally contained in the Sifre. Its presence there can easily be explained. Since the passage מעונה אלהי קדם was understood to refer to the Temple in Jerusalem, the compiler thought fit to connect with this passage a report about the three genealogical books, which were kept in that Temple. A later interpolator, however, who had already misunderstood the meaning of our report, added to it the explanatory remark about the meaning of the first book, which he copied from the Pal. Talmud, and by which he meant to account for the presence of the report in the Sifre to the passage מעונה אלהי קדם. This would explain why no remarks about the other two books are found in the Sifre, as the interpolator did not

This difficulty was felt, and so in looking for a more satisfactory explanation of the name Meoni, one of the versions had preserved the statement found in an older collection as part of R. Jose's explanation and which read ספר שנמצא במעון, shortened from ספר של מי שנמצא במעון . They took this to be a more satisfactory explanation of the term מעוני. But the error of considering these books as Torah scrolls was already too well established and could not be abandoned, and this comment, found in an older collection, had also to be adapted to the supposition that the report deals with Pentateuch copies. They accordingly assumed that this comment merely says that Meoni signifies a copy found in Maon or in the Temple, ספר עזרה 'book of the Temple'.

A later glossator, to whom it was perhaps known that Maon is sometimes used as a shorter name for Beth Maon, may have made the same mistake which Prof. Blau made, and imagined that מעון here is not the Temple but the place בית מעון, and he accordingly inserted the word בית. Thus came about the reading זהו ספר שנמצא בבית מעון, which could be explained by Blau, and perhaps also by the glossator, to mean a Torah scroll which was found or preserved in the place Beth Maon.

The above sketch of the possible developments which may have led to the false interpretation of our report is merely a suggestion offered by me to explain how our report could have been so utterly misunderstood and wrongly interpreted.

Whether the mistake came about in the manner described above or in any other way, whether it was

intend to interpret the report but merely to explain its connexion with that passage in Sifre.

committed by one or more teachers, by Amoraim, or by later interpolators, the fact remains that the interpretation is false and based upon an erroneous conception of our report. Even if this misinterpretation came from the Amoraim, it would nevertheless be wrong, and would in no way affect my main theory that our report deals, not with Torah scrolls, but with genealogical records. This theory, I trust, I have proved satisfactorily.

THE THREE SCROLLS OF THE LAW THAT WERE FOUND IN THE TEMPLE COURT

SHEMARYAHU TALMON

I

Many discussions in rabbinic literature indicate that Bible MSS current in the period of the Second Temple differed from each other textually in varying degrees. Undoubtedly some of these variations originated in scribal routine, but others preserved ancient textual traditions which had taken root in Israel at a very early time. Apparently not much thought was given to these variants during the first half of the period, in so far as they constituted mere stylistic variations, or even when they suggested some difference in views and opinions. This may explain the survival of textual variants in parallel sections of Former Prophets and Chronicles which the transmitters of the Bible did not bother to standardize.[1] In the second half of this period, however, there are to be found indications of an ever-increasing effort to consolidate a single textual tradition of the Bible in the Jewish community. But even at this stage parallel readings were viewed with relative equanimity. The exclusion of a reading from the official text did not disqualify it from being used in rabbinic discussions in the academies. This accounts for the appearance in rabbinic literature of biblical quotations that diverge from the traditional text.[2] These parallel readings persisted in the academy discussions without disparaging those who quoted them.

The preservation even in rabbinic literature of readings which differ from the *textus receptus* has prompted S. Lieberman to classify the MSS extant during the Temple period into three categories:[3] (1) authoritative books kept in the Temple ($\dot{\eta}\varkappa\varrho\iota\beta o\mu\acute{e}va$); (2) authoritative popular books used by the general public ($\varkappa o\iota v\acute{a}$); (3) inferior texts, which survived in small communities in Palestine ($\varphi av\lambda\acute{o}\tau\varepsilon\varrho a$). Only books of the first category were considered suitable for the public reading in the synagogue. The second group, representatives of which are the Torah Scroll of Rabbi Meir, the Torah

---

1. Cf. Geiger, *Urschrift und Uebersetzungen der Bibel* (Breslau, 1857) pp. 97–100; 231 ff.; see also Rashi on 1 Chronicles viii, 29.
2. V. Aptowitzer, *Das Schriftwort in der rabbinischen Literatur* (1906–1915).
3. S. Lieberman, *Hellenism in Jewish Palestine* (1950), pp. 22–23, 26–27, Cf. also Geiger loc. cit.

Reprinted from *Textus* 2 (1962).

Scroll of the Synagogue of Severus in Rome[4] and other books that emanated from Jerusalem (*P.T. Megillah*, I,9; 71d), were used for study. The rabbis strove, however, to keep the books of the third category from being used even for study purposes: "Five things did R. Akiba charge R. Shimeon b. Yochai... and when you teach your son, teach him from a corrected scroll. What is that? Said Rava—others state, R. Mesharsheya—: a new one, for once an error has entered, it remains." (*Pesaḥim* 112a; Soncino translation, ed. Epstein, p. 119). But some of these inferior MSS nevertheless found their way into the academies. This we may deduce from the dictum: "A book that is not corrected—R. Ami said: Until thirty days one is allowed to keep it, from then and further on, it is forbidden to keep it, because it is said: 'Let not unrighteousness dwell in thy tents' [Job xi,14]." (*Ketubbot* 19b; Sonc. ed. p. 106.)

According to Lieberman the popular scrolls of the Bible (κοινά or *vulgata*) were not simply corrupt MSS. They represented a variant text which lacked some of the "emendations of the Soferim and corrections of the sages" that were inserted in the normative books. This definition is marked by over-simplification, which apparently derives from Lieberman's tendency to align the modes of Bible transmission with the method that prevailed in the Hellenistic world. Surely it may be assumed that those popular texts did not reflect a single version, common to them all, but rather differed from one another in various details. They were not distinguished by a common textual tradition, but by deviating, individually and as a group, from the authoritative version which progressively crystallized in the model codices. Moreover, we should not draw a sharp line of distinction in this respect between the "popular" books and the "authoritative" books; for even the latter were not uniform throughout. For this reason the sages were occasionally called upon to decide between parallel readings which presented themselves even in the model codices that were kept in the Temple.

II

The process of selection and the criteria for the authorization of one MS and for the rejection of another are illustrated by the report on the three Scrolls of the Law found in the Temple Court, which differed from each other in several respects. The account is preserved in four sources, which differ somewhat

---

4.   P.T. Ta'anith i, 1 (64a); *Bereshith Rabba* ch. 9,5 (ed. Theodor-Albeck, p. 70), also the end of ch. 20 and ch. 94, 9; *Pesikta d'Rab Kahana* (ed. S. Buber) 68, 1; *Bereshith Rabbathi*, ed. Albeck (1940), p. 209 ff.

from each other. Our first task, therefore, is to determine the assumedly correct reading.

(1) *P.T. Ta'anith* IV, 2;68a:

Three Scrolls of the Law were found in the Temple Court: the *mĕ῾ōnā* scroll, the *za῾ăṭūṭē* scroll and the *hī'* scroll. In one of them they found written מעון אלהי קדם (Deut. xxxiii, 27) and in the other two they found written מעונה; they adopted the reading of the two and discarded the reading of the one. In one they found written וישלח את זעטוטי בני ישראל (Ex. xxiv, 5) and in the other two they found written וישלח את נערי בני ישראל; they adopted the two and discarded the one. In one they found היא written nine times, and in the other two they found it written eleven times; they adopted the two and discarded the one.

ג' ספרים מצאו בעזרה 'ספר מעוני' ו'ספר זעטוטי' ו'ספר היא'. באחד מצאו כתוב 'מעון אלהי קדם' ובשנים כתוב 'מעונה אלהי קדם'. וקיימו שנים גביטלו אחד. באחד מצאו כתוב 'וישלח את זעטוטי בני ישראל' ובשנים כתוב 'וישלח את נערי בני ישראל'. וקיימו שנים וביטלו אחד. באחד מצאו כתוב תשע 'היא' ובשנים כתוב אחת עשרה 'היא'. וקיימו שנים וביטלו אחד.

(2) *Aboth d'Rabbi Nathan*, Version B, ch. 46 (ed. Schechter, p. 129): Three Scrolls of the Law were found in the Temple Court: the *mĕ῾ōnā* scroll, the *za῾ăṭūṭē* scroll and the *hī'* scroll. The *mĕ῾ōnā* scroll: in one was written מעון אלהי קדם, and in one was written מעונה; they discarded the one and adopted the two. (Rab Yose said: This was the scroll that was found in Beth Ma῾on.) The *za῾ăṭūṭē* scroll: in one was written זעטוטי בני ישראל and in the other two was written וישלח את נערי בני ישראל. They discarded the one and adopted the two. The *hī'* scroll: wherever was written היא, they read (it) הוא. Some say: היא is written with *yod* in eleven places in the Torah. They discarded the one and adopted the two.

ג' ספרים נמצאו בעזרה, 'ספר מעונה', 'ספר זעטוטה', 'ספר היא'. ספר מעונה, באחד היה כתוב 'מעון אלהי קדם' ובאחד היה, 'מעונה'. בטלו האחד וקיימו את השנים. אמר רב יוסי זה הוא ספר שנמצא בבית מעון. ספר זעטוטי, באחד היה כתוב 'זעטוטי בני ישראל' ובשנים כתוב 'וישלח את נערי בני שיראל'. בטלו האחד וקיימו את השנים. ספר היא' בכל מקום שהיה כתוב 'היא' היו קורין (אותו) 'הוא . ויש אומרין אחד עשר יודידיות 'היא' שבתורה. בטלו את האחד וקיימו את השנים".

(3) *Sifre* II, 356 (ed. Finkelstein, p. 423; ed. Friedmann, p. 148b): Three Scrolls of the Law were found in the Temple Court, one [distinguished by readings] of *mĕ῾ōn(īm)*, one of *hī',hī'*, and one called "the *za῾ăṭūṭīm* scroll". In one was written מעון קדם, and in the second was written מעונה אלהי קדם. The sages discarded the one and adopted the two.

״ג׳ ספרים נמצאו בעזרה׳ אחד של ׳מעונים׳ ואחד של ׳היא היא׳ ואחד שנקרא ׳ספר זעטוטים׳.
באחד כתיב ׳מעון קדם׳ ובשניה כתיב ׳מעונה אלהי קדם׳. בטלו חכמים את האחד וקיימו
השנים.״

(4) *Soferim* vi, 4 (ed. Higger, p, 169):

R. Shimeon b. Lakish said: three Scrolls of the Law were found
in the Temple Court—the *mě'ōnā* scroll, the *za'ăṭūṭē* scroll and the
hī' scroll. In one they found written מעון, and in the other two was
written מעונה אלהי קדם; they adopted the two and discarded the one.
In one they found written וישלח אל זאטוטי בני ישראל and in the two
was written וישלח אל נערי בני ישראל; they adopted the two and discarded the one. In one הוא was written eleven times, and in two
היא was written eleven times; they adopted the two and discarded
the one.

״א״ר שמעון בן לקיש׳ שלשה ספרים נמצאו בעזרה׳ ׳ספר מעונה׳׳ ׳ספר זאטוטי׳׳ ׳ספר היא׳.
באחד מצאו כתוב ׳מעון׳ ובשנים כתוב ׳מעונה אלהי קדם׳. וקיימו שנים ובטלו אחד. באחד
מצאו כתוב ׳וישלח אל זאטוטי בני ישראל׳ ובשנים מצאו כתוב ׳וישלח אל נערי בני ישראל׳.
וקיימו שנים ובטלו אחד. באחד כתוב אחד עשר ׳הוא׳ ובשנים מצאו כתוב אחד עשר ׳היא׳.
וקיימו שנים ובטלו אחד.״

The subject-matter of this account evidently are three Scrolls of the Law
that had been deposited in the Temple Court[5], owing to their sanctity and
importance.[6] Even if we accept the thesis of Blau, Lauterbach and Klein,
which is rejected by others[5], that we must discern in this account between two
strata, the original discussion and an exposition of it—even then we cannot
accept the opinion of Klein and Lauterbach that the discussion here centers
on records of family genealogies rather than Torah scrolls.[7] It is true that the
text in the Palestinian Talmud is followed by references to genealogy records
that were found in Jerusalem. This juxtaposition led Rashi to discuss such
records together with the three scrolls that were found in the Temple Court

5. See M. Z. Segal, ״לתולדות מסירת המקרא״ in מנחה לדוד ילין (1935), pp. 12–22; G. Gerleman,
"Synoptic Studies in the Old Testament", *Lunds Universitets Arsskrift* N.F. Avd.
1. Bd. 44. Nr. 5. 1948, p. 4.

6. On this point, see Josephus, Ant. V, i, 17.

7. The concatenation of conjectures proffered by Lauterbach to substantiate his explanation only shows that it has no proper foundation,"The Three Books Found in the
Temple at Jerusalem", JQR 8, (1917–8), 385–423. On the arguments of Klein, ״מחקרים
בפרקי היחס שבס׳ ד״ה״, *Zion* 1 (1939), 46ff., see Segal's critique (in the appendix to
op. cit., p. 254). The opinion of L. Blau (*Studien zum althebräischen Buchwesen* (1902),
pp. 102ff.) that the מעונה codex came from Beth Ma'on near Tiberias (cf. *Aboth d'Rabbi
Nathan*), that the זעטוטי codex was an especially small book and that the היא codex
was named after its supposed owners—and that all three came into the hands of Jews
in the third century after having been carried off from Jerusalem at the time of the
destruction of the Temple—has already been refuted by Lauterbach, op. cit., p. 288 ff.

in his commentary on 1 Chronicles viii 29. But adjacency in a Talmudic treatise is not necessarily an indication of related subject matter. Furthermore, in one section *Jerusalem* is referred to, and in the other, the *Court of the Temple*.

The account is composed of four distinct parts—an introduction and three statements; the latter we shall designate A, B, and C. Each statement treats of a particular textual discrepancy, which in each instance distinguishes one scroll from the other two with which it was compared. The Introduction, which makes the three statements into a unit of subject matter, appears in all four versions, though it would seem that in none of them it has survived in its original form.

We assume that originally the three *discarded* codices were mentioned in it: ספר מעון, ספר זעטוטי, ספר היא. Against these the sages upheld in each case the readings of the codices that constituted the majority. The latter were declared authoritative: מעונה אלהי קדם (Deut. xxxiii, 27), נערי בני ישראל (Ex. xxiv, 5), and the spelling היא for the third pers. sing. fem. in eleven instances in the Pent. instead of the prevalent spelling הוא.[8]

In contrast to the relative textual uniformity of the Introduction, the statements appear in the several sources in different wordings. The version of *Aboth d'Rabbi Nathan* is distinguished by the inclusion of a comment in statement A which is not included in the other sources. This comment ascribes to R. Yose the explanation of the designation "*mě'ōnā* codex" as due to its having turned up at a place called Ma'on. There are three indications of the secondary nature of this comment: (1) According to the Introduction, the codex was found in the Temple Court and nowhere else. (2) The MS is called erroneously "*mě'onā* codex" in the Introduction, whereas the comment correctly presupposes the name "*mā'ōn* codex" (3) In the case of this codex alone an explanation of its name is offered, and this explanation bears no relationship to the Bible text, which is the sole object of the entire discussion.

The *Sifre* version is the shortest. This fact led Friedmann to assume that a section of the once fuller account had been omitted by copyists. But in fact, the author of this midrash cited only the part of the argument required for his purpose, viz. statement A, which treats of the variant readings of the phrase מעונה אלהי קדם (Deut. xxxiii, 27). We conclude that of the four versions, only that of *Sifre* fulfils a direct functional purpose. This indicates its priority over the other versions.

By analogy we may say that also the variant זעטוטי = נערי was first adduced in some midrashic or proto-massoretic treatise in connection with the verse, "*And he sent the young men of the children of Israel, who offered burnt offerings...*"

8.   We here concur with the opinion of J. Müller, *Masecheth Soferim*, 1878, p. 90.

(Ex. xxiv, 5). Similarly, the variant הוּא = הִיא first came up for consideration in the discussion of one of the eleven instances in the Pentateuch where the Massoretic Text has the exceptional spelling היא for the third person fem. pronoun, rather than the prevalent *Kethib* spelling הוּא (some 200 times) accompanied by the *Qere* היא.

It follows that the Introduction in the version of *Sifre* cannot be considered original[9]. The juxtaposition of the *mā'ōn–me'ōnā* argument and the discussion of other variant readings which are essentially unrelated to it reflects a late process of development, possibly due to a recurrent influence of the opening formula which appears in the parallel texts[10].

In the Palestinian Talmud, and especially in *Aboth d'R. Nathan*, the account of 'The Three Books' is adjacent to discussions of other subjects also arrayed in groups of three or four, such as "Upon three things the world rests..." (P.T.) There are three books of prophets, three books of Hagiographa, four (types) of wise men, three (types) of students (AdRN). In *Soferim*, the argument appears in a series of lists dealing with scribal peculiarities to be observed in the transcription of the Bible text. These lists, unrelated in their subject-matter, are couched in the form of numerical sayings, such as "There are ten dotted words in the Torah..." (vi, 3) and "Three times the word לא is written *lamed aleph* but is read *lamed waw*" (vi, 5).

It may be deduced that also the combination of the discussions concerning the 'three codices' resulted from a custom of the scribes to assemble guiding rules for the accurate transcription of Torah scrolls in accordance with a text accepted by them as standard. The juxtaposition of the three statements should therefore be considered as due to scribal techniques and does not indicate any essential relationship between them. Once the three statements were combined they became a literary unit which warranted the addition of some introductory remark. We are confronted here with a very early case of massoretic-type or proto-massoretic notation, the kind which constitutes the core of classical massoretic works.

A close examination of the textual variations between the different versions tends to confirm this hypothesis. Those in the Introduction and in the first

9.   This viewpoint contradicts the opinions of Lauterbach (*op. cit.*) and Blau (*op. cit.*), who maintain that the original substance of the account is to be found in the opening passage and that all that follows, from "in one they found" onwards, is a late exposition. S. Klein (*op. cit.*) takes up a similar position, but he considers the recurrent phrase "They adopted two and discarded one" to be part of the original discussion.

10. Thus it is possible that there is an element of historical truth in the attribution of the argument, in its complete version, to ר"ש (Rabbi Shimeon ben) Lakish, an Amora of the 3rd century. V. Aptowitzer (הקדם 2 (1908), 103) suggests the reading, ר׳ יהודאבן לקיש, assigning the dictum to a Tanna and disciple of R. Akiba.

two statements are of no importance and can be readily explained as ensuing from scribal and copyist routine. In this respect as well, the version of *Sifre* stands apart; in its introduction the enumeration of the codices follows a different order. Even its wording diverges from the almost uniform phrasing of the other three sources.

1. The variation of active and passive, "*they found* three codices" or "three codices *were found*", does not at all affect the subject matter. We find similar variants in parallel texts of the Bible (2 Sam.v, 17 משחו and 1 Chron. xiv, 8 וגמשח; 2 Kings xvii, 6 לכד and *ibid.* xviii, 10 נלכדה; and in divergencies between MT and extra-Massoretic texts (Ex. xxv, 28–MT ונשא בם, Sam., ונשאו בם ; Is. i, 26 and xiv, 3–MT יקרא and 1QIs^a, יקראו.[11]

2. The same applies to the practically synonymous expressions "was written" and "was found written" (cf. Deut. xi, 24, לכם יהיה and Josh. i,3, לכם נתתיו).

3. The wording in *Soferim*, א ל זעטוטי בני ישראל, instead of את זעטוטי בני ישראל in the other two sources, may have been influenced by the wording of Ex. xxiv, 11, וא ל אצילי בני ישראל which appears in the same context as v.5: ואת נערי בני ישראל.

4. In the designation of the codices, we find two rows of three parallel forms which undoubtedly resulted from a process of assimilation. ס׳ מיעוני (P.T.) was apparently formed by analogy with ס׳ זעטוטי (*ibid.*), unless we explain the form מעוני as an abbreviation of ס׳ זעטוטה.מעונים (AdRN) is imitative of ס׳ מעונה (*ibid.*). The form מעונים (*Sifre*), however, is probably to be explained as an allusion to the two-fold mention of מען = מעונה in the Pent. (Deut. xxvi, 15; xxxiii, 27). Analogous with it the form ס׳ זעטוטים originated in *Sifre*.

III

The variant readings in the formulations of the third statement are of greater consequence. As we have pointed out, this statement does not appear at all in the *Sifre* version, and in AdRN it has survived in a distorted form. This is clear from the replacement of the formula "In one was written... in two was written" by the wording, "The *hi*' codex—wherever היא was written, they read הוא". Now this reading is meaningless. Apparently the early expositors already sought to interpret it by adding "in eleven places in the Torah היא is written with a *yod*". The intent of this expression will be clarified by a scrutiny of the other two formulations of the statement.

Let us first examine the version of P.T. According to it, the codex that was

---

11. Cf. A. Sperber, "Hebrew Based upon Biblical Passages in Parallel Transmission", HUCA 14 (1939), 199-200, § 61a.

discarded in favour of the other two whose reading was accepted, employed in the Pent. only nine times, as against eleven in the other two, the spelling הִיא instead of the predominant spelling הוּא. Thus the difference between the majority and minority readings was only quantitative, not qualitative, and evidences the uncontrolled, unsystematic, and unequal penetration of a new phonetic spelling of the third person fem. pronoun into MSS of the Pentateuch. The penetration of this new spelling was undoubtedly gradual, reaching completion only in the Samaritan version of the Pentateuch, in which the earlier spelling הוא does not appear. This novel spelling also gained ascendancy in the Massoretic Text of the Prophets and Hagiographa, to the extent that the form הָוא has survived only three times (Ps. lxxiii, 16; Job xxxi, 11; Eccl. v, 8), while the MT of the Pent. was stabilized at a time when the spelling הִיא had become established in only eleven instances, namely: Gen. xiv, 2; xx, 5; xxxviii, 25; Lev. xi, 39; xiii, 10; xiii, 21; xvi, 31; xx, 17; xxi, 9; Num. v, 13; 14. These were counted and confirmed in the Massorah. This list marks the final stage in the process of consolidation and unification of traditions in this particular matter. The Torah Scroll of the Synagogue of Severus, for example, had הִיא also in Ex. xxxi, 13, where MT has the spelling הוא.[12] And while recension A of AdRN notes that "eleven times הִיא is written in the Torah with a yod" and recension B speaks of "eleven yod's in the Torah", the lists in the two recensions still differ in their order and even in the actual instances adduced. Version A derives only one instance, והיא, from Gen. xxxviii, 25, while Version B registers two, היא מוצאת והיא שלחה from the same verse. Version A does not list היא שבתך שבתת (Lev. xvi, 31) as does B, making up the number by counting both mentions of והיא in Num. v, 13: והיא נטמאה והיא לא נתפשה, while B counts only the second. This means that, although both recensions deal with the general rule of the "eleven היא" in the Pentateuch which are spelled with yod, their lists coincide in only nine of the cases. This seems to point to a stage of development in which the traditionists had as yet authorized a nucleus of only nine cases of the novel spelling היא. This assumption offers an explanation for the wording of our account as it appears in the Palestinian Talmud. The codex that was discarded, the one in which "they found היא written nine times" represents that intermediate stage in the penetration of the spelling היא into the text of the Pentateuch. On the other hand, the two codices which recorded "היא written eleven times" are representative of the tradition which the rabbis ultimately accepted and which took root in the majority of texts.

12. *Bereshith Rabbathi*, ed. Albeck, p. 210; A. Epstein, "Ein von Titus nach Rom gebrachter Pent. Commentar u. seine Varianten", MGWJ 34 (1885), 337-71; A. Neubauer, "Der Pent. der sogenannten Severus Synagoge" MGWJ 36 (1897), 508-509. And see A.M. Habermann's analysis of this matter (*Sinai* 32 (1953), 161–167).

Soferim deals with a more basic divergence between the discarded codex and the two whose reading was adopted. The statement, "In one was written eleven times הוא and in two they found written eleven times היא", indicates that the codex that was banished had not absorbed at all the new spelling היא but maintained throughout the Pentateuch the older spelling הוא; in other words, it stood in direct contrast to the Samaritan version of the Pentateuch, which reads היא in every instance. It is thus clear that this codex was basically different from the minority codex treated in the P.T. It did not vary from the others in the degree to which it had absorbed the novel mode of spelling, but in that it represented a textual tradition totally unaffected by the processes of textual development that had affected to some measure the codices accepted by the rabbis. The divergence in *Soferim* consequently precedes chronologically that of P.T. We may deduce from this that during the Second Commonwealth there were apparently current in Israel Torah scrolls that were completely free of the new spelling היא as a designation of the third person fem. At the same time this spelling had penetrated into other MSS without any system and in varying measure, while in yet other codices this process came to its logical and consistent conclusion, the spelling היא being accepted in every case, as in the Samaritan tradition.

IV

It is conceivable that the variant reading מעונה = מעך alludes to those texts in which no distinction had as yet been made between "closed and open" (B.T. Shabbath 103b), *i.e.* the medial and final forms of the letters מנצפ״כ [13], as we read in P.T. Megillah I,9 (71d): "Jerusalemites used to write (ה)ירושלימ — ירושלים without discriminating; similarly with צפון=(ה)צפונ and (ה)תימנ — תימן". Vestiges of that transitory stage survive in the Massoretic text: למרבה (Is. ix, 6) and המ פרוצים (Neh. ii, 13). More such readings were preserved, for example, in the Torah Scroll of the Synagogue of Severus, as recorded in *Ber. Rabbathi.*[4]

1. Gen. xxxvi, 10 MT: אליפז בן עדה
   MS. Paris: אליפז בנעדה
   Num. xxxvi, 1 MT: ממשפחת בני יוסף
   MSS Paris, Damascus: ראשי בני יוסף׳ בן יוסף כתוב
2. Gen. xxxvii, 2 MT: לא ידעתי יום מותי
   MSS P. and D.: יוממותי כתיב... והיינו שהמ״ם אינה סתומה וכתובות בתיבה אחת
   Gen. xliii, 15 MT: וירדו מצרים
   MS Prague: וירדו מצרימה

13.   N.H. Torczyner (Tur-Sinai) "מנצפ״ך צופים אמרום", *Leshonenu* 10 (1939), 98–118.

Gen. xlvii, 7 MT:	ואקברה שם
MSS Paris, Damascus:	שמ כתיב
Lev. iv, 34 MT:	ויקח הכהן מדמה
MSS Paris, Damascus:	מדמ כתיב
Deut. i, 26 MT :	ולא אביתם
MSS Paris, Damascus:	אביתמ כתיב
Deut. iii, 8 MT;	וירשו גם הם את הארץ
MSS Paris, Damascus:	גם הם׳ המ כתיב

Another explanation for the variance between the "mā'ōn codex" and the "mĕ'ōnā codex" was given by Bamberger[14], who erroneously thought that the suffix ה ָ — which distinguishes the text that was accepted [מעונה] from the one that was rejected [מעון], here indicates the locative.[15] As a result he drew an analogy to the matter under discussion from P.T. Yebamoth i,6 (3a): "Rabbi Shimeon b. Elazar taught, I told the Cuthite (Samaritan) scribes: who caused you to err? (The fact) that you do not follow the principle of R. Nehemiah: in the name of R. Nehemiah it was taught that every word which should have a prefixed (locative) lamed and does not have it, receives the suffix hē". In other words, Bamberger maintains that the "mā'ōn codex" was a Samaritan text in which the directional suffix was (erroneously) omitted without substituting for it a prefixed lamed. This opinion is untenable, since the Samaritan Version has the reading מעונה אלהי קדם, exactly as the Massoretic Text. Furthermore, the omission of the suffixed ה ָ is not one of the distinctive features of the Samaritan Version, which even adds this suffix in some instances where it does not appear in MT.[16]

As a matter of fact, the "mĕ'ōnā codex" diverged from the "mā'ōn codex" not in the inclusion or omission of the directional suffix, but in the use of an alternative form of the same word: one text has a "masculine" formation while the other employs the "feminine" formation. Actually we are dealing with two synonymous forms which may have been developed from the defective spelling: מען - מענָ, analogous to נער - נערָ[17] and ליל = לילָ (Prov. xxxi, 18). This phenomenon is quite common in diverse sets of parallel biblical texts.[18]

---

14.   "Die Bedeutung des Qeri–Kethib", Jahrbuch der Frankfurter Jüd. liter. Gesellsch., Bd. 21, pp. 46-55. See also J. Muller, Masecheth Soferim, p. 91.

15.   Segal (מנחה לדוד ילין ibid.) accepts this hypothesis, but does not accept the conclusions Bamberger draws from it.

16.   Gen. xiii, 9 and 10; xliii, 15, 18, 25; Ex. vi, 19; xxxiv, 26; Num. xiv, 25; etc. Cf. Sperber, op. cit., pp. 80-82. Gerleman, op. cit. p. 19.

17.   Gen. xxiv, 16; Deut. xxii, 15; 1 Kings v, 4 etc.

18.   See Sperber, op. cit., pp. 94-5; Also A. Sperber, "Biblical Exegesis—Prolegomena to a Commentary and Dictionary to the Bible", JBL 64 (1945), pp. 48-51.

A. MT — Samaritanus
1. Gen.   xxvii, 3 MT :   תליך   S :   תליתך
           xxxiv, 12 MT :   ומתן   ״ :   ומתנה
           xlviii, 10 MT :   מזקן   ״ :   מזקנה
     Lev.   iv, 32 MT :   כשב   ״ :   כבשה
2. Gen.   viii, 3 MT :   מקצה[19]   ״ :   מקץ
           x, 4 MT :   אלישה   ״ :   אליש[20]
     Lev.   x, 27 MT :   הגולה   ״ :   הגול

B. MT — 1QIs[a]
1. Is.   v, 11   MT :   פעל ה׳   1QIs[a] :   פעלת ה׳
       xv, 1   MT :   בליל   ״ :   בלילה
       xxxii, 12   MT :   שדי חמד׳   ״ :   שדי חמדה
2.   viii, 3   MT :   הנביאה   ״ :   הנביא[21]
       ii, 7   MT :   קצה   ״ :   קץ
       xiv, 22   MT :   שם ושארת   ״ :   שם ושאר

C. MT — 1Qs[b]
1. Is.   xxvi, 1   MT :   השיר   [= 1QIs[a]] 1QIs[b] :   השירה
       liii, 3   MT :   מכאבות   ״   ״ :   מכאבים
       lxiii, 1   MT :   בצדקה   ״   ״ :   בצדק[22]

D. Parallel readings in the MT
1. 2 Sam.   v, 9   :   במצדה   1 Chr. xi, 6   :   במצד
             xxiv, 21   :   כצדקתי   Ps. xviii 21   :   כצדקי[23]
             v, 8   :   מבטח   1 Chr. xviii, 8   :   מטבחת
     Ki.   vii, 26   :   שושן   2 Chr. iv, 5   :   שושנה
           ix, 10   :   מקצה   viii, 1   :   מקץ
     Ps.   xl, 18   :   עזרתי   Ps. lxx, 6   :   עזרי

E. Kethib–Qere
1. Gen.   xxvii, 3 Kethib: צידה   Qere :   ציד
     Jer.   xxxi, 39   ״ :   קוה[24]   ״ :   קו
     Job   xxxi, 7   ״ :   מאומה   ״ :   מאום
     Prov.   xxvii, 10   ״ :   רעה   ״ :   רע
2. Prov.   xxxi, 18   ״ :   בליל   ״ :   בלילה[25]

19.   Also in Deut. xiv, 28. Cf. further: 1 Kings iv, 10 — מקצה ; 2 Chron. viii, 1 — מקץ ; Is. ii,7, MT — קצה and 1QIs[a] — קץ.
20.   Perhaps he changed it intentionally because the subject is "the Greeks".
21.   Which is correct according to the context. It accords with the Massora which records— ב׳ הנביא.
22.   Cf. 1QIs[a] xvi, 11 — משפטית התורה. Barthélemy tends to interpret the fem. plural form as a kind of distinctive designation of the sects' basic ordinances (*QI*, p. 113).
23.   See supra, Is. lxiii, 1, MT— 1QIs[b].
24.   Cf. Zech i, 16.
25.   Cf. supra Is. xv.1, MS —1QIs[a].

The same holds true for מעון - מעונה. Both forms are found concurrently in biblical literature. To be sure, they cannot be derived with certainty from one root.[26] מעון(ה) is employed only once in the Pentateuch, in the verse discussed here (Deut. xxxiii, 27), and similarly מעון, in the phrase השקיפה ממעון קדשך (Deut. xxvi, 15). The Scroll from the Temple Court which the rabbis discarded had in both verses the reading מעון.

V

We may assume that the variants cited in our sources were not the only readings which set the minority MSS apart from the majority MSS whose text was sanctioned. But it was these variants that were used conveniently to designate those codices, until ultimately they were named after them. From this we may deduce that these variants were not mere random textual deviations, but rather were considered distinguishing signs for types of texts that the rabbis sought to remove from circulation. This we can deduce from other discussions which deal with books that deviated from the authoritative text of the Pentateuch.

Rabbinic tradition reports that "they wrote for him (King Ptolemy),

וישלח את זעטוטי בני ישראל (Ex. xxv, 5),

ואל זעטוטי בני ישראל לא שלח את ידו (xxiv, 11)".[27]

This information is recorded in a list of corrections of the *Soferim* which were entered in the Hebrew original, as it were, from which the Greek (LXX) translation of the Pentateuch was prepared for King Ptolemy. The great majority of corrections enumerated there are not to be found in any extant biblical texts.[28] This applies also to the reading זעטוטי for נערי; but the account of the "three Scrolls of the Law" gives evidence to the fact that this variant was actually current in a MS of considerable importance that was preserved in the Temple.

In fact, the report about the scroll that was prepared for King Ptolemy does

---

26. Cf. the dictionaries of Ben-Yehuda, Gesenius and Köhler. מעון : Jer, xxv, 30; Ps. lxviii, 8; Neh. ii, 12; 2 Chron. xxvi, 5. מעונה : Jer. xxi, 13; Ps. lxxvi, 3; Amos iii, 4. LXX distinguish between the two words. In Deut. xxvi, 15, it is rendered οἶκος; ib. xxiii, 27 — σκέπασις. Note further the synonymous usage of the two words in the Dead Sea Scrolls: 1QH xii, 7 — ובקץ האספו אל מעונתו ; 1QS, x, 1 ובהאספו אל מעון חוקו... למעון כבוד.

27. Megillah i, 1; Soferim i,8.

28. Exceptions to this are the following: Gen. ii, 1 ויכל אלהים ביום הששי (LXX; SAM.;P); Num. xvi, 15 לא חמור אחד מהם נשאתי (LXX:ἐπιθύμημα); Ex. xii, 40 ומושב בני ישראל אשר ישבו במצרים ובשאר הארצות ארבע מאות שנה .This reading resembles those of LXX and SAM; Ex. iv, 20, וירכיבם על נושא בני אדם (LXX); Lev. xi, 6—Deut. xiv, 7 צעירת שעירת=) רגלים) (LXX). Cf. Segal, מבוא המקרא, IV, pp. 928-9.

not really deal with corrections of the *Soferim* that were embedded in that text by the initiative and with the approval of the rabbis, but rather with variant readings which circulated amongst Jews[29], especially among groups which did not submit to the authority of the leaders of normative Jewry. The formulation, "they wrote for him", only represents an effort to camouflage the failure of the rabbis to ban these divergent readings and to remove them from circulation.[30] The representation of conditions and situations that were actually outside the sphere of the rabbis' influence as determined by them or legally authorized by them throws some light on their efforts to maintain a single central control and to attenuate the shocks of social schism which harassed Jewry in the generations between the times of Alexander and the destruction of the Second Temple.

We are unable to define precisely the nature of those dissident groups owing to the paucity of historical and manuscript evidence that has been preserved for us from that time. But by reason of the foregoing discussion we may conjecture that ס׳ הוא represents a type of manuscript accepted by extreme conservative groups, who were singularly punctilious about the text of the Bible and strove to maintain it throughout in an ancient form which resisted the intrusion of spelling novelties such as היא. The ס׳ זעטוטי, on the other hand, is a representative of those textual traditions which were open to Aramaic influences, owing to linguistic usages common in the time of the copyists. Examples of these are the complete scroll of Isaiah from the Judaean desert and the Pent. text from which the Greek translation, commonly called "the Septuagint", was made.[31]

At the outset we should expect that the reading זעטוטי would have been rejected on linguistic grounds. Whether the word is to be derived from the Zend language as suggested by Perles[32], from the Greek, as proposed by Geiger[33], or whether it be an Aramaic word, which seems most likely[34], it is

---

29. For this reason, also in rabbinic literature these readings are not associated with the book prepared for King Ptolemy. Thus, in *Sifre* 148 (ed. Friedmann 104a): ומנין אף למשתחות... כשהוא אומר ל עובד ם להביא את המשתף. The word לעובדם is not extant in MT of Deut. 17:3; it is one of the changes made for King Ptolemy. Cf. further *Mekhilta* on Ex. xii, 40, and *Bereshith Rabba* 63, 1. Aptowitzer's opinion that this constitutes evidence for a re-translation from Greek to Hebrew (הקדם, II, p. 19) is unacceptable.

30. We should interpret in similar fashion the dictum, "...they selected for Israel the Assyrian (square) script and the Holy (Hebrew) language, leaving the (old) Hebrew characters and the Aramaic language for the *hedyototh*. Who are meant by the '*hedyototh*'?—Rab Hisda answers: The Cutheans (Samaritans)." (B.T. *Sanhedrin* 21b). Cf. the comments of N.H. Tur-Sinai, כתב התורה, in הלשון והספר (1945), pp. 102-42.

31. Cf. A. Berliner, *Targum Onkelos* II (1884), S. 77. Anm. 2.

32. F. Perlies, *Beiträge zur Rabbinischen Sprach- und Sagenkunde*, S.5.

33. Ibid. p. 156: ζητήτης. The same root is often used in apocryphal literature with the meaning, "seek out God" or "seek out wisdom".

an alien, late and secondary reading, inferior to the pure Hebrew reading נערי בני ישראל. But its rejection on text-critical grounds, because of its being late and secondary, would necessitate the application of the same criteria for deciding between other divergent texts, such as ס׳ היא and ס׳ הוא. It would have been logical to prefer, from this viewpoint, ס׳ הוא, because it preserved an ancient spelling.[35] However, a decision in favour of this read ng was plainly impossible. The argument under analysis transmits a report, not about the *creation* of a *textus receptus*, but about the *confirmation* and authorization of a reading which had already been accepted by the rabbis, for unspecified reasons, and of the rejection and banishment of alternative readings which probably were current among the adherents of dissident groups. For this reason the rabbis did not attempt to correct the codex of the Temple Court whose reading was rejected, but discarded it instead. In other words, they banished it from use in their own society and abandoned it, much against their will, to those circles that were not subject to their legislation.

This sifting of readings was not an aim in itself, but rather served the normative community as a measure of self-defence against various groups of dissidents. It was intended, first and foremost, to create a stable textual tradition in those parts of the O.T. which were used as p1oof-texts in the religio-social controversies of the time.

The authorization of a reading on the strength of a fortuitous majority of two codices against one out of three found in the Temple Court was a mere formality, a sort of expedient peg on which to hang a legal decision, which accorded official recognition to a factual situation which obtained independently of this act of recognition.

---

34. Cf. E. Ben-Yehuda, *Thesaurus* s.v. זעטוטי. In the end Aptowitzer also accepted this opinion. See הקדם, III, p, 17, footnote; J. Müller, *Masecheth Soferim*, p. 92.

35. Against Gerleman, *op. cit.*, p. 4 We are not discussing the question of the relative priority of the vowel *i* in relation to *u* from a phonetic viewpoint, but the introduction of the distinctive forms הוא - היא in the Bible text. On the *u-i* transition see E. Nestle, ZAW 33 (1913); W. Gesenius — E. Kautzsch, *Hebrew Grammar* p. 73, § 32; M. Gottstein, לשונגו 14 (1945), 32.

WERE THERE THREE TORAH-SCROLLS
IN THE AZARAH?

By Solomon Zeitlin, Dropsie College

In the Palestinian Talmud a statement is found that there were three *Seforim* (Torahs) in the Azarah. In one was written מעון אלהי קדם (Deut. 33. 27); in the other two the reading was מעונה instead of מעון. The majority rule was followed; the reading of the one was disregarded the reading of the two was accepted. In one Torah, the reading was וישלח את זעטוטי בני ישדאל (Exodus 24. 5) and in the other two the reading was נערי בני ישראל instead of זעטוטי בני ישראל. The reading of the two was adopted while the reading of the one was disregarded. Again the reading in one Torah was היא with a *yod* while the reading in the other two was הוא with a *waw*. The reading of the one was disregarded and the reading of the two was accepted. [1] This statement with some minor variants is found in the Sifre, [2] Aboth d'Rabbi Nathan [3] and Soferim. [4]

The scholars who dealt with this statement accepted it as historical fact that there were three Torahs in the Temple Court and that these had different readings. The Sages, in fixing the text of the Torah, followed the majority rule, accepting the reading of the two books as against the reading of the one. The scholars were in doubt only as to the period

---

[1] שלשה ספרים מצאו בעזרה ספר מעוני וספר זעטוטי וספר היא באחד מצאו כתוב מעון אלהי קדם ובשנים כתוב מעונה אלהי קדם וקיימו שניים ובטלו אחד באחד מצאו כתוב וישלח את זעטוטי בני ישראל ובשנים כתוב וישלח את נערי בני ישראל וקיימו שנים ובטלו אחד באחד מצאו כתוב אחד עשר הוא ובשנים מצאו כתוב אחת עשרה ההיא (cf. Soferim 6.4) וקיימו שנים ובטלו אחד. Yer. Tan. 4. 2.

[2] Deut.

[3] 46. (ed. Schechter) cf. also ibid. 34.

[4] 6. 4.

Reprinted from *Jewish Quarterly Review* 56 (1966).

when the Sages fixed the reading of the three Torahs which were in the Azarah.

We are confronted with grave complexities with regard to the historicity of the entire statement. We know from tannaitic sources that there was one *Sefer*, Torah, in the Azarah. [5] It is unthinkable that there were three Torahs in the Temple which differed in their readings. On the Day of Atonement, the high priest read portions from the Torah which had been handed to him by his subordinates. [6] It is unbelievable that there were three Torahs with different readings. If there had been three Torahs, how could the overseer have known which was the Torah with the correct text to be handed to the high priest? And, if it was known that a Torah had a defective text, the question confronting us is: How could a Torah with a defective text have been kept in the Temple?

It is stated that in the two Torahs the reading was נערי בני ישראל while in the one instead of נערי was זעטוטי. In some of the texts quoting the statement זאטוטי בני ישראל was written with an *aleph* while in other texts it has an *ayin*. A story is given in the Talmud that when the seventy men translated the Pentateuch for Ptolemy they changed the reading of זאטוטי[7]. If וישלח את זאטוטי בני ישראל to וישלח את נערי בני ישראל was written with an *aleph* [8] it is an Aramaic, having the connotation small, little. If זעטוטי was written with an *ayin* [9] it is a Greek word ζητητικος meaning research, researches for wisdom. If the translators changed the word נערי they would not have substituted for it the word זאטוטי, which is Aramaic, and has the same connotation as the Hebrew word נערי. Thus we must assume that if they changed the word נערי it was to זעטוטי, researches for wisdom. If we take the state-

---

[5] M. Kelim, 15, 6, Tos. *ibid.* B.M. 15. 8, [ספר עזרה] עזרא (ספר)
M.M.K. 3. 4.

[6] M. Yoma 7. 1. חזן הכנסת נוטל ספר תורה ונותנו לראש הכנסת וראש הכנסת נותנו לסגן והסגן נותנו לכהן גדול וכהן גדול עומד ומקבל וקורא.

[7] Meg. 9. וישלח את זאטוטי בני ישראל ... ואל זאטוטי בני ישראל לא שלח ידו

[8] Meg. *ibid.*, Sof. 6. 4.

[9] Yer. Tan. 4. 2.

ment in the Talmud as a historical fact that there were or were found three Torahs and that one Torah contained the word זעטוטי instead of נערי, it would mean that a Torah with a Greek word inserted was kept in the Azarah. Such would be impossible even to contemplate.

I venture to say that the statement about the three Torahs in the Azarah has no historical basis although it is found in the Palestinian Talmud and recorded in other rabbinic literature. It is an *Aggadic* statement. Any story or legend, however, must have some historical basis. What is the historical background for the statement about the three Torahs in the Azarah?

During the Second Commonwealth the biblical books did not have the *matres lectionis*. The letters *aleph, he, waw* and *yod* were not used as vowels to define how to pronounce words. They were consonants. Nor were the five final letters of *kaph, mem, nun, pe* and *ṣade* employed in the Holy Scriptures. During the second century CE the *matres lectionis* were introduced in the Bible. A little later the five final letters were introduced into the Holy Scriptures. Some scrolls of the Bible had the *matres lectionis* while others still contained the archaic writing without the *matres lectionis*. The Sages who wanted to establish the text of the Bible with the *matres lectionis* quoted the story that three Torahs were or were found in the Azarah. In one the text had מעון and in the other two the text had a *he* appended as a vowel. They disregarded the writing without the *he* and accepted the writing with a *he*. They thereby affirmed that *matres lectionis* should be used in the Bible and cited the authority of the decision made during the Second Commonwealth.

Again during the second through the third centuries in some of the scrolls of the Torah the text had זאטוטי in place of נערי. If we accept this assumption we have to assume that this Aramaic word crept into the Torah. If, however, we accept the reading זעטוטי then we have to assume that the Greek word ζητητικος was Hebraized to זעטוטי and also crept into the

471

Torah. In establishing the text the Sages sought to eliminate the Aramaic word or the Hebraized Greek word. They substantiated this on the basis of the legend of three Torahs found in the Azarah, saying that in one the text had זאטוטי, זעטוטי while in the other two the text had נערי. The text of the one had been disregarded, considered unfit.

The word הא without a vowel had the connotation of either she or he. When the *matres lectionis* was introduced in the Bible, in many instances the word הא was written היא with a *yod*, she. In other cases it was written הוא with a *waw*, he. The Sages in establishing the correct text of the Bible brought in the story of the three Torahs found in the Azarah as authority for their text.

The *aggadah*, the story of the Torahs found in the Azarah, is not a historical fact. The Temple did not contain Torahs with different readings. The *aggadah* of the three Torahs was brought in the third century in order to give authority to the introduction into the Bible of the *matres lectionis* and the establishment of the biblical text.

C. Pre-Tiberian Evidence:
The Vocalization of the Textus Receptus.

THE PRONUNCIATION OF THE שְׁוָא ACCORDING TO NEW HEXAPLARIC MATERIAL

By Max L. Margolis

Dropsie College, Philadelphia, Pa.

On the subject of the pronunciation of the שְׁוָא (◌ְ) Ben Asher (דִּקְדּוּקֵי הַטְּעָמִים, §§ 11–14, pp. 12 ff.) lays down the following rules: (a) ◌ְ at the beginning of a word (α) unaccompanied by גְעיה (◌ְ) is sounded as a פתחה קטנה (= סֶגוֹל) pronounced quickly (בִּמְהֵרָה), e. g. בְּרוּךְ Gen. 26:29, בְּנֵי ib. 46:5, בְּרִית Num. 10:33, hence bĕrūk̆, bĕnē, bĕrīp̆; (β) with גְעיה (◌ְ) as a פתחה גדולה (= פתח, presumably in the same tempo), e. g. בְּבוֹא Ps. 51:2, לְכוּ ib. 46:9, בְּלֶכְתְּךָ Prov. 4:12, בְּשִׁכְבְּךָ ib. 6:22, בְּרֵעָתוֹ ib. 14:32, hence bābō, lākū, bālektĕk̆ă, băsŏk̆bĕk̆ă, bără'ăp̆ō; (γ) when followed by a laryngeal (אהחע), it is assimilated in pronunciation to the next following vowel, e. g. בְּהֹנוֹת Judg. 1:7, תְּאֵהֲבוּ Prov. 1:22, לְחֶלְכָה Ps. 10:8, רְעֵלְיָה Ezr. 2:2, hence bohŏnŏp̆, te'ĕhăbū, lehĕlk̆ă, re'ĕlăįă; and so without גְעיה: בְּאֵר, מְאֹד, שְׂאֵר, מְעוּכָה, מְחֵה, be'ēr, mo'ŏd, sĕ'ēr, mu'ūk̆ă, mehē; ‖ (b) in the middle of a word, of two consecutive ◌ְs the first is not sounded at all, while the second is pronounced (after the above-mentioned manner), e. g. וַיִּשְׁלְחוּ, וַיִּקְרְאוּ, וַיִּשְׁמְעוּ, uaįiš-luhū, uaįikru'ū, uaįišmu'ū; ‖ (c) in the middle of a word, when preceded by (a vowel and) גְעיה and followed by a laryngeal (and the vowel ō or ă), under ר but sporadically also under another consonant, the ◌ְ is sounded (presumably in the manner mentioned), e. g. בְּרְחוֹב Gen. 19:2, מִרְאוֹת ib. 27:1, מִרְעוֹת Ezek. 34:10, הָרְחָבָה, לְקְחָה Gen. 2:23, לְקְחִי I Ki. 17:11, שְׁמְעָה Ps. 39:13, הִשְׁחִיתוּ הִתְעִיבוּ ib. 14:1, hence bărohŏb, mēro'ŏp̆, mēro'ŏp̆, hărăhăbă, lukăhă, likihī, simă'ă, hišihīpū, hipi'ībū; contrast לִרְחוֹק, לִרְאוֹת, בִּרְאוֹת, כִּרְאוֹת lirhŏk, lir'ŏp̆, bir'ŏp̆, kir'ŏp̆; ‖ (d) ◌ְ is always sounded in the middle of a word under a geminate consonant, e. g. נִדְּהֵי, נִדְּחוּ, לְקְּחוּ, נִשְּׂאוֹ, דְּכְּאוּ, וְנִבְּאוּ,

Reprinted from *American Journal of Semitic Languages and Literatures* 26 (1909).

uĕnibu'ū, dukŭ'ū, niśo'ō, lukŭhū, nidŭhū, uĭdehē; ‖ (e) in all
other cases ־ in the middle of a word is not sounded, e. g. פִּינְחָס,
לְקָחוּ, שָׁמְעוּ, יִצְאוּ, קָרְעוּ, זָרְעוּ, נָטְעוּ, יִרְאוּ, בָּרְחוּ, hence pinḥås,
iăr'ū, năṭ'ū, zăr'ū, kăr'ū, iaṣ'ū, śăm'ū, lăkhū, bărhū; ‖ (f) ־ at
the beginning of a word followed by ־ is sounded as i (בְּחֹדָא
נְקֹדָא, ־), e. g. לְיִקִים, וְיִד, לְיוֹם, בְּיוֹם, hence biĭōm, liĭōm,
uĭiaḏ, liĭăkīm; hence also בְּיִקְרוֹתֶיךָ לְיִשְׂרָאֵל, etc., liĭisrå'ēl.
biĭikrōpekå, etc.; ‖ (g) certain scribes introduce a ־ in cases like
וְנִפְתְּחָה Gen. 43:21, שְׁמָעָה Ps. 39:13, וָאֶשְׁמְעָה Dan. 8:13,
וְנִקְרָאָה Zech. 8:3; Est. 2:14, וּנְזַרְעָה Num. 5:21, וָאֶשְׁקְלָה Ezr.
8:25, קְדַת Num. 4:2, הִקְדַּתִּי 3:27, הַקְדָתִים 10:21, הַקְעִירָה 7:85,
הַבְּרֹנֹת I Sam. 23:1, כְּתֹנֹת Exod. 28:40, מָרְדְּכַי Est. 2:5; 4:12
and many more, while other scribes write a simple ־; but the
matter is of no importance ("it has no root") and it is simply
one of scribal choice; that is to say, certainly in the examples
with a laryngeal following, the pronunciation is governed by the
rules mentioned, and the indication of the pronunciation in script
is unnecessary; ‖ (h) when ־ intervenes in the middle of a word
between two similar consonants, the Masorete Pīnḥås writes ־,
e. g. סְבֲכִים Exod. 25:20, הַמְשֹׁרֲרִים I Chr. 9:33, שׁוֹטֲטוּ Jerem.
5:1, etc.; so also under ר (preceded by one of the מַלְכִין, comp.
reference § 13, footnote f): מַרֲפִדִים Exod. 19:2, הָרְוָחָה Exod.
8:11; but also elsewhere, e. g. וְקָרֲב Ps. 58:22, וְסָגַר Dan. 6:23,
וְשֻׁבָה Judg. 5:12, בְּדֵי Exod. 23:19, קֲשִׁי Deut. 9:27, יִכְתַּבֵם Isa.
10:9. Comp. on the latter subject more fully §§ 33, 34, where
גְעִיה is mentioned as a condition; thus רְבֲבֹות Num. 10:36, but
רְבְבֹת Deut. 33:17, the ־ not being sounded in the latter instance, hence ribbōp; ־ is likewise silent in cases like יִשְׁחֲרֻנְנִי
Hos. 5:15, though גְעִיה precedes, hence iĕsahărŭnnĭ; in the case
of מ after the article, with גְעִיה preceding, we find indifferently
־ and ־, thus הַמְתַעֲבִים Mic. 3:9, but הַמְיַלְּדֹת Exod. 1:17; the
cases are enumerated in full.

Similar rules are laid down by ḤAIŪǦ in the Introduction to
his Treatise on the Weak and Geminative Verbs in Hebrew (ed.
JASTROW, Leyden, 1897, p. ٥ ff.; the passage was previously edited
and translated by the same scholar in ZAW., V [1885], 209 ff.;

comp. also the Hebrew translations in Dukes, *Beiträge zur ältesten Auslegung, etc.*, 1844, Hebrew Supplement, 4–6; 19 f.; also the passage in the ספר הנקוד, ib. 200 ff.; see also König, *Lehrgebäude*, I, 665 ff.). The following deviations (if we may speak of such in view of the unclear language of Ben Asher) may be noted: Ad *a* γ he remarks that when the vowel following the laryngeal is ◌ָ, it becomes difficult to sound the ◌ַ as a ◌ַ, and is therefore pronounced as *a* (بالفتح), e. g. הָאֱגֶה, לְהָבִים, גְּעָרָה, פְּהָדִים, hence *gāʿărā, lăhăḇīm, dăʾăẓă, păhădīm*. The same pronunciation (بالفتح, comp. Ibn Ezra, צָחוּת, ed. Ven. קלה *a:* בפתח חטף והטעם שוא עם פתח; he limits it, however, to cases where the next vowel is ◌ָ, e. g. שְׁמָרִים) he appears to assign to the ◌ַ in the cases enumerated by Ben Asher in *a a* and β (hence without regard to the גָעיה), e. g. בְּרָכָה, קְלָלָה, נְדוּדִים, דְּשֵׁנִים, גְּלִילִים, hence *bărăkă, kălălă, nădūḏīm, dăšēnīm, gălīlīm*. An obvious exception is made in the case of a ◌ַ originating in Semitic *u*, e. g. אֳנִיָּה, רְאִי, גֳרָנוֹת, קֳדָשִׁים, which is to be sounded as *ŏ*. Ad *b*, Hạyūg is explicit as to the difference between a laryngeal and a non-laryngeal following the second ◌ַ; thus יִשְׁמְעוּ is to be pronounced *iišmuʿū* (بالضم), but יִשְׁמְרוּ *iišmărū* (بالفتح); יִרְמִיָדוּ (in consonance with Ben Asher's rule under *f*) *iirmiiăhū* (بالكسر). A new rule (*i*) given by Hạyūg touches the double ◌ַ at the end of a word, e. g. וַיֵּבְךְ Gen. 46:29, יַפְתְּ ib. 9:27, שָׁמְתְּ Isa. 47:7; when occurring in the context, the second ◌ַ is vocal, but it is silent in pause. To this rule Ibn Ezra takes exception; it is clearly impossible to vocalize the ◌ַ in a combination like יַפְתְּ אֱלֹהִים Gen. 9:27. Ibn Ezra further states that in examples like בְּרָאוּבֵן, לִרְאוּבֵן, etc., the ◌ַ is silent.

Whereas Abraham Balmes gives the ◌ַ in בְּרָכָה, etc., the sound of *ă* (פתח גדול), Duran (מעשה אפוד, p. 34) is explicit in vindicating for it the sound of a very short *ĕ* (להתקרב תנושתו לתנועת הסגול אבל שהיא יותר קצרה).

Comp. also M. Schreiner, "Zur Geschichte der Aussprache des Hebräischen," in *ZAW*. VI (1886), 236–39. 245. 256. 258.

On the pronunciation of the ־ֲ in the Septuagint, particularly
the Hexaplaric remains, see FRANKEL, *Vorstudien*, § 23, p. 121 f.;
FIELD, *Hexapla*, lxxiv. The observations given there are extremely meager, and the subject requires much fuller handling.
Reserving an examination of the Septuagint and the older Hexaplaric data for a future occasion, I may be permitted to present
the evidence as far as it is based on the new and much more
copious Hexaplaric material discovered by MERCATI and others
and excerpted in the second Supplement to the Oxford Concordance.

(*a*) ־ֲ at the beginning of a word:

(*aβ*) followed by a non-laryngeal; transcribed by *a* (19 times):
βανη בְּנֵי 17:46 (where no book is named, the references are all
to Psalms); *βακααλ* בְּקָהָל 34:18; *βαμεθγε* בְּמִתֵג 31:9; *βαφιεμ*
בְּפִיהֶם 48:14; *βαχας* בְּכַעַס 30:10; *καρωθ* (*sic*) קרֹב 31:9; *κασε*
קָצֶה 45:10; *λαβαλωθ* לְבַלּוֹת 48:15; *λαμαλχη* לְמַלְכֵי 88:28;
λαμαν לְמַעַן 29:13; *λαμεσφατι* לְמִשְׁפָּטִי 34:23; *λανεγδ* לְנֶגֶד 35:2;
λαχολ לְכֹל 17:31; *μαλαμμεδ* מְלַמֵּד 17:35; *νακαμωθ* נְקָמוֹת 17:48;
σαβαωθ צְבָאוֹת 45:8, 12; *φανη* פְּנֵי 17:43; *χαμω* כְּמוֹ 88:47.
Dubious: *λαμεσαλ* (read *λεμασαλ*?) לְמָשָׁל 48:5; ‖ transcribed by
ε (10 t.): *βεκορβ* בְּקֶרֶב 35:2; *βεσανει* בְּשׁוּעִי 30:23; *βεκοδοσ*[*ι*]
בְּקָדְשִׁי 88:36; *γεδουδ* בְּדוּד 17:30; *ζερουωθαι* זְרוֹעֹתַי 17:35; *θεσω-*
βαβηνι תְּסוֹבְבֵנִי 31:7; *λερβι* (*sic*) לְרִיבִי 34:23; *μεσιω* מְשִׁיחוֹ 27:8;
σεμω שְׁמוֹ 28:2; *σερουφα* צְרוּפָה . With artificial gemination:
λεββαβεχεμ לְבַבְכֶם 30:25; ‖ by *ο* (once): *μοσανε* מְשַׁוֵּה 17:34;
‖ by *ι* (once): *χισους* כְּסוּס 31:9; ‖ unexpressed by any vowel
(50 t.): *βγηουαθω* בְּגַאֲוָתוֹ 45:4; *βδαμι* בְּדָמִי 29:10; *βδερχ*
בְּדֶרֶךְ 31:8; *βκερβα* בְּקִרְבָּהּ 45:6; *βκωλω* בְּקוֹלוֹ 45:7; *βλεβ*
בְּלֵב 45:3; *βνη* בְּנֵי 28:1; 30:20; 48:3 *bis;* 88:48; *βοωραθ* r.
βθωραθ בְּתוֹרַת 1:2; *βρεδθι* בְּרָדְתִּי 29:10; *βριθι* בְּרִיתִי 88:35;
βσαβτ בְּשֶׁבֶט 88:33; *βσαλουι* בְּשָׁלְוִי 29:7; *βσαρωθ* בְּצָרוֹת 30:8;
45:2; *βσεδκαθαχ* בְּצִדְקָתֶךָ 30:2; *βσεθρ* בְּסֵתֶר 31:21; *βσχχα* (*sic*)
בְּסֻכָּה 30:21; *βχεννωρ* בְּכִנּוֹר 48:5; *βχωρ* בְּכוֹר 88:28; *ξχορ*
זְכָר־ 88:48; *ηξχορ* (*sic*) זְכֹר 88:51; *θβουννωθ* תְּבוּנוֹת 48:4; *λβηθ*
לְבֵית 30:3; *λδανειδ*, *λδαδ* לְדָוִד 28:1; 29:1; 30:1; 34:1; 35:1;
88:50, 76; *αδωρ* r. *λδωρ* לְדוֹר 48:12; *λμαωλ* לִמְחוֹל 29:12; *λσετφ*

לְשֶׁטֶם 31:6; λσωνωθ (with a query apud REDPATH) לְשׁוֹנוֹת 30:21;
λχου לְכוּ 45:9; μσιαχ מְשִׁיחֶךָ 88:39, 52; μσουδωθ מִצְּעָדוֹת 30:3;
σμα שֹׁמֵעַ 29:11; σμην r. σμηη שֹׁמְחִי 34:26; σφωθαΐ שִׂפְתַי 88:35;
φλαγαυ פְּלָגָיו 45:5; χειλ r. χσιλ כְּסִיל 48:11; χρηε כְּרַע 34:14;
χσεδκαδ (sic) כְּצִדְקָה 34:24; χφαρδ כְּפֶרֶד 31:9.

Cases with initial ־ְ: with a (once): ιασουαθι יְשׁוּעָתִי; ‖ with ε
(once): ιεσανου יְשׁוּעֶי 17:42; ‖ with no vowel (11 t.): ιδαββερ
יְדַבֵּר (pronounced i̅daber, that is probably i̅daber) 48:4; ιδαβ-
βηρου יְדַבְּרוּ 34:20; ιμαλλετ יְמַלֵּט 88:49; ιμη יְמֵי 88:46; ιμιν
יְמִין 88:43; ιμινω יְמִינוֹ 88:26; ιριβαϊ יְרִיבֵי 34:1; ισαββουνι
יְסוֹבְּנִי 48:6; ισουβερ (sic) יְשׁוּבֵר 45:10; ισουωθ יְשׁוּעוֹת 27:8;
ισωβαβεννου יְסוֹבְבֵנוּ 31:10.

Initial וְ is transcribed ου (with no vowel following) in numerous cases.

(γ) followed by a laryngeal: with a (8 t.): βααφφω בְּאַפּוֹ 29:6;
βααμιρ בְּהָמִיר 45:3; βαανφη בְּהַנְפִּי 34:16; βαεζραθι (ε latet)
בְּעֶזְרָתִי 34:2; λααβδ לְעֶבֶד 35:1; λααραρι לְהָרְרִי 29:8; χαα
כָּאֵח 34:14; χααφαρ כְּעָפָר 17:43. As will be noticed, the vowel
following is a (־ַ, ־ָ, ־ֶ in segolate form), except in one case
which is not certain; ‖ with o (once), sequ. o: λοομ לְחֹם (read
לְהֶם?) 34:1, hence with assimilation; ‖ with ε (4 t.): βεεζδαχ
בְּחֶסְדָּה 30:8; βεειρ בְּעִיר 30:22; μεεθθα מְחִתָּה 88:41; νεουσα
נְחוּשָׁה 17:35, apparently not on the principle of assimilation; ‖
with η, clearly on the principle of assimilation (3 t.): βηηκι
בְּחֵיקִי 88:51; βηνναυ r. βηηναυ בְּעֵינֵיר 35:3; μηηρα מְהֵרָה 30:3;
‖ with no vowel (18 t.): θελαθαχ תְּהִלָּתֶךָ 34:28; λωλαμ לְעֹלָם
29:7, 13; 30:2; 48:9, 12; 88:29, 37, 38 (/ עוֹלָם), 53; λωσιηνυ
לְהוֹשִׁיעֵנִי 30:3; μωδ מְאֹד 45:2; νουμ נְאֻם 35:2; σαθι שְׁאָתִי 88:5;
σωλ שְׁאוֹל 48:15; 88:49; with initial ־ְ: ιαλληλου יְחַלְּלוּ 88:32;
ιϊδαθι יְחִידָתִי 34:17. Whether the laryngeal was sounded, it is
impossible to tell.

(bc) in the middle of a word:

(a) at the end of a closed syllable of the type מַלְכִּי, examples
αβδω עַבְדּוֹ 34:27; φααλθα פָּעַלְתָּ 31:20; ικραηνι יִקְרָאֵנִי 88:27;
φεδιων פִּדְיוֹן 48:9; λαβλωμ לִבְלוֹם 31:9; νεγδι נֶגְדִּי 88:37; οσχι
חָשְׁכִּי 17:29; χοφρω כָּפְרוֹ 48:8. A following laryngeal is of

course ignored in transcription: μαχωβιμ מִכָאוֹבִים; ιεριβου
יְרְחִיבוּ 34:21; ιεσαχα יִשָׂעֶךָ 17:36; σεμα שָׂמְחָה 29:12; μαλαμωθ
מִלְחָמוֹת 45:10; ιερε יִרְאֶה 88:49; ιερημ יִרְעֶם 48:15; νεβαλ נִבְהָל
29:8; ιθαλλαλου יִתְהַלָּלוּ; εσοκημ אֶשְׁחָקֵם 17:43. In ιεσσι יִשְׁעִי
17:47 we have actual slurring of the laryngeal and compensative
assimilation. A preceding laryngeal is equally ignored in transcription: ιδαυ יְהְדָּו 34:26; βαταθι בְּטַחְתִּי 30:7; φεθεθα פְּתַחְתָּ
29:12; ιειε יְהְיֶה 88:37, יְהְיֶה 88:49. With following ו: σαλουι
שָׁלְוִי 29:7. With following י: αδιω עֲדִיוֹ 31:9; ελιων עֶלְיוֹן
45:5; 88:28.

Note εργλαι רַגְלַי 30:9, but ρεγλαι 17:34, 39; λφνωθ לִפְנוֹת
45:6; μσωθαι מִצְוֹתַי 88:32; θου תְּדִיוּ 31:9, as if = תְּדְהוּ; ερι
(probably corrupt) יִרְאֶה 48:11. κοδος קָדְשִׁי 88:36 and οvι עָנְיִי
30:8 are perhaps to be explained on the analogy of Syriac ܡܕ̈ܝܢܬܐ
with silent ܘ and the like.

(β) at the end of a closed syllable of the type מַלְכֵי: μαλχη
מַלְכֵי 88:28; αβλη הַבְלֵי 30:7; εσρη אַשְׁרֵי 1:1; 111:1; δαβρη
דִּבְרֵי 34:20; ισρη יִשְׁרֵי 31:11; ρεγη רִגְעֵי 34:20; βαλβαβαμ =
בִּלְבָּם / בִּלְבָּם 34:25; βανγαιβ (r. -μ) בִּנְגָעִים 88:33; βαρσωναχ
בִּרְצוֹנְךָ 29:8; βαρσωνω בִּרְצוֹנוֹ 29:6; λαβνη לִבְנֵי 48:1; ρυχση
רִכְסֵי 30:21. Note, however, λεββαβεχεμ לִבַבְכֶם 30:25; αναναθαχ
עֲנֻתְךָ 17:36 (provided it comes from עֲנוּת and not עֱנוּת). Note
also βσεβ(r. μ)ωθαμ which presupposes בְּשֵׁמוֹתָם / בִּשְׁמוֹתָם 48:12
and λσαχηναυ / לִשְׁכֵנָיו 88:42. Interesting is the transcription
εκβωθ for עֲקֻבוֹת 88:52. εζαχ for הִזְקוּ 30:25 implies חֵזְקוּ, a
Syriasm.

ִ at the end of a closed syllable of the type וּבְרִיתִי is equally
unrepresented: ουβριθι וּבְרִיתִי 88:29; ουθφελλαθι וְתִפְלַתִי 34:13;
ουμσουδαθι וּמְצוּדָתִי 30:4; ουθνεελνι (an interesting form pre-
supposing וּתְנַהֲלֵנִי, comp. my "Notes on Semitic Grammar," III,
AJSL., XIX (1902), 45 ff.) / וּתְנַהֲלֵנִי 30:4; ου.βσαλη וּבְצַלְעִי
34:15; ουβμσφατι / וּבְמִשְׁפָּטִי 88:31; ουλμαν וּלְמַעַן 30:4. Note,
however, with α: ουμασανναεί וּמַשָׂנִאַי 17:41; ουβαμωτ וּבָמוֹת
45:3; with ε: ουβερωβ וּבְרֹב 48:7. Quite peculiar are: οὐαλσωνι
וּלְשׁוֹנִי 34:28; ουαρημ וּרְעֵם 27:9.

480

(γ) — — in the middle of a word. The second — may be expressed by a vowel: ουϊερογου וַיְחָרְגוּ 17:46; μεμαστ(r. γ)ω-ρωθεειμ מִמְסְגְּרוֹתֵיהֶם 17:46; so also ιεζεβου יַעֲזֹבוּ / יַעַזְבוּ 17:46. But we find examples with no vowel for the second —: μισχνωθαμ מִשְׁכְּנוֹתָם 48:12; ιεσμου יִשְׂמְחוּ 45:4; ιεμρου יָחְמְרוּ 45:4; ϊφρου יַחְפְּרוּ 34:26. Note μσχνη מִשְׁכְּנֵי 45:5; prob. r. μεσχνη. Interesting are ιεσεμου יִשְׂמְחוּ 34:24 and ικερσου יָקְרְצוּ 34:19 which I explain on the analogy of Syriac forms with the ܩ݀ܫܝܐ as segolatized forms = îisemhū, îikerṣū, comp. the parallel forms from first laryngeals: יַעֲזֹבוּ and the like.

(d) in the middle of a word under a geminate consonant. The examples available are: ζωημερου (sic) זָמְרוּ 29:5; θεσσερηνι תְּצָרְנִי 31:7; ουμασανvεαϊ וּבְמַצְנָאֵי 17:41; ουεθαζερηνι, ουθεξορηνι וַתְּאַזְרֵנִי 29:12; 17:40; φελλετηνι פַּלְּטֵנִי 30:2; without vowel: εθνηου אֶתְנֶחוּ 88:28; μεχφεριμ מְכַפְּרִים; βεσαυει בְּשַׁוָּעִי 30:23; ϊεσαυου יְשַׁוֵּעוּ 17:42; with the laryngeal ignored: χαβημωθ כַּבְּהֵמוֹת 48:13; ουνεσσημ וְנַשָּׁאָם 27:9; ουχεσσω וְכַסָּאוֹ 88:30, 37, 45.

(e) — after a vowel with מֵתֶג (—). As a rule no vowel! Thus with —: αμρου אָמְרוּ 34:21; ασσα עָשְׂתָה 30:10; σαμου שָׂמְחוּ 34:15; ταμνου טָבְנוּ 30:5; with —: ηρφου הָרְפּוּ 88:52 bis; with —: ασσωμριμ הַשֹּׁמְרִים 30:7; ιωμρου יֹאמְרוּ 34:25, 27; μεῖωρδη = מִיֹּורְדִי / מִיֹּורְדֵי 29:4; ωβρη עָבְרֵי 88:42; οιβαχ אֹיְבֶיךָ 88:52; οιβαυ אֹיְבֵיו 88:43. But we find also a vowel: ιουχαλευ יְכֻלּוּ 17:39; οϊεβαϊ, οϊεββαϊ אֹיְבֵי 17:38, 41; 29:2; with a following laryngeal: αββωτεειμ הַבֹּטְחִים 48:7; contrast σωνη (sic) שֹׁנְאֵי 34:19. On the whole therefore agreement with the tradition of the Jewish grammarians. Compare on the subject BAER, תורת אמת, p. 9, footnote **, where further proof is adduced from the system of accentuation.

(f) for — followed by י we have the following examples: βιεδ בְּיַד 30:9; βιαδαθ (sic) בְּיָדְךָ 30:6; χιαρη כִּירֵחַ 88:38, apparently without vowel.

(h) Comp. ισωβαβεννου יְסוֹבְבֵנוּ 31:10; θεσωβαβηνι תְּסוֹבְבֵנִי 31:7; αραρι הָרְרִי 29:8. Contrast εελλελεχ אֲהַלְּלֶךְ 34:18.— εμαραθ for אָמְרַת 17:31 may be explained as אָמְרַת (אָמֶרֶת).—

Examples for הְמָ: αμμααζερηνι הֲמָאֹזְרֵנִי 17:33; λαμανασση לְמִנְצֵּהַ 30:1; 35:1; 45:1; 48:1; but αμμηαλιμ הַמְיֻחָלִים.

(i) ־ְ ־ְ at the end of the word. While an example in the Hebrew covered by the new Hexaplar material does not appear to be available, numerous examples are found in consequence of two causes: (1) the ending ־ְ of the second person masc. sing. perf. is in late Aramaic and Syriac fashion transformed to ־ָ, hence arise forms like σαμθ / שַׂמְתָ 88:41; φαρασθ / פָּרַצְתָ 88:41; μαγαρθ / הִגַּרְתָה 88:45 and the like, although we also meet with ־ְ retained, e. g. σαφανθα צְפַנְתָה 30:7; 88:48; (b) the mono-syllabic form of segolates. Examples abound, e. g. αρς אֶרֶץ 34:20; 45:7; 88:28; δερχ דֶּרֶךְ 88:42; εσδ חֶסֶד 31:10; ζεχρ זֵכֶר 29:5; βοκρ בֹּקֶר 45:6 and the like (though forms like ιεθερ יֶתֶר 30:24 are also met with); with middle laryngeals: χας כַּעַס 30:10; σακ שָׂחַק 88:38; with third laryngeals: νεσ נֶצַח 88:47. Hence the Hebrews were apparently capable of pronouncing ־ְ ־ְ at the end of a syllable (word) without inserting a parasitic vowel.

The manner of transcribing the חֲטִפִין, though I have collected all the examples, need not be discussed here as it is foreign to my present purpose.

To sum up, over against the rules of Ben Asher and Ḥaiūg which no doubt represent the scholastic tradition of the Tiberian Masoretes, the Hexaplar transcriptions reveal a state of pronunciation by no means fixed. In some instances the Masoretic rules are substantiated, notably in the pronunciation of the ־ְ after מֶתֶג (ασσωμριμ הַשֹּׁמְרִים and the like); the assimilation of the ־ְ to the vowel over a laryngeal may also be witnessed as a tendency; but on the whole, a and ε are comparatively speaking by no means as frequent representations of the vocal ־ְ as is the absence of a vowel altogether. In the latter point the Hexaplar pronunciation approaches the current Ashkenazic one, which however is proved as old by Origen's transcription of the very first word of Scripture: βρησιθ (also Jerome: bresith, s. Field ad locum). Sievers (Metrische Studien, I, §§ 5, 2; 211; 212; 218; 213; 220) has on metrical grounds done away with the "Schwa medium" in הִנְנִי, וַיְהִי, לַמְלָכִים, מַלְכֵי and the "vocal schwa" in דִּבְּרוּ, דְּבַר דֶּבֶר, וַיְהִי, hence practically everywhere in the context; that it could be

missed at the very opening of the discourse is proved by βρησιθ.
The tendency toward "silencing" the "vocal" שְׁוָא is old; in
Origen's times it was on the ascendant. As the בְּעֵיה proves, the
allegro or *lento* pronunciation was dictated by the musical recitation (accentuation), which naturally varied according to the
context. The segolatization itself is but an example of *lento* pronunciation; how far it obtained in the times of Origen, has been
shown above. In a living pronunciation, not yet regulated by
rule, the old and the new will be found one by the side of the
other; compared with the Masoretic tradition, the Hexaplar pronunciation of Hebrew is in some respects more archaic, and in
others more modern.

THE DIVERGENCIES IN THE PRE-TIBERIAN
MASSORETIC TEXT*

In his well-known off-print, *On the present state of proto-Septuagint studies*,[1] Professor H. M. Orlinsky not only argued strongly for the Lagarde-Margolis approach to the reconstruction of the original text of the LXX, but also attacked the recent views of the Massoretic textual transmission as expounded by Kahle and Sperber. Professor H. H. Rowley, in a discussion of Orlinsky *versus* Alexander Sperber on the proto-LXX question, came to the conclusion that Orlinsky had put forward the stronger case[2]; it is one of the purposes of this paper to consider whether Orlinsky is equally successful in his treatment of the Massoretic Text. Naturally he devotes much less space to the argument about the M.T. than he does to the LXX, but he claims that what he says is representative of " the view which is held by practically all competent scholars to-day," viz., " that all preserved manuscripts of the Hebrew text of the O.T. go back to the one recension, which came to dominate in the first-second century A.D. at the latest."[3]

Before proceeding, it is fair to state, against Orlinsky, that among prominent modern scholars who have definitely declared themselves opposed to this view are C. Steuernagel, O. Eissfeldt, J. Hempel, A. Bentzen among continental scholars, Wheeler Robinson in this country, R. H. Pfeiffer in the U.S.A., in addition, of course, to the Kahle school, with Sperber in the U.S.A. Even C. D. Ginsburg at the beginning of the present century was not wholly given to the Lagardean view, and H. L. Strack and E. König in the 19th century were definitely opposed to it.

Orlinsky allows that the LXX does represent, in various books, textforms which differ recensionally from the Massoretic text-tradition, but states that " those text-traditions have long perished, driven out by the Hebrew text that was used by the Mishnah and Talmud, by Theodotion, Aquila, Symmachus, Origen, Jerome."[4] The key-words here are that these versions represent one recension only of the Hebrew text, which was authoritative; and that the archetype was scrupulously copied and transmitted by the Massoretes. But it is just here that Orlinsky's case appears to be weakest. As yet, there is no first-hand evidence of the existence of an archetype, and any appeal to circumstantial evidence must be admitted to be unsatisfactory. Because the argument for the existence of the archetype is mainly based on these Greek and Latin renderings and versions, the onus lies on its advocates to show that an identical archetype was the parent text in each of these versions; and an examination of each would, I think, result in a verdict of *non-possumus*. Even a superficial glance shows this adequately. Jerome is not a strong support for the hypothesis, because, not only is there the unfortunate text-history of the Vulgate, but also there is obvious vacillation in the method and purpose of St. Jerome himself. Granted that he knew sufficient Hebrew to check up on his Jewish teachers and advisers, there are also his own statements that he sometimes departed from the Hebrew text,

---

* Paper read at the Meeting of the Society of Old Testament Study held in Manchester, September, 1948.

[1] Publications of the American Oriental Society, Offprint Series No. 13. New Haven, Conn. 1941, pp. 84ff.

[2] *The Proto-Septuagint Question*, JQR, NS xxxiii (1943), pp. 497-9.

[3] *Op. cit.* p. 85.

[4] *Ibid.*

Reprinted from *Journal of Jewish Studies* 1 (1949).

preferring, e.g., either a LXX or Old Latin reading, or Symmachus, or, again, a Midrashic rendering. It would be impossible to produce textual proof that all the renderings which Jerome used represent a parent Hebrew text, much less a uniform archetype for each instance. Origen, because of his dependence in the Hexapla on other sources, must be considered later. Symmachus has strong affinities with the M.T., but that is different from a postulated identical text-form for both, for Symmachus also has affinities with the Septuagint. Aquila, still frequently regarded as a ridiculously literal rendering of the M.T., is said to contain variants from the present M.T. at the rate of one in every second verse.[5] Theodotion fails to support the supposition on two grounds : firstly, the Ur-Theodotion, generally regarded as basic to Theodotionic readings, is to be traced back to a period before that presupposed for the M.T. archetype, and therefore cannot be expected to conform with it ; secondly, a glance at the *apparatus criticus* of the text of Daniel in BH[3] shows that the divergences between the Theodotionic text and the M.T. are considerable. It follows that Origen, likewise, must be disallowed, because it was from these renderings, particularly Theodotion, that he obtained his readings when squaring his reconstructed LXX with the Hebrew text in the Hexapla. The Hexapla is further to be disallowed because of the text-form of the first two columns, the Hebrew and the Greek transcription. So far as I know, remnants of the Hebrew text in column 1 do not exist. But the transcription in column II has been carefully studied. In spite of the prolonged delay of the publication of Cardinal Mercati's treatment of the Milan palimpsest, a detailed discussion of grammatical forms has been published by Einar Brønno.[6] He observes that in 131 verses of transcribed texts of various Psalms in this 10th century palimpsest there are 88 forms which are at variance with the M.T., and of these 18 show consonantal variations which, Brønno explains, consist of the one text-form having consonants not present in the other, or having consonants which differ in both.[7] But we shall return to this list later.

The evidence of the Mishnah and Talmud for the supposed archetype is different from that of the versions, for here we deal with quotations and text-forms in Hebrew, and therefore the problems of translation and transcription do not arise. But Orlinsky's argument is again not substantiated. He refers in defence of his view to the work of Aptowitzer,[8] but it is in precisely the same work that Kahle finds adequate proof to refute the theory. Aptowitzer does show that the whole history of Rabbinic literature, down to the 8th and 9th centuries A.D., reveals divergent forms of the Hebrew text current in Rabbinic circles : variants which have also, to some extent, been established in the older versions, such as the LXX, Targumim, Peshitta. Furthermore, H. L. Strack, in his *Prolegomena*,[9] has listed 111 text-variants in Rabbinic works which provide ample illustration of the same fact.

Finally, the existence of divergent text-forms is, I think, presupposed by the persistence of Qrê and Kthibh readings throughout the period of Massoretic activity in the pre-Tiberian stages. There are frequent instances in pre-

---

[5] So BENTZEN, *Introduction to the Old Testament* (E.T. 1948), I, p. 56, after STEUER-NAGEL, *Einleitung in das Alte Testament* (1912), p. 21. It would be interesting to discover how this average was computed, for, if it is based on FIELD or HATCH and REDPATH, it is likely to be textually unsound because these works were largely based on quotations from the Fathers.

[6] *Studien über Hebräische Morphologie und Vokalismus.* Leipzig, 1943. *Abhandlungen für die Kunde des Morgenlandes.* Bd. xxviii.

[7] *Ibid*, pp. 445f.

[8] *Das Schriftwort in der Rabbinischen Literatur.* Wien, 1906-15.

[9] *Prolegomena Critica in Vetus Testamentum Hebraicum.* Leipzig, 1873.

Tiberian Hebrew manuscripts where the readings are those of the margin or *Qrê* in the Tiberian *textus receptus*. Thus far it is obvious that Orlinsky's adherence to the view of a carefully transmitted archetype cannot be justified.

But there is, I suggest, a fundamental truth in the basis of Orlinsky's argument. Kahle, and particularly Sperber, may have gone too far in the other direction when they emphasise the divergent text-forms which, they argue, are presupposed by the emergence of the M.T. By analogy, Kahle would make the divergences in the various Massoretic texts as far-reaching as those between the recensions of the LXX. He speaks of reconstructing a text-form which was " the Babylonian text of the Bible ",[10] and he interprets the reference in the colophon of the ben Asher Codex of the Prophets in 895 A.D. to the careful preservation of the consonantal text as indicating that variant readings were expunged from it.[11] Again, the numerous references in Rabbinic literature to the " corrected " manuscript, the *sefer mugah*, are explained by him as referring not merely to the correction of scribal errors but to the expunging of variant readings. Now if these explanations are correct, we may conclude the presence of major differences of text-forms in the now hidden history of Massoretic activity. But surely a more correct emphasis must be on the comparative identity and uniformity of the text-form as transmitted during the Christian era, very much in contrast to the transmission of Christian texts, both LXX and New Testament. In spite of divergences, there is an essential similarity between the M.T. and the versions mentioned by Orlinsky. Thus it is, or at least it should be, axiomatic that for the purposes of emending the M.T., in the strict sense, first importance should go to the post-1st century A.D. versions, but the very fact that these can be used but infrequently shows that there was a uniformity of the parent text. Again, Origen had a Hebrew text which he regarded as official to the extent that it was the basis of all Greek renderings to be used by the Church. Now though this text has been shown to have divergences at the rate of 88 per 131 verses in the transcription column, it does not follow that its parent was such a different recension as might be supposed at first sight. The examination by Brønno[12] shows that the variants are in the main differences of orthography, which may be explained as variation of pronunciation or dialect. A few examples might be quoted to illustrate this: Column 11 has μεσσωλ in Ps. 30.4, whereas M.T. has *min-she'ol*; it has confused *z* and *sh* in *nigrazti* in Ps. 31.23; in 32.9 it has θου for M.T. *tihyu*, which is explained, as Brønno admits after Margolis, on grammatical grounds[13]; in Ps. 35.25 Origen has λβαβ instead of M.T. *lebh*; and again in 89.38 it has λωλαμ for *'olam*, where there is also support for Origen in 16 Hebrew MSS, LXX and Peshitta.[14] As Brønno admits,[15] the only instance of a substantial change is 49.13, where Origen has βακαρ and M.T. *biqar*, and the parallelism in the passage suggests that Origen has the better reading.[16] The same general conclusion of dialect or local variations may be drawn from an examination of the transcript of Ps. 30 given by Kahle in *The Cairo Geniza*,[17] where only one word differs consonantally from the M.T., and this

---

[10] *The Cairo Geniza*. London, 1947, p. 44.

[11] *Ibid*, p. 111.

[12] *Op cit.*, especially pp. 445ff.

[13] *Ibid*, p. 45.

[14] *Bib. Heb.²*, ad loc.

[15] BRØNNO. *op. cit.*, p. 446.

[16] Cf. *Bib. Heb.³*, ad. loc.

[17] p. 88.

is to be explained on grounds other than a different recension, viz. as a textual corruption.[18]

Continuing this suggestion of variant readings as evidence of dialect forms, the following characteristics of the dialect of Origen II may be mentioned: the failure to pronounce gutturals; though this may have been a general characteristic of recited Hebrew of those days; the 2.s.m. suffixes presuppose -*ākh* or -*āt*, not -*khā* and -*tā* as in Tiberian; the omission of final -*āh*.

Subsequent centuries provide far more abundant and exact sources for an examination of the pre-Tiberian textual transmission. I refer, of course, to the manuscripts mainly from the Cairo Geniza and the two Firkowitsch collections, with texts pointed in the Palestinian and the two Babylonian vocalisations. Perhaps a word of warning might remove a wrong impression which may prevail in the treatment of these discoveries. The Geniza was the depository of discarded and unwanted manuscripts, which, though they had been used for years, were now awaiting destruction. As Kahle so frequently remarks, it was not an archive for conserving official texts, though the manuscripts conserved had, at some time, been so used. Therefore, generally speaking, Geniza fragments are related to the study of the text-transmission in much the same way as ceramics are used in the science of archæology. They are the remains of scripts which had been mainly used for the individual purposes of their owners. Our danger is to attach too great a significance to some characteristic or idiosyncrasy of a particular manuscript. There are many indications of the unofficial character of the Cairo manuscripts. Thus, the absence of consistency in the way texts are pointed shows that it is not one classical form of pronunciation that is to be presented through them, but rather that the manuscripts simply guided the person who read them. The abbreviated texts indicate the same thing, for here the manuscripts consist simply of the first word of a verse written in full, followed by those consonants which have a significance for the vocalisation or accentuation. Again, many Palestinian and Babylonian texts bear also Tiberian vowel signs, and it is thought that these are re-pointed texts which show that when the Tiberian vocalisation became official, all available manuscripts were brought into line with it. But in many instances the Tiberian vowel marks agree not with the Tiberian vocalisation but with the Babylonian or Palestinian vowels which they replace; thus, e.g., '*asher* is often pointed not with *hateph pathah* but with *pathah*, which coincides with the Babylonian vocalisation. Still another indication is that many of the manuscripts are not supplied with a Massorah. The Massoretic notes were generally attached to manuscripts which were official text-forms, and their absence from so many Geniza fragments testifies to the comparative unimportance of these manuscripts.

Thus, when Geniza manuscripts are studied, it is perhaps better to regard them as part of the domestic history of the transmission of the text, than as a standard or official text-form and vocalisation. They were aids to memory, as instanced by the abbreviated texts, aids to pointing, as in the instances of manuscripts with two kinds of pointing, or, as instanced in a later Geniza MS. in the British Museum, where the Hebrew text is given Arabic vowel marks. In these respects, the Geniza fragments are not to be regarded as equal in value with, e.g., Origen II, for the latter, in spite of its being a transcription, represents a standard, official rendering, at least sufficiently official to be placed alongside the other six columns of the Hexapla, whereas the former were simply notes or even exercises. It is probable, too, that these Geniza manuscripts were not so carefully copied as were the official texts, and contained many

---

[18] Cf. Brønno, *op. cit.*, p. 441.

more scribal errors. An interesting instance is given in Facs. 2 in *Masoreten des Ostens*,[19] viz. the Berlin MS. or. qu. 680, which shows an omission in Job 38.5, with three missing stichoi inserted in the middle and side margins by a second and third scribe.

Because they are unofficial, however, these Babylonian and Palestinian vocalised texts are of the greatest importance for the history of the pre-Tiberian textual transmission, and particularly for an understanding of the work at various centres and academies in Babylon and Palestine. The centres are to be carefully distinguished, as far as possible, for divergences of transmission are to be expected from every one. Further, Massorôth and all available Massoretic lists must be carefully distinguished, because each preserves its own individuality in the pre-Tiberian period and later, until the adoption of the ben Asher text by the decree of Maimonides.

Some divergences of transmission may be noted here. Kahle[20] emphasises that Palestinian manuscripts show variants in the consonantal text which, he says, presuppose the adherence of the scribes to divergent text-forms. One instance is his MS M.1,[21] which in Exod. 28.30 agrees with the LXX in reading מִשְׁפָּטֵי, and not the singular as in M.T. Another manuscript, H, which contains a portion of Daniel, 9.24-12.13, has numerous variants,[22] especially divergent in *scriptio plena* and *defectiva*. An examination of these and the other divergences reveal, however, that it is but seldom indeed that they are more than the addition or omission of the consonants י, ו, ה,—a characteristic by no means confined to this manuscript. Other variants are the substitution of *'al* for *'ad*, *'el* for *'al, eloha* for *ēl*. A Hithpa'el occurs instead of a Niph'al in 12.10, which is more serious. In 11.8 there is a transposition of *zahabh wakhesef*, which is paralleled by Kennicott 245, and in 11.15 we have the reading *melekh hannegebh* for *m. hassafon*,—a feature which finds its counterpart in Targumic renderings. But apart from the last substitution there is nothing in the variants which would require the drastic theory of a divergent text to account for them. They are phenomena which occur also at a period later than the emergence of the ben Asher text.

Another Palestinian manuscript has been mentioned by Kahle in *The Cairo Geniza* as bearing a variant reading. It is *ḥomez* for *ḥaron*, presumably from Ps. 58.10.[23] But the lexica show that the versions and later commentators have always found difficulty with this word, and it is not surprising that still another variant exists. That the variant is an otherwise α. λ, and does not give very good sense, is difficult to explain.

Failure to preserve a text scrupulously identical with the Tiberian *textus receptus* is found equally frequently in Babylonian manuscripts. The MS already referred to, Berlin or. qu. 680, shows that in Job 38.12 the consonantal text corresponds to the Tiberian *Qrê*, and not the *Kthibh*. On the other hand, vv. 13 and 15 show that the Massoretic rule of a suspended *'ayin* in *rᵉsha'im* was followed. Examples abound in Babylonian manuscripts of the Tiberian *Qrê* in the consonantal text. But a perusal of Ginsburg's Hebrew Bible shows that this divergence again was not confined to pre-Tiberian times, and I think it is wrong to regard their presence in pre-ben Asher texts as signs of recensions

---

[19] P. KAHLE. Leipzig, 1913.

[20] *Masoreten des Westens, II*. Stuttgart, 1930, p. 36†.

[21] *Ibid.*

[22] They are listed by KAHLE, *Mas. d. Westens II*, pp. 22†-24†.

[23] p. 54.n.1. The note gives the reference as Ps. 56.10; presumably it should be 58.10, though the text is not given in full by KAHLE.

and in post-ben Asher texts as of no significance.[24] The importance of consonantal variations in Babylonian texts is, however, not seriously advocated even by Kahle, for in his view the consonantal text had been fixed and scrupulously copied by that time. The evidence for divergent transmission is of quite a different class, and there seems to be no gainsaying its existence. The following are its main features : an independent scheme of vocalisation, with the development from simple to complex ; different Massorah, with its own technical terms ; the attaching of the Targum to every verse in the Prophets and Writings ; different division of the text into lections. Thus, the difference between the Babylonian and Palestinian Talmudim is reflected also in the differences of text-transmission between the Babylonian and Palestinian schools.

In view of this difference, the similarity of consonantal transmission is the more surprising, and should be regarded as a strong argument in favour of the traditional theory of one classic text-form for all centres. It minimises the impression left by Kahle's emphasis on an independent recensional transmission. Thus, when Kahle says that he has achieved " a broad foundation for the Babylonian text of the Bible," [25] it should mean no more than the reconstruction of the text-form transmitted there. An examination of it shows that the only real divergences are those of orthography and vocalisation. Again, the development so adequately explained by Kahle from the simple to the complex vocalisation is to be understood as a refinement of the pronunciation, not the emergence of a different recension of the text.

Thus the position regarding all known forms of the pre-Tiberian Hebrew Bible, is that the variants are, with but few exceptions, those of orthography and vocalisation, and are of very little textual significance. They do not reveal any of the usual marks of recensions ; they have no tendentiousness, such as the avoidance of anthropomorphisms ; the camouflage of the Ineffable Name had long since been adopted, though not always the same way, by all schools of tradition. Even in the matter of vocalisation there was broad uniformity, for the pronunciation was basically the same for all types of Babylonian, Palestinian and Tiberian pointing.

Is, then, Orlinsky right, and Kahle and his school wrong ? I think that the differences between them could be resolved, and both interpretations brought together, by what may be described as a less vehemently enthusiastic statement of the case. Orlinsky and the followers of de Lagarde are obviously wrong if they insist on a scrupulous transmission of an archetype ; Kahle, on the other hand, has overstated the case if we are to be persuaded that " east was east, and west was west, and ne'er the twain did meet " in the pre-Tiberian textual transmission.

But there is a major significance in Kahle's studies, which is that the pre-Tiberian vocalisations preserve for us various differences of dialect and pronunciation from the period before the fixing of the classical pointing. In such dialect forms we approach a language much nearer spoken Hebrew than is possible through the Tiberian, with the Qaraite and other influences playing upon it. For this reason we appreciate the principles of Kahle's work, and again those of Sperber, for their studies of pre-Tiberian Hebrew grammar, and likewise Brønno's treatment of the morphology and vocalisation of Origen II. On their bases a comparison of Hebrew dialects can be made which are less artificial and more akin to the real Hebrew language.

---

[24] Cf. *The Cairo Geniza*, p. 54.
[25] *Ibid.*, p. 44.

Caution is necessary if the sources to be used for such a reconstruction be extended further than the Babylonian and Tiberian vocalised texts and the transcription of Origen. Thus, transliterations in various LXX manuscripts must be scrutinised for traces of recensional influence, and all early quotations, even of Origen II, must likewise be scrutinised. This places the quotations in Hatch and Redpath's Concordance, vol. 3, on a very indifferent plane compared with the remains of the column discovered in the Mercati palimpsest. Likewise, Reider's otherwise informative *Prolegomena to an Index of Aquila*[26] suffers because of its dependence on Field. Transliterations in Jerome's works must be limited to confirmatory use : Father Sutcliffe's article in *Biblica*[27] gives adequate demonstration of this fact. At the same time, Massoretic lists of variants, such as lists of ben Naphtali readings, cannot be indiscriminately used, because it is always possible that words have been included in them which did not strictly belong to that school, but had different provenances and became so listed simply because they were variants. These reasons justify the suggestion already made that a reconstructed pre-Tiberian Hebrew grammar should confine itself to the remains in the Mercati palimpsest, and the available Hebrew manuscripts with Babylonian and Palestinian pointing, as dealt with by Kahle in *Masoreten des Ostens, Masoreten des Westens* I and II, and the invaluable collection of 70 facsimiles published by Kahle in *Zeitschrift für die alttestamentliche Wissenschaft*, NF 5, 1928, together with further manuscripts with Babylonian pointing for which the catalogue in the prolegomena to *Bib. Heb.*[3] is indispensable.

The divergences in these manuscript sources, and between them and the *textus receptus*, are the means whereby different dialect forms are to be established—but the task is by no means straightforward. According to Kahle[28] neither his own pupil, Sperber, nor Brønno can demand general acceptance for their theories. The basic fact for all such work is, I think, that the divergences of vocalisation do not imply a divergent text-form, but a different dialect or way of recitation at the various synagogues and centres of Massoretic learning.

In brief outline, the following dialect features may be said to have been established : (1) from Origen II.[29] The most important conclusions made by Brønno are :—

(*a*) Verbs : 1. the 2.s.m. ending is generally θ, sometimes θα. 2. There is not a consistent development of *ă* in the Imperfect of some ע״פ verbs. 3. The prefix of the Pi'el participle, as well as the Hiph'il is μα, 4. The perfect Hiph'il has sometimes a development which approximates to the Tiberian segholation, thus **hikhtebhet*. 5. There are frequent divergences of conjugation between Origen II and Tiberian M.T.

(*b*) Nouns : 1. Segholation of originally monosyllabic nouns does not occur. 2. Considerable difference between the pausal form here and in M.T. 3. In initial μ-nouns the prefix is usually μα, whereas in M.T., the majority are *mi* : in this feature the column is again in agreement with Babylonian manuscripts, though there are divergences in individual cases between the two. 4. Suffixes : the 2.s.m. is αχ, with an occasional *nun energicum* form having final α.

Thus far the reconstruction is comparatively simple, for the basic element is provided by the consonants. But when the column is examined for voca-

---

[26] Philadelphia, 1916.

[27] *St. Jerome's Pronunciation of Hebrew. Biblica*, 29 (1948), pp. 112-125.

[28] *The Cairo Geniza*, p. 165, note 2 ; p. 234.

[29] Cf. BRØNNO, *op. cit.*, pp. 448-463.

lisation the problems are more intricate, and conclusions must be tentative. It is obvious that the Hebrew gutturals are not represented in the column, either because the Greek alphabet could not supply the necessary letters, or, as is known from Rabbinic sources, Palestinian Jews in those times did not pronounce them. It is also impossible to establish how far the vowel values of Greek coincided with those of their contemporary Hebrew counterparts, or again how both compared with Tiberian vocalisation.   Thus Brønno's interpretation of the use of ε in certain cases brings him to the conclusion that Philippi's law, that *i* in a closed accented syllable becomes *â* before the dropping of the final vowel, does not hold for Origen II—a statement which has brought a sharp criticism from F. R. Blake.[30] This question, in turn, leads to a criticism of Brønno's work by Kahle,[31] that " he compares the transcribed forms . . . directly with the forms fixed by the Tiberian Massoretes." Whilst agreeing with Kahle that material in pre-Tiberian vocalised texts is of the greatest importance for comparison with Origen II, I think it is also true that in the last resort Brønno could do only as he did, for otherwise he would be comparing together a number of fluid and variable dialects.

(2) From Palestinian vocalised texts come the following conclusions based on facsimiles and notes in Kahle's *Masoreten des Westens*[32] :

(*a*) In MS H[33] we have the following features : 1. An *e* sound precedes the consonant, where Tiberian has *i*, e.g. Ezek. 13.22, has *hekh'abhtiv* for Tiberian *hikh'abhtiv*. 2. In Ezek. 14.3 we have *'eddārāsh* for Tib. *'iddārēsh*, a form which has its counterpart in the Babylonian vocalisation. 3. In Ezek. 14.13, a Hiph'il *teḥti'* is used where Tib. has Qal, and in 16. 25, 26, 29, the form *tirbi* occurs for Tib. *tarbi*.

(*b*) MS J. A notable feature here is that the same sign is used for the Tiberian *ṣere, seghol, vocal shewa* and *ḥateph-seghol*. This may be due, as Kahle argues, to the later refinements of the Tiberians, or, on the other hand, to the identity of the sounds in the dialect presupposed here.

(*c*) MS K. The form *ye'shshammu* in Jer. 2.3, is regarded as ע״ע, whereas Tib. *ye'shamu* makes it a normal ע״פ verb. In 2.7, there is an instance of a Hithpa'el, *wateṭṭam'u*, where Tib. reads Pi'el.[34]

(*d*) MS L. has a vowel mark which, among other usages, denotes a segholate, but with no distinction between nouns which, in Tiberian, are from *a* or *i* monosyllabic forms. Thus the Tiberian *ḥesed* (Ps. 52.5), *sedeq* (ditto), *neged* (52.11) and *'ēbher* (55.7), *sēfer* (69.29), *'ēqebh* (70.4) and others have all the same pointing. Furthermore, there is no difference here between the two vowels of the segholate.

Variant forms and grammatical features in fragments of Piyuttim with Palestinian pointing provide further examples of dialect variations.

(3) Finally, there are the Babylonian vocalised texts. When the oriental transmission is examined, the first care is that the distinction made by Kahle between simple and complex vocalisations be observed. These are not to be understood as simply forming a continuous development, with a straightforward

[30] J.N.E.S. VI 1947, pp. 192f. (Review of BRØNNO's book).

[31] *The Cairo Geniza*, pp. 232ff.

[32] Vol. II, pp. 14†-42†, esp. 35†-42†.

[33] *Mas d. Westens, II*, pp. 16† f.

[34] KAHLE objects to the form because of the inappropriate meaning, and emends by reading the *daghesh* sign over the following consonant, which would bring it into line with the Tiberian vocalisation. (*Ibid.*, p. 25†.)

transition, for they also existed alongside each other.[35] Kahle has reconstructed as follows : in certain districts of the Babylonian transmission a more exact vocalisation was undertaken, and in other districts the simple form was retained.[36] The complex Babylonian has affinities with the Tiberian, both showing the influence of the Qaraites. Simple vocalised texts are, on the whole, earlier—7th and 8th centuries, compared with the 8th and 9th for the complex. It is the former that is basic for the Yemenite vocalisation.[37]

For the present purpose of indicating dialect forms, the following features are important : 1. The present distinction between Sephardic and Ashkenazic pronunciation of *qameṣ* may be regarded as the successor of the divergence between Babylonian and Palestinian-Tiberian pronunciation of the *a* sound, with the former regarding every *qameṣ* as *a*, and the latter giving it an *ā* or *o* value. 2. The conjunction *wav*, when it occurs before a consonant without a full vowel, is always pointed with an *i* vowel, in contrast to the Tiberian, which might have *shureq*. 3. The occurrence in more than one Babylonian manuscript of a Pi'el form of the verb *'anah*, with the meaning of " to answer," " to grant,"[38] a form which does not occur anywhere in the M.T. It happens twice in the perfect with a suffix, viz., Is. 49.8, Ps. 22.22, and once in a participial form, Micah 3.7. The MSS are listed in BH[3] as Eb 10 and Ec 2. But it would be tedious to trace here all instances of this kind of variation in the Babylonian manuscripts.

Before concluding it may be permitted to return to the question of whether or not these divergences constitute recensions. We cannot allow that they are recensions in the same sense as those found in Symmachus, Theodotion or the LXX, for there is not the same significance in the variants. In this respect Orlinsky appears to be correct, and it is the M.T. itself which is a recension. On the other hand, the dialect divergences, and other considerations presuppose independent transmissions of the text-form, which retain carefully preserved traditions embodied in vocalisations and Massorôth. For this reason " recension " is, I think, the best word to use, because the alternative " text-form " would often be misleading, or at least too indefinite and colourless.

Bangor.   BLEDDYN J. ROBERTS.

---

[35] Cf. *Mas. d. Ostens*, p. 157.

[36] *ZAW* 5, *NF*, 1928, p. 117.

[37] *Mas. d. Ostens*, p. 157. The work of KAHLE on the Babylonian texts cannot be too highly evaluated for the study of pre-Tiberian Massoretic Hebrew. I refer particularly to : *Der masorethische Text des Alten Testaments nach der Überlieferung der babylonischen Juden.* (Leipzig, 1902), and the complementary chapter *Das Hebräische nach östlicher Überlieferung* in *Mas. d. Ostens*, pp. 181-199.

[38] *Mas.d. Ostens*, pp. 122 and 189.

The Masoretic Text of the Bible
and the Pronunciation of Hebrew *

IN A TREATISE on the Shwa, composed soon after the reading of
the Biblical text had been fixed by the Masoretes of Tiberias, we
have a list of Tiberian Masoretes, and a similar list is to be found in
a treatise on the accents, of which we know one folio. The Leningrad fragments, discovered by Harkavy, in which the text is partly
in Hebrew, are supplemented by Geniza fragments in London and
Oxford discovered by Mann. These belong to a manuscript written
in Arabic which is nearer to the original. But in Leningrad the whole
treatise on the Shwa is preserved. At my request, the Leningrad
texts were sent to me in Bonn and I asked Kurt Levy, one of my best
students there, to work on them. He discovered a fragment of a
second Arabic MS. from the Geniza in Frankfurt, and made an
excellent edition, with a German translation, of the treatise on the
Shwa.[1] The fact that parts of three MSS. of the treatise have been
preserved shows that the treatise must have been well known and
even famous. The list of Masoretes is important for understanding
the treatise. The author takes the list as concluded with the name of
Aaron b. Asher. But he himself is not too remote from the Ben
Asher family. The treatise makes us realise some of the problems
which the Masoretes had to face when they gave the text of the
Bible the form which was to be its final one. In its style of expression the MS. belongs to the early Arabic sources of Hebrew
grammar and it is certain that it was composed before Ḥaiyūj, in
whom we are accustomed to see the first Hebrew grammarian.

Levy, in a very fine investigation, showed how the relation of this
treatise to the *Diqduqe ha-Teʿamim* of Aaron b. Asher has to be
viewed, and in what way it is related to the " Manuel du lecteur "
published by Dérenbourg. He discusses the problem of how it can
be explained that the treatise about the Shwa disappeared later on
from the transmission, and he thinks that the cause was its language
which later generations found quaint and incomprehensible. This

---

* First Lawrence Kostoris Lecture, delivered at the Institute of Jewish
Studies, Manchester, 11th March, 1957.
[1] KURT LEVY, Zur masoretischen Grammatik. Texte und Untersuchungen
(=Bonner Orientalistische Studien, 19), Stuttgart 1936.

Reprinted from *Journal of Jewish Studies* 7 (1956).

may well be one reason. But two further causes must be considered: first, the writings deal with problems which the Masoretes had to face with regard to fixing the pronunciation of the text of the Bible and with different solutions which these problems found. One does not like to be reminded of such differences of pronunciation once the fixed text has been approved and acknowledged. The other reason is that these writings were of Karaite origin. Levy could not know this when he wrote his book, but now there can be no doubt about it.

The five generations of the Ben Asher family who are mentioned in the first list as the contemporaries of the Masoretes enable us to fix approximately when and where these Masoretes lived. The Codex of the Prophets completed in C.E. 895 in Tiberias by Moshe b. Asher proves that the work on the Biblical text was finished towards the end of the ninth century. We can go even further and suggest that the text of the Bible was copied somewhat earlier in this way. It is difficult to accept that the oldest dated manuscript of the Hebrew text of the Bible which has come down to us should have been the first one copied in this way.

Aaron b. Asher, the son of Moshe, was the great authority who in the first half of the 10th century gave to the Bible text the detailed form which it was to retain thereafter. He is explicitly named as the last of the chain of Masoretes.

We know with certainty that Moshe b. Asher and his son belonged to the community of the Karaites and it is therefore very likely that also the other members of the Ben Asher family were Karaites. How many of the Masoretes mentioned in the list belonged to the Karaites we do not know. One may suppose that there were followers of the Rabbanites among them. Furthermore we must conceive the possibility that in earlier time Karaites and Rabbanites worked together towards the carrying through of the punctuation of the Biblical text. But it seems that the Karaites were the driving force. Their founder 'Anan had already encouraged them in the study of the Biblical text. It is very conceivable that the old MSS. brought from the cave near Jericho to Jerusalem about C.E. 800 gave a new impetus to the study of the Bible.

In order to prove the Karaite affinities of the Ben Asher Masoretes from Tiberias we have to-day an abundance of material which is decisive. First there is a poem composed by Moshe b. Asher in which Israel is compared with a vine. The first part of the poem, which is in the form of verses having an alphabetical acrostic, is to be found at the end of the Leningrad Codex of the Bible B 19a dated C.E. 1009, and follows, on fol. 490 of the Codex, the *Diqduqe ha-Ṭeʿamim* of Aaron b. Asher.

In the Geniza, a second copy of the poem was discovered by Dr. Menaḥem Zulay. The first part of the poem is in the British Museum (Or 5557 I, fol. 40b) It contains the alphabetic acrostic from א to כ. The continuation is to be found in a Cambridge fragment (Univ. Collection Or 1080, Box V 1). Of these Geniza fragments photographs were made for the Research Institute for Hebrew Poetry in Jerusalem. The Cambridge fragment has the continuation with the verses from ל to ת, followed by verses beginning with the letters ש-א-נ-ב-ה-ש-מ, which indicates as author of the poem Moshe ben Asher; only the last verse beginning with ר is missing. As in the Leningrad MS. B 19a after the alphabetic acrostic a verse beginning with ק is found, it has been suggested that verses beginning with ק-ר-ה had followed at the end.

Clearly, in error the copyist of the Leningrad text passed from the ע-verse to the פ-verse, and the copyist of the Geniza-MS. passed from the פ-verse to the ר-verse. But on the whole, the two MSS. supplement each other in an excellent way.

Dr. Zulay had placed the fragments of the MS. discovered by him at the disposal of Benjamin Klar who published the poem as far as it goes in the Hebrew periodical *Tarbiṣ XV*, 1944, p. 43 f. The poem is preceded in the Leningrad Codex with the words:

> This is the adornment of Israel and the genealogy of the Prophets in which Israel is compared with a vine of which the branches are the prophets, the roots are the fathers, and the unweaned children are the wise who help the many to righteousness.

The especially important verses of this poem are, as has been shown by Dr. Naftali Wieder, verses 22 and 23. He writes: As B. Klar rightly observed, Moses b. Asher traced the chain of Karaitic tradition to the Elders of Bathyra, the spiritual ancestors of Karaism, who had inherited the prophetic traditions and transmitted them to the Karaites. The latter are thus in direct line of descent from the prophets.

As Wieder shows, it is highly significant that the epithet Moshe b. Asher conferred upon the Elders of Bathyra is precisely *the perfect ones*, which epithet was considered a sufficiently clear identification mark to indicate their religious affiliations. I confine myself here to referring to the remarks of Wieder in *JQR* XLVII, 1956, p. 97 ff.

We have come to know recently that Sa'adya Gaon polemicized against the Ben Asher Masoretes in Tiberias. From the polemic it becomes clear that these Masoretes belong to the Karaites. The first specimen of Sa'adya's polemic was discovered by Benjamin Menasseh Lewin of Haifa. It is a Piut called according to the words with which the first verse begins משלי אשא. Lewin published the specimen in *Tarbiṣ III*, 1932. A further fragment was published by Israel Davidson in *Jewish Studies in Memory of George A. Kohut* (pp. 9-24 of the Hebrew section), New York, 1935. Lewin subsequently found more material and published it in a small volume under the title אשא משלי לרבנו סעדיה גאון· ספר מלחמות הראשון כנגד הקראים (Jerusalem, 1943).

Benjamin Klar has dealt in detail with the problems arising from this polemic in two articles published in *Tarbiṣ XIV*, 1943, and *XV*, 1944. He has correctly seen that the Arabic title has to be read *ar-radd 'ala-bni Asher* " the polemic against Ben Asher." He has shown that the poem of Sa'adya contains a sharp attack on the *Diqduqe ha-Ṭe'amim* of which we know that the author was the Masorete Aaron b. Asher. So it was evident to Klar that Aaron b. Asher was the Masorete attacked by Sa'adya.

But the matter is not so simple. A great part of Sa'adya's polemic, as far as it is known, is directed against §3 of the *Diqduqe*, which bears the title *seder ha-miqra* and deals with the three night watches, identified with Torah, Prophets and Ketubim. The believers are admonished in it to observe the commandments taken from all three parts of the Bible. Rabbanite teaching ordered the believers to take precepts exclusively from the Torah with the help of the Oral Law as codified in the Mishnah. The injunction given in this paragraph of the *Diqduqe* is typically Karaitic. Against this Sa'adya directs his polemic with the utmost energy.

But precisely this paragraph of the *Diqduqe* is older than Aaron b. Asher. We find it written in a prominent way by Moshe b. Asher himself on p. 583 of the Cairo Codex of the Prophets, dated C.E. 895. It was therefore composed by Moshe b. Asher himself, if he did not take it from an older source. It is the only paragraph of the *Diqduqe* taken over by Aaron b. Asher from his father Moshe. We must therefore reckon with the possibility that Sa'adya attacked also Moshe b. Asher in his polemical Piut.

496

As is well known, Jacob Mann has proved that Sa'adya must have been ten years older than had been generally assumed, being born in C.E. 882 instead of C.E. 892. He has shown this on the evidence of a statement of Sa'adya's two sons who declared about 11 years after their father's death (10th May, C.E. 942) that when he died he was 60 years less some forty days. Mann found this statement in the Geniza, and reported on it in *JQR*, April 1921.

By this fact all the suggestions which had earlier been put forward about the first decades of his life are rendered useless. Henry Malter, in the postscript to his book *Saadia Gaon, his Life and Works* (Philadelphia, 1921) had reluctantly to withdraw all his conclusions about the early period of Sa'adya's life. What we know about Sa'adya's stay in his native country, Egypt, is that he had developed there into an excellent Arabic scholar who was far better acquainted with Arabic literature and the conditions of the Muslims than any other Jew. We further know that he had to leave his native country and was never again able to return to it. From Egypt he went to Palestine, and it seems that he stayed much longer there than was previously supposed. The only teacher in Jewish studies of whom we hear lived in Tiberias, and it is very likely that Sa'adya first came in contact with Karaites in Tiberias. If he had left his native land when he was 23, as generally supposed, he could well have met Moshe b. Asher in C.E. 905, ten years after the latter had finished the Cairo Codex of the Prophets. Moshe had by then won a high reputation. Later he may have come into contact with Aaron his son who had become the greatest authority for all matters concerning the Masorah. Against these two prominent Karaite Masoretes Sa'adya developed his polemic in the form of a Piut of which a considerable part has been found in the Geniza.

We have an important witness to Sa'adya from an Arabic contemporary al-Mas'ūdī who met him together with his former teacher. This is all the more valuable for us as our evidence from Jewish sources is very meagre and confined to two periods of his life only. Al-Mas'ūdī, an Arab historian and geographer who had seen a great part of the world in the first half of the 10th century C.E., and in his works records many interesting experiences, comes to speak in his *kitāb at-tanbīh wa'l-ishrāf* about Sa'adya and reports as follows[2]:

---

[2] The text of al-Mas'ūdī has been published by J. M. DE GOEJE in *Bibliotheca Geographorum Arabicorum*, vol. VIII, Leiden 1894, p. 113.

Concerning the Israelites, both the Ashma'ath[3] who are the many and the great mass, and the 'Ananites[4] who believe in righteousness ('adl) and monotheism (tauḥīd),[5] in their explanation of the Hebrew books, the Torah, the Prophets and the Psalms (for Ketubim) which are the 24 books, and in their translation into Arabic, rely on a number of Israelites who are held in very high esteem among them, most of whom we have personally met, amongst them Abū Kathīr Yaḥyā b. Zakarīya, the Kātib, the man from Ṭabarīya, Ashma'athī in belief who died about 320 (C.E. 932), and Sa'īd b. Ya'qūb al-Faiyūmī (i.e. Sa'adya), also Ashma'athī in belief, who had made his studies under Abū Kathīr, and whose exegesis of the Bible many of them value most highly. He had differences in 'Irāq with the Exilarch (ra's al-Jālūt) Dā'ūd b. Zaccai, from the offspring of (king) David, and opposed him. This occurred during the Caliphate of al-Muqtadir (C.E. 908-932) and the Jews were divided into two parties regarding both of them. He was present at a sitting of the Court under the Wezir 'Īsā b. 'Alī and other Wezirs and the judges and scholars for the resolution of these differences. When he had won a majority among them, the foremost part was played by al-Faiyūmī and they recognised him as leader. He died after 330 (C.E. 941).

Al-Mas'ūdī further recounts that he had many discussions with Abū Kathīr in both provinces of the land at that time, al-Filistīn and al-Urdunn, on the problem of abolishing divine laws, and the coming into existence of new conditions which could bring about alterations of previous divine commandments.

Of great interest is the report on the differences between Sa'adya and the Exilarch Dā'ūd b. Zaccai, whom Sa'adya strongly attacked in a way which led to the formation of two parties among the Jews. Their differences were heard before the High Court of Baghdād, presided over by the Wezir himself, attended by prominent judges and scholars. 'Alī b. 'Īsā Ibn al-Jarrāḥ is a well-known personality. He was several times the Wezir of the Caliph al-Muqtadir, his last term of office being January to May, C.E. 928. We may assume that in this period the first session concerned with the Jewish dispute was held. Other sessions must have taken place under his successors whose names are not mentioned by Mas'ūdī. The impression is

---

[3] Ashma'ath corresponds to the Aramaic שמעתא used in the Babylonian Talmud for tradition and used by al-Mas'ūdī collectively of the Rabbanites. A single Rabbanite is called Ashma'athī.

[4] A name given to the Karaites, derived from 'Anan their founder.

[5] The Muslim Mu'tazilites used to call themselves ahl al-'adl wat-tauḥid. Perhaps al-Mas'ūdī's authority was a Mu'tazilite who characterised the Karaites in the same way.

given that the complete hearing lasted for several years and only came to an end when Sa'adya was elected Gaon for the second time definitively.

In this eye-witness report al-Mas'ūdī refers to Abū Kathīr and Sa'adya on the basis of personal acquaintance. Tiberias was the capital of the Muslim province al-Urdunn. As Kātib, *secretary*, Abū Kathīr must have had a respected position in one of the many government offices which existed in this capital, and he must have been well informed in Jewish matters—Mas'ūdī reports discussions with him in several places, and we may suppose that he was a wealthy man. But he was certainly no expert scholar, so we can understand that nothing is to be found about him in Jewish sources. The time when Sa'adya had been his pupil was long past when Mas'ūdī met both of them.

As for Sa'adya, there can be no question that he was an unusually gifted man. Ability is inborn and cannot be learnt. But Sa'adya developed himself into an outstanding scholar. For the acquisition of scholarship even the gifted man needs quietness for study. " Sa'adya was in the habit of travelling " writes Malter (p. 37). Sa'adya had certainly travelled, but we must realise that by travelling one cannot become a scholar. To acquire scholarship one needs a home where books are available. The refugee from Egypt may have found them at the home of Abū Kathīr, and the latter may have advised him how best to make use of them. His own genius soon led him far beyond his teacher, without, however, destroying the good relations between them.

Sa'adya's polemic against the Ben Asher Masoretes of Tiberias certainly embittered the differences between Rabbanites and Karaites, to whom the Tiberian Masoretes belonged. As the text of the Bible prepared by the Tiberian Masoretes was accepted by the whole of Jewry, Rabbanites as well as Karaites, we must suppose that this occurred before the polemic of Sa'adya began and the differences came to assume such an acute form as we know they did in later times.

Benjamin Klar has given in general a correct account of Sa'adya's polemic, but one thing he completely misunderstood. The Masoretes, especially Moshe b. Asher, are greatly concerned to point out that the punctuation of the text of the Bible fixed by them is in agreement with the way in which the pronunciation of Hebrew was transmitted by Ezra through the men of the Great Synagogue. Moshe b. Asher

499

was certainly aware that the Tiberian punctuation was the work of the Masoretes of Tiberias. Nevertheless he declares that the Masoretes had not added anything to what was transmitted to them nor had they concealed anything. These points were certainly important in order that the punctuation fixed by the Masoretes of Tiberias might be generally accepted. Later speculations which tried to push back the punctuation to the time of Moses on Sinai do not interest us here. What Klar has written on the question of whether Ben Asher believed that the punctuation goes back to Moses and Sinai clearly reveals a lack of understanding.

It is of the greatest value that we have Biblical Codices which are closely connected with the last members of the Masorete family of Ben Asher. The Codex finished at Tiberias by Moshe b. Asher in C.E. 895 is the oldest dated Hebrew Codex of the Bible which has come down to us. Its preservation is to be attributed to the fact that the Codex was, for a very long time, kept and greatly revered in the Karaite Synagogue of Cairo (al-Qāhira). During my last stay in Cairo I saw the Codex at 5 p.m. on February 20th, 1956, and held it in my hands. The jeweller David Zeki Lisha יצחק אלישע דוד, president of the Karaite Synagogue community, showed it to me in the recently built Karaite Synagogue of the 'Abbāsīje (Shāri'a es-Sebīl Khāzindār). This is where the Codex was transferred a few years ago after having been kept for centuries in the old Karaite Synagogue situated in the Muski.

We are very well acquainted with the history of the Cairo Codex of the Prophets thanks to the Colophons which it contains and which I publish below in translation. We learn from a Colophon written by Moshe b. Asher himself (p. 585) that a Karaite living in Jerusalem, called Ya'beṣ b. Shelomo ha-Babli, commissioned the Codex to be made for his own use. He boasts that he had earned the money needed for the payment of the Codex with the labour of his own hands, that he did not spend inherited money on the purchase. The following is a translation of the note:

This is the Codex (*difter*) which it was granted Ya'beṣ b. Shelomo ha-Babli—may his (i.e. the father's) soul find rest—to acquire. He prepared it (the Codex) to study it himself from the reward of his work, the labour of his hands, the sweat of his face, for the honour of the God of Israel—may the Creator of souls mercifully grant him the study of it, to observe and to keep everything it contains, may He give him a good portion and a good heart and pleasant lot in this world and good reward for the world to come. May Ya'beṣ b. Shelomo—may his soul find rest—be worthy to see the grace of God and to visit His temple (*Ps.* xxvii: 4). May the God of Israel give him sons and grandsons who study the Torah and who occupy themselves with the Laws. And may all blessings which are contained in the Torah and the Prophets and the Scriptures come upon his head and that of his offspring and may the whole of Israel be included in the blessing. Amen.

From three further notes, every one of which is written by a different hand, we learn that a special place was allotted to the Codex; it was kept in the owner's grounds in Jerusalem and nobody was allowed to remove it. The Codex was dedicated to the Karaites who were to have the opportunity of reading the lessons on Sabbaths, on the festival of the New Moon, and other festivals, and it was expressly stipulated that on such days nobody should be denied access to the Codex.

The Colophon written on p. 581 in Hebrew cursive tells us that this Codex of the Prophets was dedicated to the Karaite Community in the Synagogue of al-Qāhira.

The translation of the note is:

(p. 581) This book (*sefer*), the Prophets, is consecrated to the Lord (ליני) God, the God of Israel. The great lord David, son of the great lord Yefet, known as al-Iskandari, has consecrated it after its redemption for the community of the Karaites (עדת בני מקרא) to read in it on Sabbath days and on fast days in the Synagogue in Cairo (כנסת אלא קהרה)—may it (the city of Jerusalem) be built up and established! And when he or one of his descendants is seated, the server shall set it (the book) before him. And it shall not be allowed that anyone bring it out of the Synagogue except it is done—may God prevent it!—by compulsion and he shall return it in the time of appeasement. Whoever contradicts this condition (התנאי) and donation (הקדושה), cursed be he by the Lord (יי) and all curses shall come upon him. Whoever keeps it and reads in it and puts it back into its place after the days of unrest, may he be blessed in the name of the Lord, may all the blessings and the good reward and wishes come upon his head and the head of those who have consecrated it, the lord David and his descendants, until the end of all generations and of all Israel.

The original Colophon which the writer himself added to the Codex on page 586 is the following:

I, Moshe ben Asher have written this Codex (maḥzor) of the Scriptures according to my judgement ' as the good hand of my God was upon me' (*Neh.* ii: 8), ' very clearly' (*Dt.* xxvii: 8) in

the city of Ma'azya-Ṭabarīya, ' the renowned city ' (*Ez*. xxvi: 17) as
it was understood by the congregation of Prophets, the chosen of
the Lord, the Saints of our God, who understood all hidden
things and revealed the secret of wisdom, ' the oak-trees of
righteousness ' (*Is*. lxi: 3), the men of faith, who concealed nothing
of what was given to them nor added one word to what was
transmitted to them, who have made the Scriptures powerful and
mighty, the Twenty-four Books which they established in their
integrity with explanatory accents and clear instruction as to
pronunciation with sweet palate and beauty of speech. May it
please our Creator to illuminate our eyes and enlighten our hearts
by His Torah, that we may learn and teach and act with a ' perfect
heart and a willing mind ' (1 *Chr*. xxviii: 9) and for the whole of
Israel. Amen.

It was written in the year 827 after the destruction of the
Second Temple to which may the Creator of souls be pleased to
return in mercy and build up with ' rubies, sapphires and car-
buncles' (*Is*. liv: 11 f) as a perfect building, a firmly established
building, a building which can neither be pulled down, nor
demolished nor destroyed in eternity and eternity of eternities,
speedily, in our days and in the days of all Israel. AMEN.

(The following written by another hand).

I have thoroughly discussed this colophon with Dr. M. Zucker of
New York and also with Dr. N. Wieder of Jews' College in London,
both of whom are engaged in the study of the early Karaites. There
can be no doubt whatsoever that we are here dealing with a
characteristic Karaite writing. Dr. Wieder, at my request, put at
my disposal a number of valuable remarks in a letter of the 7th
October 1956 from which I quote the following:

The expression עדת נביאים is a reference to the Karaite
scholars who maintained that divine illumination had guided
them in their exegetical work. Karaite authors of the ninth and
tenth centuries, like Daniel al-Qūmisī, Sahl b. Maṣlīaḥ, Yefet b.
'Alī, and David al-Fāsī claimed divine illumination for the later
Karaite scholars, in contrast to the first generations, including
even 'Anan, who stumbled over the exegesis of the divine laws
(al-Qūmisī). This is said to have been prophesied in the book of
Daniel where we read (xi: 35): " some of the Maskīlīm will
stumble." Al-Qūmisī refers to the Maskīlīm expressly as the
" prophets who possess knowledge " and he adds: " They know
the Bible through and through and (know) why it was thus and
not otherwise written."

That Ben Asher is referring to the Karaite scholars is quite
evident from the title אילי הצדק, the oak-trees of righteousness,
a typically Karaite way of describing Karaites. According to *Is*.

lxi: 3, it is used for those who mourn for Zion, and the Karaite scholars in the Holy Land who called themselves *the mourners for Zion* אבלי ציון applied this expression as referring to them. עדת נביאים must therefore be translated as the " Community of Prophets."

Moshe b. Asher's claim that the Karaite scholars " understood the hidden things " is quite in agreement with the corresponding claim of other Karaite authors. Dr. Wieder refers to Moshe's son Aaron who says, in *Diqduqe ha-Ṭeʿamim*, that the wise, God-fearing, perfect man knows the hidden things of the Torah.

I have already shown that from the fact that a Bible text established by Karaite Masoretes was accepted as authoritative throughout Jewry, by Rabbanites and Karaites alike, we must conclude that this acceptance must have taken place at a time when the relations between the two parties had not yet come to the critical stage that we know of at a later time. It is very unlikely that Saʿadya wrote polemical treatises against the Karaites before he left Egypt.

Since the time of the great Arab conquest in the 7th century C.E. the Jews were living in Palestine and in Babylonia, the chief centres of their activity, under Arab rule. In former times Palestine had been for centuries a part of the Byzantine empire, and Babylonia had been a part of the Sassanide territories. The frontiers had in some ways impeded the exchange of ideas and that was the reason why different shoots had grown from a common root. Based on the mainly uniform Mishna text, a Palestinian and a Babylonian Talmud had been developed. Besides the old Palestinian Targums written in an Aramaic language well understood in Palestine, official Targums to Torah and Prophets had come into existence in Babylonia. These however were not composed in the Aramaic current in that country, but in the old Aramaic as it had been used since Persian days. It was believed that in this way the widest circulation for the Targums would be secured.

That also different methods of punctuation of Hebrew had been developed in Palestine and in Babylonia we know only from the rich collection of vocalised Biblical texts preserved in the Geniza of Old Cairo.

Before developments of pronunciation parallel to the Hebrew Bible, fixed by the Masoretes from Tiberias, became known, it was hardly possible to look beyond the system established by them. This system stood before us like a " bolt from the blue." Nobody

503

could say how it came into being, nobody how it was developed. It was like a miracle for which one explanation only could be given: The pronunciation of Hebrew as fixed by the Masoretes of Tiberias was handed down by them unanimously and exactly in the form in which it was transmitted to them, and by the long chain of trustworthy transmitters every guarantee was given that they had fixed the text exactly as it had been read from time immemorial, from the golden days when the Temple was still in existence, when sacrifices were offered and services were held there, from the days of Ezra and the men of the Great Synagogue.

The Masoretes did everything in their power to foster this idea. They eliminated all remnants of earlier pronunciation so radically that no pre-Masoretic texts were allowed to be preserved. The first specimens of earlier punctuation to re-emerge were found in the Cairo Geniza, where they had been stored in order to be destroyed. It was against the will of the Masoretes that these remnants were preserved there. The Masoretes were interested to ensure that the punctuation finally fixed by them should be the only authoritative one and should alone survive. Thus it became possible to regard the text fixed by these Tiberian Masoretes as something to which, in a slightly modified form, the famous words of Vincent of Lerins could be applied,

quod semper, quod ubique, quod ab omnibus traditum erat,

as a text which in this very form had been transmitted always, everywhere, by everybody—just as the ideal text of the Koran has been regarded for more than 1200 years as its truly original form.

The material preserved in the Geniza gives us the chance to look beyond this complicated system of punctuation elaborated by the Masoretes.

Since I discovered in a Berlin MS. coming from Yemen, more than fifty years ago, the first specimen of a real Babylonian text of the Bible, a great number of such texts have been discovered chiefly in the Cairo Geniza. Recently, Professor Diez Macho of Barcelona, whilst working in the Library of the Jewish Theological Seminary of America in New York, found a great amount of new material. We have now at our disposal nearly half of the Bible provided with Babylonian punctuation. An interesting report from Qirqisānī[6] who wrote in the first half of the 10th century C.E. tells us that the

---

[6] *Kitāb al-anwār wal-marāḳib,* II, 16, (ed. Nemoy 135). Cf. GEORGES VAJDA in *REJ*, CVII, 1946-47, pp. 91 f.

Babylonian reading (*qirā'at al-'Irāq*) was used in a great part of the world from ar-Rakka on the Euphrates up to the Chinese frontiers, by most of the people living in Mesopotamia, Khurasān, Fāris, Kirmān, Iṣfahān, Yamāma, Baḥrain, al-Yaman and other countries. Qirqisānī refers for this information to a certain Ya'qūb b. Efraim ash-Shāmī of whom we unfortunately do not know anything, but it is certain that his report refers to the time before the text fixed by the Masoretes of Tiberias was known and had any authority outside Palestine. It is of a certain importance that we can expect in the near future a publication of such texts which are certainly independent of the texts fixed by the Tiberian Masoretes.

For the pronunciation of Hebrew used in Palestine at the time before the Masoretes of Tiberias began their work we can obtain some information from several texts of the Bible provided with Palestinian punctuation; a few more have recently been found by Diez Macho in America.[7] Most of these texts, however, have been influenced, in one way or another, by the work of the Tiberian Masoretes at an early stage of their history. Comparatively little influenced texts are those written on scrolls to which some Palestinian vowels and accents have been added. I have published the fragments of a scroll with the text of Ezekiel. Some fragments of a scroll with texts of the Psalms will be published by Dr. A. Murtonen. An interesting specimen of a text with Palestinian vocalisation worked over by a Tiberian Masorete was discovered by Professor Diez Macho in the Library of the Jewish Theological Seminary of America in New York. We see here how a text of the Bible to which the copyist of the MS. has added some Palestinian vowels and accents has been worked over by a method of Tiberian vocalisation which was still at the beginning of its development. It is very fortunate that such a specimen has been preserved for us.

But we have seen that the Palestinian punctuation was used in all kinds of Hebrew texts; in particular a great number of liturgical texts are preserved, and these have not been influenced by the Tiberian Masora. In the quotations from the Bible as far as they are written down in full and provided with punctuation, we have specimens of Hebrew as spoken in Palestine before the Tiberian Masoretes began their work.

---

[7] Tres nuevos manuscritos biblicos " palestinenses " in *Estudios Biblicos*, XIII, 1954, pp. 247-265.

The parchment folios of Hebrew texts with Palestinian punctuation are usually written very carefully. But they are old and were kept in the Geniza, and it is often not so easy to recognize all the details intended by the writers. Dr. A. Murtonen has now prepared an edition of some liturgical fragments together with the ancient Psalm-scroll from Cambridge. He has decided to publish only such texts of which he has carefully studied the originals in Oxford, Cambridge and Leningrad, because from photographs of such Geniza-texts the full intentions of the copyists cannot be recognized with sufficient certainty. Solely on the basis of these texts prepared by him with every care he has worked out a Hebrew Grammar in which he tries to show how Hebrew was read and recited in Palestine at a time before the Tiberian method of punctuation was invented, that is to say up to about 800 C.E. Murtonen's book is to appear in the series of publications of the Finnish Academy. The work of Murtonen on the texts with Palestinian punctuation will be very instructive and will have to be the basis for editing the available texts with Palestinian vocalisation.

It has now been established that a pronunciation of Hebrew closely resembling the one in these Palestinian texts has been used until the present day by the Samaritans. We know that a pronunciation of Hebrew has been preserved by them which is clearly different from the Hebrew used by the Jews as fixed by the Masoretes of Tiberias. However differently the pronunciation of Hebrew has developed in the different lands it is in all cases, except the Samaritan, based ultimately on the text fixed by the Masoretes as preserved in our Hebrew Bible. The pronunciation of the Samaritans is the only one which is independent of the Masoretic text, and that this pronunciation of the Samaritans goes back at least in part to a very old tradition has been evidenced by manuscripts from the Dead Sea as far as they show strong plene-writing. I have proved in my contribution to the Festschrift for Alfred Bertholet[8] that the orthography לכמה etc. found in the first Isaiah scroll has been preserved up to the present day by the Samaritans, although they do not write the ending ה in their texts. They have therefore retained a pronunciation which is clearly found in pre-Christian MSS, but was rejected by the Jews at the time of the re-organisation of Judaism after the destruction of the Temple almost 1900 years

---

[8] Tübingen 1950, pp. 281-286 (=Opera Minora, Leiden 1956, 180-185).

ago, for we find no trace of it in the transliterated texts which Origen has taken over in the *Hexapla*.

The Samaritans are firmly convinced that the way in which the Torah is read daily in their services has been handed down from father to son since time immemorial. That their pronunciation of Hebrew has not undergone an essential change in the last 600 years can be proved by a number of Samaritan MSS. of the Torah provided with vowel signs. I found four of such MSS. and entered their vowel signs in my copy of Gall's edition of *Der Hebräische Pentateuch der Samaritaner*, Giessen 1918. These entries of mine and some other material and notes by Arthur Schaade, of which I shall speak directly, were the basis for the book by Fritz Diening, *Das Hebräische bei den Samaritanern. Ein Beitrag zur vormasoretischen Grammatik des Hebräischen.* [9]

The attempt to write down the Samaritan pronunciation of Hebrew as it is spoken to-day has been made by Heinrich Petermann. During his stay in Nāblus he had asked the High-priest 'Amram to read slowly before him the Hebrew text of Genesis, and he inserted the Hebrew vowel signs into the copy of the Samaritan Pentateuch of Blayney, which he had before him. From this vocalised copy of the text printed in Hebrew letters he made, when he had returned to Germany, a transcription of the Hebrew text in Latin letters. This transcribed text he published and made the basis of his *Versuch einer hebräischen Formenlehre nach der Aussprache der heutigen Samaritaner.* [10]

This transcribed text has a certain value through the vowels which Petermann had added from the dictation by the High-priest. But it is misleading in rendering the consonants, where Petermann followed in the main the rules of the Tiberian Masoretes. Entirely useless are the texts transcribed by Petermann as he completely omitted to indicate the stress of the words which in Samaritan reading differs completely from that indicated in the text of the Tiberian Masoretes.

While I was in Nāblus myself (three days in 1906 and 2 weeks in 1908) I had to discuss other problems with the Samaritans.

In 1917 I received a letter from Hellmut Ritter from Nāblus; he knew me from his student days in Halle and knew of my interest in the Samaritans. He had visited the Samaritan High-priest, Isaak b.

---

[9] *Bonner Orientalistische Studien*, Heft 24, Stuttgart 1938.
[10] *Abhandlungen für die Kunde des Morgenlandes*, V, 1. Leipzig 1868.

'Amram, the son of Petermann's informant, whom I knew very well, and had given him my greetings. He sent me a letter from him together with 23 verses from the first chapter of Genesis, which he had copied from the dictation of the High-priest, without realizing the value of these transcriptions.

This specimen of transcription was indeed important. It reproduced, apart from the vowels as pronounced by the Samaritans (which Petermann had already recorded) also the consonants as pronounced by the Samaritans. Moreover the stress of the words was carefully recorded. The whole transcription had been done by somebody with understanding for that type of work. I asked Ritter to continue with the transcription if at all possible. He himself had no time to do it as he had to leave Nāblus shortly afterwards. But he asked Arthur Schaade, who was also serving in Nāblus at the time to take over. This was done and with great care. Schaade transcribed a large number of chapters from the Torah at the dictation of the priest 'Amram, Isaak's son.

In 1911 Schaade had become *Privatdozent* in Breslau, and in 1913-14 he was Director of the then Khedivial Library in Cairo. After the war (1919) he came to Hamburg as professor of Arabic, and there he began to copy his transcriptions of the Samaritan Pentateuch made in Nāblus. On the 27th October, 1922, he sent me at Giessen a fair copy of some specimens together with a letter describing which chapters he had recorded. I copied Schaade's fair copy, and his transcriptions were used and gratefully acknowledged by me and my pupils. My requests for further material did not meet with success. He had turned to his Arabic studies.

In the 'thirties, Schaade was again active in Cairo for a few years, this time as a professor at the Egyptian State University; there, and again in Hamburg, he was busy with other problems. On 22nd October, 1952, he died in Hamburg without having continued with his work on his transcriptions.

In connection with Hebrew Bible MSS. with strong plene-writing from the caves by the Dead Sea and in view of the special studies of Dr. Murtonen on Hebrew texts with Palestinian punctuation, I realized again the importance of Schaade's transcriptions made in 1917. I asked Mrs. Schaade about the fate of this material and was told that, together with the other remains of his scholarly work, it had gone to the State and University Library in Hamburg. The director of the Hamburger Bibliothek, Professor Dr. Tiemann, with the consent of Mrs. Schaade, kindly put them at my disposal with the permission to utilize and publish them.

Schaade had only copied a little more than he had sent to me in 1922. Based on his original transcriptions, I copied the texts as Schaade had taken them down in Nablus in 1917. The papers had suffered a little in the course of the years but in the main it was possible to read them correctly. After having received permission from Hamburg, I sent my copies with the originals to Finland to Dr. Murtonen who had recently spent nearly a year in Palestine and had discussed with the Samaritans in detail their pronunciation of Hebrew. As an expert he prepared the texts recorded by Ritter and Schaade for publication, and I hope to publish the texts in the Appendix to my *Cairo Geniza.*

There is no doubt that Schaade's transcriptions have a lasting value. They were made by a philologist who was an exact phonetician and who had a good scientific grasp of Hebrew. That he was not a specialist for problems of the Hebrew spoken by the Samaritans when he made the transcriptions does not matter. It enhances the objectivity of his work. The same applies of course to the first 23 verses of Genesis taken down by Professor Ritter. He used a slightly different method of transcription. The publication of this material will make possible a scientific exploration.

A great amount of vocalised Hebrew independent of the work of the Tiberian Masoretes is further to be found in the Hebrew text in Greek transliteration taken over as 2nd column of the *Hexapla* by Origen. The palimpsest discovered and examined by Giovanni Cardinal Mercati in the Ambrosiana in Milan in the 'nineties of the last century, which contains about 150 Psalm verses in the second to the sixth column—the first specimen of a continuous text of the *Hexapla* found so far—is now being published by the Rev. Professor G. Castellino, commissioned by the Bibliotheca Vaticana. The first volume containing the Milan fragments is printed and will come out shortly. Two further volumes will contain the extensive material which Mercati assembled in the course of years during his studies in a large number of MSS while working on the *Hexapla.* It will offer a very considerable enlargement of the material, published about 80 years ago by Field, and Mercati's commentary to the texts which he had deciphered will also be given.

Cardinal Mercati has devoted a special investigation to the second column of the *Hexapla*, containing the Hebrew text in Greek

509

transcription.[11] He tries to prove that this text transcribed into Greek comes from Origen himself or was made following his initiative. He thinks that Origen while copying the first column, containing the Hebrew text in Hebrew letters, of which no trace has been found so far, put the Greek transcription immediately next to it. Mercati admits that Origen may have had Jewish helpers for this task. Yet it would not be at all easy to produce the whole Hebrew Bible in Greek transcription with vocalisation. Even if one is prepared to grant to Origen far more knowledge of Hebrew than he himself admits, and takes into account that he learned much during the work, the task must have been an enormous one for a non-Jew.

There can hardly be a doubt that this work was done by Jews, familiar from childhood with reading the Bible and knowing it almost by heart. The Jews created this text for those of their fellow-believers who were not able to read the non-vocalised Hebrew text. Ludwig Blau[12] had already laid down the thesis that transcriptions of the Bible must have existed before Origen's time and that they were used by Jews who had some knowledge of Hebrew but were not able to read an unpointed Hebrew text and were even less able to understand it correctly.

Joseph Halévy[13] had indicated a few passages in the Palestinian Talmud and in *Canticum Rabba* from which he sought to prove that the Jews used the Hebrew text in Greek transcription also during the service in the synagogues, particularly in the synagogue of Caesarea where Origen lived. I think it is quite possible that this was the case. But it is certain that the passages indicated by Halévy do not contain what Halévy read into them. Cardinal Mercati was quite decided about that, and there can be no doubt that Cardinal Mercati is right. He is here completely in agreement with Blau who declared already in his book of 1894: " Other proofs for writing the Hebrew original with foreign characters cannot be given." We cannot expect to find in Jewish texts a clear statement on such matters. Since Christianity had become the religion of the state, the Jews'

---

[11] *Il Problema della Colonna II dell' Esaplo.* Estratto da Biblica 28, Città del Vaticano 1947, 1-30, 173-215.
[12] LUDWIG BLAU, *Zur Einleitung in die Heilige Schrift*, Budapest 1894, pp. 80-83.
[13] "L'origine de la transcription du texte hébreu en caractères grecs dans les Hexaples d'Origène," *Journal Asiatique*, IX, 17, 1901, pp. 335-41.

dislike of everything written in Greek had increased to such a degree that we may take it for granted that passages which may once have referred to such transcribed texts of the Bible were altered or omitted later.

There is no question that the transcribed text of the Bible as presented in this instance is very consistent and the text of the transcription agrees in its essentials with our Hebrew consonantal text. But recently a discovery has shed a new light on the origin and purpose of the transcribed texts. In a Greek papyrus of the fourth century, owned in part by Sir Alfred Chester Beatty and partly by the University of Michigan, a homily about Passover and Passion has been preserved which was composed by Bishop Melito who in the second century C.E. was active in Sardis. Fragments in Syriac of this homily have been known for a long time and were published by William Cureton and by Cardinal Pitra.

The homily begins with the words:

η μεν γραφη της εβραικης εξοδου ανεγνωσται και τα ρηματα του μυστηριου διασεσαφηται πως το προβατον θυεται και πως ο λαος σωζεται

> The script of the Hebrew Exodus has been read and the words of the Mystery explained, how the lamb was sacrificed and the people saved . . . .

Campbell Bonner, the editor of the Greek text, has investigated the question how the first words of the homily are to be understood.[14] Obviously one must distinguish here between the reading of Scripture, the paraphrase and the following sermon (homily). Sir Frederic Kenyon, the editor of the Chester Beatty Papyri, pointed out that the wording of the text really presupposes that the reading of the Bible was done in Hebrew.[15] Next followed the Greek translation and only then the sermon. Günther Zuntz, in a special investigation of the matter,[16] tried to show the probability that Melito's words really presuppose that it was usual to read the lessons from the Old Testament in Hebrew amongst Christian

---

[14] *Harvard Theol. Review*, XXXI, 1938, pp. 175 ff.—*The Homily on the Passion*, by *Melito, Bishop of Sardis* . . . ed. by CAMPBELL BONNER, *Studies and Documents*, XII, London 1940.

[15] *The Chester Beatty Papyri* . . . Fasc. VIII: *Enoch and Melito* by FREDERIC KENYON. Plates, London 1941.

[16] "On the Opening Sentence of Melito's Paschal Homily." *Harvard Theological Review*, XXXVI, 1943, pp. 299-315.

communities of the second century C.E. He suggests that the Christians adopted this custom from the Jews. For the reading of the Hebrew original the transcription of the Hebrew Bible in Greek letters would surely have offered every possibility in Christian circles and also extensively so for the Jews. This theory also gives a plausible reason for the existence of a Greek transcribed text; it gave the Jews and the Christians the possibility of reading the lessons from the Old Testament during the service in Hebrew, and we can understand why this transcribed text was composed so carefully and consistently and why Origen thought fit to include this transcribed text in his *Hexapla*. The texts must have been valued highly during Origen's life-time. Melito's *Homily* was composed in about C.E. 168, Origen was born in about C.E. 185. The Greek transcribed text is therefore considerably older than Origen, as Ludwig Blau correctly supposed.

Like all the texts assembled in the *Hexapla*, Origen adopted this text also from the Jews. It is very interesting to note that this transcribed text, which was obviously composed by the most official circles of Jewry and must have played an important rôle amongst the Jews at one time, should only have been preserved for us because Origen included it in his *Hexapla*. Yet this is not surprising. Many older Jewish texts in Greek have been handed down to us only because the Christians continued using them. We need only think of Philo, Josephus, the Apocrypha and Pseudepigrapha which were preserved only because the Christians went on reading and copying them. The edition of the fundamental work on these fragments by Cardinal Mercati, commissioned by the Bibliotheca Vaticana, will reveal the true value of these important texts.

I think I have shown that the work of the Tiberian Masoretes was not restricted, as Moshe b. Asher claimed, to fixing the pronunciation of Hebrew as it had been handed down from Ezra through the men of the Great Synagogue. The Masoretes corrected in many ways the pronunciation of the text in use at the time when they began their work. Nobody will pretend that the pronunciation of Hebrew at that time was ideal. It was inevitable that the language should have undergone many changes after it had been limited to the use of scholars and for Divine service. The corrections of the Masoretes must be acknowledged as such by anyone who wishes to compose a scientific Hebrew grammar. Such a grammar cannot be confined to the re-discovery of rules according to which the Tiberian Masoretes fixed the language.

I am expecting shortly a visit by Professor R. Meyer from Jena who is preparing a new Hebrew Grammar to replace the Grammar of Bauer-Leander. One may be certain that this Grammar will make use of all the Hebrew material now available.[17]

Oxford.   PAUL KAHLE.

---

[17] I have discussed the problems of this lecture with Dr. S. M. Stern in Oxford and wish to thank him for several suggestions he has made.

D. *The Masoretes and the Masorah*

LE LANGAGE DE LA MASSORE [1]

B

Lexique massorétique

ל — א

REMARQUES PRÉLIMINAIRES

I. — Si nous nous décidons à publier ce *Lexique Massorétique* dans
sa forme présente, c'est uniquement en vertu du principe que le
mieux est souvent l'ennemi du bien. Nous avons entrepris ce travail
dans le but de hâter l'éclosion des études massorétiques en fournis-
sant aux commençants les moyens de les aborder. Vouloir être com-
plet, et, à plus forte raison, vouloir faire œuvre de critique aurait été
nous exposer à manquer le but que nous nous proposions d'atteindre,
en arrivant trop tard d'abord, et peut-être aussi en paraissant avoir
épuisé le sujet. Tel qu'il est, ce lexique suffira aux besoins du moment.
D'ailleurs, nous avons pleinement conscience de son insuffisance à
d'autres égards. Si Dieu le veut, nous exploiterons nous-même, sur
une plus grande échelle, cette partie du champ de la Massore, mais,
encore une fois, nous espérons que ceux à qui nous montrons le che-
min, nous devanceront bientôt. Pour le moment nous nous déclare-
rons satisfait, si nous avons réussi à éveiller chez les autres une certaine curiosité des choses massorétiques, et à leur épargner, dans
leurs débuts, les longues heures de découragement que nous avons
connues.

II. — Ce lexique avait d'abord été rédigé presque exclusivement sur
le *Tiberias* de Buxtorf, la *Massora Magna* de Frensdorff, et la *Massorah compiled* etc., de Ginsburg. Celui-ci nous donnait les manuscrits,
ceux-là la Massore imprimée de Ben-Chayim. Mais, au dernier moment,
il nous a répugné de publier un travail, qui était de seconde main en
ce qui concerne la Massore Imprimée que nous avons principalement
en vue. Nous avons donc entrepris de le refondre entièrement, la Bible

---

(1) Voyez le n° d'octobre 1903 : PETITE INTRODUCTION A L'ÉTUDE DE LA MASSORE : II. La
langue et le langage de la Massore : I, la langue; II, le langage. — A. *Terminologie
grammaticale de la Massore.*

Reprinted from *Revue Biblique* (N.S.) 1 (1904); 2 (1905).

Rabbinique en main. Les citations marquées Mf., Mm., Mmarg. et Mp., quoique concordant, pour le plus souvent, avec celles de nos illustres prédécesseurs, sont donc le fruit de nos propres recherches, à moins d'indication du contraire, et nous pouvons en garantir l'exactitude. Quant à nos explications des termes massorétiques, qu'elles s'accordent ou non avec celles de Frensdorff et de Buxtorf, nous en acceptons la responsabilité. Il va sans dire que nous ne prétendons pas avoir enlevé toute valeur à l'œuvre de nos devanciers; nous avons, au contraire, cherché à la compléter et à la rendre plus utile. On les consultera toujours avec fruit.

III. — Explication des sigles et abréviations dont nous nous sommes servi pour désigner les ouvrages, ou les sources, auxquels nous renvoyons le lecteur.

Buxt. *Tib.* et Buxt. *Clav. Mas.* = J. Buxtorf, *Tiberias sive commentarius Masorethicus, quo primum explicatur quid Masora sit* etc., *secundo Clavis Masorae traditur* etc., etc. Publié d'abord in-folio à la fin du IV⁵ volume de l'édition du même auteur de la Bible Rabbinique, Bâle, 1619, puis séparément, in-4°, ibid., 1620. — Nous citons la première partie de cet ouvrage = Buxt. *Tib.* d'après les chapitres, la seconde = Buxt. *Cl. Mas.* d'après les mots (s. v.) qui sont disposés alphabétiquement, quoique classés en chapitres.

Buxt., *Lex.* = Johannis Buxtorfii P. *Lexicon Chaldaicum, Talmudicum et Rabbinicum* etc. (Édit. Fischer, Leipzig, 1875, 4°).

Dalm. *Gram.* = G. Dalman, *Grammatik des Jüdisch-Palästinischen Aramäisch* etc., Leipzig, 1894.

Dalm., *Wörtb.* = G. Dalman, *Aramäisch-Neuhebräisches Wörterbuch zu Targum, Talmud u. Midrasch,* Frankfurt a. M., 1901.

Fr. — Nous nous servons de cette abréviation, 1° pour le *Massoretisches Wörterbuch,* première et seule partie parue de la *Massora Magna de* S. Frensdorff, Hannover u. Leipzig, 1876. Dans ce cas Fr. est suivi d'un premier chiffre indiquant la page, d'une lettre a, b, pour la colonne, et d'un second chiffre qui représente la rubrique (et non la ligne); 2° pour les *Eigenthümliche Ausdrücke u. Abkürzungen deren sich die Massora bedient,* publié en deux chapitres à la fin du même ouvrage de Frensdorff. Comme ces deux chapitres sont arrangés alphabétiquement, nous nous sommes contenté de renvoyer au mot, ou au compendium massorétique, en ajoutant s. v. Dans notre lexique massorétique le sigle Fr. s. v. devra s'entendre du chap. ı; dans notre liste des abréviations, du chap. ıı.

Ginsb., *Introduction.* = Christian D. Ginsburg, *Introduction to the Massoretico-critical edition of the Hebrew Bible,* London, 1897.

Ginsb., *Mass.* = Chr. D. Ginsburg, *The Massorah compiled from Manuscripts* etc., London, 1880-1885, 3 vol. grand in-fol. Nous ajoutons toujours le volume, I, II, III, la page, quelquefois aussi la colonne, a, b, ou le nᵒ de la rubrique, suivant le cas.

Mf., Mm., Mmarg., Mp. — Nous citons ainsi les différentes parties de la Massore Imprimée de Jacob Ben-Chayim, publiée pour la première fois dans la deuxième Bible Rabbinique de Bomberg, Venise, 1525, et plusieurs fois réimprimée dans les éditions suivantes. — Mf. = *Massora finalis*, arrangée alphabétiquement et imprimée à la fin du IVᵉ volume, sous le titre de מַעֲרֶכֶת qui est répété en tête de chaque lettre. Les lettres sont divisées elles-mêmes en sous-titres אב, אג, etc. pour trouver la rubrique que nous indiquons par un chiffre placé après le sous-titre, le lecteur devra compter lui-même les rubriques. Le commencement de chaque rubrique est d'ailleurs imprimé en caractères plus gros que le reste. Quelquefois pourtant le sous-titre a été omis, אד par exemple. Dans ce cas le lecteur devra compter à partir de la première rubrique commençant par אד et non à partir du dernier sous-titre qui est אב. — Mm. = *Massora Magna,* dans les marges supérieure et inférieure du corps de la Bible, immédiatement au-dessus et au-dessous des deux colonnes dont l'une représente le Texte et l'autre le Targum. Rarement la Mm. a été rejetée à la marge latérale extérieure, et dans ce cas elle est invariablement annoncée par le mot מָסֹרָה, en forme de titre. — Mmarg. = *Massora Marginalis,* dans la marge latérale intérieure, à côté du Texte. — Mp. = *Massora parva,* dans la marge du milieu, entre le Texte et le Targum. Aux sigles Mm., Mmarg., Mp., nous ajoutons toujours l'indication du chapitre et du verset. Dans les Bibles Rabbiniques de Venise (qui ne sont que des réimpressions, page par page, de celle de 1525) les chapitres ne sont pas séparés, mais ils sont indiqués en lettres hébraïques dans la marge intérieure. Quelquefois pourtant cette indication a été omise et, plus souvent, elle a été placée trop haut ou trop bas. Les versets, sont marqués, en lettres hébraïques aussi, de cinq en cinq, le long du Texte. Les notes de la Mmarg. et de la Mp. sont assez régulièrement inscrites à la hauteur du passage auquel elles se rapportent. Quant à celles de la Mm., on les trouvera dans l'ordre des versets, en commençant par le haut, à la marge inférieure comme à la marge supérieure. Il en est autrement dans quelques-uns des meilleurs manuscrits (cf. *Rev. Bibl.* 1902, p. 563).

O. W. O. = *Das Buch Ochlah W'Ochlah (Massora),* édité, traduit et annoté par S. Frensdorff, Hannover, 1864, in-4ᵒ. Les chiffres, que nous avons ajoutés, se rapportent aux nᵒˢ et non aux pages.

Wickes, *Pr. acc.* = W. Wickes, *A treatise on the accentuation of the twenty-one so-called Prose Books of the Old Testament* etc., Oxford, 1887.

Wickes, *Poet. acc.* = W. Wickes, *A treatise on the accentuation of the three so-called Poetical Books of the Old Testament* etc., Oxford, 1881.

a., aram. = araméen.

déterm. = déterminé, c.-à-d. à l'état emphatique.

h., hébr. = hébreu.

q. v. = quod videas.

s. v., sb v. = sub voce.

וג׳ = וְגוֹמֵר = etc. (dans les citations de l'hébreu).

א

אַדְכְּרָא (a.), fémin. de la forme nominale 'aqṭāl (infin. 'Aph'el). Voyez Dalman, *Gram.*, p. 137. *Souvenir, mémoire, acte de prononcer le nom de quelqu'un, mention* et, par extension, 1° *Acte de prononcer le nom de Dieu*, 2° en style de Massore, le *Tétragrammaton.* Cf. Ex. iii, 15. Exemple : Deutér. xxxi, 3, la Mp. remarque qu'il y a trois versets qui commencent et finissent par la אַזְכָּרָה (forme hébr.), c.-à-d. par יהוה. C'est par erreur que dans la Mf. חג 1 on a imprimé וְאַדְכְרָא (1) לי״ו, ce qui, d'après ce que nous venons de dire, serait une tautologie. Il faut corriger avec Frensdorff s. v. לה׳ וְלֹאדכרא, avec le ה et le Tétragrammaton.

אוֹפָן וַעֲגָלָה (h.), *Roue et chariot.* Désignation de l'accent Pāzer gādhōl précédé de Galgal; ainsi dans la Mp. II Reg. x, 15. La Mm. dit en général *Pāzer gādhōl et Galgal.*

אוֹרַיְתָא (a.), forme féminine de l'infinitif 'Aph'el du verbe יְרָא = hébr. יָרָה. Équivalent araméen de l'hébr. תּוֹרָה q. v. *La Loi,* c.-à-d. *le Pentateuque.* Se dit par opposition à קְרִיָא q. v. Il est à remarquer que ce mot précédé de כָּל, *tout,* ne veut pas dire, comme תּוֹרָה dans le même cas, *toute l'Écriture,* mais simplement *tout le Pentateuque.*

אוֹת (h.), plur. אוֹתִיּוֹת, *lettre de l'alphabet.* Voyez l'équivalent aram. אָתָא.

אַזְכָּרָה (h.). Comme אַדְכְּרָא q. v.

אָחֳרִי (a.), *une autre.* Exemple : מִלָּה אָחֳרִי, *un autre mot,* O. W. O. 93; Fr. 346 a 3; Mf. כת 16. Cf. Dalm., *Gram.*, § 20, 5, a.

---

(1) ו׳׳י est l'abréviation de יהוה.

אִית (a.) = hébr. יֵשׁ, *est, il y a*. Exemple : פְּסוּקִים דְּאִית בְּהוֹן, *versets où il y a*. Fr. 373 a 6-8. Sans דְּ ibid. a 9; b 1,3.

אֲחַשְׁוֵרוֹשׁ, *Assuérus*. Désignation du livre d'Esther, par exemple Mf. שׁמ 95 (rubr. וְנִשְׁמַע). Se rencontre aussi sans le second Waw.

אַטְרוֹפֵי (a.). Ce mot qui se rencontre Mp. Gen. VIII, 11 ne peut être que le laschon אֲקְטוֹלֵי (cf. *Rev. Bibl.* 1903, p. 546) du verbe טְרַף, probablement sous l'influence du mot טַרְפָּא, *feuille*, de même que de טָרַף l'hébr. טָרַף a pris, à l'Hiph'il, le sens de *pousser des feuilles vertes*. Cf. Dalm., *Lex.* sb v.

אִיכָּא, אִכָּא, אִכָּא (a.) pour אִית כָּא, *il y a là*. אִכָּא דְאָמַר, *quelqu'un dit* (ad litter. *est hic qui [est] dicens*. Voyez aussi sous הֵיכָא).

אִילֵן, אִלֵן (a.), pron. démonstr. pluriel. *Ceux-ci, celles-ci, ceux-là, celles-là* (se rapportant à ce qui suit, aussi bien qu'à ce qui précède).

אִילָנָא (a.), *arbre*. Voyez טַרְפֵי.

אֵין (h.), *pas;* avec les suffixes pronominaux, *n'être pas*. Exemple, Fr. 384 b 4 : *Il y a 3 hés dans la Loi qui semblent interrogatifs* (נִרְאִין) *et ne sont pas* (וְאֵינָן) *interrogatifs*.

אִנּוּן, אִינוּן (a.), pron. person. com. plur. *ils, elles*. Exemple : O. W. O. 187; Fr. 339 a 1,308 a 3 ; Mf. אד 44 (rubr. מ׳ מִלִּין).

אֱנָשׁ, אֵינָשׁ (a.), *homme, personne*. Voyez שׁוֹם.

אַנְתְּתָא, אִינְתְּתָא (a.), *femme*. Voy. שׁוֹם.

אַכִּין וְרַקִּין (h.), *des mais* (אַךְ) *et des seulement* (רַק). Autre désignation des Nûns retournés appelés généralement נוּנִין הֲפוּכוֹת, ou נוּנִין מְנוּזָרוֹת. Voy. הֲפוּכָה et מְנוּזֶרֶת. Cf. Ginsburg, *Introduction*, p. 344, aussi O. W. O., *Nachweise u. Bemerkungen*, p. 39, Nr. 179. L'emploi de ces deux particules de restriction pour désigner les Nûns retournés repose vraisemblablement sur une opinion massorétique, d'après laquelle ces signes auraient été imaginés pour indiquer que certains versets doivent être transposés. Ce serait comme des parenthèses.

אַלְפָּבֵיתָא, אַלְפָא בֵיתָא (a.), plur. אַלְפָּבֵיתִין, *Alphabet*. Se dit : 1° d'une liste de mots arrangés alphabétiquement. Si une ou plusieurs lettres de l'alphabet ne sont pas représentées, on ajoute le mot דְּלוֹג q. v. On trouvera de nombreux exemples dans Fr. 327-331 ; O. W. O., 1-20; Mf. א, etc. 2° Spécialement du psaume CXIX.

Voyez אַפֵּי תְּמַנְיָא. Dans ce cas, on ajoute רַבְתִי q. v. = le *grand Alphabet*. On sait que les versets de ce psaume sont disposés alphabétiquement d'après la première lettre de chacun d'eux.

אֶמְצַע (h.), *milieu*. Par exemple dans cette expression בְּאֶמְצַע תֵּיבוּתָא, *au milieu du mot*. Fr. 361 a 7, 362 a 4; ce qui doit s'entendre de l'*intérieur* du mot (ou du verset) relativement au *commencement* ou à la *fin*. Cette expression est toujours essentiellement relative. Ainsi dans un mot de six lettres dont la troisième et la cinquième sont Taw, la troisième est dite être *au milieu* par opposition à la cinquième, Mp. Gen. xxvii, 12.

אֶמְצָעוּתָא (a.) pour אֶמְצִיעוּתָא. Même sens.

עֶמְצָעִית (a.), fém. de אֶמְצָעִי, *qui est au milieu*. Mp. Gen. xxvii, 12.

אָן (a.), *où?* אָן דְּ, *où.*

אַנְדְּרוֹגִינוֹס ('Ἀνδρόγυνος), *hermaphrodite*. Se dit d'un mot marqué à la fois du signe du masculin et de celui du féminin. Mp. Gen. xxx, 38, à propos du mot וַיֵּחַמְנָה.

אַסְחוֹפֵי (a.), infin. 'Aph'el, de la forme אַקְטוֹלֵי. Dalm., *Gram.*, p. 227. Même sens que סַחוֹפֵי q. v.

אַפֵּי (a.?). Ponctuation incertaine. Voyez תְּמַנְיָא.

אָקִים (a.). Voyez עֲקִים.

אֲרוּכָה (h.), *longue*. Voy. אָרִיךְ.

אָרִיחַ (h.), *demi-brique*. Dans la formule אָרִיחַ עַל גַּב אָרִיחַ וּלְבֵנָה עַל גַּב לְבֵנָה, *demi-brique sur demi-brique et brique sur brique*, Fr. 385 a 3. Manière d'écrire certaines portions poétiques de la Bible, de sorte que les blancs soient superposés aux blancs, les parties écrites aux parties écrites. Cette expression s'emploie par opposition à cette autre : אָרִיחַ עַל גַּב לְבֵינָה, *demi-brique sur brique* qui indique une disposition telle qu'un blanc soit superposé à une partie écrite. Ce langage est emprunté au style de la construction. Voyez pour plus de détail Fr. 385, note 1.

אָרִיךְ (a.), *long, grand*. 1° Appellatif de Waw par opposition à Yōdh qui est nommé זְעִיר, *court, petit;* par exemple dans cette rubrique Fr. 376 b 4 : *28 versets dans lesquels il n'y a ni long, ni court.* — 2° Se dit du Nûn et du Ṣādhè à la fin des mots. Ex. Mf. ב 2 : *Alphabet du Nûn* allongé (נוּן אֲרוּכָה) à la fin de mots qui ne se rencontrent qu'une fois. Cf. Fr. 386 a 8 (נוּנִין זְעִירִין) et 9 (נוּנִין אֲרִיכִין). — 3° Se dit aussi d'un verset plus long par rapport à un

autre, qui lui ressemble par le commencement, pour l'en distinguer. Ainsi dans Mm. Deuter. v, 30, le verset Jer. xxxv, 15, est
appelé *long*, par opposition à xliv, 4, ce qui épargne une trop
longue citation.

אֲרָמִית (h.) précédé de לִשׁוֹן, *la langue araméenne*. Désignation du
chaldéen de la Bible, Ginsb., *Mass.*, I, p. 272. Voyez *Rev. Bibliq.*
1903, p. 536.

אַשְׁלָמְתָּא (a.), *achèvement, ce qui vient immédiatement après*. Désignation des Prophètes; d'où נְבִיאִים רִאשׁוֹנִים = אַשְׁלָמְתָּא קַדְמֵיתָא
les Prophètes Antérieurs et נב' אַחֲרוֹנִים = אַשׁל' תִּנְיָנָא, *les Prophètes Postérieurs*. D'après Frensdorff, sb v., l'origine de cette désignation serait que, dans les synagogues, on lisait une leçon des
Prophètes immédiatement après la leçon du Pentateuque. Le sens
de *suivre immédiatement* que Fr. attribue à la forme causative de
שְׁלַם est confirmé par le passage du Talmud de Babylone, *Sabbath*, 23 b. Pour la forme nominale אַקְטַלְתָּא, voyez Dalm., *Gramm.*,
§ 34, c. 2.

אָתָא (a.), pl. אָתִין = hébr. אוֹת q. v. On trouve aussi assez fréquemment le plur. אתיין, par ex. Fr. 380 a 7 et b 6. On s'attendrait à
trouver אָתְוָן. Voyez Dalm., *Gramm.*, p. 155. Mais peut-être ce mot
est-il le pluriel d'une forme אתיא? Comp. hébr. אוֹתִיּוֹת à côté de
אוֹתוֹת. Cf. *Rev. Bibl.* 1903, p. 540.

אָתְתָא (a.). Forme assimilée pour אַנְתְּתָא q. v. Voyez שׁוֹם.

ב

בְּאֵר (h.), *puits*. Voyez שׁוֹם.

בַּהֲדֵי (a.) suivi de דְ, *pendant, tandis que*. Exemple, Ginsb. *Mass.*, II,
p. 94 (à propos d'une forme spéciale du Lāmedh).

בְּהֵמָה (h.), *bétail, animaux*. Voy. בְּעִירָה.

בְּהַעֲלֹתְךָ. Section de la Bible, Num. viii, 1-xii, 16.

בְּזוֹיִי (a.), pour בְּזוֹי (Dalm., *Gramm.*, § 12, C), contracté de בְּזוֹזִי
(ibid., § 41, 2, C). Se rencontre seulement dans l'expression
בְּזוֹיִי דְמִשְׁלֵי, *le mot* בַּז *dans le livre des Proverbes* (xi, 12; xiii, 13:
xiv, 21). On trouvera dans Ginsb., *Mass.*, II, p. 313, la rubrique générale concernant les mots בַּז, בָּר, כְּבָר, וַיְקַר et קָל. Voyez ce que
nous avons dit de ces mots, *Revue Bibl.* 1903, p. 548.

בְּלָק. Section Num. xxii, 2-xxv, 10.

בִּנְיָנָא (a.), *construction, bâtisse*. Désignation massorétique des chapitres d'Ézéchiel consacrés à la description du temple de Jérusalem, Ezech. xl et suiv. Se prend aussi dans le même sens que מִשְׁכְּנָא q. v.

בִּנְקֵבוּת (h.), *au féminin*. La Mf. אב 12 remarque que le mot אֲבִיהֶם se rencontre trois fois *au féminin*, c.-à-d. se rapportant à un sujet féminin, malgré le suffixe masculin, par exemple Num. xxvii, 7.

בְּסִפְרָא (a.), *dans le livre* (en question), c.-à-d. *dans ce même livre*. Voyez סִפְרָא.

בְּעִירָא (a.), *animal*. La Mm. Prov. i, 12, remarque que lorsque le mot תְּמִימִים est dit דִּבְעִירָא, *d'animaux*, il est écrit défectivement à la dernière syllabe. Cf. Mf. תם 12. דַּבְהֵמָה est employé dans le même sens. Cf. Fr. 207, note 6.

בְּעִקְבָא (a.), *à la fin*. Précédé de דּ, *le dernier*, Fr. 209, note 6. Alterne avec בָּתְרָא q. v. Cf. Mf. תם, 12.

בַּר נָשׁ (a.), *personne*. Voyez שׁוֹם.

בְּרוֹוִי (a.). Ainsi écrit dans la Mmarg. Thren. iii, 15 ; il faut probablement lire בָּרוֹוִי (cf. Dalm., *Gramm.*, p. 290) si, comme nous le croyons, ce mot est l'infinitif Pa'el du verbe בְּרָא = hébr. בָּרָה (cf. Dalm., *Lex.*, בְּרָא II), employé comme laschon. A l'endroit cité la Mmarg. note, à propos du mot הִשְׁבִּיעַנִי : בְּלִישׁ וא' בְרוזי ל', שְׁבוּעָה, *ne se retrouve plus* (dans le laschon) *nourrir, et* (*se rencontre*) *une fois dans le laschon* serment. On se rappelle que la Massore ne distingue pas entre שׂ et שׁ, elle ne connaît que שׁ.

בְּרוֹוִי (a.), *ses froments*, dans l'expression כָּל בָּרוֹוִי דְּיוֹסֵף, *tous les* בַּר *de Joseph* (Gen. xli, 35, 49 ; xlii, 3, 25 ; xlv, 23). Voyez בְּזוֹוִי.

בַּר מִן (a.), *excepté, sauf*. Toujours suivi d'une lettre-chiffre, les deux étant généralement compris sous une même abréviation. Ex. במ"א, sauf un.

בְּרֵאשִׁית, 1° la Genèse ; 2° la première section de la Genèse, i, 1-vi, 9.

בְּשַׁתָּא (a.). Voyez שַׁתָּא.

בִּתֵימַה (a.). Voyez תֵּימַה.

בִּתְמָהָא (a.). Voyez תֵּימַה.

בִּתְמוּה (h.). Voyez תְּמוּה.

בִּתְמִיה (a.). Voyez תְּמִיה.

בְּתַר (a.), *après*. Précédé de רְ, *qui suit*. Avec le suffixe sing. masc. de la 3ᵉ pers. וּבְתָרֵיהּ, *qui le suit*.

בָּתְרָא (a.) (pour בָּתְרָאָה?), plur. בָּתְרָאֵי. 1° *le dernier (de plusieurs)*, *le second (de deux)*. בָּתְרָאָה dans ce second sens alterne avec תִּנְיָנָא q. v. Exemples : La Mf. ר' 50 remarque qu'il y a huit versets dans lesquels il y a trois mots, le premier (קַדְמָא) et le dernier (בָּתְרָא) desquels sont précédés de Waw tandis que le second (תִּנְיָנָא) ne l'est pas. Trois rubriques plus bas (53) la même Mf. note qu'il y a six versets dans chacun desquels on trouve quatre mots dont les deux derniers (בָּתְרָאֵי) ont Waw, tandis que les deux premiers (קַדְמָאֵי) ne l'ont pas. — 2° Dans la Mf. Gen. vi, 18, on trouve aussi בָּתְרָא dans le sens de מִלְּרַע q. v.

ג

גַּב (a.), plur. גַּבֵּי, *à côté de, auprès de, dans*. Ce terme s'emploie quand on veut désigner avec précision un certain passage de la Bible qui, pour une raison ou pour l'autre, ne serait pas suffisamment désigné par l'indication du chapitre ou de la section. On ajoute alors à celle-ci גַּב ou גַּבֵּי, *dans, auprès de*, avec les premiers mots du verset où se trouve le passage en question, ou ceux du verset suivant ou précédent. Ainsi Mm. Ex. xiii, 11, le passage d'Is. xxx où se trouvent les mots שִׁבְעַת הַיָּמִים est indiqué en ajoutant à la désignation du chapitre les mots גַּבֵּי פָּסוּק וְהָיָה אוֹר־הַלְּבָנָה *dans le verset* etc. De même Mm. Ex. xx, 10 pour le passage Ezech. xviii, 6 (où l'on ajoute encore (1) דְּסִי קַדְמָא, *le premier du chapitre*, pour le distinguer du v. 15 qui commence de même, sauf עַל au lieu de אֶל).

גָּבַר, גַּבְרָא (a.), plur. גַּבְרֵי, *homme* (vir). Voyez שׁוֹם.

גּוּבְרָא (a.) = גַּבְרָא (Dalm., *Gramm.*, § 14, 2). Voy. שׁוֹם.

גְּזֵרָא (a.). Sic! Frensd. sb v. Voyez le suivant.

גְּזֵרָה (h.). Nous n'avons trouvé ce mot que dans la Mf. קו 9 qui est le seul renvoi donné par Frensdorff à propos du mot précédent. Voici la rubrique : שְׁמִיעָה לְקוֹל יֹז פֵּי הַגְּזֵרָה קְשׁוּרָה עִם למ"ד,

(1) Abréviation de סִימָן q. v. ou de סִפְרָא = סָפְרָא סִיפְרָא q. v.

entendre la voix se trouve 16 fois, c.-à-d. la gizrā (étant) reliée (au mot suivant) par Lāmedh. L'abréviation פי׳ = פֵּירוּשׁ *(explication)* que nous rendons par *c.-à-d.* montre que ce qui suit est une explication ajoutée (par un grammairien postérieur!) à la rubrique massorétique. De fait גְּזֵרָה, *coupure, retranchement* (des préformatives et des afformatives) est le terme dont les grammairiens juifs se servent pour indiquer ce que les Massorètes appellent le laschon. Cf. Buxtorf, *Lexic. Chald. Talm. etc.* sb v. Traduisez : *le laschon (en question)*, c.-à-d. le verbe שָׁמַע.

גּוּסָא, גִּיסָא *(a.)*, *côté.* מֵהָאי גִּיסָא אוֹ מֵהַאי גִּיסָא, *d'un côté ou de l'autre* (littér. *de ce côté, ou de ce côté*). Voyez sous הֶכְרֵעַ.

גְּעָיָא *(a.)*, littéralement *mugissement. Le Ga'yā,* c.-à-d. 1° *le Methegh* dans le sens d'accent tonique secondaire. Par exemple, à propos de הֶהָרָרִים la Mp. Num. v, 24, note la présence de deux Ga'yā dans ce mot. 2° *Le Methegh nécessaire.* Par exemple la Mp. I Chron. xxix, 18, remarque que שָׁמְרָה est חָטֵף q. v. ici et dans les Psaumes, sauf dans un passage Ps. cxix, 167 où il y a Ga'yā (שִׁמְרָה).

גְּרֵשׁ *(h.)* = גְּעָיָא. Voyez חָטֵף.

ד

דְּ *(a.)*. 1° *Qui.* 2° Introduit le génitif. Comme tel דְּ s'emploie fréquemment avec les noms de livres ou de sections de la Bible dans le sens de *dans.* Par exemple, דְּבְרֵאשִׁית, *dans la Genèse* (ou *dans la section בְּרֵאשִׁית); דְּבָלָק, *dans la section בָּלָק, etc. On emploie même דְּ avec un mot de la Bible pour désigner les passages qui contiennent ce mot, par ex. דְיִצֻּם les passages où se trouve יְצֻם.

דָּא *(a.)*, *celui-ci.* דָּא בָּתַר דָּא, *l'un après l'autre;* דְּדָמְיָין דָּא לְדָא (Ginsb., *Mass.,* II, p. 297), *qui ressemblent l'un à l'autre.*

דְּבְקוּ *(a.)*. Voyez le mot suivant.

דְּבֵק *(h.)*, fém. דְּבוּקָה, plur. m. דְּבוּקִין, דְּבוּקֵי, f. דְּבוּקוֹת, *adhérant.* Se dit : 1° de certaines lettres dans le sens que nous avons expliqué dans notre deuxième article, *Revue Bibl.* 1903, pp. 541, 542. Exemple, Ginsb., *Mass.,* II, p. 521 : ב׳ קוֹפִין דְּבוּקִים וְלָא זַיְנִין, *il y a deux Qôphs qui adhèrent et ne sont pas armés de picots* (voyez זַיִן). Quant à la forme דְּבְקוּ, *ont adhéré,* que nous avons mentionnée (ibid., p. 542), elle nous paraît fort suspecte. Le parfait n'est certes pas une forme que l'on s'attendrait à trouver en pareil cas. Peut-être est-ce une erreur pour דְּבֵקִי = דְּבוּקִי(1). En tout cas voici la rubrique in-extenso ה שֹׁס בְּאוֹרָיִיתָא דְּלָא דבקוּ וְאִית לְהוֹן אַרְבָּעָה קַרְנֵי, il y a dans la Loi 360 ה qui n'adhèrent pas et sont munis de quatre cornes (Ginsb., Mass., I, p. 236). — 2° Le mot דְּבוּק s'emploie aussi pour indiquer l'état construit. Ainsi la Mmarg. Ex. xv, 2 remarque qu'il y a treize mots qui ont Qāmeṣ quoique דְּבוּקִין, c.-à-d. à l'état construit (cf. Buxtorf, Lexic. sb v.).

דִּבְרֵי הַיָּמִים, les deux livres des Chroniques.

דָּגֵשׁ (a.), pl. דְּגֵשִׁין. Après ce que nous avons dit (2) sur la signification et l'usage de ce terme dans la Massore, nous pouvons nous contenter de donner ici les quelques exemples suivants. La Mm. Ex. xiv, 6 remarque qu'il y a trois וַיֹּאסֵר qui sont דְּגֵשִׁין = וַיֶּאְסֹר (et non רְפִין = וַיֶּאְסֹר). Pareillement שִׁלְּחוּ (Jud. i, 8) est appelé dāghesch, la première syllabe étant fermée par un Schewa quiescent implicite, tandis que שִׁלְחָה est rāphê (Ginsb., Mass., p. 627 a). De même encore מַעֲשֵׂר (Lev. xxvii, 30 etc.) est dāghesch, tandis que מַעְשַׂר Deut. xiv, 23 etc.) est rāphê (Mf. עשׂ 5 et 6 a fine). — En somme דָּגֵשׁ est l'opposé de רָפֶה q. v. dans ses différentes acceptions, et analogue à מַפִּיק q. v. dont il est parfois synonyme.

דּוּקָא (a.), littéralement, à la lettre. Les Massorètes emploient ce terme quand ils veulent faire porter une remarque sur un mot tel qu'il est écrit dans le passage en question et non sur les différentes autres formes que son radical pourrait revêtir en d'autres circonstances grammaticales. C'est donc le contraire du laschon. Exemple : à propos de וַיֹּאמֶר בְּלִבּוֹ (I Reg. xii, 26) la Mp. remarque : אֲמִירָה בְּלִבּוֹ דּוּקָא בְּלִבּוֹי, parler dans son cœur, littéralement dans son cœur, dix fois. Ce qui veut dire que dans dix passages on trouve n'importe quelle forme du verbe parler en combinaison avec l'expression dans son cœur (mais non à son cœur ou à mon cœur).

דָּחִיק (h.), fém. דְּחִיקָה (3), serré entre... Se dit 1° dans les traités

(1) Cette supposition nous paraît confirmée par la leçon דְּבַק que nous trouvons (Mmarg. Num. vii, 2) dans une rubrique correspondant à celle que nous avons citée d'après Ginsburg.

(2) Rev. Bibl. 1903, p. 544.

(3) Et non דְּחִיקָא comme l'a Fr. sb v.

grammatico-massorétiques du Dāghesch forte conjunctivum, quand
il se trouve immédiatement entre deux accents. Voyez les gram-
maires hébraïques; 2° d'une lettre d'un mot qui adhère à un autre
mot. Ainsi la Mm. Esdr. ɪv, 12, remarque : וְשֻׁוּרִיָא *se présente
trois fois*, Esdr. ɪv, *12, 13, 16. Dans le premier cas l'Aleph est*
דְּחִיקָה *serré contre (le mot suivant)* etc. Dans ce passage nous lisons
en effet וְשֻׁוּרִי אֹשְׁכְלֹלוֹ.

דִּין (h.), *règle*. Dans l'expression כֵּן דִּינוֹ, *telle est sa règle*, dont la Massore se sert pour confirmer une ponctuation contraire aux règles
générales. Par ex. dans la Mp. Num. xx, 17 au mot וּשְׂמֹאוּל.

דִּין (a.) *celui-ci*.

דְּכִוָתֵיהּ, דְּכִוָתְהוֹן, דְּכִוָתֵיהּ. Voyez כְּוָת.

דְּכַר (a.), *homme, masculin* (O. W. O., *Zum verständniss*, § 10, sb v.).

דִּילּוּג, דְּלוּג (h.), *saut, omission* et, au concret, *sauté, omis, contenant
une ou plusieurs omissions, défectif*. Se dit 1° d'un mot qui se
trouve de manquer dans une expression qui le contient habi-
tuellement, par exemple le mot לֵאמֹר après l'expression וַיְדַבֵּר
דְלָא, חֵסֵר = דְּלוּג *le mot le sens ce Dans* .1 ,xxxɪɪɪ Ex ,יְהוָֹה אֶל־מֹשֶׁה
נְסִיב (Fr. 20, note 1). Voyez חָסֵר. — 2° d'une liste alphabétique
de mots dans laquelle une ou plusieurs lettres ne sont pas représentées. Voyez אַלְפָא בֵיתָא.

דָּמַיִן, דָּמַיִין (a.). Le premier pourrait aussi se ponctuer דָּמִין (1). Cf.
Dalm., *Gramm.*, p. 153. *Qui se ressemblent, semblables*. Se dit des
mots (מִלִּין), des couples (זוּגִין), des versets (פְּסוּקִין) etc., qui ont
en commun une particularité que la Massore veut relever. Par exem-
ple, Fr. 374 a 7, ג׳ פְּסוּקִין דָּמַיִן אִית בְּהוֹן ו׳ מִלִּין דָּמַיִין לָא נָסְבִין ו׳
*il y a trois versets qui se ressemblent (en ce qu') ils ont (chacun) six
mots semblables qui ne prennent pas le Waw (au commencement).*
De même Fr. 374 b 1 (Mf. ד 23) 2,3 (= Mf. ד 49). L'opposé de דָּמַיִן
est מִתְחַלְפִין q. v.

דְּעַל (a.), littéralement *qui est sur..., au-dessus de..., auprès de*. En

_____

(1) Peut-être pourrait-on aussi considérer דמין comme partiç. pass., et le ponctuer
דְּמִין ou דָּמִין, Mais nous ne pouvons comprendre la ponctuation de Buxt., *Clav. Mas.*,
s. v. דְּמִין, vu que dans tous les exemples qu'il cite, comme d'ailleurs dans celui que nous
avons donné, ce mot accompagne un nom masculin, et est coordonné avec d'autres participes incontestablement masculins.

style de Massore, *qui précède ou suit.* Avec le suffixe דְּעֲלֹוִי, *que précède ou suit.* Exemples, Mm. Num. xviii, 8 : וַיְדַבֵּר יְהֹוָה אֶל־אַהֲרֹן *deux fois avec l'accent Zarqâ, à savoir* וַיְדַבֵּר וג׳ *qui précède* (דְּעַל) יַיִן וְשֵׁכָר (Lev. x, 9) *et* (וידבר וג״) *que suivent* (דְּעַלֹם) *ces mots* וַאֲנִי הִנֵּה וג״ (Num. xviii, 8). De même Mm. Num. xxxi, 13 : *Dans tout le Pentateuque* עֲרֹבת *est écrit défectivement, sauf un passage que suivent* (דְּעֲלֹוִי) *ces mots* וַיִּרָא בָלָק וג״. — Quant à דְּעַלֹם *que* nous avons rencontré dans le premier exemple et qui se retrouve encore plusieurs fois dans la Mm. Ex. vii, 8, il est bien certain que la dernière lettre représente le suffixe 3ᵉ pers. masc. plur., mais il est difficile de dire comment il faut le ponctuer. D'après l'analogie de דְּעֲלֹוִי (a.) il faudrait דַּעֲלֵיהֹון ou tout au plus דַּעֲלֵיהֹם (voyez les formes spéciales des suffixes dans le Targum de Jérusalem, Dalm., *Gramm.*, p. 79) qui, par contraction, pourrait avoir donné דְּעַלֹם.

דְּעֲלֹוִי (a.). Voyez דְּעַל.

דְּעַלֹם (a.? ponctuation incertaine). Voyez דְּעַל.

דַּרְגָּא (a.), littér. *marche d'escalier.* 1° nom de l'accent Dargā. 2° Dans la Mm. Ps. lxxi, 9 on lit דְּרִגִּין, c.-à-d. *munis de l'accent Dargâ;* mais, comme Frensdorff le remarque (sb v.), cela doit être une faute de copiste pour זֹוגִין. La même erreur se retrouve non seulement dans l'édition de la Massore de Buxtorf, mais encore dans la compilation de Ginsburg, *Mass.*, III, p. 3 a.

ה

הָאי (a.), *celui-ci.* Voyez un exemple sous גִּיסָא et sous הֶכְרֵעַ.

הֲדֵי (a.). Voyez בַּהֲדֵי.

הָדֵין (a.), *ce.* Exemple, O. W. O. 179 : *Il y a 9 versets qui ont* כְּהָדֵין סִימָן ס הָפֹוכָה, *(quelque chose) comme ce signe (c.-à-d.) un Nûn retourné.*

הֵיכָא (a.), *où.* Exemple : כָּל הֵיכָא דְאִכָּא, *partout où il y a.* Voyez אִכָּא.

הֶכְרֵעַ (h.), *certitude, décision.* S'emploie précédé de אֵין (h.) ou de לֵית (a.) pour indiquer qu'il est incertain si un mot se rapporte au précédent, ou au suivant, indépendamment de l'accentuation mas-

'sorétique qui tranche toujours la question. Exemple, Mm. Deuter.
xxxi, 16 : *Il y a cinq versets* שֶׁאֵין לָהֶם הֶכְרֵעַ אוֹ מֵהָאי גִיסָא
אוֹ מֵהָאי גִיסָא, c.-à-d. *dont on ne sait avec certitude s'ils se
rapportent à ce qui précède, ou à ce qui suit.* Un des mots visés par
cette rubrique est מְשֻׁקָּדִים (Ex. xxv, 34); voyez Wickes, *Pr. acc.*,
p. 131. Les LXX, dans ce cas-ci, ont décidé pour ce qui précède; le
Targum et la ponctuation massorétique, pour ce qui suit. Voyez
גִיסָא et הָאי.

הָלֵין (a.), *ceux-là, celles-là.* Se rapporte à ce qui suit, aussi bien qu'à
ce qui précède.

הַלֵּל (h.). Le *Hallel,* c.-à-d. les Psaumes cxiii-cxviii. Exemple, Mm.
Is. xii, 2.

הַלֵּילָא (a.). Id., quelquefois aussi le Psautier tout entier.

הִלֵּלִי (h.). *Codex) Hilleli.* Nom d'un fameux manuscrit de la Bible,
depuis longtemps perdu. Voy. Ginsb., *Introduction,* passim (consultez l'*Index*).

הָפוּךְ (h.), fém. הַפוּכָה. 1° *Marqué de l'accent Mehuppakh.* Voyez
Wickes, *Pr. acc.,* p. 24. — 2° *Retourné,* se dit du *Nûn inversum.*
Voyez la rubrique sous הָדֵין, et Ginsburg, *Introduction,* p. 342.

ו

וָי"ו, pl. וָו"ין (Mm. Esth. iv, 8), la lettre *Waw.* Exemple, Mm. Num.
x, 9 : וָי"ו לְוָי"ו וְיוֹ"ד לְיוֹ"ד, *Waw au Waw et Yōdh au Yōdh.* Phrase
mnémotechnique pour rappeler que נְתֻנִם (avec *scriptio plena* du
Waw) est accompagné de לוֹ (= לְוָי"ו) dans Num. iii, 9, tandis que
נְתוּנִים (avec *scriptio plena* du Yōdh) est accompagné de לִי (= לְיוֹ"ד)
dans Num. viii, 16.

וַדַּאי (a.), fémin. de וַדַּי. וַדָּיָה, וַדְּיָיא, וַדְּיָא, וַדְּיָא 1° *Littéralement
correct.* Se dit du mot אֲדֹנָי comme appellatif spécial de Dieu et
ainsi écrit dans la Bible, pour le distinguer de אֲדֹנָי substitut de
יהוה dans la lecture. Exemple, Mf. אד 22 : אֲדֹנָי וד' קל"ד ז' מִנְהוֹן
לַאדֹנָי, אֲדֹנָי *certain et ainsi écrit 134 fois, dont 7 avec la particule*
ל. — Cf. Mm. Is. xxxviii, 16 (où נדֹיא doit être corrigé וְדֹיא). Voyez
sur cette rubrique Fr. 333, note 1, et surtout 5, note 4. — 2° Du
suffixe ךְ = כָה. Exemple, Mf. כ 4 : כ' מִלִּין דַּמְשַׁמְּשִׁין כָה וַוְדְּיָא

בְּסוֹף תֵּיבוּ‖תָא, *il y a 20 mots qui font usage de* כָה *ainsi écrit à la fin du mot.* Cf. O. W. O. 92 (וַדְּיָה) et Fr. 365 b 5 (וַדְּיָא). Nous n'avons trouvé dans les notes auxquelles nous renvoie Fr. sb v. ni ודאי ni ודאין, les seules formes qu'il donne.

וַיְדַבֵּר. Le livre des Nombres.

וַיּוֹשַׁע. Le Cantique de la mer Rouge, Ex. xiv, 30-xv, 20.

וַיַּקְהֵל. Section Ex. xxxv, 1-xxxviii, 20.

ז

זוֹג, זוֹגָא (a. ?), plur. זוֹגִין, *paire, couple,* et par extension *trio, quatuor.* Se dit de mots ou d'expressions se représentant deux, trois ou quatre fois seulement soit absolument de même, soit avec une différence de détail. Il n'est pas nécessaire que les mots qui constituent le זוֹג aient le même sens. Pour des exemples, voyez notre premier article, *Rev. Bibl.* 1902, p. 560, et Fr. 339 et suiv. — On trouve assez souvent, à la fin d'une liste de paires, cette expression assez surprenante וְלֵית לְהוֹן זוֹגָא, *et ils ne forment pas paire,* que nous nous proposons d'examiner et d'expliquer plus loin, lorsque nous ferons l'inventaire du contenu de la Massore.

זוֹטָא (a.), *petit.* Se dit spécialement des lettres qui, d'après la Massore, étaient écrites plus petites que les autres. Cf. *Rev. Bibl.* 1903, p. 541.

זיודני (ponct. incert.). Voyez זַיִן.

זייבני (ponct. incert.). Voyez זַיִן,

זַיִן, plur. זַיְנִין. 1° La lettre de ce nom. 2° *Zayin,* un ornement analogue au תָּאג, *couronne,* dont certaines lettres sont ornées. 3° Au plur., *lettres ornées de Zayins,* comme קָמְצִין de קָמֵץ, פְּתָחִין de פֶּתַח etc. Exemple, Ginsb., *Mass.,* II, p. 521; voyez sous דִּבּוּק. Nous avons donné dans notre deuxième article, *Rev. Bibl.* 1903, p. 542, les deux mots זיודני et זייבני dans le sens de *ornés de Zayins,* sur la foi de Dérenbourg, *Journal asiatique,* Sér. VI, vol. IX, p. 242 et suiv., nous réservant de les discuter ici. Mais nous n'avons pas encore tous les éléments nécessaires pour cette discussion, et nous devons la renvoyer à une autre occasion. Le lecteur impatient pourra consulter en attendant la *Mass.* de Ginsburg, premières rubriques de chaque lettre. Quant au mot מְזֻיָּן, *orné de zayins,* nous l'avons trouvé au plur. מְזֻיָּנֵי dans Ginsb., *Mass.,* II, p. 253, 9, et I, p. 456 passim.

זְכַר (h.) = aram. זְכַר q. v.

זְעֵירָא (a.), *petit.* 1° Comme זוֹטָא q. v. — 2° Nom descriptif du Yôdh.
Voyez אֲרִיךְ 1°.

זְקִיף (a.), *droit, élevé, suspendu.* Exemple, Mm. Ex. vi, 9 : זְקִיף לְרוּמָא
substitut pour סָלֵיק לְרוּמָא (cf. Ginsb., *Mass.*, I, p. 626, ט 126 et
ט 127 b). Voyez סָלֵיק.

זָרִיז (h.), *pressé, rapide.* Se dit 1° d'un mot qui en précède un autre
immédiatement et lui est uni par le Maqqeph, tandis que dans un
autre passage de même nature, il en est séparé, ou ne lui est pas
uni par le Maqqeph. Ainsi Mm. Gen. xxiv, 14, l'expression
וְגַם־גְּמַלֶּיךָ est appelée זָרִיז pour la distinguer de גַּם לִגְמַלֶּיךָ (v. 19).
De même Mm. Ps. cv, 28, les deux passages שלח־מלך (v. 20) et
שלח חשך (v. 28) (Cf. Ginsb., *Mass.*, II, p. 626, n° 492), sont appelés,
l'un זָרִיז et l'autre מְתִין (lege מָתוּן?), c.-à.-d. *lent.* Cette différence
peut être aussi rendue par les termes חָטֵף et גֵּעְיָא q. v. — 2° D'une
expression plus brève qu'une autre à qui elle ressemble et qui est
appelée עָצֵל, *paresseux, qui s'attarde.* Exemple, Mmarg. Gen. xlii,
11, nous lisons : *les fils des justes se hâtent* (זְרִיזִין) *et ceux de la terre
de Canaan s'attardent* (עֲצֵלִין). Ce qui veut dire que la réponse des
enfants de Jacob est plus courte dans le verset 11 qui contient le mot
כֵּנִים, *justes,* que dans le verset 13 où on lit les mots אֶרֶץ כְּנַעַן, *la
terre de Canaan.*

זְרִיקָה (h.), *effusion, diffusion, aspersion.* Désignation de l'accent
Zarqā. Voy. Wickes, *Pros. acc.*, p. 19.

ח

חָבֵר · חָבֵיר (h.), *compagnon, pendant;* avec le suffixe וַחֲבֵירוֹ, *et son
compagnon.* Se dit d'un passage par rapport à un autre à qui il est
semblable, pour éviter de citer à nouveau les mêmes mots. Exemple, Mm. Gen. i, 11, le passage וְאֵת כָּל־עֹרֵב לְמִינוֹ (Deuter. xiv, 14)
par rapport au passage parallèle (Levit. xi, 15). Voyez *Rev. Bibl.*
1902, p. 561 (*Ligne c*).

חָג (h.). Le passage de la fête des Tabernacles, Num. xxix, 12 et suiv.

חַד (a.), fém. חֲדָא, *un, une.* Précédé du mot לִישָׁן, *le laschon de un,*
c.-à-d. *le singulier.* Exemple, Mf. בא 9 : *Il y a huit mots qui
sont lus au singulier* (לִישָׁן חַד) *mais qui paraissent (devoir être lus*

au) pluriel (לִישָׁן סַגִּין). — Remarquez les expressions suivantes :
1° חַד חַד, *un à un, chacun une fois seulement.* On dit dans le même
sens יְחִדָּאִין q. v. 2° חַד וְחַד, *un et un, une fois et une fois* (c.-à-d.
*deux fois seulement, une fois d'une manière et une fois d'une
autre*). On trouve dans le même sens מְיַחִדִּין q. v. sous יַחִדָּאִין.
3° חַד .... חַד *l'un, la première fois ... l'autre, la seconde fois.*
4° כָּל חַד וְחַד, *chacun.* C'est sans doute de cette expression que Buxtorf a voulu se servir Mf. ר 1 de son édition; au lieu de כל חד"ל
lisez כל חד וחד ל (cf. Fr. sous חדל).

חוֹל (h.), *profane, commun.* בְּלִישׁוֹן חוֹל, *dans le laschon de profane.*
Se dit d'un mot quand au lieu de s'appliquer à Dieu, il désigne
autre chose. Exemple, Mf. Deut. iv, 42, à propos de הָאֵל = הָאֵלֶּה :
ח בְּלִישׁוֹן חוֹל, *huit fois dans un sens profane.* Voyez לִישׁוֹן.

חוֹמֶשׁ (h.), *le nombre cinq.* — 1° Le Pentateuque par opposition à
מִקְרָא qui désigne, dans ce cas, le restant des livres de la Bible.
Exemple, Mf. II Reg. xxv, 5, à propos de la manière d'écrire le
nom de la ville de Jéricho : חוֹמֶשׁ רֵ מִקְרָא רִי; Ginsb., *Mass.*, I,
p. 740 b, a קָרְיָא au lieu de מִקְרָא. Voyez ces mots. 2° On trouve aussi
וְכָל חוּמְשָׁא pour désigner les cinq Meghilloth (Fr. sb v.).

חוּמְשָׁא (a.). Voyez חוֹמֶשׁ 2°. Cf. חֲמֵשׁ.

חָזָק (h.), *fort.* Se dit, en style sémanique, d'une voyelle primitive
par rapport à un Schewā, ou à une voyelle faible, c.-à-d. issue
d'un Schewā; par exemple le Pathach sous ל quand cette particule
contient l'article. Par contre, quand le ל ne contient pas l'article
la voyelle dont il est marqué, que ce soit une voyelle proprement
dite, ou Schewā, est dite חַלָּשׁ, *faible.* En style massorétique ordinaire, on dirait דָּגֵשׁ et רָפֵי; voyez ces mots. Exemple, Mmarg.
Lev. xxv, 30, à propos de מוֹכֵר חַלָּשׁ קוֹנֶה חָזָק : לִצְמִיתֻת, *le
vendeur* (c.-à-d. Lev. xxv, 23 où לִצְמִתֻת est précédé du verbe
vendre) *est faible, l'acheteur* (ibid. v, 30 où לִצְמִיתֻת précède le
verbe *acheter, posséder*) *est fort.*

חָטֵף (a.), *entraînant.* 1° Ce mot se dit du Schewā mobile par rapport
à une voyelle proprement dite. Par exemple la Mm. Jer. iii, 18, remarque que 7 וְיָבֹאוּ sont חֲטֵפִין pour les distinguer des autres
qui sont וַיָּבֹאוּ ou דְּיָבֹואוּ. 2° חָטֵף s'emploie aussi pour distinguer

une voyelle plus brève d'une plus longue, par exemple le Qāmeṣ chāṭuph du Qāmeṣ; voyez l'exemple sous גְּעָיָא. 2° Dans ce sens on trouve aussi גְּרֵשׁ au lieu de גְעָיָא par opposition à חָטֵף, probablement parce que l'accent Géresch avait, comme Methegh, la forme d'une barre. Ainsi dans Ginsb., *Massor.*, II, p. 645 b. Voyez Wickes, *Pr. acc.*, p. 20. — 3° Enfin le terme חָטֵף se dit, comme זָרִיז q. v., d'un mot uni au suivant par le Maqqeph, par exemple dans Ginsb., *Mass.*, II, p. 626 (n° 492), nous rencontrons cette note : שלח־מלך (Ps. cv, 20), שלח חשך (ibid., 28). *Le premier est* חָטֵף *parce qu'aucune de ses lettres ne saurait se dérober à la lecture, le second est* גְּעֶה וְלֹא נֶחְטָף, c.-à-d. *Ga'ya et non pas Chāṭeph, afin que le double* חֵית *ressorte dans la prononciation, car s'il était chāṭeph les deux* חֵית *ne seraient pas prononcés (distinctement).* Cela veut-il dire que dans le passage en question (v. 28) שְׁלֹח doit avoir un Ga'yā? Ginsburg marque ce Gay'ā dans sa Massore, mais non dans son édition du Texte Massorétique. Voyez d'ailleurs la note qu'il y donne à ce passage.

חִלּוּף, חִילוּף (h.), pl. חִלּוּפִים, *le contraire, l'opposé,* adverbialement *vice-versa.* Exemple, Mf. ב 3 : *Il y a 4 mots écrits, mais non lus, avec* ב *au commencement du mot, et vice-versa* (חִלּוּף) *1 mot lu, mais non écrit avec* ב *etc. De même, ibid.* א 4 et 5 : *Il y a 17 mots qui prononcent l'Aleph, et vice-versa* (חִלּוּפֵיהוֹן, littéralement *leurs contraires) 16 mots qui ne prononcent pas l'Aleph.*

חָלוּק (h.), plur. חֲלוּקִים, *divisé, en désaccord.* Exemple, Mm. Num. xxxiii, 49 : *Il y a trois* הַיְשִׁמֹת *qui sont en désaccord* (c.-à-d. *écrits de différentes manières)* : הַיְשִׁמֹת (Num. xxxiii, 49), הַיְשִׁימוֹת (Jos. xii, 3; xiii, 20) et הַיְשִׁימוֹת (Ezech. xxv, 9). Que ce mot vienne bien de חלק et ne soit pas une erreur pour חִלּוּף comme Fr. sb v. le soupçonne, nous paraît hors de doute. Le sens de חִלּוּף ne s'adapterait pas à cette rubrique.

חָמֵיִין (a.), partic. pass. plur. de חֲמָא, *voir.* — 1° *Paraissant.* Par exemple, la Mm. Hos. ii, 8 remarque que שָׁךְ est un des mots qui *paraissent* (devoir être lus avec) Schin (parce que écrits avec la lettre שׁ) mais qui sont lus (comme s'ils étaient écrits avec) Sāmekh (parce que Schin est quelquefois, comme dans ce cas, prononcé comme un Sāmekh). Cf. Mf. ס 2 et O. W. O. 191, aussi Fr. 307 b 3. — Voyez ce que nous avons dit du Schin, deuxième article, *Rev. Bibl.* 1903,

p. 541. Cette rubrique paraît remonter au temps où les points dia-
critiques du Schin n'avaient pas encore été inventés. — 2° Le mot
חְמִין se retrouve avec un sens plus spécial et impliquant quelque
chose comme un soupçon que la leçon reçue n'est pas correcte.
Par exemple, dans la note de Mf. בא 9 que nous avons déjà traduite
sous חַד q. v. De fait dans Ginsb., *Mass.*, I, p. 170 b, au lieu de חֲמַיִן
nous trouvons סְבִירִין q. v.

חָמֵשׁ (h.), *cinq*. Désignation des cinq Meghilloth. Voy. חוּמְשָׁא.

חָסֵר (h.), *manquant, défectif*. Se dit surtout et spécialement de la
scriptio defectiva, חָסֵר דְּחָסֵר, indiquant double *scriptio defectiva*.
Exemples,.passim dans notre premier article, *Rev. Bibl.* 1902, pp.
556-560. Dans ce sens l'opposé est מָלֵא et מָלֵא דְמָלֵא q. v. Mais le mot
חָסֵר est aussi fréquemment employé pour indiquer l'absence d'une
lettre quelconque dans un mot, par opposition à un autre mot qui
lui est, autrement, en tout semblable. Par exemple, Mf. ב 5, *Alphabet de mots se présentant deux fois seulement, une fois sans* (חָסֵר
et une fois avec (נְסִיב) *Beth*. Dans ce sens l'opposé est נְסִיב q. v.
et au lieu de חָסֵר on trouve souvent לָא נְסִיב. Voyez aussi כְּתִיב.

ט

טוּבָא (a.), *beaucoup, très.*

טַעַם (h.), *accent*. Fréquemment dans l'expression בְּטַעַם. *avec l'accent*
(tel qu'il est marqué dans le texte); le nom de l'accent suit quelquefois. Exemple, Fr. 346 b 7 : כֹּה־אָמַר ד´ בְּטַעַם זַרְקָא בִיחֶזְקֵאל. *quatre fois dans Ezéchiel* כֹּה־אָמַר *se rencontre avec l'accent Zarqa.*
Quelquefois aussi בְּטַעַם veut dire *quoique ayant l'accent*. Ainsi Mp.
Gen. xvi, 17 à propos de הַלְרֶב : *Il y a 7 mots qui ont Pathach* (1
quoique ayant l'accent (sur la même syllabe). La règle est que lorsque בֵן, *fils*, est à l'état absolu, il est accentué et s'écrit avec un Ṣērê.
tandis qu'à l'état construit il a Seghōl et se relie au mot suivant par
un Maqqeph.

טַעְמָא (a.) = טַעַם q. v. Quant à l'expression טַעְמָא לְאָחוֹר. *accent
en arrière*, que la Mm. Lev. v, 2, explique ainsi : *Paschṭa et avant lui
Yethibh*, voyez Wickes, *Pr. acc.*, pp. 19,99, 106 suiv. Qu'il suffise de

_____

(1) C.-à-d. Seghōl. Voyez *Rev. Bibl.* 1903, p. 542.

dire ici que dans certains cas le même signe ⌐ est Yethibh ou Mehuppakh suivant qu'il est placé derrière ou devant le point-voyelle.
Accent en arrière, conséquemment = *Yethibh*.

טַרְחָא (a.), *lent, lourd*. Autre nom pour l'accent טִפְחָא. Voy. Wickes,
Pr. acc., p. 18.

טַרְפֵי (a.), plur. de טַרְפָּא, *feuilles, feuillage*. Laschon araméen du
mot hébr. עָלֶה, *feuille* (cf. *Revue Bibl.* 1903, p. 547). Exemple,
Mm. Lev. xxvi, 36 : עלה, *7, dans le (sens de) feuillage, qui sont
écrits avec Yôdh, et 3 qui sont écrits avec* ה (cf. Fr. 140 b 6, et Ginsb.,
Mass., II, p. 409, צ 598). Nous n'avons trouvé nulle part la forme
טרפוי que donne Fr. sb v. Si ce n'est pas une erreur, comme
nous le croyons, pour טַרְפֵי, ce ne peut être que ce même mot avec
le suffixe 3ᵉ pers. masc. sing. טַרְפּוֹי *ses feuilles*. — Au lieu de
טַרְפֵי on trouve aussi, dans le même sens, אִילָנָא, *arbre*, par exemple dans Ginsb., *Mass.*, II, p. 409, צ 594.

י

י״ד. La lettre *Yôdh*. Voyez sous ו״ר.

יוֹשֵׁב (h.), *assis*. Autre nom, en langage sémanique, pour l'accent
Rebhia'. Exemples, Mmarg. Deuter. xi, 17 et Lev. viii, 19. Dans ce
dernier passage les termes יושב et ישן sont transposés.

יְחִידָאִין (a.), plur. de יְחִידַי, יְחִידָאָה; יְחִידִין (a.), plur. de יְחִיד; et
מְיַחְדִין (a.), plur. de מְיַחַד, partic. pass. Pa‘el. Ces trois expressions ont la même signification : *isolés, solitaires, uniques*. Elles se
disent, 1° de mots ou d'expressions qui ne se trouvent pas avec
leur entourage ordinaire. Ainsi, Mm. Gen. xix, 37, on remarque à
propos de עַד הַיּוֹם que ces mots se présentent 9 fois מְיַחְדִין, sans
leur accompagnement ordinaire, c.-à-d. sans être immédiatement
suivis de הַזֶּה, comme le dit expressément une autre version de la
même rubrique, Ginsb., *Mass.*, II, p. 374, צ 101 (1). C'est à peu près
dans le même sens que, Mp. Ex. ix, 16, il est dit que וּלְמַעַן apparaît
9 fois יְחִידָאִין, c.-à-d. sans être précédé de לְמַעַן dans le même
verset. 2° Par opposition à זוּגִין *paires*, on appelle מְיַחְדִין des
groupes de deux mots qui ne se présentent qu'une fois ensemble,
tandis que l'un de ces deux mots se retrouve deux fois avec tel

(1) Que יחידאין = מיחדין est démontré par une troisième version, *ibid.*, צ 100.

et tel autre terme, soit, les deux fois, de même, soit une fois
d'une manière et une fois de l'autre. C'est ainsi que les groupes
וְכָל־שִׂיחַ Gen. ii, 5, וְכָל־הַחַיָּה Gen. vii, 14, sont dits מְיַחְדִין (Mf. כל 1)
par opposition à des groupes comme וְכָל־שָׂה Gen. xxx, 32, le-
quel forme paire avec כָּל־שֶׂה ibid (Mf. כל 3). — 3° La Massore emploie encore le terme יְחִידָאִין pour désigner des mots qui ne se
lisent qu'une seule fois tels quels, c.-à-d. avec telles lettres serviles,
telle ponctuation, telle accentuation. Dans ce cas la Mp. se contente
de dire לֵית, *ne se retrouve plus*, mais la Mf. les enregistre sous le
titre de mots יְחִידָאִין, ou de mots חַד חַד, c.-à-d. ne se représentant
que chacun une fois (voy. plus haut sous חַד). Exemple, Mf. י 24 :
Sept mots יְחִידָאִין *qui ont à la fin Yôdh avec Pathach.* — Une
rubrique correspondante dans Ginsb., *Mass.*, I, p. 682, י 34, au lieu de
יחידאין porte חַד וְחַד, leçon fautive, sans doute, pour חַד חַד (1).
— 4° Enfin dans certains cas חַד וְחַד = מְיַחְדִין (voyez sous חַד)
et se dit des mots qui se rencontrent une fois seulement d'une manière, et une fois seulement d'une autre. Comparez Mf. אד 43 :
זוֹגִין מְיַחְדִין et la même note O. W. O. 186 : חַד וְחַד.

יָפֶה (h.), *bien, correct.* Expression dont la Massore se sert pour ap-
prouver une leçon du Texte. Exemple, Mp. Joel ii, 8, au mot לֹא.

יָשֵׁן (h.), *dormant.* Désignation de l'accent Athnach en langage sémanique. Exemple, Mmarg. Lev. viii, 15 (2).

יְתִיב (a.). En style ordinaire, l'accent Yethibh, en style sémanique
autre nom pour le Munach. Exemple, Mmarg. Ex. xxxvi, 9.

יַתִּיר (a.), pl. יַתִּירִין, *superflu.* Se dit des lettres. Exemple, Mmarg. II,
Sam. x, 9 à propos de בְּיִשְׂרָאֵל : *Il y a 4* ב *superflus au commencement du mot.* La Mp. se contente de dire קְרֵי (יְשׁ; la Mf. ב 3
porte : *4 (mots) sont écrits avec* ב *au commencement du mot et ne
sont pas lus (ainsi).* Cf. כְּתִיב.

כ

כְּבָרוֹיי, *ses* כְבָר, dans la phrase כְּבָרוֹיי דְּקֹהֶלֶת, *les* כְּבָר de l'Ecclésiaste (i, 10; ii, 15; iii, 15; vi, 10; ix, 6, 7). Voyez בָּזוֹיי.

---

(1) Il faut corriger et compléter cette rubrique d'après la note correspondante de la Mf.
que nous venons de citer.
(2) Dans ce passage les mots יוֹשֵׁב et יָשֵׁן ont été mis l'un pour l'autre.

כּוֹבַע (h.), *chapeau, le crochet par lequel commence le* ל (?); seulement Mmarg. Num. ı, 22. Voyez מְגִירָה.

כְּוָת (a.), *pareil*. Toujours avec le relatif דְּ et le pronom sing. ou plur.
de la 3ᵉ pers. masc. : דִּכְוָותֵיהּ, *comme lui;* דִּכְוָותֵיהוֹן, *comme eux.*
— Quand la Massore a noté une leçon comme exceptionnelle dans
un livre et qu'elle veut indiquer que dans d'autres livres cette leçon
est au contraire la règle générale, elle se sert à cet effet de l'expression דִּכְוָותֵיהּ ou דִּכְוָותֵיהוֹן suivant qu'elle a noté une ou plusieurs exceptions. De même, dans d'autres cas, quand l'exception
notée se limite à certaines circonstances grammaticales. Exemple,
la Mm. Gen. ııı, 11, après avoir noté deux cas de צִוִּיתִיךְ avec double
scriptio plena comme une orthographe exceptionnelle dans le Pentateuque, ajoute : וְכֹל נְבִיאִים וּכְתוּבִים דִּכְוָותֵיהוֹן, *mais tous les
Prophètes et les Hagiographes sont de même (que ces deux cas)
sauf un où le second Yōdh est écrit défectivement.* De même Mp.
Gen. ııı, 10 : אָנֹכִי ח׳ בְּטַעַם מִלְעֵיל וְכָל אַתְנַח וְסוֹף פָּסוּק וְזָקֵף
דִּכְוָותֵיהוֹן בַּר מִן א׳, *8 fois (seulement) avec cet accent sur la pénultième, mais (avec) Athnach, Sōph-pāsūq et Zāqeph c'est toujours
ainsi, sauf une (fois).*

כִּנּוּי, כִּנּוּי (h.), *sobriquet, appellation descriptive, nom patronymique*(?). Exemple Mf. יצ 38 et שח 10 : וְיִשְׂחָק ד׳ כִּנּוּי לְיִצְחָק, *Ishaq
4 (fois) patronymique d'Ishaq.* Dans les quatre passages (Jérém.
xxııı, 26; Amos vıı, 9, 16; Ps. cv, 9) auxquels cette note fait allusion, il ne s'agit pas du Patriarche lui-même; ce n'est donc pas son
nom, mais le sobriquet de sa race. Dans aucun de ces quatre passages les LXX n'ont Ισαακ. La note correspondante dans Ginsb.,
Mass., II, p. 746, dit tout simplement que Ishaq s'écrit 4 fois dans
la Bible avec שׂ. — Peut-être la substitution du שׂ au צ dans ces
passages a-t-elle été faite de propos délibéré sous l'influence du
patronymique יִשְׂרָאֵל qu'elle était destinée à rappeler?

כִּי תִשָּׂא. Section Ex. xxx, 11-xxxıv, 35.

כְּפוּפָה (h.), pl. כְּפוּפוֹת, *recourbée* (lettre). Voyez *Revue Bibl.* 1903,
p. 541. Cf. צְעִיפָה.

כַּרְעָא (a.), plur. constr. כַּרְעֵי, *jambages* (de lettres). Voy. sous מִדְלִי.

כתבין. Voyez כְּתִיב.

כתבן. Voyez כְּתִיב.

כְּתוּבִים (h.) *écrits,* c.-à-d. les Hagiographes.

כְּתִיב (a.), plur. כְּתִיבִין, *écrit.* — A. Presque toujours en combinaison avec קְרִי, *lu,* dans différentes expressions qu'il faut examiner de près.

1° כְּתִי בוּקְרִי, *Écrit et lu,* désignation technique de mots écrits avec certaines consonnes dans le texte, et avec d'autres consonnes dans la marge, le mot étant suivi de la mention קְרִי. Ce sont ces mots qui, dans les recueils de notes massorétiques, sont enregistrés sous le titre de כְּתִיב וּקְרִי. Voyez-en la liste très complète dans Ginsb., *Mass.,* II, pp. 55 et suiv. En règle générale le כְּתִיב du texte et le קְרִי de la marge ne diffèrent que par une ou plusieurs lettres que le קְרִי change, ajoute ou retranche. Et la Massore, indépendamment des listes générales, où un mot entier est substitué à un autre, n'en différàt-il que par une lettre, — la Massore, disons-nous, a dressé des listes partielle où les Kethîbhs et Qerês sont classifiés suivant la lettre qui est en jeu. Ces listes partielles sont annoncées par les expressions suivantes : a) en cas d'échange ... כְּתִיב...וּקְרִי, par ex. O. W. O. 113, ה כתיב וקריד, *écrit* ה *et lu* ד; b) en cas d'addition ...וּקְרִי כְּתִיב לָא, par ex. O. W. O. 108, לָא כְּתִיב ב וּקְרִי, *non écrit* ב *mais lu;* c) en cas de retranchement כְּתִיב ......וְלָא קְרִי, par ex. O. W. O. 107, כְּתִיב ב בְּרֵישׁ, תֵּיבוּתָא וְלָא קְרִי, *écrit* ב *au commencement du mot mais non lu.* Ces deux dernières opérations sont indiquées sommairement dans le corps de la Massore par les mots חָסֵר, *manquant,* et יָתִיר, *superflu* (voyez ces mots), et souvent même ces deux termes sont substitués dans le titre des listes partielles aux expressions לָא כְּתִיב (O. W. O. 117 etc.) et כְּתִיב (O. W. O. 132 etc.). — 2° Il ne faut pas confondre ce ...וּקְרִי לָא כתיב et ce כְּתִיב...וְלָא קְרִי avec les expressions suivantes כְּתִיב וְלָא קְרִי et קְרִי וְלָא כְּתִיב dont l'une est comme le premier avec renversement des deux termes et l'autre est en tout pareille au second, avec cette différence toutefois que les deux termes (comme d'ailleurs dans la première) se suivent immédiatement, comme nous l'avons indiqué, au lieu d'être séparés par un intervalle. כְּתִיב וְלָא קְרִי, *écrit et non lu,* et קְרִי וְלָא כְּתִיב, *lu et non écrit,* sont les désignations techniques de *mots* (jamais de lettres) qui, n'étant pas dans le texte, sont lus quand même, ou qui sont dans le texte mais sont omis dans la lecture. Ces mots sont en nombre assez restreint; on en trouvera la liste dans O. W. O. 97 et 98, et dans Ginsb., *Mass.,* II, p. 54, כ 486 et 487. Nous ne pouvons nous expliquer comment König (*Einleitung in das A. T.,* p. 36) cite des listes classifiées de Kethîbhs û-Qerês sous le titre de Qerês we-lā Kethîbhs, et Kethîbhs we-lā Qerês. Le fait est d'autant plus étrange que plusieurs des listes auxquelles il renvoie le lecteur, par exemple O. W. O. 111,117, portent en tête le mot חָסֵר au lieu de לֹא כְתִיב. Ce qui aurait dû lui ouvrir les yeux. Et ceci n'est pas la seule inexactitude que nous ayons rencontrée dans ce paragraphe d'un ouvrage excellent d'ailleurs.

B. Indépendamment de son association avec קְרִי, le mot כְּתִיב se montre encore dans la Massore pour attirer l'attention sur une orthographe extraordinaire; par exemple, à propos de אָהֳלֹה, Mp. Gen. ix, 21 : ד׳ כְּתִיב כֵּן, *4 fois écrit ainsi*, c.-à-d. avec ה au lieu de ו. Dans ce sens כְּתִיב équivaut à כֵּן דִּינוֹ (voyez דִּין) et à יָפֶה q. v.

C. Nous devons ajouter ici quelques remarques sur les formes plurielles des deux termes כְּתִיב et קְרִי. Leurs pluriels réguliers sont כְּתִיבִין et קְרַיִן. Pour קְרִי, la difficulté n'est pas considérable, car nous trouvons généralement קרין ou קריין. Quelquefois pourtant, on rencontre קרינן, par exemple, Mf. ת 3 et Fr. 329 b 3. Si ce mot n'est pas une erreur pour קריין, il n'y a qu'une manière de le ponctuer, c.-à-d. קָרֵינַן, *nous lisons*. La difficulté est bien autre pour כְּתִיב. Son pluriel nous apparaît sous quatre formes différentes : כתבן, כתבין, כתיבן et כתיבין. Tout d'abord, on serait porté à considérer les trois premières formes comme des erreurs de copiste pour כתיבין. Malheureusement les sources sont loin d'être en faveur de cette dernière. Dans six rubriques que nous avons examinées dans trois sources différentes, la Mf. O. W. O. et Fr., nous avons trouvé כתבן huit fois (O. W. O. 97, 98, 99, 162, 163; Mf. כת 12, 13, ת 4), כתבין cinq fois (Fr. 368 a 2, b 12, 369 a 1, 4; O. W. O. 100), כתיבן deux fois (Fr. 368 a 1, Mf. ת 3), כתיבין une fois (Fr. 368 b 11), enfin deux fois le singulier כתיב (Mf. כת 9 et 11). Le nombre est donc décidément en faveur de כתבן qui a encore de son côté l'autorité d'Elias Levita, celui-ci l'ayant choisi pour l'expression numérique destinée à rappeler le nombre des Kethîbhs û-Qerês קריין וכתבן (100 + 200 10 + 10 + 50 + 6 + 20 + 400 + 2 + 50 = 848). Or כתבן ne peut être qu'un partic. act. fémin. plur., aussi Buxtorf n'hésite pas à le ponctuer comme tel, כָּתְבָן (*Tiber.*, ch. xiii). De même כתיבן est un partic. pass. fémin. plur. qu'il faut ponctuer כְּתִיבָן. Il y a toutefois une objection sérieuse à ces deux ponctuations, c'est qu'elles sont en désaccord avec le genre du substantif que כתבן et כתיבן accompagnent toujours, מִלִּין (voy. מִלָּה). Quant à כתבין, ce serait un partic. act. masc. plur. כָּתְבִין que l'on peut traduire par *on écrit*, de même, d'ailleurs, qu'on pourrait ponctuer קָרְיִן et traduire : *on lit*. Nous laissons à plus habile que nous le soin d'éclaircir cette question.

כְּתִיבַיָּא (a.), plur. déterm. de כְּתִיב = כְּתוּבִים q. v.

ל

לָא (a.), *non*. Passim. בְּלָא, *sans*. Exemple, Fr. 315 a 15 : בְּלָא א'. *sans Aleph*.

לְאָחוֹר (h.). Voyez טַעְמָא. Il est étrange de trouver ce mélange d'hébreu et d'araméen dans la même expression. Peut-être faut-il lire טַעְמָא לַאֲחוֹרֵי ou טַעַם לְאָחוֹר.

לְבַד (h.), suivi de מִן, *en dehors, en outre*. Dans l'expression וּלְבַד מִמָּסָרְתָּא, *et en dehors de la Massore*, formule que les scribes emploient pour annoncer un supplément à une rubrique, par exemple O. W. O. 90. Voyez aussi *Rev. Bibl.*, p. 551, planche, ligne g, où, par erreur, nous avons imprimé לבר. Voyez מָסָרְתָּא.

לְבֵינָה (h.), *brique*. Voyez sous אָרִיחַ.

לֵית (a.), *il n'y a pas*. Exemple Fr. 376 b 4 : פְּסוּקִים [דְּ]לֵית בְּהוֹן ... *versets dans lesquels il n'y a pas etc*. Dans la Mp. toujours abrégé ל. Voyez *Revue Biblique* 1903, p. 548.

לִישָׁן, לִישָׁן (a.), déterm. לִישָׁנָא = hébr. לָשׁוֹן q. v.

לְמַטָּה (h.), *en bas (deorsum)*. Désignation en langage sémanique d'un accent placé sous la lettre, notamment Tebhir et Mehuppakh, par opposition à un accent placé au-dessus de la lettre comme Zāqeph au Zāqeph Qāton. Exemple, à propos de וְאַף Mmarg. Lev. xxvi, 39,40 : קַדְמָא וְאַף בַּעֲוֹנֹת בִּתְבִיר תִּנְיָין וְאַף אֲשֶׁר־הָלְכוּ וְאַף בְּזָקֵף : סִימָן] עֲוֹנֹת לְמַטָּא וְהָלְכוּ לְמַעְלָה, *le premier* וְאַף (v. 39) avec Tebhir, *le second* וְאַף (v. 40) avec Zāqeph. *Signe mnémotechnique : les iniquités* (= וְאַף v. 39) *en bas* (לְמַטָּה = Tebhir) *et ils allèrent* (= וְאַף v. 40) *en haut* (לְמַעְלָה = Zāqeph). — Au lieu de לְמַטָּא on trouve aussi נָחֵית לִתְהוֹמָא, *descen-*

dant à l'abîme (Mp. ibid.), comme aussi סָלֵיק לְרוּמָא, *montant au plus haut* (ibid.) ou זְקִיף לְרוּמָא, *suspendu au plus haut* (Ginsb., *Mass.*, I, p. 626, ט 127 [126?]).

לְמַעְלָה (h.), *en haut*. Désignation sémantique des accents Zāqeph et Zāqeph Qāṭon. Voyez לְמַטָּה.

מִלְּעֵיל (a.). Voyez מִלְּעֵיל

לָשׁוֹן (h.) et לִישָׁן, לְשָׁן (a.), déterm. לִישָׁנָא, pl. לִישָׁנֵי, déterm. לִישָׁנַיָּא. — A. *Ensemble des différentes formes que peut revêtir* 1° *un verbe, par suite de la conjugaison;* 2° *un nom* (singulier ou pluriel. Voyez חַד), *par suite de la préfixation des particules;* 3° *un mot quelconque, par suite de l'accentuation.* — 1° Pour le laschon du verbe nous l'avons suffisamment expliqué dans notre deuxième article, *Rev. Bibl.* 1903, pp. 545, 546, auquel nous renvoyons le lecteur. 2° Voici un exemple du laschon du nom ; la Mf. עד 20, à propos du mot כָּל־עֹלָמִים, remarque : *trois fois avec scriptio defectiva (du Waw) dans ce laschon.* Les deux autres cas visés sont הָלְעֹלָמִים et לְעֹלָמִים. 3° Exemple de laschon du mot accentué : à זָקַנְתִּי, Gen. xxvii, 2, la Mp. note : כָּל לִישָׁנָא פַּתַח, *tout le laschon a Pathach,* c.-à-d. irrespectivement de l'accent, celui-ci fût-il Athnach, Gen. xxvii, 2, ou Silluq, Gen. xviii, 13 (Buxt., *Clav. Massorae,* sb v.).

B. Indirectement לָשׁוֹן etc. a le sens de *signification.* La raison en est que, comme nous avons dit (*Rev. Bibl.* 1903, p. 546), il est essentiel, pour former un laschon, que tous les mots aient un sens commun. Ce ne peut être que par abus de langage, sinon par erreur, que, Mf. חי 17, וַיְחַיֶּה II Sam. xii, 3 est compté dans le même לָשׁוֹן que חַיָּה Prov. xxxi, 12 et בְּחַיֶּיהָ Lev. xviii, 18 (cf. Fr., p. 63, note 3).

(*A suivre.*)

Sorrente, jour de l'Assomption, 1904.

Henry Hyvernat.

LE LANGAGE DE LA MASSORE [1]

B

Lexique massorétique

מ — ס

מ

מְאוּחָר (h.), partic. Pu'al, *retardé*. L'opposé de מִיקְדָּם. *avancé*, en compagnie duquel on le rencontre pour indiquer la métathèse de deux lettres. Exemple, Mm. Prov. xiii, 20 où il est noté que הָרֹי"ךְ (קְרֵי הוֹלֵךְ) est un de 62 mots écrits מִיקְדָּם וּמְאוּחָר. *avancé* (*d'une lettre*) *et retardé* (*d'une autre*).

מָאיְילָא (arabe ڡَاِيلَ), *inclinée*. Nom d'un accent qui ressemble à un Ṭiphchā qui serait incliné à droite. On le rencontre tantôt comme serviteur de Silluq au lieu de Mērekhā (cf. Wickes, *Pr. acc.*, p. 67), et tantôt, au lieu de Mūnāch, comme serviteur d'Athnach (cf. ibid., p. 73). Exemple, Mm. Lev. xxi, 4 où, à propos de רְהֶהְלִי (et par occasion, à propos de mots comme בְּשֶׁבְעֹתֵיכֶם. Num. xxviii, 26),

il est remarqué : ה' מִלִּין בַּטַעַם לְסוֹף פָּסוּק · פֵּירוּשׁ' סוֹף פָּסוּק

לֹא יְשַׁרְתֵיהִי לְעֵילָם כִּי אִם מרכו (מֵרְכָא (sic! lisez) וּבָה מְקוֹמוֹת

ישרתיהי תִּשְׁרֵתֵהִי lisez מָאיְילָא בְּתֵיבָתִי וְסִימָן] וג' ..... וְהַמַּקֵּף

הִיא מְחַבְּרִי בְּתֵיבָה אֲחַת · וי"א בַּטַעַם לְאֶתְנַחְתָּא · פֵּירוּשׁ

הָאֶתְנַחְתָּא לְעֵילָם לֹא ישרתנה (וְיִשְׁרְתוּהּ lisez) כִּי אִם מוּנָח בַּר

כֵּן י"א מְקוֹמִות שִׁישׁרתנה (שֶׁתִּשְׁרֵתֶנָה lisez) מָאיְילָא עַל פִּי

הַמַּסֹּרָה וְהִיא דוֹמֶה לְטִפְחָא שֶׁנּוֹסָה לְצַד יָמִין וְסִימָן] וְימִינִי

---

[1] Voyez les nᵒˢ d'octobre 1902, octobre 1093 et octobre 1904.

Reprinted from *Revue Biblique* (N.S.), 2 (1905).

טִפְּחָה הַשָּׁמַיִם וג׳. *5 mots avec cet accent (devant Sôph-Pāsûq,*
c.-à-d. *Silluq).* Explication : le Sôph-Pāsûq *n'a jamais d'autre*
serviteur que Mērekhā, excepté dans 5 endroits où Māyelā le sert
dans le même mot que lui, à savoir Lev. xxi, 4 ; *Num.* xv, 21 ; *Os.*
xi, 6 ; *I Chron.* ii, 53 ; *Is.* viii, 17, *et* (dans ce dernier cas) le Maqqēph *le* (c.-à-d. le Sôph-Pāsûq) *réunit* (à la Māyelā) *en un seul*
mot. — Et 11 *mots) avec cet accent devant Athnach. Explica-*
tion : Athnach *n'a jamais d'autre serviteur que* Mûnāch *excepté*
(dans) *11 endroits où* Māyelā *le sert, suivant la Massore. Et elle*
(c.-à-d. *la* Māyelā) *ressemble à un* Tiphchā *incliné à droite et le*
signe mnémotechnique est « *et ma droite a incliné le ciel* », etc.
Cf. Mm. Num. xxviii, 26 ; II Chron. xx, 8.

Pour מָאיֵירָא *dans le sens de* Ga'yā = Methegh, *voyez* סַלְקִי
וְנָחְתֵּי.

מַאֲרִיךְ (h.). plur. מַאֲרִיכִין, *qui allonge.* 1° L'accent de ce nom,
ainsi nommé de ce qu'il prolonge la modulation (Wickes, *Pr. acc.,*
p. 24. 2° Se dit aussi de mots qui au lieu d'être unis au suivant,
comme d'habitude, par un Maqqeph, restent séparés et sont marqués d'un accent qui allonge leur prononciation. Exemple, Mm. et
Mp. Lev. i, 11 à propos de עַל : בְּסִפְרָא מַאֲרִיכִין בְּטַעַם ה׳, *8 ont*
un accent (et) *allongent la prononciation, dans ce Livre.* Dans cinq
de ces cas l'accent est Mûnāch, dans deux c'est Mērekhā (ii, 13 ; xiv,
31) et dans un autre (xxiii, 20) c'est le Petit Telischā. Cf. Ginsb.,
Mass., II, p. 390, n°s 355 et 356. De même Mp. Num. xxxiv, 14 à
propos de לִקְחוּ כִּי *où au lieu de* תֵּיבוּתָא, *il faut lire* פָּסוּק
comme dans la rubrique correspondante de la Mm. Cf. Ginsb.,
Mass., II, p. 30, n°s 130 A et 130 B. — 3° D'après Fr. sb v. et Wickes,
Pr. acc., p. 24, מַאֲרִיךְ *se dit aussi du* Ga'yā = Methegh. Voyez
מַאַרְכָא.

מַאַרְכָא (a.). De même que l'hébr. מַאֲרִיךְ q. v. Voici un exemple de ce
terme dans le sens de Methegh, Mmarg. Lev. xiii, 29 : אִשָּׁה אוֹ קַדְמָא
אוֹ בְּמוּנַּח תַּחַת אוֹ תִּנְיָין אוֹ אִשָּׁה בְּמֶקֶף וּמַאַרְכָא, *le premier*
אִשָּׁה. (v. 29) *avec* Mûnāch *sous* אוֹ, *le second* אוֹ־אִשָּׁה (v. 38) *avec*
Maqqeph *et* Mērekhā. Cf. Mmarg. ibid. 38.

מְבֻטָּל (h.) ou מְבַטֵּל (a. partic. pass. Pa'el), *empêché d'agir, con-*
traint au repos, 1° se dit en langage massorétique d'une voyelle
finale dont l'influence sur la première lettre du mot suivant (si
c'est une des lettres בגדכפת) est annulée par une consonne arti-

culée. Si, au contraire, cette consonne est quiescente, on dira que la voyelle est לָא מְבַטֵּל, *non empêchée d'agir*. Exemple, Mf. בט ד :

י״ח (מִלִּין) דְּגִשִׁים בָּתַר יה׳ו׳א בְּלָא מְבַטֵּל. *18 (mots) ont dāghĕsch (dans leur première lettre) après* א. ה. ו *ou* י (*la voyelle finale du mot précédent*) *n'étant pas empêchée d'agir.* Cf. Mm. et Mp. Dan. v. 11. Les mots visés par cette remarque sont גָּאֹה גָּאָה Ex. xv, 1 etc. (Voyez la liste complète dans Ginsb., *Mass.*, II, p. 296, n° 524).

2° Comme une voyelle finale qui est מְבַטֵּל est nécessairement brève par le fait qu'elle se trouve d'être dans une syllabe fermée, la Massore emploie la forme active du même mot מְבַטֵּל du *Dāghĕsch forte* qui enferme une voyelle quelconque dans une syllabe close et de longue la rend brève. Exemple, Ginsb., *Mass.*, II, p. 296,

n° 528 : כָּל דָּגֵשׁ מְבַטֵּל קָמֵץ בַּר מִפִּלֹּות חָמֵשׁ. *tout Dāghĕsch rend Qāmĕṣ bref* (c.-à-d. le change en Pathach) *sauf (dans) cinq mots.* Les mots en question sont לָכָה. בָּתִּים, אָנָּא, יָמָּה, שָׁמָּה. — Dans le traité massorétique *Dareché ha-niqqûdh weha-neghînôth* (1) (*voies des points-voyelles et des accents*), le terme מְבַטֵּל est dit non seulement du *Dāghĕsch forte*, mais encore de tout phénomène grammatical en vertu duquel une voyelle brève est substituée à une voyelle longue, par exemple Pathach à Qāmĕṣ, Seghôl à Sērĕ, etc.

מְגִילָּה (h.), *Rouleau (volumen).* Se dit, au pluriel, des cinq livres. Cantique des cantiques, Ruth, Lamentations, Ecclésiaste et Esther. Mais le mot peut être employé au singulier pour désigner tel ou tel de ces livres, le lecteur étant supposé savoir duquel il s'agit. C'est ainsi que Mp. Num. xi, 15, dit simplement מְגִילָּה pour désigner le livre d'Esther.

מְגֵירָה (h.), *scie* (?). Par exemple, dans cette note Mmarg. Num. i, 22 :

הַלָּמֶד הַשֵּׁנִית דְּגִלְגָּלְתָם דְּשִׁמְעוֹן עֲשׂוּיָה כִּמְגֵירָה וּזְקוּפָה וְאֵין לֹה כֹּובַע בְּרֵישָׁה לְפִי שֶׁהֹורָה נְשִׂיא בֵית אָב לַשִּׁמְעוֹנִי זְנוּת בְּיִשְׂרָאֵל בִּגִלּוּי הָרֹאשׁ וּבְקֹומֹה זְקוּפָה, *le second Lāmĕdh de* גִּלְגָּלְתָם *de Siméon est fait comme une scie, il est droit et sa tête n'a pas de chapeau, parce que le prince de la maison des Siméonites a enseigné l'impiété dans Israël (en marchant) la tête découverte et la taille redressée* (2).

____

(1) Imprimé dans les marges supérieure et inférieure de la Mf., fol. 1-33 recto.

(2) Ou *la fornication dans Israël, la tête découverte et la taille haute* (c'est-à-dire *effrontément, et avec ostentation.* Num. xxv, 6-14).

בְּמִדְבַּר pour בְּמִדְבַּר, *le livre des Nombres*. Dans la Mp. Jud. xx, 9, on trouve וַיְדַבֵּר que Buxt. a corrigé dans son édition d'après la désignation ordinaire.

מַדְנְחָאֵי (a.), plur. déterm. de מַדְנְחָאֵי. *Les Orientaux*, désignation d'une école massorétique, par opposition à celle des Occidentaux, מַעְרְבָאֵי, q. v. Se rencontre fréquemment dans la Mp., par ex. I Sam. ı, 4.

מִדְּלֵי (a.) = מִתְדְּלֵי. partic. plur. 'Ithpe'ēl de דְּלָא (cf. Dalm., *Gramm.*, § 72. 7), *qui s'élèvent*, par ex. Ginsb., *Mass.*, I, p. 321 : וֹ דְּמִדְּלֵי רֵישֵׁיהוֹן וַאֲקִים פַּרְעֵיהוֹן לְקָדָמֵיהוֹן, *Waw dont les têtes sont relevées et dont les jambes sont tordues* (אֲקִים pour אַקִימֵי?) *en avant* (littéralement *par devant elles*). Voyez *Rev. bibl.* 1903, p. 541, où le texte et la traduction de cette note doivent être corrigés d'après ce qui précède ici même.

מוּכְרַת (h.), partic. Hoph. de כְּרַת, littéralement *coupé, séparé*. 1° *état absolu* par opposition à l'état construit סָמוּךְ ou נִסְמָךְ; voyez un exemple sous נִקְדָּה. Cf. Buxt., *Lex. Chald. et Talm.* sb כְּרַת. — 2° *Pause*. Exemple, Mf. אַךְ 15 : אָכַלְתִּי, *deux fois avec Pathach à la pause* (1).

מוּקְדָם (h.), partic. Hoph. de קְדָם. Voyez מְאוּחָר.

מוֹרִיא דַלְכְרוֹת (a.). Cette expression ne se rencontre dans la Massore que dans un seul passage, Mm. Esth. ıx, 9, où à propos du mot וַיְזָתָא, on lit : וי״ו דְּוַיְזָתָא צָרִיךְ לְמִמְתְּחֵהּ כְּמוֹרִיא דַלְכְרוֹת. Il faut corriger les deux derniers mots d'après le Talmud de Babylone et lire כְּמוֹרְדְּיָא דְלַפְרוֹת. Traduisez : *Il faut prolonger le Waw comme une rame du fleuve Labros* (2). Il n'est pas clair si ce précepte se rapporte à la lecture en public ou à l'écriture. La seconde hypothèse est cependant la plus probable, la Massore ne s'occupant *ex professo* que de ce qui a trait à l'écriture. Le Labros (לְבְרוֹת suivant Buxtorf, *Lexic. Chald. et Talm.* sous רדה, II; לְבְרוּת sui-

---

(1) Les deux passages visés sont Gen. xxxı, 38 et Nehem. v, 14. Cette note toutefois ne s'accorde pas avec les éditions. Il faut lire avec Ginsb., *Mass.*, I, p. 53, א 461 : *Deux fois avec Soph-Pasûq* (= Mf. מוּבְרַת), *une fois avec Qameç et une fois avec Pathach*. Cf. Fr. 13, note 4.

(2) Et non : *le Waw est nécessaire comme une rame sur le fleuve Lafros*, traduction de Buxtorf, *Lexic. Chald. et Talm.* sous רדד, II). Cf. Fr. 384, note 4.

vant Jastrow, *Dictionary*, sb v.) serait le nom d'un fleuve, ou
plutôt d'un canal de Babylonie. Pour l'indication des sources à
consulter sur la critique de cette note, voyez Fr. 384, n. 4 et Joël
Müller, *Masechet Soferim*, Leipzig, 1878, chap. VIII, 7.

מוּתְאָמִים (h., partic. Hoph. de תָּאַם), voyez מַתְאִימִים·

מְזַיֵּן (h.), voyez זַיֵן·

מַחְזוֹרָא (a. masc.) et מַחְזָרְתָּא (a. fém.), de חְזַר· Proprement, *Cycle*,
puis, *livre de prières*, contenant le cycle des leçons qui se lisaient
pendant l'année. Ces recueils contenaient quelquefois toute la Bible, et servaient de *Codices Exemplares*. Tel était sans doute le
מַחְזוֹרָא רַבָּא· plusieurs fois cité dans la Massore. Pour plus de
détails, voyez Ginsb., *Introduction*, pp. 433-434.

מַחֱית (a.), voyez נָחֱית 2°.

מְחַלֵף (h.). 1° *Qui diffère*, équivalent de l'aram. מְשַׁנֵּי· voyez מְשַׁנְיָא·
2° *Qui fait exception à une règle*, voyez מִתְחַלֵף 2°.

מַטְעִין (h.), ou מַטְעַיִן (a.), partic. Hiph. ou 'Aph'el de טָעָה (h. ou
טְעָא (a.), *qui induisent en erreur*. Se dit des copistes officiels סָפְרֵי
quand il leur arrive d'avoir à écrire certains mots d'une manière
qui tout d'abord paraît incorrecte et qui pourrait donner à penser
que ces mots auraient dû être écrits différemment, qu'il s'agisse des
consonnes, des voyelles ou des accents. Exemples, Mp. Num. XXXIV,
2, à propos de הָאָרֶץ כְּנָעַן, la Massore remarque מַטְעַיִן בֵּיהּ סָפְרֵי·
les copistes (nous) *induisent en erreur dans cette expression*, parce
que le lecteur s'attendrait à trouver אֶרֶץ כְּנָעַן· — Mmarg. Ex. XXIII,
13, à propos de סְבִירִין וְלֹא וּקְרַיִין לֹא וּמַטְעַיִן לֹא וְיִשְׁמַע בְּהוֹן : לֹא
סָפְרֵי, 3 (*mots*) *sont pensés* (*devoir être lus*) וְלֹא *et sont lus* לֹא *et les
copistes* (*nous*) *induisent en erreur dans ces mots*. Le sujet סָפְרֵי
est fréquemment omis (comme toujours le complément direct), par
contre le complément indirect est quelquefois exprimé. Exemple,
Mmarg. Gen. XXIV, 4 : ה פְּסוּקִים דְּמַטְעַיִן בְּהוֹן אִם, *5 versets dans
lesquels* (*les scribes nous*) *induisent en erreur* (*au sujet de*) אִם
(que l'on s'imagine avoir été oublié après כִּי, parce que dans des cas
pareils à celui-ci on lit כִּי אִם)·

מְיַחְדִין (h.), voyez יְחַדְאִין·

מֵיסוֹן (μέσον), avec suffixe מֵיסֵיהוֹן, *au milieu d'eux*, O. W. O. Voyez
מְצַע·

מִירְכָא (a.) = מֵאַרְכָא q. v.

מִילָא (a.), déterm. מִילְתָא, comme l'hébr. מִלָּה q. v. Exemple,
Ginsb., *Mass.*, II, p. 12, n° 22 : כֹּל ךְ בְּסוֹף מִילְתָא בְּלָשׁוֹן אֲרָמִית
קָמְצָה בָּר מִן ךְ פַּתְחִין, *tout* ךְ *à la fin d'un mot a* (c.-à-d. dans ce
cas, *est précédé de)* Qâmès, *sauf 4 qui ont Pathach.*

מִיעוּט (h.), littéralement *diminution.* Se dit d'un mot qui ne contient
pas une certaine lettre, par opposition à un autre mot contenant
cette même lettre, celui-ci étant alors désigné par le mot רִבּוּי, littéralement *augmentation.* Exemple, Mm. Num. v, 16 à propos de
חַד מִן ז זוֹגִין מְיַחֲדִין חַד מִיעוּט וְחַד רִבּוּי : il est remarqué ,וְהַעֲמַדָה
*un de 7 couples de mots se rencontrant deux fois seulement, une
fois (avec) diminution et une fois avec augmentation (*וְהַעֲמִידָה,
Ezech. XXIV, 11). Autres couples : וּשְׁבָרָה Is. xxx, 14 et שְׁבָרֵיהָ
Ps. LX, 4; פְּתָחָהּ Zach. III, 9 et פְּתוּחֶיהָ Ps. LXXIV, 6; גְּדֵרָהּ Os. II,
8 et גְּדֵרֶיהָ Ps. LXXX, 13 et ainsi de suite (Voyez la liste complète
dans Ginsb., *Mass.*, II, p. 568, n° 157). Un examen de ces différents
exemples suggère la pensée que les mots מִיעוּט et רִבּוּי ont dû
être employés dans l'origine pour exprimer le singulier et le pluriel, et comme le pluriel se distingue généralement du singulier
par l'addition d'un Yôdh devant le suffixe du nom, on aura ensuite
étendu l'usage de ces deux termes à de simples cas de *scriptio plena*
ou *defectiva* et à d'autres cas tout aussi étrangers à l'idée de singulier ou de pluriel.

מִכָּא (a.) pour מִן כָּא, *d'ici, de là.* Exemple, O. W. O. 164 :
ז פְּסוּקִים דְּאִית בְּהוֹן ט״ו מִלִּין · חַז מִלִּין מִכָּא ז מִלִּין מִכָּא וְמִלָּה
מְצָעִית כְּתִיב, *il y a 7 versets contenant 15 mots, 7 mots d'ici
et 7 mots de là, et le mot du milieu est un Kethibh u-Qerê.*

מָלֵא (h.), plur. מְלֵאִים, *plein,* c.-à-d. avec la *scriptio plena* d'une
lettre quiescente; מָלֵא דְמָלֵא, plur. מְלֵאִים דִמְלֵאִים, *plein de
plein,* c.-à-d. avec la *scriptio plena* de deux ou de plusieurs lettres
quiescentes; opposé de חָסֵר q. v. — Ce terme s'emploie aussi de
l'affirmative verbale תָה ou תָּה et du suffixe pronominal כָה pour
les distinguer de leurs formes ordinaires תָ ou תָּ et ךְ. Exemples,
Mp. Ps. XXXI, 6 à propos de פְּדִיתָה : ל׳ מל׳ ה , *ne se retrouve plus
plein avec* ה. —Mmarg. Gen. XXVII, 7, à propos de וַאֲבָרֶכְכָה : ל׳ מל׳

בָּהּ וְחַד חָסֵר [וַאֲבָרְכֶךָ], *ne se retrouve plus plein avec* הֿ, *mais (une fois on le trouve) défectif* (à savoir Gen. XII, 3) (1).

מְלָאָה (a.), constr. מְלָא, *plénitude;* מְלָא פֿוּם, *plénitude de la bouche,* une des manières de désigner le Chôlem. Exemple, Ginsb.. *Mass.,* II, p. 296, n° 529 : מְלָא פֿוּם וְחַד קָמֵץ פֿוּם חַד זוּגִין. *paires (de mots) dont l'un a la plénitude de la bouche* (Chôlem) *et l'autre le Qāmĕṣ de la bouche* (Schûreq). Voyez *Rev. Bibl.* 1903, p. 543, note 1.

מְלָה, מִילָה (h.), plur. מִלִּין. 1° *Mot.* Elias Levita a essayé d'établir une différence entre ce terme et le terme תֵּיבָה (h.) ou תֵּיבוּתָא (a.). מְלָה serait le mot prononcé, תֵּיבָה le mot écrit (Ginsburg, *the Massoreth ha-Massoreth of Elias Levita,* p. 229). Cette distinction n'a pas été admise par Buxtorf (*Tib.,* sb v. תֵּיבָה). Sans vouloir essayer de trancher la question, nous ferons remarquer que le langage de la Massore semble donner raison à Levita. Rien de plus commun que les rubriques comme la suivante. Mf. ב 4 : כ״ט מִלִּין נָסְבִין ב בְּרֵישׁ תֵּיבוּתָא, *29 millîn prennent* ב *au commencement de la Têbhûthā.* Si תֵּיבוּתָא eût eu exactement le même sens que מְלָה, est-il probable que la Massore, toujours si laconique, l'eût employé plutôt qu'un simple suffixe ? Or ce n'est que très rarement que dans un cas pareil elle dit בְּרֵישֵׁיהוֹן, *à leur commencement.* Il semble donc que מְלָה ait un sens plus général que תֵּיבוּתָא et que ce dernier soit l'expression matérielle et visible dans laquelle le premier est comme enfermé. תֵּיבוּתָא. à proprement parler, veut dire *coffre,* peut-être, comme le pense Levy (*Chald. Wörterbuch* etc., sb v.), parce que le mot, avec ses lettres resserrées les unes contre les autres dans l'ancienne écriture, semblait être tout d'une pièce comme un coffre dont il a la forme allongée, ou peut-être parce que les anciens Juifs se représentaient les lettres comme devant être contenues dans quelque chose, sous peine d'être ex-

---

(1) Le même groupe de consonnes se retrouve encore une fois, Gen. XXVI, 3. mais ponctué autrement. La liste complète du suffixe כָה se trouve dans Mf. ה 21, sous le titre suivant : חַד כֵּן כ״א בִּילוֹן דְּכָתִיב כָה בְּסוֹף תֵּיבוּתָא וְדִיְויָא. Voyez la variante de Mf. כ 4 sous וְדִיָא. Cf. Mm. Ex. VII, 29 et Ginsb., *Mass.,* I, p. 275, n° 56 c.

(2) On trouve aussi מִלְוֹת dans Fr. 380 b 2, mais dans les deux rubriques citées par l'auteur Mf. פֿת 14 et Mm. Gen. XXXI, 18 on lit בִּילִין.

posées à s'éparpiller. Dans le Targum du Pseudo-Jonathan, Deuter. ix, 17, nous lisons que lorsque Moïse brisa les tables de la Loi les lettres s'envolèrent au vent (Levy, *op. c.*, sous אָת. Cf. Ginsburger, *Pseudo-Jonathan*, ad loc.; Talmud de Bab., *Pesachim*, 87 b fin).

2° מִלִּין se dit aussi quelquefois d'expressions consistant en plusieurs mots. Exemple, Ginsb., *Mass.*, II, p. 54, n° 485 : ג מִלִּין 1. תֵּיבוּתָא קַדְמָא (קַדְמֵיתָא) 1. נָסְבָה מִן תִּנְיָנָא (תִּנְיֵיתָא), *3 expressions où le premier mot emprunte (une lettre) du second.*

3° D'après Fr. sb v., מִלָּה se dit aussi des lettres, mais nous n'avons trouvé aucun exemple dans ce sens, pas même dans les sources auxquelles Fr. renvoie le lecteur (1).

מֶלֶךְ (h.), *roi*. Se dit 1° des accents disjonctifs (Fr. sb v.); 2° des voyelles, dans les deux cas par opposition à מְשָׁרֵת q. v. Voyez Wickes, *Pr. Acc.*, p. 9. Ce terme appartient plutôt à la grammaire qu'à la Massore proprement dite.

מַלְכַּיָּא (a.), plur. de מַלְכָּא. *rois*. Pour rappeler que le mot וְלֹא־ תַלְדְּחָמִין. I Reg. xii, 24, a le Nûn paragogique (tandis qu'il ne l'a pas dans le passage correspondant II Chron. xi, 14), la Mp. donne le signe mnémotechnique suivant : מַלְכַּיָּא אָכְלִין נוּנִין, *les Rois mangent des poissons*, jouant ainsi sur le mot לָחַם qui outre le sens de *combattre*, a celui de *manger*, et sur נוּן qui est le nom de la lettre *Nûn*, et qui veut dire aussi *poisson*.

מִלְעֵיל (a.) = מִן + לְ + עֵיל, *en haut, d'en haut*, par opposition à מִלְרַע (q. v.), *en bas*. Se dit A des accents et B des voyelles. — A. 1° De l'accent sur la pénultième par opposition à l'accent sur la dernière syllabe. Exemple, Mm. Gen. xix, 20, à propos de אִמָּלְטָה, il est remarqué : חַד מִן י״ב זוֹגִין חַד מִלְרַע וְחַד מִלְעֵיל, *une de 12 paires (dont) un (membre) est Milra' et l'autre est Mil'el* (l'autre membre de cette paire est אִמָּלְטָה. I Sam. xx, 29. Voyez la liste complète dans Ginsb., *Mass.*, I, p. 646, n° 194). — 2° Des accents placés au-dessus des lettres par opposition à ceux qui sont placés au-dessous. Exemple, Ginsb., *Mass.*, I, p. 501, col. b (= Mm. Gen. xxiii, 3) : וַיָּקָם אַבְרָהָם מֵעַל מִלְעֵיל וַיָּקָם אַבְרָהָם וַיִּשְׁתַּחוּ מִלְרַע וְסִימָן דִּסְמִיךְ מֵעַל עוֹלָה דִּסְמִיךְ יִשְׁתַּחוּ יוֹרֵד, « *et Abraham se leva de dessus* » (Gen. xxiii, 3) *est Mil'el*, « *et Abraham se leva et*

_____
(1) Le premier renvoi Mf בַּל 23 est faux.

se prosterna » (ibid., 7) *est Milra', et le signe mnémotechnique est : ce qui précède* « *de dessus* » *monte, ce qui précède* « *et se prosterna* » *descend.*

B. 1° D'une voyelle plus pleine par opposition à une voyelle moins pleine. Exemple, Mm. Gen. XXII, 2, remarque que יִדְלֹף se rencontre deux fois, une fois Milra' יִדְלָף. et une fois Mil'el יִדְלֹף (Eccl. X, 18). — Mp. Gen. XXXVII, 25, remarque, à propos de אֹרְחַת, que ce mot ne se représente plus ainsi (Milra'), mais qu'on le trouve une fois Mil'el, אֹרְחוֹת (Is. XXI. 13) (1). — De même dans Ginsb., *Mass.*, II, pp. 310, 311, n°s 606 a et 606 b (cf. Mf. א 24, sous un titre plus correct), nous trouvons Chôlem comme Mil'el relativement à Qāmēṣ-Chātùph, à Chāṭeph-Qāmēṣ et à Ṣērê; Schūreq (וּ ou ֻ) relativement à Ṣērê, à Pathach et à Qāmēṣ; Qibbùṣ relativement à Chireq; Qāmēṣ relativement à Ṣērê etc. Nous trouvons un exemple de Ṣērê Milra' (par opposition à Chireq Gādhôl) dans Mp. et Mm. Gen. IV, 12 = Mf. ט 17 (cf. Fr. 84, note 6). — 2° a) D'un mot commençant par une des particules בְּ, כְּ et לְ quand elles contiennent l'article, par opposition au même mot sans l'article. Exemples, — pour בְּ, Ginsb., *Mass.*, I, p. 159, n°s 11 a, 11 b, 11 c = Mf. ב 2 : בַּסְּבָךְ Gen. XXII, 13, relativement à בִּסְבָךְ; Ps. LXXIV, 5; בַּתַּנּוּר Lev. VII, 9, relativement à בְּתַנּוּר ibid. XXVI, 26; — pour כְּ, Ginsb., *Mass.*, II, p. 6, n° 18 = Mf. כ 1; — pour לְ, ibid., pp. 109, 110, n° 19 = Mf. ל 7. — b) D'un Waw consécutif relativement à un Waw copulatif. Exemple, Ginsb.. *Mass.*, I, p. 322, n° 10 = Mf. ו 3 : וַיְחַכְּם I Reg. V, 11 par opposition à וִיחַכְּם Prov. IV. 9. — c) D'un Waw copulatif muni d'une voyelle prétonique par rapport au Waw copulatif muni d'un Schewā (ou d'un Schūreq). Exemple, ibid., וְבֹקֶר Ps. LV, 18, mais וּבֹקֶר Ex. XVI. 7; — וְהֶגֶה Ezech. II, 10, mais וְהֶגֶה Job XXXVII, 2. — d) De la particule לְ dans les mêmes conditions. Exemple, Ginsb., *Mass.*, II, p. 110, n° 19 : לְנֶגַע Deut. XVII, 8, mais לְנֶגַע Lev. XIII, 2. Dans le sens de ce 2° מִלְעֵיל est synonyme de דָּגֵשׁ et חָזָק, מִלְרַע de רְפֵי et חָלוּשׁ; voyez ces mots.

מִלְרַע (a.) = מִן + לְ + רַע (ce dernier étant une abréviation de אֶרַע, état absolu inusité du mot אַרְעָא, *terre*), *en bas:* l'opposé dans tous les sens du mot מִלְעֵיל q. v.

---

(1) A ce même verset la Mmarg. note encore un cas de Mil'el et Milra' dans dans le sens de A 1°, à savoir בָּאָה (Gen. XXXVII, 25) et בָּאָה I Reg. II, 28,.

מְנֻזָּרוֹת (h.), pour מְנֻזָּרוֹת, apparemment partic. fémin. plur. Pu'al
du verbe נָזַר, *séparés*. Appellation des *Nûns retournés* dans Mm.

Ps. cvii, 23 : נוּנִין מְנֻזָּרוֹת וּמִקְרִין אַפִּין וְרַקִּין שֶׁבַּתּוֹרָה (lisez ט),
*il y a 9 Nûns séparés et on les appelle les mais et les seulements
qui sont dans la Loi.* Buxtorf avait déjà traduit ainsi : « separata,
scilicet per inversam formam a reliquis sejuncta et distincta » (*Tib.*,
ch. xvi). Ginsburg traduit aussi נוּן מְנֻזֶּרֶת « a separated Nûn »
(*Introduction*, p. 342), de même que Sam. Krauss, « vereinzeltes »
(*Zeitschr. für Altest. Wissensch.* 1902, p. 60). Mais ni l'un ni
l'autre n'accompagne sa traduction du moindre commentaire. Peut-
être ont-ils souscrit à l'explication de Buxtorf, qui nous paraît
quelque peu tirée par les cheveux. Hamburger est probablement
dans le vrai quand il remarque, fort laconiquement d'ailleurs, que
מְנֻזָּרוֹת vient de נָזֹרוּ אָחוֹר (1) « Zurückwenden » (*Real-Encyclo-
pädie des Iudenthums*, Abth. III, supplém. IV, p. 57). מְנֻזָּרוֹת serait donc une forme artificielle, calquée sur le modèle du Partic.
Pu'al en prenant pour point de départ (forme Qal) les consonnes
du Niph'al de נָזַר, procédé qui ne serait pas sans analogie en néo-
hébreu. Voyez Geiger, *Lehrbuch zur Sprache der Mischna*, p. 23
(Cf. Gesenius, *Hebr. u. Chald. Handwörterbuch*, 13ᵉ édit., sous נאה).
נוּנִין מְנֻזָּרוֹת est donc pour נוּנִין מְנֻזָּרוֹת אָחוֹר et doit être traduit par *Nûns qui vont en arrière*, c.-à-d. *retournés*. Cette hypothèse est d'ailleurs confirmée par l'autre expression massorétique
נוּנִין הַפוּכוֹת, *Nûns retournés*, et par une variante de la rubrique
déjà citée, que nous trouvons dans Ginsb., *Mass.*, II, p. 259, n° 15 a :
אִילוּ ט נוּנִין מְנֻזָּרוֹת וְנִכְתָּבוֹת לְאָחוֹר, *voici les 9 Nûns retournés
et qui sont écrits à rebours* (2). Plus ancienne que נוּנִין הַפוּכוֹת
et נוּנִין מְנֻזָּרוֹת paraît être l'expression אַפִּין וְרַקִּין q. v., car tandis que celles-là ne se rencontrent que dans la Massore, celle-ci se
trouve déjà dans le Talmud de Babylone, *Rösch ha-Schānāh*, 17ᵇ (3).
Que veut dire exactement אַפִּין וְרַקִּין? Faute de mieux, nous avons

---

(1) Is. i, 4. Probablement un ancien sēmān du Nun retourné.
(2) Une autre explication suggérée par Baer, *Dikduke ha-Tᵉ'āmim*, p. 47, serait l'expression יִזֹּר מֵאַחֲרָי Ezech. xiv, 7. Mais cela donnerait le sens de séparé, *détourné*, plutôt
que de *retourné*. Blau avait peut-être cette explication en vue quand il a traduit par
« Abgewandt » (*Masoretische Untersuchungen*, p. 41).
(3) Dans le même ouvrage, *Sabbath*, 115 (fin), les Nûns retournés sont appelés simplement
סִיבָּנִיוֹת, *des signes*, et dans le Siphrè (Bl. Ugolini, *Thesaurus*, XV, p. 144) נָקוּד, *point*.

adopté l'explication de Ginsburg qui est aussi celle de Blau (*Masoretische Untersuchungen*, pp. 41 et 42) (1).

מִנְיָן (h'.), *nombre* et, par extension, 1° *adjectif numéral*. Précédé de רִבּוּי, *pluriel*, ce mot désigne les nombres cardinaux de 20 à 90, qui, en hébreu, sont les formes plurielles de 10, 3, 4, etc. Exemple, Mm. Num. vii, 66 : הָעֲשִׂירִי כָּלְּהוֹן מְלֵאִין בָּר מִן ד׳ חֲסִירִין וְסִי[מָנְיהוֹן] ...., *tous les* הָעֲשִׂירִי ont la וְכָל רִבּוּי מִנְיָן מְלֵאִין בָּר מִן א׳ חָסֵ[ר] וג׳ *scriptio plena, sauf quatre qui ont la scriptio defectiva*, à savoir (Jerem. xxxix, 1, etc.) *et tout pluriel* d'adjectif numéral *a la scriptio plena, sauf un qui a la scriptio defectiva* (c.-à-d. I Sam. ix, 22, כְּשִׁלְשָׁם אִישׁ). Cf. Ginsb., *Mass.*, II, p. 235, nᵒˢ 571, 572 et Mm. Esth. ii, 16. C'est encore dans le sens d'adjectif numéral qu'il faut entendre מִנְיָן dans cette rubrique que nous reconstituons (2) d'après la Mm. et la Mp. Job xxxi, 5 : רַגְלִי ו׳ וּב לְרַגְלִי וְכָל מִנְיָן דִּכְוָותְהוֹן. Il faut évidemment suppléer après וכל les mots דִּסְמִיךְ לְ (voyez סְמִיךְ) et traduire : רַגְלִי *se rencontre six fois (sans aucun préfixe),* mais *deux fois on trouve* לְרַגְלִי, *et toutes les fois que ce mot est accompagné d'un adjectif numéral, il est de même* (c.-à-d. *sans préfixe*). En effet, outre les six cas où l'on trouve רַגְלִי sans préfixe (dans le sens de « mon pied »), on le trouve encore plusieurs fois (dans le sens de « fantassin ») également sans préfixe, mais invariablement précédé d'adjectifs numéraux, par ex. Ex. xii, 37, etc. — 2° *Nom de nombre.* Exemple, Ginsb., *Mass.*, II, p. 570, nᵒ 198 : כָּל מִנְיָן בְּלִישׁוֹן. רבע בְּסְגוֹל בָּר מִן חַד בְּחֹלֶם וְכָל שׁוֹם בַּר נָשׁ פְּוָתֵ[הוֹן] (3)

---

(1) On lira avec fruit ces deux auteurs sur la question des *Nûns retournés.* ainsi que Krauss (loc. cit.). Ce dernier, partant du mot שִׁיעוּר (désignation du Nûn retourné dans le traité *Sopherim*, vi, 1) au lieu duquel il adopte la variante שִׁיפִּיד (forme קְטִיל de שְׁפַד, *embrocher*, emprunté au grec σπόδος), démontre que le Nûn retourné n'est autre que l'obèle des Grecs. — Cette très ingénieuse théorie cadre fort bien avec le tracé du Nûn retourné qui accompagne la rubrique que nous avons citée d'après Ginsburg. C'est comme Nûn dont le crochet inférieur serait retourné en arrière, ou si l'on veut comme un Nu grec oncial qui serait retourné d'un quart de cercle de gauche à droite. Sur la signification de אָכֵן וְרַקֵּן dans l'interprétation juive, voyez Bacher, *Die älteste Terminologie der Iüdischen Schriftauslegung*, Leipzig, 1899, p. 110.

(2) Dans la Massore de Ben-Chayim (*loc. cit.* et Ps. xxvi, 12) et même dans Ginsb.. *Mass.*, II, p. 570, nᵒ 206, cette rubrique est manifestement incorrecte.

(3) Dans la rubrique telle qu'elle est dans Ginsb. חלם vient en premier lieu et כגיד en second, ce qui est manifestement incorrect.

tout nom de nombre dans le laschon de רְבַע *(s'écrit) avec Seghôl*
רֶבַע . *sauf un (qui s'écrit) avec Chôlem* (רֹבַע), *et tout nom
d'homme (dans le même laschon) est comme eux (c.-à-d. comme
ceux qui sont la règle,* רְבַע . Voyez les lexiques.

מָסוּר (h.), partic. pass. Qal dénominatif de מַסֹּרָה q. v., *qui est enregistré in extenso dans la Massore.* Exemple, Mm. Gen. XXXVII, 25,
où à propos de אֹרְחַת, il est remarqué : א״ב מִן חַד וְחַד מְשַׁמְּשִׁין
א״ת ב״ש וְלֵית דִּכְוָותְהוֹן (1 מָסוּר בְּמַסֹּרָה רַבְּתָא, *la liste alphabétique de mots ne se rencontrant qu'une fois et dont le premier commence par* א *et finit par* ת, *le second commençant par* ב *et finissant
par* ש. etc., *est enregistrée in extenso dans la grande Massore* (=
Mf.), plus généralement on trouve dans ce cas נִמְסָר q. v.

מַסֹּרָה (h.) (2), *Massore.* Dans l'édition de la Bible rabbinique par
J. ben-Chayim, ce mot se rencontre : 1° seul, en tête de la Mm. quand
elle occupe la place laissée libre par les commentaires dans les
marges latérales. 2° Suivi de רַבְּתָא i. e. *Grande Massore,* dans le
corps de la Mm., pour désigner la Mf. Voyez un exemple sous
מָסוּר (3).

מָסָרְתָּא (a.) et מְסוֹרְתָּא (a.), *tradition,* et plus spécialement, *tradition au sujet du texte de l'Écriture,* d'où 1° *rubrique contenant
une tradition relativement au Texte, note massorétique.* מְסוֹרְתָּא se
rencontre fréquemment avec ce sens dans l'expression וּלְבַד
מִמְּסוֹרְתָּא. *et en outre de (la liste donnée dans) la rubrique mas-*

---

(1) יְלֵית דִּכְוָותְהוֹן fait double emploi avec חַד יְחַד (incorrect pour חַד חַד).

(2) Ponctué aussi dans différents ouvrages מְסֹרָה, מְסֹרָה, מַסֹּרָה, מִסֹּרָה et מְסֹרָה.
Sur l'étymologie et le développement historique de ce mot et du mot מְסֹרֶת voyez Bacher,
A contribution to the history of the term Massorah (Jewish Quarterly Review, III,
pp. 785 et suiv.).

(3) Dans la préface (הַקְדָּמָה) imprimée en tête du vol. I des Bibles Rabbiniques de
Venise (et de Bâle) J. ben-Chayim mentionne plusieurs fois la מַסֹּרָה גְדוֹלָה וּקְטַנָּה, *la
Massore* Grande et Petite dans le sens que nous donnons ici à Mm. et Mp. Il appelle
aussi la Mf. מַסֹּרָה גְדוֹלָה. *Grande Massore,* ajoutant quelquefois כְּדֶרֶךְ הֶעָרוּךְ, *en manière
de lexique,* mais le plus souvent simplement בְּ׳ רַבְּתָא, équivalent araméen de גְדוֹלָה בְּ׳.
— Une fois, il dit de la Mp. הַבְּ׳ הָאֶמְצָעִית לֹא הַגְּדוֹלָה, *la Massore du milieu qui n'est
pas la Grande.* Nulle part nous n'avons trouvé une expression distincte pour Mmarg.
Peut-être est-elle comprise avec la Mm. dans l'expression סְבִיבוֹת הֶעַמּוּד, *autour de la
colonne,* qu'il emploie quelquefois en parlant de la Mm.

sorétique, qui annonce un supplément à une note de la Massore. Exemples dans O. W. O., 90, 92, 95, et *Rev. Bibl.* 1902, p. 511. Voyez לְבַד. — 2° par extension, *mot qui est l'objet, ou qui fait partie d'une remarque massorétique.* Tel est du moins le sens que, faute d'un meilleur, nous proposons pour מָסוֹרְתָּא dans cette expression מָסוֹרְתָּא מִכָּא וּמְסוֹרְתָּא מִכָּא, que la Massore emploie pour désigner un mot qui se présente deux fois dans le même verset, à savoir une fois immédiatement avant et une fois immédiatement après un autre mot. Exemple, Mf. ר ה ל מן חד : פְּסוּקִין

דְּמַיִין מָסוֹרְתָּא מִכָּא וּמְסוֹרְתָּא מִכָּא נָסְבִין ו וּמִלָּה בֵּינֵיהוֹן, *un des 35 versets qui se ressemblent, (en ce que) l'objet de la rubrique est ici, et l'objet de la rubrique est là, (tous deux prenant le Waw (copulatif), et entre les deux il y a un (autre) mot.* (Par exemple Gen. iv, 5 וְאֶל קַיִן וְאֶל...· Voyez la liste complète dans Ginsb., *Mass.,* I, p. 414, n° 95). — Autres exemples. Mm. et Mmarg. Deut. x, 21 (= Mf. ר 42, Ginsb., ibid., n° 91), Mf. ר 36 (= Ginsb., ibid., n° 90), et 38 (= Ginsb., ibid., n° 93). — Buxtorf, *Tib.,* sb v., a avancé une opinion quelque peu différente, tacitement adoptée par Worms, סְיָיג לַתּוֹרָה, fol. 28 a. Il rapproche מָסוֹרְתָּא de son équivalent hébreu מָסוֹרֶת, dans l'axiome Talmudique יֵשׁ אֵם לַמָּסוֹרֶת, *l'écriture* (1) *a une mère* (2) *(est mater scriptionis),* et conclut pour מָסוֹרְתָּא au sens de *mot écrit.* Mais dans ce sens, tous les mots de la Bible pourraient être appelés du nom de *Masoretha;* et nous ne voyons pas pourquoi, dans le cas qui nous occupe, le mot du milieu ne serait pas מָסוֹרְתָּא tout aussi bien que les deux mots qu'il sépare.

מַסְכְּתָא (a.) == מַסֶּכֶת (h.), *traité (talmudique).* Exemple, Mmarg. Ex. xvi, 29 : סִימָן תְּבוּתָא[ן] דְּפָסוּק כְּפִרְקֵי דְמַסְכְּתָא, *le signe mnémotechnique est « les mots du verset sont comme les chapitres du traité (talmudique) ».* La rubrique à laquelle ce sēmān (voyez סִימָן) se rapporte a disparu. Elle remarquait sans doute que ce verset

(1) C'est-à-dire le texte consonantal qui d'après une école rabbinique avait seul été transmis par la tradition, et qui pour cela était appelé *tradition.*
(2) C'est-à-dire qu'elle est fermement établie par une tradition certaine dont elle peut se réclamer, comme une fille se réclame de sa mère. — Dans ce sens בְּיסוֹרֶת est opposé à מִקְרָא, *la lecture.* c'est-à-dire non seulement les consonnes d'un mot mais aussi les voyelles avec lesquelles ce mot se lit. Cf. Bacher, *Die älteste Terminologie der Jüdischen Auslegung* (Leipzig, 1899), pp. 119 et suiv.

avait 24 mots, de même qu'un traité du Talmud (Schabbath) a 24 chapitres.

מסבא. Ce mot ne se rencontre que dans la Mmarg. Judic. vii, 5 où, sous le titre de לְבָד, on lit : ל זָקֵף קָמֵץ וְכָל מַשְׁכְּנָא וּמסבא וּתְרֵי עֲשַׂר דִּכְוָתֵיהּ קָמְצִין, *'ne se retrouve plus (ainsi dans ce livre avec) Zâqéph (et) Qâmés; mais tout le Tabernacle (voyez* מַשְׁכְּנָא) *et..... et les Douze* [Petits Prophètes] *sont comme ce passage, ayant (aussi) Qâmés.* La *Concordance* nous apprend que tous les passages ou לְבָד se rencontre appartiennent soit au *Tabernacle* (c.-à-d. Exod. xxvi, 9 et xxxvi, 15), soit aux Petits Prophètes (c.-à-d. Zach. xii, 12-14). Il semble donc que le mot מסבא ne puisse pas représenter une partie de la Bible comme sa position entre מַשְׁכְּנָא et תְּרֵי עֲשַׂר le donnerait tout de suite à penser. C'est sans doute ce qui a suggéré à Fr. sb v. d'y voir une erreur pour l'abréviation א״סף (אֶחָד סוֹף פָּסוּק), *et l'un est à la fin du verset,* ou encore אַתְנַחְתָּא סוֹף פָּסוּק, *Athnach et Sôph-Pâsûq).* Mais c'est supposer une bien grosse erreur; et puis la place de cette formule serait plutôt après qu'avant תְּרֵי עֲשַׂר, comme on peut s'en convaincre en examinant le texte Massorétique. Nous préférons voir dans מסבא l'erreur d'un scribe distrait ou ignorant qui ayant trouvé מסב״ (comme le porte en effet l'édition de Buxtorf) = מִסְפְּדָא, *les pleurs,* a écrit מסבא, et comme ce mot ne présentait aucun sens on aurait ajouté après coup תְּרֵי עֲשַׂר qui fait double emploi avec מִסְפְּדָא. Le terme מִסְפְּדָא est une excellente désignation de Zach. xii, 12-14, où le verbe סָפַד et le nom מִסְפֵּד se rencontrent plusieurs fois.

מַעֲרְבָאֵי (a.), plur. déterm. de מַעֲרְבָאָה, *les Occidentaux.* Nom d'une école Massorétique, par opposition à מַדִּנְחָאֵי, *les Orientaux.* Voyez ce mot.

מַפִּיק (a.), plur. מַפְקִין. *qui fait ressortir.* Après ce que nous avons dit de ce terme dans la *Terminologie de la Massore (Rev. Bibl.* 1903, p. 544), il nous suffira d'ajouter ici un exemple ou deux. Mm. Ex. vi, 24, à propos de וַאֲבִיאָסָף il est noté : י״ז מִלִּין מַפְקִין א׳לף (1 מִן חַד וְחַד, *il y a 17 mots se rencontrant chacun une fois seulement et qui font ressortir l'Aleph.* Cf. Mf. א 4 et Ginsb., *Mass.,* I, p. 11, nᵒˢ 17 a et 17 b. Et, vice versa, Mm. II Reg.

---

(1) Lisez הד הד (confusion très commune), comme dans le passage correspondant de la Mf.

xvi, 7 : ‎ז׳‎ מִלִּין בְּקִרְיָא מַפְּקִי א׳ וְלֵית לְהוֹן זוּג ‎ז״י‎, *il y a 17 mots
dans la Bible qui ne font pas ressortir l'*א *et ils ne font pas
paire* (1). Cf. Mf. א 5, et Ginsb.. ibid., n° 15.

מְצַוְּיִין (h.), plur. de מָצוּי, *se trouvant.* Se rencontre quelquefois au
lieu de l'expression plus ordinaire נִמְסַר q. v., comme renvoi d'un
endroit de la Massore à un autre. Exemple, Mm. Ex. xvii, 5 : וְסִימָן
מְצַוְּיִין בְּמִשְׁלֵי סִימָן ד׳. *et la liste* (des versets) *se trouve dans les
Proverbes, chap. 4.*

מִצִּיעִיתָה (a.), fém. de מִצִּיעָה, *qui est au milieu,* Ginsb., *Mass.*, II,
p. 54, n° 484.

מִצִּיעָא (a), *milieu, intérieur,* précédé de בְּ, *dans.* Exemple. Mp. Dan.
xi, 6 : בְּ מִצִּיעַ דְּאֶסְתֵּר, *deux se trouvent dans Esther.* Il faut
évidemment lire בְּמִצִּיעָא.

מִצִּיעְתָא (a.), fém. de מִצִּיעָא. même sens que le précédent, Mm. I
Sam. xiii, 19.

מְצַע (a.), déterm. מְצַעָא, *milieu,* O. W. O. 103, 109, 110. Peut-être
aussi, adverbialement, *au milieu,* Mm. Num. iv, 26.

מִצְעָיְתָא (a.), fémin. de מִצְעָאָה. *qui est au milieu,* Fr. 381 a, 2. Il est
à remarquer que ce mot ne se trouve dans aucune des trois sources
indiquées par Fr. pour cette rubrique. Mf. כת 10 a מִצְעוּת. Mm. I
Sam. xiii, 19 מִצְעָיְתָא, et O. W. O. 164 מִצְע. La rubrique correspondante dans Ginsb., *Mass.*, II, p. 54, n° 484, porte מִצִּיְיְתָא. Peut-
être est-ce ce dernier mot qu'il faut lire avec *scriptio defectiva*
מִצְעָיְיְתָא. Comp. מִצְעוּת pour מִצִּיעוּת.

מִצְעוּת (a.) pour מִצִּיעוּת. *milieu,* Mf. ה 5, 26, 32, Mm. Levit. viii, 26
(סמ״ך בְּמִצְעוּת תֵּיבוּתָא): Ecc. vi, 10. Peut-être aussi adverbialement (sans בְּ), *au milieu,* Mf. כת 10. *Milieu* dans cet article et les
cinq précédents doit s'entendre dans le même sens que pour
אֶמְצַע q. v. D'après Worms. סְיָג לַתּוֹרָה, il y aurait cette différence
entre les deux groupes אֶמְצַע et מְצַע que le premier ne s'emploierait que pour les lettres (*dans les mots*), tandis que le second se di-

---

(1) C'est-à-dire que ces mots ne se retrouvent pas *une autre fois seulement,* contrai-
rement à d'autres mots qui se retrouvent aussi encore une fois, et une fois seulement,
avec l'Aleph, non seulement écrit mais encore prononcé; ce qui constitue une paire,
comme תכים et תאכים. Cf. Mf. א 6 = Ginsb., *Mass.*, I, p. 11, n° 16.

rait des mots (*dans les versets*) ou des versets (*dans les sections, Li-vres* etc. de la Bible). Le court extrait de Mm. Lev. viii, 26, que nous venons de citer, prouve en tout cas que le second groupe peut aussi s'employer pour les lettres dans les mots. Fr. sb v. aurait pu être plus affirmatif sur ce point.

מַפְסִיק (a.), partic. 'Aph'el, dénominatif de פָּסִיק, *muni de la ligne Pāsēq.* Exemple, Mm. Lev. viii, 23; Is. xiii, 8; Am. i, 2 : זֹ מִלִּין

בְּטַעְמָא מַרְעִימִין וּמַפְסִיקִין, *7 mots ont l'accent Schalschéleth et Pāsēq.* Voyez מַרְעִים. Dans la rubrique correspondante Mf. טע 12 (aussi Mp. Is. xiii, 8 et Mm. Esdr. v, 15) on lit פָּסְקִין, plur. de פָּסִיק (comme קָמְצִין de קָמֵץ. Cf. *Rev. Bibl.* 1903, p. 547).

מְקוֹמוֹת (h.), plur. de מָקוֹם, *endroits, passages de la Bible.* Exemple, Mm. Lev. xxiii, 21; II Reg. xv, 16 : הַטִּפְחָא לֹא יִשְׁרְתֶנָּה מֵירְכָא בְּתֵיבָתָהּ כִּי אִם בֹּה מְקוֹמוֹת, *Mērekhā n'est serviteur de Ṭiphchā dans son* (c.-à-d. *dans le même*) *mot qu'en 8 endroits.* Voyez un autre exemple sous מָאיְילָא.

מַקֵּף (a.), partic. 'Aph'el de נְקֵף, 1° *le Maqqeph,* 2° *uni au mot suivant par le Maqqeph* (cf. *Rev. Bibl.* 1903, p. 547). Exemple, Mp. Gen. v, 19, où, à propos de וַיְחִי, il est remarqué que ce mot se trouve וֹ, מַקְּפִין בְּעִנְיָן, *6 fois uni au mot suivant par le Maqqeph dans le même contexte* (à savoir v. 6, 7, 18, 19, 29, 30).

מוּקָּף (h.), partic. Hoph'al, dénominatif de מַקֵּף q. v., *uni au mot suivant par le Maqqeph.* Exemple, Mm. Gen. xxx, 19 : כֹּל בֶּן הַמּוּקָּף פַּתַח בָּר מִן ד. *tout* בֶּן *relié au mot suivant par Maqqeph a Pathach* (c.-à-d. Seghôl, cf. *Rev. Bibl.* 1903, p. 542) *sauf 4* (qui ont Qāmeṣ, c.-à-d. Ṣērê, cf. ibid.).

מַקְרִין (h.), *qui pousse des cornes,* dans le signe mnémotechnique שׁוֹר פַּר מַקְרִין, *un jeune taureau qui pousse des cornes* (Ps. lxix, 32). On rencontre ce signe, 1° Mmarg. Ex. xxi, 39, pour rappeler que dans ce passage le mot וְאִם qui précède immédiatement le mot שׁוֹר, *taureau,* est marqué de l'accent Pāzēr qui ressemble à une paire de cornes et qui, apparemment, partageait autrefois avec Pāzēr-Gādhōl le sobriquet de קַרְנֵי פָרָה, *les cornes de la vache* (cf. Wickes, *Pr. ac.,* p. 21); — 2° Mmarg. Lev. ix, 18, pour rappeler que dans le passage וַיִּשְׁחַט אֶת־הַשּׁוֹר. *et il immola le taureau,* le premier mot est marqué du Mehuppakh, accent dont le nom com-plet est שׁוֹפָר מְהֻפָּךְ, *la trompette* (instrument en forme de corne) *retournée* (cf. Wickes, ibid., p. 24, n. 61). — Pour ne pas avoir à revenir sur cette dernière rubrique, nous mentionnerons ici deux autres signes mnémotechniques qu'elle donne comme équivalents de celui que nous avons déjà expliqué : a) שׁוֹר נַגָּח (Ex. xx, 36), *un taureau qui frappe avec la corne;* b) מָשֵׁךְ תּוֹרָא. *le taureau tire,* où la Massore joue sur le mot מָשֵׁךְ qui veut dire *tirer sous le joug* (מָשֵׁךְ בְּעֹול) et *sonner de la corne* (מָשֵׁךְ בְּקֶרֶן).

מֶרְכָא (a.), variante orthographique de מֵאֲרְכָא q. v.

מַרְעֵים (a.), 1° *qui tremblote, qui fait le trémolo, la trille.* Désignation de l'accent Schalschéleth dans le *Diqduqé ha-Ṭeʿāmîm* (édit. de Baer et Strack, p. 18 en bas). — 2° *Mot marqué de l'accent Schalschéleth;* voyez un exemple sous מַפְסִיק. Cf. Wickes, *Pr. acc.,* p. 17.

מְשׁוּנֶּה (h.), partic. Puʿal de שָׁנָה. *changer,* plur. מְשׁוּנִּים. *qui diffèrent;* voyez מִתְחַלֵּף 1°.

מַשְׁכְּנָא (a.), *le Tabernacle.* et par extension, *passages de la Bible où il est question du Tabernacle.* On distingue le מַשְׁכְּנָא קַדְמָאָה. *premier Tabernacle* (environ Ex. xxv-xxxi) du מ' תִנְיָנָא ou מ' בָתְרָאָה, *second Tabernacle* ou *T. postérieur* (ibid. xxxvi-fin). Voyez Mm. Ps. lxxv, 4 (מֶשׁ' תְנ' קַד'); Mm. Ex. xxvi, 5 et Mf. קן 9 (מֶשׁ' תנ'). Quand la Massore veut parler des deux à la fois elle se sert de l'expression כָּל מַשְׁכְּנָא, *tout le Tabernacle,* auquel cas le reste de la Bible est indiqué par כָּל קְרָיָּיא. *toute la Bible* (voyez קְרָיָּיא); par exemple, Mmarg. Ex. xxv, 20. Le *premier Tabernacle* est aussi appelé צַוְוָאָה, *l'ordre* (de bâtir); le *second T.* עֲשִׂיָּיה, *l'exécution.*

מְשַׁמֵּשׁ (a.), littéralement *qui sert* (transit. et intransit.); en langage massorétique, 1° *qui fait fonction, qui est employé,* 2° dans le sens de l'Hithpaʿel, *qui se sert de, qui emploie, qui a.*

1° D'après Fr., sb v., מְשַׁמֵּשׁ est fréquemment employé par la Massore dans le sens de *être employé, se présenter,* particulièrement avec בְּלָשׁוֹן, auquel cas il veut dire *se rencontrer dans le sens de.* Il est surprenant que Fr. n'ait cité aucun exemple de cette acception si commune. Quant à nous, nous n'avons trouvé qu'un exemple de מְשַׁמְּשִׁין בְּלִשׁוֹן, à savoir Mp. Gen. xxvi, 4, où à propos de הָאֵל

il est remarqué : ח מֹשֹׁמֹשׁין בְּלִשׁוֹן אֵלֶּה; si cette note est cor-
recte, elle ne peut qu'être traduite *est employé 8 fois dans le sens
de* אֵלֶּה. Il est à remarquer toutefois que משֹׁמֹשׁין est absent de la
Mp. aux autres passages visés par cette rubrique. On y lit invariablement ח בְּלִשׁוֹן חוֹל, *8 fois dans le sens profane* (voyez חוֹל); ainsi
Mp. Gen. xix, 25; Lev. xviii, 27; Deut. iv, 42; xix, 11; de même
Mm. Deut. xix, 11. Cf. Ginsb., *Mass.*, I, p. 57, nᵒˢ 512 et 513. Dans
Mm. Gen. xxvi, 4, au lieu de מְשַׁמְּשִׁין on lit סְבִירִין q. v. Trois passages, Gen. xix, 8; xxvi, 3 et Deut. vii, 22, ne sont rubriqués ni à
la Mp. ni à la Mm.

2ᵒ מְשַׁמֵּשׁ est au contraire très fréquent dans le sens de l'Hithpa'el. Exemples, Mf. א 9 : אִלֵּין מִלִּין דְּמְשַׁמְּשִׁין א בְּסוֹף תֵּיבוּתָא
וג". *voici les mots qui ont* א *à la fin* etc. — Mf. א 13 : אִלֵּין מִלִּין
דְּמְשַׁמְּשִׁין חַד א וְחַד וא, *voici les mots qui ont (au commencement)
une fois* א *et une fois* ואַ. — Mf. א 19 : א"ב מִן חַד חַד מְשַׁמֵּשׁ
א"ת ב"ש רֵישׁ וְסוֹף, *alphabet de mots ne se rencontrant qu'une
fois et ayant* א, ב *etc. au commencement et* ת, שׂ *etc. à la fin.*
— Mm. Job vi, 4 : חַד מִן מִלִּין דְּמְשַׁמְּשִׁין נִי בְּסוֹף תֵּיבוּתָא, *un des
mots qui ont* נִי *à la fin.* — Mf. א 12 : א"ב מִן חַד וְחַד חַד א וְחַד
ה שָׁרְשָׁהּ בִּמְעַרְכֶת אוֹת הָהֵא כִּי שָׁם בֵּיתָהּ כִּי מְשַׁמֶּשֶׁת חַד
נָסִיב הֵא וְחַד לָא נָסִיב [הֵא וג, *alphabet de mots se rencontrant
une fois (d'une manière) et une fois (d'une autre manière); on le
trouvera* (littér. *sa racine est*) *dans l'ordre de la lettre* ה, *c'est là
qu'est sa place* (littér. *sa maison*), *car il a (pour vrai titre)* : « *l'un
prend* ה (*au commencement*) *et l'autre ne le prend pas* ». Cf. Ginsb.,
Mass., I, p. 258, nᵒ 16. — O. W. O. 82 : אוֹתִיּוֹת גְּדוֹלוֹת שֶׁבַּתּוֹרָה
מְשַׁמְּשׁוֹת א"ב, *les grandes lettres de la Loi se servant de l'alphabet* (c.-à-d. *arrangées alphabétiquement*). Comparez la rédaction
plus naturelle de la rubrique correspondante dans Ginsb., *Mass.*,
I, p. 85, nᵒ 225, *Alphabet de Grandes Lettres dans la Loi.* — Dans
quelques rubriques comme la suivante, Mf. אל 100 : אִלֵּין מִלִּין
מְשַׁמְּשִׁין אֱלֹהִים וג". on est porté à attribuer à מְשַׁמְּשִׁין le sens de
se trouver à côté de. C'est ainsi que Buxtorf (*Tib.*, sb v.) a compris,
voces quae habent sibi adjunctam vocem Elohim. Mais en compa-

rant cette rubrique avec une variante que donne Ginsb., *Mass.*, I,
p. 75, n° 653 a, on voit que מְשַׁמְּשִׁין se rapporte non au mot qui
précède אֱלֹהִים, mais bien à ce mot et au mot אֱלֹהִים lui-même,
considérés comme une seule expression. Il faut donc traduire : *voici
des expressions qui ont* אֱלֹהִים (au lieu de הָאֱלֹהִים · D'ailleurs ce
n'est pas ici seulement que מִלָּה se rencontre dans le sens d'*expression;* voyez מִלָּה 2°.

מְשַׁלֵּשׁ (h.), *qui triple.* Se dit de versets où un même mot se lit
trois fois de suite. Exemple, Mm. Jer. xxii, 29 : ג פְּסוּקִין מְשַׁלְּשִׁין
בְּקְרָיָיא, *3 versets triplent (un mot) dans la Bible.* Voyez une variante de cette note sous מֻתְאָם.

מְשַׁנְּיָא (a.), fém. de מְשַׁנֵּי, plur. m. מְשַׁנְּיָין. 1° *Qui diffère.* Exemple,
Mm. Jos. vi, 4, où, à propos de שׁוֹפָרוֹת הַיּוֹבְלִים, il est remarqué :
חַד מִן י׳ זוֹגִין מִן ד׳ מִלִּין) תְּנְיָנָא (תִּנְיֵיתָא) מְשַׁנְּיָא וְסִי[מַן]
נִמְסְרָה בְּמַסּוֹרָה רַבְּתָא דְאַסְדַּרְנָא בְּרֵישׁ (?בְּסוֹף (lisez הָאי
חִבּוּרָא בְּעֶרֶךְ שִׁין, *un de dix quatuors* (littér. *de dix paires de
quatre mots*, voyez זוֹג), *le second (mot de chaque quatuor) étant
différent (des trois autres). La liste est donnée dans la Grande Massore que nous avons mise en ordre, au commencement* (à la fin?) *de
cet ouvrage, sous* (littér. *dans l'ordre de) la lettre Schin.* Le quatuor
en question se compose des quatre mots suivants : הַיּוֹבְלִים Jos. vi, 4,
יוֹבְלִים ibid. 6, היובלים ibid. 8, היובלים ibid. 13. L'équivalent
hébreu de מְשַׁנֵּי est מְחַלֵּף q. v. Voyez la variante de la rubrique
ci-dessus dans Ginsb., *Mass.*, II, p. 220, n° 431 a. — 2° *Qui diffèrent les uns des autres.* Exemple, Mm. Num. xx, 16, à propos de
וַיֹּצִאֵנוּ : ג וּמְשַׁנְיָין בִּכְתַבְהוֹן, *se rencontre 3 fois* [ici et Deutér.
vi, 21; xxvi, 8] *et (les trois) diffèrent les uns des autres dans leur
écriture* [orthographe].

מִשְׁתַּנְּיָן (a.), plur. de מִשְׁתַּנֵּי, *qui diffèrent les uns des autres.*
Exemple, Mm. Ex. xvii, 7, à propos de מַסָּה : ב שׁוֹם קַרְתָּא וּמִשְׁתַּנְיַן
חַד כְּתִיב ס׳ וְחַד כְּתִיב ש׳, *deux fois comme nom de ville, et ils diffèrent l'un de l'autre; l'un est écrit avec* ס, *et l'autre avec* ש

מִשְׁנֵה תּוֹרָה (h.), *Répétition de la Loi,* c.-à-d. *le Deutéronome.*
Exemple, Mp. Deutér. xii, 1. Voyez aussi *Rev. Bibl.* 1902, p. 561,
ligne c.

מְשָׁרֵת (h.), *servant, ministre*. Appellation générique des accents con-jonctifs. Voyez שָׁרֵת.

מָתָא (a.), plur. מְתָוָן, *localité, ville;* voyez שׁוֹם.

מַתְאָם (h.), plur. מְתָאָמִין, מְתָאָמָן, *qui se redoublent*. Exemple, Mp.

Ez. xxi, 32 : ג, מִן תְּלָת מִלִּין מְתָאָמָן, 3 (*versets*) *ayant trois mots redoublés* (c.-à-d. où le même mot se trouve trois fois de suite). Comparez la même rubrique, Ginsb., *Mass.*, II, p. 223, n° 434 : מְשַׁלֵּשׁ. Cf. ג. פְּסוּקִין דְּאִית בְּהוֹן ג מִלִּין מוּתְאָמִין.

מְתִין (a.), *lent*. Se dit dans le langage des phrases mnémotechniques d'un mot qui n'est pas uni au mot suivant par le Maqqeph, quand ailleurs il l'est, étant alors appelé זְרִיז. Ainsi Mm. et Mmarg.

Ps. cv, 28 : שְׁלוּחֵי דְמַלְכָּא זְרִיזִין שְׁלוּחֵי דַחֲשׁוֹכָא מְתִינִין, *les messagers du roi sont prompts, les messagers des ténèbres sont lents*. Ce qui veut dire que le mot שָׁלַח, verset 20, est réuni au mot sui-vant *roi* par un Maqqeph, comme dans certains exemplaires (1), ou, en tout cas, que rien n'affaiblit le pouvoir conjonctif de l'accent Mûnāch, tandis que dans le v. 28 le même mot, non seulement reste de toute manière sans Maqqeph devant le mot *ténèbres*, mais encore, comme dans certaines éditions (2), le Mûnāch y est en partie paralysé par la présence d'un Mērekhā (= Ga῾yā eupho-nique). Voyez זְרִיז 1° et חָטֵף 3°. — De même Mmarg. Lev. xxv, 55 כִּי־לִי est זְרִיז, tandis que כִּי לִי (Num. viii, 17) est מְתִין.

מִתְחַלֵּף (h.), plur. מִתְחַלְּפִין. 1° *Qui diffèrent l'un de l'autre*. Exem-ples, Mm. Lev. xxiii, 12 : י"ג זוֹגִין מִתְחַלְּפִין בְּטַעְמָא בְּעִנְיָנָא, *13 paires (de mots, les deux mots de chaque paire) différant l'un de l'autre par l'accent, dans le même contexte*. Cf. Ginsb., *Mass.*, I, p. 62, 6n° 126 et n° 127 a, où, au lieu de מִתְחַלְּפִים, on lit מְשׁוּנִּים; voyez מְשׁוּנֶּה. — Mm. Ex. v, 17 à propos de l'expression נִזְבְּחָה : חַד מִן ה זוֹגִין מִתְחַלְּפִין קַדְמָאָה אֱלֹהִים תִּנְיָן נָא יי : לַיהוָה, *une de 5 paires (d'expressions, les deux expressions de chaque paire) différant l'une de l'autre, la première ayant* אֱלֹהִים, *la seconde ayant* יהוָה. L'équivalent araméen de מִתְחַלְּפִים est מִשְׁתַּנַּין q. v. 2° D'après Fr., sb v., מִתְהַלֵּף veut encore dire *faire exception* (à

(1 Voyez l'édition de Ginsburg. *loc. cit.*, note.

2 Par exemple Mantoue, 1742. Dans la Bible Rabbinique de De Gara, il y a Tiphcha au lieu de Mērekhā; dans celle de Buxtorf, le Mûnāch est seul; de même dans l'édition de Ginsburg (et pas de note!).

une règle). Il faut remarquer toutefois que la rubrique qu'il cite Mm. Ex. xxi, 35 est certainement erronée. Au lieu de זוֹגִין ג׳׳ר מִתְחַלְּפִין qui provient d'une confusion avec une autre rubrique, Mm. Lev. xi. 12 (voyez Wickes, *Pr. Acc.*, p. 108 , il est probable qu'il faut lire, comme dans le *Dikduke ha-Ṭeʻâmîm* (édit. Baer et Strack, p. 21), מְחַלְּפִין פְּסוּקִים ר׳׳ג, *13 versets s'écartent de la règle*, c.-à-d. *y font exception*). Cette explication est d'ailleurs confirmée par la variante חוֹלְקִים עַל, *qui combattent* (la règle) que l'on trouve dans le cod. K (Copenhag., Cod. Hebr. n° 15, 4°) du *Dikduke ha-Ṭeʻâmîm* (*loc. cit.*).

מַתְחִיל (a.) et מַתְחִיל (h.), *qui commence.* Exemple, Ginsb., *Mass.*, II. p. 215, n° 422 : ז פְּסוּקִין מַתְחִילִין בְּמִלָּה דְסוֹף פָּסוּק דִּלְעֵיל מִיּנַּיהּ מוֹסִיף וַו, *il y a 7 versets qui commencent* (*chacun*) *par le mot de la fin du verset précédent* (littéral. *d'au-dessus*), *ajoutant Waw* (*au commencement*). Voyez aussi תְּחִלָּה.

מַתְקְלַיָּא (a.), plur. déterm. de מַתְקְלָא, *poids.* Exemple. Ginsb., *Mass.*. I, p. 213, n° 214. où, à propos de גֵּרָא (nom d'homme). il est remarqué : מַתְקְלַיָּא וּבְעִירָא כְתִיב הֵא, *poids et animal. écrit avec* הֵא (c.-à-d. גֵּרָה I. *rumination.* II. espèce de *poids*).

נ

נְדָרִים (h.), la section des *Vœux* dans le Pentateuque, Num. xxx, 2 suiv. Exemples, Mp. Jos. ix, 9 ; Jerem. vi, 24.

נְהַרְדְּעָאֵי, *académiciens de la ville de Nehardéa'.* Voyez סוּרָאֵי.

נְזִיקִין, les *Dommages*, nom d'un ordre de la Mischna et d'un traité du Talmud. D'après Fr., sb v., ce mot désigne, en style Massorétique. le livre de l'Exode et, en particulier, les chapitres xxi et xxii. Exemple, Mm. Gen. xxiv, 8.

נָחִית (a.), *qui descend.* 1° Dans le langage des Sēmānîn, ou expressions mnémotechniques, désignation des *accents inférieurs.* Voyez sous לְמַטָּה. Cf. Mm. Num. vi, 9, et I Chron. xviii, 3 ; O. W. O. 228.

2° *Rabattu, retourné en bas.* se dit de la couronne du Lāmedh, Ginsb.. *Mass.*, II, p. 94, n° 5 : ל דַּאֲרִיךְ קַדְלֵיהוֹן וְתַגֵּיהוֹן נָחֵית מִן קַדְלֵיהוֹן (2) וּבַהֲדֵי (1 קַדְלֵיהוֹן מַחֵית לִתְחַת כְּרֵישֵׁיהּ דִּיוֹד. *Lāmedhs dont le*

---

(1) Par erreur nous avons dit plus haut sous בַּהֲדֵי que ce mot était suivi de ד et nous avons, en conséquence, traduit *tandis que;* בַּהֲדֵי dans ce cas-ci semble être adverbe.

(2) On remarquera le fait que les adjectifs et les participes de cette note sont tous au

col est allongé et dont la couronne est rabattue de leur col, et dont
en même temps le col rabaisse (la tête?) en bas (et en avant de manière à la faire paraître *comme un Yôdh* qui suivrait le Lāmedh).
נָסִיב (a.), déterm. נָסְבָא, plur. נָסְבִין, נָסְבָן, *qui prend,* se dit 1° d'un
mot dont la première lettre appartient au mot précédent, ou la
dernière au mot suivant. Exemple Mf. 15 כת : גּ [מִלִּין] תֵּיבוּתָא
(lisez תְּנְיֵיתָא) קַדְמֵיתָא נָסְבָא מִן תִּנְיֵינָא, *il y a trois expressions*
dont le premier mot prend (sa dernière lettre) du suivant. Cf. Ginsb.,
Mass., II, 54, n° 485. Voyez sous דְּחִיק 2° une autre manière d'exprimer la même chose. — 2° De mots qui reçoivent telles ou telles lettres, généralement serviles, mais quelquefois aussi radicales, où tout
au moins faisant fonction de lettres radicales. Exemples : A. Let-
tres serviles : Mf. ר 56 : לָא קַדְמָאָ[ה] וְ בְּעִנְיָן ר' נָסֵיב תִּנְיֵינָא זוֹגִין ד'
נָסֵיב ר', *4 paires, le second (mot de chaque paire) recevant* ו, *tandis*
que le premier ne reçoit pas ו *dans le (même) contexte* (par exemple,
Gen. xiv, 1 אַמְרָפֶל, et ibid. 9 וְאַמְרָפֶל). Dans ce même sens la Massore dit aussi מְשַׁמֵּשׁ q. v., de même qu'au lieu de לָא נָסֵיב elle dit
aussi חָסֵר q. v. — B. Lettres radicales : Mmarg. Ex. v, 7, il est
remarqué que חַד מִן מ"ח מִלִּין נָסְבִין א' בְּמִצַּע תֵּיבוּתָא תֵּאסְפוּן est
לָא קָרְיַין. *une de 48 expressions qui prennent* א *à l'intérieur du*
mot (et) ne le lisent pas. Voyez Ginsb., *Mass.,* I, p. 11, n° 18 b; et
comparez le n° 18 a, où à peu près la même chose est exprimée
en d'autres termes : חֹ אַלְפִין בִּשְׁמוּאֵל כְּתִיבִין בְּמִצִיעַ מִלִּין וְלָא
קָרְיַין, *huit Alephs dans Samuel sont écrits au milieu des mots et*
ne sont pas lus. — 3° D'expressions qui contiennent un certain mot.
Ex., Mp. Gen. xvii, 24 : גּ זוֹגִין קַדְמָאָה לָא נָסֵב אֶת תִּנְיָן נָסֵב אֶת,
il y a trois paires (d'expressions), la première (expression de chaque
paire) ne recevant pas אֶת, *la seconde recevant* אֶת (par exemple :
Gen. xvii, 24 בְּהִמֹּלוֹ אֶת וגו') et ibid. 25 בְּהִמֹּלוֹ בְּשַׂר עָרְלָתוֹ).
Dans ce cas encore la Massore emploie aussi le terme מְשַׁמֵּשׁ;
voyez ce mot, 2°.

---

singulier, quoique les substantifs auxquels ils se rapportent soient au pluriel. Cette note se retrouve dans l'extrait du *Badde Aron* publié par Bargès (*Sepher Taghin,* Paris, 1866, p. 39)
sans autre différence que דנֲחִית fautif pour נֲחִית; מֻחתי fautif aussi très probablement pour
מֻחִית et לתחות plus correct que לתחת.

י׳ נְקֻדּוֹת נָקַד ‏(h.), *marquer d'un point.* Exemple, O. W. O. 96 : נָקַד
עֶזְרָא בַּתּוֹרָה וְד׳ בַּנְּבִיאִים וְא׳ בַּכְּתוּבִים, *Esdras a marqué 10 points
(extraordinaires) dans la Loi, et 4 dans les Prophètes et 1 dans les
Hagiographes.*

נְקֻדָּה ‏(h.), *point.* Se dit 1° des *points extraordinaires.* Voyez le
précédent, et cf. Mm. Num. iii, 39, Ginsb., *Mass.*, II, p. 296, n° 521 ;
— 2° des points dont sont formés certains points-voyelles. Exemples,
Ginsb., *Mass.*, I, p. 272, n° 44 : כָּל קְרִיָה (?קְרִיָה) כָּל סָמוּךְ מִתְקְרִי
בִּשְׁתֵּי נְקֻדּוֹת כְּמוֹ מַחֲנֵה אֱלֹהִים וג׳ וְכָל מוּכְרַת בִּשְׁלֹשׁ נְקֻדּוֹת
כְּמוֹ אִם־תַּחֲנֶה עָלַי מַחֲנֶה, *dans toute lecture (à haute voix)? tout
mot à l'état construit se lit avec deux points comme* מַחֲנֵה אֱלֹהִים
(Gen. xxxii, 3), *et tout mot à l'état absolu, avec trois points comme*
אִם־תַּחֲנֶה עָלַי מַחֲנֶה ‏(Ps. xxvii, 3). Voyez aussi שִׁשָּׁה.

נַקְדִּימוֹן, *Nicodème,* d'après Fr., sb v., nom d'un Massorète ou Naqdān.
N'ayant pas rencontré ce mot, nous ne pouvons qu'enregistrer
l'assertion de Fr. confirmée d'ailleurs par celle de Worms, סְיָיג
לַתּוֹרָה, sb v.

ס

סְבִיר ‏(a.), plur. סְבִירִים, partic. passif du verbe סְבַר, *comprendre,
penser.* Se dit de leçons qui paraissent suspectes et qu'on est tenté
de corriger. Ce terme est, pour cette raison, souvent accompagné
de מַטְעַיִן בֵּיהּ (בְּהוֹן) סָפְרִין ; voyez מַטְעַיִן. Exemples, Mm. Gen. xix,
22 : ג׳ סְבִירִין יָצְאָה וּקְרַיָין יָצָא. 3 *(mots) sont pensés (devoir être
lus)* יָצְאָה *mais sont lus* יָצָא. La Mp. Ex. xxiii, 13, à propos de
וּבְכֹל, remarque : ה׳ דִּמַטְעָיָן דִּסְבִירִין וְכֹל, 5 *(dans lesquels les
scribes) nous induisent en erreur, parce qu'ils* (les 6 וּבְכֹל) *sont
pensés (devoir être)* וְכֹל. — Au lieu de סְבִירִין on trouve souvent
חֲמַיִין q. v.

סַגִּין ‏(a.), plur. absol. de סַגִּי, *beaucoup, nombreux.* Précédé de לִישָׁן,
le *laschon de nombreux,* c.-à-d. *le pluriel.* Exemple, Mf. בא 9, à
propos de וַיָּבֹא, remarque : ח׳ קְרַיִין לִישָׁן חַד וּחֲמַיִין לִישָׁן סַגִּין
בְּלִישָׁנָא, 8 *sont lus au singulier, mais paraissent (devoir être lus)
au pluriel du laschon (venir).*

סֶדֶר (h.), plur. סְדָרִים, et סִדְרָא (a.), plur. סִדְרִין, *section de la Bible,*
leçon hebdomadaire. Suivant certains manuscrits provenant du Yemen (Voyez Ginsb., *Introduction,* p. 32) (1), les Sedārîm sont à proprement parler les sections de la Bible du cycle triennal qui était
en usage en Palestine, et d'après lequel le Pentateuque était divisé
en 154, 158 ou 167 leçons hebdomadaires (le nombre variait suivant
les écoles), tandis que la division en Pārāschiyōth appartenait au
cycle annuel ou babylonien où l'on divisait le Pentateuque en 54 sections. Voyez פָּרָשָׁה. La division en Sedārîm est la plus ancienne et
s'étendait à toute la Bible, tandis que les Pārāschiyōth semblent
n'avoir jamais existé que pour le Pentateuque. Toutefois, dans l'u-
sage des Synagogues, le cycle babylonien supplanta de bonne heure
celui de Palestine et la division en Sedārîm ne fut plus guère qu'un
souvenir. Jacob ben-Chayim nous apprend dans son Haqdāmā, ou
Préface à son édition de la Bible Massorétique, qu'il ne retrouva cette
division que lorsque son ouvrage était presque terminé, en sorte
que pour les renvois aux autres livres de la Bible que ceux du Pentateuque, il dut avoir recours à la division chrétienne en Chapitres, comme Rabbi Isaac Nathan l'avait déjà fait dans sa *Concordance.* Voyez סִימָן. « Cependant, ajoute-t-il, je l'ai publiée aussi de
crainte qu'elle ne fût perdue pour Israël ». On la trouvera en tête
du volume I à la suite de la division en chapitres sous le titre suivant : אִילֵין סִדְרֵי הַתּוֹרָה וּנְבִיאִים וּכְתוּבִים עַל פִּי הַמָּסוֹרָה, *voici
les sections de la Loi et des Prophètes et des Hagiographes, suivant
la Massore.* Toutefois il est à présumer que les sections palesti-
niennes n'étaient pas inconnues des Massorètes dont Ben-Chayim a
systématisé les travaux. Nous en avons là preuve dans une rubrique, Mm. Num. III, 23 où nous lisons : וְכָל סִדְרָא תְּלִיתָאָה דְּדִבְרֵי
הַיָּמִים מִן וְאַהֲרֹן וּבָנָיו עַד בְּנֵי אוּלָם, *et toute la troisième section des
Chroniques depuis* וְאַהֲרֹן וג״ (premiers mots du Sēder III = I Chron.
VI, 34 *jusqu'à* בְּנֵי וג״ (premiers mots du Sēder IV = I Chron. VII,
17). C'est probablement dans ce même sens que la Mp. Lev. III, 4,
emploie l'expression בְּסִדְרָא. *dans cette même section.* De même,
encore, Ps. LXVII, 21, où elle dit : אֵלֶּה מַסְעֵי בְּרֵישׁ סִדְרָא,
'Ellé Maseʿê, au commencement de la section, quoique ces mots

(1) On lira avec fruit sur la question des Sedarim J. Derenbourg, *Manuel du Lecteur,*
note IV (*Journal Asiatique,* Série VI, vol. XVI, p. 529).

soient aussi le commencement d'une Pārāschā babylonienne.
Le mot סֵדֶר, ou סִדְרָא, se rencontre aussi fréquemment dans les
renvois de Ben-Chayim au Pentateuque, mais toujours dans le sens
de פָּרָשָׁה q. v. Exemples, Mm. Deuter. xi, 25 : נִמְסָר בְּסֵדֶר פְּקֻדֵי,
donné dans la Pārāschā Peqūdhê (Ex. xxxviii, 21-xl, 38); Ex. xviii,
12 : נִמְסָר בְּסֵדֶר וַיְחִי, *donné dans la Pārāschā Wayechi* (Gen. xlvii,
28-l, 26); ibid. : נִמְסָר בְּרֵישׁ סִדְרָא דְנֹחַ, *donné au commencement*
de la Pārāschā de Noach (Gen. vi, 9-xi, 32). De nombreux exemples de ce genre nous autorisent à traduire encore סֵדֶר de la même
manière dans des cas comme le suivant, Mm. Deut. ix, 26 : נִמְסָר
לְעֵיל בְּרֵישׁ סִדְרָא אַחֲרִיתִי, *donné plus haut au commencement de*
l'autre [c.-à-d. *de la précédente*] *Pārāschā.*

סַחֲזוּפֵי (a.), infin. Paʿel de סָחַף, *renverser, retourner* (sens dessus
dessous); substantivement, *renversement,* nom, assez rare d'ailleurs,
de l'accent Athnach. Pour l'explication du terme, voyez Wickes.
Pr. acc., p. 16, d'après qui ce nom appartiendrait au système
d'accentuation babylonien. Exemple, Mp. Lev. xviii, 15, à propos de
כָּל סָחֹזוּפֵי בְּצֵרֵי : תִגְלֶה, *tout Athnach a Ṣêrê.* Il est étrange que
Wickes, *op. et loc. cit.,* citant ce même passage de la Massore de
Ben-Chayim, ne donne que la forme סָחְפָא. Voyez סִיחֲפָא. Peut-
être devrions-nous ponctuer סְחוּפֵי, et אַסְחוּפֵי (au lieu de אַסְחֹזוּפֵי
q. v.), comp. le syriaque ܣܘܚܦܐ. A propos de la forme אסחופי,
nous nous demandons où Fr. (sb v.) peut bien l'avoir prise.

סִיחֲפָא (a.), *renversement,* nom de l'accent Athnach dans un manuscrit de la Massore, provenant de Tchoufoutkaleh, Ginsb., *Mass.,* III,
p. 246 a. Sur d'autres exemples, consultez Wickes, *Pr. acc.,* p. 16,
note 25. Voyez le précédent.

סוֹפָא (a.) [abs. et constr. סוֹף | et סוֹף (h.), *fin* d'un mot, d'un ver-
set, etc. בְּסוֹף, *à la fin.* Exemple, Mf. ה : בְּסוֹף תֵּבוּתָא, *à la fin du*
mot; ... בְּסוֹף סֵדֶר, *à la fin de la section...* et ainsi très fréquemment. סוֹפָא peut aussi se prendre adjectivement, *qui est à la fin.*
Exemple, Mm. Eccle. i, 4 (lisez : פְּסוּקִים) מִין סוֹפֵי תֵבוֹת *mots,*
fins de versets.

סוֹפָה (h.), même sens : Exemple, Mf. ר 58 : קַדְמָאָה סוֹפָה, *le pre-*
mier (sa) *fin est* etc.

סִימָן (σημεῖον?), plur. סִימָנִין, *signe* et, en langage massorétique,
1° *Phrases mnémotechniques*. Ces phrases mnémotechniques, ou
Sēmāns, sont très variés. Quelques-uns sont en hébreu, d'autres en
araméen. Voici quelques exemples des uns et des autres. A) Sēmāns
hébreux (généralement des versets de la Bible). La Massore voulant
rappeler que les mots אֶת כָּל־עֹרֵב וג' se présentent deux fois, d'abord
sans ו (Lev. xi, 15), ensuite avec ו (Deut. xiv, 14), donne comme
signe le verset Gen. i. 1, où l'on rencontre d'abord אֵת, puis וְאֵת
(Voyez *Rev. Bibl.* 1902, p. 561, *Ligne* c. — Dans Ginsb., *Mass.*, II,
p. 346, n° 290, nous trouvons le verset Jos. ii, 9 où on lit d'abord כִּי,
puis, deux fois de suite, וְכִי, comme Sēmān des passages suivants
כִּי יָמוּךְ (Lev. xxv, 25) et וְכִי יָמוּךְ (ibid., 35 et 39). — Ibid., p. 357,
n° 464, le verset Ex. xxx, 32 qui contient les mots עַל בְּשַׂר אָדָם est
donné comme Sēmān des passages מַה־יַּעֲשֶׂה בָשָׂר לִי (Ps. lvi, 5) et
מַה־יַּעֲשֶׂה אָדָם לִי (ibid., 12). — Mmarg. Lev. xix, 5 les lettres שׁ"ת,
probablement lues שֵׁת (nom d'un patriarche), sont le Sēmān des expressions תִּזְבְּחוּ זֶבַח תּוֹדָה (Lev. xix, 5) et תִּזְבְּחוּ זֶבַח שְׁלָמִים
(ibid., xxii, 29).·— On peut classer dans cette catégorie les Sēmāns
que les Massorètes ont imaginés pour rappeler le nombre des sections dans chaque livre, et des versets dans chaque section du
Pentateuque, aussi le nombre des versets dans chaque livre de la
Bible, dans le Pentateuque et dans la Bible entière. Le Sēmān est
généralement un nom propre, hébreu ou araméen, emprunté à n'importe quel livre, ou plus rarement un ou plusieurs mots pris dans
la section même. La somme des valeurs numériques des lettres du
Sēmān donne le nombre des versets, ou des sections. Celui-ci, d'ailleurs, précède toujours le Sēmān, soit en toutes lettres, soit en lettres-
chiffres. Quelquefois le Sēmān a été perdu ; il est alors remplacé par
l'expression numérique en lettres-chiffres qui reçoit elle-même le
nom de Sēmān. Exemples, à la fin de la Genèse : חֲזַק · סְכוּם פְּסוּקֵי
דְסֵפֶר בְּרֵאשִׁית אֶלֶף וַחֲמֵשׁ מֵאוֹת וּשְׁלֹשִׁים וְאַרְבָּעָה וְסִימָן א"ך
ל"ד : וְחָצְיוֹ וְעַל חַרְבְּךָ תִחְיֶה : וּפָרְשִׁיּוֹתָיו י"ב אח"אב סִימָן
וְסִדְרָיו מ"ג יְדִידְיָה סִימָן · וְאוֹתִיּוֹתָיו ד' אֲלָפִים וּשְׁלֹשׁ מֵאוֹת
וְתִשְׁעִים וַחֲמִשָּׁה, *Bravo! Le total des versets du livre de la Genèse
est mille cinq cent trente-quatre, et le Sēmān en est 1534, et le milieu
(du livre) est (le verset) : « et de ton glaive tu vivras » (Gen.*

xxvii, 40); *et ses Pārāschiyôths sont 12,* Achab (אַחְאָב = 1 + 8 +
1 + 2) *en est le Sᵉmān; et ses Sedārim sont 43;* Yedîdyā (ידידיה
= 10 + 4 + 10 + 4 + 10 + 5) *en est le Sᵉmān; et ses lettres sont
4 mille trois cent quatre-vingt-quinze.* Il n'est pas rare qu'à la fin d'une
Pārāschā on trouve deux (ou même plusieurs) Sᵉmāns. Exemple, Pārāschā לְךָ לָךְ (Gen. xii, 1 — xvii, 27) : סִימָן מכנ״דבי נמ״לי קכ״ו
סִימָן, *126;* « ils se firent circoncire » (Gen. xvii, 27, נִמֹּלוּ = 50 +
40 + 30 + 6) *en est le Sᵉmān;* Makhnaddebhay (Esdr. x, 40, מִכְנַדְבַי
= 40 + 20 + 50 + 4 + 2 + 10) *en est le Sᵉmān.* B) Sᵉmāns
araméens. — Mp. Gen. xviii, 4, la Massore ayant remarqué que
יְקַח (ou יִקַּח) se rencontre trois fois, ajoute, pour nous rappeler
les trois passages : וְסִימָן מוֹי דְּגִבְּרָא פַּרְזְלָא. *et le Sᵉmān est :*
l'eau du brave (c'est) le fer. L'eau c'est Gen. xviii, 4 יֻקַּח־נָא מְעַט;
מַיִם; le *brave,* c'est Isaïe xlix, 25 גַּם־שְׁבִי גִבּוֹר יֻקָּח: le *fer* c'est
Job xxviii, 2 בַּרְזֶל מֵעָפָר יֻקָּח. De même Mmarg. Lev. xxvii, 18,
après avoir remarqué que dans ce verset nous lisons וְחִשַּׁב־לוֹ
הַכֹּהֵן אֶת־הַכֶּסֶף, *et le prêtre lui comptera l'argent,* avec l'accent
Azelā sur הַכֹּהֵן, tandis que dans le verset 23 on trouve וְחִשַּׁב־לוֹ
הַכֹּהֵן אֶת־מִכְסַת, *et le prêtre lui comptera le montant de la
somme,* avec Rebhîā sur le même mot, la Massore ajoute ce sᵉ-
mān : כֹּהֵן דְּכַסְפָּא אֲזַל כֹּהֵן דְּחֻשְׁבָּנָא רְבַע. *le prêtre de l'argent
a marché, le prêtre du montant de la somme s'est accroupi. A marché,* et *s'est accroupi* rappellent les accents Azelā (*le marcheur*)
et Rebhîā (*l'accroupi*). Voyez d'autres exemples sous זָרִיז, חָזַק,
et לְמַטָּה.

2° *Passages,* ou *versets auxquels s'applique une rubrique.* Du signe
à la chose signifiée la transition est toute naturelle; le mot סִימָן ou
plutôt son pluriel סִימָנִים prit bientôt le sens de *passages, versets*
où se rencontrent les exemples du mot que vise la Massore. Dans
ce sens, on le rencontre à chaque pas dans la Mm. en tête des
listes d'exemples; généralement sous la forme abrégée וסימ״
(= וְסִימָנֵיהוֹן), *et leurs sᵉmāns* (c.-à-d. leurs passages) *sont.* Souvent
on peut traduire plus commodément par *et la liste* ou *et leur liste.*
Plus souvent encore (quand les passages suivent immédiatement)
par *à savoir.* C'est dans le même sens que Jacob ben-Chayim em-

ploie le mot סִימָנִים dans le titre de la liste des chapitres chrétiens de la Bible qu'il donne en tête du volume I de sa Bible Rabbinique : (1) וְזֶה לְךָ מִסְפַּר הַפָּרָשִׁיוֹת שֶׁעֲלֵיהֶם נִרְשְׁמוּ הַסִּימָנִים, *voici* (littér. *ceci est pour toi*) *là liste des sections dans lesquelles les passages cités ont été enregistrés.*

3° *Chapitres.* De la chose signifiée, c'est-à-dire des passages cités à l'appui de la rubrique, le mot סִימָן fut ensuite étendu par Jacob ben-Chayim aux sections où les passages se trouvaient enregistrés, c'est-à-dire à nos chapitres, dont il fut obligé de se servir (voyez sous סֵדֶר) pour tous les livres de la Bible à l'exception du Pentateuque. Exemple, Mm. Ex. xii, 29 : סִימָן נִמ[וֹסָר] בִּירְמְיָ[ה] ל"ז גַּבֵּי פָּרָשַׁת וַיֵּצֵא יִרְמְיָהוּ מִירוּשָׁלַ͏ִם, *donné* (*enregistré*) *dans Jérémie, chapitre 37, au verset :* « *Et Jérémie sortit de Jérusalem* ». Et ainsi à chaque pas quand Ben-Chayim nous renvoie d'un endroit quelconque de la Bible aux Prophètes ou aux Hagiographes, ou de la Mf. à la Mm.

4° D'après Fr., sb v. (qui copie presque Buxtorf, *Tib.*, sb v.), le mot סִימָן se rencontre encore seul dans la Mp. pour attirer l'attention sur une forme particulière d'un mot ou d'une expression. Ce serait comme un point d'exclamation (*so viel als ein Ausrufungszeichen oder Gedankenstrich*) que la Massore laisserait au lecteur le soin d'interpréter. Mais après avoir examiné soigneusement chacun des exemples cités par Frensdorff et son prédécesseur, nous croyons pouvoir affirmer que ces savants sont tous les deux dans l'erreur. Le mot סִימָן a dans ce cas le sens que nous avons expliqué sous le 1° et la Mp. en l'employant tout seul nous avertit que le passage en face duquel il se trouve est l'objet d'une rubrique *accompagnée d'une expression mnémotechnique*, que l'on trouvera en général dans la Mmarg. soit un peu avant soit un peu après en face d'un autre passage analogue. Voici quelques exemples : Mp. Lev. xxiii, 19 en face de וַעֲשִׂיתֶם nous lisons סִימָן, mais Mmarg. ibid. v. 23, où ce mot s'est déjà rencontré, nous lisons sous le titre de וַעֲשִׂיתֶם une rubrique qui se rapporte à ces deux passages, suivie d'un Sēmān. De même Mp. Lev. xxvii, 23, en face de הַכֹּהֵן לוֹ, סִימָן, et Mmarg. ibid. 18 sous le titre de הַכֹּהֵן לוֹ, la rubrique et le Sēmān (voyez plus haut 1°). De même encore Mp. Num. iv, 7, en face de וּפֵרְשׂוּ, סִימָן, et

---

(1) Comparez l'explicit de cette même liste où au lieu de סִימָנִים on lit פְּסוּקִים, *versets* (*cités*).

Mmarg. ibid. 11, la rubrique et le Sēmān. Il arrive quelquefois que le Sēmān fait défaut à la suite de la rubrique; mais il est bien probable que c'est là une omission de l'éditeur ou du manuscrit qu'il a suivi, et que dans quelque autre source on trouverait le signe mnémotechnique, comme cela nous est arrivé plusieurs fois, par exemple Mmarg. Lev. xxv, 25, où la Mp. ibid. nous renvoie par le mot סִימָן, à propos de l'expression וְכִי יָמוּךְ. nous ne trouvons que la rubrique (assez fautive d'ailleurs; il faut la corriger d'après O. W. O. 239), mais dans Ginsb., *Mass.* (voyez plus haut sous 1º), nous trouvons le Sēmān qui avait été omis dans la Massore Imprimée par un copiste négligent ou ignorant. Dans d'autres cas la rubrique elle-même fait défaut dans la Mmarg.; par exemple Mp. Ps. LVI, 5 et 12, a dans les deux cas סִימָן en face de יַעֲשֶׂה וג׳. tandis que la Mmarg. est muette aux deux endroits; mais que ce soit encore une omission, on peut s'en convaincre par Ginsb., *Mass.*, où nous trouvons la rubrique et le Sēmān (voyez plus haut 1º).

Il faut avouer que cette partie de la Massore Imprimée est très défectueuse. Il semble que l'éditeur lui-même n'ait pas saisi le rapport de la Mp. à la Mmarg. et qu'il ait copié l'une et l'autre comme si elles n'eussent eu rien de commun. La *page de la Massore* que nous avons publiée en tête de ce travail, d'après un manuscrit du ixe siècle, fait foi que ce rapport est un fait ancien. Il est à regretter que Frensdorff et Ginsburg n'aient tenu, pour ainsi dire, aucun compte de la Mmarg.

סִינַי (ponctuat. incertaine), nom d'un manuscrit fameux. Exemple, Mmarg. Ex. xviii, 1, à propos de וישמע : ר״פ גְּרִישִׁין שְׁנֵי בְּטַעַם ב, בְּתוֹרָה סִינַי רְבִיעַ, *2 (fois) avec l'accent Deux-Gēreschs* (Gerschayin) *au commencement du verset* (ר״פ = פָּסוּק רֵישׁ). *dans la Tōrāh Sīnay* (?) *avec Rebhî'ā.* Voyez sur ce codex Ginsb., *Introduction*, pp. 433 et suiv.

סֵיפָא (a.), *fin;* dans le même sens que סוֹפָא q. v. Exemple. Mf. סֵף ט״ו פְּסוּקִים רֵישֵׁיהוֹן וְסוֹפֵיהוֹן מִלָּה חֲדָא · רֵישָׁא נָסֵיב ו״יו : 12 וְסֵיפָא לָא נָסֵיב ו״יו. *15 versets commencent et finissent par le même mot; (au) commencement il prend Waw, (à la) fin il ne prend pas Waw.* Cf. Mm. et Mmarg. I Reg. xxii, 48.

סוּרָאֵי (a.), *habitants, gens* (académiciens) *de Sūrā,* ville fameuse par son académie. Exemple, Mmarg. Deut. xxxii, 6, à propos de הֲלֹיהוָֹה : לְסוּרָאֵי ה׳ לְחֹד לֵיהוֹה לִנְהַרְדְּעֵי (לִנְהַרְדְּעָאֵי lisez) הֲל לְחֹד

יְהוָה לְחוֹד לְסִפְרֵי אֲחֵרִים חֲדָא מִלְתָא, *suivant les académiciens de Sûra,* ה *séparément et* לַיהוָה *séparément; suivant les académiciens de Nehardéa',* הַל *séparément et* יהוה *séparément; suivant d'autres livres,* (en) *un seul mot* (1).

סָלֵיק (a.), *qui monte.* Dans le langage des signes mnémotechniques, désignation de certains accents placés au-dessus des lettres; opposé de נָחֵית q. v. Voyez un exemple sous לְמַטָּה.

סָלְקֵי וְנָחְתֵי (a.), pluriel de סָלֵיק et de נָחֵית, *qui montent et qui descendent.* Se dit: 1° de certains versets où l'accent disjonctif Zarqā est précédé de Mērekhā comme serviteur unique, au lieu de Mùnāch. Ainsi dans Ginsb., *Mass.,* I, p. 645, n° 181 b : י׳ פִּיסוּקִין סָלְקִין וְנָחְתִין בְּטַעַם, *il y a 10 versets qui montent et qui descendent dans l'accent.* Cf. Mm. Ex. VI, 6, et voyez, en tout cas, Wickes, *Pr. acc.,* p. 109. — 2° De versets où Zarqā est précédé de Mērekhā (au lieu de Mùnāch) comme second serviteur, le premier étant Azelā. Exemple, Mm. XXXVI, 3 : חַד מִן י׳ח דְּסָלְקִי וְנָחְתֵי פֵּירוּשׁ[חַד מִן י׳ח מָאיילוֹן מָאֲרִיכִין בֵּין אָזְלָא לְזַרְקָא וג׳. *un de dix-huit qui montent et descendent, c'est-à-dire un de 18 qui ont ..... Mērekhā entre Azelā et Zarqā.* Voyez Wickes, *Pr. acc.,* p. 110. [Le mot מָאיילוֹן que nous n'avons pas traduit ne peut que vouloir dire *marqués* de Māyelā. Mais ce terme ne peut avoir ici son sens ordinaire; voyez מָאיילָא. Frensdorff sb v., si toutefois nous l'avons bien compris, affirme que dans ce cas Māyelā veut dire Gā'yā (Methegh). Mais Wickes, *Pr. acc.,* p. 27, note 77, soupçonne une erreur de copiste et suggère de lire מִלּין]. Dans une variante de la même rubrique, Ginsb., *Mass.,* I, p. 652, n° 228, nous lisons : כָּל אוֹרַיְיתָא זַרְקֵי וְסָלְקֵי בָּר מִן י׳ח זַרְקֵי וְנָחְתֵי, (dans) *toute la Loi,* (les versets) ont *Zarqā et montent, sauf 18 qui ont Zarqā et descendent.* Cela veut-il dire que par סָלְקֵי nous devons entendre Mùnāch qui est la règle, par opposition à Mērekhā qui est l'exception? Serait-ce une allusion au nom de עִלּוּי, *montée* (de la voix), que Mùnāch porte dans les cas comme celui qui nous occupe?

סָמוּךְ (h.), *qui est appuyé* sur, *qui est tout près* de quelque chose. 1° *Qui est à l'état construit;* dans ce sens, on dit aussi נִסְמָךְ. C'est

(1) Sur la situation des deux villes, et leurs académies, voyez Berliner, *Beiträge zur Geographie und Ethnographie Babyloniens im Talmud und Midrasch.* Cf. Ginsb., *Introduction,* p. 199.

l'opposé de מוּכְרַת q. v. Voyez un exemple sous נְקֻדָּה. — 2° a) *Qui précède ou suit immédiatement.* b) Avec בְּ (בִּסְמִיךְ), *immédiate-ment.* Exemple, Mmarg. Lev. xxi, 17, à propos de מוּם לֹא יִקְרָב v. 17 et מוּם לֹא יִקְרָב v. 18, il est remarqué : בְּהָדֵין עִנְיָנָא דְקוֹדְמוֹ (וְדִקְוֹדְמִי lisez) בִּסְמוּךְ מוּם לֹא יִקְרָב וּשְׁאָרָא לֹא יִגַּשׁ *dans ce contexte ce que* מוּם *précède immédiatement est* לֹא יִקְרָב (v. 17 et 18), *le reste* (c.-à-d. *les passages où* מוּם *ne précède pas immédiatement*) *est* לֹא יִגַּשׁ (v. 21, deux fois).

סְמִיךְ (a.), littéralement *appuyé*. Ce terme, en langage massorétique, se dit 1° dans le même sens que סָמוּךְ 2°. Exemple, Mmarg. xxxvi, 20; — 2° conjointement de deux ou plusieurs mots qui se suivent immédiatement dans un certain ordre. Si ces mots ne se retrouvent plus ainsi, la Massore dit, *au singulier,* de l'expression entière : לֵית דִּסְמִיךְ, *ne se retrouve plus (ainsi) appuyé.* Si, au contraire, ils se rencontrent deux fois ou plus souvent tels quels et dans le même ordre, elle dira, *au pluriel : דִּסְמִיכִין ג' וג' ב. ג. 2, 3* etc. *sont* (ainsi) *appuyés.* Exemple, Mp. Gen. i, 8 à יוֹם שֵׁנִי. remarque : לֵית דִּסְמִיךְ|ן, mais Mm. ibid. i, 2, à propos de תֹהוּ וָבֹהוּ : דִּסְמִיכֵי ב. Ce terme est très souvent sous-entendu, quand il est évident, par ailleurs, que la remarque massorétique porte sur deux ou plusieurs mots considérés comme un tout; par exemple dans notre planche (*Rev. Bibl.* 1902, p. 511), col. c, ligne 11.

סְמִיכָה (h.), *attitude, état de quelqu'un qui est appuyé, couché* (latin *reclinans*). Autre désignation de l'accent Athnach, exprimant comme ce dernier mot (cf. Wickes, *Pr. acc.,* p. 16) l'idée de *repos.* Le seul exemple que nous connaissions est celui que cite Fr. sb v., Mm. Gen. xlix, 27, à propos de עַד : בִּסְמִיכָה ב. *2 avec Ath-nach.* Comparez la note correspondante de la Mp. ...וּב בְּאַתְנַחְתָּא Le sens de *Pause* que suggère Fr. sb v. ne nous parait pas admissible. La Massore désignait la Pause par le terme מוּכְרַת q. v. Ne serait-il pas étrange qu'elle l'eût aussi désigné par un mot qui à d'autres égards est tout l'opposé du premier? Voyez מוּכְרַת 1° et סָמוּךְ 1°.

סִפְרָא (a.), סִיפְרָא, *livre.* Fréquent dans les expressions בְּסִפְרָא.

dans le livre; דְּסִפְרָא, *du livre;* כָּל סִפְרָא, *tout le livre,* ce qui doit toujours s'entendre du livre de la Bible auquel appartient le passage rubriqué. Il ne faut pas oublier que les deux livres des Rois ne forment qu'un seul livre; de même les deux livres de Samuel. Esdras et Néhémie ne comptent également que pour un seul livre, ainsi que les douze Petits Prophètes. D'après Fr., sb v., סִפְרָא s'emploierait aussi du Pentateuque tout entier, mais dans le passage qu'il cite, Mm. Gen. xxxvi, 20, au lieu de דספר קורין il faut lire דְּסֵפֶר תּוֹרָה comme plus bas dans la même rubrique, où, comme dans Ginsb., *Mass.*, II, p. 342, n° 216 : דְּקָרָיִן סֵפֶר תּוֹרָה, *où on lit le livre de la Loi.*

(*A suivre.*)

Université catholique d'Amérique, jour de la Chandeleur 1905.

Henry Hyvernat.

LE LANGAGE DE LA MASSORE [1]

B

Lexique massorétique (עׂ — ת)

ע

עׂוׂמֵד (h.), *qui se tient debout.* Désignation, dans le langage des signes mnémotechniques, des accents Schalschéleth (Mmarg. Lev. viii, 15) et Zāqēph (Mm. Deut. xi, 17; Mp. Lev. viii, 23).

עׂיטּוּר סׂוׂפְרִים (h.). Suivant Buxt., *Cl. Mas.*, sb v., *enlèvement* (de l'araméen עֲטַר), d'après König, *Einleitung,* etc., p. 34, *encerclement* (2) (de l'hébreu עֲטַר), [*d'une lettre superflue*] *par les Scribes.* Ni le Talmud de Babylone (*Nedhārîm*, 37 b et 38 a) où cette expression se rencontre pour la première fois, ni la Massore ne nous renseignent d'une manière directe et positive sur la signification du mot עׂטּוּר. L'un et l'autre se contentent de remarquer que, dans certains passages, il y a *'ittûr* (3) *Sōpherîm.* La Massore imprimée (Mm. Ps. xxxvi, 7; cf. Mf. עט 3) ne mentionne que quatre de ces passages, Gen. xviii, 5; Num. xxxi, 2; Ps. lxviii, 26 et Ps. xxxvi, 7. Mais d'après le Talmud, il y en avait un cinquième, Gen. xxiv, 55. Le Talmud et la Massore ne disent pas davantage sur quel mot, dans chacun de ces passages, porte la remarque *'ittûr Sōpherîm.* Mais les interprètes s'accordent à penser que dans Ps. xxxvi, 7, c'est sur le mot מִשְׁפָּטֶי (quoique la citation du Talmud ne commence qu'avec le mot suivant), et dans les autres passages, sur le mot אַחַר. Il paraîtrait qu'anciennement ces mots étaient précédés d'un Waw copulatif que les Sōpherîm auraient supprimé. Ce Waw se

---

(1) Voyez les nᵒˢ d'octobre 1902, octobre 1903, octobre 1904 et avril 1905.
(2) Pour la condamner.
(3) Toujours au singulier comme תִּיקוּן סׂוׂפְרִים q. v.

retrouve généralement dans les LXX et le Pentateuque Samaritain (Gen. xviii, 5; xxiv, 55; Num. xxxi, 2). Voyez pour plus de détail, Ginsb., *Introduction*, pp. 308 et 309; Strack, *Prolegomena*, p. 86, et les éditions critiques.

עַל (a.), *sur, à propos de.* Avec le suffixe 3ᵉ pers. masc. sing. עֲלֵיה et עֲלוֹהִי. Exemples, Mm. Eccl. vi, 10 : וְחַד פְּלִיגָא עֲלֵיה, *et à propos d'un (de ces cas), il y a désaccord;* Mf. ה 28 : וְחַד פְּלוּגְתָּא עֲלוֹהִי, *et à propos d'un (de ces cas), il y a désaccord* (Cf. Ginsb., *Mass.,* I, p. 270, nº 34 : בַּתְרָא פְּלִיגִין[ן] עֲלֵי[ה], *il y a désaccord sur le dernier).* Voyez aussi sous דְּעַל où nous avons enregistré la forme דַּעֲלוֹהִי = דַּעֲלוֹהִי, et avec le suff. 3ᵉ pers. masc. plur. דַּעֲלֵם = דַּעֲלֵהֹם (où, comme dans עֲלֵיה, le suffixe est ajouté au singulier עַל et non au pluriel עֲלֵי; peut-être aurions-nous dû ponctuer דַּעֲלֵם).

עַמָּא (a.), plur. indéterm. עַמְמִין, déterm. עַמְמַיָּא, *peuple.* Exemple, Ginsb., *Mass.,* I, p. 418, nº 126 : ג פְּסוּקִים אִית בְּהוֹן ז עַמְמִין קַדְמָא וּשְׁתִיתָאָה קָרְחֵי, *il y a 3 versets dans lesquels il y a 7 peuples* (c.-à-d. 7 noms de peuple) *dont le premier et le sixième sont chauves* (voyez קָרִיחַ).

[דַּ]עֲמּוֹן, le passage d'Amos (i, 13-18) relatif à Ammon.

עַנְיָא (a.), *misérable.* Dans le proverbe בָּתַר עַנְיָא עֲנִיוּתָא אָזְלָא, *après le misérable vient la misère* (1). On trouve ce proverbe Mmarg. Jerem. lii, 16, pour rappeler que le mot *misérable* est au singulier dans le premier, et au pluriel dans le second de deux versets qui ne diffèrent que par le nombre de ce mot, savoir II Reg. xxv, 12 : « Et du misérable (peuple) du pays », etc. et Jerem. lii, 16 : « Et des misérables (gens) du pays », etc. L'emploi du mot *misère* pour rappeler *misérables* repose sur sa nature de substantif abstrait qui le rend plus compréhensif que l'adjectif correspondant, surtout quand celui-ci est au singulier. — Quoique, dans la rubrique en question, ce proverbe araméen ne soit donné que pour confirmer ou éclaircir un sĕmân hébreu, il est assez vraisemblable qu'il ait inspiré ce-

(1) Comme par surcroît, c'est-à-dire que les malheurs du pauvre vont croissant. Ce proverbe est cité dans le Talmud de Babylone, *Baba Qamma*, 92 a. « Raba dit encore à Rabba ben-Mari : Quelle est l'origine de ce que les gens disent : la pauvreté suit le pauvre? Celui-ci répondit : Il est enseigné : les riches apportaient les prémices dans des corbeilles d'or et d'argent (qui leur étaient rendues), tandis que les pauvres les apportaient dans des corbeilles d'osier et remettaient celles-ci (aussi bien que les prémices) aux prêtres. » Comp. Matth. xiii : « ... *Qui autem non habet, etiam quod habet auferetur ab eo.* »

lui-ci, et même qu'il l'ait précédé dans la Massore comme signe mnémotechnique des deux mêmes versets. Voici le sᵉmān hébreu : דַּל בֶּן־הַמֶּלֶךְ דַּלּוּת יִרְמְיָה, *misérable est le fils du roi, misère est Jérémie*. Il paraît bien probable que דַּל soit la traduction de עַנְיָא et דַּלּוּת (à tort ponctué דַּלּוּת dans les éditions) soit celle de עֲנִיּוּתָא. La raison d'être de la substitution d'un sᵉmān artificiel au proverbe, serait que celui-ci, comme il arrive généralement pour les sᵉmāns tout faits empruntés à la Bible, ou à l'usage populaire, ne pouvait rappeler que l'ordre des versets et la particularité qui les distingue, tandis que le sᵉmān artificiel pouvait indiquer aussi les livres de la Bible où se trouvent les versets en question, — dans le cas présent, le livre des Rois (rappelé par les mots *fils du roi*) (1) et celui de Jérémie (rappelé par le nom de son auteur). Worms, סִיג לַתּוֹרָה, fol. 29ᵇ, affirme que les termes עַנְיָא et עֲנִיּוּתָא sont aussi l'opposé de ce qu'il a dit de עָשִׁיר q. v., mais il n'en donne aucun exemple, et Fr. sb v. qui, sur ce point comme sur quelques autres, le copie (en substance du moins et sans le citer), garde naturellement la même réserve. En tout cas, il nous paraît hors de doute que si ces mots se présentent dans la Massore avec le sens de חָסֵר, ce doit être en langage sᵉmanique.

עִנְיָן (a.), déterm. עִנְיָנָא, *chose dont il est question, sujet (argumentum)*. בְּעִנְיָן, *dans un même sujet;* בְּעִנְיָינָא, *dans ce même sujet.* 1° En général les mots ainsi qualifiés dans la Massore, se retrouvent deux ou plusieurs fois, absolument identiques ou avec quelque différence d'accentuation, d'orthographe, etc. dans une certaine partie de la Bible où il est question d'une même chose, d'un même fait, d'une même idée; 'inyān équivaut alors à *contexte*. 2° Souvent aussi ces mots appartiennent à des parties de la Bible différentes mais traitant d'une même chose, d'un même fait, etc. Dans ce cas 'inyān a le sens de *contextes,* ou *passages parallèles.* 3° Enfin le même terme s'emploie aussi, dans un sens plus large, de différentes parties de la Bible où il est question de choses, de faits ou de *concepts* différents mais *similaires,* ou *analogues.* Exemples, Mm. Lev. vﮪﮪ, 15 : י״א זוּגִין מִתְחַלְּפִין מִן תְּרֵין בְּעִנְיָין קַדְמָא רְבִיעַ וְתַנְיָנָא זָקֵף, *11 paires (de mots) différant l'un de l'autre, (chaque paire consistant) en deux (mots) dans un même 'inyān, le premier*

(1) Cette expression a été choisie, parce qu'elle se rencontre dans la Bible (II Sam. xﮪﮪ, 4) à la suite du mot דַּל.

(*mot ayant*) *Rebhîa' et le second Zâqéph.* Parmi ces onze paires nous trouvons וַיִּשְׁחָט Lev. viii, 15 et וַיִּשְׁחָט ibid. 23 (contexte);

אָמֹר I Reg. xii, 23 et אֱמֹר II Chron. xi, 3 (passages ou contextes parallèles); מְהֵרָה Deut. xi, 17 et מְהֵרָה Jos. xxiii, 16 (passages ou contextes similaires). Cf. Ginsb., *Mass.*, I, p. 653, n° 234. — La Mm. remarque encore, au passage cité, que le mot וַיִּשְׁחָט se rencontre (lisez וּבְעִנְיָנָא(?) וּבְעִנְיָין וּבְעִנְיָין קָמְצִין, ג, 3 (*fois*) *ayant Qâméṣ et dans ce même 'inyân.* Les deux autres cas sont aux versets 19 et 23 du même chapitre.

עָצֵל (h.), *lent, paresseux* (en style de signes mnémotechniques). Voyez זָרִיז 2° (1).

עָקוּם (h.), *crochu, recourbé.* Exemple, Ginsb., *Mass.*, I, p. 661, n° 3 a : עָקוּם י, *yôdh recourbé.* On trouve aussi אָקוּם, les gutturales s'échangeant volontiers en néo-hébreu (Strack und Siegfried, *Lehrbuch der Neu-hebräischen Sprache*, § 10, b), comme en judéo-araméen tant oriental (Levias, *A grammar of the aramaic idiom contained in the Babylonian Talmud*, § 17) qu'occidental (Dalm., *Gramm.*, § 10, 1).

עָקִים (a.), comme עָקוּם q. v. Exemple, Ginsb., *Mass.*, I, p. 661, n° 3 b : ג פ"כ כַּף כִּי הָעֲקִים י', בְּאוֹרַיְיתָא (*il y a*) *83 yôdhs recourbés en forme de kaph dans la Loi.* Autres exemples, ibid., II, p. 361, n°s 12 et 13. — On trouve aussi אָקִים, par exemple dans le passage correspondant du *Baddê ârôn* publié par Bargès, *Sepher Taghin*, p. 39 (2) (voyez עָקוּם; cf. *Rev. Bibl.* 1903, p. 541, n° 3) et même אוּקִים (Bargès, *Sepher Tagh.*, p. 10). Comparez תּוּמְבְנָא pour תְּמְבְנָא (Dalm., *Gramm.*, § 21, 1 et § 14, 2).

עֶרֶךְ (h.), *article* (d'un lexique), par exemple Mm. Jerem. xliv, 26 où Ben-Chayim dit : סִימָן] וּפְלוּגְתָּא תִמְצָא בְּמַסֹּ[רָה] רַבְּתָא בְּעֶרֶךְ הַגָּדוֹל, *tu trouveras le Sêmân et l'opinion différente* (*que nous soutenons*) *dans la Grande Massore* (Mf.) *à l'article* הַגָּדוֹל.

עֲשִׂיָּה (h.), *confection, construction* (du Tabernacle); en style de Massore, *passages de la Bible relatifs à la construction du Tabernacle.*

(1) D'après Worms, סִייג לַתּוֹרָה, fol. 29 b, עָצֵל contiendrait aussi une allusion à l'accent *Mûnâch* (*qui se repose*) que le passage du verset 13 a de plus que celui du v. 11.

(2) Où, par erreur, on a imprimé, comme dans plusieurs autres passages, דקאִים pour דאקים.

Voyez מַשְׁכְּנָא. Exemple, Mp. Ex. xxvi, 8 et Mmarg. ibid. xxxvi, 9 :

כֹּל אֹרֶךְ דְּצַוְּאָה בְּטַעַם וְדַעֲשִׂיָּה בְּטַעַם גֶּרֶשׁ וְסִי[מָן] דִּפְקֵיד יְתִיב וּדְעָבֵיד קָאֵים, tout אֹרֶךְ du commandement (voyez צַוְּאָה) a l'accent Mûnâch, mais (tout אֹרֶךְ) de la construction a l'accent Gé-resch, et le signe mnémotechnique est : celui qui commande est as-sis, et celui qui exécute est debout.

עָשִׁיר (h.), riche. Se dit, dans le langage des signes mnémotechniques, 1° dans le sens de מָלֵא q. v. de mots qui ont la scriptio plena par opposition à d'autres qui sont écrits defective; 2° d'une manière générale, dans le sens de יַתִּיר q. v. de mots qui ont une ou plu-sieurs lettres superflues. Pour plus de détails voyez l'article (pas très clair, à notre avis) de Worms, סְיָג לַתּוֹרָה, fol. 29 b. Il est à regretter que ce savant, notre unique source d'information sur ce point, ne nous ait pas dit en quel endroit de la Massore il a trouvé le Sēmān qu'il cite et que nous omettons pour cette raison.

פ

פִּיסוּק (h.), plur. פִּיסוּקִין, comme פָּסוּק q. v. Exemple, Ginsb., Mass., I, p. 479, n° 52 : ב' פִּיס[וּ]קִין דְּחָסֵ[ר] חֹדֶשׁ, il y a 2 versets où חֹדֶשׁ est écrit defective. Autres exemples, ibid., II, p. 450, nᵒˢ 189 et suivants.

פֵּירוּשׁ (h.), souvent abrégé פֵּירוּ', פֵּי', explication, adverbialement c'est-à-dire. Exemples sous מָאיִּלָא et sous פַּשְׁטָא.

פַּלְגָּא (a.), moitié. Exemple, Mm. Ex. xii, 15 : דִּפְלַגָּא דְּסִפְרָא, qui est, qui se trouve vers la moitié du livre. C'est là toutefois une erreur de copiste pour דִּפְלִיגִין עֲלֵיהּ סָפְרֵי, à propos duquel les copistes sont en désaccord. Cf. Fr. sb פְּלוֹג. — Par contre dans Mm. Jer. xxxix, 2, au lieu de פְּלוּגְתָּא il faut lire דִּפְלַגָּא דְּסִפְרָא, vers la moitié du livre. Voyez sous צוּר.

פְּלוּגָּה (h.), moitié. Exemple, Ginsb., Mass., I, p. 479, n° 52: פְּלוּגֵיהּ דְּסִפְ[רָא], la moitié du livre. Cette note correspond à Mm. Jerem. xxxix, 2 (voyez sous פַּלְגָּא) où on lit, par erreur, פְּלוּגְתָּא.

פְּלוּגְתָּא (a.), divergence d'opinion. Exemples, Mmarg. Gen. xxvii, 3, à propos de צֵידָה (i. e. Kethibh צֵידָה, Qerê צַיִד) : אֲבָל יַתִּיר ה' פְּלוּגְתָּא דְּרַב נַחֲמָן וְהוּא חַד מִן כ"ב תֵּיבִין כְּתִיב ה' בְּסוֹף תֵּיבוּתָא

וְלָא קְרֵי. *Le* ה *est superflu,* — *mais il y a divergence d'opinion de la part de Rabh Nachmān* — *et c'est un des* 22 *mots où* ה *est écrit à la fin du mot, mais n'est pas lu* (dans la rubrique correspondante, Ginsb., *Mass.,* I, p. 270, nº 34, au lieu de פְּלוּגְתָּא דְרַב נַחֲמָן, on lit simplement פְּלִיגֵי עֲלֵיהּ, *il y a divergence d'opinion à son sujet*); voyez פְּלִיג (1). — Mm. Ex. xiii, 16, à propos de וּלְטוֹטָפֹת, après avoir remarqué que dans Deut. xi, 18 on lit לְטֹטָפֹת tandis que Deuter. vi, 8 porte לְטוֹטָפֹת et Ex. xiii, 16 וּלְטוֹטָפֹת, la Massore ajoute : וְעַיֵּין פְּלוּגְתָּא דר״ת, *voyez la divergence d'opinion de Rabh Tām* (2). — Mmarg. Ex. xxi, 19, à propos de וְהִתְהַלֵּךְ, il est remarqué : פְּלוּגְתָּא דְבֶן אָשֵׁר וּבֶן נַפְתָּלִי, *divergence d'opinion de* (c'est-à-dire *entre*) *Ben-Aschēr et Ben-Naphtāli.* [B.-A., *Lāmēdh avec Qāmēṣ* (i. e. *Ṣērē*) *et accent Milra' sous le Lamedh,* וְהִתְהַלֵּךְ; B.-N., *Lāmēdh avec Pathach* (i. e. *Seghōl*) *et accent Mil'ēl sous la première* (*radicale?*) *et Maqqēph,* וְהִתְהַלֶּךְ. Ginsb., *Mass.,* I, p. 573 *ad loc.,* et édition Michaelis *ad loc.*]. — De même aussi la Mm. Dan. v, 11, note qu'à propos de מִי כָמוֹךְ, Ps. xxxv, 10, il y a פְּלוּגְתָּא דִבְנֵי אָשֵׁר וּבְנֵי נַפְתָּלִי, *divergence d'opinion entre les fils* (c'est-à-dire *l'École*) *d'Aschēr et ceux de Naphtāli* (3) (Cf. Ginsb., *Mass.,* I, p. 585 *ad loc. :* ב״א רְפֵי ב״נ דָּגֵשׁ). Au sujet de cette rubrique, voyez מְבַטָּל. La plupart du temps la Massore se contente de dire qu'à propos de tel ou tel mot il y a פְּלוּגְתָּא sans donner aucune autorité pour la variante, par exemple Mp. Ex. xxiv, 5 (où cependant la variante elle-même est donnée), ou quelquefois même sans indiquer la variante, quand le contexte la laisse deviner sans peine, par exemple Mm. Ex. xl, 7 où la rubrique après avoir énuméré les

---

(1) Ginsb., *Introduction,* p. 212, donne d'après Br. Mus. add. 15251 וּפְלִיג בֵּיהּ!, ce qui ne peut que vouloir dire : *on n'est pas d'accord là-dessus.* פְּלִיג se retrouverait encore plusieurs fois, dans ce sens, dans le codex Reuchlin (*op. et loc. cit.*), mais nous avons quelque raison de croire que M. Ginsburg cite de mémoire et que les manuscrits portent פְּלִיגָא = פְּלִיגִין, פְּלִיגָי ou פְּלִיג'.

(2) D'après Jacob ben-Chayim, *Haqdāmā,* 5ᵉ col. (éd. Ginsb., p. 62), cette divergence de vue paraît consister en ce que Tām croyait que le premier waw de וּלְטוֹטָפֹת devrait être entre les deux dernières lettres.

(3) Les divergences entre les deux écoles de Ben-Ascher et de Ben-Naphtali sont aussi appelées חלופים, par exemple, dans la liste imprimée par Ben-Chayim à la suite de la Mf. et dans Ginsb., *Mass.,* I, pp. 571-591.

29 cas où נָתַתָּ est écrit sans ה à la fin du mot, ajoute qu'il y a פְּלוּגְתָּא pour Nehem. ıx, 15 et 35. Il est clair que la variante est נָתַתָּה. — Voyez encore un exemple de פְּלוּגְתָּא sous עֲרֵךְ.

פְּלוּנִי (h.), *un tel.* Exemple, Mp. Num. xı, 21 (cf. ibid. xvı, 28), à propos de מֹשֶׁה וַיֹּאמֶר : בִּפְלוּנִי וַי' בַּטַעַם בְּסִיפְרָא [בַּטַעַם] ב'. *2 (fois) avec cet accent dans ce livre et 10 (fois) avec cet accent avec un tel (c'est-à-dire suivi d'un nom propre quelconque).* Autre exemple, Ginsb., *Mass.,* I, p. 93, n° 876.

פְּלִיג (a.), plur. פְּלִיגִי, פְּלִיגִין, *divisé, séparé, qui est d'opinion dif-férente,* au pluriel, *qui sont en désaccord.* Exemple, Mmarg. Num. vıı, 85, à propos de הַקְּעָרָה : הַקְּעָרָה יֹסֵף רַב וּפָלִיג ל', *ne se re-trouve plus ainsi; mais Rabh Yôsēph diffère d'opinion (et lit)* הַקְּעָרָה. — Mm. II Sam. xı, 21 : עֲלֵיהּ פְּלִיגִין דֵּין. *sur celui-ci. on est en désaccord.* Cf. Ginsb., *Mass.,* I, p. 681, n° 29. — Mm. Ex. xvıı, 16, à propos de יָהּ כֵּס : ה מַפְּקִין דְּלָא מִלִּין מִן חַד הוּא אִם פְּלִיגִין. *on n'est pas d'accord si c'est un des mots qui ne font pas ressortir le* ה (c'est-à-dire *où le* ה *est quiescent).* Voyez la liste complète dans Ginsb., *Mass.,* I, p. 709, n° 160. — עֲלֵיהּ est quelquefois omis, par exemple Mf. יד 54 (= Mm. Jon. ı, 8). — Sur le singulier פְּלִיג pris impersonnellement dans le sens de *on n'est pas d'accord* voyez פְּלוּגְתָּא, première note.

פְּלוּגָא (a.), *divergence d'opinion.* Exemple, Mm. Ezech. xxxııı, 22 : דֵּין עַל פְּלוּגָא, *il y a divergence d'opinion sur celui-ci.* (Nous ne pouvons nous expliquer pourquoi Fr. 28, note 1, lit פְּלוּגִי en citant cette même rubrique). — De même Mm. Qohel. vı, 10 : פְּלִיגָא וְחַד עֲלֵיהּ, *et sur un il y a divergence d'opinion.*

פִּנְחָס, *Pinchās,* la leçon hebdomadaire (Pārāschā) de ce nom, Num. xxv, 10-xxx, 2.

וְאָחוֹר פָּנִים (h.), *l'avant et l'après.* Désignation des mots לְפָנָיו, *avant lui* et וְאַחֲרָיו, *et après lui.* Exemple, Mp. et Mm. Ex. x, 14 : פְּסוּקִין ד' *4 versets dans lesquels il y a* לְפָנָיו *et* וְאָחוֹר פָּנִים בְּהוֹן אִית. וְאַחֲרָיו. Cf. Ginsb., *Mass.,* II, p. 448, n° 169.

פָּסוּק (h.), plur. פְּסוּקִים, פְּסוּקִין, פְּסוּקֵי. *verset.* Notez les expres-sions בַּפָּסוּק, *dans ce verset;* בַּפָּסוּק ב', *deux fois (ou le se-cond) dans ce verset;* פָּסוּק רֹאשׁ, ou פָּסוּק רֵישׁ (a.), *commencement du verset;* פ סֹוף, *fin du verset.* Exemple, Mm. Ex. xii, 30 : [ר"י פְּסוּ|קִין

אִית בְּהֹון אֵין אֵין מִצְעוּ|ת] פָּסוּק נִמְסָר בִּישַׁעְיָה סִימָן מ' גַּבֵּי

אֵין בָּעֵר דֵּי אֵין וּלְבָנוֹן וּלְבָנוֹן פָסוּק, *(il y a) 16 versets dans lesquels* אֵין

se rencontre deux fois à l'intérieur du verset; enregistré dans Isaïe, chapitre xl *au verset : Et le Liban etc.* (*v. 16*).

פְּסוּקָא (a.), même sens que פָּסוּק q. v. Exemples dans Ginsb., *Mass.*, I, p. 651, nᵒˢ 220-223, *passim*.

פֶּסַח קָטָן. *la petite Pâque.* Désignation de la section Num. xi, 1-15. Exemple, Mm. Ex. xix, 1. Dans la rubrique correspondante, Ginsb., *Mass.*, I, p. 479, nᵒ 54, au lieu de דְּפֶסַח קָטָן, *de la petite Pâque*, on trouve דִּרְחֹקָה, *du (voyage) lointain* (cf. Num. ix, 10).

פָּסִיק · פְּסִיק (a.), voyez פֶּסֶק.

פֶּסֶק (h.) (1), *division*, ou פָּסֵק (a.), *diviseur.* En Massore, 1° la ligne *Pâsêq* (2). Exemple, Mp. Lev. xi, 35, à propos de י מִנְּבֶלָתָם :

ה פֶּסֶק בְּסִידְרָא, *5 (fois) Pâsêq dans ce Sêder* (dans le sens propre, c.-à-d. chap. ix; voyez סֶדֶר). — Ibid. xxiii, 20, à propos de הַכֹּהֵן] :

ה פֶּסֶק בְּסִיפָ רָא], *8 (fois) Pâsêq dans ce Livre* (cf. Ginsb., *Mass.*, I, p. 647, nᵒ 202). — 2° *Marqué du Pâsêq.* Exemple, Mf. טע 6 : ה פְּסוּקִין

בְּטַעַם תְּלִישָׁא וּפָסְקִין], *(il y a) 8 versets avec l'accent Telischâ et marqués du Pâsêq.* Voyez la liste dans Ginsb., *Mass.*, I, p. 654, nᵒ 244. — Autre exemple sous מַפְסִיק.

פְּסָקָא (a.), plur. פְּסָקֵי. *interruption, coupure.* En Massore, 1° *Pisqâ*, espace laissé en blanc au milieu d'un verset. Exemple, Mp. Jos. iv, 1 : פְּסָקָא בְּמִצְעוּת פָּסוּק, *Pisqâ au milieu du verset.* — 2° *Qui a une*

---

(1) Ainsi ponctué par les lexicographes juifs (voyez Levy, *Neuhebräisches und Chaldäisches Wörterbuch*, sb v.; Dalman, *Lexic.*, sb v.); Wickes, *Pr. acc.*, p. 120, J. Kennedy, *The Note-Line in the Hebrew scriptures* etc., p. 1, et Baer, *Liber Genesis*, p. 91, ponctuent פָּסֵק, *qui divise, qui sépare.* Les Juifs se servent aussi, dans le même sens, du mot פָּסוּק, *divisé, séparé.* Il est à remarquer que la Massore écrit toujours פָּסֵק, jamais פָּסוּק.

(2) Nous ne pouvons entrer ici dans la question de la nature et de l'usage du Paseq. Nous renvoyons le lecteur à Wickes, *Pr. acc.*, pp. 120-129, et surtout à l'ouvrage plus récent de James Kennedy, *The Note-Line in the Hebrew Scriptures, commonly called Paseq or Pesiq*, Edinburgh, 1903. Les listes données par ces deux auteurs diffèrent beaucoup l'une de l'autre, comme elles diffèrent aussi toutes les deux de celles des Bibles Rabbiniques (Mf. après פ , de Ginsburg (*Mass.*, I, pp. 647-652) et de Baer (à la fin de chacun des livres de la Bible qu'il a publiés). La principale cause de ce désaccord est que les uns prennent pour des Paseqs ce que d'autres traitent de *Legarmehs.* D'après Kennedy il n'y a point de Legarmehs (*op. cit.*, p. 17).

Pisqā. Exemple, Mp. Gen. ɪᴠ, 8 : פְּסוּקִין פְּסָקֵי בִּמְצָעוּת פָּסוּק ‎כ״ח.
*(il y a) 28 versets (dans ce livre) qui ont une Pisqā au milieu du
verset.* — 3° D'une manière générale, *espace laissé en blanc entre
deux Pārāschās, ou entre deux sections mineures* (ouvertes ou fermées), par exemple dans une note massorétique insérée par Ginsburg
dans son édition du Texte Massorétique, Gen. xxvɪɪɪ, 10. Cf. Levita,
Massoreth ha-Massoreth (édit. Ginsburg), p. 242.

פְּסָקְתָּא, פְּסִיקְתָּא (a.), plur. פְּסִיקְתָּא. 1° Même sens que פֶּסֶק q. v.
Exemple, Mf. טע 18 (= Mm. Gen. xxx, 16 = Ginsb., *Mass.*, I,
p. 652, n° 228) : וְכָל פְּסִיקְתָּא דִכְוָותְ[הֹון, *et tout Pāsēq leur est
pareil* (c'est-à-dire *toutes les fois qu'il y a un Pāsēq il en est de
même*) (1). — Mf. (de Gara) fin de la lettre Pē : אִילֵין פְּסִקָתָא דְאֹורַיְיתָא,
voici les Pāsēqs de la Loi. — 2° *Section (fermée?)*. Exemple,
Mmarg. Num. xxxvɪ, 42 : כָּל רֵאשֵׁי פְּסִיקָתָ[א] דְעִנְיָן בְּנֵי פְלֹונִי ב״מב
וג׳, *tous les commencements de sections (fermées?) dans ce contexte
sont « Les fils d'un tel »,* *excepté 2, etc.*

פְּרַגְמָא, voyez פְּרֵיגְמָא.

פְּרֹויֵי, *ses* פַּר, dans l'expression כָּל פְּרֹויֵי דְּבָלָק. *tous les* פַּר *de Bālāq*,
c'est-à-dire le mot פַּר aussi souvent qu'il se rencontre dans la
Pārāschā (section hebdomadaire) de Bālāq (Num. xxɪɪ, 2-xxv, 10).
Pour plus de détails voyez בְּזֹויֵי.

פְּרֵיגְמָא, פְּרַגְמָא (?) (2), plur. פְּרֵיגְמֹות. désignation du *Pisqā* (voyez
פְּסְקָא) dans certains manuscrits, par exemple dans British Museum
add. 9401, Mp. Gen. ɪᴠ, 8 : פְּרֵיגְמָא (Ginsb., *Introduction*, p. 547),
et add. 21160 (3), Mp. Gen. xxxv, 22, etc. : פְּרַגְמָא בְּלָא סִלּוּק.
Pisqa sans Sillūq (Ginsb., *op. cit.*, p. 627); aussi dans une autre
rubrique Gen. ɪᴠ, 8, citée par Levita (*Massoreth ha-Massoreth*, édit.
Ginsburg, p. 262), malheureusement sans indication de la source,

---

(1) Nous nous abstenons de citer dans son entier cette rubrique obscure que nous avouons
ne pas comprendre. Voyez plus haut l'article סָלְקֵי וְנָחֲתֵי (où au lieu de Mm. xxxvɪ, 3, il
faut lire Mm. Num. xxxvɪ, 3). C'est à propos de Mm. Gen. xxx, 16 et non de Mm. Num.
xxxvɪ, 3 que Wickes suggère de lire מִלֹּין au lieu de בְּאַיְילִין. mais comme le פֵּירוּשׁ de
cette seconde rubrique est emprunté à la première, il s'ensuit que la remarque de Wickes
s'applique aux deux passages de la Massore.

(2) L'étymologie de ce terme avait déjà embarrassé Levita (*Massoreth ha-Massoreth*, édit.
Ginsburg, pp. 242 et 262). Buxtorf (*Lexic.*, sb v.) et, après lui, Ginsburg (*Introduction*,
p. 547) croient que ce mot est le grec πρῆγμα, πραγμα que Ginsburg n'hésite pas à traduire
par « break », « hiatus »! Nous réservons notre jugement.

(3) D'origine allemande.

et dans un autre, Deuter. II, 8, que Buxtorf (*Lexic.*, sb v.) dit avoir trouvé « in Pentateucho cum triplice Targum ». Nous n'avons pas trouvé ce terme dans la Massore imprimée. Suivant Levita (*op. et loc. cit.*), les לוֹעֲזִים (Juifs italiens, Buxt., *Lex.*, sb v.) appellent de ce nom avec Ṣērê sous ר tous les espaces libres entre les sections ouvertes ou fermées.

פָּרְשָׁה (h.), état construit פָּרְשַׁת (1), plur. פָּרְשִׁיּוֹת, *section*. 1° *Leçon hebdomadaire* du Pentateuque suivant le cycle annuel, ou Babylonien. Voyez סֵדֶר. Dans ce sens le mot פָּרְשָׁה se rencontre souvent dans la Massore imprimée, particulièrement dans la Mf. pour les renvois au Pentateuque. Exemple, Mf. גד 2 : בְּפָרְשַׁת וַיְחִי, *dans la Pārāschā de Wayechi*, — ibid. 5 : בְּפָרְשַׁת נֹחַ, *dans la Pārāschā de Nōach*. — Mp. Lev. IV, 24, où à propos de הוּא il est remarqué : כֹּל פָּרְשַׁת וַיִּקְרָא הוּא ב״מד הִיא, *dans toute la Pārāschā de Wayyiqrā* (on trouve) הוּא, *excepté 4 (fois)* הוּא (avec Chireq et Waw). Voyez la *Concordance* de Mandelkern à הוּא et à הוּא(הִיא). — Mm. Num. XVI, 26 : אַחֲרֵי מוֹת [וְכֹל פָּרְשַׁ]ת, *et toute la Pārāschā de Acharê môth*. Voyez des exemples du pluriel sous סִימָן 1° et 2°.

2° *Section mineure* (ouverte ou fermée). Exemple, Mm. Ex. XII, 29 : נִמְסָר בִּירְמְיָ[הוּ] סִימָן ל״ז גַּבֵּי פָּרְשַׁת וַיֵּצֵא יִרְמְיָהוּ מִירוּשָׁלַֽם, *donné dans Jérémie, chapitre* XXXVII, *dans la Pārāschā de « Et Jérémie sortit de Jérusalem »*. Cf. פָּרְשְׁתָא (2). — Plus souvent, cependant, la Massore désigne les sections mineures par leur contenu (3). Ainsi elle se contente de dire דְּעַמּוֹן, *de* (c.-à-d. *dans la section mineure qui se rapporte à*) *Ammon;* דְּנַחְשׁוֹן, *de Nachschōn;* דְּצְפַרְדְּעִים, *des grenouilles*. — On distingue les sections mineures en פְּתוּחוֹת, *ouvertes* et סְתוּמוֹת, *fermées* (Voyez *Rev. Bibl.* 1902, p. 555, note). On trouvera la liste des פְּתוּחוֹת וּסְתוּמוֹת דְּבְכָל קְרִיאָה, *(sections) ouvertes et fermées dans toute la Bible*, dans Ginsb., *Mass.*, II, pp. 478-502.

---

(1) Cette forme, à part la vocalisation que la Massore ne donne jamais, étant la même que celle de l'état construit de l'équivalent araméen פָּרְשְׁתָא q. v., tous les exemples du singulier que nous donnons dans cet article peuvent à la rigueur appartenir à ce dernier.

(2) Le mot פָּרְשָׁה se trouve déjà tant dans le sens de *leçon hebdomadaire du Pentateuque* que dans celui de *section mineure* dans la Mischna et dans le Talmud. Voyez les Dictionnaires et Strack, *Prolegomena*, pp. 74, 75.

(3) Voyez la liste des *sections ouvertes et fermées* mentionnée ci-dessous.

פַּרְשְׁתָּא (a.), état construit פָּרְשַׁת (plur. פָּרְשִׁין). Même sens que l'hébreu פָּרְשָׁה q. v. — Exemple, dans le sens de *section mineure* (ouverte), Mm. Ex. xviii, 11 : גַּבֵּי פָרָשְׁתָּא דְּהֵן אֶרְאֶלָּם צָעֲקוּ חֻצָה.
dans la section de « voici que leurs braves crient dehors » (Is.
xxxiii, 7).

פְּשׁוּט (h.), *étendu.* Se dit comme l'araméen אָרִיךְ q. v. des formes
finales de certaines lettres. Cf. *Rev. Bibl.* 1903, p. 541. Exemple,
Mm. Dan. iii, 10 : כָּל ד פְּשׁוּטָה בְלִישָׁן אֲרָמִית קָמֵץ בָּ[וֹר] מִן[וֹ] ד פַּתְחִין
(Cf. Ginsb., *Mass.*, II, p. 12, nᵒ 22), *tout Kaph final a (c'est-à-dire
est immédiatement précédé de) Qāmēṣ, sauf 4 qui ont Pathach.*

פְּשָׁטָא (a.), *extension* (de la voix), ou פָּשֵׁט (a.), *qui étend* (la voix).
1ᵒ L'accent *Paschṭā.* — 2ᵒ Suivi de צְבְחַר q. v., ce mot désigne
aussi le *Petit Pathach*, c'est-à-dire *Seghōl* (cf. *Rev. Biblique* 1903,
p. 543). Exemple, Mm. Ezech. xlv, 12, où il est dit que הַמָּנֶה appartient à חַד מִן ה זוֹגִין דְּפָשְׁטִין צְבְחַר פֵּי[רוּשׁ] בְּפַתַח קָטָן, *une
de 5 paires (de mots) qui allongent un peu, c'est-à-dire avec le
Petit Pathach* (1).

פַּתַח (2) (a. ?), 1ᵒ la voyelle *Pathach;* 2ᵒ *qui est muni d'un Pathach*,
pl. פַּתְחִין. — La Massore distingue פַּתַח גָּדוֹל, Grand Pathach
= ◌ֲ et פַּתַח קָטָן, Petit Pathach = ◌ֶ. Voyez *Rev. Bibl.* 1903,
p. 543. Exemple, Mmarg. Gen. ii, 22, à propos de הַצֵּלָע, il est remarqué : כֵּן דִּינוֹ קָמֵץ קָטָן וּפַתַח גָּדוֹל, *ainsi est sa règle : Petit
Qāmēṣ et Grand Pathach* (voyez aussi la rubrique parallèle Mmarg.
Ex. xxvi, 26 et Fr., p. 161, note 1). Mais les mots גָּדוֹל et קָטָן sont
souvent omis et le contexte seul indique s'il s'agit du Pathach proprement dit ou du Seghōl. C'est ainsi que l'on dit פַּתְחִין, *munis de
Pathach* (c'est-à-dire de Pathach ou de Seghōl, suivant le cas).
Exemples, Mp. Gen. xxviii, 10, à שֶׁבַע : חַד מִן פַּתְחִין דְּסִפְרָא, *un
des mots de ce livre qui ont (Grand) Pathach (quoique à la pause).*
Cf. Ginsb., *Mass.*, II, p. 292 (3). — Mmarg. Ex. xxii, 24, à חַד : נֶשֶׁךְ

---

(1) Cette rubrique se trouve à peu près dans les mêmes termes Mm. Ezech. vi, 9 צְבְחַר
et Mf. קמץ 3. L'expression ה זוֹגִין est probablement une erreur pour ה בְלוֹין comme on
le lit dans une rubrique correspondante, Ginsb., *Mass.*, II, p. 297, nᵒ 530 b (où même il est
dit que ces dix mots ne forment pas de paires, לֵית זוֹגִין. Cf. Mp. Ezech. xviii, 7).

(2) Ponctué aussi פֶּתַח (Ben-Yehûdhâ, *Millon,* sb v.). La ponctuation primitive était peut-
être פֶּתַח (*qui ouvre*).

(3) Où ce passage toutefois est omis.

מְן דּ פְּתָחִין דְּסִפְרָא· *un de 4 qui ont (Petit) Pathach dans ce livre (quoique à la pause)*. Cf. Ginsb., *Mass.*, II, p. 299, n° 543. — On trouve aussi quelquefois פַּתַח pour Chāṭēph-Pathach, par exemple, Mp. I Sam. xxvi, 19, où à propos de הֲסִיתְךָ il est remarqué que ce mot se rencontre aussi une fois avec *Pathach*, c'est-à-dire הֲסִיתְךָ (Job xxxvi, 16).

צ

צִבְחַר (a.) pour צְבְחַד = צִיב, *brindille* + חַד, *une, un brin, un peu* (Dalman, *Lex.*, sb v.). Ce mot ne se rencontre, que nous sachions, que dans une rubrique plusieurs fois répétée, toujours précédé de פַּשְׁטִין. Voyez פַּשְׁטָא.

צִוְּאָה (h.), *commandement, ordre*. En style de Massore, *passages de la Bible contenant les prescriptions de Dieu relativement à la construction du Tabernacle*. Voyez מַשְׁכְּנָא et עֲשִׂיָּה.

צוֹר דִּיחֶזְקֵאל, *Tyr d'Ézéchiel*, le passage d'Ézéchiel se rapportant à Tyr (et à Sidon), chap. xxvi-xxviii. Exemple, Mm. Jer. xxxix, 2 : דְּצוֹר דִּיחֶזְקֵאל, *qui se trouve dans Tyr d'Ézéchiel* (1).

צוּרַת הַבַּיִת [דִּיחֶזְקֵאל], *description de la maison (de Dieu) d'Ézéchiel*. Désignation d'Ezech. xl-fin. Exemples, Mm. I Reg. vii, 7; Ezech. xl, 41, et Mf. אמ 21. (D'après Fr., sb v., ce ne serait que par exception que dans ce dernier passage צוּרַת הַבַּיִת ne serait pas suivi de דִּיחֶזְקֵאל. Il est à remarquer toutefois que cette addition ne se rencontre pas non plus dans les deux seuls autres passages de la Massore qu'il cite et que nous avons cités avec lui). — On dit aussi dans le même sens בְּנִינָא q. v.

צְעִיפוֹת (probablement emprunté à l'arabe ضِعَافَة, *doubles, recourbées?*), équivalent de l'hébreu כְּפוּלוֹת (2) dans le sens de formes re-

---

(1) Le mot פְּלוּגְתָא qui suit cette indication ne peut être qu'une erreur pour [דְּסִפְרָא] פַּלְגָא, *à la moitié du livre*. Plus extraordinaire encore est l'erreur dans la rubrique correspondante, Ginsb., *Mass.*, II, p. 426, n° 909 : דְּפַלְגֵיהּ ר' יהזקאל. Nous avouons ne pas comprendre ce que Mons. Ginsburg a compris.

(2) Plus communément les formes כְּבֵבְץ étaient appelées כְּפוּפוֹת (cf. *Rev. Bibl.* 1903, p. 541), tandis que l'expression אָתִיוֹת כְּפִילוֹת désignait les cinq lettres doubles כמנפץ d'une manière générale. Peut-être le terme כְּפִילָה aura-t-il ensuite été étendu à la forme ordinaire de ces lettres, la forme recourbée. Mais il ne serait pas impossible que le sens

courbées des lettres כמנפץ (voyez כפול 2°), par opposition à פְּשׁוּטוֹת par lequel on désignait les formes droites des mêmes lettres (voyez פָּשׁוּט). — Suivant Fr., sb v. (qui suggère de lire צְנִיפוֹת), ce terme se rencontrerait dans la Mmarg. Soph. III, 8. Il n'existe pas dans notre exemplaire (Bragadin, 1618), mais dans l'édition de Buxtorf nous trouvons à cet endroit : אִית בְּפָסוּק א״ב בנעיפות ובִפְשׁוּטוֹת où נעיפות est probablement une erreur (facile à expliquer en raschi) pour צְעִיפוֹת. Traduisez donc : *il y a dans ce verset l'Alphabet y compris les (formes) recourbées et les (formes) droites (des lettres doubles)*. Comparez la rubrique correspondante, Ginsb., *Mass.*, II, p. 457, n° 228 : הוּא מִכָּ״ה פְּסוּ[קִין] דְּאִית בְּהוֹן א״ב וְהָדֵין יְתֵר עֲלֵיהוֹן אוֹתִיּוֹת כְּפוּלוֹת מנצפך, *c'est un des 25 versets qui ont (toutes les lettres de) l'Alphabet, mais celui-ci a de plus qu'eux les lettres doubles* מנצפך *(dans leurs deux formes)*.

צְפוּי (h.), läschōn du verbe צָפָה, cf. *Rev. Bibl.* 1903, p. 546. — Exemple, Mf. נח 31 : נְחֹשֶׁת ד׳ בְּצִפּוּי, « airain » 4 *(fois) avec (le verbe) recouvrir*. Cf. Ginsb., *Mass.*, II, p. 516, n° 182.

[דְּ]צְפַרְדְּעִים], (le passage de la plaie) *des grenouilles*, Ex. VII, 26-VIII, 12.

ק

קָאִים (a.). 1° *Qui se tient debout*, désignation de l'accent Géresch dans le langage des signes mnémotechniques. Exemple sous עֲשִׂיָּה. Fr. sb נָחֵת *semble* dire que קָאִים se rencontre aussi bien que זְקִיף comme opposé de נָחֵת, mais ni dans les trois passages de la Massore imprimée qu'il cite, ni dans les rubriques correspondantes de la compilation de Ginsburg on ne trouve קָאִים. — 2° Erreur pour צָקִים = אֱקִים q. v.

קָדְלָא (a.), *col (d'une lettre)*. Exemple sous נָחֵת.

קָדֵם (a.), plur. קָדְמִין; *qui précède*. Exemples, Mp. Lev. XV, 16 : מַיִם קָדִים לִבְשָׂרוֹ ב, « eau » *précédant* « sa chair » 2 *(fois)*. — Mm. Lev. XVI, 45 : אֲבָנִים דְּקָדְמִין לְעֵצִים, *des pierres qui précèdent des (pièces de) bois*.

---

de *plier, recourber* pour la racine כפל fût aussi ancien, et même plus ancien que celui de *doubler*.

קֶדֶם (a.), *devant, pra-devant;* avec suffixe לִקְדָמֵיהוֹן, *par-devant eux.* Exemple sous מִדִּלִי.

קַדְמָאָה (a.), souvent écrit קדמא, plur. קַדְמָאֵי, *le premier (mot, passage* etc.). Exemples sous בָּתְרָא.

קַדְמֵיתָא (a. , fém. de קַדְמָאָה, *la première.* Exemple sous נְסִיב 1°.

קְטִיעָה · קְטִיעָא (a.), littéralement *coupée, raccourcie.* C'est ainsi que, d'après Norzi, שֵׁי מִנְחַת. Num. xxv, 12 (Cf. Ginsb., *Mass.,* I, p. 37, nᵒ 229 , est qualifié le waw de שָׁלוֹם dans la Massore de certains manuscrits, conformément à la tradition talmudique, *Qiddûschîm,* 66 b. Mais on ne s'accorde pas sur le sens précis du mot קְטִיעָה, quelques-uns affirmant qu'il faut entendre *raccourcie à la base,* d'autres *coupée par le milieu.* Voyez Norzi, *op. et loc. cit.* — Dans la Mp. (imprimée) *ad loc.* ce waw est classé parmi les *Petites Lettres :* ו' זוֹטָא וְהוּא חַד מֵא"ב מֵאוֹתִיּוֹת קְטַנּוֹת, *Petit* ו *et c'est une (lettre) de la liste alphabétique des Petites Lettres.* Il paraitrait donc que קְטִיעָה dans ce cas ait exactement le même sens que קְטַנָּה, זְעִירָא ou זוֹטָא (Cf. Jastrow, *Dictionary of the Targumim* etc.,sb v.). Levita semble être de cet avis quand il dit (*Massoreth ha-Massoreth,* édit. Ginsburg, p. 231) : « Dans les rubriques massorétiques correctes le waw הַקְטַנָּה n'est pas appelé זְעִירָא, mais קְטִיעָא, c'est-à-dire un peu raccourcie par le bas ». — Le choix de קְטִיעָא, plutòt que זְעִירָא ou tout autre équivalent, semble être basé sur l'usage talmudique, et non sur une différence de sens.

קַל וָחוֹמֶר (h.). 1° *Facile et difficile.* Nom d'une règle exégétique en vertu de laquelle on conclut du facile au difficile, du moins important au plus important ou vice-versà. — 2° Cas de *Qal wā-chōmer,* plur. קַלִּים וַחֲמוּרִים (avec substitution de חָמוּר à חוֹמֶר). — Cette règle n'est pas du ressort de la Massore proprement dite et elle ne se trouve pas, que nous sachions du moins, dans la Massore imprimée de Ben-Chayìm. Mais on la trouve dans O. W. O. 182 et 183 : קַל וָחוֹמֶר ה בַּתּוֹרָה, *Qal wā-chömer,* 5 (*fois*) *dans la Loi.* Pour plus de détail, voyez la note de Frensdorff, *O. W. O.,* et Bacher, *Die aelteste Terminologie,* etc., pp. 172 et suiv.

קָלֹ· *ses* קָל, c'est-à-dire le mot קָל toutes les fois qu'il se rencontre dans le livre de Daniel. Voyez בְּזֹוִי et *Rev. Bibl.* 1903, p. 548.

קָמוּץ (h.), voyez קָמֵץ 2°.

גַ קַמְיָיתָא (a.), *première*. Exemple, O. W. O. 101 : מִלִּין תְּבוּתָא
(lisez קַמְיָיתָא (תְנְיָיתָא) נָסְבָא מִן תנינא, *3 expressions (de deux
mots), le premier mot empruntant (une lettre) du second.* Comparez la variante de cette rubrique sous נָסִיב *1°*.

קָמֵץ (a.), *qui resserre, qui fait resserrer (la bouche).* *1°* La voyelle
Qāmeṣ. La Massore distingue le קָמֵץ גָּדוֹל, Grand Qāmeṣ = ◌ָ et
קָמֵץ קָטָן, Petit Qāmeṣ = ◌ַ. Exemple de ce dernier sous פַּתַח :
des deux, Ginsb., *Mass.*, II, pp. 309 et suiv. passim. — *2° Muni
d'un Qāmeṣ.* Fém. קְמִצָה, plur. קָמְצִין, Ginsb., *op. et loc. cit.*,
passim. Dans ce sens on trouve aussi les formes hébraïques קָמוּץ
et נִקְמָץ. — *3°* On trouve encore (abusivement sinon incorrectement) קָמֵץ dans le sens de מִלְעֵיל B *1°*, de même que פַּתַח dans
le sens de מִלְרַע. C'est ainsi que tandis que Mf. א 24 nous lisons :
א״ב מִן חַד וְחַד חַד מִלְעֵיל וְחַד מִלְרַע, dans la rubrique correspondante Ginsb., *Mass.*, II, p. 310, n° 606 a, nous trouvons :
אַלְפָבֵית מִן חַד וְחַד (חַד) קָמֵץ וְחַד פַּתַח. Voyez מִלְעֵיל B *1"*.

קָרוֹיי, *ses*, [וַיִּ]קַר, c'est-à-dire le mot וַיִּקָר toutes les fois qu'il se présente dans l'histoire de Balaam (Num. XXIII, 4, 16). Voyez בָּזוֹיי et
Rev. Bibl. 1903, p. 548.

קֹרַח, leçon hebdomadaire (פָּרָשָׁה) de Qōrach, Num. XVI, 1-XVIII, 32.

קַרְחִי, probablement faute de copiste pour קְרֵיהּ q. v. Comme dans
les deux passages de la Massore où ce mot se rencontre et ou le
sens demande le singulier, ce mot est écrit ainsi, Buxt., *Clav. Mass.*,
sb v., a supposé une forme adjective en i et ponctue קַרְחִי, mais
dans son *Lex.* nous ne trouvons aucune trace de cette forme
étrange.

קְרֵי (a.), plur. masc. קָרְיָן, fém. קָרְיָן. Voyez כְּתִיב.

קְרָיָא (a.), *la lecture* (par excellence), c'est-à-dire *la Bible.* Se dit
1° de toute la Bible ; *2°* (après une remarque concernant un certain
livre) du reste de la Bible. Exemple du *1°*, Mmarg. Gen. XXXIV, 14 :
ט״ו מִלִּין נְקֻדּוֹת בַּקְרָיָא, *15 expressions sont marquées de points
(extraordinaires) dans la Bible.* Exemple du *2°*, Mm. Ex. XXV, 28 :
ו׳ בִּישַׁעְיָה ו׳ בִּקְרָיָ[א], *6 (fois) dans Isaie, 6 (fois) dans (le reste de)
la Bible.* Dans ce second sens au lieu de וְכָל קְרָיָא קְרָיָא, on trouve
souvent וּשְׁאָר, *et le reste (de la Bible)*, par exemple Mm. Ex. XXVI, 9
(édit. Buxtorf) et Mmarg. ibid. (édit. Bragadin).

קְרָיָא (a.), masc. déterm. ou fémin. indéterm., écrit aussi קִרְיָה (Mp. Ps. LXXXI, 3), *localité, village*. Voyez שׁוֹם.

קְרָיָאה (h. , comme l'araméen קְרָיָא q. v. Exemple, Mm. Gen. III, 16, où il est remarqué que אִישֵׁךְ se rencontre ב׳ בְּקְרִיָאה, *2 (fois)* *dans la Bible*. — Voyez aussi sous תִּיקּוּן סוֹפְרִים 1° et Mm. Jud. I, 14, 25, 26, etc.

קָרִיב (a.), *près, proche*. Se rencontre quelquefois dans le même sens que סְמוּךְ 2° et סְמִיךְ 1°; voyez ces mots. Exemple, Mf. אד 21

וְאִיבּוּן מ׳ מִלִּין où nous trouvons וְאִיבּוּן קְרִיבִין לְאַזְפָּרָה au lieu de סְמִיכִין לַיהֹוָה dans la rubrique correspondante, Ginsb., *Mass.*, I, p. 409, n° 81 a. Cf. *ibid.*, p. 410, n° 82 et *O. W. O.* 187.

קְרִיבָה, Mf. אד 19, erreur pour קְרָיָאה? Comparez Ginsb., *Mass.*, I, p. 23, n° 102.

קְרִיחַ (a.), plur. קְרִחִין, *chauve*. Se dit d'un mot qui n'a pas le Waw copulatif par opposition à d'autres mots qui l'ont. Exemples, Mm. Ezech. XXXI, 14 : קָדְמָא קרחי (lisez קְרִיחַ) וּתְרֵין אָחֲרָנִין נָסְבִין וי׳ו, *le premier est chauve et les deux autres prennent Waw.* — Mp. Deut. I, 15 : קָדְמָא קרחי בְלָא וי׳ו (sic!), *le premier est chauve, sans Waw.* — Mm. Ex. XVIII, 21 : קָדְמָ[אה] וְתִנְיָינָ[א] וּתְלִיתָאָ[ה] קָרְחֵי רְבִיעָ[אה] נָסֵיב וי׳ו, *le premier, le second et le troisième sont chauves, le quatrième reçoit Waw.* — Au lieu de קְרִיחַ on dit beaucoup plus souvent לָא נָסֵיב וי׳ו, *ne reçoit pas Waw.* Cf. Ginsb., *Mass.*, I, p. 417, n°s 110 et suiv.

קָרֵינַן (a.) ou קָרֵינָן (1) (partic. plur. masc. + pron. personn. enclitique, 1re pers. plur.), *nous lisons*. Exemples, Mf. ת 3, Mm. Num. XXXIV, 4 et Mm. Is. XIII, 16 (2).

קַרְנָא (a.), *corne*. Se rencontre quelquefois dans le sens de תָּאג ou de זַיִן. Exemple, Ginsb., *Mass.*, I, p. 234, n° 3 : ה׳ דְּחַד קַרְנָא וְדָבְקִין י׳ה בְּאוֹרְיְיתָא, *hés qui ont une corne et qui adhèrent, 15 dans la Loi.* — *Ibid.*, p. 236, n° 6 : ה׳ ש׳ס בְּאוֹרְוִיתָא דְלָא דבקו (lisez דָּבְקֵי) וְאִית לְהוֹן אַרְבַּע קַרְנֵי, *360 hés dans la Loi*

---

(1) Et non קָרֵינָן comme nous l'avons imprimé par erreur, *Rev. Bibl.* 1903, p. 546, ligne 21, et 1904, p. 544, C, l. 7.

(2) Nous avons donné cette rubrique sans indiquer sa provenance, *Rev. Bibl.* 1903, p. 546, ligne 21. — Le cas que nous avons cité d'après Frensdorff, *Rev. Bibl.* 1904, p. 544, C, l. 5, n'est justifié par aucune des sources qu'il indique.

qui n'adhèrent pas et ont quatre cornes. Comparez *Baddĕ ărōn* (*Sepher Taghin,* p. 38, où on lit תָּאגֵי au lieu de קַרְנֵי, et après דִּבְקִין, les mots בנהא במעהא que nous ne comprenons pas. — *Ibid.,* p. 407, n° 8 : ח כ׳ח בָּאורָיְיתָא דְתַלְתָּא קַרְנֵי תְּרֵין לְאוֹחַריהוֹן וְחַד לָקֶדָמֵיהוֹן [lisez לַאֲחוֹרֵיהוֹן] (1)], *28 chĕths dans la loi qui ont trois cornes, deux par derrière et une par devant.* Comparez *Baddĕ ărōn,* op. et loc. cit., où, au lieu de קַרְנֵי. on lit זֵיוּנֵי.

קַרְתָּא (a.), *ville, bourg.* Voyez שׁוֹם.

ר

רֵאשָׁא (a.), comme רֵישָׁא q. v. Exemple sous פְּסִיקְתָּא.

רַבָּא (a.), fém. רַבְּתָא (et רַבְּתִי q. v.). Dans une rubrique assez obscure, Mmarg. Is. xxxiv, 11, רַבָּא semble être employé dans le même sens que אֲרִיךְ q. v. pour désigner le Waw par opposition au Yôdh appelé זְעִיר q. v. La rubrique est, à propos de קַד־תַהֹו : ד דְסְמִיכִין, סְיָג לַתּוֹרָה. fol. 39 b, il faut לְיֹהֹוא רַבָּא בזעיר. D'après Worms (2), corriger et lire ainsi : ג רְפַין דִּסְמִיכִין לְיֹהֹוא רַבָּא וּזְעִיר. *3 mots (commençant par une* בֶּגֶדְכֶפֶת*) sont Râphès (à cette lettre) quoique immédiatement précédés d'(une des lettres* יֹהֹוא*, à savoir Grande (= Waw) ou Petite (= Yôdh).* — Pour le féminin précédé de מְסִירָה voyez ce dernier mot.

רִבּוּי (h.), *augmentation, pluriel, supériorité numérique.* Voyez מִיעוּט.

רְבִיעָאָה (a.), *quatrième.* Exemple sous קְרֵיחַ.

רְבַע (a.), *qui engendre.* Désignation dans le langage des signes mnémotechniques de l'accent *Rebhía'* dans cette rubrique Mmarg. Num. xxvi, 63 : אֵלֶּה פְּקוּדֵי בְּנֵי יִשְׂרָאֵל אֵלֶּה בְּטַעַם רְבִיעַ וְדֵין בִּמְהָפָּךְ [v. 51]. אֵלֶּה פְּקוּדֵי בְּנֵי יִשְׂרָאֵל *dans* סִי[מָן] רָבַע יִשְׂרָאֵל. *avec* אֵלֶּה

---

(1) Voyez pourtant Dalm., *Gramm.,* § 14, 7.

(2) Cet auteur (*ibid.,* fol. 30 a) cite, sans dire où il l'a prise, la rubrique suivante évidemment une variante de celle dont nous avons donné la traduction sous זְעִיר où, au lieu de 28, lisez 27] d'après Fr., 376, b 4 = Mmarg. Num. vii, 14; Mm. et Mp. ibid. 20; Mmarg et Mm. Ps. cv, 11; Mf. י 27. Cf. Ginsb., *Mass.,* I, p. 391, n° 32] : כ״ב פְּסִיקִים לֵית בְּהוֹן רַבָּא וּזְעִיר, *22 versets sans Grand ni Petit.*

l'accent Rebhîa', et celui-ci (v. 63 : אֵלֶּה פְּקוּדֵי מֹשֶׁה) *avec Mehup-pach, et le signe mnémotechnique (pour le v. 51) est : Israël engen-dre.* La Massore joue sur le nom du Rebhîa' (*qui est couché*), de la racine רבע à laquelle les interprètes juifs prêtaient aussi le sens de *engendrer* suggéré par l'expression רֹבַע יִשְׂרָאֵל, Num. xxiii, 10. Cf. Gesenius, *Thesaurus,* sb רֹבַע.

רַבְתִי (a.), une des formes du fémin. de רַבָּא q. v. (Cf. Dalm., *Gramm.,* § 38 fin; Levias, *Grammar of the aramean idiom contained in the Talmud* etc., § 69, n° 2, et Nöldeke [רַבְתִי], *Mandäische Grammatik,* p. 154). Seulement avec אַלְפָבֵיתָא, *le Grand Alphabet,* pour dési-gner le Psaume cxix, appelé aussi תְמַנְיָא אַפֵּי q. v.

רוּמָא (a.), *hauteur, altitude,* précédé de סָלֵיק, *qui monte,* ou de זְקִיף, *qui est suspendu, élevé,* se dit d'un mot marqué, dans un cer-tain passage, d'un accent supérieur, principalement Zāqēph, par opposition au même mot marqué, dans un autre passage, d'un accent inférieur, principalement Tebhîr, auquel cas on dit que ce mot est נָחֵת לִתְהוֹמָא. *descendant à l'abîme.* Exemple, Mp. Lev. xxvi, 41 : חַד מִן י״ח זוּגִין חַד סָלֵיק לְרוּמָא וְחַד נָחֵת לִתְהוֹמָא, *un de 18 pai-res* (*de deux mots dont*) *l'un monte au très haut et l'autre descend à l'abîme.* — Même rubrique Mmarg. Ex. vi, 9 et (avec זְקִיף au lieu de סָלֵיק) Mm. I Chron. xviii, 9. Voyez סָלֵיק et לְמַטָה.

רָזָא (a.), *mystère, secret.* Dans cette curieuse rubrique, Mp. Ex. xx, 3, à propos de עַל־פָּנָי : כֵּן דִּינוֹ לְמַאן דִּילִיף רָזָא, *ainsi est sa règle pour qui est initié au mystère* (1).

רְחֹקָה (h.), désignation de la section du (voyage) *lointain,* c'est-à-dire Num. ix, 1-15. Voyez פֶּסַח קָטָן.

רֵישָׁא (a.), état absol. et état constr. רֵישׁ, plur. רֵישִׁין, *tête, commen-cement* (d'un mot, d'un verset, d'un chapitre, d'un livre), opposé de סוֹפָא. סֵיפָא qq. v. Voyez des exemples sous סֵדֶר. סֵיפָא.

רָם 2) (h.), fémin. רָמָה. littéralement *haut, élevé,* et dans le langage des signes mnémotechniques, 1° mot *marqué d'un accent supérieur*

---

(1) Il est assez étrange que personne (à notre connaissance, du moins) ne se soit préoccupé d'éclaircir ce *mystère.* que l'on trouve pourtant dans toutes les éditions du Texte Massoré-tique.

(2. C'est ainsi probablement qu'il faut lire au lieu de דם dans la Mmarg. Ex. xxviii, 35 (cf. ibid. édit. Buxtorf) et Num. iv, 42 (cf. Worms, סָיג לַתוֹרָה, f. 36 b).

dans un certain passage, par opposition à ce même mot marqué d'un accent inférieur dans un autre endroit. C'est ainsi que la Massore, Mmarg. Num. IV, 42, voulant rappeler que le mot וּפְקֻדֵי dans ce verset (où le mot *tribus* suit immédiatement) est marqué d'un Zāqēph (tandis que dans le v. 38 il a Tiphchā), donne ce Sēmān ou signe mnémotechnique : (sic! lisez רמ = רְמוֹת) מִשְׁפְּחַת רָם. *les tribus sont élevées.* — De même Mmarg. Num. XIV, 36. le fait que dans וְהָאֲנָשִׁים, Num. XIII, 31 (où ce mot est immédiatement suivi de אֲשֶׁר עָלוּ עִמּוֹ), le Méthegh léger est remplacé par Azla (tandis que ibid. XIV, 36 il est remplacé par Mûnāch). est rappelé par ce sēmān : עָלוּ בְרָמָה, *ils montèrent (et) sont en haut lieu.* Comparez les rubriques citées sous לְמַטָּה. — 2° Écrit avec *scriptio plena.* Ainsi Mmarg. Ex. XXXVIII, 35 pour rappeler que le mot קֹולוֹ. écrit défectivement partout ailleurs dans le Pentateuque, a la *scriptio plena* dans ce passage, la Massore donne ce sēmān : קֹולוֹ רָם, *sa voix est haute* (c'est-à-dire *forte, sonore,* parce qu'elle est *pleine*). Cf. Deuter. XXVII, 14.

רָפֶה (h.), plur. רָפִים, *faible, amolli,* l'opposé de דָּגֵשׁ et מַפִּיק. Voyez ces mots et aussi ce que nous avons dit dans la *Terminologie grammaticale de la Massore,* 3-5 (*Rev. Bibl.* 1903, pp. 543 et 544). — Exemples, Mp. Gen. XXV, 31, מִכְרָה est appelé רְפִי (par opposition à מִכְרָה, Prov. XXXI, 10). — AMm. Job XV, 5 il est remarqué que deux עֲרוּמִים (*rusés*) sont רָפִים par opposition aux deux עֲרִיצִים (*ons*) qui sont דְּגֵשִׁים (Mf. עֵר 14). — On rencontre plus souvent la forme araméenne רָפִי q. v.

רְפִי (a.), pl. רְפַיִן, *amolli.* De même que l'hébreu רָפֶה q. v. Exemples, Mp. Ex. I, 19 (חָיוֹת). par opposition à חַיֹּת, Lev. XIV, 4 : Is. XXXV, 9, etc.); — Mp. Gen. IV, 9 (הֲשֹׁמֵר). par opposition à הַשֹּׁמֵר. Ps. CXLVI, 6); — Mp. Gen. IX, 15 (לְמַבּוּל). par opposition à לַמַּבּוּל; — Mp. Gen. I, 9 (וְתֵרָאֶה) et non וַתֵּרָאֶה); — Mm. Job XV, 5 (dans le Sēmān araméen, la rubrique elle-même ayant la forme hébraïque; voyez רָפֶה): — Mf. עש 5 [a fine] il est remarqué que 3 מַעֲשֹׂר sont רְפַיִן (par opposition aux trois מַעֲשֹׂר qui sont דְּגֵשִׁין Mf. ibid. 6 [a fine]) (1).

(1) Voyez, sur cette rubrique, Fr. 152, note 1.

ש

שֶׁ (h.) = אֲשֶׁר. Exemple, Mm. Ps. cvii, 23 : שֶׁבַּתּוֹרָה. *qui sont dans la Loi.*

שֶׁבֶר (h.), littéralement *rupture, cassure* (comparez תְּבִיר, *brisé*). Désignation de l'accent Tebhir dans un signe mnémotechnique, Mmarg. Num. xxxi, 54, dont le but est de rappeler que le mot הַכֹּהֵן. dans cet endroit, est marqué d'un accent supérieur (לְמַעְלָה), à savoir Azla, tandis que dans le verset 51 il est marqué d'un Tebhir. שֶׁבֶר doit avoir une valeur mnémotechnique qui nous échappe. L'opposé sémanique ordinaire de לְמַעְלָה est לְמַטָּה q. v.

שָׁוֶא (h. , fém. שָׁוָה, plur. masc. שָׁוִים, fém. שָׁווֹת, *pareil, égal (en nombre)*. Exemples, Mm. Ex. xii, 42 : ג פְּסוּקִין דְּאִית בְּהוֹן שׁוִים שְׁתֵּי תֵיבִן (lisez תֵּיבִין) וְאִית רֵאשׁוֹנָה ש (lisez שָׁווֹת), *3 versets dans lesquels il y a deux mots pareils, et dont la première lettre est* ש. Les trois versets sont Ex. xii, 42; Jud. v, 7; I Chron. vii, 24. Cf. Ginsb., *Mass.*, II, p. 601, n° 16. — Ginsb., *Mass.*, I, p. 38, n° 236 b : הָלֵין ג פְּסוּקִין] אוֹתִיּוֹתֵיהֶם שָׁווֹת בְּכָל חַד וְחַד ע״ב אוֹתִיּוֹת וג, *ces 3 versets, leurs lettres sont égales en nombre; dans chacun d'eux il y a 72 lettres* etc.

שׁוֹם (a.), שֵׁם, déterm. שְׁמָא, plur. absolu שְׁמָהָן, constr. שְׁמָהָת (voyez Dalm., *Gramm.*, pp. 159 et 160, cf. p. 63), *nom.* Exemples, 1° שׁוֹם ש : אֱנָשׁ ש, אֱנָשָׁא ש, אֲנָשָׁא ש. *nom de personne, nom propre :* par exemple, Mm. Jerem. xxii, 16, où, à propos de דָּן, la Massore remarque que cette orthographe se rencontre 3 fois dans le lâschôn de *juger* (בְּלִישָׁן דִּין) et ajoute : וְכָל שׁוֹם אֱינָשׁ וְקַרְתָּא דְּכָוָתֵיהּ]. *et tout nom de personne et de bourg est pareil.* Autres exemples, avec אֱנָשׁ Mp. Ruth iv, 20; I Chron. ii, 29,30,49; iv, 3,4, 11,12. Avec אֱנָשָׁא Mp. Esdr. vi, 15 (édit. Buxtorf); I Chron. ii, 48. — אֲנִתְתָא ש, אִינְתְּתָא ש, אִתְּתָא ש, *nom de femme.* Exemples, Mp. I Chron. ii, 26; ibid. II Reg. xviii, 2; ibid. II Sam. xvii, 20. — בְּאֵר ש, *nom de puits.* Exemple, Mp. Gen. xxvi, 33. — בַּרְנָשׁ ש, *nom de personne.* Exemples, Mmarg. Jerem. xxii, 16, à propos de דָּן ג. *3 (fois dans) le lâschôn de juger* : בְּלִישָׁן דִּין וְכָל שׁוֹם בַּרְנָשׁ דְּכָוָין דְּכָוָתֵיהּ : דָּן, *et tout nom de personne lui est pareil* (c.-à-d. s'écrit exac-

tement de même); Mp. Ps. LXXI, 3. — גְּבַר שׁ׳, גַּבְרָא שׁ׳, *nom d'homme*. Exemples, גְּבַר Mm. I Reg. I, 51; ibid. Job XXIII, 9; גַּבְרָא Mm. et Mmarg. Jos. XV, 43. — קִרְיָה שׁ׳, *nom de localité*. Exemples, Mp. Ps. LXXI, 3; ibid. I Chron. II, 46. — קַרְתָּא שׁ׳, *nom de localité*. Exemples, Mp. I Chron. V, 32; VI, 59; Mm. Ps. LXXI, 3; Mm. et Mmarg. Jos. XV, 43.

2° שֵׁם : אֱנָשׁ שׁ׳, *nom de personne*. Exemple, Mp. Neh. X, 26. — גְּבַר שׁ׳, *nom d'homme*. Exemple, Mp. II Sam. XIII, 32.

3° שְׁמָא. Exemple, Ginsb., *Mass.*, III, p. 224, col. b : שִׁבְעָא שְׁמָא דְּגַבְרָא וּמָתָא, *Schebhā, nom d'homme et de pays*.

4° שְׁמָהָן. Exemple, Mm. Num. XXVI, 33 : ו׳ פְּסוּקִין דְּאִית בְּהוֹן מִלִּין דְּדָמֵיין בִּשְׁמָהָן וּמִתְחַלְּפִין בְּאָתְוָתְהוֹן, *6 versets où se trouvent des groupes de mots qui se ressemblent par des noms (c.-à-d. qui contiennent les mêmes noms propres) mais qui diffèrent par leurs (de ces noms) lettres* (tel nom, par exemple, ayant le Waw copulatif dans un ou plusieurs groupes, et ne l'ayant pas dans un ou plusieurs autres groupes).

5° שְׁמָהָת. Exemple, Mf. ז 61 : אִלֵּין שְׁמָהָת גַּבְרֵי נָסְבִין ד׳ וג׳, *ceux-ci sont les noms d'homme qui prennent le Waw*, etc. Mm. Ex. VI, 18 : ה׳ פְּסוּקִין דְּמַיין בִּשְׁמָהָתְהוֹן וּמִתְחַלְּפִין בְּאָתְוָתְהוֹן, *5 versets qui se ressemblent par leurs noms (c.-à-d. par les noms de personne qu'ils contiennent) et qui diffèrent par leurs lettres*.

שִׁפָּה (h.), plur. שִׁפִּין, *liste* (de mots etc.). Exemple, Mf. ב 12 : שִׁפָּה חֲדָא דְּמִשְׁתַּמְּשֶׁת בָּה בְּסוֹף תֵּיבוּתָא. *une liste qui a בָּה à la fin de chaque mot* (c'est-à-dire de *mots qui finissent en* בָּה). Voyez d'autres exemples dans Fr. 381 et suiv.

שֵׁם (h.), pl. שֵׁמוֹת, *nom*. Exemple, Mp. I Chron. II, 24 : שֵׁם נִקְבָה, *nom de femme*. — Ginsb., *Mass.*, III, p. 202, col. b : וְיֵשׁ אַרְבַּע שֵׁמוֹת גּוּבְרִין שֶׁסּוֹפָן אֶל וְהָאָלֶף נָחָה, *et il y a quatre noms d'homme qui se terminent en* אֶל. *l'aleph étant quiescent*.

שְׁמָא (a.), voyez שׁוּם.

שמוש. Cette forme qu'on ne rencontre que dans une rubrique obscure, Mmarg. Gen. XXXIII, 11, est vraisemblablement à ponctuer שִׁמּוּשׁ qui ne peut que vouloir dire *action de faire fonction de lettre servile*. Voyez sur cette rubrique Worms, סְיָג לַתּוֹרָה, fol. 30 a (l'auteur, après s'être donné beaucoup de mal et avoir changé presque tous les mots de la rubrique, suggère de lire שְׁבוּשׁ).

שְׁמֵשׁ (h.), voyez מְשַׁמֵּשׁ.

שְׁנָיִין (a.), *qui diffèrent,* dans le même sens que מְשַׁנְּיָא q. v. Nous n'avons pas rencontré cette forme que nous donnons sur la foi de Fr. sb v.

שֵׁרֵת (h.), *servir.* Voyez sous מְקוֹמוֹת et מְשָׁרֵת.

שֹׁרֶשׁ (h.), *racine, radical,* c'est-à-dire le mot dépouillé de ses lettres serviles. Exemple, Mf. א 12. Voyez מְשַׁמֵּשׁ 2°.

שִׁשָּׁה (h.), *six.* En langage massorétique, *six points,* c.-à-d. deux Seghols consécutifs. Exemple, Mm. Ex. VIII, 24 : כָּל לָלֶכֶת שֶׁבַּמִּקְרָא, בְּשִׁשָּׁה במ'א לָלֶכֶת בָּקָמֵץ, *tout* לָלֶכֶת *dans la Bible s'écrit avec six (points) sauf un* לָלֹכֶת [Eccl. 1, 7] *(qui s'écrit) avec Qāmēṣ (et trois points).* Comparez la rubrique correspondante Ginsb., *Mass.,* I, p. 722, n° 348 (où au lieu de מתקרי lisez מִתְקְרִי, et לָלֶכֶת au lieu de לָלֹכֶת et vice-versà). — Voyez *Rev. Bibl.* 1903, p. 543.

שַׁתָּא (a.), *année.* Exemple, Mf. שנ 5, où il est remarqué que שְׁנוֹת se rencontre trois fois שַׁתָּא (בְּלִישָׁן) *dans (le lāschōn d')année* (1). Cf. *Rev. Bibl.* 1903, p. 547.

שְׁתִיתָאָה (a.), *sixième.* Exemples sous קְרִיח.

ת

תָּאג (persan), plur. תָּאגִים, תָּאגִין, תָּגֵי, littéralement *couronne.* Peut-être ce terme fut-il d'abord employé pour désigner le trait horizontal qui constitue la partie supérieure de la plupart des lettres hébraïques (2). En tout cas, il a servi dans la suite, comme les

---

1. Les 3 passages cités à la suite de cette rubrique sont Deuter. XXXII, 7 ; Ps. LXXVII, 6, et ibid. 11. Ce dernier, toutefois, peut être contesté (voyez la *Concordance* de Mandelkern). שָׁנוֹת dans le sens d'*années* se retrouve encore Ps. CX, 15 ; Prov. IV ; 10 ; IX, 11 et Job XVI, 22. Il est probable que dans l'origine ces quatre passages étaient cités à la suite des 3 premiers et que la rubrique portait ד au lieu de ג. Quelque copiste aura cru inutile de donner toute la liste et se sera arrêté après le troisième passage Ps. LXXVII, 11 ; assez naturellement d'ailleurs, car c'est évidemment en vue de ce passage que la rubrique a été rédigée, comme pour affirmer que là aussi, comme ailleurs, שְׁנוֹת était bien l'état construit de שָׁנוֹת, *années,* et non l'infinitif constr. de שָׁנָה, *mutatus est.* Un second copiste ne trouvant que trois citations et pensant que c'était tout, aura substitué ג à ד. (Réponse à la question de Fr. 203, note 1).

(2) Telle est l'opinion soutenue par J. Derenbourg dans la savante notice qu'il a publiée sur l'édition du *Sepher Taghin* par l'abbé Bargès (voyez la note suivante) dans le *Journal asiatique,* série VI°, vol. IX°, pp. 242-251.

termes זַיֵּין et קַרְנָא, qq. v., à désigner les picots ou crochets dont la Massore veut que certaines lettres du Pentateuque soient munies. Ginsb., *Mass.*, II, p. 681 a : ב ק״ג בְּאוֹרַיְיתָא דְלָא דְבָקִין רג׳ תָאגִין אִית לְהוֹן. *il y a 103 mêms fermés dans la Loi qui n'adhèrent pas et qui ont (chacun) trois couronnes.* On trouvera de nombreux autres exemples dans le *Sepher Taghin* (1).

תְּאוֹמִים (h.), *jumeaux.* Se dit comme מִיתְאָמִים q. v. de deux mots absolument pareils et se suivant immédiatement sans *Pisqa* (voyez פְּסְקָא). Exemple, Mf. ב ב 14 : א ב תְּאוֹמִים בְּפָסִיק. *liste alphabétique de jumeaux dans un (même) verset.* Comparez la rubrique correspondante dans Ginsb., *Mass.*, II, p. 221, n° 333 m : א ב בֵּין ב״ב (lisez דְּלוּג) דלוג [דְסְמִיךָן] דְסְמִין[וֹ]ת לֵ[יֹ]ן וְחַד חַד וְכָל מִיתְאָמִים. *liste alphabétique de deux et deux c'est-à-dire de paires de mots) jumeaux et dont aucune ne se retrouve ainsi appuyée (voyez סְמִיךְ); incomplète* (Voy. דְּלוּג).

תְּהוֹמָא (a.), *abîme.* Voyez נָחַת et רוּמָא.

תְּהִלָּה (h.), plur. תְהִלּוֹת, תְהִלִּים, תִלִּים, *louanges.* Désignation du *livre des Psaumes.*

תּוֹרָה (h.), la *Loi,* c'est-à-dire le *Pentateuque.* Fr. sb v. ajoute que ce terme, comme קְרָיא et מִקְרָא, désigne quelquefois la Bible tout entière, par exemple dans l'expression אַפִּין וְרַקִּין שֶׁבַּתּוֹרָה (voyez אַפִּין וְרַקִּין et מְנוּזְרוֹת). Nous eussions préféré un autre exemple, car nous soupçonnons fort que אַפִּין וְרַקִּין ne se disait, dans l'origine, que des נוּנִין מְנוּזְרוֹת ou *Nûns retournés* du Pentateuque et qu'on ajoutait שֶׁבַּתּוֹרָה pour les distinguer d'autres אַפִּין וְרַקִּין dont nous ne savons plus rien.

תּוֹרַת הַכֹּהֲנִים (h.), la *Loi des Prêtres,* c'est-à-dire le Lévitique. Exemples, Mm. Lev. xi, 3; Gen. xxxii, 14 et Ps. xcvi, 7. Voyez aussi notre planche (*Rev. Bibl.* 1902, p. 551), lignes c et d.

---

(1) Le *Sépher Taghin* a été publié pour la première fois par l'abbé Bargès, à Paris, 1866, sous le titre de סֵפֶר תַּגִּין, *Sepher Taghin, Liber coronularum,* etc. L'éditeur y a ajouté, comme traitant du même sujet, 1° trois chapitres du sixième livre du *Baddé aron (les bâtons de l'Arche)* et 2° un midrasch attribué à Rabbi 'Aqibha. — Ginsburg, *Mass.*, II, pp. 680 et suiv., a publié sous le titre de תָּאגִים une autre recension de ce même ouvrage, où, au lieu de donner après chaque lettre tous les passages qui s'y rapportent dans tout le Pentateuque, on a distribué ces passages en cinquante-deux séries correspondant aux cinquante-deux Sedârin. — Nous aurons probablement à revenir sur ce traité curieux qui, en outre des תָאגִין et דַּיְינִין, a encore pour objet les formes extraordinaires dans le tracé des lettres. En attendant, voyez ce que nous avons dit, *Rev. Bibl.* 1903, pp. 541 et 542.

תְּחִלָּה (h.), *commencement*, d'où les verbes dénominatifs néo-hébreu הֵחֵל et araméen תְּחַל, employés l'un et l'autre à la forme causative dans le sens de *commencer*.

תֵּיבָה, תֵּבָה (h.), plur. תֵּיבוֹת, תֵּיבִין, littéralement *coffre, arche* et, en langue massorétique, 1° *mot, mot écrit, en tant qu'assemblage de lettres*. Voyez מִלָּה 1°. — 2° Suivant Worms, סְיָיג לַתּוֹרָה, fol. 30 b, תֵּיבָה. « *voyelle avec la consonne*, par exemple dans עָשִׁיר il y a deux tébhôth ». Si l'auteur, comme nous le supposons, veut dire que תֵּיבָה a aussi le sens de *syllabe*, il ne s'est pas exprimé assez clairement; il est regrettable d'ailleurs qu'il n'ait pas cru nécessaire de renvoyer le lecteur à la Massore. — 3° Selon Fr. sb v., תֵּיבָה se dit non seulement des mots et des syllabes (pas d'exemple!), mais aussi des *lettres*. A l'appui de ce dernier sens il cite la rubrique Mm. Gen. xxxvii, 25 à propos de וּצְרִי : ב זוֹגִין בִּתְרֵי לִישָׁנֵי וב' תֵּיבִין קַדְמָאֵי יצ. Frensdorff, p. 341, note 1, lit קַדְמָאֵי et traduit : *2 paires de mots avec deux significations et dont les 2 premières lettres sont* צו. Les deux paires sont 1° וּצְרִי, *et la résine*, Gen. xxxvii, 25, et וּצְרִי, *et Serí*, I Chron. xxv, 3 ; 2° וְצַרְתִּי, *et je poursuivrai*, Ex. xxiii, 22, et וְצַרְתִּי, *et j'assiégerai*, Is. xxix, 3. — Cette interprétation toutefois nous semble devoir être écartée, ne fût-ce que parce que, les deux mots en question ayant en commun les trois premières lettres, la Massore aurait certainement dit *3* et non *2* si elle eût voulu attirer l'attention sur le nombre des lettres communes. D'ailleurs ce n'est pas צו que nous lisons dans la Massore, comme Frensdorff l'imprime, mais bien וצ' = וצר. Il nous paraît donc plus naturel de prendre תֵּיבִין dans son sens ordinaire et traduire le commencement de la note : *2 paires avec deux sens et deux mots*, c'est-à-dire *avec un sens différent pour chacun des deux mots pareils formant chaque paire* (Comparez la rubrique correspondante, Mf. א 22 : א״ב מן ב״ב וְתַרְוַיְהוֹן בִּתְרֵי לִישָׁנֵי, *liste alphabétique de mots se rencontrant* deux et deux [c'est-à-dire *par paires*] *et les deux mots de chaque paire dans deux sens*). Quant à la seconde partie de la rubrique, nous avouons qu'elle nous embarrasse un peu. Peut-être קדמ' est-il pour קַדְמְהוֹן = רֵישְׁהוֹן et faut-il traduire : *et le commencement des mots* (dans les deux paires) *est* וצר.

תֵּיבוּתָא (a.). pl. תֵּיבוּתָן, comme תֵּיבָה q. v. Exemple, Mf. ן 11 : א״ב מן חַד חַד מן תַּרְתֵּין תֵּיבוּתָן לָא נָסְבִין ו׳ יו בְּרֵישׁ תֵּיבוּתָא

דְּמַטְעֶה דְלֹוּג, *liste alphabétique d'expressions ne se rencontrant qu'une fois et consistant en deux mots qui ne prennent pas Waw au commencement, ce qui induit en erreur. Incomplet.*

תֵּיבְתָּה (h.), peut-être erreur pour תֵּיבְתָא (a.) = תֵּיבוּתָא (Voyez Dalm., *Lex.*, sb v.). Même sens que תֵּיבָה. Exemple, Mm. Ezech. XXXVI, 25.

תֵּימַה (h.), *étonnement, admiration* et, en langage massorétique, *interrogation.* Exemple, Mm. Gen. XVIII, 25 : ג הֵהִין בַּתּוֹרָה דְנִרְאָין תְּמוּהוֹת וְאֵינָן תְּמוּהוֹת וְסֵימָנֵיהוֹן וג׳ ..... וְכֹל הֵא תְמוּהָה פַּתַח כְּשֶׁהַתִּימַה בְּהֵא כְמֹו ..... אֲבָל אֵלּוּ הַתֵּימַה אֵינוּ בְהֵא אָכֵן בָּא אַחֲרֵי כֵן, *(il y a) 3 Hês qui paraissent interrogatifs et qui ne sont pas interrogatifs et ce sont etc..... et tout Hē interrogatif a Pathach lorsque l'interrogation est sur le Hē comme..... mais dans ces cas-ci l'interrogation n'est pas sur le Hē, mais vient après. Voyez sur cette rubrique Fr. 384, note 3.*

תִּיקּוּן סֹופְרִים (h.), *correction de scribes* (1). 1° La Massore donne ce nom, toujours au singulier, à une liste de dix-huit passages qui ont été modifiés, apparemment pour faire disparaître autant de manières de parler, ou d'expressions choquantes « offensivæ aurium piarum ». Cette liste est donnée Mm. Num. I, 1 (autour du titre) : י״ח מִלִּין תִּיקּוּן סֹופְרִים וְסֵימָנֵיהוֹן] וג׳. *18 expressions [sont (2) correction de scribes, à savoir, etc.* — Ibid. Ps. CVI, 20 : ח״י חַד מִן מִלִּין בְּקְרִיאָה תִיקּוּן סֹופְרִים, *une de 18 expressions dans l'Écriture (qui sont) correction de scribes.* Le nom d'Esdras, avec ou sans celui de Néhémie, est quelquefois ajouté ou substitué à סֹופְרִים. Exemple, Mp. Num. XII, 12 : י״ח תִּיקּוּן עֶזְרָא, *18 (expressions sont) correction d'Esdras.* Ginsb., *Mass.,* II, p. 710, n° 206 (3) : (sic!) י״ח דבר

---

(1) Et non, comme on le trouve quelquefois traduit, *corrections des Scribes*, — « *Emendations of the Sopherim* », Ginsb., *Introduction*, p. 347, « *Verbesserungen der Schriftgelehrten* », Buhl, *Kanon und Text des Alten Testamentes*, p. 103. Ce savant écrit même *Tiqqune Sofrim !* expression que nous n'avons jamais rencontrée dans la Massore, et qui semble avoir été déjà employée par Fr. Hoedelhofer dans un ouvrage cité par Strack, *Prolegomena*, p. 87. — Au lieu de *correction de Scribes*, peut-être faudrait-il traduire *correctoire de Scribes.* Comparez le 2° de ce présent article et תִּיקּוּן ס״ת.

D'une manière générale sur le תִּיקּוּן סֹופְרִים voyez Buxtorf, *Lexic.*, sb v.; Strack, *Prolegomena critica in Vetus Testamentum* etc., Lipsiæ, 1883, pp. 86 et suiv.; Fr. Buhl, *Kanon und Text des Alten Testamentes*, Leipzig, 1891, p. 103 et suiv.; Ginsburg, *Introduction*. pp. 347-363.

(2) Ou bien, en sous-entendant אִית בְּהוֹן. *dans lesquelles il y a.*

(3) D'après trois manuscrits du British Museum provenant du Yémen.

דְּבָרִים? תִּיקוּן סוֹפְרִים וְאִית דְּאָמְרִין עֶזְרָא וּגִ' *18* (*expressions* דְּבָרִים *sont*) *correction de scribes et il y en a qui disent d'Esdras.* Ginsb., *Introduction,* p. 351 (1), en tête de la liste : תִּיקוּן סוֹפְרִים עֶזְרָא, וּנְחֶמְיָה, *correction de scribes, Esdras et Néhémie.* Voyez aussi sous תַּקֵּן·

2° Un traité massorétique, probablement un *correctoire* (2) comme le nom l'indique, cité dans la Mp. d'un manuscrit du British Museum (Add. 15282). Ginsb., *Introduct.,* p. 602, fin de la note.

תִּיקוּן עֶזְרָא, voyez תִּיקוּן סוֹפְרִים 1°.

תִּיקוּן ס'ת = תִּיקוּן סֵפֶר תּוֹרָה, *correction du livre de la Loi,* nom d'un manuscrit modèle, ou plutôt d'un traité massorétique, d'un correctoire du Pentateuque (Cf. תִּיקוּן סוֹפְרִים 2°). Exemple,

Mmarg. Gen. XLIX, 21, à propos de הַנֹּתֵן : lisez חַד מִן ה' מלֹי (מל') מְלֵאִים (= וּבְסֵ[פֶר] אַ[חֵר] נִמְסָר עָלָיו ד' חָסֵר וְכֵן הוּא בְּתִיקוּן ס'ת וּבְרוֹב הַסְּפָרִים, *un de 5 plenes, et dans un autre livre il est noté à propos de ce mot : « 4 (sont écrits) defective », et il en est ainsi dans la « correction du Pentateuque » et dans la plupart des livres* (3).

תִּיקוּן ר'ס, *correction de Rabbi S***?* titre d'un traité massorétique, mentionné dans la Mp. d'un manuscrit du British Museum (Add. 15282) décrit par Ginsburg, *Introduction,* p. 602, fin de la note.

תָּלוּי (h.), fém. תְּלוּיָה, *suspendue.* Se dit de certaines lettres écrites un peu au-dessus de la ligne et dépassant d'autant les autres lettres par le haut. Exemples, Mp. Job XXXVIII, 12 : ד' אֹתִיּוֹת תְּלוּאוֹת, *4 lettres suspendues;* Mm. *ibid.* : חַד מִן ד' מִלִּין דְּאִית בְּהוֹן אוֹת תָּלוּי. *un de 4 mots dans lesquels il y a une lettre suspendue.* — De même, Jud. XVIII, 30, Mf. תל' 2 (4). — Voyez, sur les *lettres suspendues,* Ginsb., *Introduct.,* pp. 334-341 et ailleurs, passim (consultez l'Index).

תִּלִּים (h.), voyez תְּהִלִּים.

תִּמְהָא (a.), état absolu תִּמַהּ, *étonnement, interrogation* (Cf. תִּימַהּ).

(1) D'après Cod. or. 1425 du British Museum.

(2) Correctorium, Ἐπανορθωτής.

(3) Sur cette rubrique, voyez Norzi, בִּנְחַת שַׁי *ad locum,* et cf. Ginsburg, *Mass.,* II, p. 294, n° 502.

(4) Le dernier passage cité, II Sam. XVIII (10), appartient à תל' 1.

Exemple, Ginsb., *Mass.,* I, p. 257, n° 11 c : אָלֶף בֵּית מִן חַד וְחַד

בִּתְמִהָא (lisez חַד), *liste alphabétique de mots se rencontrant cha-*
cun une fois avec l'interrogation.

תְּמוּהַּ (h.), fém. תְּמוּהָה, *interrogatif.* Exemple sous תֵּימָה. Voyez
un autre תמוה sous תְּמִיָּה.

תְּמִיהָא (a.), fém., *interrogatif.* Exemple, Ginsb., *Mass.,* I. p. 258,
n° 12 : כָּל הֵא תְּמִיהָא, *tout hē interrogatif.* Cf. la rubrique correspondante Mm. Gen. XVIII, 25, sous תֵּימָה.

תְּמִיָּה (h.), contracté de תְּמִיהָה (Buxtorf, *Lex.,* sb v.), *admiration, in-*
terrogation. Exemple, Mf. ה 3 : א״ב מִן חַד חַד ה׳ בְּרֵישׁ תֵּיבוּתָא
בִּתְמִיָּה, *liste alphabétique de (mots) un et un* (c'est-à-dire *se ren-*
contrant chacun une fois seulement) et ayant au commencement
du mot Hē avec interrogation. C'est aussi, probablement, תְּמִיָּה
qu'il faut lire, au lieu de תמוה, dans la rubrique correspondante.
Ginsb., *Mass.,* I, p. 257, n° 11 c; autrement il faudrait suppléer ה׳
et ponctuer בה׳ תְּמוּהַּ. Voyez תְּמוּהַּ.

תְּמָנְיָא אַפֵּי (a.), *huit faces,* précédé de בּ, *à huit faces,* c'est-à-dire
octuple. Désignation du Psaume CXIX (qu'on appelait aussi quelquefois א״ב רַבָּתִי, *le grand alphabet,* par ex. Mf. ר 57 voyez ci-
dessous], et Mm. Ps. LXXXVI, 16). Exemples, Mmarg. Ps. CXIX. 52
(où il faut lire, comme dans les passages suivants. ח׳ דּיִין יג. au
lieu de ר״ג). et 131; Mp. *ibid.,* 158 et 167; Mm. *ibid.,* 158 : ה׳ דּיִין
קָמְצִין ב״אב (sic!) בִּתְמָנְיָא אַפֵּי, *8 waws ont Qāmēs* (au lieu de
Schewā) dans l'alphabet à huit faces (1) (*octuple* . — On disait
aussi par abréviation תְּמָנְיָא אַפֵּי, *l'(alphabet) octuple.* Exemple, Mf.
ה 57 : ו מִלִּין נְסָבִין י קָמְצִין בִּתְמָנְיָא אַפֵּי בְּא״ב רַבָּתִי וְסִימָנֵיהוֹן ו
ו׳ שָׁם בְּתִלִּים בְּא״ב רַבָּתִי אוֹת נ, *8 mots prennent Waw. avec*
Qāmēs dans l'octuple, (c'est-à-dire) *dans le grand alphabet. et leurs*
signes (c'est-à-dire *leurs passages) sont là dans les Psaumes, au*
grand alphabet, à la lettre נ (verset 106). — Mmarg. et Mm. Ps. CXIX.
106 (où nous renvoie la Mf.), on lit : בִּתְמָנְיָא אַפֵּי בְּא״ב. D'après la

---

(1) Quelque fortement que nous inclinions vers cette manière de rendre l'expression בא״ב
בתמ׳ אפ׳, nous ne tenons pas pour impossible que בתמ׳ אפ׳ puisse être considéré comme
étant en apposition avec בא״ב, comme ailleurs (voyez ci-dessous) nous trouvons בא״ב en
apposition avec בתמ׳ אפ׳, auquel cas il faudrait traduire : *dans le (grand) Alphabet* (c'est-
à-dire) *dans l'Octuple.*

rubrique de la Mf. que nous venons de donner, il faut évidemment ajouter רַבְתִי et traduire : *dans l'Octuple, dans le Grand Alphabet.* D'ailleurs, dans la Massore de ce Psaume (comme aussi ailleurs, par ex. Mp. Ps. LXXXVI, 16; Mm. Is. XIII, 11), on le trouve souvent désigné par א״ב (ou tout au long, אַלְפָּא בֵיתָא) tout seul, par ex. Mm. 51 et 54.

L'expression תְּמַנְיָא אַפִּין se rencontre déjà dans ce même sens dans le Talmud de Babylone, *Berâkhôth,* 4 b (1).

תִּקֵּן (h.), *corriger, rectifier.* Exemple O. W. O. 168 : י״ח מִלִּין תִּקֵּן עֶזְרָא וְסֵ יְמָנֵיהוֹן וג׳. *Esdras a corrigé 18 expressions, à savoir* etc. (variante de la rubrique que nous avons donnée sous תִּקּוּן סוֹפְרִים 1°).

תַּרְגּוּם (h.), *traduction,* et en particulier, la traduction araméenne de la Bible, d'où l'expression si fréquente pour introduire un sēmān en araméen, בִּלְשׁוֹן תַּרְגּוּם, *dans la langue du Targum,* par exemple Ginsb., *Mass.,* II, p. 294, n° 499; p. 295, n° 506.

תְּרֵין (a., *deux* (masc.); avec le suffixe 3e pers. masc. plur. תְּרַוֵיהוֹן, *les deux.*

תְּרֵיסַר (a.) = תְּרֵי עֲשַׂר. *douze,* et en particulier *les Douze* (Petits Prophètes). Exemple, Mm. Ex. XXXV, 12 : וְכָל תְּרֵיסַר[וּתְהִלּוֹ[ת] וג׳, *et tous les Douze et les Psaumes* etc.

תַּרְתֵּין (a., *deux* (fém.). Exemple O. W. O. 3, Mf. ה 11 : א״ב מִן חַד וְחַד וּמִן תַּרְתֵּין תֵּיבוּתָ[ן יג׳. *liste alphabétique (d'expressions se rencontrant) une fois (d'une manière) et une fois (d'une autre manière) et (consistant en) deux mots* etc.

Sorrente, en la fête des SS. Apôtres Pierre et Paul, 1905.

H. HYVERNAT.

(1) Dans un manuscrit (voyez l'édition de Goldschmid) on trouve la variante תְּמַנְיָא אָלֶף בֵית, les *huit alphabets*, probablement par le fait d'un copiste qui n'a pas compris le sens de אפ׳ dans ce cas. Fr. sb v. *semble* tomber dans la même erreur et pour la même raison quand il traduit « 8 Alphabete ».

W. BACHER

A Contribution to the History of the Term "Massorah."
—In the first chapter of his *Commentarius Massoræ Historicus*
(Tiberias, Part I.), Buxtorf says that the pronunciation now
generally in use among the Jews of the name of the Tradition
that dealt with the biblical text is מְסוֹרָה (after the form of
בְּגוֹדָה Jer. iii. 7), and as *samech* has a sharp sound, the word is
written with a double *s*, Massorah. This manner of spelling the
word, although it was not adopted by Buxtorf himself, is still everywhere in vogue ; at the same time, however, one generally recalls the
possibility referred to by Buxtorf that the form of the word may be
מְסוּרְדָה (with a dagesh in the ס). Buxtorf also mentions that the
word was by many read מְסָרָה or מַסָּרָה and even מִסְרָה (by Pagninus), while he himself adduces the form מְסוּרְדָה (compare בְּשׁוֹרָה
עֲבוֹדָה) as possible. This remarkable fluctuation in the pronunciation of a word of such frequent use, as well as in the grammatical
explanation of its form, still prevails. Compare F. Buhl, *Kanon und
Text des alten Testaments* (Leipzig, 1891), page 95 *seq.* The very
foundation upon which the use of the word itself rests is extremely
uncertain. In the oldest sources (Talmud and Midrash) it is not to be
found at all, as in these only its equivalent מסורת is to be met with.
Similarly, later authorities speak only of the מסורת, which expression
is very often employed to indicate the Massorah in its written form,
as, for example, by Abulwalîd (see quotations in my *Life and Works
of Abulwalîd, Merwan Ibn G'anah*, etc., p. 52). *Elias Levita* speaks
onstantly of the מסורת not of the מסורה, both in the title and in
he body of his great work dealing with the subject ; the Massorites
are with him, as with Ibn Ezra, אנשי המסורת. I am not in possession of the requisite data to be able to explain how, in spite of all
this, the expression מסורת; for which alone there is foundation in
ancient usage and literature, has been displaced by the other terms.
Elias Levita himself makes use of the other expression, מסורה,
(mostly written *defective*, מסרה), in order to indicate both the
Massorah as "written down by the sages of the city of Tiberias," as
well as the written Massorah which is to be found in Bible MSS. (see
beginning of the Third Introduction ed. Ginsburg, p. 103, ומהם
לחכמי טבריה אשר כתבוה וקראו לה מסרה, and towards the end
of the same Introduction, p. 138, המסרה הגדולה and מסרה קטנה
seq.)'. He thus appears to recognise the name מסרה as applicable

---

' Instead of Ginsburg's כל המסורה הנדפסת p. 138, the edition 1538,
p. 28, line 4, has כל המסורת הנדפסת.

Reprinted from *Jewish Quarterly Review* (O.S.), 3 (1891).

only to the concrete form of the written Massorah, not to the Massorah in general.[1] Jacob ben Chayim, the first editor of the Massorah (in Bomberg's Bible, 1518), speaks in the Preface as well as in the prefatory remarks to the Massorah finalis, mostly of מסרה (always without ו), but also of מסורת, while he calls the written Massorah consistently מסרה, *defective*. His example will certainly have been of the greatest influence in the further use and general adoption of the word מסרה. As regards its pronunciation, the word מסורת, resting, as it did, upon better testimony, was decisive, both words being considered as similar substantive forms, distinguished only by the feminine endings ת ָ and ה ָ ; and, as Buxtorf asserts, the word was pronounced מָסוֹרָה. The question, however, arises whether this was the original pronunciation of the form of the word written with ה. This may be doubted, since both Jacob ben Chayim and Elias Levita, unquestionably relying upon MS. sources, always write the word without a ו ; while מסורת is always written with a ו. This doubt is strengthened by several very significant facts in the cognate literature. I have already pointed out (*Life and Works of Abulwalid*) that one of the two Oxford MSS. of *Kilāb-al'-Luma* (No. 1,462) very often instead of מסרת (or מסורת) writes מוסרת, which spelling is also found in an exegete of the fourteenth century. Since then I have discovered that this variant spelling of such a well-attested word as מסורת can be explained by the influence of the form מוֹסֵרָה. This form of the word is used almost exclusively to indicate the Massorah in the so-called "Massorah from Teman," which Ginsburg has edited in the third volume of his great work on the Massorah (p. 53 *seq.*). Here מסורת is only now and then to be met with (in Gen. xliv. 6 ; Exod. xxix. 15), elsewhere, המוסרה, also רברא מוסרה and מוסרה קטנה. This pronunciation is attested from very ancient times. The Karaite exegete, Japheth ben Ali (end of the tenth century) says in his commentary on Daniel ix. 29 (ed. Margoliouth, p. 101, line 3), וצבטת במוסרות "it is fixed in the M."; and the same plural form of the word is also to be found in the renowned St. Petersburg *Biblecodex* of the year 1010, where in the superscription of a Massoretic section, the expression occurs ולא נאמר בְּמְסְרוֹת גדלות ולא במֹסְרוֹת קטנות, the vocalisation being as here given, where, however, strange to say, the word is written once with cholem and once with kometz (see Baer and Strack, *Dikduke Ha-Teamim*, p. xxvi.).

---

[1] In Tishbi sub voc. מסר he does not mention the form מסרה at all, but only says in reference to Aboth iii. 13, והיא המסורת הכתובה סביב ספרי המקרא.

A further proof of the age of the form of spelling מוֹסֵרָה is furnished by the circumstance that the Karaite lexicographer *David ben Abraham*[1] calls the Massorah in Arabic אלמאסרה, מאסרה (see my treatise: *The Grammatical Terminology of Jehudah ben David ibn Chajjag*, p. 36); he thus forms the participle of the first conjugation of the verb מסר after the Arabic manner, corresponding to the Hebrew construction מוסרה as Kal participle. The Massora Magna he also calls in Arabic אלמאסרה אלכבירה (see Pinsker, *Sikkute Kadmonijoth*, p. 140 of the text). It is therefore proved that the word מסרה has been pronounced מֹסֵרָה since the tenth century, and one may assume that this is not an arbitrary pronunciation, but that it was the original pronunciation of the form מסרה, which grew up in addition to the older form מסורת. The above-mentioned lexicographer, David ben Abraham, also uses the Hebrew form מסרה (אל) without ו (see Neubauer: *Notice sur la Lexicographie Hebraïque*, p. 100, l. 13), as in the St. Petersburg *Biblecodex*.

It follows from the preceding that the form מסרה is not a later invention of the Massorah-scribes, but is to be regarded as an ancient term of the Massorites. I believe that the employment of this ending was determined by the fact that one of the encampments of Israel in the wilderness was called מוֹסֵרָה (Deut. x. 6), and מֹסֵרוֹת (Numb. xxxiii. 30 and 31). Nothing was more natural than that this name should be used as a synonym for מסורה, whose plural מסורות also occurs.[2] It is, however, remarkable, that מסרה is written *defective*, while מוסרה in Deut. x. 6 is *plene*; but perhaps this is owing to מסרות being *defective* in Numb. xxxiii.[3]

---

[1] Formerly regarded as belonging to the tenth century. A later date has, however, been assigned to him. (See P. F. Frankl, Article "Karäer" in *Ersch und Grubers Allgemeine Encyclopædie*, 2 Section, xxxiii. 17.)

[2] Ibn Ezra in one place calls Ben Asher and Ben Naphtali שני שרי המסורות (see my *Ibn Ezra als Grammatiker*, p. 38, note 13), and his contemporary, the Karaite, Jehudah Hadassi, likewise speaks, referring to Ben Asher, of the מסורות (see Baer und Strack, *Dikduke Ha-Teamim*, p. xiii., note 14; comp. *Ibid.*, p. xxviii., line 6 from the end; *Ibid.* page 79, line 8). In *Midrash Tanchuma*, ואתחנן, *fin.*, R. Jonathan (third century) says · · · · · ניטלו מסורות החכמה ממשה, for which passage the Midrash Petirath Mosheh (Jellinek's *Beth-Hamidrash*, vol. i., p. 127) has ניטלו אוצרות החכמה, perhaps a mistake in transcription from מוסרות החכמה. See also *Bab. Megillah*, 3a; *Nedarim*, 37b; אלו המסורות, for which *Jerus. Megillah*, 74d, *fin.* has זה המסורת.

[3] It should also be observed that מוֹסֵרוֹת, מוֹסֵרָה in the sense of *vinculum*, band (comp. Psalm ii. 3; cvii 14; cxvi. 16), was a very general

The pronunciation of מסורת is likewise not free from doubt. True, Buxtorf (Tiberias, *loc. cit.*), referring to the spelling מָסוֹרֶת, says, " *Quæ pronunciatio itidem communis est*," and at the present day also this mode of spelling is almost universally adopted as the correct one. Levy (*Neuheb. Wörterbuch*, iii. 178) adopts this punctuation, so also Strack in the *Dictum of Akiba, Aboth*, iii. 13 (*die Sprüche der Vater*, 2, Auflage, p. 38). But in reality the spelling מָסוֹרֶת, which has been emphasized by Buxtorf, and which is based upon the expression בְּמָסֹרֶת הברית (Ezek. xx. 37), appears to be more accurate. For although the word in Ezekiel is not exactly derived from מסר, but from אסר, to bind to fetter (=מֶאְסֹרֶת), as Abulwalîd already perceived (*Kilâb-al'-Luma*, p. 244, line 17 ; *Rikma*, p. 146), and as, following him, David Kimchi explains, yet the traditional rendering of the word seems to have assigned to it the meaning " Tradition, Handing down," in agreement with which Rashi explains בברית שמסרו לכם. As a fact, the Targum retains the Hebrew word, together with the corresponding Aramaic term (במסורת קימא), and Theodotion translates, ἐν τῇ παραδόσει τῆς διαθήκης (see Field, *Hexapla II.*, 820a). Aquila, it is true, translates ἐν δεσμοῖς τῆς διαθήκης, and, following him, Hieronymus in *Vinculis Fœderis*. Still, for the dominant conception of the word in the time of the Tanaim and Amoraim, the Targum, when it is unopposed by any other explanation in the literature of tradition, is sufficiently convincing, especially as its translation is supported by Theodotion, and as Rashi gives evidence for the maintenance of the traditional view.

It is now more than probable that if the Tanaim employed the expression מסורת, not only for the text of the Scripture but also for the traditions relating to it, they did not introduce a newly-formed word into the terminology of the schools, but adopted the word from the Book of Ezekiel as a welcome substantive to the verb מסר, which latter occurs only twice in the Bible (Numb. xxxi. 5 and 16), but has passed from Aramaic into New-Hebrew, and which became, in *constructio pregnans*, an expression in common use in the schools (see Mishnah, *Aboth*, i. 1). For it is difficult to see why, for the purpose of expressing the idea of " Tradition," a word of such rare occurrence, even in biblical Hebrew, as מָסֹרֶת (after the model of כֻּצֶּרֶת, בִּפֹּרֶת), should have been formed from the verb מסר[1] instead of

---

expression in the language of the Mishnah (see *Levy*, iii., 53b), and was even brought into connection with מסר by the Babylonian Amorah Raba (see *Baba Meziah*, 8b.)

[1] In New-Hebrew there is no substantive of this form so far as I know, and Siegfried, in his *Lehrbuch der Neuhebraïschen Sprache* (1884) is only

מְסִירָה or מְסוֹרָה; even מְסְרָה (comp. עֲבֵרָה), מְסוּרָה (comp.
סְעוּדָה), and מִסְרָה (comp. דְּרָשָׁה), would have been more con-
formable to analogy. The linguistic process probably took the following course : on the one hand מסר, having become a familiar
verb, led to Ezekiel's word מָסֹרֶת being used in the sense of
Tradition.[1] On the other hand, the word was admitted into the
terminology of the schools in order to form a substantive corresponding to the verb מסר. Had the word in Ezekiel not reached
us with the Massoretic punctuation, it could certainly have been
read מַסֹּרֶת quite as well as מָסֹרֶת, after the analogy of
מַכֹּלֶת (from אכל), 1 Kings v. 25, as indeed Abulwalîd also remarks
(loc. cit.) that in מסרת the א of the root has become softened,
quiescent, but has not assimilated with the ס. As, however, we must
assume that the word in Ezekiel was already read in the manner in
which we find it punctuated in the earliest periods of the transmission
of the text, it follows that the New-Hebrew expression based upon
the word in Ezekiel must also be so pronounced, viz., מָסוֹרֶת. He
who speaks and writes מְסוֹרֶת is therefore guilty of no inaccuracy,
as the word in Ezekiel might also sound thus, but he has against him
the facts as above presented in their historical development. Under
no circumstances may מָסוֹרֶת be regarded as a direct noun-form
derived from מסר, and independent of the biblical word.

I wish further to draw attention to the interesting fact that Elias
Levita, in the explanation of the word מסרות, at the beginning of
the third introduction to his *Masoreth Hamasoreth*, points only to the
verb מסר, but makes no mention whatever of the passage in Ezekiel,[2]
no doubt because he explained the biblical word according to its right
meaning of fetter, band, and he therefore saw in it no connection with
the end-form מסורת.

The following may serve as a brief summary of the results of the
above investigations into the history of the name of the Massorah :—
1. From Ezek. xx. 37 the noun מָסוֹרֶת, as if it was derived from

---

able to adduce as examples of the ground-form *qattôl* the " Fem. מְסוֹרָה,
מְסוֹרֶת " (p. 44.) The form had long lost its propagative power, and even
among the Payetanim, who had the courage to revive many a rare form,
it is not represented by a single example. See the register of noun-forms
in Zunz, *Die Synag. Poesie des Mittelalters*, pp. 383-409.

[1] Comp. opinion of Raba referred to above, p. 787 note 3.

[2] What Levy (*Wörterbuch*, iii. 179 b) cites in the name of Levita
appears to rest upon some confusion with another author.

the verb מסר, was adopted as the expression to designate oral tradition,[1] but especially the tradition fixing the pronunciation of the biblical text. (Compare specially the expression אם למקרא אם למסורת.) The term is also used in the plural.

2. In post-Talmudic times another substantive, also a biblical word, was applied with a similar meaning to the verb מסר, viz., מַסֹּרֶת, pl. מֹסְרוֹת. It was regarded as participle *kal*, and accordingly was cast in Arabic form. Under the influence of this word arose also the form מוסרת instead of מסורת.

3. The form מסורת remained until modern times, and even with Elias Levita, as the usual term to designate the Massorah. The form מסרה or מסורה, its pronunciation מְסוֹרָה being copied from מְסֹרֶת, gradually became the customary designation of the Massoretic discussions (first edited by Jacob ben Chayim), and displaced the expression Mâsôreth.

4. The pronunciation מַסֹּרֶת has no historical justification.

5. For מסרה the pronunciation מוֹסְרָה alone is attested from ancient times; the forms of spelling מְסוֹרָה and מְסוּרָה rest only upon the analogy of the two styles of spelling מסורת.

6. The transliteration Massorah or Masorah owes its right to further existence only through its having been long naturalised in scientific literature.[2]

W. BACHER.

---

[1] It is to be observed that halachic tradition is never indicated by this expression. See the examples in Levy, iii. 178 *seq.*

[2] So also one may continue to write "Agadah" as the transcription based upon long and general usage for הגדה=אגדה (Haggadah, Aggadah) just as foreign proper names are retained in the transliteration in which they have become usual, although they be not scientifically correct. Zunz, in his great work on the history of the Aggadah (*Die Gottesdienstlichen Vorträge*) writes Hagada (with one *g*), and similarly in his later works which is even less correct than Agada, as one may suppose a root אגד for אנדה, and may punctuate the word אֲגָדָה.

MASSORETIC STUDIES.

I.

The Number of Letters in the Bible.

ACCORDING to the well-known Talmudical passage, T. B. Kiddushin, 30 a, the name Sofer derives its origin from the fact that the scholars of Scripture *counted* all the letters of the Bible [1]. The same explanation of the term Sofer occurs also in Chagiga, 15 b [2]. It follows, unquestionably, from these passages that the counting of the letters took place at least in Tanaitic times; for the passage in Kiddushin seems to be extracted from a Boraitha. But even if it be assumed that the author of the anonymously mentioned etymology was an Amora, it may, nevertheless, be deduced with absolute certainty, that already at that time the counting of the letters passed for a very ancient tradition, for otherwise no Amora would have hit upon such a derivation.

It may be inferred, from this circumstance alone, that the determination of the number of letters in the Pentateuch and Psalms, which is the subject dealt with in the passage referred to, must be regarded as a pre-Tanaitic, or, at least an early Tanaitic, production. If the letters began to be counted for the first time at the flowering time of tradition, after the destruction of the Temple, it would never have occurred to an Amora living (even in Babylon) 150 years later—the passage in Kiddushin must be ascribed, at latest,

---

[1] לפיכך נקראו ראשונים סופרים שהיו סופרים כל האותיות שבתורה שהיו אומרים וא"ו דגחון חציץ של אוהיות של ס"ת דרש דרש חציץ של תינות וההגלח של פסוקים יכרסמנה חזיר מיער עי"ן דיער חציים של תהלים והוא רחום יכפר עון חציו דפסוקים.

[2] איה סופר (Isa. xxxiii. 18) שהיו סופרים כל אותיות שבתורה (Cf. also B. Sanhedrin, 106 b.) The Jerusalem Talmud gives a different etymology, Shekalim, 5, 1 (ed. Krotoschin, 48 c): אמר ר' אבהו כתיב משפחות סופרים יושבי יעבץ (1 Chron. ii. 55) מה ת"ל סופרים אלא שעשו את התורה ספורות ספורות חמשה לא יתרומו ה' דברים חייבין בחלה וכו'. The counting is, therefore, not referred to the letters, but to the traditional ordinances.

Reprinted from *Jewish Quarterly Review* (O.S.) 8 (1896); 9 (1897).

to about the year 300—to assign this operation to the Sofrim[1]. Such an ante-dating is only intelligible on the assumption that the real period of origin lies so far back in the past that the memory of it is completely obliterated—a condition which supposes an interval of at least two centuries.

There is another consideration which leads us to the same conclusion as to the antiquity of this counting of the letters. In the synagogue scrolls, the middle letter of the Pentateuch (Lev. xi. 42) is indicated by a Vav maiusculum. If the letter-counting, and consequently the indication of the middle of the Pentateuch, was not yet known in the second century of our present era, or only then became a subject of notice, then that fact would not have been made outwardly perceptible in the text of the Bible, not even in the shape of a littera maiuscula, for at that time the holy text was already fixed and *consciously* no further change in it was taken in hand.

To which Biblical books this counting in the earliest period extended, cannot, with the data which have come down to us, be determined. As, in the passage in question, only the Pentateuch and the Psalter are mentioned, and as, further, in these two books alone the middle letter is indicated by large letters, we shall certainly hit the truth if we assume that the process of enumerating the letters was applied, in the first instance, to the Pentateuch as the law-book, and then to the Psalter as the prayer or hymn-book. The Massoretes, at all events in post-Talmudical times, unquestionably counted the letters of the other Biblical books also, as they did also the single letters of the alphabet, the numbers of whose occurrences in the *whole Bible* are given in the well-known poem ascribed to Sᵉadyah. But, strange to say, on this point no specific statement has come down to us ; I have nowhere found one.

Another, and indeed more difficult question is, how many letters were counted in the Torah and how many in the other books ? The results which have been handed down to us differ considerably from each other. The Pentateuch alone, according to Elias Levita (*Masoreth Ha-masoreth*, III, Preface, ed. Ginsburg, p. 136), has 600,045 ; according to Joseph del Medigo (*Nobloth Chochma*, at the end), 600,000 in round numbers ; according to Ben Asher (*Dikduke Ha-teamim*, p. 55), 400,945 ; according to Manuel du lecteur (ed. Derenbourg, p. 150), 400,900 ; according to an old Bible codex of Dr. Curtiss, 305,607

---

[1] Cf. Sabbath, 49 b, where it is stated : מי לא אמר רגה בר בר חנה משום רבי יוחנן לא זזו משם עד שהביאו ספר תורה ומנאום which Rashi connects with our passage. Kiddushin, 30 a, is in all probability a Boraitha ; but we will make our demonstration independent of this hypothesis.

(in *Baer-Strack Dikd. Ha-team*, p. 55, note 1); according to Norzi (*Minchath Shai*, ed. Mantua), in the Massoretic concluding note to the Torah, 304,805; according to Ch. D. Ginsburg's edition of the Massora, 290,136. I have arrived at this last figure by adding together the different estimates showing the number of times each letter of the alphabet occurs in the Torah—which estimates are to be found at the beginning of each letter in the Massoretic Dictionary, *The Massorah*. Ginsburg has, unfortunately, omitted to mention the sources of his Massoretic data, and we therefore do not know whence these important figures have been taken.

If we disregard the smaller differences and only consider round numbers, we get three different estimates: (1) 600,000; (2) 400,000; (3) 300,000. These variations cannot possibly have resulted from actual enumerations; in view of the exactness and extreme accuracy of the Massoretes such gross blunders are entirely out of the question. How, then, is this confusion in the statement of the figures to be explained?

In order to gain a solid standpoint from which these difficulties may be considered, there is no better and simpler means than a re-count. But as in our case the matter to be dealt with is not so much the determination of the exact number of letters, as the accounting for an error of at least 100,000 letters, this re-count can best be effected by working out some comparative estimates of the number of letters contained in various editions of the Pentateuch. For this purpose I select from the editions of the Bible which are accessible to me, three in particular, which contain the text of the Torah without any addition whatsoever; and of these, the stereotype edition of the Bible Society commends itself to the first place.

In my pocket edition (Berlin, 1886) the Pentateuch occupies 150 pages (+ 7 lines); each page has two columns, making altogether 300; each *full* column has 38 lines. A full column which occurs on p. 120 a has 1,072 letters; on the other hand, a column on p. 2 a, which contains 37 lines, and is printed less closely, has only 997 letters. Page 2, containing 74 incomplete lines has 1,997, the more closely printed page 120, with 74½ lines, numbers 2,087 letters; thus, the two together have 148 lines and 4,084 letters. Hence, a column of 37 lines has, on an average, 1,020 letters. In the 300 columns of the Pentateuch there would be, if fully printed, 11,400 lines (300 × 38). But at the beginning and end of each single book, as well as at the chapters, and at the Sedarim and Parashim, a larger or smaller space is always left blank. According to my calculation at least 644 lines are thus missed: viz. 129 in Genesis, 116 in Exodus, 137 in Leviticus, 173 in Numbers, and 89 in Deuteronomy, and the

result is therefore 11,400−644 or **10,756** lines. If we add to this
7 lines, which are on p. 151 of this edition of the Bible, and divide
the number thus obtained, viz. 10,763, by 37, we get just 291 columns.
As one such column numbers, on an average, 1,020 letters, we obtain,
as the total number of letters in the Torah, 1,020 × 291 or **296,820.**

Substantially the same result is yielded by a calculation based on
ed. Amsterdam, 1734, which bears the title חמשה חומשי תורה, and
which presents the Torah to us without any addition. The whole
Pentateuch embraces 266½ pages, each full page has 32 lines. About
217 lines = 7½ pages, are incidentally missed; there thus remain
259 pages. Page 20 b, where scarcely a single blank place has been
left, contains 1,179 letters; 56 b 1,148; 92 a 1,193. On the average,
therefore, there are $\frac{3,520}{3} = 1,173$ letters to a page, and the total
number of letters would therefore be 1,173 × 259 = **303,807.** If we
make a deduction on account of letters missed at the closed Parashim,
which are indicated by a ס, and at the poetical passages, which we
have not taken into consideration, we shall arrive, on this calculation
also, at a total sum of about 300,000 letters.

A third test is afforded by the Biblia Hebraica sine punctis, &c.,
Amstelaedami, 1701. The Pentateuch occupies 148½ pages; each
page has two columns, and each *full* column 51 lines. If there were
no blank spaces, the Pentateuch would thus contain 15,147 (297 × 51)
lines; but, according to my calculation, 610 of these must be
deducted; there remain, therefore, 14,537 lines, which, divided by 50,
gives 290·7 columns. The two columns on 9 b (= 100 lines) have
2,250 letters, those on 10 a (likewise with 100 lines) have 2,152;
a column would, therefore, on an average contain 1,050 letters.
Total, 290·7 × 1,050 = **305,235.** If the omissions of letters, as indicated
above, are deducted, there remains a round sum of about 300,000.

That the type is uniform, and that, consequently, every page contains very nearly the same number of letters, may be deduced from
the fact that the traditional centre of the letters of the Pentateuch
occurs almost exactly on the page where it is expected. נחן, Lev.
xi. 42, occurs on page 76 (= 150 ÷ 2) in the edition of the Bible
Society; in the Amsterdam edition of 1734, which contains 133½
double pages, it appears on page 68 b; and in the Amsterdam edition
of 1701, which has 74½ double pages, it is found on page 39 a. That
in all three editions the recognized centre of the letters appears
one or two pages later than the exact half of the number of pages
would presuppose, is explained by the circumstance that comparatively larger blank spaces occur in the first half of the pages
than in the latter half.

Reckon how one will, by pages, by columns, by lines, if several pages be reckoned out and the average number of letters per page and line be ascertained, the minimum total never sinks below 290,000 and the maximum total never rises above 310,000. We may even go beyond the wildest dreams of the boldest Bible critics, and, at the expense of the correctness of our text, generously place at their disposal several thousands of letters, which may, at pleasure, be added to or subtracted from the total number, without materially altering thereby the final result. In no case will a sum of 400,000 be arrived at, still less of 600,000.

According to our investigation, then, it admits of no doubt that the approximately correct statement can only be that which is furnished by Norzi and the old Bible codex of Dr. Curtiss, according to which the number of letters amounts to 305,607. But the question arises how the remaining, mutually contradictory, traditions have arisen? I am in the happy position of being able to solve this difficulty satisfactorily.

The statement, just alluded to, reads as follows:

1. וסכום האותיות של תורה שלשים רבוא וחמשת אלפים ושש מאות ושבע (*D. H.* p. 55, n. 1).

In Levita (*Mas. Ham.* ed. Ginsburg, p. 136), the statement takes the following form:

2. ומספר אותיות של כל התורה ששים רבוא וארבעים וחמשה

Similarly, in Joseph del Medigo (*Nobl. Chochmah*, at the end):

2 a. ואמרו יש ס' רבוא אותיות לתורה כר"ת ישׂרׂאׂל שהוא סוף התורה

Norzi, *Minchath Shai*, at the end of Deuteronomy, has:

3. מנין אותיות של ספר תורה שׂדׂ אלפים ותת מאות וחמשה

The identity of these three statements as regards the main quantity is strikingly evident. In Levita, or rather in the sources from which he drew his estimate, we must read שלשים רבוא instead of ששים רבוא. The words שלשים רבוא arose from the device ש"ר—a mistake arising from its resemblance to the ש"ר, which is found in Norzi. Thus all the estimates can be traced back to Norzi's. From ש"ר (= 304,000), ש"ר arises, which in the old Bible codex becomes שלשים רבוא; and in Levita ששים רבוא.

The next question that arises is how the estimate of Ben Asher and Manuel arose? From the digits 45, it may be concluded with certainty, that here too the same statement lies before us, but in a corrupt form. If the enumerations had been independent, the same number 45 would not have been obtained in both cases, while at the same time, a round difference of 100 (300:400) resulted in the thousands. We may, with great probability, assume that Ben Asher, or his copyists, resolved רש (= שר = 304,000) into (ר =) אלף ארבע מאות וחשע מאות (= ש = תשע). According to this hypothesis the original statement of the number would have been: ש"ד ר"ה מ"ה, which = 304,045; this becomes in Levita ששים רבוא וארבעים וחמשה; in Ben Asher ארבע מאות אלף ותשע מאות (= דש = ש"ד) וארבעים וחמשה; in Manuel, likewise ארבע מאות אלף ותשע מאות with the omission of ארבעים; in the Curtiss codex שלשים רבוא; while in the words וחמשת אלפים ושש מאות ושבע, which are expressed by the letters ה' ו' ז', lie Norzi's 805. Perhaps from ה (= 800) ה' or חמשת אלפים has arisen, and has been referred to the thousands instead of to the hundreds, while after the resolution of ש"ר into שלשים רבוא for the thousands, no units remained.

These conjectures regarding the minor figures may no doubt be accepted or rejected; but every one, it is to be hoped, will assent to the main proposition, viz. the view that the different estimates are corrupt variations of a single statement. If this be the case, there can be no doubt that this statement contained 300,000 or 304,000 in its total. As a matter of fact the Pentateuch numbers about 300,000 letters, as our calculation showed. The only evidence that conflicts with this result is furnished by the estimates for single letters in Ginsburg's *Massorah*, the sum of which amounts to only 290,136.

It can, however, easily be proved that errors have crept into these detailed estimates. For the figures which are there given as specifying the number of times each letter of the alphabet occurs in the Pentateuch, are in many instances so low that they cannot possibly be right. Especially striking are: ב = 1,634; ג = 2,105; ז = 2,200; ס = 1,843. In order to judge of these figures correctly, let us compare them with the figures which are given for the same letters in the case of the *whole Bible*[1]. The relation between the two is represented by the following ratios, in which the numbers for

---

[1] These latter numbers, as is well known, are furnished in the poem אהל מכן בניני which is ascribed to S°adyah. The poem has often been printed, cf. C. D. Ginsburg, *The Massoreth Ha-massoreth of Elias Levita*, London, 1867, p. 269, n. 1; (also Ginsburg, III, 299); more especially, J. Derenbourg, *Manuel du lecteur*, Paris, 1871, pp. 139 ff. and 234 ff, where, for the first time, an attempt is made to elucidate the unintelligible rhymes. The same numbers are given by Ginsburg in *The Massorah*, at the beginning of each single letter; they therefore emanate from this source.

611

the whole Scriptures are placed first: ב 38,218:1,634; ן 29,537:2,105; ף 22,867 : 2,200; ם 13,580 : 1,843. Now the Pentateuch hardly forms more than a fourth part of the Bible; it is, therefore, quite inconceivable that it should contain only the twenty-fourth part of the total number of Beths, and in respect of the letters נ, ן, and ם, the proportion is similarly unfavourable in a greater or less degree. The fact must not be concealed that in the case of ר a contrary proportion is found, viz. Bible 22,147, Torah 18,106. But if even the latter number is pitched too high, it nevertheless does not seem large enough to cover the deficiencies in the case of the other letters, and we may therefore, with great probability, add from 10,000 to 15,000 letters to the total number, whereby here too a result of 300,000 to 305,000 is reached.

This final result is, on the whole, confirmed also by a consideration of the number of *words* in the Pentateuch. This, according to *Dikduké Ha-teamim* (p. 55), and *Manuel du lecteur* (p. 150), as well as Ginsburg, III, 301 a, amounts to 79,856; according to Norzi (end of the Pentateuch), 79,976, or in round numbers, 80,000. Accordingly there would be, on an average, four letters to a word, while on a hypothesis of 400,000 letters, each word would contain at least five letters, and on a hypothesis of 600,000, the number of letters to a word would be $7\frac{1}{2}$. In view of the tri-literal basis of Hebrew, the two latter averages are in the highest degree improbable, for even supposing five letters to a word, it would be necessary to assume that the suffixes, matres lectionis, &c., entirely swamped the radical letters, which is not the case.

It is certainly a question how the words were counted; whether every particle was taken to be a separate word or whether it was regarded as belonging to the following word. E. g., Gen. i. 1 to ii. 3 has 469 words, of which 60 are connected with a Makkef, and among these several words, in reality independent, are found joined to the following word. There can hardly be a doubt that these are counted as separate words [1]. As the section referred to contains 1815 letters, we get a result of four rather than of five letters, as the average number for each word. It is not without purpose that we have selected this section as the basis of our calculation. For we find it here once more exemplified how uncritically Massoretic data are treated even by real savants. In Introduction, no. III to *Massoreth Ha-massoreth*, Levita says (Ginsburg, p. 135) that the weekly section Bereshith has 1,915 letters [2]—which number is de-

---

[1] Cf. on this point, *infra*, II.

[2] S. Baer .והאותיות בפרשת בראשית אלף והשע מאות וחמשה עשר סימן א''ק ט''ו
(*Orient.* XII [1851], 202, note) perverts אותיות into תיבות and א''ק ט''ו into

scribed already by Buxtorf as being too small (*Tiberias*, c. 18, p. 43).
Now there can be no doubt that this estimate refers not to the
Babylonian, but to the Palestinian weekly section Bereshith, which
ends at chapter ii. 3, and contains 1,815 letters[1]. This fact escaped
Buxtorf as well as Levita, as may be gathered from the context.
There were figures in existence for both kinds of Sedarim. In
Buxtorf's edition of the Bible there is a specification at the end
of Genesis, according to which the number of letters amounts to
4,395. This number can only refer to the section Vayechi, as Buxtorf
(*Tiberias*, 43) already correctly observes.

We see to what misconceptions and confusions the traditional
numbers have given rise. Keeping this fact steadily before our
eyes, we proceed to an examination of the statement specifying the
total number of letters in the Holy Scriptures. In the Seadyah poem
already referred to, the amount is given as 792,077[2]. As Derenbourg
has already rightly observed (*Man.* p. 150, n. 10) this number is
incompatible with the statement which fixes the number of letters
in the Torah at 400,000, since the Pentateuch forms not much
more than a fourth of the whole Bible. This discrepancy between
the two figures is increased if 600,000 letters are allotted to the
Torah alone, but neither is it removed, if, according to one demonstration, only an approximate number of 300,000 is adhered to,
for after subtracting this sum, there would remain for the Prophets
and Hagiographa only 492,077, whereas they are together almost
thrice as large as the Pentateuch, and would, therefore, alone contain
792,077 letters.

And this is in fact the case. A glance at the various editions which
contain the text without any addition, convinces us of the fact.

א"ץ יהיה. This sum is made to represent the number of words in בראשית;
the number of letters, on the other hand, is given as 7,213, with the
symbol או"ר אחר. It is a pity that Baer leaves his readers in obscurity
as to the source of his information.

[1] Instead of א"ץ מ"ו we must read א"ץ מ"ו. How easily ף may be
confounded with ץ is seen from the fact that even Baer (loc. cit.) once
puts ף for ץ.

[2] *Manuel*, p. 149: כלל מנין האותיות שבמקרא כולם הכפופות והפשוטות שבע מאות
אלף ושנים תשעים אלף ושבעה ושבעים אות סימן ת"ש וצ"ב אלף וז"ז אות. This total
sum results mainly from the separate figures for single letters which are
also to be found in Ginsburg's *Massorah*. On I, 613, however, י"א אלף נג
is a printer's error for נ"ב; further, in *Manuel*, p. 144, l. 4, in the סירוש
the words חמשה וארבעים are wanting. Anschel Worms סיג לתורה Frankfurt
a. M., 1766, p. 15, has 815,280, but he counts one of the component
numbers twice over. Cf. *Manuel*, p. 148, n. 16.

According to the method already employed with the Pentateuch, the calculation, based on the edition of the Bible Society, appears as follows:

Of the 605 pages, 150 are occupied by the Pentateuch, and 8 are quite blank; there remain, therefore, for the Prophets and Hagiographa 447 pages = 894 columns. At the beginning and end of the books, at the chapters, &c., if my calculation is correct, about 2,180 lines = 58 columns of 38 lines each are missed. The Prophets and Hagiographa, therefore, occupy 894 – 58 = 836 columns. Many pages, however, have but 37 lines, occasionally only 36; further, unprinted places in the middle of the lines have not been taken into account. If we reckon the loss on these accounts at one line per column on an average—which is rather too little than too much—and subtract the 900 lines thus obtained, we get in round numbers 830 columns of 37 lines each as the contents of the Prophets and Hagiographa. Each such column, as has been already remarked above, contains an average of 1020 letters, and the total capacity of the Prophets and Hagiographa is therefore $1,020 \times 830 = 846,600$. This calculation is not, by reason of its nature, an exact one; a difference of tens of thousands may be assumed, but not one reaching to hundreds of thousands. But if the *whole Bible* had approximately 800,000 letters, there would remain for the Prophets and Hagiographa only 500,000, which is entirely out of the question.

The calculation in the case of the Biblia Hebraica sine Punctis (Amsterd. 1701) appears much simpler and more exact. The whole of the books occupy a space of $292\frac{1}{2}$ double pages = 585 pages, of which, between the three divisions of Scripture and elsewhere, 10 pages are left blank; therefore 585 – 10 = 575 pages = 1,150 columns. Of these 1,150 columns, 298 belong to the Pentateuch, and 852 to Prophets and Hagiographa. Speaking in round numbers, the Pentateuch has been found to contain 300,000 letters; consequently, the Prophets and Hagiographa would number 850,000. But in the case of the Prophets and Hagiographa, comparatively more unprinted spaces must be allowed for, since there are here 34 books, counting Samuel, Kings, Ezra, and Chronicles, as two each, and the Minor Prophets as 12; besides this, in most of the books the chapters are much smaller than in the Pentateuch, for which reason a larger quantity of blank space is taken up in dividing them. These two circumstances demand a deduction of about 40 to 45 columns, whereby a net result of approximately 800,000 is reached. Hence the proportion of the size of the Pentateuch to that of the Prophets and Hagiographa is expressed by the ratio 3 : 8, and not by 3 : 5.

We arrive, therefore, at the astonishing result that in the rhyme referred to above, the total number of figures mentioned relates only to the Prophets and Hagiographa, exclusive of the Pentateuch. The whole Bible has, not 800,000, but 1,100,000 letters. The source of the error is probably the word מקרא. As is well known, this term was not only used to designate the whole Scriptures, but also to describe the Torah in contradistinction to the Prophets and Hagiographa[1]. The words אותיות של מקרא, then, have been understood to refer to the whole Bible instead of to the Prophets and Hagiographa. With whom the enumeration of the single letters of the alphabet originated, is unknown; it is equally uncertain who is the author of the rhyme[2]. Hence, it cannot be decided whether the versifier regarded the figures handed down to him as referring to the whole Bible or only to the Prophets and Hagiographa. Moreover, as regards the main problem this is a matter of indifference. In Manuel du lecteur the number is held to represent the whole 24 books[3].

If the separate component numbers are placed in juxtaposition, we shall find our assertion, that the final sum, viz. 792,077, only gives the number of letters in the latter two divisions of the Bible, fully established. We append them here according to Ginsburg's *Massorah*, where the two sets of figures, those for the whole Bible and those for the Torah, are recorded, whereas the other sources at our disposal contain only the figures of the poem.

	Bible.	Torah.			Bible.	Torah.
א	42,377	27,055		ה	47,754	28,148
ב	38,218	1,634		ו	76,922	30,419
ג	29,537	2,105		ז	22,867	2,200
ד	32,530	7,034		ח	23,447	7,187

[1] On the expression תורה ומקרא, cf. my *Introduction to the Holy Scriptures*, p. 26; the word was used in the same sense even as late as Ben Asher (cf. *Massoretic Investigations*, p. 50). This nomenclature finds an analogy in the *Massorah*; e. g. on Exod. xii. 39: צו ה כל אורייתא חסר וכ' קרי' מלא במ''ב. How this expression is to be understood is shown by the antithesis of וכל אורייתא and וכל שאר קריא (Frensdorff, *Massoretic Dictionary*, p. 336, col. b). According to this, מקרא = תורה ומקרא. That the הורה ושאר מקרא specialized meaning lies in the omitted word שאר, and not in the meaning of מקרא, is proved by Ochla ve-Ochla, No. 60: א''ב חד בהלים וחד בקריא; the antitheses, therefore, are תלים and מקרא, which is only intelligible by the addition of שאר to מקרא.

[2] Cf. *Manuel*, p. 234 ff.

[3] P. 139: וזה הוא מספר כל האותיות שמקרא שהוא ארבעה ועשרים ספרים. The last four words give the impression of being an explanatory gloss of the compiler.

	Bible.	Torah.		Bible.	Torah.
ט	11,052	1,812	ע	20,175	11,244
י	66,420	31,522	פ	20,750	3,975
כ	37,272	8,616	ף	1,975	831
ך	10,981	3,362	צ	16,950	2,929
ל	41,517	21,612	ץ	4,872	1,033
מ	52,805	14,474	ק	22,972	4,701
ם	24,973	10,616	ר	22,147	18,106
נ	32,977	9,873	ש	32,148	15,592
ן	8,719	4,352	ת	36,140 [1]	17,960
ס	13,580	1,843			

We have already spoken of ב, ג, ז, ם, and ר. The first four are credited with far too low figures, while ר exhibits far too high an

[1] In Ginsburg, *Massorah*, I, 33 b. ff, the poem is given with the same numbers, and yet 792,145 is given as the total. This figure has arisen from the erroneous סימן in the case of ר. It is rightly stated : מנין כל דלה מנין כל דלה. But then follows ל"ב סימן להם. שבמקרא שנים ושלשים אלף וחמש מאות ושלשים אלף הקצה instead of תקל. The difference of 68 raises the total amount from 77 to 145. Another error in the MS. or in the printing occurs with נ, where instead of טֹ we find ע"י אלף, which, however, has had no effect on the final result. The accuracy of these numbers was already called into question by R. Jair Bacharach (p. 272 a). He says : כאלו רוח "ה. דבר בו יי אבל מה נעשה והרוש מכחיש פרטי המספרים. Prof. Kaufmann has drawn attention (JEWISH QUARTERLY REVIEW, VII, p. 291) to this fact, and has also referred to the divergent numbers communicated by Shapira in the *Athenaeum*, No. 2,626 (Feb. 23, 1878). As this note only came into my hands during the correction of the proof of this article, I have been unable to refer to this issue of the *Athenaeum*. Lazarus de Viterbo's words *Litterae omnes ipsius Genesis fuerunt 4,395* are passed over by Prof. Kaufmann without comment, as is also the statement that Genesis contains 1,915 (א"ץ מ"ו) letters, while, on the other hand, he rightly corrects *Versus omnes totius Pentateuci 5,045* into 5,845 ; Ghimel 29,637 he corrects into 29,537 ; and the number of verses in Genesis, previously given as 1,634, he corrects into 1,534. It is evident, however, that the admission that the numbers 4,395 and 1,915 are false—a fact which, as we observed above, Buxtorf and Baer perceived—is of the utmost importance for forming a judgment concerning L. de Viterbo, because the admission shows that, in spite of his differing as to the age of the vowels and accents, he followed Levita slavishly. Otherwise, he would not have adopted the figures in question, referring to the book of Genesis and the first section thereof respectively. Other proofs might be adduced to show the slavish dependence of Viterbo on Levita ; these, however, do not come within the scope of this article. (On p. 291, for 60,045 read 600,045.)

estimate. If the figures of the first column referred to the whole Bible, then for Resh there would remain only 4,041 letters for the Prophets and Hagiographa, while the Pentateuch would have 18,106, which is manifestly impossible. Similarly, for א there would remain 15,322, while the Pentateuch would have 27,055! Again, on this supposition, the Pentateuch would have more ה, ל, and ע's than the Prophets and Hagiographa. The sums of most of the other letters only correspond to the proportion between the sizes of the two divisions, Pentateuch and the Prophets and Hagiographa; if the single letter estimates for the Pentateuch are not deducted from the corresponding estimates for the מקרא, of which fact any one can convince himself by comparing the corresponding sets of figures. We do not know from what sources C. D. Ginsburg has collected, in his great work on the *Massorah*, the data in question, nor whether the systematic arrangement of them is also to be found in those sources. In the latter case, there is nothing to prevent the conception that the constant forms: שבמקרא ... כל מנין and ... כל מנין שבתורה, indicate the numbers for the Pentateuch on the one hand, and the numbers for the Prophets together with those for the Hagiographa on the other: תורה = Pentateuch; מקרא = Prophets and Hagiographa. One feels in this instance also, how important it is in the case of the *Massorah*, to mention one's sources. The Massoretic works of Jacob ben Chayim, S. Frensdorff, and C. D. Ginsburg are invaluable aids, but the *Massorah* can as little be studied by means of them alone, as the Talmud by means of Maimun's *Mishna Torah*, as the Halacha by means of Joseph Karo's *Shulchan Aruch*, or as the literature of the Bible by means of Gesenius', or any one else's, lexicon. All information as to Massoretic sources must be made fully and entirely accessible to research, for a true understanding of it can only be achieved by means of a sifting of all the circumstances, including time, place, and authors.

The process of counting the letters was carried out, not only with the separate books, but also with single sections, at all events, those of the Pentateuch; and that, too, according to the Palestinian division as well as the Babylonian, as has been shown by the examples already cited. Unfortunately, with the exception of those already adduced, no record of these figures is anywhere to be found, so far as I know. And yet these figures, especially those of the Palestinian divisions, would be of importance for the text criticism of the Bible. A few examples are met with in the Talmud and Midrash. A well-known instance is the Baraitha, Sabbath 116 a, according to which the small Parasha, Num. x. 35, 36, contains 85 letters. According to Targum Jonathan and Targum Jerushalmi

on Deut. xxxii. 3, the verses from xxxii. 1 to שם, in verse 3, contain
21 words, comprising 85 letters, whence Norzi infers that כשעירם
must be written with only one *yod*. Deut. iv. 34, from לבוא to
ובמוראים גדלים, with the omission of the second גוי, numbers 72 letters[1]. The decalogue from אנכי to אשר לרעך has 613 + 7 letters[2];
the blessing of Isaac, Gen. xxvii. 28, 29, has 100 letters[3]; the priestly
blessing, Num. vi. 24–26 has 60 letters[4]. It is certain that the Massoretes counted the letters of every single verse, as many comparisons
show[5]. From these data, which make no pretensions to completeness[6], it is evident that the counting of the letters was a practice
of very ancient origin. But it was probably not till much later
that it was used for agadic interpretations.

I cannot close this chapter without calling attention to the related
phenomenon in the Greek and Latin Bibles. The counting of the
letters and stichs was in ancient times peculiar to these translations
also. What data are still accessible in the MSS. I am, unfortunately,
unable to state, since the literature in question is not at present
at my disposal. I should merely like to suggest the question,
whether the letter-counting of the Hebrew Bible did not give the
students and copyists of the Septuagint the first impulse towards
a similar proceeding? The Greek translators and the first people
to use and disseminate this version were of course Jews, and the
possibility that the Greek text of the Bible had its Massoretes as

---

[1] Judah II in Leviticus Rabbah, c. 23 at the beginning (ed. Wilna, 64 b
at the bottom) and parallel places; Deut. Rabbah, c. 1 (196 a), incorrectly
מלבוא עד סוף הפסוק.

[2] Numbers Rabbah, c. 13 (p. 108 a); c. 18 (152 b).

[3] Ibid., c. 18 (152 b); this result can only be arrived at artificially.

[4] Ibid.   [5] Cf. e. g. Frensdorff, *Massoretic Dictionary*, 377 b.

[6] Gen. xlix. 16, 17 has 70 letters (Numbers Rabbah, c. 14, fol. 121 a);
Judges xv. 19, from עין to בלחי, 15 letters. It was here overlooked by the
mediaeval authors; that c. 14 of Numbers Rabbah, in which most of the
data in question occur, might be very late (cf. also, ibid., c. 14, fol. 126 a).
The names of the tribes engraved on the breast-plate of the High
Priest contain (according to Jerus. Sota, VII, 4, 21 d 29, and Bab. Sota,
36 a) fifty letters. This statement is of interest in this connexion from
the answer given by R. Jochanan to the objection (in the Jerusalem
Talmud) that the letters in question only amount to 49. He answers:
בנימן דוחולדותם מלא. The names of each six tribes contain 25 letters.
How this division was effected is a subject of controversy (cf. the commentators, ad loc.). The Aruch (s. v. מאה, Kohut, V, 64 b) cites וי"א שכל
עולה למנין מאה אותיות [Deut. x. 12] הפסוק הזה, from which Norzi infers
שאל מלא, but in the ordinary editions the word is printed *defective*.

well as the Hebrew, is therefore not *a priori* to be rejected. According to Grause, the Grecian stichometry, and consequently also the counting of the letters which was connected with it, goes back to the habits of the booksellers of classical antiquity, who paid the copyists on a scale of this sort[1]. Contrariwise, the conjecture is also worth considering, whether among the Jews it was not originally the fixing of the transcribers' remuneration that gave rise to the system of recording the number of the letters of the Bible, of its single books and their parts and divisions. It is of course known that the copyists and revisers were paid out of the Temple treasury.

It will be interesting for our purpose to see the estimates of the number of letters contained in the Biblical books as mentioned by Berger (p. 323 f), and we quote a few of them for purposes of illustration and in confirmation of the assertions which we have put forward on this point. The Pentateuch has 523,063 letters, the Octateuch (= Pentateuch, Joshua, Judges, Ruth) 663,027, the whole Bible without the Apocrypha 2,105,515. Hence the Prophets and Hagiographa have 1,582,452. We see then from these specifications of the letters in the Vulgate, that the Pentateuch forms just a fourth of the whole Bible. Hence, in the Hebrew original also, the proportion cannot be other than about 1 : 4. If, therefore, the Pentateuch has approximately 300,000 letters, the Prophets and Hagiographa must have at least 800,000. We see, further, from the figures 523,063 for the Pentateuch, that in the Hebrew, where no vowels are written, 600,000 is an impossible number, for the Hebrew cannot have more letters than the Latin. The total number of letters in the Vulgate amounts to about 2,100,000. If in the Hebrew there were altogether only about 800,000, then we should have to assume that on account of the vowels the number of letters increased in Latin nearly threefold, which is a sheer impossibility. Thus, the results reached by us as regards the total of letters in the Pentateuch on the one hand, and in the Prophets and Hagiographa on the other, are corroborated in this direction also in the most gratifying manner.

II.

The Number of Words in the Bible.

We have, above, already touched upon the question whether the particles were regarded as separate words. This question is all the

---

[1] Cf. Samuel Berger, *Histoire de la Vulgate pendant les premiers siècles du moyen âge*, Paris, 1893, p. 316 ff.

more justified, because, not only are these little words often, sometimes consistently, marked as belonging to the following word by means of a Makkeph, but also frequently make their appearance deprived of their independence, in the paraphrases of the Hexapla[1]. In order to solve this problem, we have submitted the smallest of the sections, regarding which the number of words contained therein has been transmitted to us, to a re-count. For we find in Ginsburg, *Massorah*, II, p. 714 ff, the following data: (1) מקץ, 2,000 words; (2) קרח, 1,462; (3) חקת, 1,454; (4) בלק, 1,450; (5) ואתחנן, 1,870; (6) עקב, 1,746. Furthermore, Baer observes in the *Orient*, XII (1851), p. 202, note, that בראשית has 1,930 words: סימן א׳ צ׳ יה״יה. Whether this statement is old or whether it originates with Baer, I do not know. According to our computation the section Balak has 1,454 words[2], consequently the particles are counted independently.

In our traditional literature only the following passages are known to me, in which the number of words is spoken of; and among these only two are of importance for our problem. In Sanhedrin, 10 b, some Amoraim of the second half of the third century point to Num. vi. 24–26 as containing 3 + 5 + 7 words. In Numbers Rabbah, Naso, sect. 13 (ed. Wilna, 108 b–109 a), it is stated that Ps. xix. 8–10 has five words to every half verse[3], that in Deut. xxxiii. 18 the blessing of Moses consists of five words[4]; that, on the other hand, the blessing of Jacob in Gen. xlix. 13 consists of ten words[5]. In the last-named verse עלי־ציד is connected with a Makkeph and is yet taken as two words[6]. Decisive, also, are the passages in Numbers Rabbah,

---

[1] Dillmann says in his article, "Text of the Old Testament" (*Protestant Real-Encyclopedia*[2], II, 391), speaking of the Greek translations of the Bible, that they "differ indeed very frequently from the present text as regards the division of words, but still this is more the case with words which in sense belong together more closely (Cappell. II, 685–693, 839–842; Eichorn, §§ 73, 76)." Cf. the transliteration in Field, *Hexapla*, LXXIII, θεσαμηώθ = חצץ מאות.

[2] Possibly I have miscounted to the extent of 4, or the Massoretic statement תנ אלף should be emended so as to read תנר אלף.

[3] אילים חמשה שתורים חמשה כבשים בני שנה חמשה (Num. vii. 23) כנגד ג׳ פסוקים של תורה שבהם ו׳ סדרי משנה והן שתים פסקה וכל פסקה ופסקה מן חמשה תיבות ואלו הם תורת ה׳ תמימה וגו׳.

[4] נגד ה׳ תיבות שהם בפסוק שביך משה שותפוחם.

[5] משרה והב מלאה קשרת כבגר ׳י תיבות שיש בברכת זבולן.

[6] In Sanhedrin, 22 a, R. Jehuda says, in the name of Rab: באוחה שזה קנחה בת שבע בשלש עשרה מצות, on which Rashi observes that in 1 Kings i. 15, 13 words are to be found. This enumeration is only correct, if

ch. 14 (117 b), where it is stated that Gen. xlviii. 14 וישת—xlviii. 20 has 130 words; ibid. 121 a, that Num. vi. 13-20 also contains 130 words; ibid., that Num. vi. 8-12 contains 70 words; ibid. 118 a, that Gen. xlviii. 14 to והצעיר has ten words; and that in xlviii. 20, from וישם to מנשה, there are five words. According to a citation in the Aruch from the *Yelamdenu* the Shema contains 248 words [1].

It is a question indeed how old the passages here cited are; nevertheless, this much is proved by them, that at the time when the enumeration of the words enjoyed a certain amount of attention, every word which in our texts appears separately, was regarded as independent, which was, indeed, from the outset to be expected. The outward separation of the words, as carried out in written Bible texts is very ancient, and springs from pre-Talmudic times, as can be proved from several considerations [2]. The variations found in the Greek translators are explained by the small size of their copies of the Bible, which offered opportunity for confusion in doubtful cases. Nevertheless, this antiquity of the division of words did not result in the removal of all doubt, for as late as the second century, differences of opinion prevailed as to the proper way of writing certain words [3].

The total number of words in the Pentateuch, as has already been mentioned above, amounts, according to Ben Asher (*Dikd. Hat.*, p. 55 supra) to 79,856; according to Norzi in his concluding observation to the Pentateuch, to 79,876. It is evident that both transmit the same estimate: either נ״ו (= 56) has been corrupted to ע״ו (= 76)

את המלך is counted as one word. It is inconceivable that there is here a miscount, for Rashi quotes the whole verse. Hence את would not be regarded as a separate word. It is, however, possible that Rashi took the name בת־שבע as *one* word. This passage cannot under any circumstances furnish a proof for the period of Rab, because it remains doubtful whether Rab really took the number 13 from the number of words in the quoted verse, since 13 is well known to be a favourite and frequently-used number in our Tradition.

[1] Aruch, ed. Kohut, V, 64 b, Art. מאה : רמ״ח תיבות יש בקרית שמע שמצ שמשמרות. רמ״ח איברים שבאדם גילמדנו פרש׳ כי אם שמר השמרמך. Kohut remarks hereon that the citation cannot be verified.

[2] Cf. Dillmann, l. c.; Menachoth, 30 a: ובין תיבה לתיבה כמלא אות קטנה.

[3] Cf. Pesachim, 117 a supra; Chullin, 65 a supra. Whether כרלצמר and כסיה form one or two words, could have been decided by the number of words in the Pentateuch; nevertheless, we find no proposition with respect to counting the words (similar to that in Kiddushin, 30 a), because the contending Amoraim probably declared themselves incompetent to decide a question involving a point as to the division of the words.

or the opposite has taken place. It is noticeable that no numerical statement as to the words in the Prophets and Hagiographa has been recorded, whereas such has been the case as regards the letters of the alphabet. There exists, therefore, no mention of the middle word either of the Prophets and Hagiographa or of the whole Bible, as there does of the Torah. In the familiar passage, Kiddushin, 30 a, already quoted, there is no allusion to an enumeration of the words, only to a counting of the letters. For division by words was only an external feature; it was therefore not necessary that, like the quantity of letters, it should be fixed by a number. They rested satisfied with having done this with the most important book—the Torah. The counting of the letters is unquestionably older than the counting of the words. From the preceding, too, the fact is explained why in Tradition the letters are so often spoken of and the words so seldom.

LUDWIG BLAU.

BUDAPEST.

(To be continued.)

MASSORETIC STUDIES.

III.

The Division into Verses.

1. *Age of the Division into Verses.*

It is known that the older form of the Biblical text is contained in the scrolls as used in the Synagogues; all external additions which were not admitted in such scrolls are of comparatively later origin. The text of the Torah authorized to be used in the Synagogal service shows the division into books and sections, but not the division into verses. The former division, the *Parashas*, are therefore of greater age than ⌐ne latter, the *Pesukim*. The text had first been divided into sections according to the contents, and afterwards subdivided into sentences; the division progressed from the greater to the smaller. For the same reason it may be confidently asserted that the subdivision of the verses themselves into smaller portions, according to the sense, has followed, and not preceded, the division into verses; the complete verse is older than the half-verse. The analysis of the text has progressed gradually from a division into books to one into sections, verses, and half-verses.

As the books and sections of the Pentateuch are severally marked in the scrolls used in the Synagogues by empty spaces, and the various verses are not so distinguished, there can be no doubt that the former division hails from pre-Talmudic times, otherwise it would not have been introduced in these scrolls; just as little as the division into verses, which was already known to the oldest traditions that have come down to us. From an historical point of view the *Parashas*, and the division into five books of the Pentateuch, must therefore be called pre-historic. From this it by no means follows, however, that the division into verses first arose in historical times, which, in this case, means the first century of the common era. A distinction must be made between the division into verses and its external indication. The beginning and end of each verse have been marked by external signs only in post-Talmudical times, and yet we find the older Tanaites already speak of separate verses, and there can be no question that even the oldest Tanaites were acquainted with them. It is pure chance that no maxims have been handed down in their name in evidence of this fact. The counting of the verses, and, consequently, the division into verses, is in Kiddushin, 30 a, attributed to the Soferim. It is therefore beyond doubt that this process took place at a period to which the tradition of the Tanaites does not reach up. The proofs of these assertions will be adduced in the course of our inquiry.

The information afforded by tradition cannot, therefore, fully answer this question. A. Dillmann has condensed the results of the previous investigations in the following sentence: "There is no evidence to show whether larger or smaller sentences were separated in writing; it was certainly not done regularly; but probably occasionally, and in special cases (on the Mesha stone), by means of a vertical stroke, and in poetry verses and parts of verses seem to have been usually marked by distinct lines, for even at a later time poems were written always after that fashion; and with other nations, for instance the Arabians, this mode of writing poetry dates from antiquity [1]." D. H. Müller, in his latest work [2], expresses himself much more confidently: "I believe myself able to maintain, and in certain cases also to prove, that the Prophets in writing down their speeches divided them in lines or verses."

Even if Dillmann's and Müller's opinions be correct, the question remains, whether in Hebrew prose also the text was divided into separate verses? The idea that this might have been effected by means of a vertical stroke, must, I think, be discarded, for no trace of such distinction can be found either in the text of the Bible, or in the older traditional literature. If the text of the Torah had ever possessed such signs to divide the sentences, they could not have been so thoroughly eliminated from it as not to leave some reminiscence at least in the tradition. It is true M. Friedmann [3] wanted to infer from Soferim, 3, 7 (vi. ed. Müller = Sefer Tora, 3, 4), the existence of a division by means of a vertical stroke, but without sufficient ground. For, in the first place, שפסקו ספר does not necessarily mean a stroke, it means merely a division, which might have been effected by an empty space; and, secondly, this prohibition, which is to be found neither in the Talmud, nor in the Midrash, may have originated only at the time when the signs for the vowels and accents came to be developed, and cannot therefore serve as an evidence of antiquity.

---

[1] Herzog-Plitt, *Protestantische Real-Encyclopaedie*[2], II, 383.

[2] *Die Propheten in ihrer ursprünglichen Form*, Vienna, I, 61. Müller holds that the פהרוחות and סתומות, and the formation of stanzas, date from the oldest times.

[3] Literaturblatt of the *Menorah*, I (1891), No. 3. Cp. on this point, Pinsker, *Einleitung in das hebräisch-babylonische Punktationssystem*, p. 133, n. 1.

For the same reason is the expression ושניקר ראשי פסוקים not to be understood as referring to a division in the oldest time by means of points[1].

In the absence of all historical evidence, nothing remains, as far as the oldest time is concerned, except turning to the text of the Bible itself and drawing conclusions from it. Not desiring to enter upon the frequently discussed question of Hebrew metres, stanzas, and versification[2], this being beyond the scope of our investigations, I bring forward only one proof for the pre-Massoretic, or, more exactly, the pre-Talmudic origin of the division into verses[3]. I allude to the alphabetical portions of Holy Writ[4]. It is especially Psalms xxv, xxxiv, and cxix, with their symmetrical half-verses, and the third chapter of the Lamentations of Jeremiah, with its short verses, which seem to me to supply a proof that the division into verses was not a product of theological knowledge, but had its origin in the very thought and speech of the ancient Hebrews. These short sentences cannot be considered as *strophae;* if we were to designate them as such, it would amount only to giving another name to the same thing. In the same manner I believe Psalms cxi and cxii to afford a proof for the primitive nature of the half-verses. Dichotomy is an inherent law of ancient Hebrew literature. The application of the alphabet to denote the commencement of verses bears ample evidence that the authors appreciated the separate nature of sentences; it may, therefore, be justly assumed, that the authors of the Bible had such consciousness of a division of the speech according to sentences, not only in poetry but also in prose. The melodious mode of recitation on solemn occasions, which is mentioned in the Talmud[5], may be

---

[1] There were scrolls of the Torah in the Middle Ages in which a space of the size of one letter was left empty between the verses. Isaac ben Shesheth says in his *Responsae*, No. 286 : מה שמצאת בספר תורה אחר אויר מלא אות "אחר בין פסוקא לפסוקא וכו", and permits the questioner the use of the scroll.

[2] Besides the works of Dillmann and Müller, already cited, cf. Delitzsch, *Psalms*, 1st ed., Preface x, part II, p. 394 sqq.; 3rd ed., I, p. 17 sqq.; Budde, *Zeitschrift für die Alttestamentliche Wissenschaft*, II (1882), p. 1 sqq.; *Das Hebräische Klagelied*, XI (1891), p. 234 sqq., and the literature quoted there. Especially important for the subject of versification is S. Berger, *Histoire de la Vulgate*, Paris, 1893, p. 316 sqq. and p. 363 sqq.

[3] I see from Delitzsch, *Psalms*[3], I, p. 20, n. 2, that Hupfeld and Riehm adopted this assumption (*Luth. Zeitschrift*, 1866, p. 300).

[4] Pss. ix, x, xxv, xxxiv, xxxvii, cxi, cxii, cxix, cxlv ; Lam. i–iv.

[5] Megilla, 32 a : הקורא בלא נעימה והשונה בלא זמרה. Whether the intonation in use at the present day is identical with this נעימה remains an open question.

of very ancient origin; it certainly is pre-Talmudic. I think that no stronger proof than this for the pre-Talmudic origin of the division into verses can be adduced. Sufficient proofs are only given by the tradition.

2. *The Division into Verses in the Talmud and the Midrash.*

In order to be able to form a judgment on the division into verses by the authorities of Tradition, it is necessary to make a complete collection and examination of the material referring thereto; a thing which has not hitherto been done[1]. The attempt shall therefore be made here to reconstruct a sort of mosaic picture out of the occasional, and widely scattered utterances of the doctors of the Talmud and Midrash.

The word פסוק is of the same formation as the word כתוב; both require the noun דבר as their complement[2]. The root פסק does not occur in Biblical Hebrew, but in the Aramaic dialect it denotes various things[3]. But the way the word is applied in new-Hebrew sufficiently explains the technical meaning of the word פסוק. Only the two following meanings need be considered: (1) "to cleave asunder," (2) "to interrupt." Friedmann, in his aforementioned essay, decides for its derivation from the former meaning, and concludes from it that the separation was marked, either by a vertical stroke at the end, or by a dot at the beginning of the verse. But, as we have already explained, the term פסוק is older than any written designation of the beginning or the end of the verses. We therefore prefer the second meaning; פסק means "to interrupt the reading," "to make a pause." In the Mishna Sheviith we read: מלאכה שהיא פוסקת בשביעית משמטת אינה פוסקת וכו' "Labour, which rests in the seventh year," &c. In the same sense the term הפסיק is applied in innumerable passages; for instance, Mech. to 12, 6 (6 a 2): הפסיק הענין; Tosifta Megillah, 4, 10: ממקום שפוסקין שחרית משם מתחילין במנחה וכו' ר' יהודה ממקום שפוסקין שבת שחרית שם מתחילין שבת הבאה. Similarly we read in Mechilta to 15, 23 (45 a 19): קורין בשבת ומפסיקין באחד בשבת וכו'. Single passages from the Bible are either called כתוב, after the Writing, or מקרא, after the Reading. Now it is probable that the expression to denote separate verses was taken from the Reading,

---

[1] Strack, *Prolegomena critica in Vetus Testamentum hebraicum*, pp. 78–80, 122 ; Harris, JEWISH QUARTERLY REVIEW, I (1884), pp. 224, 231 ; Friedmann, Literaturblatt of the *Menorah*, I, No. 3. They have dealt with very small fragments only of Talmudical data.

[2] Blau, *Zur Einleitung in die Heilige Schrift*, p. 18.

[3] Cf. Elia Levita, *Methurgeman*, s. v. פסק.

because the reader paused for rest, and not from the Writing, where no external sign marked the division of verses.

A distinction must be sharply drawn between מקרא and כתוב on the one hand, and פסוק on the other hand. The former expressions denote any passage from scripture, without regard to its length; the latter term applies exclusively to a verse. This use of the terms is the predominant one in the older traditional literature. In the Thirteen Rules of R. Ishmael, in which the Torah in its written shape was foremost in the mind of the Tanaite, the term כתוב only is used, because there is no question of verses. The words כתוב and מקרא occur in the same sense in no end of passages; the word פסוק, however, mostly, when it is not so much intended to lay stress on the contents, but rather on the length of the quotation. The portion of the פרשה is therefore called פסוק, e. g. Sifre, II, 4 sub fin.: "מי ששמע פסוק אחד ‧‧‧‧‧ מי ששמע פרשה אחת וכו'". Just as, in the same passage, פרק is divided into הלכות, thus פרשה is divided into פסוקים. In Aboth, 6, 3 והלומד מחברו פרק אחד או הלכה אחת או, the word פרשה is perhaps missing. Sifra to 16, 23 פסוק [1]. כל הפרשה אמורה על הסדר חוץ מן הפסוק הזה (82 b Weiss): can also be used as "part of a book"; e. g. Boraitha Sanh. 99 a 38: ת"ר הקורא פסוק של; ib. 101 a 4: כל התורה כולה מן השמים חוץ מפסוק זה; שיר השירים ועושה אותו כמין זמר; Tosifta Megilla, 2, 2 (223, Zuckerm.): הקורא את המנלה וטעה והשמיט בה פסוק אחד. פסוק is also used when a certain number of verses is given, e. g. Mishna Megilla, 4, 5: הקורא בתורה לא יפחות מג' פסוקים. These instances we shall give completely later on.

We are, however, in a position to show, that in our texts the word פסוק has frequently taken the place of מקרא or כתוב, and this not only in texts of a later origin, but already in the oldest, in the Tanaite Midrashim. Mechilta, 19, 1 (61 b 3), verse 1, 8 of the Song of Solomon is introduced by Johanan ben Zaccai with the following formula: כל ימי הייתי מצטער על פסוק זה; but in the otherwise identical parallel passage of Sifre, II, 305 sub fin. (130 a 12), we find: וכל ימי בקשתי מקרא זה; Tosifta, Kethuboth, 5, 10 (26, F 10), is said in the name of Eleazar bar Zadoc: וקראתי עליה את המקרא הזה, similar to Kethuboth, 67 a 7; it occurs in the same form in Echa Rabba, I, 16

---

[1] Ed. pr., Malbim, the parallel passages Joma, 32 a and 71 a, all have פסוק; Jer. Joma, 7, 2 (44 b 33), the word פסוק is omitted. Besides this passage פסוק occurs only twice more in Sifra: at the end of ג' מדות where most likely וכך הכתוב אומר ought to be read, instead of הפסוק; and to 11, 29 (52 b) כשהיה ר' עקיבא מגיע לפסוק זה = Chullin, 127 a. מקרא and כתוב occur, of course, hundreds of times.

627

(34 b 20), Jerush. Kethuboth 5, 13 (30 e 2), and Pesikta Rabbatai, ed. Friedmann, 140 a, with the difference that פסוק is read instead of מקרא. In Aboth de R. Nathan, ed. Schechter, I, c. 17 (p. 33, l. 5), we read : רי״בז . . . כל ימי הייתי קורא מקרא זה. Besides other differences in the wording we find in the same sentence three times פסוק, and four times מקרא; the latter reading is certainly the original one, for there is no question of the length, but of the contents of the passage. Another instance is this. The contradiction and harmonization of two scripture passages is in numerous cases expressed by the following formula : כתוב אחד אומר וכו״ וכתוב אחד אומר וכו״ כיצד יתקיימו שני כיצד יתקיימו (מקראות) כתובים. Thus Mechilta, 20, 7 (p. 69 a 1) : הללו כתובים אלו ד׳; 20, 17 (70 b 2); 20, 24 (73 b 9); 23, 11 (100 b 9). Somewhat differently Mechilta, 22, 8 (92 b 4) : ר׳ שמעון אומד קורא אני עליו כאן וכו״ וקורא אני להלן וכו״ כיצד יתקיימו שני מקראות הללו. Without regarding the variation of כתוב and מקרא, on which point Mechilta, 12, 5 (4 b), is important, as after ב׳ מקראות the rule is cited with the expression שני כתובין; cf. Mech. 13, 6=20 b 4 and 12, 15=8 b; and also Sifre, II, 134 = Menachot, 66 a, we maintain, that in Mech. 15, 4 (38 a 7) the strange formula : כתוב אחד אומר ירה וכתוב אחד אומר אומר רמה כיצד יתקיימו ב׳ פסוקים הללו is undoubtedly corrupt, for one word, ירה or רמה, cannot be called פסוק. As a matter of fact I do not think that there is any other passage in which the words כיצד יתקיימו ג׳ פסוקים של צדוק הדין שני פסוקים הללו occur. In the same way in Sifre, II, 307 (133 a) is a corrupted reading, for in the parallel passage in Aboda Zara, 18 a 20, we read correctly שלש מקראות של צדוק הדין. I learn from my notes that the subtle distinction between פסוק and כתוב or מקרא was disregarded after some time, so that in Echa and Koheleth Rabba the word פסוק is generally used without any notice of its original meaning being taken. This occurs so frequently that it is unnecessary to quote passages from these and other Midrashic works, such as Pesikta de Rab Kahana, &c.[1]

The important question has next to be considered, whether Tradition knew of a fixed division into verses, and of what nature such may have been. We can answer both questions from the tradition, and will therefore quote our sources first. The existence of a fixed division of verses is borne out by the fact that certain numbers of verses are mentioned. The previously quoted Mishna Megilla says : " Not *less*

---

[1] Baba Bathra, 82 a : א״ל רב אחא בריה דרב אויא לרב אשי מכדי פסוקי נינדו ולקרי. Here פסוקים are equivalent to מקראות; it is an Amora of the fifth century who speaks. Sabbath, 118 b 31, פסוקי דזמרא. There are, besides, numerous other instances from the later tradition.

than *three* verses of the Torah must be read [1]." The Tosifta (ibid.
4, 17, 18) on the other hand says : "No *more* than *three* verses are read
without interruption ; if it is a Parasha of *four* or *five* verses, it is all
read ; if it is a Parasha of *five* verses, *three* are read and *two* are left,
and the next person reads these *two* and *three* more from the next
Parasha, but if this one had *four* or *five* verses, it was all read.
As Haftara from the Prophets not more than *three* verses are read ;
if the Parasha had *four* or *five* verses, all of it is read ; if it is a small
Parasha, as, for instance, Isa. lii. 3, it is read by itself. At the end
of a book (of the Torah), not less must be left than would suffice for
seven persons [2]." From the Babylonian Talmud we quote the following
Baraithot : Berachoth, 22 b, R. Meir teaches that one who is unclean
may read only three verses from the Torah [3]; in the Synagogue not
less than ten verses must be read [4]; as Haftara not less than twenty-one
verses may be read [5]; if a slave had read in the Synagogue he was
not yet declared free [6]; if one had betrothed a wife asserting that he
was a Reader, it was enough that he had read three verses in the
Synagogue [7].

---

[1] Deuteronomy Rabbah, c. 7 (227 b) : למה התקינו שלא יפחות משלשה פסוקים כנגד
אברהם יצחק ויעקב ד"א כנגד משה ואהרן ומרים שניתנה התורה על ידיהן. This is, of
course, an Agadic interpretation ; such also is that given in Megilla, 21 b :
כנגד כהנים לוים וישראלים or כנגד תורה נביאים וכתובים. The law that not less
than three verses be read shows that it had been done before ; perhaps
the reading of one verse is meant. Jer. Kethuboth, 2, 10 (26 D 21) : א"ר וטירא
א"ר ירמיה העגר שלה משבעה קריות וידבר עולה מג' פסוקים.

[2] אין קורין בתורה יותר משלשה פסוקין בנכך אחד · אם היתה פרשה של ארבעה ושל
חמשה הרי זה קורא את כולה · אם היתה פרשה של חמשה קורא שלשה והניח שנים ועומד
אחריו לקרות קורא אותן שנים ועוד שלשה מפרשה אחרת · אם היתה של ארבעה ושל חמשה
הרי זה קורא את כולה · אין מפטירין בנביא יותר משלשה פסוקים בנכך אחר · היתה פרשה
של ארבעה ושל חמשה הרי זה קורא את כולן · אם היתה פרשה קטנה כגון כה אמר ה'
חנם נמכרתם קורין אותה בפני עצמה · אין משיירין בסוף הספר אלא כדי שיקראו שבעה · שייר כדי
שיקראו שבעה וקראו ששה וטד שבעה מחומש אחד וכו". The apparent contradiction
can be solved in this way, that a difference is made in case other persons
have still to read ; for then two verses of the Parasha can remain for the
next person. Cf. on this rule Jer. Megillah, 4, 5 in (75 b).

[3] אמר ר' מאיר אין בעל קרי רשאי לקרות בתורה יותר משלשה פסוקים.

[4] Megilla, 21 b 22 : אלא הא דתני רב שימא אין פוחתין מעשרה פסוקים בבית הכנסת וירבר
עולה מן המנין.

[5] Baraitha in Megilla, 23 a : המפטיר בנביא לא יפחות מעשרים וא' פסוקים כנגד שבעה
Ibid. 23 b 6 : וכי הוי קרינן טשרה פסוקיא אמר לן (ר' יוהנן) אפסיקו. שקראו בתורה.

[6] Kethuboth, 28 b 2 : או שקרא (העבר) שלשה פסוקים בבית הכנסת הרי זה לא יצא
לחירות.

[7] Kiddushin, 49 a : ח"ר על מנת שאני קריינא כיון שקרא שלשה פסוקים בב"ה הרי זו
מקורשת רבי יהודה אומר עד שיקרא ויתרגם.

These figures presuppose a fixed division into verses. So do those sentences in which single verses are mentioned. The aforementioned Mishna in Megilla, 4, 5, reads: "No more than one verse at a time is read to the interpreter, but three verses from the Prophets[1]." To this rule belongs also the observation of the Amoraite R. Chisda: "The interpreter may not commence before the reader has finished the verse, nor must the reader commence before the interpreter has finished his interpretation[2]." "One who reads the book of Esther, either letter by letter, or verse by verse," &c.; "he who wrote and read the Megilla verse by verse[3]." "The threats in Leviticus xxvi and Deuteronomy xxviii must not be read without break, together with the verse preceding them and the verse following them[4]." "The reading of a verse which is not found in the twenty-four books of the Bible is equivalent to the reading of a verse from the Apocrypha[5]."

As a third proof that the verses and their parts bore a fixed distinction, the decisions about the commencement and middle of verses may be cited: "Simeon ben Gamaliel says that on Sabbath the commencement of the verses may be arranged for children by lamplight[6]." Best known is the interpretation given to Neh. viii. 8, according to which ויבינו במקרא means the beginning of the verses[7]. The king Ahab appears to the Amoraite Levi, who had

---

[1] ולא יקרא לתורגמן יותר מפסוק אחד ובנביא שלשה.

[2] Sota, 39 b: ואמר רבי זירא אמר רב חסדא וכו" ואין המתרגם רשאי להתהיל בתרגום עד שיכלה פסוק מפי הקורא ואין הקורא רשאי להתחיל בפסוק אחר עד שיכלה תרגום מפי המהרגם.

[3] Megilla, 18 b: ת"ר השמיש בה סופר אותיות או פסוקין וקראן הקירא כמתורגמן המחרגם יצ"א—ת"ר השמיש בה הקורא פסוק אחד לא יאמר אקרא את כולה ואה"כ אקרא אורו פסוק אלא קורא מאותו פסוק ואילך—אלא כתב פסוקא פסוקא יקרי ליה. Cf. on the second sentence, the above cited Tosifta Megilla, 2, 2; and on the Talmudical question "אלא רכתב וכו", Megilla, 25 a, ראמר פסוק פסוק (of the Sh'ma), Berachot, 13 b (cf. Succah, 42 a), פסוקא קמא of the Sh'ma is mentioned.

[4] Megilla, 31 b 23: תנא כשהוא מהחיל (ברכות וקללות) מתחיל בפסוק שלפניהן וכשהוא מסיים מסיים בפסק ק שלאחריהן.

[5] Numbers Rabbah, c. 14 (117 a): כל מי שקורא פסוק שאינו מ"כר ספרים כאלו קורא בספרים החצונים. In Kohelet Rabbah, sub fin., Ben Sira and Ben Laana are named as examples. Mention may also be made of Jer. Erubin, 10, 3 (26 b 9), זבוקיא as contrasted with ספר; Jer. Succa, 5, 1 (55 b 20), Jer. Sabbath, 6, 1 (8 b 18): אין קורין פסוק על גבי מכה בשבת והדין דקרי על יברוחה אסור בוא וקרי את. Cf. הפסוק הזה על בני שהוא מתבצח הן עליו ספר הן עליו הפל בשביל שיזן אסור also Sabbath, 103 b 30: ובלבד שיכתוב את הפסוק נולו.

[6] Jer. Sabbath, 1, 4 (3): תני רשב"ג אומר התינוקות מתקינין להן ראשי פסוקיהן לאור הנר; and a little before, מהוא מחקן ראשי פרק"ם פסקין.

[7] Jer. Megilla, 4, 1 (74 d 50): ושום שכל אלו . . . רבי זעירא בשם רב חננאל הטעמים רבינו במקרא ז' המסורות וש אומרים אילו ההכרגים וש אומרים.

VOL. IX.   K

been wont to interpret 1 Kings xxi. 25 to his disadvantage, and says to him: "Thou only hast regard to the beginning, but not to the conclusion of the verse [1]." Samuel bar Nachmann says of Num. xxiii. 19, and Simon ben Lakish of Ps. cii. 18 that the beginning of the verse contradicts its latter part [2]. The middle of the verse is also mentioned [3]. Long and short verses are distinguished [4], and even half-verses have a special name [5]. In writing most verses occupied two, three, or four lines [6]. From all these data it is sufficiently clear *that the texts of the Bible as possessed by the Tanaites and Amoraites had an established division* of verses. If therefore the Talmud, Kiddushin, 30 a, attributes the division into verses to the Soferim, it is only meant to express the

אילו ראשי פסוקים. In accord with this, but more accurately, Genesis Rabbah, c. 36 (149 b Wilna): ושום שכל אלו המטעמים · יבינו במקרא אלו ראשי הפסוקים · רב הינא בן לוליאני אימר אלו דהכרעות והראיות (?) · רבנן דקסרין אמרי מכאן למסורת. In Megilla, 3 a, and Nedarim, 37 b, this important passage reads thus: דאמר רב איקי בר אבין אמר רב חננאל אמר רב ... ושום שכל אלו הפסוקים יבינו במקרא זה פיסוק מטעמים ואמרו אלו המסורות. It seems that מטעמים is the same as פסוקים, and פסקי מטעמים the same as הכרעות. Both expressions mean, respectively, complete and half-verses. The preceding note shows that ראשי פסוקים, which, according to Soferim, 3, 7, were, at a later period, also externally marked, were of importance in Palestine. I know of no passage in the Babylonian Talmud in which ראשי פסוקים, nor in the Palestinian Talmud in which פסקי מטעמים, occurred. Whether in Jer. Chagiga, 2, 4 (77 a 45), בתחלה רבו פוהח לו ראשי פסוקים ומסכים is not corrupted from ראשי פרקים I should not like to decide. The question is, מצטה מרכנה and פסוקים may be correct, although afterwards פרק is mentioned. On ראש פ' and סוף פ' cf. Rappoport, Erech Millin, 110 b.

[1] Jer. Sanhedrin, 10, 2 (28 b 18): איח לך רישיה דפסוקא ולית לך סופיה; similarly Levit. Rabbah, c. 36 (96 a): רישיה והרין פסוקא או סיפיה; Berachoth, 10 a 7: שפיל לסיפיה דקרא, referring to Isa. liv. 1 b; ibid. is Ps. civ. 29 in its relation to civ. 1, called סיפא דענינא, and not דקרא?

[2] Genesis Rabbah, c. 53 (215 b 2), and Pesikta de R. Kahana, ed. Buber, 181 a 1. The same words occur in both passages: הפסוק הזה לא ראשו סופו ולא סופו ראשו. Benjamin ben Levi speaks similarly of Ps. lxix. 34 (Gen. Rabbah, c. 71 init.), and Jose bar Chanina of Song of Solomon vi. 2 (Shir. Rabbah, s. v. = 65 a); cf. *Pesikta Rabbathi*, Friedmann, 8 b.

[3] Jer. Berachoth, 2, 1, sub fin.: באמצע הפרשה ואפילו באמצע הפסוק.

[4] Zebachim, 28 b. Lev. vii. 18 is called קרא אריכא in contrast to xix. 7. In Bamidbar Rabbah, c. 4 (27 b), Num. vii. 9 is called פסוק קטן שהתינוקות קורין.

[5] Numbers Rabbah, c. 13 (108 b), פסקה. This chapter and chapter 14 are from a later date.

[6] Jer. Megilla, 71 c 10: מעה והשמיש פסוק אחד אם יש בו שתים שלש שיטין מהקנו וקורא בו ארבע אינו קורא בו. There were, of course, also verses of only one line, and of more than four lines.

fact generally known and recognized at that period, that this division was ever so old, and its origin lost in the remotest antiquity[1].

Having settled this point we now approach the important question whether the division of verses, known to the doctors of the Talmud, was different from the one we possess? It is only by the production of the direct and indirect testimonies contained in the Talmud and. Midrash that idle speculation and gratuitous conjecture can be put a stop to. The material is much more ample than is commonly assumed, and quite sufficient to enable us to come to a decision on the question. For the purpose of greater lucidity we shall produce the proofs in several groups, and commence with those which contain evidence as about certain numbers of verses.

According to the Mishna Taanith, 4, 1. those Israelites whose Mishmar was on service in the temple, had throughout the week a religious service in their towns, in which the history of the creation was read in the following order[2]: first day, Gen. i. 1-8; second day, Gen. i. 6-13; third day, i. 9-19; fourth day, i. 14-23, &c. The Talmud, 27 b, observes in reference to this: בראשית has five verses, יהי רקיע three verses[3], together eight verses[4]; i. 6-13 has 8 verses[5]. Therefore, already at the time of Rav and Samuel, who are the disputants in that passage, the section Gen. i. 1-13 had the same division as in our time. This is the more noteworthy, because ויהי ערב וגו' 1 3, 19, 23 form a verse by itself, whereas these words are in ver. 5 and 8 only a part of another verse. Indeed, the Palestinian Talmud[6] says that, according to the opinion of those who allow one verse to be severed into two, these words at the reading formed a separate verse.

Numbers Rabbah c. 14 (123 b), and Midrash Tadshe, c. 11 (Epstein,

---

[1] This view also finds expression in the well-known maxim: כל פסוקא דלא פסקיה משה אנן לא פסקינן; instead of כל פסוקא, Berachot, 12 a, reads כל פרשה.

[2] וקורין במעשה בראשית ביום הראשון בראשית ויהי רקיע · בשני יהי רקיע ויקוו המים · בשלישי יקוו המים ויהי מאורות · ברביעי יהי מאורות וישרצו המים וכו'. This can serve also as an example of the mode in which, in ancient times, biblical passages were cited.

[3] Cf. Megilla, 22 a.

[4] Jer. Megilla, 4, 2 (75 a) = Taanith, 4, 3 (68 b): והא לית בהון אלא תמניא.

[5] This follows from: ודא הנינן נשנ יהי רקיע ויקוו דמים · מן דמר חוור חוור בפסוקים · וכן דמר חותך אפילו חותך אין בו.

[6] L. c. ומן דכר חותך ויהי ערב ויהי בקר פסוק בכנ עצמו. Rashi, Megilla, s. v. פוסק, says that verse 1, 3 was divided into two, which Samuel perhaps did not mean. In Babli, Rav and Samuel dispute whether פוסק or וולג; in Jerushalmi, Kahana and Asi whether חוור or חותך.

K 2

Beiträge zur jüdischen Alterthumskunde, p. xxv), bears testimony that Gen. i. 1 to iii. 14 contained seventy verses [1]. That the section about Amalek, Exod. xvii. 8-16, did not have ten verses is testified by Jer. Megilla, 4, 2 (75 a), on which point compare Tosafoth, s.v. אין פותחין in Megilla, 21 b. The Mishna Sota, 37 b, and the Talmud, 40 a 7, declare that the blessing of the priests, Num. vi. 24-26 (ברכת כהנים), contained three verses [2].

Our division of verses of Numbers xxviii. 1-15 is borne out in all its parts by Megilla, 21 b [3], so is our division of the Shema, Deut. vi. 4-6, Jer. Berachoth, 1, 5 (3 b 9) [4]. The last eight verses of the Pentateuch are, as is well known, mentioned in the old Boraitha Baba Bathra, 14 b [5], and by a Tanaite of the middle of the second century in Makkot, 11 a 12 [6].

The Prophets and Hagiographa were not revered in the same degree as the Torah, and were not, therefore, as assiduously studied. Consequently they afford less proofs for our theory; yet they are not entirely missing even in these books.

1 Kings i. In Koheleth Rabbah, 8, 8 (44 a), R. Levi says : "Almost fifty-two times we find the expression 'the king David,' but in the narrative of his death it is only said 'David' (ii. 1), because 'there is no sovereign on the day of death.'" The strange

---

[1] Numbers Rabbah : א"ר פנחם מראש ספר בראשית עד קללת נחש שב:ים פסוקים שני אויבים לא נאררו עד שהשלים עליהם שבעים פסוקים הנחש והם הרשע מבראשית עד ארור אתה מכל הבהמה שבעים פסוקים · הם מאחר הדברים האלה גרל המלך וג'" שבעים פסוקים (ibid. vii. 10) עד ויהלו את המן (Esther iii. 1): Midrash Tadshe similarly, but shorter. The Pinchas mentioned here is Pinchas ben Jair, to whom the book of the Jubilees was attributed. If Epstein's conjecture is correct, that the passages are quoted from the book of Jubilees in the name of Pinchas ben Jair, this date would be old enough; but even if the Hebrew rendering of the book of Jubilees belongs to a later period, the date would still be pretty old.

[2] Cf. also Numbers Rabbah, c. 11 (86 a) and c. 14 (126 a).

[3] בעא מיניה עולא בר רב מרבא פרשת ראש חדש כיצר קורין אותה צו את בני ישראל ואמרת אליהם את קרב:י לחמי דהויק המניא · · · פש: להו שבעה דביום השבת הויק חרי ובראשי חדשיכם הויק חמשה וכו'"

[4] א"ר מני וכו' ג' פסוקין הראשונים צריכק כונה · מן גו דאינון ציבהר מיכין Vide 2, 1 (4 a, at the bottom) בר קשרא; Sabbath, 1, 1 (3 a 9, at the bottom); 2, 1 (4 b 1) and Babli Berachoth, 61 b = Jer. Berachoth, 9, 5 (14 b 15, at the bottom) = Jer. Sota, 5, 7 (20 c) לעקיבא, Deut. vi. 5. These passages leave no doubt that שמ: ישראל was divided in the same manner as we have it.

[5] יהושצ כתב ספרו ושמנה פסוקים שבתורה Vide ibid. 15 a; Menachoth, 30 a : (74 b 63) Jer. Megilla, 3, 8; אמר רב גידל אמר רב שמנה פסוקים שבתורה יהיר קורא אותן רבי יוסי בי רבי בון הומנתי פסוקייא אחרייא רמשנה הורה מעינין ברכה לפניהן ולאחריהן.

[6] פליני בה ר' יהודה ור' נרהמיא ח"א שמנה פסנקים וח"א ער מקלמ.

expression, "almost fifty-two times," can only be understood thus, that Levi counted in the first chapter of I Kings fifty-two verses, and means to say that the words "the king David" occurs in almost every verse, but immediately after, when David's death is mentioned, he is called "David" only[1].

Leviticus Rabbah, c. 6 (20 b 1) ascribes the authorship of the two verses, Isa. viii. 19, 20, to Beeri, the father of Hosheah, and says that they were embodied in the prophecy of Isaiah because they afforded too little material for a separate book[2]. Of the prophets, three verses were read consecutively to the interpreter, but if such three verses constituted three separate sections, in that case they were read separately. The Talmud, Megilla, 24 a, says in explanation of these words of the Mishna, "for instance, Isa. lii. 3-5," which verses we also have as two Parashas[3].

Psalm xix. 8-10 are called three verses in Numbers Rabbah, c. 13 (108 b)[4]; that the people responded Ps. ciii. 20-22 to the blessing of the priests is mentioned in Jer. Berachoth, 1, 1 (2 c 25), and Babl. Sota, 39 b, and that text is called expressly three verses in Numbers Rabbah, c. 11 (86 a, at the bottom), in the name of Amoraites[5]. Of less importance is the evidence of the tradition that Threni i. 1-5 formed five verses[6], and that the third chapter of the same book had a threefold alphabet of verses[7]. Numbers Rabbah, c. 14 (114 b,

---

[1] The Agadah reads : א״ר לוי קרוב לחמשים ושתים פעמים כתיב והמלך דוד כיון (I Kings ii. 1). שנכתב למות דוד ויקרבו ימי דוד למות משום ואין שלבון ביום המות. Verbal communication by Prof. Bacher. In our text the chapter has fifty-three verses.

[2] א״ר סימן באירי לא נתנבא אלא שני פסוקים ולא היה בהם כרי ספר ונטפלו בישעיה ואלו הן וכי וחברו. In the parallel passage, c. 15 (40 b, at the bottom), we read דברים instead of פסוקים.

[3] ולא יקרא למתורגמן יותר מפסוק אחד ובנביא שלשה · היו שלשהן שלש פרשיות קורן אחר אחר. The Talmud mentions as an instance of this Isa. lii. 3-5. Baer, in his edition of Isaiah, restores also the third Parasha, but only on the ground of our passage from the Talmud, which is inadmissible, as Baer wanted to give the Massoretic text.

[4] כנגר ג׳ פסוקים של תורה (i. e. Bible) שבהם ו׳ סדרי משנה.
פליגי בה רב מארי ורב זביד חר אמר פסוק כנגר פסוק וחר אמר בכל פסוק אומר לכל ג׳ הפסוקים.

[6] Jer. Moed Katon, 3, 7 (83 b 44), says, in reference to Jer. xxxvi. 23 : מהוא שלש ולהות וארבעה הלת ארבע פסוקן · כיון שהגיע לפסוק החמישי כי ה׳ הונה. Parallel passages : Genesis Rabbah, c. 42 (169 a) ; Leviticus Rabbah, c. 11 (32 a), and others. The identification of ולהות and פסוקים is interesting ; it is possible.

[7] Echa Rabbah, prooemium No. 28 (15 a) : שהוא מן תלתא תלתא פסוקא באלפא ביתא.

at the bottom), says that 2 Chron. vi. 18-41 consisted of twenty-four verses[1]. That Esther iii-vii numbered seventy verses, has already been mentioned above, when we spoke on Genesis. According to S adyah, *Emunoth Weduoth*, c. 7 (ed. Cracow, p. 147), Daniel xi. 2-xii. 3 had forty-seven verses; and details are given as to groups of these verses, entirely in accord with our division of verses.

The allegations as to the number of verses of whole books can also be taken advantage of in proof of the division of verses. It is known that the principal passage is in Kiddushin, 30 a, where a statement is made as to the number of verses of the Pentateuch, the Psalms, and the Chronicles. On account of the importance of the subject we shall devote a special chapter to the number of verses of the Pentateuch, and in connexion therewith, to those of the Psalms and the Chronicles; and shall, therefore, mention here only Samuel bar Nachman's statement as to the number of verses of the Proverbs. He says, in Shir Rabbah, I, I (5 b), in agreement with our Massorah, that he had not found in the whole book of Proverbs more than nine hundred and fifteen verses[2]. Midrash Tadshe, c. 20 (p. xxxviii), says of Threni that it consisted of one hundred and fifty-four verses[3], which agrees with our number. This statement would, of course, be of importance for ancient times, only if we knew that it emanated from an ancient source.

[1] כ"ד פסוקים. This is a later interpretation, after כ"ד רננות, as older sources interpret it.

[2] אמר ר' שמואל בר נחמני חזרנו על כל ספר משלי ולא מצינו שנכתב בו אלא תשע מאות ומ"ו פסוקים ואת אומר נ' אלפים משל (?) אלא שאין לך כל פסוק וכסוק שאין בו ב' וג' טעמים. Pesikta, 34 b; Pesikta Rabbathi, 60 a; Koheleth Rabbah, 7, 23; Tanchuma חקת, 14; Numbers Rabbah, c. 19 (156 b): אלא קרוב לשמונה מאות פסוקים. Although this latter reading had already been possessed by Kimchi (Commentary to 1 Kings v. 12), I believe, nevertheless, that only Shir Rabbah has preserved Samuel bar Nachman's statement in its authentic form. It was easy for התקמו' (915) to be turned into תת קרו' = קרוב לשמנה מאות. Strack, *Prolegomena*, p. 12, assumes the figure 915 to be a correction of the copyist, in order to obtain agreement with the Massorah. We do not share this opinion, because there can be no question of another system of division into verses; and it is, therefore, impossible to cause 115 verses to disappear. The term טעמים will have to be taken to mean the single sentences in the middle of the verse, equal to the פסקי טעמים in the Babylonian Talmud. He therefore says only that in each verse two or three טעמים were contained, although 915 × 3 still does not give 3,000. If he had meant what Bacher assumed in *Agada der Paläst. Amoräer*, I, 501, that each verse had several meanings, this limitation would be out of place. Friedmann, n. 55, ad loc., thinks that Samuel bar Nachman had merely counted the משלים, and found 800 (?).

[3] פרשיות הן בספר הוה ויש בהן קנ"ד פסוקים ר'. (?)

We shall now adduce passages from the Talmuds and Midrashim demonstrating to certainty that single verses commenced and terminated with the authorities of the tradition in the same way as in our Massorah. For the sake of shortness we shall content ourselves, in most cases, with indicating the sources, without communicating the matter itself. In by far the greater portion it is quite impossible to have any doubt as to their demonstrative value. In order to facilitate the survey as much as possible, we have, as far as our exposition allowed it, retained the order of the Biblical passages. We do not claim to have been exhaustive; on the contrary, we are convinced that a careful study would be rewarded by a rich gleaning. We omit several allegations already given in reference to other points.

Our division of verses is testified: for GENESIS ii. 16 in Pesikta, 100 b[1]; for iv. 23, 1 Kings i. 33, Esther viii. 8 in Genesis Rabbah, c. 51 (209 a); for xiii. 7 in Pesikta Rabbathi, 9 b[2]; for xix. 24, 25 in Pesikta, 170 a[3]. For EXODUS ii. 4 in Sota, 11 a 17[4]; the full and half verses of chap. xv, in Mechilta, 15, 1, Tosifta Sota, 6, 23 (303[16]), Mishna Sota, 5, 6, Jer. Sota, 20 c 9, Babli Sota, 30 b[5]. LEVITICUS: we have already spoken of the "long verse," vii. 18, in contrast to xix. 7 (Zebachim, 28 b 14). Pesikta R. interprets the whole verse, Lev. xxiii. 24, when it says בו בפסוק "in the same verse;" xxiii. 27, 32; xvi. 29, 31, Num. xxix. 7, are entirely quoted in

[1] ר' יוסי בר סימן פתר · · · וכולם בפסוק אהד.

[2] א"ר יהורה בר סימן קרא סופו של פסוק והכנגני והצריוי או יושב בארץ.

[3] Two commencements of verses, with omission of the rest, in one quotation.

[4] אמר ר' יצחק פסוק זה כולו על שם שכינה נאמר, followed by an interpretation of the *whole* verse.

[5] An exposition of the different readings, and an explanation of the passage, would occupy too much space, and we must therefore leave the reader to do it for himself. For our purpose the following words of the Mechilta are already sufficient: ר' אליעור בן תראי אומר משה היה פותה ברבריו החלה וישראל שונין אחריו וגומרין עמו · משה היה פותח ואומר אשירה לה' כי גאה גאה וישראל אמר סוס ורוכבו רמה בים · משה היה אומר עוי וומרת יה וישראל שונין אחריו ויהי לי לישו:ה · משה היה פותה יי' איש מלחמה וישראל שונין אחריו וגומרין עמו יי' איש מלחמה יי' שמו. Thus the passage reads without Friedmann's correction. It seems that Moses intoned the first half-verse, whereupon Israel responded with the second half, so that they concluded the verse at once together with Moses. I would, therefore, strike out the second יי' איש מלחמה. The short ver. 3 is particularly conclusive. I would give it as a conjecture that one of the controversies of the disputing Tanaites was whether each sentence (= ענין) formed a separate verse. The שירת הים is, as is known, written, according to the Massorah, in separate verses.

Joma, 76 a. NUMBERS viii. 19 is testified in Leviticus Rabbah [1], c. 2 (8 a 8); xxiii. 19 in Genesis Rabbah, c. 53 (215 b 2); xxiv. 9 in Talmud Berachoth, 12 b (in the middle). DEUTERONOMY viii. 8 is testified in Berachoth, 41 a, and parallel passages; xvi. 14 in Pesikta, 100 a. The first words of xxxii. 1, 7, 13, 19, 27, 39, are abbreviated and composed into a mnemonic in Rosh Hashanah, 31 a 16 [2]; xxxiii. 18 is testified in Numbers Rabbah, c. 13 (109 a).

For the division into verses of the second portion of Holy Writ the following passages are of importance: 1 Sam. xxv. 32 is testified in Jer. Sanhedrin, 2, 3, at the end (20 b); 1 Sam. i. 11 in Pesikta Rabbathi, 18 a [3]; i. 16, 18 in Sanhedrin, 93 a, at the bottom [4]; 2 Sam. xii. 3 in Megilla, 13 a 29, where it is quoted in full; 1 Kings xxi. 25 in Jer. Sanhedrin, 10, 2 (28 b 18); Isa. iv. 6 in Sukka, 6 b, at the bottom (quoted in full); lxv. 24 in Exodus Rabbah, c. 21 (79 b) [5]; Jer. ii. 2 in Sanhedrin, 110 b 18 (quoted in full by Jochanan); xv. 2 in Baba Bathra, 8 b 6; Ezek. viii. 16 (a long verse), x. 2, 7, 9, 11, 1 Kings ii. 26 (long verse) are fully quoted, neither less nor more, Joma, 77 a, at the top.

Of the Hagiographa, the Psalms are most frequently quoted, and for the division of their verses the most proofs can be adduced; which is of special importance for the double mode of division into verses, of which we shall speak later on. For the examples to be cited prove that the ordinary division into verses was the one we have. We have made the following notes. The well-known Baraitha in Sukka, 55 a, cites in full Ps. xxix. 1, l. 16, xciv. 16, xciv. 8, lxxxi. 7, lxxxii. 5 b. The last verse seems to have commenced with ימוטו. The single verses of this Psalm have, indeed, two parts each, with the exception of ours. Ps. xxi. 9 is testified in Esther Rabbah, 1, 1 (6 a); xxxi. 6, Berachoth, 5 a, at the top; xxxix. 2, Gittin, 7 a 11 [6]; xlv. 8 in Pesikta

---

[1] The same in Pesikta d. R. Kahana, 17 a: א״ר יודן בוא וראה כמה חיבב. הק״בה לישראל שהוא כזכירן המשה פעמים בפסוק אחד. The verse has thirty words, and there is no verse of similar length near it.

[2] במוסזי דשבתא מה היו אומרים (?) אמר רב חנן אמר רב הוי״ו ל״ך [ה=האוינו · 1.=זכר וכו׳] ואמר רב חנן אמר רב כורך שחרל״ין כאן כך חולקין בבית הכנסת. The first four sections consist, according to Rashi, of six verses each, the last two of eight verses each, which does not answer; for then there would be only forty verses, whilst האוינו has forty-three verses. Even if Rashi meant that the last three sections had eight verses each, there still remained a superfluous verse, namely, between 27 and 39.

[3] א״רב יהודה אמר רב כל הפסוק הזה.

[4] א״ר שמואל בר נחמני שלשה פעמים כהוב בפסוק זה אָמָרָך אמתך כנגד שלש מצות וכו״.

[5] שני פעמים בפסוק הוא אומר אני ואני.

[6] שרטט וכתב ליה (ר״א למר עוקבא)

Rabbathi, 150 a[1]; xlvi. 8 (and 12), Jer. Berachoth, 5, 1 (8 d 47); l. 7, Sanhedrin, 110 b 11 ; lxix. 34 in Genesis Rabbah, c. 71, at the commencement (277 a)[2]; civ. 31 in Chullin, 60 a, at the bottom; civ. 35 and Isa. liv. 1 in Berachoth, 10 a 7.

The other books of the Hagiographa are also represented by some verses : Prov. xiv. 34 in Pesikta d. R. Kahana, 13 b ; xxx. 4 in Pesikta Rabbathi, 15 a; Job xxxvi. 3 in Leviticus Rabbah, c. 14 (38 b 2, at the bottom); Koheleth ii. 12 in Exodus Rabbah, c. 2, at the commencement (33 b); Esther i. 14 in Megilla, 12 b 30[3]; Dan. iv. 34 in Leviticus Rabbah, c. 13 (38 a 3); 2 Chron. vii. 3 in Shebuoth, 16 b; xv. 3 in Leviticus Rabbah, c. 19 (52 a 5, at the bottom).

There is yet another formula which furnishes an unmistakable proof for the division of verses, and which occurs often enough. We allude to the favourite sentence that "three things are contained in one verse[4]." If the ancients had had a division of verses different from ours, there should be cases of passages of scripture having now two verses of which it was said that "all three things occurred in one verse." But no such case occurs in the passages noted by me, and which follow here. That there is no question here of the opinions of single individuals is proved by the circumstance that many a statement in reference to this occurs several times, in the most different sources, and in the name of many authorities, as will be clearly seen from our list: Gen. iii. 6 in Genesis Rabbah, c. 19 (84 b), Jose ben Zimra=Koheleth Rabbah, 5, 10 (30 b); Exod. xv. 13 in Numbers Rabbah, c. 12 (97 a), which same interpretation is applied to another biblical passage in Jer. Megilla, 3, 7 (74 b 39); Deut. xiv. 7[5] in Leviticus Rabbah, c. 13 (37 b); xxxiii. 23 in Jer. Berachoth, 7, 6 (11 d, at the top) ; Isa. li. 16 in Jer. Taanith, 4, 2 (68 a, at the bottom, bis)[6]=Jer. Megilla, 3, 7 (79 b 39); Zech. x. 1 in Jer. Taanith, 3, 2 (66 c 18, 28) in the name of Eleazar (ר' לעזר)=Leviticus Rabbah,

---

[1] Introduced by the words שהפסוק הזה, and fully indicated. When we make no remarks, the reader should carefully consider the cited passage before doubting its demonstrative value.

[2] לא ראשו של פסוק הזה סופו ולא סופו ראשו, already quoted before, as is also the following passage. But the passages, already adduced before in proof of the designation of the portions of the verses, are not all repeated.

[3] אמר ר' לוי כל פסוק זה על שם קרבנות נאמר.

[4] ושלשתן בפסוק אחר.

[5] Not Lev. c. 11, where these three significant words are scattered over vers. 4, 5, 6. The original place of the Agadah was in Deuteronomy, whence it was taken over. We cannot, therefore, agree with Harris, J. Q. R. I, 140. It seems that Harris allowed himself to be carried away by Strack, *Prolegomena*, p. 80.

[6] The whole verse is interpreted.

c. 35 (103 b); Koheleth xii. 1 in Jer. Sota, 2, 2 (18 a) in the name of Levi; 2 Chron. vii. 14 in Jer. Taanith, 2, 1 (65 b 3), Eleazar[1].

On recapitulating our investigations thus far, we find that an innumerable amount of data testify to the high—we may safely say the pre-Talmudic—antiquity of *our* division of verses[2]. We will now do what hitherto has been exclusively done, namely, to look at the reverse of the medal, and look for those statements which speak against our division of verses. In order to prevent misunderstandings, we observe at the very beginning that here only the information given by the tradition and the oldest Jewish commentators shall be taken notice of, as these can also be regarded as the Massoretes of their age. On the other hand, the views of the modern commentators who differ from the Massorah shall not be taken into account, because the subject of inquiry is, above all, to establish the historical conditions of the question, but not to investigate the correctness of the views of the Massoretes. We have no reason to believe in the infallibility of the Massoretes; for, with all our admiration for their truly grand achievements, we cannot close our eyes to the fact that they have made now and then serious mistakes[3]. Historical importance would attach to the conceptions of the ancient versions when contradicting those of the Massorah, especially to those of the LXX and the Peshita; there is, however, as yet a want of more modern special inquiries[4].

Only a small number of verses divided in a different way from that of the Massorah can be pointed out; we shall adduce them in as far as we know them.

[1] The Agadah occurs also: Jer. Sanh. 10, 2 (28 c 9); Koheleth Rabbah, 5, 6 (28 b); Pesikta Rabbathi, 200 a, 200 b 16, ח״ר, as if it were a Baraitha; Genesis Rabbah, c. 44 (180 b).

[2] Vide Frankel, *Vorstudien zu der Septuaginta*, p. 217, holds that the "present division of verses" is younger than the Talmudical period. We return to that question in the course of our essay.

[3] Vide my *Massoretische Untersuchungen*, and my *Zur Einleitung in die Heilige Schrift*, pp. 100-120.

[4] Important observations on the stichometry of the Old and New Testaments have been made by Graux, Martin, Sanday, Zahn, Harris, Berger, and E. Klostermann. But detailed investigations would be required for our purpose. Such have not been made, to our knowledge, to such an extent as to enable the question as to the relations of the division of verses of the LXX, the Peshita, and other versions to be discussed. We shall, as soon as possible, devote a special inquiry to this subject. Azaria de Rossi, *Meor Enayim*, II, c. 8, at the commencement, has already drawn attention to the different division of verses between the LXX and the Massorah.

Rashi to Gen. xix. 18 connects אדני to the following verse, at which Norzi, ad loc., expresses his surprise. Ib. xxxv. 22, we have a פסקא באמצע פסוק, whilst Pinsker, *Einleitung in das babylonische Punktationssystem*, p. 48, states that, in an old code of the Bible, this passage formed two verses, which Geiger had already assumed (*Urschrift*, 373). The Massoretes differ about it, as Norzi observes ad loc. From Megilla, 25 b 22, it might be inferred that this text had been taken as *one* verse; for we read there that when, during the reading at the synagogue, the passage ויהי בשכן ישראל was read, Chanina ben Gamliel called out to the Meturgeman, "Translate only the last[1]." If the verse had terminated with the words וישמע ישראל, the Meturgeman, to whom it was not allowed to read more than a verse at a time, would have had nothing to translate. At any rate, the possibility that in reference to this verse Massorah and tradition were in conflict is not excluded. Similarly, the *possibility* of a contradiction must be admitted in reference to Gen. xlix. 7. It is known that this verse belongs to one of the five passages, the division of which is doubtful, so that ארור of the following verse is brought in connexion with the preceding one[2]. It is true the Massorah had to decide for one of the two modes of division. All scholars who dealt with the division of verses, take their stand on the Talmudical passage in Kiddushin, 30 a (=Nedarim, 38 a), according to which, in Palestine, Exod. xix. 9 was divided into three verses. We should have, therefore, historical evidence for the discrepancy between the Babylonian and the Palestinian division of verses. We shall soon have occasion to speak about this.

Numbers xii. 2, 3 was read as one by Nathan, Sifre I, 100[3]. This is not, however, to our mind, a proof for any difference in the division of verses from ours, for such license was admissible in interpreta-

---

[1] אל תהרגם אלא אחרון.

[2] Mechilta, 17, 9 (54 a, at the top); Jer. Aboda Zara, 2, 8 (41 c, at the bottom); Babl. Joma, 52 a; Genesis Rabbah, c. 80 (303 b), and elsewhere: חמשה דברים יש בתורה שאין להם הכרע. The other examples and the divergence in the sources do not concern us here. I must confess I cannot understand how a Tanna could have had any doubt whether Gen. iv. 7, שאת ואם לא תישיב, was to be read. The matter is very obscure. Cf. also יד מלאכי, No. רצח. On the הכרעות in the middle of a verse, vide Minchat Shai to Gen. xxxiv. 7, Exod. xxiv. 5, xxv. 34, Deut. xxxi. 16. In this connexion the saying of Raba's becomes of interest: א"ל רבא סכינא חריפא מפסקא קרא (Menachoth, 74 a; Baba Bathra, 111 b; Arachin, 26 a). Geiger, *Urschrift*, p. 143, tries to explain why they wanted to connect ארור with the preceding verse.

[3] ר' נתן אומר ... שנאמר וישמע ה' והאיש משה.

tions[1]. Deut. iv. 30, 31 is introduced in Pesikta, ed. Buber, 162 b 2, with the words הפסוק הזה. It is, however, possible that originally only the first verse was cited here, and that afterwards the second verse was added to it; or also, that הפסוק is equivalent to הכתוב, since the difference between these two expressions was no longer felt in the idiom of the later Midrashim, as we noted above[2]. It is not impossible that Sifre took Deut. xviii. 12, 13 to be one verse, as both verses are treated in one Piska; it is true, in a short one (II, 173)[3]. The majuscle Tav in תמים would, in that case, have to be considered as a polemical sign against the connexion of the two verses. Deut. xxv. 2 terminates, according to the Massorah, with במספר, and ver. 3 commences with ארבעים. According to the Mishna, Makkoth, 22 a, as also Sifre, II, 286[4], these two words belong together. The Septuagint concurs *with this*, for there ver. 3 commences καὶ ἀριθμῷ τεσσαράκοντα[5]. Josh. xiii. 3 concludes with והעוים. This is also assumed in the Talmud, Chullin, 60 b, where the question is asked and answered, why five Philistine princes are mentioned and six enumerated. But, at the same time, it is recorded that Rab and a Baraitha are of a different opinion, and maintain that the עוים came from Teman[6], to which Tosafoth correctly observes that, according to this conception, והעוים must be drawn to the following verse. Ps. lxxxii. 5 b was perhaps the commencement of a new verse; this has already been conjectured before, after Sukka, 55 a. In the Mishna, Aboda Zara, 2, 8, there is a controversy between Joshua and

---

[1] In the Halachic Midrashim we found several, but did not note them down. Cf. Strack, l. c., pp. 78 and 155.

[2] Jer. Sanhedrin, 10, 2 (28 c), also has הפסוק הזה, and likewise cites both verses required by the context. The possibility of a divergence between Massorah and tradition may therefore be admitted.

[3] There are, of course, many Piskas that treat on several verses. But in this passage a connexion of the two verses meets with no difficulty, so that the possibility may be admitted.

[4] יכול ארבעים שלימות ת"ל במספר ארבעים מין סמוך ל' מ' ר' יהודה אומר ארבעים שלימה. The controversy is perhaps based on a discrepancy in the division of the verses. 23 a 19, Rabba Kahana cites כרי רשעתו במספר.

[5] This was already pointed out by Azaria de Rossi, *Meor Enayim*, II, c. 8, at the commencement; but it escaped him that in this case the Tradition with the LXX gave evidence against the Massorah.

[6] ופלינא ורב דאמר רב עוים מהימן באו · חניא נמי הכי עוים כתימן באו וכו'. The Vulgate accords with the Talmudic division, which might be referred back to Jerome (Geiger, *Jüdische Zeitschrift*, X, 277). But the Talmudic passage shows also that our division was not only known, but also generally adopted; otherwise the question, "five are named and six enumerated," could not have been raised at all.

Ishmael about Song of Solomon, i. 2, which has been much discussed. A. Perls tried to prove [1] with arguments, some of which are plausible enough, that the difference of opinion turned on the question, whether מיין has to be drawn to the next verse; and that Joshua negatived it by citing the Song of Solomon iv. 10, where מיין could not be combined with וריח. Accordingly, in the Mishna, וריח שמניך would have to be read instead of לריח שמניך, and טובים to be struck out, as being a later addition. In post-Talmudical time, Seadyah has, in ten passages, adopted a termination of the verses different from the traditional [2]. The Orientals and Occidentals differ about Deut. xvi. 3; according to the former כי בחפזון is ראש פסוק, according to the latter מצעות פסוק [3]. They also differ about Isa. xx. 2, which the Orientals divide into two verses [4]. Ps. xlvi. 6 terminates, according to the St. Petersburg Codex, as also the Peshita, with the first word of ver. 7 [5].

Only ten of the passages discussed here belong to the Talmud and Midrash, and I have my doubts about them, whether they really contradict the Massorah; since only Deut. iv. 30, 31 and Ps. lxxxii. 5 b have been handed down by the tradition without controversy, and it is not at all clear that they are contradictory. Exod. xix. 9, which is considered by the scholars to clinch the question as to the divergence in the division of verses, proves at the same time that this passage formed one verse in Babylonia; consequently, that our Massorah is based upon the Babylonian traditions. The Massorah

---

[1] In the Hungarian Magazine, *Magyar Zsidó Szemle*, XI, 158 sqq. One of his chief arguments is taken from Jer. Aboda Zara, 2, 8 (41 c, at the bottom) : אם יהפליגו בדברים היה מבקש היה לו להשיא בחמש השיאות שבתורה. This interpretation is disputed by A. Sidon, l. c., p. 266 sqq.

[2] Cf. on this point, Bacher, *Abraham Ibn Ezra als Grammatiker*, pp. 38, 39, where also the opinions of Jehuda Halevi (*Kusari*, III, 21), Ibn Ezra, and Efodi (*Maasse Efod*, c. 7, p. 41) on the distribution of verses are given. It is held to be the work of either Ezra or the Ecclesia Magna. Samuel ben Meir, in accordance with Shocher Tob (ed. Rosin, p. 46), connects also והמנע, Gen. xxxvi. 12, with the preceding verse. In our copies of Shocher Tob, the passage is not found (vide Rosin, ad loc., n. 10), Jad Maleachi, n. 283.

[3] Vide Baer, *Liber Genesis* (Lipsiae, 1869), p. 81, n. 1.

[4] Baer, *Liber Jesaiae* (Lipsiae, 1872) ; Pinsker, *Einleitung in das babylonisch-hebräische Punktationssystem* (Vienna, 1863), p. 4.

[5] Pinsker, l. c., p. 133, corrects at the same time פני after xlii. 12 and xliii. 5, into פַנַי. Pinsker expresses himself there on the division of verses and accentuation in general ; he gives several conjectures about Biblical passages in contradiction to the Massorah, and quotes such also from older and newer works. We also refer to Buhl, *Kanon und Text des A. T.*, pp. 233 sqq. and 241 ; Dillmann, *Hiob*[4], XXIV, on xi. 6 and xvi. 4.

has thus made a choice out of two traditional opinions, but there is no question of a conflict with tradition. Besides, there seems also to have been a Massorah, which followed the Palestinians, which we shall try to show in the chapter on the number of verses of the Pentateuch. Too far-reaching conclusions have been drawn from the passage in Kiddushin, 30 a. It was overlooked that there the question is that of fixing the exact half of the number of verses of the Pentateuch, namely, whether Lev. xiii. 33 belongs to the first or the second half. A decision on this point can be arrived at by counting, only when there is no doubt about any one verse of the whole Pentateuch in reference to number. It can, therefore, be understood why R. Joseph *in a dispute about words* declines a proposal to count the verses of the Pentateuch by referring to the statement of an Amoraite as to the division of Exod. xix. 9. But this does not show yet that in Babylonia the division of verses was carried on in an arbitrary manner, or that there had been greater differences of opinion about the same. Just the contrary. Since R. Joseph refers to a Palestinian and not to a Babylonian controversy, we may conclude with confidence that in Babylon there was no difference of opinion on the point. R. Joseph, in saying, " We are not conversant with the division of verses," means, as may be gathered from the context, that there may be some verse or other which was divided in Palestine into two verses, as the example he refers to shows ; but he never thought of a different system of dividing the verses, or even of one that was divergent in a number of instances. On the other hand, in asking the question whether the Massoretic and Talmudic mode of dividing the verses were identical, we do not mean to say that every single verse of the twenty-three thousand must concur. The identity of both modes of dividing the verses is established even if—and this is not the case—in some ten or twenty of the five thousand eight hundred and forty-five verses of the Pentateuch an essential discrepancy between Talmud and Massorah could be shown. Even between Madinchaë and Maarbaë differences are shown to exist on this point, and yet nobody will think of maintaining that these schools had two different modes of dividing the verses.

We were not able to oppose anything to the numerous decisive proofs for the concurrence of Talmud and Massorah, even after a diligent investigation of the sources and the literature, except a few uncertain passages. The proofs in favour of the identity emanate both from Palestinian and Babylonian sources, and belong to various periods ; and this *testifies to the same division of verses in the divers lands during the course of centuries.* This disposes also of Rappoport's conjecture (*Halichoth Kedem*, Amsterdam, 1846, pp. 10 and 17) that in Palestine, where the whole Pentateuch was read in three years, most verses were divided into two or three[1]. It is also groundless, when Friedmann, in the final note to *Sifre Numeri* and the *Litteraturblatt* of the *Menora*, I, No. 3, speaks of an uncertainty in reference to the division of verses having crept in at some period, so that we no longer know which verses were formerly divided. We have traced our division of verses from the most ancient time up to the conclusion of the tradition, and shall find the same again in the various statements of the Massorah. The far-reaching inference, which Grätz (*Monatsschrift für Geschichte und Wissenschaft des Judenthums*, XX, 52) draws from a Gaonic expression is also unjustified, and must be rejected[2]. If we look without prejudice upon the age of the division of verses, we must consider the differences that have arisen in the course of centuries in various countries as rather too few than too numerous, and, in opposition to most scholars, take them as exceptions to the rule, tending to confirm the high age of the division we possess.

3. *The Division of Verses of the Massorah.*

In the preceding investigations it was presumed that the division of verses of the Massorah was known, and that, with very few exceptions, it was identical with that of our editions of the Bible. This identity is, in the first instance, based upon the tradition; for our editions flowed from manuscripts in which the division of verses was marked. It is further based on the concurrence of the numbers of the verses of separate sections (Pentateuch), and of the sums of the verses of the separate books and of the three parts. That also the separate verses in respect to their magnitude, i.e. the division of verses, in a narrower sense, are the same in our copies as those which the Massorah hands down and demands, follows from the diversified statements about the "Pesukim," which can be verified by the "Pesukim" of our copies. It is for the purpose of establishing

---

[1] Baer also, *Orient*, XII (1851), p. 263, rejects Rappoport's opinion without attempting the proof given by us as to the verses mentioned by the tradition. Cf. also Luzzatto's *Letters*, p. 345 seq.

[2] ואפיל׳ במקראות · · · יש שנוי בהם בין בבל לארץ ישראל בחסרות ויהרות ובפתוחות וסתומות ונפסקי הטעמים ובחיתוך הפסוקים. From this it follows that in only a few passages there existed a difference between Madinchaë and Maarbaë; but there is no question of different systems or of numerous differences. Pinsker, *Punktationssystem*, p. 133 seq., also speaks of the division of verses as of something changeable. Cf. also at the end of the fifth chapter the confutation of Grätz's conjecture about the division and the middle of the verses of the Pentateuch.

this assertion, and, at the same time, of illustrating what importance the Massoretes attached to the division and limitation of verses, and what amount of labour they consequently bestowed on them, that we will produce here a few characteristic data from the Massoretic material extant. For this object we shall make use of the *Massora marginalis* and *finalis*, such as Frensdorff's Massoretic works (*Ochlah We-Ochlah*, Hanover, 1864, and *Massoretisches Wörterbuch*, Hanover and Leipzig, 1876), and Ginsburg's *The Massorah* (3 parts). In the latter books the reader can find the further explanations of the data we produce, and, of course, a great number of other data on this point [1].

We commence with the proofs for whole verses. There are three verses (Gen. ii. 5, Num. xxvi. 8, Josh. xi. 14) which number eighty letters (*Ochla*, No. 316, cf. *M. W. B.*, p. 377 b); three verses commence and terminate with שׁ (*Massora Exodus*, 29, 30; *M. W. B.*, p. 378 b; Ginsburg, שׁ, No. 17). Eleven other verses begin and terminate with נון (Ginsburg, II, נ, No. 13 = Lev. xiii. 9; Num. xxxii. 32, &c.). There are ten verses each word of which contains a שׁ (*Massora*, Num. xxvi. 24; *Mf.*, שׁ, 8; Ginsburg, שׁ, 18); the whole alphabet (Ginsburg, פ, 277; *M. W. B.*, p. 381 b; for instance, Zeph. iii. 8: cf. *Minchat Shai*; Ezek. xxxviii. 12, &c.). Five verses have forty words each: Jer. xxxviii. 4, Dan. iii. 15, v. 23, Esther iii. 12 (*Massoret. Wörterbuch*, 380 and 381, No. 1). The fifth verse was unknown to Frensdorff; it is, as Ginsburg, פ, 442, correctly states, Dan. vi. 13. Fourteen verses of the Pentateuch contain three words each (*Massora Exodus*, 28, 13, &c.; *Mf.* ר, 1; *M. W. B.*, p. 381, No. 4; Ginsburg, פ, 439). Four verses have each seven words consisting of four letters (*Mp.*, Psalm lxxiii. 2, Prov. xvii. 3). Ps. cxix has four verses—namely, 15, 47, 113, and 146—having four words each (*Massora*, Ps. cxix. 47: *Mf.* עי, 17).

LUDWIG BLAU.

(To be continued.)

---

[1] Vide particularly Ochla, Nos. 39, 164, 171-175, 179, 194, 225-230, 268, 274-282, 286-288, 296-360, 362-365, 374; *Massoretisches Wörterbuch*, pp. 373-381. The Massorah follows, on the whole, in its arrangement the *Masora finalis*; the above-mentioned book, the *Massoretisches Wörterbuch*, can therefore be used. It is rather more difficult, as we have done, to look out the needful passages from the register to vol. II. But, having regard to the space at our disposal, we can only give a small fragment. After some study of the Massoretic material, the corresponding data can easily be found in these four collections. We, therefore, refer to this only occasionally. Ochla is the handiest of them, but contains, comparatively, the fewest data; which proves that, in the course of centuries, the Massoretic material has increased also in this respect. We do not especially cite Frensdorff's notes.

MASSORETIC STUDIES.

IV.

The Division into Verses (continued).

3. *The Division of Verses of the Massorah.*

IN the preceding investigations it was presumed that the division of verses of the Massorah was known, and that, with very few exceptions, it was identical with that of our editions of the Bible. This identity is, in the first instance, based upon tradition; for our editions flowed from MSS. in which the division of verses was marked. It is further based on the concurrence of the numbers of the verses of separate sections (Pentateuch), and of the sums of the verses of the separate books and of the three parts. That also the separate verses in respect to their magnitude, i.e. the division of verses, in a narrower sense, are the same in our copies as those which the Massorah hands down and demands, follows from the diversified statements about the "Pesukim," which can be verified by the "Pesukim" of our copies. It is for the purpose of establishing this assertion, and, at the same time, of illustrating what importance the Massoretes attached to the division and limitation of verses, and what amount of labour they consequently bestowed on them, that we will produce here a few characteristic data from the Massoretic material extant. For this object we shall make use of the *Massora marginalis* and *finalis*, such as Frensdorff's Massoretic works (*Ochlah We-Ochlah*, Hanover, 1864, and *Massoretisches Wörterbuch*, Hanover and Leipzig, 1876), and Ginsburg's *The Massorah* (3 parts). In the latter books the reader can find the further explanations of the data we produce, and, of course, a great number of other data on this point[1].

---

[1] Vide particularly *Ochla*, Nos. 39, 164, 171-175, 179, 194, 225-230, 268, 274-282, 286-288, 296-360, 362-365, 374 ; *Massoretisches Wörterbuch*, pp. 373-381. The Massorah follows, on the whole, in its arrangement the *Masora finalis* ; the above-mentioned book, the *Massoretisches Wörterbuch*, can therefore be used. It is rather more difficult, as we have done, to look out the needful passages from the Index to vol. II. But, having regard

We commence with the proofs for whole verses. There are three
verses (Gen. ii. 5, Num. xxvi. 8, Josh. xi. 14) which number eighty
letters (*Ochla*, No. 316, cf. *M. W. B.*, p. 377 b); three verses commence
and terminate with ‎ש‎ (*Massora Exodus*, 29, 30; *M. W. B.*, p. 378 b;
Ginsburg, ‎ש‎, No. 17). Eleven other verses begin and terminate with ‎נון‎
(Ginsburg, II, ‎נ‎, No. 13=Lev. xiii. 9; Num. xxxii. 32, &c.). There
are ten verses each word of which contains a ‎ש‎ (*Massora*, Num. xxvi.
24; *Mf.*, ‎ש‎, 8; Ginsburg, ‎ש‎, 18); the whole alphabet (Ginsburg, ‎פ‎, 277;
M. W. B., p. 381 b; for instance, Zeph. iii. 8: cf. *Minchat Shai*; Ezek.
xxxviii. 12, &c.). Five verses have forty words each: Jer. xxxviii. 4,
Dan. iii. 15, v. 23, Esther iii. 12 (*Massoret. Wörterbuch*, 380 and 381,
No. 1). The fifth verse was unknown to Frensdorff; it is, as Ginsburg,
‎ם‎, 442, correctly states, Dan. vi. 13. Fourteen verses of the Pentateuch
contain three words each (*Massora Exodus*, 28, 13, &c.; *Mf.* ‎ד‎, 1;
M. W. B., p. 381, No. 4; Ginsburg, ‎ם‎, 439). Four verses have each
seven words consisting of four letters (*Mp.*, Ps. lxxiii. 2, Prov. xvii. 3).
Ps. cxix has four verses—namely, 15, 47, 113, and 146—having four
words each (*Massora*, Ps. cxix. 47: *Mf.* ‎עד‎, 17). So has Ps. cxix,
verses 43 and 128, ten words each (*Mp.* cxix. 128). Seven verses have
fifteen words each, of which the middle word, i.e. the eighth, form
a Ketib and Keri: 1 Sam. xiii. 19, xxx. 24, Jer. xxxiii. 8, &c. (*Ochla*,
No. 164). Eleven verses of the Torah begin and end with the same
word, for instance, Lev. xxiii. 42 (*Massora*, Lev. vii. 19; *M. W. B.*, p. 381,
No. 3). Ginsburg, ‎ם‎, 424, mentions, in accordance with the Massorah
to Lev. vii. 19 cited by him, only ten, but in the index he correctly
notes ‎י"א‎. In other places, also, there are discrepancies between
Ginsburg's text and the index, which were not noted by Baer in his
review of Ginsburg's work in the *Zeitschrift der Deutschen Morgenländischen Gesellschaft*, XL, 743 sqq. Cf. about the notation in question
Ginsburg, III, p. 221 a, where thirty-three verses of that kind are
adduced; also ‎ו‎, 98. Three verses begin and terminate with the
Tetragrammaton (Deut. xxxi. 3; *Mf.* ‎אר‎, 50; *M. W. B.*, p. 338, *sub fin.*).
We also refer briefly to several numbers of the *Ochla*, where various
combinations of the same particle in *one* verse are noted: 230 (‎אֶת‎),
298-315 (‎כֹל‎), 317, 318 (‎מִן‎), 321-324 (‎עַד‎), 328-333 (‎אִין‎), 334 (‎בָּם‎),

to the space at our disposal, we can only give a small fragment. After
some study of the Massoretic material, the corresponding data can easily
be found in these four collections. We, therefore, refer to this only
occasionally. *Ochla* is the handiest of them, but contains, comparatively,
the fewest data; which proves that, in the course of centuries, the
Massoretic material has increased also in this respect. We do not
especially cite Frensdorff's notes.

335-337 (שָׁמָה), 339 (הִנֵּה), 340-342 (וְהוּא), 346 (אִם), 349-355 (עַל), 356 (וְגַם), 362, in three verses of which לֹא occurs once, and וְלֹא occurs four times. These references occur also in Ginsburg's work and elsewhere, e.g. א, 517, in three verses of which, after אֶל. וְאֶל occurs four times, again followed by אֶל. This very small collection of data is sufficient to give an idea of the host of indications contained in the Massorah towards the fixing of the division of the verses.

A number of data give certainty about the COMMENCEMENT of verses: *Ochla*, Nos. 39, 171-175, 319, 320, 327, 338, 343, 345, 360, 368. In order to enable the reader to gain a correct idea of the amplitude of such data, I shall give a selection out of the less accessible work of Ginsburg, *and only such notes about the commencement of verses as are noted under* א: 88, Abraham commences a verse five times; 805, אָמַר ה' three times; 1469, אַתָּה ה' three times; 869, וַיֹּאמֶר ה' אֵלָיו three times; 193, וְאוּלָם five times; 340, וְאַיֵּה three times; 365, וְאֵיךְ three times; 418, אִישׁ ten times in the Pentateuch and twice in Job; 452, אַךְ eight times (cf. 457); 650, אֱלֹהִים thirty-one times; 735, 736, אִם seventeen times in Exodus and seven times in Leviticus; 813, אָמַרְתָּ three times; 82, לֵאמוֹר nine times; 957, וַאֲנִי thirty-three times; 1096, אֶרֶץ thirteen times; 1109, וְהָאָרֶץ eight times; 1182, וַאֲשֶׁר twelve times. And to give a few more instances of other letters: ה, 93, וְהוּא thirty-three times; ז, 49, וְזֹאת seventeen times; י, 196, וַיְהֹוָה five times in Genesis; ע, 920, עַתָּה twenty-five times.

On the MIDDLE OF VERSES (מֶצְעוּת פסוק), see *Ochla*, Nos. 325, 326, 345, 346, 363; Ginsburg, א, 320, אַחֲרֵי כֵן twice; 384, אֵין sixteen times (cf. ibid., 387, 390, 394); ב. 370, וּבְנֵי יִשְׂרָאֵל fifteen times; כ, 250, וכל ישראל thirty-five times, &c.

On the TERMINATION OF VERSES (סוֹף פסוק) see *Ochla*, Nos. 357, 268 (cf. ibid., note); Ginsburg, א, 808, אָמַר ה' twenty times in the Prophets; 945, אֲנִי ה' twenty times in Leviticus; 949, אֲנִי ה' אֱלֹהֵיכֶם seventeen times; 750, אִם לֹא seven times; ד, 147, לְדֹרֹתֵיכֶם five times; ה, 255, הֵם twelve times; י, 123, וִידַעְתֶּם כִּי אֲנִי ה' (in the index erroneously וְיָדַע) eleven times in Ezekiel.

It is noteworthy that the notes about the commencement of verses are considerably more numerous than those about the middle or termination of verses. We remind the reader of our previous observations as to the much greater significance attached, in the Talmud, to the commencement of verses than to their middle or termination. The latter is not mentioned at all, and for very good reasons. A knowledge of the beginning of the verses was useful in the schools and in the study of the Scriptures, because it called to memory the whole verse, which could then be read correctly to the end. Thus it was allowed to arrange on Friday evenings the beginnings of the verses for children. But we do not hear anything about the terminations of verses, because these only gained a significance later, after the verses had not only received their limitations by accentuation, but had also become fixed for recitation by means of written signs. The Massoretic notes on the beginnings of verses, which are more natural intersections of the text than the terminations of verses, were, for the reasons stated above, already deemed worthy of attention in remote times, and therefore the number of such notes is greater. This becomes evident by a comparison of the data contained in *Ochla*, where the notes about the beginning of verses form by far the majority. The circumstance that *we* speak frequently of סוף פסוק, and hardly ever of ראש פסוק, rests, as already mentioned, on our system of accentuation, which knows no ראש פסוק, but only a Silluk, usually called סוף פסוק. The alphabetical portions of Holy Writ prove that the beginnings of verses had already a significance in Biblical times: for the terminations of verses not even a rhyme exists.

The hosts of data contained in the Massorah make an accurate limitation of the individual verses possible; and thus the discrepancies are not numerous, either in the Massoretic works or in the editions. What we know about this, we have given in the previous chapter. *The result is, that Tradition, Massorah, and the Editions of the Bible are in perfect harmony on this point.*

4. *Division into verses and Stichometry.*

The verses of classical antiquity differ essentially from those of the Alexandrine Bible. In secular writings, the "verses" served the purpose of fixing the remuneration of the copyists: they wrote lines of a certain length—thirty-six to thirty-eight letters to the line—without any attention being paid to the contents; but in Holy Writ the sections or lines were, at the same time, sections in reference to the contents. Every sentence formed a line, a στίχος or versus[1]. A פסוק can have, therefore, several verses (lines), as well as several כתוב, מקרא, קרא. We can identify *stichos* with דָּבָר, or, better still, with the טעמים of the Jerusalemite, or the פסקי טעמים of the

[1] Cf. Berger, *Histoire de la Vulgate*, p. 316 sqq.; E. König, *Einleitung in das alte Testament*, p. 462, and the works quoted in these books. We have made mention already, II, 1, of more recent works. It would be worth while to make a thorough comparative study of the division into verses and the Biblical *Stichometry*, and we recommend such study to those to whom the literature in question is accessible.

Babylonian Talmud. The question is whether the Hebrew Bible knew of *Stichoi*.

Hupfeld[1] answered this question in the affirmative in respect to the poetical pieces. We assent to this opinion, without, however, wishing to decide whether such sentences made a line each. We consider it as certain that such sentences formed a unity, and were recognized as such. People knew that the individual sentences in the poetical pieces, Exodus xv, Deut. xxxii, Judges v, and 2 Sam. xxii, were complete in themselves, and were reproduced also in writing in accordance with such limitation[2].

Another question, which does not concern us here, is, how this limitation of individual sentences was expressed in writing. It is known that the three books of Psalms, Job, and Proverbs were, as late as the Middle Ages, written as שירה, although the linear representation in the MSS. is no longer the original one. It is, therefore, beyond doubt, that the Talmud, Kiddushin, 30 a, when giving the number of the פסוקים of the Psalms as 5,896, means such *stichoi*[3]. Consequently, *the number of stichoi is found in the Talmud in the same manner as*, on the other hand, *the number of Massoretic verses in the non-Hebrew codices*. A distinction (mentioned also elsewhere) is found in Cod. Erlangen, 770, 8 *sub fin.*, which gives the number as 2,606 : "Ter quinquagenos David canit ordine psalmos Versus bis mille sexcentos sex canit ille[4]." Still more remarkable is the account given in a fragment of the Psalms in the Royal Library in Copenhagen, in which the number of the verses of the Psalms is given as IIDXXVII. *This is the figure given by the Massorah*, which seems to have escaped Berger[5]. I am fortunate enough to be able to point out the Massoretic number of verses for the Pentateuch in a MS. of the Vulgate. For Exodus, Berger, p. 363, gives "*Mille ducenti et novem*: compl.[1]," and this agrees with the Massorah to the letter[6].

[1] *Ausführliche hebr. Grammatik*, 1841, pp. 84–114, König, 461.

[2] Vide Megilla, 16 b, and Minchat Shai to Deut., c. 32.

[3] Luzzatto, *Hebrew Letters*, ed. Gräber, p. 346 ; Hupfeld, *Grammatik*, § 20 ; Delitzsch, *Psalms*, II, 398, 3rd edition ; I, 21. Luzzatto, in accordance with Joel Brill's edition with commentary, really obtained the number 5,896, but not without some artifices. The Massorah counts in the Psalms only 2,527 verses. By adding the number of verses of the individual chapters, I get for the Peshitta 4,793 ; in Berger, p. 365, I find 5,000, and from MSS. of the Vulgate, 5,500.

[4] Delitzsch, *Psalms*, II, 398, the same is cited by Berger (p. 365), from B, No. 10,420.

[5] *Histoire de la Vulgate*, p. 365 ; for the description of the MS. in "Nouveau fonds royal," No. 1, vide ibid, p. 380.

[6] For a description of the Codex Compl.[1], vide Berger, p. 392. The

The same Codex gives for Genesis: *Mille* LXXXIIII. This figure cannot possibly refer to *stichoi*, the numbers of which vary between 3,070 and 4,900 (Berger, p. 363). The Massoretic number of verses for Exodus being attested, it is not too hazardous to assume that for Genesis also the Massoretic figure was originally given, and we really obtain it if we substitute D for L = 1,534. Three sets of figures of *stichoi* are preserved for Leviticus, namely, 2,300, 2,400, and 2,600,— tens and units are neglected. A fourth record gives MCCC (= 1,300). This figure cannot possibly refer to *stichoi*. On the ground of the information given by the Massorah about the number of verses, and previously pointed out by me, I venture to conjecture, by the figure as given in this MS., which hails from the tenth century, and which, according to Berger, exhibits the Spanish text of the Vulgate, that the number of verses as given by the Massorah is meant. It is only necessary to put D instead of M,— DCCC = 800, the figure given by the Massorah. As in the other codices, tens and units are neglected. The assumption that in Kiddushin, 30 a, the *stichoi* of the Psalms are given bears a high amount of probability. It is, therefore, plausible that figures giving the number of verses of the Chronicles, which is handed down together with that of the Psalms, also refers to the number of *stichoi*. The Chronicles have, according to the Talmud, 5,880 verses; the figure given by the Peshitta, which is of Jewish origin[1], is only slightly less, namely, 5,630[2].

The passage in the Talmud, frequently mentioned but not explained, is protected against far-reaching conjectures by the evidence of a Gaon. In the *Responsa of the Geonim*, edited by Harkavy (Berlin, 1885), No. 3 a, the question occurs how the sums of the verses of our

MS. is in the library of the Central University at Madrid, No. 31: "Première Bible d'Alcala: Nombreuses notes hébraïques en margo." The MS. hails from the ninth century. If it is possible to venture making a conjecture on the ground of the ample description (l. c., p. 22 sqq.), Jews must have had a part in the translation, or, at least, in the correction. Might not the Hebrew marginal notes be by Alfonzo de Zamora, about whom Neubauer wrote in this REVIEW, VII, 398 sqq. ?

[1] Rappoport, *Halichoth Kedem*, p. 16 ; Perlos, *Meletemata Peschittoniana*.
[2] ראיתוהי סתהׁמא חמשׁׁא אלפין ושתמׁאא ותלתא ; *Vulgate* (Berger, p. 364), 1 Chron. 2,040, 2 Chron. 2,100. The figure given by the Peshitta refers, perhaps, to the Chronicles together with Ezra and Nehemiah; although 2,361 is given as the number of Ezra only (to which Nehemiah, of which no figure is given, probably belongs also). In reference to Proverbs, Peshitta (1,863) and Vulgate (IDCCCXL = 1,840) almost entirely concur, especially if XL is altered to LX. Rappoport's conjecture can be called a happy one in that particular point, that the Jews also occasionally used the word פסוקים in the sense of στίχοι.

Baraitha were to be understood, as they were contradictory to the facts. The Gaon answers: Your question is well-founded; we have quite different figures, namely, Torah 5,884, Psalms 2,524, Chronicles 1,970: the Baraitha refers to a Bible found in Jerusalem, which differed from other Bibles in respect to writing and number of verses. The three books in question have at present the afore-mentioned numbers [1].

I shall give another conjecture on the *stichoi* in Jewish literature in the last note of the next chapter.

5. *The number of verses of the Pentateuch* [2].

Before entering upon the question of the sum total of the verses of the Torah, we must first bring some order in the detailed information about · the separate Sedarim, in which many variations show themselves. It is fortunate that, besides the Editions (= E), there are five lists at our disposal, which correct each other reciprocally. Four occur in Ginsburg's work,—ii. 450 sqq. (= A); iii. 6 sqq. (= B); iii. 269 sqq. (= D); iii. 301 sqq. (= F); and one in the *Manuel du lecteur*, pp. 111 sqq. (= C). The last (C) is identical with the first (A);

---

[1] The words in the Responsum read : יפה הוקשה לכם וראי דלא האוי דכין · הווה יפה הוקשה לכם וראי דלא האוי דכין · הווה
חמשת אלפים ושמונה ושמונים וארבעה פסוקי · וספר תילים שני אלפים וחמש מאות ועשרים
וארבעה פסוקין · דברי ימים אלף והשע מאות ושבעים אלא כך שמעונו מפי חכמים הראשונים
שאמרו בריתא הדא בספרים מסנהא (?) באותו ספר תורה שמצאו אותו בירושלים שהיה משונה
בכתב ובמנין פסוקין שלו וכן ספר תלים וכן ספר דברי ימים אבל עכשיו אין הורה אלא כך ואין
חלים אלא כך ואין דברי ימים אלא כך. It is remarkable that the Gaon gives the Massoretic figure only for the Psalms. The variation 24 instead of 27 is easily explained by a corruption from ז into ר, which was natural by the Arabic pronunciation of the Dzal, and which occurs elsewhere also. In the case of the number of verses of the Pentateuch ושמונים וארבעה is perhaps a corruption of וארבעים 'ושמונ' (= ושמונה וארבעים). As we shall endeavour to show in the next chapter, the Pentateuch has 5,842 verses, if the Decalogue is reckoned for ten verses; but if the Gaon reckoned it for thirteen verses, he would obtain 5,848: but perhaps מ"ח was read instead of ה"מ. It is more difficult to reconcile the Gaon with the Massorah in reference to the verses of the Chronicles. The latter have, according to Ginsburg, II, p. 453 (1,765 V), אלף ושבע מאות וששים וחמשה; according to Norzi, ed. princeps (1,787), אלף ושבע מאות ושמונים ושבעה; according to Baer (*Orient*, XII, 262), 1,764. It is, therefore, probable that in the *Responsum* of the Gaon שבע מאות must be read instead of חשע מאות, so that only a surplus of five or six verses remains.

[2] This subject has been treated by Baer, *Orient*, XII, 202 sqq.; I. Derenbourg, *Manuel du lecteur*, note iv; Geiger, *Jüdische Zeitschrift*, X (1872), 22 sqq.

I i 2

we nevertheless reckon them for two, for three variations[1] seem to prove that Ginsburg had not taken that list from the *Manuel*. The Arabic list, B, accords with these, and is, in cases of difference, the most precise one. D and F belong together; both show the same corruptions, and differ only in two cases, which are obviously errors of the copyists[2].

A comparison of all the lists, including those which are afforded by the editions of the Bible, show to demonstration that they flow, one and all, essentially from the same source, i. e. that they are all based upon the same numbering of verses. In by far the most cases they agree with each other, and their origin is obvious in spite of the comparatively few discrepancies. The latter are, for the most part, errors in copying or in reading, which are easily recognized and explained. A conclusive proof of the correctness of this assertion lies in the fact that the total sums of all are equal, without, however, even in one single list, according with the results offered by the detailed data. If we have here different methods of counting the verses, we must needs ascribe this harmony to the strangest possible errors of addition.

We shall now make such comparison for the purpose of proving the above proposition, and of fixing the correct figure for the number of verses, and for many sections of verses. We shall give *seriatim* the numbers of verses of our weekly portions—no tradition existing to my knowledge about the Palestinian Sedarim—according to A, and compare them with those of the other lists, and with what other data there are. No discrepancy is noted whenever all lists and all references concur. For the sake of brevity the names of the portions are not given[3].

---

[1] קדושים has, according to A, ארבעה ושׁשׁים סֿו וסימן נוד; C has the same note, only more correctly סֿו for סֿו. Ginsburg, strangely, marks נוד with a query, instead of סֿו. Now if he had taken his list from the *Manuel*, ס, which is protected by the query against misprint, would be unintelligible. נדר has, according to A, fifty-seven verses (= חֲטִיל); according to C, שׁבעה וחמשׁים נר נגד המכן הֹצֹיל. Here we should have to assume a tacit correction by Ginsburg, which is improbable in view of the previous example. שׁטׁים has, according to A, ninety-seven; according to C, שׁשׁה וחשׁים צו ניר המכן צֹבֹוֹיֹהֹוֹ צו. It is true צו=צו and שׁשׁה=שׁבצה; nevertheless, a tacit correction cannot be assumed. This very capable Massorete will, perhaps, shortly give an account of his sources; for in that case only his work will be of real service to science.

[2] D has תוריע, 66, F 67 (סו=סו); כי חצא D 110, F 106 (קֹ=קֹ).

[3] For another comparison, vide Baer, *Orient*, XII, 205. Has not Baer coined several mnemonics himself?

Genesis : 146 + 153 + 126 + 146 + 105 + 106 + 148 + 154 + 112 + 146 + 106 + 85. D F have 84 instead of 85 (Vayechi). Vayerah has in B E 147, which is the correct figure, for otherwise the sum total for Genesis would not be 1,534, as given everywhere, but only 1,533. לְמֹו was turned into קְמֹו. and afterwards the mnemonic יִחְזְקִיָהוֹ was invented. Accordingly, B has another mnemonic, כונניהו, which is correct. E, although giving here correctly 147, furnishes, nevertheless, 1,533 as the sum total of the book ; for it gives only 153 as the number of וישלח. A פסקא באמצע פסוק, Gen. xxxv. 22, was undoubtedly taken for two verses, which is not the case in our editions of the Bible [1]. The two verses do not belong together, and were only read as one to enable the reader to omit the first without its being noticed [2]. xxvii. 40 is given as the middle of the verses. The book numbers 767 verses up to this verse, if Vayera numbers 147 verses. This follows also from the note that Genesis numbers 1,000 verses up to xxxiv. 20 (*Man. d. l.* 149 and elsewhere) : if Vayera had only 146 verses, there would only be 999. The figures are exclusive of xxvii. 40, resp. xxxiv. 20 ; this follows from the data on the next thousand, on which we shall have to dwell again.

Exodus : 124 + 121 + 106 + 116 + 72 + 118 + 96 + 101 + 139 + 122 + 92. D F show the following corruptions : וארא, 118 (D also 98); בא, 129 (D also correction, 106) ; פקודי, 96. The first error may be accounted for by erroneous addition, — 118 instead of 121. The second error may have arisen in this way : that the fourth Palestinian סדר of בוא was taken in full, i. e. twenty verses of בשלח (xiii. 17– xiv. 14) also ; for B C first give the Palestinian Sedar of each week. This would produce מאה ועשרים וששה, which then became מאה ועשרים ותשעה. In the third instance צֹו=צב,'ש תשעים=וששה תשעים. The other sources produce identical figures. The main difficulty consists in this : how is the figure 1,209, which is universally handed down as the sum total, to be accounted for ? The addition of the separate figures produces only 1,207. The half of the number of verses of the book is fixed at xxii. 27, exclusive (Ginsburg and *Manuel*); and up to that verse there are only 602 verses, and not 604 ($= \frac{1209}{2}$), whilst, as a matter of fact, there are 604 verses from xxii. 17 to the end. The two missing verses must therefore be looked for in the first half. Besides, according to the *Manuel* (p. 149), there are from Gen. xxxiv. 20 to Exod. xvii. 15 one thousand verses : this statement

---

[1] Cf. S. Baer, *Orient*, XII, 202, and Geiger, *Urschrift*, p. 373.

[2] Mishna, Megilla, 25 a ; Shabbat, 55 b. According to another interpretation of the Talmudical passage, which we gave above, the Talmud assumes here only one verse ; but the Massorah numbers two, and explains the Talmudical passage in the way given here.

proves to be correct, both according to the separate verses and the editions. The two verses in question must therefore be looked for in chapters xviii-xxii. This closer limitation at once suggests the decalogue.

It is known that the decalogue can be divided into two sets of verses. If it is divided according to the commandments, we find ten verses; if no regard is had to the commandments, there are thirteen verses[1]. In the former case, the weekly portion, Jethro, has seventy-two verses, and seventy-five in the second case. The number of verses is, therefore, either one too many or two too few. The larger figure is usually adopted, and the number 1,209 upheld by the elimination of one verse[2]; but some correct the Massorah, e. g. S. J. Reggio[3]. The statement of the Massorah cannot be upheld, once the decalogue is held to contain thirteen verses. But we reject this mode of reconciling the two statements, and for an important reason. All lists agree in assigning to the weekly portion, Jethro, seventy-two verses; all of them have, therefore, divided the decalogue into ten verses. The decalogue in Deuteronomy is, in all lists, also stated to have ten verses; for they assign to Vaetchanan 119 verses, our editions numbering 122[4]. But if the decalogue is counted as ten verses, then two verses are missing from the sum total both of Exodus and Deuteronomy. Exodus would have 1,207 verses instead of 1,209, and Deuteronomy 953 instead of 955.

I believe I shall be able to trace the two missing verses in Exodus xix. 9 in accordance with Kiddushin, 30 a. It is stated in this Talmudical passage that the Palestinians divided the verse in question into three

---

[1] Cf. W. Heidenheim's *Meor Enayim*, Appendix to Exodus. The stereotype edition erroneously counts sixteen verses, by dividing ch. xx. 13-16, על שקר · · · לא תרצה, into four verses. This is admissible only when the division is made according to commandments, but in that case vv. 3-6 and 8-11 would be only one verse each. In Deut. v. 17 these commandments count correctly as one verse.

[2] Vide Baer, "Die Verszählung des Pentateuch," *Orient*, XII (1851), 200 sqq. A. Geiger, *Jüdische Zeitschrift*, IV, 265 sq., takes xx. 2-3 as one verse. Cf. also, on the division of the verses of the decalogue, Geiger, *Wissenschaftliche Zeitschrift für jüdische Theologie*, III (1837), 153, 463.

[3] Igroth Jaschar, p. 30.

[4] A proof that the decalogue was counted as ten verses can be found in Chizkiyah's words, according to which, the reason why in the synagogue no less than ten verses should be read, was in order to correspond to the ten commandments : חזקיה אמר כנגר עשרה הוברות. (J. Taanith, 4, 3, fol. 68 a at the bottom = J. Megilla, 4, 2, fol. 75 a ; cf. b. Meg., 21 b, in the name of רב יוסף.) It would have been remarkable if they had satisfied themselves with ten verses for the sake of a decalogue of thirteen verses.

verses; and as the same tradition assigns the origin of the fixing of the numbers of the verses to the Soferim, which would mean that it had come from the Palestinians to the Babylonians, there could not be anything remarkable in the circumstance that in fixing the figure 1,209, Exod. xix. 9 was counted as three verses. The Massoretic notes must be sifted according to their original sources. The sum total, 1,209, dates from time immemorial, and has its origin in Palestine; the detailed figure seventy-two is either of Babylonian origin, or has been changed from seventy-four after the Babylonian division of verses had already counted xix. 9 as one verse. The fact that several contradictory statements occur in the Massorah side by side is also proved by this, that two notes, quoted by Heidenheim, *Exodus*, p. 80 b, contradict the division of the decalogue into ten verses.

As to the two missing verses in Deuteronomy, I believe that they must be looked for in Haäzinu, for in the lists F D, fifty-four verses, instead of fifty-two, are given as the number of that weekly portion. I do not venture to decide how these two verses are to be got at, but it is not impossible to do so, for this weekly portion contains several verses consisting of four parts. The middle verse of Deuteronomy is, according to the *Manuel*, p. 149, xvii. 10. According to the separate figures, the book numbers up to this passage only 475 verses, instead of the required number, 477 $(=\frac{954}{2})$. But this information cannot be used as an argument against our assumption, for it is also contradictory to the assertion of the *Manuel* and the other lists, that Veatchanan numbered 119 verses. The designation of this middle verse is based on the decalogue being counted as thirteen verses, but is not quite correct even then, for a verse remains superfluous if the number is given exclusive of the middle verse, as is usually done.

Leviticus has $111 + 97 + 91 + 67 + 90 + 80 + 64 + 124 + 57 + 78 = 859$ D F gives for צו, צֹו, which is a slip for צֹו; in the same way D has for תזריע, סֹו instead of סֹו. We have already noticed that in A, in קדושים, כֹו is an error for סֹו, just as in C, in בהר, הטיל for חטיל. D F have further, in בחקתי, עה instead of עֹח. The middle verse is xv. 7. This is correct, for up to this verse (exclusive) there are 429 verses $= \frac{859}{2}$. The note that Exod. xvii. 16 to Lev. xi. 7 contains a thousand verses is also correct. That בהר has fifty-seven verses and not fifty-four, a thing evident in itself, follows also from the note that the fourth thousand is contained in Lev. xi. 8 to Num. x. 16.

Numbers. The unanimous information of all sources produces: $159 + 176 + 136 + 119 + 95 + 87 + 104 + 168 + 112 + 132 = 1,288$. The middle verse is xvii. 20 (exclusive) $= 644 = \frac{1288}{2}$. The *Manuel* shows

1,289 verses, because there xxv. 19 and xxvi. 1 are taken as two verses each, although they are real cases פסקא באמצע פסוק. This is also shown by the note that Num. x. 17 to Deut. iii. 29 contain a thousand verses. פנחס must, therefore, have only 168 verses, and not 169, as correctly given by Heidenheim, and S. D. Luzzatto, *Il Pentateuco* (Padova, 1875).

Deuteronomy: 105 + 119 + 111 + 126 + 97 + 110 + 122 + 70 (נצבים וילך) + 52 + 41. We have already dwelt upon ואתחנן; also on D F, which give 127 in ראה, where קְבֹו = קְבֹו: on D, 106 in כי תצא = קֹו = קֹי (110), which is passed over by Ginsburg; on C in שפטים, where צו=צו; and on D F, in reference to האזינו, 54. These figures give 953, and not 955 of the usual tradition. Everything that was required to be said on this point, as also on the middle verse, xvii. 10, has already been remarked above. Deuteronomy, from iv. 1 to the end, has 845 verses. Consequently, ואתחנן is counted as 122 and not 119 verses, and שפטים as 97 and not 96.

The whole of the Pentateuch contains, both according to the Massoretic works[1] and the editions[2], 5,845 verses. The figure 5,835, which is twice met with in the Massorah of Tshufut-Kale[3], is not an independent statement, but merely an error of the copyist; for it is not based on special detailed information, and is, moreover, in direct conflict with previous statements. It is frequent in the Massorah that numbers expressed by letters are easily corrupted, and that the erroneous statements that have thus arisen are further transmitted after having been transcribed in words. We have already given several instances of that kind in the course of these articles; in the present case הֻף מה was turned into הֻף לה. We are convinced that there exists no rival information in the copies of the Massoretic notes. Our investigation leads to the conclusion that, in spite of the many discrepancies that these notes show, we may confidently assign all information of the Massorah referring to the number of verses in the Pentateuch to the same source.

---

[1] Ben Asher, *Dikduke Hat'amin*, p. 55; *Manuel du lecteur*, p. 179, h. D Ginsburg, *The Massorah*, II, p. 338 b, at the top; II, p. 452 b.

[2] E. g. Minchat Shai, ed. Mantua; W. Heidenhein, *Meor Enayim*, Rödelheim, 1818 sqq., and in the concluding Massoretic remark on the Torah. In Bomberg's Rabbinical Bible of 1526, and in Buxtorf's Bible of 1665, the figure 5,245 is the error either of the copyist or of the printer, for the addition of the separate numbers at the end of each book produces 5,845.

[3] Ginsburg's *Massorah*, III, 269 b and 301 b, at the end of the two lists D F discussed above. I cannot find any reason why Ginsburg should have printed twice the same list.

But the information given in b. Kiddushin, 30 a, which states the number of verses in the Torah to be 5,888, seems to be of a different character[1]. It is not impossible that there was a time when forty-three more verses were counted in the Torah. There was, perhaps, another division of verses in the poetical portions of Exod. xv and Deut. xxxii, which produced forty-three additional verses. This figure could be arrived at from Heidenheim's two MSS. Heidenheim observes at the end of Deuteronomy, in the repeatedly-quoted edition, that the separate figures of the weekly portions amount to 992, and not to 955. Add this difference of thirty-seven to 5,845, and we obtain 5,882. For the sake of reconciling the two figures, we should have to read in Kiddushin, שמונים ושנים instead of שמונים ושמנה. But Baer (*Orient*, XII, p. 204, n. 3), and, after him, Geiger (*Jüd. Zeitschrift*, IV, 265) observe, that the separate figures in Heidenheim's MSS. were not correct; the harmony between the two figures is, therefore, merely accidental. It would be very peculiar indeed if the Tanna as well as the Massorete had first counted the total of נצבים וילך, and then again the verses of נצבים separately. The many " eights " in the Baraitha are suspicious from a Massoretic point of view. Otherwise we should be led to assume that 8,888 should be read instead of 5,888 (ח=ה), as Isaiah Berlin corrects Berachot, 7 a. This figure would then be connected with another, which refers to the definition of the moments. A פסוק would certainly be too much for a רגע.

A third information is that of the Yalkut, i. 855, which gives 15,842 as the number of verses of the Pentateuch[2]. Rappoport wanted to conclude boldly from this passage that the Palestinians had divided most verses into three, and that the enormous figure had thus arisen[3]. But in all probability we have here only a wrong interpretation of the letter ה used as a figure. The words הי אלפים were taken for 15,000[4]. We then should get the figure 5,842, which we consider

---

[1] ה"ר חמשת אלפים ושמנה מאוה ושמונים ושמנה פסוקים הוו פסוקי ספר תורה יהר עליו הלים שמונה חסר ממנו ר"ה שמונה.

[2] וחשבון פסוקים של תורה ש"ו אלפים תתמב.

[3] G. Pollak, *Halichot Kedem* (Amsterdam, 1846), p. 10. Cf. supra, c. 2, *sub fin.*, the refutation of that opinion.

[4] Cf. J. Müller, *Sopherim*, p. 135, n. 9. In the Massorah הי is usually written, not הא; vide *Manuel*, 35, 7, 9; 37, 6; 126, 6; Ginsburg, *Massorah*, I, p. 234 a at the commencement, p. 224 b and 289 b several times; also b. Menachot, 29 b. Other instances, taken from the Talmuds, are found in Berliner, *Beiträge der Hebräischen Grammatik im Talmud und Midrash*, p. 19. From the Jerushalmi, the form הא only is quoted there. In Ginsburg,

the most correct. In discussing the number of verses of the Pentateuch
we have already endeavoured to prove that the decalogue counted
only as ten verses. We conjectured that the missing two verses were
contained in Exod. xix. 9. The number of verses of Deuteronomy
seemed to be in conflict with that assertion, because it amounts to
955 only, if the decalogue counts as thirteen. But the Yalkut gives,
as a matter of fact, only 5,842 (not 5,845), and the decalogue must,
therefore, have been taken to contain only ten verses; and this, as we
have seen, was really done in the detailed amount of Vaetchanan.
It is noteworthy, also, that Levita, *Massoret Hammassoret*, III. Preface
sub fin., counts 5,842, and not 5,845. The exact Massoretic number
of the verses of the Pentateuch may, therefore, be 5,842. The identity
of the hundreds, tens, and units in Yalkut and Massorah goes to prove
that the discrepancy in the thousands owes its origin to a corruption,
provided that we have, in our editions, the original reading, and not
a reading corrected in conformity with the Massorah [1].

III, 70 a, הא occurs repeatedly. פי is also written like הי in *Manuel*, 35, 2;
39, 2, 7, and elsewhere. Ginsburg, II, 429, has פא only in the heading
emanating from Ginsburg; the four notes cited there have פי. The mode
of writing הוא and פף is of a more recent date; and it seems to me that
it was not used at all in ancient times.

[1] מדרש is given as the source of this Agada. This points to a younger
Midrash, as Zunz, *Gottesdienstliche Vorträge*, 302, note, observes. Since
Simeon Kara, as Zunz assumed, and A. Epstein again proved in his
treatise: ר' שמעון קרא והילקוט שמעוני (Cracow, 1891), lived in the thirteenth
century, the Midrash in question must be very recent. It is not impossible that this Agada was taken from the collection of Midrashim
of Moses Hadarshan, who embodied in his work also non-Jewish Agadas,
and even such as are opposed to Jewish conceptions, as Epstein proved
in his *Beiträgen zur jüdischen Allerthumskunde*, XI, *Moses ha-Darshan aus Narbone*
(Vienna, 1891), p. 9, and *Revue des études juives*, XXI, p. 80 sqq. I am led
to assume this, in the first place, by the calculation of the days of seventy
years and of the two verses that fall to each year; the figure seventy and
the Gematrias belonging to the favourites of Moses Hadarshan. In the
second place, the mentioning of verses from the Apocrypha is most
remarkable, לבר מספר החיצונים; this can only have been done by Moses
Hadarshan, who did not keep himself free from Christian conceptions.
Nor is the computation of the seventy years according to the solar cycle
Jewish. Add to all this the number of the eighteen ימי החג, which do not
accord with the number of the festival days of the Diaspora, and refer
perhaps to the eighteen days on which the individual in *Palestine* could
recite the complete Hallel (Taanith, 28 b, י"ח ימי החג = י"ח ימי ההלל י"ח, for
which reason the recitation of the two verses is omitted). All these
considerations suggest the assumption that this Agada has issued from

Grätz (*Monatsschrift*, XXXIV, 97 sqq.), arguing from the number of verses as given in the Talmud and Yalkut, endeavoured to establish important discrepancies in reference to the division of verses. In this he looks for support also in the threefold information about the middle verse of the Torah, which is given in Kiddushin, 30 a, as Lev. xiii. 33; in Masechet Soferim, IX, 3 (ed. Müller, XVI) as Lev. viii. 23; and in the Massorah and *Dikduke Hat'amim*, p. 55, as Lev. viii. 8. Grätz argues that the first indication referred to the Babylonian, the second to the Palestinian, and the third to the Karaite division of verses, and that the latter had become solely and universally adopted. The three figures given as the sum total of the verses of the Pentateuch are explained by Grätz in the same way, namely, that 5,888 was the figure of the Babylonians, 15,842 that of the Palestinians, and 5,845 that of the Karaites. The Baraitha in Kiddushin, 30 a, which is introduced by the words חנו רבנן, must, in that case, be of *Babylonian* origin; further, in a division of verses which gives for the whole Pentateuch an overplus of forty-three verses only, and which, therefore, almost entirely agrees with ours, the middle verse must be moved forward by 152 verses (Lev. viii. 8 to xiii. 13), from which it would follow that they had made their verses longer than ours in the first half of the Pentateuch, and shorter in the second half. Nothing of this can be entertained. Grätz attaches too much importance to the expression בעלי מקרא, which he considers to refer, like בני מקרא, to the Karaites; but the expression is frequently enough applied in Talmud and Midrash to those who have a great knowledge of the Bible [1]. We can, however, in complete refutation of Grätz's assumption, adduce the numerous data, quoted from the Talmudim and Midrashim in the second chapter of this inquiry, which constitute irrefragable evidence for the division of verses as possessed by us. From these data, being partly of Babylonian and partly of Palestinian origin, there can be no doubt that, barring insignificant differences which can have no weight in deciding this question, essentially the

an extraneous, non-traditional source. If this be the case, the enormous number of verses, which according to this computation must be the result, can also be understood. For according to this calculation, there must be at least 41,160 verses; for seventy years have 20,580 week-days, every day two new verses should be given to God = 41,160. The Hebrew Canon containing in round figures 23,000, the Apocrypha must supply the still missing 18,000. Or Moses Hadarshan counted the *stichoi* as Biblical verses; in that case the number of verses required can be accounted for. I believe that the enigmatical Agada could be solved after this method, although not strictly in the way indicated here.

[1] Erulim, 21 b; Baba Mezia, 33 b; Sanhedrin, 101 a, and elsewhere.

same division of verses existed in both countries. In the face of this fact we can dispense with all other, however obvious, refutations.

Turning to the question of the divergent information about the middle verse, the one given in the treatise Soferim, namely, Lev. viii. 23, can be explained in two ways. Up to Lev. viii. 8 there are 2,922 verses; the verse indicated as the middle verse belongs, therefore, neither to the first nor to the latter half, but stands between, for $2,922 \times 2 = 5,844$, and there are 5,845 verses. Now suppose a Massorete had in the Talmud the reading 5,882 (שמונה = שנים), and considered this the correct number, either from having omitted to check it, or on the ground of a different numbering of the verses of Deut. xxxii, in that case he had to count till he reached the half of that figure, $\frac{5882}{2} = 2,941$. If he, further, took the decalogue to contain thirteen verses — a thing not at all impossible, considering what we said before on the subject — then on reaching Lev. viii. 8 he had 2,925 verses, and sixteen more verses brought him to Lev. viii. 23 = 2,941 verses. Another explanation would be this: that the abbreviation ויש (= וַיִּשָּׂם), Lev. viii. 8, was turned into וַיִּשְׁחָם, Lev. viii. 23. The information about the middle verse as given in the Talmud is more difficult to explain. It cannot have been based upon an essentially different division of verses, for the very same Baraitha gives the sum of the verses of the Pentateuch as only forty-three verses more than that of the Massorah, but there are 152 verses between Lev. viii. 8 and xiii. 3. I admit I can propose nothing in explanation, except that the ancient Massorete made a mistake in counting, or that he failed to understand the note about the middle verse. It is also possible to conjecture that the big נ had been originally an indication of the middle letter, which indication was erroneously transmitted to the middle verse, the ו in נחון serving for this purpose. I do not attach much value to this conjecture; I give it merely as a suggestion.

6. *The Number of Verses of the Prophets, the Hagiographa, and the whole Bible.*

The sums of the separate books of the Prophets and the Hagiographa are given, besides the editions, which cannot be relied on[1], by Ginsburg, ܦ, 195-215, and partly by Baer, *Orient*, XII, 262. We give here Ginsburg's list, and add Baer's variations in brackets. A " B " is added where both agree; where Baer has given no figure nothing is added.

[1] In the stereotype edition of the Bible Society the figure for the Chronicles is 1,656.

Prophets.		Middle.
Joshua	656 [1].	xiii. 26.
Judges	618 [1].	x. 8.
Samuel	1506.	I, xxviii. 24.
Kings	1536 B.	I, xxii. 6.
Isaiah	1292 [1] B.	xxxiii. 21.
Jeremiah	1365 [2] [1364]	xxviii. 11.
Ezekiel	1273 [1272] [3]	xxvi. 1.
XII Prophets	1050.	Micah iii. 12 [4].
	9296	

In spite of the separate figures, the sum total is given by Ginsburg as 9,294; and by Baer, who has only two verses less, as 9,292 [5]. In another Massorah (Ginsburg, II, p. 338 at the top), the figure 9,298 occurs. *Dikduke Hat'amim* gives, in agreement with the first figure, 9,294. Isa. xvii. 3 is indicated as the half of the Prophets (חצי הנביאים), *Dikduke*, 56, Ginsburg, II, 338 a 6; this accords both with the figure 9,294 and the figure 9,296. In the former case xvii. 3 belongs to the second half, and in the latter case, to the first; for up to Isa. xvii. 3 there are 4,647 verses=9,294 : 2. If 9,298 verses are counted, the two additional verses would be equally divided between the two halves, and the middle verse would remain the same.

Hagiographa.		Middle.
Psalms	2527	lxxviii. 36.
Proverbs	915 (914)	xvi. 18.
Job	1075	xxii. 16.
Song of Solomon	117	iv. 14.
Ruth	85	ii. 21.
Lamentations	154	iii. 34 (32 misprint).
Kohelet	222	vi. 10.
Esther	167 B	v. 7.
Daniel	357 B	vi. 12 [6].
Ezra (Nehemiah)	688 (686)	iii. 32 [7].
Chronicles	1765 (1764) [8]	I, xxvii. 25.
	8072	

[1] The same in Baer's edition.
[2] In the סימן : אסתה the ס is a misprint for ש.
[3] Baer gives, in his edition of Ezekiel (Leipsic, 1884), the figure 1,273.
[4] [5] [6] [7] [8] For these notes see next page.

The sum total is not given by Ginsburg in this place, but is found 338 b, as 8,063; *Dikduke*, p. 55, has 8,064. This figure can be reconciled with the separate items only by subtracting five verses from Job, two from Ezra, and one each from Proverbs and the Chronicles; this would give 8,063. Was not Baer induced by the addition to subtract, against the Massorah, a verse each from Proverbs and Chronicles? The remaining eight or nine verses can only be accounted for by eliminating five verses from Job, two from Ezra, and one from Esther (according to Norzi). Psalm cxxx. 3 is marked as the middle verse of the Hagiographa (Ginsburg, 338 a, and *Dikduke*, 56). The sum total being 8,063, there must be 4,032 to Ps. cxxx. 4. The Chronicles and Psalms have 1,765 + 2,527 = 4,292. From Ps. cxxx. 3 to the end of the book there are 259 verses; therefore 4,292 − 259 = 4033, which is not quite correct. A total of 8,064 must therefore be assumed, and Ps. cxxx. 3 must be counted to the second half [1].

The sum total of the whole Bible amounts, according to Ginsburg, II, 453, and *Dikduke*, p. 55, to 23,203. This sum can only be arrived at by keeping, according to Ginsburg and against the separate figures

[4] Ginsburg, it is true, gives the same verses, but persistently gives in his reference of chapter and verse the one that precedes. For Joshua, cf. Minchat Shai. For Ezekiel, the second verse of ch. xxvi was given by Baer (*Orient*, XII, 262), but in his edition he notes xxvi. 1. Norzi always notes the middle verses, and they agree with those given.

[5] 9,292 being expressed in words (השעים ושנים), נסמך מ"ר צ"ר must be a misprint and not vice versa.

[6] Ginsburg, v, 29, וחציו בה בליליא קטיל, but up to v. 30 there are only 167 verses. Norzi and Baer mark correctly vi. 12. Has Ginsburg obtained his reference from some MS.? The Bible, ed. Brescia, 1493, marks Ps. lxxviii. 38 as the middle of the book, as Berliner observes: *Ueber den Einfluss des ersten hebräischen Buchdrucks auf den Cultus und die Cultur der Juden*, p. 28. He could have added, that Kiddushin, 30 a, also marks this verse as middle verse. Cf. Norzi, end of צו.

[7] There are 343 up to this verse = 686 : 2. According to the figure 688, one verse must be sought before and one after the middle.

[8] Norzi has Proverbs and Ezra 915, 688 respectively, Esther 166, Chronicles 1,787. Job has, according to Norzi, and Baer in his edition, not 1,075, but 1,070. The latter figure is verified by the addition of the verses. In Baer, ch. 5, the number of the last verse is missing, but the section is indicated. Ginsburg's figure, which is protected against misprint by its repetition in letters אזה, is consequently wrong. Whence has Baer 914 instead of 915, a figure already given in the Midrash? The same applies to Chronicles.

[1] For references on the Fourths of the Pentateuch and the Hagiographa, vide *Dikduke*, p. 56.

for the Prophets, to the traditional figure 9,294, and by supplying 8,064 for the Hagiographa. These figures are expressly preserved in *Dikduke*. Accordingly, 5,845 (Torah) + 9,224 (Prophets) + 8,064 (Hagiogr.) = 23,203. For the three divisions of Holy Writ, Ginsburg has, II, 338 b, the following figures: 5,845 + 9,298 + 8,063. This amounts to 23,206. Baer, *Orient*, XII, 262, gives 23,202, having adopted for the Hagiographa the figure 8,063. These differences can be explained. But the following formulae also occur:

(1) פסוקים שתי רבואות ושני אלפים ושבע מאות וארבעים ושבעה לא פחות ולא יותר (Ginsburg, II, 338).

(2) תרתין רבוון) ותרתין אלפין ושבע מאות וארבעין ושבעה וחכו).

(3) שתי רבוא ו····· אלפים ויבע מאות וארבעים ושבעה לא יתר לא פחות.

(4) שתי רבוא) ושלשה אלפים ושתי מאות וארבעים וׁשבע (*Dikduke*, p. 56, note).

The identical introductory and concluding formula shows that we have to deal here with the same Massoretic note. On comparing these corrupted readings, we are struck by the fact that they have, besides the myriads, only the figure 47 in common. Although we are justified in considering the thousands and hundreds as errors of the copyists, we cannot do so with the figure 47. It would be incomprehensible indeed how ג could have become מ"ז, or שלשה have been turned into ארבעים ושבעה. It seems to me that we have here an intentional correction by an overwise copyist. who, instead of the Massoretic sum of verses of the Pentateuch (5,845), took that of the Talmud (5,888). Thus he obtained an overplus of forty-three verses, which added to 23,203 (4) gives 23,247. This different sum total is, therefore, the correction of the sum of the verses of the Pentateuch made by a copyist who had read the Talmud.

The Massoretic sum total is, however, the correct one. This is shown by the indicated middle verse of the whole Bible, which is Jer. vi. 7. There are, up to this verse, 5,845 (Pentateuch) + 5,608 (Joshua–Isaiah) + 149 (Jer. i. 1–vi. 6) = 11,602. This multiplied by two makes 23,204. It follows that the sum total of the Prophets is 9,296 (not 4). and the sum total of all the verses of the Bible is 23,205 (or 6). Without arithmetic one cannot find his way even in the Massorah.

We have described the history of the division into verses within the circle of Rabbinical Judaism, without entering upon the grounds upon which such divisions were based. The examination of its justification on internal grounds has been undertaken by the commentators, especially in respect to the poetical and prophetic. As to the prose writings, the Pentateuch only has been subjected to an investigation from this point of view in the repeatedly-quoted essay by Friedmann (*Menora*, I), not reckoning occasional remarks by commentators. We do not wish to pronounce a judgment about this essay. We only express the wish that commentators may give their attention to this neglected branch of Biblical studies, in order to evolve the laws by which the division into verses are ruled. It may be advantageous to Exegesis. and may give many a clue or hint towards the elucidation of some obscure passages.

Budapest.   LUDWIG BLAU.

The Rise of the Tiberian Bible Text[1]

*To N. H. Tur-Sinai—master and friend—on his
seventy-fifth birthday*

By M. H. GOSHEN-GOTTSTEIN

I. INTRODUCTION

1. There can be little doubt that one of the major problems to be tackled
afresh in connection with the new critical edition of the Bible, now in
progress at the Hebrew University Bible Project, is our understanding of
the growth of the Tiberian Bible text. While establishing the authentic
character of the renowned Aleppo Codex was the first necessary step,[2]
it seems that further study of all the evidence may enable us to get at some
broader implications of the discovery of this codex. Much, of course, still
remains to be done in furthering our understanding of details of the Masoretic vocalization and accentuation. But the preparation of the new edition
also forces us to try to see the forest, not only the manifold trees.

1. The gist of the present paper (finished in July 1961) was read in different stages
before various learned audiences during my stay in the United States. While it has been
reworked for publication, the original oral manner of presentation is very much in evidence. This will also explain the sometimes unwieldy size of the footnotes. As it stands,
the paper contains the backbone of the argumentation of a number of chapters in a forthcoming volume, tentatively termed *Nosah ha-Miqrā ha-Tavrāni*, to be published by the
Hebrew University Bible Project. While the present study stands in its own right, many
additional issues have been hinted at in the notes to this paper; they will be discussed
in detail in that volume.

This paper was written concurrently with my "Biblical Manuscripts in the United
States," *Textus* 2:28f. (1962). A number of problems concerning Biblical manuscripts
have been dealt with in that paper, and to that extent the two studies will complement
each other. Some other points which have been developed here have already been mentioned as "theses" in the introduction to my *Text and Language in Bible and Qumran*
(Jerusalem–Tel Aviv, 1960).

While I am fully aware that in my work I have somewhat strayed from the teaching of
my masters, I still venture to dedicate this effort to the Nestor of Israeli Hebraists,
Professor N. H. Tur-Sinai (Torczyner), whose productivity and brilliance remain an
ever-present challenge to his erstwhile students.

2. See Goshen-Gottstein, "The Authenticity of the Aleppo Codex," *Text and Language*, pp. 1f., and also D. S. Löwinger, *Textus* 1:59f. (1960).

Reprinted from *Biblical and Other Studies*, Cambridge (Mass.), 1963.

2. For the purpose of the present study I should like to use as a starting point the results arrived at earlier. I hope that in the study of the Aleppo Codex I have already shown:

- (a) that the manuscript now under investigation at the Hebrew University Bible Project and scheduled to be printed as the basic text is, indeed, the famous Aleppo Codex;
- (b) that the text of that manuscript turns out to conform to the accepted characteristics of a Ben Asher text better than any other known early manuscript, so that it must be taken as the superior representative of the tradition of Aaron Ben Asher;
- (c) that what was supposed for a century to be a pious legend of the Jewish community of Aleppo and was disbelieved by most scholars— namely, that the Aleppo Codex is the selfsame model codex declared "authoritative" by Maimonides in his great halakhic compendium (the *Code*) with regard to certain fundamental questions of preparing Torah scrolls—is true. The Aleppo Codex *is* the codex of Maimonides, and as such became the halakhically binding model for later generations.

3. In the light of these earlier results with regard to the status and character of the Aleppo Codex we may now try to picture afresh on a broader canvas the history of what has become our *textus receptus*, before the emergence of the Aleppo Codex and after it. However, before turning to our main task on this occasion some general remarks may not be out of place.

The present study is an inquiry into a subject matter, not an analysis of scholarly theories. But trying to gain an understanding of the growth of the Tiberian Bible text means of necessity coming upon the theories of P. Kahle. For almost half a century Kahle's name has been synonymous with the study of the Hebrew Bible text, and what is found today in handbooks on the subject mostly reflects his ideas. Whether directly or indirectly, every student of the Bible text is in Kahle's debt. Only by standing on his shoulders can we try to perceive new vistas.[3]

By the same token, however, it is mainly Kahle's theses that our findings will question. While other scholars have dealt with certain details in most valuable monographs, only Kahle has put forward a general hypothesis of the emergence of the Tiberian Bible text through working into a

---

3. I should like to use this opportunity to express my gratitude to Professor Paul Kahle for his unfailing courtesy and helpfulness. I am especially in his debt for his permission to use his own transcripts from the fragments of the *ḥillufim* of Mishael. See below, Section V.

whole the results of various studies, carried out since the end of the last century.[4]

4. It was therefore inevitable that our results finally amount almost to an alternative general hypothesis, differing in many respects from the picture painted by Kahle. As such it is to be judged solely by its ability to accommodate the known facts. I would not claim that each particular detail of our thesis has been proved convincingly and that each proof is as sound as, I hope, the proof of the character of the Aleppo Codex itself—our starting point. Certain details will become clearer only after much further work (see below, §50). What I submit at present is that the over-all picture I try to convey allows for the inclusion of a larger number of known details and for a less forced interpretation of many facts than does the picture Kahle has presented. Or, to be less ambitious, the hypothesis to be outlined here is not less probable than his.

By the customary rules of formulating general hypotheses I shall be obliged to accommodate facts only and am not answerable for any theory of Kahle's (or others). At the same time, our hypothesis must allow for later modification of details, and it should not be taken as a final statement of opinions, to be defended stubbornly henceforth.[5]

5. Having grown up, like most of my contemporaries, under the impact of Kahle's teaching, I admit that all this sounds almost sacrilegious. Furthermore, the fate of Kahle's critics in another field of textual studies, the Septuagint text—where practically all the specialists who have investigated the subject on their own stand united against him, while his theories loom largely in the handbooks—does not make my task more enviable. To be sure, I take some comfort from the fact that the teaching of the young Kahle in its time also necessitated a frontal attack on the established authorities on the Hebrew Bible text of those days, such as Baer, Ginsburg, and Strack.[6] Even so I am conscious of embarking on a dangerous undertaking.

---

4. Kahle has now summed up his views in *Cairo Geniza*, 2nd ed. (Oxford, 1959), and in his German series of lectures, *Der hebräische Bibeltext seit Franz Delitzsch* (Stuttgart, 1961). As far as possible, the most recent statements of his position will be referred to as reflecting his opinions.

5. It is only human that as we advance in our work, we all try to fit new facts into our old patterns rather than to change our theories. Having rechecked Kahle's work as it developed over the decades, I feel—if I may venture such a remark—that his holding fast to the theories submitted in his brilliant pioneer studies (until 1930) has prevented him from much necessary revision.

6. Cf. especially Kahle's introduction to his *Masoreten des Ostens* (Leipzig, 1913), pp. xivf. His attack has not diminished; see *Der hebräische Bibeltext*, pp. 13f.

However, having reached the conclusions on the subject which I have reached, I could not honestly deal with all those questions without getting involved in a major discussion with Kahle and without submitting my findings to all scholars in general and to him in particular. If there is someone alive today who could show the basic fallacy of my position, it surely should be the *Altmeister* of this subject himself. It is in this spirit that I dare to outline my hypothesis. It would be folly to expect that I am completely right; I hope that I am not wholly wrong.

II. Tiberian and Non-Tiberian Traditions

6. Bearing in mind that our point of departure is the new edition of the Bible, no justification is needed for taking the Tiberian Bible text as our central theme. To be sure, the trend of research in Hebrew Bible traditions during the past decades, largely thanks to Kahle's work, has been to concentrate heavily on the study of traditions outside the Tiberian Bible text.

The nineteenth century had witnessed an increasing understanding of Hebrew in the light of Comparative Semitics, and the facts of the Tiberian Bible text, practically the only tradition known then, seemed, so to speak, "exhausted." Nothing was more natural for scholars than to turn to virgin soil. By concentrating their efforts on non-Tiberian traditions—written as well as oral[7]—a new perspective was gained for analyzing the development of Hebrew.

This gain of a new comparative dimension within the realm of Hebrew is one of the fundamental gains of this century in the field of Hebrew and Bible studies. All scholars will accept, therefore, the necessary corollary that every text-form of our Hebrew Bible, including the text of Aaron Ben Asher, represents only a synchronic cut in the flow of diachronic evolution (see my "Authenticity of the Aleppo Codex," §7).

7. But there is another side to the picture, somehow neglected through our preoccupation with non-Tiberian traditions (see also below, §47)—which reminds one of the truism that with all due respect to the side that lost, we should not ignore the fact that there was a winner.[8] It was a particular

7. It would seem that only the few studies undertaken by European scholars on the Samaritan reading tradition have come to Kahle's notice. I should therefore like to stress that the present essay relies in its general outlook on the results of many studies on Masoretic and dialectical questions, especially those by A. Ben David, Z. Ben Ḥayyim, J. Garbell, S. D. Goitein, Y. G. F. Gumpertz, D. S. Löwinger, S. Morag, H. Yalon, and J. Yeivin. See Notes 39, 43, and 54.

8. The question of the neglect of Tiberian Biblical manuscripts has been dealt with in my "Biblical Manuscripts."

Tiberian text-form that became our *textus receptus*, and ninety-nine per cent of the readers of the Hebrew Bible are interested in this form exclusively. In spite of our fullest awareness of the historic circumstances and in spite of the absorbing scholarly interest of other text-forms, our Tiberian Bible text still commands the paramount attention of scholars (see also my "Authenticity of the Aleppo Codex," 1).

Indeed, the great editors of Masoretic Bibles—from the First Masoretic Bible, connected with the name of Jacob Ben Ḥayyim[9] in 1524, to Seligmann Baer, Christian David Ginsburg,[10] and Paul Kahle—saw their task in printing what they believed was the Tiberian Ben Asher text.[11] The recovery of Aaron Ben Asher's model codex is therefore an event which calls for a new attempt to put the Tiberian Bible text into the center of our attention and to trace its emergence and rise to victory.

8. Apart from a new evaluation of the previously known facts, our attempt is based on three lines of inquiry:

(a) the study or perusal of all the Hebrew Bible codices and of most Geniza fragments (outside Russia; see my "Biblical Manuscripts in the United States");

(b) the study of the whole of Mishael Ben ʿUzziel's treatise on the "differences" (*ḥillufim*) between Ben Asher and Ben Naftali in comparison with the codices mentioned under (c);[12]

(c) a new study of the codices customarily connected today with the

---

9. I use this formulation in order not to enter the problem of Jacob Ben Ḥayyim's dependence in his *text* (as opposed to the *Masora*) on the work of Felix Pratensis. There seems to be no generally accepted way to make it clear that the First Masoretic Bible is the Second Rabbinic Bible.

10. It has been stressed repeatedly by Kahle (see *Cairo Geniza*, 2nd ed., p. 130) that C. D. Ginsburg was the only one among the editors of the *textus receptus* in recent times who endeavored to reprint exactly the text of Ben Ḥayyim. But Ginsburg did not fully carry out his promise (quite apart from the question of the declared differences between his editions). Any sample collation over a few chapters will reveal this. As far as I can see, only A. Sperber, "Hebrew Phonology," *HUCA* 16:42⁸ ˙ 11), is aware of this fact.

11. This statement needs some qualification. In spite of Kahle's statement (at the moment of writing I find my reference to his chapter in L. Goldschmidt's *Earliest Editions of the Hebrew Bible* [New York, 1950], p. 46; but it probably also appears elsewhere), I cannot find the place where Ben Ḥayyim states that his aim is to print the text of Ben Asher. He intended to print what seemed to him the "correct Masoretic text" (which follows, as he surely believed, the tradition of Ben Asher). This is a slight difference, but still noteworthy. See §44.

12. The results from the analysis of the collations will be given in my *Nosaḥ ha-Miqrā*. I am greatly indebted to Mr. J. Yeivin, assistant at the Hebrew University Bible Project, who took upon himself to copy all the quotations from the various codices and also sent them to the States. In Note 3, above, I expressed my appreciation of Professor Kahle's generosity in making his transcripts available.

Ben Asher family: that is, the Aleppo Codex (A), the codex British Museum Or. 4445 of the Pentateuch (B), the Cairo Codex of the Prophets (C), and the Leningrad Codex B 19a (L).

9. In order to sketch our picture of the rise of the Tiberian Bible text we have to pay attention to the following major problems:[13]

(a) the relationship of Aaron's codex to other "Tiberian" traditions in general and to the Cairo Codex in particular;

(b) the nature of the Ben Naftali tradition—or what is widely accepted as such;

(c) the reason for the victory of Aaron's system.

III. The Position of the Aleppo Codex

10. A study of the Aleppo and Cairo codices[14] and their Masoras, leaf by leaf, gives one the impression, perforce subjective, that these codices are very much personal and individual achievements. The way in which Masoretic notes are put together and corrections introduced is different from that of the twelfth- and thirteenth-century codices. The Aleppo and Cairo codices impress us not as stereotyped copies but as first-hand creations, still bearing marks of occasional changes, not just mistakes,[15] in the light of evidence the author seems to have gathered in the course of his work. Each codex shows its own arrangement and choice of the Masora—substantially different in character from the carefree attitude and "choice" of later copyists. They often offer materials in their margins other than those in the text itself (and sometimes apparently representing an "earlier" stage). Furthermore, the considerable number of Babylonian signs[16] leads us back to a stage when the Tiberian tradition was still under "foreign influence" with regard to the graphic notation, and the extremely rare *ḥaṭaf-ḥiriq* vowels (compare Löwinger, *Textus* 1:83f.) reveal a momentary glimpse of an "experiment" which was immediately discarded.

---

13. The questions are interconnected and have not influenced the structure of this paper.

14. All Ben Asher manuscripts were studied from photographs, but the Aleppo Codex and British Museum Or. 4445 were also verified from the originals.

15. Completely different from the erasures in the Leningrad Codex (see below, §30). All the codices, of course, have their fair share of "ordinary" mistakes and corrections.

16. Kahle was clearly aware of the significance of this phenomenon in the very early codices (see especially *Theologische Rundschau*, N.S., 5:330f. [1933] reprinted in *Opera Minora* [Leiden, 1956], pp. 70f.). This was stressed again by F. Diez Esteban, *Sefarad* 14:317f. (1954), and with regard to the Aleppo Codex by Löwinger, *Textus* 1:82f.

In short, the codices around ʿ,00 C.E. show, so to speak, no stereotype; the last touches of the masters are still fresh. What we see is not the work of copyists, with a tradition of generations of copying the same text, but something which had only just then become fully fledged.[17]

11. In other words: in our submission the early codices which we possess are not only the oldest ones known to us, but they seem to belong to the altogether earliest stratum of codices of the fully developed prototype of the Tiberian Bible text. This impression, gained from working on the codices, tallies exactly with the feeling we get from the unique colophon of the Cairo Codex, written by Moses Ben Asher at the very end of the ninth century.[18] We cannot help noticing the satisfaction of the Masorete that something novel has been achieved, not necessarily by him personally, but through the then-recent common effort of a whole group, something not achieved in the same fashion until that time (see below, §18f.).

12. Third, and hardly less important: not only are these the earliest known codices,[19] but among all the known Biblical Geniza fragments[20] which have now been perused for the first time, there is not one that can be said to represent basically the Tiberian Bible text and yet be earlier than the ninth- and tenth-century codices.[21]

13. All this is circumstantial evidence and must remain argument from silence. Also, as I stressed elsewhere,[22] the treasures kept in Russia may

17. The chronological implications in the light of the "List of Generations" of the Masoretes (K. Levy, *Zur masoretischen Grammatik* [Stuttgart, 1936], ʋ) will be dealt with in *Nosaḥ ha-Miqrā.* See below, Notes 65, 112.

18. See *Cairo Geniza*, pp. 8of. See below, Note 57.

19. *Mutatis mutandis* matters apply also to a manuscript like the Sassoon Codex 507 (S).

20. I do not think I exaggerate if I put the number of these fragments, including the very small ones, at ten thousand and above. Selections from these have been photographed by the Hebrew University Bible Project for further study. Only the Russian material and those fragments of the so-called "New Series" in Cambridge which are still in the large wooden crates have not been examined. See my "Biblical Manuscripts," chap. ii.

21. On the basis of my work on Geniza material, both Biblical and non-Biblical, I tend to endorse J. L. Teicher's warning (*JJS* 1:158 [1949]) that in general we should not expect in the Geniza any material antedating that period (see Notes 40, 65, 1.12). But because of the basic character of the Geniza as well as the type of writing materials used, one might have expected that a few Bible manuscripts, a century or two old, should have been ready for the Geniza by the tenth century. In fact, it has been generally held that the Geniza contains much older material (but cf. below, Note 112). Yet no part of an eighth- or ninth-century Tiberian Masoretic manuscript has come to light so far. I include in this statement MS. JTS 226, possibly the earliest Geniza fragment of the Tiberian Bible text, which has not entered the literature so far. See my "Biblical Manuscripts," p. 38. Publication will take place in *Nosaḥ ha-Miqrā* and in forthcoming volumes of *Textus.*

22. See for this matter my *Text and Language*, p. x.

still provide a surprise.[23] Yet from all the indications there emerges, in my opinion, something which we could not suspect until now, something which also throws a completely new light on the astounding action of Maimonides (see my *Text and Language*, pages 43f., especially 46, and below, my Section IX). It sounds, indeed, unbelievable because of its very simplicity.[24] In my submission it has become very probable that the Aleppo Codex was not only one early manuscript out of a few; it was the great event in the history of the Tiberian Bible text. It was preceded, no doubt, by other codices. But this was the *first codex of the complete Bible* with full Masoretic annotation, exhibiting what was to be regarded as the prototype of the Tiberian Bible text. It was the final achievement of the continued work of generations of *the* dynasty of Masoretes,[25] the descendants of "the Old Asher."

14. The stress is on the complete Bible. For our thesis also takes into consideration the fact, often ignored, that for centuries to come codices of the complete Bible remained very rare, and it must have taken a very long time until such a codex was first attempted.[26] Maimonides' description of

23. Although the examination of the Russian collections remains a high-priority desideratum, I am afraid that to some extent our inability to examine them at this moment makes us expect more than there might be. To be more specific: the Günzburg collection does not, to my knowledge, include old Bible codices, and it hardly stands to reason that the Geniza material in the Antonin collection is basically different from the material which came to other countries.

In other words, our main hope is undoubtedly the Firkowich collections. But most of that material was examined at the time by H. L. Strack (who was interested in the Ben Asher question; see his pioneer article, "Die biblischen und die massoretischen Handschriften zu Tschufut Kale in der Krim," *Zeitschrift für die Lutherische Theologie und Kirche* 36:585f. [1875]). However, Strack's examination was, according to his own words, rather cursory. Furthermore, we may judge matters differently nowadays. Kahle's own discoveries (*Masoreten des Westens*, vol. I [Stuttgart, 1927], pp. 56ff.), on the other hand, turn out to depend rather heavily on the notes of his predecessors. It is, therefore, not easy to form a picture of what to expect from the manuscripts kept in Russia. See also Note 81.

24. I have wondered for a long time whether any thesis which depends in the last analysis on argument from silence may be suggested. It can never be fully proved and can hardly be disproved. Furthermore, one feels reluctant to assume that the earliest item known is in actual fact the earliest item. Yet the evidence pointing in the direction of our thesis seems so strong that I am personally convinced it is true. Nevertheless, I should like to stress that the other theses of this study—and especially my argument with Kahle— are not dependent on this.

25. This attribute is not based on the ultimate victory of this tradition, but results from the analysis of medieval material (such as that alluded to in Note 17).

26. The only codex of a complete Bible about which we hear the claim that it was earlier than our earliest Tiberian Bible text codices is the legendary Codex Hilleli, long lost. That claim is contained in Zacuto's note which is patently fictitious (dated at the sixth or seventh century!). As a reference I suggest H. L. Strack's *Prolegomena critica in Vetus Testamentum* (Leipzig, 1873), p. 16; all later handbooks seem to have copied their information from him.

the Aleppo Codex as containing the complete Bible[27] thus becomes much
more significant than we could imagine. Parts of the Bible were copied
much more often, because there was a practical need for them. Such codices
with full Tiberian Masoretic annotation may already have been current
during the ninth century, and the Cairo Codex may have been spared the
fate of other such codices because of its prestige and its superb workman-
ship. But the idea of a complete model codex,[28] to serve as final arbiter for
scribes and scholars, with full Masoretic annotation according to the then
most reliable tradition—this idea had yet to be conceived of. Apart from
everything else, it must have been extremely expensive,[29] because its author
spent many years on it. The Aleppo Codex was the first model codex
of this textual type.[30]

15. Although the vicissitudes of Jewish life in the Middle Ages brought
about the destruction of many Bible codices, there is no reason on earth
why only the codices from before 900 C.E. should have disappeared completely.[31] If there were such codices, some kind of trace should have been left.

It seems therefore much more reasonable to assume that a model codex
of the complete Tiberian Bible was attempted only as a crowning undertaking in the mature stage of Masoretic activity. In other words: all the
facts known indicate that the practically uniform medieval tradition should
be taken at its face value. It was Aaron Ben Asher who was recognized
almost universally as the Masorete who had the final word,[32] it was he to

27. *Code*, Book ii, *Ahabha, Hilkhoth Sefer Thora*, viii, 4: הספר הידוע במצרים שהוא כולל
ארבעה ועשרים ספרים ("The codex known in Egypt which contains the whole Bible"). For
a translation of the whole note, see my "Authenticity of the Aleppo Codex," n. 1.

28. For information on differences among the various types of codex, see my "Biblical
Manuscripts," pp. 36f. See also below, Notes 136, 138.

29. I understand that information on this subject from Geniza documents will be given
by S. D. Goitein in a forthcoming publication.

30. It is useful to remember that there is no such thing as a scroll of the whole Bible.
The ancient tradition knows only of parts as the scribal entity.

31. If we may judge at all by the contents of present-day collections and the ratio
between the numbers of manuscripts from before and after 1200 C.E., codices of the
complete Bible remained very rare, but they are in existence as from the tenth century.
It is also illuminating to find that the rarity of complete Bible codices is in evidence
elsewhere. Thus from the whole period between the fifth century (the time of the first
known codex) until the twelfth century, we possess only four complete codices of the
Peshitta. See my "Prolegomena to a critical edition of the Peshitta," *Text and Language*, p. 200. On the other hand, codices of various parts of the Peshitta run into
dozens. Furthermore, it took the Syrian punctuators and Masoretes some five hundred
years after the invention of diacritic signs before anything faintly resembling a "Masoretic
manuscript" was attempted (*Text and Language*, p. 201). For a similar situation with
regard to the Vulgate, see S. Berger, *Histoire de la Vulgate* (Paris, 1895), p. 3.

32. היה אחרית השלשלה=כאן אכ׳ר אלסלסלה ("He was the last link in the chain")
(Levy, *Zur masoretischen Grammatik*, p. י). For the importance of the facts mentioned
here, see below, Note 91. For the development after him, see below, §43f.

whom the collection of Masoretic material, probably partly current in his family for some generations, known as *Dikduke Ha-ṭeamim* was attributed; it was he who was named as the authority in polemic teasings between Rabbanites and Ḳaraites (see below, Note 51); it was his codex that Maimonides relied upon (see below, my Section IX).

As far as our knowledge goes, Aaron Ben Asher did not bring about any revolution in Masoretic notation[33] which would justify his status. Had his father succeeded in preparing a complete Bible codex he would, in all probability, have carried off the palm. In my opinion, then, all the facts point in one direction. *The Aleppo Codex is not only the oldest complete codex of the Tiberian Bible text known to us, but it is altogether the earliest complete codex of that Masoretic subsystem which had been perfected by the Ben Ashers.*

16. This claim does not ignore the possibility that Aaron Ben Asher himself also prepared codices of *parts* of the Bible,[34] probably before the Aleppo Codex was written. But it seems improbable, contrary to what has been believed until now without any positive evidence, that there ever existed another codex of the complete Bible prepared by him. If we bear in mind that even *copying* a codex like the Aleppo Codex, with its ten thousands of annotations, is perforce a matter of years, it seems that the original *preparation* of such a model codex was almost by definition a goal reached once in a lifetime. Being something novel in its execution, even though based on earlier work, it was by necessity the crowning event of many years of endless toil—and we might assume that Aaron began his codex only when his father had laid away his pen forever. Again and again over the years, he introduced slight corrections, just as was hinted by Maimonides (see Note 27) and as was the habit of many authors.[35]

17. To sum up the position so far: in my submission all the facts are

---

33. For the problem of Aaron versus Moses, see below §33f.

34. The expression הספרים המוגהים והמבוארים אשר עשה המלמד אהרן בן משה בן אשר ("The correct and clear codices prepared by the master Aaron Ben Moses Ben Asher") in the colophon of the Leningrad Codex (fol. 479a) would fit this assumption well, although this is not the only possible explanation. At the same time such an assumption would offer a possible explanation for some differences between the Aleppo and Leningrad codices. See, for the matter, also note 81, below. As far as I can see, no attention has been paid to the wording in the Leningrad Codex as regards its possible relationship with the Aleppo Codex. See also below, §30.

35. Mishael Ben ʿUzziel testifies when dealing with the *gaʿyas* of לא יהיה לך (Exod. 20:3; Mishael יב) that such a change of position on the part of Ben Asher took place. The fact of this special mention can, of course, be interpreted in two opposite ways. Unfortunately we do not know the reading of the Aleppo Codex in this instance. (The verse is not mentioned in Jacob Sapir's list; see my "Biblical Manuscripts," chap. v).

interpreted best by assuming that the Aleppo Codex was, indeed, the greatest event in the history of the Tiberian Bible text, the first complete codex of the Bible according to the tradition later to be accepted as *the* Tiberian Masoretic Bible. It is not only the superior manuscript connected with the name of Aaron Ben Asher, but also it is the only complete Bible codex prepared by him (see below, §§31, 43f., 45f.). Its "victory" was due to these circumstances, to its inherent obvious perfection as the acme of achievement of *the* dynasty of Masoretes.

IV. Lower Bible Criticism and Oral Tradition

18. The stress I have put on the unique and novel aspect of Aaron Ben Asher's achievement approaches so dangerously the formulation of Kahle, "dass die tiberische Punktation erst eine Schöpfung der Ben Ascher-Masoreten gewesen ist . . ." (*Der hebräische Bibeltext*, page 51) and similar statements, that our next step must be to try to outline the way which led up to the creation of the Aleppo Codex.[36] This is all the more necessary because the discussions of the last decades have often become reminiscent of the theological feuds of the sixteenth and seventeenth centuries in the wake of Levita's discovery of the late provenience of the vowel points. The analogy is quite striking. Just as Levita's correct critical insights led to the monstrous disregard of facts by later scholars and their cavalier attitude to the Masoretic text,[37] so the modern theories about the development of the Tiberian Bible text, as propounded by Kahle, seem the almost natural outcome of our better acquaintance with non-Tiberian systems, mainly thanks to his work.

19. In order to introduce our point, we may start by looking back at the history of the so-called "Higher Bible Criticism" since Kahle's early days. The theory of evolution was still all-pervading, and it was the aim of

36. With regard especially to the following sections, which develop my main discussion with Kahle, I should like to stress that the arguments are given in greater detail in my *Nosaḥ ha-Miqrā*.

37. The best accounts of these discussions are still those written in the second half of the nineteenth century which deal with the subject in different ways. S. D. Luzzato is still a party to the discussion (*Dialogues sur la Kabbale et le Zohar et sur l'antiquité de la ponctuation et de l'accentuation dans la langue hébraïque* [in Hebrew; Gorice, 1852, pp. 79ff.]). C. D. Ginsburg has written a detailed survey in his introduction to Elia Levita, *Massoreth ha-Massoreth* (London, 1867) while G. Schnedermann has highlighted *Die Controverse des Ludovicus Capellus mit den Buxtorfen* (Leipzig, 1879). I have not found it pointed out that, ironically enough, it was the "discoverer" of the Aleppo Codex himself who again took up the cudgels for the defense of the antiquity of the vowel points (Jacob Sapir, *Even Sapir*, p. ii, end [1874]).

scholars, at least unconsciously, always to detect the line of development. Different phenomena were conceived of as stages in a developmental sequence; the question was only: which preceded which and why.[38]

Whatever our attitude to some extreme contentions of the so-called "oral tradition" school, there is no doubt that during the past quarter of a century it has made scholars aware again of the power of "oral tradition" in Near Eastern cultures. Furthermore, we are much more willing today to acknowledge the existence of traditions side by side, and do not telescope them by force into an evolutionary chain.

20. The discussion of all the details of Kahle's theories on the Tiberian Bible text must be left for *Nosaḥ ha-Miqrā*. For the moment, I would suggest that it is precisely by practically negating the role of oral tradition and by forcing the facts into a developmental Procrustean bed, that Kahle was able to build his hypothesis. Since the Tiberian forms are different[39] from those of other traditions they are more recent,[40] and since the Hebrew language had long become extinct, the Tiberian Bible text is really no true tradition at all.[41] It is the invention of the Tiberian Masoretes. They

---

38. For the general attitude involved see my *Text and Language*, pp. 157ff.

39. See above, Note 7. Kahle, whose revolutionary stressing (since 1902!) of non-Tiberian traditions has made others aware of the problems of dialect traditions in the transmission of Hebrew, apparently never seriously considered the possibility of a plurality of traditions—none of which is necessarily per se inferior to any other—side by side with what may all the time have been the mainstream of tradition. For the present writer this way of explaining facts is an attitude basic both to his viewing the Masoretic consonantal text vis-à-vis the Bible Versions, the Dead Sea Scrolls, variants in Rabbinic literature, and so on, and to his estimation of the Tiberian Bible text vis-à-vis other reading traditions. See my *Text and Language*, pp. ix f., 51f., 156f., 161, and below, Note 43 and §49.

40. Recently Kahle has claimed that A. Murtonen, *Materials for a Non-Masoretic Hebrew Grammar*, I (Helsinki, 1958), has shown that "die Aussprache des Hebräischen in Palästina in der Zeit, ehe die Masoreten von Tiberias mit ihrer Arbeit begannen, im wesentlichen so gewesen ist, wie die Samaritaner heute noch in ihren Gottesdiensten die Tora rezitieren" (*Hebräischer Bibeltext*, p. 29). Furthermore (p. 68), this "palästinische Punktationsmethode . . . die heute noch bei den Samaritanern gebraucht wird [sic], von der Dr. Murtonen nachgewiesen hat, dass sie im wesentlichen identisch ist mit der Aussprache des Hebräischen, die . . . in liturgischen Texten [Only ?—*M.G.*] mit palästinischer Punktation . . . einst auch bei rabbanitischen Juden [sic] in Palästina bis zum 8/9 Jahrhundert üblich gewesen ist."

I cannot find the slightest basis for this claim in Murtonen's study, nor do I find that Murtonen has claimed this. What Murtonen's investigation of "Palestinian" texts has shown are, in my opinion, certain "Palestinian"–Samaritan isoglosses in addition to those previously known. *Vive la petite différence!* Cf. also below, Notes 65, 112.

41. Having rightly stressed the importance of the non-Tiberian traditions, Kahle went to extremes—in what might have been "discoverer's enthusiasm" at the time. In spite of what purported to be a rejoinder (Marti Festschrift, *BZAW* 41:167f. [1925], collected in *Opera Minora*, pp. 48f.), Kahle never succeeded in answering G. Bergsträsser,

invented, "restituted," and changed arbitrarily (see below, Note 49). Their model was, *horribile dictu*, no one else but the Qoran readers![42]

21. It is not my fault if this sounds like a caricature of critical method (see Note 44). In my submission Kahle's theory does not merely start from outdated ideas.[43] It is contrary to sound historical criticism. It postulates a textual situation unparalleled in the history of philology, and turns into reckless deceivers generations of Masoretic scholars who spent their lives to safeguard the "correct tradition" of the Bible, to the very best of their ability.[44] Even were we to possess what looks like a perfect proof, not just

who had protested (*OLZ* 19:582f. [1924]) that Kahle "lässt nur die nicht-'massoretischen' Vokalisationen überhaupt als Überlieferung gelten, so dass schon aus äusserem Grund das von ihnen Gebotene zu bevorzugen, die tiberienische Vokalisation also wie eine nachweislich entstellte Handschrift zu behandeln wäre." Bergsträsser's attitude is, of course, different from that of M. Kober (*Jeschurun* 17:149 [1930]). For Kober, the Tiberian Bible text is obviously the main tradition and the others are "only" dialects. For the problem (cf. also Note 39) see my *Nosaḥ ha-Miqrā*.

In order to prevent any misunderstanding, I should add that becoming aware of the non-Tiberian traditions is of vital importance for understanding the history of Hebrew (see above, §6), but they should not make us turn history upside down. Understanding a problem in historic-comparative linguistics and explaining the history of the Bible text are not necessarily the same thing. Especially with regard to the latter problem Kahle has overplayed his hand and has, besides, ignored any statement to the contrary by specialists. Thus, for example, he continuously adduces Origen's *Secunda* as one of the pillars of his theory. Apart from the fact that, in my opinion, his argument is doubtful, he never refuted in detail the result of what must still be regarded the most thorough monograph on that tradition, E. Brønno's *Studien über hebräische Morphologie und Vokalismus* (Leipzig, 1943), p. 462: "Die grosse Bedeutung der SEC [the Hebrew transcription column in Origen's Hexapla] für die hebr. Sprachwissenschaft liegt u.a. darin, dass diese alte Überlieferung deutlich zeigt, dass das tiberische Formensystem in seinen wesentlichen Hauptzügen eine alte Tradition hinter sich hat." One need not accept Brønno's verdict, but one might at least take the trouble to refute it.

42. Cf. Kahle's summary, *Cairo Geniza*, p. 170: "There need be no doubt that the impetus for revising the reading of the Hebrew text was given to the Masoretes by the Arab readers of the Koran." Not only do I not admit Kahle's claims with regard to the tradition of the Qoran itself, but in all his writings there is not the slightest evidence connecting the activity of the Masoretes with that of the Qoran readers. His whole argument is based on alleged analogy—no doubt a favorite way of proof with Kahle, brought to perfection in his treatment of the Bible versions.

43. Cf. above, Notes 7 and 39, and my *Text and Language*, pp. 157f. It is astonishing that Kahle, who stressed the pluralism of sources with regard to the Bible versions (cf. *Text and Language*, pp. 65f.), did not allow for this possibility with regard to the Hebrew reading traditions. I should like to use this opportunity to stress that while I firmly believe in the pluralism of traditions—and in our inability always to recover the first source *in practice* (*Text and Language*, pp. 156f.)—I do not accept Kahle's thesis that by necessity there was no "*Ur*-Septuagint" (as Strugnell, *JBL* 80:200 [1961], seems to have inferred). My wording in *Text and Language*, p. 160, is deliberate.

For another important aspect of the problem cf. S. Talmon's studies in *Textus* 1:144f., and *Scripta Hierosolymitana* 8:335f. (1961).

44. Cf. Note 50. Statements like those quoted there are painfully reminiscent of what Paul A. de Lagarde in his weak moments had to say about the "Jewish Masoretes."

theories, that the Tiberian Masoretes did what Kahle attributes to them—and what has entered since into most handbooks—we should rather disbelieve our "proofs."

22. One point of detail ought to be made now. Kahle has recently made much of the alleged Ḳaraite beliefs of the Ben Ashers (in both *Cairo Geniza* and *Der hebräische Bibeltext*). He has never paused to ask seriously: Given the relations between Ḳaraites and Rabbanites in the ninth century, is it at all conceivable that anyone could have interfered with the tradition of the Bible text in a way even remotely similar to Kahle's suggestions without causing an immediate outcry by his opponents? Whether the culprits were Rabbanites or Ḳaraites, the other party would have raised a storm.

The polemic literature of that time is not a total blank. Some of it was written very soon after the activity of the younger Ben Ashers, and it contains a good number of teasing remarks on textual and Masoretic matters. There is no doubt that neither side ever suspected the other of any tampering with the text—which according to Kahle was then of very recent occurrence. The very fact that there still exist doubts as to the creed of the Ben Ashers[45] should, indeed, suffice to highlight this point. Ḳaraites and Rabbanites alike must have hushed up their crime—presumably to please the Qoran readers.

23. What Kahle wishes us to assume on this subject is possible only if we completely ignore history.[46] According to him,[47] "from the fact that a Bible text established by Ḳaraite Masoretes [*sic*] was accepted as authorita-

---

It gives some food for thought that the type of Bible criticism prejudiced by evolutionary theory has ended, both in the "Higher" and the "Lower" field, by practically turning our only witnesses into deceivers, even if it was only *pia fraus*. Usurping the attribute "critical" for these theories becomes, of course, a mighty weapon against all "uncritical" dissenters. Cf. below, Notes 89 and 96 and §§ 33 and 47.

45. In "The Authenticity of the Aleppo Codex" I have repeatedly (cf. its § 33 and Notes 16 and 52) spoken of the *alleged* (my italics here) Ḳaraite creed of Ben Asher. This was intended to keep me out of the discussion (a full century old, begun with S. Pinsker's *Lickute Quadmonioth* [Vienna, 1860], pp. 32f.) about the creed of the Ben Ashers, because it was completely immaterial to my subject. On the basis of this expression, however, N. Alloni (*Ha-Aretz*, October 28, 1960) attacked me for my belief that the Ben Ashers were Rabbanites! I ought to state, therefore, that I do not hold such a belief. Although the issue may be included in *Nosaḥ ha-Miqrā* (I have tentatively prepared a chapter on the subject), the interesting fact for me at present is that a good case can be made out for each theory. It is this aspect that is of importance for our discussion.

46. For our argument we do not even have to invoke Bergsträsser's remark (*OLZ* 19:582f.): "Ist in diesen traditionsgebundenen Jahrhunderten eine solch kühne Reform, wie Kahle sie voraussetzt, denkbar?"

47. Cf. *JJS* 7:143 (1956).

tive throughout Jewry, by Rabbanites and Karaites alike, we must conclude that this acceptance must have taken place at a time when the relations between the two parties had not yet come to the critical stage that we know of at a later time."

When, then, did this happen? How did those Rabbanites pronounce "before" and how should we picture the development? I quote from Kahle's latest statement (*Der hebräische Bibeltext*, page 68): "Die Samaritaner haben eine Aussprache des Hebräischen bis auf den heutigen Tag festgehalten, welche die palästinische Punktation in alten Geniza-Fragmenten einst auch für die Aussprache des Hebräischen bei den rabbanitischen Juden bezeugt hat. [Cf. above, Note 40.] Bei diesen rabbanitischen Juden ist diese Aussprache aber abgelöst worden durch eine solche, die von den Masoreten ausgebildet worden ist, die ihren Sitz in Tiberias gehabt haben. Diese haben der im Laufe des 9. Jahrhunderts mächtig aufblühenden Gemeinde der Karäer angehört. Diese Aussprache ist dann [*sic*, necessarily not earlier than 900 C.E.—*M.G.*] aber von den rabbanitischen Juden übernommen und hat sich bei ihnen so vollständig durchgesetzt, dass jede Erinnerung an eine frühere Art der Aussprache des Hebräischen vollständig in Vergessenheit geraten war.[48] Man hat sich sogar mit Erfolg bemüht, alle Spuren zu verwischen, die uns Kunde davon gaben, dass die karäischen Masoreten eine neue Aussprache des Hebräischen ausgebildet und durchgeführt haben [*sic*] und auch den karäischen Ursprung der tiberischen Punktation hat man zu vergessen sich bemüht."

24. According to Kahle's picture, for which we are not offered a scrap of direct evidence,[49] we are requested to believe that there was a unique case of conspiracy between Rabbanites and Karaites in order to falsify

---

48. To keep chronology straight: according to this hypothesis, all this happened near the lifetime of people like Menahem Ben Saruq in Spain and Rabbenu Gershom in Germany—not to mention R. Saʿadya.

49. In order to give what seems a typical example of Kahle's argumentation, I adduce the following reasoning (*Hebräischer Bibeltext*, p. 67): "Wir müssen also damit rechnen, dass die tiberischen Masoreten eine neue Methode der Andeutung der Betonung der hebräischen Worte durchgeführt haben [Agreed—*M.G.*], die für die hebräische Grammatik, wie wir sie kennen, von grundlegender Bedeutung geworden ist. Das will aber besagen [*sic*], dass die Aussprache des Hebräischen wie wir sie auf Grund der tiberischen Punktation kennen, überhaupt erst eine Schöpfung der tiberischen Masoreten gewesen ist, des prominentesten unter ihnen, insbesonderer erst des grossen Masoreten Mosche ben Ascher, von dem der Kairoer Prophetenkodex eine der ganz grossen Leistungen ist." A perfect example of Kahle's *non sequiturs*. [May 1962: In *Textus* 2:2 (1962) we read that what "became the official language in Tiberias" is a "form of Hebrew created by the Tiberian Massoretes" (*sic*).]

purposely[50] the Bible text, hushed up by all concerned.[51] This took place almost at the height of the anti-Ḳaraite polemic trend (around 900 C.E.), and was accepted by authorities all over the world within a generation or two. Its aim was to enforce (against whom?) a text against live tradition, which had been modeled under the influence of Qoran readers. *Sapienti sat!*

25. I think that for the moment, leaving further details for the forthcoming Hebrew study, I made it clear that I think Kahle's widely accepted theories unfortunate, and that I should not like the stress I put on the novel character of the Aleppo Codex as a *written* document to be interpreted along the lines of Kahle's hypothesis.

In my opinion, the work of the Masoretes, which reached a peak in the Aleppo Codex, is to be understood as the invention and perfection of an ever more refined graphic notation for an age-old oral tradition[52] which endeavored to note down with the greatest possible exactness[53] the smallest details of the customary liturgical way of reading the Bible.[54]

---

50. Kahle, *Hebräischer Bibeltext*, p. 10: "Schliesslich kann es heute keine Frage mehr sein, dass die Masoreten von Tiberias *absichtlich* [My italics—M.G.] Änderungen der Aussprache des Hebräischen vorgenommen haben." (By the way, this is completely different from what some non-specialist *Haskala*-writers who sometimes expressed themselves similarly have meant.)

It is in the same vein that Kahle suggests (*JJS* 7:144 [1956])—again leveling his accusations without any evidence—that in order to hush up their fraudulent conspiracy, the Masoretes committed what by law was a heinous crime (when in fact they would rather have died than have committed it): "The Masoretes eliminated all remnants of earlier pronunciation so radically that no pre-Masoretic texts were allowed to be preserved. The first specimens of earlier punctuation to re-emerge were found in the Cairo Geniza [*sic*] where they had been stored *in order to be destroyed* [My italics—M.G.]."

51. In reality, even seemingly insignificant problems formed the subject of "teasing questions" and caused remarks in the polemical literature between Ḳaraites and Rabbanites; each party would surely have seized upon the smallest evidence of doubtful procedure in order to tease the other and to accuse it. These remarks are known in the literature for almost a century. They were republished by Strack in 1879 and 1897 and have appeared on numerous occasions since. Kahle prefers to ignore all this. See my *Nosaḥ ha-Miqrā*.

52. The explanations by medieval grammarians are not to be dismissed without eliciting some information (see Note 55). The need for writing down the tradition was, in my opinion, primarily an *inner* problem (dangers of sectarianism, deviating traditions over the centuries, didactic needs, etc.). Although this assumes that the main reasons were not *exterior* circumstances, which used to be thought responsible, I believe the invention of diacritic notation by the Syriac scribes was of greater importance than, e.g., S. W. Baron, *Social and Religious History of the Jews*, VI (New York, 1958), 241, wishes to allow. Cf. also my remarks on "The Diacritic Points in Syriac," *Tarbiz* 24:105f. (1955).

53. As shown by different opinions on methegs, erasures, and changes. Cf. §§ 10, 27, 30.

54. It should be made quite clear that in this case also, writing down a tradition is not the end of *oral tradition*, a fact not appreciated sufficiently by most European (and American) scholars. Thus the original custom of "indicating the accents" by movement

Critical scholarship should, no doubt, refrain from accepting at their face value the statements of the Masoretes (always including here the early punctuators) about their activity. But it is necessary to find out what those views were. Their testimony is largely identical with our view—with the necessary difference that for them the "tradition from time immemorial" was identified with the Revelation on Sinai,[55] with Ezra, with the Temple, and so on. Our thesis, to be sure, maintains solely that theirs was basically a living tradition (which probably had undergone slight diachronic

---

of the hand continued long after th invention of the signs (which, to be sure, were never introduced into the scrolls). Cf. Rashi's note on the Talmudic dictum (*Berakhoth*, 62a): מפני שמראה בה טעמי תורה ("for one uses it [i.e., one's right hand] for indicating Torah accents"): "One moves one's hand according to the cantillation accent; I have seen readers [doing] this who came from Palestine." Similarly S. Baer and H. L. Strack, *Dikduke*, § 17 (*Die Dikduke Ha-Te'amim des Ahron ben Moscheh ben Ascher* [Leipzig, 1879]), speak of an accent יוצאת ביד ברעדה ("going tremblingly forth from the hand"). J. Qâfih mentions (*Sinai* 29:262 [1951]) that this custom is still alive in Yemen.

The relationship between quoting by heart and melodious accentuation was well realized in the Middle Ages; cf. *Tosafoth* on *Megilla* 32a. Cf. J. Yeivin, *Leshonenu* 24:48 (1960), who quotes Saʿadya's justification for the use of accents in his writings: ליכון אסהל לקראתה ואמכן לחפט׳ה ("so that it is easier to read and to memorize").

It would also seem that the famous fragments from the Cairo Geniza of so-called "Short-hand Bibles" (published first, I think, by A. Neubauer, *JQR* 7:361ff. [1894] and analyzed first by M. Friedländer [*ibid.*, p. 564]) throw an interesting sidelight on the relationship between written text and oral tradition. [May 1962: See also the material published by Yeivin, *Textus* 2:120f.] Another aspect of the problem, merely to be hinted at, is the non-Tiberian reading habits of various Jewish communities in disregard of their Tiberian Bible text (see above, Note 7; see especially—also for non-Biblical texts—S. Morag, *Leshonenu La-ʿAm* 73:22f. [1957], and the literature there and in *Leshonenu La-ʿAm* 74:73; also *Tarbiz* 30:121 [1960]). Furthermore, the fate of texts written by scribes of different traditional reading habits—such as "Sefardis" (see below, Notes 65 and 112) and Yemenites who ostensibly tried to reproduce the Tiberian Bible text (see my "Biblical Manuscripts," pp. 39ff.) shows the power of traditions long after the Tiberian Bible text had become "officially" accepted.

55. The varying details as to the origin of the oral tradition and its subsequent graphic fixation are of considerable interest, but they are outside our scope. The usual picture of medieval grammarians—not by necessity identical with that of the Masoretes and punctuators themselves—runs somewhat like this: וכאן אלסייד אלרסול יתלי עליה אלנץ ויחכמהם קראתה באלרפע ואלצ׳אם ואלנצב ואלכפט׳ ואלמסך ואלמפתח ואלקטע ואלוצל וכל אלאעראב. וכאנת כלהא ענדהם חרכאת אללסאן ואליד איצ׳א כמא קאלו ״לא יקנח בימין שמראה בה טעמי תורה״ (ברכות סב, ע״א). והד׳א הו אלחכם אלחקיקי. וכאן ד׳לך ענדהם תלקין מן צדר אלי צדר. פלמא ראוא אבתדא אלגלות ותשתת אללגה אלי שוא כ׳שוא עלי אנקטאעה ודת׳ורה מן אלמלה פקאמוא ושכלוא וצווררא ..... (A. Neubauer, *Petite Grammaire hébraïque* [Leipzig, 1891], p. 23)—"And Moses used to read the text before them and securely taught them all the different ways of vocalization. All these were movements of the mouth and also of the hand, as the Sages put it: 'One should not wipe oneself with the right hand, because one uses it for indicating the Torah accents.' This is the true custom, and this used to be the way of dictating all of it. But once they saw that the Diaspora had started and that the language had become confused [literally: torn to parts], they were afraid that [the language] might become cut off and forgotten by the Nation. So they started to put signs and marks." To be sure, this is a standard explanation for the change-over from oral tradition. Cf. Rashi *ad Bābā Məṣiʿā* 33a.

changes).[56] The Masoretes were convinced, rightly in their way, that they
were keeping up an ancient tradition, and interfering with it purposely
would have been for them the worst crime possible. Yet they were extremely proud, quite justifiedly, of their own achievement:[57] the graphic notation
and its perfection, so as to safeguard the ancient tradition for all future
generations.[58] It was this double belief in the antiquity of the tradition and

---

The ideas as to when the fixation in writing occurred are clearly expressed in "Manuel
du Lecteur," ed. J. Dérenbourg, *JA* 16:361 [1870]: ‏ואם יאמר אדם מי חבר אלה המלכים וכן‎
‏הטעמים והתקין צורתן כמו שהן עתה בידינו, ידע תחלה כי צורתן הוא ממה שחברו עליו האחרונים‎
‏ואמרו: זו היא צורת הקמצה וזו היא צורת הפתחה וכו'... וכולן הסכימו על זה ועשו אותן סימנין ללמוד‎
‏וללמד בהן. יש מי שאומר מימות עזרא הן שכתבו אותן והעלו להן אלו הצורות... ויש מי שאומר מקודם‎
‏עזרא,וזה שאמרנו: בצורתן ושמוחן. אבל עניינם ממשה מסיני כמו תורה שבעל פה, והיו על פה כותבין תיבות‎
‏הפסוק בלא מלכים ולא טעמים וקורין אותו כתקון כמו ששמעו ממשה... וכן קבלו איש מפי איש. וכיון‎
‏שראו שהתחילה הגלות ונתבלבלה הלשון עמדו וסמנום וחקקום ונקדו בהן החומשין כדי שילמדום הכל במהרה‎
‏ותהיה הלשון הכל צחה בלשון הקדש על פי הדקדוק ששמעו ממשה מסיני.‎" (My emphasis—*M.G.*)
"If someone says: Who invented these vowels and accents and who fixed the forms as
we have them now—let him know, to begin with, that their form was decided on by the
later generations who said: This is the form of a *qamaṣ* or a *pataḥ* . . . So they all agreed
and made the signs for learning and teaching purposes [*sic*]. Some say that the writing
down and invention of graphic signs occurred in the days of Ezra . . . and some say before
him. But the matter itself comes from Moses on Sinai and was oral tradition like the Oral
Law. One wrote without vowels and accents, but read them, just as one heard it from
Moses . . . and they handed them from generation to generation. But once they saw that
the Diaspora had started and that the language had become confused [Because of ‏נתבלבל‎
in this text I slightly twisted the translation of ‏תשתח‎ above—*M.G.*], they began to mark
them and to fix them and they vocalized the codices so that everyone could quickly learn
them and use a correct language according to the exact way they had heard from Moses
on Sinai."
    Allowing for the difference of eleven or twelve centuries, these medieval descriptions
are truer to the substance of the facts than the theories of Kahle. For another interesting
aspect of medieval attitudes I refer meanwhile to the text in Levy, *Zur Masoretischen
Grammatik*, ‏לה‎.
    56. I need not add that the emphasis on the true traditional character of the Tiberian
Bible text does not in any way detract from the value of other oral traditions—"dialects,"
so to speak—whether they were written down or not (see above, §6). That the other traditions finally bowed to the Tiberian Bible text and that the superiority of ‏קראה אלשאמי‎
became universally recognized (cf. Yaʿqūb al-Qirqisānī, *Kitāb al-ʾAnwār*, I, 139) is
the outcome of historical circumstances, although the feeling that the Babylonian tradition was less accurate (‏תנבסת קראתהם‎, *loc. cit.*) is noteworthy. But the fact that it *did* happen
seems to me another important indication against Kahle's thesis. See below, Note 118.
    57. As is evident from many passages in Baer-Strack, *Die Dikduke*, etc., and from
Moses Ben Asher's remarks. See also above, Note 18.
    58. This point ought to be stressed because even in the latest discussion of this apparent
contradiction (M. Zucker's refutation of B. Klar, *Tarbiz* 27:63f. [1958]) the matter has
not been fully explored. As for the views of the Masoretes themselves on the graphic
notation, the analysis of the sources adduced by Klar (*Tarbiz* 14:156f. [1943]; 15:36f.
[1944], collected in his posthumous *Meḥqārim wǝ-ʿIyyūnīm* [Tel-Aviv, 1954], pp. 276ff.),
A. Dothan (*Sinai* 41:280f., 350f. [1957]), Zucker (*Tarbiz* 27:63f.) and Kahle (*JJS*
7:140 [1956]) make me definitely side with all the latter against Klar's contention that the
Masoretes themselves believed the graphic signs to be old. (This does not mean that I
accept, for example, all the details of Dothan's remarks.) What the Masoretes believed
was that the *accents* and so on were old, but not so their *signs*. No quotation adduced

the novelty of the graphic notation[59] which explains, in my opinion, all contemporaneous statements on the subject.[60]

26. In order to avoid unnecessary discussions, let us state that our understanding of the activities of the Masoretes does not deny that the very process of fixing a final graphic notation possibly necessitated certain very minor adjustments which might have been sometimes against the oral custom (of a minority or the majority of Masoretes?). In certain matters of accentuation—especially with regard to *ga'yas*, the vast majority of the *hillufim* (see below, Note 109)—the *Systemzwang* might have been strong.[61] But it is precisely the fact ignored until now that such minute differences were noted down with unbelievable exactness and that different Tiberian graphic notations turn out on examination to represent identical phonetic systems (see below, Section VII) that proves the underlying practically uniform[62] oral tradition, common to all, which is the basis of our Tiberian Bible text.

To my knowledge it has never been spelled out that all the much publicized differences in graphic habits[63] among all the Tiberian Masoretes, as far as our knowledge goes, never amounted to more than shades of

necessitates Klar's assumption and, as a personal conviction, I would never assume without clinching arguments that scholars did not know what had happened a few generations before their time. After all, the matter was known in roughly contemporaneous Responsa (cf. Klar, *Tarbiz* 14 : 170, who raises the problem of the authorship of certain Responsa).

59. A good formulation is given by the anonymous author quoted in *Mahzor Vitry* (cf. Klar, *loc. cit.*, p. 170). While it is continuously quoted in connection with the three vocalization systems its main subject is easily neglected: שטעמי נגינות הם שנאמרו למשה. ... אבל סימני הנגינות סופרים הוא שתקנום, ולפיכך אין נקוד טברני דומה לנקוד שלנו ולא שניהם דומים לנקוד ארץ ישראל. "The cantillation *accents* were, indeed, revealed to Moses ... but the *signs* [My italics—M.G.] were arranged by the Scribes, and for this reason the Tiberian vocalization is not like ours and are both different from the Palestinian one."

60. The Karaite attitude remains to be discussed (see my *Nosah ha-Miqrā*). For the moment suffice it to state (with a reference to Qirqisānī) that the belief in the antiquity of the graphic signs was by no means the accepted Karaite theory around 900 C.E.

61. To give another example: I think it possible that some adjustments were made in questions of the realization of the *zero vowel* after faucals. This is a very far cry from Kahle's theory of "restitution." See Note 64.

62. In certain cases the fixation in writing, accepted by all, surely tended to obscure traditional differences in pronunciation. The *locus classicus* is for me the document republished in Levy, *Zur masoretischen Grammatik* (cf. his pp. 20 and 31 and, earlier, J. Mann, *The Jews in Egypt and in Palestine*, II [London, 1922], 43) that the spelling שתי obscured the tradition of pronouncing *aštē* etc., as pronounced by Ben Asher himself and all other "Tiberians": וגמיע אהל טבריה הד׳א מעהם באלתלקין ואן כאן עלתה לא יערפונהא ולא יעלמון מא הי—"All Tiberians have this by oral teaching even if they do not know its reason."

63. This includes what I think is a Ben Naftali text as well as what Kahle thinks it is. See below, Section VII. Our statement does not deal, of course, with the classical issue of *Inconsequenzen der hebräischen Punktation.*

phonetic realization,[64] one vowel-phoneme (possibly)[65] and the "famous contraction" to *wī, lī, yē*.[66] To that degree did the Masoretes succeed in disguising the origins of their "artificial invention," until they were unmasked by Kahle.

V. Mishael's *Ḥillufim* and the Ben Asher Codices

27. Having dealt with the origins out of which the work of the Ben Ashers grew, we now have to turn to the codices themselves which are linked

64. The vast literature on the problem of pronouncing *shəva/ḥaṭaf*—i.e., the question of free variants of the zero vowel—makes it clear that this was regarded as the gravest problem. In number, of course, the differences on the *gaʿya* overshadowed everything else. See Note 109.

65. I am paraphrasing mainly the statement about the differences between the Masoretes (Levy, *Zur masoretischen Grammatik*, י): קד אכ׳תלפוא פי אשיא כת׳ירה מן קמץ ופתח ותנתין ולת׳לת׳ה ושוא סאכן ושוא מתחרך. "They differed in many matters with regard to *qamaṣ* and *pataḥ*, *ṣere* and *segol*, quiescent and mobile *shəva*."

While the opposition of the graphemes .. versus ·· cannot be said to be phonemic in the Tiberian Bible text—although there are signs of a beginning phonemization—the opposition - versus ᴛ certainly is. It is conceivable that some of the early Tiberian Masoretes tried, indeed, to represent graphically another tradition which did not have the opposition [å]:[a]—a tradition later on to be labeled "Sefardi"; see Notes 54, 109, and 112. But I doubt that this was felt as a problem within the Tiberian Bible text, or that within that earlier tradition out of which the Tiberian text grew there was a problem as to the phonemic opposition between these vowels. However, although the question does not seem to have been studied until now, I should like to point out that a case can be made out for the Tiberian Bible text type of vocalization being secondary to a "Tiberian grapheme" system which in fact was "proto-Sefardi"; for the way in which all ancient manuscripts write the *qamaṣ* (ᴛ) gives some food for thought. Cf. also Notes 109, 112.

I doubt, however, that this whole problem did exist within the Tiberian Bible text tradition. That is, although I have taken care to indicate the possibility in the text, I believe that within the Tiberian Bible text tradition there were no phonemic oppositions. The text adduced before would hardly have mentioned this matter in such an incidental fashion; moreover, arguments about such a problem would have left their mark in quite a different way. In my opinion, these differences within the Tiberian Bible text refer to exactly the type of *hillufim* quoted for Ben Asher–Ben Naftali, mainly dependent on the degree of stress. See below, Note 109.

To the problem hinted at above, I should like to add that the question of a "proto-Sefardi" vocalization—not merely a reading tradition, which would be obvious—has been on my mind for some time. "Proto-" is to be understood in a similar way to the now already fashionable "Proto-" traditions of the "Latter" Greek versions. (For the Syriac versions see my *Text and Language*, p. 198.) The question is tied up with the "Palestinian" use of graphemes, but our "Tiberian" manuscripts known at present are of too late a date, and arguments are bound to lead to a vicious circle. Were our paleographic knowledge larger, we might at least find out a little more about the vexing question: in what places did reading habits conflict with the intention of scribes to reproduce the "official" Tiberian Bible text? While "geographical paleography" is still a dream, it need not be pointed out—especially after the work of scholars like H. Yalon and Y. G. F. Gumpertz—that "Sefardi" is simply an a posteriori label, both in the historic and in the "prehistoric" (i.e., before 900 c.e.) dimensions. For the whole issue—also with regard to Sperber's claims in *HUCA* 16:450 (1941)—see my *Nosaḥ ha-Miqrā*. See also above, Notes 17 and 21 and my "Biblical Manuscripts," pp. 42f., 47f.

66. The *hilluf wəyi > wī, yəye > yē* etc. is, of course, the major phonetic difference between Ben Asher and Ben Naftali. See below, Note 108.

with their name, as well as to Mishael Ben ʿUzziel's famous treatise on the differences (*ḥillufim*) between Ben Asher and Ben Naftali.

For the last quarter of a century Mishael's treatise had become the proof-stone used by Kahle—especially thanks to the investigations of his student Lipschütz[67]—and others to investigate the possible Ben Asher character of a manuscript. There can be no doubt that Mishael's treatise is largely superior to other lists of differences between the versions of Ben Asher and Ben Naftali[68] and in the first days of our investigation of the Aleppo Codex it was a most welcome help. I feel therefore guilty of ingratitude if I have to stress now that the readings of Mishael prove in no way a rival to the Aleppo Codex. In fact, as regards our knowledge of the Ben Asher text, it has practically become superfluous through the Aleppo Codex.[69] This does not mean that the details of Mishael's list are not instructive or need not be published.[70] But the main importance of the list lies now in its Ben Naftali readings (see Notes 68 and 87). Since the character of the Aleppo Codex has been established, the procedure must be reversed. It is the Aleppo Codex that is now our yardstick for judging the character of other manuscripts—and for judging Mishael.[71]

28. This claim has to be explained. Given the result that the treatise of Mishael has been shown to be generally correct in its quotations of Ben Asher readings, we must ask: "Do these readings practically reflect the text of the Aleppo Codex, or do they differ considerably from it?" If the latter were the case, we would have to explore seriously the possibility that there was in existence *another* text attributed to Aaron Ben Asher,

67. In his introduction and edition of *Ben Ašer–Ben Naftali* (1935). Owing to the persecution in Germany, the dissertation was never published in full. See Note 70.

68. Cf. also H. Yalon, *Kiryat Sefer* 30:258 (1955). To my knowledge, no one has ever seriously troubled to find out whether all the other lists of *ḥillufim*—many of which were published in Ginsburg's *Massorah*, *s.v.* חלופים—are really as worthless as they were made out to be (cf. Lipschütz, *Ben Ašer–Ben Naftali*, pp. 2f.). The main problem is that we have few means of finding out which of the *ḥillufim* contained in these and not contained in Lipschütz are true ones and whether they have been handed down correctly. However, with the help of the Aleppo Codex some material can probably be salvaged. This would by now be important mainly for the readings of Ben Naftali.

69. The *ḥillufim* remain of practical interest for the Ben Asher text only in the part which is already published—because it is missing in the Aleppo Codex—and in its few readings in the end of the Hagiographa.

70. I understand that the original editor, Lipschütz, who was forced to discontinue his publication (see Note 67), is now ready to publish the whole treatise. [May 1962: Published just recently through the Hebrew University Bible Project, *Textus* 2: אff. (Jerusalem, 1962); see below, Note 109.] In *Hebräischer Bibeltext*, p. 16, Kahle announced that Lacave also is preparing an edition—which seems unnecessary duplication. However, at this stage it is the checking of Mishael's list against the Aleppo Codex on which all the results depend. The data as analyzed by me will be given in *Nosaḥ ha-Miqrā*.

71. I have hinted at this in *Text and Language*, p. x.

apart from the Aleppo Codex, considered equally authoritative, so that a Masoretic scholar like Mishael could use it for his list. That would be a strong indication against the unique position we claim for the Aleppo Codex and might mean that we cannot reach the archetype of the text of Aaron Ben Asher (see my *Text and Language*, pages 156f.)

29. The opposite is the case. A comparison of the whole of Mishael's text to the Aleppo Codex yields about one to two per cent discrepancies. It would be, indeed, against sound practice to make these astonishingly few differences bear the weight of such a far-going hypothesis as suggested above (for argument's sake only). The solution is self-evident: the Aleppo Codex is an original autograph. Mishael's list, as we possess it, is as good a tool as we can hope for. But it is a *copy of a secondary compilation.*[72]

Because of possible future arguments I would like to add that in all publications by Kahle the tenth or eleventh century has been given as the time for Mishael's treatise.[73] It is, however, customary in investigating documents to comment on both the possible date of authorship and of the copy itself. For some reason I do not find that Kahle ever commented on the latter point. A final statement could be made only after examining the original fragments which Kahle used. But a careful analysis of Kahle's transcription makes me suggest that the copy is hardly earlier than the thirteenth century—at least three centuries after the Aleppo Codex.[74] So much for our claim that in spite of its superiority to other lists Mishael's

---

72. It is difficult to know whether Mishael's original list looked different from the copy we possess. But the astonishing unevenness in adducing readings—sometimes one reading for a large number of chapters leaving serious lacunae, make one wonder what degree of exhaustiveness the author had intended. Or was it just a checklist for scribes? The fact as such as been noted by Lipschütz, *Ben Ašer–Ben Naftali*, pp. 6f.

It certainly strikes one as ironical that the first *ḥilluf* quoted in the "official" technical literature on the Pentateuchal text is not included in Lipschütz. It is quoted by Mena-ḥem di Lonzano, *'Or Torah* (Homburg, 1738) on Gen. 1:14 יהי מארת. See below, Note 121.

73. There is no proof for that date but also none against it. Cf. A. Ben David in *Beth Miqrā* 3:17f. (1958). The eleventh century is possible as a *terminus ante quem*, but is not proved. Kahle's suggestion of the tenth century (since *Masoreten des Westens*, II, 60*) is a guess which has not gained force from repetition.

74. My claim is mainly based on the following fact. In Kahle's transcript I find a number of interchanges of *segol-pataḥ*, e.g.:

אֶל בֵּאפֶך (Jer. 10:24), וּנבוכדרצר (Dan. 3:2; Jer. 34:1), וַאתן נום (Ezek. 16:12) וַאקח לי (Zech. 11:7), אשתחוה (Ps. 5:8) וַאל תאסר, (Ps. 69:16) etc.

[May 1962: None of these is given in the edition of Lipschütz; see above, Note 70, and below, Note 109.] They are too numerous to be simple mistakes and he must have copied these from the manuscripts (without being aware, at the time, of their importance as evidence). If so, the fragments must be of Yemenite provenance. This leaves the thirteenth century as *terminus post quem* for our copy. This analysis disposes of all exaggerated claims which anyone might care to put forward with regard to our copy of Mishael.

treatise is obviously far from being perfect.[75] In any event we are not entitled to assume because of the few discrepancies that Mishael's list bears witness to another Ben Asher tradition.

30. Our next step is to find out whether our claim for the Aleppo Codex is invalidated by the only other complete codex of the Bible connected with Aaron Ben Asher's name in a colophon: the Leningrad Codex.

If we follow Kahle's pronouncements on the subject carefully, there can be no doubt that he accepted the Leningrad Codex, in the first place, as a basis for the third edition of the Stuttgart Biblia Hebraica only *faute de mieux*. Even though he had never seen more than the photograph of the one page of the Aleppo Codex, he would have preferred to use the Aleppo Codex.[76] However, once the Leningrad Codex had to be chosen, its value rose slowly but steadily in consecutive descriptions, until it became the primary Ben Asher text.[77] But for our recovery of the true Ben Asher text, the Leningrad Codex would have stood unchallenged and all other manuscripts of the Tiberian Bible text would have been judged by it.[78]

Our earlier study[79] left no doubt that the Leningrad Codex is no rival to the Aleppo Codex and that it should not be used as a yardstick to measure other manuscripts. In the best case we might take its colophon at its face value and make the codex a copy harmonized with the Ben Asher text according to some copies which bore Ben Asher's name.[80] But it is clear by now that the Leningrad Codex was basically not a Ben Asher codex. It was secondarily brought into harmony with a Ben Asher *Vorlage* by

75. From a different angle Ben David (*Beth Miqrā* 3:17f.) has come to a similar result, without any connection with the problem of the Aleppo Codex.

76. See the introduction to the Biblia Hebraica, p. vi.

77. In Kahle's *Hebräischer Bibeltext*, p. 9, we finally come upon the unbelievable statement that the Leningrad Codex is the "älteste vollständige Ben Ascher–Handschrift." Or does Kahle wish to elevate the Leningrad Codex to that position because the Aleppo Codex has recently been mutilated by vandals? (See President Ben-Zvi's description, *Textus* 1:1f. [1960].)

78. This is not quite correct. Without having the Aleppo Codex at his disposal, Yalon had become suspicious of the many erasures in the Leningrad Codex (*Kiryat Sefer* 30:259 [1955]; cf. *ibid.* 32:100 [1957]). See also F. Perez-Castro, *Sefarad* 15:27f. (1955). Kahle says now (*Hebräischer Bibeltext*, p. 77) that the corrections and erasures were known to the editors of the Biblia Hebraica. It might have been useful to state all the facts thirty years ago. From R. Kittel's introduction to the Biblia Hebraica (p. iv) these could hardly be inferred.

79. See my "Authenticity of the Aleppo Codex," § 13f. See also Löwinger, *Textus* 1:64f. (1960).

80. See above, Note 34. For the moment I do not wish to press the point that the Leningrad Codex has a colophon in the first person singular which does not put forward the claim of connection with Ben Asher (fol. 474a). It is the colophon in the third person (fol. 479a) that does this. At the time of writing I have no means of checking on the question of handwriting.

endless erasures and changes. This procedure is, in my opinion, of great importance as proof for the status which Aaron's text must have had in the generation after he passed away and should be taken as strengthening our claims as to his position (see below, Note 91). The Leningrad Codex was turned very successfully into a Ben Asher codex and was not too bad a substitute. But it stands to reason that if no direct copy can be a rival to the archetype, a harmonized manuscript can do this even less well. We have no way of knowing whether the deviations of the Leningrad Codex from the Aleppo Codex can even be taken to represent the readings of Ben Asher codices (assumed for argument's sake) of *parts* of the Bible.[81] But surely they challenge the unique position of the Aleppo Codex.

As matters stand today we have no right to assume that the Leningrad Codex represents in any way a genuine Ben Asher tradition where it differs from the Aleppo Codex.[82] Needless to add, that this makes its reproduction as the basic text of a new scholarly edition of the Bible an anachronism.[83]

31. None of our sources, then, disproves the unique position we have claimed for the Aleppo Codex—although I should like to stress that there is naturally no possibility of obtaining clinching positive proof. While the codices of *parts* of the Bible are still of interest, we can study at the moment only British Museum Or. 4445[84] and have to wait until the Leningrad

81. It should be stressed that for my general hypothesis I do not have to assume that there was no other authentic Ben Asher tradition apart from the Aleppo Codex. It happens to be a fact that there remains no basis for such an assumption and, as far as we can see now, there is no text which clearly represents such a tradition. Were we to find such a manuscript, it could be taken as representing other codices by Ben Asher of parts of the Bible. Note that the colophons speak of ספרים מוגהים in the plural, and the copyist surely did not intend to present an eclectic text-edition of Ben Asher codices! I speak of colophons in the plural because of the codex from Tschufutkale (allegedly written in 989 C.E.; referred to in Baer-Strack, *Dikduke*, p. xxvii). For the time being the matter of the genuineness of that codex from Firkowich's collections must naturally be left in abeyance. (This question should not be confused with the completely different issue of fifteenth-century Yemenite manuscripts; see below, Note 133, and my "Biblical Manuscripts," pp. 47f.)

At the moment it is anybody's guess whether any other manuscript in the Firkowich collections puts forward similar claims and whether the suspiciously similar wording is a sign of early widespread esteem for Aaron Ben Asher—or whether it indicates Firkowich's tampering with the colophon. See above, Note 23, and my "Biblical Manuscripts," p. 50.

82. I need hardly add that this is different from the negative judgment passed on the Leningrad Codex by A. Harkavy and later by J. L. Teicher. Cf. A. E. Harkavy and H. L. Strack, *Catalog der hebräischen Bibelhandschriften der Kaiserlichen Öffentlichen Bibliothek in St. Petersburg* (St. Petersburg, 1875), pp. 263f.; Teicher, *JJS* 2:20f. (1950). See also below, Note 89.

83. Just as an eclectic edition of the text of the "Ben Asher family" would be. See my "Authenticity," n. 55, and below, Note 90.

84. The most exhaustive study of sample passages of that codex is the somewhat unknown article of A. Ramírez, *Biblica* 10:200ff. (1929), 11:108ff. (1930), 14:303ff. (1933). On this occasion I should like to query the statement, copied by one author from

material mentioned by Kahle in *Masoreten des Westens* (I, 56f.) becomes available again.

After examining the British Museum codex in the original I have no doubt that this is not a harmonized manuscript—there are, of course, the normal few erasures. But I am afraid I cannot agree that it could be a substitute for the missing part of the Aleppo Codex. To be sure, it is very close to the subsystem of Ben Asher, and if we put the (wrong) alternatives: Ben Asher or Ben Naftali—according to Lipschütz's *Mischael*—it definitely looks like Ben Asher.[85] But one of the valuable aspects of Mishael's list is that it also lists cases where Ben Asher and Ben Naftali agree against some other Masorete who, generally speaking, belonged to the same tradition. In a certain number of cases British Museum Or. 4445 agrees with such a reading which is neither Ben Asher nor Ben Naftali.[86]

In this case our investigation leads, indeed, to a clear result which is no less astonishing: as far as our present knowledge of manuscripts goes, the Aleppo Codex is not just the superior known representative of Aaron Ben Asher's text; *it is the only known true representative.*

VI. Moses Ben Asher and Moses Ben Naftali

32. The next step must be to examine anew the relationship of the Aleppo Codex—and the codices which are similar to it—with the Cairo Codex of the Prophets written by Aaron's father, Moses Ben Asher. This question is inextricably bound up with the age-old problem of the so-called Masoretic rival systems of Ben Asher and Ben Naftali.

Even though we objected (above, §29) to any possible claims for absolute correctness on the part of Mishael's list, we nevertheless found it to be an excellent working tool. If its quotations from Ben Asher are, in

---

the other (Ramirez, 10:203), that the Masoretic annotator of that manuscript must have lived during the lifetime of Aaron Ben Asher. The alleged reason is the lack of the eulogistic formula when Ben Asher is mentioned in the margin. In my opinion this is an unsatisfactory criterion to prove the age of a document. No one has ever shown that a note, supposedly written in the tenth century, mentioning somebody's name in the margin (not in a colophon!) should have added the formula if the person mentioned was no longer alive.

85. I hinted at this in *Text and Language*, p. x, by calling both the Leningrad Codex and British Museum Or. 4445 *codices mixti* from the point of view of the Aleppo Codex. See also below, §42f.

86. Perez-Castro (*Sefarad* 15:27f.) seems to have neglected this necessary part of the examination. For this reason the British Museum Codex seemed to him more of a Ben Asher text than it actually is. I understand from J. Yeivin that he has meanwhile come to similar conclusions with regard to the character of the British Museum manuscript, whereas Löwinger (*Textus* 1:93) takes the latter as the best possible Ben Asher text to serve as a complement to the Aleppo Codex.

the main, correct, it stands to reason that a similar degree of correctness should be assumed for its quotations from Ben Naftali. The latter we must, for the moment, accept solely on the authority of Mishael,[87] since we possess no manuscript which claims, or is proved to represent, the text of Ben Naftali.[88] Mishael's list is then by necessity our sole proven criterion.

33. It is precisely this decisive document that seems to cast suspicion on the oldest dated Biblical manuscript in our possession: the Cairo Codex of the Prophets. For, judging by Mishael's list, the Cairo Codex is much more a Ben Naftali manuscript than a Ben Asher manuscript. In fact, but for the colophon, the Cairo Codex would have surely been acclaimed as the outstanding distinguished representative of the Ben Naftali tradition. Hence we are led, so it seems, to the logical conclusion that the colophon of this earliest dated Hebrew Bible manuscript is a forgery.[89]

87. Hence our statement above (§ 27) that the main importance of Mishael's list now lies in its quotations from Ben Naftali.

88. See my statement in *Text and Language*, pp. ix f. No one seems to have considered the possibility that there was never such a thing as a "pure" Ben Naftali manuscript and that Ben Naftali's main contribution was to compile his dissenting annotations on the Ben Asher tradition, to which he adhered in general (see below, Note 117). There is nothing to prove such an assumption, but for that matter nothing to disprove it either, and we should at least be aware of the possibility. In fact, I doubt very much whether Ben Naftali ever produced a model codex of the complete Bible comparable in its scope to the Aleppo Codex. See below, Note 100.

On the other hand, the fragment (Strack, *Zeitschrift für die Lutherische Theologie*, 36:617; in Baer-Strack, *Dikduke*, p. xii) of which Kahle (*Masoreten des Westens*, II, 50*) tried to dispose in order to develop his own theory (see below, Section VII), and on which Ben Naftali's name apparently occurs, is still a possibility as a Ben Naftali text. However, the matter cannot be proved. The whole issue hinges on exactly one accent, and this is hardly enough to go by. Yeivin has recently discussed the problem (*Tarbiz* 29:346 [1960]), and his conjecture as to that one accent is borne out by Mishael's list.

Incidentally, I would think that after Mishael we must finally accept Moses Ben David Ben Naftali as the correct name (not Jacob Ben Naftali, as accepted especially on the authority of Levita, who, in any case, did not know too much about Ben Naftali; see below, Notes 109, 133). The above fragment is obviously defective, and to call Ben Naftali David Ben Naftali, as Yeivin does, may cause additional confusion.

All the other manuscripts recently suggested as possibly from Ben Naftali's hand are by necessity at best *codices mixti*. Cf. Yalon, *Kiryat Sefer* 30:258f.; Perez-Castro, *Homenaje a Millas-Vallicrosa*, II (Barcelona, 1950), 141f., and Yeivin, *Tarbiz* 29:346. See also Ben David, *Beth Miqrā* 3:15 (1958). Sassoon Codex 507 may come nearest to the subsystem connected with Ben Naftali's name. See below, §42f.

89. For the most recent accusations along these lines and my position, see my "Authenticity," nn. 55, 15. Löwinger (*Textus* 1:93) tries to solve the problem by assuming that the Cairo Codex is "a secondary copy made on the basis of a manuscript written at the time by Moses ben Asher, but that during the process of copying, fundamental changes in punctuation and accents were made on the basis of considerations unknown to us." This is nothing else but denying the colophon of the Cairo Codex. It should be stated that during the last decade only Kahle has stood up against this trend.

For our purpose it is immaterial whether we assume a forgery or the transfer of the colophon from another manuscript. These doubts with regard to the Cairo Codex are, of course, again materially different from those of nineteenth-century scholars who denied

In my opinion, this type of solution to our difficulties should never be suggested except as a very last resort, the more so since scholars are apparently prone by nature to prove their critical acumen by casting suspicions on our most distinguished and ancient sources (see above, Note 44). My own thesis is, I submit, a bit less drastic. To my mind it is our own habit of talking of a "Ben Asher text"—without qualifying *which* Ben Asher, and tacitly assuming the identity of the texts of father and son[90]— that has created this problem which has led, in the last instance, to accusations of forgery or willful tampering.

34. Medieval scholars talking of Ben Asher were exclusively referring to the one whose text had become the final authority. Once history had been changed through the great achievement of a complete Bible codex, all earlier attempts became prehistory, and no one bothered much about Aaron's father.[91]

---

the Ben Asher relationship because the early codices did not fit the Baer–Wickes rules on the *metheg*. See above, Note 82, and my "Authenticity," §3f. For that view see A. Neubauer, *Studia Biblica et Ecclesiastica*, 3:25 (1891). In this case, too, Strack did not accept the judgment, but again gave no reasons; see my "Authenticity," n. 14.

I cannot help directing the reader's attention to the commonsense remark of Richard Gottheil (*JQR* 18:566 [1906]), who never claimed to be an authority on the Masora, against the absurd results of critics (see above, Note 44). According to the authorities of the day, he muses, the same strange fate has overcome our two most ancient Hebrew Bible manuscripts. Both the codex of the father (Cairo Codex) and the codex of the son (Aleppo Codex) have turned out to have forged colophons!

90. This tacit assumption has, in my opinion, misled Cassuto and made him attempt a reconstruction of a text which never existed (see my "Authenticity," n. 55, and Note 83, above). Kahle, on the other hand, wishes to minimize the differences between the Aleppo and Cairo codices so as to make Aaron into almost the copyist of his father's work. Although he allows for slight changes of mind—Or. 4445 is for him a "Text aus Ahron ben Ascher's früherer Zeit" (*Hebräischer Bibeltext*, p. 77)—the Ben Asher text is basically one entity, and the Cairo Codex is just a "Ben Ascher Kodex aus noch früherer Zeit." See also next note.

91. This does not mean that all authors knew who was who and that some nonspecialist did not sometimes confuse the two. Such mistakes can also happen to modern scholars (see my "Authenticity," nn. 2, 24). For the general problem of the Cairo Codex, see "Authenticity," §20f.

I should, however, like to voice strongest dissent from a remarkable position recently adopted by Kahle. While everyone will agree that Moses Ben Asher was "one of the prominent Masoretes," as Kahle used to call him (my reference at the moment is to his chapter in Goldschmidt, *Earliest Editions of the Hebrew Bible* [1950], p. 49), it seems an extraordinary coincidence that since the Aleppo Codex was made available to serve as the basis for the new edition of the Bible, Kahle insists on repeatedly referring to Moses as "*the prominent* Masorete" and practically turns his son into his amanuensis. In *VT* 10:35 (1960), Moses has become the "Hauptmasoret von Tiberias" and in *Hebräischer Bibeltext*, p. 76, the "Prominenteste der Masoreten."

This flies in the face of all the evidence (cf. above, §15). Kahle cannot get rid of the judgment of generations by a mere stroke of his pen. Similarly he might have learned from the volume of *Textus* (which he quotes, *Hebräischer Bibeltext*, p. 83) that the opposite is true of what he claims: "Eine genaue Gegenüberstellung der beiden Texte hat ergeben,

We have stated before (above, §10f.) that the ninth century was (at least until 900 C.E. and slightly after that) a time of *individual* creations, each Masorete refining the notation and sifting the material assembled before him. These were not yet stereotyped works of copyists who worked from accepted models, but the very personal creations of "Masters of the Masora" on the basis of their lifelong studies. The graphic notation was in a constant process of refinement.[92] Even though the founder of the Ben Asher dynasty and his contemporaries—a century and more before Aaron Ben Asher—had taken decisive steps toward refining the notation and had taught their system to their sons and disciples, yet the "young" Ben Ashers, Moses and Aaron, were still busy perfecting it. Both were masters in their own right, and nothing on earth could stop them from holding certain different opinions as regards some minutiae—and minutiae they were.[93] It was Moses' bad luck that only his son, standing no doubt on his father's shoulders, made the final step and produced the complete model codex.

We have no reason to doubt the tradition that the scribe[94] of the Cairo Codex was the father of the scribe of the Aleppo Codex. But there is no reason whatsoever why the son should merely have copied his father,[95] nor why the father should have written his codex according to the sub-system finally perfected and adopted by his son.

35. In our view there is no need to expect the Cairo Codex to conform in

---

dass der Aleppo Kodex in allen Einzelheiten [*sic*] von Text und Vokalisation genau mit dem Kairoer Prophetenkodex übereinstimmt. Das ergab aber mit Sicherheit, dass der Aleppo Kodex im wesentlichen auf die Fassung des Kairoer Prophetenkodex zurückgeht und auf ihm beruht und dass als der *massgebende Mann für den tiberischen* Bibeltext durchaus der Vater Mosche ben Ascher anzusehen ist" [My italics].
In order to avoid any misunderstanding of my position, I should stress that I regard the Cairo Codex as a most valuable source, the importance of which for our understanding of the history of the Tiberian Bible text is perhaps, in its way, equal to that of the Aleppo Codex. But the Cairo Codex *was not the model for our textus receptus.* (Cf. below, §42f.) It was the bad luck of Moses Ben Asher that he did not succeed where his son was to succeed—which would have made him into The Masorete. But this was not what happened, and in the judgment of later generations it was Aaron who was regarded as "the most prominent Masorete." Kahle will have to explain away all the facts before his claim will be acceptable.
92. The developments which we can trace in Babylonian punctuation may give an idea of the developments which led up to the Cairo and Aleppo codices. But this is no more than a possible illustration.
93. See for this issue, Note 64f. above and Note 109 below.
94. For our purpose it is immaterial whether we speak of scribe, author, etc., and whether the Masorete also wrote the consonantal text.
95. See above, §15. The formulation in the text Levy, *Zur masoretischen Grammatik,* p. ט, קבלה מן אבוה וריקאט ריקאט אברהם ("Abraham Riqaṭ and his father Riqaṭ before him") might provide an interesting parallel.

all its details to the system of the Aleppo Codex. Consequently, all the suspicions raised against the Cairo Codex are baseless.[96]

Yet one question remains. If the Cairo Codex need not conform to the Ben Asher column of Mishael's list, it seems extraordinary that it conforms so much better to the Ben Naftali column. How, then, can we account for what seems the Ben Naftali character of the Cairo Codex?

36. This alleged character of the Cairo Codex is, in my opinion, history turned topsy-turvy. The tiny differences between Aaron Ben Asher and Moses Ben Asher were not their inventions. They handed on, each in his own slightly different way, some earlier tradition. What finally became crystallized and connected to the name of Ben Naftali was essentially the tradition of his predecessors, among them Moses Ben Asher, even though Ben Naftali probably deviated in some minutiae. But for the fact that history made that subsystem finally stick to the name of Ben Naftali—just as it happened with Aaron Ben Asher—it would not be too far from the truth to speak of the two subsystems inside the Ben Asher family and to term the contrast of readings: *Ben Asher versus Ben Asher*.[97]

Both Aaron Ben Asher and Ben Naftali mark, so to speak, final steps,[98] slightly apart, in the development of that subsystem of Masora, in which the last stage but one has left us only one known representative: the codex of Moses Ben Asher. For illustration's sake one may picture both Aaron and Ben Naftali being educated in the old tradition of the Ben Ashers,[99] both ripening and developing and refining their work, but Ben Naftali in the last instance remaining more faithful to that subsystem to which Aaron's father adhered.[100] Only once the contrast had become finally

96. I am not concerned for the present with the kind of criticism which allows itself any kind of liberty because the author of the document concerned cannot rise from his grave to testify. See also above, Note 44.

97. I have hinted at this in *Text and Language*, p. ix. The formulation here is meant to be provocative, but I think I made it clear that there was, in my opinion, a development from the Cairo Codex to Ben Naftali. My position is therefore different from that of Yeivin (*Tarbiz* 29:345 [1960]) who formulates: "The Ben Naftali text is represented, to a smaller or larger extent, by manuscripts like the Cairo Codex."

98. But we should not forget for a minute that this final development among the master Masoretes does not mark the final development of the text itself, as is shown by the immediate rise of what from their point of view were *codices mixti*—the direct ancestors of our *textus receptus*. See below, §43.

99. And those Masoretes whose system was similar. Cf. Levy, *Zur masoretischen Grammatik*, v.

100. For argument's sake we could work out a theory which would make Ben Naftali a "master Masorete" in the generation before Moses Ben Asher. Certain details would then have to be changed, but the general thesis would not be affected. The possibility is remote. Because of the picture of later sources and the absence of Ben Naftali's name

crystallized into the Ben Asher–Ben Naftali "controversy," could we be misled in retrospective to mistake the Cairo Codex for a manuscript which could not have been written by "a" Ben Asher.

VII. RECEPTUS AND NON-RECEPTUS TRADITIONS

37. Our theory assumes that the two traditions, crystallized into the pigeon-hole opposition Ben Asher–Ben Naftali, which seemed two major rival systems of the Tiberian Masora, are basically alike. This is exactly what is borne out by the facts, and it is only on this basis that many readings attributed to Ben Naftali slipped into our "Ben Asher" *textus receptus* (see Note 98 and below, §43).

Without going here into all the details[101] I therefore have to add that the type of manuscript accepted on Kahle's authority[102] by practically all scholars to this day as Ben Naftali manuscripts has been wrongly labeled so.[103] These manuscripts—the best known of which is, of course,

---

in the list of Masoretes (cf. Levy, *Zur masoretischen Grammatik*), the only reasonable theory is to make Ben Naftali roughly contemporaneous with Aaron Ben Asher.

We may speculate, of course, on why it was not the subsystem of the Cairo Codex and Ben Naftali that carried off the palm—supposing, for the sake of argument, that Ben Naftali did produce a model manuscript similar in its way to the Aleppo Codex (see Notes 88, 128) and that our assumption about the novel character of the Aleppo Codex is wrong. It may be, then, that Aaron benefited from his descent from Ben Asher forefathers, while Ben Naftali was an outsider. For all we know, Aaron may have taken after his grandfather and returned to the "original" family tradition. All this is idle speculation. One point, however, already seems quite clear to me (although I should not like to say much before completing the analysis for *Nosaḥ ha-Miqrā*): Ben Naftali's "defeat" is not due to any inherent difference between his system and that of Aaron Ben Asher. (For such a theory, see Ben David, *Tarbiz* 26:384f. [1958].)

101. This subject will be dealt with in a special chapter.

102. Kahle, *Masoreten des Westens*, II, 45*. Much of the work seems to have been carried out by Edelmann.

103. Lipschütz must have realized that Kahle's identification was wrong, but in the published part of his book which I use I cannot find any protest on his part. (However, he was Kahle's student, and this was his dissertation!) A. Sperber obviously did not accept Kahle's idea and finally called those manuscripts "pre-Masoretic." See his "A Grammar of Masoretic Hebrew," *Corpus Codicum Hebraicorum Medii Aevi*, II (I use the 8vo edition of his treatise, Copenhagen, 1958; see below, Note 112). S. Morag, *JSS* 4:234 (1959), is clearly against calling the Codex Reuchlinianus a Ben Naftali manuscript, while he regards the problem of Ben Naftali manuscripts in general as outside the scope of his paper (see below, Note 108). Ben David, *Beth Miqrā* 3:415 and *Tarbiz* 26:384f. and Yeivin, *Tarbiz* 29:345 (1960) are the only ones clearly to criticize Kahle. A. Diez-Macho (since *Estudios Biblicos* 15:187f. [1956]) has tried to build his understanding of the issue around the problems of certain "Palestinian" fragments. (To be sure, the possible existence of such a "proto-Ben Naftali" need not have prevented anyone from continuing to talk about Ben Naftali manuscripts. See Note 65, above.)

On the other hand, the latest and most competent summary of our subject (H. Rabin's article on Ben Naftali in *Encyclopedia 'Ivrith*, IX [Jerusalem, 1958], *s.v.* "Ben Naftali") accepts Kahle's view, and Yalon (*Kiryat Sefer* 1957:108) leaves the question open for

the Codex Reuchlinianus 3 (CR = Kennicott 154)[104]—were declared by Kahle to be Ben Naftali manuscripts in the face of the only existing criterion, the very same manuscript which Kahle had used correctly for proving the genuineness of the Ben Asher manuscripts. This refers, it goes without saying, to Mishael's list.

38. For the present suffice it to say that at the very moment when Kahle fully realized the fallacy of medieval compilers of Masoretic lists who reduced variants indiscriminately to the stereotyped contrast Ben Asher– Ben Naftali (see also below, Note 121), and when he recognized the value of Mishael's treatise, he committed a similar error with regard to what he termed Ben Naftali manuscripts. Taking up hints dropped by earlier scholars[105] and closing his eyes to the most conspicuous[106] marks of those manuscripts,[107] he identified them as Ben Naftali manuscripts on the basis of little more than one phonetic isogloss.[108]

---

discussion but neither discusses it nor opposes Kahle. For this reason it seems that Yeivin (*Tarbiz* 29:345) is rather optimistic when he claims that "today the accepted view is that these manuscripts are not by Ben Naftali and not by his school." Agreed—but just by three or four scholars, and it will take some time until Kahle's mistaken identifications will be dropped from the handbooks.

104. To the manuscripts listed by Kahle we have not only to add Prijs, *ZAW* 69:171 (1957), as noted by Yeivin, but also J. Hempel's "Codex Wolters" (*Nachrichten der Göttingen Gesellschaft der Wissenschaften*, 1937, *Phil.-Hist. Klasse, Fachgruppe III*:227f.), which seems to have disappeared from the recent literature. By the way, Hempel naturally accepts Kahle's authority, but with a cautionary note: "Darf man diese Gruppe mit Kahle für Ben Naftali in Anspruch nehmen, so hätten wir im Codex Wolters eine BN-Handschrift zu sehen. . ." For fragments see also my "Biblical Manuscripts."

105. Ginsburg in particular had dealt with the subject (not just "auch bereits"; cf. Kahle, *Masoreten des Westens*, II, 51*f.) The idea of that identification was apparently "in the air" after the Delitzsch-Baer edition of Jeremiah in 1890 (cf. Kahle, *loc. cit.*). Graetz wrote about this type of vocalization in 1887 (*MGWJ* 36:489) and did not know of such a theory.

106. In *Masoreten des Ostens* (1913), p. xvi, he was much more aware of these marks and spoke correctly of "eine besondere Gruppe . . . die, wie es erscheint, weder mit Ben Ascher noch mit Ben Naftali zu tun hat."

107. Because of the importance of the practical unity of all Tiberian systems from the phonetic (and certainly phonemic) point of view (see above, Notes 64f.), it should be stressed again that these are only graphic differences, but most conspicuous ones indeed. See next Note and Note 112.

108. In spite of his wording—which indicates the difference between him and me— Morag was aware of the linguistic question involved when he wrote (*JSS* 4:234): "This comparison shows that only a small number of CR [Codex Reuchlinianus] features in this table can be defined as belonging to the school of Ben Naphtali." In my opinion, there is a clear structural difference between the case of the *dagesh* in בֵּן־נֻין—a completely isolated instance in the system of Ben Naftali which may or may not link up with the system of some other manuscripts (see Note 116)—and the perpetual syllable indicator in the Codex Reuchlinianus and kindred manuscripts. This leaves us, then, with the haplological contraction *yəye > yē*, etc. (see above, Note 66), which must have been quite widespread as a phonetical phenomenon and was certainly not restricted to one particular type of tradition. In other words: the one isogloss is far from being significant.

39. If we, however, leave these alleged Ben Naftali manuscripts aside and turn to the only admissible evidence of Ben Naftali's readings—Mishael's list—there remains no doubt that the two systems are practically one. The judgment of scholars before Kahle, that the lists of *hillufim* are, on the main, lists of minutiae, is correct.[109] Although there are a few items

---

The question may, of course, be asked whether this type of contraction was a general phenomenon in Ben Naftali texts (as I believe it was) or whether its notation is meant to indicate that the phenomenon was sporadic and could be found only in the places indicated. If I see correctly, there are fewer than ten places where the *hilluf* is attested; cf. Jud. 19:6, 9—Ben Asher, וַיִּיטַב; Ben Naftali, "וְיִטַב ''לֹא יכ'רג אליוד" (the *yodh* is not pronounced). There is only one case of haplology with identical consonants, and this is the only case in which the phenomenon does not occur at the juncture after a syntactical prefix; this is (ו)יְלִיל/יְיְלִיל in Isa. 16:7 and Hos 7:14. (All other cases after copulative *waw* except Ps. 119:38: לִירַאתֶךָ.) See next Notes.

109. Cf. above, §26, and below, Note 120. The judgment of Ginsburg (*Introduction* [1897], p. 278) is not far from the truth: "It is the presence or absence of the *metheg* or *gaya* which constitutes fully nine-tenths of the differences between these two redactors of the text." (Ben David has echoed this sixty years later in *Beth Miqrā* 3:1f.). Against this basically correct judgment Kahle's identification had assumed much larger differences, which, in their way, although substantially different, were as large as those presupposed some hundreds of years ago. For the idea that Ben Naftali was actually the representative of the readings of the "Orientals"—still echoed by Ginsburg, mainly introduced into scholarly literature on the authority of Levita, *Massoreth ha-Massoreth*, p. 114, but in existence at least as early as Ibn Balᶜam (cf. Baer-Strack, *Die Dikduke*, p. 83)—assumed considerable differences by necessity.

For this reason Ginsburg, although he had already become aware of the character of the *hillufim* (while still allowing the evidence of certain marginal notes which claimed real textual variants; *Introduction*, p. 246), could still speak of Ben Asher and Ben Naftali as "two rival textual critics, engaged in the redaction of two rival recensions of the Hebrew Bible" (*Introduction*, p. 241).

Nevertheless, there may be a few real textual differences not recorded in Lipschütz, *Ben Ašer Ben Naftali*, but noted in the margins of ancient codices. The problem is to find out and to prove how trustworthy these are. A good example is the note recurring in the margins of ancient codices (adduced by Strack, *Zeitschrift für die Lutherische Theologie* 36:611 on Jer. 29:22: וכאהב כתיב בן אשר; בן נפתלי: כצדקיהו וכאהב כתיב וכאחיו קרי; וכן קרי. But it is this expression which is recorded elsewhere as part of the *hillufim* between "Orientals" and "Occidentals"; cf., e.g., the discussion, in this connection, of S. Pinsker, *Einleitung in das babylonisch-hebräische Punktationsystem* (1863), p. 126. See also C. D. Ginsburg, *The Massorah*, I (London, 1880), p. 595. While such a case illustrates the old (erroneous) identification of the Ben Naftali readings as "Orientals," it also illustrates the difficulties in reclaiming *hillufim* not recorded in Mishael.

In general, however, the analysis of all the material in Mishael's list shows that Levita, *Massoreth ha-Massoreth*, p. 114, was actually not wrong in his description of the differences, but his lack of quantitative differentiation between the phenomena (which is indicative of the whole issue) was misleading. He describes: והפלוגתות שביניהן בטעמים אינן אלא בטעמים הקטנים, כגון מתג ומקף ומונח ובפשטא אחד ורב' פשטין ... גם הפלוגתות שביניהן בנקודות אינן אלא בחולם ובקמץ חטוף ובקמץ גדול ופתח ובשוא ובחטף פתח וכן בדגשין ורפין ומלעיל ומלרע ("The differences of opinion between them in matters of accent only appear in minor accents, such as *metheg* ... Also the differences in matters of vocalization are only questions of *holam* and *qamaṣ ḥatuf*, etc.")

where the two Masoretes differ in text or vocalization, I am afraid—without being very facetious, I hope—that the vast majority of present-day Bible scholars would not notice without special study any difference in a Ben Naftali manuscript (if there were one in existence).

To give a first idea of the material I summarize the following notes from the list of Mishael.

(a) Addition and omission of *waw* (of course there are always other sources which show the same change): Jer. 7:25: Ben Asher עד היום, Ben Naftali ועד היום; Jer. 11:7 Ben Asher—ועד היום, Ben Naftali—עד היום; Dan. 9:8: Ben Asher למלכינו לשרינו, Ben Naftali—למלכינו ולשרינו.

(b) Change of Tetragrammaton: Lam. 5:21: Ben Asher—והוה, Ben Naftali—אדני.

(c) Change identical with *qere*/*ketibh* in other sources: Job 6:21: Ben Asher—הייתם לא Ben Naftali—לו.

(d) Orthography in one or two words: Isa. 54:9: Ben Asher—כימי, Ben Naftali—כי־מי; Ps. 48:15: Ben Asher—על־מות, Ben Naftali—עלמות; Cant. 8:6: Ben Asher—שלהבתיה, Ben Naftali—שלהבת־יה.

(The question of the Aleppo Codex versus the Leningrad Codex in these cases needs special discussion.)

(e) Odd differences in matters of *dagesh* which cannot be reduced to a common denominator: Jer. 9:3: Ben Asher—יַעֲקֹב Ben Naftali—יַעֲקֹב, (like the Cairo Codex!) reminds us of the tendency to insert a *dagesh* after syllable-final faucals (see Note 116). But it should be stressed that one example in Ben Naftali—supposing that he accepted all the other readings indicative of this tendency which are in Ben Asher—is not really of a sign. I Sam. 16:7: Ben Asher—כי לֹא, Ben Naftali—כי לֹּא with *dagesh* (like the Cairo Codex!) is interesting because of the accentuation pattern *in loco* Job 20:26: Ben Asher—לצפוניו (thus the Aleppo and Leningrad codices, not as in Biblia Hebraica), Ben Naftali—לצפוניו (no *dagesh*) may illustrate a grammatical point. Why Ben Naftali in II Chron. 31:7 has החלו without *dagesh* in the *lamedh* I cannot figure out at the moment.

(f) In connection with the *hilluf* discussed in the preceding note, Neh. 11:25: Ben Asher—וביקבצאל (with *dagesh* against Ben Naftali) seems important. This kind of indication surely cannot be divorced from Ps. 45:10: Ben Naftali—בִּיקְרוֹתֶיךָ (I cannot make out from the transcript whether the Ben Asher form is written with a *dagesh*; cf. Biblia Hebraica). The problem whether there is a Ben Naftali system in this case and whether also in Mishael the two Masoretes could "exchange places" remains to be discussed.

(g) The largest group among the non-accentual *hillufim* are changes of vowels, practically all in connection with stress conditions. Well known already are Gen. 41:50; Ben Asher—וליוסף יֻלַּד, Ben Naftali—יֻלָּד and the strange Deut. 31:21: Ben Asher—אשר נשבעתי (in pause), Ben Naftali—נשבעתי. Cf. also my "Biblical Manuscripts," pp. 56ff. Ezek 15:15: Ben Asher—ושכלתה, Ben Naftali—ושכלתה. Ez. 27:13: Ben Asher—תֵּבֶל, Ben Naftali—תּוּבֶל, seems a problem of a proper name.

There seems to be only one case with *e*-vowels: Job 9:33: Ben Asher—יֵשׁ בינינו, Ben Naftali—יֵשׁ בינינו (with *segol*). All the other cases deal with the *holam-qamas* series and are to be found, curiously enough, in the three poetic books (Psalms, Proverbs, Job). In this case there is a discernible pattern: an "imperfect"-imperative *qal*-form connected to a complement with *maqqef* is read by Ben Asher with *qamas* and by Ben Naftali with *holam*. Thus: Ps. 49:25: Ben Asher—שפָך־עליהם, Ben Naftali—שפֹך עליהם;

The very fact that these minutiae were recorded in Mishael's treatise—together with a listing of cases where Ben Asher and Ben Naftali agree (against some other Masorete [see above, §31 and below, Note 117]) proves to me that what had seemed, after Kahle's identifications, a major difference between basically different graphic systems, are nothing but the very last minute differentiations between the exponents of the same school.[110]

40. In the light of what we found I would therefore suggest the following picture of the rise of the Tiberian Bible text.

The earliest stages of the "Tiberian" attempt—as opposed to the "Palestinian"—to note down the oral tradition are unknown to us. We can only assume that the Masoretes, about most of whom we know nothing but their names (see Note 117), gradually refined their system of notation. By the end of the ninth century (?) two main Tiberian systems had emerged, each of which presented the same reading tradition in a graphically different way, by using the same "Tiberian" signs: the one I propose to term *proto-receptus*, the other *non-receptus*.

41. The *non-receptus* tradition is the one used by the Reuchlinianus and kindred manuscripts.[111] While there are obvious differences among these

---

Ps. 121:8: Ben Asher—צֵאתְךָ־יִשְׁמָר, Ben Naftali—צֵאתְךָ־יִשְׁמֹר, and so on. Similarly, Job 3:5: עָלָיו־תִּשְׁכָּן, 24:14: עָנִי־יִקְטָל, Prov. 4:4: דְבָרַי־יִתְמָךְ. Only in Ps. 10:15, do we find that it is Ben Naftali who has a *qamaṣ* without *maqqef*! The remaining case is also apparently one of *matres*-orthography: Ben Asher spells in both Job 13:27 and 3:11 אָרְחוֹתִי with *qamaṣ*, whereas Ben Naftali spells it with a *waw*.

These are almost all the differences in Mishael with regard to text and vocalization, as far as they can be made out from Kahle's transcript. [May 1962 (see above, Note 70): Between Kahle's transcript and the text now published by Lipschütz there are certain slight differences. The most important one is the lack of the telling vocalization, mentioned above, Note 74. The differences will be discussed, together with the full evaluation of the material, in *Nosaḥ ha-Miqrā*. For the moment I should like to point out that the suspicious *plene* אוֹרְחוֹתִי of Ben Naftali in Job 13:27, 33:11, is not borne out by the text of Lipschütz. On the other hand, the alleged צִיצַת of Ben Naftali, in Isa. 28:4 in Lipschütz' text, seems a simple misprint.]

110. That is to say: Ben Naftali is basically an exponent of the tradition of the Ben Ashers (in the plural), and developed in particular the subsystem of which Moses Ben Asher was the outstanding exponent in the generation before him. See also above, Note 100.

111. Just as the ancient codices of the Tiberian Bible text type show clear connections with the Babylonian system (see above, Note 16), it stands to reason that we should search for parallel connections of the *non-receptus* tradition. At present I merely want to hint at the fact that certain features of "Babylonian" manuscripts—including the Codex Petropolitanus of the Prophets (ed. Strack, 1876) and noticed in part already in their own right by Pinsker, *Einleitung*, esp. p. 111—show certain affinities with the *non-receptus* tradition (and kindred types). I suppose that the hint dropped by Ben David (*Leshonenu* 22:21 [1958]) is meant to refer to such features. However, as they stand, the manuscripts of the *non-receptus* tradition have to be regarded as a *Tiberian* system, and not just as a

manuscripts which remain to be analyzed in order to establish possible subsystems, their common features are conspicuous enough to justify our term as a unity—at least for the time being.

These are neither Ben Naftali manuscripts nor are they *pre-Masoretic* or *post-Masoretic*[112] or *non-Masoretic*.[113] They were, in their way, as

---

"Tiberian" counterpart to the opposite phenomenon symbolized by the existence of the Codex Petropolitanus. See below, Note 118.

112. This is to say I agree with Kahle (*Cairo Geniza*, p. 123) and Morag (*JSS* 4:216f.), who do not admit Sperber's claims. On the other hand, I do not agree with Morag when he—perhaps somewhat in a polemical vein—regards these manuscripts as *post-Masoretic* (*JSS* 4:229, 237). While the thesis that a more developed phonetic notation is not only a typological but also a chronological criterion is valid in general (this is not Morag's phrasing, but I think that is what he means), I cannot see why "the *CR* [Codex Reuchlinianus] *vocalization system is far more phonetic in its principles than the usual Tiberian system*" (p. 229, his italics). To be sure, it uses certain graphic devices much more than does the Tiberian Bible text, but this does not make it necessarily "more phonetic." The relationship as regards the graphemic complexity between the two Tiberian systems is *not* similar to the ostensibly parallel problem of the Babylonian systems. I have not found in the tradition of the Codex Reuchlinianus any graphic notation indicative of a phonetic phenomenon not known from the Tiberian Bible text. (If anything, the only partial notation of the *patah furtivum* might have been taken to point to the opposite.)

While I take the *non-receptus* tradition as a whole as chronologically neither earlier nor later than the emergence of the Tiberian Bible text (for this whole issue see also Notes 17, 21, 40, 65), I agree that the particular subsystem as shown by the Codex Reuchlinianus exemplifies a comparatively later stage inside that tradition. My main reason is (but cf. above, Note 65) that the Codex Reuchlinianus does not differentiate between certain vowel graphemes (- : ⸗, etc.) which stand in opposition within other manuscripts of that tradition. In my opinion (cf. also Prijs, *ZAW* 69:180 [1957], against Yeivin, *Tarbiz* 29:347), the Codex Reuchlinianus is an example of a particular, comparatively later, subsystem, which is to be judged in accordance with what we have remarked on the "Sefardi" codices (see above, Notes 54, 65). But the *non-receptus* tradition in general is typologically (and probably chronologically) neither pre- nor post-Tiberian Bible text.

This whole problem is bound up not only with the question of early reading traditions in general, but also especially with that of the "Palestinian" vocalization. I might therefore add (see my *Nosah ha-Miqrā*) that because Kahle's claims were widely accepted, the problem of typological versus chronological evaluation, with regard to the Palestinian vocalization, has never been tackled seriously. Kahle's "High chronology" for the Palestinian fragments—which are a decisive part of his theory on the Tiberian text (see above, Note 41)—is exclusively based on a priori evolutional reasoning. Paradoxically, he has always claimed dates but never dealt convincingly with the question of dates of Geniza fragments (see above, Note 21)—presumably because he did not bother much about the Geniza material apart from the fragments with non-Tiberian vocalization (as can be seen from his book entitled "Cairo Geniza"). I am not aware of any paleographical study ever having been carried out by him (or by his followers). Even though the fragments may not be as late as suggested by Ben David (*Kiryat Sefer* 33:484), who has sharply criticized Kahle, also this part of Kahle's theories is without the slightest factual basis. Perhaps the Geniza may yield some further "Palestinian"–Tiberian fragments to help us to solve this problem and to base claims on a sounder paleographical basis. See also "Biblical Manuscripts," pp. 35ff.

113. As Yeivin terms them (*Tarbiz* 29:345f.). Since Mr. Yeivin has been kind enough to arrange for me various collations within the framework of the Hebrew University Bible Project and since we have had the opportunity to discuss many questions of

Masoretic as "our" Tiberian Bible text and were in use, it seems, especially in the Franco-German area, until the thirteenth or fourteenth century.[114] Although they must always have been very rare,[115] it is not impossible that they were finally doomed only by the advent of printing. All this will explain that the least misleading term at the moment seems to be "Tiberian *non-receptus* tradition."

VIII. Prehistory and History of the Tiberian Bible Text

42. No typology can get rid of borderline phenomena. There were, no doubt, mutual influences between the traditions,[116] and yet we can clearly

---

common interest, I might stress, that as regards this subject, each of us has come to his conclusions on his own, both where we differ and where we agree.

114. This is already obvious from the descriptions by Ginsburg, *Introduction*, pp. 556f., 605f., 632f.

115. Since I suspect that there is a local preference, one cannot really judge from the scarcity of fragments of this tradition in the Cairo Geniza. I would estimate that the fragments of *non-receptus* material in the Geniza are less than half of one per cent. For this reason the few ones in existence deserve careful study. See also my "Biblical Manuscripts," pp. 43f.

116. Those manuscripts which consistently put a *dagesh* after a syllable-final faucal and/or in the second of two similar letters need special investigation; see above, Note 108. (The question whether this dot is a *dagesh* should be left open for the moment.) Ben Naftali does not have this system, and the one or two cases in which the Ben Naftali reading has such a "*dagesh*" which is not in the Ben Asher text should not really be taken as suggesting any definite connection. Since Ginsburg's *Introduction* (see also below), this type of manuscript becomes somewhat mixed up with the "pure" *non-receptus* and as far as I can make out at the moment, Yeivin's fragment (*Tarbiz* 29:345f.) also does not belong to the "pure" type. Whatever term we use, in my opinion, these manuscripts which put a *mappiq* in consonantal *alefs* and mark the beginnings of syllables as a constant rule—not just in a very special case—have to be taken as a group by themselves. The importance of the *mappiq* as the essential sign of a certain group was first stressed by L. Prijs, *ZAW* 69:171f. (1957). But Prijs never questions Kahle's identification as such. Whether we can establish any connection between the *non-receptus* manuscripts and those which have a special "*dagesh*" (as mentioned in the beginning of this note) remains to be seen. Certainly, talking of the two systems as "primitive" and "elaborate"—if I interpret some recent suggestions rightly—might again lead us into creating a new evolutional chain without any real basis.

Furthermore, the connection—if there is any—with certain "*dageshes*" of Tiberian Bible text manuscripts has to be examined. What I refer to is the kind of dot which since the time of Michaelis (and later through W. Gesenius' *Lehrgebäude* [Leipzig, 1817] §§3, 19) has been sporadically introduced into grammars under such promising names as *dagesh neutrum, orthophonicum, orthosyllabicum*, etc., sometimes with some censoring remarks of the author that this is an "Übertreibung" (F. Böttcher, *Lehrbuch* [Leipzig, 1866], §227) or "purism" (Ginsburg, *Introduction*, pp. 556f., 605f., 632f.).

The "academic" Hebraists do not seem to be aware of the fact that the Jewish grammarians have had remarks to make on manuscripts of the *non-receptus* type and have been alert to some of its characteristics—at least since the eighteenth century. It is fascinating to follow up this lead which—this much I shall say here—seems to go back to the famous punctuator, Yequtiel Hakohen, who is supposed to have flourished in Prague in the thirteenth century. (To be sure, our term is not meant to indicate that the *non-receptus*

distinguish between the *non-receptus* and the (*proto*)-*receptus* traditions. The *proto-receptus* tradition may for the moment be identified with that of the dynasty of the Ben Ashers (and their adherents), including the *Vorlagen* of what seem to us Ben Naftali manuscripts as well as codices which contain readings which are neither those of Aaron Ben Asher nor of Ben Naftali (like the Cairo, Sassoon, and British Museum codices, et cetera).[117] The differences between all those must have been rather small. All these belonged to *one* tradition, even though a particular subsystem, represented by the Aleppo Codex, was finally to gain fame.

43. By the end of the ninth century this tradition was fully developed,[118] and the Aleppo Codex emerged out of it as a perfect specimen, crystallizing the tradition in a model codex of the complete Bible. But it was part and parcel of that tradition. In spite of its unique prestige it remained near the other subsystems. It could serve as a model. But scribes, while ostensibly reproducing it, could easily keep deviating readings to which they had been accustomed. In contradistinction to the *non-receptus* codices these minute deviations amounted to very little.

---

vocalization is found in Biblical manuscripts only. This fact should have been clear at least since M. Zulay's *Meḥqəre Yannai* [Berlin, 1936], p. 326.) For the whole problem see my *Nosaḥ ha-Miqrā*.

117. There are only a very few cases where tradition has elaborated on the question of *three* different readings within the *proto-receptus* tradition. The classical example remains, of course, the proper name יששכר (since Pinsker's *Lickute Qadmonioth*, pp. 98f.; cf. Ginsburg, *Introduction*, p. 252, and Ben David, *Beth Miqrā* 3:415). The Masoretes who apart from the Ben Ashers come alive somewhat through our sources, are Pineḥas, head of the Academy, and especially Moshe Moḥa (Moḥe). See my *Nosaḥ ha-Miqrā*.

But only very seldom can we find out against whom Mishael stressed the agreement between Ben Asher and Ben Naftali. One example must suffice here: for Exod. 3:8 Mishael stressed their agreement very strongly: והד׳א מא לם יכ׳חלף פיה בתה .... ואדד להציל̇ו ... ("There was absolutely no *ḥilluf* on these"). To my mind this means that some earlier listing of differences—there must have been such a listing against which Mishael stressed his better tradition!—mistakenly quoted some difference of opinion on this subject and attributed it to Ben Asher and Ben Naftali (as happened throughout the Middle Ages). There was no such difference between them, says Mishael. But if we happen to look up Pinsker's *Lickute Qadmonioth*, p. 30, we find who *did* differ: R. Pineḥas' reading is like our Ben Asher version: להצילו, while R. Ḥabib read להצילו, with *gaʿya*. See also Pinsker, *Lickute Qadmonioth*, p. 30, for another case.

Such instances account, in my opinion, for the existence in the *proto-receptus* period of what in our eyes are *codices mixti*, containing also readings which are neither Ben Asher nor Ben Naftali. Of course we should not expect at that stage that there were *three* codices, each exhibiting a "pure" subsystem of *proto-receptus*. It will be clear that my position agrees to some extent with that of Yalon, *Kiryat Sefer* 32:101 (1957). See also above, Note 88.

118. Geiger has already suggested (*Urschrift* [Breslau, 1857], p. 169) that around 900 C.E. the Tiberian system conquered areas which had previously used the "Babylonian"

It is this basic similarity between the "model" Aleppo Codex and other codices of the *proto-receptus* tradition—some of which may have been esteemed codices of certain parts of the Bible—which explains in my submission that in spite of the immense prestige which was accorded to Aaron Ben Asher very soon after his death (see above, §15), ostensible copies of his text were, in fact, *codices mixti* from the point of view of the Aleppo Codex.[119]

The Aleppo Codex was not the absolutely final step. It was the peak which marks the transition from the *proto-receptus* to the *receptus* period. This was a completely smooth transition, hardly noticeable at the time, and yet there was a distinct later development, as can be seen especially by the use of methegs.[120] Those *codices mixti* were, indeed, the direct continuation

---

system. This idea has now been taken up in detail by Morag, *Sefer Tur-Sinai* (Jerusalem, 1960), pp. 234f. I admit that I hesitate somewhat to believe that one system yields to another because of some relative decline in the life of the community. The decline in Babylonia in the ninth century was not so sharp and the upward trend in Palestine not that decisive. Furthermore, I suspect that the very term "Babylonian system" has been too much identified in this case with the system of Babylonian Jewry—contrary to our sources.

But the whole history of the victory of the "Tiberian" system becomes more comprehensible to me if we assume that it was precisely in the ninth century that the Tiberian system had been finally perfected. Its system of accentuation (not of vocalization!) must have been recognized as vastly superior to the "Babylonian" system, and was taken by the users of the "Babylonian" system as the true and "original" Palestinian tradition for liturgical recitation. As a further suggestion, just as the "Tiberians" had tried, as an "experiment," to enhance the utility of their graphic vowel-notation by such an invention as the *ḥataf-ḥiriq*, obviously drawing on Babylonian custom (see above, §10), so the other side tried to combine the achievements of both Tiberian and Babylonian systems; both experiments failed. But it seems to me extremely significant that we possess a specimen like the Codex Petropolitanus of the Prophets from exactly that time. See above, Note 111.

In my submission, it was this recently achieved perfection which was a decisive factor in the victory of the Tiberian system—allowing, of course, for the possible "prestige appeal" of the Palestinian tradition. See Benjamin Klar, *Meḥqārim wə-ʿIyyūnim* (1954), pp. 45f. See also above, Note 56.

119. This consideration may force us again to discuss the problem whether in the Masora apparatus of a critical edition (see *Text and Language*, p. x) we should not really also include those manuscripts written prior to the thirteenth century which are actually *codices mixti*—but lean heavily toward the *non*–Ben Asher subsystems of the *receptus* tradition. If we include the Cairo Codex in the apparatus, there is little sense in leaving the Sassoon Codex out!

120. Having repeatedly called questions of *gaʿya* "minutiae" (see, e.g., Note 93 above, and especially Note 109), I should add that this is only a relative evaluation within the system. In point of fact, the *gaʿya* fulfilled a considerable task in exact phonetic notation. Its neglect by many modern students of Hebrew can be explained only by the fact that the attempts inside the *receptus* tradition after Ben Asher to remedy what seemed like deficiencies in the Tiberian system finally led to the worst confusion in our *receptus* prints, with editors trying to bring order into the system according to what they thought that order was. Yeivin's forthcoming study of the subject (cf. *Textus* 1:211) should help to remedy the situation.

of the *proto-receptus* tradition, with the one difference that the vast majority were now leaning heavily toward that subsystem which had been the basis of the Aleppo Codex (not toward the Cairo Codex, and so on).[121]

44. This is, in my opinion, the story of the rise of the Tiberian Bible text, and these manuscripts are the ultimate basis of our *textus receptus* prints, basically similar to the Aleppo Codex, and yet slightly removed from it.[122]

According to our picture it becomes obvious, for the first time, why generations took those *codices mixti*, which were finally used by Jacob Ben Ḥayyim, to represent the Ben Asher tradition. Looking back in our secure possession of the Aleppo Codex, we might even allow for a broadness of terminology and say that calling these *receptus* manuscripts "Ben Asher codices" was not really as wrong as scholars were led for the past generation to believe.[123]

IX. MAIMONIDES AND THE BEN ASHER TEXT

45. A final word may be permitted now on the role of Maimonides in

---

121. See my "Authenticity," §§1, 8. To put it differently: in the self-estimation of scribes and writers, the text of the "in-group" was declared to be a Ben Asher text, and the readings of the "out-group" were often termed Ben Naftali! Thus, e.g., the first example of a *ḥilluf* given by Lonzano (see above, Note 72) is very illuminating because he terms one reading, the one of *this area* (הגלילות האלו), the "correct" one, the reading of Ben Asher; whereas the other reading is that of the Ashkenazi codices (ספרי אשכנזים) which are unreliable (אין לסמוך עליהם)—and that is the reading of Ben Naftali! See also above, Note 11.

122. It appears from the picture I have tried to present that there is a kernel of truth in Sperber's grossly nihilistic and misleading dictum (*Grammar of Masoretic Hebrew*, p. 51): "*There never existed The Masoretic Text, and consequently never will be*" (his italics). To be sure, there never was a "canonization" (see below, Note 130). But when all is said and done, it is misleading to create the impression that the "Masoretic text" is practically the invention of Jacob Ben Ḥayyim (see above, Note 11). Sperber is one of the few scholars who were privileged to study Bible codices by the hundreds, and it must have occurred to him that—allowing for the differences often mentioned in this study—the *receptus* tradition emerges clearly from the vast majority of the codices. It would seem that only by disregarding the position of each phenomenon in its structural context and by treating the overwhelming majority and the hardly noticeable minority alike in his system, could Sperber reach his results which have—in his words (*Grammar of Masoretic Hebrew*, p. 17)—"reduced to shambles" all the work of other Hebrew grammarians.

123. See for this problem my "Authenticity," n. 17. [May 1962: In the light of these facts we need not wonder that N. H. Snaith could recently have published an edition of the Hebrew Bible (London, 1958) on the basis of fourteenth- and fifteenth-century manuscripts, being convinced that he had discovered a "way of obtaining the Ben Asher text independently of Leningrad Codex B 19 a." His understanding of the facts is highlighted by his judgment that the Aleppo and the Leningrad codices on the one hand and the "first hand of the best Sephardi MSS" (!) on the other hand are all equally "sound representatives of the true Ben Asher tradition." See *Textus* 2:11ff. (1962) and *Vetus Testamentum* 7:207f. (1957). Kahle has rightly hinted (*Cairo Geniza*, 2nd ed., p. 140, and *Hebräischer Bibeltext*, p. 17) that if Snaith had at least reproduced the thirteenth-century manuscript used by Norzi, his edition would have had value.]

connection with the "victory" of the Ben Asher text. In spite of the importance of Maimonides' authoritative acceptance of the Aleppo Codex for certain halakhic questions, I have already expressed doubts[124] as to the assumption, constantly repeated by Kahle[125] and others,[126] that it was the authority of Maimonides to which the victory of Ben Asher was due. I now submit that that view is untenable in every respect.

46. In view of the apparently ineradicable mistake reiterated by scholars,[127] it should be stressed first that Maimonides never dealt in as much as one word with the text of Ben Asher—and certainly not with Ben Naftali.[128] None of the textual problems which were of interest to medieval grammarians—let alone to modern students of the Bible—was of interest to him.[129]

Furthermore the assumption of the victory of Ben Asher in the wake of Maimonides' "decree" comes dangerously near to what can only be called a canonization. It looks as if on the authority of Maimonides and by some apparently arbitrary act, a text hitherto not accepted by the whole of Jewry became all of a sudden authoritative for all Jewish communities—two and a half centuries after Aaron Ben Asher (and a century and a half, according to Kahle's theory, after the "Tiberian pronunciation" had been "substituted" for the "original" one).

This is completely off the mark. There was never any "decree" which

124. For "Authenticity," §1, I did not have to investigate this point. But I felt uneasy even then about this accepted theory.

125. While in most of Kahle's statements on the subject Maimonides is simply made responsible for the victory of Ben Asher, he admits in *Hebräischer Bibeltext*, p. 69, that Aaron Ben Asher was in Maimonides' eyes the long-established Masoretic authority.

126. In lieu of many examples I choose the formulation in one of the most widely used handbooks on the Bible text (B. Roberts, *The Old Testament and Versions* [Cardiff, 1951], p. 64): "During the first half of the tenth century A.D.[!] there flourished in Palestine two main families of Massoretes, that of ben Asher and that of ben Naphtali [!], and it was not until the twelfth century that it was decided, by the decree of Maimonides[!], that the text and vocalization of the former family was to be regarded as standard."

127. See my "Authenticity," §8. I cannot rid myself of the suspicion that most scholars copying this myth from somebody else never troubled to look up the statement of Maimonides in its context in the *Code*. The "Urtext" is nowadays possibly Kahle, *Masoreten des Westens*, I, 12: "Freilich möchte ich darauf hinweisen, dass Maimonides in dieser viel zitierten Stelle in erster Linie [sic] auf die in diesem Kodex vorliegende massgebend korrekte Schreibung des Konsonantentextes der Tora hinweist [sic] und auf die Minutiae der Punktation [sic] nur nebenher Bezug nimmt." The Maimonides text bears no relation to what is imputed to it in this statement.

128. As far as I can see, only Prijs, *ZAW* 69:180 (1957) and Rabin, *Encyclopedia 'Ivrith*, IX (1958), s.v. "Ben Naftali," correctly stress that the decline of Ben Naftali cannot be attributed to the decision of Maimonides.

129. For the issue see my "Authenticity," §8.

had the character of a "canonization"[130] and it is impossible that in the halakhic literature of the twelfth and thirteenth centuries there should be no trace of it—had it existed. But it is completely out of the question that anything like that could have happened around 1200 C.E. Great as Maimonides' authority was, he would never have dared to do such a thing nor would he have dreamed of doing it. Had he done so, all other halakhists would have put him under ban.[131] But it was not in the power of any one person at that stage of history to make all communities accept a text contrary to their age-old traditions.

To be sure, Maimonides did not succeed too well in settling those (comparatively minor) halakhic questions of certain details in writing Torah scrolls, for which he had invoked the authority of the Aleppo Codex[132]— he would have been less successful in questions which he never tackled. The most that can be said is that through his reliance on the Aleppo Code as a model codex for those halakhic purposes, he indirectly strengthened the prestige of the *receptus* codices—which were the vast majority anyhow— that were held to represent the Ben Asher tradition.[133]

130. For the crime allegedly committed already earlier by the Masoretes see above, Note 50. It might still be useful to point out that it is not a Jewish way to "canonize" a text by declaring that as from now, such and such a text is "holy."

131. While Maimonides is the one all-round genius known to the gentile world, too, he was not at all regarded as the undisputable halakhic authority neither in his time nor later on. This position was accorded to him only by the Yemenite Jews. See below, Note 133.

132. See the discussion in my "Authenticity," esp. §33.

133. Later scholars never credited Maimonides with having brought about the general acceptance of a textual tradition (see next Note). Although I cannot check the text at present, I remember having been struck while working on ha-Meiri's *Kiryat Sefer* (cf. "Authenticity," §31f.) by the fact that he deals at great length with Maimonides' views without mentioning Ben Asher in that context; on the other hand, when discussing the widespread acceptance of the *receptus* ha-Meiri does not allude to Maimonides. I would suspect that modern scholars were perhaps misled by their usual source for Masoretic information. We have seen that Levita, *Massoreth ha-Massoreth*, p. 114, is not too well informed about the Ben Asher–Ben Naftali problem (see above, Note 88). He is the first one to mention the decision of Maimonides and the acceptance of Ben Asher's readings in one breath, implying some faint causal connection: ‏וכתב הרמב״ם . . . ועליו סמכתי בספר‏ ‏תורה שכתבתי כהלכתו״. וכן אנחנו סומכין על קריאתו בכל הארצות האלה ואנשי מזרח סומכין על קריאת‏ ‏בן נפתלי‏ ("Maimonides wrote . . . And similarly we rely on his [Ben Asher's] reading in all these countries, whereas the 'Orientals' rely on Ben Naftali.") Only for one community did Maimonides' decision mean a real change of their habits, precisely because they had still a completely different type of codex (according to the "Babylonian" system; these were the Yemenites). Cf. on this issue and the importance of Maimonides in this respect Qafiḥ, *Sinai* 29:262f. (1951). The only way for the Yemenite Jews to implement their full acceptance of Maimonides' authority was to change their type of codex altogether, and the analysis of Yemenite codices in the libraries leaves no doubt that the changeover to Tiberian tradition started with the Hebrew text of the Pentateuch. As late as the sixteenth century a certain school of Yemenite scribes used to stress

Scribes, grammarians, and Masoretic scholars became more conscious of the facts and started stressing the point that their tradition was the tradition of Ben Asher—whether that claim was justified or not (see above, Note 121). This trend may also have hastened the final decline of other traditions, especially that of *non-receptus*. But it was a gradual and natural process,[134] not an active and conscious suppression.

47. But on the whole—and this is the main point—the excellence of Aaron Ben Asher's textual achievement was acknowledged[135] for two centuries before Maimonides. The *receptus* tradition, which the Aleppo Codex had helped to bring about and into which it had merged again, had already become by 1200 C.E. the accepted form of the Hebrew Bible for the vast majority of Jewry.[136] Only by speculating on the Bible text *in vacuo* and by neglecting what we know from the pulsating Jewish literature of those days, only by concentrating exclusively on the few fragments of non-Masoretic texts kept in libraries—important as they are in their own right (see above §6f. and Note 112)—and by ignoring the evidence, up to the thirteenth century, accumulated in collections all over the world, only thus could history be turned upside down.

In my opinion, Maimonides' act—rather drastic from the halakhic point of view, even though of minor consequence—can be understood only on the assumption that he did exactly as he said. Also in this case Maimonides

---

that their codices were according to the halakhic tradition declared authoritative by Maimonides. But this had absolutely nothing to do with the details of the Ben Asher vocalization and accentuation, and the comparison of those codices shows clearly that they had no access to the Aleppo Codex or to any direct copy from it. No special claims in this respect— as put forward by Morag (May 26, 1961, and June 16, 1961)—seem plausible, and it will take some skill to convince us that the Aleppo Codex should be judged by the yardstick of these late Yemenite manuscripts. See above, Note 81, and my "Biblical Manuscripts," pp. 47f.

134. The formulation I find given by Lonzano, *'Or Thora*, on Gen 1:3 mirrors precisely the correct feeling people had about the issue and can be taken as classsic: ונהגו כל ישראל בגלילות האלו לסמוך על קריאת בן אשר כאלו יצאה בת קול ואמרה: בן אשר ובן נפתלי הלכה כבן אשר. ("And the whole of Israel in these countries got accustomed to rely on the reading of Ben Asher, as if a Divine voice [not Maimonides!—*M.G.*] had declared: The decision is always according to Ben Asher.")

135. The colophon of the Leningrad Codex (and other codices? See above, Note 81) and the fact that the scribe of the Leningrad Codex took upon himself the trouble to harmonize the manuscript are good indications (see above, §30). To be sure, while the literature shows that Aaron's tradition carried most prestige, it was not yet towering high above everyone else's as happened later on. A fair example of the prestige, yet not absolutely binding, of Ben Asher can be found in Levy, *Zur masoretischen Grammatik*, p. 39. Cf. also Ben David, *Beth Miqrā* 3:12f.

136. What is decisive in this respect is the nature of the "Masoretic model codices," not the "teaching" or "private" codices. Cf. my "Biblical Manuscripts," chapter iii.

had his usual excellent information about valuable ancient manuscripts.[137] The Ben Asher text and the Aleppo Codex did not become authoritative because Maimonides chose them, but Maimonides chose the codex, because he considered it authoritative! This is what he says,[138] and again it might be useful to listen to our source before engaging in speculative criticism (see above, Note 44).

48. The Aleppo Codex was accepted as a model codex—as is quite obvious from the note which was appended to it[139]—long before Maimonides. By referring to it he tried to remedy a halakhically disturbing situation by going back to what he took to be—most justifiedly, as it has turned out—the best ancient codex available. Indirectly his act raised the prestige of Ben Asher and of the Aleppo Codex as a whole, not only in those matters with which he had dealt. But, generally speaking, the act of Maimonides is additional and extremely important evidence for our thesis as to the status of the Aleppo Codex.

49. As I said at the outset, scrutiny of all the facts known today has led me, against the teachings I used to take for true, to formulate a general hypothesis which differs in its decisive aspects from the picture accepted on Kahle's authority by many students of the Bible. Where he sees abrupt changes, artificiality, invention, and what amounts to fraudulent tampering, I see a live tradition, endless toil for safeguarding a sacred text, and gradual development. Where he speculates about the Bible text without properly taking into consideration the data of Jewish history and non-Biblical documents, I have tried to paint the picture of the rise of the Tiberian Bible text within living communities, listening to what history tells us about Karaites and Rabbanites, about Masoretes and grammarians, about Maimonides and his contemporaries. Where he sees life in every tradition except the "official" Tiberian one, I see plurality around the ancient mainstream which finally led to our Masoretic *textus receptus*.

137. His use and acceptance of certain ancient manuscripts is well known in halakhic literature. While the discussion of the assumed Karaite creed of Ben Asher will be dealt with in *Nosaḥ ha-Miqrā* (see above, Note 45), I should like to say meanwhile that the argument of the acceptance of the Aleppo Codex by Maimonides against the assumption of Ben Asher's Karaite leanings has been grossly overplayed. Cf. Dothan, *Sinai* 41:307.

138. The full quotation has been given in my "Authenticity," n. 1.

139. Most recently published by President Ben-Zvi (*Textus* 1:13f.) and in Kahle, *Hebräischer Bibeltext*, pp. 84f.

What I claim is that my general hypothesis accommodates all the facts no worse—and I venture to hope better—than does his.

50. Many details, however, are still in need of further examination,[140] and I pray that my colleagues and I may be allowed to continue our work, filling in what is missing and correcting what is wrong. Meanwhile it will be left to fellow scholars to decide which picture they wish to accept.

140. I need not repeat that only certain details known already have been given in the footnotes to this paper. See *Nosaḥ ha-Miqrā*.

האמנם היה בן־אשר קראי?

שנים רבות העסיקה את החוקרים השאלה המטרידה: מה היתה אמונתו
של בן־אשר? האם היה קראי או רבני? למן שנות השׁשׁים של המאה הקודמת,
כשהועלתה לראשונה ההשׁערה שׁבן־אשׁר קראי היה, ניטש ויכוח חריף בשׁאלה זו,
ויכוח שׁלא חסרו בו האשׁמות הדדיות בכפירה ובקנאות לקראות. ולא לפלא
ייחשׁב הדבר, שׁכן היתה זו שׁאלה עדינה, שׁבה הצד ההיסטורי טפל וכמעט נטול
חשׁיבות לעומת הצד התיאולוגי.

בן־אשׁר נחשׁב לבר־סמכא בכל הנוגע לנוסח המקרא המסורתי, בעיקר
בניקוד, בטעמים, במלא וחסר, בפרשׁיות סתומות ופתוחות וכדומה. אמנם בתחילה
לא היה הוא בבחינת דן יחידי, ויעידו על כך רשׁימות החילופים בינו ובין בן־
נפתלי, אך מאז סמך הרמב״ם את ידו על נוסחו, הרידו בחזקת פוסק אחרון לגבי
נוסח המקרא.

והנה כשׁטעננו הטוענים שׁבן־אשׁר היה קראי, ערערו בכך את אחד היסודות
החשׁובים ביותר שׁעליו נשׁען נוסח המקרא שׁבידינו. ובמוחם של כל המשׁתתפים
בויכוח, שׁנתעורר בעקבות טענה זו, ניקרה השׁאלה: הייתכן, שׁאלו הכול, שׁנוסח
המקרא שׁלנו התבסס במשׁך כל הדורות על נוסח של מין? המתנגדים לטענה
החדשׁה ביססו את פרכתם על העובדה, שׁהרמב״ם לא היה סומך ידו
על נוסח של קראי. ואילו הראשׁונים מצאו צידוק לרמב״ם ואמרו, שׁלא ידע דבר
על אמונתו של בן־אשׁר, והסתפקו בהערה, שׁאכן קרה לו דבר מפתיע.

הויכוח הגדול על קראיותו של בן־אשׁר נמשׁך עד שׁלהי המאה הקודמת, וכדין
כל ויכוח, שׁהצדדים המשׁתתפים בו אין בידם להוסיף טענות חדשׁות על מה
שׁכבר נאמר, שׁכך ודעך. אולם הבעיה לא נתיישׁבה. כל צד העמיד את ראיותיו
שׁלו, אך לא תמיד עלה בידו לבטל ביטול גמור את ראיות הצד שׁכנגד. אעפ״כ
לא מצאה לה ההשׁערה החדשׁה אזניים קשׁובות, ורוב מעניינם של הכותבים בעניין
זה הסתייגו ממנה; דומה היה, שׁהדף מוכרעת לצד המתנגדים.

אולם משׁהצליח קלאר לקרוא את השׁם בן־אשׁר בכתובת שׁבראשׁ כתב־יד
של ״אשׁא משׁלי״ לרס״ג, נכנסה השׁאלה כולה למפנה חדשׁ. לאור תגליתו בחן
קלאר את הטענות הישׁנות, ביסס אותן מחדשׁ והשׁלים ע״י כך את התמונה
המשׁקפת את דמותו של בן־אשׁר. קלאר קבע באופן מוחלט שׁבן־אשׁר היה קראי.
על דעה זו, שׁהיתה מאז הדעה השׁלטת בחוגי המלומדים, לא קמו מערערים.

כשׁבאים אנו לבחון היום בעיה זו מחדשׁ, לא נוכל להתעלם מתולדותיה.
בייחוד במקרה זה, שׁהבעיה לא היתה קיימת כלל ורק נולדה וההריפה בעיצומו
של ויכוח ועל ידיו, דין הוא שׁנבדוק בדיקה חדשׁה את טענות המתווכחים אחת
לאחת, לפני שׁנאמר את דברינו *.

---

* תודתי נתונה לפרופ׳ ז׳ בן־חיים, שׁקרא את כתב היד של מאמר זה והעיר לי הערות
חשׁובות, ולמר מ׳ מדן, שׁסייעני בהדפסתו.

Reprinted from *Sinai* (1957).

קיצורים וראשי תיבות

אבן אלהיתי — G. Margoliouth, Ibn Al-Hiti's Arabic Chronicle of Karaite
Doctors, JQR IX (1897), 429—443.

אפנשטיין, גאונים — S. Eppenstein, Beiträge zur Geschichte und Literatur im
geonäischen Zeitalter, Berlin, 1913.

אשא משלי — ב"מ לוין, "אשא משלי לרס"ג" ב"רב סעדיה גאון, קובץ תורני־מדעי,
בעריכת הרב י"ל מישמן, ירושלים, תש"ג, עמ' תקה—תקלב.

אשה"כ — ספר אשכל הכפר ליהודה הדסי בן אליהו הדסי, גוזלוו, 1836.

גוטלובר, ביקורת — אברהם בער גאטטלאבער, בקרת לתולדות הקראים, וילנא, 1865.

גרץ, בא"מ — H. Graetz, Die beiden Ben-Ascher und die Masora, MGWJ
XX (1871), 1—12, 49—59.

גרץ, התחלות — H. Graetz, Die Anfänge der Vocalzeichen im Hebräischen,
MGWJ XXX (1881), 348—367, 395—405.

גרץ, תוה"י — H. Graetz, Geschichte der Juden, 5. Band, 3. verbesserte Auflage,
Leipzig, 1895.

המהדורה הראשונה של כרך זה נדפסה בשנת 1860 ולא עלה בידי לראותה.

דודזון, מלחמות — ישראל דודזון, ספר מלחמות ה' כולל טענות הקראי סלמון בן ירוחים
נגד רב סעדיה גאון, נויארק, תרצ"ד.

דקה"ט — ספר דקדוקי הטעמים לרבי אהרן בן משה בן אשר, מהדורת בער ושטראק,
ליפסיא, 1879.

חילוק הקראים — חלוק הקראים והרבנים, נדפס בלקוטי קדמוניות לפינסקר, עמ' 99—106.

כי"ל — כתב־יד תנ"ך מס' B19a בספרייה הציבורית ע"ש סלטיקוב־שצ'דרין, לנינגרד.
השתמשתי בתצלום שבספרייה הלאומית, ירושלים.

כי"ק — כתב־יד נביאים משנת 895 בבית הכנסת של הקראים בקהיר. השתמשתי בתצלום
שבספרייה הלאומית, ירושלים.

ליפשיץ, חילופים — L. Lipschütz, Der Bibeltext der tiberischen Masoretenschulen,
Ben Ašer — Ben Naftali, Mukačevo, 1935.

ל"ק — שמחה פינסקער, לקוטי קדמוניות לקורות דת בני מקרא והליטעראטור שלהם,
וויען, 1860.

מאן, היהודים — J. Mann, The Jews in Egypt and in Palestine under the Fāṭimid
Caliphs, Volume I (1920), Volume II (1922).

ספיר א' — יעקב ספיר, אבן ספיר, חלק ראשון, ליק, 1866.

ספיר ב' — יעקב ספיר, אבן ספיר, ספר שני, מגנצא, 1874.

פוזננסקי — S. Poznański, The Karaite Literary Opponents of Saadiah — KLOSG
Gaon, London, 1908. (JQR של XVIII—XX מן הכרכים מקובצת הדפסה)

פירסט, תוה"ק א' — J. Fürst, Geschichte des Karäerthums bis 900 der gewöhnlichen
Zeitrechnung, Leipzig, 1862.

פירסט, תוה"ק ב' — J. Fürst, Geschichte des Karäerthums von 900 bis 1575 der
gewöhnlichen Zeitrechnung, Leipzig, 1865.

קלאר, בחקרים — בנימין קלאר, "בן־אשר", מחקרים ועיונים בלשון, בשירה ובספרות, תל־אביב,

תשי"ד, עמ' 276—319. המאמר נדפס ראשונה בתרביץ יד (תש"ג), עמ' 156—173 ;
טו (תש"ד), עמ' 36—49.

L. Nemoy, Kitab al-Anwar wal-Maraqib, Code of Karaite Law, — קרקסאני
by Yaʾqub al-Qirqisāni, New York, Volume I, 1939.

פרק ראשון: הטענות לקראיותו של בן־אשר

כדי להקל על ההבנה של השתלשלות הבעיה, נפריד את הטענות זו מזו
ונחלקן לשלושה שערים, אע״פ שבדברי המתווכחים קשורות הן ואחוזות זו בזו.
השער האחד — דברי חכמים בספרות הקרובה קרבת זמן לבן־אשר, השני —
דקדוקי הטעמים, והשלישי — הקולופונים של כתבי־יד המיוחסים לבן־אשר.

א. ראיות מן הספרות

ראשון עורר את הבעיה שמחה פינסקר בשנת 1860. וכה דבריו[1] : „ואני
איני חש לחוות דעתי שכל אלה בעלי מסורה ודקדוק ונקוד וטעמים (בצירוף
ב"א ו ב"נ) שהיו מבלים כל ימיהם במלאכות כאלה ולא נמצא מהן ממקום
אחר שום סימן שהתעסקו גם בתלמוד, אלה כולם חשודים אצלי
בקראית או עכ״פ אם לא היו קראים בפרהסיא, מידי ריח קראית והנטיה
אליה לא יצאו... וכן דעתי ג״כ על אותם שעסקו רק באגירת האגרונות ופרושי
המקראות עפ״י פשט חשודים אצלי בכך, אך להתודע ולהגלות שזה החשד נופל
ממני רק על אותן מבעלי מלאכה כאלה שהיו בין התגלות ענן ובין כמו חמשים
שנה אחר הרס״ג, אבל אחר זה הזמן נמצאים מתעסקים כאלה גם בין הרבנים,
אעפ״י שלא נודע מהם זולת זה דבר״[2].

כבר טען „שור״[3] על פסקנותו השרירותית של פינסקר במשפט זה, שהרי
אי אפשר לחשוד בקראיות כל מי שאין עליו ראיה שהיה רבני. אולם את ההוכחות
להנחה אכסיומאטית זו של פינסקר הביא גרץ. הוא קיבל את ההנחה, שבן־אשר
היה קראי, אף ביסס אותה בראיות מרובות. מתוכן נביא בשער זה רק את הארבע
שעניינן לכאן[4] :

א. בן־אשר נזכר פעמים אחדות בכינוי „המלמד". כך בכי"ל[5] „המלמד
אהרן בן משה בן אשר נוחו בגן עדן" וכן בכתבי־יד אחרים. וכינוי זה מצוי רק
אצל קראים.

ב. דונש מעיד[6] שרס״ג השיב על בן־אשר, והרי רס״ג לא השיב אלא
על קראים ומינים, גם לא נהג בו כבוד בתשובתו[7], מכאן שבן־אשר היה קראי.

---

1 ל״ק עמ' לב. הפיזור בהבאה מידי הוא.　　2 עי' גם ל״ק, עמ' 163.

3 י״ה שור, בקורת ס' לקוטי קדמוניות להחכם ר"ש פינסקער, החלוק, מחברת ששית,
תרכ"ב (1861), עמ' 67.

4 גרץ תוה"י, עמ' 479־480. ראיותיו האחרות ר' להלן בשערים הבאים.

5 בקולופון שבעמ' 479 א'. גרץ ציטט ע״פ ה־ Prospectus של Pinner (אודיסה,
1845), עמ' 86.

6 ספר תשובות דונש הלוי בן לברט על רבי סעדיה גאון (ברסלאו, 1866), עמ' 21,
סי' 72.

7 זאת למד גרץ כנראה, אע״פ שלא אמר זאת בפירוש, מדבריו של שד"ל, בית האוצר,

ומתוך שרס״ג פונה בתשובתו אל בן־אשר בגוף שני „תֵּלַף", הרי שהתשובה
מכוונת אֶל בן זמנו, היינו אל א ה ר ן בן־אשר [8].

ג. ‏דונש ותלמידו יהודי בן ששת אינם מזכירים את בן־אשר בתשובותיהם
על מנחם ותלמידיו, שכן היה דונש בן ארץ־ישראל, וכבן דורו הצעיר של אהרן
בן־אשר, ידע שהוא קראי [9].

ד. הקראי יהודה הדסי מדבר בבן־אשר כבבן עדתו, שכן הוא מזכירו
בברכת „רוח ד' תניחנו" [10].

נשקול טענות אלה אחת אחת :

א. על הטענה הראשונה כבר השיבו [11], שגם בין הרבניים היו מלמדים,
מלמדי תינוקות, שעיסוקם בכך. ומסתבר שראשוני העוסקים בדקדוק ובמסורה
היו מלמדים, שהתפרנסו מהוראת המקרא והקריאה לתינוקות [12].

ולגופה של הטענה יש לומר : ברוב המקומות, שבהם נזכר אהרן בן־אשר
בכינוי „המלמד", משתמע מתוכם התוכן המקצועי הטמון בכינוי זה. כך בכי״ל [13],
כך בכ״י חאלב [14] „המלמד הגדול", „ראש המלמדים" [15], כך בראש ספר החילופים
של מישאל בן עזיאל [16] „אלכלף אלד״י אכתלף פיה אלמעלמין" ותרגומו [17]
„החלוף אשר נתחלפו בו שני המלמדים" וכך בדברי בעל מאמר השוא [18] „גם
היו עם אלו הזקנים המלמדים הגדולים הנזכרים למעלה מלמדים אחרים והיו
חכמים גדולים על קריאת ארבע ועשרים ובקיים בכל הנקודים והטעמים והמסורות
וכל שמושיהם" [19] — בכל אלה, ובייחוד בשני האחרונים, ברורה המשמעות

לשכה א', יא ע״ב, שניקד „תֵּלַף תֵּלֶף האותות" ופירש : „ראוי שתלמד למוד האותיות קודם
שתכתוב מה שכתבת". עוד אפנשטיין, גאונים, עמ' 72, הע' 1, מחזיק בפירוש זה, אע״פ
שאינו מסכים למסקנה שמבסס עליו גרץ.

      8 ‏גרץ, בא״מ, עמ' 9.   9 ‏גרץ, שם, עמ' 57־58.

10 ‏אשה״כ, א״ב קסג, אות ל' (דף ס ע״ב) : „בן אשר ר י י ״ ת המדקדק במסורות
מכתבך". ובא״ב קעג, אות נ' (דף ע ע״א) מזכירו בברכת „נ״ע".

11 ‏גוטלובר, ביקורת, עמ' 125, בשולי תרגום דבריו של גרץ ; הרכבי בהערתו לדברי
ימי ישראל (תרגים שפ״ר לגרץ, תוה״י) חלק ג' (1893), עמ' 488, הע' קפו.

12 ‏על עיסוק זה עי' אפנשטיין, גאונים, עמ' 43־45 ; מאן, היהודים, כרך א' עמ' 270 ;
ש' אסף, תקופת הגאונים וספרותה (תשט״ו), עמ' קיד ועוד.

13 ‏ר' לעיל בגוף טענתו של גרץ. אף הוא עצמו מפקפק אם כי״ל נכתב ע״י סופר
קראי ובשביל קראי (עי' גרץ, בא״מ, עמ' 58).

14 ‏הוא ה„כתר" המפורסם שבארם צובה, וביטויים אלה הם מן הקולופון הארוך
שבסופו. ועי' על כ״י זה להלן בשער ג של פרק זה.

15 ‏והשוה את הביטוי „ראש המדברים" בראש ספר מאזנים לראב״ע (הוצ' אופיבאך,
תקנ״א], דף ב ע״א].

16 ‏ליפשיץ, חילופים, עמ' ג'.

17 ‏בעדת דבורים לר' יוסף הקסטנדיני (הרכבי, חדשים גם ישנים, חלק א' חוב' ב',
עמ' 12].

18 ‏K. Levy, Zur Masoretischen Grammatik (Stuttgart, 1936)   עמ' י.

19 ‏לדעת מאן, היהודים, כרך ב' עמ' 48, לא רק שושלת בן־אשר אלא אף כל חכמי
המסורה הנגמנים שם בסמוך — רבניים הם.

713

המקצועית של התואר „מלמד", היינו מורה, ובמקצוע זה אין לקראים, ומעולם
לא היתה להם, זכות יחיד.

זהות התפקידים של המלמד־המורה ושל הסופר ידועה היא, אעפ״כ ראוי
לבסס אותה כאן לגבי התקופה שאנו דנים בה[20]. מפורסמת היא עדותו של רס״ג
על המעשה באשה, שפנתה אל המלמד („אלמעלם") של בנה בבקשה לשחררו:
„יא ס פ ר א א פ נ י ב ר י"[21] — והרי זו עדות של משיח לפי תומו וראיה היא
לסמוך עליה, שכן מביא רס״ג מעשה זה לעניין אחר. גרף עצמו מביא בהערה
לדברי טענתו זו[22] קטע מכתב־יד, שנזכרת בו דעתו של „ ה מ ו ר ה יעקב בן
נפתלי ה ס ו פ ר". ובקולופון של כ״י חאלב מכונה אהרן בן אשר בשם „אדון
הסופרים... וראש ה מ ל מ ד י ם", ובמקום אחר „ ה מ ל מ ד ה ג ד ו ל ר' אהרן
בן משה בן אשר... הוא א מ ן ג ד ו ל ב ת ק ו ן הסופרים"[23], ואין „אמן" כאן אלא
סופר ו„ה א ו מ נ י ם הראשונים"[24] הם „הסופרים הראשונים"[25].

ולא זו בלבד, שמלאכת הסופרים־המלמדים מעצם טיבה בוודאי אינה
מיוחדת לקראים, אלא אף שנמצא כינוי זה מצורף לשמותיהם של חכמים, שאין
ספק ברבניותם: „מרנא ורב' אפרים... ברבי שמריה ה מ ל מ ד"[26], „...בן
מ ל מ ד י... מרנא ורבנא עובדיהו הכהן ה מ ל מ ד"[27], ועוד רבים. ובמכתב מאת
ראשי ישיבת ירושלים אל קהילות ארץ־ישראל פונים הכותבים, בין יתר מנהיגי
הציבור, אף אל ה מ ל מ ד י ם[28].

בכך בטלה אפוא הטענה המסתמכת על הכינוי „מלמד".

ב.   אמנם, אין להביא ראיה ממה שנראה לגרף פניי זלזול של רס״ג אל
בן־אשר, שהרי שלוש המלים, המובאות בדברי דונש, כבר נתפרשו בדרך
אחרת[29], ואין הזלזול משתמע מתוכן. אבל טענתו של גרף, שרס״ג כתב תשובות
רק נגד קראים ואפיקורסים ולכן בן־אשר המותקף הוא קראי, שרירה וקיימת,

---

20   לגבי תקופות קודמות יוזכר כאן, דרך משל, רב שמואל בר שילת שהיה מלמד
תינוקות ושבאו ממנו ובשמו אמירות רבות בהלכות כתיבת ספר תורה ומזוזה (כגון בירושלמי
מגילה פ״א הי״א), או מאמר המדרש: „קורות בתינו [ארזים] אלו ה ס ו פ ר י ם רהיטנו
[ברותים] אלו ה ת י נ ו ק ו ת " (ילקוט שמעוני, תתקפ״ה, לשיה״ש א, יז), ועוד הרבה.

21   פירוש ספר יצירה לרס״ג, פ״ב ה״ב (מהדורות למברט, החלק הערבי, עמ' 45).

22   גרף, תוה״י, עמ' 480, הע' 1.

23   דקה״ט עמ' XXXVIII (מתוך כ״י F 88 שבספרייה הציבורית בלנינגרד).

24   שטראק, ספר הזיכרון לאלכסנדר קוהוט (1897), עמ' 572 (מתוך כ״י נייר
צופוט־קלעה מס' 1 שבספרייה הנ״ל).

25   דקה״ט § 19.   26   מאן, היהודים, כרך ב', עמ' 119.

27   מאן, שם, עמ' 279.

28   אסף, מקורות ומחקרים בתולדות ישראל (תש״ו), עמ' 30. וע׳ גם בקרובה
„אותותיך" לשביעי של פסח, לר' שמעון בר יצחק : „מלמדי ומשכילי וסופרי" (בסיום
הפסקה „תמך במעגלותיו"). ועוד ע׳ להלן הע' 96 בראיה מדברי קרקסאני, שבהם „מורים"
אינו אלא מלמדים.

29   ופירושן האמיתי „תֵּלֵף תֵּלֶף הָאֹתֶת" — הזדיין בנשקך כותב הזיכרונות לעתיד.
ע׳ ב' אלוני, לשוננו טז (תש״ח־תש״ט), עמ' 180, וסיני כרך כח (תשי״א), עמ' קמד ואילך,
ובייחוד עמ' קנח־קנט והספרות הנזכרת שם.

אע״פ שבאבר [30] אינו מוכן להסתפק בראיה כזו, כדי לקבוע על פיה שבן־אשר היה קראי. ועוד נשוב לדבר בענין זה.

ג. טענתו השלישית של גרץ אי אפשר לקבלה כלל. אם דונש ותלמידו אינם מזכירים את בן־אשר, עדיין אין מכאן ראיה שהיה קראי. גם מנחם, שלא היה בן ארץ־ישראל, אינו מזכיר את בן־אשר, ולעומתו דוד בן אברהם, שהיה קראי וישיב בארץ־ישראל [31] והיה בן דורו הצעיר של בן־אשר, אף הוא אינו מזכירו. בדרך זו לא נוכל להוכיח דבר : לא שהיה בן־אשר קראי ולא שהיה רבני. העובדה שגרץ מסתמך עליה אין בה אלא כדי ללמד, שבתקופה זו, היינו בדורי ובמאה העשירית בכלל, עדיין לא יצא שמו של בן־אשר [32].

ד. טענה זו כבר הופרכה [33]. אין הקראים מבחינים בברכות המתים בין בני בריתם ובין רבניים במקום שהמריבה אינה מקלקלת את השורה. וכן מצאנו בדברי הדסי גם „יהודה בן דוד חיוג הספרדי ז״ל ויונה בן גנח נ״ע״ [34]. ובסידור התפילה של הקראים נזכרים בין ראשי הקראים גם שלושה מחכמי הרבניים בברכת „זכרונם לברכה ולתחייה״, ורבנים אלה נקראים שם אפילו „שלושת הצדיקים הנוחלים בגן עדן״. ובמקומות הרבה שאינם ענין למחלוקת ולקנאת הדת מכנים הקראים את הרבניים „אחינו״ [35]. יתר על כן, ברכת „רי״ת״ נוסח קדמון היא ומשתמשים בה בין השאר גם יהודי תימן ובבל ואף על רס״ג נאמרה [36]. עכ״פ אין ראיה זו של גרץ ראיה כלל.

ראינו אפוא שמן הראיות לקראיותו של בן־אשר, הנסמכות על הספרות הקרובה לו קרבת זמן, נשארה רק אחת, טענה ב׳, שלא הופרכה.

ב. ראיות מדקדוקי הטעמים

אלה טענותיו של גרץ [37] :

א. מן האמור בדקדוקי הטעמים (§ 3) „סדר הנביאים האשמרת התיכונה, שלום התורה כמעמד התורה, ומורים מהם הוריה כתורה״ [37a] ברור שבן־אשר

---

30   Die Massora בספרם של Winter ור־„Die Jüdische Literatur, Wünsche”, חלק ב׳ (1894), עמ׳ 131.

31   עי׳ ש״ל סקוז במבואו למהדורת כתאב ג׳אמע אלאלפאט׳ לדוד בן אברהם, כרך א׳, עמ׳ XXXVI — L.

32   ועי׳ על כך עוד להלן בפרק השלישי.

33   עי׳ גוטלובר, ביקורת, עמ׳ 124, בשולי תרגום דבריו של גרץ.

34   אשה״כ, א״ב קמ״ג, אות צ׳ (דף ע״ב).

35   אברהם פירקוביץ העיר בספרו הנ״ל של גוטלובר (שם), שהדסי נוהג להבדיל בין קראים ורבנים ע״י נטיית הכינוי : חכמי הקראים בגוף ראשון, כגון „משכילי״, וחכמי הרבניים בגוף שני, כגון „יהודה חיוג ויונה בן גאנח ואבן עזרא ז״ל ושאר בעלי הלשון מדקדקיך״ (אשה״כ, א״ב קסז, אות ש׳, דף סג ע״ב). ואולם פירקוביץ לא דק פורתא וראיתו היא, לדעת גוטלובר, ראיה לסתור, שכן אומר הדסי על בן־אשר „המדקדק במסורות מכתבך״ (עי׳ לעיל הע׳ 10) בכינוי של גוף שני, הרי שבן־אשר המדקדק היה רבני דוקא.

36   ספרי א׳, עמ׳ קצא.   37   גרץ, תוה״י, עמ׳ 480־479.

37a   גרץ מצטט כאן ע״פ קונטרס המסורת המיוחס לבן־אשר, הוצ׳ ליב דוקעס (טיבינגען 1846), עמ׳ 37־36.

חשב את הנביאים והכתובים כחלק מן התורה וכהשלמה לה. והרי זו שיטתם של
הקראים. פירסט [38] הבהיר טענה זו ביותר והציג זו למול זו את עמדתם של
הרבנים ושל הקראים לגבי נביאים וכתובים: הראשונים לומדים הלכה מן התורה:
נביאים וכתובים הם רק בגדר קבלה ואסמכתה ו„דברי תורה מדברי קבלה לא
ילפינן". [39] ואילו האחרונים לומדים הלכה מכל התנ״ך וכל התנ״ך „תורה" הוא
לדידהו, וכמותם סבור גם בן־אשר, שנביאים וכתובים הם „שילום התורה" או
„אשלמתא" [40] ו„מורים מהם הוריה כתורה".

ב. עקרונות הלימוד הראשיים להלכה הקראית הם בדרך כלל שלושה:
הכתוב (לשון המקרא), ההיקש (האנאלוגיה) והקיבוץ (נקרא גם עדה, הסכמה) [41]
— וכולם שווים ללמוד מהם דבר הלכה. בן־אשר מזכיר בדקדוקי הטעמים את
אחד מעקרונות הלימוד, ההיקש (,המוקש" — § 3), ואף מעיד עליו שהוא נחשב
כמו הכתוב גופו. [42]

ג. לשון בן־אשר בדקדוקי הטעמים (§ 9) „על שלשה דרכים אמורה.
רבם בדעה קשורה... ומהם בצווי אסורה ומהם בעדה עצורה" מעידה על קבלה
מלאה של עקרונות הלימוד הקראיים: ,דעה" היא ההיקש או הידיעה, ו,עדה"
(ובכ״י אחר „כנסת") היא ההסכמה, הקיבוץ. [43]

ד. הלשון „משכיל" מוסב פעמים אחדות על בן־אשר. כך, למשל,
„המשכילים והמזהירים יזהירו כזהר הרקיע בגן עדן". [44] במקום אחר משתמש
הוא עצמו בביטוי „והמשכילים יבינו". [45] וכינוי זה, „משכיל", מיוחד לקראים
בלבד.

נבחן עתה גם טענות אלה:

א. דווקא „שילום" ו„אשלמתא" מתאימים לשיטת הרבנים, שכן רואים
הם בנביאים ובכתובים וגם בתורה שבעל־פה ה ש ל מ ה לתורה, ואילו לשיטת
הקראים, נביאים וכתובים תורה ממש הם ולא „אשלמתא". ולכן דווקא הביטוי
„שילום התורה", כפי שהוא מתפרש ע״י גרץ, הוא ראיה לסתור. יתר על כן:
בדקדוקי הטעמים מוסב „שילום" רק על הנביאים ולא על הכתובים, ועל הכתובים
לא נאמר שהם „כמעמד התורה". והרי ההבחנה בין רמת קדושתם של הנביאים
והכתובים אינה קיימת אצל הקראים. [46]

---

38 פירסט, תוה״ק א', עמ' 113—115.   39 חגיגה י ע״ב, בבא קמא ב ע״ב.

40 לדעת גרץ, שם, קיבלו מהם הרבנים בתמימותם את השם „אשלמתא" ככינוי
לנביאים (אשלמתא קדמיתא — נביאים ראשונים, אשלמתא בתריתא — נביאים אחרונים), ולא
הרגישו שהם סוטים בזה מדרך התלמוד.

41 על מונחים אלה והקרובים אליהם — העתקה, סבל הירושה, והם „הגדת אב לבן",
מסורת הקבלה הקראית — ע״י לאחרונה צ' אנקורי, Some Aspects of Karaite-Rabbanite
Relations in Byzantion on the Eve of the First Crusade, PAAJR, XXIV (1955)
עמ' 10–11.

42 כדי ללמוד דבר זה מדקה״ט חייב היה גרץ לתקן את הנוסח ולהוסיף מלים. ועי'
על כך להלן עמ' רצ.   43 גרץ, התחלות, עמ' 366, הע' 1.

44 דקה״ט § 1. גרץ השתמש בנוסח שבמקראות גדולות, ויניציא רע״ח, ובקונטרס
המסורת, עמ' 2.   45 דקה״ט § 3. גרץ מצטט ע״פ קונטרס המסורת, עמ' 36–37.

46 עי' גוטלובר, ביקורת, עמ' 126־127, בשולי תרגום דבריו של גרץ.

מצד שני נראה שגם הלשונות "שילום", "אשלמתא" אין פירושם השלמה
אלא מסירה [47], וכן שימושו של הפועל "שלם" במדרשים ובפיוטים [48] ואף בלשונות
הקרובות (בסורית "משלמנותא" = מסורת). ועל כן שילום־אשלמתא מתאימים
ל"קבלה"; ואמנם כך, "דברי קבלה", נקראים ספרי הנביאים בתלמוד, ובתקופה
מאוחרת יותר נקראו גם "אשלמתא", משום שהשם המקביל, מסורה או מסורת,
נתפס לעניינים אחרים.

ודייק יעקב ספיר [49] מן הלשון "ולמדים ממנו הורייה כתורה" [50], שדווקא
מדברי נביאים לומדים הלכה אבל לא מדברי כתובים [51]. והמאמר "דברי תורה
מדברי קבלה לא ילפינן" כוונתו, שאין לומדים גזרה שווה מדברי קבלה [52], כי
לשון תורה לחוד ולשון נביאים לחוד, אבל דין תורה למדים מן הנביאים [53].
וכך מוכרע גם מן הלשון: לא נאמר "דין תורה... לא ילפינן" אלא "דברי
תורה... לא ילפינן" [54]. אופנהיים הוסיף דוגמאות הרבה לעניין זה [55], כגון, "דבר
זה מתורת משה לא למדנו עד שבא יחזקאל ולימדנו" (יבמות כב ע"ב, פג ע"ב), או
"דברי קבלה כדברי תורה דמו" (ראש השנה יט ע"א), שהוא מאמר מקביל ממש
ל"שלום התורה כמעמד התורה". אף הוא מדייק מן הלשון "ומורים בה [56] הורייה".

<hr/>

47   כבר עמד על כך צ"מ פינילים, המגיד, שנה ד' (1860), גיליון 40, עמ' 163. —
ואע"פ שלשנה האחרת חזר בו וקיבל דעת גרץ בעניין קראיותו של בן־אשר.

48   ועי' צונץ, Literaturgeschichte der synagogalen Poesie (ברלין, 1865), עמ'
641-642; מילון בן־יהודה ערך "שלם" (בכרך ט"ו ההולך ונדפס, עמ' 7182-7183). אחרים
פירשו "שילום" ע"ש ההפטרה שנקראה אשלמתא (קלאר, מחקרים, עמ' 308, הע' 198).

49   ספיר א', טז ע"א ; ספיר ב', עמ' קפז-קפח.

50   כך הנוסח בכי"ק (עמ' 583) והוא שהיה לעיני ספיר.

51   חוץ מחליפין דבועז, אבל שם כתוב "וזאת לפנים בישראל" (רות ד, ז), משמע
שדין תורה זה קדום הוא. עי' ספיר ב', עמ' קפח. ועי' רש"י חולין קלז ע"א ד"ה אנן דברי
קבלה נינהו : "תורת משה קרויה תורה לפי שנתנה תורה לדורות ושל נביאים לא
קרי אלא קבלה...".

52   וחיזוק לכך גם מן הנוסח העברי "דין ד ב ר י ת ו ר ה מ ד ב ר י ת ו ר ה
ואין דנין דברי תורה מדברי קבלה" (נדה כג ע"א). ועי' גם פוזננסקי, Anan et ses écrits
REJ, XLIV (1902), עמ' 179, הע' 2.

53   אך רק מדברי נביאים האמורים בדרך ציחי, כגון, ערל שפסול לעבודה (מיתזקאל
מד, ט : כל־בן־נכר ערל לב וערל בשר לא יבוא אל־מקדשי), ובדיקת הסכין מן התורה (משמואל
א' יד, לד : ושחטתם בזה ואכלתם), וחתימת עדים בשטר (מירמיה לב, מד : וכתוב בספר
וחתום והעד עדים), ועוד הרבה.

54   ועי' סקירתו ההיסודית של ש' פדרבוש באזכרה להרב א"י קוק, מחלקה ד' (תרצ"ז),
עמ' סט־ע.

55   D. Oppenheim, Ben-Ascher und der angebliche Differenzpunkt in
Betreff der Heiligkeit der Bibel zwischen Rabbinismus und Karäismus
ב־ Zeitschrift של גייגר, XI (1875), עמ' 84. ואע"פ שלא ירד לעומקו של עניין כיעקב ספיר.

56   לא דייק אופנהיים בהבאת דברי הקטע. כאן (במאמרו עמ' 84) הביא "בה", לפני כן
(עמ' 81) הביא "בו", וזה גם זה אינו ידוע לי מכתבי־יד, אלא או "ממנו" או "מהם". אך אין בכך
נפקא מינה לעניינו.

דווקא הוריה ולימוד מן הנביאים ולא מצוות, ושלא כקראים, השואבים את מצוותיהם מכל התנ״ך.

וכראיה אחרונה: בניגוד לתפיסה הקראית שכל חלקי המקרא שווים הם בערכם, וכולם תורה ממש, מכנה בעל דקדוקי הטעמים את הכתובים „ק ב ל ה של אמת" (§ 3).

ב. יסוד מידת ההיקש הוא אצל הרבניים ובוודאי איננו סימן קראי מובהק [57]. פירסט הרגיש כנראה, שהיקש ל ע צ מ ו עדיין אינו יסוד קראי כל זמן שלא נזכרו בצדו עקרונות הלימוד האחרים של הקראים, ולכן ביקש למצוא באותו מקום בדקדוקי הטעמים „להודיע שכל הכתוב והבטוי והמוקש" את כל שלושת עקרונות הלימוד. לשם כך נדחק לפרש [58] „בטוי" — Mittheilung, כלומר, עקרון ההעתקה (!).

ונתפלגו דעות החכמים אף לגבי הנוסח שעליו יש לסמוך לביסוס טענה זו או לביטולה. גרץ ומצדדיו הסתמכו על אותו קטע מדקדוקי הטעמים כפי שנדפס ב„קונטרס המסורת" [59], ואילו המתנגדים, ספיר, אופנהיים ואחרים, הסתמכו על הנוסח שבכתב-יד קהיר [60]. ומאחר שכתב-יד זה קדום בלי ספק והוא מכתיבת ידו של משה בן אשר ואין בו תיבת „המוקש", הרי, כך טענו המתנגדים, שנוסחאי של גרץ, דהיינו קונטרס המסורת וחבריו, מאוחר ומוטעה ואין משגיחים בו. וכיוון שמשה בן אשר רבני היה, לדעתם, לא ייתכן שבנו, אהרן, היה קראי.

כדי לברר עניין זה לאשורו, נביא כאן את סופו השונה של הקטע מתוך שני המקורות הללו ונברר את היחס ביניהם:

כתב-יד קהיר	קונטרס המסורת
...וכל זה להודיע	...להודיע
לכל באי העולם	
כבוד קדושתם וגודל שבחם ועוצם תפארתם	
שכל הברוי וכל [61] העליונות והתחתונות	שכל הכתוב והבטי והמוקש לכתב הקדש
5 והעתידות והקדמניות והחדשות	והנקוד והטעמים ואותיות תלויים ואותיות
	קטנים וגדולים יעקומים והנקודות והחצונות
	וסתומות [62] ופתוחים ונכתב ולא נקרא ונקרא 5
	ולא נכתב ואותיות מנוזרות
שהן על סידורן ועל חלקם ועל גבולם	כי הם על חלקם ועל גבולם ועל סדורם
וכן העליונים והתחתונים	ועל שנונם
אם רבו בשמות ובמיניהם	אם רבו בשמות ובמנין [63]
הם שבים לסידור הזה	הם שבים לסדר הזה 10
10 בבית קדש הקדשים והקדש וחצר אהל מועד.	בבית קדש הקדשים וחצר אהל מועד.

---

57   עי׳ גוטלובר, ביקורת, עמ׳ 126־127, בשולי תרגום דברי גרץ של גרץ.

58   פירסט, תוה״ק א׳, עמ׳ 115, והע׳ 407 (בעמ׳ 179).

59   עמ׳ 35־37. ונוסח זה קרוב לנוסח שבדפוס ויניצ׳יא רע״ח ולנוסח של דקה״ט § 3.

60   ע״פ מה שנדפס ע״י ספיר, ב׳, עמ׳ קפז. ובדקתי ע״פ התצלום (עמ׳ 583).

61   תיבת „וכל" נכפלת בכתב-היד.

62   בדפוס ויניצ׳יא: „וסתומים".   63   שם: „ובמיני" (= ובמינים).

הקטע המובא כאן מכתב־יד קהיר דן בזיקתה של הבריאה כולה **אל המקרא.**
עליונים ותחתונים, עבר ועתיד, הכול נאמר במקרא ונרמז בו והכול מושתת על
המקרא, אשר לו שלוש דרגות קדושה (או חשיבות) : תורה, נביאים וכתובים,
שהם בבחינת קודש הקדשים, הקודש, וחצר אוהל מועד [64]. זה בקירוב תוכנו של
הקטע. ואם גם יש בו פרטים שאינם ברורים ואף גלויים [65] בין
נסתרים, בכל זאת כולו אחדותי ועשוי מקשה אחת. ויעיד על כך החוט המשולש
העובר בו בתיאור הבריאה. בתיאור המקום : הברוי, העליונות והתחתונות —
בחינת האדם (הברוי העיקרי, שלמענו נברא העולם), העולם העליון והעולם
השפל ; בתיאור הזמן : העתידות, הקדמוניות והתחדשות — בחינת עתיד, עבר
והווה [66]. ומכאן תובן יפה אף ההדרגה המשולשת של ספרי המקרא, שעליו כל
אלה עומדים. גם ביטויים אחרים, שאין בהם מטבע החלוקה הזאת, אף הם
נשלשים : כבוד קדושתם, גודל שבחם, עוצם תפארתם ; על סידורן, על חלקם,
על גבולם [67].

לעומת קטע זה בולט חוסר הקשר והעדר הרציפות בקטע שבקונטרס
המסורת. כאן הושמט כל העניין האוניברסאלי, הדן בזיקתה של הבריאה אל
המקרא, והפונה משום כך „לכל באי העולם". ובמקומו באה הנחיה טכסטואלית
לקורא וללומד. והנחיה זו תלושה מן הקודם לה [68] — שלושת חלקי המקרא, ומן
הסיום — הַדְרָגַת הקדושה, המתיחסת אף היא אל שלושת חלקי המקרא, כפי
שהסברנו. יש על כן מקום לשער, שהפסקה החדשה (שו' 2‏־6) שובצה כאן, אולי
ע״י בעל דקדוקי הטעמים, כדי לשוות לקטע כולו אופי מסרני. עד כאן לבירור
היחס בין שני הנוסחים.

מבלי לברר לעת עתה את מובנה של השורה הראשונה שבפסקה החדשה
בקונטרס המסורת (שו' 2), נראה תחילה מה נמנה בפסקה זו. ארבעה עניינים יש

---

64   על הסבר זה של שלוש דרגות קדושה עי׳ ספרי ב', עמ' קפט ; אופנהיים במאמרו
(הנ״ל הע' 55), עמ' 90, המביא מקבילה לדימוי המקרא למקדש מן הדרש על תהלים עג, יז
בבבא מציעא פו ע״א ומ„מעשה אפד" לפרופיאט דוראן, עמ' 11 (ניסיונו של אופנהיים להסביר
את הנוסח ושבכי״ק כמדובר בניקוד עליון ותחתון אל עלה יפה) ; וכן עי׳ בער, דקה״ט, עמ' 2,
בפירוש, סימן h. — לעניין הקשר שבין „דביר" ו„ספר" השווה שופטים א, יא ו„שם דביר
לפנים קרית ספר" והדרשות שבגמרא על פסוק זה, ועי׳ לאחרונה י׳ בן־צבי, „מקדש י ה׳
הירושלמי וכתרי־התורה שבבתי־הכנסת הקראים בקושטא ובמצרים", קרית ספר לב (תשי״ז),
עמ' 366.

65   כגון „ובמניניהם" (שו' 8) שצ״ל „ובמנינים" או „ובמנין". ואולי אף המלים „וכן
העליונים והתחתונים" (שו' 7) נכפלו משו' 4.

66   הדברים ה מ ת ח ד ש י ם בכל יום. — וכל התיאור הוא בבחינת מה למעלה
מה למטה מה לפנים ומה לאחור. — איני עומד על פרטי הפירוש המוצע כאן, אך נראה,
שהדרך להבנת הקטע היא בכיוון זה ובקירוב לתפיסה זו. אפשרות אחרת, הראויה למחשבה,
היא אולי על דרך כלל ושני פרטים : כלל הבריאה — העולם העליון והעולם השפל ;
העתיד (כלל) — הנוהג מנהג קדמון (שבדרך הטבע) והמתחדש (שלמעלה מדרך הטבע).

67   איני יודע פירושם המדויק כאן, ועניינם — הנהגה.

68   לא רק תלישות בתוכן, אלא אף השמטת ביטוי הזיקה „וכל זה", כלומר, כל
שנאמר עד כאן, — ביטוי המסמיך את הקטע אל שלפניו.

719

כאן: הוספות בגוף הטכסט של המקרא (ניקוד, טעמים, אותיות נקודות, אותיות
מנוזרות), הוספות מחוץ לטכסט (חיצונים[69], כתיב ולא קרי, קרי ולא כתיב),
זרויות בכתיבת אותיות (אותיות תלויות, קטנות וגדולות ועקומות[70]) וסידור
השורות (פרשיות סתומות ופתוחות).

חסר במניך זה עיקר העיקרים — הטכסט הקונסוננטי, והוא גרמז בוודאי
במשפט הראשון במלים "הכתוב והבטוי". שתי המלים האלה מקבילות ממש
לדרכי הלימוד הנזכרות בתלמוד "יש אם למסורת", "יש אם למקרא". הכתוב,
או לפי כתבי־יד אחרים "הכתב", הוא המסורת (של האותיות), והבטוי הוא
המקרא (הקריאה המסורה של הטכסט). ושתי הדרכים הללו הן דרכי האינטרפרטציה
של הטכסט אצל ה ר ב נ י י ם[71].

ובהקשר עניינים זה, כשלפניו "הכתב והבטוי" ואחריו ההוספות השונות
על הטכסט, בוודאי אין מקום לפרש "מוקש לכתב הקדש" כהקש של קראים.
אף גרץ הרגיש, שפירושו אינו כשורה, ו"תיקן" והוסיף מדעתו "והמוקש ד ו מ ה
לכתב הקודש"[72]. ותוספת שרירותית היא ואינה מתאשרת אף מתוך אחד מן
הדפוסים ומכתבי־היד הרבים, לא אלה שגרץ ידע עליהם ואף לא אלה שנתגלו
מאז כתב את דבריו[73]. אין לנו אלא לראות מלים אלה כעין כותרת לכל הנמנה
בסמוך, ולפרשן כמו בער: מקושר ומחובר לכתב הקודש[74], דהיינו, כל אמצעי
העזר הטכניים של שתי האפליקציות להבנת הטכסט.

עוד נשאר לנו לעיין במשפט הסיום "הם שבים לסדר הזה בבית קדש
הקדשים וחצר אהל מועד". העובדה שבמשפט זה נשמטה תיבת "והקדש" בנוסחאות
הגורסות את הנוסח המתוקן[75], היינו בקונטרס המסורת וחבריו, היא עצמה מעידה,

_____

69 תיבה זו עוד לא נתפרשה, עד כמה שידיעתי מגעת, ונראה לי שהיא מכוונת להערות
המסורה הנכתבות מ ח ו ץ לטכסט, בגיליון. והשווה לכך את הסברו של בעל דקדוקי הטעמים
לתופעה של קרי וכתיב: "וצוה לכתוב אחד מ ב ח ו ץ ואחד מבפנים" (§ 8).

70 עי' על אותיות עקומות בתקון הסופר והקורא ליצחק בער, מהדורה שנייה (רעדעלהיים,
1875) בנספח עמ' 18 ואילך. ומה שהוא קורא "הפוכות", אף הן בכלל "עקומות".

71 ושמדובר כאן בהבנה ובפירוש נרמז גם בתוספת "בעניו ובמשפטו", המצויה
בקצת כתבי־יד אחרי תיבת "והבטוי". ור' עוד להלן (בפרק השני, שער ב) על גישתם של
הקראים לענין זה, שהיא שונה לגמרי.

72 גרץ, תוה"י, עמ' 480. ופירסט תוה"ק א', הע' 407 (בעמ' 179), מעתיק את
הנוסח המתוקן ע"י גרץ בלי שום הערה, כאילו כך כתוב במקור, בקונטרס המסורת.

73 ולמעשה לא הועיל גרץ אף לשיטתו, ותיקונו הוא בבחינת כל המוסיף גורע, שכן
המשפט המתוקן "הכתוב והבטוי והמוקש דומה לכתב הקודש" איננו הגיוני: הכתוב — —
דומה (!) לכתב הקודש !

74 דקה"ט, עמ' 2, בפירוש, סימן ε, ובלשונו: Das mit der heil. Schrift Verknüpfte,
Zusammenhangende. או אפשר כבאכר, (1895) ZAW, XV, עמ' 300, "מושחה לכתב
הקודש", דהיינו, מה שאינו שייך לו אלא רק מושווה אליו.

75 כך בכל כתבי־היד להוציא כ"י האלב, שבידיעותינו אודותיו עליונו לסמוך על
עדותו של בער, בחילופי הגרסאות שבדקה"ט. ושמא יש בו בכ"י זה תיקון מוטעה לתיקון
הראשון. והטעה בער במהדורת דקה"ט, שהכניס תיבת "והקדש" לגוף הטכסט על סמך כתב־יד
אחד בלבד ובניגוד לכל המקורות האחרים, כתבי־יד ודפוסים, שהיו בידו, או אולי, וזו אפשרות

שיש כאן המשך לתיקון הקטע כולו, וההשמטה השמטה מכוונת היא, הבאה ללמד
על הכלל ולאשר אותו. שכן אחרי שניטל מן הקטע תוכנו האוניברסאלי וניתן לו
תוכן מסורתי־דקדוקי, שוב אין מקום למנות בו שלוש דרגות של קדושה, כי אם
שתיים בלבד : הכתב והביטוי, דהיינו הטכסט הקונסוננטי, שהוא בבחינת קודש
הקדשים, ולעומתו המוקש לכתב הקודש, דהיינו כל יתר ההוספות, שהן בבחינת
חצר אוהל מועד.

ראינו עכ״פ שאף טענת ה„היקש״ של גרץ אין לה אחיזה ויסוד.

ג. נגד טענה זו של גרץ עדיין לא נאמר דבר, וראויה היא לבחינה
מדוקדקת. אמנם נכון הדבר, ש„דעה״ ו„עדה״ משמשות בפי הקראים לציון
עקרונות הלימוד [76], אך, כמו למעלה בעניין ההיקש, לא נוכל אף כאן לעקרן מתוך
ההקשר, שבו הן באות, ולפרשן לעצמן. אם רצה גרץ להראות, שבעל דקדוקי
הטעמים בא למנות כאן את עקרונות הלימוד של הקראים, ועקרונות אלה הם
לפחות שלושה, חייב היה למצוא גם עיקרון שלישי. אך בתיבת „ציווי״ לא נמצא
לו עיקרון שלישי, גם אם נתעלם משינוי הנוסח בכתבי־יד „כנסת״ (במקום „עדה״),
שאיננו שם של עיקרון בשום מקור קראי. וכל זמן שלא פירש תיבה זו, תיבת
„ציווי״, אין טענתו טענה [77].

קלאר בא למלא אחרי גרץ ופירש „ציווי״ כמו „מצווה״, שמשמעו „לשון
הכתוב״ [78]. וכך נמצאו לו במשפט זה שלושה עקרונות : דעה, ציווי (=כתוב),
עדה (=קיבוץ, הסכמה). אך הרי מידת ההיקש היא האופיינית לקראים ועל שמה
נקראה עדתם „אלקיאסין״ [79] (=בעלי ההיקש). איך אפשר, שדווקא מידה חשובה
ואופיינית זו נשמטה כאן ? [80] וכנראה הרגיש בכך גרץ ומשום כך לא הכריע
בפירוש תיבת „דעה״ [81] וכתב ההיקש או ידיעה [82]. פתח פתוח הניח לפרש דעה —
היקש. אבל נוסף על מה שפירוש זה מוקשה מצד הלשון, איך ייתכן, שפעם קרא

רחוקה, הושאר המשפט על מכונו בסיום כסיום לקטע השלם כולו, ובלי קשר אל הפסקה החדשה
שבסמוך לו לפניו. ואם כך גם אפשר, שאל סיום זה נמשכת ראשיתו של הסעיף הבא בדקה־ט
(46) „עוד בשלשה נמשלה תורה״, כלומר, נוסף על המשל הראשון, הממשיל את
המקרא לשלושה דברים, הרי לך עוד משל של שלושה. אך דומני שסדר זה, שבו בא סעיף 4
אחרי סעיף 3, מיוחד הוא למהדורה ואיננו במקורות שהשתמש בהם בער.

76 עי׳ על זה פוזננסקי, REJ, XLIV (1902), Anan et ses écrits, עמ׳ 179
ואילך, וכן קלאר, מחקרים, עמ׳ 308־303.

77 ועי׳ גם אפשטיין, גאונים, עמ׳ 51, הע׳ 4.

78 קלאר, מחקרים, עמ׳ 309.

79 כוזרי, מאמר שלישי, מט (מהד׳ הירשפלד, עמ׳ 198), ותרגם יהודה אבן תבון
„אנשי הסברא״ (שם, עמ׳ 199). וכן ידוע כינוים „המתקוששים״, כגון בפירוש עשרת הדברים
לנסי בן נח (ל״ק, עמ׳ 9, ועוד הרבה שם ובמקומות אחרים).

80 אמנם יהודה הדסי, אשה״כ, א״ב קסט, אות ב׳ (דף סד ע״ב), מעיד על מי שאינו
מודה בהיקש והוא יוסף בן נח, וכפי הנראה הוא בן ראשית המאה הי״א (עי׳ ש״ל סקון
The Arabic Commentary of Ali ben Suleiman the Karaite on the Book of Genesis
פילדלפיה, 1928, במבוא עמ׳ 9).

81 גרץ מעתיק שם פעמים „דעת״ במקום „דעה״.

82 בלשונו Die Analogie oder die Erkenntnis.

בן־אשר להיקש „דעה" ופעם אחרת (לעיל טענה ב') „מוקש", שהוא, לשיטתו
של גרץ, היקש. והרי אין מדובר כאן במליצות העשויות להתחלף, אלא במתחים
קבועים ובעקרונות, ומה גם שהמונח „דעה" משמש למושג אחר באותה מסגרת
של ערכים. אי אפשר אפוא לפרש דעה — היקש.

וכאמור פירש קלאר „דעה" כפשוטו, ולשיטתו נמנים כאן עקרונות הלימוד:
דעה, כתוב, קיבוץ. אך איך נניח שבעל דקדוקי הטעמים גרס שלושה עקרונות
לימוד זולת ההיקש, והרי הוא מזכיר היקש במקום אחר [83]. ואם ארבעה עקרונות
בתלמודו, מדוע אין הוא מזכיר את הארבעה, ובכלל היקש, כאן, כשהוא בא
למנות את עקרונות הלימוד במרוכז? איך יכול הוא לומר „על שלושה דרכים
אמורה", כשבאמת ארבעה דרכים אתו? [84]

יתר על כן: אם באמת כיוון בעל דקדוקי הטעמים ב„דעה" לעקרון לימוד קראי,
איך יכול הוא לומר „רובם בדעה קשורה"? הרי עקרון ה„דעה" איננו מפרנס
את רוב המצוות, ודאי לא יותר מאשר העיקרון הראשי — לשון הכתוב.
אדרבא, רבים מחכמי הקראים באותו זמן, ואולי חלקם הגדול, אינו גורס כלל
את עקרון ה„דעה" [85]. וכן אי אפשר לומר על מצוות הנלמדות בדרך ה„דעה",
שהן „לא ישתנו עד בלתי שמי שפרה"; הרי זוהי עצם מהותו של עקרון ה„דעה",
שכל אחד מחכמיהם יכול להיסמך על דעתו שלו, וללמוד חוקים ומצוות כפי ראות
שכלו. לכן לא רק שאין שייך בהן, במצוות הקראים, „לא ישתנו עד בלתי שמי
שפרה", אלא אפילו אותו קראי עצמו רשאי לחזור בו מדעתו ולשנות או לבטל
מצווה, שלמדה ע״פ סברה, ושהיה מקיימה עד ששינה את דעתו [86].

ולבסוף, נוסף על כל האמור, גם פירוש תיבת „ציווי" כלשון הכתוב איננו
נכון. פירוש זה [87] מסתמך על הביטוי „מצווה" בדברי נסי בן נח, ונביא את דבריו
לעניין זה [88]:

„דעת התורה ועשיית מצוותיה מתחלקת על ב' חלקים. א' מהם מצוה
שצוה אל שדי בתורה לעשותה ולשמרה, והיא ברורה וגלויה, כשמור את יום
השבת לקדשו, וכבד את אביך ודומיהן... והשנית מצוה צפונה [89] וסתורה והיא
מתחלקת על ב' פנים. א' מהם מצות שזכר ואמר מעט מהרבה לחייבנו להקיש
כמותם, כמו שצוה אל שדי ואמר לא תחרוש בשור ובחמור יחדו להקיש ולחייב
המריא והפרד. וכמו שאמר ונפל שמה שור או חמור להביא הכבש והסוס, ששור
וכל מיני בהמה טהורה, וחמור וכל מיני בהמה טמאה בהקש. והשנית מצות דברים
שאינם ברורים וגלוים ולא מפורשים ומבוארים בתורה ואין כמותם להקיש עליהם
ולהסבירה, ואין אנחנו יודעים אותם אלא (כצ״ל) בהגדת אב לבן וראשון לאחרון...".

---

83   וקלאר מקבל את פירושו של גרץ שם.

84   ויש מן הקראים הגירסים ארבעה עקרונות לימוד, כגון סהל בן מצליח, בן המחצית
השנייה של המאה העשירית, ואף יהודה הדסי (אשה״כ א״ב קסח, אות ב' — סד ע״ב).

85   עי' קלאר, מחקרים, עמ' 307-308.

86   ר' דברי ראב״ע לעניין זה המובאים להלן בעמ' שג.

87   קלאר, מחקרים, עמ' 309, הע' 205.

88   מתוך פירושו לעשרת הדברים (ל״ק, עמ' 11).

89   קלאר (מחקרים, עמ' 308, הע' 196) העתיק את טעות הדפוס „אפונה" מגרץ,
תוה״י, עמ' 444, ונדחק לפרשה „מסופקת".

הפירוש „מצווה" = לשון הכתוב מסתמך על האמור בראשית הדברים „מצוה שצוה אל שדי בתורה... והיא ברורה וגלויה". אך עיון קל בלבד בדברים מראה, שעקרון ה„כתוב" נרמז במלים „ברורה וגלויה", כלומר מצוות הברורות וגלויות בלשון הכתוב, להבדילן ממצוות צפונות ונסתרות, שלא נאמרו בפירוש במקרא ושיש ללמוד אותן בעקרונות הלימוד האחרים. ושאין „מצווה" מורה על עקרון ה„כתוב" דווקא, מתברר גם מתוך כך שגם בשני העקרונות האחרים נאמרה „מצווה": הן בכללם „מצוה צפונה וסתורה", כלומר שאיננה מפורשת בכתוב, והן בפירוטם „מצות שזכר ואמר מעט מרבה לחייבנו להקיש כמותם", היינו היקש, ובסמוך „מצות דברים שאינם ברורים וגלוים... אלא בהגדת אב לבן", היינו סבל הירושה. אי אפשר להוציא מלת „מצווה" כאן מידי פשוטה, ואינה יכולה אפוא לשמש אסמכתא לפירוש „ציווי" שבדקדוקי הטעמים כעקרון ה„כתוב".

ראינו שהנסיון למצוא בדקדוקי הטעמים את עקרונות הלימוד הקראים לא עלה יפה. ננסה עתה להסביר את אותו משפט בדרך אחרת. לשם כך נביאו בהקשרו ונפרשו :

„תחלה תנחיל אל דברות עשרה, ועוד משפט ואזהרה, וגם קלה וחמורה, בְּאֵר הֵיטֵב מְבֹאָרֶה, על שלשה דרכים אמורה, רֻבָּם בדעה קשורה, ויפה ברורה, ומהם בצווי אסורה, ומהם בְּעֵדָה (נ״א בכנסת) עצורה, לא ישתנו עד בלתי שְׁמֵי שְׁפָרָה" (§ 9).

פירוש הדברים כך הוא בקרוב : על עשרת הדיברות נוספו עוד מצוות עשה (משפט) ומצוות לא תעשה (אזהרה), קלות וחמורות a89, מבוארות היטב ואמורות על שלושה דרכים: רובן קשורות בדעה ובשכל וטעמן ברור יפה, חלקן אסורות וקשורות בציווי ובגזרת הכתוב (ואינן מתבארות בעזרת השכל) וחלקן עצורות ושמורות בעדת ישראל (או בכנסת ישראל) והן מצוות התורה שבעל־פה 90, ומצוות אלה לא ישתנו לעולם.

המשפט הנדון מכוון אפוא יפה לחלוקה המקובלת של מצוות התורה למצוות שכליות (דעה) 91 ומצוות שמעיות (ציווי) 92 ונוספו עליהן מצוות מדברי סופרים, השמורות בעדה.

---

89 a   ואולי בא „קלה וחמורה" לא להבחנה המקובלת של מ צ ו ו ת קלות וחמורות, אלא ע״ד המאמר בבבלי (עירובין כא, ע״ב) : „חדשים גם ישנים דודי צפנתי לך (שיה״ש ז, יד) אלו מצות קלות ואלו מצות חמורות... הללו מדברי תורה והללו מדברי סופרים". והוא ברוח הפירוט המובא מיד בסמוך : מצוות קלות הן דברי תורה (דעה וציווי) ומצוות חמורות הן דברי סופרים (עדה).

90 השווה מגילה יט ע״ב : „ועליהם ככל הדברים אשר דבר ד' עמכם בהר (דברים ט, י) מלמד שהראהו הקב״ה למשה... מ ה ש ה ס ו פ ר י ם ע ת י ד י ן ל ח ד ש".

91 ויש לתת את הדעת במיוחד על הלשון „ויפה ברורה", והוא הסבר מתאים למצות השכליות, שהן מסתברות מאליהן (כגון לא תרצח) והשכל היה מחייבן גם אילולא נכתבו בתורה (עי' ספר האמונות והדעות לרס״ג, מאמר שלישי).

92 ור' שימוש זה של ציחי בהוראת מצווה שמעית בדברי רס״ג, אשא משלי, עמ' תקכה : „צִוּויו לא יכתב לנו שרשם".

ד. גם אם נתעלם מכך שהלשון „משכיל" בא במקומות שציין גרץ
במסגרת של כתובים מן המקרא [93], הרי כינוי זה גם כשהוא לעצמו מקובל הוא
אצל הרבניים, וגם אם נטלוהו הקראים לעצמם, אין ספק שגם הרבניים לא נמנעו
מלהשתמש בו. רבים הביאו ראיות לכך משימושם של בני דורות שונים [94]. וראיה
מכרעת ביותר לכך [95] גם מבן־דורו של אהרן בן־אשר ודווקא מעדותו של קראי:
קרקסאני מעיד בפירוש, שהרבניים טוענים על עצמם שהם הם ה מ ש כ י ל י ם
ו ה מ ו ר י ם [96]. וכן מצאנו ביטוי זה בדברי רס״ג ב„אשא משלי" [97]: „מצדיקַי
ומשכילַי ומזהירַי", ורבני עלום שם בעל „שאלות עתיקות בתנ״ך" קורא לשבעת
החכמים העומדים בראש הישיבה „שבעה החברים משכילי דברים עתיקים" [98].

נראה אפוא שהלשון „משכילים" היה מקובל על הכול, וכבר עמד על כך
מאן, שגם לשון זה וגם חברו „אבלי ציון" שאולים הם בידי הקראים ומן הרבניים
באו להם [99]. לתופעה, שהקראים יחדו כינוי זה לחכמיהם, מסתברת הסיבה בכך,
שראו למעט ככל האפשר בלשון „רבנים", שהיה בו שמץ פסול לגביהם בגלל
ייחודו ה„רבני".

דומה שבזאת נדחו כל הטענות שהובאו להוכחת קראיותו של בן־אשר
ע״פ דקדוקי הטעמים [100]. ולפני שניגש לשער הבא, עוד הערה כללית: כל
המתווכחים הסתמכו על ספר דקדוקי הטעמים [101] כעל חיבור של בן־אשר,
והתייחסו אל כל מלה כתובה בו, כאילו מעטו של בן־אשר יצאה. אך דבר זה

---

93   ע״פ דניאל יב, ג, י.

94   שפע דוגמאות מביאים: גוטלובר, ביקורת, עמ' 125־126, בשולי תרגום דבריו של
גרץ; שטראק במבואו לדקה״ט, עמ' XIII — XIV; רוזין בביקורתו על דקה״ט, MGWJ, XXX
(1881), עמ' 517, מביא (ע״פ עמ' 66, הע' 1 בחיבורו R. Samuel b. Mëir als Schrifterklärer)
דוגמאות ממחברת מנחם בן סרוק, ויש להוסיף על אלה עוד (מהד' פיליפאווסקי) מעמ'
4 א, 15 ב, 16 ב, 33 א, 33 ב העוד; מילון בן־יהודה, ערך „משכיל" (כרך ז', עמ' 3431).

95   הביאה הרכבי במקום המצוין לעיל בהע' 11.

96   קרקסאני (מאמר א', סוף שער ג') עמ' 31: وهم... يزعمون انهم ناقلة وانهم اخذوا
من النبوة وانهم اصحاب اللغة وانهم هم المشكيليم والموريم. — ותרגומו: והם
(הרבניים)... טוענים שהם בעלי הקבלה ושהם קיבלו מן הנבואה ושהם בעלי הלשון ושהם
הם המשכילים והמורים. — ו„מורים" כאן מקביל ל„מלמדים" שדברנו בהם למעלה בעמ'
רמד.

97   אשא משלי, עמ' תקיט, שו' 18־19 (— אם נכונה שם ההשלמה).

98   יהודה רוזנטאל, שאלות עתיקות בתנ״ך, (1948) HUCA, XXI, חלק עברי
עמ' נא (חרוזי שה, שו' 7). הע' עוד במה שהובא לעיל, בהע' 28, מן הקרובה של ר' שמעון
בר יצחק.

99   מאן, היהודים, כרך א', עמ' 49, הע' 2, ועמ' 141, הע' 1. ולעניין „אבלי ציון"
עי' גם אסף, תקופת הגאונים וספרותה, עמ' צא.

100   ראיה נוספת של קלאר תידון להלן בפרק הבא במסגרת הדיון בתפיסת הניקוד
בדקדוקי הטעמים.

101   קודם בנדפס במקראות גדולות דפוס ויניציא רע״ח ובקונטרס המסורת, ואח״כ
במהדורת בער ושטראק.

לא הוכח, וגם המהדירים מעירים על כך [102]. גם אם יימצאו ראיות ברורות, שבן־
אשר הוא מחבר הספר, בכל זאת אין מלים וביטויים בודדים בספר זה, שאינו
עוסק בהלכה ובתיאולוגיה, עשויים לשמש אסמכתה מכרעת לעניינים דקים כל כך
כאמונתו של המחבר. שהרי קשה ומעורפלת היא לשונו גם במקום שהעניין ברור,
ואין ספק ששיבשו ונשתבשו המעתיקים בהעתקת לשונות לא מובנות להם. גם
מה שהגיע לידינו מספר זה הרי הוא מפוזר ומפורד ; מעטים הספרים, שהועתקו
בדרך כה מקרית כספר דקדוקי הטעמים, שכן העתיקו מתוכו הסופרים חלקים
חלקים לפי ראות עיניהם, אם מתוך עניין בפרק זה או אחר, אם מתוך רצון
בעלמא לעטר את ספריהם בתוך שאר רשימות מסורה גם בטכסט מסורתי קדום
ומיוחס [103], ועובדה זו מכבידה על קביעת היקפו המקורי של הספר, וקשה לאין
ערוך להוציא את יקר המקור מן הזולל שנטפל אליו במשך הדורות. על כן, גם
אילו לא היינו מצליחים להפריך בכל מקום את דברי הטוענים לקראיותו של בן־
אשר, במידה שהסתמכו על דקדוקי הטעמים, עדיין היו דבריהם עומדים על יסוד
רעוע ביותר, כל זמן שלא הוכח, שקטעי ההסתמכות שייכים לטופס המקורי של
ספר זה, כל זמן שלא הוברר שבן־אשר חיברו. מה גם שכל טענותיהם הובאו רק
מתוך שניים מעשרות פרקי דקדוקי הטעמים [104].

ג. ראיות מן הקולופונים

נפנה עתה אל העדויות שהביא גרץ מתוך הקולופונים שבכתב־יד קהיר
ושבכתב־יד חאלב.

1. כתב־היד המפורסם של נביאים שבבית הכנסת הקראי בקהיר נכתב,
בעדות אחד הקולופונים שבסופו, בידי משה בן־אשר, הוא אביו של אהרן. גרץ [105]
הוכיח תחילה, שמשה האב היה קראי, וממילא נוסף לו חיזוק לטענת קראיותו
של אהרן הבן.
ואלה טענותיו :

א. מן הלשון „כתבתי זה ה מ ח ז ו ר שלמקרא" [106] ברור, שכתב־היד

102　עי׳ בדברי דוקעס במבוא לקונטרס המסורת עמ׳ 4, ובדברי שטראק במבוא לדקה״ט
עמ׳ XVII־XIV.

103　לא מעטים כתבי־היד שבהם נרשמו קטעים מדקדוקי הטעמים בגליון סביב סביב,
ממש כמסגרת וכעיטור לגוף העמוד.

104　והם §§ 3, 9. — קלאר, מחקרים, עמ׳ 309־308, ניסה למצוא סמוכין גם
ב־§ 65. אולם פרק זה הוא פירוש וסיום (אולי באמת קראי) לפרק שלפניו „פירוש כתיב ולא
קרי" (§ 64). גם אינגו בכתבי־היד החשובים של דקדוקי הטעמים, וסגנונו, סגנון שקלא וטריא,
אינגו לשון בעל דקדוקי הטעמים, וודאי שאינו שייך לספר זה, כשם שגם הפרק „פירוש כתיב
ולא קרי" והפרק שלפניו אינם שייכים לו. ואכמ״ל. וקלאר, שקיבל העת ליפשיץ (חילופים,
במבוא עמ׳ 8, הע׳ 1), המייחס לבן־אשר רק את החלקים המחוזרים שבדקדוקי הטעמים, והעיד
על עצמו (קלאר, מחקרים, עמ׳ 291, הע׳ 89), שכך נהג בהבאת דברי בן־אשר במאמרו,
תימה שהתעלם מכך והביא את פסקה זו, שאינה חרוזה כל עיקר, ואף הסתמך עליה.

105　גרץ, בא״מ, עמ׳ 55־56.

106　כי״ק, הקולופון שבעמ׳ 586. — הקולופונים שבסוף כי״ק נדפסו ע״י קאלה,
The Cairo Geniza, עמ׳ 114־110.

הוא חלק מטופס שלם של תנ"ך. טופס זה היה מיועד לקריאה בבית הכנסת "בשבתות ובחדשים ובמועדים" [107]. ומתוך שהרבנים אינם קוראים בבית הכנסת מטופס שלם של מקרא, הרי שנכתב כי"ק לשימושם של קראים בלבד [108].

ב. בעליו של כתב-היד, יעבץ בן שלמה, הקדיש אותו לא לסתם קראים, אלא לקראים מובהקים "העושים את המועדות על ראיית הירח" [109]. מכאן שהיה יעבץ מופלג בקראיותו, וקראי כזה לא היה מזמין סופר רבני שיכתוב לו ספר תנ"ך. אמור מעתה: אף הסופר, משה בן אשר, קראי הנהו.

ג. לשון אחד הקולופונים "...עדת נביאים... המבינים כל נסתרות... לא כיחדו דבר ממה שניתן להם ולא הוסיפו מאמר על מה שנמסר להם..." [110] מעידה על ההשקפה, שהובעה גם בדקה"ט (§ 3), שהנביאים וכתובים הם ההשלמה לתורה, וע"י כך נעשית תורה-שבעל-פה מיותרת.

2. אחר שהוכח, שהאב משה היה קראי, מסתבר שגם בנו אהרן דבק באמונתו. אך לגביו, לגבי אהרן בן-אשר, הוסיף גרץ ראיות והסתמך בכך על כתב-היד של תנ"ך שבארם צובה (חאלב), שלפי עדות הקולופון שבסופו "נקד ומסר אותו" אהרן בן אשר.

גרץ טען [111]:

א. כתב-היד נמסר לשמירתה ולחסותם של שני האחים "הנשיא יאשיהו והנשיא יחזקיהו בני כבוד קדושת הנשיא דוד בן הנשיא בעז", שהם נשיאי הקראים מזרעו של ענן.

ב. בעל הקולופון מתיר אמנם לרבניים לראות את כתב-היד, אולם רק להגהת ספרים ולא לקריאה.

ג. ישראל מבצרה, המקדיש את כתב-היד, היה קראי, כפי שמתברר מתוך הקולופון.

ד. "ההערה לפני הקולופון שבראש כתב-היד "קודש לה' על ישראל הרבנים וכו'" היא מאוחרת, שכן בתיקון הסופרים שהותעק בשנת ש"ל (1570) בשביל הרמ"א מקראקא לא נכתבה הערה זו. מכאן שנוספה אחרי סוף המאה הט"ז, כשעבר כתב-היד לידי הרבניים.

דבריו אלה של גרץ טעונים עיון מדוקדק:

1. א. אילו היה כי"י קהיר חלק מכי"י של תנ"ך שלם, היה הסופר מסתפק בקולופון בראשית כתב-היד השלם או בסופו, היינו לפני התורה או אחרי הכתובים, שכן רחוק הוא להניח שנכתב קולופון מפורט כל כך באמצעו של כתב-יד. ומתוך שהקולופון נכתב אחרי הנביאים, ברור עכ"פ שכתב-היד לא כלל את ספרי הכתובים. אם כלל כתב-היד במקורו גם את התורה, קשה לדעת. אין דבר זה מתחייב כלל מתוך עיון בתצלום, שכן לפיו מתחיל כתב-היד בראשית ספר יהושע [112]. אדרבא מתוך השוואת דברי הקולופונים המאוחרים, שלא מכתיבת

---

107   בי"ק, הקולופונים שבעמ' 582, 583.

108   גרץ חזר על הציון זה גם במאמרו, התחלות, עמ' 366, הע' 1.

109   כי"ק, הקולופון שבעמ' 583. הנוסח בכתב-היד הוא "המועדים על ראות", וגרץ העתיק מספיר א', טו ע"א, אלא ש"המועדות" הוא תיקון שלו.

110   כי"ק, הקולופון שבעמ' 586.   111   גרץ, בא"מ, עמ' 57.

112   גוטהייל, שראה את סה"י גופו, מעיד (JQR XVII [1905], עמ' 639, הע'

ידו של משה בן-אשר, שנאמר בהם „זה הדפתר שמונה נביאים שהקדיש וכו'" [113], אל דברי הקולופון של משה בן-אשר עצמו „זה הדיפתר מה שזכה וכו'" [114], יש ללמוד שהדפתר [115] הזה כלל גם במקורו רק את הנביאים. ולא רק מהיקש הלשון אפשר ללמוד זאת, אלא אף מכך : אין זה מסתבר שבעל כתב-היד, יעבץ בן שלמה, פירק כתב-יד שלם, שכלל תורה ונביאים, והקדיש לקראים בירושלים רק את הנביאים [115a].

גם מן הלשון „מחזור" אין ללמוד דבר. אין ביטוי זה מורה על ט ו פ ס ש ל ם של מקרא דוקא, והוא משמש כאן במשמעות החדשה של המלה „מהדורה", המצויה כבר בלשון חז"ל בהוראה קרובה, בתלמודים של בני המערב בצורת „מחזירה" [116], ובתלמודם של בני בבל בצורה הארמית „מהדורא" [117]. וכשהמכוון הוא לטופס שלם של תנ"ך אומר, למשל, בעל הקולופון בכי"ל „מחזור מ ק ר א ש ל ם".

אולם גם אילו היה כי"ק טופס שלם של תנ"ך, המיועד לקריאה בבית הכנסת, אי אפשר לתלות קראיות במשה בן אשר. שהרי מתוך ששת הקולופונים, הבאים בסופו של כתב-היד, רק שניים הם בכתיבת ידו של סופר כתב-היד, ואילו האחרים, ובכללם שלושת הקולופונים המדברים בהקדשת כתב-יד לקראים בירושלים, כתובים בכתב שונה ודחוקים בשולי הדפים מעשה סופר מאוחר. ומכך התעלם גרץ לחלוטין [118] וייחס לכל הקולופונים מידה שווה של אותנטיות בן-

גם ספיר א', יד ע"א), שכה"י אינינו שלם בתחילתו ; מכאן למדו אחרים, שכה"י כלל גם ספרים נוספים על ספרי הנביאים, ואולי אף תנ"ך שלם. ואולם בתצלום נראים כל הדפים מתחילתו של ספר יהושע ואילך, ואין דפים לפניו. גם קאלה חושב שכי"ק כלל מעיקרו רק את הנביאים, עי' מאמרו The Ben Ascher Text of the Hebrew Bible ב-Donum Natalicum H. S. Nyberg Ablatum, עמ' 166.

113   כי"ק, הקולופון שבעמ' 583. וכן בקולופון שבעמ' 582 : „זה הדפתר הנביאים שהקדיש וכו'".

114   כי"ק, הקולופון שבעמ' 585.

115   פירושו כאן מחברת, קונטרס (עי' ירושלמי, פיאה פ"ב ה"ו, יז ע"א וחגיגה פ"א ה"ח, עו ע"א). ושלא כקאלה, The Cairo Geniza, עמ' 57, 110.

115a   קשה לקבל דעת קצת שקמו לערער על מהימנות הקולופון של משה בן-אשר ע"פ גורמים חיצוניים. הסתמכותו של ש. י. ח. סוקר („תנ"ך הוצאת ירושלים (תשי"ג)", בית מקרא, שנה ב' (תשי"ז), עמ' 5 (ג)) על העובדה שרדב"ז שותק מכי"ק אינה ראיה, שכן היה כי"ק באותו זמן בידי הקראים (שלא להזכיר את הקשיים הפאליאוגראפיים שמעוררת השערתו המאוחרת). אף טייכר במאמרו The Ben Asher Bible Manuscripts ([1950] JJS, II), עמ' 25-17), מנסה לבטל את מהימנותו של כי"ק של בן-אשר ; הנחותיו לוקות באי-דיוקים רבים, ועיקרי ראיותיו מופרכים להלן בגוף המאמר ובהערות. — אמנם ריבוי הגעיות והמתגים בכי"ק ודרכי ניקוד אחרים הזרים לשיטת בן-אשר עשויים לעורר ספקות לגבי „טהרתו" של גוף הטכסט המנוקד. וכבר העיר ח' ילון (פרשת שלח לך, קרית ספר, ל' (תשט"ו), עמ' 261) : „נביאים כ"י קהיר ודאי שזיקתו לב"א מרופה", והכוונה, ל ש י ט ת אהרן בן-אשר. אך אין להטיל ספק, לדעתי, בקולופונים.

116   ירושלמי, שבת פ"א, ב ע"ד.   117   בבלי, בבא בתרא, קנז ע"ב.

118   גרץ אמנם לא ראה את כתב-היד והסתמך על ההעתקה שבספסיר א', יד ע"ב —

אשרית. ולא רק התעלם, אלא אף הרכיב ביודעין קולופון חדש ע״י צירוף מלים
וקטעי משפטים מתוך ארבעה קולופונים שונים. וכך הוא ״מצטט״ [119] מן הקולופון
של כי״ק: ״אני משה בן אשר כתבתי זה המחזור של מקרא... [120] מה שזכה יעבץ
בן שלמה הבבלי... [121] אשר הקדיש ללקראין בירושלים... [122] העושים את המועדים
על ראית הירח יקראו בו כלם בשבתות ובחדשים ובמועדים״ [123].

לאור הבחנתנו נראים פני הדברים כך: משה בן אשר כתב, ניקד ומיסר
את מחזור הנביאים ויעבץ בן שלמה ק נ ה [124] אותו ממנו. יעבץ הקדיש אותו
לקראים בירושלים, ונראה שכתב־היד נשאר בידיו בחייו [125], וכוחה של ההקדשה
היה יפה לאחר מותו. בין שהיה יעבץ רבני בשעת הקנייה ושינה את טעמו אחר-
כך, בין שקנה את כתב־היד באמצעות שליח ומתווך, שלא גילה למוכר את
אמונתו של הקונה — ותיווך בקניין זה מסתבר, שכן ישב משה בן־אשר בטבריה
ויעבץ בירושלים או בבבל [126] — ובין שמכר משה בן־אשר את כתב־היד ביודעין

ט״ו ע״א, אך גם ספיר מבחין שם בפירוש בין ״כתב יד הסופר בעצמו ו ב ד י ו ש ל ו ״
ובין ״כתיבה אחרת״.   119   גרץ, התחלות, עמ׳ 366, הע׳ 1.

120 מן הקולופון שבעמ׳ 586, שהוא בכתבית ידו של משה בן אשר.

121 מן הקולופון שבעמ׳ 585, שאף הוא בכתבית ידו של משה בן־אשר.

122 מן הקולופון שבעמ׳ 588, בכתיבה שונה לחלוטין. כאן השמיט גרץ אחרי תיבת
״הקדיש״ את המלים ״יעבץ בן שלמה״, שנעשו מיותרות אחרי שנזכרו כבר פעם בקולופון שלו.

123 מן הקולופון שבעמ׳ 583, אף הוא בכתיבה מאוחרת ודחוקה בגיליון. יצוין שגרץ
לא העיר כלל על מעשה ה״איסוף״ שעשה כאן. וידועה דרכו של גרץ בהתאמת ציטטות מדברי
אחרים לצרכיו. ר׳ דברי ג׳ דייטש בחיברתו ״היינריך גרץ, תקופת מאה שנה״, בסוף ספרו של
א׳ שמרלר ״חיי גרץ״ (ניו יורק, 1921), עמ׳ 134־135.

124 ״זכה״ פירושו כאן בלי ספק קנה, רכש (עי׳ מילונים) וכך גם פירוש ההמשך
״ ו ע ש ה א ו ת ו ל ע צ מ ו להגות בו מעמלו ומיגיע כפיו ומזיעת אפו״ (ולא כפירושו
של קאלה במקום הנזכר לעיל בהע׳ 115). והשווה לכך גם את לשון הקולופון שבראש כי״ל:
״זה המחזור מקרא שלם נכתב ונגמר בנקודות ובמוסרות ומוגה יפה... מ ה ש ז כ ה מבורך
בן יוסף בן נתנאל הידוע בן וזדאד הכהן ו ע ש ה א ו ת ו ל ע צ מ ו להגות בו מעמלו
ומיגיע כפיו ומזיעת אפו...״. כאן הרי ידוע לנו שסופר כי״י זה היה שמואל בן יעקב (כעדות
הקולופונים שבסוף כי״י) ומבורך בן יוסף בוודאי לא כתב את כה״י אלא רק קנה אותו.
— ולפירוש זה של ״קנה״ עי׳ תרגום אונקלוס ותרגום יונתן לבראשית לא, א ולדברים ח, יז
וכן רש״י וראב״ע לבראשית יב, ה. והשווה אף בכתב־יב במכתב הידוע אל בגוהי פחת יהודה
(Cowley, Aramaic Papyri of the Fifth Century), עמ׳ 112 — גומא מס׳ 30, שו׳ 13)
״ולנפשהום עבדו״, אמנם בהוראה שונה במקצת (וקרבת ההוראות עבד / עשה כקרבת לקח — נטל
אל לקח — קנה). ועי׳ לאחרונה גם ש׳ אברמסון, מלשון חכמים, לשוננו כ״א (תשי״ז), עמ׳ 99־100.

125 על כך מעידים הלשונות ״ולא יוצאו אותו מ ב י ת ו ״ (הקולופון שבעמ׳ 588),
״וכל מי אשר יוציא אותו מחצר י ע ב ץ ב ן ש ל מ ה ״ (הקולופון שבעמ׳ 582) ועוד,
וכן מעידה על כך העובדה, שיעבץ בן שלמה אינו נזכר בקולופונים בברכת המתים. ואולי
הכוונה לבית כנסת ע״ש יעבץ, שנקרא ״חצר יעבץ בן שלמה״, ו״מביתו״ מכון לביתו הקבוע
של הדפתר.

126 בשעת הקנייה. — אם הכינוי ״הבבלי״ בקולופון שבעמ׳ 585 מוסב גם על יעבץ
ולא רק על אביו.

לקראי, כפי שקרה לא אחת [127], אין לכך שום זיקה לאמונתו של משה בן־אשר.
די לנו בדבריו המפורשים, שמכר את הספר כדי „להגות בו", כלומר ללמוד
מתוכו ולא לקרוא ממנו בבית הכנסת, ועל כן ניקדו ומיסרו. וההועדה של כתב־
היד המנוקד לשם קריאה בציבור לא משל משה בן אשר היא, אלא משל המקדיש
הקראי.

ב.   באמור לעיל נתיישבה אף טענה זו, השנייה, של גרץ.

ג.   לבירור הטענה השלישית נביא כאן את ראשית הקולופון של משה
בן־אשר, שעליו מסתמך גרץ לעניין זה [128]:

„אני משה בן אשר כתבתי זה המחזור שלמקרא על פי [129] כיד אלהי הטובה
עלי באר היטב במדינת מעזיה טבריה העיר ההוללה כשהבינו [130] עדת נביאים
בחורי ד' קדושי אלהינו המבינים כל נסתרות והמשפירים סוד חכמה אילי הצדק
אנשי אמנה לא כיחדו דבר ממה שניתן להם ולא הוסיפו מאמר על מה שנימסר
להם והעצימו והגדילו המק' עשרים וארבעה ספרים וייסדום באמונתם בטעמי
שכל בפירוש דיבור בחיך מתוק ביופי מאמר...".

גלוי וברור שהמשמעות שגרץ מסתמך עליו אין בו אפילו רמז של התנגדות
לתורה־שבעל־פה ואינו אומר אלא, שדברי הנביאים לא על דעת עצמם כי אם
ברוח הקודש נאמרו, מעין דברי חז"ל „מה שהנביאים עתידים להתנבאות בכל
דור ודור קבלו מהר סיני" (שמות רבה פכ"ח, ו), או „ואתנה לך את לוחות האבן
והתורה והמצוה אשר כתבתי להורותם (שמות כד, יב)... אשר כתבתי אלו נביאים
וכתובים... מלמד שכולם נתנו למשה מסיני" (ברכות ה ע"א). גם הביטוי „אילי
הצדק" אינו אלא מליצה מקראית (ישעיה סא, ג) ואינו בא לרמז כאן רמז קראי.
כבר ראינו ביטויים אחרים (מלמד, משכיל), המשמשים אמנם גם בפי הקראים,
אך ידועים ומקובלים הם גם בקרב הרבניים. אף ביטוי זה משמש אצל רבניים [131]
ומתאים כאן יפה: תיאור הנביאים במליצה של נביא [132]. ועל דרך כלל יש לומר:
ביטוי מקראי שהקראים קבעוהו כמטבע לאחר זמן, עדיין אין הוא מעיד על כל
מי שמשתמש בו שקראי הוא, ודאי לא בדורות הראשונים.

בטלה אפוא האפשרות להיאחז בקראיותו של האב, כדי להוכיח שגם הבן
אהרן היה קראי.

2.   נבחן עתה את הטענות שהביא גרץ על סמך הקולופון של כתב־יד חאלב.
כל דבריו של גרץ לעניין זה נראים נכונים. אל נכון נמסר כתב־היד
לחסותם של נשיאי הקראים (טענה א), אל נכון היה ישראל מבצרה קראי (טענה

---

127 ובכל הדורות. עי' ספיר ב', עמ' קפו ; אסף, לתולדות הקראים בארצות המזרח,
ציון א' (תרצ"ו), עמ' 230, ובייחוד הע' 138 ; י' בן־צבי, קרית ספר, כרך ל"ב (תשי"ז),
עמ' 368.   128 כי"ק, הקולופון שבעמ' 586.

129 כינוי גוף ראשון.   130 = כמו שהבינו.

131 עי' למשל „אילי הצדק", פתיחת הסדר בקרובה „אותותיך" לשביעי של פסח,
לר' שמעון בן יצחק.

132 ותמוהה הסתמכותו של קלאר (מחקרים, עמ' 314) על יפת בן עלי, המכנה את
חכמי הקראים „אילי הצדק". גם הביטוי „אבלי ציון", שיפת מכנה בו את הקראים, אף
הוא מקורו באותו פסוק בישעיה, וכינויי שאול אף הוא מן הרבניים. עי' לעיל עמ' רצד והע' 99.

ג) ואל נכון מאוחרת היא התוספת „קודש לה' על ישראל הרבנים וכו'" (טענה ד).
אולם שוב התעלם גרץ מ„פרט" אחד: כל הדברים הללו נלמדים מתוך קולופון,
שנכתב אחרי מותו של אהרן בן אשר והמזכיר אותו בברכת המתים. אין אפוא
ליחס לאהרן את אמונתו של בעל הקולופון. ואם לגבי כי״ק העלינו שלוש דרכים
להסביר איך הגיע כתב-היד לידי קראי עוד בחייו של סופרו הרבני, הרי כאן
אין כל צורך בכך. כתבי-יד של מקרא עברו מיד ליד, מידי רבנים לידי קראים
ולהיפך.[133] ובין אם נתגלגל כתב-היד לידי הקראים אחרי מותו או עוד בחייו,
אהרן בן אשר לא היה חייב לדעת על כך דבר.[134]

ושהיה כתב-יד האלב לכתחילה בידי רבנים מסתייע מן התנאי המפורש
שמתנה המקדיש „ואם יחפץ איש מכל זרע ישראל מבעלי הבינה מהרבנים בכל
ימות השנה לראות בו דברי יתר או חסר או סתור או סדור או סתום או פתוח
או טעם מהטעמים האלו יוציאהו אליו לראות ולהשכיל ולהבין לא לקרות ולדרוש
וישיבוהו למקומו...".[135] כלומר, אע״פ שכתב-היד היה מיועד לקריאה בבתי-
הכנסת של קראים בשלוש רגלים בלבד, כאמור בקולופון קודם לכן, בכל זאת
חייבים להראותו, לשם השוואה והגהת ספרים, לרבנים בכל ימות השנה. מסתבר
שדברים אלה אינם תוצאה של „רצון טוב" מצד הקראים, אלא תנאי שהותנה
מפורש בשעת המכירה.

והדיוק „לראות ולהשכיל ולהבין לא לקרות ולדרוש" מלמדנו גם על
התפקיד, שמילא כתב-היד אצל הרבניים, ועל הצורך שלשמו נכתב. ספרים
מקובצים, מנוקדים ומוטעמים, כמו כ״י האלב וכ״י קהיר, שימשו לרבניים לא
לקריאה ולדרישה בציבור, אלא ללימוד בלבד, ולשם כך נכתבו. אך לשווא
רואה גרץ (טענה ב) הגבלה בכך, שבעל הקולופון התיר לרבניים את השימוש
בכתב-היד רק לעיון ולהגהה. לא הגבלה היא, אלא עיקר השימוש. ובכך בטלה
ממילא טענתו של גרץ,[136] שרבני לא היה כותב תנ״ך בכרך אחד מנוקד ומוטעם
לקריאה בבית-הכנסת. ולא זו בלבד אף זו: רבני לא היה כותב תנ״ך על גבי

---

133 וגם כתב-יד האלב, אחרי שעבר לידי הקראים, חזר ובא לידי הרבניים. לקאלה
(Masoreten des Westens), חלק א', עמ' 7-12) דעה שונה במקצת על גלגוליו של כתב-
היד, כיון שהוא קובע את זמנה של הכתובת „קודש לה' על ישראל הרבנים וכו'" במחצית
הראשונה של המאה הי״א, ולא התחשב בקביעתו הנכונה של גרץ בענין זה (ר' לעיל טענה
ד', עמ' רצו).

134 איני נוגע כאן בשאלה, אם עדות הקולופון במה שנוגע לבן-אשר אמת היא.
כידוע קמו מערערים על כך. ראשון להם W. Wickes ב-A Treatise on the Accentuation
of the twenty-one so-called Prose Books of the Old Testament (אוקספורד,
1887, עמ' VII-IX. הרכבי, חדשים גם ישנים, חלק א', חוברת 6, עמ' 7-8, מאחר את כתב-היד
כולו במאתיים שנה. — לצורך הדיון הנחתי שדברי הקולופון אמת; ואם אינם אמת, ולא
אהרן בן-אשר ניקד את כתב-היד, בטלות ראיותיו של גרץ מעיקרא.

135 הנוסח הוא ע״פ הרכבי, שם, עמ' 7. והוא מעיד על עצמו שבדק את הקולופון
הזה „בעיון גדול ארבע פעמים". ואיני משגיח בסינתיזה שעושה קאלה (שם, עמ' 3-5) ע״פ
פרסומיהם של אחרים ומבלי שראה את כתב-היד גופו.

136 שחזר עליה גם במאמרו, התחלות, עמ' 366, הע' 1.

מ צ ח ף לקריאה בציבור [137]. רק שימוש אחד היה למצחפים המנוקדים והמסורים — הגהת ספרים וקריאה של לימוד וכמכשיר לימוד והוראה בידי המלמדים.

בזאת תמה פרשת הדיון בראיות העיקריות, שהובאו כדי להוכיח שבן־אשר היה קראי [138].

פ ר ק   ש נ י :   ה ר א י ו ת   ל ר ב נ י ו ת ו   ש ל   ב ן ־ א ש ר

א.   יחסם של הרבנים

1. הראיה־שכנגד היסודית והחזקה ביותר, שהועמדה לעומת טענות הקראיות של בן־אשר, היתה העובדה, שהרמב"ם סמך את ידו על תנ"ך שהגיהו בן־אשר וממילא גם על בן־אשר.

וכך כתב הרמב"ם בהלכות ספר תורה (ח, ד) :

„וספר שסמכנו עליו בדברים אלו [139] הוא הספר הידוע במצרים שהוא כולל ארבעה ועשרים ספרים שהיה בירושלים מכמה שנים להגיה ממנו הספרים ועליו היו סומכין לפי שהגיהו בן אשר ודקדק בו שנים הרבה והגיהו פעמים רבות כמו שהעתיקו ועליו סמכתי בספר התורה שכתבתי כהלכתו".

על הסתירה הגלויה והעקרונית הזאת, שהתריעו עליה רבים [140], יכלו הטוענים לקראיותו של בן־אשר להשיב אחת משתי תשובות : א) הרמב"ם לא ידע שבן־אשר היה קראי ונכשל בשגגה, ב) הרמב"ם ידע והתיר לסמוך על נוסח של מין־קראי.

לתשובה הראשונה מרמז גרץ בחצי פה, באמרו שאכן קרה לרמב"ם דבר מוזר [141]. אך הרי לא ייתכן שעובדה כזאת היתה נעלמת מעיני הרמב"ם, ספרים בניקודו של בן־אשר היו נפוצים באותם הימים, ומסתבר שגם אישיותו של בן־אשר ידועה היתה ומפורסמת. אילו היה מתעורר רק שמץ של פקפוק באמונתו ואף צל צלו של חשד של נטייתו לקראות, לא היה הרמב"ם סומך עליו.

גם פינילייש, הנאחז בתשובה השנייה, פוסל את הראשונה מכול וכול. לא ייתכן, אף לדעתו, שכל ספרי התורה שלנו מאז ועד היום סומכים ב ש ג ג ה על נוסחאות של מין. אך אע"פ שבתחילה התנגד פינילייש לדברי גרץ, והיה הראשון שיצא נגד אחדות מטענותיו [142], שב ושינה את טעמו [143]. הוא קיבל את דעתו של גרץ בעניין קראיותו של בן־אשר וניסה להוכיח, שלא בשגגה סמך הרמב"ם על בן־אשר, אלא ביודעין. גלוי וידוע היה לרמב"ם, שבן־אשר קראי היה, ואעפ"כ העתיק ממנו, כיוון שלא ראה בקראיותו פסול לעניין כתיבת ספר תורה ומסירתו.

---

137   ותמיה שגרץ לא השגיח בכך ולא טען טענה זו, לא הוא ולא יתר התומכים בקראיותו של בן־אשר.

138   תמה ולא נשלמה. בפרק השני ובפרק הרביעי אדון בטענות חדשות ביחס.

139   פרשיות פתוחות וסתומות וצורת השירות.

140   בהם שור, גוטלובר, ספיר, שטראק, באכר — במקומות שצויינו בהערות קידמות, וכן דב"מ במקום הנזכר להלן הע' 145.

141   ובלשונו   etwas Wunderliches passiert   (גרץ, בא"מ, עמ' 58).

142   עי' לעיל הע' 47.

143   בספרו „דרכה של תורה", וינא 1861, עמ' 268-269 מתעלם הוא ממה שכתב הוא עצמו שנה קודם לכן נגד גרץ בעניין „שילום התורה".

פיניליש הביא ראיות מצד ההלכה והסתמך בכך בייחוד **על** ל**דברי ר׳ שמעון בן**
גמליאל „כל מצוה שהחזיקו בה כותים הרבה מדקדקין בה **יותר מישראל״** (גיטין
י׳ ע״א ועוד). וכבר השיבהו אחד המשיבים[144] דברים קו**לעים המתקבלים** על
הדעת והראה, שאין שום אפשרות להסיק מסקנות כשל פינילי**ש מן הדין,** וב**ודאי**
לא היה הרמב״ם מעתיק מבן־אשר אילו ידע שהוא קראי[145].

ועוד יש לומר: הרמב״ם שידוע הוא בהקפדתו לשרש **כל שריד וזכר** של
השפעה קראית והמבקש לעקור מנהגים קראיים שהסתננו אל **עדת הרבנים בקצת**
מקומות, כגון בדיני יולדת, נידה וטבילה[146], לא ייתכן שב**בעניין חשוב כל כך**
ועקרוני כמו נוסח המקרא היה מסתמך על קראי.

לסתירה יסודית זו לא נמצא מענה משכנע; **וכנגד כל הטענות, שהובאו**
להוכחת קראיותו של בן־אשר, שהן טענות בלבד, עומדת כאן **העובדה ההיסטורית**
הברורה והבלתי ניתנת לערעור, שהרמב״ם, שחי רק כשתי **מאות שנים אחריו,**
סמך ידיו על בן־אשר וקיבל ממנו. והרי היו לו לרמב״ם מתנגדי**ם רבים, שהדרחרו**
מחלוקת וביקשו מומים בתלמודו, אך איש מהם לא נתלה **בעניין זה ולא תקפו**
על שסמך על נוסח בן־אשר.

גם בכל הדורות לא קם אף אחד ויחיד מקרב הרבניים **לחתריע על קראיותו**
של בן־אשר או לערער בגללה אף במקצת על סמכותו בעניי**ני ניקוד ומסורה,**
ואיש מן הרבנים המזכירים והמסתמכים על בן־אשר, מדקדקים **ושאינם מדקדקים,**
אינו מכנה אותו קראי. ומזכירים אותו רבים מן הקדמונים: ר׳ **האיי גאון**[147], **אבן**
ג׳נאח[148] וביותר רד״ק[149], וכמוכן גם הרמב״ם. ובין שהיה זה **חיבורו הנודע לנו**
דקדוקי הטעמים, שהשתמשו בו חכמים אלה ואחרים, בין שהיה זה **חיבור אחר**[150],

---

144   החותם דב״ב, ולא ידעתי מי הוא.

145   החיכוח הממושך בין פינילי**ש ודב״ב בשאלה צדדית זו ובמסתעף ממנה אינו**
מעניינני. והרוצה יעיין ב„המגיד״ של השנים 1860־1862 ובספרו הנ״ל **של פינילי**ש.

146   ע׳ משנה תורה, הלכות איסורי ביאה פי״א הט״ו: „**אין זה מנהג אלא טעות**
הוא באותן התשובות ודרך אפיקורסות באותן המקומות ומן הצדיקים (**ואין צדוקים בדורו של**
הרמב״ם אלא קראים. — א״ד) למדו דבר זה״. וכל תשובות הרמב״ם ב**„ספר פאר הדור״**
(אמשטרדם, 1765), תשובה קנ״ב (לא ע״א): „ונהגו מנהג מינות עד שהן רוח**צות במים שאובין**
(מנהג קראי מפורסם. — א״ד) וחושבין כי בזה טהרו ממקור דמיהן ובזה הותרו לבעליהן
ואין זה כי אם מינות גמורה והדבר אשר לא דברו ד׳״. ובתשובות הרמב״ם ליוסף **בן גאבר**
מאנשי בגדד ב„טעם זקנים״ לא׳ אשכנזי (פרנקפורט ענ״מ, 1854), עמ׳ 74: „**אבל אנשי מצדים**
מצינו אותם בזה נוטים לדברי מינות והולכים אחר סדור הקראים״, ושם בסמוך: „**והיה**
החרם (הוא החרם הנזכר ב„פאר הדור״, שם. — א״ד) שארירה כל אשה שלא תמנה שבעה
נקים או תבטל הטבילה או תרחוק בלבד כמו שעושים הקראים״. ואגב, מתשובות **אלה תשובה**
ניצחת לבא להפריד בין מין לקראי בדברי הרמב״ם.

147   ע׳ מאן, JQR, סדרה חדשה XI (1920-1921), עמ׳ 470.

148   ע׳ ספר הרקמה, מהדורת וילנסקי, במפתחות.

149   ע׳ ספר השרשים, ערכים „דרך״, „דרבן״ ועוד; עט סופר (ליק, 1864) עמ׳ **לא**;
פירושו לשופטים ו׳, יט, ליחזקאל טז, יח ועוד; ובמכלול במקומות הרבה.

150   אולי „מחברת בן אשר״ הנזכרת בפירוש רד״ק לשופטים ו׳, יט.

מסתבר שלא היו חכמים אלה נזקקים לו, לפחות בלא הסתייגות מפורשת, אילו
מצאו בו רמז של קראות.

ואין לטעון שהרבניים ראו בקראים בני־סמכא בעניני דקדוק ולכן לא
חששו לסמוך על בן־אשר. כי דבר מומחיותם של הקראים בדקדוק ובלשון המקרא
היה מקובל אמנם בקרב הקראים עצמם ושימש יסוד להתפארותם, אך הרבניים
לא הודו בכך כלל. כך למשל מתריס כנגדם בעל "שאלות עתיקות" ולועג
להתמסרותם לפרטים חיצוניים, טכניים (מכנה אותם "עוגבי הטעמים" [151]), בעוד
שהם חסרים הבנה מעמיקה במקרא ובפירושו. אף רס"ג כופר בידיעתם של
הקראים בעניני דקדוק מסורה [152], ורבני אחר מקנטרם בדברים ופונה אליהם בשאלות
דקדוק שאין עליהן תשובה : "...ואם אין ישובה לשתי המלין איך תקראו נפשכם
בעלי המקרא ומלמדים ומורים כי אתם לא תדעו עלילות הנקוד והטעמי' ולא
חילוף עשרים וארבעה ספרים" [153]. ובדורות מאוחרים יותר התפתחה השקפה זו
והגיעה לכלל כפירה מוחלטת בידיעתם בלשון. וכך אומר ראב"ע בהקדמתו
לפירוש התורה: "הדרך הב' בחרוה פתלתולים... וזאת דרך הצדוקים כענן ובנימין.
וכן [154] משיח וישועה וכל מין. אשר בדברי מעתיקי הדת [155] לא יאמין. והוא
נוטה להשמאיל או להימין. וכל איש כרצונו יפרש הפסוקים. גם במצות ובחקים.
והם מדעת תוצאות לשון הקודש ריקים. על כן יתעו גם
בדקדוקי'. ואיך יסמכו למצות על דעתם. וכל רגע יהפכו מצד אל צד כפי
מחשבותם... [156]."

לא ייתכן אפוא להעלות על הדעת שהרבניים הסכימו לקבל שיטתו של
קראי בנוסח המקרא, לא רק בגלל החשש מפני סטיותיו הדתיות, אלא גם בגלל
היותו נטול סמכות לשונית ודקדוקית בעיניהם.

---

151 יהודה רוזנטאל, שאלות עתיקות בתנ"ך, (1948) HUCA, XXI, חלק עברי,
עמ' לז, שו' 6. א' שייבר פרסם קטע נוסף (שאלות עתיקות Unknown Leaves from
(1956) HUCA, XXVII, עמ' 291-303) ולמד מתוכו שבעל השאלות תוקף את
בעלי המסורה. אף הפליג ואמר, בהסתמך על הדעה המקובלת ש"אשא משלי" נכתב נגד בעל
המסורה אהרן בן־אשר, שבעל השאלות מתפלמס עם בן־אשר ! אולם בדברי הקטע הנוסף אין
כל התקפה על בעלי המסורה. ואני מקוה לדון בו במקום אחר.

152 עי' אשא משלי, עמ' תקט, שו' 36-29, ומדגיש שם שרק הרבניים מבינים את עניני
המסורה.

153 כ"י F 88 בספרייה הצבורית שבלנינגרד. נתפרסם בדקה"ט, עמ' XXXVIII-
XXXIXA, וגם אצל מאן, היהודים, כרך ב', עמ' 48-49. וטעה מאן והעתיק בראשית הקטע (שלא
הובאה כאן) "בעלי לשון המקרא" במקום "בעלי (!) המקרא". ואולי תיקן מדעתו,
אך לא העיר על כך. — כל הקטע נושא אופי של שאלת קנטור ולא של שאלת חכם, והשואל
רואה את בן־אשר כבר־סמכא ומתגרה בקראים ודורש שיסבירו את ניקודו של בן־אשר. ושלא
כקלאר (מתקרים, עמ' 294), הרואה בשאלה ערעור סמכותו של בן־אשר.

154 צ"ל : "ובן משיח". — משפט זה מן "וכן" עד "מין" משובש בכמה דפוסים,
והשתמשתי בחמשה חומשי תורה, הוצ' שוקן, תרצ"ז.

155 חכמי הקבלה, "אלנאקלין" (= המעתיקים), כלשון ריה"ל בכוזרי, מאמר שלישי,
מט (מהדורת הירשפלד, עמ' 198).

156 לרעיון שבמשפט האחרון עי' הנאמר לעיל, עמ' רצב.

ב. יחסם של הקראים

מדרכם של הקראים בכל הדורות ובייחוד בדורו של רס״ג. דור פריחה
ושגשוג להם. שלא להעלים את קראיותם. אלא להתריע עליה בריש גלי ולהתפאר
בה בכתביהם. אף להבזות את הרבניים ולתקוף אותם בכל הזדמנות ובכל חיבור.
אף שאיננו עוסק בהלכה. אפילו דוד בן אברהם. שאינו עוסק אלא בפרשנות
לשונית ובדקדוק. אף הוא אינו מושך ידיו מללעוג לרבניים[157] ומלגלות את
גאוותו על קראיותו. אילו היה בן-אשר קראי. לא היה חושש להתפאר בכך או
לפחות לרמוז על כך רמז מפורש בחיבורו.

ומן הקראים לא נודע לנו אף אחד בכל הדורות. שהעיד על בן-אשר
שקראי הוא. לא ברשימות חכמיהם[158] ולא בנוסח הזכרת הנשמות שבסידור
תפילתם.[159] והרי ידוע עד כמה השתדלו הקראים לייחס לעצמם חכמים רבניים
ולהתכבד בהם. עד שפרשו את כנפי אמונתם גם על יהודה בן קריש ואחרים.[160]
אבל ליטול לעצמם את בן-אשר — זאת לא עלתה על דעתם. וכשבא הקראי כלב
אפנדופולו (בסוף המאה הט״ו) להכריע בין הקריאות של שני המלמדים. אין הוא
מערב בהנמקתו שיקולים שבדת. אלא מסתמך על הסמכות הייחודית שקנה לו
בן-אשר במרוצת הדורות ואומר[161]: ״ולהיות שדעת בן אשר יותר אמתית מדעת
בן נפתלי. אע״פ שבקריאת קצת מלות ובקצת מן הנקוד והטעמים אנחנו נמשכין
אחרי דעת בן נפתלי. אמנם על הרוב מאוד אנחנו נמשכים אחרי דעת בן אשר
בין בקריאה בין בניקוד בין בטעמים״. ותומך את דבריו בסיוע של דרש: ״כי
מלת אשר מן מאשרי העם (ישעיה ט. טו) ענין יושר ודבר אמת. ונפתלי מן עקש
ופתלתול (דברים לב. ה)״. ובדורות שאחר כך מכריע החכם הקראי מרדכי בן
ניסן (בסוף המאה הי״ז) את הכף לטובת בן-נפתלי דווקא. ואומר[162]: ״וקריאת
בן נפתלי אנחנו תומכים בקריאתינו. כך קבלנו במדרשי מלמדינו דזר מדור״.
אולי משום שבן-אשר כבר נחשב בעיניו אותוריטה רבנית. והמלומד הקראי
אברהם פירקוביץ. בן המאה הקודמת. לא העלה תחילה במחשבתו שבן-אשר היה
קראי. ורק כשיצאו פינסקר וגרץ בהשערה זו. שש לקבל דעתם ולספח בכך חכם
חשוב נוסף אל בני עדתו.

ברם עדות קראית אחת ב״חילוק הקראים והרבנים״. המיוחס לאליה בן

---

157 קורא להם ״אלאגביא״ (= הכסילים. הבורים). עי׳ כתאב ג׳אמע אלאלפאט.
מהדורת סקוז. כרך א׳. עמ׳ 254. שו׳ 148.

158 כגון חילוק הקראים (עמ׳ 106) ומאוחר יותר אבן אליהיי ואחריו מרדכי בן
ניסן בעל ״דד מרדכי״ (ווין. 1830). יא ע״ב) ושמחה בן משה הלוצקי בעל ״אורח צדיקים״
(כנ״ל). כא ע״א וע״ב) ואחרים. אף הדסי באשה״כ לא כינה את בן-אשר ״משכיל״ כדרך
שהוא נוהג בחכמי הקראים.

159 כידוע מזכירים הקראים מדי שבת בשבתו. אחרי השלמת התפילה. את נשמות
החכמים שעמדו להם מימי ענן ועד הורם. עי׳ סדר תפלות הקראים. הוצ׳ יצחק איסכוויץ
(וינה. 1854). חלק ראשון. עמ׳ שג״שו.

160 ואף פינסקר הלך בדרכם. ועשה גם את מנחם בן סרוק לקראי. (עי׳ ל״ק עמ׳
קטז. ובייחוד עמ׳ 163-164).

161 עי׳ דקד״ט במבוא. עמ׳ X בהערה.   162 דד מרדכי. טו ע״ב.

אברהם, קראי בן המאה הי״ב [163], נחלקו חכמים בפירושה. יש שראו בה הודאה ברבניותו של בן־אשר [164], ויש שהבינו מתוכה את ההיפך [165]. כדי לברר דבר לאשורו מן הראוי להביא את הקטע הנדון במלואו [166] ולדון בו:

„ועוד ראו [167] חלופי מערבאי ומדנחאי בתורה זה אומר בכה וזה אומר בכה, מה שילמוד זה חסר ילמוד זה מלא, ומה שילמוד זה מלא ילמוד זה חסר, מה שילמוד זה תיבה אחת ילמוד זה שתי תיבות, מה שילמוד זה במסורת ילמד זה בטעם, וכן מסורת הרבה אחד למערבאי ואחד למדנחאי, מענינו לבן אשר ולבן נפתלי, וראה במלת ישׂשכר כי בן אשר יקראו יִשָּׂשׂכָר, ובן נפתלי יִשָּׂשׂכָר ומשה (בכ״י ובן משה) בן מוחה יִשָּׂשׂכָר וכאלה רבים, וכמו כן נכתבים דביונים חריונים, עפולים טחורים, וכאלה רבים, עתה אם בדברים הנכתבים ונמסרים מפי הנביאים נתחלפו, א״כ שאר הדברים והתורות אשר לא נכתבו מפי נביאים וחוזים, ק״ו שלא יכתבו וישתבשו כאלה וכאלה, אף מקובל לומר יש אם למקרא ויש אם למסורת, ופירשו לא תענה על ריב, על פי, על רב, על פה, אותם אתם, לעולם לעלם, ציצת ציצית וכאלה רבים, ויכשר לתמים דעים שיתן לנו תורה עומדת בשתי הסעפים ולשתי דיעות, והאם למסורת תהדוף והמסורת לאם...״.

בעל החילוק בא לערער את יסודותיה של תורת הרבניים בטענה העקרונית: כיצד תיתכן מחלוקת בכתוב ובפירושי הכתוב [168], וכי „יכשר לתמים דעים שיתן לנו תורה עומדת בשתי הסעפים ולשתי דיעות״? הרי הרבניים מפרשים את הכתוב על שתי פנים, עתים על דרך יש אם למקרא ועתים על דרך יש אם למסורת, כגון הדוגמאות שהוא הולך ומונה. ומסקנתו: תורתם של הרבניים משובשת בידם ואין לההאמין להם. והוא מוסיף בסמוך: „ולנו לא תאמינו [169] (נ״א האמינו [170]) כי אנחנו בני הנאנחים והנאנקים וקדמונים אנחנו מאחיכם״.

כך לגבי פירוש הכתוב וכך לגבי נוסח הכתוב. כידוע, לא הודו הקראים בגרסאות שונות של נוסח המקרא, ועמדו על כך שרק נוסח אחד הוא הנכון. קרקסאני הרחיב את הדיבור בעניין זה ועמד על כך, שאי אפשר ששתי הקריאות, של מערבאי ושל מדנחאי, גם יחד נכונות, אלא רק קריאת בני המערב, ארץ־ישראל, היא האמיתית, והקריאה הבבלית, המדנחאית, מוטעית [171]. גם בעל

---

163   נראים הדברים שזמנו של בעל החילוק לא היה מאוחר מן המאה הי״ב (עי׳ פוזננסקי, KLOSG, עמ׳ 72), אך לגבי זהותו לא נתיישבו הדברים כל צורכם, ועי׳ גוטלובר, ביקורת, עמ׳ 158, בהערה.

164   עי׳ שור בההלוץ, מחברת ששית (תרכ״ב, 1861), עמ׳ 67 ; גוטלובר, ביקורת, עמ׳ 143.

165   פינליש, דרכה של תורה, עמ׳ 277-276 ; א׳ פירקוביץ, בהערה בספרו של גוטלובר, שם.

166   חילוק הקראים, עמ׳ 103-102.   167   קרא : ראו.

168   דרכם של הקראים בפולמוסיהם מפורסמת : לא לראות את מומיהם שלהם ותלותם בזולתם. וידוע, שמחלוקותיהם בינם לבין עצמם לא רק בפירושי הכתוב, אלא אף ביסודות קיום המצוות הלכה למעשה.

169   בתמיהה.   170   לשון ציווי.

171   קרקסאני (מאמר ב׳, שער יז), עמ׳ 140-138. ותרגום הקטע במאמרו של קלאר,

החילוק מלגלג על הרבניים באותו עניין „זה אומר בכה אומר בכה וכו'"[171]
ומראה עד כמה נשתבש עליהם, על הרבניים, מקראם. וכאן לומד הוא קל וחומר:
ומה בתורה שבכתב (״בדברים הנכתבים ונמסרים מפי הנביאים") נתחלפו הרבניים,
בתורה-שבעל-פה (״שאר הדברים והתורות אשר לא נכתבו מפי נביאים וחוזים")
לא כל שכן נתחלפו ונשתבשו.

אך בדבר אחד טעה בעל החילוק, ואיננו יחיד בטעותו, בזהותו את חילופי
מערבאי ומדנחאי בחילופי בן-אשר ובן-נפתלי. ונראה שלא היה כוחו גדול
בעניני דקדוק ומסורה, וכשרצה להביא דוגמה מחילופי מערבאי ומדנחאי, כשם
שהביא בסמוך דוגמאות לאם למקרא ואם למסורת, פירש „מענהו לבן אשר ולבן
נפתלי", והביא דוגמה מחילופיהם של אלה, והרי עיקר חילופיהם של אלה לא
בעניינים שמנה בעל החילוק — מלא וחסר, תיבה אחת ושתי תיבות וכד' —
אלא בעיקר בעניני ניקוד וטעמים. גם עצם ניקודן[173] של התיבות שבדוגמה[174],
וכן פרשת קרי וכתיב (דביונים חריונים וכו') שכרכה כאן[175], גורמים לנו שנטיל
ספק בבקיאותו בעניינים אלה.

אולם מטעות זו של בעל החילוק נמצאנו נשכרים, שכן מראה היא לנו
בבירור יתר את יחסו אל בן-אשר ובן-נפתלי. מתוך שזיהה אותם במערבאי
ומדנחאי, שחילופיהם הם לדידיה סמל ההשתבשות של הרבניים, נתגלתה לנו
ממילא עמדתו כלפיהם: הוא ראה בהם רבניים מובהקים.

ג. שיטות במסורה ובדקדוק

מן הראוי להשוות את ההשקפות המקובלות על הקראים בעניני מסורה
ודקדוק אל השקפתו של בעל דקדוקי הטעמים.

א. גישתם של הקראים אל הניקוד והטעמים ידועה, והביעה יהודה
הדסי[176]: „וספרי התורות ראויין להיות ננקדים בנקוד וטעמים... כי בלא נקוד
וטעמים לא נתנם אלהינו... על כי מכתב אלהינו חרות על הלוחות ככה מלאים
בכתיבתן בנקוד וטעמים ולא חסרים מנקודים וטעמם...".

„עניני מסורה ומבטא אצל קרקסאני", עניני לשון בעריכת חנוך ילון, תש״ג, עמ' 36־34
(= מחקרים ועיונים, עמ' 326־324).

172 ובאותה מליצה משתמש גם במקום אחר, חילוק הקראים עמ' 101, כשבא ללגלג
על מחלוקת הרבניים במשנה ובתלמוד.

173 אם לא חלו בו ידי מעתיקים, ובכללם המהדיר סינסקר.

174 על מסורות ניקודה של תיבת יששכר ע״י לאחרונה דברי ח' ילון, קרית ספר,
ל (תשט״ו), עמ' 258, הע' 7.

175 ויש לבדוק אם לא הייתה נטייה בספרי הקראים בזמנו של בעל החילוק לכתוב
את הקרי בכל מקום ולהתעלם מן הכתיב, כדי להימנע מכפל נוסחאות במקרא. מצויים כתבי-
יד רבים הנוהגים כך לפעמים; עי' בתנ״ך מהדורת גינצבורג, למשל, שתי המלים שהביא
בעל החילוק. ועי' גם עדות קרקסאני על שיטתו של אסמעיל אלעכברי, שאינו גורס את הקרי
כלל וקורא בכל מקום את הכתיב. קרקסאני (מאמר א', שער טו), עמ' 56: אן אסמעיל
אלעכברי אבטל אלכתיב ואלקרי וזעם אן אלקראה יג״ב אן תכון עלי מא הו מכתוב. ועי'
גם מאמר ב', ריש שער כג (שם, עמ' 161).

176 אשה״כ א״ב קעג, אות ס' וע', דף ע ע״א. וכיו״ב במקומות אחרים.

כשנשווה לכך את התפיסה המרומזת בדקדוקי הטעמים נמצאנה רחוקה מדרך זו, הן באשר לניקוד והן באשר לטעמים.

ה נ י ק ו ד. — בעל דקה״ט חוזר ומדגיש פעמים אחדות שכ״ב האותיות „נתונות משמי שפרה, מפי הגבורה, על יד עֶנֶו נקרא״ (§ 4), או „משמים אתויות, על יד עֶנֶו עֲנֶו קנויות״ (§ 5), או „ממשה קנויות״ (שם), ואינו כולל בכלל מה שניתן בסיני את הניקוד והטעמים. אדרבא, בפרק הדן באותיות (§ 5), כשהוא בא לדון בתכונתן המיוחדת של אותיות אחה״ע, העשויות להינקד בשני סימני ניקוד (החטפים), מקפיד הוא להדגיש, שתכונה זו באה להן לאותיות אלה לא מצד עצמן אלא מצד תוספת הניקוד שבהן, שהוא לימוד נביאים וסופרים; ובלשונו: „כי כל אותיות, אשר ממשה קנויות, כל אות מלך אחד לבדו לו, משרתו בדרך אחד שבילו, בנועם דבור מלולו, חוץ מן אחה״ע הידועים, אשר במקרא קבועים, כי שני כתרים, נחלו בארבעה ועשרים ספרים, כלמוד נ ב י א י ם ו ס ו פ ר י ם ״ (§ 5), הוי אומר, אותיות אחה״ע נחלו שני כתרים, שני סימני ניקוד, שהם לימוד נביאים וסופרים. אף במקום אחר, בפתיחה למניין התנועות: „שבע נקדות, למאד כבדות, מקרא מלמדות, וחכמות מגידות, כעטרות ענודות, מ נ ב י א י ע ת י ד ו ת...״ (§ 10).

קשה לקבוע על סמך הנאמר עד כאן למי במיוחד ייחס בעל דקדוקי הטעמים את קביעת הניקוד, אם לנביאים או לסופרים (ור׳ עוד להלן), אך מסתמנים בדבריו שני קווי עיקרון, המנוגדים ניגוד גמור לתפיסה הקראית:

1. ה אותיות והניקוד לא ממקור אחד ניתנו.   2. ה ניקוד לא ניתן בסיני.

קלאר[177] מצא סמך לכך שבן אשר האמין בקדמות הניקוד מסיני בדברי דקה״ט (§ 9): „ידע הדורש בדעה גמורה... כי כל המקרא שלם בלי חֶסְרָה, כי נקדה זעירה תעמוד במקום האות כקורה, תועיל וסבר תסבירה, וחסרון האות תגדורה״, היינו גם התיבות הנכתבות חסר אינן חסרות בעצם, כי הניקוד בא במקום אימות הקריאה החסרות, כגון עָצֵר, חָצָה, נֵב, שֵׁלָֹה וכיו״ב. ועל השאלה הטבעית המתעוררת כאן „מה טעם נקדה על מלה יתרה כמו דרך מלה חסרה״ — היינו, אם בא הניקוד למלא את חסרון אימות הקריאה, מפני מה נקדו גם תיבות כתובות מלא — משיב בעל דקה״ט: „כי הנקודה למוד ואזהרה, לתלמידי תורה, למען לא ישגו במקרא, בין נורא לנורא (דניאל ג, ו) ובין שׁוֹרה (ישעיה כח, כה) לסׁוּרָה (שופטים ד, יח) ובין צור לצור העירה ובין עוּר (דניאל ב, לה) לעוֹר אדם הנבראׁ״. וקלאר מסיים „אמנם התשובה אינה תשובה, שכן אם אנו סומכים על הניקוד, היתה כל התורה יכולה להיכתב חסר, אבל אין לזה חשיבות לעניננו״.

ולא היא. יש לזה חשיבות לעניננו והתשובה תשובה היא, ורק המסקנה אינה נכונה, משום שהיא נסמכת על ההנחה שבעל דקה״ט האמין בניקוד מסיני. אבל דווקא מתוך תשובתו למדים אנו שהנחה זו מוטעית היא, שכן אילו היה בעל דקדוקי הטעמים מאמין בניקוד מסיני, לא היה יכול לתת תשובה כזאת. כל הדיון בניקוד לא בא כאן אלא כדי להאיר באור נכון את המונח „חסר״, המצוי בדברי בעלי המסורה והנזכר קודם לכן „בה ח ס ר ה ויתרה, כאמר זקני חבורה״, ולהוציאו מהוראתו המילולית, המשמיעה כאילו חסר כאן משהו, וללמדך שהניקוד בא מצד אחד במקום אימות הקריאה שאינן כתובות,

177 קלאר, מחקרים, עמ׳ 290־291.

ומצד שני כדי למנוע טעויות בקריאות הכתיב המלא ("למוד ואזהרה, לתלמידי
תורה[178], למען לא ישגו במקרא "בין נורא לנורא"). הניקוד אינו אפוא שוה ערך
לטכסט הקונסוננטי; הוא בא רק להשלים אותו. ולכך נתכוון בעל דקדוקי
הטעמים בתשובתו. כל הגישה בסוגיה זו מנוגדת לתפיסתם של הקראים: קראי
אינו צריך להסביר את מטרת הניקוד ולהצדיק את נחיצותו; לגביו אותיות ונקודות
חד הם.

גם מן המשפט "באותיות ותיבות מסורה, ונקדות עד לאין ספירה, ובטעמים
ובדקדוק גדורה" (§ 9) הסיק קלאר[179] שהתורה נמסרה באלה ובאלה, היינו גם
ניקוד וטעמים מסיני. ושלא בדין הסיק כך. אין משפט זה שייך לראשיתו של
הפרק "תחילה הנחיל אל דברות עשרה וכו'", ואין הכוונה שבאותיות ובנקודות
נמסרה התורה מסיני; דבר זה לא נאמר כאן, ולא זה הדבר שבא בעל דקדוקי
הטעמים להשמיענו. הוא דן בטופס המקרא המעסיק אותו כבעל מסורה, כלומר
במקרא על אותיותיו ונקודותיו וטעמיו ("בטעמים ובדקדוק[180] גדורה, ובשבעה
מלכים אזורה"[181] (§ 3) ועל
טופס זה אומר הוא שהוא מסור, לא מסיני, אלא "כאמר זקני חבורה, זמאמר
סופרי תורה" (§ 9), כלומר, במאמר בעלי המסורה.

הטעמים. — אף כאן ברורה עמדתו של בעל דקדוקי הטעמים. הטעמים
לא ניתנו למשה מסיני אלא "מפי מבינים וסופרים" (§ 16) הם. רעיון זה מובע
פעמים אחדות בהסתמכות ברורה על דרשת חז"ל על הפסוק בנחמיה ח, ח "ושום
שכל — אילו הטעמים" (ירושלמי, מגילה פ"ד ה"א, עד ע"ד). וכה דבריו: "עוד
שנים עשר טעמים, המשולים במי אגמים... נגון נואמים, שיר מנעימים, בשום
שכל חתומים, מפי נבונים וחכמים..." (§ 4). וכן במקום אחר: "שער הטעמים
שנים עשר רשומים... בפי נבונים וחכמים, בשום שכל חתומים" (§ 17). וכן
מכנה אף משה בן־אשר בקולופון שלו בכי"ק[182] את הטעמים "טעמי שכל", ביטוי
המיוסד אף הוא על דרשת חז"ל הנזכרת. ולא רק הסתמכות על דרשת חז"ל בדברי

---

178 ואין להסתמך על ביטוי מעין "תלמידי תורה" ולקבוע שהוא "מונח קראי" (קלאר,
שם, הע' 79) רק מפני שסהל בן מצליח מכנה בו את הקראים באחת מאיגרות התוכחה שלו
(ל"ק, עמ' 33), וזאת לא ככינוי עצמאי אלא ככפיל מליצי של כינוים הרגיל "בני מקרא"
(או "בעלי מקרא"). ואין "תלמידי תורה" כאן בדקה"ט אלא לומדי תורה, שהרי אף התמים
שבקראים לא יתיימר שהניקוד ניתן רק לקראים "למען לא ישגו במקרא".

179 קלאר, מחקרים, עמ' 298.

180 וזה, יהא פירושו אשר יהיה, ודאי אינו מסור מסיני.

181 וגם שם מסיק קלאר (מחקרים, עמ' 299-298), שהניקוד מסיני, מן הלשון:
בלם שבים לסדור הזה בבית קדש הקדשים והקטש וחצר אהל מועד" (§ 3), שכחנתו, לפי
קלאר, שהכתב והניקוד והטעמים אינם המצאה של הסופרים, אלא הם שבים לסידור (= ספר
תורה) שהיה בבית המקדש. אך מה פירוש "הסדור הזה"? ולשם מה "קדש הקדשים
והקדש וחצר אהל מועד"? וכי בשלושתם היה ה"סידור"? והיכן אמר בן־אשר "שכל חלקי
המקרא שוים בערכם" (שם, הע' 147)? ופירושו גם אינו מתאים לנוסח שבכי"ק. ועי' הנאמר
על ענין זה לעיל בעמ' רפה.

182 כי"ק, עמ' 586.

דקדוקי הטעמים, אלא שוב רמז למסירתם של הטעמים „מפי נבונים וחכמים״,
ולא כדעת הקראים, הלכה למשה מסיני.

וכנראה מבחין בעל דקדוקי הטעמים בין מסורת הטעמים, שהם
„בחונים מזקקים, מפי נביאים וחכמים, ויודעים ומשכילים,
חתומים בחותם נביאי אל״ (§ 16)[183], ובין „תיכונם״ של סימני
הטעמים, שהם מזקני הסנהדרין : „שמונה למעלה עקודים, וארבעה למטה קדים,
נותנים טעם ולא פוחדים, ומגביהים ורדים, מתכנים מזקני עגלה, נביאי שרי
גולה״ (§ 16). מתוך י״ב סימני הטעמים המפסיקים שבכ״א ספרים, שמונה נכתבים
מעל לתיבה וארבעה תחתיה, היינו הסימנים הגראפיים, מתוכנים מזקני עגולה.

וללשון „זקני עגולה״ יש להשוות „סנהדרין היתה כחצי גורן עגולה״
(סנהדרין ד, ג), וכן „אשר בעגולה גידל דורשים״ (סופרים יט, ט). ביטוי זה נהג
אף בתקופה הגדונה. כך מכנה אותו רבני עלום־שם את הסנהדרין דרך כבוד
„חכמי גורן עגולה, חבורת הצדק הקדושה, שוקדים על דלתות תלמוד ומשנה״[184],
ואף בקינה קדומה על חורבן הקהילות בארץ־ישראל מסופר „מישראל כבוד גלה
ושבתו זקני עגולה״[185]. ובדקדוקי הטעמים אין זה אלא כינוי של כבוד לחכמי
הסנהדרין, שאין לו מקום בדברי קראי.

בהתאם לנאמר על הטעמים אפשר להניח, שגם הייחוס הכפול של
הניקוד לנביאים מכאן ולסופרים מכאן[186] שורשו בהבחנה בין ההגייה המסורה
(או מסורת הניקוד) ובין קביעת הסימנים הגראפיים של הניקוד בכתב.

ההשקפה שסימני הניקוד והטעמים ניתנו בסיני הכרחית היא לקראים, לא
רק בגלל הקדושה והסמכות ההלכתית שהם מייחסים לניקוד השווה בערכו לטכסט
הקונסוננטי, אלא גם כדי לקיים בידם את הטענה ההיסטורית שלהם, שהם נחלקו מן
הרבניים לפני עידן המשנה והתלמוד. כי, אם יסכימו שהניקוד והטעמים נקבעו
בעידן זה, כדבריו המפורשים של בעל דקדוקי הטעמים לגבי הטעמים, או אחריו,
ומאחר שבניקוד וטעמים אין חילוף ביניהם ובין הרבניים, שוב לא יוכלו לפרנס
את טענת קדמותם[187]. ודעת בעל דקדוקי הטעמים בענין זה ברורה, ובהכרח
רבנית היא.

ב. ענין אחר שבו נבדלת דרכו של בעל דקדוקי הטעמים מדרכם של
קראים : ראשוני המדקדקים הקראים נהגו להתייחס אל צורת הציווי כצורה
היסודית של הפועל. סיבתה של תופעה זו לא נתבררה כל צרכה[188], אך מציאותה
אינה מקרית, אלא עוברת היא כחוט השני בחיבוריהם של המדקדקים והפרשנים

183   מעין הדברים שאומר משה בן אשר בקולופון שלו (עי׳ לעיל, עמ׳ רצז), שעדת
     ה נ ב י א י ם   יסדו את ספרי המקרא „בטעמי שכל״ וכו׳.

184   שאלות עתיקות בתג״ך, (1948) HUCA, XXI, חלק עברי, עמ׳ נא.

185   אסף, מקורות ומחקרים, עמ׳ 15.   186   עי׳ לעיל, עמ׳ שז.

187   דברים אלה ממש טוען בעל „דד מרדכי״, טו ע״א.

188   ושיער א״ז רבינוביץ ב„גנזי הדקדוק״ לבאכר, בהערה לעמ׳ 59 (הערת המתרגם),
שתופעה זו קשורה בתפיסה ההיסטורית של הקראים, אשר לפיה העתיד הוא העיקר והעבר
חשיבתו פחותה. והרי הציווי נחשב לאחת הדרכים (modi) של העתיד. ואין הסברו נראה,
שכן הפרידו הקראים בפאראדיגמות בין הציווי ובין העתיד ; והעתיד בא אחרי העבר. ועי׳
בהערה הבאה.

מבני מקרא: דוד בן אברהם [189], יפת בן עלי [190], אבו אלפרג' האראן [191], עלי בן סלימאן [192]. וכן פרסם הרכבי [193] קטע מכתב־יד שבו דוגמאות של פעלים בצורת הציווי ודוגמאות נטיה שביסודן צורת הציווי [194].

נשווה עכשיו לתפיסה דקדוקית זו את שיטתו של בעל דקדוקי הטעמים ונראה, שהיא שונה לחלוטין משיטתם זו של הקראים. וכה דבריו על התהוות צורות הפועל: „...או זמן יפול על השם וְיֵעָשֶׂה פּוֹעֵל, ויבדיל בו עבר מן הנצב [195] ומן העתיד, כי הזמן על שלשה דרכים, עבר ונצב ועתיד... כן תאמר בעבר דִבַּרְתִּי... ותאמר על הזמן הנצב דּבֵר... ותאמר על הזמן העתיד [196]... דָּבָר... יָדַבָּר...″ (36 §). הציווי־עתיד אחרון בשורה אצלו. ובכך סטייה עקרונית מתפיסתם של הקראים.

המסקנות, העולות מבירור ההשקפות הרבניות המשוקעות בדקדוקי הטעמים, יש בהן כדי ללמדנו שבעל דקדוקי הטעמים לא היה קראי. ואם בעל דקדוקי הטעמים הוא אהרן בן־אשר [197] — הרי שאהרן בן־אשר אינו קראי אלא רבני.

ג.   מתוך הערות הגיליון שבכתב־יד הנביאים של משה בן־אשר ראיה גם לרבניותו של זה.

בכתב־יד זה מובאת במקומות שונים הערת גיליון „י״ח מלין (בקר') תיקון סופר' וחכמ'″ [198], ורשימת י״ח מלים אלו מקורה במדרשי חז״ל [199] ואין הקראים מודים בה. אמנם ניסה גרץ [200] לטעון, שי״ח תיקוני סופרים מסורת

---

189   כגון בכתאב ג'אמע אלאלפאט', שורש „בט″ (מהדורת סקוז, כרך א', עמ' 212), שורש „עשה″ (כרך ב', עמ' 413), ועוד הרבה. ואפילו כשהוא מביא צורות פועל על שם הדוגמת וענין אחר (למשל הצטרפות וי״ו החיבור) הוא פורט אותן בסדר ציווי, עבר, עתיד: עֲשֵׂה וְעָשָׂה וְיַעֲשֶׂה; רְאֵה וְרָאָה; צֵא וְיָצָא וְיֵצֵא (כרך א', עמ' 2), — בהפרדה גמורה בין ציווי לעתיד.

190   כגון בקטע שפרסם מונק Notice sur Abou'l-Walid, עמ' 21. ועי' הערת מונק שם. וכן בנספח לפירושו על הושע הביא בו עלי הסברים לצורות דקדוקיות קשות, ובהסבריו לצורות הפועל הנטויות חוזר הוא תמיד אל הציווי כצורה היסודית. נספח זה פרסם ר״י R. Schroeter ב־ Archiv של Merx, כרך II (1871), עמ' 25־29 (עם תרגום לגרמנית), ע״פ כתב־יד מספריית בודלי שבאוקספורד. אחריו פרסמו הירשפלד ע״פ כתב־יד מן המוזיאון הבריטי, בספרו Literary History of Hebrew Grammarians and Lexico- graphers (לונדון, 1926), עמ' 103־105.

191   עי' דברי באכר, (1895) REJ ,XXX, עמ' 242, הע' 3.

192   כגון בפירושו לבראשית ו, ג, מהדורת סקו The Arabic Commentary of Ali ben Suleiman the Karaite on the Book of Genesis (פילדלפיה, 1928), עמ' 129.

193   זכרון לראשונים, חלק א', מחברת ה', עמ' עד ואילך.

194   ולדברי באכר (נצני הדקדוק, עמ' 55 הע' 1 ועמ' 59 הע' 4) קטע זה של קראי הוא.

195   = החזה.   196   „הזמן העתיד″ כולל גם ציווי. ועי' לעיל, הע' 188.

197   עי' ההסתייגות בעניין זה לעיל ועמ' רצה.

198   כגון בעמ' 89 לכתוב „מקללים להם″ (שמואל א' ג. יג), ובעמ' 580 לכתוב „קבעים אתי″ (מלאכי ג. ח) ועוד.

199   עי' ספרי ח', יז ע״א, וכן ציונים שמציין באר (דקה״ט עמ' 44) כמקורות ל־§ 57.

200   גרץ, בא״מ, עמ' 56, הע' 1.

עתיקה הם ונהגו להעתיקם בכתבי־יד של מקרא עוד לפני היות הקראים,
והקראים לא שינו מן המנהג והוסיפו להעתיקם. אך תשובה קלושה היא, שכן
תמוה ביותר שסופר כמשה בן־אשר היה מעתיק בתנ"ך שלו מתוך שגרת ההעתקה
דברים שאינו מקבל אותם ואינו מאמין בהם, מעשה מעתיק עם־הארץ. ועוד :
מאמיתי נהגו הקראים כבוד במסורת עתיקה ? וכיצד דחו מעל פניהם את התורה־
שבעל־פה, שמסורתה עתיקה לא פחות מתיקוני הסופרים ? ועדות מפורשת מפי
קראי על דחייתם של הקראים את תיקוני הסופרים נמצאת לנו בספרו של
קרקסאני, המקדיש שער שלם „בביאור הפסד טענתם" [201] של הרבנים בעניין זה.
והערת המסורה בסיום רשימת תיקוני הסופרים „אלו י"ח דברים תקון סופרים
ודקדוקיהן משובחים, ומארה תבא על כל מי שעליהם שטנה כותבים" [202] מוסבת
בלי ספק על הקראים ועל דברי שטנה מעין אלה של קרקסאני.

ד. מטבעות לשון

עם כל הזהירות שיש להתייחס בה אל הקבלה לשונית ואל המסקנות
שאפשר להסיק ממנה, אי אפשר להתעלם משפעת דפוסי הלשון, המליצות
והביטויים של לשון חז"ל השזורים בלשון דקדוקי הטעמים. כבר הצביעו חכמים
על מקבילות לשוניות רבות, שאפשר להכיר מהן עד כמה היה בן־אשר מעורה
בלשון חז"ל. נביא כאן לדוגמה רק אחדות מעשרות המקבילות האלה: [203]

החשובה שבהן היא המליצה „והבטוי כהררים תלוים בשערה כשלהבת
קשורה בגחלת" (§ 71), שראשיתה ע"פ חגיגה א, ח וסופה ע"פ ספר יצירה א,
ז [204]. המאמר „ובמסורות אשר הם ׳סיג לתורה" (§ 9) הוא ע"פ מאמר ר׳ עקיבא
„מסורת (נ"א מסורות) סיג לתורה" (אבות ג, יג) [205]. הבטוי התלמודי „זקני
עגולה" (§ 16) כבר נזכר. אוסיף לדוגמה גם את אזהרת בעל דקדוקי הטעמים:
„ומן הדרך הזאת לא יסורה, ועל דברי חכמים לא יעבורה, ומצה

201 „פי איצ׳אٴת פסאד דעואהם". זאת כותרתו של שער כ"ב (במאמר ב׳) הדן בעניין
זה. עי׳ קרקסאני, עמ׳ 153־161.

202 מסורה קטנה לבמדבר א, א.

203 עי׳ ספיר א׳, טז ע"ב ־ יז ע"א ; דוד אפפענהיים, המגיד, שנה יד (1870), גיליון
46, עמ׳ 365, וביותר מאמרו ב־ Zeitschrift של גייגר, XI (1875). עמ׳ 79־90 ; באכר,
Rabbinisches Sprachgut bei Ben Ascher, (1895) XV, ZAW. עמ׳ 293־304.

204 על שאילת רעיונות בדקה"ט מספר יצירה עי׳ רווין, (1881) XXX, MGWJ,
עמ׳ 521 ; באכר, נצני הדקדוק, עמ׳ 28. — אמנם גרץ טען (בא"מ, עמ׳ 58, הע׳ 1), שספר
יצירה אינו נוטה לשום צד והוא ניטרלי מבחינה דתית (בלשונו Confessionslos), אך הרי
ידוע שהקראים בזו ולעגו להתעסקות בקבלה ובתורת הסוד. עי׳ אפנשטין, גאונים, עמ׳ 51.
ועי׳ התקפתו החריפה של סלמון בן ירוחים על ספרות הסוד של הרבנים, כגון ספר רזים,
ספר שם בן נח, אותיות דר׳ עקיבא, שעור קומה (דודזון, מלחמות, שער יד, עמ׳ 111, 113,
ור׳ הערות המהדיר שם). אף קרקסאני מתריס כנגד ספרות זו (קרקסאני, מאמר א׳, שער ג׳
וד׳, עמ׳ 15, 31. ועי׳ על ספרים אחרים במפתח של המהדיר, כרך ה׳, עמ׳ 042־043).

205 והוא קרוב אל הכלל „יש אם למסורת" (עי׳ פירוש רע"ב למקום). הרעיון נרמז
אף במקום אחר בדקדוקי הטעמים (עי׳ לעיל עמ׳ רצ), וכבר ראינו את התנגדותו של בעל
החילוק לכלל זה (לעיל עמ׳ שה).

וריב יסירה, כי זאת דרך ישרה..." (9 §). הקרובה אל מאמרי חז"ל "וכל העובר
על דברי חכמים חייב מיתה" (ברכות ד ע"ב) או "כל העובר על דברי סופרים
חייב מיתה" (עירובין כא ע'ב) הן מצד הלשון והן מצד התפיסה. הרי דרך הקראים
לחפש ולחקור בעצמם, ואין שייך בהם "לעבור על דברי חכמים", שכן דברי
חכמיהם אינם קבועים, אלא משתנים לבקרים ע"פ סברה[206]. ודרכם זו הרבתה
אצלם מצה ומריבה, ושמא בא הלשון "ומצה וריב יסירה" לרמז על מריבות
הקראים, שיש לסור מהן כדי לדבוק בניגודן — בדרך הישרה והסלולה של דברי
חכמים.

ומעין זה אף במה שנרשם בכתב ידו של משה בן־אשר בכי"ק, אחרי שהוא
מונה ע"פ סדר חז"ל את "הנביאים שנתנבאו על ישראל"[207] : "כל נביאי ישראל
ממשה רבינו... עד דניאל ומלאכי מאה ושבעה עשר מכן והלך ולחתם חזון ונביא
מכן והלך הט אזנך ושמע דברי חכמים"[208]. הרי שאף הוא מודה
בתורה־שבעל־פה. גם במקום אחר בקולופון מכתיבת ידו[209] משתמש הוא בביטוי
תלמודי מובהק "מצורע מוסגר" (מגילה א, ז)[210].

(הסיום יבוא)

---

206 עי׳ לעיל עמ׳ רצב, וכן דברי ראב"ע המובאים לעיל עמ׳ שג : "וכל איש כרצונו
יפרש הפסוקים. גם במצות ובחקים... וכל רגע יהפכו מצד אל צד כפי מחשבותם...".
207 כי"ק, עמ׳ 584.
208 וסיום זה מובא כאן כלשונו בסדר עולם רבא, ל׳ (מהדורת ראטנער, חילנא
תרנ"ז, עמ׳ 140).
209 כי"ק, עמ׳ 586.   210 עי׳ ספיר א׳, טז ע"ב.

האמנם היה בן־אשר קראי? *

פרק שלישי: מי הוא בן־אשר הקראי?

מאז שכך הוויכוח על אמונתו של בן־אשר, בשלהי המאה הקודמת, נתרחבה ידיעתנו בספרותם של הקראים במידה מרובה. כתבי־יד של חיבורי קראים בפרשנות ובהלכה, אגרונים, קטעי דקדוק ויכוצא בהם, שהיו עלומים בגנזים ובספריות, ראו אור ולראיה למהדורות ביקורתיות ובכך נפתח פתח למחקרים מקיפים יותר ולראיה רחבה וכוללת יותר של הספרות הקראית. נתגלו גם כתבי־יד של חיבורי פולמוס נגד הקראים ואף אלה נתפרסמו ותרמו תרומה חשובה לקידום חקר הקראות. בין אלה ידוע ומפורסם חיבורו הפיוטי של רס"ג "אשא משלי", העוסק בפולמוס עם הקראים, ואשר עניין מיוחד לו בפרשה שאנו דנים בה.

משהחלו מתגלים ומתפרסמים קטעים שונים מחיבור זה, נמצאה רשומה בראש אחד הקטעים, לפני שם החיבור, כתובת באותיות ערביות, שהחוקרים התקשו בקריאתה ובפירושה. בשנת תש"ג הצליח בנימין קלאר ז"ל לקרוא נכונה את הכתובת הערבית והיא "אלרד עלי בן אשאר עבראני", ותרגומה: "התשובה על בן־אשר, עברית" [211], הווי אומר: "אשא משלי" הוא תשובה של רס"ג על בן־אשר. הוסף לכאן את עדותו של דונש [212] "שהשיב (רס"ג) על בן אשר" ונמצאת למד ש"אשא משלי" הוא אותה תשובה של רס"ג, הנזכרת בדברי דונש. וחיבור זה הריהו רצוף התקפה רבתי על הקראים, מכאן טענה חזקה שבן־אשר, שנגדו נכתב החיבור, היה קראי. לכאורה סתירה מפורשת למסקנה שהגענו אליה בדברינו עד כאן.

הבה נתעלם לרגע מן המסקנה הזאת וננסה לבחון את העובדות הנוספות הללו לאור הידוע לנו עד כה על בן־אשר. מיד מתעוררות תמיהות אחדות:

א. אף לדברי הטוענים שבן־אשר היה קראי, הרי כל פעלו בשדה הקראות אינו משתקף, אלא ברמזים בודדים בחיבורו הקצר דקדוקי הטעמים. ואף רמזים אלה אינם נושאים אופי פולמוסי, ולא כדי להוכיח את צדקת הקראים אמרם אומרם, אלא כמסיח לפי תומו, ואינו אלא כאומר את דבריו על ענייני המסורה לפי השקפת עולמו. האפשר להעלות על הדעת, שרס"ג יכתוב חיבור גדול כל כך [213] ומפורט כל כך [214] בתשובה על רמזים בודדים כאלה? הרי, אף לדעת

---

* ראשיתו של מאמר זה בחוברת הקודמת, עמ' רפ—שי"ב.

211 קלאר, מחקרים, עמ' 276—281.

212 עי' לעיל עמ' רפד. אם נניח שהכוונה בשניהם, היינו בכתובת של "אשא משלי" ובעדות דונש, לאותו חיבור. ועי' סיכום השיקולים בעד ונגד הנחה זו, אלוני, סיני, כרך כח (תשי"א), עמ' קמו.

213 ואמנם גדול הוא ומקיף למעלה מ־500 בתי שיר בני 3—5 שורות כ"א. מה שנתגלה עד כה מגיע לכדי שליש מן החיבור כולו ונתפרסם במקובץ ע"י ב"מ לוין בספר רס"ג, עמ' תקה—תקלב.

214 נוסף על דברים כלליים נגד הקראים נכנס רס"ג לפרטי פרטים בהלכה הקראית.

הטוענים לקראיות, לא בא בעל דקדוקי הטעמים להטיח דברים נגד הרבניים [215],
ולמה אפוא יתקוף הרס"ג דווקא אותו, וביחוד בתקופה משופעת בקראים
מפורסמים בעלי מענה־לשון חריף ובעלי השפעה ?

וכבר כתב לוין [216] : "קשה מאוד להחליט, שכל הדברים הקשים שבאשא
משלי, והמה מרובים ושונים מאוד, נכתבו כנגד בן אשר לבד, ואף על פי שלא
היה סומך ב"דקדוקי הטעמים" שלו על דרשות חז"ל". ובסמוך הוא דוחה את האפשרות
שבן־אשר היה קראי, שאילו כן לא היתה המסורת שלו מתקבלת על הרבניים
כנגד בן־נפתלי, אך מתוך שהלך לוין בדרך קודמיו, נדחק ליישב שלכתחילה אמנם
כתב רס"ג את "אשא משלי" כנגד בן־אשר בעל המסורה, ומכאן הכתובת שבשער
החיבור, ואולם אח"כ חזר וכתב מהדורות חדשות והוסיף והרחיב את החיבור
גם על הקראים. ותמיהני איך לא שם לב לכך, ש"אשא משלי" הוא חיבור
בעל תכנית ערוכה מראש ומכוונת ל־572 בתי שיר, האסורים בכבלי ברזל
של סדר א"ב מורכב ומסובך [217], ואיך ייתכן בו הוספה והרחבה ?

ב. תמוה הדבר : כל עיסוקו של בן־אשר הוא במסורה ובדקדוק, אך
ב"אשא משלי" [218] לא ראה רס"ג להזכיר ענייני מסורה אלא במעט מן המעט [219],
וגם כשהוא מזכירם אין הוא טוען טענות ענייניות מפורטות, אלא מדבר באופן
כללי ביותר על הדבקות הפורמאלית המוגזמת של הקראים בסימני המסורה.
ואפילו דברים אלה נאמרים בצורה סתמית ובלשון נסתרים, ובהכרח אינם מכוונים
אל הנתקף המסוים שבחיבור, אלא אל בני אל בני עדתו בכלל. והרי נגד בן־אשר בעל
דקדוקי הטעמים היה לו לרס"ג לומר הרבה, לפחות לפי דעת הטוענים שבן־אשר
האמין בניקוד מסיני : זוהי סטיה חמורה שראוי היה להתריע עליה.

ג. אילו חלק רס"ג על תורתו של בן־אשר בדקדוק ובמסורה, באשר
היא תורתו של קראי, איך לא הזכירו אף ברמז באחד מחיבורי הדקדוק שלו ?

כל עצמו של "אשא משלי" נתחבר כהתרסה נגד קראי טיפוסי, שעסק
בקראות לשמה ושהיה מראשי המדברים נגד הרבניים ומבוזי שמם של חכמי
התלמוד, ש"כתב כי התעו איומה למען בצוע בצע בתרמה" [220], ועל כן היה
מקום והיה צורך להשיב עליו ולהראות את הבלותו שלו ושל אחיו הקראים עמו.
ולא בא רס"ג להאשימם על עצם עיסוקם במסורה ובדקדוק — הרי גם הוא עסק

_____

כגון ציצית, מזוזה, תפילין, ברכת המזון, סגנין התפילות, חשבון השנה, שיטת הרכוב, דיני
יבום ונידה וכיו"ב.

215 וכך כותב פיניליש, דרכה של תורה, עמ' 276 : "כי הם (בן־אשר ובן נפתלי. —
א"ד) לא היו קראים מתעצמים ומתעסקים בויכוח נגד הרבנים, כי אם מדקדקים מסורנים עושי
מלאכתם באמונה".

216 לוין, ספר רס"ג, עמ' תצז.

217 ובמאמרו הנ"ל, עמ' תקה, אף הביא לוין טבלה מפורטת של תכנית זו.

218 לפחות במה שהגיע לידינו.

219 רק שמונה מתוך מאות השורות בקטעים שנתגלו דנות במסורה.

220 אשא משלי, עמ' תקין, שו' 7‎-8. ורס"ג הולך ומונה את טוהר לבם ומידותיהם
של חז"ל.

בכך וביסודיות מרובה, ואין פסול בכך — אלא על חוסר הבנתם בעניינים אלה
ועל האבסורד שבעיסוקם זה, שאין לו טעם, כשאין הם מודים בדרשות חז"ל,
המיוסדות על הקוריוזים שבמסורה ומסבירות אותם [221]

אך קריאתו הנכונה של קלאר „אלרד עלי בן אשאר" ועדותו של דונש,
שרס"ג השיב על בן־אשר, במקומן עומדות ואינן משאירות צל של ספק, ש„אשא
משלי" אמנם נכתב כתשובה על בן־אשר. על כן, בהכרח יש לומר: ל א ע ל
א ה ר ן ב ן ־ א ש ר א ו ע ל מ ש ה א ב י ו, ה מ ל מ ד י ם ה ג ד ו ל י ם, נ כ ת ב
ח י ב ו ר ז ה, א ל א ע ל ב ן ־ א ש ר א ח ר, ב ן ־ א ש ר ק ר א י ש ק ר א ו ת ו
א ו מ נ ו ת ו. שהרי גם בדברי דונש וגם בכתובת של „אשא משלי" אין נזכר שמ'
הפרטי של בן־אשר זה, וההנחה, שאיש לא פקפק בה עד היום הזה, אך איש גם לא
טרח להוכיח אותה, ששתי עדויות אלה מוסבות דווקא על בן־אשר בעל המסורה, אין
לה על מה שתסמוך [222], באשר היא מושתת בעיקרה על דעה קדומה מוטעית,
שסתם בן־אשר בדורו של רס"ג הוא בעל המסורה הידוע [223]. „הידוע" כאן הוא
תיאור אנאכרוניסטי, שכן נראה, שפרסומו של בן־אשר בעל המסורה נתפשט רק
בדורות שלאחריו, ואילו בחיבורי בני דורו אין לו זכר כלל [224].

מי אפוא היה בן־אשר הקראי הזה שרס"ג השיב עליו?

עלינו לחפשו בין בני־דורו של רס"ג, שהשיבות עליו, שמא יימצא ביניהם.
החכם הקראי סהל בן מצליח מונה, באחת מאיגרות התוכחה שלו אל ר' יעקב בן
שמואל תלמיד רס"ג, את בני הפלוגתה של רס"ג מבין הקראים. אביא קטע זה
בשלמותו [225]:

„ואתה עתה הטוב טוב אתה [226] מן סעדיה הפיתומי [227] ראש הישיבה הרוב
רב עם בני [228] מקרא יֵצ"ו [227] אם נלחום נלחם עמהם והלא חכמיהם ותלמידיהם
היו תובעים [229] ממנו לצאת אליהם ולשבת עמם [230] במלחמת [231] ה' ולערוך עמם
משפטיהם לדעת אי זה דרך הטוב מדרכיהם ואומרים משפט נבחרה לנו נדעה [232]
מה טוב בדבריהם, ולא רצה ומנע [233] נפשו לצאת [234] אליהם ובא חדר בחדר
להחבא, וגם לא היה מביא אליו כי אם את [227] אשר הוא חפץ, וגם [227] לא [235]

<hr>

221   עי' „אשא משלי, עמ' תקכ, שו' 29—36. ולא שהיא פוסל את העיסוק בכך מעיקרו,
אלא כופר היא ביכולתם של הקראים להתעסק בכך.

222   אחת הטעויות הראשונות הייתה בפירוש תיבת „האותות" במובאה של דונש
מתוך דברי רס"ג, שהבינוה, לפי פירוש שד"ל (בית האוצר, לשכה א', יא ע"ב), כמדברת
באותיות, ועל כן ראו בה תשובה על בן־אשר המדקדק. ואינו כן, ופירושה האמיתי ר' לעיל
הע' 29.

223   עי' לוין, ספר רס"ג, עמ' תצד ; קלאר, מחקרים, עמ' 288.

224   סמי מכאן קולופונים, שאינם ראיה לפרסום.

225   ל"ק, עמ' 37, ומשם העתיקו מאן, Texts and Studies II (1935). עמ' 25,
הע' 46. ונדפס לראשונה ע"י שטיינשניידר, Catalogus Codicum Hebraeorum Bibliothecae
Academiae Lugduno-Batavae (1858). עמ' 403. בהערות להלן אביא חילופי נוסח
שבמהד' שטיינשניידר (= ש"ש).

226   וְאתה.   227   (אין תיבה זו).   228   בעלי.
229   מבקשים.   230   עמהם.   231   במלחמות.
232   נדעה ב נ י נ ו מה טוב.   233   ומנה.   234   לבלתי צאת.   235   ולא.

יכלו בני מקרא להקבץ עמו בשבת מפני הנר, ובן משיח הקציר נפשו מביניהם
והביא אותו חדר בחדר עד שצעק ואמר מה לי ולך לך מעלי, והספרים אשר כתב
לא הוציאם בחייו מתחת ידו על בני מקרא ואחד מהם נפל ביד בן משיח והשיב
עליו בחייו, וכן שלמון בן ירוחים [236] ע״ה [227] השיב עליו בלשון הקדש על אשר
כתב עליו [237], נשא [238] משלו [239] ואמר [240], ואחרי מותו כמות [227] נבל [227] נפלו
ספריו ביד בני מקרא [241] בכל מקום ומקום וישיבו עליו [242] תשובות בדברים
נבוחים כמסמרות [243] נטועים בספרים הרבה, כמו שעשה אבו אל טייב
הנודע אל גבלי [244], וכן [245] עלי בן חסון [246] וכן בן משיח ובן
ירוחם הנודע בן רוחים, ואבו עלי חסן [247] אלבצרי
ווולתם, וגם אני כתבתי תשובה לדבריו כאחד מהם,
ואם תבקש להתבונן היטב בספריהם עד אשר תמצא אמונת [248] הדבר ותדע כי
האמת אתם.

מבין החמישה הנזכרים כאן, נוסף על סהל בן מצליח עצמו, יש בידינו
ידיעות ברורות, פחות או יותר, על שלושה. שניים הנותרים, אבו אלטייב אלגבלי
ועלי בן חסון, ידיעותינו עליהם קלושות למדיי.

עלי בן חסון, או בן אלחסן, הוא כנראה אביו של יפת בן עלי המפורסם
והרא נזכר ע״י נכדו לוי הלוי בן יפת במקדמא שלו לפרשת דברים [249].

אבן אלטייב אלגבלי לא היה ידוע כלל עד שפרסם ג׳ורג׳ מרגליות [250]
את רשימת חכמי הקראים של אבן אלהיתי. וברשימה זו נזכר אבו אלטייב אלגבלי
בשמו העברי: „שמואל בן אשר בן מנצור".
הרי הקטע שבו הוא נזכר [251] :

„ואלשיך שמואל בן אשר בן מנצור אלמערוף באבו אלטייב אלג׳בלי כאן
פי זמאן אלשיך אבו [252] אלפרג׳ האדון ותנאט׳רא [253] פי אלאביב ואלסנה אלשרעיה

---

236 ירוחם. — לצורת השם ועי׳ דורון, מלחמות, עמ׳ 1, הע׳ 1.

237 (אין תיבה זו). — וזה עיקר, ועי׳ ועל כך מאן, תרביץ ג (תרצ״ב), עמ׳ 382
והספרות המצוינת שם. 238 אשא. 239 משלי. 240 צ״ל : ואחוד.

241 בני מקרא יצ׳ ו. 242 עליהן. 243 כמסמרים.

244 אלנבלי. — וטעות. 245 וגם. 246 כיסון. — וטעות.

247 חוסן. 248 ש״ש מציע לקרוא „אמתת".

249 ל״ק, עמ׳ 64. — פוזננסקי (KLOSG), עמ׳ 17) מפקפק בייחוס זה, משום
הספק במהימנות המקדמא. אך ספק זה נתעורר לגבי המקדמא של סלמון בן ירוחים, וייחוס
זה נזכר במקדמא של לוי הלוי בן יפת, שאיש מלבד פוזננסקי (-Zur jüdisch
arabischen Litteratur, ברלין 1904, עמ׳ 49. — בלי הנמקה) לא פקפק באמיתותה.
ומסכימים לייחוס זה גם פינסקר, ל״ק עמ׳ קיא ; פירסט, תוה״ק ב׳, עמ׳ 46 ; גוטלובר,
ביקורת, עמ׳ 207 ; שטיינשניידר, Die arabische Literatur der Juden (פרנקפורט ענ״מ,
1902), עמ׳ 85, § 46. ואחרים. הזמן שקבע פוזננסקי (KLOSG, שם) לעלי בן חסן מתמיה
ביותר, אם נשווה לכך את הזמן שקבע לבנו (שם, עמ׳ 20).

250 JQR, IX (1897), עמ׳ 429—443.

254 אבן אלהיתי, עמ׳ 435. 252 כך יש להגיה ע״פ מרגליות. בכה״י „אבר".

253 בכה״י „ותנאצ׳רא". וחילופי ט׳ —צ׳ בכתבי־יד — מפורסמים.

וכאן עלי ראי אלמולי אבו עלי רחֹ אתֹ ולהו מקאלה פי אפסאד אלמחזור וחסאב אלמולד ורד [254] עלי מנחם ראש מתיבא ענד וקופה עלי רקעהֹ בן מנחם אלי אביתֹאבת איידה אתֹ״.

ותרגומו [255]: והחכם שמואל בן אשר בן מנצור הידוע ב(שם) אבו אלטיב אלג׳בלי היה בזמן החכם אבו אלפרג׳ האֹרון, והתוכחו זה עם זה ב(ענין) האביב והשנה (כפי שהיא נקבעת) בהלכה, והיה (מסכים) על דעת החכם אבו עלי ירחמהֹ עליון, ולו מאמר ב(ענין) הפסד המחזור וחשבון המולד, והשיב על מנחם ראש ישיבה כשנודעה לו [256] איגרת בן מנחם אל אבו תאבת יסעדהו עליון.

לא נוכל לסמוך על עדות-הזמן של אבן אלהיתי, שכן, כאמור, נזכר אלג׳בלי כבר באיגרתו של סהל בן מצליח, ואילו היה אלג׳בלי בן זמנו של אבו אלפרג׳ האֹרון (השלים את כתאב אלמשתמל שלו בשנת 1026 [257]), ספק גדול אם היה סהל יודע עליו בכלל. על כורחנו נעדיף את עדותו של סהל בן מצליח, הקרוב אל אלג׳בלי קרבת זמן, מעדותו המאוחרת של אבן אלהיתי, בן שלהי המאה הי״ד וראשית הט״ו. בדרך השערה אפשר לומר, שאבן אלהיתי מצא חיבור של אבו אלפרג׳, שבו הוא מתווכח עם דעותיו של אלג׳בלי, והסיק מכך שהיה בן זמנו.

יש לתת את הדעת גם על קושי בדבריו של סהל בן מצליח בקטע הנ״ל. אבו אלטיב אלג׳בלי נמנה שם עם הקראים שהשיבו על רס״ג א ח ר י מ ו ת ו. לא ייתכן, אפוא, שהוא פתח בוויכוח ורס״ג, כעדות הכותרת של ״אשא משלי״, כתב ת ש ו ב ה ומענה לדבריו. [258]

אולם אין כאן כל סתירה והדברים מתיישבים יפה, אם נזכור שני דברים:

א. גם ״רד״ וגם תרגומו ״תשובה״ אין פירושם רק מענה והשבת דברים לשואל או למתקיף, אלא גם תגובה, הכחשה וסתירה לדברים, שלא נאמרו בלשון שאלה דווקא או בדרך׳ של פתיחת ויכוח. כך, למשל, כתב דונש ספר ״תשובות״ על רס״ג, ובוודאי לא פ ת ח רס״ג בוויכוח אתו. ומה לנו דוגמה טובה יותר מחיבורו של רס״ג עצמו ״כתאב אלרד עלי ענן״ (=ספר התשובה על ענן). ענן, שחי למעלה מ־150 שנה לפני רס״ג, ודאי לא פתח בוויכוח עמו ולא הפנה אליו שאלות. אם כך, יכול להיות שרס״ג כתב תגובה לאלג׳בלי, אם לאחד מחיבוריו אם להטפתו הקראית, וזה השיב עליו, לדברי סהל, רק לאחר מותו.

ב. קיימת גם אפשרות שנייה. אלג׳בלי פתח בוויכוח עם רס״ג וה״רד״ של רס״ג עליו הוא תשובה ומענה ממש. כדי להניח אפשרות כזאת, עלינו לבחון פרטים אחדים בדברי סהל. אין ספק שעדותו של סהל מושתתת על יסודות של אמת בכל הנוגע לעצם העובדות, היינו שהחכמים שמנה אמנם השיבו על רס״ג. אך

---

254 כך יש להגיה עֹפֹ מרגליות. בכה״י ״ורדה״.

255 תודה לד״ר י׳ בלאו על עזרתו בכמה דיוקי תרגום.

256 ״כשעמד עלֹ״.

257 עי׳ באכר, REJ, XXX (1895), עמֹ 253.

258 בטענה זו דוחה קלאר (מחקרים, עמֹ 288, העֹ 60) את האפשרות, שרס״ג כתב נגד אלג׳בלי.

ניסיונו להסביר עובדות אלה בכך, שרס״ג „בא חדר להחבא" מפני חמת
פולמוסם של הקראים, בא לעטוף במעטה של שקרים את גרעין האמת ההיסטורית
שבדבריו, אמת מרה כלענה לגאות עליונותם של הקראים, והיא, שחכמיהם, להוציא
את שני עזי המצח שבהם, לא העזו להשיב על רס״ג בחייו. הגוזמה והתהללות
השוא האופיינית לקראים, אף סהל לא ניקה מהן והן מורגשות בדבריו ביותר,
ומתוך כך יש לחשוש, שגם הדיוק לקה במקצת. ביחוד רופפת החלוקה בין
המשיבים על רס״ג בחייו ובין המשיבים עליו לאחר מותו.

נראה שסדר המניה של החכמים בדברי סהל הוא כרונולוגי, והדבר מתקבל
על הדעת. אבו עלי חסן אלבצרי — הוא יפת בן עלי המפורסם — וסהל בן
מצליח עצמם הם הצעירים שבתבורה ונזכרו בסוף. לפניהם חסן (או חסון) בן
משיח וסלמון בן ירוחים הם מבני דורו של רס״ג, והם חולקים עליו בחייו [259]
אף לפי עדות סהל [260], והאחד אף מתוכח או מנסה להתוכח עמו פנים אל פנים.
ואילו מבני הזוג הראשון האחד הוא עלי בן חסון, אביו של יפת בן עלי [261] והוא
ודאי זקן מן הנגמנים אחריו, והשני, אבו אלטייב אלג׳בלי, עומד בראש הרשימה;
ואם באמת סדר כרונולוגי כאן, כפי שניסינו להראות, קרוב לוודאי שהוא הזקן
שבהם.

ועל כן מוזרה היא החלוקה של סהל למשיבים לפני מותו ואחרי מותו
של רס״ג ויש לקבל אותה בספקנות מרובה. שכן, אם בן משיח וסלמון, הצעירים
מאלג׳בלי, השיבו על רס״ג בחייו, מתקבל על הדעת שגם אלג׳בלי השיב עליו
והתקיף אותו בחייו, ועל כך השיב רס״ג ב„אשא משלי". אי־דיוק כזה בדברי סהל
אף אינו חייב להיות מכוון. לא ייפלא אם שגה סהל בראשה, שכן היו החכמים
שמנה מפוזרים ורחוקים מירושלים עיר מושבו [262], והיו יושבים בבבל [263],
בסוריה [264] ובפרס [265]. אין זה מן הנמנע שטעה במועד החיבור של דברי אחדים מהם.

---

259 מסתבר שתשובת סלמון על „אשא משלי" נכתבה בחיי רס״ג, שכן אילו השיב
עליו רק לאחר מותו, די היה לו לסהל למנותו פעם אחת בלבד — ברשימה הרצופה של
המשיבים לאחר מות רס״ג. וע' דודזון, מלחמות, במבוא, עמ' 2.

260 לפי עדויות קראיות אחרות, שלא נתאשרו, היה סלמון זקן מרס״ג ואף רבו ומורו
(ע' דודזון, מלחמות, עמ' 1 ; לוין, ספר רס״ג, עמ' תקא). אבן אלהיתי (עמ' 434) אף יודע
לספר, שרס״ג השתתף בהלוויתו של סלמון והתאבל עליו מרה. וזה בוודאי מוגזם.

261 ע' לעיל עמ' שגג והע' 249.

262 כך באיגרתו הנדונה אל יעקב בן שמואל : „אני מבית המקדש באתי" (ל״ק, עמ'
27, וכן בעמ' 30) וכוונתו : בית אלמקדס — אלקדס — ירושלים. וע' אסף, מקורות ומחקרים,
עמ' 40, הע' 53, המביא דוגמאות מרובות לשימוש זה של „בית המקדש".

263 בן משיח ישב בבגדד (ע' אבן אלהיתי, עמ' 434). אבו עלי חסן אלבצרי,
כלומר יפת בן עלי, ישב אמנם רוב ימיו בירושלים, ו„אלבצרי" הוא כינוי למוצאה של
משפחתו (ע' פ' בירנבוים, The Arabic Commentary of Yefet ben 'Ali the Karaite on
the Book of Hosea, פילדלפיה, 1942, עמ' VII). ואולי אביו, עלי בן חסן, הנזכר אף הוא
ברשימת סהל, ישב וחי בבצרה.

264 סלמון בן ירוחים חי כנראה בחאלב. לפי אבן אלהיתי (עמ' 434) נפטר שם.

265 לפי מאן (Texts and Studies), כרך II, עמ' 25, הע' 46) אלג׳בלי הוא מן
Media = ג׳באל. אך וע' גם פינסקר, ל״ק עמ' 37, הע' 1 ; פירסט, תוה״ק ב':

738

זמנו של אלג׳בלי בלי טעון עיון נוסף. פוזננסקי קבע את זמנו מסביב לאמצע
המאה העשירית 266. אך קביעה זו מבוססת על זיהוי של „מנחם ראש מתיבא״,
הנזכר ברשימת אבן אלהיתי, עם מנחם בלתי ידוע, שהציג שאלות לרב סעדיה
בזמן היותו גאון 267, ועל עדות־הזמן הנזכרת של סהל. אך מהימנותו של פרט
זה בעדות סהל מתערערת כאן, וגם הזיהוי של „מנחם ראש מתיבא״ הוא מפוקפק
ביותר 268, שכן אין ראש ישיבה בשם מנחם בזמנו של רס״ג ואחריו לא בסורא
ולא בפומבדיתא. על כן נראית ביותר הנחתו של מרגליות 269 ש„מנחם ראש
מתיבא״ הוא גאון פומבדיתא במחצית השנייה של המאה הט׳. ואם כך, יבוא הכול
על מקומו בשלום: אלג׳בלי חי בזמן בנו של מנחם זה, היינו בסוף המאה התשיעית
—תחילת העשירית. הוא כותב תשובה נגד מנחם האב 270 ומפרסם חיבורים
שונים בהלכה הקראית, כגון אלה שמנה אבן אלהיתי. ואולי אף ספרי פולמוס
וויכוח. פעולתו הספרותית למען הקראות חייבה תשובה ומענה של רס״ג, וזו ניתנה
ב„אשא משלי״ 271.

עמ׳ 48, הע׳ 159 ; פוזננסקי, Jewish Encyclopedia כרך VII, עמ׳ 16, ערך
Jabali, Abu al-Tayyib al-.

266 עי׳ פוזננסקי, שם, וכן KLOSG, עמ׳ 17. ועי׳ גם שטיינשניידר, -Die ara
bische Literatur der Juden, עמ׳ 79 (42 §). אמנם פירסט (תוה״ק ב׳, עמ׳ 48) מקדימו
לשנת 935.

267 הרכבי פרסם את חרוזי הפתיחה העבריים לשאלות אלה, הגורן א׳ (1897), עמ׳ 91.

268 וגם פוזננסקי מדגיש זאת (עי׳ בערך הנזכר ב־Jewish Encyclopedia).

269 JQR, IX (1897), עמ׳ 442, הע׳ 8.

270 ואין הדבר מתויב, שמנחם היה אותו זמן בחיים. השווה את הנאמר לעיל עמ׳ שנד
על תשובות רס״ג על ענן.

271 יורשה נא לי להעמיד כאן על אפשרות שלא עמדו עליה החוקרים. אסף פרסם
(תרביץ ד׳ (תרצ״ג), עמ׳ 35—53, 193—206) „דברי פולמוס של קראי קדמון נגד הרבנים״,
ושיער שהם חלק מחיבור של אבן סאקויה, שנכתב כתשובה לחיבורו של רס״ג „כתאב אלרד
עלי אבן סאקויה״. דודזון (מלחמות, במבוא עמ׳ 27) הסכים עמו לייחס את הדברים לאבן
סאקויה, אך שיער שהם תשובה לחיבור אחר של רס״ג „כתאב אלרד עלי אלמתכאמל״. ואולם
מאן (תרביץ ו׳ (תרצ״ה), עמ׳ 67, הע׳ 199) פקפק בעצם ייחוס הדברים לאבן סאקויה. מן
הראוי להעיר על רמיזות אחדות ב„אשא משלי״ הנראות כתשובה ממש על אחת ההאשמות
של אותו קראי קדמון. וכה דברי הקראי: „ספר לנו על קדמוניך הראשונים כמו שמאי והלל
העקביא ועקיבא ודוסא ויהושע ושאר התלמידים, אשר הודו קדמוניך והודית שמפני שלא שמשו
כל צרכן רבתה מחלוקת...״ (התרגום העברי במאמרו של אסף, שם, עמ׳ 194). ועל כך ב„אשא
משלי״ (עמ׳ תקיז) : „תפלצתך אטמה אזנך, והשיא אותך זדונך, ותשא מרום עיניך, על ה ל ל
ו ע ק י ב ה״, ובסמוך : „אולת עדת חנף ומרית, כי בחכמי אל התגרית...״, ולהלן (עמ׳ תקיח) :
„טורף נפשו באפו, חכמי אלוה בחרפו, ואליהם ידו נטה... כתב כי התעו אימומה, למעז בצע
בצע בתרמה...״, והולך ומונה מידותיהם הטובות של חז״ל, ובהם איתם חכמים, שהקראי
מאשימם בכך שלא שימשו כל צורכם. האפשר לחפש קשר בין שני חיבורים אלה ? הייתכן
שאבו אלטייב אלג׳בלי הוא אותו קראי קדמון, ושחיבורו הוא הוא שנגדו כתב רס״ג את „אשא
משלי״ ? התשובה לשאלות אלה קשה כל עוד לא נתגלה חומר נוסף על אלג׳בלי, אך דומה
שראויה אפשרות זו לתת עליה את הדעת.

הדברים שאמרנו לעיל [272] על זיקתו של אלג'בלי אל אבו אלפרג' האֻרון
בעיני אבן אלהיתי נכונים אף לגבי זיקתו אל יפת בן עלי, הנזכר בדברי אבן
אלהיתי „אלמולי אבו עלי". מדברי הכרוניקן אין ללמוד שהיו בני זמן אחד, אלא
שמה שראה הוא מחיבורו של אלג'בלי מתאים לדעתו של יפת בן עלי. אבן אלהיתי
לא ידע הרבה על אלג'בלי, וכשבא לתאר את תורתו ציין אותה לפי ה„מגדיר"
הפשוט שהיה בידו : תיאר את האחד הבלתי ידוע (אלג'בלי) על פי השניים
הידועים (אבו אלפרג' ויפת); אלג'בלי חלק על אבו אלפרג' האֻרון והסכים עם
יפת בן עלי, אע״פ שלמעשה ספק גדול אם ראו השלושה זה את זה.

על כל פנים ראינו בבירור, ששמואל בן אשר הנודע בשם אבו אלטייב אלג'בלי
היה קראי „מתעצם ומתוכח" בקראות ובן דורו של רס״ג (ואולי אף זקן ממנו),
ומכל מה שידוע לנו עליו אין כל מניעה להניח, שהוא הוא בן־אשר אשר נגדו
כתב רס״ג את „אשא משלי". אין ספק שהיה אלג'בלי חשוב בדורו וכדאי להשיב
עליו ולהגיב על דבריו [273].

פרק רביעי : שירת הגפן

מחקר זה לא יהיה שלם, אם לא ניתן את הדעת על עוד עדות אחת,
שהובאה להוכיח ש מ ש ה בן־אשר היה קראי. בסופו של כי״ל הועתק שיר על
„ישראל שנמשלו בגפן". השיר הוא בן 23 שורות : 22 ראשונות שבהן פותחות
באותיות הא״ב כסדרן ואחרונה פותחת באות קו״ף, שהיא כנראה שורת חתימה
של אקרוסטיכון „חזק". זולאי גילה שני כתבי־יד אחרים של שיר זה, באחד מהם
11 השורות הראשונות של השיר ובשני המשכו, משורה 12 עד 22 ועוד נוספו

---

272 עמ' שנד.

273 יֵּם סיומו של פרק זה, שנגעֵנו בו ב„אשא משלי", מן הראוי להסתייג, בהתאם
למסקנתנו, מזמן חיבורו של חיבור זה, שהוגבל ע״י קלאר (מחקרים, עמ' 314 ואילך) בשנים
915—921 זמן זה הוא קובע משני טעמים : א) מכיוון ש„אשא משלי" נכתב נגד אהרן בן־
אשר איש טבריה, קרוב להניח שנתחבר בשנת שבתו של רס״ג בארץ ישראל ובטבריה, היינו
בשנים הנ״ל. ב) דונש בתשובותיו על רס״ג מביא משמו את ההרוז „ברקת וזהב ויהלם, וראמות
וכדכד ואחלום, חבורת צדק הקדושה" (ספר תשובות דונש על רס״ג, עמ' 23, סי' 87), כדי
לחלוק על הצורה „אחלום", שרס״ג טבעה לצורך החרוז במקום „אחלמה". קלאר שיער, שהרוז
זה מקורו בחרוזי „שֶׁה" שב„אשא משלי" ועל סמך השערה זו הניח, שהחיבור כולו לא נכתב
אחרי שנת 921, היא השנה שבה פרצה מחלוקת הלוח בין רס״ג ובן־מאיר, שכן אחרי שנה זו,
בעיצומה של מחלוקת, אין להעלות על הדעת ביטוי ביטוי כזה של כבוד מצדו של רס״ג כלפי „חבורת
צדק הקדושה", חבורת הסנהדרין שבארץ ישראל, שבראשה עמד או בן־מאיר הסורר.
לפי דרכנו סר כוחו של הטעם הראשון. ועל השני יש לומר : אם נכונה ההשערה על
מקורו של החרוז, הרי מסתבר שרס״ג כתב את „אשא משלי" קודם 921. אך הדעת נותנת,
שחיברו בבבל דווקא, בסמוך לג'באל, מקומו של שמואל בן־אשר. והרי ידוע לנו, שרס״ג יצא
את מצרים למשך זמן קצר עֵוד קודם לעלייתו הידועה לארץ בשנת 915, ושהה אז בסוריה
ובבבל (עֵי' מאלטר, Saadia Gaon, his Life and Works, עמ' 425 ; שמחוני, התקופה, כרך
כ״ב, עמ' 497). וֵעל כן פתח פתוח גם לאפשרות, שחיבר את שירו בצעירותו, סמוך לשנת 905,
בבבל או לאחר מכן בשובו מבבל מצרימה. והרי גם את חיבורו הנודע „כתאב אלרד עלי ענן"
חיבר בשנת 905, משמע שכבר התחיל באותם ימים את מלחמתו בקראים ובקראות.

בו 7 שורות חדשות שאינן בכי״ל (וחסרה האחרונה שבכי״ל) [274]. בראשן של 7 השורות הנוספות חתום „משה בן אש״. קלאר פרסם את השיר ע״פ שלושה כתבי־יד אלה [275], ומתוך שהשיר מדבר גם בעניני טעמים ומסורה הסיק, שהחתום בראשי השורות אינו אלא בעל המסורה משה בן־אשר אביו של אהרן. מתוכנו של השיר למד שמחברו היה קראי, והסתמך לשם כך על הנקודות הבאות [276]:

א. אע״פ שהפייטן סוקר בשיר את גדולי ישראל מאברהם אבינו עד החשמונאים, לא הזכיר לא את אנשי כנסת הגדולה, לא את שמעון הצדיק ולא את הזוגות.

ב. הוא „מעלה ומרומם את בני בתירה, שלא שימשו את שמעיה ואבטליון וחלקו על הלל הזקן, שנוא נפשם של הקראים, למדרגת יורשי הנביאים ומיחס להם קביעת טעמי המקרא והמסורות, בניגוד לחז״ל שמיחסים פיסוק טעמים ומסורות לעזרא וסיעתו (נדרים ל׳, ע״ב)״. בכך רואה קלאר „שיטה שאחזו בה הקראים מאז ומתמיד, היינו לבחור להם מתוך התלמוד דעות יחידים שאין

---

274 השיר כולו פורסם לראשונה ע״י קלאר, מחקרים, עמ׳ 311־310.

275 עיינתי בתצלומים של שלושת כתבי־היד, היינו כי״ל, כ״י המוזיאון הבריטי (= ב״מ) וכ״י קמברידג׳ (= ק׳). תיאוריהם וציוניהם של כתבי־היד ע׳ בדברי קלאר, שם, הע׳ 209. וע״פ קריאתי הריני מביא כאן תיקונים (להוציא סטיות כתיב מלא וחסר) לנוסח שפרסם קלאר. מחזיק אני טובה לספריית שוקן ולספרנה מר א״מ הברמן על הרשות שניתנה לי לקרוא ולהשתמש את תצלומי הספרייה של כ״י ב״מ וכ״י ק׳.

שו׳ 1 : כי״ל : נטעתה (ולא ככלאר, שם, הע׳ 210). כי״ל : הגפנים (ואין נוסח „גפנים״).

שו׳ 2 : כי״ל : אֶרֶן. הניקוד כך — וּדַאי, הַנּ׳ו׳ן הסופית — ספק. ואולי היא בכל זאת וּ׳י׳ן. או שמא היא נו׳ן וְעֵירָא ע״פ ישעיה מד׳, יד׳ „אֹרֶן״. (עי׳ תנ״ך מהדורת קיטל־קאהלה, היינו כי״ל, ובקצת גרסאות במהד׳ גינצבורג. גרסאות אחרות שם הן בזי״ן קרי בנו״ן).

כי״ל : ה י ת ה בתוכה.

שו׳ 7 : כי״ל : זְמָרוֹת. — כך מנוקד, וב׳מ : זמירות (מלא), ואין כלל נוסח זְמִרות. וכאן זמיר או זמירה בהוראת ענף (ואין במילונים).

שו׳ 12 : כי״ל : לוֹלְבֵּי. — כך מנוקד.

שו׳ 15 : כי״ל : סְמָדְרֵי. — כך מנוקד.

שו׳ 16 : כי״ל : עֲנָבֵי. — כך מנוקד.

שו׳ 17 : כי״ל : כְּנַרוֹתֵיהֶם. — כך מנוקד.

שו׳ 19 : כי״ל : סָמוּךְ. — כך מנוקד.

שו׳ 22 : „בתירה״ — ר׳ להלן בהע׳ 286.

שו׳ 27 : ק׳ : ולהגדיל.

שו׳ 29 : ק׳ : בתיבת „נתעוררו״ קו תחתון מטושטש לרגל ריש תנינא, ואפשר לקרוא „נתעורטו״.

שו׳ 30 : כי״ל : ותמלוך. (ובל״ק, עמ׳ קכא בהערה — טעות דפוס).

ולא נראה לי שכי״ל ק׳ וב״מ שייכים לכתב־יד אחד (כהשערת קלאר, שם, הע׳ 209), שכן : בב״מ הכתב שונה במקצת, השורות והכתב צפופים יותר, מספר השורות בעמוד רב יותר, וביחוד שינה דרך כתיבת שם הוי״ה. בב״מ שתי יודי״ן, בק׳ שתי יודי״ן היו בינוהן.

276 קלאר, מחקרים, עמ׳ 312—314.

הלכה כמותם, כדי לתלות עצמם בחכמים ראשונים".

ג. בכי"ל באה לפני השיר כותרת בפרווזה וסיומה: „ויונקותיה (של הגפן. — א"ד) הם החכמים מצדיקי הרבים", ומעין לשון זה חוזר אף בגוף השיר (שו' 27): „להצדיק [ר]בים להגדיל תורה". ביטויים אלה משמשים בפי קראים, כגון יפת בן עלי, כינוי לחכמי הקראים.

אך כל הטענות האלה אין בהן כדי לקבוע, שהמחבר היה קראי. ויש להשיב עליהן:

א. נראה שהפייטן לא נתכוון למצות בסקירה כרונולוגית לא את שלשלת הנביאים והחכמים בישראל, שכן חסר בה, למשל, עזרא וכן רבים מן הנביאים הנזכרים ברשימת הנביאים שהביא משה בן־אשר עצמו בסיום כתב־יד קהיר[277], ולא את האישים הבולטים האחרים בתולדות ישראל, כגון שאול ושלמה ומלכי ישראל וכן גיבורי הכתובים, נחמיה, מרדכי ועוד. הרי גם אילו היה הפייטן קראי, ראוי היה לו למסור את השתלשלות הקבלה של הקראים. העדר הרציפות בשלשלת קשה היא לקראי לא פחות משהיא קשה לרבני. ואין ללמוד מכאן אלא שהמחבר לא נתכוון לסקירה היסטורית ולא שהיה קראי או רבני.

כוונתו בשיר זה לדמות את ישראל לגפן בדרך הדרש[278], והבסיס לדרושו אינו ידוע לנו. וכל עוד נעלם מאתנו בסיס זה ומקורו, אין לטעון שיש כאן התעלמות מכוונת מאישים מסוימים. ואין ללמוד דבר לא משמות הנראים לנו חסרים (אם לא באו בהמשך השיר שאינו לפנינו), ולא משמות יתרים, כגון יואב ושני אחיו, שחשיבותם בעינינו קטנה יחסית, וכגון בני בתירה (ר' בסמוך).

ב. הקראים מאמינים שהניקוד והטעמים נמסרו למשה מסיני, ועכ"פ אין עיקרי דתם מרשים להם ליחס את הניקוד והטעמים לדור אחרוני הזוגות[279]. ולכן עצם הראיה, שהפייטן מייחס את קביעת הטעמים והמסורה לזקני בתירה[280], בני דורו של הלל, היא ראיה לסתור. קראי לא יכול היה לכתוב זאת.

אמנם נכון הדבר שהקראים נוהגים להתלות בחכמים שאין הלכה כמותם בתלמוד, אולם בני בתירה אינם דוגמה לכך. בני בתירה לא חלקו על הלל, אלא, להיפך, שאלוהו הלכה שנעלמה מהם. וכשלימדם הלל קיבלו ממנו ו„מיד הושיבוהו בראש ומינוהו נשיא עליהם" — כך לפי נוסח הבבלי (פסחים סו ע"א). ולפי נוסח הירושלמי (פסחים פ"ו ה"א, לג ע"א) התוכחו עמו ו„לא קיבלו ממנו עד שאמר להן יבא עלי כך שמעתי משמעיה ואבטליון". אמנם נכון שלא שימשו את שמעיה

---

277 עי' לעיל עמ' שיב והע' 207.

278 שפע כתובים רמוזים בשיר. השווה את שיר הגפן בישעיה ה' וכן את המשלים ביחזקאל יז, ו"ח ; יט, י"ד. והשווה במיוחד : בראשית מט, יא, ישעיה ה, ב (לשורה 1) ; ישעיה ה, ז (לשו' 3) ; יחזקאל יז, ח, יט, א (לשו' 5) ; יחזקאל יז, ז, תהלים פ, יב (לשו' 6) ; תהלים קו, טז, ישעיה סא, ו (לשו' 16) ; יואל ב, טז (לשו' 18) ; דניאל יב, ג, ישעיה מב, כא (לשו' 27), ועוד.

279 עי' לעיל עמ' שט. הרי לפי המסורת הקראית המאחרת ביותר היה הפילוג בין הרבנים והקראים בימי יהודה בן טבאי (המקורות ידועים). ואולם יש המקדימים אותו עד רתבעם בן שלמה המלך (עי' חילוק הקראים, עמ' 100, אורח צדיקים, עמ' יז).

280 ואגב, מתוך דברי השיר אין כלל הכרח להבין דווקא כך. ור' להלן עמ' שסא (ב).

ואבטליון, אבל כיבדו את דבריהם ולא חלקו עליהם. אדרבא, „כיון ששמעו ממנו
כן עמדו ומינו אותו נשיא עליהן" (ירושלמי, פסחים, שם). ורבי אמר עליהם [281]:
„כל מה דיימר לי בר נשא אנא עביד חוץ ממה שעשו זקני בתירה לזקני דשרון
גרמון ומנוניה". ועל ענוותנותם מעיד הירושלמי [282]: „ג' הניחו כתרן בעה"ז
וירשו חיי העה"ב. ואילו הן יונתן בן שאול. ואלעזר בן עזריה וזקני בתירה. יונתן
בן שאול א"ר לא אפי' נשים מאחורי הקוריין יודעות היו שדוד עתיד למלוך.
אלעזר בן עזריה תניין הוה לית לך כהדא דזקני בתירה דשרון גרמון דשרון נשייות
ומנוניה נשיא".

ואף את הדברים שבנוסח הירושלמי יש להבין לאשורם. אין כאן
מ ח ל ו ק ת, שכן מזקני בתירה נעלמה ההלכה כליל ורק היססו לקבלה מהלל על
סמך ראיות משלו; אין הם אפוא בחינת יחיד שאין הלכה כמותו. ומה גם שהלל
היה אותו זמן סתם „בבלי אחד", ולא נשיא, שיש לקבל את דעתו, ואילו דוקא
הם היו נשיאים. ואע"פ שהיו הם שניים והוא אחד, קיבלו ממנו בסופו של דבר [283].

זאת ועוד. שיטות שונות לשלשלת הקבלה הקראית: יש המתחילות
ברתבב"ם בן שלמה [284], ויש המתחילות בבני הזוגות [285], יהודה בן טבאי, שמעיה,
שמאי, ואחריהם ר' יוחנן בן זכאי ור' אליעזר בן הורקנוס ואחרים, אך לא נמצא
אף קראי אחד המייחס לבני בתירה חשיבות כל שהיא או הנתלה בהם לאיזה עניין
שדרא [286].

ג. הדברים שאמרנו לעיל לגבי הלשונות „מלמד" [287], „משכיל" [288]
ו„אילי הצדק" [289], ראויים להיאמר אף כאן לגבי „מצדיקי הרבים". אין ביטוי
מקראי זה „מונופולין" של קראים גם אם משתמש בו יפת בן עלי פעמים אחדות;
וכן נמצא מעין ביטוי זה „מצדיקי" גם בדברי רס"ג ב„אשא משלי" [290] — וכולם
אינם אלא על דרך הכתוב בדניאל יב, ג. ובביטוי זה ממש מתכנה ר' שרירא

---

281   ירושלמי כתובות פי"ב ה"ג (לה ע"א) וכלאים פ"ט ה"ד (לב ע"ב).

282   במקום הנזכר בפסחים. ועי' אף בבלי, בבא מציעא פה ע"א.

283   אף המעשה שבבבלי, ראש השנה כט ע"ב, מעיד על מתינות וויתור, ובשום פנים
אי אפשר להיתלות בהם כנושאי נס המחלוקת בתלמוד, ואין לומר שדעתם „דעת יחידים שאין
הלכה כמותם". הרי אף כאן לא ידעו את הדין וביקשו לדון. ועי' תוספתא, פסחים ג, ט
(צוקרמאנדל, עמ' 162).

284   עי' לעיל סוף הע' 279.

285   עי' דף מרדכי י' ע"א, ע"פ מטה האלהים למשה בן אליהו בשיצי.

286   אף מתעוררים ספקות לגבי הקריאה „בתירה" בכי"ל. תיבה זו כתובה שם בוי"ו
בין התי"ו והרי"ש וכתולם דהוי במקצת, וכן בפתח דהוי מתחת לבי"ת ובדגש דהוי בתי"ו,
ובכן בַּתּוֹרָה (?) (ואם כך, אין כאן אלא כינוי כולל לחז"ל „זקני בתורה") ; אבל מאידך גיסא
נראים בבירור גם חירק מתחת לתי"ו וסימני הרפה מעליה וכן נוסף מעין קו אלכסוני קצר
החוצה את הוי"ו באמצעה (והחירק והקו האלכסוני נראים חזקים ובולטים יותר מן הרגיל —
ואולי הם שינוי ותוספת מאוחרת ?), ובכן בִּתִירָה, (ואולי בְּחִירָה ?).

287   לעיל עמ' רצד.   288   לעיל עמ' רפג.

289   לעיל עמ' רצט.   290   עי' לעיל הע' 97.

גאון במכתב של בני פוסטאט אל בנו ר' האיי גאון [291]: "פאר הישיבה שלגולה
העתיק במחצות מצדיקי הרבים".

ובדרך עיקרון יש לומר: אי אפשר להסתמך על מלים בודדות, שהן כביכול
ולמראית עין מונחים קראיים, ולקבוע שהמשתמש בהן הוא קראי. רק עיון בתוכנו
של השיר עשוי לשמש יסוד להשערה כזאת או להיפוכה.
ומה מתקבל מעיון בתוכנו של השיר ?

נראה לי, שהשורות שבראשיהן חתום "משה בן אש" (שו' 29־23) אינן
שייכות כלל לשירת הגפן, כלומר ל־22 השורות הראשונות ולשורת הסיום, אע"פ
שהן רשומות בכתב־יד אחד כהמשך להן. ואלה ראיותיי בקצרה:

א. אין נזכרת בהן אף פעם אחת מלת "הגפן", שהיא נושא השורות
הקודמות ובאה כמעט בכל אחת מהן.

ב. כל האמור ב־7 השורות הנוספות מוסב על נושא אחד ויחיד, אך נושא
זה אינו נאמר בהן בפירוש. ובמקומן זה, כהמשך לשירת הגפן, מוסבים הדברים
בהכרח על הנושא שבשורה האחרונה של השירה (שו' 22), היינו זקני בתירה.
אך השורות 30־27 מדברות בדור המכבים ("אפפום צרות ממלכי יְוָנִים") ולא ייתכן
שנושאן הוא זקני בתירה.

ג. כשם שהשורות הנוספות אינן מתקשרות לשירת הגפן בתוכנן, כך אינן
מתקשרות במבנן. השירה רצופה דימויים, כמעט בכל שורה, בין אגודים בין
שאינם אגודים; אך בשורות הנוספות אין דימויים כלל וסגנונן סגנון הסיפור.

ד. להרכבה המלאכותית של שני השירים מקבילה הרכבה דומה של
הכותרת שבכי"ל עם שירת הגפן. אף זו אינה מתאימה לשירה, שכן: בכותרת
שורשי הגפן הם האבות, ובשירה הם "יואב ואבישי ועשהאל" (שו' 21), ואילו
האבות הם "זמירוֹת [292] הגפן" (שו' 7); בכותרת יונקות הגפן הם החכמים,
ובשירה אין יונקות כלל, ואילו חכמי הגפן הם "משה ואהרן ומרים אחותם"
(שו' 8).

כאמור [293], אין אנו יודעים דבר על הבסיס, שעליו מושתת הדרוש של
שירת הגפן (שורות 22־1, 30), ומתוך כך גם על מחברה. אך לגבי 7 השורות
הנוספות, נוטה אני להאמין שמחברן הוא משה בן אשר. וזאת לא רק ע"פ
האקרוסטיכון, ואע"פ שחסרה בו האות האחרונה, אלא גם בגלל דמיון הלשון ללשונו
של משה בן אשר בקולופון שלו לכ"י קהיר [294]: "...והעצימו והגדילו [295] המק'
עשרים וארבעה ספרים ויסדום באמונתם בטעמי שכל בפירוש
דיבור בחיך מתיק ביופי מאמר..." — ובשירנו: "באמונתם יסדו פרוש
מקרא..." (שו' 26), וכן "שעשועים התקינו טעמי מקרא בשום
שכל וניב מפֹרש" (שו' 24).

291   עי' מאן, JQR, סדרה חדשה VII (1917־1916), עמ' 478, הע' 22.

292   עי' לעיל הע' 275 בתיקוני הקריאה.

293   לעיל עמ' שנט.

294   עי' לעיל עמ' רצט והע' 128. וקלאר עמד על דמיון זה.

295   לשון "יגדיל תורה ויאדיר" (ישעיה מב, כא).

בין אם נכונה השערה זו בין אם איננה נכונה, ברור עכ״פ שהקטע הנוסף,
היינו השורות שבראשיהן חתום ״משה בן אש״, בידי מחבר רבני נכתבו, והדברים
שנאמרו בהן לא מפי קראי יצאו. ואלה העדויות לכך:

בשורה ״נפשם נתנו על תורת אלהינו להצדיק [ר]בים להגדיל
תורה״ (שו' 27) המדובר הוא בלי ספק במסירות נפשם של ישראל בימי החשמונאים,
כאשר ״אפפום צרות ממלכי יונים״ (שו' 28). וכי יש מקום להאשים כאן את
הפייטן שהתכוון לרמוז ל״מונה״ הקראי ״מצדיקי הרבים״? גם לפי המסורות
הקראיות המקדימות את הקרע לתקופת המקרא אין שום יסוד להשתתפות קראית
במאורע היסטורי מסוים זה. ״להצדיק רבים״ אין פירושו כאן אלא את
הרבים ולהגדיל תורה (השווה ישעיה מב, כא), כשם ש״מצדיקי הרבים״ בכותרת
שבכי״ל אינו אלא מלמדים, על דרך דברי הבבלי [296]: ״ומצדיקי הרבים ככוכבים
לעולם ועד (דניאל יב, ג) אלו מלמדי תנוקות״.

הפייטן מקבל את התפיסה שבדברי רבי עקיבא ״מסורת (נ״א מסורות)
סיג לתורה״ והוא אומר: ״הקיפו גדר לתורת אלהינו מסורות סדורות ל[החכי]ם
פתי״ (שו' 25). וכן הוא מכיר בדרשת חז״ל על הכתוב ״ושום שכל״ [297] ומסתייע
בה: ״שעשועים התקינו טעמי מקרא בשום ש כ ל וניב מפרש״ (שו' 24).

ועל הכול ובעיקר מעידות על כך השורות האחרונות בקטע (שו' 27–29):

״נפשם נתנו על תורת אלהינו   להצדיק [ר]בים להגדיל תורה
אפפום צרות ממלכי יונים   והגלו[ם] ונפצום [לנ]א ובנותיה
שבטי קדושים נתעוררו עליהם   וחנכו נרות על נפילתם״.

מדובר כאן בלי כל ספק במרד המכבים, שמסרו נפשם על תורת ד', ומלכי
היוונים שלחצו אותם הוגלו והופצו [298] ל״נא ובנותיה״ [299], אחרי שנתעוררו (או
נתערכו [300]) עליהם למלחמה שבטי קדושים, ״וחנכו נרות על נפילתם״ של
מלכי היוונים. מה לנו רמז ברור מזה לחג החנוכה? והקראים אינם מכירים
ואינם מודים בחג זה. הרי שורות אלה מעידות כמאה עדים, שמחברן
רבני היה ולא קראי.

ראינו אפוא לא רק שאין להביא ראיה משירת הגפן לקראיותו של משה
בן־אשר, אלא אדרבא שיש יסוד מספיק ללמוד ממנה, לפחות מן השורות ששמו
חתום בראשיהן, שמשה בן־אשר היה אף הוא רבני.

296   בבא בתרא ח ע״ב, במעשה רב שמואל בר שילת. וע׳ אף בפירוש המיוחס לרס״ג
     על פסוק זה בדניאל.

297   עי' לעיל עמ' שח.

298   נפצום כמו הפיצום, בחילוף השכיח של ע״ו — פ״נ.

299   ההשלמה [לנ]א, וכן יתר ההשלמות שהובאו כאן בסוגריים מרובעים, הן משל קלאר.
     ואם נכונה השלמה זו, עי' י' פרס, אנציקלופדיה ארץ־ישראל, כרך ג', עמוד 624, ערך ״נוה״
     (גרסה אחרת: נוא) — והיא עיר עתיקה בבשן.

300   מלשון מערכה, ערך מלחמה. וע' לעיל הע' 275 בתיקוני הקריאה.

E. *Masoretic Bibles.*

THE BEN ASHER BIBLE MANUSCRIPTS

The study of the Massora of the Hebrew Bible pursued by Professor Kahle with sustained vigour for many years and embodied in such outstanding works as the *Masoreten des Westens, Masoreten des Ostens*, and recently *The Cairo Geniza*, as well as in the last edition of the *Biblia Hebraica*, has exerted a great influence in the field of Massoretic research. It may, therefore, not be inopportune to consider one of Kahle's conclusions in a dispassionate and critical manner in order to assess whether, and if so to what degree, it may ￩e regarded as a lasting acquisition for scholarship.

The most important conclusion reached by Professor Kahle in his research on the Ben Asher text of the Bible is that this text was not definitely fixed from the start but underwent a gradual process of development, and that the single stages of this development are still preserved in various manuscripts, either written by members of the Ben Asher family or by scribes closely connected with them. The line of ￩development of the Ben Asher text is traced by Kahle in the following manner :—

> The Cairo Ben Asher Codex represents a text from which Ahron b. Asher started. The British Museum MS. (Or. 4445) is a specimen of the development of the text in the earlier time of Ben Asher's activity ; in the text from which the Leningrad Codex (B. 19a) was copied we have a type of the Hebrew Biblical text in the later time of Ben Asher's activity. It is very likely that the Aleppo Codex is another type of this text, in which the Masora was further developed.[1]

The contention that there was a process of development of the Ben Asher text which can still be reconstructed rests, obviously, on the assumption that we have in our possession genuine Ben Asher codices different in their nature from other Biblical manuscripts that also claim to represent the Ben Asher text. Grave doubts as to whether the Cairo and the Aleppo codices— two of the four codices singled out by Kahle—represent the genuine Ben Asher text had been raised by scholars before Kahle. But their arguments, based on an examination of the contents of the codices, are met by Kahle with the counter-argument that these scholars applied to the codices a preconceived notion of what a Ben Asher text ought to be, but, in fact, had no idea of what a real Ben Asher text is.[2] Such a text could be established only by an examination of the original Ben Asher manuscripts, and Professor Kahle and his pupils devoted themselves with the utmost diligence to this task. The first step was to identify the original Ben Asher codices on the basis of the data contained in the manuscripts examined, and the four codices, Cairo, Aleppo, Leningrad B.19a, and British Museum Or. 4445, were declared to

---

[1] *The Cairo Geniza (The Schweich Lectures of the British Academy, 1941)*, London, 1947, p. 68. All these codices, except the Aleppo one, were used as basis for the last edition of *Biblia Hebraica*.

[2] op. cit., p. 66 : " Under these conditions we need not wonder that William Wickes also was impressed with Baer's acquaintance with the Massora in such a way that he declared the colophons of valuable old Biblical MSS., to be *fabrications*, because the texts of these MSS. did not follow the rules which Baer believed to be those of Ben Asher, and that Neubauer did not dare to say anything against these authorities."

Reprinted from *Journal of Jewish Studies* 2 (1950).   c

represent genuine Ben Asher texts. It is perhaps unfortunate that, although the data contained in the manuscripts have such an important bearing on the problem of their identification, Kahle's description of these manuscripts scarcely satisfies the required standard of exactitude in such matters. But even in the light of the information made available about these manuscripts it is very doubtful whether the claim that they represent genuine Ben Asher texts has really been substantiated. Let me now examine *seriatim* the codices which 'Professor Kahle identifies as original Ben Asher texts :—

(a) THE CAIRO CODEX OF THE EARLIER AND LATER PROPHETS

This codex, according to one of its colophons, was written by Moses b. Asher in 895 C.E., which would make it the oldest dated Hebrew Bible manuscript. This date is accepted by Kahle together with its implication that the text of the Prophets was actually written by Moses b. Asher. There is, however, another colophon in this codex, in which the name of Ya'beṣ b. Solomon is mentioned, and the interpretation of its contents and their relation to the Ben Asher colophon offers some difficulties. The beginning of this colophon reads as follows [1] :—

זה הדיפתר מה שזכה יעבץ בן שלמה הבבלי...ועשה אותו לעצמו להגות בו
מעמלו...

Professor Kahle translates this passage thus :—

This is the Parchment which Ya'beṣ b. Shelomo ha-Babli . . . has acquired, and he has prepared it for himself, for studying in it, by his work . . .[2]

He interprets the passage in conjunction with the first colophon in the sense that Moses b. Asher wrote the Cairo codex " for Ya'beṣ b. Shelomo, a Karaite who had himself prepared the parchment for the codex ".[3]

The key-word in Ya'beṣ's colophon is the expression, *diftar*, which in colophons of manuscripts always means *codex*, and there is no evidence that it has also the meaning of *parchment*. In Talmudic literature *diftar* often means *not properly tanned hide*, but never *parchment*, and, in any case, the writing of Bibles on *diftar* is not allowed.[4] The material of the Cairo codex is, in fact, parchment and not *diftar*. The natural meaning of the beginning of Ya'beẓ's passage would be :—

This is the codex which (through the grace of God) it was granted to Ya'beṣ son of the late Solomon, the Babylonian, to write for himself . . .

The implication of this passage is that Ya'beẓ copied for himself the text of the Bible from an original which had the Moses b. Asher colophon, and he copied both the text and the colophon—a feature by no means rare in manuscripts.[5] The script of Moses b. Asher's colophon is certainly not earlier

---

[1] op. cit., p. 110.   [2] Ibidem.
[3] op. cit., p. 56.   [4] *Masseket Soferim*, i, 5.

[5] It could be objected that if this explanation is correct the colophon with Ya'abeẓ's name should have come after, and not before, Ben Asher's colophon, but, according to KAHLE (*Cairo Geniza*, pp. 110 and 111), the latter is to be found on p. 586 of the MS., while the former is on p. 585. It is not very difficult to meet this objection : the Cairo codex, when examined by KAHLE, consisted of loose pages and was bound afterwards. The present position of the folio bearing Ya'abeẓ's colophon is, obviously, due to the binder who placed it before the folio with the Ben Asher colophon.

than the eleventh century,[1] and this bears out the conclusion that the colophon was not written by a ninth century scribe.

This interpretation of Ya'bez's colophon meets, however, with an obstacle. In the Leningrad codex B.19a a note on the first page states that *Meborak b. Josef b. Natan'el zakah . . . we'asah oto le'azmo*,[2]—exactly the same phrase as that used in Ya'bez's colophon in the Cairo codex. But in the case of the Leningrad codex it cannot be interpreted that Meborak wrote the text, for the scribe of the codex, Samuel b. Jacob, clearly states in the colophons at the end of the manuscript that he himself wrote it for Meborak. It is true that the Leningrad codex passed through Firkowicz's hands and there is always a suspicion that the colophons may have been tampered with ; but if they are genuine the meaning of Meborak's note would be that " it was granted to him to procure for himself this codex ". The meaning of Ya'bez's colophon in the Cairo codex may perhaps also be the same, namely, that he procured for himself this codex, although in this case there is no mention of the scribe having written it expressly for him.[3] The handwriting of both the Moses b. Asher and the Ya'bez colophons is, apparently, the same—though this has never been stated explicitly by those who have dealt with the Cairo codex—but there is no evidence to show that the scribe who wrote them was Moses b. Asher. All the evidence is to the contrary. The handwriting of the colophons is, as mentioned above, much later than the ninth century, and corroborating evidence can be easily found on examining the contents of the Cairo codex itself.

This codex contains, in addition to the colophons and the text of the Prophets (incomplete), two more fragmentary items, which are mentioned by Jacob ibn Saphir,[4] but not by Kahle. One is a fragment of the *Seder 'Olam Raba* and the other a fragment of Aaron b. Moses b. Asher's *Diqduqē ha Te'amim*. Both these fragments are written apparently in the same hand as the colophons, and it is highly improbable, if not impossible, that Moses b. Asher should have copied his son's work in 895, when, as likely as not, it did not yet then exist. But even if we were determined, despite all these considerations, to ascribe the colophons and the fragments to Moses b. Ahser, nothing would be gained for the matter at issue. For the text of the Prophets in the Cairo codex was

---

[1] A. NEUBAUER, in *Studia Biblica*, iii, Oxford, 1891, p. 25.

[2] A. HARKAVY UND H. L. STRACK, *Katalog der Bibelhandschriften der Kais. Oeffent. Bibliothek in St. Petersburg*, I–II Theil, St. Petersburg, 1875, p. 266.

[3] If Ya'bez was not the scribe but only the owner of the codex, the question arises as to what state the codex was in when it was acquired by him. Moses b. Asher's colophon refers to the complete Bible ; but the dedication note also contained in this codex and published in KAHLE's *Geniza*, p. 112, mentions that the *diftar*, containing eight prophetical books, was dedicated by Ya'bez to the Karaites in Jerusalem. Does this indicate that Ya'bez acquired an incomplete copy, or that he had bought originally the complete Bible, parts of which were lost while in his possession ? Probably neither alternatives is true or, as it will be shown later in this essay, the text of the eight Prophets contained to-day n the Cairo codex has no connection with the colophons of this codex. Ya'bez's original Bible—except for the colophons—was appa ently replaced at a later date by an incomplete text of the Prophets.

[4] *'Eben Sapir*, Lyck, 1866, vol. i, p. 15., and vol. ii (Mainz, 1874), pp. 187a and 221a.

certainly written by a hand different from, and later than, that which wrote the colophons. A facsimile of the colophon with Moses b. Asher's name and another of a page of the book of Samuel were published by Gottheil,[1] and the *ductus* in each of them is so different that it is difficult to understand how they could ever have been attributed to the same scribe.

The Cairo codex appears to be composed of two different parts which were subsequently joined ; one containing the colophons and the fragments of *Seder 'Olam* and *Diqduqē ha Te'amim*, and the other the incomplete text of the Prophets and the colophons. These two parts were written by two different scribes, neither of whom was Moses b. Asher.

These results are confirmed by the evidence of the text of the Prophets, the modes of accentuation of which—as it has been repeatedly pointed out—contradict the rules laid down by Ben Asher. To plead, as Kahle does, that such divergences from the Ben Asher rules represent an early stage in the development of the Massora is to stretch the notion of development to a breaking point and to use it to cover up even palpable contradictions. Such a conception might be entertained only if there were unimpeachable evidence that the Cairo codex was actually written by Moses b. Asher. This, however, is not the case.

(b) THE ALEPPO CODEX

The vicissitudes of this codex, pointed, as it is generally stated, by Aaron b. Moses b. Asher, are described by Professor Kahle,[2] who follows in the footsteps of ibn Saphir and Graetz in his account.

According to Kahle the codex, written by the scribe Solomon b. Buya'a, was provided with punctuation and Massora by Aaron b. Moses b. Asher. A Karaite from Basra, Israel b. Saadya b. Ephraim, gave it to the Karaites in Jerusalem, where it was kept until it was seized by the Crusaders in the capture of the town in 1009. A few years later it was released, together with other Hebrew manuscripts, by King Baldwin and brought to Old Cairo, where it served as the model codex for scribes, and Maimonides himself copied from it the text of the Torah. Subsequently, at an unspecified date, the codex was transferred to Aleppo, where it was seen in the fifteenth century by Saadya b. David al-'Adani. In the sixteenth century David b. Zimra also mentions that this codex had been transferred from Egypt to Aleppo, and finally, in the same century, Joseph Karo supplied Moses Isserles in Cracow with a copy of the Pentateuch made from this codex.

Let me begin the examination of these data with the last point. Joseph Karo supplied Moses Isserles not with a copy of the Pentateuch from the Aleppo codex, but with a copy of *Tiqqun Soferim*, in accordance with which

---

[1] *JQR*, xvii (1905). The facsimiles face pp. 609 and 657 respectively (at least in the copy used by me). These facsimiles are much better than those published by NEUBAUER in *Studia Biblica*.

[2] *Masoreten des Westens*, i, pp. 1–12 ; *The Cairo Geniza*, pp. 57–60.

Isserles wrote his Pentateuch.[1] This may seem to be a trifling matter, but it is important because it shows that the Aleppo codex contains other matter beside the Bible. This is confirmed by the description of the Aleppo codex which Jacob Ze'ebh sent to ibn Saphir,[2] according to which, the Aleppo codex contains on the first page two notes, one in Hebrew stating that the codex belongs to the Rabbanites in Jerusalem, and another in Arabic to the effect that this codex was transferred to the Palestinian Synagogue in Cairo after it had been redeemed from the " Jerusalem booty ". Then follows the *Tiqqun Soferim*, and finally the text of the Bible, at the end of which there is a colophon conveying the information that the codex, written by Solomon b. Buya'a and pointed by Aaron b. Asher, was dedicated to the Karaites in Jerusalem by Israel of Basra.

It is possible, although in a rather roundabout way, to establish what this *Tiqqun Soferim* in the Aleppo codex is. Ibn Saphir tells us that Firkowicz went to Aleppo in order to see the codex of the Bible. While failing in this, he succeeded in obtaining a copy of all the items in the codex preceding the text of the Bible as well as of the colophon following it. This copy was examined by ibn Saphir.[3] Now after Firkowicz's death his son gave to Strack a manuscript, which had belonged to his father, written in an Oriental hand and containing Aaron b. Asher's *Diqduqē ha-Te'amim*. Strack's description of this manuscript,[4] which he utilized for the edition of the *Diqduqē ha-Te'amim*, tallies exactly with Jacob Ze'ebh's description of the Aleppo codex and with ibn Saphir's description of the manuscript which Firkowicz brought back from Aleppo. It appears to be beyond doubt that Firkowicz's copy was taken from the Aleppo codex, and that the *Tiqqun Soferim* preceding the text of the Bible in the Aleppo codex is no other than Aaron b. Asher's *Diqduqē ha-Te'amim*.

Strack considers Firkowicz's manuscript of the *Diqduqē ha-Te'amim* to be " werthvoll " in that it contains many excellent readings and also some sections not available in other sources.[5] But he also notices that two of its prose sections, corresponding to paragraph 53 of the edition of the *Diqduqē ha-Te'amim*, not only differ from each other but also from the other known rhymed version of this section. The presence in the Aleppo codex of a double version of the same section creates the presumption that the *Diqduqē ha-Te'amim* in the Aleppo codex does not go back to a Ben Asher original. There is, however, both on paleographical and other evidence, more than a presumption that the Bible contained in this codex was neither written by Solomon b. Buya'a nor pointed by Aaron b. Asher. Harkavy, who examined the codex in Aleppo, ascribes it to the eleventh to twelfth century, and the facsimile of a page of the codex published by Wickes [6] bears out this opinion.

---

[1] See WEISSMANN, in *Magid*, 1857, No. 47.
[2] See the account in *'Eben Sapir*, p. 12a.
[3] op. cit., p. 12b, n. 1.
[4] p. xxi of the preface to the edition of *Diqduqe ha-Te'amim*.
[5] Ibidem, p. xxiii.
[6] *A Treatise on the Accentuation of the twenty-one so-called Prose Books of the Old Testament*, Oxford, 1887. The facs. faces the title-page.

Moreover, we have a specimen of Solomon b. Buya'a's handwriting in the Pentateuch codex preserved in Leningrad,[1] a page of which is reproduced in facsimile by Kahle,[2] and it is enough to compare this facsimile with that of the Aleppo codex published by Wickes in order to see the difference of the *ductus* in both cases and to conclude that the same scribe did not write the Aleppo and the Leningrad codices. Finally, as Wickes points out, the punctuation of the Aleppo codex is at variance with Ben Asher's known practice and contrary to his own rules or the Palestinian Massora.[3]

Little weight can be attached to the statement in the colophon of the Aleppo codex that it was written by Solomon Buya'a and pointed by Aaron b. Asher. This colophon is, in fact, neither the colophon of the scribe nor that of the Massorite, but a " dedication " note, obviously written later than the codex itself, which may, or may not, embody a reliable tradition. I should like to suggest, however, that the writer of the note—as is usual in such cases—incorporated into it the data which he found in the colophon of the codex he had received, but there is no evidence that this codex is the Aleppo codex, which has no colophon of the scribe or of the Massorite. The dedication note of the Aleppo codex probably belonged to, or was transcribed from, another manuscript.

The examination of the data concerning the Aleppo codex has shown that there is no basis for connecting it with Aaron b. Asher, and this result disposes of the theory that this codex is the Ben Asher model codex, which was transferred from Jerusalem to Old Cairo where it was used by Maimonides. Wickes was surprised that he could not find in the Aleppo codex " the Parasha marked in the margin, for it was expressly to note these divisions that Maimonides consulted a text written and pointed by Ben Asher ".[4] Indeed, from Maimonides' reference to this codex we may form an idea of what its colophon contained. Maimonides writes [5] :—

> Everybody relied on it (Ben Asher's model codex), for it was corrected by Ben Asher who for many years applied himself carefully to it and corrected it many times, as it is recorded by the scribe (lit. : as they have copied it).[6]

I suggest that all this information about Ben Asher was contained in the colophon of this model codex. Only if a manuscript of the Bible containing a colophon of such a description comes to light, may we presume that we have recovered the Ben Asher model codex.

It remains now to examine the references to the existence in Aleppo of the Ben Asher model codex. The first author to connect the Aleppo codex with the Ben Asher model codex is Saadya b. David of Aden, who, in his commentary on Maimonides' *Mišneh Torah*, states that he saw in Aleppo the

---

[1] 2, Firk. No. 17.
[2] *Masoretan des Westens*, i, facs. No. 17/1.
[3] op. cit., pp. viii–ix.
[4] Ibidem, p. viii, n. 7.
[5] *Mišneh Torah, Hil. Sefer ha-Torah*, cp. viii.
[6] The Hebrew reads : *kemo šehe'etiqu*, which is translated by KAHLE (*Mas. d. Wes.*, i, 11) " wie man es überliefert. hat ", but this meaning of the verb is only in use, as far as I know, among Karaite authors.

codex used by Maimonides and that he read at the end of it : " It is I, Aaron b. Asher, who corrected it." [1] But none of those who examined the Aleppo codex or obtained copies of its colophon ever mentions a colophon with the name of Ben Asher in the first person, and we must conclude that Saadya either saw a codex other than our Aleppo Bible, or—what is more likely—that he saw the Aleppo codex but misread its colophon, or rendered its contents inaccurately.

David b. Zimra's reference to this matter was first mentioned by Ibn Saphir, who states in vague terms that David b. Zimra says in one of his *Responsa* that Maimonides' model codex was transferred from Egypt to Aleppo and that "it is still there to-day ".[2] Unfortunately, nobody as yet has been able to trace this reference in the collection of b. Zimra's *Responsa*,[3] and it is probably a slip of memory on the part of Saphir, who mistook the frequent references in those *Responsa* to a corrected copy of Maimonides' *Mišneh Torah* preserved in Aleppo for references to the corrected Ben Asher model codex of the Bible.

Finally, the statement in the note on the first page of the Aleppo codex to the effect that this codex was redeemed in Cairo from " the Jerusalem booty " [4] is quoted in support of the theory that the Aleppo codex is identical with the Ben Asher Bible which had been previously in Egypt. But this piece of information in the note could be utilized for the history of the Ben Asher model codex only if it had been previously established that this codex is identical with that in Aleppo. This identification lacks, as we have seen, any basis.

(c) THE LENINGRAD CODEX, B.19A

This codex is considered by Kahle to represent a genuine Ben Asher text, for, according to him, its scribe, Samuel b. Jacob " copied a MS. prepared by Aaron b. Asher ".[5] In fact, the scribe states merely that " he wrote, pointed and provided with Masŝora this complete (*maḥzor*) Bible from the codices corrected and provided with Massora, which the Master, Aaron b. Asher, had written ".[6] This clearly implies that the scribe had no Ben Asher model text,

---

[1] See *The Cairo Geniza*, p. 58. KAHLE published Saadya's note from Bodl. Ms. Hunt. 372, to which his attention was drawn by Dr. N. WIEDER. This information had already been published by ASSAF in *Qirjath Sepher, Bibliographical Quarterly of the Jewish National and University Library*, Jerusalem, vol. xxii (1946), p. 241.

[2] *'Eben Sappir*, p. 12a.

[3] See *Mas. d. West.*, i, p. 12, n. 3.

[4] KAHLE refers this expression to the release by King Baldwin of Hebrew manuscripts which had been seized by the Crusaders in Jerusalem. This information is derived from a colophon of a Karaite Bible, but MANN, following HARKAVY and DEINARD (see *Texts and Studies*, ii, 137, n. 12) regards it as one of Firkowicz's numerous forgeries. KAHLE (*Geniza*, 60, n. 1) thinks that MANN's doubts in this matter are " certainly not justified ". But it may be pointed out, in support of the contention that the colophon in question is not genuine, that, if it were true that King Baldwin released the Hebrew manuscripts in Jerusalem, there was no need to redeem them in Cairo.

[5] *The Cairo Geniza*, p. 60.

[6] See *Katalog . . . St. Petersburg*, p. 269 ; *Geniza*, p. 50, n. 4, where for *mebo'ar* read *mebo'arim*.

but several codices, from which he compiled an *eclectic* text. How far he succeeded in this task cannot be stated, for the essential factors that would enable us to form a judgment on his work, namely the degree of his critical acumen and the measure of the reliability of the codices which he had used, are unknown to us.[1] It is significant, however, that the text of this codex diverges from the Massoretic rules established by Aaron b. Asher,[2] and it could be credited to him only if there were compelling reasons for doing so.

(d) THE BRITISH MUSEUM CODEX, OR. 4445

This manuscript is singled out by Kahle because it is " connected with the name of Ben Asher, in so far as on the margin ' the great master Ben Asher ' is mentioned several times ".[3] According to Ginsburg the text of this manuscript " belongs to a period when the superfine speculations about the *Metheg* and the *Gaya* had not yet asserted themselves ", that is to say, to the first half of the ninth century, and the Massora on the margin to a century later, within the life-time of Aaron b. Asher, whose name is mentioned without eulogy for the deceased.[4] Kahle believes that both the text and the Massora belong to Aaron b. Asher's period.[5] But is it a sound method to date manuscripts on the basis of their contents ? From the paleographical point of view this manuscript seems to be older than the tenth century, and the lack of eulogy after Ben Asher's name is not a cogent reason for assigning it to an earlier date. Again, is it quite certain that the manuscript represents the Ben Asher text, as asserted by Kahle ? It is significant that the Massora on the margin of the page, reproduced in facsimile on Plate I of the British Museum Catalogue of Hebrew and Samaritan Manuscripts, mentions the accentuation of the " great master Ben Asher " and also an accentuation that diverges from it. But the text of the manuscript itself (Lev. xx, 17, to which the massoretical note refers) follows neither of these contrasting views. Finally, the British Museum MS. Or.4445 diverges considerably—as Margoliouth pointed out in the Catalogue—from the commonly accepted Massoretic rules with regard to the open and closed sections of the Pentateuch. The Ben Asher model codex consulted by Maimonides conformed, however, as has been mentioned above, to these rules.

It may be convenient to sum up briefly the results of this examination of the Ben Asher manuscripts :—

---

[1] The scribe of this Leningrad codex is also its illuminator, who wrote the Massoretic rules in beautiful geometrical patterns (see the description of this magnificent codex in PINNER, *Prospectus*, etc., Odessa, 1845, p. 81). In the centre of one of the geometrical patterns we find the words *'ani Shemu'el ḥaqaqti*, which is probably the oldest signature of a Jewish illuminator. Unfortunately, the accuracy of a scribe is sometimes in inverse proportion to his artistic accomplishments.

[2] See STRACK, *Katalog . . . St. Petersburg*, p. 264, " Gegen diese Behauptung (i.e. that the scribe copied a Ben Asher text) sprechen die zahlreichen Abweichungen von der durch den genannten Massoreten aufgestellten (befolgten) Regeln, z.B. in bezug auf des Meteq, Chateph Patah, das Dagesh lene."

[3] *Geniza*, p. 67.

[4] CH. GINSBURG, *Introduction*, p. 470 and p. 474.

[5] *Mas. d. West.*, i, 17 ; *Geniza*, p. 68.

(*a*) The Cairo codex was not written by Moses b. Asher and does not represent a genuine Ben Asher text. The colophons with the names of Moses b. Asher and of Ya'beẓ b. Solomon were written by a scribe, who copied the colophon with M. b. Asher's name from another codex ; this scribe may have been Ya'beẓ himself or a scribe working for him. Another scribe wrote the text of the Prophets, which was subsequently joined to the colophons. The writing of both the text of the Prophets and of the colophons is not earlier than the eleventh or twelfth century.

(*b*) The Aleppo codex was not written by Solomon b. Buya'a, nor pointed by Aaron b. Asher. The text of the Bible was written not earlier than the eleventh or twelfth century, and the colophon at the end of it refers probably to another manuscript. The Aleppo codex has no connection whatever with Ben Asher's model codex consulted by Maimonides in Cairo. It does not represent the genuine Ben Asher text.

(*c*) The Leningrad codex, B.19a, was not copied from a text of the Bible corrected by Aaron b. Asher ; it represents an *eclectic*, not a genuine, Ben Asher text.

(*d*) The British Museum codex, Or.4445, does not follow the genuine Ben Asher tradition, and is probably later than the tenth century.

(*e*) None of the above codices can be regarded as representing diverse stages in the development of the Ben Asher Massoretic activity.

The implication of this critical survey of the Ben Asher manuscripts seems to me to be that, though Kahle's conception of the development of the Massora may still remain intact, his attempt to pin down the stages of this development to a selected number of manuscripts has not been successful. As a heuristic principle Kahle's hypothesis may become fruitful in the field of Massoretic research when it will be applied with a discriminating caution in the handling of the manuscript source material.

J. L. Teicher.

Cambridge.

THE CODEX OF BEN ASHER*

Izhak Ben-Zvi

I

The United Nations resolution in favour of the establishment of a Jewish State was immediately followed by a wave of anti-Jewish riots in the neighbouring countries. In attacks by mobs on ancient Jewish places of worship, the Old Synagogue at Aleppo, traditionally identified with the Biblical Aram-Zobah, suffered especially severe damage.

Great, therefore, was the apprehension felt for the safety of the historic Bible Codex (*Kether Torah*) which, collated and pointed in Palestine more than a thousand years ago by the Massorete Ben Asher, had since been preserved in this synagogue in Aleppo. After numerous investigations and enquiries, it transpired that, though desecrated and pillaged, this venerable MS had been rescued from complete destruction and was hidden in a secret place.

It is my privilege and pleasure to inform the Jewish public and the world of Biblical scholarship that the precious MS has been found and is now in safe keeping.

This Codex has held the interest of students of the Bible for the past hundred years. Jewish and non-Jewish scholars have travelled great distances in order to see and use it, though for the most part without success. What then is its special importance? First of all, it is one of the oldest complete texts of the Hebrew Old Testament now extant. But even its antiquity is less important than its having been pointed, collated, and provided with a Massorah by one of the most outstanding Massoretes, Aaron Ben Asher, who made a detailed study of all contemporary MSS of the Old Testament and devoted his whole life to establishing the correct text.

Many such Great Codices are known to us. In former generations, the most important and most ancient of them were found mainly in the Oriental Jewish communities in Palestine, Syria, and Egypt, but not many have survived to the present day. Written on parchment, these Codices usually contained only the Old Testament without Targum and Commentaries, though in a few the Targum appears after each verse of the Biblical text. The text itself is framed by the Massorah, and is written on both sides of the parchment and bound in

---

* Revised and enlarged translation of a Hebrew article in *Sinai* 43 (1957-8) pp. 5-13.
Reprinted from *Textus* 1 (1960).

book form, not in scrolls like a *Sefer Torah*. In the more ancient Codices there are three columns to a page, while the later ones have only two. The Books of Job, Proverbs, Psalms and other poetical passages are written in two columns in the older as well as the later MSS.

Unfortunately we possess no exact description of the Aleppo MS under discussion, since the scholars who endeavoured to examine it were not permitted to photograph it, but only to look at it. Hence, up till now, our information has been of a very general nature. Now at last, for the first time, we can give a complete description of the MS from what remains of it.

The Codex of Aleppo contained all the books of the Old Testament. On each page there are three columns, except for the Books of Job, Proverbs and Psalms and other poetical passages, which are written on pages of two columns. Every column contains 28 lines. The size of the leaf is 33 by 26,5 cm. As a result of the violence done to the MS during the pogroms, about one quarter of it is missing, so that today it contains only 294 folios out of the presumable original number of about 380.

A.   Pentateuch:
     Missing: Gen. i, 1 — Deut. xxviii, 16.

            The Codex thus begins with Deut. xxviii, 17.

B.   Former Prophets:
     Joshua — complete
     Judges — complete
     Samuel — complete
     Kings   — missing: 2 Kings xiv, 21 — xviii, 13.

C.   Latter Prophets:
     Isaiah — complete
     Jeremiah — missing: xxix, 9 — xxxi, 35 (torn page also xxxii, 2–4, 9–11, 21–24).
     Ezekiel — complete
     Minor Prophets — missing: Amos viii, 12, Obadiah, Jonah, Micah v, 1;
                           Zephaniah is extant except for the last verse;
                           Haggai i, 1 to Zech. ix, 17.

D.   Hagiographa:
     Chronicles — missing: 2 Chron. xxxv, 7 — xxvi, 19
     Psalms — missing xv, 1 — xxv, 2
     Job — complete

Proverbs — complete

Ruth — complete

Song of Songs — up to iii,11; Ecclesiastes, Lamentations, Esther, Daniel
Ezra are all missing.

From this list it is evident that, in our MS, the books of the O.T.were arranged
in a different order from that laid down by the Sages (B.T. Baba Bathra 14b).[1]
What is still more significant is that this order is the same as in the Leningrad
MS B. 19, written in 1008, i.e. nearly at the same time as the Aleppo Codex and
also pointed according to Ben Asher.

II

The Jews of Aleppo believed that this Codex was written by Ezra the Scribe
himself. This tradition is an expression of the special awe felt by the community
for this book, which no mere mortal dared to look upon. At the beginni. g and
the end of the book were recorded the date when it was written and its subsequent fortunes. These sections have, unfortunately, been lost, and all tnat has
come down to us are copies of them made at various times, most of which are
inaccurate. An exception is the copy of R. Meir Neḥmad of Aleppo, who in
1933 published at Aleppo a small booklet called מאמר חקירה על הכתר היקר
הנקרא כתר ארם צובה.Although he does not touch on the bibliographical and
scientific problems involved in any historical study of the Codex, Neḥmad
was nevertheless the only one who approached the MS critically. His copying
was done with accuracy and great care, and some of his comments are worth
reading.

The colophon, which was written at least one hundred years after the MS,
makes it clear that this Codex was copied out by the scribe Solomon Ben
Buyā'ā, a member of a well-known family of copyists. Where this scribe lived
and when he worked at copying out the Codex is uncertain. What is known
is that in the town of Čūfut-Kale ("Jews' Rock") in the Crimea, there was a
copy of the Pentateuch written by the same R. Solomon Ben Buyā'ā. The
colophon to that MS bears no date, but it does contain further biographical
details about the copyist. A section of it is worth quoting here:

אני] שלמה הלוי בר בויאעא
תלמיד סעיד בר פֿרגוי המכונה
בלקוק כתבתי זה ספר תורת
משה כיד אלהי הטובה עלי לרבנ׳

1. On the order of the books in the Bible see Abinoam Yellin, "The 'Crowns' of Damascus",
   Mizraḥ u-Ma'arav 1 (1919) pp. 23–127.

ברהון ולרבנא צליח בנוהי דרבנא
מימון יהיה עליהם סימן טוב...

"[I], Solomon Halevi the son of Buyā'ā,
the disciple of Sa'īd the son of Pargoi, called
Balqūq, have written this Book of the Law of
Moses, according to the good hand of my God upon me[2], for our Rabbi
Barhūn[3] and for our Rabbi Ṣāliḥ, the sons of our Rabbi
Maimūn, may it be a good omen for them . . . . . ."[4]

In another colophon of the same MS, there are data which can provide us
with information about R. Solomon ben Buyā'ā. The MS was pointed and
provided with a Massorah by another member of the same family, R. Ephraim
ben Buyā'ā, who has left us some interesting details about his work:

אני אפרים בן רבי בויאעא
נקדתי ומיסרתי וכללתי את
התורה הזאת ובדקתי אותה
כיד אלהי הטובה עלי ואם
יש בה שגגה אל יחשב
לי יוי עון השלמתי ביום ו
ח בח כסלו שנת אלף
ומאתים ארבעים ואחת
שנה למנין שטרות
לרבנא אברהם ולרבנא
צאליח בנוהי דרבנא מימון...".

"I, Ephraim the son of Rabbi Buyā'ā
have pointed and provided with a Massorah and perfected
this Torah and examined it
according to the good hand of my God upon me; and if
there be any unintentional error in it, let it not be accounted
to me a sin by the Lord. I completed (the work) on Friday
the eighth day of Kislev in the year one thousand
two hundred and forty one
according to the counting of the documents[5]
for our Rabbi Abraham and for our Rabbi
Ṣāliḥ the sons of our Rabbi Maimūn. . . . . ."[6]

2. Cf. Neh. ii, 8.
3. i.e. Abraham, v. infr.
4. Baer and Strack, *Dikduke ha-Teamim*, Leipzig 1879, p. XXXVI.
5. i.e. the Seleucid era.
6. Ibid., p. XXXVII.

From this several important conclusions may be drawn concerning the problems which we are discussing: a) The copyist of the Čūfut-Kale MS used to copy out the Hebrew text, leaving the pointing, accents and Massorah to be added by a specialist in those matters. b) The vocalizer finished his work in the year 1241 of the Seleucid Era, i.e. 930 C.E., no doubt a few years after the scribe had copied the text. Hence it can confidently be assumed that the writing of this Codex was begun in the twenties of the 10th century. c) It would appear that the Aleppo Codex was copied before that of Čūfut-Kale, since the vocalizer of the Aleppo Codex was Ben Asher — who had perhaps died in the meantime —, while in the Čūfut-Kale Codex it was a relative of the scribe. From this we may draw the important inference that the Aleppo Codex was written at the end of the ninth century, at any rate not later than the year 910.

These colophons can also provide a solution to an important question which has greatly exercised the minds of scholars — namely, whether the Aleppo Codex is of Karaite or Rabbanite origin. The colophons leave no room for further doubt that the family of Buyā'ā were all Rabbanites. As a general rule the Rabbanites, being the majority, did not go out of their way to proclaim their identity, and therefore any text of the O.T. which contains no specific indication of its being Karaite may be presumed to be Rabbanite, unless proved otherwise. Now, in the colophons under discussion there is no reference to בעלי מקרא, or other distinctively Karaite features, such as would certainly be found in a Karaite MS, since the Karaites never missed an opportunity to proclaim their sectarian allegiance.

As regards the question of where the MS was written, we apparently have to fall back on conjecture. Here two facts may provide us with a clue. In the colophons frequent mention is made of Jerusalem and its rebuilding; and shortly after it had been written, the Codex was, as we shall see below, in Jerusalem.

Hence, we may assume that the family of Buyā'ā lived in Palestine, either in Jerusalem itself or in Tiberias.

Some scholars maintain that the Codex is Karaite on the ground that some of the plene and defective spellings in it do not accord with the traditional readings of the Sages as recorded in the Talmud.

To refute this argument it is sufficient to remark that even in those Codices which are indisputably non-Karaite we find variants from the traditional readings of the Sages. Moreover, if it can be proved, as in our case, that the scribe who wrote the MS was a Rabbanite, then the whole argument falls to the ground.

Scholarly opinion is also divided as regards the denomination of the author of the Massorah and the pointing of our Codex — "Master (מר) Rab Aaron the son of Master Rab Asher". We aᵣe not here concerned with the details of the discussion of this question, on which an exhaustive article has recently been published by Aaron Dotan.[7] Suffice it to say that I accept his conclusion — that Ben Asher was not a Karaite. It is confirmed by what I have already said above and the further evidence that will come to light below.

It should be remarked here that the name "Rab Aaron the son of Rab Asher" does not mean that R. Asher was his father. The name of R. Aaron's father was R. Moses ben Asher, who lived in Tiberias. We know his approximate date from a Codex which was in the possession of the Karaites in Egypt[8], where the date "827 after the Destruction" (i.e. 895–897 C.E.) appears. It follows from this that R. Aaron lived in the first part of the tenth century.

III

Since the original colophons of the copyist and vocalizer are not extant, we do not know for whom the Codex was written. The first piece of information we have is that, many years after it had been written, it was purchased by the "prince" (*sar*) Israel ben Simḥa, a Karaite from Basra, who presented it to the Karaite synagogue in Jerusalem, entrusting it to the keeping of the two great "*nesi'im*"Josaiah and Hezekiah. Since we know that Hezekiah was alive in the year 1064[9], it follows that the Codex came into the hands of the Karaites only in the eleventh century. It was a common occurrence for non-Karaite scribes to sell texts of the Bible to the Karaites. Even the מקדשיה in the Karaite synagogue in Jerusalem was undoubtedly of Rabbanite origin. Altogether the relations between Rabbanites and Karaites were, at that time, far less strained than in later generations.[10]

The Codex did not remain in Jerusalem long. In 1071, after the sack of Jerusalem by the Seljuks, it was carried off to Egypt as part of the booty.[11] It was ransomed by the Jewish community and placed in tne Synagogue of the

7.   "האמנם היה בן-אשר קראי?", *Sinai* 41 (1957) pp. 280–312, 350–362.

8.   See Jacob Sapir, אבן ספיר, I, 14b. Cf. R. Gottheil, "Some Hebrew Manuscripts in Cairo", JQR 17 (1905) p. 639.

9.   See J. Mann, *The Jews in Egypt and Palestine under the Fatimid Caliphs*, Oxford 1920, II, 213 and I, 178.

10. See I. Ben-Zvi, "מקדשיה הירושלמי" in the Hebrew Memorial Volume for R. Abraham Isaac Kook, (אזכרה), Jerusalem 5697, pp. 556–8; id., מקדשיה הירושלמי לבתרי התורה id., Jerusalem 5697, pp. 556–8; id., שבכתי הכנסת הקראיים בקרשטא ובמצרים, *Kiriath Sefer* 32 (1957) p. 366. R. David b. Zimra and R. Moses Galante permitted the sale even of a Scroll of the Law to the Karaites if it was unfit for liturgical use. There could thus be no objection to the sale of a Bible in book form. See S. Assaf, באהלי יעקב, Jerusalem 1943, p. 202.

11. Kahle, however, adopts a later date. He holds that the Codex was carried off to Egypt by the Crusaders in 1099 and returned to Jerusalem in 1105. Cf. *Masoreten des Westens*, I, Stuttgart 1927, pp. 9–11.

Jerusalemites in Cairo, which was a Rabbanite synagogue. Shortly afterwards Maimonides saw the Codex in Egypt and used it as his authority for the correct Hebrew text for the Scroll of the Law copied out by himself, since he found that it was the most accurate version. This is what he writes in the *Code*, *Hilkhoth Sefer Torah*, viii:

"Since I found great confusion in these matters in all the manuscripts that I saw, and since I found that the Massoretes who write and compose works to show which paragraphs are to be 'open' and which 'closed' differ no less in their opinions in these matters than do the manuscripts on which they rely — I decided to write down here all the sections of the Law, both the open and the closed ones as well as the correct way of writing the poems, for the purpose of revising existing books by them and collating new ones. My authority in these matters was the well-known codex in Cairo which contains the twenty-four books and which was in Jerusalem several years ago. This book was referred to by all as an authority for the correct text, since it was collated by Ben Asher, who worked on it for many years and collated it many times. It has been my own authority in the correct Torah scroll which I have written".

It is worth quoting the comment of R. Shem-Tob Gaon (1283–1330), one of the greatest Massoretic authorities, on these words of Maimonides in his מגדל עז [12]: "(Maimonides) took the text of Moses Ben Asher as his authority and, in my opinion, was quite right in his choice". R. Shem-Tob thus identifies Maimonides' "Ben Asher" (wrongly) as Moses Ben Asher.

Prof. M.D. Cassuto[13] has expressed doubt as to whether the book referred to by Maimonides really was the Codex of Aleppo, but has not given reasons for his skepticism. In any case, whether we believe that Ben Asher actually pointed and collated this MS or not, there is no disputing the fact that in the colophon attached to the "Crown" when it was in Cairo it was recorded that this book was so pointed and collated by Ben Asher, and Maimonides considered the information of the colophon authentic. Moreover, all the rest of the data is in keeping with the statement of the colophon. It may be objected that, according to Maimonides, Deut. xxxii should contain seventy verses, whereas in the Aleppo MS it has only sixty-seven. However, a careful examination of the earliest MSS and editions of the *Code* has revealed that Maimonides also wrote the poem in *sixty-seven* verses, in accordance with Ben Asher, and that his text was subsequently altered by the printers and copyists.[14] This is a further confirmation of what has been surmised above.

12. First published Constantinople 1509.
13. *Ha'aretz* 2.1.1948.
14. This problem and its solution will be discussed by Dr. M. Goshen-Gottstein in his article appearing in this volume.

When was the Codex removed from Egypt to Aleppo? For an answer to this question the scholars of Aleppo refer us to R. David b. Zimra (1479–1574) who in his *Responsa* stated that the Codex used by Maimonides as his authority in writing his Scroll of the Law was brought to Aleppo in his own lifetime. Scholars have searched in vain for this particular responsum. It has recently been proved by N. Ben-Menachem[15] that David b. Zimra was not referring to a Bible Codex, but to a copy of the *Code*, which was copied by a professional scribe and revised by Maimonides himself, and that the scholars of Aleppo confused the two books.

The most likely time for the transference of this Codex to Aleppo would seem to be the end of the 14th century. It is known that in the year 1375, Rabbi David the son of R. Joshua, the son of R. Abraham, the son of R. David, the son of R. Abraham the son of Maimonides, left Egypt and, travelling to Syria by way of Palestine, settled first in Damascus and then in Aleppo, where he lived, apparently, till his death (c. 1410). R. David the younger took with him many MSS, including the commentary of Maimonides to the Mishnah in the author's own hand[16], and it is quite possible that amongst them was the Codex of Ben Asher which his ancestor had used as his authority. Or else the MS may have been brought by one of two other scholars who moved to Aleppo in the same period. To-day we have clear proof that a hundred years before the time of R. David b. Zimra, even before the expulsion of the Jews from Spain, the Codex was already in Aleppo.

Saadiah ben David of Aden, who visited Aleppo, no doubt in the course of his pilgrimage to Safed, before the year 1478–9, mentions the Codex in his commentary to *Seder Ahabah* of Maimonides' *Code*, a MS of which is in the Bodleian Library[17]:

הספר שסמך עליו הגאון ז״ל עדיין הוא היום במדינת צובא והיא חלב ויסמוה אלתאג׳ ומכתוב עלי רק בכל ורקה תלאת דפאת ומכתוב פי אכ׳רה אני אהרן בן אשר שהגהתיו וכו׳.

"The book which the Gaon of Blessed Memory used as his authority is still today in the town of Zobah, i.e. Aleppo, and is called 'the Crown'. It is written on parchment with three columns of writing to every page. At the end is written: "I, Aaron ben Asher collated it, etc.".[18]

Thus there is a gap in our knowledge of only about one hundred years from

15. N. Ben-Menachem "A missing responsum of Ben Zimra", in *Studies in Bibliography and Booklore*, 3 (1957) p. 51–52.
16. S. David Sassoon, *Introduction to Maimonides' Commentary to the Mishnah*, photostat edn., Copenhagen 1956, pp. 29–30.
17. Dated 28 Tebeth 5239 (Jan. 1479); Neubauer's Cat. No. 619.
18. Quoted by S. Assaf, ״מפירושו של סעדיה בן דוד אלעדני על הרמב״ם״, *Kiriath Sefer*, 22 (1946) p. 241.

the year 1375 when R. David ha-Nagidh left Egypt to the time of R. Saadiah of Aden who was in Aleppo before the year 1478. Less than a hundred years later one of the most famous scholars of Safed, R. Joseph Ashkenazi "the Tannaite", declares that he, too, consulted the Codex of Ben Asher in Aleppo on the subject of the open and closed paragraphs of the Law, in connection with the above ruling of Maimonides. He writes as follows:

מצאתי הספר עצמו של בן־אשר שהעתיק הוא ממנו פרשיות הפתוחות והסתומות כמו שכתב בספרו, ומצאתי בו שפעמי׳ רבות לא כתב אלא תיבה אחת בשיטה והתחיל כנגדה בשיטה שתחתיה, ואלו היתה דעתו כדעת הרב שקראה סתומה, הלא היה אפשר לו לעשותה סתומה מכל צד שהרי נשאר חלק הרבה.....וגדולה מצאתי כי הסופר כתב בסוף הספר: וכל מי שירצה לראות אות מתוכו חסר או יתר פתוח או סתום סדור או סתור. . . ולפי דרכו לא ידעתי מה היתה דעת הסופר בכל אלה שהזכרנו.

"I found the actual manuscript of Ben Asher from which he (Maimonides) copied the open and closed sections, as he wrote in his book. I found there that many times he wrote no more than a single word (at the beginning of a line) and then began the following section on the line below. If his (Ben Asher's) opinion had been like that of Maimonides who read it as a closed section, he could easily have written it as such[19], since there was plenty of space left . . . . . Moreover, the scribe wrote at the end of the book:'Whoever wishes to see from it which words have the full and which the defective spelling, which sections are open and which closed, where a new *sedher* begins and where the text goes on'. . . According to his (Maimonides') system I did not know what the opinion of the scribe was in all these matters that we have mentioned."[20] This is exactly the version found in the colophon of our Aleppo Codex.

IV

For two hundred years after this we have no further information about the Codex in Aleppo. Then the Rabbi of the community, R. Raphael Solomon Laniado (died in 1783–4) mentions it in one of his responsa:

ומנהג העיר שמי שאומר כן צריך להשבע על כתר התורה כמה יש לו והוא יתן כפי שבועתו ומנהג ותיקין הוא...

19. If a 'closed' section ends before the middle of a line, the first word of the following section is written at the end of the same line, otherwise the same blank space is distributed between this and the following line. An 'open' section requires in any case restarting on another line, and if the section ends after the middle of the line, the following line is left blank (Maimonides, *Code, H. Sefer-Torah* viii, 1–2).

20. Oxford MS Neubauer 1664, p. 123b. I have reproduced the text as printed by G. Scholem, "Fresh Information about R. Joseph Ashkenazi, the Tanna from Safed", *Tarbiz* (Hebrew), 28 (1959) p. 75. After the publication of my Hebrew article, Scholem, too, stated that Rabbi Joseph's remarks referred to the Aleppo Codex discussed here.

"It is a custom in our city that he who says so[21] must swear by the 'Crown of the Law' how much he has and then he pays according to his oath. . . . . and this is an ancient custom".[22]

About this time, before 1753, an English traveller, Alexander Russell, who visited Aleppo, was allowed to see the Codex. In the record of his travels, *The Natural History of Aleppo* (second edition, London 1794) Russell devoted a whole chapter to the Jews and their customs. At the end (Vol. II, pp. 59, 399) he refers to this ancient MS which was kept in the Old Synagogue in Aleppo and which the Jews of Aleppo believed to be from the time of the Second Temple[23]:

"They have one synagogue, situated in what is called the Jews' Street, where a manuscript of the Old Testament is preserved, which, as they pretend, is of very high antiquity.

"(Note) The Jews assign two reasons for ascribing such high antiquity to the M.S. Bible preserved in the synagogue at Aleppo. The one, the concurrent tradition of their Rabbis, and their submission to its authority in the various readings of disputed passages: they produce instances of deputations sent from Europe on purpose to consult it.

The other that at the end of the M.S. there is a prayer for the preservation ot the Temple: whence they conclude it must have been written before the expedition of Titus; because after that period, their prayers were offered up for the restauration, not preservation of the Temple of Jerusalem. A specimen of this M.S. was transmitted to Dr. Kennicot, who did not find reason to ascribe such high antiquity to it as the Jews do."

The tradition of swearing by this Codex has persisted in Aleppo down to the present day. There can thus be no doubt that Laniado's words refer to the famous Codex copied by R. Solomon ben Buyā'ā, as will be corroborated by further evidence to be brought below. Such being the case, this MS must have been in Aleppo many years before the lifetime of R. Solomon Laniado.

The Codex was kept in one of the seven "shrines"[24] of the Old Synagogue. There is extant a description of this repository written in the year 1847–8 by one of the scholars of Aleppo, R. Abraham the son of R. Isaiah Dayan. He writes as follows: "In the shrine on the south-eastern side there is a niche containing four Crowns of the Law, some being texts of the whole Bible, some only of the Pentateuch, and on one of them it is written *that it was found among the booty*

---

21. i.e. who does not accept the assessment made of his means for the purpose of the con-gregational tax.
22. In his responsa collection כסא שלמה, Jerusalem n.d., Par. 2, fol. 9a.
23. This source was brought to my notice by Mr. Ben-Zion Luria. Dr. Michael Davis was kind enough to lend me his copy of the book. I hereby express my thanks to both of them.
24. For a description of this synagogue and its shrines, see the article of Alexander Dothan, "לתולדות בית הכנסת הקדמון בחלב", *Sefunoth* 1 (1957) pp. 25–61.

taken from Jerusalem (may it be rebuilt and restored). There is no date on them, but they appear to be ancient. He who incurs an oath by the Law swears there upon the Codices. The administration of the oath is the sole prerogative of the Dayan family. There is also a cave there in which tradition relates that Elijah the prophet appeared. It is customary to light lamps there in time of trouble, and also women do so when they start their ninth month of pregnancy. Also on the eve of the Day of Atonement, at the time of the *Minḥah* prayer, the women leave their ovens and cooking fires, change their garments and join the throng to place oil (lamps) in that cave."[25]

Subsequently, the Codex was removed from this shrine. Rabbi Isaac Sh'ḥey-bar, one of the scholars of Aleppo (now living in Buenos Aires), has given me the following information about it by letter:

היה מונח בקרן זוית בארגז עץ בבית השמן של ביה״כ הגדולה, בלי שירהיב שום יהודי לגשת אליו ובזה היה שמור מפני חומר קדושתו ההמונית כל הימים, עד שלבסוף מפני מקרה דלקה שהיתה בבית השמן נכנס הספר הנ״ל בסכנה ונצל בדרך נס, וגם מפני החשודים, שהיו באים מארצות שונות בתור תיירים ואנשי מדע לעיין בספר הנ״ל, וחששו אנשי הקהילה פן יגנב, וגם חששו פן יצלמו אותו שום פעם, לזה החליטו בשנים האחרונות ויחדו לו ארגז גדול מברזל והניחוהו שמה עם שאר כתבי יד של התנ״כים האחרים שהיו נמצאים שמה למשמרת. לארגז הזה היו שני מפתחות. לא היו נמסרים ביחד לגבאי אחד אף שהיה הנאמן הגדול ביותר, רק היו נמסרים לשני אמידים וחשובים שלא יפתח הארגז הנ״ל אלא בנוכחות שניהם יחד ותחת השגחת ועד הקהילה. את הארגז שמו במערת אליהו הנביא בבית הכנסת הגדולה על מצבת אבן גדולה, וכל העם מקדישים ומעריצים את מקום מושבו.

"It stood in a wooden case in a corner of the oil store of the Great Synagogue, and no Jew had the presumption to go near it. Thus its great sanctity in the eyes of the masses preserved it intact all the time. Eventually, however, there was a fire in the oil store and it was saved from destruction only by a miracle. In addition some suspicious-looking people in the guise of tourists and scholars came from various countries to look at the book, and the members of the community feared that they would steal or photograph it. For these reasons they decided in recent years to make a special iron box for it, and they put it in this box with the other manuscripts of the Bible that were kept in the synagogue. There were two keys to this box. Both of them were not given even to the most trusted *gabbai*, but one key was given to each of two wealthy and important members of the community, so that the box could only be opened in the presence of both of them together and under the supervision of the council of the congregation. The box was placed on a large stone slab in the cave of Elijah the Prophet in the Great Synagogue and all the congregation regard the place where it stands with awe and reverence."

25. See Abraham Dayan, הולך תמים ופועל צדק, Leghorn 5610, fols. 67b–68a.

I have quoted the evidence of the scholars of Aleppo at length, because of the most interesting light that it throws upon the development of a tradition. The special sanctity attaching to the Codex goes back no further than to the time when it was placed in the Cave of Elijah. Shortly afterwards, the Jewish masses had forgotten the source of the cave's sanctity and attributed it to the Codex. But it is clear from the words of R. Abraham Dayan that a hundred years ago the Jews of Aleppo used still to prostrate themselves in worship and light candles not to the Codex, which was then in another place, but to the Prophet Elijah. R. Solomon Laniado, too, does not regard the Codex as particularly holy, nor does he attribute it to Ezra the Scribe: he simply writes that his contemporaries used to swear upon it. Thus it is clear that these later legendary embellishments grew up around the Codex only after it had been transferred to the Cave of Elijah.

The tradition described by Rabbi Sh'heybar appears to be inaccurate in certain particulars. The codices were certainly not kept in the oil store, but in the south-eastern "shrine". It is possible that the oil for replenishing the lamps was also placed there, as is done in several Oriental congregations and was the case in the "Istambulis" synagogue in Jerusalem. Our Codex was transferred to the Cave of Elijah after 1850 and before 1899, since in the latter year the collector Elhanan Nathan Adler from London, on a visit to Aleppo, already found it in the cave.[26]

V

The high esteem in which this Codex was held by scribes may be gauged from the fact that, in many Codices, the later scribes also copied out the colophon attached to it, as proof of having taken their text of the Bible from this accurate source. In the synagogue of the Rema (Rabbi Moses Isserlis) at Cracow there was a Codex sent to him in 1558–9 by R. Joseph Caro of Safed (author of the *Shulḥan ʿArukh*) which had been bought for one hundred ducats. Isserlis copied the text of his own Scroll of the Law from this MS because it contained the colophon of the Codex of Aleppo.[27] At the end of the מקדשיה which was in the Karaite synagogue in Jerusalem, this same colophon was added in a modern Karaite script which was no part of the original MS; this was apparently the work of the notorious Karaite scholar Firkovich who introduced various

---

26. See his *Jews in Many Lands*, London 1905, p. 162.
27. The colophon has been reproduced in the Hebrew periodical *Ha-Maggid*, 1 (1856–7) No. 47. The copyist was unable to read all the letters. The fate of this Codex after the European holocaust and its present whereabouts are unknown to me. *Any one who possesses such information is requested to communicate with me. B-Z.*

changes and distortions into the original version in order to prove its Karaite origin. At the head of this colophon he states:

אמרתי להעתיק רשימה היקרה מסוף התני־ך היקר הנקרא מקדש יי־ה בתוככי ירושלם
הנעתקת בו מספר הנקרא כתב הירושלם שהוקדש למצרים לכנסת הירושלם.

"I set myself to copy the precious note from the end of the precious Bible known as the מקדשיה in Jerusalem, which was copied into it from a Codex called כתב הירושלם that was dedicated to the Jerusalemite Synagogue in Cairo".[28] There is no point in commenting here on all the errors in this copy, but the differences which prove his tendentious distortions should be mentioned. Instead of giving the name of the scribe as "Solomon known as Ben Buyā'ā", the Karaite writes "Our Master and Teacher Solomon the son of Jeruḥam the deft scribe", thus hoping to mislead the reader into thinking that the MS was copied by the Karaite Solomon ben Jeruḥam (b. ca. 910). At the same time it is interesting to note that the name of Ben Asher appears in Firkovich's copy in its correct form (and not as it is wrongly written in our MS): "Our Master Aaron the son of our Master Moses the son of Rab Asher". In the genealogy of the "Princes" (נשיאים) he adds the name of the Prince Solomon, son of the Prince David.[29]

We shall now quote in full the lost colophon at the end of the Codex, as copied by R. Meir Neḥmad[30]:

זה המצחף השלם של כ־ד ספרים שכתב אותו מרנא ורבנא שלמה הנודע ב בן בוי־
א ע א הסופר המהיר, רוח ה׳ תניחנו, ונקד ומסר אותו באר היטב המלמד הגדול החכם הנבן
אדן הסופרים ואבי החכמים וראש המלמדים והמהיר במעשיו המבין במפעליו ויחיד בדו־
רותיו מר אהרן בן מר רב אשר תהי נפשו צרורה בצרור החיים עם הנביאים והצדיקים
והחסידים. הקדיש אותו השר הגדול האדיר האביר מרנא ורבנא ישראל, תפארת כל ישראל,
החכם והנבון החסיד הישר הנדיב ירים ה׳ דגלו ויציץ נזרו ויגביה עוזו וממדינת בצרה בן מר
רב שמחה בן מר סעדיה בן מר רב אפרים רוח ה׳ תניחם לירושלים עיר הקודש על זרע ישר־
אל קהלת יעקב עדת ישורון בעלי המדע סגולת החכמים השוכנים בהר ציין, אלהים ישמרם
עד עולם סלה. קודש לה׳, לא ימכר ולא יגאל על מנת שלא יצא מתחת יד שני הנשיאים הגדו־
לים כבוד גדולת קדושת הוד הדר הנשיא יאשיהו והנשיא יחזקיהו בני כבוד גדולת קדושת
הנשיא דוד בן הנשיא בעז תהי נפשם צרורה בצרור החיים בגן עדן תחת עץ החיים כדי שיו־

28. Cf. note 10.
29. Since the copy of the colophon in the Cracow Codex contains the additional name Solomon, it may be presumed that the name was inadvertently omitted from the copy of R. Meir Neḥmad.
30. כתר ארם צובה Aleppo, 1933. I found R. Meir Neḥmad, whom I met on visits to Cairo and Aleppo, to be a scholar of vast knowledge and scientific acriby. The translation has been set out in paragraphs so as to guide the reader through the labyrinth of names and eulogies.

ציאוהו אל המושבות והקהלות שבעיר הקודש בשלשה רגלים חג המצות וחג השבועות וחג
הסכות, לקרות בו ולהתבונן וללמוד ממנו כל אשר יחפצו ויבחרו, ואם ירצו אלו שני הנשיאים
הגדולים, מר רב יאשיהו ויחזקיהו, יהיי צורם בדרך הצלחה, ויפקידו אותו עם שני אנשים
צדיקים ונבונים וידועים יראי אלהים אנשי אמת שונאי בצע יעשו בחכמתם ובחזקתם, ואם
יחפוץ איש מכל זרע ישראל מבעלי הבינה מהרבנים בכל ימות השנה לראות בו דברי יתר
או חסר או סתור או סתום או פתוח או טעם מהטעמים האלו, יוציאהו אליו לראות ולהשכיל
ולהבין לה(ם) לקרות ולדרוש וישיבוהו למקומו וישמרוהו ולא יתפרד בו איש אין בו אמונה,
וה' אלהי ישראל ישים אותו סימן טוב סימן ברכה עליו ועל זרעו ועל כל ישראל ויתקים עליו
מקרא שכ(תוב) כי אצק מים על צמא ונחלים על יבשה, אצק רוחי על זרעך וברכתי על
צאצאיך וצמחו בבין חציר כערבים על יבלי מים זה יאמר לה' אני וזה יקרא בשם יעקב וזה
יכתוב ידו לה' ובשם ישראל יכנה וכל הברכות האמורות בו יחולו ויבואו ויאתיו ויאמרו עליו
ועל זרעו ועל כל מי שישמע ויאזין ויקשיב ויעשה כדברים האלה ולא יחליפם ולא ימירם
לעולם ולעולמי עולמים ברוך ה' לעולם אמן ואמן.

"This complete copy of the Twenty-four Books, which was written by our
Master and Teacher Solomon known as Ben Buyā'ā, the deft scribe, (may the
spirit of the Lord rest him), and pointed and given a full Massorah by the
great scholar and wise sage, lord of the scribes and father of the sages, and
chief of the scholars, who was deft in his deeds, knowledgeable in his under-
takings and unique in his generation — Master Rab Aaron the son of Master
Rab Asher (may his soul be bound up in the bundle of life with the prophets,
the righteous and the pious ones)

"was dedicated by the great, exalted, mighty prince, our Master and Teacher
Israel, the glory of all Israel, the sage and wise, the pious, upright and noble one
(may the Lord raise high his standard and cause his crown to flourish[31] and his
strength to increase) from Basra, the son of Master Rab Simḥa, the son of
Master Saadiah, the son of Master Rab Ephraim (may the spirit of the Lord
rest them)

"to Jerusalem the Holy City, into the keeping of the seed of Israel, the
congregation of Jacob, the community of Jeshurun, the possessors of knowledge
and the chosen ones of the wise ones[32] who dwell upon Mount Zion, may God
preserve them forever, Selah,

"as a thing holy unto the Lord[33]: it shall not be sold or redeemed[34], that it
may not pass out of the hands of the two great Princes, their honoured and
glorious highnesses and holinesses the Prince Josiah and the Prince Hezekiah,
the sons of his honoured highness the Prince David, the son of the Prince

31. Cf. Ps. cxxxii, 18.
32. R. Meir Neḥmad remarks that this word is written in place of a previously erased word
which, in his opinion, was "the Karaites", הקראים.
33. Cf. Lev. xxvii, 21.
34. i.e. made available for profane use by paying a sum of money to the synagogue's treasury.

Boaz (may their souls be bound up in the bundle of life in the Garden of Eden beneath the tree of life)

"so that they may bring it out to the study-houses (מושבות)[35] and the congregations in the Holy City on the three pilgrim-festivals, on the Feast of Passover and the Feast of Pentecost and the Feast of Tabernacles, (for the people) to read therein and to study and to learn therefrom all that they wish and choose.

"If these two great Princes, Master Rab Josiah and Hezekiah (may their Rock grant them happy lives) so desire and entrust it to two righteous and wise men, known to be God-fearing and true and haters of ill-gotten gain, they shall act in their wisdom and according to their prerogative.

"And if, on any day of the year, anyone of the seed of Israel from amongst the possessors of understanding from[36] the Rabbanites desire to check in it words with *plene* or *defective* spelling, or whether a passage runs on without break or is open or closed, or any accents, they shall produce it for him to see and study and to explain to them, to read and interpret, and afterwards they shall restore it to its place and keep watch over it; and no untrustworthy person must be left alone with it.

"The Lord, the God of Israel, will set it as a good sign, a sign of blessing, for him and for his seed and for all Israel, and there will come to pass for him the words of the prophet: 'For I will pour water on the thirsty land, and streams on the dry ground; I will pour my spirit upon thy descendants and my blessing on thine offspring. They shall spring up like grass amid waters, like willows by flowing streams. This one will say, I am the Lord's, another will call himself by the name of Jacob, and another will write on his hand, The Lord's, and surname himself by the name of Israel'.[37] And all the blessings written in this volume shall be fulfilled and come to pass and be said concerning him and his seed and everyone who shall hear and listen and give ear and do according to these words and shall not change and alter them for all eternity. Blessed be the Lord for evermore. Amen. Amen."

At the end of the first page the following words are written:

אנתקל בחכם אלאפתיכאק מן נהב ירושלים עיר הקודש תבנה ותכונן לקהל מצרים לכניסת ירושלים תבנה ותכונן בחיי ישראל ברוך שמרו וארור גבו וארור ממשכנו לא ימכר ולא ינאל לעד ולעולמי עולמים.

---

35. Ibn Sapir reads ישיבות. The Karaite מושב seems to have been something like a בית־מדרש, cf. Ben-Yehuda, *Thesaurus* p. 2866b, s.v. מושב, par. ח.

36. This word, too, is written over an erasure where, in the opinion of Nehmad, the reading had been "from amongst the Karaites (בעלי המקרא) and from the Rabbanites".

37. Isa. xliv, 3-5.

"Transferred by force of ransom (*al-iftikāk*)[38] from the booty of Jerusalem the Holy City (may it be rebuilt and restored) to the congregation of Cairo to the Synagogue of Jerusalem (may it be rebuilt and restored in the lifetime of Israel). Blessed be he who keeps it and cursed be he who steals it, and cursed be he who gives it in pledge. It shall not be sold or redeemed for all eternity."

VI

One further point remains to be discussed. As stated by Rabbis Abraham Dayan, Adler, Neḥmad and Sh'ḥeybar, there were four codices in the Great Synagogue in Aleppo. One of them, containing only the Pentateuch, was rescued together with the Codex of Ben Asher. This MS was completely undamaged, apart from the last page on which the colophon was written. Thanks, however, to the particulars noted down by Adler, we know that it was completed on the 15th of Tammuz in the year 5111 A.M. (1341 C.E.) apparently in Italy. The other two Codices were an illuminated double-column Pentateuch with the *Haphtaroth* and the Five Scrolls, which Adler describes as being even then in bad condition; and another Pentateuch with a colophon stating the name of the dedicator: קדש כה״ר אברהם דקדיש כהן בכ״ר יצחק כהן. "Dedication of his honour, Rabbi Abraham, dedicated by a *Kohen*, son of his honour Rabbi Isaac the *Kohen*."[39]

We fervently hope that these two copies of the Pentateuch may also come to light again in due course.

The last in time, but by no means the least in importance, who was privileged to see the Codex of Ben Asher in its entirety and to note down particulars about its contents, was the late Prof. M.D. Cassuto. Following the decision of the Hebrew University to publish a scientific edition of the Hebrew Bible, Prof. Cassuto travelled to Aleppo for the specific purpose of examining the Codex of Ben Asher. Unfortunately, the Aleppo congregation did not permit him to spend there more than a few days. He thought of basing his Hebrew text on this MS, and later, when he heard of the fire in the Aleppo Great Synagogue, he lamented the destruction (as he thought) of the Codex in a special article.[40] It is our hope that what was denied this scholar will be granted to his pupils and disciples who will have the advantage of being able to refer to this ancient MS when restoring the exact Hebrew text of the Bible.

38. Cf. R. Baruch Toledano, "על התנ״ך ״כתר״ של חלב", *Ha'aretz* 2.X.1949.
39. Adler, op. cit. (note 26), p. 163.
40. *Ha'aretz* 18.XII.1947.

THE AUTHENTICITY OF THE ALEPPO CODEX*

MOSHE GOSHEN-GOTTSTEIN

I

§ 1   For almost a century Bible scholars have been aware of the fact that the
Jewish community of Aleppo claimed to be in possession of the very
codex which had served Maimonides as a basis for setting out the exact rules
for writing Scrolls of the Law, as stated in his *Code*. The overwhelming authority
of Maimonides as the first great systematizer of Jewish law explains why his
pronouncements on this subject, too, could hardly be brushed aside by later
halakhists. In other words: in all those details which were not already regulated
by Talmudic law, later generations were, according to theory, trying to follow
the system of the "model codex" as described by Maimonides. Most of these
rules were not made absolutely binding; but it certainly was meritorious to
follow them.

We cannot say for sure whether the Massoretic school of Ben Asher would

---

* With the following study I have returned to what may be regarded as the *pièce de résis-
tance* of any work on the Bible text: the Massoretic *textus receptus*. There can be no end to
our work in this field, and the very attempt to translate the results of our previous studies
into editorial practice is bound to bring with it new insights. Yet I may be excused for looking
upon this study as the end of a decade of preliminary work which in one way or another
centered around the problem of how to gain a deeper understanding of the questions of the
Bible text and its language.

While I feel that with this chapter I may hand the first volume of my attempts in this field —
as far as they are not written in Hebrew — to the binders, the exterior circumstances which
forced me to publish the material chapter by chapter will explain why I would like to refer
those readers who do not read this study within the framework of my *Text and Language in
Bible and Qumran* at least to: *Biblica* 35 (1954), pp. 429 f., VT 7(1957) pp. 195 f., JJS 8
(1957), pp. 5 f., *Scripta Hierosolymitana* (Volume VIII, 1960).

The special abbreviations in this paper are as follows:

A	= Aleppo Codex of Aaron ben Asher
BA	= Ben Asher
BH	= *Biblia Hebraica*, third edition
C	= Cairo Codex of Moses ben Asher
Hil.S.T.	= Hilkhot Sefer Torah in Maimonides' *Code*
HUBP	= Hebrew University Bible Project
L	= Leningrad Codex, after Aaron ben Asher
MT	= Massoretic Text
SM	= Song of Moses (Deut. xxxii)
Sof.	= Tractate Soferim

Reprinted from *Textus* 1 (1960).

[1]

have won the day without Maimonides taking sides. In any case, what seems to have been the final crown of the work of generations of Massoretes, the only codex containing the whole Bible procured through infinite labour by the latest scion of this dynasty, Aaron ben Asher, was accepted by Maimonides as the model copy for all future generations.[1] This made our Hebrew *textus receptus* largely identical with Ben Asher's text.

§ 2   If it is true that the so-called Aleppo Codex was the manuscript used by Maimonides and if he was right in accepting the tradition of Ben Asher's authorship[2], then his manuscript would, indeed, have a unique claim upon our attention. However, no modern scholar was able to study it properly, nor was the Aleppo Jewish community ever willing to make it available in photographs.[3] Thus this codex — allegedly the most important single manuscript of the MT — remained practically a hidden treasure. The supposed loss of this manuscript during the pillage of the Aleppo synagogue, shortly after the

---

1.   As we shall have occasion to return to the statement of Maimonides, I shall quote it here in full (*Code*, Book II, *Ahabah, Hilkhoth Sefer Torah* viii, 4):

   ולפי שראיתי שבוש גדול בכל הספרים שראיתי בדברים אלו, וכן בעלי המסורת שכותבין ומחברין להודיע הפתוחות והסתומות נחלקים בדברים אלו במחלוקת הספרים שסומכין עליהם, ראיתי לכתב הנה כל פרשיות התורה הסתומות ופתוחות וצורות השירות, כדי לתקן עליהם כל הספרים ולהגיה מהם. וספר שסמכנו עליו בדברים אלה הוא הספר הידוע במצרים שהוא כולל ארבעה ועשרים ספרים, שהיה בירושלים מכמה שנים להגיה ממנו הספרים, ועליו היו הכל סומכין; לפי שהגיהו בן אשר ודקדק בו שנים הרבה והגיהו פעמים רבות כמו שהעתיקו. ועליו סמכתי בספר התורה שכתבתי כהלכתו.

   "Since I have seen great confusion in all the Scrolls [of the Law] in these matters, and also the Massoretes who wrote special works] to make known [which sections are] open and closed, contradict each other, according to the books on which they base themselves, I decided to write down here all the sections of the Law, closed and open, and the forms of the Songs [viz. Ex. xv, Deut. xxxii], so as to correct the scrolls accordingly. The copy on which we based ourselves in these matters is the one known in Egypt, which contains the whole Bible, which was formerly in Jerusalem (serving to correct copies according to it), and everybody accepted it as authoritative, for Ben Asher corrected it many times. And I used it as the basis for the copy of the Pentateuch which I wrote according to the Law."

2.   By the time Maimonides wrote his *Code*, the colophon, attributing the Massoretic part and the pointing to *Aaron ben Asher*, formed already part of the codex. Although Maimonides speaks of *Ben Asher* only, there is no reason to doubt that if the colophon turns out to be correct as regards the "Ben Asher" character, it may be also taken as trustworthy in attributing the manuscript to the son, *Aaron*, the more so since it agrees in its character with other MSS which are connected with *Aaron*, while it is opposed to the Cairo Codex attributed to *Moses* (cf. also below, §15). It is well known that many authors did not distinguish carefully between the father, *Moses* and the son, *Aaron*. The fact, to which E. E. Urbach kindly drew my attention, that the commentary *Migdal 'Oz* on the *Code ad loc.* happens to insert the name of *Moses* (שסמך על ספר משה בן אשר) is one of these instances and is not backed by any manuscript or other authority (see also below, n. 24).

3.   On alleged copies cf. below, §11 and n. 34. Cf. also next par. and below, n. 20.

[2]

UNO decision in 1947 to establish a Jewish State, seemed therefore irretrievable.

It is, therefore, extremely fortunate that through the good offices of H. E. the President of the State of Israel, Mr. I. Ben-Zvi, a manuscript, unfortunately mutilated, alleged to be the said Aleppo Codex, has come to light and been made available for study. In connection with the Bible Project, carried out at present at the Hebrew University (HUBP), it has been the great privilege of the present writer to carry out a first investigation of the main problems posed by this unique codex. Being confronted with this task, I was forced to venture far into fields which the student of Semitic and Biblical philology is rarely called upon to enter. I cannot but hope that my findings will stand up to the acid tests to be applied by experts on Rabbinic law, upon whose territory I have trespassed.[4]

§ 3   No manuscript of the Hebrew Bible, apart from those discovered among the Dead Sea Scrolls, has been the subject of so heated a discussion as our Codex. Ever since the first information about it was published almost a century ago[5], the controversy has been raging, on and off. Now that the manuscript is available, the discussion must perforce be reopened.

On the one hand, there are the few followers of Graetz, the first European scholar to discuss the Codex, who endeavoured to justify the local tradition of the Aleppo community.[6] On the other hand, there are the much more numerous opponents of this tradition who reasserted the position taken up by Wickes.[7]

4.   But for the fact that Professors Lieberman and Urbach were good enough to read this paper before publication, I would have felt much more hesitant about presenting my findings. I am most grateful indeed to these two masters of Rabbinics for their kind encouragement. I would like to use this occasion to offer my sincerest thanks also to those who were instrumental in enabling the HUBP to study the text of this precious codex: H. E. Mr. I. Ben-Zvi, President of the State of Israel; Professor B. Mazar, President of the Hebrew University; Professor E. E. Urbach, Dean of the Institute of Jewish Studies; Mr. M. Benayahu, Director of the Ben-Zvi Institute: last, but not least, to my esteemed colleague and co-editor, Professor C. Rabin, without whose comments the present paper would have been even less readable.

5.   By R. Jacob Berlin in the first volume of the weekly *Libanon* (הלבנון) 1863. pp. 23, 31, 76 (copies of which are extremely rare), and in the famous travel account of R. Jacob Sapir, אבן ספיר I (1866), 12b ff.

6.   Cf. MGWJ 22 (1871), p. 52 f. It was, apparently, he who coined the term *Aleppo Codex*.

7.   W. Wickes, *A Treatise on the Accentuation of the Twenty-One so-called Prose Books of the Old Testament* (Oxford 1887), p. vii f.
       Kahle is correct in maintaining, in his analysis of the development of the discussion until the present time (cf. *Cairo Geniza*, 1947,p. 62f., [1959,p.111f.] and after that in V.T. 1 (1951), p. 163), that according to his own admission Wickes was more than a little influenced by the opinion of Seligmann Baer. This also applies to Neubauer, who

If one retraces today the stages of the discussion and the arguments advanced, one sometimes wonders how it was possible. Yet, our amazement may be less great if we bear in mind that no modern scholar was able to investigate the Codex or to photograph it, so that the whole discussion was based on the photograph of one single page (cf. below, note 20), on a few variant readings[8], and on a colophon in which quite a number of details had been purposely erased and rewritten.[9]

§ 4   On the basis of this exceedingly meagre material, the discussion was fervently pursued, and the opponents finally won the day. Today their reasons appear rather strange. But in those days there was little familiarity with ancient Hebrew MSS and palaeography, so that scholars could with impunity put forward the opinion that the Codex (=A) was centuries later than Ben Asher![10] In the light of our present, one hopes somewhat more consolidated, knowledge of palaeography, and in the light of the extension of our field of view as a result of the publication of comparative material[11], such arguments hardly seem acceptable.

As regards the alleged lack of agreement between certain readings of A and the supposedly "true" text of BA — that is to say, the one which Baer and his followers considered to be the original BA text — it can no longer be doubted today that those scholars turned the facts upside down: they regarded late "syncretistic" readings as the true BA text, and consequently judged the early authentic readings to be late and untrustworthy (cf. esp. Kahle, *op. cit.*).

pronounced on the issue already in MGWJ 36 (1887), p. 302, four years before his much-quoted statement in *Studia Biblica et Ecclesiastica* (Oxford 1891), p. 25 f. Nevertheless it should be emphasized that it was not Baer who pronounced against the genuineness of the Codex: in 1879 he only expressed a slight doubt (cf. Introduction to *Dikduke ha-Te'amim*, p. xiii).Furthermore, a scholar who happened to make a thorough study of treatises on the Massorah at that time mentions only Wickes as holding the opinion that the tradition about A is untrue. Cf. Harris, "The Rise and Development of the Massorah", JQR, O. S. 1 (1889), p. 249.

8.   Since these passed various hands until they appeared in *Libanon* (see above, note 5), it may be doubted whether they were printed correctly. In any case, for the last seventy years no one troubled to analyze them.

9.   Cf. the discussion in Kahle's *MdW* I, 1 f. The most recent publication of the text is by President Ben-Zvi (cf. above, p. 13) who based himself on the treatise of Meir Neḥmad, מאמר חקירה על הכתר היקר הנקרא כתר ארם צובה "A study of the precious Codex called the 'Crown' of Aleppo" (Aleppo 1933).

10.   As is well known, Lagarde went so far as to claim that the Codex was a German MS of the fourteenth century; Kahle, *MdW* I, 14, already tried to explain the origin of this egregious error, which was unfortunately widely accepted because of Lagarde's prestige in other fields of research.

11.   Most useful to all who deal with this subject are the tables published by S.A. Birnbaum, *The Hebrew Scripts*, Part Two, London 1954, etc.

Even stranger seems to us the argument — the origin of which is once again to be sought in the lack of familiarity with ancient MSS on the part of 19th century scholars — that because the open and closed sections in A were not marked with the letters פ and ס, it was impossible that this should have been the MS which Maimonides saw. For how could he have ruled on the matter of open and closed sections if these letters are missing! We have meanwhile learnt that this marking was not at all the prevalent custom in early MSS; rather the difference between open and closed sections was indicated by the size of the blank space left between the sections and by the manner in which the new section was started (cf. below, n. 112). To those early scholars, however, the arguments against the antiquity of A and its identity with Maimonides' "Ben Asher codex" appeared formidable, and they consequently pronounced against acceptance of the local tradition of Aleppo Jewry.

§ 5   The only scholar who contradicted the view which by then had become well-nigh universally accepted on the authority of Wickes[12], was Kahle. Whatever has been said in favour of A in more recent studies of the subject, is entirely due to Kahle, who since 1926[13] has fought to refute the view generally held until that time.[14]

Kahle's refutation of the arguments put forward by Wickes and his followers could however do no more than restore the traditional *status quo*, as accepted more than half a century earlier by Graetz. The reasoning of Wickes and his followers was shown to be fallacious; and we should add that those same arguments of Kahle hold good in this respect also as regards the claims of

12.   To be sure, the only independent argument ever to be put forward after Wickes was advanced by Harkavy, *Ḥadhashim gam Yeshanim* VI (available to me in *Ha-Pisgah* 1 (Vilna 1891), p. 61 (offprint, p. 7)). Although Harkavy was a much more competent connoisseur of Hebrew MSS, he also sought to date the MS two hundred years later than BA on palaeographic grounds. It was he who put forward the explanation that the colophon may originally have been part of another MS. Since Harkavy, one of the few scholars who actually saw the Codex, does not advance any reason for this suggestion from what he actually saw, it carries little weight, because a remark of that nature might obviously be advanced as regards many colophons (cf. also above, note 2).

13.   As far as I know, Kahle assumed this point of view at that time, and it first appeared in the abstract of his lecture at the Deutscher Orientalistentag, Hamburg 1926 (cf. ZDMG, N. F. 6 (1927), liii, and the following year in *MdW* I, 1 f. In 1922 (*apud* Bauer-Leander, *Histor. Gramm. d. hebr. Sprache*, p. 89) he still believed that the Rabbinic Bible of Jacob ben Ḥayyim (1524/5) really represented the BA text.

14.   The only scholar before Kahle sufficiently qualified to judge Hebrew manuscripts who was not convinced by Wickes — though he only expressed his doubts without adding any reasons — was apparently Strack, "Ueber verlorengegangene Handschriften des Alten Testaments", in *Semitic Studies in Memory of A. Kohut* (Berlin 1897), p. 563, and in Hastings, *Dictionary of the Bible* IV (1902) p. 728.

Teicher, who maintained nothing less than that *none* of the manuscripts attributed today to the family of Ben Asher are in fact BA MSS.[15]

§ 6   However, neither Kahle nor anyone else did or could produce positive proof for the correctness of this tradition, since no one had access to anything but the same meagre material published in the last century. Thus by the end of World War II (cf. below, § 17, f.) the status of A among Biblical manuscripts rested on the authority of one single advocate, who himself had no positive proof to offer. The most Kahle could do was to make it plausible that A belonged to the BA family of MSS. Even this one pillar was soon, as we shall see (cf. below § 18 f.), to give way.

Considering the possibly unique importance of A, this state of affairs is more than lamentable. After all, should the local "legend" of the Aleppo Jews turn out to be true, our Codex would be one of the oldest massoretic MSS — and the oldest MS of the whole Bible at that — and one of the few MSS att ibutable to the BA family; possibly even more than that: it would be *the ideal model codex*, unique in its completeness, of the Massoretic *textus receptus*.

§ 7   To prevent at once any misrepresentation: this characterization is not oblivious of the fact that the text of Aaron ben Asher was the outcome of a gradual process of evolution in time, and that he himself most certainly changed many details in it during his lifetime. Nor do we ignore the fact that his Codex became a new starting point of further evolution, once other MSS were brought into some harmony with it or were copied from it (or its descendants). From the point of view of historical development, BA's codex is only one stage in the evolution of the Massoretic text, one text amongst others. Even if scholars are agreed on the eminence of BA, we possess no criterion for adjudging to it absolute immanent superiority from the point of view of the Massorah embodied in it.

This truth from the realm of *Textgeschichte*, however, does not prevent us from looking at the problem from another angle. If the Aleppo tradition is true, A is the one and only MS which without exaggeration may be said to represent a unique event in the history of the Massoretic text. Inasmuch as Maimonides declared it authoritative, he invested a text-form which otherwise might have been a momentary crystallization with a character both permanent and absolute.[16]

15.   Teicher's paper "The Ben Asher Manuscripts", JJS 2 (1950), pp. 20, 35, unfortunately happened to be published soon after the rumour was accepted that the Aleppo Codex had fallen a prey to rioters. As far as A is concerned, Teicher adds nothing to the statements of his predecessors. See Kahle, V. T. 1 (1951), p. 163 f., and cf. below, note 112.

[6]

§ 8   This point allows for some further elaboration. There is no doubt that Maimonides never intended to pronounce on those questions which are of interest to the student of the Bible text, *viz.* plene and defective spellings, punctuation, and accentuation in their various aspects. Nor, as we shall see later, did A become "canonized" in such a way as to oust all other traditions. Since practically all of the rules without talmudic basis which were recommended on the basis of A were not binding in halakhah, and since it was only meritorious to act according to them (cf. above, § 1), compromises became inevitable.

Matters developed rather differently from what Maimonides appears to have intended. On the one hand, those rules which he had phrased on the basis of A were not exactly followed, and the confusion he had intended to remedy became perhaps even greater. On the other, the BA tradition became (finally?) recognized as the text to be followed. But correcting existing manuscripts according to some copy of a BA text resulted necessarily in the development of a new tradition, more or less akin to A.

In other words: from the historical point of view, A is not exactly the archetype of our *textus receptus*, although it had (together with its sister codices) a decisive influence on the development of the latter. In theory, however, or in the "ideological" (*sit venia verbo*) assumptions of the editors of our printed Bibles — from Jacob ben Ḥayyim down to Baer and Ginsburg — the "true" BA text, as sanctioned by Maimonides — has become the ultimate goal, and each scholar in turn believed that he had practically reached it.[17] If the "legend" of the Aleppo community be true, A would therefore be destined to take from now on its honoured place as our most trustworthy guide.[18]

§ 9   The object of this article is to determine whether the Codex we are studying here is, indeed, that ultimate goal; or whether, even though

16.   There is no need to dwell once more on the fact that Maimonides' acceptance of BA's work as authoritative went a long way towards complicating the discussion on the alleged Karaite leanings of that Massorete. Cf. now Dothan, *Sinai* 41 (1957), mainly p. 301 f. (against him Allony, *Ha'aretz* 25.X.57) and Zucker, *Tarbiz* 27 (1957), p. 61 f.
17.   It may be due to discoverer's enthusiasm that Kahle and his assistants, in connection with the publication of the Leningrad MS (=L), emphasized the differences between the Rabbinic Bible of Ben Ḥayyim and the BA text to an extent which is likely to deceive those who have not themselves compared the two texts. Yet the importance of the differences should not be minimized, as was done by Sperber in his introduction to *The Pre-Masoretic Bible* I, p. xxii, Copenhagen 1956.
18.   In view of the excitement which has gripped Bible publishers in Israel (see Yalon's scathing remarks in *Hatzofeh* 10.IV. 59), it should be stressed that our remarks must not be interpreted to mean that the text of our common Massoretic Bible editions is

Wickes and his followers erred in their reasoning, they did not err in their view that the legend surrounding the Aleppo Codex is really nothing but a legend, one of those tales which are sometimes woven around ancient manuscripts.[19]

In order to decide our issue, the following claims have to be proved:

1. That the manuscript discussed here is, in fact, the Aleppo Codex. Since the famous colophon, on which its claim to be a BA text mainly rested, was lost together with a considerable part of the Codex, the identity of our manuscript cannot simply be taken for granted.
2. That the Aleppo Codex is really a BA manuscript.
3. That this is, indeed, the MS on which Maimonides based his rules. This is, of course, the mos important point, and by far the most difficult one to prove.

II

§ 10   It is comparatively easy to show that the MS before us really is the Aleppo Codex. First of all, the identity of the two MSS became obvious immediately on comparing the two pages photographed side by side in the President's first article (*Sinai* 43 (1957), p. 8). This impression becomes certainty when one places additional pages of the MS next to the photograph of the one page of the Aleppo Codex hitherto known.[20] One could assume, of course, for the sake of argument, that our Codex is a twin of the Aleppo Codex. But all the MSS originally kept in Aleppo have been known for a long time and there exists no MS even faintly resembling A — let along resembling it like two peas in a pod. Since the provenience of our MS from Aleppo is a fact, such an assumption is void.

Moreover, Wickes mentions amongst the sparse information at his disposal (*op. cit.*, p. VII, n. 4) that the height of a column in A is 23 cm. and the width 6 cm. These are the exact measurements of the MS before us. The combination of these facts is perforce unique. The MS before us can be none other than the Aleppo Codex, as maintained by witnesses, and its identity is beyond doubt. We may add that once we prove the identity of our MS with the codex used by Maimonides, this should be further proof of this point, if such were needed.

"wrong", God forbid, or that from now on all the printed Bibles in existence had better be quickly discarded!

19.   It is, of course, true that the existence of a tradition for a number of centuries does not in itself constitute proof. Still, some weight it does bear (cf. below, § §25 and 42).
20.   Cf. above §3. The photograph had been published at the time as frontispiece to Wickes' book. Great consternation was caused among the heads of the Aleppo community when they learned from the late Prof. Cassuto that such a photograph existed (cf. *Ha'aretz*, 2.I.48).

§ 11 On the other hand, we have to note that in its present state the identity cannot be proved by any known variant readings, for the list of readings published in the name of Jacob Berlin (cf. above, note 5) terminates at the end of Exodus (*ib.* p. 76).[21]

One might, on the other hand, have assumed that the late Prof. Cassuto's working copy of the Bible, on the margin of which he had noted the readings for the new edition he was planning, would contain notes of variants from A. This is not so. I am much beholden to Dr. A. Hartom, who supervised the printing of the edition which was based on Cassuto's notes, for informing me that in Cassuto's own copy not a single variant from A was noted.[22] This would explain why Cassuto was so careful, whenever he mentioned A, to talk only of his having "examined" or "studied" that codex. It seems therefore hardly accidental that no variant readings from A have been found among the papers left by this scholar (cf. below, notes 35, 48).

The last possible source of material for comparing our MS to A would be the alleged copy of A which was sent in the 16th century from Palestine to R. Moses Isserlis.[23] But even assuming that it has not been irrevocably lost, we cannot know to what extent it was, indeed, an exact copy of A.[24]

All these possible sources might have furnished confirmation for our conclusion; but the identification of our MS with A seems beyond dispute in any case. We may therefore turn our attention to the MS itself.

21. Even assuming that all the readings were printed correctly — they appeared in a weekly! — they all concern minor points of accents, methegs and vowels, which by their very nature do not lend themselves to generalizations that could be verified from other passages in the same MS.
     However, when I finally ran to earth a copy of that rare volume of *Libanon* (probably the only copy existing in this country), my attention was caught by the many places where A has Ḥateph Pataḥ instead of a Shewa in the Heidenheim edition used by J. Berlin (cf. above n. 5). In the light of the findings in our MS (see Loewinger's article in this volume of *Textus*), this point should not be ignored.
22. Correct accordingly Eissfeldt, *Einleitung*², p. 843 [and Kahle, *Cairo Geniza*², p. 135]. Completely unjustified therefore is Brownlee's recent statement, that the so-called "Jerusalem edition" is "a correction of the Ginsburg edition in the light of Cassuto's collation of the famous Aleppo MS" (cf. "*The Text of Habakkuk in the Ancient Commentary from Qumran*", *JBL Monograph Series* XI (1959), p. 5).
23. See President Ben-Zvi's article in this number and expecially his request that anyone who knows anything about this matter should publish it. Cf. above, n. 3.
24. In the literature on this subject it is sometimes stated that the copy of R. Moses Isserlis was made from C (written by *Moses* ben Asher). It needs to be emphasized that this information is based on a misunderstanding which spread on the authority of C. D. Ginsburg, *Introduction*, etc. (1897), p. 242. His error was repeated by Strack, in Hastings, *Dictionary of the Bible* IV, 728. Already Kahle, *MdW* I, 12, has pointed out that the statement is erroneous. A confusion of facts of a different order occurs in the latest comprehensive work on the Bible text, Roberts, *The Old Testament Text and*

§ 12   The problem we just tried to solve would not have existed, had scholars had the opportunity to investigate A properly while it was still complete and safe in the hands of the Aleppo community. Our second question, however, is posed by A itself: can we take the colophon at its face value? The tradition about Maimonides using A may be a legend; yet the colophon's information about BA may be correct. What has to be examined first of all is whether the colophon attributing A to BA is spurious or not.

The criteria according to which a MS does or does not represent a BA text have been established and generally accepted during the last thirty years, thanks to the labours of Kahle and his pupils. On the basis of the one known page, it has been assumed that A is indeed a BA MS. This was also the conclusion arrived at by the only scholar who succeeded in looking at the MS itself, namely Cassuto (cf. below, n. 42). It did not take many hours of studying to convince ourselves that these claims are justified, and a fairly comprehensive comparison with the relevant data from Mishael ben Uzziel's treatise conclusively proved that impression to be correct.[25]

§ 13   Not only is the BA character of the MS obvious, but it can already be established that it differs so decisively from the only other known BA MS of the whole Bible, *viz.* the Leningrad Codex (L) that it is quite out of the question to argue that it is directly connected with it. A is not the immediate *Vorlage* of L, nor are they both derived from one *Vorlage*. In other words: even if, for the moment, we would not claim superiority for A on the basis of internal criteria, we are already justified in maintaining that A is, at the very least, an alternative BA manuscript.

I would claim, however, that we may at once go one step further. Even without a full-scale investigation of A and its Massorah, accents, vowels, etc., as compared with L (cf. above, n. 25), it seems that we already possess distinct indications that of the two complete BA Bible codices, A and L, A is the superior one, and is consequently to be preferred as the basic manuscript in future critical editions of Aaron ben Asher's text.[26]

Versions (1951), p. 81. According to him the Codex is housed "in the Qaraite synagogue at Aleppo and the Qaraites have always regarded it as their most costly treasure".

25.   The special character and place of A, according to internal criteria, within the framework of MSS attributed to BA, will be discussed in detail by D. S. Loewinger in this volume. Dr. Loewinger, with the aid of the assistant in the Massorah Departement of the HUBP, Mr. Yisrael Yeivin, has already carried out a first summary study of the whole MS. On the subject of Mishael ben Uzziel's treatise, taken to be the most reliable touchstone for examining a BA MS, cf. also Lazar Lipschütz, *Ben-Asher — Ben-Naftali, Eine Abhandlung des Mischael b. Uzziel* (Bonn 1935); F. Pérez Castro "Corregido y correcto", *Sefarad* 15 (1955), pp. 3 ff.

26.   This superiority of A over the *Vorlage* of L may, perhaps, be inferred from the

§ 14   A few examples will illustrate this claim, but their full importance can be only evaluated later on in this paper (cf. below, §30 f.).

It should be remembered, first of all, that the problem which troubled Maimonides and which caused him to specify the MS on which he based himself (cf. above, n. 1) was that of open and closed sections. Even from those few chapters of A from the end of Deuteronomy which have escaped destruction, it is clear that this MS *agrees in every instance with the statements of Maimonides* while L diverges from them not less than four times.[27]

Maimonides = A			L
Dt. xxx, 11 (כי המצוה) :	ס		פ
xxxi, 7 (ויקרא משה) :	ס		פ
xxxi, 16 (ויאמר ה' ... הנך) :	—		ס
xxxiii, 8 (וללוי) :	פ		ס

Assuming that readers will wish to look up these passages in their copies of the *Biblia Hebraica*, I have to add, unfortunately, that also in this respect[28] the text as printed there is not reliable.[29]

§ 15   The superiority of A over L does not only express itself in complete agreement with Maimonides' statements on the subject of the sections, but also as regards the beginnings of the lines after the Song of Moses (SM = Deut. xxxii) — a question of utmost importance, as we shall see later on.[30] Additional proof of A's superiority is the layout of SM itself and the method of filling up the lines ("*Zeilenfüllung*"). Also these questions will demand our attention later on (cf. also below, n. 75, 81).

Since A's superiority over L seems rather obvious, it may not be superfluous

wording of Kahle *Cairo Genizah*, p. 61 [slightly changed in the 2nd edition, p. 111]. For the ranking of MSS attributed to BA (apart from A, of course) cf. also Castro, *op. cit.*, p. 27.

27.   If we were to extend the examination of L over the whole Pent., we would find many deviations in the matter of sections; cf. below, n. 113.

28.   Cf., in connection with another problem regarding Hebrew MSS, *Biblica* 35 (1954), p. 429 f. The *caeterum censeo* of Orlinsky concerning the apparatus of the BH is too well known to need mentioning. However, it is only fair to add that in any extensive project based on collations carried out mainly by assistants, in spite of the editor's formal responsibility, errors even on major points can hardly be avoided.

29.   In the first two passages quoted, BH has closed sections, while in xxx, 15 (ראה נתתי) the sign of the closed section has been omitted, so that one gets the erroneous impression that the MS deviates from Maimonides' rule. For my comparisons I have used photostats of L belonging to the National and University Library of Jerusalem (cf. also n. 31).

30.   For this subject cf. below, §30 f. and n. 85. As against A's agreement with the ruling of Maimonides., L deviates as follows: ויבא — לדבר — אשר — התורה — האדמה

to add that there seem to be also considerable divergencies between A and L
in plene and defective spellings.[31]

To sum up: without basing ourselves on the colophon of A, we maintain
that A is, indeed, a BA MS, and that of the two known BA codices of the
whole Bible, A seems the superior one.[32] Once we have come to that conclusion, we are allowed to take the colophon as further evidence. It will, inevitably,
remain our sole witness for the claim that A is not only a BA MS, but was
actually vocalized, accented, and embellished with the Massorah by R. Aaron
ben Asher himself.

III

§ 16   We now come to our last and most crucial problem: Is A only the best
        BA codex available to us? Is it only an additional step nearer the
desired goal? For even if we assume for the moment that the difference between
the superior BA MS before us and the model codex which was before Maimonides, and which has become hallowed in the mind of later generations, is
minimal, yet a gnawing doubt will persist for ever that we have before us
nothing but a substitute, though a rather perfect one. In fact, all hope ever to
find that codex would have to be abandoned. If A cannot be plausibly shown
to be that model codex itself, no other candidate is likely to emerge.

On the other hand, if we were able to prove that A is indeed the MS used by
Maimonides, we would not only have in our hands the model codex which
generations tried in vain to reach, but this historical sanctity would coincide
with our textual findings, according to which this MS is in fact the superior
one of the known representatives of the BA text.

31.   As an example we shall quote the differences in the fifty odd verses from Deut. xxviii
        which now form the beginning of A (note the defective spelling):

	L	A
18:	ועשתרות	ועשתרת
49:	מרחוק	מרחק
52:	הגבהות	הגבהת
58:	הכתובים	הכתבים
59:	גדלות	גדלת

        Verse 63 להיטב as printed in BH is an error for the actual להיטיב of L = A.
        Cf. above, n. 29, and below, n. 114.

32.   For details cf. Loewinger's discussion. According to this claim, it would seem that
        from now on, L should not be used as a test for judging the BA character of other
        MSS, since it has to be regarded as a MS which has not been too well harmonized
        with its BA *Vorlage*. Cf. also Yalon's queries (*Kiriath Sefer* xx (1955), p. 261) on L,
        which Castro, *Sefarad* 15 (1955), p. 6 f., has tried to rebut. Unfortunately we cannot
        compare A with BM Or. 4445 at this stage, since that MS breaks off long before
        Deut. xxviii.

§ 17   To start with, our prospects to prove this identity appear practically nil. The status of A in modern Biblical scholarship rests, as we saw, on the sole authority of Kahle. Kahle, however, who in any case had very little to go by, never pronounced on this problem. He was exclusively interested in our previous question, *i.e.* the BA character of A.

On the other hand, any identification of A with the model codex of Maimonides will have to be based on the Pentateuch only, since all the remarks of Maimonides concern that part of the Bible exclusively. No more than ca. 4% of the Pentateuch have escaped the rioters, so that there is hardly any possibility left to come to a positive conclusion.[33]

Whatever shred of a possibility remains was, however, torn apart by the most decisive blow of all: the only modern scholar who was ever privileged to study A while it was still complete[34], the late Prof. Cassuto, stated unequivocally that *A is not the Codex used by Maimonides.* Since Cassuto started out with the belief that A was that codex and later on, after having seen it, repudiated that assumption, our attempt looks hopeless. Still,, it is imperative to investigate, before deciding to break off, whether Cassuto's view must be accepted without further discussion.

33.   Cf. in the light of this below, §22 f.
34.   Though modern scholars had no access to A, others apparently sometimes had, and even succeeded in obtaining copies of it, if we can believe their tales. Thus I note that R. Samuel Solomon ben R. Moses Meir claims in his עמודי שש (Jerusalem 1892, Excursus, p. 1) that he possessed a copy; but he reveals nothing of its contents.
I was even more pleased when I discovered that R. Ḥayyim Hacohen Finfer in his book מסורת התורה והנביאים (Vilna 1906), p. 98 f. (who is known to have taken much trouble, in his own way, to collect material on the problem of open and closed sections) also used a copy of A. But there again: he talks at great length about the price he paid; of the MS itself he reveals nothing.
In spite of this, we may note the tradition which was related to him by the person who obtained the copy for him, namely, R. Isaac Moses Abulafia. For this is the only place where we find an allegedly direct tradition about the time when the Codex was written. This is how Finfer quotes the tradition: ס' תנ״ך ישן נושן כתוב על קלף מזה הזמן תרמ״ד שנה [לאלף החמישי, ונכתב לפני אלף ועשרים שנה] ככתוב תוך הספר "A very ancient copy of the Bible, written on parchment 644 years ago (*i.e.* in the year 644 of the fifth millenium [= 883–4 C.E.], written 1020 years ago — sic!) as is written in the Codex." Without dwelling too long on this piece of information, we may remark that Finfer's(?) explanation of the statement "644 years ago" as "in the year 644" could be based on some authority. Anyhow, it would not be too far out, although we can hardly believe that the codex written by Aaron Ben Asher is ten years older than the Cairo Codex written by his father. Also the fact that Ibn Buyā'ā wrote another MS some fifty years later (cf. *MdW* I, 7) almost precludes the claim. The main trouble is that all of Finfer's statements on that whole subject (cf. *ib.*, p. 100–101) are so confused and that he apparently used a number of doubtful copies of MSS, so that one has to approach his information with skepticism. It is even possible, as E. E. Urbach suggested to me, that the number 644 goes to show that Finfer was, in fact, handed a copy of a different MS altogether.

§ 18   There obtains not the slightest doubt that Cassuto, indeed, declared
         himself against A, although the opposite view was sometimes
attributed to him after his death.[35] Kahle himself, when lately summing up the
discussion, made scholars acquainted with Cassuto's real verdict and concluded
that we have no alternative but to accept it[36], for no one, — so it seemed then —
would ever again have the opportunity to study the codex.

Cassuto's decision was first announced in 1946, in the following statement[37]:

הוצאת ספר זה מבוססת על כתב היד של ספרי הנביאים שנכתב בעיר טבריה בידי
משה בן־אשר, אחד מחכמי המסורה החשובים ביותר, בשנת שמונה מאות ועשרים ושבע אחר
חרבן הבית השני... כתב יד זה, הנשמר עכשיו בקאהיר, היה כולל מעיקרו גם את התורה
ואת הכתובים ואולי הוא הספר שעליו סמך הרמב״ם כשקבע את
הפרטים שבפרק ח׳ מהלכות ספר תורה. אמנם לפי הדעה הרווחת הספר
שעליו סמך הרמב״ם היה ה־כתר־ של אהרן בן־משה בן־אשר, הנשמר עכשיו בעיר חלב;
אבל מתוך בדיקה מדוייקת ב־״כתר־ זה מצד המנהל המדעי הנ״ל,
שנסע לחלב לשם כך בשנת תש״ד, יצא לו בבירור שדעה זו אינה נכונה.

"The edition of this Book is based upon the codex of the Prophets which was
written at Tiberias by Moses Ben Asher, one of the most outstanding Massoretes,
in the year 827 after the destruction of the Second Temple. . . This codex, now
preserved at Cairo, originally comprised also the Pentateuch and the Hagiographa. It may well be that *this is the manuscript upon which Maimonides relied
in formulating the details in chapter viii of Hilkhoth Sefer Torah.* Admittedly,
it is widely believed that the manuscript upon which Maimonides relied was
the 'Crown' of Aaron ben Moses ben Asher, now preserved at Aleppo; however,
*a thorough examination of that 'Crown' by the above-mentioned Scientific
Director*[38], who visited Aleppo for this purpose in 1944, *made it quite clear
to him that this view is wrong.*" (My italics, M.G.).

Cassuto never changed his view on this matter. He both published it himself[39],
and mentioned it in his letters to Kahle, who later quoted from the contents of

35.   It is not impossible that the Introduction of the so-called "Jerusalem (Bible) Edition"
      (1953), which singles out for mention A only, contributed to the spreading of this
      erroneous view. Yet the actual words used in that introduction are correct, since it
      does not state that Cassuto *used* A, but only that he *studied* it! Cf. above, §11 and n. 48.
36.   After quoting Cassuto (cf. immediately below), Kahle felt obliged to sum up (VT
      1 (1951), p. 163 f.): ". . . . He is the first modern scholar who had the opportunity
      of doing so [of studying the Codex], and he will have been the last one if the news of
      the destruction of the Codex is confirmed. We are therefore dependent for this Codex
      on the information Cassuto has to give, and everything that has been said before on the
      Codex has to be regarded in the main as antiquated...."; "There is no point in discussing
      these matters again. We will have to await the information that Cassuto is able to give us.
37.   The statement accompanies the sample edition of the Book of Jonah which the Hebrew
      University of Jerusalem Press published in the summer of 1946.
38.   *i.e.* Cassuto.
39.   The earliest reference to it by Cassuto himself is in *Ha'aretz* 2.I.1948.

this correspondence in various scholarly periodicals.[40] Cassuto may possibly have experienced doubts concerning the "positive" part of his theory, *viz.* his elevation of C to the rank of Maimonides' model codex (cf. below, §20 f., and esp. note 46). But he did not retract his negative judgment of A, which has already been admitted into text books[41] as the last word on our subject.

§ 19   It would not have been too much to expect that the attempt to deprive
A of the position which it was accorded by the Jews of Aleppo[42], and which had been accepted by scholars on Kahle's authority, should be accompanied by decisive or at least reasonable proof. It is therefore rather amazing that Cassuto did never find it necessary to justify his damning verdict.

A thorough search throughout Cassuto's writings and public utterances, and even questioning those who were connected with his Bible edition from 1944 onward, produced no result whatever. All that can be discovered is the kind of statement he published in *Ha'aretz* (2.I.48):

רגילים לחשוב שהספר שסמך עליו הרמב־ם היה דוקא ה־כתר־ של ארם צובא.
ולכאורה נראה הדבר קרוב מאד. ואולם מרשה אני לעצמי להטיל בזה ספק, מפני
טעמים טכניים שאין כאן המקום ליחד עליהם את הדיבור.

"One usually assumes that the book on which Maimonides relied was the Aleppo Codex. Ostensibly, this seems likely enough. Yet I permit myself to doubt it for *technical reasons which this is not the place to set out in detail*". (my italics — M.G.). What a pity that these technical reasons were never set out elsewhere. Similarly, in his letter to Kahle, written at the same time (cf. VT 3 (1953), p. 418): "This tradition [about A] which you regard as indubitable is certainly very old, but it is not proved, and there are some reasons for querying it".

One may take it for granted that Cassuto pondered his decision a great deal: his explanation to Kahle (see below, §21) gives the impression that he himself was not quite convinced. Perhaps it is for this reason that he refrained from publishing his reasons. Our suggestion advanced below (§23, esp. notes 51, 55) may provide a solution to this riddle.

§ 20   In any event, there is no doubt that as a result of his negative attitude
towards A, Cassuto went one step further, and a decisive one at that.

40.   In VT 1 (1951), p. 164, as well as in his article "The Ben Asher Text of the Hebrew Bible", in *Donum Natalicium H.S. Nyberg oblatum* (1955).
41.   Cf. M. H. Segal, *Mevo' Ha-Miqra'* IV (1950), p. 898; Z. Ben-Ḥayyim, s.v. "Ben-Asher" in *Encyclopaedia 'Ivrith* IX (1958), col. 41.
42.   I should like to stress that Cassuto did not recognize A as being the MS which Maimonides used, yet repeatedly upheld the view that it is BA MS (cf. above § 12). Kahle sums up his correspondence with Cassuto (VT 1, p. 164) as follows: "Cassuto has not any doubt that the Aleppo Codex is a real Ben Asher codex".

Obviously Cassuto could have arrived at his negative decision as regards A only because it did not agree with Maimonides' rules in some detail in its Pentateuchal part. In assuming now C to be Maimonides' MS, Cassuto accorded this honour to a codex which does not contain the Pentateuch at all! Consequently there was no possibility that it might disagree with the ruling of Maimonides. The claim of C, so it must have seemed to him, could not be disproved. But then there was no possibility ever to prove it.

The Cairo MS of *Moses* ben Asher was elevated by Cassuto, though with the proviso "perhaps"[43], to the rank of "the MS which Maimonides used", and thus was chosen to assume in the Bible edition which he was then planning the central position originally reserved for A.[44]

§ 21   To invalidate Cassuto's hypothesis as regards C does not automatically mean promoting the case of A. Yet I must point out that also in our view (cf. above, n. 43), this hypothesis is contrary to all available evidence. The very possibility of proving it being absent from the start, it could not be more than a guess, and we would be entitled to dismiss it without hesitation. But even on its own merits it lacks all foundation. We have no right to assume that C ever was a codex of the complete Bible, so that it would at least on this point fit in with the statement of Maimonides that he used a codex of the whole Bible (cf. above, n. 1). On the contrary, all the signs point in the opposite direction, especially the existence of the extremely full colophon after the Prophets, which would be out of keeping in a MS where originally the Hagiographa still

43. Kahle convincingly summed up his doubts concerning C in *Donum. . . Nyberg*, p. 165 f., and especially emphasized that there is no justification to suppose that this MS, at any time, formed part of a complete Bible codex, as is implied by Maimonides' statement (cf. below, §21). On the other hand, the objection advanced by B. Toledano (*Ha'aretz* 2.X.1949), that Cassuto's hypothesis is contrary to the evidence of R. David ben Zimra (the great Rabbinic authority in the 16th century who allegedly testified in favour of A) — whose testimony ought to be accepted blindly — is hardly convincing even if the whole matter of the responsum of Ben-Zimra were not based on an error (cf. Ben-Zvi's article, above p. 8). Although we now possess alternative information concerning that tradition from the pen of R. Joseph Ashkenazi (cf. Scholem, *Tarbiz* 28 (1958), p. 75), all information of this type must be taken as the foundation of the "legend" woven around A, and certainly does not prove it. Moreover, none of it is early enough to enable us to dispense with further investigation [cf. *Cairo Geniza*[2], p. 94].
44. I do not wish to join the discussion about the so-called "Jerusalem (Bible) Edition". But I consider it my duty to emphasize that I have no doubt that the decisive step — namely, to accord pre-eminence to C for the Books of the Prophets (that is as far as this MS goes) while using MSS of different character as a basis for the text in the rest of the Bible — was entirely Cassuto's own. The confusion which was the necessary outcome of giving preference to C, and which resulted in a change of vocalization in the one part (the Prophets) of this edition as against the rest, was remarked upon especially by Yalon in *Ha'aretz* 16.IV.1954 and later by Kahle, *Donum . . . Nyberg*, p. 162 f.

followed.[45] The contents of the colophon, the dedications[46], and the additional evidence of the Ashkenazi Rabbi of Cairo at the beginning of this century[47], all these deprive Cassuto's hypothesis — which he apparently adopted rather rashly,", on the rebound", after A disappointed him — of any verisimilitude.

In addition Cassuto seems to have gone a long way towards retracting his hypothesis. In his article in *Ha'aretz* of the 2.I.48 he did not even mention it. And in his last article in which he summed up this subject (*Ha'aretz*, 15.IV.1949) he made no reference to C, while mentioning again A[48].

Moreover, he expressly wrote to Kahle at that time (cf. V.T. 3 (1953), 418): "That the codex used by Maimonides is that of which the part containing the Prophets [*sic!* — M.G.] is preserved today at Cairo, is mentioned only in a tentative way in the prospectus attached to the edition of Jonah, *and is not more than a conjecture* [my italics — M.G.]. All the same, the reasons which you advance to the contrary are not so strong as to exclude this possibility." But again, even to fellow scholars, not so much as a hint about the reasons for his far-reaching decision.

In spite of these rather discouraging circumstances, I hope that the discussion presented in the following chapters will lead us in the right path. Our argumentation will perforce be neither simple nor direct. It is, however, precisely the extraordinary facts I intend to marshal here which have imbued me with the faith that our solution is correct.

IV

§22 At first sight the few pages of the Pentateuch preserved in A offer conclusive proof that the Codex is not identical with the MS which Maimonides used. Maimonides states (cf. above, n. 1) that he noted down the open and closed sections as well as the layout of the two Pentateuchal songs according to that model codex. In his own words *(loc. cit.,* end of chapter viii):

45. Cf. also Dothan, *Sinai* 41 (1957), p. 296.
46. The whole of the colophon refers only to the Prophets. It is, furthermore, rather improbable that, had C ever been a codex of the whole Bible in Maimonides' time, just one part of it would have been singled out later on for dedication in such an elaborate form, with the other parts disappearing — and the legend adhering to another BA MS. It is really too much to postulate all these vicissitudes without very strong reasons. Cf. also Kahle (above, n. 43).
47. After an examination of the MS he decided that there is no sign that it ever contained more than the Prophets or that there are pages missing at the beginning, as might erroneously be assumed from Sapir's note on this MS. This information was given to Finfer cf. *op. cit.* note 34, p. 99 f.).
48. לא רציתי ליהר על העיון בספר חשוב זה, "I did not wish to forgo the examination [*sic,* M. G.] of this important MS." This formulation agrees perfectly with the somewhat amazing text of the introduction to the "Jerusalem Edition" (cf. above, §11 and n. 36).

צורת שירת האזינו: כל שיטה ושיטה יש באמצעה רווח אחד כצורת הפרשה הסתומה,
ונמצאת כל שיטה חלוקה לשתים. וכותבין אותה בשבעים שיטה.

"The layout of the Song of Moses: Every single line has a space in its middle like a closed section, so that every line is divided into two. And it is written *in seventy lines*." In what follows, with a degree of precision never attempted before, he faithfully writes out all the words which start each one of the 140 hemistichs cf. also below, §31 f.).

Maimonides' statement is unequivocal. The number of lines, namely 70, as mentioned in the heading to that paragraph, agrees with the number of words we find written down there, no matter whether we consult the first or the latest edition of Maimonides' *Code*.[49] This is Maimonides' apparent decision on the basis of the BA MS to which he gave his approval, and this decision was accepted by all later decisors (cf. *Shulḥan 'Arukh, Yoreh De'ah*, cclxxv, 5). Such is the rule to the present day, as can easily be seen from the usual Bible editions.

Nothing easier, therefore, than to arrive at a conclusion on our issue. Counting the lines in A, we immediately see that SM (=Song of Moses, Deut. xxxii) is portioned off in *sixty-seven lines*. By necessity a number of the words which Maimonides mentions as being the beginnings of hemistichs do not tally either.

This would seem to be conclusive proof against the proposed identification; even though we found A to be a superior BA MS, it cannot possibly be the model codex which Maimonides used and which we hoped to discover. The facts, so to speak, stare one in the face, and one cannot help coming up against them at the first serious comparison. Though Cassuto did not intimate his reasons for disqualifying A from being the MS which Maimonides used[50], I feel that when he saw the MS at Aleppo, he was struck by this discrepancy and considered it such definite proof against the identification that he entertained no further doubts. Since the facts are so unambiguously presented in all the editions of the *Code* as well as later in the authoritative *Shulḥan 'Arukh*, it would not be fair to ask why Cassuto accepted what he found printed and did not continue his enquiry; all the more so since the conditions under which he worked at Aleppo made any further enquiry almost impossible (cf. his description of the difficult conditions in *Ha'aretz*, 2.I.48).

§23   We have stressed that we must assume that Cassuto disqualified A solely because it did not agree with one of the data specified by Maimo-

---

49.   I use the first edition (Rome 1480, p. 72) according to the photographic reproduction published by Mosad ha-Rav Kook, Jerusalem 1955, and have compared the edition *Rambam la-'Am*, Mosad ha-Rav Kook, Jerusalem n. d. [1957], p. 206.
50.   Stressing at the same time the fact that he considered A a true BA MS; cf. above, n. 42. This is a very important point, as we shall see presently.

nides (who dealt with the Pentateuch only). In other words: Cassuto's consideration was perforce of a *halakhic* nature.[51]

The above paragraph of the *Code* (cf. note 1) deals with three major items: 1) The open and closed sections, 2) The Song of Moses (Deut. xxxii), 3) The Song of the Sea (Ex. xv).

As regards the open and the closed sections, it is well known that errors and doubts already arose in the first generation after Maimonides, as can be seen from a statement of R. Meir ben Todros Ha-Levi Abulafia (Toledo, ca. 1170–1244), as quoted by R. Menaḥem ha-Meiri (Perpignan, ca. 1249–1306) in the latter's work *Kiriath Sefer* (II, 2, ed. Hirschler, Jerus. 1946, p. 46 f., cf. n. 106, 109). Again, ever since that time the Decisors are known to have been in doubt as to Maimonides' position with regard to certain details in the layout of the beginning of the Song of the Sea (Ex. xv). That is to say: we cannot rule out that in the part of A now lost, Cassuto may have found a contradictory detail with regard to these points. But since such possible contradictions were to be expected, on the basis of the existing literature, we doubt that Cassuto would have taken so fatal a step with so little apparent reason. Any divergency on the part of A in that respect could easily have been interpreted away. More decisive still: were the reason some disagreement, say, in the matter of open and closed sections, this would certainly not have been too technical a matter for mention. There would have been nothing easier for Cassuto than to state that A does not agree in its treatment of the sections with the *Code*. Why then should he have avoided giving his reason on the ground that it was too technical?

The position is totally different as regards SM. In every edition of Maimonides' *Code* which Cassuto could have consulted, he would have found the same evidence against the identification of A. Nor does the usual halakhic literature (which he might have consulted as an additional precaution) contain any reference to doubts as to Maimonides' position with regard to the layout of SM (cf. below, chapter V). In other words: Cassuto's reason was halakhic, and the only halakhic item which justifiably could have appeared divergent enough to base on it a negative verdict on A, and which, at the same time, would be too technical to be mentioned in passing, was the problem of SM.

To sum up: Cassuto never explained his reasons, neither those against A, nor those in favour of C. As regards C, we have already seen that his claim is totally void. As regards A, we are in no position to disprove an argument which has never been advanced and, in any event, we need not be detained by it. Yet it seems to me likely that we have discovered the only obvious reason for rejecting A, Cassuto could have had.

51. That his reason was halakhic was confirmed to me also, to the best of his recollection, by Mr. A. Even-Zahav, who accompanied Cassuto on his journey to Aleppo.

§ 24   Precisely because the facts against A are so obvious, I dare to ask
        all the more for serious consideration of my contention, which is
no less than this: *All that has been stated in our editions of the Code on the
subject of the writing of SM (and which is binding halakhah) in fact never
was the ruling of Maimonides, as evidenced by the MSS of the Code.* The opposite
is the case: Maimonides' decision is identical with the layout of A, and is
thus contrary to the widely accepted tradition of writing SM in seventy lines,
which found its main formulation in the tractate *Soferim.* Through a remarkable
process of harmonization and as a result of halakhic objections and reasonings
raised against Maimonides' true decision[52], his ruling was altered until it
became identical with the accepted tradition of writing the song in seventy lines.
*This apocryphal decision was the one which found its way into the first printed
edition of the Code* and, as we shall see, convinced later generations that they
acted on Maimonides' ruling when they accepted the layout in seventy lines as
binding halakhah (cf. below, n. 98).

        Maimonides' true decision, however, as regards SM itself as well as the
arrangement of the page and the writing of the lines before and after SM
(cf. below § 30 f., 35 f.), a ruling which to later Decisors seemed unbelievable —
and according to their assumptions rightly so — *becomes intelligible from the
one and only existing MS whose method completely tallies with the statements of
Maimonides. This is the very MS which according to tradition was used by him,
viz. the Aleppo Codex.*

§ 25   It is obvious that one must not rely on the sole evidence of tradition
        or a colophon (as Kahle perforce did). But when these are confirmed
by study of the MS itself (and under such amazing circumstances, as we shall
see), that tradition may be taken as corroborative evidence (cf. also below,
§42).[53] The very text which according to internal criteria was shown to be the
most reliable representative of the Ben Asher tradition will turn out on all

52.   Cf. below, §36 f., n. 97. It seems that the substitution was facilitated by the fact that
       Maimonides decided expressly on the basis of one MS and took no account whatsoever
       of other traditions already hallowed for generations (as embodied in *Sof.*). With much
       reservation, I would add that it is not impossible that doubt was cast on the authoritative
       character of the MS as such. But we have no right to put this point forward in any
       discussion of Ben Asher's alleged Karaite leanings (cf. below, §33).
53.   It might be claimed with some ingenuity that at this moment, when at long last we
       have found *one* MS which is in complete agreement with Maimonides' rulings, we
       found in fact only an identical twin of the MS which Maimonides saw. Such a possible
       argument for argument's sake would hardly deserve our attention. However, not only
       are such completely identical twins quite unknown in the history of Bible MSS, and
       it would be necessary to confirm such assumption with convincing proof; but it would
       be more than strange that the tradition — which obviously knew nothing of the
       internal evidence that we can detect — should single out just the Aleppo Codex and

the internal and external evidence available to be the model codex used by Maimonides. Its text bears, therefore, the stamp of authority for which generations have searched in vain. *The legend is true.*[54]

§ 26   Having outlined our claim in general terms[55], we shall now set it out in detail. We begin with the question of the layout of SM in seventy lines. As mentioned (cf. above, § 22), this is the reading of the printed editions ever since the *editio princeps*. However, when we turn to the MSS of the *Code*, especially the Yemenite and Spanish as distinct from the Ashkenazi ones (cf. below, §§27, 37), we find a different tradition holding the field almost exclusively.

Of decisive importance, of course, is the famous MS Ox. Hunt. 80.[56] Not only the catch-line וכותבין אותה בשבע ושׁשׁים שׁיטות *"and it is written in sixty-seven lines"* agrees with the facts of A, but also the enumerated beginnings

claim it to be that MS. In addition, we shall still see that A was apparently rather unique even in Maimonides' time (cf. below, n. 80 and §§31, 33).

54.   Dean Lieberman kindly drew my attention to a further point. The Aleppo community boasted in former times not only the possession of A: it also owned a copy of Maimonides' *Code*, the accuracy of which was guaranteed by the master's own signature [on this point as well as on our witnesses for this matter, cf. N. Ben-Menaḥem, *Studies in Bibliography and Book-Lore* 3 (1957), p. 52, who mentions that this is the copy known to scholars as Oxford Hunt. 80 (cf. below §26) — M. G.]. While the learned Rabbis of Aleppo were perhaps no experts on BA MSS, any obvious discrepancy between A and that copy of the *Code* would certainly have struck them.

55.   According to my conclusions I have no choice but to infer that Cassuto erred in his decision as regards A — and I have tried to show how he was led into error (cf. above, end of §23). Had there still been a shred of doubt as regards his erroneous claim in favour of C — which I believe to be the result of his disappointment with A — this doubt will be dispelled by our restoring A to its position of honour. This, of course, also removes the last vestige of justification for publishing an eclectic edition, prepared "as closely as possible to the form fixed by the school of Massoretes of the Ben Asher family" (cf. Cassuto's last public formulation of the issue, *Ha'aretz* 15.IV.1949); cf. also above, n. 44.

In order to prevent any misunderstanding, I would like to add that all I have stated as regards C should not be construed so as to support Yalon's claim, (*Ha'aretz*, 16.IV.1954), who doubts that C is the codex of *Moses* ben Asher. We have just found out, to our great dismay, how irritating is this habit of scholars to deprive our most distinguished MSS of their status without setting out their reasons — without which one cannot, of course, discuss the matter. Since much importance is, deservedly, accorded to Yalon's statements in the field of Massorah studies, it is to be hoped that he will not content himself with casual remarks on so important a subject. The fact that in *Hatzofeh* of 10.IV.1959 he did not repeat this opinion of his against C, while mentioning others who doubted the genuineness of its colophon, is liable to increase the confusion even further.

56.   Cat. Neubauer 577 (cf. above, n. 54). This is the most highly regarded MS of the book *Ahabah* of the *Code*, and that not only on account of Maimonides' signature at its end. For the authority of this MS cf. now also Goldschmidt in ידיעות המכון לחקר השירה

of each hemistich. In order to facilitate the comparison, I arrange here the beginnings of the hemistichs as quoted in the MS of the *Code*.[57]

1. האזינו – ותשמע	35. ותלהט – אספה
2. יערף – תזל	36. חצי – מזי
3. כשעירם – וכרביבים	37. וקטב – רשן
4. כי – הבו	38. עם – מחוץ
5. הצור – כי	39. גם – אמרתי
6. אל – צדיק	40. אשביתה – לולי
7. שחת – דור	41. פן – פן
8. הלה' – עם	42. ולא – כי
9. הלוא – הוא	43. ואין – לו
10. זכר – שאל	44. יבינו – איכה
11. בהנחל – בהפרידו	45. ושנים – אם
12. יצב – למספר	46. וה' – כי
13. כי – יעקב	47. ואיבינו – כי
14. ימצאהו – ובתהו	48. ומשדמת – ענבמו
15. יסבבנהו – יצרנהו	49. אשכלת – חמת
16. כנשר – יפרש	50. וראש – הלא
17. ה' – ואין	51. חתום – לי
18. ירכבהו – ויאכל	52. לעת – כי
19. וינקהו – ושמן	53. וחש – כי
20. חמאת – עם	54. ועל – כי
21. בני(!) – עם	55. ואפס – ואמר
22. ודם – וישמן	56. צור – אשר
23. שמנת – ויטש	57. ישתו – יקומו
24. וינבל – יקנאהו	58. יהי – ראו
25. בתועבת – יזבחו	59. ואין – אני
26. אלהים – חדשים	60. מחצתי – ואין
27. לא – צור	61. כי – ואמרתי
28. ותשכח – וירא	62. אם – ותאחז
29. מכעס – ויאמר	63. אשיב – ולמשנאי
30. אראה – כי	64. אשכיר – וחרבי
31. בנים – הם	65. מדם – מראש
32. כעסוני – ואני	66. הרנינו – כי
33. בגוי – כי	67. ונקם – וכפר
34. ותיקד – ותאכל	

העברית VII (Jerusalem 1959), p. 187. On the question of adding the author's *khaṭṭ*, cf. Blau, *Tarbiz* 27 (1958), 542; Stern and Sassoon, *ib.* 29 (1960), 266.

57.   Because of spelling differences in the various MSS of the *Code*, I quote all the words according to the spelling of A.

§ 27   This version would have been of the greatest importance, even if
unsupported by other MSS. The fact is that practically all the MSS
which ʒ had the opportunity to consult, and apparently all the Spanish and
Yemenite ones (cf. below, §37 f. and n. 71, 102 a), support it.[58]

For instance: MS Budapest Kaufmann 77[59], Vienna 57[60], London BM
Har. 5698[61], Casanatense 3203, Angelica 76, Rovigo 209[62], Padua 549[63],
Vatican 172[64], as well as all the Yemenite MSS housed in the above-mentioned
libraries in Jerusalem.[65]

§ 28.   There exists another group of MSS of the *Code* which also mentions
"sixty-seven lines" in the catch-line, but is set apart from the first
group by an error which must be regarded as stemmatic: the word יפרש
(line 16) is quoted as opening the first as well as the second hemistich! To this
group — the majority, if not all, of which are Ashkenazi MSS — belong,
inter alia, Oxf. Seld. Arch. B 2[66], Sassoon (the photostat has no number and
I was not able to identify it), Tübingen 12/7[67], and Nuremberg Fen. V 58,20.[68]
This common error seems to be based on a mishap in copying marginal
corrections, similar to that in the peculiar MS Oxf. Can. Or. 78 (Neubauer
568). It is not impossible that this MS itself forms the actual basis of the mistake.
This is one of the very few MSS where, though the original reading was "seventy
lines", a second hand corrected the text so as to make it agree with the system

58.   Since in this article I am not engaged in classifying the MSS of Maimonides' *Code*,
I have mainly restricted myself to collating MSS to which I could gain access in Jerusalem and Rome without too much trouble. I wish to express my sincere thanks to the
National and University Library and to the Mosad ha-Rav Kook in Jerusalem, as well
as to the other libraries I have mentioned below, who placed their treasures at my
disposal.
59.   Written in 1295, according to the catalogue of M. Weisz (1906).
60.   According to the catalogue of Zachariah Schwarz, a German MS of the fourteenth
century.
61.   No. 486, written in 1472, according to the catalogue of G. Margoliouth.
62.   In the *Biblioth. dell' Acad. dei Concordi Silvestriani* according to a note on the photostat.
63.   In the *Biblioth. del Seminario*, according to a note on the photostat.
64.   The photostat is marked as Vat. 175. This seems improbable, bearing in mind Assema-
ni's description. I failed to check the reference while using the original. Because of the
absence of catalogues, I cannot give more exact data as regards the MSS just mentioned.
65.   As for the MSS in the National and University Library of Jerusalem, Jer. Heb. 8°
1183 was written in 1382; Jer. Heb. 4° 444 in 1657; and 4° 445 seems to hail from the
same period. Sometimes one of the words is omitted in a MS ; these are the usual
scribal mishaps. The overall number is always correct.
66.   Neubauer 569 has no date; the MS seems to be of the 15th cent.
67.   Formerly no. 7 in Steinschneider's catalogue of the Berlin Hebrew MSS (Or. Fol. 12).
According to him it was written in the 14th–15th cent.
68.   Details about this MS, the photostat of which has a note to the effect that it is now
kept at the Landeskirchliches Archiv, are not known to me.

of sixty-seven lines. According to the system of seventy lines, the word יפרש
stands at the beginning of a first hemistich. The corrector added a cancelling
sign and the word was added as opening of a second hemistich. Thus (or in
some such way) the enumeration of hemistichs in these MSS became corrupted.[69]

Except for this last MS, which originally read "seventy lines", every MS
I have seen[70] — the most important one being, of course, Hunt. 80 — supports
the 67-line system.

§ 29   In §22 above I mentioned that the *Shulḥan 'Arukh* perpetuated the
        method of writing SM in seventy lines as a binding rule. But this rule
is obligatory only on scribes of Pentateuch scrolls for ritual use; it does not
necessarily apply to the writing of Pentateuchal codices. Here we find various
types, among them old MSS which still bear witness to the tradition of sixty-
seven lines.[71]

In general, the possibilities are more varied than one would imagine in the
first moment.[72] The number of lines is not fixed: sometimes they fall below
sixty-seven[73], while other MSS have even more than seventy.[74] But by no means

69.   It is difficult to obtain a clear picture of the true nature of this MS which, according
       to the statement of its scribe in the colophon, was written in 1184/85, that is to say,
       within the lifetime of Maimonides. This date appears very unlikely from the palaeographic
       point of view and it has been questioned before. I have no doubt that the colophon
       was written by the scribe himself; cf. the page in Neubauer, *Facsimiles of Hebrew
       Manuscripts in the Bodleian Library*, etc. (Oxford 1886), pl. XXIII. To correct the date
       (claiming that there is a small line which was erased) and to read 1045 (תתרמ־ה
       instead of תתקמ־ה) would be, of course, pointless, because that year would simply
       have been written as ח־מ This MS altogether has some amazing errors, and also
       the text of the colophon, which speaks of רבנו משה ן׳ מימון תנצב־ה, "Our Teacher
       Moses son of Maimon, may his soul be bound up in the bundle of life" (without
       adding the word *Rabbi* to the name of his father) seems rather peculiar. Altogether I
       would suspect intentional mystification rather than a case of copying the colophon
       from a *Vorlage*.
70.   Since our choice of examples is random, depending on the MSS which happened to
       be accessible, it may be assumed that the numerical relationship is not without interest.
       I did not see a MS which reads "seventy lines" without any marginal correction;
       but no doubt there are such.
71.   E. g. the sumptuous MS Casanatense 21 (= Ken. 447, Spanish square script, 12th–13th
       cent.); Vat. Ross. 363. According to my — by no means exhaustive — investigations,
       the author of *Iggereth Soferim* (cf. below, §27) had good reason for maintaining that
       this is a tradition prevalent in Spanish MSS — and one ought to add, Yemenite
       (cf. also above, beginning of §27, and below, n. 102a).
72.   Again, I can only exemplify, but in this case I have gone over hundreds of MSS pre-
       served in Italian libraries. The subject as such deserves more that the summary treatment
       which can be accorded to it in this paper.
73.   E. g. Vat. 475 which has sixty-six lines, since the words גם בחור...אגור are written
       in one line; on the other hand, Vat. 503 has sixty-eight lines.
74.   E. g. Firenze pl. I 30 (written in 1290).

[24]   796

should we imagine that all MSS come near that number[75], because the scribe may simply write the song in two columns (לבנה על גבי לבנה, "like bricks one on top of the other") as exemplified by L.[76] Of special interest are those MSS which still exemplify a custom declared impermissible by the halakhah[77], viz. writing SM in the same manner as the "Song of the Sea".[78]

75. It should be stressed that L, which until now served as a kind of substitute for A, is not written according to this system, and the number of lines in that MS is only slightly more than half the number of lines mentioned by Maimonides. Only the separation of hemistichs reveals the character of the Song, but (unlike the printed layout in BH) the division does not correspond to any poetical or contextual criterion. Thus, e.g., line 1 ends with תזל, line 3 with ואין, line 5 with עשך, etc. It is superfluous to add that this is an important point in considering the question of the connection between L and A. Cf. above, §15 and below, note 81.

76. From the statement of Rabbenu Tam, for instance, it may be deduced that writing the Song in two equal hemistichal columns was not yet an accepted practice at his time (vid. Hil. Sefer Torah in Wertheimer, Ginze Yerushalayim I, 18 f. = Maḥzor Vitry (cf. below, note 87).
    It should be noted that Jacob ben Ḥayyim in his Rabbinic Bible (1525) still printed SM after the fashion of writing the "Ten Sons of Haman" in Esther Scrolls, that is, a broad column on the one side and a narrow one on the other (לבנה על גבי לבנה ואריח על גבי אריח).
    MSS which contain also the Targum often have three columns, one of them reserved for the Targum; cf., for instance, Vat. Ebr. 439–440.

77. Cf. below, note 98.

78. This pattern of "broken lines" is not easily described in words, and is best comprehended by looking up Ex. xv in any printed edition of the Pentateuch. As an example for writing SM after this fashion cf. the following layout from Barb. Or. 161 (13th cent. ?). (In the following quotations I have not tried to reproduce the actual plene and defective spellings of each MS.)

	האזינו	השמים ואדברה ותשמע הארץ
אמרי פי יערף כמטר לקחי	אמרתי כשעירם	תזל כטל
עלי דשא		וכרביבים עלי עשב כי שם ה'
אקרא הבו גדל לאלהינו הצור	פעליׄ כי כל דרכיו משפט אל אמונה ואין עול	תמים
צדיק		וישר הוא שחת לו לא בניו מומם
דור עקש ומ...לתל הלה' תגמלו	עם נבל ולא חכם הלוא הוא אביך קנך הוא	זאת
עשך וגו'		

The basic idea is the same in Vat. Heb. 5 (an Ashkenazi MS which, in my view, is centuries later than the specified date, 840 C. E.):

	האזינו	
ואדברה		השמים
	ותשמע הארץ	
יערף		אמרי פי
	כמטר לקחי	
אמרתי		תזל כטל
	כשעירם עלי	
בים עלי		דשא וכרבי
	עשב כי שם וגו'	

In a slightly different execution, Firenze pl. III, 4 (Spanish square script, 13th-14th cent.):

Very rarely the Song is written without any external distinction, "like the rest of the Pentateuchal text" כשאר הכתב.[79]

Yet, among all the many and diverse MSS, we have not found another MS which agrees with the ruling of Maimonides both as regards the number and incipits of the hemistichs of SM, and the lines following it (cf. immediately), as does the Aleppo Codex.[80]

§ 30   At this juncture we must briefly deal with the lines preceding and following SM. Maimonides leaves us in no doubt (*Hil. Sefer Torah* vii, 10) that also as regards this question he had no formulated *halakhah* before him. But this was one of those rules שלא נאמרו בתלמוד ונהגו בהם הסופ־ רים, וקבלה היא בידם איש מפי איש "which are not stated in the Talmud, but the scribes practised them, each generation receiving it by word of mouth from its predecessors". In the light of Maimonides' remarks (ib. viii, 4) on the BA Codex, it is obvious that his rules concerning the beginnings of the lines before and after SM are based on the authority of that same MS. The following are the incipits of the lines preceding SM (Deut. xxxi, 28 f.):

ואעידה

אחרי

הדרך

באחרית

להכעיסו

קהל׳

After the poem Maimonides mentions only *five* lines, beginning, respectively (Deut. xxxii, 44 f.):

ויבא

לדבר

אשר

הזאת

אשר

note 78 contd.   האזינו השמים ואדברה

פי יערף כמטר   ותשמע הארץ אמרי

לקחי תזל כטל אמרתי כשעירם עלי

עשב כי שם ה׳   דשא וכרביבים עלי

אקרא הבו גדל לאלהינו הצור וגו׳

For this type cf. also Vat. Borg. 17 (13th–14th cent.), Vat. Ross. 554, (14th–15th cent.).

79.   E. g. Firenze, pl. III, 3, written apparently in 1291. On the problem of כשאר הכתב cf. below, notes 97–98.

80.   As the Hebrew saying goes: " 'Not having seen' is no proof." But if among hundreds of MSS examined by me there was not a single one which agreed with A — neither amongst early, nor among later ones — this fact may be added as cumulative evidence

On consulting A in the facsimile, we not only see that such is indeed the case, but we also understand how the scribe achieved this adaptation of the text to the given width of his page: by filling in the lines with meaningless shapes resembling the ductus of letters (*Zeilenfüllung*). As we shall see presently, this is a matter of major importance.

§ 31   Not only is A the only MS known today which agrees in all these details (cf. § 36) with all of Maimonides' rulings on the writing of SM and the adjacent verses[81]; it must have been, to say the least, extraordinary, if not unique, in Maimonides' own time. For this reason his decision was bound to arouse surprise, especially as it was opposed to a different and apparently universally accepted tradition.[82] On this subject we have the express evidence of *ha-Meiri*, quoting R. Meir ben Ṭodros of Toledo, who asked the translator, R. Samuel ibn Tibbon, to verify the wording of Maimonides' ruling from his copy.[83] This is how R. Meir summed up his efforts: אך ענין "ויבא משה- לא יכולתי להכריע בו דבר ותמה אני אם אינו טעות סופר. ואני בספרי לא כתבתי כן, זולתי כאשר נמצא בכל הספרים הישנים המדוייקים הנמ־ צאים בארצות האלה, שהם: ובא (=ויבא) – הדברים – לכתבם (=לבבכם) – אשר – התורה.

"Regarding the matter of ויבא משה I was not able to come to any decision, and *I wonder whether it is not a scribal error*. In my own scroll of the Law I have not written in this way, but as it is found *in all the old and exact scrolls found in these lands*, namely: – ובא (= ויבא) – העם – הדברים – לכתבם (=לבבכם) – אשר התורה.

The testimony of R. Meir cannot be valued highly enough. The data, as quoted by ha-Meiri — both as regards SM itself (*Kiriath Sefer*, p. 41) and as regards the lines followings it (p. 38) — fit those quoted in the MSS of Maimo-

for the apparent uniqueness of the Aleppo Codex, which can already be inferred from the statement of R. Meir; cf. below, §31 and end of §36.

81.   Besides the many disagreements between L and Maimonides' statements, the secondary nature of L is also apparent in that it has simplified the method of filling in the lines before SM. Instead of the letter-like shapes for filling any empty space, which can be seen clearly in the photograph of A, L uses within the line dots only. At the end of the line one finds a different sign. Cf. above, §15 and note 75, and below, note 93.

82.   Yet, Maimonides' ruling concerning the lines after SM was at least not opposed to an early written and definite tradition like that of the seventy lines as regards the Song itself. Hence, after R. Meir's hesitation, as we shall see, a "compromise" was reached. Maimonides' ruling on writing SM was explained away, while his tradition concerning the lines following it was accepted and became fixed practice! (The fact that through some scribal mishap the *Ṭur* and the *Shulḥan 'Arukh* quote וידבר in place of לדבר, is not part of our issue here; cf., for instance, the commentary *Sifthe Kohen* to *Shulḥan 'Arukh, Yoreh De'ah*, end of §275).

83.   R. Menaḥem ha-Meiri, *Kiriath Sefer* (ed. Hirschler, 1956), p. 46 f.

nides' *Code*, and are identical with the system of A. In fact, R. Meir expressly justifies himself for deviating from Maimonides as regards the lines *after* the poem.[84] Nevertheless he felt compelled to reject what he found written down as Maimonides' ruling because of the strong tradition of "all the old and exact scrolls".[85] He considered Maimonides' arrangement, after all his enquiries, as an individual idiosyncrasy, so much so that he thought it to be a scribal error![85a] We may ask ourselves why R. Meir went to such lengths in deciding this small point. The answer is obvious: it seemed impossible to him that Maimonides should have ruled, as was (quite correctly) handed down in his name, that there are only five lines after SM, for this would mean, as *ha-Me'iri* calculated, that "those lines would have to be much too long" (שהרי יצטרכו השטין להיותם גדולים יותר מדי; *op. cit.*, p. 38; cf. below, § 35 f.).

§ 32   In order to comprehend more fully the halakhic aspect involved, we shall try provisionally to sum up the facts as we have so far established them: The tradition which entered the standard halakhic treatises as well as our printed editions of Maimonides' *Code* assumes that Maimonides decided that SM itself should be written in *seventy* lines and the verses of the following prose

84.   His justification: ונשענתי על דברי הרב הגדול ההוא שכתב, שכל הדברים האמורים בענין ראשי השטות אינן אלא למצוה מן המובחר ואם שנה לא פסל "And I relied on the words of that great Rabbi, who wrote that all the statements with regard to the beginnings of the lines are only a meritorious practice, and deviation does not disqualify." As against this, cf. Ḥassan's and Lonzano's views on the one hand (below, §36 and n. 97), and those of the later Decisors on the other (note 98).

85.   It should be noted that earlier, while dealing with the prescriptions for writing SM (*op. cit.*, p. 38), ha-Meiri himself rules differently and notes for the beginning of the sixth line הזה (=הזאת?) in place of התורה. I would suggest that the main part of the tradition only went as far as fixing the number of lines (*six*), while as far as the details were concerned, there were apparently slight differences. This is also borne out by Pentateuch codices. For instance, six lines and at their end התורה, e.g. in the sumptuous MS Casanat. 21 (written in 1243) and Jer. Heb. 8° 1401 (written in 1341). In the famous *Miqdashiah* (now Jer. Heb. 4° 780; cf. Ben-Zvi, KS 32 (1957), p. 366 f.) the beginnings are: ויבא – העם – הדברים – לבבכם – תצוום – הזאת. That the number *six* is fixed while the incipits change, I found borne out on examining a fair number of ancient Sephardi scrolls of the Law, kept in various synagogues in Safed. As for L, cf. above, n. 30.

85a.   E. E. Urbach rightly pointed out to me that the uniqueness of Maimonides' readings in R. Meir's eyes should be taken at its face value only as regards the situation in western Europe (and North Africa). Although later Decisors were mainly influenced by the state of affairs in these countries, we have no means of saying whether A was unique in its own time also in Palestine or Egypt. Even so R. Meir seems to have gathered information from various places, and still found A unique.
       On the other hand nothing can be inferred from the term *Akhū maṣḥaf al-tāj* ("The Brother of the Crown Codex"), by which a certain MS kept at Fostat (Old Cairo) in Maimonides' time was apparently known. I am indebted for this reference to S. D. Goitein, who discussed that MS in *Homenaje a Millàs-Vallicrosa* I (1954). p. 713 f.

section in *five* lines; while ha-Meiri held that the correct way is *sixty-seven* lines for the Song and *six* lines for the closing section; though there is no doubt that he was well aware that on the last point he decided contrary to what he found transmitted in the name of Maimonides, namely sixty-seven and five. On this latter point we possess the additional evidence of R. Meir ben Ṭodros, who can almost be called a younger contemporary of Maimonides. On the strength of this we can conclude that the evidence in early halakhic sources fits the tradition of the MSS of the *Code*, which in turn reflect the system of A.

V

§ 33   With this consideration we have already started on the last part of our study, namely, the development of Maimonides' ruling in the treatises of the Decisors. The quotation from R. Meir apprehended us of the important fact that A was apparently unique in its way of writing. This fact, together with the opposition of those used to the *Sof.* tradition, suffices to explain the tendency to bring Maimonides' ruling into line with the older seventy-line tradition.[86]

This apparent identity between the tradition of *Sof.* and the ruling attributed to Maimonides was made even more striking by the fact that later Decisors expressly stressed that on one point only we find a difference between *Sof.* and Maimonides, namely, that the latter starts line 23 with בני בשן, while *Sof.* starts it with ואילים.[87]

At first sight one feels tempted to ask why it was Maimonides' view that was

---

86.   In the printed editions it is found in *Sof.* ch. xii Hal. 9 (ed. Higger (1936): Hal. 8). The number *seventy* in *Sof.* is above doubt, being established by the aggadic linking of "seventy plus two" (the two empty lines above and below the Song) with the seventy-two elders (cf. *Sof.* ii, 6; xii, 8).

87.   Cf. *Naḥalath Ya'aqob* on *Sof. ad. loc.* Similarly commentators understood (justifiedly, it seems) the statement of Rabbenu Asher (הרא״ש) (*Hil. S. T.* xiv = *Ṭur Yoreh De'ah* §275): והתחלת ראשי השיטות כתובים במסכת סופרים וגם הרמב״ם ז״ל כתבן ושינה בהן קצת "And the commencements of the lines are stated in *Sof.*, and also Maimonides, of blessed memory, recorded them and *changed them a little*". Cf. *Ma'adanne Yom-Ṭov, ad. loc.*, and below, note 97.
Since this incidental controversy does not form part of the main problem of the *sixty-seven* as against *seventy* lines, it is not difficult to understand that in this case the need for harmonization was not felt, all the more so since on this point Maimonides seems to have been supported by some other tradition (cf. the note of Wertheimer, *Ginze Yerushalayim*, p. 18, on the tradition attributed to R. Tam; printed later in *Maḥzor Vitry* (available to me in ed. Nuremberg 1923, p. 656 f.). But here, too, there were attempts at explaining away the express statements of Maimonides (cf. Lonzano's remarks following on the quotation given below, §36). It is, indeed, a widespread custom to follow *Sof.* also on this point.

rejected. After all, harmonization could also have been achieved in the opposite
direction. This, however, is hardly a real problem. Not only was the tradition
to which Maimonides' ruling was opposed, invested with the authority of a
much earlier and well-established halakhic source, but Maimonides did not
trouble to give any reason for his decision against that source (*i.e. Sof.*), but
solely decided on the basis of one MS which he considered authoritative. As
it turned out, the history of Halakhah took its revenge. We have no right to
assume that there were any other reasons for reversing Maimonides' ruling,
such as the alleged Karaism of BA (cf. above, n. 52).

§34   It may, however, be that a very weak echo reached us, indeed, of an
       effort to strengthen the ruling of Maimonides, in a story related by R.
Azariah de'Rossi (ca. 1512–78), which he found written at the end of an ancient
Pentateuch.[88] According to this, Maimonides travelled to France in order to
compare the Scroll of the Law he had written for himself according to the BA
Codex, with the Scroll of Ezra the Scribe (ספר עזרא) which was reputedly
preserved there (!), and found that everything corresponded perfectly:

והבאתי עמי תקון סופרים פתוחות וסתומות וסדורות שהעתקתי מספר העשרים וארבע אשר
הובא מירושלים ומצאתי בגויל כל פתוחות וסתומות מכוונות יחד עם הספר אשר הבאתי עמי.

"And I brought with me the Bible text, indicating the various sections, which
I had copied from the complete Bible which was brought from Jerusalem, and
I found on the parchment all the open and closed sections agreeing with the
scroll which I had brought with me."[89]

§ 35   We have mentioned above (§31 f.) that the ruling on sixty-seven lines was
       known to ha-Meiri[90]; nor was it forgotten long after the process of harmo-
nization had taken place.[91] Later Decisors, however, were very much amazed at
ha-Meiri's statement, so much so that they claimed that he must have happened

---

88.   *Me'or 'Enayim, Imre Binah,* end of ch. 9 (in the Vilna edition 1863, p. 135.). R. Azariah
      de'Rossi himself already expressed doubts regarding the truth of the story. I suggest
      it is simply a rehash of the story told in ha-Meiri's *Kiriath Sefer,* p. 46, about the MSS
      of the *Code* and the correspondence between R. Meir ben Ṭodros of Toledo and the
      scholars of Burgos.
89.   The purpose of this piece of information is obvious, for the apocryphal story makes
      Maimonides end with the words: אומר הכתוב עליו יחליף ולא באלה והמדקדק ...
      "And he who follows these rules exactly and makes no change in them is the one
      whom Scripture means when it says...".
90.   Note the softening of his formulation (*op. cit.,* p. 41): שטין בס״ז לכתבה ונהגו,
      "and according to custom it is written in sixty-seven lines", instead of Maimonides'
      original וכותבין, "and it is written".
91.   It is still found in the *Tiqqun Soferim* by R. Solomon Dubno, composed at the time of
      Mendelssohn (I have used the edition of נתיבות שלום, Berlin 1783, *ad. loc.*).

to have used a corrupt copy of the *Code* (cf. below, §37). There would have been no need to examine the "evidence" of the Decisors against ha-Meiri, were it not that our thesis receives additional support from it.

We have already seen (§31 f.) that ha-Meiri saw himself compelled to assume that the section after SM should be written in *six* lines, contrary to what he knew to be Maimonides' ruling (*i.e.* five lines). His reason was: "Otherwise the lines would have to be too large" (*Kiriath Sefer*, p. 38).

This argument, finally put forward with more elaborate reasoning by the great Massoretic scholar, R. Menaḥem di Lonzano (16th–17th century) was based on the following assumption: the width of the lines in the column is perforce determined by four factors: a) the beginnings of the lines before SM, b) the beginnings of the lines after it, c) the first words of the hemistichs, d) the minimum space between the two hemistichs within the Song, which was taken to be equal to the blank space of a closed section.

With pencil in hand it can be worked out that it is practically impossible to compose a column taking into consideration all these factors if Maimonides' ruling of 6+67+5 lines is taken as a basis. For that very reason Decisors found it easy to uphold, finally, the tradition of *Sof.* which was passed off as Maimonides' ruling. In the time of ha-Meiri the true ruling of Maimonides was still too well known, and ha-Meiri had to admit that he consciously contravened it as regards the last five lines. However, by the time of Lonzano the substitution of the seventy-line system of *Sof.* had already been accepted to such a degree that only a final blow was needed. Since that system enabled the scribe to compose a column somewhat more easily, it provided — so to speak — internal evidence against the original ruling of Maimonides. The 67–line tradition was officially declared spurious, and the 70–line tradition became the only recognized one.

§ 36   Because of its decisive bearing on the history of our problem, Lonzano's reasoning deserves to be quoted in full (ed. in שתי ידות, Venice 1618, *ad. loc.*):

בענין צורת השירה הזאת כתב הרמב״ם ז״ל שכותבין אותה בששים ושבע שיטות. וזה אמנם כפי מה שמצאתי בשלושה רמב״ס כתיבת יד וכפי מה שכתב רבי דוד כוכבי ז״ל בספר בית אל בשמו ולזה הסכים המאירי ז״ל. ואולם בספרי רמב״ם הדפוס׳ כתוב שכותבין אותה בשבעים שיטות, וכך מצאתי ברמב״ם אחד כתיבת יד (!) וכן מצאתי בהללי ובספר... ובספרי הירושלמיים הקדמונים ביותר מן ת״ק שנה וכן כתוב במסכת סופרים פרק יב (!) ... וספרי ספרדיים נחלקו בזה, קצתם כסברא ראשונה וקצתם כסברה אחרונה; וכן נראה לי עיקר, ולא עוד אלא שנראה לעניות דעתי שכל ס פ ר תורה שכתוב כ ס ב ר א ראשונה פסול לפי שבאמצע כל שיטה משירה זו צריך רווח כצורת פרשה סתומה, ואם

שינה פסול ... כמו שכתב המאירי ז״ל בהדיא, וכן דעת הרמב״ם. ובעלי הסברה הרא־
שונה צריכים בג׳ מקומות... להכניס בשיטה אחת מה שהוא שתי שיטות לסברא האחרונה
ולכן לא יוכלו להניח באמצע שלשת השיטות ההן רווח כשיעור פרשה, כי קצר המצע.
וכי תאמר: אפשר לתקן זה... ומתחילה ירחיב עמוד השירה הרבה כדי שיוכל להכניס
שתי שיטות בשיטה אחת וגם יישאר באמצע כשיעור, הא לאו מילתא היא, דאם כן יהיה
הספר תורה פסול ממקום אחר, לפי שצריך למעלה משירה זו שש שיטין וכלן שיטות קצרות
ואיך יעשה הסופר? אם יתחילם בימין העמוד שוה להתחלת שיטות השירה יישאר משמאל
העמוד רווח בסוף כל שיטה, וכשתסתכל היטיב תמצא שכל השיטין זולת הראשונה הרי
הם כדין פרשה פתוחה שקודם לה רווח בסוף שיטה והיא מתחלת בריש שיטה, ונמצא שעשה
חמש פרשיות פתוחות במקום שאין בו אחת. ואם יתחילם באמצע העמוד בין שיעשה סופן
שוה לסופי שיטות השירה ויניח כל הרווח מימין העמוד, בין שינית חצי הרווח מימין וחציו
משמאל ושטת השיטות באמצע – סוף סוף כיון שיש בראשן רווח הרי הם ששה פרשיות
סתומות וכן לא יעשה. וקושיא זו לא יימלטו ממנה בעלי סברא זו אף אם היה מותר להם
שלא להניח רווח באמצע השיטה העשירית והשש עשרה והשלושים ושמונה, כי אלו יותר
ארוכות בלא רווח מהישאר עם הרווח! הא למדת כי הטוב והישר לעשות לעשות שירה
זו שבעים שיטות וראשיהן הראשונים והאמצעים הנם כתובים בספר
רי הרמב״ם הדפוסים...

"As regards the layout of SM: Maimonides wrote that it is written in
sixty-seven lines. And this, indeed, is what I found in three Maimonides MSS
and it is in accordance with what R. David Kokhavi wrote in his *Beth El*
in his name and ha-Meiri agreed with it. However, in the printed Maimonides
editions it states that it is written in *seventy* lines, and I found the same in one
Maimonides MS (!), and in the *Hilleli* and in. . . . and in scrolls from Jerusalem
more than five hundred years old, and thus it is written in the *Tractate Soferim*
XII (!) . . . . Spanish scrolls, however, differ in this matter, some go according
to the former view and some according to the latter, and this latter seems to
me to be the better opinion. Moreover, in my humble view *every scroll written
according to the first view is unfit for ritual use*. This is because in the middle
of every line of this song there must be a space, the size of a closed section,
and if the scribe changes this, the scroll is unfit . . . . . as ha-Meiri stated
expressly, and this is the view also of Maimonides. However, those holding
the former view must in three places. . . admit into one line what is two lines
in the latter view and therefore they cannot leave in the middle of those three
lines a space the size of a section since the width of the page is too small. You
could say: this can be arranged. . . . and from the start one could widen the
column of the Song a great deal so that one can admit two lines in one line
and still in the middle there will remain enough blank space — but this is no
solution. Because if so, the scroll would be unfit for another reason, since there
needs to be above this Song six lines, all of them short lines; what then should
the scribe do? If he begins them at the very right of the column, equal to the

beginnings of the Song's lines, there will remain a space at the end of every line on the left hand of the column. And if you look carefully into the matter you will find that all the lines, except the first one, would become 'open sections', which are defined as sections preceded by a space at the end of the previous line while the section itself starts at the beginning of a new line. That would mean that such a scribe made five open sections where there is not even one! If on the other hand, he begins them in the middle of the column, either making their ends even with the ends of the lines of the Song (so that the whole blank space is on the right hand of the column) or leaving half the space at the right and half of it at the left, and thus placing the six lines in the middle — whatever way he does it there will be six closed sections, and this he must not do. Those holding the first view will not escape this difficulty even were it permitted not to leave any space in the middle of the tenth, sixteenth, and thirty-eighth line; for these are longer without a space than the rest of the lines with a space! Thus you have learnt *that it is right and proper to write this Song in seventy lines; and the beginnings of the hemistichs are indeed those indicated in the printed editions of Maimonides...*"

Nevertheless, Lonzano felt that matters were not quite smooth. Dealing with the problem of the "five lines" after SM (which had troubled ha-Meiri, who consequently accepted another tradition) he suggested a solution based on the rather modern principle that such discrepancies should be explained through successive corrections which Maimonides made in his *Code*:

ונראה לעניות דעתי שכתב כן הרמב"ם ז"ל לפי סברתו הנמצאת בספריו כתיבת יד שכת־
בתי למעלה, שכותבים השירה ששים ושבע שיטות ונמצא בהן שלש שיטות ארוכות מאד וב־
עבורן צריך להרחיב כל העמוד, לכן כתב בסופם שיטות ארוכות אלו. אלא שאם תיקן
הרב בזה הסוף, לא תיקן הראש, ר"ל כי ששת השיטין שלמעלה מהשירה קצרות מאד ויקשה
מה שהקשיתי למעלה. לכן נראה שחזר בו הרמב"ם ז"ל וחזר ואמר שכותבין אותה בשבעים
שיטות והיינו שנמצא בספריו הדפוסים – אלא שנראה שלא זכר הרב לתקן גם השיטות
שלמטה ונשארו כשהיו...

"In my humble view Maimonides wrote this according to his view found in the MSS of his Code which I mentioned above, namely, that the Song is written in sixty-seven lines, so that there are three very long lines and on their account the whole column has to be widened. That is why after the Song he has these long lines. However, if the Master managed to get the final lines right, he did not do justice to the initial ones; for the six lines before the Song are very short, and the same difficulty arises as I pointed out above. It therefore seems that Maimonides retracted his former view, and now stated that the Song is written in seventy lines (*i.e.* as it is found in the printed editions of the

Code), but apparently he did not remember to correct also the lines after the Song, so they remained as they were....."[92]

Lonzano's decision is the final word on this issue, no matter whether the Decisors also accepted his radical view that writing SM in sixty-seven lines disqualifies a scroll for ritual use or whether in practice they were not so strict (cf. below, §37 and note 98). Lonzano's argument was, under the circumstances, fully convincing. After all, no one could have known — as has now been revealed to us — that in the MS which Maimonides used *there was no problem whatsoever, due to the system of "filling-in signs"* in the section before the Song.[93] The only MS which agrees with all of Maimonides' data — and which alone could agree with it on account of this system (which was unknown to the later Decisors) — is the Aleppo Codex.

§37   We have anticipated the historical development by mentioning the final step, Lonzano, next to the initial one, ha-Meiri. Lonzano's authority was accepted by everyone, and no later Decisor dared to contest his ruling.[94] In order to fill in the picture, we shall now try to catch some glimpses of what happened before that final decision.

The most important connecting link between ha-Meiri and Lonzano is to be found in a treatise which was almost exclusively devoted to our subject. It seems, however, that it was soon forgotten, and in any case it did not directly influence later Decisors.[95] I am referring to *Iggereth Sofer* ("An epistle for the Scribe") by R. Abraham Ḥassan.[96] With great ingenuity and unbearable

---

92.   I have asked Dean Lieberman whether it is to his mind possible for this to be one of the cases in which Maimonides introduced changes in his "editions" of the *Code* (cf. Lieberman's *Hilkhoth ha-Yerushalmi*, New-York 1947, p. vi). He feels that this is quite possible — of course exactly in the direction opposite to that assumed by Lonzano, *i.e.* that Maimonides' final ruling (as evidenced by the "last edition", Ox. Hunt. 80) was based on the 67 lines which he found in A. I would, however, add that such an assumption is not at all necessary and does not agree too well with the relationship between MSS and printed editions as known to us.

93.   For the originality of the signs in A as opposed to L, cf. above, note 81. It should be noted that the signs serve for filling in spaces not only in the lines before the Song, but also in the lines of SM itself (as well as elsewhere in that MS; cf. §41 below). It would seem that a most precise system obtained. Thus, for instance, the one sign used throughout the whole chapter is changed for another, so-to-say final, sign in the last hemistich of SM.

94.   Lonzano's statement became known to later generations mainly through being quoted by R. Jedidiah Solomon of Norzi in his famous *Minḥath Shay*. Norzi does not add anything new, and expressly states that he is "like one who gleans after the harvesters" (כמלקט שבלים אחרי הקוצרים). Cf. *Minḥath Shay, ad loc.*

95.   Lonzano does not mention it; but a few of his phrases let one suspect that he knew it.

96.   The author, who worked as a corrector of scrolls of the Law in Salonica (about 1500), addressed this epistle in the form of a halakhic question to one of the greatest authorities

---

longwindedness he attempts to prove that ha-Meiri was led astray by corrupt copies of Maimonides' *Code*, and that there could be no possible doubt whatever that Maimonides actually ruled there were to be *seventy* lines. Any scroll written otherwise is in his view so severely corrupt that there is no remedy but the removal and replacement of the whole length of parchment on which SM is written![97]

However, we are interested in the evidence he mentions by the way rather than in his tortuous argumentation. Not only (cf. *Ha-Segullah*, no. 54, p. 7) do we learn that in all Spanish scrolls "for the last three hundred years [*i.e.* since the days of Maimonides! — M.G.] it has been written in only sixty-seven lines" — בלבד שיטין ס״ז בס אותה שעושין שנה מאות משלש קרוב לנו זה – as opposed to the scrolls of the 'Ashkenazi' Jews who always write the Song in seventy lines according to the Halakhah (!) (*ib.* p. 11), but he also informs us that almost all MSS of Maimonides' *Code* at his time were "corrupt", for they, too, contained the reading 'sixty-seven lines'!

One can hardly wish for more explicit evidence for the practically universal tradition of sixty-seven lines in the Spanish scrolls (cf. above n. 71), as late as three hundred years after Maimonides. R. Abraham is well aware of the

of his day, R. Elijah Mizraḥi; the latter did not deal himself with the actual subject matter, but only answered politely that he was certain R. Abraham was right, and thus it should be decided. The epistle is not yet to be found in the Jerusalem 1938 edition of the *Responsa* of R. Elijah Mizraḥi (which is only a reprint of the Constantinople edition, 1560), but was published in the same year in *Ha-Segullah*, nos. 53–56).

97.   It would lead us too far from our issue to go into the niceties of his halakhic reasoning. In addition to his reliance on R. Asher, the printed editions, *Soferim*, the *Hilleli* (sic) etc., he proves his view as follows: In writing sixty-seven lines instead of seventy, three lines of SM are, so to say, erased. Halakhically speaking, that means that instead of writing those lines in the form of a Song, "one writes the Song like the rest of the text" (הכתב כשאר שירה עשה). That, according to the halakhah, is a completely disqualifying blemish (cf. also below, note 98). Furthermore, every line of SM has in its middle the space of a closed section. Now, if we write three lines less, we change perforce also the number of sections in the Pentateuch, which are definitely fixed. This again is one of the things which would make a scroll unfit, etc.
       Moreover: Rabbenu Asher explained (according to the *Ba'al ha-Ṭurim*) that an alteration in the beginnings of the lines of the Song of the Sea does not disqualify a scroll. But he did not state the same thing as regards SM — which means that there one has to be strict, all the more so since Rabbenu Asher was even amazed at the slight change in the matter of בשן בני and איילים (cf. above, note 87). A more serious change he would, no doubt, have regarded as disqualifying. Moreover, the fact that Maimonides dealt separately with the case of the lines above and below the Song on the one hand and the problem of the number of lines of the Song itself on the other, proves that he intended to make this distinction: a change in the first ruling does not disqualify; but changing the lines of the Song itself is, indeed, disqualifying. These are all obvious reasons that a Torah Scroll in which SM is written in sixty-seven lines is completely unfit for ritual use.

origin of the tradition but he, too, is forced to prove, like Lonzano after him, that it is a mistake to attribute that tradition to Maimonides, since Maimonides' "true" tradition is identical with that in *Sof.* Therefore, writing SM in sixty-seven lines disqualifies the Torah Scroll![98]

§ 38   We possess additional evidence from the same period, which I consider hardly less important, though it, too, was not used by Lonzano in his decisive discussion of this matter. Its particular interest derives from two facts: that it is not part of a halakhic discussion — in which the views of earlier sources might have affected the picture —, and that it establishes a direct connection between the facts of the Aleppo Codex and the rulings in Maimonides' *Code.*

98.   The position at which the halakhah was finally settled is not part of our subject, and we shall only mention it in passing. According to the *Shulḥan 'Arukh (Yoreh De'ah* §275,5), the rule is seventy lines, and no doubt this decision was intended to represent Maimonides' view as well as the ruling according to *Sof.* (in spite of disagreements on certain other laws concerning the writing of scrolls of the Law, it appears that the Decisors intended to follow Maimonides; cf. the remark of R. Moses Isserlis, *loc. cit.,* subsection 2).

As regards SM, no divergent tradition seems to have got as far as the commentaries on the *Shulḥan 'Arukh.* One almost wonders whether they were at all aware of the divergent tradition, which was so well known to those who specialized in the laws governing the writing of Torah Scrolls. But they may simply have ignored the remarks of the specialists and regarded the matter with less severity than R. Abraham Ḥassan. In any case, the accepted view was that expressed already by ha-Meiri (*Kiriath Sefer,* p. 41), ואם שנה בראשי השטין ובראשי אמצעיתה לא פסל "if one alters the beginnings of the first or second hemistichs, this does not disqualify the scroll". Thus we read: ומנין השטין של השורות נראה דגם כן אם שינה לא פסל "With regard to the number of the lines of the Songs, it also appears that if one deviates from the rule, the scroll does not become disqualified" (*'Arukh ha-Shulḥan* §275, 18). This decision seems in the last instance to be based on Maimonides' own conclusions (*Hil. S. T.* x, 1; cf. also *ib.* vii, 11), that the only blemish which renders a scroll unfit is writing the Song like a prose text (cf. B. T. *Shabbath* 103b; *Menaḥoth* 31a), but keeping to the special form for each poem is only a matter of special merit. Cf. also *Shulḥan 'Arukh, Yoreh De'ah* 275, 3).

Also from this latter point we must deduce that it was Maimonides whom the Decisors intended to follow, for this approach is opposed to the stricter halakhah of *Sof.* i, 10 (11 in ed. Higger): האזינו שעשאה שירה, שירה שעשאה האזינו, רצוף שעשאה מסורג, מסורג שעשאה רצוף...אל יקרא בו "If one writes SM like the Song of the Sea, or the Song of the Sea like SM, a continuous text like a broken text, or a broken text like a continuous text. . . . one must not read from that scroll. . .". Many ingenious suggestions were advanced in order to get away from that difference between *Sof.* and Maimonides (and Rabbenu Asher after him), so much so that the expressions מסורג and רצוף were given a meaning different from their real one (cf. especially the effort of Azulai, *Kisse' Raḥamim,* Leghorn 1803, *ad loc.*). But such an attempt is in obvious contrast to the ancient tradition which explains what is said in *Sof.*:

ספר שכתבו כמין שירה, שירה שכתבה כמין ספר לא יקרא בו... רצוף שעשה מסורג... אל יקרא בו. ואיזה רצוף? זה שכתוב כהלכתו. מסורג — כגון האזינו וספר תילין ואיוב; ושמעינן מינה תיקון שירת האזינו שצריכה להיות מסורגת לשני סטרים ...

I am referring to the statement of R. Saadya ben David of Aden (Ha-'Adani, ca. 1480). Steinschneider already pointed out[99] the statement of this Saadya in his commentary on Maimonides' *Code*, that he saw in Aleppo the MS on which Maimonides based himself.[100] Immediately following this important remark, Saadya writes[101]:

למה שירת האזינו כותבין אותה על ש ב ע ה ו ש ש י ם שיטה? אלגיואב: קאלו ז״ל כדי
לזכור שם המוכיח הוא משה שנ׳ והוכח >כמהב< (!) במכאוב על משכבו וג׳. מנין 'במכ-
אוב' שבעה וששים. במכאוב שם משמותיו של משה שאמרו: עשרה שמות למשה.

"Why is SM written in *sixty-seven* lines? The answer: The sages said, in order to allude to the name of the reprover [=the author of the poem of reproof], *i.e.* Moses, as is written: 'He is reproved [A.V. chastened] also with pain upon his bed', etc. (Job xxxiii, 19). The numerical value of the letters במכאוב is sixty-seven. במכאוב is one of the names of Moses, as they said: Moses had ten names."[102]

"A scroll [where the prose] is written like a Song, or a Song written like a [prose] scroll is unfit for reading... a continuous text written like a broken text is unfit for reading. What does 'continuous' mean? The normal writing. And what 'broken'? Such as SM and the books of Psalms and Job. Thus we learn that the proper way of writing SM is to be broken up into two lateral columns...." (cf. the Geniza fragment attributed to R. Judah ben Barzilai of Barcelona, published by E. N. Adler, JQR 1897, p. 703). Also to be compared is the text of the Palestinian tractate *Sefer Torah* (cf. שבע מסכתות קטנות, ed. Higger, New-York 1930, Introduction, p. 11), which, however, raises other problems: האזינו שעשו רצוף או שעשו את המסורג שלא כהלכתו אל יקרא בו: A] השירת Scroll in which] SM is written continuously, or in which the broken text is not written according to its particular way, is unfit for reading' (cf. also n. 78 above).

99.   *Catalogus Librorum Hebr. in Bibl. Bodleiana*, col. 1936. Cf. also his *Arab. Literatur der Juden* (1902), §202.

100. Steinschneider quoted this fact from Ox. Hunt. 372 (an autograph?), and the statement itself was published by Assaf, KS 22 (1946), p. 241:

הספר שסמך עליו הגאון ז״ל עדיין הוא היום במדינת צובה והיא חלב, ויסמוה אל תאג׳ ומכתוב עלי רק, בכל
ורקה תלאת דפאת ומכתוב פי אכרה 'ואני אהרן בן אשר שהגהתיו וכו''. ואני ראיתיו וקראתי בו.

"The codex upon which the Master based himself exists still today in Aleppo, and it is called 'the Crown', and it is written on parchment, on every page three columns, and at its end it says: 'It is I, Aaron b. Asher who corrected it, etc.' And I have seen it and read in it."
This same information was published a year later by Kahle, *The Cairo Genizah*, p. 58, who apparently knew neither of Steinschneider's note nor of Assaf's publication. [2nd ed. unchanged!] Kahle already pointed out that the quotation is not literal.

101. I came upon this (unpublished) statement while verifying the preceding quotation in MS Jer. Heb. 8° 1179, fol. 102a. This is a later MS than the Bodleian one, but it can be taken to be exact, as turned out on comparing other quotations from the above Bodl. MS.

102. This is, obviously, a rather weak argument to explain a custom for which no reason had been given (as opposed to the tradition of *Sof.* about seventy lines, cf. above, n. 86). As far as the supposed numerical value of במכאוב is concerned, it seems that already the scribe failed to understand how במכאוב equals 67.
With regard to the numerous traditions concerning the names of Moses, cf. now the note of Margalioth on *Lev. Rabba* i, 3 (Jerusalem 1953, p. 11). I did not find in the

Thus the only commentator of the *Code* who informs us that while commenting on *Hil. S. T.* he took the trouble of consulting the Aleppo Codex, attests at the same time to the tradition of writing SM in sixty-seven lines. This tradition, which he found confirmed on examining the Codex, must have been the one known to him: while he tries to account for it, he certainly takes it for granted that this was the authentic ruling of Maimonides. In any case he did not find it necessary to state that there was also another tradition.[102a]

§ 39   This is sufficient to show that the evidence garnered from the MSS of the *Code* is confirmed and explained by the development of the matter in halakhic literature. Maimonides' original decision always remained known to those Decisors who dealt specifically with the laws for writing Torah Scrolls, but they finally saw themselves compelled to uphold the spurious tradition.[103]

§ 40   Having completed our main inquiry, we may add a number of minor details culled from the writings of the Decisors. Now that A lies before us, these are perhaps not without interest.

We saw the difficulties encountered by the Decisors, from R. Meir and ha-Meiri to Lonzano, with regard to the actual layout of the column on which SM is written. According to their assumptions they were quite justified in maintaining that only a layout of seventy lines enables one to write a ritually correct page, on which the scribe could leave in the middle between the two hemistichs a blank space the size of a closed section (cf. above § 36). We saw that the problem solved itself once we realized that the model codex used dummy signs for filling up certain lines. This simple device was not taken into account by all the calculations of the Decisors, since it was apparently unknown to them (and since, in any case, it could not be used in scrolls).

We may, however, be able to discover even more, It seems that the Decisors started out from an additional wrong premise. A glance at the facsimile will show that there always remains a space between the two hemistichs even in the long lines of SM. But this space is definitely not always of a size to allow for the writing of nine letters, which is the measure of a closed section as generally accepted by the Decisors.

---

literature mentioned there any parallel to the explanation offered by Saadya al-'Adani.

102a.   As mentioned, this seems to be the common tradition in Yemenite MSS; cf. above, beginning of §27 and n. 71.

103.   The only one whose wording leaves one with the suspicion that he might have felt some misgivings about Lonzano's decision (though he upheld it) is Azulai (cf. *Kisse'*, *Rahamim*, Leghorn 1803, fol. 46b). In any case his words contain at the utmost a bare hint, and no conclusions must be draw from them.

104.   Mainly two, three and five; cf. the conclusion in *Tosafoth* on B. T. *Menahoth* 32a and also the fragment mentioned in note 98.

We know that formerly there used to be traditions which assumed a smaller number of letters for fixing the size of the blank space in a closed section[104], and the scribe of A may have followed one of these. But in any event it must be stressed that it was not Maimonides who formulated the ruling that the blank space should equal the measure of nine letters; it rather seems that only later his statements were interpreted as though that was his intention.

The exact words of Maimonides regarding the closed section are: מניח רווח כשעור i.e. "one leaves a space to the proper measure" (*Hil. S. T.* viii, 2). As regards SM, however, he expressly formulates: יש באמצעה רווח אחד, כצורת הפרשה הסתומה "in the middle one leaves a space *similar to the form of a closed section*", which may simply refer to the form in general, but not to the exact width. Ha-Meiri still differentiates exactly. Only later the difference of formulation became blurred, and Maimonides' statement was reworded in a more absolute form so as to stress the identical width between a closed section and the blank between two hemistichs in SM.[105] Thus a further difficulty was added in understanding the words of Maimonides as they were meant, which no doubt helped in spreading the apocryphal ruling, as finally promulgated by Lonzano.[106]

§ 41   Another point which is clearly demonstrated in A — more than in any other known MS — concerns the way in which Maimonides developed the ruling on writing words at the end of the line (cf. B.T. *Menahoth* 31a-b).

---

105.   R. Asher formulates as follows: ובצורת שירת האזינו מפורש במסכת סופרים באמצע כל שיטה רוח כשעור הפרשה הסתומה, "And the form of SM is expressly stated in *Sof.*: in the middle of every line a space the measure of a closed section" (*Hil. S. T.*, 14; and similarly *Tur, Yoreh De'ah* §275). Even though his words give the impression that they were taken from *Sof.*, they must have been derived, in fact, from Maimonides' wording.

106.   I hardly like to remark on matters of practical halakhah, but I cannot help feeling that Maimonides himself does not seem to have stated expressly what constitutes the space of a closed section. Even so it seems accepted in halakhic literature, apparently already by ha-Meiri (*Kiriath Sefer*, p. 51), that as regards the closed section (Hil. S. T. viii, 2), Maimonides' phrase כשעור ("to the proper measure") intends the same measurement as that which he gave (ib. 1) for the open section —i.e. nine letters. In the light of the divergent traditions on this subject (cf. note 104), I am not fully convinced that this really was his intention. I would suggest, with all due caution, that the certainty of the late Decisors in their interpretation was perhaps unconsciously strengthened by their desire to "enable the God-fearing to satisfy all views" (ויראי שמים יצא את כלם). Since with regard to certain sections, there were other traditions than those accepted by Maimonides' (cf. *Yoreh De'ah* §275, 2, and cf. below, note 109), and since these could not be brushed aside, it must have been imperative to keep at least the same size for both types in order to "satisfy all views" (as suggested in detail by commentators). In connection with this problem, it is worth while to have a look at the photograph of A so as to realize what could be, in fact, the size of a closed

It would seem at first that Maimonides only developed the system of the Talmud in deciding (*Hil. S. T.* vii, 5) that, if there is not enough space left in the line to write three letters, the scribe should leave the space empty (מניח מקום פנוי) and start from the beginning of the next line. However, the commentators already voiced their surprise why Maimonides did not mention the scribal custom of dilating the letters אהלת״ם so as to avoid blank spaces (explicitly: *Shulḥan 'Arukh, Yoreh De'ah* §273, 3; also *Haggahoth Maimoniyoth* on our passage).

The method of filling up the lines with dummy signs (cf. n. 93) offers a simple solution, even if we may assume that Maimonides knew the different customs of Scroll scribes. This method of filling up lines is, of course, not peculiar to A and cannot serve as evidence to prove our main contention.[107] But we know of no other MS which has developed this method to the extent that A did, and when Maimonides formulated the rule about leaving empty spaces, he may well have had in mind the system of A.[108]

We cannot close this chapter of sidelights without a brief mention of the controversies on the form of the open and closed sections (*Hil. S. T* .viii, 1–2). Undoubtedly there were varying traditions as to what these sections should look like.[109] It would, of course, be wrong to say that on this major subject Maimonides relied on anything but a very early talmudic tradition[110], but it

section; *e.g.* the space before ולאשר אמר (Dt. xxxiii, 24). Even though a nine-letter space may have been usually observed in this MS, it was not obligatory, as assumed by later Decisors.

107.   The method is customary to a more limited extent also in other MSS attributed to BA (cf. note 81). Cf. now S. A. Birnbaum, V. T. 9 (1959), p., 123 concerning a column of a Torah Scroll which, he claims, precedes BA. Since his statement is not accompanied by a photograph, it is impossible to comment on it.

108.   With all due reserve, I would suggest that there may be some connection between those blank spaces of two to three letters which are less than the measure demanded for a section (cf. note 104) and the problem of a פרשה סדורה, about which already our earliest sources are uncertain. On the other hand, this problem may find its solution if we bear in mind the various spaces found in pre-massoretic MSS (compare the Dead Sea Scrolls). Those spacings, which were later not recognized as sections in the halakhic sense (פתוחה/סתומה) may for some time have lingered on as סדורה until they were finally rejected.

109.   The main summary on this subject: *Ṭur, Yoreh De'ah* §275 and *Beth Joseph* and other commentaries *ad loc.*; *Tosafoth* on B. T. *Menaḥoth* 32a. Cf. the literature cited by Higger, *Sof.*, end of chapter i (p. 110). It should be mentioned that R. Abraham, the son of Maimonides, expressly recognized the existence of the divergent traditions; he decided that scrolls following such traditions are ritually fit unless the sectioning of a scroll did not agree with any tradition at all. Cf. his Responsa, ed. Freimann-Goitein (1938), §91, and also R. Moses Isserlis, *apud Shulḥan 'Arukh, Yoreh De'ah* §275, 2, and above, note 106.

110.   The classic formulation as regards the halakhic problem in P. T. Megillah i, 9 (=11) is that of *Mar'eh Panim ad loc.*:

should be emphasized that Maimonides' statements as well as the exact drawing of the forms of the sections he added[111], completely agree[112] with the way he found these sections executed in A.[113]

The points which we have raised just now may throw some further light on our subject[114], but our identification of the MS and our tracing of the development of the halakhah in respect of Maimonides' ruling as regards SM, do not depend on them.

§ 42   It remains to sum up our findings: all our evidence goes to prove that the system of A as regards SM is identical with the ruling adopted by Maimonides. Not only is A the only extant MS of that period which fulfils all the conditions, but on examining the history of Maimonides' ruling until its rejection, we found that the MS on which Maimonides based himself was apparently unique even in his time. The very way in which Maimonides' ruling

הנה ראינו כמה דיוות משתפכין וכמה קולמוסין משתברין... ולכולן נזדמנו להם ספר מוטᵉᵉ ᵗ וגרסה
משובשת מלבד הרמבᵚם, שהיה לפניו הגרסא הנכונה והאמיתית כמו שהיא לפנינו בדפוס ויניᵎᵎᵎᵎ ומתפרשת
כפשטה וכדברי הרמבᵚם בלי פקפוק.

"Behold we have seen much ink being spilt and numerous reeds being broken... and they all happened to use an incorrect book and a spurious reading, except for Maimonides, who had in front of him the correct and true reading as we have it in the Venice edition (of the P.T.). Its meaning is plain, and according to the words of Maimonides it should not be doubted." Cf. also *Tractate Sefer Torah* i, 13 and the explanations of Higger, שבע מסכתות קטנות, Introduction, p. 14, and ha-Meiri, *Kiriath Sefer*, p. 50, note 184.

111.   The drawing was, of course, already omitted in the Rome edition (though the space for it is still visible), but it is found in absolute precision in all the MSS I saw, beginning with Ox. Hunt 80.

For an open section   _____   or   פנויה

For a closed section   ____ ____   or _____   or   ____

112.   It is superfluous to stress that with regard to such an ancient MS, one cannot query the omission of the words "open" and "closed", as Wickes erroneously believed when he w... to disqualify A (cf. above, §3), and as Teicher objected after him (JJS 2 (1950), p. 20). The nature of the sections was, of course, recognizable beyond all doubt from the very form of the spaces left in A as well as in other early MSS.

113.   In the light of what we have seen of harmonization whenever there are conflicting traditions, it is not unreasonable to assume that the difference between the open and closed sections as they are noted in MS Ox. Hunt. 80 and in other MSS of the *Code* and what appears in our printed editions, is not accidental. So long as we do not possess the missing pages of A, there can be no complete certainty. In any case, this subject deserves a separate investigation, if ever those pages should become available.

114.   Since we have dealt with SM, I shall use the opportunity (cf. above, note 31) to add the differences in the plene and defective spellings between A and L as regards SM.

	L	A
xxxii, 7	דור ודור	דר ודר
27	ידינו	ידנו (!)
34	חתם	חתום

was replaced may be taken to strengthen our contention. In addition, A is the BA MS *par excellence*, and from a purely textual point of view is superior to all MSS of that school known to us. These findings, moreover, do not refer to an unknown MS in some obscure library, but to the very MS which according to ancient tradition is the one which Maimonides saw.

On the eve of the establishment of our State, one of the outstanding teachers of the Hebrew University was the first to recognize the value of the oldest MSS of the Hebrew Bible discovered so far, the now famous Dead Sea Scrolls. Ten years later, with the help of H. E. the President of Israel, we are able to discuss the value of a manuscript which — though from a different point of view — is of hardly less importance to Bible scholars. I cannot but hope that also in this case the evaluation will be found sound and that it is not an act of rashness if I claim that the "legend" believed in by Aleppo Jews for many centuries is true.

The Vulgate Chapters and Numbered Verses in the Hebrew Bible.

PROFESSOR G. F. MOORE.

ANDOVER, MASS.

THE division into chapters which is now universally adopted was first made in the Latin Bible in the thirteenth century.[1] It was employed in the concordances of the Vulgate which gave Rabbi Isaac Nathan[2] (about 1440) the idea of the first Hebrew concordance. In his concordance he cites, first, by the number of the Vulgate chapter, and second, by the number of the Massoretic verse in the chapter, precisely as we do.[3] To make possible the application of this system to the Hebrew Bible, he appended a table giving the Hebrew words corresponding to the beginning of each chapter of the Vulgate, and the whole number of Massoretic verses in each chapter.[4] For convenience of reference, however, it was necessary that the beginning of each chapter should be indicated by its number in the margin of the Hebrew Bible, and those who used Rabbi Nathan's concordance or adopted his convenient method of citation by chapters, doubtless made such notes in their copies.[5]

[1] Probably by Stephen Langton. See Gregory, *Prolegomena*, etc., 164–166; also Schmid, *Ueber verschiedene Eintheilungen der heiligen Schrift, insbesondere über die Capitel-Eintheilung Stephan Langton's im XIII. Jahrhundert.* 1892.

[2] On the title page of the first edition of his Concordance, Venice, 1523, he is called R. Mordechai Nathan, but in the preface he calls himself Isaac Nathan. See Buxtorf, Preface to his edition of the Concordance.

[3] The following is his own account of his procedure: ולמה שראיתי שהמעתיק ספרי הקדש בלא"טין חלק הספרים למספר הפרשיות מה שאין כן בספרינו רשמתי הפסוקים כלם לפי מספרם למין הפרשיות גם רשמתי מספר הפסוקים לפי מה שהם אצלנו למען ימצאו בנקלה על מקומותדם.

[4] This table is reprinted in the Concordances of Calasius and Buxtorf.

[5] For some deviations from the accepted division of chapters in Athias's edition of 1667, he professed to have the authority of a Hebrew manuscript; this could only be a copy in which the beginning of the chapters had been noted from R. Nathan's apparatus. See Leusden, *Philologus Hebræus*, Dissert. iii. § 14. On the advantages of this method of citation see Elias Levita, Preface to *Bachur* (1518).

Reprinted from *Journal of Biblical Literature* 12 (1893).

The chapters were not marked in the earliest printed editions. It is commonly said that they were first introduced in the second quarto edition published by Daniel Bomberg, Venice, 1521.[6] This is an error; they appear in both the preceding Bomberg editions, the folio of (1517–) 1518 (the first Rabbinical Bible, edited by Felix Pratensis) and the first quarto, of 1518.[7]

In the books of Samuel, Kings, Ezra-Nehemiah, and Chronicles, the numbering of the Vulgate chapters follows the usage of the church, which divides each of these books into two.[8] Accordingly, in the folio of 1518 the numeration begins anew at 2 Sam. i., 2 Ki. i., Neh. i., 2 Chron. i.; but the division is not in any way recognized in the text. Thus, while Samuel (1 Sam.) has an ornamental title, 2 Sam. i. runs on without a break after 1 Sam. xxxi., and so in the other cases. The beginning of Nehemiah is indicated by the numeral i., but the running title, Ezra, is carried on. Only at 2 Ki. i. is there a marginal note, כאן מתחילין הלועזים ספר מלכי׳ רביעי, "Here the Greeks and Latins begin the Fourth Book of Kings," and at 2 Chron. i., the note ספר שני. With this the quarto of 1518 exactly agrees. In the quarto of 1521,[9] we find at 2 Ki. i. the marginal note, ספר ד׳; at Neh. i., ספר נחמיה (but still with the running title עזרא); at 2 Chron. i., ספר שני. Separate titles or head-pieces for 2 Sam., 2 Ki., Neh., 2 Chron., do not appear in the Hebrew Bible till a much later time.

We have seen that Rabbi Nathan in his concordance cites by the number of the Vulgate chapter and the number of the Massoretic verse in the chapter.[10] After it became usual in editions of the Hebrew Bible to designate the beginning of each chapter by a numeral, it was not a long step to the introduction of numerals for the verses

---

[6] See Buhl, *Kanon und Text des A. T.*, 1891, p. 229; Ryle, *Canon of the O. T.*, p. 238. The root of the error is probably Le Long-Masch, I. 19, where in enumerating the differences between the Bomberg edition of 1521 and the Brescia Bible, Masch writes: " 5. capita librorum litteris hebraicis sunt numeratæ." As nothing of the kind is said about its predecessors, some one inferred that these numbers were introduced for the first time in 1521.

[7] I possess a copy of the folio; the quarto I have examined in the library of Union Theological Seminary, New York. Elias Levita, in the Advice to the Reader, prefixed to his Massoreth ha-Massoreth (Venice, Bomberg, 1538), says that Bomberg introduced the Latin chapters, and implies clearly enough that this was done in the first folio and the first quarto. The passage is strangely mistranslated by Ginsburg in his edition, p. 85.

[8] See Elias Levita, Preface to *Bachur*, 1518.

[9] In the library of Union Theological Seminary.

[10] See also Pagninus, Preface to his Hebrew Lexicon (1529).

also, thus saving the necessity of counting, at every reference, from the beginning of the chapter. At first, a numeral was affixed only to every fifth verse (1, 5, 10, 15, 20, etc.) ; subsequently each verse was designated by a numeral. No one seems ever to have investigated the origin of the verse numeration ; [11] writers on the history of the text have gone on copying the mistakes of their predecessors with increase of their own. The climax is reached in a recent English book in which we read : "The division into verses, which appeared in the *Editio Sabioneta* [12] of the Pentateuch (1557), does not seem to have been applied to the whole Hebrew Canon before the edition of Athias (1661)" ; and again, " If the principle of the division into verses be ultimately of Jewish origin, the *numeration* adopted was borrowed from Rob. Stephen's Edition of the Vulgate (1555)." [13]

It would be impossible to condense more misinformation into the same compass ; every statement in these sentences is erroneous. It is not merely "the principle of the division into verses" which " is ultimately of Jewish origin " ; the existing verses are the basis of the whole system of accents ; they are carefully enumerated in the oldest Massora, for example, in the St. Petersburg codex of the Prophets (A.D. 916) ; the verse divisions appear in every codex, and in every edition that was ever printed. Professor Ryle has confounded the division into verses with the marginal numeration of the verses, which is commonly, though erroneously, believed to have been first employed in the Sabbioneta Pentateuch of 1557. [14]

The ultimate source of the statement that the verses were numbered for the first time in this edition is G-B. De Rossi, who in his description of it writes : [15] " In editione hac non solum capitibus sed

---

[11] See Eichhorn, *Einleitung*[4], I. 266 n.

[12] The name of the town is Sabbioneta; see De Rossi, *Annali ebreo-tipografici di Sabbioneta*, 1780; Lagarde, *Mittheilungen*, II. 166 n. If it were necessary to write "Sabbioneta edition" in Latin, *Editio Sabioneta* is hardly the way most scholars would prefer to write it, even with the example of Berliner and Buhl (1885) before them.

[13] H. E. Ryle, *The Canon of the Old Testament*, 1892, p. 238. Compare Horne's Introduction, 10 ed. (S. Davidson) II. 29: "The introduction of verses into editions of the Hebrew Bible proceeded from Athias, . . . in the first edition, 1661. They had been previously in the Vulgate so early as 1558." (!)

[14] So Buhl, *Kanon und Text*, 229: "Die Numerierung der Verse setzt natürlich die Kapiteleintheilung voraus. Sie findet sich zum ersten Male in der Sabbionetaausgabe des Pentateuchs 1557, im ganzen A. T. erst 1661 (Athias)."

[15] *Annali ebreo-tipografici di Sabbioneta*, Parma, 1780, p. 23 = *Annales Typographicæ Ebraicæ Sabionetenses*, etc. Ex Italicis Latinos fecit M. Jo. Frid. Roos, Erlangen, 1783, p. 27. I quote the translation.

quinto etiam cujuscunque capitis versiculo numerus additur; et me quidem judice prima omnium hæc est editio, saltem primarum una, in quibus hoc obvium est." Later writers transformed this cautious statement into the positive assertion that this was the first edition in which the verses, or more properly, every fifth verse (א, ה, י, טו, etc.), were designated by numerals.

In reality the verses were numbered throughout in this way in Bomberg's Great Bible of 1547–1548 (4 vols. fol.) ; [16] and as they were not so numbered in any of the preceding Bomberg editions,[17] we may affirm with some confidence that the system was first introduced in this second (or, if that of 1518 be counted in the series, third) Rabbinical Bible. The convenience of this method of numeration was soon recognized ; Bomberg's example is followed in the Sabbioneta Pentateuch (1557), the Plantin Bible of 1566,[18] the octavo Bible of De Gara, Venice, 1568–1572,[19] etc. It was not, however, universally adopted ; the edition of Manasseh ben Israel, Amsterdam, 1635 f., and the Mantua Bible, 1742–1744, for example, have no verse numerals.

That the numeration of the verses was first extended to the whole Bible by Athias in 1661, is, of course, an absurd blunder. Aside from the Great Bible of 1547–1548, several of the best known editions of the sixteenth century are numbered throughout. The currency of this error is the more remarkable because the preface to the edition of 1661 (by Leusden) contains a perfectly clear account of the innovation which Athias made.[20] A somewhat fuller statement is found in Leusden's *Philologus Hebræo-Græcus*, Dissert. iii., § 10, which I transcribe. Leusden argues that the division into verses dates from the authors of the Old Testament ; "Sed olim in Bibliis Hebraicis ad marginem non solebant exprimi literæ Hebraicæ, denotantes distinctionem versuum ; ut videre est in antiquis Bibliis Hebraicis Bombergi, Munsteri, aliorumque editionibus. Postea circa medium fere præcedens seculum quintus quilibet versus ad marginem fuit annotatus literis Hebraicis א, ה, י, טו, כ, etc. Tandem anno 1660 singuli versus Latinis numericis notis (excepto quinto quolibet versu, qui more antiquo literis Hebraicis exprimitur) in Bibliis Hebraicis editionis Amstelodamensis (me suadente et instigante) ad bonum

---

[16] I have a copy of this edition in my library.
[17] See Carpzov, *Critica sacra*, 2 ed. (1748), p. 420–421.
[18] In my library.
[19] Le Long-Masch, I. 30.
[20] Compare also the preface to the edition of 1667.

publicum a Josepho Athia distinctæ sunt ; quales notæ numericæ numquam antehac ulli textui Hebraico appositæ fuerant." Leusden thus claims for himself the credit of an improvement in the method of numbering introduced in Athias's edition, by which verses 2, 3, 4 ; 6, 7, 8, 9 ; etc., were designated by Arabic numerals, as in our common editions.

The assertion, however, that such numerals had not previously been affixed to any edition of the Hebrew text, requires qualification, if not correction.[21]   In the Antwerp Polyglott (1569–1572), Vols. I.–IV., every verse of the Hebrew text has its Arabic numeral ; and this is the case also in the separate edition of the Hebrew text with interlinear Latin translation which forms a supplemental volume (sometimes numbered VII., sometimes VIII., more properly perhaps, VI.) to that Polyglott (1571). This usage is followed also in the numerous later editions and reprints of this volume, including the octavo Bible " ex officina Plantiniana Raphelengii," 1610–1615, and the Leipzig reprint of 1657 in folio. The verses of the Hebrew text are numbered throughout by Arabic numerals in the Commelin Polyglott also (1586, 1599, 1616).

Professor Ryle is equally unfortunate in his remaining assertion, that " the *numeration* adopted was borrowed from Rob. Stephen's [*sic*] Edition of the Vulgate (1555)." Aside from the fact that the numeration is found in the Hebrew Bible eight years earlier, it is well known that the numbering of the (Massoretic) verses in the margin of the Latin Bible was not first introduced by Robert Stephens in his Vulgate of 1555.[22]   In 1509 Henry Stephens printed Le Fèvre d'Étaples' *Quincuplex Psalterium* with Arabic numerals for every verse. In 1528 the whole Bible, in the Latin version of Pagninus, was published at Lyons, with the verses indicated in the same way ; and in the Old Testament the numeration of the Massoretic verses in the Vulgate chapters is identical with that which we use.

To sum up, then : the Vulgate chapters were introduced into the Hebrew Bible in the first two Bomberg editions, the folio and the quarto of 1518 ; the numeration of the verses was introduced in Bomberg's Great Bible of 1547–1548, in which every fifth verse (1, 5, 10, etc.) is designated by the Hebrew numeral ; the use of

---

[21] In the preface of 1661 he says only : Sed nulla Biblia, quod scio, hactenus edita sunt, in quibus ita distincte versus discernuntur.

[22] See W. Wright in Kitto's Cyclopædia, *s.v.* Verse; Ezra Abbot in Gregory's *Prolegomena* to Tischendorf's Greek New Testament, *Editio octava critica maior,* p. 167 *sqq.,* or his *Critical Essays*, Boston, 1888, p. 464 *sqq.*

Arabic numerals for the intervening verses (2, 3, 4 ; 6, 7, 8, 9 ; etc.) was introduced by Leusden–Athias in 1661, though there were older editions (in Polyglotts or with interlinear Latin version) in which *every* verse was indicated by an Arabic numeral.

THE HEBREW BIBLE SINCE 1937[1]

THE 1937 third edition of *Biblia Hebraica* was hailed as a turning-point in the history of the printed Hebrew Bible, paralleled only by the production of its early progenitor, the Ben Asher text in the genuine Ben Asher scrolls of the 11th century. Since 1937 we have had two new Hebrew Bibles, those of Cassuto[2] in 1953 and the British and Foreign Bible Society, edited by N. H. Snaith,[3] in 1958. Two other projected editions are being widely discussed, namely that of the Hebrew University Bible Project[4] and the revised fourth edition of *Biblia Hebraica*.[5] In view of the claims made and universally accepted about the uniqueness of *B.H.*[3], with its first-time publication of a Ben Asher text, it is remarkable that the only one of the four subsequent texts that does not constitute a challenge to it is its own immediate successor. It looks as if we need to stand aside and consider the significance of this challenge, and ask whether or not we should modify our assessment of *B.H.*[3] Thereby, too, we might be able to understand better than hitherto the phase represented by the Ben Asher text in the general history of the Massoretic transmission. The textual criticism of the nineteenth century, and the publication of various texts such as Delitzsch–Baer on the one hand and Ginsburg and *B.H.*[1 and 2] on the other were marked by clashes of opinion and standpoints which now appear to be pathetically pointless; we might become involved in similar turbulent conflicts as new controversies and issues become more bitterly argued, and conflicting and extravagant claims are made by the participants of the new

[1] The Presidential Address to the Society for Old Testament Study at King's College Hostel, London, 1 Jan. 1964.

The following abbreviations are used:

    B.H.   = *Biblia Hebraica.*
    C.G.   = P. Kahle, *The Cairo Geniza* (2nd ed., 1959).
    H.D.B. = *Hastings Dictionary of the Bible* (1904).
    Txt.   = *Textus*, vols. i (1960) and ii (1962).
    V.T.   = *Vetus Testamentum.*

[2] *Torah, Nebi'im, Kethubim* (Jerusalem, 1953).

[3] Ibid. (London, 1958).

[4] Cf. the Prolegomena issued in *Txt.*

[5] Cf. two papers delivered at the 1962 Bonn Congress of the International Organization for the Study of the Old Testament and published as *Supplement to V.T.* ix (1963): G. E. Weil, 'La nouvelle édition de la Massorah (*B.H.K.* iv) et l'histoire de la Massorah' (pp. 266–84), and A. Jepsen, 'Von den Aufgaben der alttestamentlichen Textkritik' (pp. 332–41).

[Journal of Theological Studies, N.S., Vol. XV, Pt. 2, October 1964]

Reprinted from *Journal of Theological Studies* 15 (1964).   S

ventures. One safeguard that might be effective is that the non-textualist professional Hebraist should familiarize himself with the issues, and thereby, possibly, obtain and advocate a perspective which might save the protagonists from unnecessary and unseemly invective.

The main objective of *B.H.*³ still stands unchallenged, and the substitution of a Ben Asher text for the Ben Chayim text is fully vindicated. No one now, or apparently in future, would dream of departing from a Ben Asher text in favour of any text-form short of an authenticated earlier text. Nevertheless, the text of *B.H.*³, or rather its basis in the Leningrad Codex has become the subject of criticism and our first inquiry is to consider the nature of the attack on it. All three editions have made the attack each in its own way.

In the first place the Cassuto text has claimed to be tantamount to a Ben Asher text-form although it is conveyed in the Ben Chayim text-form as it appeared in the Ginsburg printed Bible. The publication has been given a notoriously poor reception, and I would not wish to hold any brief for it or defend it in detail. On the other hand, it is fair to concede that, in principle, it constitutes an interesting and even an important experiment. Cassuto was convinced that his new Jerusalem Bible must bear the Ben Asher text-form and he took steps to reconstruct this text by collating with *B.H.*³ (i.e. the Leningrad Codex), the British Museum manuscript of the Pentateuch (Or. 4445), and the Cairo Codex of the Prophets. When the text was finally published, after Cassuto's death, scholars were amazed to find that it consisted merely of a photographic edition of the Ginsburg Bible, shorn of its textual marks and corresponding *apparatus criticus* and incorporating Cassuto's own vocalic changes based on his collations. Critics were quick to fall on some unfortunate anomalies which were bound to occur, and we are given a list of inconsistent vocalizations by Kahle.[1] Professor Kahle, probably more than any other, has maligned the publication in a number of places, and he became so vituperative in his review of the work in *Vetus Testamentum* for 1953[2] that a polite but very effective rejoinder appeared in the next number of that Journal by the Chairman of the Publishers of the Bible, Sir Leon Simon, and its edge was not blunted by Kahle's retort that he had received nice letters from Mrs. Cassuto and her daughter.[3] Kahle had implied that the publication was a gross injustice on Cassuto's work, for which guilt attaches to those who published it after Cassuto's death. Sir Leon's reply is significant, and forms

---

[1] 'The Ben Asher Text of the Hebrew Bible' (*Donum Natalicum H.S. Nyberg Oblatum* (1960), p. 162).
[2] 'The New Hebrew Bible' (*V.T.* iii (1953), pp. 416–20).
[3] *Der Hebräische Bibeltext seit F. Delitzsch* (1961), p. 88.

the basis of the present assessment of the Cassuto Bible: it is that the publishers were acting on Cassuto's own suggestion, and it was he himself who had chosen the Ginsburg edition 'as the one into which his alterations were to be carried'.[1] Cassuto had concluded that, for practical purposes, the Ginsburg Bible could be the vehicle to convey the Ben Asher text, and the correspondence between Cassuto and Kahle as published by Kahle himself makes the point quite clearly. To Kahle, it was unthinkable that a Ben Asher text could be produced independently of an actual Ben Asher manuscript, but Cassuto had certainly such an aim before him when he said, 'my intention is to reconstruct as far as possible the text of Ben Asher in its definitive form by a collation of the different manuscripts, those of Cairo, Aleppo, Leningrad, London 4445 and some other fragments of the same school'.[2] The fact is that Cassuto assumed that the Ben Asher text was a reconstructable text, and acted accordingly. This is the purport, too, of the rejoinder by Sir Leon Simon and the publishers. All that we regret, and possibly attribute to the posthumous nature of the publication, are the anomalies of the type mentioned above which had not been ironed out of the vocalization before publication. Concerning the above list of manuscripts collated for the Ben Asher text, Professor Goshen-Gottstein[3] goes out of his way to convince his readers that the Cassuto Bible does not include variants from the Aleppo Codex although the editor had been able to consult that codex, and wishes to correct the false impression which has been spread abroad because of Kahle's original mistake. It is important to note in this context, however, that Cassuto himself once more explains this decision,[4] and states that he did not wish to make substantial use of the Aleppo text because he was not convinced of its Ben Asher nature. The Cassuto text is, indeed, a deliberate, scientifically conceived reconstruction of Ben Asher according to the lights of the editor, who was by general consent no mere amateur in this field of study. In some ways, it was a more consistent effort than B.H.[3], as may be seen from the following instance. In the preface to B.H.[3] Kahle expresses gratitude to the British Museum for photographs of Or. 4445 to facilitate the preparation of the edition, but nowhere is this 'important London manuscript' referred to in the list of 'sigla et compendia', nor, so far as I can see, is it used at all in the apparatus criticus. I would suggest that,

---

[1] 'The Jerusalem Bible' (V.T. iv (1954), pp. 109 f.). Cf. also Goshen-Gottstein, 'The Authenticity of the Aleppo Codex' (Txt. i (1960), p. 32).
[2] Letter sent to Kahle in 1950, qu. Kahle, 'The New Hebrew Bible' (V.T. i:i (1953), p. 418).
[3] 'The Authenticity of the Aleppo Codex' (Txt. i (1960), p. 25).
[4] Cassuto's letter, cf. above, n. 2.

despite its obvious and few infelicities, Cassuto's Bible makes an important contribution to the post-1937 study of the history of Hebrew Bibles.

The second example is again a case of producing a Ben Asher text without, as it were, a Ben Asher pedigree; it is the Snaith edition published by the British and Foreign Bible Society in 1958. Like Cassuto, Snaith was convinced that his text should be Ben Asher, but, apparently, he was unable to use the Leningrad Codex and he, differing from Cassuto, would not embark on an eclectic text. But he looked around for other sources[1] and found one in the first-hand of a Sephardi manuscript in the British Museum, Or. 2626–8, dated 1483. He also used, for confirmation, Norzi's *Minḥath Shai*, the *kethubim* of a Yemenite manuscript also in the British Museum (Or. 2375), and, for checking purposes, *Shem Tob* from the David Sassoon Library. We note that, compared with the Ben Asher texts, they are all late (*Minḥath Shai*, 1626; Or. 2626–8, 1483; Or. 2375, 1460–80; *Shem Tob*, 1312), and one of them is even of non-Spanish provenance. But Snaith[2] can claim that by means of these manuscripts he has found 'a way of producing the true Ben Asher text independently of the Leningrad Codex'. He explains this by saying that 'accurate Ben Asher MSS. must have been introduced into Spain at a comparatively early period of the time when Spain became the great centre of Jewish learning'. Of course, it is necessary to stress the other point made by Snaith that only the first hand of Or. 2626–8 is relevant, whereas the corrections in this manuscript were extraneous, having been introduced in order to bring the text into line with the Ben Chayim text and thus rendering it valueless from the Ben Asher point of view.

It is significant that the claim made by Snaith has not as yet, so far as I know, been basically challenged. The one criticism that has been made,[3] namely that he should have gone one step further back and used the same manuscript as was used by Norzi himself rather than a copy, rather loses point in view of the basic importance of the other, Sephardic manuscript, and the assumption that the copy is a replica of the earlier manuscript. Furthermore, by tacitly confirming the bona fides of Snaith's edition, it would appear to me that Kahle[3] has himself made an important concession, namely by permitting the possible survival of Ben Asher manuscripts which must have been copied in Spain with great care. Consequently, an edition based on such manuscripts can legitimately be claimed as Ben Asher without, however, showing lineal Ben Asher descent. In other words, provided he is familiar with the Ben Asher text-form an editor of a Hebrew Bible is not restricted in his choice to the actual Ben Asher manuscripts themselves. Whether or not

---

[1] 'The Ben Asher Text' (*Txt.* ii (1962), pp. 8–13). Cf. *V.T.* vii (1957), p. 207.
[2] Ibid., p. 12; cf. *C.G.*, p. 140.   [3] Cf. Kahle, *C.G.*, p. 139.

Snaith has actually produced such a text, correct in all details, remains to be seen, and it is possible that the acknowledged presence of accidental printers' errors might so complicate the research that the task might be long delayed.[1] Nevertheless the principle seems to be established that a judicious use of medieval, post-Ben Asher manuscripts might indeed result in the production of the Ben Asher text-form.

The next on our list is the Bible of the Jerusalem Bible Project, with its basis firmly laid on the Aleppo Codex. The preliminary studies already make it clear that the project involves a direct challenge to the claims made for the Leningrad Codex. In common with the Cassuto and Snaith Bibles, it is recognized by the Jerusalem team that only a Ben Asher text can satisfy the demands of a modern Hebrew Bible, but it is now further claimed that it is only the Aleppo Codex that supplies it. The Aleppo Codex is unique, the sole bearer of the real Ben Asher text. I quote Professor Goshen-Gottstein:[2] 'The Aleppo Codex was, indeed, the greatest event in the history of the Tiberian Bible text, the first complete codex of the Bible according to the tradition later to be accepted as *the* Tiberian Massoretic Bible. Its "victory" over other Ben Asher texts was due to its inherent obvious perfection as the acme of achievement of *the* dynasty of Masoretes.'

In order to establish this superiority it has appeared necessary to deny Ben Asher recognition to all other texts which have hitherto qualified. This is particularly true of the Leningrad Codex which has attracted fire from all quarters.[3] Codex L, they say, was copied from a manuscript far removed from Ben Asher, and later brought to conform with it by means of 'endless erasures and changes'. One might interpose here to say that this conclusion seems to place both Cassuto and Snaith in the respectable company of the Leningrad correctors!

A corollary of this conclusion is to introduce a new assessment of Ben Naphtali readings. We know that Kahle argued that one strong point in favour of the authenticity of L was the agreement between it and the list of Ben Asher readings in Mishael Ben Uzziel; it now transpires that not only was L subjected to erasures and corrections in order to secure this

---

[1] The Bible Society representative who was present when this paper was read informed me that substantial corrections have already been made in a recent reprint of the Snaith text, and another reprint already under way will contain still further corrections.

[2] 'The Rise of the Tiberian Bible Text' (*Biblical and Other Studies* (ed. A. Altmann), i (1963), p. 89).

[3] It is right to add here that the attack has been already in part anticipated, at least by implication, by members of the team preparing the new *B.H.*⁴, particularly by G. E. Weil. Cf. 'La nouvelle édition de la Massorah (*B.H.K.* iv) et l'histoire de la Massorah' (*V.T.*, suppl. ix, pp. 266–84).

agreement, but also that Mishael's list of Ben Asher–Ben Naphtali readings is not as genuine as had been assumed. It is, says Goshen-Gottstein,[1] a copy of a secondary compilation, and from a putative date 'hardly earlier than the 13th century' (this, despite Kahle's frequently stated but, says G.-G., purely conjectural estimate of the tenth or eleventh century). The completion of Lipschütz's[2] publication of Mishael in *Textus* 1962 becomes important not because, as was intended by the editor, it presents 'true' Ben Asher readings but because it provides the means of reconstructing the Ben Naphtali variants. The document is further relevant because it proves to a large extent that one of the texts hitherto regarded as an important Ben Asher text, namely the Cairo Codex of the Prophets, is much more Ben Naphtali than Ben Asher. Such a conclusion is disconcerting until, however, we read in Goshen-Gottstein's treatment that the distinction between Ben Asher and Ben Naphtali does not amount to divergent traditions, for it is possible that the Ben Asher father (i.e. Moshe) could have written the Ben Naphtali and the son (Aaron) could nevertheless have written the Ben Asher text *par excellence*. There is a further indication of drastic revision of traditional theories on this point in the analysis by Díez-Macho,[3] from quite a different approach, where he shows that many manuscripts hitherto accepted as Ben Naphtali should in fact be reckoned as proto-Tiberian, deriving from the Palestinian tradition.

To revert to the Aleppo Codex. It is urged against Cassuto and others that it was this Codex that received the commendation of Maimonides in the thirteenth century, but Goshen-Gottstein,[4] having taken endless trouble to prove this, feels constrained to argue elsewhere[5] that it was not Maimonides's decree that gained the 'victory' of the Ben Asher text over its rivals but that it merely attests to its superiority in the Aleppo Codex. The conclusion is an important one in view of the significance hitherto attached to this decree, though one might also wonder whether or not this, again, is but a thinly veiled attack on Kahle's conclusions. It is significant that Ginsburg[6] in his Introduction makes no mention of the Maimonides statement, and all that Strack[7] does in his article in

[1] 'The Authenticity of the Aleppo Codex', op. cit., p. 26.
[2] L. Lipschütz, *Kitab al-Khilaf, Mishael Ben Uzziel's Treatise on the Differences between Ben Asher and Ben Naphtali.* Part i (1935); Part ii (*Txt.* ii, 1962 (Supplement)).
[3] 'A new list of so-called "Ben Naftali" manuscripts' (*Hebrew and Semitic Studies presented to G. R. Driver* (ed. D. W. Thomas and W. D. McHardy, 1963), pp. 16–52).
[4] Cf. 'The Authenticity of the Aleppo Codex', op. cit., pp. 22 ff.
[5] 'The Rise of the Tiberian Massoretic Text', op. cit., pp. 117–21.
[6] *Introduction to the Massoretico-Critical Edition of the Hebrew Bible* (1897).
[7] 'The Text of the Old Testament' (*H.D.B.* iv, p. 730).

H.D.B. on the Old Testament Text is to refer to the scribes of the Leningrad Codex, Maimonides and Kimchi as prominent authorities in which the prestige of Aaron Ben Asher was recognized. Kahle, in *Masoreten des Westens*,[1] refers to Sappir and Graetz as having mentioned that Maimonides saw the scroll, but that signifies little except as a hint that here, as so often, Kahle adopted a suggestion by earlier scholars and worked it up to make it appear pivotal in his own reconstruction.

Despite the disclaimer of Goshen-Gottstein, it appears right to assert that it is the Maimonides decree that signifies the adoption of Ben Asher in medieval times and indicates to us the significance of that act. I shall not repeat the contents of Maimonides's statement[2] which is given in his *Hilkoth Sepher Torah*, viii. 4; the relevant point is that he used the standard codex which he found in Cairo for the correct division of open and closed paragraphs in his copy of the Torah, since all was confusion in the available scrolls and Massoretic works. Goshen-Gottstein[3] rebukes some people for having exaggerated the significance of Maimonides's decree by making it tantamount to 'canonization', and since I have been singled out for special mention—rather as a whipping-boy—I shall restate my reasons for making this assessment.[4] Actually, Goshen-Gottstein has not helped matters by telling his readers what he thought I meant, and reading into my interpretation—it is really Kahle's interpretation—that Maimonides's decree has the character of a 'canonization'. Of course, I have never used the word in this context. What Maimonides did, and what I think is the importance of Maimonides, was to single out the Aaron Ben Asher text—the Aleppo Codex—from the welter of chaos and confused texts, and to accept it as the authoritative text. In this sense I think it is correct to talk of a 'victory' of one text-form over a number of competing texts which had caused confusion. But this is not 'canonization'. Furthermore, I would venture to suggest to the Hebrew University Bible Project that the Aleppo Codex could well have become just another Ben Asher text were it not for Maimonides. These scholars might persuade one another that there was no other really Ben Asher text, but I would think, despite the array of special pleading, that the existence of other Ben Asher texts must be admitted by them, otherwise what are they using to fill in the lacunae—the very extensive lacunae—in the Aleppo manuscript? And in any case, it is stretching the evidence very far to say that there is no Ben Asher text except that of Aaron.

[1] Vol. i (1927), pp. 2 f.
[2] Four translations are now readily available; two of them in *Txt.* i, p. 7 and p. 18; *C.G.*[2], p. 107; *Masoreten des Westens*, i, pp. 11–12.
[3] 'The Rise of the Tiberian Text', op. cit., p. 118.
[4] Cf. *The Old Testament Text and Versions* (1951), pp. 64 f.

Let us look again at the Maimonides decree, and note that what Maimonides gained from the Aaron Ben Asher text was safe guidance in the matter of paragraphs, and similar items of information. It is this that helps us to put the whole matter in perspective. Jerusalem appears to be saying: 'Away with the Leningrad Codex, and, of course, *B.H.*[3] Pour scorn on the ill-begotten bastard Bible of Cassuto and the pitiful effort of the British and Foreign Bible Society. It is only the unique Aleppo Codex that can serve the Project. This is the only text with the right paragraphs, divided in the right way, open and closed!' I am not mocking the Jerusalem scholars—they are very able people, and their Bible will be a notable achievement—but I am anxious that we should all know what is involved by their insistence on the Aleppo Codex. It is that the Codex embodies the necessary official information about the use of the text for synagogue purposes. Furthermore, I would suggest that the actual value of all Ben Asher studies relates more to the history of Jewish liturgies than to the history of textual transmission in the usual sense of this term.

In one way Professor Goshen-Gottstein has himself, it appears to me, pointed to the same conclusion, and yet has again possibly overstated the case. When discussing the Ben Naphtali–Ben Asher divergences[1] he says, 'if we leave aside the alleged Ben Naphtali manuscripts (the Reuchlin Codex and others used by Kahle) and turn to the only admissible evidence of Ben Naphtali's readings, Mishael's list, there remains no doubt that the two systems are practically one. And in this', he continues, 'the vast majority of present-day Bible scholars would concur.' But the fact remains that Ben Asher and Ben Naphtali variations have always loomed large in all the histories of Massoretic works and in many of the medieval manuscripts. I think, for instance, of the 1958 edition by Cecil Roth[2] of the superb Aberdeen Codex from the late fifteenth century which devotes thirteen pages to lists of Ben Asher–Ben Naphtali variants. Nevertheless, I would urge that the variants are of much more interest to the Jewish liturgiolist than to the textual critic. The point is well taken in a recent article in *Z.D.M.G.* by Rudolf Meyer[3] of Jena in which he deals with the grammatical significance of the Ben Naphtali codices on the basis of the use of the various forms of *daghesh*, and their treatment by Sperber.[4] He explains that there is an inherent homogeneity to the Ben Asher texts whether they be those represented

---

[1] 'The Rise of the Tiberian Text', op. cit., p. 110.
[2] *The Aberdeen Codex of the Hebrew Bible* (1958), cf. pp. 23–25.
[3] 'Die Bedeutung des Codex Reuchlinianus für die hebräische Sprachgeschichte dargestellt am Dageš-Gebrauch' (*Z.D.M.G.* (1963), Hft. i, pp. 51–61).
[4] A. Sperber, *Codex Reuchlinianus, with a General Introduction; Masoretic Hebrew* (1956).

by the Leningrad Codex or Ben Chayim, whereas the Ben Naphtali texts represent a divergent tradition. Nevertheless, he explains, the outstanding feature of the latter is that their relevance is mainly for the pronunciation of Hebrew. This, it appears to me, points to the liturgical use of the texts, and concerns the recitation of Scripture rather than its textual transmission.

From a textual point of view, the finer distinctions between various Ben Asher texts, and the superiority of the Aleppo Codex over all others, and also the divergences of the Ben Naphtali and Ben Asher traditions, are mainly of academic interest—for, although we have been traditionally taught that the *daghesh* and the *ḥateph* vowel marks have a grammatical significance, it is now becoming clearer that they function more effectively as aids to intoning. Of course, we appreciate that the difference between what we call grammar and what the Massoretes regarded as pronunciation is often artificial, and not recognized by the actual Massoretic lists; nevertheless for the purpose of textual study it is a distinction we must draw and, as often as possible, observe.

This same assumption might be drawn from the use made of medieval manuscripts which do not conform, even textually, to the class of texts conventionally called Ben Asher. I think particularly of the variants listed in Kennicott and de Rossi, and to a lesser extent in the Ginsburg Bible.[1] Apart from the superabundance of divergent *scriptio plena* and *defectiva* probably the most striking feature, especially in Kennicott and de Rossi, is the apparently inconsequential interchange between the uses of the Divine Names. The Babylonian Talmud *Menaḥoth* 29[b]–30 contains rules about the writing of the Divine Name, but in a context which is concerned with its inadvertent omission by a scribe. But what we have in the manuscripts is the substitution of one name for another. In the past this phenomenon has been noted but very irregularly used and has led to confusion especially in the *apparatus criticus* of *B.H.*[3], where, it might appear, the main source of entries was the Ginsburg Bible, but even this was only sporadically used.

Simply as examples of the feature I have in mind I quote some cases of interchange, and their treatment by the editors of *B.H.*[3] I looked up the variants given by Kennicott for Genesis vi–vii: in vi. 5 *Elohim* stands for *Yahweh* in one manuscript and is added in LXX, but is not mentioned in *B.H.*[3]; in vi. 13 *Yahweh* is added to *Elohim* in one manuscript, and again not mentioned in *B.H.*[3]; in vii. 1 *Elohim* stands for *Yahweh* in one, whereas in vii. 9 the reverse takes place, and also in vii. 16 (the first, with further Version evidence, is included in *B.H.*[3], but not the last

---

[1] London (1927).

two, despite the interesting though irrelevant fact that these verses are from the Priestly document). I turned to the Elohistic Psalter to find ample evidence that Kennicott might have raised difficulties for the theory of an 'Elohistic recension'! I shall ignore for the moment the very common substitution of *Adonay* for *Yahweh* and vice versa, and note that in Ps. xlvii. 9 *Yahweh* is given for *Elohim* in 34 MSS. and neither Ginsburg nor *B.H.*[3] mentions it. Other failures to mention similar substitutions in *B.H.*[3] are in xlvii. 7; xlviii. 9, 11; l. i, 16; li. 17: a substitution is entered wrongly in lii. 10, omitted from liii. 3, mentioned in liii. 5, omitted from liii. 6, and mentioned in liii. 7. In Isa. vii. 13 *Elohai* occurs for *Yahweh* in one MS., but is omitted from *B.H.*[3], whereas in vii. 14 the substitution of *Yahweh* for *Adonay* is included: in viii. 18 the whole gamut of changes, from *Yahweh* and *Adonay* to *Elohim* is recorded in a large number of MSS. by Kennicott but there is no mention of these in *B.H.*[3]

Such a sporadic annotation of divergences is obviously unsatisfactory, but, if it is to be included at all, what should it be made to convey? We cannot dismiss it as a peculiarity of post-Ben Asher textual vagaries, because it is not in keeping with the known textual history of the period when textual innovations are no longer to be expected. Furthermore, it can be proved by reference to Genizah fragments that such interchange of the Divine Names was quite common long before the so-called emergence of the Ben Asher text. And, of course, a superficial knowledge of both Qumran and Septuagint texts is enough to demonstrate the still greater antiquity of the phenomenon. I would suggest that here, just as in minor variations of vocalization, we are dealing with synagogue usage rather than with text-transmission in the strict sense of the term. It would appear that apart from certain rules about the Divine Name, no mistake rendered a codex 'unfit', but whatever those rules denote, it is certainly true that it was common practice to ring the changes with Divine Names according to some, to us, indefinable principle.

Another kind of problem is posed by the Cairo Geniza fragments. They do figure in *B.H.*[3] but only according to Kahle's interpretation. The fact remains, however, that we do not really know how to assess their textual significance. There are literally thousands of them still unexamined, as far as is known, and it is precarious to base any far-reaching hypothesis on what has hitherto been discovered. On the negative side, I would suggest that any claim that they provide textual evidence of immediate significance must be carefully scrutinized. I have myself looked at a few hundreds of fragments from Cambridge to find only divergences of *scriptio plena* and *defectiva* and in the Divine Names. I have suggested above that such divergences are synagogal rather than textual. Goshen-Gottstein[1] has looked at thousands, and assesses their textual importance as small, though he hopes to find an occasional textual variant. I quote his opinion because I find it confirms in a way the suggestion I make: 'The freedom in copying out these texts is of vital importance for our understanding of Hebrew reading traditions and linguistic habits. But its textual importance is, as a rule, to be doubted unless specifically proved for a given fragment.' I take this to mean that for Jewish liturgical studies they are significant, for the Hebrew grammarian they have a use which must be judiciously applied, for the textualist they might produce an occasional note. With this view I would concur, and in consequence stress that Hebrew liturgiologists be invited to assess their value.

Finally, I would mention the vexed question of the relevance of the Dead Sea Scrolls. Obviously the textualist will make a clear distinction between Qumran and other texts and place Murabba'at and its parallel texts from the Bar Cochba period in a group apart. The distinction between them is basic, for the latter, of course, belong to the Massoretic tradition—and the former do not. The main problem about Murabba'at is the relevance of the *scriptio plena* and *defectiva* variations in the few instances where they occur. The Qumran material, however, is a very different proposition. In the first place I think it is quite illogical to deal with it as if it formed part of the Massoretic transmission. No one would act in this way with the Septuagint, and, for textual purposes, the cultural affinities of Qumran lie more in that direction than in the direction of the Massoretic text, despite the fact that so many Qumran texts agree with the latter. Rabbi Akiba had harsh things to say about the Christians, and I doubt whether he would be any more kindly disposed to the Qumranites and their texts. In the second place, the whole problem of the relationship of the scrolls to one another needs to be faced, for, again, it is quite as illogical to use the evidence of the scrolls indiscriminately as it is that of the Geniza Fragments. A great deal of useful material has been assembled by the one scholar who has examined the scrolls systematically from this point of view, namely Father Martin in his two volumes on *The Scribal Character of the Dead Sea Scrolls*,[2] but his conclusion has been simply to push further back the question of unification of diverse sources. There is in the scrolls generally, he maintains, a consistently true copying of compilations, without, however, any attempt to introduce a unified orthography. Basically this is also true of the biblical scrolls from Qumran. Obviously the problem still remains of how we are to understand the relationship of these diverse

[1] 'Biblical Manuscripts in the United States' (*Txt.* ii (1962), pp. 36–44).
[2] 1958.

forms *vis-à-vis* a reasonably uniform text which I call, simply for convenience, a proto-Massoretic text. I think the existence of such a text can be postulated on two grounds, namely the evidence of DSIb and of numerous Qumran fragments which coincide with M.T., or which have but very few orthographic variations, and secondly, what I think is the clear indication of Rabbinic teaching that the Massoretes were concerned about preserving tradition and not changing it, much less creating a new one.[1] For the time being, however, all one can do is to enter a caveat against an indiscriminate use of the scrolls especially as evidence to bolster an hypothesis about the early history of the Massoretic text-form.

It is with great joy and satisfaction that we greet the information about the new Jerusalem Bible Project and the fourth edition of *Biblia Hebraica*. The significance of the Cassuto and Snaith texts, however, is not thereby diminished, for not only have they given us each its own independent text but also jointly they have helped considerably in placing the Ben Asher text-form in its appropriate setting. Such a perspective, however, serves only to show that the real problem of the Hebrew Bible is to be tackled in the *apparatus criticus*. We would not move far from the text-form of Ben Asher, but we realize that this was conditioned by the need of the Jewish synagogue in medieval times. Our needs in general do not, however, fall into this category, and consequently the Hebrew Bible must be supplied with a competent annotation. The nature of this *apparatus criticus* could provide the theme for another excursus in this wide-ranging topic.   BLEDDYN J. ROBERTS

[1] Cf. B. J. Roberts, 'The Old Testament Canon: A Suggestion' (*Bulletin of the John Rylands Library*, xlvi (1963), pp. 164–78).

PROLEGOMENON:
The Masoretic Text:
A Critical Evaluation

HARRY M. ORLINSKY

The ways of scholarship, no less than those that the author of Proverbs 30.18-19 had found too wonderful to fathom, are passing strange. Who would have thought in 1897, when C. D. Ginsburg's monumental *Introduction to the Mas-soretico-Critical Edition of the Hebrew Bible* appeared, that within about a quarter of a century a new discipline in biblical research would come into being, in the guise of archeology, that would push out the classical approach to the study of the text of the Bible? And no less marvelous, who would have imagined in the Twenties that about a quarter of a century later new archeological discoveries, in the guise of the Dead Sea Scrolls, would help to restore something of that classical approach? And so it has come to pass that Ginsburg's *Introduction*, standard in its field for several decades until it lapsed into neglect and was permitted to run out of print, is now experiencing revival.

Toward the end of the nineteenth and early in the twentieth century, biblical studies generally dealt with philology, that is, with the grammatical and textual analysis of the Bible.

Reprinted from Prolegomenon to KTAV reissue of C.D. Ginsburg's *Introduction to the Massoretico-Critical Edition of the Hebrew Bible*, N.Y., 1966.

Also, the biblical scholar tended to study in the greatest possible detail each section and each chapter, and often each
verse, of each biblical Book, with the view to determining
their authorship and their relative, or absolute, date of composition. Since extrabiblical data were then available in but
rather meager quantity and quality, it was chiefly the biblical
writings themselves that were closely analyzed. This was the
period when the great introductions to the Bible were composed, e.g., those by J. Wellhausen (—F. Bleek) and S. R.
Driver; when the standard grammars, dictionaries, and en-
cyclopedias were worked up, e.g., the grammars of F. E.
König and Gesenius-Kautzsch-Cowley, the dictionaries of
Brown-Driver-Briggs and Gesenius-Buhl, and the encyclope-
dias of J. Hastings and Cheyne-Black; nor should C. Brockel-
mann's comprehensive *Grundriss der vergleichenden Grammatik der semitischen Sprachen* go unmentioned. [1]

In the midst of this heyday of philology and textual
criticism, the massive *Introduction* of Christian David Ginsburg (1831 - 1914) made its debut, marking the climax of a
flourishing period of masoretic research. Wolf Heidenheim
(1757-1832) had compiled his instructive little book of 132
pages on משפטי הטעמים (Rödelheim, 1808), and had edited the
Pentateuch מאור עינים (5 vols., Rödelheim, 1818-21;   מדויק
בתכלית הדיוק ומסודר בשלימות הסדור), which included on every
page the עין הקורא of Jekuthiel Ha-Naqdan ("the Punctuator"; 13th century); Abraham Geiger (1810-74) had achieved
his important study of *Urschrift und Uebersetzungen der Bibel,*
etc. (Breslau, 1857); Simḥah Pinsker (1801-64) had published
his epoch-making מבוא אל הנקוד האשורי או הבבלי *Einleitung
in das Babylonisch-Hebräische Punktationssystem,* etc. (Vienna, 1863; together with Abraham ibn Ezra's   ספר יסוד
מספר *Grammatik der hebräischen Zahlwörter* of XLIV
pages), not to mention his revolutionary לקוטי קדמוניות לקורות
דת בני מקרא והליטעראטור שלהם *Zur Geschichte des Karäismus
und der karäischen Literatur* three years earlier; following on
his edition of דרכי הנקוד והנגינות *Fragmente aus der Punkta-*

tions- und Accentlehre der hebräischen Sprache (Hannover, 5607/1847; attributed to Moses ben Yom-Ṭob Ha-Naqdan, English Masorete and grammarian of the 12th century), Solomon Frensdorff (1803-80) had edited two basic works, *Das Buch Ochlah W'ochlah* (*Massora*) (Hannover, 1864) and *Die Massora Magna: I. Massoretisches Wörterbuch* (Hannover und Leipzig, 1876); Joseph N. Derenbourg (1811-95) had published the *Manuel du Lecteur, d'un Auteur Inconnu,* etc. (Paris, 1871; reprinted from Series VI of *Journal Asiatique,* 16 [1870], 309-433,; see L. Lipschütz, *Textus,* 4 [1964], pp. 2, 27. On the title of the *Manuel,* מחברת התיגאן "Treatise on the Crown" (i.e., the Bible), see, e.g., Baer-Strack, *Diqduqe Ha-Ṭe'amim,* Einleitung, XX, §4; Wickes טעמי כ"א ספרים, p. xiv and n.27; or F. Buhl, *Canon and Text of the Old Testament* [Edinburgh, 1892], 98); the excellent *Prolegomena Critica in Vetus Testamentum Hebraicum* (Lipsiae, 1873) by Hermann L. Strack (1848-1922) had appeared, as well as his edition of *Prophetarum Posteriorum Codex Babylonicus Petropolitanus* (St. Petersburg, 1876) in photographic reproduction; Seligman Baer (1825-97)—he and Ginsburg were the most active and important "Masoretes" in our time — had analyzed in 1869, in vol. 1 of *Archiv für wissenschaftliche Erforschung des Alten Testament* (ed. A. Merx), pp. 55-67, 194-207, "Die Metheg-Setzung nach ihren überlieferten Gesetzen dargestellt." In the same year his *Liber Genesis* appeared, the first fruits of his projected *Textum Masoreticum* of the whole Bible (see further below). And in 1879 he published (in association with Strack) ספר דקדוקי הטעמים לרבי אהרן בן משה בן אשר עם מסורות עתיקות אחרות להבין יסודות המקרא ודרכי ישר לשונו, מסודר בשלמות בפעם ראשונה על פי העתקות רבות כתבי יד ישנים גם מבואר היטב... (Leipzig, 1879); W. Wickes (dates unknown to me) had published טעמי אמ"ת, *A Treatise on the Accentuation of the Three So-called Poetical Books of the Old Testament: Psalms, Proverbs, and Job* (Oxford, 1881) and טעמי כ"א ספרים,*A Treatise on the Accentuation of the Twenty-one So-called Prose Books of the Old*

Testament (Oxford, 1887); Samuel Rosenfeld (dates unknown to me) had published his useful משפחת סופרים (Wilna,
1883); and Ludwig Blau (1861-1936), precocious scholar,
had published his *Masoretische Untersuchungen* (Strassburg,
1891) and *Zur Einleitung in die Heilige Schrift* (Budapest,
1894), as well as "Massoretic Studies" in *Jewish Quarterly
Review, O.S.,* 8 (1896), 343-59; 9 (1897), 122-44, 471-90,
where he dealt with the number of letters and words in the
Bible and with the division into verses. [2]

For Ginsburg, the *Introduction* was the culmination of
much prior work of his own—even though some of his results
would not be published for some years to come. In 1867 he
had published *The Massoreth Ha-Massoreth of Elias Levita,
being an Exposition of the Masoretic Notes on the Hebrew
Bible, or the Ancient Critical Apparatus of the Old Testament
in Hebrew, with an English Translation and Critical and
Explanatory Notes* (London), two years after putting out
*Jacob ben Chayim ibn Adonijah's Introduction to the Hebrew
Bible, Hebrew and English; with Explanatory Notes* (London,
1865), both works of great significance for the correct understanding of how the modern, so-called masoretic Bible editions
have come into being.

About 1895 Ginsburg published an 88-page preliminary
Essay on the Massorah. He began with the blunt statement,
"For the past seven years I have been engaged in a critical recension of the text of the Hebrew Scriptures . . . Now, although
almost every Introduction to the Bible speaks about the Massorah, and although the *textus receptus* of the Hebrew Scriptures is technically called 'the MASSORETIC Text,' yet I
venture to say, without intending to give offence, but without
fear of contradiction, that with the exception of a few Jews
and one or two Christians, all those who have edited the Hebrew text, or written upon its Massorah in their respective
Introductions, could neither master nor describe the entire domain of this ancient critical apparatus." This *Essay* was to
reach much greater proportions in the *Introduction* as chapter

XI, "The Massorah; its Rise and Development" (pp. 287-468).

The two works which have given Ginsburg lasting fame, in addition to the *Introduction,* are his edition of the Hebrew Bible and his edition of *The Massorah.* In 1894 there appeared in two volumes, under the sponsorship of the Trinitarian Bible Society, his עשרים וארבעה ספרי הקדש/מדויקים היטב על פי המסורה / ועל פי דפוסים ראשונים / עם חלופים והגהות / מן / כתבי יד עתיקים ותרגומים ישנים / מאת / דוד גינצבורג / לונדון / בשנת / ת' ר' נ' ד' לפ"ק / 1894 / בראשית - מלכים, ישעיה - דברי הימים / על ידי חברת מוציאי לאור תורת יהוה תמימה; this edition of the *Massoretico-Critical Text of the Hebrew Bible* was reproduced in one volume in 1906 by the Society for the Circulation of Uncorrupted Versions of the Word of God.³ While only reproducing essentially the text published in 1524-25 by Jacob ben Chayim, Ginsburg made available very considerable new data from old manuscripts and other early printed editions, providing the knowing reader with a critical apparatus of some significance.⁴

The same, essentially Jacob ben Chayim text served subsequently as the basis for Ginsburg's four-volume edition of the Bible published by the British and Foreign Bible Society. The Pentateuch appeared in 1908,⁵ and the *Prophetae Priores* and the *Prophetae Posteriores* in 1911 (with the assistance of R. Kilgour); *The Writings* were put out in 1926, twelve years after Ginsburg's death, by H.E. Holmes, "under the oversight of the Rev. Professor A. S. Geden."⁶

Ginsburg's four-volume edition of *The Massorah. Compiled from Manuscripts, Alphabetically and Lexically Arranged,* imperial folio (London, 1881-1905), is a truly monumental work; a pity that the fifth and last volume, which would have constituted part 2 of vol. 4, never appeared. Ginsburg gathered together masoretic notes from numerous manuscripts and early printed editions of the Bible, rearranged them in alphabetical order, and translated them into English, frequently introducing annotations of his own; in addition, he made available other masoretic tractates. It is no diminu-

tion of Ginsburg's massive contribution that there are now
available many more masoretic notes, and that it is even possible to distribute some of them, up to a point, among the
schools of Ben Asher, Ben Naftali, and other Masoretes in
Palestine and Babylonia.

There were several useful by-products of Ginsburg's intensive researches. In 1897 there appeared *A Series of Fifteen
Facsimiles of Manuscripts of the Hebrew Bible with Descriptions;* and in the following year he issued an enlarged *Series
of XVIII. Facsimiles,* etc., adding three facsimiles (XVI-
XVIII) to the fifteen reproduced previously. (Incidentally,
the photography is excellent, and it is a pleasure to work
directly from the reproductions; see the nice review by I.
Harris in *JQR,* 10 [1898], 190-4.) In 1899 Ginsburg published in the Chwolson Volume לחם חמדות ‏/לדניאל איש חמדות
*Recueil des travaux rédigés en mémoire du Jubilé Scientifique
de M. Daniel Chwolson* [Prof. at the University of St. Petersburg, 1846-96], Berlin, on pp. 149-88, a fine statement "On
the Relationship of the so-called Codex Babylonicus of A.D.
916 to the Eastern Recension of the Hebrew Text." Thus
Ginsburg recognized that " . . . the simple fact that this Codex has the Babylonian system of punctuation can no longer
be adduced by itself as proof that the consonantal text is also
that of the Babylonians . . . " (p. 150) ; indeed, " . . . there
are one hundred and twenty-eight passages in which the Babylonians deviate from the Palestinians. Of these the St. Petersburg
Codex has thirty-three only which are peculiar to this Codex.
Twenty-two others it has simply in common with Palestinian
MSS. and early printed editions. Eight of its readings in passages where these variations are recorded neither coincide with
the Babylonians nor with the Palestinians; whilst in no fewer
than sixty-five instances this Codex most undoubtedly follows
the Palestinian text. In some instances the Codex exhibits the
Palestinian readings where even the Palestinian Standard MSS.
themselves and the early printed editions have the Babylonian
readings . . . " (p. 188). In short, as we shall see below, this

old manuscript, just like all other manuscripts and printed editions of the Hebrew Bible, without a single exception, is a mixed text.[7]

While Ginsburg was working on the Masorah and producing his critical edition of the masoretic text, Seligman Baer, with the encouragement and assistance of Franz Delitzsch, was busy putting out his version of the masoretic text, *Textum Masoreticum Accuratissime Expressit, e fontibus Masorae Variae Illustravit, Notis Criticis Confirmavit* — each Book with valuable "Additamenta Critica et Masoretica" (Leipzig, 1869-95; only the last four Books of the Pentateuch, Exodus-Deuteronomy, failed to appear, due to Baer's death). Ginsburg and Baer each claimed that only his edition truly represented the correct masoretic text; thus Ginsburg (*Introduction*, Preface, p. V), "When compiling the notes to the Hebrew Bible, I at first gave the results of my collation without regard to the work of others who also profess to edit the Hebrew Text according to the Massorah. It was, however, pointed out to me that as sundry parts of Dr. Baer's edition of the text had been accepted by students as exhibiting the Massoretic recension, and since my edition differs in many respects from that of Dr. Baer, it was my duty to specify the authorities when my readings are in conflict with his . . . " And in his chapter (X) on "The Differences between Ben-Asher and Ben-Naphtali" (241-86) he had some specific criticism to make of Baer's approach to matters masoretic; thus, "As regards the separate Treatise called in some MSS. *Dikdukē Ha-Teamim* which has come down to us in several Codices and in the name of Ben-Asher, its text in the different MSS. and in the *editio princeps* is as hopelessly irreconcilable as that of the official Lists . . . As far as my collation of the numerous MSS. goes I can safely state that I have not found a single MS. which uniformly follows the rules about the vowel-points and accents propounded in the name of Ben-Asher in the Treatise which Drs. Baer and Strack have compiled and have named '*The Dikdukē Ha-Teamim of Ben Asher*' . . . If, therefore, Codices which in their Massoretic Appendices exhibit Rubrics ascribed to Ben-Asher, do not follow his rules in the text, it shows that either the rules do not belong to Ben-Asher or that they were not generally accepted and that the opinions of other Massoretic Schools were more popular. And . . . It is most uncritical to correct the definite statements in the official Lists which tabulate the precise nature of the differences between Ben-Asher and Ben-Naphtali by the uncertain utterances in these highly artificial Rubrics. The reverse process is far more critical. Any views expressed in the conglomerate Treatise which do not harmonise with the official Lists must not be taken as proceeding from Ben-Asher" (pp. 278-86). (In this connection it is good to learn that Dr. Aharon Dothan of Tel-Aviv University, who is well aware of these fundamental pitfalls, has announced a new, critical edition of *Diqduqe Ha-Ṭe'amim*, to be published by Israel's Hebrew Language Academy; see *Tarbiẓ*, 34 [1965], 138, n. 13.) I shall return below to the full significance of Ginsburg's strictures.

Baer and his supporters replied in kind. Already in 1879 — long before *The Massorah* had begun to appear — Baer-Strack commented in their *Dikduqe Ha-Ṭe'amim* (Einleitung, p. V), "*Ch. D. Ginsburg* druckt gegenwärtig ein grosses Werk 'The Massorah,' welches dem Prospect zufolge in vier Foliobänden enthalten soll . . . Endlich hat der mitunterzeichnete *S. Baer* schon vor Jahren den ganzen Text der Massora nach Handschriften berichtigt und besser geordnet. Seine Arbeit wird in der durch den russisch-turkischen Krieg aufgehaltenen, jetzt aber wieder in Angriff genommenen neuen Ausgabe der Rabbinischen Bibel (מקרא גדול), welche die Firma Witwe und Gebr. Romm in Wilna edirt. abgedruckt werden." Baer himself published a detailed critical review of vols. 1 and 2 of *The Massorah* in the *Zeitschrift der Deutschen Morgenländischen Gesellschaft*, 40 (1886), 743-56, with a "Nachschrift" on vol. 3 on pp. 756-8; it was on the basis of these and other critiques that Richard Gottheil has given what may be regarded as the consensus of scholarly opinion in the matter (Jewish Encyclopedia, II [1902], s. Baer, Seligman (Sekel), 433a-434b): "In general Baer's text has been accepted as representing the [sic!] Masoretic tradition; even though exception may be taken to his view on individual points or to his too extensive generalization from insufficient manuscript evidence. Christian Ginsburg . . . has criticized a number of these faults with some severity. He points out, among other things, that Baer has indicated the open and closed sections in the Prophets and the Hagiographa, a thing not usually done in Masoretic manuscripts . . . that he has introduced a number of anti-Masoretic pauses . . . that his division of the Sedarim is faulty . . . that he has introduced the dagesh into the first letter of words when the preceding word ends with the same letter . . . as well as the dagesh which follows upon a guttural with silent shewa and a ḥatef-pataḥ under the first of two similar letters . . . all of which are not warranted by the best manuscripts. The Masoretic notes at the end of Baer's edition are also criticized . . . especially the lists of various readings . . . Many of these faults were due to Baer's inability to consult manuscripts in the large European collections; yet, in spite of this, his edition will remain for some time to come the [*sic!*] standard Masoretic text." (I shall return below to the utterly gratuitous and misleading use of the definite article "the" in reference to Baer's, or anyone else's, "Masoretic text.")

Paul E. Kahle, *The Cairo Genizah* (London, 1947; *The Schweich Lectures of the British Academy*, 1941), pp. 41 ff., 60 ff., has subjected both Ginsburg and Baer to most trenchant (and even personal) criticism; ironically, however, his criticism applies fully to much of his own work on the so-called masoretic text (e.g., manuscript B19a of *Biblia Hebraica*[3]), reminding one of the pot that insisted on calling the kettle black; in chap. VIII of his "Problems of the Masora" (pp. 347-56) Sperber has had a few things to say about "The Ms. B19A of the Public Library in Leningrad (according to the

Biblia Hebraica ed. Kittel-Kahle)." L. Blau wrote a very fair review of "Dr. Ginsburg's Edition of the Hebrew Bible [and *Introduction*]" in *JQR*, O.S., 12 (1900), 217-54; I note one of his statements (p. 217, n. 2), "Baer does not even mention the main defect: — the omission of the sources of these Massoretic Notes."

Let us go back a bit and review the history of the printed editions of the Hebrew Bible. When printing was invented, it was hailed in the Jewish community as a God-given gift to man wherewith to spread the Sacred Scriptures. From 1477, when the book of Psalms was published, to 1521, when the second quarto edition of the Bomberg Bible appeared (Venice, in one vol.), no less than twenty-two printed texts of the Hebrew Bible — eight of them containing the entire Bible — had seen the light of day. Some of these were more important than others, e.g., the first edition of the entire Bible (Soncino, 1488), the Complutensian Polyglot (Alcalá, 1514-17; 6 vols.), the first edition of the Bomberg Rabbinic Bible, ed. Felix Pratensis (Venice, 1516-17, 4 vols.; 1517-18, one vol.), and the first edition of the Bomberg Bible in quarto (Venice, 1516-17, 4 vols.; 1517-18, one vol.), and the first edition of the Bomberg Bible in quarto (Venice, 1516-17, one vol.; 1517, 2 vols.). None of these, however, attained the significance of the second edition of the Bomberg Rabbinic Bible that was edited by Jacob ben Chayim (Venice, 1524-26; 4 vols.). In concluding his most informative chapter (XIII) on the "History of the Printed Text of the Hebrew Bible" (pp. 779-976), which constitutes a detailed analysis of the first twenty-four such texts, Ginsburg has noted (p. 976) that "All subsequent editions are in so far Massoretic as they follow the Standard edition of Jacob b. Chayim. Every departure from it on the part of editors who call their texts Massoretic has to be explained and justified on the authority of the Massorah and MSS. which exhibit the Massoretic recension of the text."[8]

Of course Ginsburg was fully correct in the first of these two assertions. (I shall deal below with the second assertion.) Thus the well-known Bibles of Johannes Buxtorf (the Elder), both the handbook edition (Basle, 1611) and the Rabbinic Bible in four folio volumes (Basle, 1618-19; IV, 2 consists of the Masorah), exhibited a somewhat different text from that of Ben Chayim only because he had made use also of the text of the Complutensian Polyglot. Buxtorf's text was used by Joseph ben Abraham Athias (died 1700) — and his meticulous proofreader, John Leusden — for his beautiful edition of the Bible (Amsterdam, 1661; 2nd ed., 1667), upon which, in turn, Daniel Ernest Jablonski (1660-1741) based his text of the Bible (Berlin, 1699; 4 vols.); and the latter served Johann Heinrich Michaelis (1668-1738) well when he worked up — with the aid of nineteen printed editions and five Erfurt manuscripts (including Erfurt 3; see below) — his own critical edition of the Bible (Halae Magdeburgicae, 1720; frequently reprinted).[9]

The most popular edition of them all, even now a pleasure to use, was that of Everard van der Hooght (Amsterdam, 1705; 2 vols.), essentially because of its attractive, clear-cut type; it was little more than a reprint of the Buxtorf-Athias-Leusden Bible. Van der Hooght was frequently reprinted not only in its own right but also in the form of editions by Benjamin Kennicott (1718-83; the famous *Vetus Testamentum Hebraicum cum variis lectionibus*, 2 vols., Oxford, 1776, 1780), August Hahn (1792-1863; *Biblia Hebraica secundum editiones . . . Leusden . . . Simonis aliorumque imprimis Everardi van der Hooght . . . addidit Augustus Hahn*, Lipsiae, 1831; frequently reprinted), and Meir Halevi Letteris (1800-71; 2 vols., Vienna, 1852). In the United States, van der Hooght's text — unvocalized! — constituted the first Hebrew Bible published (Philadelphia, 1814; 2 vols.), and it served Isaac Leeser in association with his English translation of the Bible (Phila., 1849); as put by Gottheil ("Bible Editions," in *Jew. Enc.*, III, 154a-162a), " . . . the Van der

Hooght was considered to be a sort of 'textus receptus' . . . " [10]

The Letteris Bible became a world-wide phenomenon in the form prepared for the British and Foreign Bible Society and published in 1866.[11] Norman H. Snaith, in his article on "The Ben Asher Text" (in *Textus: Annual of the Hebrew University Bible Project*, 2 [1962], 8-13), has now drawn attention to the fact that "Actually this 1866 Letteris Bible seems to be based to a marked extent on MS Erfurt 3 [= Or fol 1213 in Berlin's Preussischen Staatsbibliothek], readings of which are to be found in the Michaelis 1720 Bible. Whether Letteris actually consulted this MS I do not know, but he often has the same reading where the MS varies from printed editions. This MS is now known as Berlin MS Or fol 121 and is kept in the Westdeutsche Bibliothek in Marburg. It is important because there is to be found in its margins the text of *Okhlah we-Okhlah,* an ancient collection of Massoretic notes, apparently the only such study to which the famous Jacob ben Hayyim had access. Since it was held in the last century that the true Massoretic text of Ben Asher was to be found in the Second Rabbinic Bible of 1524-5, printed by Bomberg in Venice and edited by Jacob ben Hayyim, it could then be said that the Letteris Bible was a good, sound text. It is closely allied to the text of Jacob ben Hayyim because of its closeness to MS Erfurt 3."

Rudolf Kittel, too, made available "the" masoretic text of the Bible. His edition of *Biblia Hebraica* (Stuttgart, 1905-6; 2nd ed. 1912) provided the reader with essentially the text of the second Rabbinic Bible; cf. p. VI of the Prolegomena, "Ceterum praeter exceptiones sub 2 [pp. IV-VI] enumeratas et sub 4-6 [pp. VI-VIII] enumerandas textus masoreticus Bibliorum secundum *principem editionem* JACOBI BEN CHAJJIM (anni 1524/5) in apparatu littera B (*Bomberg*) significatam exscribi potuit. Bibliis enim Hebraicis a GINSBURG secundum B (cf *Introd.*, p. III) editis — quorum magnas et varias virtutes gratissimis animis omnes aestimant — etiam obiter percursis codicem B denuo consulendum esse apparuit . . . "

Max L. Margolis (1866-1932), it is known, denied final authority to all extant "authoritative" editions of the masoretic Bible. (It was common knowledge that Margolis wanted very much to produce for the Jewish Publication Society the definitive edition of the masoretic text of the Bible, one that would go well with the new English version that the Society was then sponsoring [1917] with Margolis as its editor-in-chief.) In his learned and stimulating essay on "The Scope and Methodology of Biblical Philology" (*JQR*, N. S., 1 [1910], 5-41), Margolis touched on this perennial problem in the sections "Definition of the Masoretic Text" and "How the Masoretic Text is to be Reconstructed" (pp. 19-21): " . . . Equally the reconstruction of the Biblical text, not yet the original but the Masoretic form thereof [84], awaits consummation at the hands of a master trained in the school of philology. And much even then will remain doubtful . . . "; with n. 84 (on p. 40) reading: "The efforts of Baer and Ginsburg (not to mention their predecessors) notwithstanding."

Several Bibles designated as "masoretic" have appeared since the days of World War I. In 1936 the third edition of Kittel's *Biblia Hebraica* appeared, with much fanfare; for was not its "masoretic" text unique and definite by virtue of the fact that it was supposed to represent the pure text achieved by Aaron ben Moses ben Asher, the great Masorete of the tenth century? The manuscript upon which B(iblia) H(ebraica)[3] was based was the well-known Leningrad Codex designated B 19a of the early eleventh century (= Ginsburg's Codex A.D.1009; cf. the *Introduction*, Index of Manuscripts, p. 1005a). More about this edition below.

The less said about the so-called "Jerusalem Bible" the better. In 1953 the Magnes Press of the Hebrew University in Jerusalem issued, תורה נביאים וכתובים הוצאת ירושלים, מוגהים לפי המסורה עפ"י בן-אשר, על יסוד כתב היד שהתקין משה דוד קאסוטו ז"ל, והגיהו אליהו שמואל הרטום, ירושלים, תשי"ג — *Hebrew Bible: Jerusalem Edition, Corrected by M. D. Cassuto on the basis of the Masora of Ben Asher*. Strange as it may

seem, this highly publicized edition — it is even now adver-
tised as הטפסט המסורתי והמדויק ביותר בעולם — is nothing
more than a photographic reproduction of Ginsburg's Bible
published in 1908 but without the very valuable footnotes
(and without the little circles over these words in the text
which drew attention to these footnotes)! And Ginsburg's text
— reference to which was suppressed in the Jerusalem edition
— was "corrected" on the basis of sundry notes compiled by
Cassuto in the margin of his copy of a Letteris Bible. There
were other shortcomings; see the notice by N. H. Snaith in
Book List (of the Society for Old Testament Study), 1954
(= pp. 564-5 in *Eleven Years of Bible Bibliography,* ed. H. H.
Rowley, 1957). After reading the exchange in *Vetus Testamentum,* 3 (1953), 416-20 and 4 (1954), 109-10, one can appreciate Snaith's opening sentence, "This edition of the Hebrew
Bible is tragedy almost unrelieved." This Bible edition should
be withdrawn from the market and be permitted to rest in
peace. (See B. J. Roberts, "The Hebrew Bible since 1937,"
Journal of Theological Studies, 15 [1964], 253-64.)

In the same year (1953) there had appeared in Jerusalem
*The Hebrew Bible with English Translation edited by M.
Friedlander, Sanctioned by the Rabbinate* (תורה נביאים וכתובים
עם תרגום לאנגלית ערוך ע"י מ. פרידלנדר ומאושר ע"י הרבנות).
This edition has no scientific value whatever; and it is difficult
to comprehend exactly what it was that was "authorized"
(מאושר), and by what real authority such sanction was given.

In 1958 the British and Foreign Bible Society published
a new masoretic text of the Bible, edited by N. H. Snaith:
ספר/תורה נביאים וכתובים/מדויק היטב על פי המסורה/ הוגה
Norman Henry Snaith בעיון נמרץ על ידי/, London. The edition was based on the first hand of a Sephardic manuscript (British Museum Or 2626-27-28) completed in Lisbon in 1483;
another manuscript in the same Museum (Or 2375), a Yemenite manuscript written during 1460-80 and covering only the
Ketubim, was found by the editor to be as accurate and trustworthy as Or 2626-27-28; and with the aid of certain readings

in Jedidiah Solomon Norzi's *Minhat Shai* (seventeenth century) — readings which went back to the first hand of much older Sephardic manuscripts — and in the *Or Torah* of Menahem di Lonzano (late seventeenth century). In Snaith's judgment, "the Ben Asher text was . . . to be found [not only] in the Aelppo Codex [but also] . . . in the first hand of the best Sephardi MSS, and that Norzi had access to it in 1626 C.E." (p. 13 of his above-mentioned article on "The Ben Asher Text."). In a brief preliminary notice of his "New Edition of the Hebrew Bible" (*Vetus Testamentum*, 7 [1957], 207-8), the editor asserted, " . . . in every way I have tried to follow the Masoretic tradition." But I do not comprehend the expression "the (Masoretic tradition)." Was there ever any? As an example of *a* masoretic text, Snaith's is as good as any other; but none can lay claim to being *the* masoretic text   (על פי המסורה).

To accompany "Yehoash's Yiddish Translation of the Bible" (see my article in *Journal of Biblical Literature,* 60 [1941], 173-7), a masoretic Hebrew text was worked up by Rabbi Chaim M. Brecher and published in 1941 (2 vols., New York). The text (see the הקדמת הרב המגיה on p. א at the end of vol. 1) was based upon Jacob ben Chayim's Rabbinic Bible, the editions of Heidenheim, Baer, Letteris, Kittel, etc.

The most recent edition of the Bible that may be regarded as masoretic — the claim is made specifically not in the volume itself but in a four-page brochure — is that produced in 5722/1962 by Qoren Publishers in Jerusalem: תורה נביאים כתובים הוצאת קורן ירושלים. D. Goldschmidt, A. M. Haberman, and M. Medan arrived at the text on the basis of a close scrutiny of previous editions, both manuscript and printed, and masoretic lists; the Torah was based on Heidenheim's edition. In the beautiful folio edition of the Torah, published in 1959, the simple and proud statement is made: התנ"ך הראשון המסודר ומודפס בנקודות וטעמים בארץ ישראל ("The first Bible worked up and printed with vowels and accents in the

Land of Israel"). Page שעט at end of the whole Bible reads
הגהת מהדורה זו נעשתה בעיון רב ובבדיקה מדוקדקת, עד כמה שיד
אדם מגעת, על יסוד חוות דעתם של בעלי המסורה ושל המדקדקים
והמפרשים ועל פי מה שנמצא ברוב כתבי היד והדפוסים המקובלים
;כבני סמכא, ולא כהעתקה משועבדת לדפום או לכתב יד מסוים
and this is followed (pp. שעט-שעיג) by a list of חילופי
נוסחאות... שיש בהם שינוי של ממש לגבי הנוסח המודפם בפנים...
שמקורם מוסמך, כגון עדויות מפורשות של המסורה ושל גדולי
המפרשים והמדקדקים (ת"י, רש"י, ראב"ע, רד"ק, מנחת שי, רו"ה,
ועוד) או הנוסח שברוב כתבי יד והדפוסים הראשונים. On the
superiority of the Qoren Bible in the matter of Kethib-Qere,
see below.

It is too early to include here specific reference to the
Hebrew Bible projected by the Hebrew University. In a "Brief
Report on the Hebrew University Bible Project" (*Textus*,
I [1960], 210-211), it is stated that "The aim of the Project
is to edit the Massoretic text according to the most authentic
MS of the Ben Asher school, viz. the Aleppo Codex, and to
provide this text with critical apparatuses . . . " Yet serious
misgivings may already be felt on this score alone, in that it
is becoming increasingly doubtful just how authentically Ben
Asher this Codex really is — apart from the extremely important question, to which I shall return below: What
is so definitive and authoritative about an authentic Ben
Asher manuscript?

In a sober discussion of "The Aleppo Codex and the Ben
Asher Tradition" (pp. 59-111 in *Textus*, I [1960]),S. L. Loewinger ("responsible . . . for Massorah studies" in connection
with the Hebrew University Bible Project; see ibid., p. 211
bottom) is careful to conclude (p. 94): " . . . For the present,
this MS is superior to all the MSS which we have mentioned.
This superiority cannot as yet serve as complete evidence that
this MS was in fact written by Aaron by Moses ben Asher. It
might be the work of an earlier punctuator or an exact copy
made on the basis of his model MS . . . " Aharon Dothan, in a
recent important article, "Was the Aleppo Codex Actually

Vocalized by Aharon ben Asher?" (*Tarbiz*, 34 [1965/5725], 136-155), raised two questions: "Do the vocalization and the Massora of the *Aleppo Codex* correspond systematically to each other, or are they inconsistent to the point that there is no reasonable justification to look upon them as being written by the very hand of Aharon ben Asher? Do the vocalization and the Massora of the Codex correlate with what we know of Ben Asher's method from other sources?" (ibid., Summaries, p. II).

As a result of his close study, based largely on a considerable number of photographic reproductions, the data offered in Loewinger's article, and the masoretic rules which originally stood at the beginning of the Aleppo Codex (the *Diqduqe Ha-Te'amim*), Dothan was able to conclude that "the method of the *Aleppo Codex* differs from that of *Diqduqé Hatte'amim* (MS Leningrad B 19a is closer to it in some respects) and that the marginal Massora is contradicted by the vocalization of the biblical text. Moreover, the vocalization is very inconsistent especially as regards the markings of *hatefs* and *ga'yas*. In some places, readings which are Ben Naftali's *par excellence* are also found. All these factors taken together do not permit us in any manner whatsoever to ascribe the vocalization to the master Massorite Aharon ben Asher, as the colophon wishes to do . . . The paleograhical evidence brought by M. H. Goshen-Gottstein (Tarbiz XXXIII) as to the authenticity of the colophon at the end of the Codex — the identity of the handwriting of the scribe Shelomo ben Būyā'ā—is also contradicted here on both paleographical and other counts: the arrangement of the lines in the section following the poetics of 'Ha'azinu' in the codex of the scribe Ben Būyā'ā differs from the arrangement found in the *Aleppo Codex* (Cf. photograph)."

One has the feeling that he is reading here, all over again, a criticism of the work of Jacob ben Chayim in the sixteenth century and of Baer and Ginsburg in the late nineteenth century. In short, we are right back to where we had started,

849

working with manuscripts that are late and inadequate and self-contradictory; and it is improper and misleading, at this late date, to attribute to such manuscripts — Aleppo, B 19a, Erfurt 3, et al. — authority that they simply do not merit. But more on this below

We are now ready to deal with the crux of the whole matter, something that the numerous editors of "masoretic" editions of the Bible have overlooked, namely: There never was, and there never can be, a single fixed masoretic text of the Bible! It is utter futility and pursuit of a mirage to go seeking to recover what never was.

What scholars have done is to confuse the fixing of the Canon of the Bible with the fixing of the Hebrew text of the Bible. The Bible was fixed so far as the three main Divisions (Torah, Prophets, Writings) and the Books in them were concerned. Even if only twenty-two Books were canonized shortly after the mid-first century and the other two Books, Koheleth and Esther, recognized only subsequently—as argued persuasively by S. Zeitlin, "An Historical Study of the Canonization of the Hebrew Scriptures" (in *Proceedings of the American Academy for Jewish Research,* 3 [1931-32], 121-58) —the fact is that the Canon of the Bible was closed by the time that the Mishnah was codified, not to be reopened and enlarged, or reduced, thereafter.

But the order of the individual Books in the last Division was never really fixed. Thus there are three different sequences of the Five Scrolls, depending on whether Nisan is treated as the first month of the year (Song of Songs — Passover; Ruth-Shabu'ot; Lamentations — Tishah be-Ab; Koheleth—Succot; and Esther—Purim) or Tishri (whence Koheleth, Esther, Song of Songs, Ruth, and Lamentations), or whether chronology, traditionally reckoned, is the factor (Ruth—period of the Judges; Song of Songs—Solomon as a young man; Koheleth

—Solomon as an old man; Lamentations—destruction of the First Temple; and Esther—Persian Period); and there are some "lapses" from these sequences (e.g., when Esther heads the list). Who is to say which is the original order? Indeed, there is no reason to believe that there ever was an "original" order of the Megillot. The Writings, in general, also, show a lack of fixed order; some of the data are given in Ginsburg's *Introduction,* chap. I, "The Order of the Books," pp. 1-8; also pp. 802, 868-9.

As a matter of fact, there is some problem with the order even within the second division, the Prophets. Everyone knows that the Babylonian Talmud (Baba Bathra 14b) has the order: Jeremiah, Ezekiel, and Isaiah; and several manuscripts actually have this order. Most manuscripts and the printed editions in general have the order: Isaiah, Jeremiah, and Ezekiel (see Ginsburg, pp. 4-6). Which is the original? Different Jewish communities in different (or even contemporaneous) periods decided the order of the Books for themselves, and no single Jewish community can claim exclusive authority in the matter. But since the accident of history had the first important printed editions of the Bible follow manuscripts which had the order Isaiah, Jeremiah, Ezekiel, etc., that will probably remain the order henceforth for all "masoretic" texts—even though there is nothing masoretic about this order.

In this connection it is of more than passing interest to note that it may well be that the Christian, essentially fourfold division of the Bible (Torah, Historical Writings, Wisdom Books, and Prophets) and the Christian names of the penta-teuchal Books (Genesis, Exodus, etc.) are actually Jewish in origin. Old Jewish tradition knew the name of the first of the pentateuchal Books to be ספר מעשה בראשית (on יצירת העולם see W. Bacher, *ZAW,* 15 [1895], 308), as well as בראשית, which is the pre-Christian term *Genesis* that Philo used; again, Philo's (pre-Christian)'Εξαγωγή (also *Έξοδος) = Exodus* corre-sponding to ספר יציאת מצרים (alongside שמות [ואלה]); ספר תורת כהנים (alongside ויקרא) is the equivalent of

851

Λευιτικόν *Leviticus;* the expression חומש הפקודים (alongside ספר וידבר or במדבר) belongs with the term Ἀριθμοί
Numbers; and the title *Deuteronomy* corresponds to ספר
משנה תורה (alongside אלה ה[דברים]).. These are patently (if
only because of chronolgical considerations) terms that the
Jewish community did not take over from the Christians. As
for the Christian fourfold division of the Bible, it is hardly
likely that the Church would have taken an original threefold
division, one in which the Prophets followed immediately
upon the all-important Torah, and transformed it into a fourfold division, one in which the all-important Prophets were
relegated to the fourth division; and why should the Christians have bothered to divide the Bible into four instead of
three main divisions? It would seem not unreasonable to believe that there were two "original" orders (as well as titles
of the Five Books of Moses), both Jewish—perhaps one
Judean and the other Alexandrian (as reflected in the Septuagint); the former continued as the Jewish tradition, the latter
as the Christian. But this whole matter, interesting and important as it is, may not be pursued here.[12]

So far as the Hebrew text of the Bible is concerned —
the consonantal (unvocalized) text—that too was never fixed
for all Jewry for all time. During the Second Jewish Commonwealth, numerous scrolls of the individual Books of the Bible
circulated in the learned Jewish circles of Judea, Egypt, Syria-
Babylonia, and other regions. And in the rabbinic literature
of the first several centuries there are numerous references to
the existence of biblical texts with faulty readings. Not only
that, the rabbinic literature itself, in quotations from the
Bible, exhibits more frequently than is generally realized readings that differ from those preserved in our so-called "masoretic" texts, readings that are not due to faulty memory and that
crop up in Hebrew manuscripts and/or biblical quotations in
Mechilta, Sifra, Sifre, the Gemara, the grammatical work of
ibn Janaḥ, etc. Thus, e.g., Num. 34.2 reads in our printed
"masoretic" editions, צַו אֶת־בְּנֵי יִשְׂרָאֵל וְאָמַרְתָּ אֲלֵיהֶם כִּי־אַתֶּם)

852

בָּאִים) אֶל־הָאָרֶץ כְּנַעַן (זֹאת הָאָרֶץ אֲשֶׁר תִּפֹּל לָכֶם בְּנַחֲלָה אֶרֶץ כְּנַעַן לִגְבֻלֹתֶיהָ). The Sifre (ed. M. Friedmann, Wien, 1864), p.1, line 17, reads אֶל אֶרֶץ כנען. That this is not simply an "easy" (even unintentional) correction of ungrammatical אל הארץ כנען " is clear from the fact that 4 Kennicott manuscripts and the reading designated Sebir (indicating that this was a recognized variant reading) likewise read ארץ כנען. How is one to decide — leaving aside the question as to which of the two readings is correct and/or original (for the older reading may already have been the corrupt one) — which of the two is the correct masoretic reading? On what decisive evidence would the argument be based in favor of the one and against the other?

Again, in B. T. Berakot 54b we read (וַיְהִי בְנֻסָם) מִפְּנֵי בְנֵי יִשְׂרָאֵל (הֵם בְּמוֹרַד בֵּית חוֹרֹן וַיהוה הִשְׁלִיךְ עֲלֵיהֶם אֲבָנִים גְּדֹלוֹת . . .). The "masoretic" text in our printed editions, at Josh. 10.11, is simply . . . (וַיְהִי בְנֻסָם) מִפְּנֵי יִשְׂרָאֵל). The reading מפני בני ישראל is attested by the Septuagint (see M. L. Margolis, *The Book of Joshua in Greek* [Paris, 1931], Part II, p. 177) and by 2 de Rossi manuscripts. Clearly, then, מפני בני ישראל is a most legitimate variant — and perhaps even the original — reading. On what grounds would an editor decide that מפני ישראל is the "masoretic" reading and that מפני בני ישראל is not? None of the Aleppo Codex, Leningrad B 19a, Erfurt 3, etc., or any of the printed editions, can have any decisive merit in determining here what is masoretic and what is not.

The preserved text of II Ki. 3.15 reads (וְעַתָּה קְחוּ־לִי מְנַגֵּן וְהָיָה כְּנַגֵּן הַמְנַגֵּן וַתְּהִי עָלָיו) יַד יהוה. In his excellent grammatical work סֵפֶר הרקמה (ed. M. Wilensky, 2 vols. [Berlin, 1928-30]), I, p. 67, line 10, ibn Janah quotes this verse(וַתְּהִי עָלָיו . . .) רוּחַ יהוה. That this is a genuine variant, and not a slip of memory, is evident from the fact that more than a score of Kenn and de Rossi manuscripts likewise read רוח. Not only that, the Targum too (ed. A. Sperber, 1959), ושרת עלוהי רוח נבואה מן קדם יי, derives from רוח; it is not uncharacteristic of BH[3] that both parts of its critical apparatus pass over this important datum in silence. Indeed, who is to say, after a full study of the expression (וַתְּהִי עָלָיו יָד/רוּחַ יהוה), that the so-called "variant" reading רוּחַ is not only "masoretic" but even original, with יָד, *the* universally accepted "masoretic" reading, being secondary and merely a variant reading — though still also *a* masoretic reading?

Or what will the editor of "the masoretic text of the Bible" do with this clear statement in Berakot 61a: אָמַר ר' נ(חמן) מנוח עם הארץ היה דכתיב וַיֵּלֶךְ מָנוֹחַ אַחֲרֵי אִשְׁתּוֹ. מתקיף לה ר' נ(חמן) בר יצחק, אלא מעתה גבי אלקנה, דכתיב וַיֵּלֶךְ אֶלְקָנָה אַחֲרֵי אִשְׁתּוֹ, וגבי אלישע דכתיב וַיָּקָם וַיֵּלֶךְ אַחֲרֶיהָ ... "Rabbi Nahman said, 'Manoah was a boor,' since it is written (in Scripture, Jud. 13.11), 'And Manoah walked behind his wife.' But Rabbi Nahman son of Isaac objected: in that case one would have to say the same of Elkanah, since it is written (in Scripture), 'And Elkanah walked behind his wife,' and of Elisha, since it is written (in Scripture, II Ki. 4.30), 'And he (Elisha) arose and walked behind her' ... " Already the Tosafot commented: אלא מעתה גבי אלקנה דכתיב וילך אלקנה אחרי אשתו שבוש הוא, שאין פסוק זה בכל המקרא ולא גרסינן ליה, "Except that the expression ... as it is written (in Scripture), 'And Elkanah walked behind his wife,' is in error, for there is no such passage in the whole of Scripture; and it should be deleted."

But apart from the fact that this is hardly the kind of error which the two talmudic sages would commit — after all, this was not simply a slip of the memory; they would both be guilty, in this case, of having actually created in the Bible a passage that did not exist!—there is another simple fact, long recognized, that the Septuagint of Samuel at this point, as elsewhere in the Book, not only fails to coincide with our preserved, so-called masoretic text, but is often clearly superior to it. Thus at I Sam. 1.21-23 it is clearly stated that Elkanah made the annual pilgrimage to Shiloh while his wife Hannah remained at home with the baby; only after she had weaned Samuel did she go to Shiloh to leave the boy in the service of

the Lord (vv. 23-28). But after Hannah's moving "magnifi-
cat" of God in 2.1-10, we read most unexpectedly in v. 11a,
וַיֵּלֶךְ אֶלְקָנָה הָרָמָתָה עַל־בֵּיתוֹ,   "Then Elkanah went to Ramah,
to his home" — "unexpectedly" because Elkanah had not been
mentioned at all in connection with Hannah's latest pilgrimage to Shiloh. The Septuagint, in place of "masoretic"
וַיִּשְׁתַּחוּ שָׁם לַיהוה at the end of chap.1(v.28b)and וַיֵּלֶךְ אֶלְקָנָה
הָרָמָתָה עַל־בֵּיתוֹ at 2.11a, reads at 2.11a, "and she left him
there before the Lord and she went to Ramah" (καὶ κατέ-
λιπον αὐτὸν ἐκεῖ ἐνώπιον κυρίου καὶ ἀπῆλθον εἰς Αρμαθαιμ
(וַתַּנִּיחֵהוּ/ וַתַּעַזְבֵהוּ שָׁם לִפְנֵי יהוה וַתֵּלֶךְ הָרָמָתָה. Scholars (e.g., S.R.
Driver, *Notes on . . . Samuel* ², ad loc.) generally have pre-
ferred the Hebrew text underlying the Septuagint to the preserved Hebrew text. But we can go farther now, due to the
discovery of the Dead Sea Scroll fragments of Samuel. Even
from the bit published so far, covering parts of I Sam. 1.22b-
2.6 and 2.16-25 (F.M. Cross, Jr., *Bulletin of the American
Schools of Oriental Research,* No. 132, 1953, pp. 15-26), it is
clear that in this third version of the Hebrew text of Samuel
the role of Elkanah was greater than indicated in the preserved
"masoretic" Hebrew text, and specifically so at this very point;
cf. pp. 19-20 and nn. 6, 10. There can be no doubt, in the
light of the preserved Hebrew text, the Septuagint, and the
Samuel fragments, that Rabbi Nahman bar Isaac (died 356)
still knew in the fourth century of the — quite original! —
reading וַיֵּלֶךְ אלקנה אחרי אשתו. And since the Gemara
justifies this reading, how could an editor of "the masoretic
text of the Bible" justify exclusion of these four words?

In fine, any such contention as "But we are editing as
'masoretic' only the Hebrew text of the Masoretes (or, of Ben
Asher)" immediately falls to the ground of its own accord.
There never was and there can never be *"the* masoretic text"
or *"the* text of the Masoretes." All that, at best, we might
hope to achieve, in theory, is *"a* masoretic text," or *"a* text of
the Masoretes," that is to say, *a* text worked up by Ben Asher,
or by Ben Naftali, or by someone in the Babylonian tradition,

or a text worked up with the aid of the masoretic notes of an
individual scribe or of a school of scribes. But as matters
stand, we cannot even achieve a clear-cut text of the Ben
Asher school, or of the Ben Naftali school, or of a Babylonian
school, or a text based on a single masoretic list; indeed, it is
not at all certain that any such ever existed. All that an editor
can claim with justification is that he has reproduced the text
of a single manuscript, be it Aleppo (Hebrew University
Bible Project), or Leningrad B 19a (BH³), or British Museum
Or 2626-27-28 (Snaith), and the like; and the editor should
tell the reader forthrightly—as he has not been wont to do—
exactly at what points he has departed from the manuscript,
and the reasons for departing. At the same time, it cannot be
emphasized too strongly that none of these manuscripts or of
the printed editions based on them has any greater merit or
"masoretic" authority than most of the many other editions
of the Bible, than, say, the van der Hooght, Hahn, Letteris,
Baer, Rabbinic and Ginsburg Bibles.

An excellent justification of this viewpoint may be gained
from the manner in which the various just-mentioned editions
of the Bible—each of them claiming the last word in masoretic authority — treated the important aspects of masoretic activity which the Kethib-Qere system constitutes.

It is now scarcely possible to deny that the system of Kethib-Qere readings had its origin in variant readings; by the
same token, the theory that the Qere readings are but corrections (really a euphemism for "emendations") of the Kethib
readings has no real justification.[14]

If one reads Num. 23.13 (...לְךָ־נָא אִתִּי) and II Chron.
25.17 (לְךָ נִתְרָאֶה פָנִים) in the texts of van der Hooght, Hahn,
Baer (lacking in Numbers), Ginsburg, the Rabbinic Bible
(*Mikra'ot Gedolot;* ed. Vilna-Romm on Numbers; ed. Warsaw on the entire Bible), BH²(= essentially Jacob ben Chayim),
Snaith, and Qoren, he will find the reading לך, without any
variant reading indicated (except that Snaith at Num. notes:
חסר ה'). In Jud. 19.13 (לְךָ וְנִקְרְבָה / לְכָה), however, the texts of

Ginsburg, BH², and Snaith break with the other editions: whereas all the latter give לְךָ only, the former three record a Kethib-Qere, the K pointed לְךָ (by Ginsburg and BH²; Snaith unvocalized לך), the Q לְכָה. The "masoretic" text of BH³ goes farther than any of the other editions: it records לְכָה as the Qere not only in Judges but also in Numbers and II Chronicles, and vocalizes the Kethib in the Judges passage as לְךָ. (In the Numbers passage the critical apparatus reads "Q לְכָה" with the K left unvocalized, and in the Judges and Chronicles passages the critical apparatus says nothing whatever about our word. If Leningrad B 19a did not really offer the editor of BH³ these capricious data, this leaves unanswered the very important question: when is BH³ not really B 19a, and why?)

From sundry sources it is now known that the earliest orthography of our word was לך, which in time gave way to the spelling לכה; see the argument and references in my article on "The Import of the Kethib-Ḳere and the Masoretic Note on לְכָה, Judges 19.13" (*JQR*, 31 [1940-41], 59 ff.). Accordingly, the spelling of verbal-interjectional "go; come let us . . . " — perhaps aided by the desire to distinguish more readily from prepositional לְךָ "to you" — became normally לכה (some thirty cases in all), with only three instances of the older spelling לך. But even in the case of thrice-occurring לך, the original spelling began to give way at the hands of some scribes to the more usual לְכָה; and once לך became in one or more manuscripts, or groups of manuscripts, לכה, it is not surprising that a Kethib-Qere arose in some scribal circles, exactly as happened in the case of K שת Q וְחָיִיתָ, K וחייתה Q וְאַתָּה, K ואת Q שַׁתָּה. K לכן Q לֶכְנָה, and the like.[15]

In the case of לך in Judg. 19.13, the older spelling was preserved in those manuscripts that served as the basis of most printed editions of the Bible; no לכה had crept in there, and so no K-Q variants were known or introduced. So it is not surprising that David Qimḥi (died 1235), unaware

of any K-Q, simply notes in his commentary, ad. loc.,
לך. כמו לכה הכתיב בה"א. וכמוהו לך נתראה
לכה "לך" is like — ,פנים הכתוב בד[ברי] ה[ימים]
which is written with a ה; compare the passage לך
נתראה פנים which is found in Chronicles." In other manuscripts, however (Kennicott lists about a dozen; de Rossi is
content with "Multi codices לכה"), לכה came to be introduced for לך, the two became K-Q variants (cf. Kennicott,
"marg. habet לכה ק' 154, 155"), and in time they found
their way into the editions of Jacob ben Chayim, Ginsburg,
BH³, etc.

In the case of Num. 23.13 and II Chron. 25.17, on the
other hand, לך became לכה in even fewer manuscript-tra-
ditions; Kennicott, e.g., lists a few individual manuscripts as
reading לכה in these two passages, but with no ק' recorded.
So that only the "masoretic" text in BH³ offers a K-Q לכה/לך
in these two verses; unfortunately, the editor has not told us
whether it was his manuscript (Leningrad B 19a) that gave
him these data or whether he himself, acting secretly as a
modern-day masorete, created these two K-Q himself.

It is evident, then, that in this particular instance, the uncritical "masoretic" text of *Miqra'ot Gedolot* (with no K-Q
for any of the three occurrences of לך) is superior as a "masoretic" text to the critical "masoretic" texts of Jacob ben
Chayim (the basis of BH²) and Ginsburg (with a K-Q for
Judges only), and these two, in turn, to that of BH³ (with
K-Q on all three passages).

There are more than one hundred and fifty instances in
the Bible where nouns and prepositions with the third person
masculine suffix constitute members of the K-Q system, the
Q being written *plene* (and of course pointed) and the K
defective, without the *yodh*. Thus the Q is written and vocalized יָדָיו "his hands" in such instances as וְסָמַךְ אַהֲרֹן אֶת־
כִּי הוּא . . . יִמְחַץ) וְיָדָיו תִּרְפֶּינָה (Lev. 16.21) and שְׁתֵּי יָדָיו
Job 5.18), while the K is written ידו (and of course unpointed).
Similarly one finds such forms as וַיֵּלֶךְ דָּוִד) וַאֲנָשָׁיו; I Sam.

23.5) as the Qere, with ואנשו as the Kethib. And, finally, such forms as אַחֲרָיו, אֵלָיו, עָלָיו, and תַּחְתָּיו constitute Qeres, with אחרו, אלו, עלו, and תחתו constituting their respective Kethibs, vocalized by some editors of "masoretic" Bibles and even by grammarians and lexicographers אַחֲרוֹ, אֵלוֹ, עָלוֹ, and תַּחְתּוֹ.

It is self-evident that no one could possibly have read K ידו as יָדוֹ "his hand" with שְׁתֵּי and תִּרְפֶּינָה! Or how could anyone vocalize ואנשו as וְאֶנְשׁוֹ when the singular form of אֱנוֹשׁ is not declined in the singular? However, the problem becomes especially acute, and clear, in the matter of the prepositions, some 150 cases of K-Q in all.

According to the masoretic tradition preserved in S. Frensdorff's edition of *Ochlah W'ochlah* (Hannover, 1864), listed as § 128 (pp. 104 f.), there are 56 words that only once in the entire Bible lack the *yodh* of the plural masculine suffix in the third person singular in writing, but which are pronounced nevertheless as if the *yodh* were really there.[16] To the best of my knowledge, the Masoretes never connected two words of different morphologic character unless they distinctly specified that difference. Now if the Masoretes, for whatever reason, had decided to make note of a form כַּפּוֹ "his palm," they would not refer to it as the form כַּפָּיו "his palms" written defectively, without the *yodh*.[17] Nor, in the opposite direction, would they make a masoretic note on a form like יָמָיו "his days" by referring to it as the form יָמוֹ "his day" written *plene*, with a *yodh*.[18] Accordingly, when the 56 words listed in § 128 of *Ochlah W'ochlah* are stated to be *defective* forms read just like their *plene* correspondents, they cannot possibly be singular-suffixed כַּפּוֹ, or יָמוֹ, or עָלוֹ,[19] but merely the plural-suffixed defectively-written (without the *yodh*) כַּפָּו, and יָמָו, and עָלָו. Consequently—and this is of utmost significance — Kethib forms like כפו, ימו, and עלו were not yet recognized in the period of the Masoretes.

Coming back to alleged תַּחְתּוֹ as the pointing of Kethib

תחתו, List 128 will not have included it since it is found more than once in the Bible—four times to be exact. But on II Sam. 2.23, which is the first of the four passages in which the K form occurs, Jedidiah Solomon Norzi's masoretic work, *Minḥat Shai,* reads as follows, תחתו, תחתיו ק' ומסורת כ"י תחתו ד' חסר וסימנהון..., i.e., according to the tradition of the Masorah, Q תחתיו is found written in the Bible 4 times defectively, without the *yodh.* Both *per se* and in the light of the above, it is clear that the Masoretes did not have in mind any such word as תַּחְתּוֹ differing morphologically from תַּחְתָּיו — for they would not refer to a form תַּחְתּוֹ by identifying it with the form תַּחְתָּיו written defectively. All that they had in mind, and all that they stated, was that the form תחתיו was written 4 times defectively, without the *yodh,* though of course pronounced the same as the plena form, i.e. תַּחְתָּיו=תַּחְתָּו in morphology and pronunciation.

Now, as to when such alleged forms as אַחֲרוֹ,אֵלוֹ, עָלוֹ, תַּחְתּוֹ, and the other 150 or so cases of K-Q of the same kind first came into existence, even if incorrectly and without proper authority, it would appear that they originated after the time of David Qimḥi, who died in 1235. In common with such earlier grammarians as ibn Janaḥ (died 1040),[20] and ibn Ezra (died 1167),[21] Qimḥi knows no form תַּחְתּוֹ; cf., e.g., his statement in *Sefer Ha-Shorashim,* p. 410, תחת... יחובר עם תחת",הכנויים יהיה בלשון רבים... בלשון רבים כולם..when joined with suffixes it is in the plural . . . all of them in the plural . . . " The earliest reference to such a form, so far as I am aware, is to be found in the early sixteenth century, in the masoretic work of Elijah Levita, *Massoreth Ha-Massoreth* (ed. C. D. Ginsburg, Introduction III, pp. 102 ff., pp. 182 f. and n. 4), who arrived at this form through an erroneous comprehension of the import of the caption of List 128 in *Ochlah W'ochlah.* While not referring to K תחתו itself, since the 56 words that he discusses occur but once each written defectively, whereas תחתו occurs 4 times as such, the fact that he pointed Kethibs of this kind as וֹ-(Levita did not recognize *scriptio plena* and *defectiva* as a factor in the K-Q system), and the fact that the strictly analogous עָלוֹ (occurring but once among the 56 words in List 128) is pointed עָלוֹ, and the fact that the Kethib was considered by him an integral part of the sacred text, all resulted in gratuitously assumed תַּחְתוֹ coming to be regarded by later, and modern, grammarians and lexicographers as an original and genuine alternate of תַּחְתָּיו. Yet in fairness to Levita, it should be pointed out that he himself considered the K as anomalous in the context and the Q as a substitution for it, on the authority, direct or indirect, of the various authors of the Bible. Consequently, Levita himself probably did not consider forms like תַּחְתוֹ and עָלוֹ to be as authoritative as תַּחְתָּיו and עָלָיו. And that may be why he made no mention at all in his edition of and commentary on Moses Qimḥi's little grammatical treatise, מהלך שבילי הדעת, of the form אֵלוֹ (אלו occurs three times as a K) as a variant of the אֵלָיו listed by Qimḥi (see at the end of the grammar). In his own grammatical work, ספר הבחור, Levita did not concern himself with prepositional forms.

In summary: none of the "masoretic" editions of the Bible published to date has genuinely masoretic authority for hundreds of the Kethib-Qere that they offer the reader." [22]

The vast majority of the scholars who have attempted to work up "the" masoretic text of the Bible have scarcely bothered with the system of Ben Naftali; they have reproduced what has come down to them, by way of manuscripts and/or printed editions, and these happened to be generally the product of the school of Ben Asher. A few scholars, e.g., Ginsburg and Baer, did pay attention to Ben Naftali, even if they usually preferred Ben Asher's readings; Ginsburg has a chapter on this in his *Introduction* (X: "The Differences between Ben-Asher and Ben-Naphtali," pp. 241-86) and other references (see Index IV, p. 1016), and Baer included in his "Appendices Criticae et Masoreticae" a very useful section on חלופי נקוד... בין בן אשר ובין בן נפתלי / *Loci* ... *a Ben-Ascher et Ben-Naphtali diverse punctis signati* in every biblical Book that he edited. More recently, L. Lipschütz published *Ben Ascher-Ben Naftali. Der Bibeltext der tiberischen Masoreten. Eine Abhandlung des Mischael b. Uzziel, veröffentlicht und untersucht* (Bonner Orientalische Studien, Heft 25; Stuttgart, 1937); and see now especially his edition of "Mishael ben Uzziel's Treatise on the Differences between Ben Asher and Ben Naphtali" as Supplement in *Textus,* 2 (1962), pp. א-נח; with the valuable analysis in 4 (1964), 1-29.

But the question asks itself: What is there inherently in the masoretic work of the Ben Asher school that gives it greater authority than that of the Ben Naftali school? Why should the vowels, the dagesh, the maqqef, the raphe, the metheg-ga'ya, the accents, the hataf, and the like, as used by Ben Asher's school be more acceptable to an editor of "the" masoretic text than their use by Ben Naftali's school? (Had the matter been left to Saadia Gaon to decide, this tenth century scholar would have ruled vigorously in favor of Ben Naftali as against Ben Asher; see the data in Lipschütz, *Textus,* 4 [1964], 9 and nn. 1-3.) Surely Maimonides, authority that he was in matters of halacha and philosophy, was in no position to deal adequately with the problems of the rise of the Masorah and the achievement of a masoretic text; so that if this notable halachist and philosopher is said to have designated a certain manuscript, said to have derived from the school of Ben Asher, as one upon which everyone could depend, even if that manuscript could be identified with full confidence, it would still have to be treated the same as every other manuscript of the Hebrew Bible.[28] Unfortunately, it is not easy to identify the codex in question; despite the confident and even dogmatic statements made to the contrary, Aharon Dothan has advanced cogent arguments against the popular view that it was the Aleppo Codex that Maimonides saw and used and praised (*Tarbiz,* 34 [1964-65], 147 ff.). In addition, Dothan has shown that the Aleppo manuscript is not pure Ben Asher at all, containing as it does some readings which are characteristically Ben Naftali.

Let us cite some specific cases in point. According to Baer, *Liber Chronicum* (חלופי נקוד בספר... בין בן אשר ובין בן נפתלי, p. 131), at I Chron. 15.2, Ben Asher vocalizes וּלְשָׁרֵתֽוֹ, Ben Naftali וּלְשָׁרְתֽוֹ; Ginsburg's text reads וּלְשָׁרְתֽוֹ, with the note "so Ben Asher; Ben Naftali וּלשרתו, with the ga'ya" (כן ב"א, ב"נ וּלשרתו געיא); BH³ reads וּלְשָׁרְתֽוֹ; Miqra'ot Gedolot, Snaith, and Qoren agree with Ginsburg (without, of course, his rafeh sign over ת). Regardless of which reading is genuinely Ben Asher and which Ben Naftali, on what basis is that of Ben Asher more truly "masoretic" than that of Ben Naftali? What are the criteria that an editor would employ, and with what justification?[24] Again, in I Chron. 16.12, what is more "masoretic" about Ben Asher's (...מִפְתָיו) וּמִשְׁפְּטֵי־פִיהוּ—the reading employed also in Baer, Ginsburg (with the note: ס"א ומשפטי ובלא מקף וכן ד"ב, ד"ג, ד"ו, ד"ט, די"ב, ודי"ד, i.e., other editions וּמשפטי, and without the maqqef; and similarly the 1488 Soncino Bible, the 1491-93 Naples Bible, the 1494 Brescia Bible, the 1511-17 Pesaro Bible, the 1517 Felix Pratensis Bible, and the 1521 Bomberg Bible), Miqra'ot Gedolot, BH³, Snaith, and Qoren—than about Ben Naftali's וּמִשְׁפְּטֵי פִיהוּ ?[25] In II Chron. 2.13, according to Baer (p. 132), Ben Asher reads בַּזָּהָב־וּבַכָּסָף, and Ben Naftali בַּזָהָב וּבַכָּסָף. But Baer and Qoren point בַּזָּהָב־וּֽבַכָּֽסָף (note extra telisha), BH³ and Snaith point בַּזָהָב־וּבַכָּסָף (note metheg on וּֽ!), leaving only Ginsburg with Ben Asher's reading (with addition of the rafeh sign: בַּזָהָב־וּֽבַכָּסָף) and Miqra'ot Gedolot with Ben Naftali's—to which may be added the note in Ginsburg: ס"א בזהב וכן ד"ג, ד"ו, ד"ט, די"ב ודי"ד, i.e., other edd. בזהב; and similarly all the Bibles mentioned by Ginsburg at I Chron. 16.12 above, except the 1488 Soncino Bible. Again then, how is a scholarly editor to decide which pointing, that of Ben Asher or that of Ben Naftali or that of the other edi-

tions, is the true "masoretic" reading? Why should Ben Naftali be regarded as less "masoretic" than Ben Asher, and why
should either of them be accorded greater "masoretic" authority than either of the two readings presented in Baer, BH³,
Snaith, and Qoren?

Or take the Hebrew form for Issachar. Ginsburg
(*Introduction*, pp. 250-55 and notes) has brought together
considerable data which offer no less than six possible "masoretic" readings of the word: יִשָּׂשכָר (with dagesh in first
sin: Yissachar), יִשָׂשכָר (without dagesh in first *sin*: Yi-
sachar), יִשְׂשכָר (first *sin* silent), יִשָּׂשָכָר (both
sins vocalized), יִשָּׂשכָר, and יִשָׂשָכָר (first sibilant
shin rather than *sin*). I do not know—regardless of which is
the original reading—how those who claim to be editing
the masoretic text determined the correct "masoretic" reading
here.[26]

It would be all too easy to go on in this vein; there are
literally thousands of readings in the Hebrew text of the Bible
involving the elements that go to make up the masoretic text
that no one can point to and say: this is, or this is not, "the"
masoretic reading. For there never was any such thing as "the
masoretic text" in existence.

A word is in order here about the differences in pronunciation among the schools of Ben Asher, Ben Naftali, Babylonia,
etc. I regard it as fundamentally wrong to look upon any of
the בעלי המסורה as innovators in phonology, as though one
Masorete after another invented a pronunciation of Hebrew.
All the Masoretes, from first to last, were essentially preservers
and recorders of the pronunciation of Hebrew as they heard
it.[27] If the Ben Ashers vocalized וּלְשָׁרֲתוֹ, and the Ben Naftalis
וּלְשָׁרְתוֹ, then those were the pronunciations current in their
circles. If the Ben Ashers vocalized לִירְאָה, בְּיִרְאָה, לְיִשְׂרָאֵל,
בְּיִשְׂרָאֵל, etc., as against the Ben Naftalis' לִירְאָה, בִּירְאָה,
לְיִשְׂרָאֵל, בְּיִשְׂרָאֵל, etc. (see the data in Ginsburg, *Introduction,*
267-8 and n. 1; Lipschütz,*Textus,* 2 [1962], ד, and 4 [1964],

18 and nn. 16-17), it was simply because words with initial — יְ
when prefixed with בְּ or לְ were pronounced — לְ / בִּ **in**
one region and — לְ / בִּ in another. The same is true of several
verbal forms of אכל, e.g., Ben Asher יְ / תֹּאכְלֶנָּה vs. Ben
Naftali יְ / תֹּאכְלֶנָּה (see the data in Ginsburg, 255-64; Lip-
schutz, ג, and 17, nn. 7-9) and of גרש, e.g., Ben Asher
אֲגָרְשֶׁנּוּ vs. Ben Naftali אֲגָרְשֶׁנּוּ (see Ginsburg,
264-7; Lipschütz, ג, and 17, nn. 10-12). To the same category
belong the hundreds of instances of the kind אֶשְׁתַּחֲוֶה–אֶשְׁתַּחֲוֶה,
יָאנַף–יָאֶנַף, הַנֶּחְמָדִים [28] הַנֶּחֱמָדִים, עוֹלְלִים–עוֹלֵלִים (these
instances taken at random from Baer, *Liber Psalmorum*, 136 ff.,
(חלופי נקוד ... בין בן אשר ובין בן נפתלי);or Ben Asher's
(... מְשָׁרְתָיו) וּמַאֲכַל (שֻׁלְחָנוֹ וּמוֹשַׁב עֲבָדָיו) וּמַעֲמַד (I Ki 10.5//
II Chron. 9.4) as against Ben Naftali's וּמַעֲמָד [28] ... וּמַאֲכָל.
In the opposite direction, editors have generally preferred Ben
Naftali's וְהִתְפַּלְלוּ (Ginsburg, BH³, Snaith, Qoren; at I Ki.
8.33, 35, 44, 48) and וְהִתְחַנְנוּ, (Ginsburg, BH³ Snaith, Qoren;
at 8.33, 47) and וַיְבָרְכוּ (Ginsburg, Snaith, Qoren;at 8.66)
to Ben Asher's וְהִתְפַּלֲלוּ (Baer), וְהִתְחַנֲנוּ (Baer), and וַיְבָרֲכוּ
(Baer,BH³). [29]   In all these instances, one pronunciation was employed in some circles, the other in other circles; and all these
pronunciations are equally traditional and correct and "masoretic," and provide no authority to anyone to exclude the one
in favor of the other. [30]

With all this in mind, one can appreciate the full significance of the following statements in Lipschütz's article on the
ḥillufim between Ben Asher and Ben Naftali (*Textus*, 4
[1964], 3f., 12f.), "Although Mishael [ben Uzziel] reports
fully on the differences and congruences of BA and BN, he
does not mention anywhere whose reading deserves priority.
Today we know positively that he was not the first to compile
such a list of differences. Already the learned Karaite author
Levi ben al-Ḥassan [early eleventh century] . . . had drawn up
a list of *ḥillufim* . . . [and] speaks very highly of both Masoretes . . . and their versions of the Bible . . . but neither he
drops a hint as to which of the two should be given preference.

"At first, apparently only the Massoretic scholars, especially among the Karaites, took interest in these differences. For some time BA and BN obviously enjoyed equal authority and reputation. Thus, an anonymous author, most probably of the 11th century, in discussing the controversy between BA and BN on the placing of the *dagesh* in בגד כפ״ת after the word ויהי concludes: 'And the reader should conform to one of these two opinions.' Another unidentified author of that time, but beyond all doubt a Karaite . . . states that Jews everywhere adopted the Bible codices of BA and BN, and that Massoretic scholars went from Tiberias to Babylon and other countries . . .

"But gradually the majority of Hebrew grammarians and scholars gave preference to the readings of BA . . . Maimonides accepted as authoritative a copy of the Bible that had been vocalized, collated and provided with Massorah by BA [— but see Dothan's *caveats* in his *Tarbiz* article quoted above! —] . . . Maimonides made his statement with regard to the marking of the open and closed sections in the Torah. As this did not constitute a matter of dispute between our Massoretes, we should not be surprised that he does not mention the name of BN at all. But . . . Maimonides' reliance on that MS raised the prestige of BA and not only in matters with which he had been directly concerned. Simultaneously, it caused the decline of the BN tradition. As far as we know, David Qimḥi (died 1235) . . . was the first who, in reporting on the differences between the two Massoretes, decided in favour of BA. Now a widespread demand was felt to get acquainted with the readings of BA and . . . BN. More than thirty different lists of *ḥillufim* originating from the 14th and 15th century are known. These lists have a very limited value. They differ from each other substantially, and the later a list the more *ḥillufim* it shows. The Bible MSS that contain such lists are not in agreement either with the readings of BA or with those of BN quoted in their attached lists. Any variation in punctuation and accentuation that a MS showed, automatically was ascribed to BN because people were aware only of differences between BA and BN. But today we know . . . that there lived a considerable number of Massoretes in Tiberias . . . (pp. 3-4)

"Due to the efforts of the Tiberian Massoretes their system of punctuation had displaced all the others by the end of the 9th century. But by this no absolutely uniform text of the Bible was yet established. These Tiberian Massoretes among themselves continued to hold different views on many issues . . . About the beginning of the eleventh century the readings of many Massoretes, such as . . . were almost displaced. There were left mainly the systems of BA and BN. These two Massoretes agreed in many things, and the differences between them were only of minor significance. Both enjoyed great esteem and held the same high reputation. Although the readings of BN showed more system, in both vocalization and the rules of accentuation, BA in the end achieved greater recognition . . . The final decision in favour of BA came only at the end of the 12th century . . ." (pp. 12-13).

While it is impossible *a priori* to achieve "*the* masoretic text" when none ever obtained, it would seem possible in theory to produce a Hebrew text of the Bible with the claim that it is derived from "*a* masoretic text," that is, that it is based on some such manuscript as Codex Petropolitanus, or British Museum Orient. 4445, or British Museum Or 2626-27-28, or Erfurt 3, or Leningrad B 19a, or the Aleppo Codex, and the like. But in that case, the text of the manuscript that is reproduced should either be left wholly unchanged or else every single change that is introduced, no matter how slight, should be indicated clearly, and justified— as is done, e.g., when the Septuagint is edited on the basis of Codex Vaticanus, or Codex Alexandrinus, etc. At the same time, however, it should not be claimed that the text published is that of Ben Asher, or of Ben Naftali, or of Babylonian provenance, or the like, not only because none of these is *a priori* any more au-

thoritative or "masoretic" than any other but also because no
such text is in existence; the Aleppo Codex, Leningrad B 19a,
Erfurt 3, et al., are full of Ben Naftali readings.[31] Indeed, it
may well be that all these manuscripts exhibit a "mixed" text
not because any of them were "pure" to begin with, until
"contaminated" by foreign readings, but because they were
"mixed" (from our point of view) already at the outset.[32]
After all, what do we know about the masoretic appendage to
the purely consonantal text (apart from the rabbinic and other
earlier references, especially Jerome, to the inverted *nun,* the
Fifteen Extraordinary Points, the Tiqqune Soferim, the Suspended Letters, and the like) in the various Jewish centers of
Western Asia up to about the ninth-tenth centuries?

Furthermore, if a masoretic list is attached to the text,
then the reader should be advised clearly not only as to which
list it is but also that there are several different lists with
variant and various comments, sometimes quite contradictory,
and that no one list is *a priori* more authoritative or "masoretic" than another; not only that, but also that we no longer
are able to match a list to the text on which it was based.[33]
From the very outset there were different lists compiled by
different scholars on the basis of different manuscripts; it is
no longer possible to reconstruct the time and place and circumstances of this process.

In fine, any editor of the Hebrew text of the Bible who
claims that his edition is based upon and carefully and dili-
gently corrected according to הַמְּסוֹרָה *"the* Massorah" is em-
ploying an expression that is utterly without meaning; he has,
in reality, simply reproduced a form of the preserved, or traditional, or received Hebrew text (*textus receptus*),[34] a form
whose provenance — especially in the period preceding the
invention of printing — is generally unknown to us.

There is much, very much work to be done in the specialized area of masoretic research. The happy thought to re-

issue Ginsburg's *Introduction,* and thus make readily available once again to scholars the enormous material compiled and elucidated in this classic, will surely stimulate the renewed study of the Masorah in its several aspects.

June 1, 1965
Harry M. Orlinsky
Professor of Bible
Hebrew Union College —
Jewish Institute of Religion
New York

NOTES

1. Cf. H. M. Orlinsky, "Old Testament Studies," chapter II in *Religion*, ed. P. Ramsey (in series *Humanistic Scholarship in America: The Princeton Studies;* Prentice-Hall, Englewood Cliffs, N. J., 1965), pp. 51-109 and Index.

2. Useful data may be found, e.g., in F. Buhl, *Canon and Text of the Old Testament* (Edinburgh, 1892); the article on "Masorah" by C. Levias in *Jewish Encyclopedia*, VIII (1904), 365a-371b; P. Kahle, §§6-9 of "Lehre von den Schriftzeichen" (pp. 71-162) in vol. I of H. Bauer-P. Leander, *Historische Grammatik der hebräischen Sprache des Alten Testamentes* (Halle, 1918); E. Ehrentreu, *Untersuchungen über die Massora, ihre geschichtliche Entwicklung und ihren Geist* (=Heft 6 in *Beiträge zur semitischen Philologie und Linguistik*, ed. G. Bergsträsser; Hannover, 1925); S. Lieberman, *Hellenism in Jewish Palestine*, 2nd ed. (New York, 5722/1962), e.g., 28 ff., 38ff., 43 ff.; and, of course, the chapter on "The Massorah" in Ginsburg's *Introduction* (287-468). There has now come to hand *Textus*, 4 (1964), with a fine discussion of masoretic matters by Lazar Lipschütz (pp. 1-29). Of particular interest is the fuller appreciation of Menahem di Lonzano (author *Or Torah*; Venice, 1618) and especially of Jedidiah Solomon Norzi, author of the masoretic commentary on the Bible, *Minḥat Shai* (completed 1626, but not printed until 1742): " . . . Norzi's authority was accepted by everyone, Jews and non-Jews alike . . . the work of Norzi must be regarded as a most valuable contribution to the exploration of the Massorah. But . . . its importance has been over-rated by some modern scholars, such as Derenbourg, Strack and Snaith" (pp. 13-15).

3. The full English title of the reprint is *Biblia Hebraica, Massoretico-Critical Text of the Hebrew Bible, carefully revised according to the Massorah and the early printed editions of the Hebrew Bible with the Variations and marginal Annotations of the ancient Manuscripts and Targums*. It is of interest that in this missionary work the "Christian" part of Ginsburg's name did not appear in Hebrew; and the date of publication included the Jewish reckoning (according to the traditional date of Creation) as well as the Christian-secular.

4. It has long been known that Jacob ben Chayim himself proceeded "According to the eclectic method. But we are at a complete

loss, when searching for the underlying principles" (A. Sperber, "Problems of the Masora," *Hebrew Union College Annual,* 17 [1942-43], chap. IX, "The Biblia Rabbinica, Venice 1524/5" and chap. X, "Jacob ben Chayim as Editor," pp. 350-77. This study as a whole can be used only with great reserve). Scholars who have been quick to criticize Ginsburg's reliance on Jacob ben Chayim have failed to note that Ginsburg himself had pointed out several serious shortcomings in ben Chayim's procedure as editor; see *Introduction,* 958-60, 963-74.

5. ‏חמשה חומשי תורה / מדוייקים היטב / על פי המסרה ועל פי‎
‏דפוסים ראשונים / עם חלופים והגהות / מן כתבי יד עתיקים ותרגומים‎
‏ישנים / מאת כ' ד' גינצבורג / לונדון / בשנת תרס"ט לפ"ק‎ 1908
Pentateuchus. Diligenter Revisus juxta Massorah atque Editiones principes cum variis lectionibus e MSS. atque antiquis versionibus collectis. The "Advertisement" on p. IV reads: " The text presented in this book is that of the first edition of Jacob ben Chayim's Massoretic Recension, printed by Bomberg at Venice in 1524-5. No changes have been made in it beyond the correction of obvious errors as indicated by the MSS. collated. But at tht foot of each page are placed all the variations from that text, including its accents, which are to be found in a larger number of ancient MSS. and early printed editions than were ever before collated so minutely and fully."

6. See Alfred S. Geden and R. Kilgour, *Introduction to the Ginsburg Edition of the Hebrew Old Testament* (= *Bible House Paper* No. XIII of British and Foreign Bible Society, London, 1928); also the very critical review by L. Blau in *Journal of Theological Studies,* 31 (1930), 216-22.

7. See Sperber's analysis of the Masora Parva in Codex Petropolitanus in chap. VII of "Problems of the Masora" (pp. 334-46); and Lipschütz has noted (*Textus,* 4 [1964], 6), with reference to the detailed studies by H. Yalon and F. P. Castro, "that the close agreement of Cod. L(= B 19a) with Mishael (ben Uzziel)'s list was achieved, to some extent, by erasures, addition and alterations . . . "

8. R. Gottheil, (depending apparently on Ginsburg) offers a useful chart on the "Pedigree of Hebrew Bible" in *Jewish Encyclopedia,* III, 161; more recently, Lazarus Goldschmidt discussed *The Earliest Editions of the Hebrew Bible,* etc. (New York, 1950. "Limited to 330 Copies Only"). Stanley Rypins has made available interesting data in *The Book of Thirty Centuries* (New York, 1951), e.g., in chap. VII, "The Printed Bible" (pp. 174 ff.; the Notes on 332 ff.),

which is headed by a quotation from Thomas More: "Though an angel should write, still 't is devils must print;" B. J. Roberts, "The Hebrew Bible since 1937," *JTS*, 15 (1964), 253-64.

A general warning is in place here: not all scholars who have written on this aspect of the subject have really bothered to check their data carefully at the source when they could and should have done so; too often errors have been repeated and new ones created.

9. On the Hebrew Bibles edited by Jablonski, H. Opitius (Kiel, 1709), and Michaelis, Wickes wrote (טעמי אמ״ת, 1881, p. ix), "The three . . . edd. are all much more correct, as far as the accents are concerned, than our common edd. Modern editors (excepting of course Heidenheim and Baer [to whom Wickes was uncritically partial, as against Ginsburg]) have one and all gone on perpetuating the errors of the Van der Hooght text, without taking the trouble of enquiring whether more correct texts were not available." The Michaelis edition, Wickes noted (ibid.), "is valuable to the student because of the various accentual readings, taken from the Erfurt MSS."

10. The 1884 edition of van der Hooght-Hahn had the *"Key to the Massoretic Notes, Titles, and Index . . . translated from the Latin of A. Hahn, with many additions and corrections,"* by Alexander Meyrowitz, A.M., Prof. of the Hebrew Language and Literature in the University of New York.

11. The title of the 1870 (Vienna) edition was: ספר תורה נביאים וכתובים/מדויק היטב על פי המסורה/הוגה בעיון נמרץ/על ידי/ החכם המובהק מהור״ר/מאיר הלוי לעטעריס/שנת התר״ל ליצירה — *The Holy Scriptures of the Old Testament, Hebrew and English.*

12. Thus, too, the term Pentateuch (alongside νόμος — תורה) corresponds to חמשה חומשי תורה; and the term Hagiographa (alongside Writings — כתובים) may well correspond to the expression כתבי הקודש used in antiquity for Books of the Third Division — so that both "Writings" and "Hagiographa" are originally Jewish titles of the Third Division. Or cf.   Θρῆνοι   — *Lamentations* with קינות (alongside איכה). The best collection of data on "Die Namen der Heiligen Schrift" may be found in L. Blau's *Zur Einleitung in die Heilige Schrift* (Budapest, 1894), Part I, pp. 1-47.

A good case has been made recently for an Alexandrian as against a Judean order for two of the Ten Commandments: the latter is the traditional "You shall not murder. You shall not commit adultery," with the Alexandrian order being the reverse. Both orders are equally Jewish and well known already during the last centuries of the Second Temple. Who is to decide which order is the original? Cf. D. Flusser, *Textus*, 4 (1964), 220-4.

13. Ibn Ezra, it is true, comments, ‏אל הארץ כנען. כמו והנבואה‎
‏עודד הנביא, הנבואה נבואת עודד הנביא. והטעם אל הארץ ארץ כנען.‎
However, one has but to look at II Chron. 15.8 to realize that the
text there is hardly original precisely at this point, and, consequently,
offers ibn Ezra no real support. Our verse is patently clumsy and has
suffered conflation.

14. See, e.g., Chapter V of my "Studies in the Septuagint of the
Book of Job": "The Hebrew *Vorlage* of the Septuagint of Job: the
Text and the Script," § B The Kethib and the Qere (in *Hebrew
Union College Annual*, 36 [1965], 37-47); "The Origin of the
Kethib-Qere System: A New Approach" (*Supplement to Vetus Testa-
mentum*, 7 [1960], 184-192); and "Problems of Kethib-Qere"
(*Journal of the American Oriental Society*, 60 [1940], 30-45). I.
Yeivin has discussed "The Vocalization of Qere-Kethiv in A (leppo
Codex)" and related material in *Textus*, 2 (1962), 146-9.

15. Contrary to all students of the Masorah and editors of the
"masoretic" text, the Kethib forms are all simply orthographic
(*defective*) variants of the Qere, i.e., they are to be vocalized exactly
as the Qere: ‏וְאַתְּ‎ (just like the *scriptio defectiva* Q ‏וְחָיִיתְ‎), —not
‏וְאַתְּ!‎ —, ‏שַׁתְּ‎, ‏לֵכְןָ‎, etc. Thus, e.g., where no K-Q variants were involved,
we have ‏בְּךָ‎ in the Psalms (18.30) version of David's Hymn of Triumph
as against ‏בְּכָה‎ in the Samuel (II: 22.30) version; ‏גָּלְיָת‎ (1 Chron.
17.25) alongside ‏גָּלְיָתָה‎ (II Sam. 7.27); ‏וְהָיִיתְ‎ (I Chron. 19.12)
along with ‏וְהָיִיתָה‎ (II Sam. 10.11); ‏וְנָתַתְּ‎ (I Ki. 8.39) together
with ‏וְנָתַתָּה‎ (II Chron. 6.30); and so on. What is involved in all
these instances is merely variation in orthography, in no way, as
scholars have erroneously assumed, in morphology. For the data and
argument, see "The Import . . , " pp. 60 f. And see the statement
by Raphael Chayim Bazila (18th cent.), " . . . Qere and Kethiv involve the letters, and not the accents and vowel signs" (*apud* I. Yeivin, *Textus*, 2 [1962], 147 and n.1).

In reference to the Qoren Bible, one of its Editors, Dr. A. M.
Haberman, has advised me (in a letter dated 12 Iyyar 5725 = May 14,
1965): ‏בענין קרי וכתיב נהגנו כך : אם על ידי כתיב שונה מן המקובל‎
‏לא נשתנה הקרי, הדפסנו אותו בפנים מבלי להביא קרי בצד...‎
Hence ‏תַּחְתָּו, אֵלָו, יָדָו, לָךְ‎, etc.

16. ‏נ"ו מלין חסר י' במצע' תיבות' וקרין וכל חד לי'‎.

17. In II Ki. 4.34, with reference to Elijah, ‏(וַיַּעַל וַיִּשְׁכַּב עַל־‎
‏הַיֶּלֶד וַיָּשֶׂם פִּיו עַל־פִּיו וְעֵינָיו עַל־עֵינָיו וְכַפָּיו עַל־)כַּפּוֹ‎, vocalized ‏כַּפּוֹ‎ in
List 128 — as though a reading ‏כַּפּוֹ‎ were possible here in context
‏(וְכַפָּיו עַל־)‎. Yet BH³ vocalizes the Kethib as ‏כַּפּוֹ‎ (—עַל־ ‏וְכַפָּיו!‎.

In all these instances, Kahle, unlike Ginsburg, suppressed the fact that he vocalized the Kethib on his own (arbitrary and insufficient) authority.

18. In Jer. 17.11, with reference to the godless one, ‏(. . . עֹשֶׂה‎ ‏עֹשֶׂר וְלֹא בְמִשְׁפָּט) בַּחֲצִי יָמוֹ יַעַזְבֶנּוּ (וּבְאַחֲרִיתוֹ יִהְיֶה נָבָל:)‎ vocalized ‏יָמוּ‎ in List 128. Yet BH³, e.g., with its K ‏ימו‎ Q ‏יָמָיו‎, actually vocalizes K ‏יֹמוֹ‎! Did BH³'s "masoretic" editor get the authority for this from B 19a?

19. In I Sam. 2.10 (Hannah's prayer),‏(עלו) יהוה יֵחַתּוּ מריבו (. . .‎ ‏בַּשָּׁמַיִם יַרְעֵם‎, vocalized ‏(מְרִיבָו) עָלָו‎ in List 128. No one would have thought of ‏(מְרִיבוֹ) עָלוֹ‎.   In v. 9a preceding, ‏(יִשְׁמֹר) חֲסִידוֹ (רַגְלֵי)‎ ‏וּרְשָׁעִים בַּחֹשֶׁךְ יִדָּמּוּ)‎ is a K-Q in BH³, K ‏חסידו‎ Q ‏חֲסִידָיו‎; but the "masoretic" editor vocalized the K as ‏חֲסִידוֹ‎! This vocalization of the Kethib is, of course, not only non-masoretic and even anti-masoretic—lacking, as it does all masoretic justification and running counter to the import of List 128— it is also nonsense in its own right in context. This word will not be found in List 128, since it occurs not once but twice in the Bible, here and in Prov. 2.8 (where BH³ again points the Kethib as ‏חֲסִידוֹ‎). It may be that only in Deut. 33.8 is ‏חָסִיד‎ declined in the Bible in the singular; there ‏לְאִישׁ חֲסִידֶךָ‎ is the equivalent of ‏לְאִישׁ־חָסִיד שֶׁלְךָ‎ ("Your faithful one").

20. Ibn Janaḥ has nothing to say about the manner of adding pronominal suffixes to ‏תַּחַת‎; but concerning ‏אַחַר‎ and ‏אֶל‎ (see under these roots in his dictionary, Kitāb al-Usūl, ed. Ad. Neubauer) he is very explicit, viz., the suffixes are added to ‏אחרי‎ and ‏אלי‎.

21. Cf. e.g., his comment on ‏תַּחְתֶּנָּה‎ at Gen. 2.21; Sefer Ṣaḥōt (Berlin, 1768), fol. 23a; Moznayim (Offenbach, 1791), fol. 30a, 38b, 39b.

22. For a more detailed analysis, see my article on "The Biblical Prepositions ‏תַּחַת, בֵּין, בַּעַד‎, and Pronouns ‏אֲנוּ‎ (or ‏אָנוּ)‎, ‏זֹאתָה‎" in Hebrew Union College Annual, 17 (1942-43) 267-292.

23. Maimonides' statement (Mishneh Torah, Hilchot Sefer Torah, 8:4) runs as follows, ‏וספר שסמכנו עליו בדברים אלו הוא‎ ‏הספר הידוע במצרים שהוא כולל ארבעה ועשרים ספרים שהיה בירושלים‎ ‏מכמה שנים להגיה ממנו הספרים ועליו היו הכל סומכין לפי שהגיהו בן‎ ‏אשר ודקדק בו שנים הרבה והגיהו פעמים רבות כמו שהעתיקו ועליו‎ ‏סמכתי בספר התורה שכתבתי כהלכתו‎. In the same vein, David Qimḥi: ‏ואנחנו סומכים על קריאת בן אשר‎.

24. Interestingly, editors of masoretic texts have tended to disregard Ben Asher on such vocalizations in favor of Ben Naftali. Thus the "masoretic" editor of BH³, boasting as he did that his text (B 19a) is purest Ben Asher, disregarded Ben Asher and adopted Ben Naftali

but with an additional metheg, borrowed from Ben Asher, וּלְשָׁרְתוֹ —
without telling his readers that he did so, and why. Masoretically
speaking, the allegedly "Ben Asher masoretic" text of BH³ is all too
often a hodge-podge, possessing no greater authority as *the,* or *a,*
masoretic text than any other on the market. On p. 61 of his *Cairo
Geniza,* Kahle blamed Kittel for adding "some Methegs which were
not found in the [B 19a] MŜ"; but Kittel himself wrote (p. IV of
his "Prolegomena" to BH³)" . . . Ich habe nach mehrfacher Durch-
beratung mit Paul Kahle Meteg überall da gesetzt oder weggelassen . ."

25. The problem of which, if either, is more "masoretic" than the
other, is not to be confused with the fact that anyone with a feeling
for the meter of the poem (//Psa. 105.5, פִּיו(־)וּמִשְׁפְּטֵי מִפְּתָיו) will
prefer Ben Naftali and grant the second half of the verse a 3 (rather
than Ben Asher's mouthful of a 2) meter; the first half reads
זִכְרוּ נִפְלְאוֹתָיו אֲשֶׁר־עָשָׂה.

26. The "masoretic" editor of BH³ has brought this material
together in the form of a bewildering mish-mash; his note on יִשָּׂשׂכָר
at Gen. 30.18 reads: "Q יִשְׂכָר (pro יִשְׂכָּר ? cf. min. et sab. וישכראל),
1 c K יִשְׂשָׂכָר (= אִישׁ שָׂכָר); ben Naft יִשְׂשָׂכָר, al יִשָּׂשׂכָר
(= *affert praemium*)." On what basis was his Kethib vocalized
יִשָּׂשׂכָר ?   —this apart from the fact that the origin of the K-Q here
requires careful investigation, especially in the light of the data
brought together by Lipschütz in *Textus,* 2 (1962) p. ג and n.3 and
4 (1964), 9 and 16f.

27. Blau (*JQR,* O.S., 12 [1900], 241) put it this way, "The
Soferim were the editors and revisers of the text; the Massoretes are
the conservators of the tradition, not the revisers." I put it this way,
in dealing with "The Origin of the Kethib-Qere System: A New
Approach" (*Supplement to Vetus Testamentum,* VII, 1960; the
Oxford Congress Volume), p. 186, " . . Clearly the Masoretes were
neither correctors nor selectors; i.e., they did not deal with the
Hebrew text of the Bible subjectively, *ad hoc,* deciding each reading
within its context. That is why the very first Kethib-Qere in the Bible,
in Gen. viii 17, exhibits the anomalous, quite incorrect form הַיְצֵא,
the alleged hiph'il imperative of the root יצא, as the Qere, and
the patently correct and expected form, הוֹצֵא, as the Kethib . . .." ;
or cf. my chapter (IV) on "The Hebrew Text and the Ancient
Versions of the Old Testament" in *An Introduction to the Revised
Standard Version of the Old Testament* (New York, 1952), 24 ff.

28. The dot in the *mem* is not really a dagesh; it was used to
indicate—before the system of vocalization was introduced — that

the preceding shewa was silent (עְ–;חָ–) rather than vocal (–ֱעֲ;–ֱחֲ).
There are scores of instances of this use of the dot, erroneously
"explained" by grammarians as one kind of dagesh or another.

29. In Lipschütz's edition of ben Uzziel's treatise on the differences between Ben Asher and Ben Naftali (*Textus*, 2 [1962]; כתאב
אלכלף אלדי בין אלמעלמין בן אשר ובן נפתלי), differences which
revolved about the vocalization and accentuation of the Hebrew
Bible, our words והתפללו and והתחננו will be found listed under
ספר מלכים, ad loc. (p. כט); but the reader will see there only:
והתפללו; והתפללו והתחננו־אשר והתחננו־נפתלי.Max L. Margolis ("Accents in Hebrew," *Jew. Enc.*, I [1901], 149b-158a) and E. Werner
("Masoretic Accents," *The Interpreter's Dictionary of the Bible*,
3 [1962], 295a-299a) have written exemplary articles on the accents.

A careful reading of Lipschütz's analysis of the *Kitāb al-Khilaf*
(*Textus*, 4[1964]) makes it more than amply clear how little we
really know of the rise and nature of the numerous schools of thought
on the part of masoretes in Babylonia and Palestine; we are far from
knowing as much as we should even of the quantity and quality of
the differences between the groups that came to be designated Ben
Asher and Ben Naftali. And it is not helpful when scholars denigrate
and dismiss the work of others, as Kahle (and subsequently some of
his students) was wont to do; I have in mind the derogatory remarks
casually made of such scholars as Baer and Ginsburg—as though
they should have perceived all the problems and achieved their solutions, problems and solutions which we today continue to
find perplexing.

30. Much important work in this area has been done by Israeli
scholars, e.g., Z. Ben-Hayyim, Y. Kutscher, S. Morag, and H. Yalon.

31. Sheldon H. Blank made a very fine study of "A Hebrew
Bible MS. in the Hebrew Union College Library" (*HUCA*, 8-9
[1931-32], 229-55), an interesting Spanish manuscript of about the
thirteenth century; in a fine piece of detective work he identified
other portions of the original in Leningrad. The text of the "HUC
MS. represents a late development of the ben Naftali tradition . . "

32. I am not sure that it is really facetious to ask whether some
of the allegedly Ben Asher manuscripts that contain numerous Ben
Naftali readings may not actually be Ben Naftali manuscripts that
contain numerous Ben Asher readings. Blank (see preceding note),
p. 246, has noted also the consonantal text as a possible basis for distinguishing between these two groups, though "According to Mishael
(ben Uzziel), BA and BN differed only in eight instances concerning

the consonantal text" (Lipschütz, *Textus*, 4 [1964], 16, and n 2);
but more study of this aspect is needed.

33. Everyone who has worked with masoretic lists knows how
true this is; cf., e.g., Sperber, "Problems of the Masora" chaps. VIII-
X, the sections that deal with "The Text contradicts the Masora,"
"The Text is Revised so as to Conform to the Masora," and the like.
Or see Ginsburg, *Introduction*, 965 ff., with reference to Jacob ben
Chayim's text and its Masorah. G. E. Weil and Israel Yeivin
have been publishing and analyzing new lists and related
material in volumes of *Textus* and elsewhere; important and
clarifying contributions. See e.g., G.E. Weil, "La nouvelle édition
de la Massorah (BHK iv) et l'histoire de la Massorah," in *Supplements to Vetus Testamentum*, IX (1963), 266-84.

34. Out of deference to tradition, the title page of the new
translation of *The Torah* (Jewish Publication Society, Philadelphia,
1962) reads " . . . according to the Masoretic text"; the dust-jacket,
however, reads more correctly, " . . . according to the traditional
Hebrew text."

877